PRINCIPLES OF SCOTTISH
PRIVATE LAW

PRINCIPLES OF SCOTTISH PRIVATE LAW

By

DAVID M. WALKER

M.A., LL.B. (Glas.), Ph.D. (Edin.), LL.D. (Edin. & Lond.),
One of Her Majesty's Counsel in Scotland,
Of the Middle Temple, Barrister-at-Law,
Regius Professor of Law in the
University of Glasgow

VOLUME II

CLARENDON PRESS · OXFORD

1970

Oxford University Press, Ely House, London W.1
GLASGOW NEW YORK TORONTO MELBOURNE WELLINGTON
CAPE TOWN SALISBURY IBADAN NAIROBI DAR ES SALAAM LUSAKA ADDIS ABABA
BOMBAY CALCUTTA MADRAS KARACHI LAHORE DACCA
KUALA LUMPUR SINGAPORE HONG KONG TOKYO

Made and printed in Great Britain by
William Clowes and Sons, Limited, London and Beccles

CONTENTS

VOLUME II

PART 3

OBLIGATIONS OF RESTITUTION

PART 4

PARTICULAR OBLIGATIONS OF RESTITUTION

PART 5

OBLIGATIONS OF REPARATION ARISING FROM DELICT GENERALLY

PART 6

THE PARTICULAR DELICTS

BOOK V
LAW OF PROPERTY

PART 1
PROPERTY IN GENERAL

PART 2
CORPOREAL HERITABLE PROPERTY

PART 3
INCORPOREAL HERITABLE PROPERTY

PART 4
CORPOREAL MOVEABLE PROPERTY

PART 5

INCORPOREAL MOVEABLE PROPERTY

BOOK VI

LAW OF TRUSTS

BOOK VII

BANKRUPTCY

BOOK VIII
SUCCESSION

BOOK IX
CIVIL REMEDIES

AUTHORITIES AND ABBREVIATIONS

A.A. Act of Adjournal.
A.Ass. Act of the General Assembly of the Church of Scotland.
A.P.S. Acts of the Parliaments of Scotland, 1124–1707, ed. Cosmo Innes and Thomas Thomson, 11 vols. in 12, 1814–1875.
A.S. Act of Sederunt.
Anton. Professor A. E. Anton, *Private International Law*, 1967.
Balf. Sir James Balfour of Pittendreich, *Practicks: or a System of the more Ancient Law of Scotland*, 1754 and (Stair Socy.) 1962–3.
Bankt. Andrew McDouall, Lord Bankton, *Institute of the Laws of Scotland in Civil Rights*, 3 vols., 1751–3.
Begg. J. Henderson Begg, *Law of Scotland relating to Law Agents*, 2nd ed., 1883.
Bell, *Arb.* J. M. Bell, *Law of Arbitration in Scotland*, 2nd ed., 1877.
Bell, *Comm.* Professor G. J. Bell, *Commentaries on the Law of Scotland and the Principles of Mercantile Jurisprudence*, 7th ed., 1870.
Bell, *Conv.* Professor A. Montgomery Bell, *Lectures on Conveyancing*, 3rd ed., 2 vols., 1882.
Bell, *Dict.* William Bell, *Dictionary and Digest of the Law of Scotland*, 7th ed., 1890.
Bell, *Prin.* Professor G. J. Bell, *Principles of the Law of Scotland*, 10th ed., 1899.
Borthwick. J. Borthwick, *Law of Libel and Slander in Scotland*, 1826.
Broun. J. C. C. Broun, *Law of Nuisance in Scotland*, 1891.
M. P. Brown. M. P. Brown, *Law of Sale*, 1821.
Brown. Richard Brown, *Sale of Goods Act, 1893*, 2nd ed., 1911.
Burn-Murdoch. H. Burn-Murdoch, *Interdict in the Law of Scotland*, 1933.
Burns. John Burns, *Conveyancing Practice*, 4th ed., 1957.
C. Code (Corpus Juris Civilis).
C.L.J. Cambridge Law Journal.
Cheshire. G. C. Cheshire, *Private International Law*, 7th ed., 1965.

Clark. F. W. Clark, *Law of Partnership and Joint Stock Companies*, 2 vols., 1866.

Cooper. F. T. Cooper, *Law of Defamation and Verbal Injury*, 2nd ed., 1906.

Craig. Sir Thomas Craig, *Jus Feudale*, 3rd ed., 1732, and trs. Lord President Clyde, 2 vols., 1934.

D. Digest (Corpus Juris Civilis).

Dallas. George Dallas of St. Martin's, *Styles of Writs*, 2nd ed., 1774.

Dicey and Morris. A. V. Dicey and J. H. C. Morris, *Conflict of Laws*, 8th ed., 1967.

Dickson. W. G. Dickson, *Law of Evidence in Scotland*, 3rd ed., 2 vols., 1887.

Dirleton. Sir George Nisbet, Lord Dirleton, *Doubts and Questions in the Law, especially of Scotland*, 1698.

Dobie. W. J. Dobie, *Manual of the Law of Liferent and Fee in Scotland*, 1941.

Dobie, *Prac.* W. J. Dobie, *Law and Practice in the Sheriff Court*, 1948.

Duff, *Deeds.* A. Duff, *Treatise on Deeds, chiefly affecting moveables*, 1840.

Duff, *Feudal.* A. Duff, *Treatise on Deeds and Forms used in the Constitution Transmission and Extinction of Feudal Rights*, 1838.

Duncan and Dykes. G. Duncan and D. Oswald Dykes, *Principles of Civil Jurisdiction as applied in the Law of Scotland*, 1911.

Encyc. *Encyclopaedia of the Laws of Scotland*, 18 vols., 1926–52.

Ersk. Professor John Erskine of Carnock, *An Institute of the Law of Scotland*, 8th ed., 2 vols., 1871.

Ersk., *Prin.* Professor John Erskine of Carnock, *Principles of the Law of Scotland*, 21st ed., 1911.

Ferguson, *Roads.* J. Ferguson, *Law of Roads, Streets, Rights of Way, Bridges and Ferries*, 1904.

Ferguson, *Water.* J. Ferguson, *Law of Water and Water Rights in Scotland*, 1907.

Forbes. Professor William Forbes, *Institutes of the Law of Scotland*, 2 vols., 1722–30.

Fraser, *H. & W.* Patrick, Lord Fraser, *Husband and Wife according to the Law of Scotland*, 2nd ed., 2 vols., 1876–8.

Fraser, *M. & S.* Patrick, Lord Fraser, *Master and Servant, Employer and Workman, Master and Apprentice*, 3rd ed., 1882.

Fraser, *P. & Ch.* Patrick, Lord Fraser, *Law of Scotland relative to Parent and Child and Guardian and Ward*, 3rd ed., 1906.

Gibb. Professor A. Dewar Gibb, *International Law of Jurisdiction in England and Scotland*, 1926.

Gibb and Dalrymple. *Scottish Judicial Dictionary*, 1946.

Gloag. Professor W. M. Gloag, *Law of Contract*, 2nd ed., 1929.

Gloag and Henderson. Professor W. M. Gloag and Professor R. C. Henderson, *Introduction to the Law of Scotland*, 7th ed., 1968.

Gloag and Irvine. Professor W. M. Gloag and J. M. Irvine, *Law of Rights in Security, Heritable and Moveable, and Cautionary Obligations*, 1897.

Goudy. Henry Goudy, *Law of Bankruptcy in Scotland*, 4th ed., 1914.

Gow. J. J. Gow, *Mercantile and Industrial Law of Scotland*, 1964.

Graham Stewart. J. Graham Stewart. *Law of Diligence*, 1898.

Halsbury. Laws of England, 3rd ed., 43 vols., 1952–64.

Henderson. Professor R. C. Henderson, *Principles of Vesting in the Law of Succession*, 2nd ed., 1938.

Hope, *Major Prac.* Sir Thomas Hope, *Major Practicks*, 1608–33, 2 vols. (Stair Socy.), 1937–8.

Hope, *Minor Prac.* Sir Thomas Hope, *Minor Practicks*, 1726.

Hume. Baron David Hume, *Decisions*, 1781–1822, 1839.

Hume, *Comm.* Baron David Hume, *Commentaries on the Law of Scotland respecting Crimes*, 4th ed., 2 vols., 1844.

Hume, *Lect.* Baron David Hume, *Lectures on the Law of Scotland*, 6 vols. (Stair Socy.), 1939–58.

Hunter. R. Hunter, *Law of Landlord and Tenant*, 4th ed., 2 vols., 1876.

I.C.L.Q. International and Comparative Law Quarterly, 1952–.

Inst. Institutes (Corpus Juris Civilis).

Irons. J. Campbell Irons, *Judicial Factors*, 1908.

J.R. Juridical Review, 1889–.

Kames, *Eluc.* Henry Home, Lord Kames, *Elucidations respecting the Law of Scotland*, 1777.

Kames, *H.L.T.* Henry Home, Lord Kames, *Historical Law Tracts*, 4th ed., 1817.

Kames, *Equity.* Henry Home, Lord Kames, *Principles of Equity*, 5th ed., 1825.

L.Q.R. Law Quarterly Review, 1886–.

Mor. W. M. Morison's *Dictionary of Decisions*, 22 vols.

M.L.R. Modern Law Review, 1937–.

Mackay, *Manual.* Aeneas J. G. Mackay, *Manual of Practice in the Court of Session*, 1893.

Mackay, *Prac.* Aeneas J. G. Mackay, *Practice of the Court of Session*, 2 vols., 1877–9.

Mack. Sir George Mackenzie of Rosehaugh, *Institutions of the Law of Scotland*, 1684.

Mack., *Crim.* Sir George Mackenzie of Rosehaugh, *Laws and Customs of Scotland in Matters Criminal*, 2nd ed., 1699.

Mackenzie Stuart. Professor A. Mackenzie Stuart, *Law of Trusts*, 1932.

Maclaren. J. A. Maclaren, *Court of Session Practice*, 1916.

McLaren. John, Lord McLaren, *Law of Wills and Succession*, 3rd ed., 1894; Supplement by Dykes, 1934.

Menzies. Professor Allan Menzies, *Lectures on Conveyancing according to the Law of Scotland*, revised ed., 1900.

Menzies, *Trs.* A. J. P. Menzies, *Law of Scotland affecting Trustees*, 2nd ed., 1913.

Millar. J. H. Millar, *Handbook of Prescription according to the Law of Scotland*, 1893.

More, *Lect.* Professor J. S. More, *Lectures on the Law of Scotland*, ed. McLaren, 2 vols., 1864.

More, *Notes.* Professor J. S. More, *Notes to Stair's Institutions*, in fifth edition thereof, 1832.

Napier. Mark Napier, *Law of Prescription in Scotland*, 2nd ed., 1854.

Nov. Novels (Corpus Juris Civilis).

Paton and Cameron. G. C. H. Paton and J. G. S. Cameron, *Law of Landlord and Tenant*, 1967.

Q.A. *Quoniam Attachiamenta.*

R.C. Rules of the Court of Session, 1965.

R.M. *Regiam Majestatem*, ed. Skene, 1609, and ed. Cooper (Stair Socy.), 1947.

Rankine, *Bar.* Professor Sir John Rankine, *Law of Personal Bar in Scotland*, 1921.

Rankine, *L.O.* Professor Sir John Rankine, *Law of Land Ownership in Scotland*, 4th ed., 1909.

Rankine, *Leases.* Professor Sir John Rankine, *Law of Leases in Scotland*, 3rd ed., 1916.

Ross, *Lect.* Walter Ross, *Lectures on the History and Practice of the Law of Scotland relative to Conveyancing and Legal Diligence*, 2nd ed., 2 vols., 1822.

S.L.R. Scottish Law Review, 1886–1963.

S.L.T. (News). Scots Law Times, News portion.

Skene, *D.V.S.* Sir John Skene, *De Verborum Significatione*, 1597.

Smith, *British Justice*. Professor T. B. Smith, *British Justice—The Scottish Contribution*, 1961.

Smith, *Precedent*. Professor T. B. Smith, *Doctrines of Judicial Precedent in Scots Law*, 1952.

Smith, *Studies*. Professor T. B. Smith, *Studies Critical and Comparative*, 1963.

Smith, *Sh.Comm*. Professor T. B. Smith, *A Short Commentary on the Law of Scotland*, 1963.

Spotiswoode. Sir Robert Spotiswoode, *Practicks of the Laws of Scotland*, 1706.

Stair. Sir James Dalrymple, Viscount Stair, *Institutions of the Law of Scotland*, 5th ed., 2 vols., 1832.

Steuart. Sir James Steuart, *Answers to Dirleton's Doubts in the Laws of Scotland*, 1715.

Thoms. G. H. Thoms, *Judicial Factors*, 2nd ed., 1881.

Umpherston. F. Umpherston, *Master and Servant*, 1904.

Walker, *Damages*. Professor D. M. Walker, *Law of Damages in Scotland*, 1955.

Walker, *Delict*. Professor D. M. Walker, *Law of Delict in Scotland*, 2 vols., 1966.

Walker, *S.L.S*. Professor D. M. Walker, *The Scottish Legal System*, 3rd ed., 1969.

Walkers. A. G. Walker and N. M. L. Walker, *Law of Evidence in Scotland*, 1964.

Wallace. G. Wallace, *System of the Principles of the Law of Scotland*, 1760.

Walton. F. P. Walton, *Handbook of the Law of Husband and Wife in Scotland*, 3rd ed., 1951.

Wood. Professor J. P. Wood, *Lectures on Conveyancing*, 1903.

PART 3

OBLIGATIONS OF RESTITUTION

CHAPTER 57

THE OBLIGATION OF RESTITUTION IN GENERAL

In many circumstances law imposes an obligation on persons, independently of their will and of agreement or contract, entitling the one to recover, and obliging the other to repay or restore, money or goods to the first. In the Roman law the second class of obligations, those arising *quasi ex contractu*,[1] included obligations arising by law not by agreement, yet not founded on any wrongdoing by one party to another, and the categories there recognized have been accepted in Scots law also as founding an obligation to restore, independently of contract.[2] Fundamentally similar obligations are also recognized in maritime law, in the claims for salvage and general average, and in the law of trusts, to restore to the trust benefits which it would be unjust for the trustee to retain for himself.

The principle underlying all the categories is the unwillingness of the law to countenance the unjustified enrichment of one party at the expense of another, expressed in the maxim *nemo debet locupletari ex aliena jactura*.[3]

The justification for imposition of this obligation is natural justice and equity,[4] so that, in general, no obligation will arise where restitution would be contrary to justice and equity.

[1] Inst. 3, 13 and 27; see also Dig. 12, 4–7; 44, 7, 5.
[2] Stair I, 3, 2; I, 7 and 8; Bankt. I, 8 and 9; Ersk. III, 3, 51; Bell, *Prin.* §437–46; 525–41; Ch. 58, *infra*.
[3] cf. Balf., *Prac.* 333; *Somerville* v. *Hamilton* (1541) Mor. 8905; Ersk. I, 7, 33; *Edinburgh Trams* v. *Courtenay*, 1909 S.C. 99, 105; *Cantiere San Rocco* v. *Clyde Shipbuilding Co.*, 1922 S.C. 723, 737; 1923 S.C. (H.L.) 105, 117.
[4] Kames, *Equity*, I, 1, 3, 2(3); *Edinburgh Trams.*, *supra*; Walker, 'Equity in Scots Law' (1954) 66 J.R. 103, 138.

PART 4

PARTICULAR OBLIGATIONS OF RESTITUTION

CHAPTER 58

DUTIES OF RESTITUTION AND COMPENSATION

RESTITUTION

A PERSON who comes into possession of moveable property without any title to retain custody thereof is obliged to restore it to the person truly entitled to the possession thereof.[1] Thus the finder of straying animals must intimate the fact, and the finder of lost property must disclose his finding and deposit the thing found with the police.[2] A person to whom goods have been mistakenly delivered must restore them for proper delivery.[3] A thief, or person who has obtained goods by fraud, acquires no title to the property,[4] and should restore it to the true owner, who can reclaim the property. Moreover property so acquired is affected by an inherent *vitium reale* which prevents the thief or fraudulent person from conferring a good title on anyone, even on a taker from him in good faith, who has given value and taken without notice of the thief's defective title;[5] such a taker must return the property to the true owner, or pay compensation therefor.[6] A bona fide purchaser of stolen or fraudulently acquired property who has resold the goods before his title is challenged is liable only for any profit he made on the

[1] Stair I, 7, 1; More, Note F; Bankt. I, 8, 1; Ersk. III, 1, 10; Bell, *Comm.* I, 281; *Prin.* §527.

[2] Burgh Police (Sc.) Act, 1892, S. 412; Lost Property (Sc.) Act, 1965; cf. *Lawson* v. *Heatley*, 1962 S.L.T. 53.

[3] *Findlay* v. *Monro* (1698) Mor. 1767; *Pride* v. *St. Anne's Bleaching Co.* (1838) 16 S. 1376; *Caledonian Ry.* v. *Harrison* (1879) 7 R. 151.

[4] *Morrisson* v. *Robertson*, 1908 S.C. 332; contrast *Macleod* v. *Kerr*, 1965 S.L.T. 358 where purchaser's title voidable only; see also *Todd* v. *Armour* (1882) 9 R. 901; cf. *Ingram* v. *Little* [1961] 1 Q.B. 31.

[5] cf. *International Banking Co.* v. *Ferguson, Shaw & Sons*, 1910 S.C. 182; *McDonald* v. *Provan (of Scotland St.)*, 1960 S.L.T. 231.

[6] *Bp. Caithness* v. *Edinburgh Fleshers* (1629) Mor. 4145; *Fergusson* v. *Forrest* (1639) Mor. 4145; *Forsyth* v. *Kilpatrick* (1680) Mor. 9120; *Henderson* v. *Gibson*, 17 June 1806, F.C.

resale, and that only if the goods cannot be recovered.[1] An exception to the rule of *vitium reale* exists in the cases of money, bank notes and negotiable instruments, where even a thief or holder by fraud, though himself having no title and legally obliged to make specific restitution or compensation,[2] may pass a good title to a third party if the latter takes in good faith, for value, and without notice of the defective title of the giver. In that event the true owner's only claim is against the thief or fraudulent person for damages for the loss; he has no claim against the innocent third party.

Termination of limited title to possess

Similarly, where a temporary or otherwise limited title of possession, as that of pledgee, borrower,[3] despositary, hirer or custodier,[4] has terminated, the possessor must restore the goods transferred to him, or he will be liable in compensation for their value.[5] *Vitium reale* attaches also to goods wrongfully retained in such circumstances.

The obligation of restitution extends also to property transferred where the contemplated purpose of the transfer has failed, such as gifts given in contemplation of a marriage which does not take place,[6] and to property purchased at a sale following a poinding later held to have been irregularly conducted.[7]

No restitution is due where the property has been transferred *ob turpem causam*; if both parties be *in culpa*, *melior est conditio possidentis* and there is no restitution,[8] but if they are not *in pari delicto* the less guilty may have a claim for restitution.

Ineffective contracts

Where a contract is held ineffective any money paid or property transferred thereunder must be restored, as where a contract is

[1] Stair I, 7, 11; *Scot* v. *Low* (1704) Mor. 9123; *Wallace* v. *Spence and Carfrae* (1765) Mor. 12802.

[2] *Crawford* v. *Royal Bank* (1749) Mor. 875; *Swinton* v. *Beveridge* (1799) 10105; *Lambton* v. *Marshall* 21 June 1799, F.C.; *Scott* v. *Kilmarnock Bank*, 27 Feb. 1812, F.C.; *Walker & Watson* v. *Sturrock* (1897) 35 S.L.T. 26; *Gorebridge Cooperative Socy.* v. *Turnbull* (1952) 68 Sh. Ct. Rep. 236; cf. *Lawson, supra*; see also *Kinniburgh* v. *Dickson* (1830) 9 S. 153.

[3] *Forsyth* v. *Kilpatrick* (1680) Mor. 9120; *Lockhart* v. *Cunningham* (1870) 8 S.L.R. 151.

[4] *Ramsay* v. *Wilson* (1666) Mor. 9113; *Pringles* v. *Gribton* (1710) Mor. 9213.

[5] cf. *Wright* v. *Butchart* (1662) Mor. 9112; *Ramsay* v. *Wilson* (1666) Mor. 9113; *Sc. Central Ry.* v. *Ferguson* (1863) 1 M. 750.

[6] Stair I, 7, 7.

[7] *Beveridge* v. *Cupar Inhabitants* (1583) Mor. 9111.

[8] Stair I, 7, 8.

reduced on the ground of minority and lesion,[1] or as entered into under error induced by misrepresentation,[2] or as not having been constituted in proper form.[3] Similarly if a contract is justifiably rescinded by one party for material breach by the other he must make restitution of any property acquired under the contract, or its value, if consumed.[4]

COMMON PROPERTY

Where two or more persons become proprietors in common of the same subject with no intention of partnership they become mutually obliged to share the profits and losses of the subject so long as held in common. Thus one owner of a common gable may recover half of the cost of building or repairing it from the other proprietor in common.[5] From this follows the obligation to divide the common property if any one proprietor in common desires to have his own part.[6] This arises particularly where property has been acquired in common, or passes on succession to parties in common, or boundaries require to be settled.

If the parties are partners they are by statute owners in common of the partnership property[7] and on dissolution the partnership property falls to be divided among the partners in the proportion in which profits were shared.[8]

REPETITION OF MONEY

A particular case of restitution is the repetition of money.[9] Where money has been paid by one party to another in error, or for a consideration which has failed, the law imposes on the payee an obligation to repay and confers on the payer a right of

[1] *Scoffier* v. *Read* (1783) Mor. 8936; *Harkness* v. *Graham* (1833) 11 S. 760; (1836) 14 S. 1015.

[2] *Boyd & Forrest* v. *G.S.W. Ry.*, 1915 S.C. (H.L.) 20 (where restitution, and therefore reduction of the contract, impossible); *Spence* v. *Crawford*, 1939 S.C. (H.L.) 52; cf. *Hay* v. *Rafferty* (1901) 2 F. 302.

[3] *Goldston* v. *Young* (1868) 7 M. 188.

[4] *McCormick* v. *Rittmeyer* (1869) 7 M. 854, 858; *Pollock* v. *Macrae*, 1922 S.C. (H.L.) 192; *Mechans* v. *Highland Marine Charters, Ltd.*, 1964 S.C. 48.

[5] *Stark's Trs*, v. *Cooper's Trs.* (1900) 2 F. 1257; cf. *Robertson* v. *Scott* (1886) 13 R. 1127; but contrast *Innes* v. *Hepburn* (1859) 21 D. 832.

[6] Dig. 3, 5, 21; Stair I, 7, 15; More, Note F; Bankt. I, 8, 36; Ersk. III, 3, 56; Kames, *Equity*, I, 1, 3, 2; *Milligan* v. *Barnhill* (1782) Mor. 2486; cf. *Forbes* v. *Ross and Paterson* (1676) Kames Fol. Dic. II, 318.

[7] Partnership Act, 1890, Ss. 20–22.

[8] Ibid., Ss. 39, 44.

[9] Stair I, 7, 7 and 9; More, Note F; Bankt. I, 8, 23; Ersk. III, 1, 10; Bell, *Prin.* §530.

recovery. Following the Roman law the remedies in these cases are known as *condictio indebiti* and *condictio causa data, causa non secuta*;[1] both are equitable remedies and will not be granted if it would be contrary to equity and justice to do so.[2]

Condictio indebiti

Money paid may be recovered by action, if paid under error of fact,[3] or error of law which affects the parties only, such as the misinterpretation of a document,[4] but not under error of general law.[5] The error may be as to the creditor's identity,[6] a clerical error as to amount,[7] an unfounded belief in a person's death,[8] an unfounded belief as to compensation due on the expiry of a mineral lease,[9] an erroneous belief as to title to heritage,[10] ignorance that the pursuer's predecessor had paid,[11] or belief that a condition would be satisfied.[12] It may be uninduced, or have been induced by the payee.[13] Similarly a conditional payment may be recovered if the condition is not satisfied.[14]

Recovery will not, however, be decreed where the payment, though not exigible in law, had in fact been made, as where a claim had prescribed or was otherwise legally unenforceable, yet was due in honour and equity.[15] Nor is payment recoverable where payment not due is made in the full knowledge of that fact,[16] nor

[1] Dig. 12, 4; Cod. 4, 6.

[2] *Haggarty* v. *Scottish T. & G.W.U.*, 1955 S.C. 109; *Scott* v. *York Trailer Co.* 1969 S.L.T. 87.

[3] Stair I, 7, 9; Bankt. I, 8, 23; Ersk. III, 3, 54; *Wallet* v. *Ramsay* (1904) 12 S.L.T. 111; *Haggarty, supra*; cf. *British Oxygen Co.* v. *S.S.E.B.*, 1959 S.C. (H.L.) 17, 48.

[4] *Baird's Trs.* v. *B.* (1877) 4 R. 1005; *Armour* v. *Glasgow R.I.*, 1909 S.C. 916 (interpretation of will); *British Hydro-Carbon Chemicals and B.T.C. Petrs.*, 1961 S.L.T. 280 (interpretation of contract).

[5] *Rowan's Trs.* v. *R.*, 1940 S.C. 30; *Glasgow Corpn.* v. *Inland Revenue*, 1959 S.C. 203, 215. Older Scots law probably allowed recovery in this case also.

[6] *Credit Lyonnais* v. *Stevenson* (1901) 9 S.L.T. 93.

[7] *Wallet* v. *Ramsay* (1904) 12 S.L.T. 111.

[8] *Masters and Seamen of Dundee* v. *Cockerill* (1869) 8 M. 278; *N.B. and Mercantile Ins. Co.* v. *Stewart* (1871) 9 M. 534.

[9] *Duncan, Galloway & Co.* v. *Duncan, Falconer & Co.*, 1913 S.C. 265.

[10] *Cairns* v. *Howden* (1870) 9 M. 284.

[11] *Moore's Exors.* v. *McDermid*, 1913 1 S.L.T. 298.

[12] *Semple* v. *Wilson* (1889) 16 R. 790.

[13] *Duncan, Galloway & Co., supra.*

[14] *Semple* v. *Wilson* (1889) 16 R. 790; cf. *Glasgow Gas Light Co.* v. *Barony Parochial Board* (1868) 6 M. 406.

[15] Bell, *Prin.* §532.

[16] *Brownlie* v. *Miller* (1880) 7 R. (H.L.) 66, 80; *Dalmellington Iron Co.* v. *G.S.W. Ry.* (1889) 16 R. 523; cf. *Balfour Melville* v. *McDermid* (1903) 41 S.L.R. 149; *Agnew* v. *Ferguson* (1903) 5 F. 879; *Moore's Exors.* v. *McDermid*, 1913 1 S.L.T. 298.

where payment was made with the intention to make a gift, confer a benefit,[1] or compromise a claim, or where the payer has acquiesced in a challengeable payment,[2] or acted under an agreement approved of by the court.[3]

Nor will repayment be ordained where the payment has been made for an illegal or immoral consideration, save that a *bona fide* assignee of bonds evidencing a debt is not barred from claiming against the assignor.[4]

Condictio causa data, causa non secuta

Under the principle of this claim, where money has been paid and the agreed consideration therefor has not been received, the payment is recoverable,[5] as where money has been advanced and the work not performed,[6] or money advanced by the charterer of a ship to the master and the voyage not performed,[7] or money paid for apprenticeship and the master died,[8] or money was given in contemplation of a marriage which did not take place,[9] or money has been paid but the contract has been frustrated.[10] But where the contract or consideration was illegal, no recovery is permitted: *in turpi causa melior est conditio possidentis*.[11] But even in this last case if the payment was made under unfair pressure and in the knowledge that it was not due it may be recovered.[12]

If the contract is partially performed, partial recovery is competent, the payer being bound to pay only so far as benefited by the payee's actings.[13] Similarly if one party justifiably rescinds a contract, he may recover any money paid thereunder.[14]

1 *Masters of Dundee* v. *Cockerill* (1869) 8 M. 278; *McGaws* v. *Galloway* (1882) 10 R. 157.

2 *Johnston* v. *J.* (1875) 2 R. 986; cf. *Assets Co.* v. *Guild* (1885) 13 R. 281.

3 *Mackintosh* v. *Rose* (1889) 26 S.L.R. 450.

4 *Ferrier* v. *Graham's Trs.* (1828) 6 S. 818.

5 Dig. 12, 4; Code, 4, 6; Stair I, 9, 7; Bankt. I, 8, 23; Ersk. III, 1, 10; Bell, *Prin.* §530; *Watson* v. *Shankland* (1871) 10 M. 142, 152.

6 *Watson, supra,* 152.

7 *Watson, supra*; affd. 11 M. (H.L.) 51.

8 *Ogilvy* v. *Hume* (1683) 2 B.S. 34.

9 Stair, Ersk., *supra*; *Cantiere San Rocco, infra.*, 124.

10 *Dewar and Primrose* v. *Clyde Shipbuilding Co.*, 1917 1 S.L.T. 297; *Cantiere San Rocco* v. *Clyde Shipbuilding Co.*, 1923 S.C. (H.L.) 105.

11 Stair I, 7, 8; *Bruce* v. *Grant* (1839) 1 D. 583; *Cantiere, supra,* 122.

12 Sometimes called *condictio ob turpem causam*: see Ersk. III, 1, 10; cf. *Jack* v. *Fiddes* (1661) Mor. 2923.

13 *Watson, supra,* 152; cf. *Ogilvy* v. *Hume* (1683) 2 B.S. 34; *Cutler* v. *Littleton* (1711) Mor. 583; contrast *Shepherd* v. *Innes* (1760) Mor. 589.

14 *Lawson* v. *Auchinleck* (1699) Mor. 8402; *Paterson* v. *P.* (1897) 25 R. 144, 191; *Edgar* v. *Hector*, 1912 S.C. 348.

RECOMPENSE OF OUTLAYS

Where one party has benefited from the expenditure of another and the other has lost thereby, without intention of donation, the former must compensate the latter for and to the extent of the benefit.[1] A claim for recompense is incompetent so long as the one party's payments to the other are regulated contractually, and the principle does not justify a claim for payment in excess of the contract price even for extra work or other benefit.[2] Where, however, a contract has been so departed from that an inference of common intention to depart from its provisions regulating payment may be drawn, a claim founded on recompense may be competent.[3] So, too, where a contract has been declared void for technical reasons,[4] or is unenforceable for lack of the requisite kind of proof[5] but not where the contract is *pactum illicitum*.[6]

Claims for recompense have been upheld where a party had done work under a contract but had so departed from the contract that his work could have been rejected and that he could not have sued for the price, but the work had been accepted for what it was worth;[7] or where a party, though in fundamental breach of contract, had benefited his employers;[8] or an agent obtained a bank overdraft without authority and the executors had the benefit thereof.[9]

Incidental benefit to defender

No claim for recompense lies where the one party has benefited merely incidentally from expenditure by another made for another purpose,[10] or for his own benefit,[11] or in the hope of other benefit,[12]

[1] cf. Stair I, 8, 3; Bankt. I, 9, 4; Ersk. III, 1, 11; Bell, *Prin.* §538, criticized *Edinburgh Trams.* v. *Courtenay*, 1909 S.C. 99.

[2] *Wilson* v. *Wallace* (1859) 21 D. 507; *Tharsis Sulphur Co.* v. *McElroy* (1878) 5 R. (H.L.) 171; *A/S Heimdal* v. *Noble* 1907 S.C. 249; *Boyd and Forrest* v. *G.S.W. Ry.*, 1915 S.C. (H.L.) 20; cf. *Menzies, Bruce-Low & Thomson* v. *McLennan* (1895) 22 R. 299.

[3] *Mackay* v. *Lord Advocate*, 1914 1 S.L.T. 33; cf. *Mackenzie* v. *Baird's Trs.*, 1907 S.C. 838; *Parkinson* v. *Commrs. of Works* [1949] 2 K.B. 632; *Head Wrightson Aluminium Co.* v. *Aberdeen Commrs.* 1958 S.L.T. (Notes) 12.

[4] *Cuthbertson* v. *Lowes* (1870) 8 M. 1073; *Duncan* v. *Motherwell Bridge Co.*, 1952 S.C. 131.

[5] *Bell* v. *B.* (1841) 3 D. 1201; *Hamilton* v. *Lochrane* (1899) 1 F. 478 (on which see *Gilchrist* v. *Whyte*, 1907 S.C. 984); *Mackay* v. *Rodger* (1907) 15 S.L.T. 42; *Newton* v. *N.*, 1925 S.C. 715; see also *Gray*, *infra.*

[6] *Jamieson* v. *Watt's Tr.*, 1950 S.C. 265.

[7] *Ramsay* v. *Brand* (1898) 25 R. 1212; *Steel* v. *Young*, 1907 S.C. 360; see *Forrest* v. *Sc. County Investment Co.*, 1916 S.C. (H.L.) 28.

[8] *Abrahams* v. *Campbell*, 1911 S.C. 353; *Graham* v. *U.T.R. Ltd.*, 1922 S.C. 533.

[9] *Commercial Bank* v. *Biggar*, 1958 S.L.T. (Notes) 46.

[10] *Edinburgh Trams.* v. *Courtenay*, 1909 S.C. 99.

[11] *Rankin* v. *Wither* (1886) 13 R. 903; *Wallace* v. *Braid* (1900) 2 F. 754.

[12] *Gray* v. *Johnston*, 1928 S.C. 659.

unless it can be shown that the other had reasonably expected that he would be repaid his outlays.[1] A tenant has no claim against his landlord for improvements made by him on the subjects let save under statute or express contract.[2]

Indirect benefit to defender

A claim for recompense does not lie against a person indirectly benefited by the pursuer's actings, such as a security holder benefited by the repair of the security subjects by the debtor; the latter alone is liable to the tradesman.[3] So too where a firm is benefited by goods obtained by a partner on his own credit.[4]

No benefit to defender

No claim for recompense lies, even if the pursuer has expended time or money and lost thereby, if the defender has not been benefited and is not *lucratus*.

Pursuer's loss

It is a general requisite of a claim for recompense that the pursuer should show that he has suffered loss by fruitless expenditure, or by rendering services unrewarded, in either case without the intention of donation.[5] If the expenditure was necessarily made there is no claim for recompense merely because the other party has benefited or avoided loss thereby.[6] A common case of this is where a person has spent money in the *bona fide* but mistaken belief that the property on which he spent it was his own; in such a case he is entitled to recompense therefor from the true owner who vindicates his property.[7] No such claim lies

[1] *Halliday* v. *Gardine* (1706) Mor. 13419; *Morgan* v. *M's J. F.*, 1922 S.L.T. 247; cf. *Nelson* v. *Gordon* (1874) 1 R. 1093.

[2] *Thomson* v. *Fowler* (1859) 21 D. 453; *Walker* v. *McKnight* (1886) 13 R. 549.

[3] *Selby's Heirs* v. *Jollie* (1795) Mor. 13438; *Cran* v. *Dodson* (1893) 1 S.L.T. 354. It is of course, otherwise if the debtor in instructing the repairs were acting as agent for the security holder.

[4] *White* v. *Macintyre* (1840) 3 D. 334; *Lockhart* v. *Brown* (1888) 15 R. 742.

[5] *Stewart* v. *Steuart* (1878) 6 R. 145; *Chisholm* v. *Alexander* (1882) 19 S.L.R. 835; *Kennedy* v. *Glass* (1840) 17 R. 1085; *Knox & Robb* v. *Scottish Garden Suburb Co.*, 1913 S.C. 872.

[6] *Buchanan* v. *Stewart* (1874) 2 R. 78; *Ruabon S.S. Co.* v. *London Assurance* [1900] A.C. 6; *Edinburgh Trams.* v. *Courtenay*, 1909 S.C. 99; *Cameronia* v. *Hauk*, 1928 S.L.T. 71.

[7] *York Buildings Co.* v. *Mackenzie* (1795) 3 Paton 378; *Selkirk Mags.* v. *Clapperton* (1830) 9 S. 9; *Duff, Ross & Co.* v. *Kippen* (1871) 8 S.L.R. 299; *McDowal* v. *McD.* (1906) 14 S.L.T. 125; *Edinburgh Life Assce. Co.* v. *Balderston*, 1909 2 S.L.T. 323; *Newton* v. *N.*, 1925 S.C. 715; see also *Anderson* v. *A.* (1869) 8 M. 157; *Fernie* v. *Robertson* (1871) 9 M. 437; *McIntyres* v. *Orde* (1881) 18 S.L.R. 604; *Robertson* v. *Scott* (1886) 13 R. 1127.

where the belief was *mala fide* or known to be unjustified.[1] This principle has sometimes been applied to persons spending money on improvements to property held on a temporary title only, such as on lease,[2] or liferent.[3] But loss by itself, as by expenditure incurred in reliance on expressions by the other party, not amounting to promises or representations, gives no ground for recompense.[4]

Expenditure for common benefit

Where one party has incurred expenditure in promoting an object of common interest, but the enterprise fails or is discontinued, the party disburser must be recompensed by the others, as where expenditure was made under an arrangement to board children which was prematurely terminated,[5] or expenses were incurred in establishing a claim to property in which others had an interest.[6]

Property used without authority

Where a person obtains possession of property without authority or by mistake and uses it instead of making restitution, he must pay therefor on the basis of recompense. Thus goods delivered unordered, if kept, must be paid for, as must goods delivered by mistake and consumed,[7] or goods bought in good faith from a thief, and used.[8]

Value of claim

Where a claim for recompense lies, the claim is measured *quantum lucratus*, by the extent of gratuitous benefit which would

1 *Barbour* v. *Halliday* (1840) 2 D. 1279; *D. Hamilton* v. *Johnston* (1877) 14 S.L.R. 298; *Waugh* v. *Nisbett* (1882) 19 S.L.R. 427; *Sones* v. *Mill* (1903) 11 S.L.T. 98; *aliter*, Stair I, 8, 6; *Steuart's Trs.* v. *Hart* (1875) 3 R. 192; *Yellowlees* v. *Alexander* (1882) 9 R. 765.

2 *McIntosh* v. *Ogilvy* (1806) Hume 822; *Officer* v. *Nicolson* (1807) Hume 827. In general a tenant apart from statute, has no claim: *Scott's Exors.* v. *Hepburn* (1876) 3 R. 816.

3 *Reedie* v. *Yeaman* (1875) 12 S.L.R. 625; *Morrison* v. *Allan* (1886) 13 R. 1156; *Morgan* v. *M's Factor*, 1922 S.L.T. 247. In general a liferenter is presumed to expend money for his own benefit: *Rankin* v. *Wither* (1886) 13 R. 903; *Wallace* v. *Braid* (1900) 2 F. 754. So too the fiar or landlord executing improvements is presumed to do so for his own benefit and to have no claim for recompense.

4 *Gilchrist* v. *Whyte*, 1907 S.C. 984.

5 *Dobie* v. *Lauder's Trs.* (1873) 11 M. 749; *Allan* v. *Gilchrist* (1875) 2 R. 587; contrast *Patmore* v. *Cannon* (1892) 19 R. 1004.

6 *Forbes* v. *Ross* (1676) Mor. 13414; *Campbell* v. *Creditors on the Equivalent* (1725) Mor. 9276; *Cowan's Tr.* v. *C.* (1888) 16 R. 7; *Sawers' Factor* v. *S.* (1889) 17 R. 1; see also *Bennett* v. *McLellan* (1891) 18 R. 955.

7 *Findlay* v. *Munro* (1698) Mor. 1767.

8 *International Banking Co.* v. *Ferguson, Shaw & Co.*, 1910 S.C. 182; cf. *Oliver & Boyd* v. *Marr Typefounding Co.* (1901) 9 S.L.T. 170.

otherwise be obtained by the defender.[1] But the extent of benefit derived by a person from goods or services furnished can only generally be measured by their market price. Also the gratuitous benefit cannot exceed the expenditure by the pursuer.[2]

Implied contract

Akin to recompense are cases of implied contract, as where persons incapable of contracting have had necessaries sold to them,[3] or where work has been done under a contract making no express provision for payment,[4] or extra work has been done under a contract,[5] or an employer used an employee's invention,[6] or land was occupied under an arrangement not proved to be gratuitous,[7] or work was done under an arrangement though a contract was ultimately not concluded.[8] In all such cases a reasonable remuneration is due for the goods supplied or services rendered or land occupied, measured *quantum meruit*, by their fair market value, whether they have proved beneficial or not.[9] It may be a narrow question in some circumstances whether a reward is due as recompense or on the basis of implied contract.[10]

NEGOTIORUM GESTIO

A person who, without authority, takes it on himself to administer the affairs of another who, by reason of absence or incapacity, cannot do so himself, in circumstances where it is reasonable to assume that authority would have been granted if circumstances had permitted it being sought, is a *negotiorum gestor*.[11] There is

[1] *Fernie* v. *Robertson* (1871) 9 M. 437, 440; *Ramsay* v. *Brand* (1895) 25 R. 1212; *Edinburgh Trams* v. *Courtenay*, 1909 S.C. 99, 102.

[2] *Binning* v. *Brotherstone* (1676) Mor. 13401; *Edinburgh Life Assce. Co.* v. *Balderston* 1909 2 S.L.T. 323.

[3] Sales of Goods Act, 1893, S. 2; *Scott's Tr.* v. *S.* (1887) 14 R. 1043; cf. *Henderson* v. *Dawson* (1895) 22 R. 895; *Laing* v. *Provincial Homes Co.*, 1909 S.C. 812.

[4] *Hardinge* v. *Clarke* (1856) 18 D. 612; *Pinkerton* v. *Addie* (1864) 2 M. 1270; *Landless* v. *Wilson* (1880) 8 R. 289.

[5] *Wilson* v. *Wallace* (1859) 21 D. 507; *Tharsis Sulphur Co.* v. *McElroy* (1878) 5 R. (H.L.) 171; cf. *Head Wrightson Aluminium, Ltd.* v. *Aberdeen Harbour Commrs.*, 1958 S.L.T. (Notes) 12.

[6] *Mellor* v. *Beardmore*, 1927 S.C. 597.

[7] *E. Fife* v. *Wilson* (1864) 3 M. 323; *Glen* v. *Roy* (1882) 10 R. 329; *Cooke's Circus Bldgs. Co.* v. *Welding* (1894) 21 R. 339.

[8] *Pillans & Wilson* v. *Castlecary Fireclay Co.*, 1931 S.L.T. 532.

[9] *Pinkerton, supra.*

[10] *Anderson* v. *A.* (1869) 8 M. 157; *Mellor, supra.*

[11] Inst. 3, 27, 1; Dig. 3, 5; Code, 2, 18; Stair I, 8, 3; Bankt. I, 9, 2; Ersk. III, 3, 52; Bell, *Comm.* I, 287; *Prin.* §540; *Johnston* v. *M. Annandale* (1726) Mor. 9281.

no place for this intervention if there is no necessity, or a person on the spot is actually authorized to act. Thus persons acting on behalf of a minor,[1] a person abroad,[2] or in prison,[3] or insane,[4] or absent,[5] have been held to be *gestores*.

A gestor has a claim for reimbursement of expenditure reasonably made in acting as such. Having set his hand to the task a gestor must complete it and may not relinquish it unless the principal relieves him or a duly authorized person supersedes him. If he gives up he may be liable in damages for resulting loss.

A gestor must exercise reasonable diligence in his conduct and take reasonable care in the circumstances, and he will be liable for gross omissions or neglect of care,[6] though in cases of necessary interference or emergency he will more readily be excused than when he has been officious and interested.[7] He must account for his intromissions with the beneficiary's property and restore all that he received on the conclusion of his *gestio*.

A gestor has no claim for reward but is entitled to be reimbursed for outlays necessarily and usefully incurred in the reasonable course of acting, even though they should not have proved beneficial,[8] and to be relieved of all liabilities reasonably undertaken. An agent reasonably and properly employed by the *gestor* has a claim for remuneration directly against the beneficiary,[9] and his heir.[10] Many cases of agency of necessity[11] could be treated as cases of *negotiorum gestio*.

SALVAGE

The term salvage is applied to voluntary services which save or contribute to the saving of a ship, her apparel, or cargo, or to the lives of persons belonging to her, when endangered by perils of the sea, shipwreck, fire or capture, and also to the reward

1 *Paterson* v. *Greig* (1862) 24 D. 1370; *Fulton* v. *F.* (1864) 2 M. 893.
2 *Bannatine's Trs.* v. *Cunninghame* (1872) 10 M. 319.
3 *Gemmell* v. *Annandale* (1899) 36 S.L.R. 658.
4 *Ker* v. *Graham* (1757) 2 Pat. 13; *Fernie* v. *Robertson* (1871) 9 M. 437; *Dunbar* v. *Wilson & Dunlop's Tr.* (1887) 15 R. 210.
5 *Kolbin* v. *Kinnear and United Shipping Co.*, 1931 S.C. (H.L.) 128.
6 *Kolbin* v. *Kinnear and United Shipping Co.*, 1931 S.C. (H.L.) 128.
7 *Bannatine's Trs.* v. *Cunninghame* (1872) 10 M. 319; *Kolbin, supra*, 1930 S.C. 724, 757.
8 Stair I, 8, 3; Ersk. I, 7, 28; hence reimbursement to a *gestor* may be larger than the recompense to a person who has benefited another: cf. *Paterson, supra*, 1381.
9 *Fernie* v. *Robertson* (1871) 9 M. 437; *Dunbar* v. *Wilson & Dunlop's Tr.* (1887) 15 R. 210.
10 *Fernie, supra*.
11 Ch. 50, *supra*.

due to salvors for such services.[1] The obligation to pay salvage reward is founded on principles of equity recognized at common law and adopting a principle long recognized by the general maritime law of Western Europe. The principle does not apply to similar services on land.

The right to salvage reward is independent of contract[2] and salvage services rendered by themselves entitle the salvor to reward.[3] Where a vessel is wrecked, stranded or in distress at any place on or near the coasts of, or any tidal water within the limits of the United Kingdom and services are rendered by any person in assisting that vessel or saving the cargo or apparel of that vessel or any part thereof, and where services are rendered by any person other than a receiver in saving any wreck, a reasonable amount of salvage is payable to the salvor by the owner of the vessel.[4]

Subjects of salvage services

Salvage applies only to vessels,[5] their apparel, cargo, or wreck, and freight in the course of being earned, and to aircraft and their apparel and cargo,[6] in on or over the sea, tidal waters, or the shore.

The saving of life at sea is a statutory duty[7] and a title to salvage award exists where services have been rendered wholly or partly in British waters in saving life from any British or foreign vessel,[8] and outside British waters in saving life from any British vessel,[9] or saving life from any aircraft anywhere.[10] But apart from this and from special agreement, no claim for life salvage lies unless some property has also been preserved,[11] whether or not due to any salvage service.[12] A claim for life salvage takes priority over all other salvage claims.[13]

[1] See generally, Stair I, 8, 3; Bankt. I, 8, 5; I, 9, 40; Bell, *Comm.* I, 638; *Prin.* §443, 541; Maclachlan on *Merchant Shipping*; Kennedy on *Civil Salvage*.

[2] *Five Steel Barges* (1890) 15 P.D. 142; *Cargo ex Port Victor* [1901] P. 243.

[3] *The Vandyck* (1882) 5 Asp. M.L.C. 17.

[4] M.S.A., 1894, S. 546. This provision applies also to aircraft: Civil Aviation Act, 1949, S. 51(2).

[5] As to what are 'vessels' see Merchant Shipping Act, 1894, S. 742; *The Mac* (1882) 7 P.D. 126; *Wells* v. *Gas Float Whitton (No. 2)* [1897] A.C. 337; *The Harlow* [1922] P. 175; *Marine Craft Constructors, Ltd.* v. *Erland Blomquist Engineers, Ltd.* [1953] 1 Ll. Rep. 54.

[6] Civil Aviation Act, 1949, S. 51(1).

[7] M.S.A., 1894, S. 422; Maritime Conventions Act, 1911, S. 6.

[8] M.S.A., 1894, S. 544; *Jorgensen* v. *Neptune Steam Fishing Co.* (1902) 4 F. 992.

[9] M.S.A., 1894, S. 544.

[10] Civil Aviation Act, 1949, S. 51.

[11] *The Renpor* (1883) 8 P.D. 115.

[12] *Cargo ex Schiller* (1877) 2 P.D. 145.

[13] M.S.A., 1894, S. 544.

Modes of rendering salvage services

Modes of rendering salvage services include standing by[1] or piloting[2] a vessel in danger; refloating a stranded vessel;[3] fetching assistance to a vessel in danger;[4] giving advice to save a vessel from a local danger;[5] supplying crew or tackle to a vessel in need;[6] rescuing persons who have taken to the boats;[7] removing a vessel or cargo from danger;[8] rescuing a vessel, cargo or persons on board from pirates or revolutionaries;[9] towing a disabled ship[10]; raising a sunken vessel or cargo;[11] trans-shipping or landing cargo from a vessel in danger;[12] saving a derelict or wreck;[13] and extricating a vessel from danger.[14]

Conditions of claiming salvage award

Not only must salvage services have been rendered, but the subject of the services must have been in real danger,[15] and it or some part of it must have been ultimately saved, whether by the salvage services or otherwise;[16] if none be saved, no salvage reward is payable, save by express agreement.

The salvor's services must be voluntary, though they may be the subject of a special agreement, and not rendered in pursuance of official duty, solely in the interest of self-preservation, or under a general contractual obligation.[17] Hence services rendered by the master and crew, a tug towing under a towage contract,[18]

[1] *Walker* v. *N. of S.S.N. Co.* (1892) 19 R. 386; *The Guernsey Coast* (1950) 83 Ll. L. Rep 189.

[2] *The Tafelberg* (1942) 71 Ll. L. Rep. 189.

[3] *The Cayo Bonito* [1904] P. 310; *The Queen Elizabeth* (1949) 82 Ll. L. Rep. 803.

[4] *The Sarah* (1878) 3 P. D. 39; *The Margaret Molinos* [1903] P. 160.

[5] *The Strathnaver* (1875) 1 App. Cas. 58; *The American Farmer* (1947) 80 Ll. L. Rep. 672.

[6] *The Skibladner* (1877) 3 P.D. 24.

[7] *The Carrie* [1917] P. 224.

[8] *The Vandyck* (1882) 5 Asp. M.L.C. 17; *The Demosthenes* (1926) 26 Ll. L. Rep. 99.

[9] *The Erato* (1888) 13 P.D. 163; *The Lomonosoff* [1921] P. 97.

[10] *Vulcan* v. *Berlin* (1882) 9 R. 1057; *The Madras* [1898] P. 90; *Swanney* v. *Citos*, 1925 S.L.T. 491; *The Troilus* [1951] A.C. 820.

[11] *The Cadiz and The Boyne* (1876) 3 Asp. M.L.C. 332.

[12] *The Erato, supra.*

[13] *The Janet Court* [1897] P. 59.

[14] *The Port Caledonia and The Anna* [1903] P. 184.

[15] *The Strathnaver* (1875) 1 App. Cas. 58; *The Aglaia* (1888) 13 P.D. 160; *The Lomonosoff* [1921] P. 97; *The Tower Bridge* [1936] P. 30.

[16] *Cargo ex Sarpedon* (1877) 3 P.D. 28; *Cargo ex Port Victor* [1901] P. 243.

[17] *Cargo ex Schiller* (1877) 2 P.D. 145; *Clan Steam Trawling Co.* v. *Aberdeen Steam Trawling Co.*, 1908 S.C. 651; *Newton* v. *Maatschappij Steam Trawlers*, 1913 1 S.L.T. 72; *The Lomonosoff, supra.*

[18] *Akerblom* v. *Price* (1881) 7 Q.B.D. 129; *The Glenmorven* [1913] P. 141.

government officials acting in the course of their duties, and passengers, do not generally rank as salvage services.[1]

The salvor's services must have been, at least in part, successful, the reward being not for services rendered but for benefit conferred.[2] It is sufficient to show material contribution to the ultimate saving.[3] But where the service is rendered at the request of the master of the vessel in danger in circumstances implying a promise to pay, salvage reward is payable even if the salvor did not make a material contribution to the vessel's ultimate safety.[4]

Parties entitled to claim salvage

The parties entitled to claim reward for salvage services are the owners of the salving vessels,[5] the master, officers, and crew of the salving vessels,[6] and, exceptionally, crew[7] and passengers[8] of the salved vessel. The Crown is entitled to claim salvage in respect of salvage services rendered by or on behalf of Her Majesty.[9] Tugs under towage contract may claim if circumstances have converted towage into salvage services.[10] Salvage may be claimed even though the salving vessel belongs to the same owners as the ship which, as by collision, caused the danger.[11]

Parties liable to contribute to salvage

All property benefited by the salvage services, the owners of the salved ship,[12] owners of the cargo, and parties entitled to freight, but excepting clothing and personal effects of crew and

[1] Crew may claim as salvors if, before rendering the services, their contracts had been terminated by capture or bona fide abandonment of the vessel: *The San Demetrio* (1941) 69 Ll. L. Rep. 5; *The Albionic* [1942] P. 81.

[2] *Steel & Bennie* v. *Hutchison*, 1909 2 S.L.T. 110; *Melanie* v. *San Onofre* [1925] A.C. 246. But see *Ross & Marshall* v. *Davaar* (1907) 15 S.L.T. 29.

[3] *The Hestia* [1895] P. 193; *The Kangaroo* [1918] P. 327.

[4] *The Tarbert* [1921] P. 372.

[5] *The Enchantress* (1860) Lush. 93; *The Gipsy Queen* [1895] P. 176.

[6] *The Martin Luther* (1857) Sw. 287. A seaman is prevented by the M.S.A., 1894, S. 156, from abandoning by any agreement any right he may have or obtain to salvage, but this does not affect any agreement by a seaman on a ship to be employed on salvage service, as to his salvage remuneration, if equitable and honestly made: *Nicholson* v. *Leith Salvage & Towage Co.*, 1923 S.C. 409.

[7] Only if, prior to the salvage services, their contracts of employment had been terminated: *The San Demetrio* (1941) 69 Ll. L. Rep. 5; *The Albionic* [1942] P. 81.

[8] *The Vrede* (1861) Lush. 322; *The Merrimac* (1868) 18 L.T. 92.

[9] Crown Proceedings Act, 1947, S. 8(2). As to Northern Lighthouses Commrs., see *Swanney* v. *Citos*, 1925 S.L.T. 491.

[10] *Akerblom* v. *Price* (1881) 7 Q.B.D. 129; *The Liverpool* [1893] P. 154; *The Glenmorven* [1913] P. 141.

[11] *The Kafiristan* [1938] A.C. 136; *The Susan V. Luckenbach* [1951] P. 197.

[12] If the owner is a foreign sovereign he may decline the jurisdiction and so escape liability: *Grangemouth Towing Co.* v. *Netherlands E.I. Government*, 1942 S.L.T. 228.

passengers[1] and bottomry and respondentia bonds,[2] contribute rateably according to their values to the salvage award.[3] For the saving of life, ship, cargo and freight contribute rateably, so far as preserved.[4] Salvage reward for saving life is payable in priority to other claims for salvage.[5]

Salvage awards

The amount of an award for salvage services is in the discretion of the court, subject to the limitation of the value of the property or interest in the property salved. The court has regard to the danger,[6] the duration and difficulty of the services rendered,[7] the skill and seamanship involved in rendering them,[8] and the value of the property saved,[9] and seeks to reward meritorious services liberally.[10] Risk to the salving ship,[11] and losses and expenses incurred by it[12] are relevant to enhance an award, but misconduct or negligence[13] diminish the award. The court is reluctant to interfere with the assessment made by a judge of first instance.[14]

Recovery

A salvor has a maritime hypothec over salved property,[15] and also a possessory lien over it.[16] He may enforce his claim by action *in rem*[17] or action *in personam*[18] against the owners of property salved to the extent of the property saved for that owner and of

[1] *The Willem III* (1871) L.R. 3 A. & E. 487; *Duncan* v. *Dundee, etc. Shipping Co.* (1878) 5 R. 742.
[2] *The Fusilier* (1865) Br. & Lush. 341.
[3] *The Longford* (1881) 6 P.D. 60; *The Chateaubriand* [1916] W.N. 105.
[4] M.S.A., 1894, S. 544–6.
[5] M.S.A., 1894, S. 544.
[6] *The Krypton* [1954] 2 Lloyd's Rep. 451.
[7] *The Strathgarry* [1895] P. 264.
[8] *The William Beckford* (1801) 3 C. Rob. 355.
[9] *Vulcan* v. *Berlin* (1882) 9 R. 1057; *The City of Chester* (1884) 9 P.D. 182; *The Glengyle* [1898] P. 97.
[10] See *The William Beckford* (1801) 3 C. Rob. 355; *The London Merchant* (1837) 3 Hag. Adm. 394; *The Werra* (1886) 12 P.D. 52; *The City of Chester* (1884) 9 P.D. 182; *The Glengyle* [1898] P. 97; *Greenock Towing Co.* v. *Anchor Line* (1801) 9 S.L.T. 221.
[11] *The Werra* (1886) 12 P.D. 52.
[12] *Bird* v. *Gibb* (1883) 8 App. Cas. 559; *Baku Standard* v. *Angèle* [1901] A.C. 549; *Marburg* v. *Strathbogie* (1903) 11 S.L.T. 314; *The Fairport* [1912] P. 168.
[13] *The Capella* [1892] P. 70; *The Clan Sutherland* [1918] P. 332; *The Kenora* [1921] P. 90.
[14] *Jorgensen* v. *Neptune Steam Fishing Co.* (1902) 4 F. 992.
[15] *The Fusilier* (1865) Br. & Lush. 341; *Cargo ex Schiller* (1877) 2 P.D. 145.
[16] M.S.A., 1894, S. 552; *Walker* v. *Mitre Co.*, 1913 1 S.L.T. 67.
[17] *Hatton* v. *A/S Durban Hansen*, 1919 S.C. 154.
[18] *Duncan* v. *Dundee, Perth and London Shipping Co.* (1878) 5 R. 742.

the value of his interest therein. Claims by competing salvors may be conjoined.[1]

Apportionment

The court may apportion the salvage award in such manner as it thinks just,[2] to the owners, in respect of the risk to and services of their vessel,[3] the master, in respect of his responsibility,[4] and the officers and crew, in respect of their efforts, proportionately to their ratings.[5] Where several vessels or sets of salvors are involved apportionment among them similarly has regard to their respective contributions to the salving.[6] An agreement among salvors for apportionment is binding, so long as fairly and honestly made.[7]

Salvage agreements

An agreement may be made settling the reward due to a salvor for his services, either subject to the usual conditions for a salvage award[8] or making it payable whether or not any property is ultimately saved.[9] Or there may be an agreement to render salvage services, the reward to be settled by agreement or arbitration.[10] It need not be in writing or any set form but must be clearly proved.[11] The owner is normally bound by an agreement made by the master, such being within his ostensible authority,[12] but not where it was not reasonably necessary[13] or the master could have, but did not, obtain authority[14] or where the agreement was not for the shipowner's benefit.[15] The owner of cargo is not bound by a salvage agreement made by the master and may challenge its reasonableness.[16]

1 *Wilson* v. *Rapp*, 1911 S.C. 1360; *Boyle* v. *Olsen*, 1912 S.C. 1235. As to claims in the Sheriff Court see M.S.A., 1894, S. 547.

2 M.S.A., 1894, S. 556; *Fraserburgh Steam Trawling Co.* v. *Glen* (1901) 8 S.L.T. 438. See also *Boyle* v. *Olsen*, 1912 S.C. 1235.

3 *The Enchantress* (1860) Lush. 93.

4 *The Charles* (1872) L.R. 3 A. & E. 536.

5 *The Birnam* (1907) 10 Asp. M.L.C. 462; *The Empire Gulf* [1948] P. 168.

6 *The Clarisse* (1856) Sw. 129.

7 *The Afrika* (1880) 5 P.D. 192.

8 *The Hestia* [1895] P. 193.

9 *The Alfred* (1884) 5 Asp. M.L.C. 214.

10 *Nicholson* v. *Leith Salvage & Towage Co.*, 1923 S.C. 409.

11 *The Graces* (1844) 2 Wm. Rob. 294.

12 *Anderson* v. *Ocean Steamship Co.* (1884) 10 App. Cas. 107.

13 *The Mariposa* [1896] P. 273.

14 *The Elise* (1859) Sw. 436.

15 *The Mariposa, supra.*

16 *The Friesland* [1904] P. 345.

Such an agreement may be set aside if induced by fraud or material misrepresentation,[1] or if inequitable, the reward agreed being inadequate or excessive,[2] particularly if the vessel in danger was driven to conclude the agreement.[3] It is not binding if supervening circumstances render performance of salvage services impossible, or if the services actually rendered are wholly different from those agreed upon.[4] An agreement as to salvage award may be made after the services have been rendered, but such may be set aside if the sum agreed is grossly inadequate and the salvor did not appreciate the value of his services or the circumstances in which it was made are not properly explained or indicate that it was unauthorized.[5]

Towage

An agreement by one vessel to tow another which, though not in any material danger at the time, is unable to make steerage way or to proceed under her own power, justifies a reward similar to though less liberal than salvage.[6] An agreement for towage may be transferred into a claim for salvage by change in circumstances.[7] Service which begins as salvage is not transformed into towage merely because the ship is towed past, or into, ports wherein she would be safe.[8]

GENERAL AVERAGE

When goods are carried by sea any damage or loss sustained by ship, cargo, or freight, if not total, falls on the particular interest affected and is a particular average loss. But where the loss arises in consequence of extraordinary sacrifice deliberately made or expense incurred for the preservation of the several interests involved, it is a general average loss and must be borne in proportion by all the interests affected. This principle, recognized in the sea law of Rhodes and the Mediterranean, was adopted in the Roman law and the general maritime law of

[1] *The Kingalock* (1854) 1 Ecc. & Adm. 263; *The Canova* (1866) L.R. 1 A.& E. 54.

[2] *The Henry* (1851) 15 Jur. 183; *The Phantom* (1866) L.R. 1 A. & E. 58; *Akerblom* v. *Price* (1881) 7 Q.B.D. 129; *The Strathgarry* [1895] P. 264.

[3] *The Altair* [1897] P. 105; *The Port Caledonia and the Anna* [1903] P. 184.

[4] *The Westbourne* (1889) 14 P.D. 132.

[5] *The Macgregor Laird* [1867] W.N. 308; *The Hermione* [1922] P. 162.

[6] *Lawson* v. *Grangemouth Dockyard Co.* (1888) 15 R. 753.

[7] *Bennet* v. *Henderson* (1887) 24 S.L.R. 625; see also *Duke of Portland* v. *Ahdeek Shares Co.* (1900) 8 S.L.T. 81.

[8] *Troilus* v. *Glenogle* [1951] A.C. 820.

Western Europe[1] and accepted in Scots law.[2] The obligation to compensate so as fairly to share the loss arises *ex lege*, independently of agreement.[3] There is no authority for application of the principle to circumstances other than a maritime adventure.[4]

Conditions of right to general average contribution

The conditions which must be satisfied before a claim for general average contribution arises are that both interests involved, that claiming and that claimed against, must have been exposed to a common danger;[5] the danger must have been real and actual;[6] it must not have been attributable to the actionable[7] default of the interest claiming contribution, such as to the ship's unseaworthiness,[8] negligence of the master or crew,[9] or unjustified deviation,[10] or to the dangerous nature of the goods shipped;[11] the property sacrificed must have been intentionally[12] and reasonably sacrificed for the common benefit of the interests involved in the adventure;[13] the sacrifice must have been made on an extraordinary occasion, of extraordinary and abnormal peril,[14] and the property claimed against must have been saved by reason of the sacrifice.[15]

1 Dig. 14, 2, 1; Maclachlan on *Merchant Shipping*; Lowndes and Rudolf on *General Average and The York-Antwerp Rules.*

2 Stair, I, 8, 6; Bankt. I, 8, 5; I, 9, 3, and 29; Ersk. III, 3, 55; Bell, *Comm.* I, 547, 629; *Prin.* §437. An early instance in Scotland is *Lesley and Miller* v. *Weir* (1680) Mor. 13417; cf. *Strang, Steel & Co.* v. *Scott* (1889) 14 App. Cas. 601; Marine Insurance Act, 1906, S. 66; York-Antwerp Rules, 1950, Rule A.

3 *Burton* v. *English* (1883) 12 Q.B.D. 218; *Milburn* v. *Jamaica Fruit Co.* [1900] 2 Q.B. 540.

4 *Falcke* v. *Scottish Imperial Ins. Co.* (1886) 34 Ch. D. 234, 248.

5 *R.M.S.P. Co.* v. *English Bank of Rio de Janeiro* (1887) 19 Q.B.D. 362.

6 *Watson* v. *Firemen's Fund Ins. Co.* [1922] 2 K.B. 355.

7 This principle does not apply if the default were an excepted peril and would *not* have been actionable: *Strang, Steel & Co.* v. *Scott* (1889) 14 App. Cas. 601; *The Carron Park* (1890) 15 P.D. 203; *Milburn* v. *Jamaica* [1900] 2 Q.B. 540.

8 *Goulandris Bros.* v. *Goldman* [1957] 1 Q.B. 74.

9 *The Ettrick* (1881) 6 P.D. 127.

10 *Dreyfus* v. *Tempus Shipping Co.* [1931] A.C. 726; *Hain S.S. Co.* v. *Tate and Lyle, Ltd.* [1936] 2 All E.R. 597; *Reardon Smith Lines, Ltd.* v. *Black Sea and Baltic Ins. Co.* [1939] A.C. 562.

11 *Pirie* v. *Middle Dock Co.* (1881) 4 Asp. M.L.C. 388.

12 *Shepherd* v. *Kottgen* (1877) 2 C.P.D. 585; *The Seapool* [1934] P. 53; *Athel Line* v. *Liverpool etc. Assoc. Ltd.* [1944] K.B. 87.

13 *R.M.S.P. Co., supra*; *The Leitrim* [1902] P. 256.

14 *Societe Nouvelle d'Armement* v. *Spillers and Bakers* [1917] 1 K.B. 865.

15 *Chellew* v. *Royal Commn. on Sugar Supply* [1921] 2 K.B. 627; [1922] 1 K.B. 12. See also Marine Insurance Act, 1906, S. 66(2): 'There is a general average act when any extraordinary sacrifice is voluntarily and reasonably made or incurred in time of peril for the purpose of preserving the property imperilled in the common adventure.'

General average loss

General average losses may be sustained in respect of the ship and her equipment, as by jettison of stores, slipping an anchor or cable, cutting away a boat, straining the engines to force a ship off the ground,[1] or scuttling to extinguish fire;[2] or in respect of the cargo, as by jettison,[3] save in the case of deck cargo, jettison of which does not give rise to a general average claim, unless it was carried on deck by agreement of all parties concerned or in accordance with a custom of trade,[4] or by damage by water used to extinguish a fire,[5] or by sale of part of the cargo at a port of refuge, if necessary to complete the voyage and if it is in the interest of the rest of the cargo that the voyage be completed;[6] or in respect of the freight, where the shipowner to avert a danger so damages part of the cargo as to render it unfit to be carried to its destination, and so sacrifices his entitlement to freight thereon,[7] though not where by reason of inherent defect of the cargo the shipowner has had to put into a port and abandon the attempt to carry the cargo and has thereby lost the freight.[8]

Extraordinary expenditure

Among general average sacrifices may be included extraordinary expenditure incurred for the safety of the whole adventure,[9] such as the cost of discharging the cargo and landing it, but not necessarily of refloating the ship,[10] and expenses incurred in putting into a port of refuge;[11] the cost of repairs may or may not, depending on circumstances, be a general average expenditure.[12] The reward for salvage services is not, but remuneration under a salvage contract and life salvage are, treated as general average expenditure.

[1] *The Bona* [1895] P. 125; see also *Austin Friar Co.* v. *Spillers & Bakers* [1915] 3 K.B. 586; *The Seapool* [1934] P. 53.

[2] *Whitecross Wire Co.* v. *Savill* (1882) 8 Q.B.D. 653.

[3] *Strang, Steel & Co.* v. *Scott* (1889) 14 App. Cas. 601.

[4] *Wright* v. *Marwood* (1881) 7 Q.B.D. 62; *Burton* v. *English* (1885) 12 Q.B.D. 218; *Strang, Steel & Co., supra.*

[5] *Whitecross Wire Co., supra.*

[6] *The Gratitudine* (1801) 3 C. Rob. 240; *Hallett* v. *Wigram* (1850) 9 C.B. 580.

[7] *Pirie* v. *Middle Dock Co.* (1881) 4 Asp. M.L.C. 388; *Iredale* v. *China Traders Ins. Co.* [1900] 2 Q.B. 515.

[8] *Iredale, supra.*

[9] *Anderson* v. *Ocean S.S. Co.* (1884) 10 App. Cas. 107; *Rose* v. *Bank of Australasia* [1894] A.C. 687.

[10] *Job* v. *Langton* (1856) 6 E. & B. 779.

[11] *Svendsen* v. *Wallace* (1884) 13 Q.B.D. 69.

[12] *Hallett* v. *Wigram* (1850) 9 C.B. 580; *Svendsen, supra.*

Liability to contribute

The parties liable to contribute to a general average sacrifice or expenditure are all those whose interests in the common adventure have been benefited thereby,[1] namely, the shipowner, in respect of ship and chartered freight,[2] the charterer, if any, in respect of bill of lading freight, the cargo owner in respect of the cargo,[3] and any other person liable under an express term in the contract of carriage. Passengers' luggage and effects, and crew's effects and wages, do not contribute.[4]

The shipowner usually enforces the liability on behalf of all interests concerned; he has a lien over the cargo for its contribution.[5] Other parties must enforce their claim by action.

Adjustment

The adjustment of the amount to be contributed by the different interests must be effected within a reasonable time; the shipowner frequently employs a professional average adjuster, but a statement prepared by him does not bind the persons concerned in the absence of contract.[6] The amount due, if due to the shipowner, is based on the cost of repairing the ship or making good the equipment sacrificed;[7] if due to the cargo-owner, it is based on the probable state of the cargo if it had arrived;[8] and if due to the party entitled to freight, it is based on the amount of freight lost, after deduction of the charges the shipowner would have incurred to earn it, but not incurred by reason of the sacrifice.

Enforcement of claims

The shipowner has a possessory lien over the cargo for its share of general average,[9] which he may relinquish if the cargo-owner gives an average bond and cash deposit or guarantee in lieu thereof.[10] It is the shipowner's duty to exercise the lien on

1 *Fletcher* v. *Alexander* (1868) L.R. 3 C.P. 375.

2 *Strang, Steel & Co.* v. *Scott* (1889) 14 App. Cas. 601; *Greenshields, Cowie & Co.* v. *Stephens* [1908] A.C. 431.

3 *Strang, Steel & Co.*, *supra*.

4 Bell, *Comm.* I, 636.

5 *Svendsen* v. *Wallace* (1885) 10 App. Cas. 404; *Strang, Steel & Co.*, *supra*.

6 *Wavertree Sailing Ship Co.* v. *Love* [1897] A.C. 373; see also *Robinow & Marjoribanks* v. *Ewing's Trs.* (1876) 3 R. 1134.

7 *Aitchison* v. *Lohre* (1879) 4 App. Cas. 755; *Henderson Bros.* v. *Shankland* [1896] 1 Q.B. 525.

8 *Fletcher* v. *Alexander* (1868) L.R. 3 C.P. 375.

9 *Hingston* v. *Wendt* (1876) L.R. 1 Q.B.D. 367.

10 *Svendsen* v. *Wallace* (1885) 10 App. Cas. 404.

behalf of any other persons entitled to claim contribution and he is himself liable to them if he fails to do so.[1]

The owners and master have powers of enforcing the lien for freight or other charges, by landing and warehousing the goods, or depositing them with a wharfinger, and giving him notice in writing requiring him to retain the goods subject to the claim for freight or other charges. The owner of the goods can only obtain delivery by depositing with the warehouse owner a sum equal to that demanded.[2]

A cargo owner whose cargo has been sacrificed has no right of lien, but may claim damages if the shipowner fails to exercise his lien by requiring payment or the giving of reasonable security for payment before delivery of the surviving cargo.[3]

Shipowner and cargo-owner may each sue to recover contribution from other interests concerned. A cargo-owner liable to contribute in general average may recover from the owner of another ship, whose collision with his ship caused the general average sacrifice.[4]

York–Antwerp Rules

International uniformity in determining what losses must be regarded as general average, and in the manner of calculating the losses and determining how they shall be borne, is desirable, and contracts of affreightment commonly incorporate a provision that questions of general average are to be determined by the York–Antwerp Rules.[5] The Rules consist of a preliminary Rule of Interpretation, Rules lettered A. to G., and Rules numbered 1 to 23.[6] The Rule of Interpretation of 1950 provides that the Rules, if incorporated in the contract of affreightment, apply to the exclusion of any law and practice inconsistent therewith, and, except as provided by the numbered rules, general average is to be adjusted according to the lettered rules.[7]

1 *Strang, Steel & Co.* v. *Scott* (1889) 14 App. Cas. 601.

2 M.S.A., 1894, Ss. 492–501; see *Miebrodt* v. *Fitzsimon* (1875) L.R. 6 P.C. 306; *Smailes* v. *Hans Dessen* (1906) 12 Com. Cas. 117.

3 *Crooks* v. *Allan* (1879) 5 Q.B.D. 38; *Strang, Steel & Co.* v. *Scott* (1889) 14 App. Cas. 601; *Nobel's Explosives* v. *Rea* (1897) 2 Com. Cas. 293.

4 *Morrison S.S. Co.* v. *Greystoke Castle* [1947] A.C. 265.

5 The Rules have their origin in an international Conference held in Glasgow in 1860, and were developed largely at Conferences at York in 1864 and Antwerp in 1877. The rules were revised in 1890, 1924, and 1950. They are not legislation, nor even an international convention, but only a statement of agreed international practice which is effective only if incorporated by reference in the contract.

6 Full text in Lowndes and Rudolf on *General Average*.

7 This in effect reverses the interpretation of the 1924 Rules reached in *Vlassopoulos* v. *British and Foreign Mar. Ins. Co.* [1929] 1 K.B. 187, followed in *Athel Line* v. *Liverpool and London War Risks Ins. Assoc.* [1944] 1 K.B. 87.

PART 5

OBLIGATIONS OF REPARATION ARISING FROM DELICT GENERALLY

CHAPTER 59

THE NATURE OF DELICT AND REPARATION THEREFOR

THE third and fourth branches of the Roman law of obligations dealt with obligations arising *ex delicto* and *quasi ex delicto*.[1] Delicts were harmful conduct done intentionally (*dolo*) or culpably (*culpa*), particularly theft, robbery, *damnum injuria datum*, redressed by the *actio legis Aquiliae*, and *injuria*, redressed by the *actio injuriarum*; certain praetorian delicts were also recognized. Of the delicts the most important were the claims for wrongful damage to proprietary right, (*damnum injuria datum*) and for affront to personality (*injuria*) and from them much of the modern Scottish law of delict has developed.

Quasi-delicts were kinds of conduct similar to delicts, differing as being cases of vicarious liability, i.e. liability for the fault of another, or of strict liability, i.e. liability without proof of fault (*dolus* or *culpa*). Four cases are mentioned, liability of the unfair judge, liability for things thrown or poured down, liability for the fall of things suspended on high, and the liability of shipmasters and tavern or stablekeepers for loss of property in their care.

The terms delict and quasi-delict have been adopted in Scots law[2] but the distinction has come latterly[3] to be equated to that between wrongs of intention, punishable also, or even primarily, criminally, as well as civilly actionable for damages, and wrongs of negligence involving only civil liability. In modern law the distinction is superfluous and the modern law of delict includes categories of wrong developed from both delicts and quasi-delicts, and others derived from other sources.

[1] Inst. 3, 13; 4, 1; cf. Stair I, 3, 2; Mack. III, 1; IV, 1 and 4; Bankt. I, 4, 25–7; Ersk. III, 1, 19; Hume, *Lect.* II, 3; III, 186; *Campbell* v. *Kennedy* (1864) 3 M. 121, 125; Stein, 4 I.C.L.Q. 356.

[2] Bankt. I, 4, 26–7; Ersk. IV, 4, 2; Hume, *Lect.* III, 120, 186; cf. Stair I, 9, 5.

[3] Bell, *Prin.* §543–4, probably following Heineccius; *Palmer* v. *Wick & Pulteneytown S.S. Co.* (1894) 21 R. (H.L.) 39, 43; cf. Stein, 4 I.C.L.Q. 356.

Purpose of delictual obligations

The purpose of the rules as to delictual liability is, in appropriate circumstances, to shift loss from the person suffering it to the person responsible for causing it or allowing it to happen. The legal obligation, conferring the right to compensation for harm suffered and imposing the duty to compensate,[1] arises when harm has been done to another in circumstances where a rule of law had imposed a duty not to cause or permit a harm of that kind. If the duty has been breached a consequential duty to make reparation to the person injured by the breach arises. The duty to make reparation by paying compensation does not arise merely because harm has befallen a person, or been done him by another, but only if that other in causing or permitting the harm to happen was in breach of duty imposed by law on him to the injured person.

Nature of delict

A delict is accordingly conduct, by act or omission, done or allowed to happen by a person, in breach of a general legal duty incumbent on him by force of law and independent of his volition, and owed to, *inter alios*, the injured person, not to do or permit conduct of that kind, thereby causing unjustifiable loss or harm to the injured party and importing a consequential obligation to make reparation to the injured person therefor. Whether in particular circumstances the law does impose a duty not to do or permit potentially harmful conduct and what in particular circumstances the duty is, is a question of law, determined, failing authority of statute or precedent, by consideration of whether a reasonable person in the position of the alleged wrongdoer should have foreseen the possibility of harm, of the general kind which happened, befalling a person in the position of the injured person. In the case of intentional conduct, foresight of the natural and probable consequences of their conduct is attributed to all reasonable persons; in the case of unintentional conduct it is frequently more difficult to determine whether it can fairly be said that a reasonable person in the wrongdoer's place should have foreseen, and prevented or taken care against, the possibility of harm.

In Scots law there is recognized the general duty under the law to refrain from causing persons with whom one comes in contact

[1] In some cases, e.g. nuisance, it is possible to seek interdict to restrain a threatened, or the continuance or recurrence of, a delict.

legally unjustifiable harm of many kinds, and the consequential obligation to make reparation for delict, for wrong or conduct causing unjustifiable loss, injury, or damage.[1] Most of the categories of wrong now recognized are instances or developments of the *actio legis Aquiliae* or the *actio injuriarum*. The purpose of this obligation is to protect the legally recognized interests of individuals in the inviolability of their bodies and minds, in their domestic relations, and in their economic relations and property.[2]

Damnum sine injuria

Loss befalling one person without legally wrongful conduct, i.e. without conduct in breach of duty on the part of another, is not actionable as delict.[3] Loss alone is not actionable, and in some cases, as of trade competition, a man may, even deliberately, cause loss to another without being in breach of duty, and consequently without liability for delict,[4] or may cause loss or injury for which there is legal justification in the circumstances.[5] Again loss caused to another by conduct purely involuntary and beyond a person's control cannot be said to be in breach of duty, and does not subject to liability.[6] Nor is there liability for harm resulting from inevitable accident, an event beyond foresight or counter-precautions.[7]

Injuria sine damno

Conduct in breach of duty which does not cause any identifiable loss is not actionable at all if the wrong is a derivative of the *actio legis Aquiliae*, causing patrimonial loss,[8] but if it is a derivative of the *actio injuriarum* and sounds in hurt feelings damages are due for at least the affront, even if no substantial loss or damage be proved.[9]

[1] Generally Stair I, 9, 1; Mack, III, 1; Forbes, III, 1, 10; Bankt. I, 10, 1; Ersk. III, 1, 2, and 12; Hume, *Lect.* III, 186; Bell, *Prin.* §543; More, *Lect.* I, 331; Walker, *Delict, passim.*

[2] cf. Stair I, 9, 4; Ch. 65–73, *infra.*

[3] *Crofter Co.* v. *Veitch*, 1942 S.C. (H.L.) 1, 7; *Bourhill* v. *Young*, 1942 S.C. (H.L.) 78, 89; *Kenyon* v. *Bell*, 1953 S.C. 125, 128.

[4] *Mogul* v. *McGregor* [1892] A.C. 25; *Ajello* v. *Worsley* [1898] 1 Ch. 274.

[5] *Findlay* v. *Blaylock*, 1937 S.C. 21; *Crofter Co., supra.*

[6] *Ryan* v. *Youngs* [1938] 1 All E.R. 522; *Waugh* v. *Allan*, 1964 S.C. (H.L.) 102.

[7] cf. *Tennent* v. *Earl of Glasgow* (1864) 2 M. (H.L.) 22; *Rothes* v. *Kirkcaldy Waterworks Commrs.* (1882) 9 R. (H.L.) 108.

[8] *Graham* v. *D. Hamilton* (1868) 6 M. 965; *Hay's Trs.* v. *Young* (1877) 4 R. 398; *L.A.* v. *Glengarnock Iron Co.*, 1909 1 S.L.T. 15; *Rankin* v. *Waddell*, 1949 S.C. 555; cf. *Aarons* v. *Fraser*, 1934 S.C. 137, 143, which is too wide.

[9] *Mackay* v. *McCankie* (1883) 10 R. 537; *Stuart* v. *Moss* (1885) 14 R. 299.

Delict and contract

The duty to refrain from causing unjustifiable harm arises *ex lege* and independently of agreement or consent, but a contract, as of employment, may bring persons into such proximity that the one thereby comes to owe the other a duty not to cause him harm,[1] and in some circumstances, as of carriage, one party owes the other duties both by contract and by law,[2] and in others again one party owes another a duty under contract and to a third a duty imposed on him by law.[3] It is sometimes uncertain whether a pursuer is complaining of a breach of contractual duty or of a breach of a general legal duty owed to him *inter alios*.[4]

Delict and restitution

Claims for restitution and claims for reparation for delict both arise by force of law, independently of agreement, but in cases of restitution the fundamental idea is of restoring for the avoidance of unjust benefit whereas in cases of delict the fundamental idea is of making reparation for harm unjustifiably done.

Delict and crime

The same set of facts may amount to both a delict and a crime, but the different aspects of the conduct are treated separately, in different courts, by distinct procedures. Hence delicts are frequently called civil wrongs, as contrasted with criminal wrongs. Civil action and criminal prosecution are, in general, concurrent and independent.[5] Conduct which is criminal at common law is normally, possibly always, also an actionable delict against the injured person. Conduct which is criminal by statute is not automatically, but may be, also actionable as a delict. But many recognized delicts are not crimes. It is irrelevant, in determining whether conduct is delictual or not, to consider whether it is criminal, or 'wrongful' by any social, moral or other non-legal standard, or whether it is 'illegal' or 'unlawful'; it is delictual only if it is done in breach of legal duty; if it is, it may then loosely be called wrongful or even unlawful.[6] Wrongfulness is a

[1] *Donoghue* v. *Stevenson*, 1932 S.C. (H.L.) 31, 64.

[2] e.g. *Williamson* v. *N. of S.S.N. Co.*, 1916 S.C. 554.

[3] *Donoghue, supra*; cf. *Edgar* v. *Lamont*, 1914 S.C. 277.

[4] e.g. *Drinnan* v. *Ingram*, 1967 S.L.T. 205.

[5] Bell, *Prin.* §548, 551; for exceptions see Game (Sc.) Act, 1832, S. 16; Game Laws Amdt. (Sc.) Act, 1877, S. 11.

[6] cf. *Ward* v. *Abraham*, 1910 S.C. 299, where the court approached the problem from the wrong end, and said: conduct not unlawful, *ergo* not delictual.

consequence, not a cause or a prerequisite, of conduct being held to be delictual.

Physical factors in delict

The physical factor in all cases of delict is human conduct, by act or omission, which is subject to the doer's voluntary control, is in breach of legal duty, and which has harmful consequences for the complainer. Events of nature,[1] or happenings uncontrollable by the will of the person involved,[2] do not amount to delictual conduct. Also, the physical factor in delict includes not merely the bare act or omission, but also its immediate consequences;[3] reckless or careless conduct gives no right of action unless there is harm, and only to someone who is injured thereby. Liability for delict is founded on wrongful harm, not on bare conduct.

Mental factors in delict

Conduct in breach of duty, by act or omission, may be done, or allowed to happen, by a person with differing mental states in different circumstances. It may, firstly, be done deliberately, intentionally, maliciously, *dolo* or *animo injuriandi*, with which state of mind falls to be equated[4] reckless conduct, or the conduct of one who 'takes a chance' or is indifferent to obvious risks.[5]

Or, secondly, it may be done unintentionally but in breach of duty, negligently, i.e. culpably carelessly, or *culpa*.[6] Negligence in law connotes not merely neglect or carelessness, but unintentional breach of the duty incumbent by law,[7] which may take

[1] e.g. lightning killing a person. But events of nature, e.g. rainfall, if interfered with by a person, may subject him to liability: e.g. *Kerr* v. *Earl of Orkney* (1857) 20 D. 298.

[2] e.g. a vehicle injuring a pedestrian, the driver having unforeseeably died at the wheel: *Waugh* v. *Allan*, 1964 S.C. (H.L.) 102. But conduct which could, and should, have been, but was not, controlled, e.g. letting a car get out of control, does amount to delictual conduct; cf. *Balmer* v. *Hayes*, 1950 S.C. 477 (driver, who had previously had fits, having fit while driving); *Mathieson* v. *Dunbartonshire C.C.*, 1926 S.C. 795; *Caminer* v. *Northern & London Inv. Tr. Ltd.* [1951] A.C. 88 (fall of trees).

[3] A bare act or omission without resultant harm, e.g. careless driving, may result in criminal liability, but not normally in civil liability.

[4] cf. *Callendar* v. *Milligan* (1849) 11 D. 1174, 1176.

[5] A person's intention or his recklessness fall to be determined by his conduct and the circumstances in which it is done; he must be assumed to foresee those risks which all reasonable persons foresee: cf. *Crofter Co.* v. *Veitch*, 1942 S.C. (H.L.) 1, 28.

[6] The terms *culpa* and 'fault' are sometimes used very widely as including all mental elements relevant to infer liability.

[7] In English law negligence is also the name of a specific tort or category of actionable wrong, corresponding to the Scottish delicts of negligent harm to person, to domestic relations, and to property. In the phrase 'contributory negligence', however, negligence means merely carelessness and does not involve any breach of legal duty of care.

place notwithstanding the taking of care, if the care was deemed inadequate in the circumstances; *culpa* or legal negligence is absence of, or inadequate, care or diligence to implement the legal duty not to cause or permit harm.[1] Indeed if in the circumstances there was no legal duty to take care a person may be careless with impunity, even though harm results.[2]

Or, thirdly, in the cases known as cases of strict liability,[3] the conduct may be culpable only in having failed to prevent the harm, the occurrence of which, in the absence of one of the limited defences recognized in such cases, infers liability for delict.

Or, lastly, in the cases of absolute liability sometimes imposed by statute, the conduct may be culpable and infer liability if the harm directed to be prevented is allowed to happen at all, entirely irrespective of care and diligence.[4]

Some kinds of wrongs can be caused by conduct with only one or another of these concomitant states of mind, while others can be done, in different circumstances, sometimes with one, sometimes with another, concomitant mental state.[5]

Fault liability and risk liability

Intentional and negligent wrongs are both comprehended under the idea of liability for fault, in that not merely is the conduct in breach of the duty imposed in the circumstances by law but the fact that harm has resulted carries an underlying idea of moral blameworthiness, *culpa* or fault, in having caused or permitted the breach.

In the cases of strict liability and of absolute liability under statute there is little or no underlying idea of moral fault; the law in fact imposes a duty to prevent harm in cases where the defender is deemed to have created or permitted a risk of harm; if the risk eventuates he is held liable for the resultant harm,

[1] 'Negligence *per se* will not make liability unless there is first of all a duty which here has been failure to perform through that neglect'; *Clelland* v. *Robb*, 1911 S.C. 253, 256.

[2] cf. *Mathieson* v. *Dunbartonshire C.C.*, 1926 S.C. 795; *Hedley Byrne & Co.* v. *Heller & Partners* [1964] A.C. 465.

[3] Sometimes called cases of liability without fault. The recognized cases of strict liability are: harm to person or animal by a dangerous animal; nuisance; escape of a danger from one's land; and cases under statutes where there is liability unless a limited defence can be invoked.

[4] e.g. *Millar* v. *Galashiels Gas Co.*, 1949 S.C. (H.L.) 31; *Hamilton* v. *N.C.B.*, 1960 S.C. (H.L.) 1.

[5] It is convenient, though logically unjustifiable, to treat the happening of a harm which the person should have taken effectual precautions to prevent, or should have absolutely prevented from happening, as akin to letting it happen by not taking adequate precautions.

independently of fault or moral blameworthiness. He may have striven hard to prevent or avoid or minimize the risk, but he is deemed to have created the risk and to be liable if harm results.

Older cases sometimes stated that *culpa* was the indispensable basis of delictual liability,[1] but this view cannot now be supported and there are several recognized categories of cases of liability without fault.

Motive and malice

The motive underlying conduct i.e. the ultimate purpose or object sought, is not generally relevant to liability;[2] in general a good motive does not exculpate, nor a bad one inculpate; exceptionally, bad or malicious motive is relevant.

Malice in the sense of intention to injure[3] is synonymous with with intentional or deliberate wrongdoing, and need not be separately proved in any case of intentional conduct causing harm. Malice in the sense of hatred, spite, malevolence or ill-will,[4] is relevant only exceptionally, in those cases where a malicious motive is relevant, namely, defamation (to rebut the defences of qualified privilege or fair comment), malicious prosecution, conspiracy to injure, malicious falsehood, use of land *in aemulationem vicini*, and wrongful use of diligence.

[1] e.g. *Laurent* v. *Lord Advocate* (1869) 7 M. 607, 611; *Moffat* v. *Park* (1878) 5 R. 13, 17; *McLaughlan* v. *Craig*, 1948 S.C. 599, 610; *Hester* v. *Macdonald*, 1961 S.C. 370, 390; *Henderson* v. *John Stuart (Farms) Ltd.*, 1963 S.C. 245, 248.

[2] *Crofter Co.* v. *Veitch*, 1942 S.C. (H.L.) 1.

[3] Sometimes called malice in law; see also *Crofter Co.*, *supra*, 24.

[4] Sometimes called actual malice or malice in fact.

CHAPTER 60

PARTIES AND MODES OF LIABILITY

Title to sue for reparation for delict

THE pursuer in an action of delict must satisfy the court that he has both a title to sue, connoting that he is the person, or one of the persons, to whom the alleged duty in issue was owed, and one entitled to complain of its breach,[1] and an interest to sue, in that he has lost or will lose by that breach. These are separate but connected factors, but a pursuer having a title is generally presumed also to have an interest to sue.[2] If a pursuer does not have both title and interest his action falls to be dismissed; whether he has or has not title and interest is a question of law.[3] The pursuer must have title to sue when the action is brought.[4] Absence of, or defect in title cannot be cured by the consent of the person entitled.[5] Title can frequently be established by showing that the pursuer was one of a group, e.g. employees, passengers in a vehicle, relatives of a deceased, to whom a duty was owed. Interest is usually established by allegations of pecuniary loss resulting from the alleged delict:[6] Cases of *damnum sine injuria* are cases of interest without title, cases of *injuria sine damno* of title without interest.

Title to defend

A person called as defender always has a title to defend to try to exculpate himself, to contend that the pursuer was himself solely or partly to blame, and to bring in another party who, he contends, was also, or alternatively, to blame. Other parties may also have title and interest to defend and may seek to be sisted so that their rights may not be prejudiced;[7] the court will normally allow them to be sisted if the action would affect their rights.[8]

[1] *Nicol* v. *Dundee Harbour Trs.*, 1915 S.C. (H.L.) 7, 12.

[2] *Pyper* v. *Christie* (1878) 6 R. 143; but see *Rankin* v. *Waddell*, 1949 S.C. 555.

[3] e.g. *Eisten* v. *N.B. Ry.* (1870) 8 M. 980; *McLachlan* v. *Bell* (1895) 23 R. 126; *Bourhill* v. *Young*, 1942 S.C. (H.L.) 78; *McKay* v. *Scottish Airways*, 1948 S.C. 254; *Agnew* v. *Laughlan*, 1948 S.C. 656.

[4] *Symington* v. *Campbell* (1894) 21 R. 434; *Bentley* v. *Macfarlane*, 1964 S.C. 76.

[5] *Hislop* v. *MacRitchie's Trs.* (1881) 8 R. (H.L.) 95.

[6] *Rankin* v. *Waddell*, 1949 S.C. 555.

[7] *Gas Power Co.* v. *Power Gas Corpn. Ltd.*, 1911 S.C. 27; *Zurich General Accident Ins. Co.* v. *Livingston*, 1938 S.C. 582.

[8] *Keiller* v. *Dundee Mags.* (1886) 14 R. 191; see also *McDermott* v. *Western S.M.T. Co.*, 1937 S.C. 239.

Capacity to pursue or defend

The capacity of particular parties to sue or defend actions arising *ex delicto* is an aspect of the legal capacity of persons of particular status, and of associations and corporations.[1]

Liability of alleged wrongdoer

A defender's liability to make reparation for delict depends on proof that he is the person immediately or mediately in breach of a recognized legal duty owed in the circumstances to the pursuer, which breach has caused the pursuer the harm of which he complains. The defender actually sued is not necessarily the wrongdoer truly liable and a defender may not be liable on the ground of fault alleged though he might have been liable on some other ground.

Personal liability

An actual wrongdoer is always personally liable, unless protected by special privilege or immunity: *culpa tenet suos auctores*.[2] This is so even though the actual wrongdoer was acting under instructions,[3] unless he were acting merely as a channel of communication.[4] Similarly the person who instructs a wrong is personally liable, though he does not personally commit it.[5] In general one person is not liable for the fault of another; one spouse is not liable for the other's delict.[6]

Joint and several liability

Where two or more persons have contributed, either equally or in varying proportions, to the commission of a delict, they are liable jointly and severally therefor, i.e. all are liable jointly, and each is also liable for the whole wrong.[7] The injured person may

[1] See Chs. 19–28, *supra*.

[2] Ersk. III, 1, 15; *Woodhead* v. *Gartness Mineral Co.* (1877) 4 R. 469; *Grieve* v. *Brown*, 1926 S.C. 787.

[3] *Dobbie* v. *Halbert* (1863) 1 M. 263; *Miller* v. *Renton* (1885) 13 R. 309; cf. Bankt. I, 10, 27; *Mackenzie* v. *Goldie* (1866) 4 M. 277.

[4] *Wilson* v. *Purvis* (1890) 18 R. 72; *Crawford* v. *Adams* (1900) 2 F. 987.

[5] Ersk. III, 1, 15; *Dobbie, supra*; *Stephen* v. *Thurso Police Commrs.* (1876) 3 R. 535; *Cameron* v. *Fraser* (1881) 9 R. 26; *Miller, supra*; *Peffers* v. *Countess of Lindsay* (1894) 22 R. 84; *Crawford, supra*; *Fleming* v. *Gemmill*, 1908 S.C. 34.

[6] *Barr* v. *Neilsons* (1868) 6 M. 651; *Milne* v. *Smith* (1892) 20 R. 95; *Hook* v. *McCallum* (1905) 7 F. 528; *Bruce* v. *Murray*, 1926 S.L.T. 236.

[7] Stair I, 9, 5; Bankt. I, 10, 4; Ersk. III, 1, 15; IV, 1, 15; Hume, *Lect.* III, 124; Bell, *Prin.* §56, 550.

sue any one or more or all, and recover his full loss from the one, or those, sued.[1]

Such liability exists both where the wrongdoers acted in concert or in pursuance of a common plan,[2] and where wrongdoers, by actings quite separate and distinct, have contributed to one single common harmful result,[3] but not where separate wrongdoers have committed distinct wrongs causing separate harms to the same person, though the wrongs are of the same type, and close in space and time.[4] Joint and several liability exists also where other wrongdoers who cannot be identified or over whom the court has no jurisdiction were involved in the wrongdoing along with those actually called as defenders,[5] and where some defenders are absolved.[6] By statute partners are jointly and severally liable for delicts committed by the firm or any partner, or a servant or agent of the firm, against a third party, but only subsidiarily to the liability of the firm.[7]

Allocation of responsibility and contribution

Where a court finds two or more defenders jointly and severally in fault, it must, without prejudice to the pursuer's right to a joint and several decree, allocate the responsibility, by stating the proportion or percentage of fault applicable to each defender.[8] If it cannot allocate with precision, it should allocate responsibility equally; the allocation should be made on the basis of causation.[9] Where, in pursuance of a joint and several decree, a pursuer recovers damages or expenses from one defender, the latter may recover from the other defenders against whom decree passed, a contribution in proportion to their respective shares of responsibility as found by the court or jury.[10] A defender who has paid damages or expenses may also by separate action

[1] *Ross* v. *Baird* (1848) 10 D. 1493; *Palmer* v. *Wick and Pulteneytown S.S. Co.* (1894) 21 R. (H.L.) 39; *Ellerman Lines* v. *Clyde Nav. Trs.*, 1909 S.C. 690.

[2] *Smith* v. *O'Reilly* (1800) Hume 605; *Ware* v. *Abraham*, 1910 S.C. 299.

[3] *Belmont Laundry* v. *Aberdeen Steam Laundry Co.* (1898) 1 F. 45; *Fleming* v. *Gemmill*, 1908 S.C. 340; *Arneil* v. *Paterson* 1931 S.C. (H.L.) 117; *Drew* v. *Western S.M.T.*, 1947 S.C. 222; *N.C.B.* v. *Thomson*, 1959 S.C. 353.

[4] *Barr* v. *Neilson* (1868) 6 M. 651; *Sinclair* v. *Caithness Flagstone Co.* (1898) 25 R. 703; *Conway* v. *Dalziel* (1901) 3 F. 918; *Hook* v. *McCallum* (1905) 7 F. 528; *Turnbull* v. *Frame*, 1966 S.L.T. 24.

[5] cf. *Duthie* v. *Caledonian Ry.* (1898) 25 R. 934.

[6] *Fleming* v. *Gemmill*, 1908 S.C. 340.

[7] Partnership Act, 1890, Ss. 10, 12; *Mair* v. *Wood*, 1948 S.C. 83.

[8] Law Reform (Misc. Prov.) (Sc.) Act, 1940, S. 3.

[9] *Drew* v. *Western S.M.T. Co.*, 1947 S.C. 222, 240.

[10] *Palmer* v. *Wick and Pulteneytown S.S. Co.* (1894) 21 R. (H.L.) 39; Law Reform (Misc. Prov.) (Sc.) Act, 1940, S. 3(1).

recover from any other person who, if sued, might also have been held liable, such contribution, if any, as the court may deem just.[1] The defender's claim for relief must be founded on a debt to the pursuer constituted by decree, not on a settlement reached with the pursuer.[2] Alternatively he may blame that other party and bring him into the pursuer's action as a third party.[3] Alternatively he may bring an action of relief against that other party and recover total or partial relief.[4] A defender may also have a contractual right of relief against another party entitling him to total or partial relief.[5]

Several liability

Where disconnected wrongs, even of the same kind, are done to a person by two or more wrongdoers, they are severally liable, i.e. each is liable for his own wrong only.[6]

In cases of doubt defenders may be sued 'jointly and severally, or severally',[7] but even under a conclusion against defenders 'jointly and severally' it is competent to find fault by one or other or some and not by both or all defenders.[8]

Vicarious liability

Vicarious liability exists where one person may be sued and held liable for a wrong actually committed by another.[9] It is justified on various bases, that 'he doth, that causeth do',[10] because it ensures vigilance in selecting and superintending servants,[11] because the servant is identified with his master,[12] or by the maxims *qui facit per alium facit per se* and *respondeat superior*,[13] but the only real justification is expediency, the need

[1] 1940 Act, S. 3(2); *N.C.B.* v. *Thomson*, 1959 S.C. 353.

[2] *Duncan's Trs.* v. *Steven* (1897) 24 R. 880; *Glasgow Corpn.* v. *Turnbull*, 1932 S.L.T. 457; *N.C.B., supra*.

[3] R.C. 85 and Form 7; *Bush* v. *Belling*, 1963 S.L.T. (Notes) 69. This is now the preferable procedure. See also *Aitken* v. *Norrie*, 1967 S.L.T. 4; *Travers* v. *Neilson*, 1967 S.L.T. 64.

[4] cf. *Lister* v. *Romford Ice Co.* [1957] A.C. 555; *N.C.B., supra*, at 373.

[5] *Hamilton* v. *Anderson*, 1953 S.C. 129; *N. of S. Hydro-Electric Board* v. *Taylor*, 1956 S.C. 1.

[6] *D. Atholl* v. *Dalgleish* (1822) 1 S. 511; *Barr* v. *Neilsons* (1864) 4 M. 651; *Taylor* v. *McDougall* (1885) 12 R. 1304; *Hook* v. *McCallum* (1905) 7 F. 528; *Sinclair* v. *Caithness Flagstone Co.* (1898) 25 R. 703; *Conway* v. *Dalziel* (1901) 3 F. 918; *Fleming* v. *McGillivray*, 1946 S.C. 1.

[7] *Ellerman Lines* v. *C.N.T.*, 1909 S.C. 690.

[8] *Fleming* v. *Gemmill*, 1908 S.C. 340; *Ellerman Lines, supra*.

[9] See generally Atiyah, *Vicarious Liability*.

[10] Stair I, 9, 5; cf. Bankt. I, 10, 47.

[11] *Gregory* v. *Hill* (1869) 8 M. 282, 288.

[12] *Baird* v. *Hamilton* (1826) 4 S. 790; *Gregory, supra*, 284.

[13] *Gregory, supra*, 287.

to impose liability on a defender who usually can pay and who is frequently insured.[1]

Where vicarious liability exists it is not alternative or substituted liability, as the actual wrongdoer still remains liable, but is a special instance of joint and several liability where one defender is being sued rather than both or all of the possible defenders.[2] Whether vicarious liability exists or not in a particular case is a question of law. If a pursuer sues a defender other than the actual wrongdoer he must aver and prove facts importing vicarious liability of the defender for the wrongdoer, and the defender may disprove those facts.[3]

Vicarious liability of the Crown

The Crown is subject[4] to the liabilities of a private person in respect of delicts committed by its servants[5] or agents, including independent contractors,[6] and for infringement by a servant or agent of a patent, trade mark or copyright, if committed with the authority of the Crown,[7] but not for anything done or not done by an officer of the Crown in the exercise of judicial duties,[8] for anything done or not done in relation to post or telephone services, save as provided by Post Office regulations,[9] nor for the death of or injury to a member of the armed forces on duty in circumstances attributable to service for pension purposes.[10]

Vicarious liability of corporations

A corporation is vicariously liable for the wrongs of its agents and servants,[11] whether wrongs of intention[12] or of negligence,[13]

[1] cf. *Baird, supra*; *Gregory, supra*; *Mair* v. *Wood*, 1948 S.C. 83, 87.

[2] *Jones* v. *Manchester Corpn.* [1952] 2 Q.B. 852; *Lister* v. *Romford Ice. Co.* [1957] A.C. 555.

[3] *Power* v. *Central S.M.T. Co.*, 1949 S.C. 376.

[4] Crown Proceedings Act, 1947, S. 2(1).

[5] Defined, S. 2(6); The definition excludes local authorities and their officials, hospital boards and most public corporations and bodies, and the police; the chief constable is vicariously liable for his constables: Police (Sc.) Act, 1967, S. 39 (not yet in force).

[6] S. 38(2).

[7] S. 3.

[8] S. 2(5).

[9] S. 9.

[10] S. 10; *Adams* v. *War Office* [1955] 3 All E.R. 245.

[11] *Beaton* v. *Glasgow Corpn.*, 1908 S.C. 1010, 1013.

[12] *National Exchange Co.* v. *Drew & Dick* (1855) 2 Macq. 903; *Jardine* v. *Carron Co.* (1864) 2 M. 1101; *Clydesdale Bank* v. *Paul* (1877) 4 R. 626; *Houldsworth* v. *City of Glasgow Bank* (1880) 7 R. (H.L.) 53; *Citizens Life Assce. Co.* v. *Brown* [1904] A.C. 423.

[13] *Mersey Docks and Harbour Board* v. *Gibbs* (1866) L.R. 1 H.L. 93; *Virtue* v. *Alloa Police Commrs.* (1873) 1 R. 285; *Percy* v. *Glasgow Corpn.*, 1922 S.C. (H.L.) 144; *Kilboy* v. *S.E. Fire Area Joint Cttee.*, 1952 S.C. 280; *Macdonald* v. *Glasgow Western Hospitals*, 1954 S.C. 453.

done within the scope of the agent's authority or the course of the servant's employment.

VICARIOUS LIABILITY OF INDIVIDUALS

(a) FOR AGENT

A principal is vicariously liable to an injured person for a wrong actually done by his agent or mandatary, if the principal expressly authorized the conduct,[1] or subsequently ratified it,[2] or if the act were within the ostensible or usual authority of the agent,[3] whether it were done for the principal's benefit,[4] or for the agent's own benefit,[5] or even was expressly forbidden,[6] but not if the conduct falls wholly outside the scope of the agent's authority.[7]

For the purposes of delict 'agent' is interpreted widely and covers many cases of acting for another in a matter in which the latter has an interest.[8] If the conduct is within the scope of the agent's authority the principal is liable even though the agent made a mistake of fact or of law in doing what he did.[9] The agent remains personally liable,[10] and he can probably not avail himself of any immunity which protects the principal.[11] Under this general principle a firm is vicariously liable for the wrongs of its partners to third parties,[12] but not for the wrong of a partner to another partner.[13]

1 *Monaghan* v. *Taylor* (1886) 2 T.L.R. 685; *Crawford* v. *Adams* (1900) 2 F. 987.

2 *Buron* v. *Denman* (1848) 2 Ex. 167; *Eastern Counties Ry.* v. *Broom.* (1851) 6 Ex. 314.

3 *Makin* v. *Union Bank* (1873) 45 Sc. Jur. 323; *Neville* v. *C. & A. Modes*, 1945 S.C. 175; *Ormrod* v. *Crosville Motor Services* [1953] 2 All E.R. 753; *Carberry* v. *Davies* [1968] 2 All E.R. 817.

4 *Barwick* v. *English Joint Stock Bank* (1867) L.R. 2 Ex. 259.

5 *Lloyd* v. *Grace, Smith & Co.* [1912] A.C. 716; *United Africa Co.* v. *Saka Owoade* [1955] A.C. 130.

6 *Yeo* v. *Wallace* (1867) 5 S.L.R. 253; *Sinclair, Moorhead & Co.* v. *Wallace* (1880) 7 R. 874; *Nicklas* v. *New Popular Cafe Co.* (1908) 15 S.L.T. 735.

7 *Wardrope* v. *Hamilton* (1876) 3 R. 876; *Hockey* v. *Clydesdale Bank Ltd.* (1898) 1 F. 119; *Beard* v. *L.G.O.C.* [1900] 2 Q.B. 530; *Percy* v. *Glasgow Corpn.*, 1922 S.C. (H.L.) 144, 151.

8 cf. *Horn* v. *N.B. Ry.* (1878) 5 R. 1055; *Monaghan*, *supra*; *Ormrod*, *supra*; see also *Mair* v. *Wood*, 1948 S.C. 83.

9 *Percy*, *supra.*

10 *Sinclair, Moorhead & Co.*, *supra*; *Smith* v. *Taylor* (1882) 10 R. 291.

11 cf. *Adler* v. *Dickson* [1955] 1 Q.B. 158.

12 Partnership Act, 1890, Ss. 5, 10; Bell, *Prin.* §356; *Jardine's Trs.* v. *Drew* (1864) 2 M. 1101; *Trail* v. *Smith's Trs.* (1876) 3 R. 770; *Gordon* v. *British and Foreign Metaline Co.* (1886) 14 R. 75; *New Mining and Exploring Syndicate Ltd.* v. *Chalmers & Hunter*, 1912 S.C. 126.

13 *Mair*, *supra.*

(b) FOR SERVANT

A person is vicariously liable for wrongs committed by his servant or employee, done when acting in the course of his employment, but not if done when acting outwith the course of his employment.[1]

Wrongdoer must be servant

The relationship must be that of employment (*locatio operarum*) and not *locatio operis faciendi*. Whether the relationship in a particular case is that of master and servant or not is in each case a question of fact, the onus of proof of which is on the pursuer.[2] Traditionally the main factor in determining this was whether the employer had the power of detailed control of the employee's work,[3] but today persons may be servants or employees though exercising professional skill and independent judgment and having a large measure of discretion in performing their duties,[4] and the power to select and dismiss, the mode of payment, the duration and place of employment and other considerations are also relevant.[5]

A superior servant is not vicariously liable for an inferior;[6] the employer is vicariously liable for both.[7]

If the servant of one employer is lent to or hired by another, the presumption is that the permanent employer, rather than the temporary master, is vicariously liable,[8] but it may be shown that

[1] *Baird* v. *Hamilton* (1826) 4 S. 790; *Duncan* v. *Findlater* (1839) MacL. & Rob. 119; *Bartonshill Coal Co.* v. *Reid* (1858) 3 Macq. 266, 276, 283.

[2] *Stephen* v. *Thurso Police Commrs.* (1876) 3 R. 535; *Scottish Ins. Commrs.* v. *Edinburgh R.I.*, 1913 S.C. 751; *Dow* v. *McNeill*, 1925 S.C. 50; *Reidford* v. *Aberdeen Mags.*, 1933 S.C. 276.

[3] *Bartonshill Coal Co.* v. *Reid* (1858) 3 Macq. 266, 283; *Stephen*, *supra*; *Lavelle* v. *Glasgow R.I.*, 1932 S.C. 245.

[4] *Macdonald* v. *Glasgow Western Hospitals*, 1954 S.C. 454; cf. *Mersey Docks & Harbour Board* v. *Coggins & Griffith, Ltd.* [1947] A.C. 1; *Stevenson, Jordan & Harrison* v. *Macdonald and Evans* [1952] 1 T.L.R. 101.

[5] *Malley* v. *L.M.S. Ry.*, 1944 S.C. 129, 136; *Short* v. *J. & W. Henderson*, 1946 S.C. (H.L.) 24; *Kilboy* v. *S.E. Fire Area Joint Committee*, 1952 S.C. 280. Contrast *Lavelle*, *supra*; *Reidford* v. *Aberdeen Mags.* 1933 S.C. 276 with *Macdonald*, *supra*; see also *Gold* v. *Essex C.C.* [1942] 2 K.B. 293; *Collins* v. *Hertfordshire C.C.* [1947] K.B. 598; *Cassidy* v. *Min. of Health* [1951] 2 K.B. 343; *Bullard* v. *Croydon Hospital Cttee.* [1953] 1 Q.B. 511; *Roe* v. *Ministry of Health* [1954] 2 Q.B. 66; *Fox* v. *G. & S.W. Hospitals Board*, 1955 S.L.T. 337.

[6] But a chief constable is liable for the wrongs of constables: Police (Sc.) Act, 1967, S. 39.

[7] cf. *Wilson* v. *Merry & Cuninghame* (1868) 6 M. (H.L.) 84; *Connolly* v. *Young's Paraffin Oil Co.* (1894) 22 R. 80.

[8] *Century Ins. Co.* v. *N.I. Road Tpt. Bd.* [1942] A.C. 509; *Malley* v. *L.M.S. Ry.*, 1944 S.C. 129; *Mersey Docks & Harbour Bd.* v. *Coggins and Griffiths, Ltd.* [1947] A.C. 1.

control has been so far transferred to the temporary employer as to make the servant *pro hac vice* his employee and render him liable.[1] The onus of showing that the temporary employer had become the master *pro hac vice* is heavy.[2]

Course of the employment

The employer is liable only if the employee, when he committed the wrong, was acting in the course of his employment.[3] This is a question of fact, and the pursuer must aver and prove facts enabling the court to determine whether the conduct was within or outwith the course of the employment. Course of employment includes conduct ordered or authorized[4] or subsequently ratified,[5] but also actings reasonably incidental to the due performance of the servant's work,[6] doing work the servant is employed to do but in a way unknown and unauthorized,[7] or in an improper way or carelessly,[8] and misconduct in the performance of the work.[9]

The employer is not, however, liable for wrongs done by the employee when acting outwith the course of his employment. Conduct outwith the course of the employment has included persons arrogating duties to themselves in breach of statutory regulations,[10] conduct prohibited by statute and punishable criminally,[11] pursuing a private quarrel with the injured person,[12] doing work other than that which alone the servant is employed to do (rather than merely doing an authorized act in an improper way);[13] using the master's time, place or tools for his own

[1] Transfer: *Wilson* v. *Caledonian Ry.* (1887) 24 S.L.R. 541: *Elliott* v. *Beattie*, 1926 S.L.T. 588; *Fulton's Tutors* v. *Mason*, 1927 S.L.T. 428; *Bowie* v. *Shenkin*, 1934 S.C. 459; *McGregor* v. *Duthie*, 1966 S.L.T. 133. No transfer: *Anderson* v. *Glasgow Tramways Co.* (1893) 21 R. 318; *Burgoyne* v. *Walker*, 1908 S.C. 321; *Connelly* v. *C.N.T.* (1902) 5 F. 8; *Ainslie* v. *Leith Dock Commrs.*, 1919 S.C. 676; *Mersey Docks, supra.*

[2] *Century Ins. Co., supra*; *Malley, supra*; *Mersey Docks, supra.*

[3] *Baird* v. *Hamilton* (1826) 4 S. 790; *Miller* v. *Harvey* (1827) 4 Mur. 385; *Baird* v. *Graham* (1852) 14 D. 615; *Woodhead* v. *Gartness Mineral Co.* (1877) 4 R. 469.

[4] Bell, *Prin.* §547; *Hill* v. *Merricks* (1813) Hume 397; *Kirby* v. *N.C.B.*, 1958 S.C. 514, 532.

[5] *Hilbery* v. *Hatton* (1864) 2 H. & C. 822.

[6] *Mulholland* v. *Reid & Leys*, 1958 S.C. 290; *Bell* v. *Blackwood Morton & Co.*, 1960 S.C. 11; *Staton* v. *N.C.B.* [1957] 2 All E.R. 667.

[7] *Jefferson* v. *Derbyshire Farmers* [1921] 2 K.B. 281; *Century Ins. Co.* v. *N.I. Road Tpt. Board* [1942] A.C. 509; *Kirby, supra*, 533.

[8] *Limpus* v. *L.G.O.C.* (1862) 1 H. & C. 526.

[9] *Central Motors* v. *Cessnock Garage Co.*, 1925 S.C. 796.

[10] *McAulay* v. *Dunlop*, 1926 S.C. (H.L.) 35; *Alford* v. *N.C.B.*, 1952 S.C. (H.L.) 17.

[11] *Kirby* v. *N.C.B.*, 1958 S.C. 514.

[12] *Power* v. *Central S.M.T. Co.*, 1949 S.C. 376.

[13] *C.P. Ry.* v. *Lockhart* [1942] A.C. 591; *Kirkby, supra*, 533.

purposes;[1] going to a prohibited place;[2] going to a place purely for the employee's own purposes.[3]

Deviation from the course of employment

A deviation from the course of employment, as where a driver makes a detour for his own purposes,[4] does not take him outwith the course of his employment, but it is otherwise if the divergence amounts to an independent expedition, as where he goes off 'on a frolic of his own'.[5]

Servant's conduct in breach of orders

A servant's conduct is not necessarily outwith the course of his employment because it is in breach of instructions given to him. A distinction exists[6] between prohibitions which limit the sphere of employment and prohibitions which only deal with conduct within the sphere of employment; the former may,[7] but the latter do not, exclude the employer's liability.[8]

Servant's actings on own initiative

If an employee does something unauthorized on his own initiative and intended to further his employer's interest, such as endeavouring to protect his employer's property which he reasonably believes to be in danger, the employer is liable therefor unless the conduct is such that no employee could have contemplated it as within the scope of the employment.[9]

Servant's conduct in breach of duty

The master is only vicariously liable if the servant's conduct was in breach of some duty which the latter owed in the circumstances to the injured person, i.e. the servant must have been in

[1] *Goh Choon Seng* v. *Lee Kim Soo* [1925] A.C. 550; *Kirby, supra*, 533.

[2] *Donnelly* v. *Moore*, 1921 S.C. (H.L.) 41.

[3] *Kirby, supra.*

[4] e.g. *Joel* v. *Morrison* (1834) 6 C. & P. 501; *Sleath* v. *Wilson* (1839) 9 C. & P. 607; *Wallace* v. *Morrison*, 1929 S.L.T. 73; *Williams* v. *Hemphill*, 1966 S.C. (H.L.) 31, *sed quaere.*

[5] *Joel, supra*; *Storey* v. *Ashton* (1869) L.R. 4 Q.B. 476; *Coupé Co.* v. *Maddick* [1891] 2 Q.B. 413; *Rayner* v. *Mitchell* (1877) 2 C.P.D. 357; *Sanderson* v. *Collins* [1904] 1 K.B. 628; cf. *McIntosh* v. *Cameron*, 1929 S.C. 44.

[6] *Plumb* v. *Cobden Flour Mills Co. Ltd.* [1914] A.C. 62, 67.

[7] *Rand* v. *Craig* [1919] 1 Ch. 1; *Twine* v. *Bean's Express Ltd.* (1946) 175 L.T. 131.

[8] *C.P. Ry.* v. *Lockhart* [1942] A.C. 591; *Young* v. *Box* [1951] 1 T.L.R. 789; *L.C.C.* v. *Cattermoles (Garages) Ltd.* [1953] 2 All E.R. 582;

[9] *Poland* v. *Parr* [1927] 1 K.B. 236; cf. *Neville* v. *C. & A. Modes*, 1945 S.C. 175.

fault.[1] If not, the master is not liable vicariously for the servant, though he may be personally liable on some other ground.[2]

(c) FOR INDEPENDENT CONTRACTOR

An employer is not vicariously liable for a wrong committed by an independent contractor employed by him under a contract *locatio operis faciendi*;[3] the contractor alone is personally responsible to the injured person,[4] or may be vicariously liable for his employees, because he is not subject to direction or control by the employer in the execution of what he has undertaken to do. Similarly an employer is not liable for harm caused by a failure of equipment supplied by a reputable independent contractor.[5]

Personal liability for wrong of contractor

An employer is sometimes, however, held personally, not vicariously, liable for wrong done by an independent contractor or the latter's servants, on grounds of personal fault on the employer's part. This arises where the duty is incumbent on the employer personally; where he is under a statutory duty,[6] or a duty of strict liability when he is bound to take stringent precautions against risk;[7] where the contractor was instructed or authorized to do what is in fact a delict;[8] where the contractor is unqualified, incompetent, or not adequately skilled and experienced for the work;[9] where the contractor is employed to carry out an inherently or specially dangerous operation;[10] where the

[1] *Baxter* v. *Colvilles, Ltd.*, 1959 S.L.T. 325.

[2] cf. *Collins* v. *Hertfordshire C.C.* [1947] K.B. 598.

[3] Bell, *Prin.* §547; *McLean* v. *Russell, Macnee & Co.* (1850) 12 D. 887; *Stephen* v. *Thurso Police Commrs.* (1876) 3 R. 535; *Reidford* v. *Aberdeen Mags.*, 1933 S.C. 276, 280 (where words 'operis' and 'operarum' should be transposed).

[4] *Phillips* v. *Britannia Laundry Co.* [1923] 2 K.B. 832; *Grieve* v. *Brown*, 1926 S.C. 787, 791.

[5] *Davie* v. *New Merton Board Mills* [1959] A.C. 604; *Sullivan* v. *Gallagher & Craig*, 1959 S.C. 243.

[6] *Stephen* v. *Thurso Police Commrs.* (1876) 3 R. 535.

[7] *Stephen, supra*; *Cameron* v. *Fraser* (1881) 9 R. 26; cf. *Hole* v. *Sittingbourne Ry.* (1861) 6 H. & N. 488; *Rylands* v. *Fletcher* (1868) L.R. 3 H.L. 330; *Dalton* v. *Angus* (1881) 6 App. Cas. 740; *Matania* v. *N.P. Bank* [1936] 2 All E.R. 633.

[8] *Ellis* v. *Sheffield Gas Co.* (1853) 2 E. & B. 767; *Cameron* v. *Fraser* (1881) 9 R. 26; *Miller* v. *Renton* (1885) 13 R. 309; *Stewart* v. *Adams*, 1920 S.C. 129.

[9] *Wolfson* v. *Forrester*, 1910 S.C. 675; *Lavelle* v. *Glasgow R.I.*, 1932 S.C. 245; *Reidford* v. *Aberdeen Mags.*, 1933 S.C. 276; *MacDonald* v. *Reid's Trs.*, 1947 S.C. 726.

[10] *Rankine* v. *Dixon* (1847) 9 D. 1048; *Bower* v. *Peate* [1876] 1 Q.B. 321; *Dalton* v. *Angus* (1881) 6 App. Cas. 740; *Paterson* v. *Lindsay* (1885) 13 R. 261; *Penny* v. *Wimbledon U.D.C.* [1899] 2 Q.B. 72; *Sanderson* v. *Paisley* (1899) 7 S.L.T. 255; *Stewart, supra*; *Honeywill & Stein* v. *Larkin* [1934] 1 K.B. 191; *Balfour* v. *Barty-King* [1957] 1 Q.B. 496.

employer has retained direction and control of the operations;[1] and where the employer's operations may interfere with the public highway.[2]

There is, however, no liability on the employer where the employer was not himself personally in fault and the contractor alone was in breach of duty.[3] Nor is the employer ever liable for merely casual or collateral negligence by the contractor or his servant, which is merely incidental to, and not a risk inherent in, the performance of the contractor's work.[4]

[1] *Stephen, supra.*

[2] *Hardaker* v. *Idle District Council* [1896] 1 Q.B. 335; *Penny* v. *Wimbledon Urban Council* [1899] 2 Q.B. 72; *Holliday* v. *National Telephone Co.* [1899] 2 Q.B. 392.

[3] *McLean* v. *Russell, Macnee & Co.* (1850) 12 D. 887; *Phillips* v. *Britannia Laundry Co.* [1923] 2 K.B. 832; *Grieve* v. *Brown*, 1926 S.C. 787, 791; *Davie* v. *New Merton Board Mills* [1959] A.C. 604.

[4] *Penny* v. *Wimbledon U.D.C.* [1899] 2 Q.B. 72; *Padbury* v. *Holliday* (1912) 28 T.L.R. 494; *McKeman* v. *Renfrewshire Educ. Authy.*, 1930 S.N. 72.

CHAPTER 61

LIABILITY AT COMMON LAW FOR HARM

At common law liability to make reparation for harm caused by act of commission or omission depends on its having been done in breach of a legal duty not, by act or omission, to cause harm of such a kind. Harm caused in the absence of legal duty not to cause or permit such harm is *damnum sine injuria* and affords no remedy.[1] Liability accordingly exists where an individual, on whom there was at the material time incumbent by operation of law a duty, which was in the circumstances owed to the complainer, not intentionally, or by failure to take reasonable care, or by failure to take effectual precautions, as the case may be, to cause harm of some general kind, has, by conduct in breach of that duty, been the effective cause of, and a cause not too remotely connected with, at least some of the harm of that general kind complained of by the complainer. While the factors of duty, breach of duty, causation of harm, and remoteness of injury from breach are distinguishable and some cases turn on one of these factors, more than on others,[2] all are truly merely elements of the single but complex concept of liability for harm.[3] To succeed in a claim at common law a pursuer must satisfy the court on all of the factors; the pursuer fails if the defender's contentions on any one of the factors is accepted by the court. Some of the factors (duty, causation, and remoteness) are questions of law, or of mixed fact and law but others (breach, and harm suffered) are questions of fact and evidence.

(1) LEGAL DUTY

To cause another harm, injury, or loss is not actionable as a civil wrong unless done in breach of legal duty.[4] It must appear from the pursuer's averments what legal duty he contends was in the circumstances incumbent on the defender.[5] Whether that

[1] *Le Lievre* v. *Gould* [1893] 1 Q.B. 491, 497.

[2] cf. *Muir* v. *Glasgow Corpn.*, 1943 S.C. (H.L.) 3, 11, 12, 18.

[3] *Roe* v. *Minister of Health* [1954] 2 Q.B. 66, 85.

[4] *Clelland* v. *Robb*, 1911 S.C. 253, 256; *Donoghue* v. *Stevenson*, 1932 S.C. (H.L.) 31, 43; *Bourhill* v. *Young*, 1942 S.C. (H.L.) 78.

[5] *Oliver* v. *Saddler*, 1928 S.C. 608, 613 (revd. 1929 S.C. (H.L.) 94); *Donoghue* v. *Stevenson*, 1932 S.C. (H.L.) 31.

duty is legally recognized is a question of law, determined by precedent or judicial acceptance. The duties which commonly arise, such as to refrain from assaulting or defaming another, to drive carefully and at a reasonable speed, or to take reasonable care for the safety of one's employees, are well settled,[1] but cases may occur raising the question of the recognition or not of certain other alleged duties or of the extension of recognized existing duties to fresh sets of circumstances.[2] The categories of legal wrongs are never closed and the courts may always recognize a new duty.[3] If no such duty as is impliedly contended for by the pursuer's allegations of fact is recognized by law, the defender is not liable even if he has caused harm by his conduct.[4] Harm resulting from deliberate, or careless, conduct does not impose any liability unless there was a legal duty not deliberately or carelessly to have done or permitted that kind of conduct, which has in fact caused harm.[5] In cases of intentional conduct such as assault, defamation, damage to property, infringement of patent, etc., it is usually clear from precedent and on grounds of public policy that there is a legal duty not to perpetrate or permit such conduct, the danger of harm being obvious. In cases of unintentional conduct causing harm the duty is frequently clear, e.g. to drive carefully, but sometimes doubtful.

In default of precedent or analogy the court may hold that a duty exists where, in its view, a reasonable person in the defender's position should have foreseen that conduct by him of the kind in issue would be likely to harm a person who should reasonably have been contemplated by the defender as being likely to be affected by such conduct.[6] It is not necessary that the defender should actually have foreseen injury, or the precise kind of injury which happened; it is enough if, in the view of the court, he should reasonably have foreseen the risk of harm of the general

[1] See Chs. 65–72, *infra*.

[2] e.g. *Hedley Byrne & Co.* v. *Heller & Partners* [1964] A.C. 465.

[3] *Donoghue*, *supra*; *Candler* v. *Crane, Christmas & Co.* [1951] 2 K.B. 164; *Hedley Byrne*, *supra*.

[4] *Le Lievre* v. *Gould* [1893] 1 Q.B. 491, 497; *Deyong* v. *Shenburn* [1946] K.B. 227; *Candler* v. *Crane, Christmas & Co.* [1951] 2 K.B. 164, 177 (on which see *Hedley Byrne & Co.* v. *Heller & Partners* [1964] A.C. 465).

[5] *Mogul* v. *Macgregor* [1892] A.C. 25 (intentional harm to another's trade); *Clelland* v. *Robb*, 1911 S.C. 253, 256 (negligent death); *Donoghue*, *supra*.

[6] *Donoghue* v. *Stevenson*, 1932 S.C. (H.L.) 31, 44, 70; see also *Heaven* v. *Pender* (1883) 11 Q.B.D. 503; *Kemp and Dougall* v. *Darngavil Coal Co.*, 1909 S.C. 1314; *Reilly* v. *Greenfield Coal Co.*, 1909 S.C. 1328; *Lamond* v. *Glasgow Corpn.*, 1968 S.L.T. 291; *Robertson* v. *Bell*, 1969 S.L.T. 119.

kind which in fact happened.[1] Nor will a duty be held imposed because of a remote possibility of harm, or a small or negligible risk,[2] nor because hindsight and the experience of what happened have shown that precautions were necessary or inadequate.[3] And when an accident is of a different type and kind from anything that a defender could have foreseen, he is not liable for it.[4]

(2) DUTY INCUMBENT ON DEFENDER

To attach liability to the defender the duty alleged must have been one incumbent, at the material time, on the defender and not only on another person or persons. If incumbent only on another person, that other may be liable, but the defender called is not liable.[5] If the duty of avoiding or preventing the harm was not incumbent on the defender, he is not at fault even if care is not taken and the harm has resulted.

Different duties may be incumbent on different defenders. If an employee is sent to do work on another's premises and is injured, the fault may be that of his employer, or of the occupier of the premises, different duties being incumbent on each.[6] If two or more defenders are sued jointly and severally, one may escape by showing that the duty in question in the circumstances was incumbent only on the other defender or defenders.[7]

(3) DUTY OWED TO THE INJURED PERSON

The duty on the defender must, at the material time, have been owed to, *inter alios*, the injured person, in that he must have been within the ambit of the duty, or the area of risk of harm resulting from its non-implement. A duty does not extend to everyone, nor necessarily to anyone who is in fact injured, but only to those persons who might in the view of the court, reasonably foreseeably

[1] *Miller* v. *S.S.E.B.*, 1958 S.C. (H.L.) 20, 34; *Harvey* v. *Singer Mfg. Co.*, 1960 S.C. 155, 167; *Hughes* v. *Lord Advocate*, 1963 S.C. (H.L.) 31, 42, 44, 46, 48.

[2] *Fardon* v. *Harcourt Rivington* (1932) 146 L.T. 391; *Bolton* v. *Stone* [1951] A.C. 850.

[3] *Hall* v. *Brooklands* [1933] 1 K.B. 205, 225; *Marshall* v. *Lindsey C.C.* [1935] 1 K.B. 516, 549; *Muir* v. *Glasgow Corpn.*, 1943 S.C. (H.L.) 3, 8; *Baker* v. *Bethnal Green B.C.* [1944] 2 All E.R. 301, 307; *Carmarthenshire C.C.* v. *Lewis* [1955] A.C. 549, 562, 569.

[4] *Hughes*, *supra*, 48.

[5] *McLachlan* v. *Peveril S.S. Co.* (1896) 23 R. 753; *Laing* v. *Paull & Williamsons*, 1912 S.C. 196; *McPhail* v. *Lanarkshire C.C.*, 1951 S.C. 301; *Durie* v. *Main*, 1958 S.C. 48; cf. *Mooney* v. *Lanarkshire C.C.*, 1954 S.C. 245 (different duties on defenders as landlords and as contractors).

[6] cf. *Macdonald* v. *Reid's Trs.*, 1947 S.C. 726.

[7] e.g. *Leckie* v. *Caledonian Glass Co.*, 1957 S.C. 89; *Sullivan* v. *Gallagher & Craig*, 1959 S.C. 243.

be injured by a breach thereof.[1] It may be owed at the time of the occurrence to some persons, but not to others.[2] A duty may be owed to a person whose presence is unknown if such presence was foreseeably likely.[3] The question is not whether the defender did or did not foresee possible injury to a person in the pursuer's position, but whether a hypothetical reasonable man in the defender's position would have so foreseen.[4]

A duty to the pursuer is not imposed, nor is its standard enhanced, by any peculiarity or disability of the pursuer,[5] unless the defender actually knew that the pursuer was infirm, or peculiarly susceptible to injury, or unduly sensitive,[6] or should in the circumstances have foreseen the possible presence of persons so disabled.[7]

(4) CONTENT AND STANDARD OF DUTY

What the legal duty requires the defender to do or not to do is a question of law. In determining the content of the duty in a particular case the court has regard to precedent, to the state of knowledge at the time as to the danger,[8] to the degree of risk of harm attaching in the circumstances,[9] to the expense and difficulty of taking precautions,[10] and to any emergency or exceptional circumstances which may justify running a greater risk.[11]

The standard of duty is also a question of law. In the case of duties not to commit intentional aggressions on other persons, as by assault, defamation, or wrongful use of diligence, the duty is

[1] *Heaven* v. *Pender* (1883) 11 Q.B.D. 503; *Kemp & Dougall* v. *Darngavil Coal Co.*, 1909 S.C. 1314, 1319, 1327; *Donoghue, supra.*, 44, 59, 71; *Bourhill* v. *Young*, 1942 S.C. (H.L.) 78, 83, 85, 88, 90, 98; *Woods* v. *Duncan* [1946] A.C. 401; *Farrugia* v. *G.W. Ry.* [1947] 2 All E.R. 565; *King* v. *Phillips* [1953] 1 Q.B. 429; *Carmarthenshire C.C.* v. *Lewis* [1955] A.C. 549; *Electrochrome* v. *Welsh Plastics* [1968] 2 All E.R. 205.

[2] *Bourhill, supra* (duty to persons in other vehicle, but no duty to B.)

[3] *Carmarthenshire C.C.* v. *Lewis* [1955] A.C. 549 (duty to any driver who might come along).

[4] *Bourhill, supra*; *Waugh* v. *Allan*, 1963 S.C. 175, 189.

[5] *Walker* v. *Pitlochry Motor Co.*, 1930 S.C. 565, 569; *Bourhill, supra.*, 92.

[6] *Paris* v. *Stepney B.C.* [1951] A.C. 367; *Porteous* v. *N.C.B.*, 1967 S.L.T. 117 (one-eyed man).

[7] *McKibbin* v. *Glasgow Corpn.*, 1920 S.C. 590; *Haley* v. *London Electricity Board* [1964] 3 All E.R. 185 (blind).

[8] *Dominion Natural Gas Co.* v. *Collins* [1909] A.C. 640.

[9] *Fardon* v. *Harcourt Rivington* (1932) 146 L.T. 391 ('not bound to guard against fantastic possibilities'); *Bolton* v. *Stone* [1951] A.C. 850 (negligible chance of that kind of injury).

[10] *Henderson* v. *Carron Co.* (1889) 16 R. 633, 637.

[11] *Daborn* v. *Bath Tramways, Ltd.* [1946] 2 All E.R. 333; *Roe* v. *Min. of Health* [1954] 2 Q.B. 66.

absolute and breach is constituted by the defender doing the conduct at all.[1] Short of full legal justification, care or precautions to prevent the breach are irrelevant.

In the case of duties not unintentionally to cause harm, failure in which is accounted negligence or negligent harm, the standard of duty is normally only to take reasonable care not to do or permit what will foreseeably likely cause harm.[2] Reasonable care is the notional standard of care expected of a man of ordinary care and prudence, the hypothetical reasonable man, and is independent of the idiosyncrasies of the particular person whose conduct is in question.[3] It varies with the circumstances,[4] being higher where the danger is obvious, the operation dangerous, or the risk great.[5] It is judged objectively, being not what the defender deemed reasonable but what care a reasonable man in those circumstances would have taken. Reasonable care demands a high standard towards persons of known susceptibilities to injury, such as children.[6] In the case of practitioners of a recognized profession or trade, reasonable care and skill is that reasonable for a qualified member of the profession in question.[7]

In the particular cases of unintentional harm known as cases of strict liability, as for injury by animals,[8] harm by nuisance,[9] or escape of a danger from one's land,[10] the standard of duty required is to take effectual precautions against the foreseeable harm, and liability will attach if the harm occurs, unless one or other of certain limited defences can be invoked. Reasonable

[1] *Rae* v. *Linton* (1875) 2 R. 669; *Morrison* v. *Ritchie* (1902) 4 F. 645; *Hulton* v. *Jones* [1910] A.C. 20.

[2] *Muir* v. *Glasgow Corpn.*, 1943 S.C. (H.L.) 3, 10.

[3] *Blyth* v. *Birmingham Waterworks Co.* (1856) 11 Ex. 781, 784; *Mackintosh* v. *M.* (1864) 2 M. 1357, 1362; *Smith* v. *L.S.W. Ry.* (1870) L.R. 5 C.P. 98; *King* v. *Pollock* (1874) 2 R. 42, 45; *McLean* v. *Warnock* (1883) 10 R. 1052, 1055; *Paterson* v. *Kidd's Trs.* (1896) 24 R. 99, 103; *Grant* v. *Baird* (1903) 5 F. 459, 463; *Donoghue* v. *Stevenson*, 1932 S.C. (H.L.) 31, 44; *Hunter* v. *Hanley*, 1955 S.C. 200, 206, 207.

[4] *Caswell* v. *Powell Duffryn Collieries* [1940] A.C. 152.

[5] *Gilmour* v. *Simpson*, 1958 S.C. 477; *Lloyds Bank* v. *Ry. Executive* [1952] 1 All E.R. 1248, 1253; *Porteous* v. *N.C.B.* 1967 S.L.T. 117 (one-eyed man).

[6] *Taylor* v. *Glasgow Corpn.*, 1922 S.C. (H.L.) 1; *Mourton* v. *Poulter* [1930] 2 K.B. 183; *Excelsior Wire Rope Co.* v. *Callan* [1930] A.C. 404; *Yachuk* v. *Oliver Blais Co.* [1949] A.C. 386; *Paris* v. *Stepney B.C.* [1951] A.C. 367, 385; *Miller* v. *S.S.E.B.*, 1958 S.C. (H.L.) 20; *Hughes* v. *L.A.*, 1963 S.C. (H.L.) 31.

[7] *Hunter* v. *Hanley*, 1955 S.C. 200; *Stewart* v. *Brechin*, 1959 S.C. 306; cf. *Philips* v. *Whiteley* [1938] 1 All E.R. 566; *McLaughlan* v. *Craig*, 1948 S.C. 599; *Wells* v. *Cooper* [1958] 2 Q.B. 265.

[8] e.g. *McDonald* v. *Smellie* (1903) 5 F. 955.

[9] e.g. *Watt* v. *Jamieson*, 1954 S.C. 56.

[10] e.g. *Kerr* v. *Earl of Orkney* (1857) 20 D. 298; *Caledonian Ry.* v. *Greenock Corpn.*, 1917 S.C. (H.L.) 56.

precautions are inadequate. The defences available in such cases are *damnum fatale*, or circumstances which no human foresight can provide against, of which human prudence is not bound to recognize the possibility, and which when they occur are calamities which do not infer liability,[1] deliberate intervention by a third party,[2] and the pursuer's voluntary act or assumption of risk.

(5) BREACH OF DUTY

Whether in the circumstances the defender has implemented the duty incumbent on him, or been in breach thereof, is a question of fact and depends on whether the court or jury thinks the defender has, or has not, satisfied the standard of care or precautions appropriate in the circumstances. Evidence is normally required of care not taken, or precautions omitted. Where alleged negligence consists in omission, proof of the failure must normally be that the common practice of precautions was not adhered to, or that the precaution neglected was one so obviously wanted that it would be folly in anyone to neglect to provide it.[3] The lack of care proved must, to justify a finding for the pursuer, be in respect of the grounds of fault averred in the pursuer's pleadings. A pursuer cannot obtain a decree by proof of some fault, but only by proof of the breach of duty alleged in his summons, or a variation, modification, or development thereof but not something new, separate and distinct.[4]

The onus of proof is on the pursuer initially,[5] but may shift during a proof.[6] It is satisfied by showing preponderance of probability in favour of his case.[7] Where there is conflict of evidence the court must decide which view to adopt, having regard to which is more consistent with surrounding circumstances.[8] In some cases very little evidence of fault is sufficient

[1] *Tennent* v. *E. Glasgow* (1864) 2 M. (H.L.) 22, 26; see also *Nichols* v. *Marsland* (1876) 2 Ex. D. 1; *Kerr*, *supra*; *Caledonian Ry.*, *supra*.

[2] *Rickards* v. *Lothian* [1913] A.C. 263.

[3] *Morton* v. *Nixon*, 1909 S.C. 807, 809; *Barkway* v. *S. Wales Tpt. Co.* [1950] A.C. 185; *Paris* v. *Stepney B.C.* [1951] A.C. 367, 382; *Quinn* v. *Cameron & Roberton*, 1957 S.C. (H.L.) 22, 28, 35; *Brown* v. *Rolls-Royce Ltd.*, 1960 S.C. (H.L.) 22, 26.

[4] *Burns* v. *Dixon's Ironworks*, 1961 S.C. 102, 107; *O'Hanlon* v. *Stein*, 1965 S.C. (H.L.) 23.

[5] *Barrie* v. *Kilsyth Police Commrs.* (1898) 1 F. 194, 197; *Port-Glasgow & Newark Sailcloth Co.* v. *Caledonian Ry.* (1898) 25 R. (H.L.) 75; *Hendry* v. *Clan Line Steamers*, 1949 S.C. 320.

[6] e.g. *Clyde Nav. Trs.* v. *Barclay Curle* (1876) 3 R. (H.L.) 44; cf. *Brown* v. *Rolls-Royce, Ltd.*, 1960 S.C. (H.L.) 22.

[7] *Hendry*, *supra*; *Cleisham* v. *B.T.C.*, 1964 S.C. (H.L.) 8.

[8] *Davison* v. *Henderson* (1895) 22 R. 448.

to establish at least *prima facie* liability, which is sufficient in the absence of other explanation of the happening.[1] Corroboration of evidence is no longer essential in actions of damages for personal injuries, though it remains necessary in all other civil proceedings.[2] The onus of proof of a substantive defence, such as contributory negligence, is on the defender.[3] The verdict in a prior Fatal Accident Inquiry is not admissible evidence,[4] but a conviction in a prior criminal trial is admissible and establishes that the person concerned committed the offence unless the contrary is proved.[5] In defamation cases a conviction of a criminal offence is conclusive evidence that the person concerned committed that conduct.[6]

The court is not entitled to presume fault from the mere happening of an accident, in default of evidence,[7] but it may draw an inference of fault from the whole proven circumstances of the case.[8]

Res ipsa loquitur

Where the thing which causes an accident is within the exclusive control of the defender and his servants and would not have caused harm if proper control had been exercised or proper care taken, the bare accident is evidence of lack of due precautions, unless explained consistently with due precautions being taken.[9] The principle is inapplicable where the real cause of the happening can be ascertained,[10] or where the happening is a neutral event, consistent with fault or absence of fault.[11]

Where it applies the maxim raises a *prima facie* case of fault, but it may be rebutted by a reasonable explanation of the happening, showing how it could equally have happened without fault

[1] *O'Hara* v. *Central S.M.T. Co.*, 1941 S.C. 363.

[2] Law Reform (Misc. Prov.) (Sc.) Act, 1968, S. 9.

[3] *Barrie, supra*; *Wardlaw* v. *Bonnington Castings, Ltd.*, 1956 S.C. (H.L.) 26.

[4] Fatal Accidents and Sudden Deaths Inquiry (Sc.) Act, 1895, S. 6; cf. *Docherty* v. *Niddrie and Benhar Coal Co.*, 1911 1 S.L.T. 396.

[5] Law Reform (Misc. Prov.) (Sc.) Act, 1968, S. 10, altering *Devlin* v. *Earl* (1895) 3 S.L.T. 166.

[6] 1968 Act, S. 12.

[7] *Macfarlane* v. *Thompson* (1884) 12 R. 232; *Wakelin* v. *L.S.W. Ry.* (1886) 12 App. Cas. 41; *Barrie* v. *Kilsyth Police Commrs.* (1898) 1 F. 194; *Dillon* v. *Clyde Stevedoring Co.*, 1967 S.L.T. 103.

[8] *Milliken* v. *Glasgow Corpn.*, 1918 S.C. 857; *Craig* v. *Glasgow Corpn.*, 1919 S.C. (H.L.) 1; *Mersey Docks & Harbour Bd.* v. *Procter* [1923] A.C. 253.

[9] *Byrne* v. *Boadle* (1863) 2 H. & C. 722; *Scott* v. *London Docks* (1865) 3 H. & C. 596; *Watson* v. *N.B. Ry.* (1876) 3 R. 637; *Clerk* v. *Petrie* (1879) 6 R. 1076; *Milliken* v. *Glasgow Corpn.*, 1918 S.C. 857; *Ballard* v. *N.B. Ry.*, 1923 S.C. (H.L.) 43.

[10] *Macfarlane* v. *Thompson* (1884) 12 R. 232; *Milne* v. *Townsend* (1892) 19 R. 830.

[11] *Wing* v. *L.G.O.C.* [1909] 2 K.B. 652; *Ballard, supra.*

on the defenders' part, which leaves the onus of proof of actual fault still on the pursuer; but in cases where the happening has been caused by voluntary action the defender must justify his conduct by legal proof.[1]

Cases of strict liability

In cases of strict liability it is sufficient to prove the happening, against the risk of which stringent precautions should have been taken, and the resultant harm, which casts on the defender the onus of excusing himself, if he can, by proving one or more of the limited recognized defences.[2]

(6) CAUSATION OF HARM

The pursuer must further satisfy the court that the breach of duty alleged was in fact the real, predominant, or effective cause of the event which caused him loss, injury and damage, or at least a materially contributing causal factor.[3] It is not sufficient to show breach of duty and harm, if the latter was not brought about by the former.[4] Causal connection must be proved, or at least be the reasonable inference from established facts.[5]

The courts distinguish between a causal factor which was merely a prerequisite of, or essential for, the harm which resulted, known as *causa sine qua non*, and a causal factor regarded as the real, dominant or effective cause of the resultant harm, known as *causa causans*.[6] A *causa sine qua non* may be essential in that, without it, the harm would not have happened, but it is not necessarily the dominant cause of that harm.[7] Any cause the influence of which has been exhausted before another causal factor supervenes is merely *causa sine qua non*.

[1] *Mars* v. *Glasgow Corpn.*, 1940 S.C. 202; *O'Hara* v. *Central S.M.T. Co.*, 1941 S.C. 363; *Ballingall* v. *Glasgow Corpn.*, 1948 S.C. 160; *Doonan* v. *S.M.T. Co.*, 1950 S.C. 136; *Barkway* v. *S. Wales Tpt. Co.* [1950] A.C. 185; *Devine* v. *Colvilles*, 1967 S.L.T. 89; 1969 S.L.T. 154.

[2] *Chalmers* v. *Dixon* (1876) 3 R. 461; *Caledonian Ry.* v. *Greenock Mags.*, 1917 S.C. (H.L.) 56.

[3] *Craig* v. *Glasgow Corpn.*, 1919 S.C. (H.L.) 1, 6; *Wardlaw* v. *Bonnington Castings Ltd.*, 1956 S.C. (H.L.) 26; *Quinn* v. *Cameron & Roberton*, 1957 S.C. (H.L.) 22; *Nicholson* v. *Atlas Steel Foundry*, 1957 S.C. (H.L.) 44; *McWilliams* v. *Arrol*, 1962 S.C. (H.L.) 70, 83.

[4] *Gray* v. *N.B. Ry.* (1890) 18 R. 76; *Barrie* v. *Kilsyth Police Commrs.* (1898) 1 F. 194; *Bradley* v. *Wallaces, Ltd.* [1913] 3 K.B. 629; *McWilliams*, *supra*.

[5] *MacDonald* v. *Smellie* (1903) 5 F. 955; *Craig* v. *Glasgow Corpn.*, 1919 S.C. (H.L.) 1.

[6] *Harvey* v. *Singer Mfg. Co.*, 1960 S.C. 155, 171.

[7] e.g. *Carse* v. *N.B. Steam Packet Co.* (1895) 22 R. 475 (deceased's presence a prerequisite of accident, but not real cause). cf. *Harvey* v. *Singer Mfg. Co.*, 1960 S.C. 155, 171.

The choice of the real or dominant cause from a number of causal factors has to be made by commonsense standards;[1] the dominant cause is not necessarily the nearest in time to the harm; it may be an early factor, though others supervened and made the harm worse,[2] and may be the real causal factor though separated substantially in space and time fom the ultimate harm.[3] The real or dominant cause is sometimes called the proximate cause, but it is proximity in efficiency as an operating factor, or in causal potency, not in space or time, that is important.[4]

Breach of causal connection

The connection between cause and natural consequence may be diverted or broken by a fresh intervening factor, usually called a *novus actus* (or *nova causa*) *interveniens*, which may be held to be a merely collateral causal factor, or to be a cause equally with the original cause, or to be the real and effective cause of the actual harmful consequence, superseding the original cause and reducing it to merely a *causa sine qua non*.[5] There is a presumption against a fresh intervening factor being regarded as the dominant cause, so that the defender whose conduct started the chain of events will normally be held liable for the ultimate consequences, despite the intervention of a new factor,[6] and the onus is on that defender to persuade the court that the new factor has superseded his fault as the dominant cause.[7]

To break the chain of causation started by the initial breach of duty, the *novus actus* must be something ultroneous, unwarrantable, extraneous or extrinsic, not merely something which follows naturally or inevitably.[8] The kinds of acts and events which may amount to *novus actus interveniens* may be acts by the pursuer himself, acts of a third party, or external natural events.

Acts by the pursuer himself, if voluntary and unnecessary, may break the causal chain,[9] but voluntary acts in pursuance of legal

[1] *Yorkshire Dale S.S. Co.* v. *M.O.W.T.* [1942] A.C. 691, 706.

[2] *Leyland S.S. Co.* v. *Norwich Union Fire Ins. Co.* [1918] A.C. 350; *Grant* v. *Sun Shipping Co.*, 1948 S.C. (H.L.) 73, 94.

[3] *The City of Lincoln* (1889) 15 P.D. 15; *Leyland S.S. Co., supra*; *Yorkshire Dale S.S. Co., supra.*

[4] *Leyland S.S. Co., supra.*

[5] See e.g. *Leyland S.S. Co., supra*; *Weld-Blundell* v. *Stephens* [1920] A.C. 956; *Liesbosch* v. *Edison* [1933] A.C. 449.

[6] *Marshall* v. *Caledonian Ry.* (1899) 1 F. 1060; *Martin* v. *Stanborough* (1924) 41 T.L.R. 1; *The Oropesa* [1943] P. 32.

[7] *Baron Vernon* v. *Metagama,* 1928 S.C. (H.L.) 21, 26.

[8] *The Oropesa, supra,* 39.

[9] *Cutler* v. *United Dairies, Ltd.* [1933] 2 K.B. 297.

or moral duty, such as seeking to rescue a person in danger,[1] or property in danger,[2] instinctive reactions to danger,[3] and action in emergency,[4] or action to avoid or minimize the damage done by the defender, so long as reasonable, even if unsuccessful and even if not ultimately thought to have been the best course,[5] do not normally break the chain of causation.

Acts by a third party, particularly if deliberate and foreseeable, such as maliciously frightening horses left unattended,[6] causing flooding,[7] or causing a fire,[8] may amount to *novus actus interveniens*, but other actings by third parties which result naturally, such as improper medical treatment of the pursuer, unless amounting to unskilful or professionally negligent treatment,[9] a crowd rushing to see a balloonist descend,[10] a thief taking advantage of building operations to steal,[11] are much less likely to be held to break the chain, particularly when the intervention by the third party is of a kind which naturally and probably happens. An act by a third party is less likely to be held to break the causal connection if the third party were a person of lesser responsibility such as a child, and particularly if the intervention of inquisitive or meddlesome persons should have been anticipated.[12]

An external natural event, such as storm, flood or lightning is rarely held to amount to *novus actus* even though it would have been avoided but for the defender's original wrong.[13]

[1] *Wilkinson* v. *Kinneil Coal Co.* (1897) 24 R. 1001; *Haynes* v. *Harwood* [1935] 1 K.B. 146; *D'Urso* v. *Sanson* [1939] 4 All E.R. 26; *Morgan* v. *Aylen* [1942] 1 All E.R. 489; *Hyett* v. *G.W. Ry.* [1948] 1 K.B. 345; *Baker* v. *Hopkins* [1959] 3 All E.R. 225; *Videan* v. *B.T.C.* [1963] 2 Q.B. 650.

[2] *Steel* v. *Glasgow Iron & Steel Co.*, 1944 S.C. 237.

[3] *Woods* v. *Caledonian Ry.* (1886) 13 R. 118; *Wilkinson, supra*; *Brandon* v. *Osborne Garrett & Co.* [1924] 1 K.B. 548.

[4] *The City of Lincoln* (1890) 15 P.D. 15.

[5] *Jones* v. *Boyce* (1816) 1 Stark. 493; *Wilkinson, supra*; *Baron Vernon* v. *Metagama*, 1928 S.C. (H.L.) 21; cf. *Wallace* v. *Bergius*, 1915 S.C. 205; *The Oropesa* [1943] P. 32; *The Guildford* [1956] P. 364.

[6] *Haynes* v. *Harwood* [1935] 1 K.B. 146.

[7] *Rickards* v. *Lothian* [1913] A.C. 263.

[8] *Philco Radio* v. *Spurling* [1949] 2 All E.R. 882.

[9] *Bloor* v. *Liverpool Derricking Co.* [1936] 3 All E.R. 399; *Rothwell* v. *Caverswall Stone Co.* [1944] 2 All E.R. 350; *Hogan* v. *Bentinck West Hartley Collieries* [1949] 1 All E.R. 588, 596.

[10] *Scott's Trs.* v. *Moss* (1889) 17 R. 32.

[11] *Marshall* v. *Caledonian Ry.* (1899) 1 F. 1060; cf. *Stansbie* v. *Troman* [1948] 2 K.B. 48.

[12] *Campbell* v. *Ord & Maddison* (1873) 1 R. 149; *Latham* v. *Johnson* [1913] 1 K.B. 398, 413; *Martin* v. *Stanborough* (1924) 41 T.L.R. 1; *Shiffman* v. *Order of St. John* [1936] 1 All E.R. 557; *Wells* v. *Metropolitan Water Board* (1937) 54 T.L.R. 104; *Cuttress* v. *Scaffolding (G.B.) Ltd.* [1953] 2 All E.R. 1075; *Perry* v. *Kendricks Transport* [1956] 1 All E.R. 154.

[13] *Leyland Shipping Co.* v. *Norwich Union Fire Ins. Socy.* [1918] A.C. 350; *Boiler Inspection Co.* v. *Sherwin Williams* [1951] A.C. 319.

Co-operating causes

A supervening causal factor may be held to be neither collateral, nor *novus actus*, but to become a co-operating cause of the ultimate harm along with the original cause, in such proportions as the court may apportion to each. The fact that subsequent negligence has been the immediate cause of loss does not necessarily wholly exonerate the original wrongdoer.[1] A common case of co-operating causes is where the pursuer has been contributorily negligent, i.e. where he has himself been careless and this has in part caused the harm.[2]

(7) INJURY OR HARM SUFFERED

The pursuer must also establish that the consequence of the defender's breach of duty to him was some injury or harm to one or more of his legally protected interests.[3] If the claim is one based on the *actio legis Aquiliae*, for patrimonial loss, the pursuer must prove what loss, measurable in money, he has suffered.[4] If the claim is one based on the *actio injuriarum*, for hurt feelings, a nominal award is justifiable, where conduct of a hurtful character is proved,[5] and a substantial award where there is evidence of substantial pain.[6]

(8) BREACH AND HARM NOT TOO REMOTELY CONNECTED

Not only must the breach of duty have been a main cause of the harm complained of, but it must have been an immediate or proximate cause and not one deemed too remotely or distantly connected with the harm complained of. If the alleged breach of duty and the ultimate injury are deemed too remotely causally connected the defender is held not liable at all, because conduct may set off a long chain of consequences and at some point the law must intervene to cut off the defender's liability and hold his initial fault spent. The principle *alterum non laedere* does not impose liability for every injury which conduct may occasion however far separated in space and time. Legal liability is limited to those consequences of acts which a reasonable man of

[1] *Grant* v. *Sun Shipping Co.*, 1948 S.C. (H.L.) 73; *Miller* v. *S.S.E.B.*, 1958 S.C. (H.L.) 20.
[2] Ch. 63, *infra*.
[3] As to what are legally protected interests see Chs. 65–73.
[4] e.g. *Gilmour* v. *Simpson*, 1958, S.C. 477.
[5] *Mackay* v. *McCankie* (1883) 10 R. 537; *Cassidy* v. *Connochie*, 1907 S.C. 1112. In *Rankin* v. *Waddell*, 1949 S.C. 555, no such evidence was given.
[6] *McKinlay* v. *Glasgow Corpn.*, 1951 S.C. 495.

ordinary intelligence and experience so acting would have in contemplation.[1] Whether, even if there has been conduct in breach of duty to the pursuer causing him injury, the injury is legally too remote from the breach of duty for the court fairly to hold him liable therefor is the problem of remoteness of injury.[2] The problem of remoteness of injury is one aspect of the problem of liability or culpability and for the court to hold that an injury was too remote is one way of finding that the defender is not liable at all, for any of the harm allegedly sustained by his fault.

The test for determining whether an injury is too remote from allegedly wrongful conduct is whether the injury followed naturally and directly from the conduct alleged to be in breach of duty, or was a reasonable and probable consequence of the initial alleged negligence, or was reasonably foreseeable by a person in the wrongdoer's position.[3] Thus, even if there was breach of duty, injuries have been held too remote to give rise to any liability for the harm which befell where a carrier misdelivered petrol, which caused an explosion, a fire, and personal injuries to the storekeeper when trying to extinguish the fire;[4] where a painter negligently set a house on fire and a guest tried to save property and collapsed and died from the exertion;[5] where by an engine fitter's alleged negligence it was necessary for an engine driver to extinguish the fire and he died from the exertion.[6] Harm of the general kind which was reasonably foreseeable may be or may not be too remote,[7] but if of a different kind from that foreseeable it is certainly too remote.[8]

[1] *Eccles* v. *Cross & McIlwham*, 1938 S.C. 697, 705; *Muir* v. *Glasgow Corpn.*, 1943 S.C. (H.L.) 3, 10.

[2] This question is frequently confused with that of remoteness of damage; remoteness of injury or culpability is concerned with the existence or not of liability for some of the harm alleged; remoteness of damage or compensation is concerned, if liability for some harm is admitted or proved, with the extent of that liability. The terms 'remoteness' or 'remoteness of damage' are frequently applied to both problems, and cases dealing with the one problem too frequently cited in regard to the other.

[3] *Allan* v. *Barclay* (1864) 2 M. 873; *Couper* v. *Macfarlane* (1879) 6 R. 683, 690; *Woods* v. *Caledonian Ry.* (1886) 13 R. 1118, 1123; *Scott's Trs.* v. *Moss* (1889) 17 R. 32, 37; *McGarrot* v. *Addie's Collieries* (1894) 2 S.L.T. 11; *Wilkinson* v. *Kinneil Coal Co.* (1897) 24 R. 1001; *Cooper* v. *Caledonian Ry.* (1902) 4 F. 880, 882; *Ross* v. *Glasgow Corpn.*, 1919 S.C. 174, 177; *Ross* v. *McCallum's Trs.*, 1922 S.C. 322, 327; *Fraser* v. *Pate*, 1923 S.C. 748, 753; *Muir* v. *Glasgow Corpn.*, 1943 S.C. (H.L.) 3, 8, 10.

[4] *Macdonald* v. *Macbrayne*, 1915 S.C. 716.

[5] *Malcolm* v. *Dickson*, 1951 S.C. 542; contrast *Gilmour* v. *Simpson*, 1958 S.C. 477, where damage to house was foreseeable and not too remote.

[6] *Blaikie* v. *B.T.C.*, 1961 S.C. 44.

[7] *Miller* v. *S.S.E.B.*, 1958 S.C. (H.L.) 20; *Harvey* v. *Singer Mfg. Co.*, 1960 S.C. 155; *Hughes* v. *Lord Advocate*, 1963 S.C. (H.L.) 31.

[8] *Doughty* v. *Turner Mfg. Co.* [1964] 1 All E.R. 98.

REMOTENESS OF DAMAGE

As in cases of contract, a defender who is held to be in breach of duty to a pursuer is not necessarily liable for all the loss, injury, or damage which actually results as a consequence of his breach of duty.[1] In delict cases also the problem of remoteness of damage arises, but only if liability for some of the harm which has happened is admitted or proved. But the defender is not necessarily liable for all the damage alleged by him to have flowed from the original wrong, particularly where a chain-reaction of consequences has followed, and both immediate and consequential damage have been suffered.[2] For reasons of justice the court must at some point draw a line as limiting the extent of the defender's liability.[3]

The problem of liability or no liability (including the issue of remoteness of injury)[4] is logically prior to that of remoteness of damage; if there is no liability at all, no question of remoteness of damage can arise; only if there is admitted or proven liability for at least some of the harm which has befallen the pursuer can there be any question of remoteness of damage.[5]

The test for determining, if there is admitted or proved liability for at least some of the harm sustained, how far it extends, and whether any of the damage claimed for is too remote to be fairly chargeable against the defender is now clearly settled after much argument in older cases. If the defender is liable for at least some of the harm which has actually happened, he is liable for all the damage which naturally and directly arises out of the negligence.[6] Reasonable foreseeability of some harm is relevant in determining whether a defender is liable at all or not. It has no relevance once liability is established and the extent

[1] cf. Ch. 36, *supra*; *The Heron II* [1967] 3 All E.R. 686, 692, 708.

[2] On this problem see Walker, *Delict*, I, 248; Walker 'Remoteness: Culpability and Compensation', 1967 J.R. 245.

[3] cf. *Liesbosch* v. *Edison* [1933] A.C. 449, 460.

[4] Sub-head (8), *supra*.

[5] *Bourhill* v. *Young*, 1942 S.C. (H.L.) 78.

[6] Bankt. I, 10, 7; Hume, *Lect.* III, 192; *Lord Keith* v. *Keir*, 10 June 1812, F.C.; *Robertson* v. *Connolly* (1851) 13 D. 779; 14 D. 315; *Baird* v. *Graham* (1852) 14 D. 615; *Smith* v. *L.S.W. Ry.* (1870) L.R. 6 C.P. 14; *Main* v. *Leask*, 1910 S.C. 722; *H.M.S. London* [1914] P. 72; *Nautilus S.S. Co.* v. *Henderson*, 1919 S.C. 605; *Re Polemis and Furness Withy & Co.* [1921] 3 K.B. 560; *Hambrook* v. *Stokes* [1925] 1 K.B. 141; *Reavis* v. *Clan Line*, 1925 S.C. 725, 738; *Baron Vernon* v. *Metagama*, 1928 S.C. (H.L.) 21; *Liesbosch* v. *Edison* [1933] A.C. 448; *Thurogood* v. *Van den Berghs* [1951] 2 K.B. 537; *Pigney* v. *Pointers Transport Services, Ltd.* [1957] 2 All E.R. 807; *Oman* v. *McIntyre*, 1962 S.L.T. 168; *McKillen* v. *Barclay Curle & Co.*, 1967 S.L.T. 41; *McKew* v. *Holland & Hannan & Cubitts (Sc.) Ltd.*, 1969 S.L.T. 101.

of the liability is being considered.[1] It follows that the wrongdoer must take his victim as he finds him, and may, by reason of the victim's unusual susceptibility to injury, be liable for greater loss than might have occurred in the case of another victim, or than anyone might have expected.[2] An alternative view was that the defender, if liable, was liable only for the reasonably foreseeable consequences of his wrongful conduct,[3] which are generally assumed to be less extensive than the direct consequences. A third view, that the defender's liability depends on the reasonable foreseeability of the consequent damage, and that his liability is in respect of that damage and no other,[4] depends on a confusion between existence of liability or remoteness of injury and extent of liability or remoteness of damage, and is not sound law in Scotland.[5] There is no liability for consequences deemed to be not the natural and direct consequence of the initial injury,[6] nor for indirect consequences of the initial injury, such as those brought on by a subsequent *novus actus*.[7]

QUANTIFICATION OF DAMAGES

Once the question of the defender's liability has been established and the court has determined whether any part of the loss claimed must be excluded from consideration as being too remote to justify compensation, the court may proceed to the practical problem of the quantification of damages or assessment of the sum which is proper in the circumstances. In cases of pecuniary loss or damage, a reasonably accurate assessment may be made, but in cases of sentimental loss (pain, hurt feelings) the court has regard to the factors which previous cases have fixed as relevant and to the general level of awards currently being given for losses of that kind and degree.[8]

[1] *McKillen, supra.*

[2] *Clippens Oil Co.* v. *Edinburgh and District Water Trs.*, 1907 S.C. (H.L.) 9, 11, 14; *Bourhill* v. *Young*, 1942 S.C. (H.L.) 78; *Smith* v. *Leech Brain & Co.* [1962] 2 Q.B. 405; *McKillen, supra.*

[3] *Rigby* v. *Hewitt* (1850) 5 Ex. 240; *Greenland* v. *Chaplin* (1850) 5 Ex. 243; *Cory* v. *France* [1911] 1 K.B. 114; disapproved for Scotland by *McKillen* v. *Barclay, Curle & Co.*, 1967 S.L.T. 41.

[4] *Overseas Tankship (U.K.) Ltd.* v. *Morts Dock and Engineering Co.* (*The Wagon Mound*) [1961] A.C. 388 (P.C.), disregarded by the Court of Session in *McKillen, supra.*

[5] Many of the dicta, it is thought, proceed on confusion between questions of culpability or liability or remoteness of injury and questions of compensation or remoteness of damage.

[6] *McKillen, supra.*

[7] *McKew* v. *Holland & Hannen & Cubitts (Sc.) Ltd.*, 1969 S.L.T. 101.

[8] See further Ch. 115, *infra.*

CHAPTER 62

LIABILITY UNDER STATUTE FOR HARM

MANY statutes impose duties on individuals to avoid, or take precautions against, dangers and potential harms. Breach of such a duty is normally punishable criminally, but in many cases the courts have held that the statute impliedly also gives an injured person a right, enforceable by common law action, to claim damages for injuries resulting from the breach of statutory duty.[1] Statutory duties may be different from common law duties, but are frequently similar to and cumulative therewith. In many cases circumstances give rise to claims for breach both of common law and of statutory duties, and in such cases both claims may be brought in one action, and the pursuer may succeed in one claim and fail in the other.[2] But liability for breach of statutory duty frequently goes beyond liability for breach of common law duty because the statutory duty normally cannot be delegated, and the scope and standard of the duty are fixed by the statutory provision.[3]

As in the case of common law duty, a pursuer, to be successful in a claim for breach of statutory duty, must satisfy the court on all the elements of liability; if he fails on any one or more the defender succeeds.

(1) STATUTORY DUTY (A) IN FORCE

The pursuer must satisfy the court that, at the material time, a statute or statutory instrument was in force and imposed a duty of compliance, rather than merely enabled, permitted, or directed certain conduct.[4] It must also have been applicable to the place or premises on which,[5] and to the operation in which, the harm was suffered.[6]

[1] Ersk. III, 1, 14; *Kelly* v. *Glebe Sugar Refining Co.* (1893) 20 R. 833, 835; *Black* v. *Fife Coal Co.*, 1912 S.C. (H.L.) 33, 45; *McMullan* v. *Lochgelly Iron Co.*, 1933 S.C. (H.L.) 64; *Caswell* v. *Powell Duffryn* [1940] A.C. 152.

[2] e.g. *Millar* v. *Galashiels Gas Co.*, 1949 S.C. (H.L.) 31.

[3] *McMullan*, *supra*; *Hamilton* v. *Anderson*, 1953 S.C. 129, 137.

[4] *Monaghan* v. *Glasgow Corpn.*, 1955 S.C. 80.

[5] e.g. *Wood* v. *L.C.C.* [1940] 2 K.B. 642; *Riddell* v. *Reid*, 1942 S.C. (H.L.) 51; *Thomson* v. *B.T.H. Co.* [1953] 1 All E.R. 29; *Elliot* v. *N.C.B.*, 1956 S.C. 484; *Gardiner* v. *Admiralty*, 1964 S.C. (H.L.) 85.

[6] *Mortimer* v. *Allison*, 1959 S.C. (H.L.) 1.

(2) STATUTORY DUTY (B) INCUMBENT ON DEFENDER

For the defender to be liable, the statutory duty must have been incumbent on the defender, or on him among others.[1] It may be incumbent on the injured person, or on a third party.[2] It is a general principle that a statutory duty imposed on a person is personal and non-delegable to a subordinate or to an independent contractor.[3] It is, however, sometimes competent to delegate a statutory duty, even to the person who is later injured; in such a case the onus of proving the delegation is heavy.[4]

(3) STATUTORY DUTY (C) INTENDED TO PROTECT, INTER ALIOS, THE PURSUER

An injured person has no title to sue for harm caused by breach of statutory duty unless the duty was imposed for protection of such persons as himself, and not only for others.[5] Duties are frequently held imposed for the benefit of whole classes of persons, such as mineworkers,[6] and may even protect any person legitimately present on the premises.[7] If the statute is held intended to protect the public, it will not normally, however, be held to give a right of action to any individual members of the public, but will be enforceable by prosecution only.[8] The duty may be owed to employees of an independent contractor employed by the defender.[9]

(4) INTENTION THAT IT BE ENFORCEABLE BY CIVIL ACTION

The Court must be satisfied that the statutory provision in issue was intended to impose a duty enforceable by an injured person by civil action and not merely a duty enforceable by

1 *Gallagher* v. *Wimpey*, 1951 S.C. 515; *Solomons* v. *Gertzenstein* [1954] 2 Q.B. 243; see also *Black* v. *Fife Coal Co.*, 1912 S.C. (H.L.) 33; *Harrison* v. *N.C.B.* [1951] A.C. 639.

2 cf. *McCafferty* v. *Brown*, 1950 S.C. 300.

3 *Groves* v. *Wimborne* [1898] 2 Q.B. 402; *McMullan* v. *Lochgelly Iron Co.*, 1933 S.C. (H.L.) 64, 68, 70, 73, 77; *Mulready* v. *Bell* [1953] 2 Q.B. 117.

4 *Vyner* v. *Waldenberg Bros.* [1946] K.B. 50; *Smith* v. *Baveystock* [1945] 1 All E.R. 531; *Barcock* v. *Brighton Corpn.* [1949] 1 All E.R. 251; *Manwaring* v. *Billington* [1952] 2 All E.R. 747; *Ginty* v. *Belmont Building Co.* [1959] 1 All E.R. 414.

5 e.g. *McCarten* v. *McRobbie*, 1909 S.C. 1020; *Hillen* v. *I.C.I. Ltd.* [1934] 1 K.B. 455; *Knapp* v. *Ry. Exec.* [1949] 2 All E.R. 508; *Hartley* v. *Mayoh* [1954] 1 Q.B. 383; *Bollinger* v. *Costa Brava Wine Co.* [1960] Ch. 262.

6 e.g. *Britannic Merthyr Coal Co.* v. *David* [1910] A.C. 74; *Black* v. *Fife Coal Co.*, 1912 S.C. (H.L.) 33; *Watkins* v. *Naval Colliery Co.* [1912] A.C. 693.

7 *Ward* v. *Coltness Iron Co.*, 1944 S.C. 318.

8 e.g. *Phillips* v. *Britannia Laundry* [1923] 2 K.B. 832; *Balmer* v. *Hayes*, 1950 S.C. 477.

9 *McWilliams* v. *Arrol*, 1962 S.C. (H.L.) 70.

prosecution. The answer depends in every case on the interpretation of the particular statutory provision.[1] Interpretation does not necessarily lead to the same result in all sections of one Act.[2] Relevant factors are the state of the pre-existing law,[3] whether the duty has been imposed for the benefit of a class which includes the pursuer, or for the protection of the public generally,[4] the nature and extent of any penalty imposed for contravention,[5] and the provision of any alternative remedy.[6]

(5) INTENTION TO GUARD AGAINST THE RISK OF THE KIND OF HARM WHICH HAS RESULTED

The pursuer must show that the harm suffered was among the kinds of harm against which the statute was intended to protect him, and that it was not directed only against other evils.[7] Hence a provision requiring fencing to keep operators out of machinery cannot be founded on if the machine ejects material and thereby injures the operator.[8]

(6) CONTENT AND STANDARD OF STATUTORY DUTY

What duties the statute imposes is a question of interpretation in each case.[9]

The standard of the duty is in each case also a question of interpretation; it may be a duty not intentionally to cause harm, or to take reasonable care to prevent harm.[10] It may, however, be more stringent, such as to take all practical measures, or to ensure safety so far as practicable.[11] In some cases the duty has been held to be absolute, in which case the happening by reason of non-compliance of a harm of the kind sought to be prevented

[1] *Cutler* v. *Wandsworth Stadium, Ltd.* [1949] A.C. 398.

[2] Contrast *Monk* v. *Warbey* [1935] 1 K.B. 75; *Houston* v. *Buchanan*, 1940 S.C. (H.L.) 17 with *Balmer* v. *Hayes*, 1950 S.C. 477.

[3] *Phillips* v. *Britannia Laundry* [1923] 2 K.B. 832; *Clarke* v. *Brims* [1947] K.B. 497; *Balmer, supra.*

[4] *Groves* v. *Wimborne* [1898] 2 Q.B. 402; *Black* v. *Fife Coal Co.*, 1912 S.C. (H.L.) 34; *Solomons* v. *Gertzenstein* [1954] 2 Q.B. 243 citing earlier cases.

[5] *Groves, supra*; *Black, supra*; *Cutler, supra.*

[6] *Pullar* v. *Window Clean, Ltd.*, 1956 S.C. 13.

[7] *Gorris* v. *Scott* (1874) L.R. 9 Ex. 125; *Grant* v. *N.C.B.*, 1956 S.C. (H.L.) 48.

[8] *Carroll* v. *Barclay*, 1948 S.C. (H.L.) 100; *Kilgollan* v. *Cooke* [1956] 2 All E.R. 294; cf. *Nicholls* v. *Austin (Leyton) Ltd.* [1946] A.C. 493; *Close* v. *Steel Co. of Wales* [1961] 2 All E.R. 953. Contrast *Grant, supra*; *Boryk* v. *N.C.B.*, 1959 S.C. 1.

[9] cf. *O'Hanlon* v. *Stein*, 1965 S.C. (H.L.) 23.

[10] e.g. *Keogh* v. *Edinburgh Mags.*, 1926 S.C. 814; *Gemmell* v. *Glasgow Corpn.*, 1945 S.C. 287; *Ghannan* v. *Glasgow Corpn.*, 1950 S.C. 23; *O'Hanlon* v. *Stein*, 1965 S.C. (H.L.) 23, 37.

[11] *Sharp* v. *Coltness Iron Co.*, 1937 S.C. (H.L.) 68; *Street* v. *British Electricity Authy.* [1952] 2 Q.B. 399; *Hall* v. *Fairfield Shipbuilding Co.*, 1964 S.C. (H.L.) 72.

evidences breach, despite all attempts at compliance with the duty.[1] An absolute duty is also normally a continuing one, to maintain the apparatus safe as well as to make it safe initially.[2]

(7) BREACH OF THE STATUTORY DUTY

As at common law the onus is on the pursuer to prove that the statutory duty was in fact breached.[3] If the statutory duty is a qualified one[4] the onus of proof of the exception is on the defender.[5] If the duty is an absolute one, the pursuer need only prove the happening of the event, the risk of which should have been prevented.[6]

(8) CAUSATION OF HARM COMPLAINED OF

Causal connection between breach and harm must be proved, by the ordinary standard of proof in civil actions, that on the balance of probabilities the breach of duty caused or materially contributed to the injury.[7] An inference of causation may be drawn from breach of duty coupled with the occurrence of the kind of injury the statutory provisions were intended to prevent.[8] The breach is not the cause if the injured person would not have availed himself of the required protection even if it had been available,[9] nor if the injury were caused by his own failure or refusal to use a safety device.[10]

1 *McMullan* v. *Lochgelly Iron Co.*, 1933 S.C. (H.L.) 33; *Smith* v. *Cammell Laird & Co.*, [1940] A.C. 242; *Carroll* v. *Barclay*, 1948 S.C. (H.L.) 100; *Millar* v. *Galashiels Gas Co.*, 1949 S.C. (H.L.) 31; *Latimer* v. *A.E.C. Ltd.* [1953] A.C. 643; *Hamilton* v. *N.C.B.*, 1960 S.C. (H.L.) 1.

2 *Millar, supra*; *Close* v. *N.C.B.*, 1951 S.C. 578; *Hamilton, supra*; contrast *Mazs* v. *N.C.B.*, 1958 S.C. 6, where no continuing absolute obligation of maintenance.

3 *Wardlaw* v. *Bonnington Castings, Ltd.*, 1956 S.C. (H.L.) 26.

4 e.g. to exclude risks 'so far as practicable'.

5 *Sharp* v. *Coltness Iron Co.*, 1937 S.C. (H.L.) 68; *Edwards* v. *N.C.B.* [1946] 1 K.B. 704; *Brown* v. *N.C.B.* [1962] A.C. 574; *Sinclair* v. *N.C.B.*, 1963 S.C. 586.

6 *Smith* v. *Cammell Laird & Co.* [1940] A.C. 242; *McMullan* v. *Lochgelly Iron Co.*, 1933 S.C. (H.L.) 33; *Millar* v. *Galashiels Gas Co.*, 1949 S.C. (H.L.) 31; *Hamilton* v. *N.C.B.*, 1960 S.C. (H.L.) 1; *Harkness* v. *Oxy-Acetylene Welding Co.*, 1963 S.C. 642; the only defence is to show that the event did not cause the injury, or that it was entirely due to the pursuer's own fault.

7 *Caswell* v. *Powell Duffryn Assoc. Collieries* [1940] A.C. 152, 168; *Balfour* v. *Beardmore* 1956 S.L.T. 205; *Wardlaw* v. *Bonnington Castings Ltd.*, 1956 S.C. (H.L.) 26; *Quinn* v. *Cameron & Roberton*, 1957 S.C. (H.L.) 22; *Nicholson* v. *Atlas Steel Co.*, 1957 S.C. (H.L.) 44.

8 *Lee* v. *Nursery Furnishings* [1945] 1 All E.R. 387; *Smithwick* v. *N.C.B.* [1950] 2 K.B. 335.

9 *Nolan* v. *Dental Mfg. Co.* [1958] 1 W.L.R. 936; *Qualcast* v. *Haynes* [1959] A.C. 743; *McWilliams* v. *Sir Wm. Arrol & Co., Ltd.*, 1962 S.C. (H.L.) 70.

10 *Ginty* v. *Belmont Supplies, Ltd.* [1959] 1 All E.R. 414; *McMath* v. *Rimmer Bros.* [1962] 1 W.L.R. 1.

The defence of *novus actus interveniens* is available in a statutory case as at common law.[1]

(9) INJURY OR HARM SUFFERED

A breach of statute may be actionable without need to prove actual resultant injury or harm,[2] but normally it is necessary to prove that some actual injury, harm or damage was sustained by reason of the breach.

(10) BREACH AND HARM NOT TOO REMOTELY CONNECTED

Questions of remoteness of injury may, but rarely do, arise in cases of breach of statutory duty.

REMOTENESS OF DAMAGE

Questions of remoteness of damage, once liability for some harm has been admitted or proved, are probably determined by the same principles as apply in cases of breach of common law duties.

QUANTIFICATION OF DAMAGES

Damages are assessed in the same way and on the same principles in actions based on breach of statutory duty as in actions based on breach of common law duty.

[1] *Groves* v. *Wimborne* [1898] 2 Q.B. 402; *Northwestern Utilities Ltd.* v. *London Guarantee Co.* [1936] A.C. 108.

[2] e.g. *E. Kinnoul* v. *Ferguson* (1843) 5 D. 1010.

CHAPTER 63

DEFENCES TO ACTIONS FOR DELICT

THE defences competent in an action of reparation for delict may be defences in law, or in fact, or both. Defences in law include pleas to the jurisdiction, to the pursuer's title or interest to sue, to the competency of the remedy sought, as to the relevancy of the action in respect of any of the necessary legal elements of liability,[1] that the matter is *res judicata*, or the action excluded by lapse of time, and pleas of positive legal defences, such as contractual exclusion of the claim, or justification in particular circumstances.

Defences in fact include challenging the pursuer's evidence, or leading counter-evidence, on any of the necessary factual elements of liability,[1] and evidence supporting any of certain positive defences on the facts, such as contributory negligence.

Immunity from liability—heads of state

Certain persons, for reasons of public policy, are wholly or partially immune from action for delict.

The Queen in her personal capacity is immune.[2]

The Crown, and its servants and agents, are immune from liability for any 'act of State', which is an act of the executive done as a matter of policy in the course of relations with another state or its subjects who are not, unless temporarily, within allegiance to the Crown.[3] It does not extend to acts done within the realm, or to a British subject or one temporarily owing allegiance to the Crown anywhere,[4] and the act must have been authorized, or ratified, by the appropriate minister on behalf of the Crown.[5]

Foreign sovereigns are immune in respect both of personal conduct,[6] and of property and commercial transactions.[7] A

[1] i.e. the elements discussed in Chs. 61 and 62.

[2] Crown Proceedings Act, 1947, S. 40(1).

[3] Crown Proceedings Act, 1947, S. 2; *Salaman* v. *Secy. of State for India* [1906] 1 K.B. 613; *Johnstone* v. *Pedlar* [1921] 2 A.C. 262; *Commercial and Estates Co. of Egypt* v. *B.O.T.* [1925] 1 K.B. 271.

[4] *Walker* v. *Baird* [1892] A.C. 491; *Johnstone, supra*; *Netz* v. *Ede* [1946] Ch. 224; *R.* v. *Bottrill, ex. p. Kuechenmeister* [1947] K.B. 41.

[5] *Buron* v. *Denman* (1848) 2 Ex. 167.

[6] *Mighell* v. *Sultan of Johore* [1894] 1 Q.B. 149; *Statham* v. *S.* [1912] P. 92.

[7] *The Parlement Belge* (1880) 5 P.D. 197; *The Porto Alexandre* [1920] P. 30.

certificate from the Foreign or Commonwealth and Colonial Office is conclusive as to the status of a foreign sovereign.[1] A department of State of a foreign country operating in this country is also immune.[2] The immunity may be waived, but only by deliberate submission.[3]

Diplomatic and similar immunity

Diplomatic agents of other states in this country have certain privileges agreed in the Vienna Convention on Diplomatic Relations of 1961,[4] including immunity from criminal, civil, and administrative jurisdiction, with certain exceptions,[5] though this may be expressly waived by the sending state.[6] Members of the family of diplomatic agents enjoy the same privileges, members of the administrative and technical staff of the mission lesser privileges, members of the service staff of the mission more restricted privileges and private servants of members of the mission privileges only to the extent admitted by the receiving state.[7] Privileges and immunities may in certain circumstances be restricted.[8]

International organizations and persons connected therewith,[9] chief representatives in this country of Commonwealth countries and the Republic of Ireland and their staff and families,[10] officials of the International Development Association,[11] and representatives of the governments of Commonwealth countries and the Republic of Ireland attending conferences in the United Kingdom[12] are also entitled to certain privileges and immunities. Consuls have certain privileges and immunities,[13] but official agents under a trading agreement are not privileged.[14]

Visiting forces enjoy certain privileges and immunities.[15]

[1] *Mighell, supra*; *Duff Development Co.* v. *Govt. of Kelantan* [1924] A.C. 797; *Engelke* v. *Musmann* [1928] A.C. 433.

[2] *Krajina* v. *Tass Agency* [1949] 2 All E.R. 274; *Baccus S.R.L.* v. *Servicio Nacional del Trigo* [1957] 1 Q.B. 438.

[3] *Mighell, supra*; cf. *Rosses* v. *Bhagvat Sinhjee* (1891) 19 R. 31; *Sultan of Johore* v. *Abubakar Tunku Aris Bendahar* [1952] A.C. 318.

[4] Diplomatic Privileges Act, 1964, Ss. 1, 2, and Sched. 1.

[5] Sched. 1, art. 31.

[6] Sched. 1, art. 32.

[7] Sched. 1, art. 37.

[8] S. 3.

[9] International Organizations (Immunities and Privileges) Act, 1950.

[10] Diplomatic Immunities (Commonwealth Countries and Republic of Ireland) Act, 1952.

[11] International Development Association Act, 1960.

[12] Diplomatic Immunities (Conferences with Commonwealth Countries and Republic of Ireland) Act, 1961.

[13] Consular Relations Act, 1968.

[14] *Fenton Textile Assoc. Ltd.* v. *Krassin* (1921) 38 T.L.R. 259.

[15] Visiting Forces Act, 1952, S. 12.

Judicial immunity

Judges and officers of courts of justice are totally immune from civil action in respect of judicial actings,[1] nor is the Crown liable for their actings,[2] even though they act in excess of jurisdiction,[3] in bad faith,[4] oppressively[5] or maliciously,[6] but an inferior court judge is liable for acting without or in excess of jurisdiction,[7] if he knew or had the means of knowing this fact, but a mere misconstruction of a statutory power does not take a magistrate outwith protection.[8]

Judicial immunity does not extend to ministerial actings, such as issuing illegal or irregular warrants,[9] but liability is conditional on proof that the defender acted from malicious motive.[10]

Certain statutes also provide a measure of protection for inferior court judges in certain circumstances.[11]

Persons and bodies exercising quasi-judicial functions enjoy immunity only in the absence of fraud, collusion or malice.[12]

Statutory authority

Statutory authority for harm done is a defence if the statute in question is imperative and ordered the conduct alleged to be harmful,[13] or if it is permissive and authorized the conduct irrespective of whether it harmed persons or not,[14] or if it merely authorized the conduct, and in fact no other or greater harm was done in the exercise of the authority than was inevitable and

[1] *Haggart's Trs.* v. *L. P. Hope* (1824) 2 Sh. App. 125; *Hamilton* v. *Anderson* (1858) 3 Macq. 363; *Watt* v. *Thomson* (1870) 8 M. (H.L.) 77; *Watt* v. *Ligertwood* (1874) 1 R. (H.L.) 21; *Everett* v. *Griffiths* [1921] 1 A.C. 631; *McPhee* v. *Macfarlane's Exor.*, 1933 S.C. 163.

[2] Crown Proceedings Act, 1947, S. 2(5).

[3] *Scott* v. *Stansfield* (1868) L.R. 3 Ex. 220; *Anderson* v. *Gorrie* [1895] 1 Q.B. 668; *McCreadie* v. *Thomson*, 1970 S.C. 1176.

[4] *Hamilton* v. *Anderson* (1858) 3 Macq. 363; *Anderson, supra.*

[5] *Ewart* v. *Strathern*, 1924 J.C. 45; *Learmonth* v. *Salmon*, 1926 J.C. 103; *McCulloch* v. *McLaughlin*, 1930 J.C. 8.

[6] *Anderson* v. *Gorrie* [1895] 1 Q.B. 668.

[7] *Pollock* v. *Clark* (1829) 8 S. 1; *Murray* v. *Allan* (1872) 11 M. 147; *McCreadie* v. *Thomson*, 1907 S.C. 1176.

[8] *McPhee, supra.*

[9] *Pollock* v. *Clark* (1829) 8 S. 1; *Ferguson* v. *Kinnoull* (1842) 1 Bell 662; *Carne* v. *Manuel* (1851) 13 D. 1253; *Watt* v. *Thomson, supra*; *Beaton* v. *Ivory* (1887) 14 R. 1057.

[10] *McPherson* v. *McLennan* (1887) 14 R. 1063.

[11] Justices Protection Act, 1803; Circuit Courts (Sc.) Act, 1828, S. 26; Criminal Law (Sc.) Act, 1830, S. 13; Summary Jurisdiction (Sc.) Act, 1954, S. 75.

[12] *Royal Aquarium Soc.* v. *Parkinson* [1892] 1 Q.B. 431.

[13] e.g. *L.A.* v. *Sinclair* (1872) 11 M. 137; *Gray* v. *Fife C.C.*, 1911 S.C. 266.

[14] *Hammersmith Ry.* v. *Brand* (1869) L.R. 4 H.L. 171.

reasonably necessarily incidental to its exercise.[1] Statutory authority is normally permissive, and conditional on the taking of all reasonable precautions to avoid or prevent harm from the exercise of the powers.[1] An action lies for doing what Parliament has authorized if it be done negligently.[2] Authority does not extend to conduct which need not have been done at all,[3] the doing harmfully of what could have been done harmlessly,[4] the negligent doing of the authorized conduct,[5] nor to the doing of more damage than the necessity of the case requires.[6]

Common law authority

Harmful conduct, if authorized by common law, is not actionable as wrongful. Such authorized harms include the reasonable use of force in effecting arrest,[7] or restraining a patient,[8] or administering chastisement to children, pupils or members of a ship's crew,[9] or ejecting persons misbehaving[10] or who are trespassing on the premises.[11] The defence fails if the force used was unreasonable or unnecessary[12] or if the person acted outwith the scope of his authority.[13]

Justification

In exceptional cases it may be justifiable, even deliberately, to commit a delict to avoid or prevent some greater wrong or harm, and to preserve a higher moral value than that infringed. Thus a person may deliberately induce a breach of contract to strike at

[1] *Hunter* v. *Glasgow Union Ry.* (1870) 8 M. (H.L.) 156; *Metropolitan Asylum District* v. *Hill* (1881) 6 App. Cas. 193; *Clyde* v. *Glasgow City & District Ry.* (1885) 12 R. 1315; *Edinburgh Water Trs.* v. *Sommerville* (1906) 8 F. (H.L.) 25; *Manchester Corpn.* v. *Farnworth* [1930] A.C. 171.

[2] *Geddis* v. *Bann Reservoir Proprs.* (1878) 3 App. Cas. 430.

[3] *Tilling* v. *Dick, Kerr & Co.* [1905] 1 K.B. 562.

[4] *Lord Advocate* v. *N.B. Ry.* (1894) 2 S.L.T. 71.

[5] *Northwestern Utilities Ltd.* v. *London Guarantee Co.* [1936] A.C. 108.

[6] *Manser* v. *N.E. Counties Ry.* (1841) 2 Ry. & Can. Cas. 380.

[7] *Mason* v. *Orr* (1901) 4 F. 220; *Baillie* v. *Edinburgh Mags.* (1906) 14 S.L.T. 344.

[8] *Knight* v. *Inverness District Board of Control*, 1920 2 S.L.T. 157.

[9] *Reekie* v. *Norrie* (1842) 5 D. 368; *Muckarsie* v. *Dickson* (1848) 11 D. 4; *Ewart* v. *Brown* (1882) 10 R. 163; *Scorgie* v. *Lawrie* (1883) 10 R. 610; *Wight* v. *Burns* (1883) 11 R. 217.

[10] *Highland Ry.* v. *Menzies* (1878) 5 R. 887; *Apthorpe* v. *Edinburgh Tramways* (1882) 10 R. 344; *Wallace* v. *Mooney* (1885) 12 R. 710; *Scott* v. *G.N.S. Ry.* (1895) 22 R. 287; *MacRaild* v. *N.B. Ry.* (1902) 10 S.L.T. 348; *Cook* v. *Paxton* (1910) 48 S.L.R. 7; *Coutts* v. *MacBrayne*, 1910 S.C. 386.

[11] *Bell* v. *Shand* (1870) 7 S.L.R. 267.

[12] *Mason* v. *Orr* (1901) 4 F. 320; *Wilson* v. *Bennett* (1904) 6 F. 269; *Downie* v. *Connell Bros.*, 1910 S.C. 781.

[13] *Mason, supra*; *Baillie* v. *Edinburgh Mags.* (1906) 14 S.L.T. 344.

moral degradation,[1] or to prevent an unsuitable marriage,[2] or to cause economic harm incidentally to furthering a legitimate economic purpose.[3] The justification disappears if it appears that the conduct was done *in mala fide* or with any malicious or improper motive.[2]

Necessity

The doing of what would otherwise be a delict is justifiable for the avoidance of some greater evil, particularly in emergency. Thus a person may trespass on another's property and even break into his building in the exercise of public right,[4] to prevent a crime or in pursuit of a criminal,[5] to save life or property,[6] to escape from imminent serious danger,[7] to recover goods or animals taken or straying on another's land,[8] or in pursuit of foxes so as to save poultry from destruction,[9] but not for the purposes of picketing.[10] Prison officers may forcibly feed a prisoner if necessary to preserve his life.[11] Similarly a person may take steps to preserve himself or his property from imminent harm even though it results in harm to another's property, as by embanking his lands against flooding.[12]

Defence of person or property

A person may use reasonable force in defence of himself against assault,[13] or unlawful arrest,[14] and probably also in defence of a member of his family, or of any person requiring protection.[15] If the force used is excessive in nature or amount it may be a counter-assault.

A person may also use reasonable force to prevent interference with or damage to his property, as by resisting an unauthorized

1 *Brimelow* v. *Casson* [1924] 1 Ch. 302.
2 *Findlay* v. *Blaylock*, 1937 S.C. 21.
3 *Mogul S.S. Co.* v. *McGregor* [1892] A.C. 25; *Crofter Co.* v. *Veitch*, 1942 S.C. (H.L.) 1.
4 *Shepherd* v. *Menzies* (1900) 2 F. 443.
5 Bell, *Prin.* §957.
6 *Cope* v. *Sharpe* [1912] 1 K.B. 496.
7 Rankine, *Landownership*, 139.
8 *E. Morton* v. *Macmillan* (1893) 1 S.L.T. 92.
9 *Colquhoun* v. *Buchanan* (1785) Mor. 4997.
10 *Merry & Cuninghame* v. *Aitken* (1895) 22 R. 247.
11 *Leigh* v. *Gladstone* (1909) 26 T.L.R. 139.
12 *Gerrard* v. *Crane* [1921] 1 A.C. 395; contrast *Whalley* v. *L. & Y. Ry.* (1884) 13 Q.B.D. 131; see also *Young* v. *Bankier Distillery* (1893) 20 R. (H.L.) 76.
13 *Dowie* v. *Douglas* (1822) 1 Sh. App. 125; *Reekie* v. *Norrie* (1842) 15 Sc. Jur. 151; *Hallowell* v. *Niven* (1843) 5 D. 759; *Aitchison* v. *Thorburn* (1870) 7 S.L.R. 347; cf. *Owens* v. *H.M. Advocate*, 1946 J.C. 119.
14 *Codd* v. *Cabe* (1876) 1 Ex. D. 352.
15 Bell, *Prin.* §2032; cf. *H.M.A.* v. *Carson*, 1964 S.L.T. 21.

person[1] or ejecting a trespasser,[2] or shooting a dog which is frightening or killing sheep if there was actual or imminent danger of harm, no other practicable means of stopping or preventing the attack, and the act was in the circumstances reasonably necessary.[3]

Provocation

Provocation is a defence in cases of assault, provided the assault is not excessive retaliation for the provocation given.[4] Verbal provocation may be relevant only in mitigation of damages.[5]

Ignorance

Ignorance of law is no excuse for delict.[6] Ignorance of fact may be a defence if the fact is one which makes the taking of precautions incumbent,[7] but not if the fact is as to the customary or necessary standards or kinds of precautions.

Mistake

Mistake of law, or the unfounded belief that conduct was not actionable, is no defence.[8] Mistake of fact, as by defaming a person accidentally,[9] or arresting the wrong person, or the belief that the precautions taken were adequate, is not a defence.

Inevitable accident

An inevitable accident is a casual happening, neither intended nor avoidable by any such precautions as any reasonable man could be expected to foresee as necessary in the circumstances or to take. If accordingly all such care and precautions as prudence and foresight would suggest to the reasonable man as desirable in the circumstances have been taken, but harm befalls, the

[1] cf. *Strong* v. *Bradbury* [1952] 2 All E.R. 76.

[2] *Bell* v. *Shand* (1870) 7 S.L.R. 267; *Wood* v. *N.B. Ry.* (1899) 2 F. 1.

[3] *Miles* v. *Hutchings* [1903] 2 K.B. 714; *Cope* v. *Sharpe* [1912] 1 K.B. 496; *Gott* v. *Measures* [1948] 1 K.B. 234; *Creswell* v. *Sirl* [1948] 1 K.B. 241; *Hamps* v. *Darby* [1948] 2 K.B. 311; *Goodway* v. *Becher* [1951] 2 All E.R. 349.

[4] *Haddaway* v. *Goddard* (1818) 1 Mur. 148; *Beatson* v. *Drysdale* (1819) 2 Mur. 151; *Dowie* v. *Douglas* (1822) 1 Sh. App. 125; *Miles* v. *Finlayson* (1829) 5 Mur. 85; *Brown* v. *Gibson-Craig* (1834) 13 S. 697; *Hallowell* v. *Niven* (1843) 5 D. 759.

[5] *Thom* v. *Graham* (1835) 13 S. 1121; *Anderson* v. *Marshall* (1835) 13 S. 1130; *Falconer* v. *Cochran* (1837) 15 S. 891.

[6] cf. *Clark* v. *Syme*, 1957 J.C. 1.

[7] e.g. the dangers inherent in particular work. But if the reasonable person would or should have known of the dangers, the defence must fail.

[8] *Shields* v. *Shearer*, 1914 S.C. (H.L.) 33; cf. *Clark* v. *Syme*, 1957 J.C. 1.

[9] *Morrison* v. *Ritchie* (1902) 4 F. 645; *Hulton* v. *Jones* [1910] A.C. 20.

defender is not liable.[1] Inevitable accident is not, however, a defence in a case of absolute statutory duty, where liability attaches even though all reasonable precautions have been taken.[2]

Damnum fatale

Damnum fatale, *vis major*, or act of God is a happening which no human foresight can provide against and of which human prudence is not bound to recognize the possibility; such an event is accordingly a calamity which infers no obligation to make reparation.[3] An earthquake might be, but an extraordinary downpour of rain is not, in Scotland, a *damnum fatale*.[4]

Limitation or exclusion of claim by contract

Save in certain cases,[5] a party may by contract limit or exclude liability for loss or harm caused by his fault to the other contracting party. The exclusion may be total[6] and even exclude the claim of a surviving relative in the event of the contracting party's death.[7] To be effective the exemption must be incorporated in the contract at the time of contracting and not be apparent only afterwards.[8] Incorporation in an oral contract is possible but difficult of proof. A notice may be a mere warning and not a term of the contract,[9] but may import a term into a contract if so visible that a contracting party must have seen it when he contracted,[10] or if referred to in any document evidencing the contract.[11]

If any document is handed over it must be obviously a con-

[1] cf. *Stanley* v. *Powell* [1891] 1 Q.B. 86; *Fowler* v. *Lanning* [1959] 1 Q.B. 426.

[2] *Millar* v. *Galashiels Gas Co.*, 1949 S.C. (H.L.) 31.

[3] *Tennent* v. *Earl of Glasgow* (1864) 2 M. (H.L.) 22, 26.

[4] *Kerr* v. *Earl of Orkney* (1857) 20 D. 298; *Tennent, supra*; *Caledonian Ry.* v. *Greenock Corpn.*, 1917 S.C. (H.L.) 56; see also *Samuel* v. *Edinburgh & Glasgow Ry.* (1851) 13 D. 312; *Pirie* v. *Aberdeen Mags.* (1871) 9 M. 412; *Kidston* v. *Caledonian Ry.* (1894) 1 S.L.T. 576; *Niven* v. *Ayr Harbour Trs.* (1898) 25 R. (H.L.) 42; *St. George Co-op. Soc.* v. *Glasgow Corpn.*, 1921 S.C. 872; contrast *Nichols* v. *Marsland* (1876) 2 Ex. D. 1.

[5] Carriers Act, 1830, S. 4; Railway and Canal Traffic Act, 1854, S. 7; Carriage of Goods by Sea Act, 1924, Sched., Art. III, s. 8; Law Reform (Personal Injuries) Act, 1948, S. 1(3); Hotel Proprietors Act, 1956; Road Traffic Act, 1960, S. 151; Carriage by Air Act, 1961, Sched. I, Ch. III, Art. 23.

[6] *Henderson* v. *Stevenson* (1875) 2 R. (H.L.) 71; *Beaumont-Thomas* v. *Blue Star Line* [1939] 2 All E.R. 127; *Curtis* v. *Chemical Cleaning Co.* [1951] 1 K.B. 805; *Adler* v. *Dickson* [1954] 3 All E.R. 397; *Spurling* v. *Bradshaw* [1956] 2 All E.R. 121.

[7] *McKay* v. *Scottish Airways*, 1948 S.C. 254.

[8] *Olley* v. *Marlborough Court, Ltd.* [1949] 1 K.B. 532; *McCutcheon* v. *MacBrayne*, 1964 S.C. (H.L.) 28.

[9] *Jude* v. *Edinburgh Corpn.*, 1943 S.C. 399, 402.

[10] *Wright* v. *Howard Baker & Co.* (1893) 21 R. 25; *Olley, supra*; *Harling* v. *Eddy* [1951] 2 K.B. 739.

[11] *Watkins* v. *Rymill* (1883) 10 Q.B.D. 178; *Thompson* v. *L.M.S. Ry.* [1930] 1 K.B. 41.

tractual document evidencing the contract on which conditions may be and often are stated, and not merely a receipt, admission ticket or other document not *ex facie* contractual.[1]

A condition exempting one party from liability will be held incorporated in the contract if the other party signed the contract, in which case he is bound whether he read the conditions or not,[2] if it were signed by his agent,[3] or even if he could not read[4] or understand the conditions,[5] but not if the signature were obtained by fraud or innocent misrepresentation.[6]

Or it will be held incorporated if the party relying on the exemption took reasonably adequate steps to bring the condition to the notice of the other party; the latter is bound if he knew that there was writing on the document and knew or believed that it contained conditions, or if he knew that there was writing on the document but did not know that it contained conditions but if document and the mode of delivery to him gave reasonable notice that the document contained conditions.[7] The condition will not be held incorporated if the document does not give reasonable notice of the conditions.[8] It is sufficient notice if notice is given of the existence of conditions by reference to where they may be seen.[9] Or a condition may be held incorporated by a previous course of dealing between the parties.[10]

The scope of any limitation or exclusion depends on the interpretation of the condition. Such clauses are construed strictly and *contra proferentem*;[11] if not clearly expressed they may be disregarded.[12]

[1] *Parker* v. *S.E. Ry.* (1877) 2 C.P.D. 416, 422; *Skrine* v. *Gould* (1912) 29 T.L.R. 19; *Chapelton* v. *Barry U.D.C.* [1940] 1 K.B. 532; *Taylor* v. *Glasgow Corpn.*, 1952 S.C. 440; *McCutcheon* v. *MacBrayne*, 1964 S.C. (H.L.) 28.

[2] *Parker, supra*; *Hood* v. *Anchor Line*, 1918 S.C. (H.L.) 143.

[3] *G.T. Ry. of Canada* v. *Robinson* [1915] A.C. 740.

[4] *Thompson* v. *L.M.S. Ry.* [1930] 1 K.B. 41.

[5] *Parker, supra.*

[6] *Curtis* v. *Chemical Cleaning Co.* [1951] 1 K.B. 805.

[7] *Parker* v. *S.E. Ry.* (1877) 2 C.P.D. 416; *Marriott* v. *Yeoward Bros.* [1909] 2 K.B. 987; *Hood* v. *Anchor Line*, 1918 S.C. (H.L.) 143; *Nunan* v. *S. Ry.* [1923] 2 K.B. 703; *Thompson* v. *L.M.S. Ry.* [1930] 1 K.B. 41; *Penton* v. *S. Ry.* [1931] 2 K.B. 103.

[8] *Henderson* v. *Stevenson* (1875) 2 R. (H.L.) 71; *Richardson* v. *Rowntree* [1894] A.C. 217; *Grieve* v. *Turbine Steamers* (1903) 11 S.L.T. 379; *Hooper* v. *Furness Ry.* (1907) 23 T.L.R. 451; *Williamson* v. *N. of S. S.N. Co.*, 1916 S.C. 554; *Lewis* v. *Laird Line*, 1925 S.L.T. 316; *Morris* v. *Laird Line*, 1925 S.L.T. 321.

[9] *Parker, supra*; *Richardson, supra.*

[10] *Spurling* v. *Bradshaw* [1956] 2 All E.R. 121; *McCutcheon* v. *MacBrayne*, 1964 S.C. (H.L.) 28.

[11] *Horsley* v. *Baxter* (1893) 20 R. 333; *Moor Line* v. *Distillers Co.*, 1921 S.C. 514; *Van Til Hartman* v. *Thomson*, 1931 S.N. 30; *Lee* v. *Ry. Exec.* [1949] 2 All E.R. 581; *White* v. *Warwick* [1953] 2 All E.R. 1021.

[12] *Alison* v. *Wallsend Slipway Co.* (1927) 43 T.L.R. 323; *Rutter* v. *Palmer* [1922] 2 K.B. 87.

No exemption clause, however widely framed, will protect a party who was in breach of any of the fundamental obligations of his contract when his fault caused the loss or harm complained of, as when a contract of carriage is being performed by an unroadworthy vehicle or an incompetent driver.[1]

Consent or voluntary assumption of risk

A person has no right of action if he has expressly consented to conduct to him which would otherwise be actionable, or to run the risk of unintentional harm. Unwilling consent, if voluntary, is valid[2] but consent obtained by force, fear or misrepresentation is invalid.[3] In emergency necessity may be held to justify acting in the absence of consent, and a tutor or curator may consent on behalf of a ward. An inference of implied consent may be drawn from conduct, acquiescing in what is later objected to as a wrong, or participation without objection. To be a defence the consent must cover the kind of conduct complained of, and is no defence to conduct other than or going beyond that consented to.[4] The common cases are of consent to surgical treatment,[5] medical treatment or examination, and alleged indecent assault or rape.[6]

Voluntary assumption of risk—volenti non fit injuria

A pursuer may be held in particular circumstances to have voluntarily assumed the risk of the harm which befell and caused him the injury complained of.[7] The basis of this plea is that he consented in the circumstances to waive the duty of care otherwise incumbent on the defender towards him, rather than that he consented to absolve the defender from liability for breach of that duty.[8] The plea is probably inapplicable in all cases of breach of statutory duty.[9] If the plea is upheld the pursuer's case fails

[1] cf. *Alexander* v. *Ry. Executive* [1951] 2 K.B. 882; *Spurling* v. *Bradshaw* [1956] 2 All E.R. 121; *Karsales (Harrow) Ltd.* v. *Wallis* [1956] 2 All E.R. 866.

[2] *Latter* v. *Braddell* (1880) 50 L.J.Q.B. 448.

[3] cf. *Muir* v. *Hamilton Mags.*, 1910 1 S.L.T. 164; *Adamson* v. *Martin*, 1916 S.C. 319.

[4] cf. *Reid* v. *Mitchell* (1885) 12 R. 1129.

[5] cf. *Marshall* v. *Curry* [1933] 3 D.L.R. 260.

[6] *Murray* v. *Fraser*, 1916 S.C. 623, 635.

[7] *Wallace* v. *Culter Paper Mills* (1892) 19 R. 915; *Murphy* v. *Stewart* (1906) 14 S.L.T. 336; *Robertson* v. *Primrose*, 1910 S.C. 111; *Stewart's Exrx.* v. *C.N. Trs.*, 1946 S.C. 317; *Rowand* v. *Saunders & Connnor Ltd.*, 1953 S.C. 292.

[8] *Dann* v. *Hamilton* [1939] 1 K.B. 509; *Kelly* v. *Farrans, Ltd.* [1954] N. I. 41; *McCaig* v. *Langan*, 1964 S.L.T. 121; see also *Bankhead* v. *McCarthy*, 1963 S.C. 263.

[9] *Baddeley* v. *Granville* (1887) 19 Q.B.D. 423; *Davies* v. *Owen* [1919] 2 K.B. 39; *Wheeler* v. *New Merton Board Mills* [1933] 2 K.B. 669; *Alford* v. *N.C.B.*, 1952 S.C. (H.L.) 17, 22.

entirely because there was no duty for the defender to breach and any harm is *damnum sine injuria*.[1]

For the plea to apply it must be shown that the pursuer freely and voluntarily, with full knowledge of the nature and extent of the risk he ran, impliedly agreed to incur it;[2] it must be not merely some risk, but the risk of the particular kind of harm which in fact befell him.[3] A person is not *volens* merely because he was present, or continued at work, or did not object to the defender's actings.[4]

In landlord and tenant cases tenants have sometimes been held barred by taking or remaining in a house in the knowledge of the defect and without objection,[5] but not if they had objected and, sometimes, had been assured it would be remedied.[6]

In employment cases the defence is inapplicable to even known risks, particularly if objected to,[7] and requires the clearest evidence of consent by the pursuer to the conduct involving the risk to him and consent to take the risk on himself.[8]

In road accident cases the plea may apply to passengers riding in a vehicle in the knowledge of the driver's diminished capacity to drive.[9]

In the case of spectators at sports meetings the plea applies to injuries incidental to the fair playing of the game but not

[1] As to the appropriate counter issue for a jury trial see *Rowand, supra.*

[2] *Letang* v. *Ottawa Electric Ry.* [1926] A.C. 725.

[3] *Stewarts Exrx., supra*; *Andrews* v. *Colvilles*, 1947 S.N. 10; cf. *Ward* v. *Revie*, 1944 S.C. 325.

[4] *Reid* v. *Mitchell* (1885) 12 R. 1129; *Smith* v. *Baker* [1891] A.C. 325; *Stewart's Exrx., supra.*

[5] *Henderson* v. *Munn* (1888) 15 R. 859; *Webster* v. *Brown* (1892) 19 R. 675; *Russell* v. *Macknight* (1896) 24 R. 118; *Smith* v. *School Board of Maryculter* (1898) 1 F. 5; *McManus* v. *Armour* (1901) 3 F. 1078; *Davidson* v. *Sprengel*, 1909 S.C. 566; *Wolfson* v. *Forrester*, 1910 S.C. 675; *Hislop* v. *Murphy*, 1924 S.L.T. 796; *Proctor* v. *Cowlairs Co-op. Soc.*, 1961 S.L.T. 434. The defence is still competent under the Occupiers' Liability (Sc.) Act, 1960, S. 3.

[6] *Shields* v. *Dalziel* (1894) 24 R. 849; *Hall* v. *Hubner* (1897) 24 R. 875; *Caldwell* v. *McCallum* (1901) 4 F. 371; *McKinlay* v. *McClymont* (1905) 13 S.L.T. 427; *Grant* v. *McCafferty*, 1907 S.C. 201; *Cameron* v. *Young*, 1907 S.C. 475 (revd. 1908 S.C. (H.L.) 7); *Dickie* v. *Amicable Property Inv. Bldg. Soc.*, 1911 S.C. 1079; *Dickson* v. *St. Cuthbert's Co-op. Assoc.*, 1922 S.L.T. 116; *Mullen* v. *Dunbarton C.C.*, 1933 S.C. 380.

[7] *Smith* v. *Baker* [1891] A.C. 325; *Wallace, supra*; *Smith, supra*; *Robertson, supra*; *Stewart's Exrx. supra.*

[8] *Williams* v. *Birmingham Battery Co.* [1899] 2 Q.B. 338; *Monaghan* v. *Rhodes* [1920] 1 K.B. 487; *Baker* v. *James* [1921] 2 K.B. 674; *Bowater* v. *Rowley Regis Corpn.* [1944] K.B. 476; *Staveley Iron Co.* v. *Jones* [1956] A.C. 627.

[9] *Dann* v. *Hamilton* [1939] 1 K.B. 509 (expld. *Slater* v. *Clay Cross Co.* [1956] 2 Q.B. 264; *Dawrant* v. *Nutt* [1960] 3 All E.R. 681); cf. *Bankhead* v. *McCarthy*, 1963 S.C. 263; *McCaig* v. *Langan*, 1964 S.L.T. 121.

to injuries caused by reckless disregard of the spectator's safety.[1]

The plea has repeatedly been rejected in rescue cases, where an individual has deliberately taken a known risk to save life or property from imminent danger. The compulsion of social or moral duty to attempt rescue makes such intervention and the taking of the risk less than wholly voluntary.[2]

Contributory negligence

Contributory negligence is carelessness on a pursuer's part which is a co-operating cause, along with the negligence of the defender, of the harm the pursuer sustains.[3] Negligence, to be contributory, need not amount to breach of a legal duty of care; it need only be lack of reasonable care for oneself.[4] The onus of proof of contributory negligence is on the defender.[5] The plea is competent both in actions based on common law fault and in those based on breach of statutory duty.[6]

At common law contributory negligence by the pursuer, to any extent at all, defeated his claim entirely.[7] This result was modified by the 'last opportunity' rule that the party was to blame who had the last clear chance of avoiding the accident but failed to do so by not taking reasonable care,[8] though latterly,

[1] *Hall* v. *Brooklands Auto Racing Club* [1933] 1 K.B. 205; *Meldrum* v. *Perthshire Agricultural Soc.* (1948) 64 Sh. Ct. Rep. 89; *O'Dowd* v. *Frazer Nash* [1951] W.N. 173; *Murray* v. *Harringay Arena, Ltd.* [1951] 2 K.B. 529; cf. *Wooldridge* v. *Sumner* [1962] 2 All E.R. 978.

[2] *Haynes* v. *Harwood* [1935] 1 K.B. 146; *D'Urso* v. *Sanson* [1939] 4 All E.R. 26; *Morgan* v. *Aylen* [1942] 1 All E.R. 489; *Steel* v. *Glasgow Iron & Steel Co.*, 1944 S.C. 237; *Baker* v. *Hopkins* [1959] 3 All E.R. 225; *Videan* v. *B.T.C.* [1963] 2 All E.R. 860.

[3] *Moffat* v. *Park* (1877) 5 R. 13, 17; *Robinson* v. *Wm. Hamilton (Motors) Ltd.*, 1923 S.C. 838, 841.

[4] *McLean* v. *Bell*, 1932 S.C. (H.L.) 21, 28; *Davies* v. *Swan Motor Co.* [1949] 2 K.B. 291, 308, 324; *Nance* v. *B.C. Electric Ry.* [1951] A.C. 601; *Jones* v. *Livox Quarries, Ltd.* [1952] 2 Q.B. 608, 615.

[5] *Hayden* v. *Glasgow Corpn.*, 1948 S.C. 143. See also *McMartin* v. *Hannay* (1872) 10 M. 411; *Potter* v. *N.B. Ry.* (1873) 11 M. 664.

[6] *Caswell* v. *Powell Duffryn Collieries* [1940] A.C. 152.

[7] *Heaney* v. *Glasgow Iron & Steel Co.* (1898) 25 R. 903; *Driscoll* v. *Partick Burgh Commrs.* (1900) 2 F. 368; *Maxwell* v. *Caledonian Pottery Co.* (1902) 10 S.L.T. 160; *Campbell* v. *United Collieries*, 1912 S.C. 182; *Baikie* v. *Glasgow Corpn.*, 1919 S.C. (H.L.) 13; *Holland* v. *Glasgow Educ. Endowments Bd.*, 1923 S.L.T. 687; *Jude* v. *Edinburgh Corpn.*, 1943 S.C. 399.

[8] *Butterfield* v. *Forrester* (1809) 11 East 60; *Davies* v. *Mann* (1842) 10 M. & W. 546; *Radley* v. *L.N.W. Ry.* (1876) 1 App. Cas. 759; *Mitchell* v. *Caledonian Ry.*, 1909 S.C. 746; *Gibb* v. *Edinburgh Tramways.* 1913 S.C. 541; *Taylor* v. *Dumbarton Tramways*, 1918 S.C. (H.L.) 96; *Barty* v. *Harper*, 1922 S.C. 67; *Mitchell* v. *McHarg*, 1923 S.C. 657; *Robinson* v. *Hamilton*, 1923 S.C. 838; *McLean* v. *Bell*, 1932 S.C. (H.L.) 21.

where both parties had been in fault, the question was said to be whose fault had been the decisive and immediate cause.[1]

The Maritime Conventions Act, 1911, provided that where damage or loss was caused by the fault of two or more vessels, their liability should be in proportion to the degree in which each was in fault.[2] This principle was applied generally by the Law Reform (Contributory Negligence) Act, 1945, which provides that in a case of joint fault, a claim does not wholly fail by reason of the pursuer's contributory negligence but damages are reduced in proportion to the pursuer's share in responsibility for the damage. The court or jury can therefore now find that the faults of both parties caused the harm, and allocate responsibility between pursuer and defender.[3] Liability is to be apportioned on the basis of responsibility, not of causation.[4] Where there are two or more defenders the court must first make any reduction in respect of the pursuer's own fault and then allocate responsibility between the defenders.[5]

Alternative danger, or the agony rule

If the defender's fault has placed the pursuer in a position of danger, he is not guilty of contributory negligence if he adopts the wrong course of action and thereby suffers injury which he might in fact have avoided, or suffers greater injury.[6] The pursuer's conduct must not be judged too critically by the defender who has caused the emergency.[7]

The dilemma principle

Nor is the pursuer guilty of contributory negligence if, having been placed in a dilemma by the defender's fault, he elects what proves to be a harmful, or the harmful, course.[8]

[1] *Taylor, supra*; *Swadling* v. *Cooper* [1931] A.C. 1; *Caswell* v. *Powell Duffryn Collieries* [1940] A.C. 152; *Boy Andrew* v. *St. Rognvald*, 1947 S.C. (H.L.) 70, 76.

[2] See *Admiralty Commrs.* v. *S.S. Volute* [1922] 1 A.C. 129; approved *Sigurdson* v. *British Columbia Electric Ry.* [1953] A.C. 291, as still a suitable direction for a jury.

[3] *Davies* v. *Swan Motor Co.* [1949] 2 K.B. 291; *Jones* v. *Livox Quarries, Ltd.* [1952] 2 Q.B. 608. As as to the appropriate counter-issue in a jury case see *Hayden* v. *Glasgow Corp.*, 1948 S.C. 143; *Maclean* v. *Admiralty*, 1960 S.C. 199.

[4] *McLean* v. *Bell*, 1932 S.C. (H.L.) 21, 29; 1945 Act, S. 1(1); *Davies, supra.*

[5] Law Reform (Misc. Prov.) (Sc.) Act, 1940, S. 3.

[6] *Jones* v. *Boyce* (1816) 1 Starkie 493; *The Bywell Castle* (1879) 4 P.D. 219.

[7] *Laird Line* v. *U.S. Shipping Board*, 1924 S.C. (H.L.) 37, 40; cf. *Baron Vernon* v. *Metagama*, 1928 S.C. (H.L.) 21.

[8] *Clayards* v. *Dethick* (1848) 12 Q.B. 439; cf. *Sayers* v. *Harlow U.D.C.* [1958] 2 All E.R. 342.

Contributory negligence of children or infirm persons

Children and infirm persons will be less readily held guilty of contributory negligence than normal adults. Young children may be too young to appreciate danger and it is always a question of circumstances whether a child is old enough to have appreciated the danger and avoided it,[1] but sometimes the danger is so obvious that even a young child will be contributorily negligent if he takes the risk and is injured.[2]

A person suffering from physical infirmity should take greater care for his own safety[3] and may be held contributorily negligent if he has attempted to do what only a normal person can safely do, or has not disclosed his susceptibility and thereby contributed to his own injury.[4]

Defences special to particular kinds of wrongs

In many cases particular defences are competent in the circumstances of particular kinds of wrongs only; among such are provocation and self-defence in assault, *veritas*, privilege, fair comment, fair retort and *rixa* in defamation. These are dealt with in the context of those particular wrongs.

[1] *Fryer* v. *N.B. Ry.* (1908) 15 S.L.T. 886; *Campbell* v. *Ord & Maddison* (1873) 1 R. 149; *Fraser* v. *Edinburgh Tramways* (1882) 10 R. 264; *McGregor* v. *Ross & Marshall* (1883) 10 R. 725; *Devine* v. *Aitken* (1905) 13 S.L.T. 736; *Crawford* v. *Edinburgh Mags.* (1906) 14 S.L.T. 383; *Reilly* v. *Greenfield Coal Co.*, 1909 S.C. 1328; *Yachuk* v. *Oliver Blais Co.* [1949] A.C. 386; *Hughes* v. *Lord Advocate*, 1961 S.C. 310, 323 (affd. 1963 S.C. (H.L.)) 31.

[2] *Balfour* v. *Baird & Brown* (1857) 20 D. 238; *Thomson* v. *Lanarkshire Ry.* (1897) 24 R. 1025; *Pollock* v. *Glasgow Corpn.*, (1901) 39 S.L.R. 1; *Cass* v. *Edinburgh Tramways*, 1909 S.C. 1068; *Plantza* v. *Glasgow Corpn.*, 1910 S.C. 786; *Allison* v. *Langloan Iron Co.*, 1917 2 S.L.T. 162; *Shillinglaw* v. *Turner*, 1925 S.C. 807.

[3] *Clerk* v. *Petrie* (1879) 6 R. 1076; *Pollock* v. *Glasgow Mags.* (1895) 3 S.L.T. 156; *Rennie* v. *G.N.S. Ry.* (1905) 12 S.L.T. 667; *McKibbin* v. *Glasgow Corpn.*, 1920 S.C. 590; cf. *Bourhill* v. *Young*, 1942 S.C. (H.L.) 78, 92; *Paris* v. *Stepney B.C.* [1951] A.C. 367; *Haley* v. *London Electricity Bd.* [1964] 3 All E.R. 185.

[4] *Cork* v. *Kirby MacLean Ltd.* [1952] 2 All E.R. 402.

CHAPTER 64

TRANSFER AND EXTINCTION OF CLAIMS AND LIABILITIES

Voluntary assignation of claim

A CLAIM of damages for delict may be assigned *inter vivos* by the claimant, at any time when he could claim, to the effect of entitling the assignee in his own name to sue the wrongdoer, on any ground on which the assignor could have sued, and to recover such damages as the assignor could have recovered.[1] The assignor cannot thereafter sue unless a retrocession is effected before action is raised.[2] Any defences competent against the assignor may be pleaded against the assignee.[3] An injured person may also raise an action and then assign his claim,[4] or assign a decree obtained to a third party.[5] Assignation is useful where one party has settled a claim and wished to claim relief from another alleged to be also in fault.[6]

Subrogation

Where an insurer has indemnified his insured for a loss for which another party is legally liable he is without express assignation proportionately subrogated to the insured's right to recover from the wrongdoer, and may sue in name of the insured,[7] or is entitled to the benefit of compensation recovered from the wrongdoer by the insured.[8]

By the Third Parties (Rights against Insurers) Act, 1930, if an insured becomes bankrupt or unable to pay, the rights of the insured against the insurer are transferred to any third party

[1] *Milne* v. *Gauld's Tr.* (1841) 3 D. 345; *Mein* v. *Call* (1844) 6 D. 1112; *Thom* v. *Bridges* (1857) 19 D. 721; *Neilson* v. *Rodger* (1853) 16 D. 325, 329; *Gardiner* v. *Main* (1895) 22 R. 100, 104; *Traill* v. *A/S Dalbeattie* (1904) 6 F. 798; *Ryan* v. *McBurnie*, 1940 S.C. 173; *Cole-Hamilton* v. *Boyd*, 1963 S.C. (H.L.) 1.

[2] *Symington* v. *Campbell* (1894) 21 R. 434; *Bentley* v. *Macfarlane*, 1963 S.C. 279.

[3] *Cole-Hamilton, supra*, 14.

[4] *Cole-Hamilton, supra*, 12.

[5] *Palmer* v. *Wick & Pulteneytown S.S. Co.* (1894) 21 R. (H.L.) 39; *Steven* v. *Broady, Norman & Co.*, 1928 S.C. 351.

[6] cf. *Traill, supra*; ; *Ryan, supra*; *Coyle* v. *N.C.B.*, 1959 S.L.T. 114; *N.C.B.* v. *Thomson*, 1959 S.C. 353, 359.

[7] *Castellain* v. *Preston* (1883) 11 Q.B.D. 380; *King* v. *Victorian Ins. Co.* [1896] A.C. 251; *Edwards* v. *Motor Union* [1922] 2 K.B. 249; *Lister* v. *Romford Ice Co.* [1957] A.C. 555.

[8] *Castellain, supra.*

to whom liability covered by the insurance has been incurred and he may recover from the insurer.[1]

By the Road Traffic Act, 1960, S. 201, motor vehicles must be insured against the risk of liability for injury to or death of third parties caused by the driver's negligence. Insurers must (S. 208) satisfy judgments against persons insured notwithstanding that the insurer may be entitled to avoid or cancel, or may have avoided or cancelled, the policy.[2]

Assignation of decree

A decree obtained for damages may be assigned to a third party.[3] A joint and several decree enforced against one defender may then be assigned to him to enable him to claim relief from a joint delinquent,[4] though express assignation is no longer necessary.[5] The sum paid for the assignation is relevant only if paid by way of damages as it must then be taken into account in settling the rights of the wrongdoers *inter se*.[6]

Transmission of claim on death

Where a person has suffered actionable injury and later died the claim, if for solatium for infringement of personal rights, in his person, or honour, or domestic relations, dies with him, and cannot be initiated by his executor.[7] If, however, the claim were for compensation for infringement of patrimonial rights, involving damage to his property or loss to his estate, it passes to his executor, who may initiate an action therefor.[8]

In either case if the injured person had actually commenced an

[1] *Greenlees* v. *Port of Manchester Ins. Co.*, 1922 S.C. 383; *Rutherford* v. *Licences and General Ins. Co.*, 1934 S.L.T. 31; *Cunningham* v. *Anglian Ins. Co.*, 1934 S.L.T. 273.

[2] By an agreement of 1946 with the Ministry of Transport the Motor Insurers' Bureau will satisfy unsatisfied judgments of a court in respect of a liability required to be covered by insurance, provided notice is given within 21 days after proceedings are commenced.

[3] *Steven* v. *Broady, Norman & Co.*, 1928 S.C. 351.

[4] *Palmer* v. *Wick & Pulteneytown S.S. Co.* (1894) 21 R. (H.L.) 39.

[5] Law Reform (Misc. Prov.) (Sc.) Act, 1940, S. 3(2); *Central S.M.T. Co.* v. *Lanarkshire C.C.*, 1949 S.C. 450; *N.C.B.* v. *Thomson*, 1959 S.C. 353.

[6] *Cole-Hamilton* v. *Boyd*, 1963 S.C. (H.L.) 1, 17.

[7] *Bern's Exor.* v. *Montrose Asylum* (1893) 20 R. 859; *Boyce's Exor.* v. *McDougall* (1903) 5 F. 452; *Stewart's Exrx.* v. *L.M.S. Ry.*, 1943 S.C. (H.L.) 19; *Smith* v. *Stewart*, 1960 S.C. 329; 1961 S.C. 91.

[8] *Milne* v. *Gauld's Trs.* (1841) 3 D. 345; *Davidson* v. *Tulloch* (1860) 3 Macq. 783; *Garden* v. *Davidson* (1864) 2 M. 758; *Auld* v. *Sharp* (1874) 2 R. 191; *Bern's Exor.* v. *Montrose Asylum* (1893) 20 R. 859; *Borthwick* v. *B.* (1896) 24 R. 211; *Stewart's Exrx.* v. *L.M.S. Ry.*, *supra*; *Smith* v. *Stewart*, 1961 S.C. 91; *McGhie* v. *B.T.C.*, 1964 S.L.T. 25.

action before his death, his executor can continue that action,[1] but can recover only such damages as the deceased could have recovered, down to the date of his death. Any damages recovered by an executor belong to the deceased's estate, not to any particular surviving relative unless by right of succession to part of the estate.

Transmission of liability on death

In all cases a wrongdoer's liability is enforceable against his executors *quantum lucrati*.[2] A widow or other relative is not, as such, liable for a wrong done by the deceased.[3]

Transmission of claim on bankruptcy

A bankrupt retains a title to sue for damages for wrongs personal to himself;[4] the trustee has no title to sue alone[5] but may sist himself in an action brought by the bankrupt and take any award of damages for the creditors.[6] The trustee alone has a title to sue for patrimonial loss to the bankrupt's estate.[7]

Transmission of liability on bankruptcy

A bankrupt's liability for damages for delict transmits against the estate in the trustee's charge and any decree granted may be ranked for *pari passu* with other unsecured claims against the estate.

Transmission of claims and liabilities on liquidation

When a company goes into liquidation all rights of action may be enforced by the company (in liquidation) and the liquidator for the benefit of the creditors and shareholders.[8] Claims against the company may be constituted against the company and the liquidator thereof[9] and ranked for in the liquidation as an

[1] Bell, *Prin.* §546; *Neilson* v. *Rodger* (1853) 16 D. 325; *Borthwick* v. *B.* (1896) 24 R. 211; *Darling* v. *Gray* (1892) 19 R. (H.L.) 31; *Reid* v. *Lanarkshire Traction Co.*, 1934 S.C. 79; *Stewart's Exrx., supra.*; *Smith* v. *Stewart*, 1960 S.C. 329, overruling *Leigh's Exrx.* v. *Caledonian Ry.*, 1913 S.C. 838; *Smith* v. *Stewart*, 1961 S.C. 91; *Russell* v. *B.R.*, 1965 S.C. 422.

[2] Ersk. III, 1, 15; Bell, *Prin.* §544; *Auld* v. *Shairp* (1874) 2 R. 199; *Evans* v. *Stool* (1885) 12 R. 1295; *Bourhill* v. *Young's Exrx.*, 1942 S.C. (H.L.) 78; *Stewart's Exrx.* v. *L.M.S. Ry.*, 1943 S.C. (H.L.) 19, 24.

[3] *Thomson* v. *Duggie*, 1949 S.L.T. (Notes) 53.

[4] *Scott* v. *Johnston* (1885) 12 R. 1022; *Bern's Exor.* v. *Montrose Ayslum* (1893) 20 R. 859; *Muir's Tr.* v. *Braidwood*, 1958 S.C. 169.

[5] *Jackson* v. *McKechnie* (1878) 3 R. 130, 133.

[6] *Thom* v. *Bridges* (1859) 19 D. 721; *Jackson* v. *McKechnie* (1875) 3 R. 130.

[7] *Muir's Tr., supra.*

[8] cf. *Munro* v. *Hutchison* (1896) 3 S.L.T. 268.

[9] cf. *Steven* v. *Broady Norman & Co.*, 1928 S.C. 351.

unsecured claim. A claim constituted by decree before liquidation may be lodged in the liquidation.[1]

Transmission of claims and liabilities with property

A claim for damages for injury done to property does not transmit to a purchaser without assignation.[2] Nor does a wrongdoer rid himself of liability by disposing of the property involved in the wrongdoing.

Relief

A person who satisfies a claim of damages may claim relief from another who, he avers, was the real, or a co-operating, cause of the loss, and is therefore liable to relieve him in whole or in part. Right of relief may arise by contract,[3] or by statute, against a joint delinquent,[4] or against one who, if sued, might also have been held liable along with the claimant,[5] to such extent as the court may deem just.[6] The damages against which relief, total or partial, is sought must have been judicially constituted against the claimant, not ascertained by settlement or compromise.[7]

A right of relief also exists at common law against an actual wrongdoer for whom the claimant has been held vicariously liable to a third party,[8] and against any party whose initial fault caused the claimant to become liable to a third party in damages.[9] There is no right where the claimant compromised the claim against him or did not make the payment under decree,[10] still less where he was held liable for his own fault.

Discharge of claim by decree, absolvitor or dismissal

A claim for damages for delict is totally discharged by grant of decree and satisfaction of that decree; the cause becomes *res*

1 Companies Act, 1948, S. 316.

2 *Symington* v. *Campbell* (1894) 21 R. 434; cf. *Blumer* v. *Scott* (1874) 1 R. 379; *Craig* v. *Blackater*, 1923 S.C. 472.

3 *Binnie* v. *Parlane* (1825) 4 S. 122; *Hamilton* v. *Anderson*, 1953 S.C. 129; *N. of S. Hydro-Electric Bd.* v. *Taylor*, 1956 S.C. 1.

4 Law Reform (Misc. Prov.) (Sc.) Act, 1940, S. 3(1).

5 Ibid., S. 3(2); cf. *Glasgow Corpn.* v. *Turnbull*, 1932 S.L.T. 457; *Wimpey* v. *B.O.A.C.* [1955] A.C. 169.

6 This may amount to a complete indemnity; cf. *Jones* v. *Manchester Corpn.* [1952] 2 Q.B. 852; *Harvey* v. *O'Dell* [1958] 2 Q.B. 78.

7 *N.C.B.* v. *Thomson*, 1959 S.C. 353.

8 *Ryan* v. *Fildes* [1938] 3 All E.R. 517; *Jones* v. *Manchester Corpn.* [1952] 2 Q.B. 852; *Semtex* v. *Gladstone* [1954] 2 All E.R. 206; *Lister* v. *Romford Ice Co.* [1957] A.C. 555.

9 *Gilmour* v. *Clark* (1853) 15 D. 478; *Colt* v. *Caledonian Ry.* (1860) 3 Macq. 833; *Ovington* v. *McVicar* (1864) 2 M. 1066; *McIntyre* v. *Gallacher* (1883) 11 R. 64; *Baxter* v. *Boswell* (1899) 6 S.L.T. 278; *Wood* v. *Mackay* (1906) 8 F. 625; *Buchanan and Carswell* v. *Eugene*, 1936 S.C. 160.

10 *Gardiner* v. *Main* (1894) 22 R. 100.

judicata. A further action cannot then be brought, whether on the ground that the damages are inadequate, or on the ground that further and greater loss has subsequently been found to have been sustained by reason of the wrong; a claim must cover all loss alleged, past and future, certain and contingent, direct and consequential.[1] Nor can a further action be brought against another defender who is alleged to have been in part the cause of the loss,[2] unless the decree in the first action has been worthless.[3]

But if there is a continuing cause of action such as nuisance a fresh action may be brought for each fresh incident causing loss, damages being given for that alone and not prospectively.[4]

Also if a single incident gives rise to more than one distinct cause of action, as to claims for personal injuries and also for property damage, separate actions are competent.[5] Claims based on breach of common law duty and of statutory duty are not separate causes of action, though arising from one set of facts.[6]

Decree of absolvitor similarly totally extinguishes a right of action against the defender sued on the ground of action founded on, even if based on an agreement to settle the claim.[7]

Decree of dismissal only excludes a future action against the same defender based on the same point of law; the pursuer may bring another claim on the same ground of action but on a different ground in law.[8] The dismissal of an action on relevancy can never be *res judicata*.[9]

Discharge of claims

A person may discharge a claim he has against another on any terms they may agree, frequently in return for a payment made to settle the claim though without admission of liability. It may be in any form and may be proved by any evidence.[10] A *pactum de non petendo* in unqualified terms imports a discharge of the claim[11]

[1] *Brunsden* v. *Humphrey* (1884) 14 Q.B.D. 141; *Stevenson* v. *Pontifex and Wood* (1887) 15 R. 125; *Darley Main Colliery* v. *Mitchell* (1886) 11 App. Cas. 127.

[2] Ersk. III, 1, 15; *Balfour* v. *Baird*, 1959 S.C. 64.

[3] *Steven* v. *Broady Norman & Co.*, 1928 S.C. 351.

[4] *Hole* v. *Chard Union* [1894] 1 Ch. 293; see also *Jackson* v. *Cowie* (1872) 9 S.L.R. 617; *Cameron-Head* v. *Cameron*, 1919 S.C. 627.

[5] *Brunsden*, *supra*.

[6] *Matuszczyk* v. *N.C.B.*, 1955 S.C. 418.

[7] *Matuszczyk* v. *N.C.B.*, 1955 S.C. 418; *Young* v. *Y's Trs.*, 1957 S.L.T. 205.

[8] *E. Perth* v. *Willoughby d'Eresby's Trs.* (1875) 2 R. 538, 545 (affd. 5 R. (H.L.) 26); *D. Sutherland* v. *Reed* (1890) 2 F. 754.

[9] *Menzies* v. *M.* (1893) 20 R. (H.L.) 108.

[10] *N.B. Ry.* v. *Wood* (1891) 18 R. (H.L.) 27; *Davies* v. *Hunter*, 1934 S.C. 10; cf. *Macvean* v. *Maclean* (1873) 11 M. 506.

[11] *Thin & Sinclair* v. *Arrol* (1896) 24 R. 198; cf. *McLean* v. *Hassard* (1903) 10 S.L.T. 593. Contrast *Muir* v. *Crawford* (1875) 2 R. (H.L.) 148.

and acceptance of insurance benefits from an employer has been held to imply a discharge.[1] A discharge can be founded on only by the party in whose favour it was granted.[2]

The effect of a discharge granted to one of several co-delinquents sued jointly and severally depends on whether it discharges the liability of the grantee only, in which case the pursuer's right to proceed against the other delinquents for the balance of the sum sued for, is unimpaired.[3] or is a discharge of the whole claim as a ground of action.[4] If several delinquents are sued severally only, a discharge of one imports a discharge of the others.[5] A decree against one of several delinquents sued jointly and severally does not operate as a discharge of the others if it is not satisfied.[6]

In the interpretation of a discharge general words are limited to what was contemplated by the parties at the time it was granted.[7] If the wards of the discharge do not exclude it a claim on another legal ground of action, though arising from the same facts, is competent.

A discharge may be reduced by the granter if he can establish minority at the time of granting and lesion,[8] or impetration by fraud, or essential error induced by misrepresentation,[9] but not merely because the granter did not understand the full significance of the discharge,[10] nor because it had been granted in ignorance of an offer made,[11] nor because the consideration was inadequate.[12]

[1] *Wright* v. *Howard, Baker & Co.* (1893) 21 R. 25. Acceptance of National Insurance benefits does not carry any such implication.

[2] *Dillon* v. *Napier, Shanks & Bell* (1893) 30 S.L.R. 685; *Douglas* v. *Hogarth* (1901) 4 F. 148.

[3] *Western Bank* v. *Bairds* (1862) 24 D. 859, 912; *Cormie* v. *Grigor* (1862) 24 D. 985; *Campbell* v. *Morrison* (1891) 19 R. 282; *Delaney* v. *Stirling* (1893) 20 R. 506; *Douglas, supra*; *Robinson* v. *Reid's Trs* (1900) 2 F. 928; *Steven* v. *Broady Norman & Co.*, 1928 S.C. 351; *McNair* v. *Dunfermline Corpn.*, 1953 S.C. 183.

[4] *Delaney* v. *Stirling, supra.*

[5] *Douglas, supra.*

[6] *Steven* v. *Broady Norman & Co.*, 1928 S.C. 351; cf. *Houston* v. *Buchanan*, 1937 S.C. 460; 1940 S.C. (H.L.) 17.

[7] *McAdam* v. *Scott*, 1913 1 S.L.T. 12.

[8] *Robertson* v. *Henderson* (1905) 7 F. 776; *McFeetridge* v. *Stewarts and Lloyds*, 1913 S.C. 773.

[9] *Dornan* v. *Allan* (1900) 3 F. 112; *Ellis* v. *Lochgelly Iron Co.*, 1909 S.C. 1278; *McGuire* v. *Paterson*, 1913 S.C. 400; *Park* v. *Anderson*, 1924 S.C. 1017; *Davies* v. *Hunter*, 1934 S.C. 10; *McGuire* v. *Addie's Collieries*, 1950 S.C. 537.

[10] *N.B. Ry. Co.* v. *Wood* (1891) 18 R. (H.L.) 27; *Mackie* v. *Strachan, Kinmond & Co.* (1896) 23 R. 1030; *Mathieson* v. *Hawthorns* (1899) 1 F. 468; contrast *McDonagh* v. *McLellan* (1886) 13 R. 1000; *Macandrew* v. *Gilhooley*, 1911 S.C. 448.

[11] *Welsh* v. *Cousin* (1899) 2 F. 277; cf. *Russell* v. *Farrell* (1900) 2 F. 892.

[12] *N.B. Ry. Co.* v. *Wood* (1891) 18 R. (H.L.) 27; *McGuire, supra.*

Compromise or settlement of claim

A claim may be compromised or settled by the parties on whatever terms they may agree, without the leave of the court, by extra-judicial offer before litiscontestation, by such an offer thereafter, or by tender or judicial offer made thereafter and duly accepted. An advocate may,[1] but a solicitor cannot,[2] compromise a claim without authority.

A compromise may be entered into orally and proved *prout de jure*;[3] once agreed it is not revocable[4] but is reducible if obtained unfairly,[5] and not merely under error in fact[6] or in law.[7] The authority of the court is unnecessary[8] but if an action has been commenced it must be abandoned or dismissed of consent or decree for the agreed sum consented to or authority granted to a joint minute craving decree in terms of the settlement.

Settlement may also be based on a tender of a sum by the defender made on record or by separate minute.[9] It may be amended, or withdrawn,[10] or lapse.[11] It must include an offer in respect of the expenses of process; it remains open for a reasonable time unless definitely refused. Where there are several pursuers there must be a tender of separate sums to each pursuer.[12] A tender by one of several joint delinquents may be accepted and the action continued against the others.[13] In defamation cases a tender must contain a withdrawal of the alleged slander.[14] If the tender is accepted, a minute of acceptance is lodged and decree

1 *Duncan* v. *Salmond* (1874) 1 R. 329; *Batchelor* v. *Pattison and Mackersy* (1876) 3 R. 914.

2 *Thoms* v. *Bain* (1888) 15 R. 613.

3 *Thomson* v. *Fraser* (1868) 7 M. 39; *Love* v. *Marshall* (1872) 10 M. 795; *Dobie* v. *Lauder's Trs.* (1873) 11 M. 749; *Downie* v. *Black* (1885) 13 R. 271; *Gow* v. *Henry* (1899) 2 F. 48; *Anderson* v. *Dick* (1901) 4 F. 68.

4 *Dewar* v. *Ainslie* (1892) 20 R. 203.

5 Bell, *Prin.* §535; *Stewart* v. *S.* (1836) 15 S. 112; cf. *Henderson* v. *Stewart* (1894) 22 R. 154.

6 *Welsh* v. *Cousin* (1899) 2 F. 277.

7 *Johnston* v. *J.* (1859) 3 Macq. 619; *Kippen* v. *K's Tr.* (1874) 1 R. 1171.

8 *McAthey* v. *Patriotic Investment Socy., Ltd.*, 1910 S.C. 584.

9 *Bissett* v. *Anderson* (1847) 10 D. 233; *Gunn* v. *Breadalbane* (1849) 11 D. 1046; *Low* v. *Spences* (1895) 2 S.L.T. 170; *Thomson* v. *Dailly* (1896) 4 S.L.T. 172; *Smeaton* v. *Dundee Corpn.*, 1941 S.C. 600; *Avery* v. *Cantilever Shoe Co.*, 1942 S.C. 469.

10 *McMillan* v. *Meikleham*, 1934 S.L.T. 357.

11 *Macrae* v. *Edinburgh Street Tramways* (1885) 13 R. 265; *Bright* v. *Low*, 1940 S.C. 280; *Sommerville* v. *N.C.B.*, 1963 S.C. 666.

12 *Flanagan* v. *Dempster*, 1928 S.C. 308; *Peggie* v. *Keddie*, 1932 S.C. 721; see also *Wilkinson* v. *Richards*, 1967 S.L.T. 270.

13 *McNair* v. *Dunfermline Corpn.*, 1953 S.C. 183.

14 *Mitchell* v. *Nicoll* (1890) 17 R. 795; *Sprott* v. *Walker* (1899) 2 F. 73; *Hunter* v. *Russell* (1901) 3 F. 596; *Sturrock* v. *Deas*, 1913 1 S.L.T. 60; *Davidson* v. *Panti*, 1915 1 S.L.T. 273.

granted for the agreed sum, or the defender is assoilzied of consent,[1] the settlement being enforceable as a contract.

Limitation on right of action

Statutes sometimes exclude or place limitations on rights of action in particular circumstances; among such provisions are the power to prohibit the initiation of actions believed to be frivolous, vexatious or ill-founded;[2] exclusion of actions of damages founded on alleged irregularities in procedure leading to small debt decrees;[3] exclusion of liability for irregularities by officers[4] or for anything done by the Department of Health, a local authority or hospital authority in the execution of the Public Health Act, 1897, or the National Health Service (Sc.) Act, 1947;[5] limitation of liability for proceedings under the Summary Jurisdiction (Sc.) Act, 1954,[6] the Food and Drugs Act, 1938,[7] the Local Government (Sc.) Act, 1947,[8] and the Mental Health (Sc.) Act, 1960.[9]

Limitations on time for bringing actions

Statutes also sometimes impose limitations on the time within which actions under those statutes must be brought.[10] The most general limitation is under the Law Reform (Limitation of

1 *Murphy* v. *Smith*, 1920 S.C. 104. See also *Hamilton & Baird* v. *Lewis* (1893) 21 R. 120.

2 Vexatious Actions (Sc.) Act, 1898: *L.A.* v. *Arnold*, 1951 S.C. 256.

3 Small Debt (Sc.) Act, 1837, ss. 30, 31; *Crombie* v. *McEwan* (1861) 23 D. 333; *Gray* v. *Smart* (1892) 19 R. 692; contrast *Clark* v. *Beattie*, 1909 S.C. 299.

4 *Edwards* v. *Parochial Bd. of Kinloss* (1891) 18 R. 867; *Mitchell* v. *Aberdeen Mags.* (1893) 20 R. 253; *Sutherland* v. *Aberdeen Mags.* (1894) 22 R. 95; *Glasgow Corpn.* v. *Smithfield Meat Co.*, 1912 S.C. 364; *Davis's Tutor* v. *Glasgow Victoria Hospitals*, 1950 S.C. 382.

5 1897 Act, S. 166; 1947 Act, S. 70; *Gillilan* v. *Lanarkshire C.C.* (1902) 9 S.L.T. 432; *Duncan* v. *Hamilton Mags.* (1902) 5 F. 160; *Brash* v. *Peebles Mags.*, 1926 S.C. 995; *Baker* v. *Glasgow Corpn.*, 1916 S.C. 199; *Davis's Tutor*, *supra*; *Morris* v. *Caithness Hospitals Bd.*, 1950 S.C. 390; *Callaghan* v. *Greenock Hospitals*, 1950 S.L.T. (Notes) 68; *McGinty* v. *Glasgow Victoria Hospitals*, 1951 S.C. 200; *Walker* v. *Greenock District Hospital Bd.*, 1951 S.C. 464.

6 S. 75; *Hastings* v. *Henderson* (1890) 17 R. 1130; *Lundie* v. *MacBrayne* (1894) 21 R. 1085; *Ferguson* v. *McNab* (1885) 12 R. 1083; *Rae* v. *Strathern*, 1924 S.C. 147; *Graham* v. *Strathern*, 1924 S.C. 699.

7 S. 94. 8 S. 103. 9 S. 107.

10 *Two months*: Summary Jurisdiction (Sc.) Act, 1954, S. 75: cf. *Alston* v. *Macdougall* (1887) 15 R. 78; Licensing (Sc.) Act, 1959, S. 195, amd. Licensing (Sc.) Act, 1962, S. 26; cf. *Boyd* v. *Hislop* (1902) 9 S.L.T. 466.

Three months: Seditious Meetings Act, 1817, ss. 30 and 38: *Capaldi* v. *Greenock Mags.*, 1941 S.C. 110; *Coia* v. *Robertson* 1942 S.C. 111; *Pompa's Trs.* v. *Edinburgh Mags.*, 1942 S.C. 119.

Six months: Game (Sc.) Act, 1832, S. 17; Foreign Jurisdiction Act, 1890, S. 13: Trade Disputes Act, 1965, S. 1(2).

Actions) Act, 1954, which provides (S. 6) that no action of damages where the damages consist of or include damages or solatium shall be brought unless commenced within three years[1] of the act neglect or default giving rise to the action,[2] or the date when it ceased, or the date of death if caused by the default.[3] A pursuer under legal disability at the date when his cause of action accrued may claim within two years of his ceasing to be under disability. An action commenced within three years may be amended[4] but not fundamentally altered[5] outwith that period.

The Limitation Act, 1963,[6] extends the time for bringing actions, if it is proved that material facts relating to that right of action were or included facts of a decisive character which were at all times outside the knowledge, actual or constructive, of the pursuer until a date either after the end of the three-year period or within a year of the end thereof and not earlier than a year before the action was brought.

Mora

Delay short of the prescriptive period does not cut off a claim but an action may be excluded by delay if prejudicial to the defender and justifying an inference of acquiescence by the pursuer in the wrong,[7] or if there has been unreasonable and

Twelve months: Criminal Procedure Act, 1701; Limitation of Actions and Costs Act, 1842, S. 5; Maritime Conventions Act, 1911, S. 8; Carriage of Goods by Sea Act, 1924, Sched., Art. III, 6; Limitation (Enemies and War Prisoners) Act, 1945, S. 4(a); Crown Proceedings Act, 1947 S. 9(2), amd. Law Reform (Limitation of Actions) Act, 1954, S. 5(3).

Two years: Limitation of Actions and Costs Act, 1842, S. 5; Habitual Drunkards Act, 1879, S. 31 (any act in execution of the Act); Merchant Shipping Act, 1894, S. 178(2) (creditor's claim against deceased seaman's estate); Maritime Conventions Act, 1911, S. 8 amd. Crown Proceedings Act, 1947, S. 30(1); Law Reform (Limitation of Actions) Act, 1954, S. 5(2) (claim for damage to vessel or loss of life or property or salvage services); see *Birkdale S.S. Co.*, 1922 S.L.T. 575; *Reresby* v. *Cobetas*, 1923 S.L.T. 492, 719; *Dorie S.S. Co.*, 1923 S.C. 593; Carriage by Air Act, 1961, S. 5 amd. Limitation Act, 1963, S. 10 (3) and (5) (injury or damage in air carriage).

Three years: Prescription (Ejections) Act, 1579; Criminal Procedure Act, 1701 (wrongful imprisonment and delays in trial).

1 *Miller* v. *N.C.B.*, 1960 S.C. 376.

2 *Watson* v. *Fram Concrete Co.*, 1960 S.C. (H.L.) 92; *Ellis* v. *Brand*, 1969 S.L.T. (Notes) 14.

3 *Emslie* v. *Tognarelli's Exors.* 1969 S.L.T. 20.

4 *Coyle* v. *N.C.B.*, 1959 S.L.T. 114; *McCluskie* v. *N.C.B.*, 1961 S.C. 87; *Mackenzie* v. *Fairfields*, 1964 S.C. 90; *O'Hare's Exrx.* v. *Western Heritable Investment Co.*, 1965 S.C. 97.

5 *Dryburgh* v. *N.C.B.*, 1962 S.C. 485; *Aitken* v. *Norrie*, 1967 S.L.T. 4.

6 Ss. 7–9, as applied to Scotland by S. 13.

7 *Cook* v. *N.B. Ry.* (1872) 10 M. 513; *Assets Co.* v. *Bain's Trs.* (1904) 6 F. 676; revd. (1905) 7 F. (H.L.) 104; cf. *Murdoch* v. *Wallace* (1881) 8 R. 855; *Barclay* v. *G.N.S. Ry.* (1882) 10 R. 144; *Maloy* v. *Macadam* (1885) 22 S.L.R. 790.

unjustifiable delay in proceeding further with an action.[1] Delay may also be a ground for the court refusing jury trial, if evidence has become confused or lost.[2]

Prescription

A claim of damages for delict is extinguished under the long negative prescription[3] by the lapse of, formerly, 40 and now of 20 years[4] from the date of the wrongdoing.[5] A person's right is extended if during part of the prescriptive period he was *non valens agere*, i.e. legally disabled from suing.[6]

Under the Nuclear Installations Act, 1965, S. 15, claims for compensation for injury or damage caused by breach of duty under that Act must be brought within twenty, or in certain cases, thirty years of the occurrence giving rise to the claim.

[1] *Russell* v. *McKnight's Tr.* (1900) 2 F. 520; *Smith* v. *Dixon*, 1910 S.C. 230.

[2] *Woods* v. *A.C.S. Motors*, 1930 S.C. 1035; *Ewart* v. *Ferguson*, 1932 S.C. 277; *McLellan* v. *Western S.M.T. Co.*, 1950 S.C. 112; *Milne* v. *Glasgow Corpn.*, 1951 S.C. 340; *Devine* v. *Beardmore*, 1955 S.C. 311; *Halley* v. *Watt*, 1956 S.C. 370; *Hunter* v. *John Brown & Co.*, 1961 S.C. 231.

[3] Ersk. III, 7, 8; Bell, *Prin.* §608; *Young* v. *Y.* (1903) 5 F. 330, 331.

[4] Conveyancing (Sc.) Act, 1924, S. 17; *Sutherland C.C.* v. *Macdonald*, 1935 S.C. 915.

[5] *Harvie* v. *Robertson* (1903) 5 F. 338.

[6] *Harvie, supra*; *Campbell's Trs.* v. *C's Trs.*, 1950 S.C. 48.

PART 6

THE PARTICULAR DELICTS

CHAPTER 65

WRONGS IN RESPECT OF THE PERSON

A PERSON has a legally protected interest in the immunity of his person from harm or injury, whether caused intentionally, negligently, in breach of a duty of strict liability, or in breach of a statutory duty.[1] If the harm is of the nature of affront or insult it is actionable under the principle of the *actio injuriarum* and an award of solatium is competent even if no actual loss be established, but if patrimonial loss is proved further compensation is due under the principle of the *actio legis Aquiliae*.[2]

INTENTIONAL HARMS

In intentional harms the requisite *animus injuriandi* is inferred from the deliberate or reckless doing of something naturally likely to cause affront or actual injury.[3]

Assault

Assault is an overt physical act intended to insult or affront or harm another, done without lawful justification or excuse.[4] It covers notional assaults such as threats, insulting behaviour, affronts, and conduct causing a person danger or reasonable alarm even without physical contact or harm.[5] It also extends to actual assaults, in the shape of deliberate contacts causing insult or actual harm,[6] which might be punished as criminal assaults.

[1] Bell, *Prin.* §2028; cf. Stair I, 9, 4; I, 10, 22.

[2] *Macnaughton* v. *Robertson*, 17 Feb., 1809, F.C.

[3] Bell, *Prin.* §2032; cf. *Wilson* v. *Bennett* (1904) 6 F. 269; *H.M.A.* v. *Phipps* (1905) 4 Adam 616.

[4] Bankt. I, 10, 22; Hume, *Lect.* III, 120; Bell, *Prin.* §2032; More, *Lect.* I, 347.

[5] *Cook* v. *Neville* (1797) Hume 602; *Macnaughton*, *supra*; *Hyslop* v. *Staig* (1816) 1 Mur. 22; *Lang* v. *Lillie* (1826) 4 Mur. 82, 86; *Tullis* v. *Glenday* (1834) 13 S. 698; *Ewing* v. *Mar* (1851) 14 D. 314, 330; *Robson* v. *Hawick School Board* (1900) 2 F. 411; *Macdonald* v. *Robertson* (1910) 27 Sh. Ct. Rep. 103.

[6] Distinguished by Bankton, I, 10, 22, as 'batteries' rather than assault, but commonly called assaults: cf. *Jamieson* v. *Corrie* (1833) 11 S. 1027; *Anderson* v. *Marshall* (1835) 13 S.

Medical examination or treatment without the patient's consent is an assault.[1] Persons may not be searched by the police unless they consent or have been apprehended,[2] nor have their finger prints taken.[3] Physical tests are permissible only where the individual has been cautioned and charged,[4] and in certain cases, also consented.[5]

The defences of unavoidable accident, consent, self-defence or defence of another are competent,[6] and provocation may at least mitigate damages.[7] Damages may be increased by the enormity of the insult or affront,[8] or the gravity of the harm done,[9] or the concomitant circumstances.[10] Reasonable force in controlling crowds, ejecting a trespasser or disturber of the peace, or in making a lawful arrest does not make the conduct an assault, but otherwise if the force were unnecessary or unreasonable in the circumstances.[11]

Indecent assault or rape

These are aggravated assaults and actionable as such.[12] Consent, if genuine,[13] is a defence. Rape of a married woman also gives her husband a right of action.[14]

1130; *Gordon* v. *Stewart* (1842) 5 D. 8; *Reekie* v. *Norrie* (1842) 5 D. 368; *Gillespie* v. *Hunter* (1898) 25 R. 916; *Bryce* v. *Glasgow Tramways Co.* (1898) 6 S.L.T. 49; *Wilson* v. *Bennett* (1904) 6 F. 269; *Stevenson* v. *Glasgow Corpn.*, 1922 S.L.T. 185; *Gordon* v. *O'Hara*, 1931 S.C. 172; *Houston* v. *McIndoe*, 1934 S.C. 362; *McGregor* v. *Shepherd* (1946) 62 Sh. Ct. Rep. 139; *McGeever* v. *McFarlane* (1951) 67 Sh. Ct. Rep. 48; *Marco* v. *Merrens*, 1964 S.L.T. (Sh. Ct.) 74.

[1] *Thomson* v. *Devon* (1899) 15 Sh. Ct. Rep. 209.

[2] *Jackson* v. *Stevenson* (1897) 24 R. (J.) 38; *Adair* v. *McGarry*, 1933 J.C. 72; *McGovern* v. *H.M.A.*, 1950 J.C. 33.

[3] *Adamson* v. *Martin*, 1916 S.C. 319; *Adair*, *supra*.

[4] *Forrester* v. *H.M.A.*, 1952 J.C. 28.

[5] *Reid* v. *Nixon*, 1948 J.C. 69; *Farrell* v. *Concannon*, 1957 J.C. 12; *McKie* v. *H.M.A.*, 1958 J.C. 24.

[6] Bell, *Prin.* §2032; *Hallowell* v. *Niven* (1843) 5 D. 759.

[7] *Seymour* v. *McLaren* (1828) 6 S. 969; *Thom* v. *Graham* (1835) 13 S. 1129.

[8] *Gordon*, *supra*.

[9] *Kerr* v. *Anderson* (1837) 15 S. 928.

[10] *Thom* v. *Graham* (1835) 13 S. 1129.

[11] *Anderson* v. *Barr and Cavens* (1847) 9 D. 929; *Hanlon* v. *G.S.W. Ry.* (1899) 1 F. 559; *Wood* v. *N.B. Ry.* (1899) 2 F. 1; *Mason* v. *Orr* (1901) 4 F. 220; *Cook* v. *Paxton* (1910) 48 S.L.R. 7.

[12] *Hill* v. *Fletcher* (1847) 10 D. 7; *Armstrong* v. *Thomson* (1894) 2 S.L.T. 70; *A.* v. *B.* (1895) 22 R. 402; *E.T.* v. *T.B.M.* (1905) 21 Sh. Ct. Rep. 156; *A.* v. *C.* (1919) 35 Sh. Ct. Rep. 166; cf. *Moorov* v. *H.M.A.*, 1930 J.C. 68.

[13] cf. *H.M.A.* v. *Montgomery*, 1926 J.C. 2; *H.M.A.* v. *Logan*, 1936 J.C. 100.

[14] *Black* v. *Duncan*, 1924 S.C. 738.

Intentional mental harm

Intentional conduct likely to cause serious nervous shock is actionable.[1]

Contravention of lawburrows

A person who has been required to find caution not to harm another[2] may, if he contravenes the court order not to molest the other, be sued in an action of contravention of lawburrows for forfeiture of the caution.[3]

Deforcement

It is actionable, as well as criminal, forcibly to prevent an officer of law from executing a legal warrant of a competent court.[4]

Breach of arrestment

It is similarly actionable for an arrestee to disregard the arrestment and pay the common debtor. The claim is for the debt attached by the arrestment.[5]

Battery pendente lite

This wrong consisted in slaying, wounding, or attacking the other party while a litigation was pending. The conduct would probably now be treated merely as assault.[6]

NEGLIGENT HARMS

Negligent harm to the person of another is actionable in many circumstances. In every case the question is whether the defender was, in the circumstances, in breach of a general legal duty, incumbent on him and owed to, *inter alios*, the injured person, to take reasonable care to avoid or prevent harm of the general

[1] *Wilkinson* v. *Downton* [1897] 2 Q.B. 57; *Janvier* v. *Sweeney* [1919] 2 K.B. 316; *Pollok* v. *Workman* (1900) 2 F. 354; *Conway* v. *Dalziel* (1900) 3 F. 918; *Hughes* v. *Robertson*, 1913 S.C. 394; cf. also *A.* v. *B.* (1906) 12 S.L.T. 830; *Finburgh* v. *Moss' Empires*, 1908 S.C. 928.

[2] Stair I, 9, 30; IV, 48, 1; Bankt. I, 10, 157; Ersk. IV. 1, 16; Lawburrows Acts, 1429 and 1581; Civil Imprisonment Act 1882; see also *Mackenzie* v. *Maclennan*, 1916 S.C. 617; Dobie, *Sheriff Court Practice*, 510.

[3] Walker, *Delict*, 505–7.

[4] Stair I, 9, 29; IV, 49, 1; Mack. IV, 4, 17; Bankt. I, 10, 190; Ersk. IV, 4, 32; *McConnell* v. *Brew* (1907) 23 Sh. Ct. Rep. 261.

[5] Stair I, 9, 29; IV, 50, 30; Bankt. I, 10, 190; Ersk. III, 6, 14; IV, 4, 36; Hume, *Lect.* VI, 112; see also *McEwen* v. *Blair & Morrison* (1822) 1 S. 313; *Inglis & Bow* v. *Smith & Aikman* (1867) 5 M. 320.

[6] Bankt. I, 10, 179; Ersk. IV, 4, 37; *Annand* v. *Ross* (1790) Mor. 1379; *Cadell* v. *Northland* (1799) Mor. 16789.

kind which occurred,[1] and whether his breach was the proximate and not too remote cause of at least some of the harm or injury sustained by the complainer. The precise duties of care vary with the circumstances and the facts of particular cases.

Injuries caused negligently on roads

In every case the question is whether the defender has failed to take reasonable care for the safety of other road-users. There is no liability merely because there has been an accident,[2] nor for an inevitable accident.[3] Road-users should obey the customary rules of the road and the injunctions of the Highway Code, though failure to obey the Code is not automatically fault, nor will compliance necessarily exculpate.[4] Fault is frequently constituted by excessive speed,[5] failure to keep adequate lookout,[6] or to be able to pull up in time[7] or to give signals,[8] failure to have a vehicle in roadworthy condition,[9] or to exhibit lights.[10] Drivers of vehicles must be on their guard against carelessness of other road-users,[11] obstructions in the road, and other foreseeable obstacles and eventualities.[12] A person having control of a vehicle owes to persons entering thereon the duty of taking reasonable care to see that the passenger will not suffer injury or damage by reason of any danger due to the state of the vehicle.[13]

Injuries caused negligently on railways

The railway authority must take reasonable care to provide and maintain safe stations,[14] permanent way[15] and rolling-stock[16] and

[1] *Bourhill* v. *Young*, 1942 S.C. (H.L.) 78; *Miller* v. *S.S.E.B.*, 1958 S.C. (H.L.) 20; *Harvey* v. *Singer Mfg. Co.*, 1960 S.C. 155; *Hughes* v. *Lord Advocate*, 1963 S.C. (H.L.) 31.

[2] *Alexander* v. *Phillip* (1899) 1 F. 985.

[3] *Waugh* v. *Allan*, 1964 S.C. (H.L.) 102.

[4] Road Traffic Act, 1960, S. 74; *Croston* v. *Vaughan* [1938] 1 K.B. 540.

[5] *Cowan* v. *Robertson*, 1941 S.C. 502; as to fire engines, ambulances, and police vehicles, see R.T.A. 1960, S. 25; *Gaynor* v. *Allen* [1959] 2 Q.B. 403.

[6] *Muir* v. *L.N.E. Ry.*, 1946 S.C. 216; *Drew* v. *Western S.M.T. Co.*, 1947 S.C. 222.

[7] *Scott* v. *McIntosh*, 1935 S.C. 199; *Cowan* v. *Robertson*, 1941 S.C. 502; *McGeown* v. *Greenock Motor Services, Ltd.*, 1943 S.C. 33; *Drew, supra.*

[8] *Davies* v. *Swan Motor Co.* [1949] 2 K.B. 291.

[9] *Phillips* v. *Britannia Laundry Co.* [1923] 1 K.B. 539; 2 K.B. 832; *Stewart* v. *Hancock* [1939] 2 All E.R. 578.

[10] *Gibson* v. *Milroy* (1879) 6 R. 890; *Pressley* v. *Burnett*, 1914 S.C. 874; *West* v. *Lawson*, 1949 S.C. 430.

[11] *L.P.T.B.* v. *Upson* [1949] A.C. 155.

[12] *Adamson* v. *Roberts*, 1951 S.C. 681.

[13] Occupiers' Liability (Sc.) Act, 1960, Ss. 1, 2.

[14] *McGregor* v. *Glasgow Dist. Subway Co.* (1901) 3 F. 1131; *Fraser* v. *Caledonian Ry.* (1902) 5 F. 41; *McCallum* v. *N.B. Ry.*, 1908 S.C. 415; *Wilson* v. *G.S.W. Ry.*, 1915 S.C. 215; Occupiers' Liability (Sc.) Act, 1960, Ss. 1, 2.

[15] *Stewart* v. *Caledonian Ry.* (1870) 8 M. 486; *Smyth* v. *Caledonian Ry.* (1897) 24 R. 488.

[16] *Inglis* v. *L.M.S. Ry.*, 1941 S.C. 551; Occupiers' Liability (Sc.) Act, 1960, Ss. 1, 2.

to maintain a safe system of operation of trains.[1] The occurrence of an accident is *prima facie* evidence of fault,[2] but this may be rebutted by proof of latent defect,[3] or that the accident was caused by the wrongful act of a third party.[4] Passengers must, however, take reasonable care for their own safety.[5]

Injuries caused negligently on shipboard or by ships

Shipowners owe duties of care, both at common law and under statute,[6] to passengers in ships, while embarking or disembarking,[7] and for their safety and health while on board,[8] and may be in breach by negligence of the crew, defect in the ship, or by its mismanagement resulting in collision,[9] stranding or other casualty.[10] Injuries may similarly be caused to persons in another ship[11] or on the quay.[12]

Shipowners may also be liable both at common law[13] and under statute[14] for injuries to stevedores, workmen and others, who come on board or about the ship in connection with fitting, repairing, or loading her, and, as employers, owe duties of care to their crew and shore staff.

Injuries caused negligently in aircraft

Aircraft operators owe duties of care to persons on the ground[15]

[1] *Gray* v. *Caledonian Ry.*, 1912 S.C. 339; *Smith* v. *L.M.S. Ry.*, 1948 S.C. 125.

[2] *Ayles* v. *S.E. Ry.* (1868) L.R. 3 Ex. 146; *Watson* v. *N.B. Ry.* (1876) 3 R. 637.

[3] *Readhead* v. *Midland Ry.* (1869) L.R. 4 Q.B. 379.

[4] *Latch* v. *Rumner Ry.* (1858) 27 L.J. Ex. 155; *Daniel* v. *Metropolitan Ry.* (1871) L.R. 5 H.L. 45.

[5] *Roe* v. *G.S.W. Ry.* (1889) 17 R. 59; *Pirie* v. *Caledonian Ry.* (1890) 17 R. 1157; *Abbott* v. *N.B. Ry.*, 1916 S.C. 306.

[6] Temperley, *Merchant Shipping Acts, passim*; Occupiers' Liability (Sc.) Act, 1960, Ss. 1–2.

[7] *Monaghan* v. *Buchanan* (1886) 13 R. 860; *Grieve* v. *Turbine Steamers* (1903) 11 S.L.T. 379; *O'Brien* v. *Arbib*, 1907 S.C. 975; *Adler* v. *Dickson* [1955] 1 Q.B. 158.

[8] *Andrews* v. *Little* (1887) 3 T.L.R. 544; *Jones* v. *Oceanic S.N. Co.* [1924] 2 K.B. 730; *Rudd* v. *Elder Dempster* [1933] 1 K.B. 566; *Beaumont-Thomas* v. *Blue Star Line* [1939] 3 All E.R. 127.

[9] *MacLean* v. *Clan Line*, 1925 S.C. 256; *Reavis* v. *Clan Line*, 1925 S.C. 725, 740; *Lewis* v. *Laird Line*, 1925 S.L.T. 316.

[10] *Hood* v. *Anchor Line*, 1918 S.C. (H.L.) 143.

[11] *Haglund* v. *Russell* (1882) 9 R. 958; *The Bernina* (1888) 13 App. Cas. 1; *Carse* v. *N.B.S.P. Co.* (1895) 22 R. 475; *Kendrick* v. *Burnett* (1897) 25 R. 82; *Leadbetter* v. *Dublin S.P. Co.*, 1907 S.C. 538; *Rodger* v. *Glen-Coats*, 1913 1 S.L.T. 434.

[12] *Clark* v. *Glasgow S.P. Co.* (1901) 3 F. 991; *Craig* v. *Aberdeen Harbour Commrs.*, 1909 S.C. 736.

[13] e.g. *Jordan* v. *Court Line*, 1947 S.C. 29; *Grant* v. *Sun Shipping Co.*, 1948 S.C. (H.L.) 73.

[14] Occupiers' Liability (Sc.) Act, 1960, Ss. 1–2; Factories Act, 1961, Ss. 125, 175; Docks Regulations, 1934; Shipbuilding Regulations, 1960.

[15] *Billings* v. *Reed* [1944] 2 All E.R. 415; *Waring* v. *East Anglian Flying Services* [1951] W.N. 553; *Blankley* v. *Godley* [1952] 1 All E.R. 436; Civil Aviation Act, 1949, S. 40.

and to passengers in their own[1] or other aircraft not to cause them harm. They also, as employers, owe duties of care to their air and ground crew.

EMPLOYERS' LIABILITY TO EMPLOYEES

Personal liability

At common law an employer has long been held bound to take reasonable care for the safety of his own employees.[2] As developed, this principle has been held to be a threefold obligation,[3] comprehending the provision of a competent staff of men,[4] adequate plant and materials,[5] and a proper system of working and effective supervision.[6] This duty is personal to the employer and not discharged by delegation;[7] it is not absolute but is fulfilled by the exercise of due skill and care, by taking reasonable care.[8] Though the standard demanded is high, it is not strict or absolute.[9] It may vary according to the danger of the operation in question,[10] and the known peculiarities of the employee.[11] It normally involves taking the precautions normal and customary in doing such work, but may require the taking of further or

1 *Fosbroke-Hobbes* v. *Airwork* [1937] 1 All E.R. 108; *Ludditt* v. *Ginger Coote Airways* [1947] 1 All E.R. 328; *McKay* v. *Scottish Airways*, 1948 S.C. 254; Occupiers' Liability (Sc.) Act, 1960, Ss. 1–2; Carriage by Air Act, 1961.

2 *Dixon* v. *Rankin* (1852) 14 D. 420; *McNeill* v. *Wallace* (1853) 15 D. 818; *Paterson* v. *Wallace* (1854) 1 Macq. 748; *Marshall* v. *Stewart* (1855) 2 Macq. 30; *McNaughton* v. *Caledonian Ry.* (1858) 21 D. 160.

3 *Bett* v. *Dalmeny Oil Co.* (1905) 7 F. 787; *Black* v. *Fife Coal Co.*, 1912 S.C. (H.L.) 33; *McMullan* v. *Lochgelly Iron Co.*, 1933 S.C. (H.L.) 64; *English* v. *Wilsons & Clyde Coal Co.*, 1937 S.C. (H.L.) 46.

4 *Wilson* v. *Merry & Cunningham* (1868) 6 M. (H.L.) 84; *Flynn* v. *McGaw* (1891) 18 R. 554; *McCarten* v. *McRobbie*, 1909 S.C. 1020; *Black* v. *Fife Coal Co.*, *supra*.

5 *Macfarlane* v. *Thomson* (1884) 12 R. 232; *Fraser* v. *Hood* (1887) 15 R. 178; *Weems* v. *Mathieson* (1861) 4 Macq. 215; *Moore* v. *Ross* (1890) 17 R. 796; *Tyrrell* v. *Paton & Hendry* (1905) 8 F. 112; *Gordon* v. *Pyper* (1892) 20 R. (H.L.) 23; *Sullivan* v. *Gallagher & Craig*, 1959 S.C. 263; *Harvey* v. *Singer Mfg. Co.*, 1960 S.C. 155.

6 *McKillop* v. *N.B. Ry.* (1896) 23 R. 768; *Bain* v. *Fife Coal Co.*, 1935 S.C. 681, 692; *English* v. *Wilsons & Clyde Coal Co.*, 1936 S.C. 883, 904; affd. 1937 S.C. (H.L.) 46; *Speed* v. *Swift* [1943] K.B. 557; *Kerr* v. *Glasgow Corpn.*, 1945 S.C. 335; *Ramsay* v. *Wimpey*, 1951 S.C. 692; *Brown* v. *Rolls Royce, Ltd.*, 1960 S.C. (H.L.) 22.

7 *Wilson* v. *Merry & Cunningham* (1868) 6 M. (H.L.) 84; *Thomson* v. *Edinburgh Collieries Co.*, 1934 S.C. 217; *Bain* v. *Fife Coal Co.*, 1935 S.C. 681; *English*, *supra*, 65.

8 *English*, *supra*, 66; *Sneddon* v. *Summerlee Iron Co.*, 1947 S.C. 555; *Millar* v. *Galashiels Gas Co.*, 1949 S.C. (H.L.) 31; *Winter* v. *Cardiff R.D.C.* [1950] 1 All E.R. 819; *Grace* v. *Stephen*, 1952 S.C. 61.

9 *Grace* v. *Stephen*, 1952 S.C. 61, 66; *Latimer* v. *A.E.C.* [1953] A.C. 643; *Smith* v. *Austin Lifts* [1959] 1 All E.R. 81.

10 *Paterson* v. *Wallace* (1854) 1 Macq. 748.

11 *Paris* v. *Stepney B.C.* [1951] A.C. 367; contrast *Cork* v. *Kirby Maclean & Co.* [1952] 2 All E.R. 402.

other precautions where it would be folly not to do so.[1] The ultimate test of negligence is lack of reasonable care for the safety of the workman in all the circumstances of the case.[2] There is no breach of duty if plant has been obtained by the employer from a reputable supplier, though by reason of a latent defect it causes injury to an employee.[3] Faulty system is distinct from mere casual negligence, not attributable to defective organization of the work.[4] Not only must a safe system be established but it must be enforced and supervised.[5] It must be shown that the breach of duty was the cause of the injury complained of.[6]

Vicarious liability

An employer is also at common law vicariously liable to employees for injuries caused them by the fault of another employee,[7] if acting in the course of his employment with the employer,[8] even though the negligence was merely incidental to the work,[9] but not if the fellow employee were acting outwith the course of his employment,[10] in which case the negligent employee alone remains personally liable to the injured fellow-employee.[11] The employee must be shown to have been in breach of a duty of care to the injured employee, and thereby to have

[1] *Morton* v. *Dixon*, 1909 S.C. 807; *Sneddon* v. *Summerlee Iron Co.*, 1947 S.C. 555; *Gallagher* v. *Balfour Beatty & Co.*, 1951 S.C. 712; *Cavanagh* v. *Ulster Weaving Co.* [1960] A.C. 145.

[2] *Brown* v. *Rolls Royce, Ltd.*, 1960 S.C. (H.L.) 22.

[3] *Davie* v. *New Merton Board Mills* [1959] A.C. 604; *Sullivan* v. *Gallagher & Craig*, 1959 S.C. 243. Contrast *Thomson* v. *Wallace*, 1933 S.N. 15.

[4] *Maguire* v. *Russell* (1885) 12 R. 1071; *Winter, supra*; *Grace* v. *Stephen*, 1952 S.C. 61.

[5] *Clifford* v. *Challen* [1951] 1 K.B. 495; *General Cleaning Contractors* v. *Christmas* [1953] A.C. 180; *Crookall* v. *Vickers-Armstrong* [1955] 2 All E.R. 12.

[6] *Wardlaw* v. *Bonnington Castings, Ltd.*, 1956 S.C. (H.L.) 26; *McWilliams* v. *Arrol*, 1962 S.C. (H.L.) 70.

[7] During the years 1858 to 1948, under the doctrine of 'common employment' or collaborateur, enunciated in *Priestley* v. *Fowler* (1837) 3 M. & W. 1, applied to Scotland in *Bartonshill Coal Co.* v. *Reid* (1858) 3 Macq. 266, and *Bartonshill Coal Co.* v. *McGuire* (1858) 3 Macq. 300, the employer was held not vicariously liable for the fault of one employee which caused injury to a fellow-employee. See e.g. *Macfarlane* v. *Caledonian Ry.* (1867) 6 M. 102; *Wilson* v. *Merry & Cunningham* (1868) 6 M. (H.L.) 84; *Woodhead* v. *Gartness Mineral Co.* (1877) 4 R. 508; *Miller* v. *Glasgow Corpn.*, 1947 S.C. (H.L.) 12; *Neilson* v. *Pantrini*, 1947 S.C. (H.L.) 64. The doctrine was abolished by the Law Reform (Personal Injuries) Act, 1948, S. 1, which accordingly restores the authority of pre-1858 decisions, e.g. *Sword* v. *Cameron* (1839) 1 D. 493; *Dixon* v. *Rankin* (1852) 14 D. 420; *Baird* v. *Addie* (1854) 16 D. 490; *Cook* v. *Duncan* (1857) 20 D. 180.

[8] *Lindsay* v. *Connell*, 1951 S.C. 281; *Lister* v. *Romford Ice Co.* [1957] A.C. 555; *Mulholland* v. *Reid & Leys*, 1958 S.C. 290; *Baxter* v. *Colvilles*, 1959 S.L.T. 325; *Bell* v. *Blackwood Morton & Sons*, 1960 S.C. 11.

[9] *Lindsay, supra.*

[10] *Kirby* v. *N.C.B.*, 1958 S.C. 514.

[11] cf. *Lees* v. *Dunkerley* [1911] A.C. 5; *Lister, supra.*

caused the injury. The employer is negligent if he delegates to an employee a task requiring special skill and the employee fails to perform with the requisite standard of skill or care.[1]

Statutory liability

Numerous statutory duties are incumbent on employers to take care for the safety, health or welfare of employees.[2] These are frequently cumulative with common law duties, though often imposing a more stringent standard of duty,[3] but may sometimes impose a duty where common law does not do so.

Liability of third parties to employee

Where the employee of one has to work on the premises of another, or with the servants of another, or use the plant of another, his claim for injuries may, depending on the ground of fault, lie against his employer,[4] or against the other employer, or some third party,[5] or against both his employer and another party.[6] Other parties may owe him duties of care as their employee *pro hac vice*,[7] or as a legitimate visitor on their premises,[8] or as a person whom they should have had in contemplation and for whose safety they should have taken care,[9] but the employer is not automatically absolved because the employee is working on another's premises,[10] though he is not bound to make a detailed inspection of those premises.[11]

OCCUPIERS' LIABILITY TO VISITORS

The occupier of premises owes to visitors a duty to take reasonable care that they do not suffer injury from anything

[1] *Stokes* v. *G.K.N., Ltd.* [1968] 1 W.L.R. 1776.

[2] See also *infra*.

[3] e.g. *Smith* v. *Cammell Laird & Co.* [1940] A.C. 242; *Millar* v. *Galashiels Gas Co.*, 1949 S.C. (H.L.) 31; *Latimer* v. *A.E.C., Ltd.* [1953] A.C. 643; *Matuszczyk* v. *N.C.B.*, 1953 S.C. 8; *Hamilton* v. *N.C.B.*, 1960 S.C. (H.L.) 1.

[4] e.g. *General Cleaning Contractors* v. *Christmas* [1953] A.C. 180.

[5] e.g. *Muirhead* v. *Watt & Wilson* (1895) 3 S.L.T. 71; *MacDonald* v. *Reid's Trs.*, 1947 S.C. 726; *Durie* v. *Main*, 1958 S.C. 48.

[6] e.g. *Grant* v. *Sun Shipping Co., Ltd.*, 1948 S.C. (H.L.) 73; *Sullivan* v. *Gallagher & Craig*, 1959 S.C. 243; *McWilliams* v. *Arrol*, 1962 S.C. (H.L.) 70.

[7] cf. *Malley* v. *L.M.S. Ry.*, 1944 S.C. 129.

[8] Occupiers' Liability (Sc.) Act, 1960, Ss. 1–2.

[9] cf. *Heaven* v. *Pender* (1883) 11 Q.B.D. 503; *Donoghue* v. *Stevenson*, 1932 S.C. (H.L.) 31; *Billings* v. *Riden* [1958] A.C. 240.

[10] *Harkness* v. *Oxy-Acetylene Welding Co.*, 1963 S.C. 642.

[11] *Durie* v. *Main*, 1958 S.C. 48.

due to the state of the premises.[1] The duty is incumbent on persons occupying or having control of land or other premises, whether or not they are owners,[2] and is owed to persons entering on the premises, in respect of dangers due to the state of the premises or to anything done or not done on them and for which the occupier is in law responsible.[3]

It applies to 'premises', which at common law covers land and buildings[4] but under the 1960 Act the principle applies also to a person occupying or having control of any fixed or moveable structure, including any vessel, vehicle or aircraft, and to persons entering thereon,[5] and to an occupier of premises or a person occupying or having control of any such structure and to property thereon, including the property of persons who have not themselves entered on the premises or structure.[6]

The duty is to take such care as in all the circumstances of the case is reasonable to see that a person entering will not suffer injury or damage by reason of any danger due to the state of the premises or anything done or not done thereon.[7] This duty may be extended, restricted, modified or excluded by agreement.[8] A higher standard may be due under some other rule of law.[9] No duty is owed to a visitor in respect of risks which he has willingly accepted as his.[10]

[1] Occupiers' Liability (Sc.) Act, 1960, Ss. 1, 2; between the decision of *Dumbreck* v. *Addie's Collieries, Ltd.*, 1929 S.C. (H.L.) 51, and 1960 the Scottish courts, under English influence, accepted the rigid classification of visitors to premises into (a) invitees, persons expressly or impliedly invited to be on the premises, (b) licensees, persons permitted to be on the premises, and (c) trespassers, persons present uninvited and without any right. To each class of visitor defined duties were owed. These principles are elaborated in many cases. In 1960 the Occupiers' Liability (Sc.) Act restored the former Scottish rule, exemplified by *McKinlay* v. *Darngavil Coal Co.*, 1923 S.C. (H.L.) 34, and *Shillinglaw* v. *Turner*, 1925 S.C. 807, under which the duty was always one of reasonable care, the standard of care varying according to the visitor's degree of entitlement to be on the premises.

[2] Occupiers' Liability (Sc.) Act, 1960, S. 1(2); *Devlin* v. *Jeffray's Trs.* (1902) 5 F. 130; *Mellon* v. *Henderson*, 1913 S.C. 1207; *Murdoch* v. *Scott*, 1956 S.C. 309.

[3] S. 1(1). The category of 'persons' certainly includes everyone who would have been classed as an invitee or as a licensee under the pre-1960 law, and may include trespassers.

[4] *Dumbreck* v. *Addie's Collieries*, 1929 S.C. (H.L.) 51. See also *Carney* v. *Smith*, 1953 S.C. 19.

[5] S. 1(3)(a). This covers passengers on ships, vehicles and aircraft, and probably persons on scaffolding or cranes; cf. *Nicolson* v. *Macandrew* (1888) 15 R. 854; *Paterson* v. *Gardiner* 1924 S.L.T. 63.

[6] S. 1(3)(b). This may cover dangerous goods in shops, or on a vessel or vehicle.

[7] S. 2(1); this restores the authority of older Scottish decisions, decided prior to *Dumbreck* v. *Addie's Collieries*, 1929 S.C. (H.L.) 51, e.g. *McKinlay* v. *Darngavil Coal Co.*, 1923 S.C. (H.L.) 34, 37; *Shillinglaw* v. *Turner*, 1925 S.C. 807.

[8] S. 2(1). The duty cannot be excluded merely by notice or warning.

[9] S. 2(2); e.g. duty of employer to employee to maintain safe premises.

[10] S. 2(3); i.e. the defence of *volenti non fit injuria* is competent. But a person is not *volens* when he knowingly runs a risk in the course of his duty, e.g. *Merrington* v.

The duty of reasonable care is probably higher to legitimate visitors than to trespassers; at common law the duty to trespassers was merely not to do them deliberate harm[1] but in exceptional circumstances some precautions were demanded against readily foreseeable harm even to trespassers.[2] Under the Act precautions must be taken but probably less than are due to the legitimate visitor.[3]

Reasonable care probably demands a higher standard where children, blind or infirm persons may be expected to come, and particularly if there is any kind of trap or allurement.[4]

It is doubtful whether the occupier is liable for risks created by his independent contractor.[5] The independent contractor may be an 'occupier' and accordingly be directly liable.[6]

In the special case of landlord and the tenant or sub-tenant or temporary occupier occupying his premises, if the landlord is responsible for the maintenance or repair of the premises, it is his duty to show the same care for any persons who or whose property may be on the premises as is required of an occupier for a visitor.[7] This duty is without prejudice to any other duty owed by a landlord.[8] The landlord owes the ordinary duty of care to all legitimate visitors in respect of closes, stairs, and common parts of a building kept under his own control.[9]

The 1960 Act covers damage to property occasioned by the occupier's fault as well as injury to persons; in this respect it probably does not alter the common law.[10]

Ironbridge Metal Works [1952] 1 All E.R. 1101 (fireman), or when acting under moral duty, e.g. *Baker* v. *Hopkins* [1959] 3 All E.R. 225 (doctor).

1 *Prentice* v. *Assets Co.* (1890) 17 R. 484; *Devlin* v. *Jeffray's Trs.* (1902) 5 F. 130; *Holland* v. *Lanarkshire*, 1909 S.C. 1142; *Melville* v. *Renfrewshire C.C.*, 1920 S.C. 61; *Dumbreck*, *supra*.

2 *Prentice*, *supra*; *Dumbreck* v. *Addie's Collieries*, 1928 S.C. 547, 552; *Donald* v. *Dixon*, 1936 S.L.T. 429; *Miller* v. *S.S.E.B.*, 1958 S.C. (H.L.) 20.

3 *McGlone* v. *British Railways*, 1966 S.C. (H.L.) 1.

4 *Forbes* v. *Aberdeen Harbour Commrs.* (1888) 15 R. 323; *Cooke* v. *Midland G.W. Ry. of I.* [1909] A.C. 229; *Taylor* v. *Glasgow Corpn.*, 1922 S.C. (H.L.) 1; *McGlone*, *supra*. See also *Grant* v. *Fleming*, 1914 S.C. 228.

5 cf. *Cremin* v. *Thomson*, 1956 S.L.T. 357, probably superseded by *Davie* v. *New Merton Board Mills* [1959] A.C. 604. See also *Cook* v. *Broderip* [1968] C.L.Y. 2690.

6 cf. *Miller* v. *S.S.E.B.*, 1958 S.C. (H.L.) 20.

7 1960 Act, S. 3; this overrules *Cameron* v. *Young*, 1908 S.C. (H.L.) 7. See also *Haggarty* v. *Glasgow Corpn.*, 1964 S.L.T. (Notes) 95.

8 e.g. under statute, or under an express or implied term of the lease.

9 cf. *Mellon* v. *Henderson*, 1913 S.C. 1207; *Gaunt* v. *McIntyre*, 1914 S.C. 43; *Grant* v. *Fleming*, 1914 S.C. 228; *McIlwaine* v. *Stewart's Trs.*, 1914 S.C. 934.

10 cf. *Caledonian Ry.* v. *Greenock Sacking Co.* (1875) 2 R. 671.

INJURIES DUE TO THE STATE OF ROADS AND STREETS

Liability for injury to persons on roads or streets by reason of defect therein depends on the defender's possession and control thereof,[1] and his failure to take reasonable precautions to maintain the road or street in a reasonably safe condition,[2] or to remove obstructions or dangers,[3] or to fence dangers.[4] By implication a road or street authority must inspect for defects or dangers.[5] Statutory undertakers who execute works on streets must take precautions by fencing and lighting.[6]

INJURIES CAUSED BY DANGEROUS GOODS

Quite apart from any possible contractual liability,[7] the manufacturer,[8] repairer,[9] installer[10] or consignor[11] of goods, who puts out goods in a form intended to reach the ultimate user or consumer in the form in which they were issued, with no reasonable possibility of examination by an intermediate party, owes a duty to the ultimate user or other person likely to be affected by them to take reasonable care that they can be used or consumed without harm to him.[12] A builder of heritable property may be subject to the same duty.[13]

This duty applies to a wide variety of goods and many kinds of defects; it is excluded where the goods should have been tested or examined by an intermediate party,[14] or the ultimate user has

[1] *Laurie* v. *Aberdeen Mags.*, 1911 S.C. 1226; *Laing* v. *Paull & Williamsons*, 1912 S.C. 196; *Taylor* v. *Saltcoats Mags.*, 1912 S.C. 880; *Black* v. *Glasgow Corpn.*, 1959 S.C. 188.

[2] *Nelson* v. *Lanarkshire C.C.* (1891) 19 R. 311; *Alexander* v. *Dundee Corpn.*, 1950 S.C. 123.

[3] *Stephen* v. *Thurso Police Commrs.* (1876) 3 R. 535; *Cameron* v. *Inverness C.C.*, 1935 S.C. 493 (snow).

[4] *Greer* v. *Stirlingshire Road Trs.* (1882) 9 R. 1069; *Strachan* v. *Aberdeen* (1894) 21 R. 915; *McIntyre* v. *Lochaber Dist. Cttee.* (1901) 4 F. 188.

[5] *Keenan* v. *Glasgow Corpn.*, 1923 S.C. 611; *Rush* v. *Glasgow Corpn.*, 1947 S.C. 580.

[6] Public Utilities Street Works Act, 1950; cf. *McNair* v. *Dunfermline Corpn.*, 1953 S.C. 183; *Hughes* v. *Lord Advocate*, 1963 S.C. (H.L.) 31.

[7] e.g. under Sale of Goods Act, 1893, S. 14.

[8] *Donoghue* v. *Stevenson*, 1932 S.C. (H.L.) 31; *Grant* v. *A.K.M., Ltd.* [1936] A.C. 85; *Lockhart* v. *Barr*, 1943 S.C. (H.L.) 1; *Davie* v. *New Merton Board Mills* [1959] A.C. 604; cf. *Oliver* v. *Saddler*, 1929 S.C. (H.L.) 94, 103.

[9] *Herschtal* v. *Stewart & Ardern, Ltd.* [1940] 1 K.B. 155; *Haseldine* v. *Daw* [1941] 2 K.B. 343.

[10] *Eccles* v. *Cross & McIlwham*, 1938 S.C. 697; *Paine* v. *Colne Valley Elec. Co.* [1938] 4 All E.R. 803.

[11] *Cramb* v. *Caledonian Ry.* (1892) 19 R. 1054; cf. *Macdonald* v. *MacBrayne*, 1915 S.C. 716.

[12] *Donoghue*, *supra*, 44, 57.

[13] *Gallagher* v. *McDowell, Ltd.* [1961] N.I. 26; *Sharpe* v. *Sweeting* [1963] 2 All E.R. 455.

[14] Unless, probably, the defect would not have been discovered by any test reasonably expected.

used the goods in the knowledge of a defect,[1] or the damage is due to supervening defect[2] or to some peculiarity of the user[3] or to some unintended use of the goods,[4] or where warnings given have not been adhered to.[5]

The duty is of reasonable care only but fault is readily inferred where the whole process of manufacture or repair has been under the defender's control and a pursuer is not obliged to prove exactly how the defect arose.

A duty of care, cumulative with but wider than contractual duty,[6] is owed by a donor, retailer,[7] lessor[8] or lender of goods,[9] to take reasonable care that the goods supplied by him do not suffer from discoverable defects which are not disclosed and which cause foreseeable injury. He is not liable for defects not discoverable by him by any reasonable or practicable examination,[10] nor if the recipient had full opportunity to examine for himself.[11]

Persons having control of dangerous things, such as guns,[12] vehicles,[13] blowlamps,[14] petrol,[15] poison,[16] explosives,[17] radioactive substances,[18] and the like, must take reasonable care in the use and control of them to prevent injury to persons who might foreseeably be injured by them.

INJURY BY ANIMALS

The person in charge of an animal must take reasonable care that it does not cause injury, or damage to property.[19] Similarly a

1 *Farr* v. *Butters Bros.* [1932] 2 K.B. 606; *Grant, supra.*

2 *Donoghue, supra*, 72.

3 *Griffiths* v. *Conway* [1939] 1 All E.R. 685; *Ingham* v. *Emes* [1955] 2 Q.B. 366.

4 *Kubach* v. *Hollands* [1937] 3 All E.R. 907.

5 *Holmes* v. *Ashford* [1950] 2 All E.R. 76.

6 Wider in that it is owed not only to the other contracting party but to any foreseeable user.

7 *Marshall* v. *R.O.P.*, 1938 S.C. 773; *Yachuk* v. *Blais* [1949] A.C. 386.

8 *Edwards* v. *Hutcheon* (1889) 16 R. 694; *Andrews* v. *Hopkinson* [1957] 1 Q.B. 229; *Sullivan* v. *Gallagher & Craig*, 1959 S.C. 243.

9 *Heaven* v. *Pender* (1883) 11 Q.B.D. 503; *Oliver* v. *Saddler*, 1929 S.C. (H.L.) 94.

10 *Gordon* v. *McHardy* (1903) 6 F. 210.

11 *Gavin* v. *Rogers* (1889) 17 R. 206; *McGill* v. *Bowman* (1890) 18 R. 206.

12 *Lynch* v. *Nurdin* (1841) 1 Q.B. 29; *King* v. *Pollock* (1874) 2 R. 42.

13 *Campbell* v. *Ord & Maddison* (1873) 1 R. 149; *McGregor* v. *Ross & Marshall* (1883) 10 R. 725; *Morrison* v. *McAra* (1896) 23 R. 564; *Hendry* v. *McDougall*, 1923 S.C. 378; *Ballantyne* v. *Hamilton*, 1938 S.L.T. 468.

14 *Malcolm* v. *Dickson*, 1951 S.C. 542; *Gilmour* v. *Simpson*, 1958 S.C. 477.

15 *Ross* v. *McCallum's Trs.*, 1922 S.C. 322.

16 *Fitzpatrick* v. *Melville*, 1926 S.L.T. 478.

17 *McWilliam* v. *Hunter & Clark*, 1926 S.L.T. 676.

18 Radioactive Substances Act, 1960.

19 *Gilligan* v. *Robb*, 1910 S.C. 856; *Pitcher* v. *Martin* [1937] 3 All E.R. 918; *Henderson* v. *John Stuart (Farms), Ltd.*, 1963 S.C. 245.

person bringing an animal on to, or driving it along, a road, must take care for the safety of persons and property thereon.[1] There is no liability for harm arising without negligence, or by unforeseeable happening.[2] But the occupier of farmland is not liable if tame farm animals escape on to the highway;[3] he is not bound to fence his land or to keep his animals in.[4] In certain circumstances[5] a person in charge of an animal may be under a strict liability to keep it under control and be liable if his control is ineffectual, even without negligence.

MENTAL INJURIES

Negligent infliction of nervous shock

Injury by shock sustained without contact is as much actionable as physical injury.[6] The duty of care on a person is as much not to cause nervous shock as not to cause physical lesion. To be actionable as nervous shock there must be an actual physical disorder of the nervous constitution of the body producing intellectual or emotional stress and resulting in incapacity in varying degree.[7] Claims are competent for nervous shock caused by reasonable fear of immediate bodily injury to the pursuer,[8] possibly by reasonable fear for a relative or close friend,[9] possibly if caused by seeing or hearing harm caused to another,[10] but possibly not if caused by hearing the report of an accident to another,[11] or a report about oneself.[12]

[1] *Phillips* v. *Nicoll* (1884) 11 R. 592; *McEwan* v. *Cuthill* (1897) 25 R. 57; *Milne* v. *Nimmo* (1898) 25 R. 1150.

[2] *Shaw* v. *Croall* (1885) 12 R. 1186; *Harper* v. *G.N.S. Ry.* (1886) 13 R. 1139; *Smith* v. *Wallace* (1898) 25 R. 761; *Hogg* v. *Cupar District Cttee.*, 1912 1 S.L.T. 57.

[3] *Heath's Garage, Ltd.* v. *Hodges* [1916] 2 K.B. 370; *Fraser* v. *Pate*, 1923 S.C. 748; *Sinclair* v. *Muir*, 1933 S.N. 42, 62.

[4] *Searle* v. *Wallbank* [1947] A.C. 341; *Wright* v. *Callwood* [1950] 2 K.B. 515.

[5] See, *infra*.

[6] *Brown* v. *Watson*, 1914 S.C. (H.L.) 44; *Cowie* v. *L.M.S. Ry.*, 1934 S.C. 433; *Bourhill* v. *Young*, 1942 S.C. (H.L.) 78.

[7] *Bourhill* v. *Young*, 1941 S.C. 395, 432.

[8] *Dulieu* v. *White* [1901] 2 K.B. 669; *Cooper* v. *Caledonian Ry.* (1902) 4 F. 880; *Wallace* v. *Kennedy* (1908) 16 S.L.T. 485; *Gilligan* v. *Robb*, 1910 S.C. 856; *Fowler* v. *N.B. Ry.*, 1914 S.C. 866; *Campbell* v. *Henderson*, 1915 1 S.L.T. 419; *Ross* v. *Glasgow Corpn.*, 1919 S.C. 174; *Brown* v. *Glasgow Corpn.*, 1922 S.C. 527; *Walker* v. *Pitlochry Motor Co.*, 1930 S.C. 565; *Cowie* v. *L.M.S. Ry.*, 1934 S.C. 433; *Bourhill*, *supra*; *King* v. *Phillips* [1953] 1 Q.B. 429.

[9] *Hambrook* v. *Stokes* [1925] 1 K.B. 141; *Currie* v. *Wardrop*, 1927 S.C. 538; cf. *Dooley* v. *Cammell Laird* [1951] 1 Lloyd's Rep. 271.

[10] *Smith* v. *Johnson* [1897] 2 Q.B. 61; *Campbell* v. *Henderson*, 1915 1 S.L.T. 419; *Brown*, *supra*; *Bourhill*, *supra*; *King*, *supra*; *Schneider* v. *Eisovitch* [1960] 2 Q.B. 430; *McLinden* v. *Richardson*, 1962 S.L.T. (Notes) 104.

[11] *Bourhill*, *supra*, 399; *Gray* v. *Sun Publishing Co.* (1952) 2 D.L.R. 479. Contrast *Schneider*, *supra*.

[12] *Furniss* v. *Fitchett* [1958] C.L.Y. 2284.

PROFESSIONAL NEGLIGENCE

A practitioner of a profession owes a contractual duty to his employer to exercise the skill and care expected of a normally competent practitioner of that profession or trade[1] and a similar duty *ex lege* to any person who may be personally injured by his failure to attain that standard of skill or care.[2] Liability is only for failure to attain the standard of skill and care reasonably to be expected,[3] not for failure of the treatment.[4] Conformity to general and approved practice of the profession at the time will normally exculpate.[5] Similar principles apply to persons exercising a skilled trade.[6] By custom, however, an advocate is not legally liable for professional mistake or fault.[7]

Persons in charge of others

Teachers, hospital staff, prison officers, and others having the care of persons must take reasonable care for the safety of the persons in their charge and may be liable if they cause personal injury by failure to take reasonable precautions against foreseeable harm. The liability may be on the authority,[8] directly or vicariously, or the member of staff personally in fault.[9]

STRICT LIABILITY FOR PERSONAL INJURIES

Quasi-delictual liability

A person may be strictly liable if he has placed or suspended something over a public way and it has caused damage by falling, on the basis of the *actio de positis vel suspensis*.[10] Similarly he may be

[1] Bell, *Prin.* §154; *Dickson* v. *Hygienic Institute*, 1910 S.C. 352, 356.

[2] *Farquhar* v. *Murray* (1901) 3 F. 859; *Edgar* v. *Lamont*, 1914 S.C. 277.

[3] *Lamphier* v. *Phipos* (1838) 8 C. & P. 475; *Harmer* v. *Cornelius* (1858) 5 C.B. (N.S.) 236; *Rich* v. *Pierpont* (1862) 3 F. & F. 35; *Hunter* v. *Hanley*, 1955 S.C. 200.

[4] *Fish* v. *Kapur* [1948] 2 All E.R. 176; *Cassidy* v. *Ministry of Health* [1951] 2 K.B. 343; *Roe* v. *Ministry of Health* [1954] 2 Q.B. 66, 76.

[5] *Hunter*, *supra.*

[6] *Eccles* v. *Cross & McIlwham*, 1938 S.C. 697; *McLaughlan* v. *Craig*, 1948 S.C. 599; *Malcolm* v. *Dickson*, 1951 S.C. 542; *Waddell's C.B.* v. *Lindsay*, 1960 S.L.T. 189; *Morrison's Assoc. Companies* v. *Rome*, 1964 S.C. 160.

[7] *Purves* v. *Landell* (1845) 4 Bell 46; *Batchelor* v. *Pattison & Mackersy* (1876) 3 R. 914; *Rondel* v. *Worsley* [1967] 3 All E.R. 993.

[8] *Gow* v. *Glasgow Education Authy.*, 1922 S.C. 260; *Macdonald's Tutor* v. *Inverness C.C.*, 1937 S.C. 69 (schools); *Jones* v. *Manchester Corpn.*, [1952] 2 Q.B. 852; *Macdonald* v. *Glasgow Western Hospitals Board*, 1954 S.C. 453 (hospitals); *Pullen* v. *Prison Commrs.* [1957] 3 All E.R. 470; *Keatings* v. *Secy. of State for Scotland* (1961) 77 Sh. Ct. Rep. 113 (prisons).

[9] cf. *Hunter* v. *Hanley*, 1955 S.C. 200 (doctor).

[10] Bankt. I, 4, 32; Hume, *Lect.* III, 186; cf. *Cleghorn* v. *Taylor* (1856) 18 D. 664; *Campbell* v. *Kennedy* (1864) 3 M. 121; *Laurent* v. *L.A.* (1869) 7 M. 607.

strictly liable if any substance has been thrown or poured down on the complainer from a house of which he is the occupier, on the basis of the *actio de effusis vel dejectis*.[1] The strict liability imposed on innkeepers, shipmasters, and stablekeepers under the edict *nautae, caupones, stabularii* has been accepted, with variations, in Scots law.[2] These last heads of liability though quasi-delictual in origin have now been absorbed into the law of contract.[3]

Animals

Apart from liability for injuries caused by negligence in handling or controlling an animal,[4] the person in charge of an animal which is, or is deemed, dangerous is strictly liable for it and must take, not reasonable, but effectual precautions to ensure that it does not get out of control and do harm to person or beast.[5] This strict liability attaches only where the custodier had, or is deemed by law to have had, knowledge of the animal's dangerous propensities.[6] This knowledge may be actual, based on experience, information or knowledge, that his animal, though of a domesticated nature and of a non-dangerous species, has at least once previously exhibited vice of the kind now in issue,[7] or knowledge imputed to him that his animal is dangerous by its belonging to a species not domesticated in Britain and accordingly legally deemed wild and dangerous. The distinction between animals not dangerous or *domitae naturae* and those dangerous or *ferae naturae*[8] is one of law; the former class includes cats,[9] dogs,[10]

[1] Bankt. I, 4, 27; Kames, *Equity*, I, 1, 1; Hume, *Lect.* III, 186; *Gray* v. *Dunlop*, 1954 S.L.T. (Sh. Ct.) 75; Stein, 4 I.C.L.Q. 356.

[2] Stair I, 9, 5; I, 13, 3; IV, 44, 4; Bankt. I, 16, 1; Ersk. III, 1, 28; Bell, *Comm.* I, 495; *Prin.* §235; Hume, *Lect.* III, 417; *Mustard* v. *Paterson*, 1923 S.C. 142; Mackintosh, 3 J.R. 306.

[3] Vide Ch. 38, *supra*.

[4] *Supra*.

[5] *Burton* v. *Moorhead* (1881) 8 R. 892; *Hennigan* v. *McVey* (1882) 9 R. 411.

[6] cf. Stair I, 9, 5; *Clark* v. *Armstrong* (1862) 24 D. 1315; *Milligan* v. *Henderson*, 1915 S.C. 1030; *Fraser* v. *Pate*, 1923 S.C. 748.

[7] Hence the maxim that every dog is allowed one worry with impunity is good law, as the first worry serves only to fix the owner with knowledge of the dog's vicious propensity; cf. *Fleeming* v. *Orr* (1853) 15 D. 486, 487 (revd. 2 Macq. 14); *Renwick* v. *Von Rotberg* (1875) 2 R. 855; *Burton* v. *Moorhead* (1881) 8 R. 892, 895.

[8] *Fraser* v. *Pate*, 1923 S.C. 748, 751; *Behrens* v. *Bertram Mills Circus* [1957] 2 Q.B. 1, 14.

[9] *Buckle* v. *Holmes* [1926] 2 K.B. 125.

[10] *Fleeming* v. *Orr* (1855) 2 Macq. 14; *Milligan* v. *Henderson*, 1915 S.C. 1030. Contrast *Renwick* v. *Von Rotberg* (1875) 2 R. 855; *Burton* v. *Moorhead* (1881) 8 R. 892; *Fraser* v. *Bell* (1887) 14 R. 811; *Macdonald* v. *Smellie* (1903) 5 F. 955; *Baker* v. *Snell* [1908] 2 K.B. 825; *Gordon* v. *Mackenzie*, 1913 S.C. 109.

fowls,[1] sheep,[2] horses,[3] cattle,[4] and sows.[5] The latter class includes lions,[6] elephants,[7] bears,[8] boars,[9] monkeys,[10] and zebras,[11] and it matters not that the particular animal is a tamed one.[12] In animals of the former class actual knowledge of the beast's vicious propensities must be proved; in the latter class knowledge is assumed and imputed to the person in charge. Knowledge of vice is not attached by proof that an animal, not of a dangerous nature, had done something natural to it, such as chasing birds,[13] or had been playful.[14] If knowledge of vicious propensities, actual or imputed, is established the injured person need only establish that the animal escaped from control and caused harm to person or beast; he need not prove negligence.

The defender is not however liable if the pursuer provoked the animal[15] or was materially imprudent or negligent in approaching it,[16] nor if the animal is still under control,[17] nor if the animal was improperly loosed by a third party.[18] *Damnum fatale* is doubtless a defence.[19]

Nuisance

Nuisance consists in so using heritable property as to cause continuing or repeated material disturbance or inconvenience to, and interference with, the reasonable use of adjacent property by the complainer.[20] Neither intention to hurt nor negligence need be

1 *Hadwell* v. *Righton* [1907] 2 K.B. 345.
2 *Heath's Garage, Ltd.* v. *Hodges* [1916] 2 K.B. 370; *Fraser* v. *Pate*, 1923 S.C. 748; cf. *Jackson* v. *Smithson* (1846) 15 M. & W. 563.
3 *Glanville* v. *Sutton* [1928] 1 K.B. 571; *Clelland* v. *Robb*, 1911 S.C. 253.
4 *Clark* v. *Armstrong* (1862) 24 D. 1315; *Ellis* v. *Banyard* (1911) 28 T.L.R. 122; contrast *Hudson* v. *Roberts* (1851) 6 Exch. 697; *Phillips* v. *Nicoll* (1884) 11 R. 592.
5 *Higgins* v. *Searle* (1909) 100 L.T. 280.
6 *Pearson* v. *Coleman Bros.* [1948] 2 K.B. 359.
7 *Filburn* v. *People's Palace Co.* (1890) 25 Q.B.D. 258; *Behrens* v. *Bertram Mills Circus* [1957] 2 Q.B. 1.
8 *Wyatt* v. *Rosherville Gardens Co.* (1886) 2 T.L.R. 282.
9 *Hennigan* v. *McVey* (1881) 9 R. 411.
10 *May* v. *Burdett* (1846) 9 Q.B. 101.
11 *Marlor* v. *Ball* (1900) 16 T.L.R. 239.
12 *Behrens, supra.*
13 *Buckle* v. *Holmes* [1926] 2 K.B. 125.
14 *Fitzgerald* v. *Cooke Bourne (Farms)* [1963] 3 All E.R. 36.
15 *Daly* v. *Arrol* (1886) 14 R. 154; *Gordon* v. *Mackenzie*, 1913 S.C. 109.
16 *Sycamore* v. *Ley* [1932] All E.R. Rep. 97.
17 *Rands* v. *McNeil* [1955] 1 Q.B. 253; *Behrens, supra.*
18 *Fleeming* v. *Orr* (1855) 2 Macq. 14.
19 *Nichols* v. *Marsland* (1875) L.R. 10 Ex. 255, 260.
20 *Watt* v. *Jamieson*, 1954 S.C. 56. See further Ch. 70, *infra.*

proved.[1] It may justify a remedy where not merely inconvenience but personal injury results.[2]

Escape of danger from land

Where a person has introduced to or accumulated on his land anything which, if it escapes, will obviously do serious damage, he is strictly liable to keep it in, and liable without proof of negligence if it does escape and cause damage.[3] This liability is certainly applicable to damage to property, but may apply to personal injuries also.[4]

STATUTORY LIABILITY FOR PERSONAL INJURIES

Numerous statutes, and sets of regulations made under authority thereof, impose liability, expressly or by interpretation, under some of their sections, for injuries caused by breach of the statutory duties thereby imposed.[5] This liability is frequently cumulative with liability for criminal penalties and with liability for breach of common law duty constituted by the same harmful conduct.

The standard of care imposed by a statutory duty is determined by the interpretation of the particular section in question. It may be a duty to refrain from intentional harm, or to take reasonable care against foreseeable risks,[6] or a duty qualified in the manner stated in the section, e.g. 'so far as is reasonably practicable',[7] or a rather higher duty to take 'all practicable measures',[8] or to take precautions 'except in so far as . . . impracticable',[9] or the

[1] *Sedleigh-Denfield* v. *O'Callaghan* [1940] A.C. 880, 897.

[2] cf. *Fleming* v. *Hislop* (1886) 13 R. (H.L.) 43, 45; *Castle* v. *St. Augustine's Links* (1922) 38 T.L.R. 615; *Gray* v. *Dunlop* (1954) 70 Sh. Ct. Rep. 270.

[3] See further Ch. 70, *infra*.

[4] *Kerr* v. *Earl of Orkney* (1857) 20 D. 298, 302; *Western Silver Fox Ranch* v. *Ross C.C.*, 1940 S.C. 601, 605; cf. *Miles* v. *Forest Rock Granite Co.* (1918) 34 T.L.R. 500; but see *Paterson* v. *Lindsay* (1885) 13 R. 261; *Reynolds* v. *Lanarkshire Tramways Co.* (1908) 16 S.L.T. 230; *Read* v. *Lyons* [1947] A.C. 156; *McLaughlan* v. *Craig*, 1948 S.C. 599.

[5] The principal statutes are Merchant Shipping Acts, 1894 to 1968; Railway Employment (Prevention of Accidents) Act, 1900; Civil Aviation Act, 1949 and Carriage by Air Act, 1961; Mines and Quarries Act, 1954; Agriculture (Safety, Health, and Welfare Provisions) Act, 1956; Road Traffic Acts, 1960 to 1966; Factories Act, 1961 and Dangerous Trade Regulations made thereunder; Offices, Shops, and Railway Premises Act, 1963; Radioactive Substances Acts; and certain Police and municipal Acts.

[6] e.g. *McCarthy* v. *Daily Mirror* [1949] 1 All E.R. 801; *Marshall* v. *Babcock & Wilcox*, 1961 S.L.T. 259; *Brown* v. *N.C.B.* [1962] A.C. 574; *O'Hanlon* v. *Stein*, 1965 S.C. (H.L.) 23.

[7] *Sharp* v. *Coltness Iron Co.*, 1937 S.C. (H.L.) 68; the onus of proof of practicability may be on the pursuer: *Hall* v. *Fairfield*, 1964 S.C. (H.L.) 72.

[8] *Balfour* v. *Beardmore*, 1956 S.L.T. 205.

[9] *Buchan* v. *Hutchison*, 1953 S.L.T. 306.

duty may be absolute,[1] in which case there is no defence save to prove that the breach did not cause the harm complained of, or that the injured person's own conduct was entirely the cause of the harm.[2]

The Consumer Protection Act, 1961, S. 3, created the statutory delict of contravening or not complying with any regulations made under that Act imposing requirements as to goods to prevent or reduce risk of death or personal injury therefrom. The Resale Prices Act, 1964, S. 4, created the statutory delict of contravening any of the provisions of that Act, which avoids conditions seeking to maintain the resale price of goods.

1 *Millar* v. *Galashiels Gas Co.*, 1949 S.C. (H.L.) 31; *Hamilton* v. *N.C.B.*, 1960 S.C. (H.L.) 1.

2 cf. *Knight* v. *Colvilles*, 1963 S.C. 26.

CHAPTER 66

WRONGS IN RESPECT OF THE DOMESTIC RELATIONSHIPS

A PERSON has a right of action where his domestic relations with spouse and family have been unjustifiably broken or infringed by another. Some of the infringements may be done intentionally, others negligently or by breach of a duty of strict liability or breach of statutory duty.

Enticement

A person has a right of action against another, even a relative, who without justification entices his or her spouse to break cohabitation and to leave.[1] The enticement need not be for adultery. A husband may be enticed,[2] or a child.[3] Exceptionally enticement might be justifiable.

Adultery

Adultery with a married person renders the paramour liable to an action at the instance of the married person's spouse for the hurt to his honour and feelings.[4] It is unnecessary to prove enticement, seductive wiles, or interference with matrimonial life.[5] The claim may be by separate action, or conjoined with a conclusion for divorce on the ground of the adultery,[6] or after divorce for adultery;[7] it is not barred by condonation of the adultery,[8] nor by the spouse's death,[9] but is by connivance[10] or collusion.[11] It is probably necessary to prove that the defender

[1] Hume, *Lect.* III, 131–2; *Duncan* v. *Cumming* (1714) 5 B.S. 104; *Adamson* v. *Gillibrand*, 1923 S.L.T. 328; cf. *Place* v. *Searle* [1932] 2 K.B. 497.

[2] *Gray* v. *Gee* (1923) 39 T.L.R. 429; *Newton* v. *Hardy* (1933) 49 T.L.R. 522; *Place*, *supra*.

[3] *Hutchinson* v. *H.* (1890) 18 R. 237; *Edgar* v. *Fisher's Trs.* (1893) 21 R. 325; *Begbie* v. *Nichol*, 1949 S.C. 158; cf. *Delaney* v. *Stirling* (1893) 20 R. 506; *Delaney* v. *Edinburgh Children's Aid* (1889) 16 R. 753; *Delaney* v. *Colston* (1891) 19 R. 8.

[4] *Kirk* v. *Guthrie* (1817) 1 Mur. 271.

[5] *Baillie* v. *Bryson* (1818) 1 Mur. 317, 334.

[6] *Fraser* v. *Fraser and Hibbert* (1870) 8 M. 400.

[7] *Steedman* v. *Coupar* (1743) Mor. 7337; *Baillie*, *supra*; *Glover* v. *Samson* (1856) 18 D. 609.

[8] *Collins* v. *C.* (1882) 10 R. 250; *Macdonald* v. *M.* (1885) 12 R. 1327.

[9] *Kent* v. *Atkinson* [1923] P. 142.

[10] *Thomson* v. *T.*, 1908 S.C. 179; *Gallagher* v. *G.*, 1928 S.C. 586.

[11] *Fairgrieve* v. *Chalmers*, 1912 S.C. 745; *Riddell* v. *R.*, 1952 S.C. 475.

knew or should have known that his partner was married,[1] but immaterial that the spouses were separated or living apart. The damages are for hurt to feelings, loss of the spouse's society, and have regard to her qualities as wife and housekeeper.[2]

Rape or indecent assault

Rape of or indecent assault on a married woman gives her husband an action for the affront to him and the hurt to his feelings.[3]

Physical or mental injury to relative

No action lies for physical or mental injury to a relative, not resulting in death, nor for loss of that relative's services.[4] Where, however, such injury has caused the pursuer pecuniary loss for medical treatment or extra housekeeping expenses in consequence of the relative's injury, a claim is competent therefor.[5]

Assythment—death caused criminally

A claim for assythment or reparation lies at the instance of the wife, children and next of kin of a person killed by the defender's criminal conduct.[6] Such a claim is doubtless still competent, though practically unknown in modern practice, having been superseded by the so-called *actio injuriarum*.[7]

Death caused negligently

An action[8] lies at the instance of certain surviving relatives where the defender's fault or negligence, not amounting to

[1] cf. *Miller* v. *Simpson* (1863) 2 M. 225; *Kydd* v. *K.* (1864) 2 M. 1074; *Laurie* v. *L.*, 1913 1 S.L.T. 117; *Heggie* v. *H.*, 1917 2 S.L.T. 246.

[2] Fraser, *H. & W.* II. 1203; *Baillie, supra*; *Butterworth* v. *B.* [1920] P. 126.

[3] *Colonel Charteris* (1723) Hume on *Crimes*, II, 123; *Black* v. *Duncan*, 1924 S.C. 738.

[4] *Allan* v. *Barclay* (1864) 2 M. 873; *Reavis* v. *Clan Line*, 1925 S.C. 725, 739; *Quin* v. *Greenock Tramways*, 1926 S.C. 544; *Burgess* v. *Florence Nightingale Hospital* [1955] 1 Q.B. 349; *Gibson* v. *Glasgow Corpn.*, 1963 S.L.T. (Notes) 16.

[5] *Soutar* v. *Mulhern*, 1907 S.C. 723; *Murphy* v. *Baxter's Bus Service*, 1962 S.C. 589; *Thomson* v. *Angus C.C.*, 1962 S.C. 590; *McBay* v. *Hamlett*, 1963 S.L.T. 18; see also *Robertson* v. *Glasgow Corpn.*, 1965 S.L.T. 143; *Edgar* v. *P.M.G.*, 1965 S.C. 67, *sed quaere*.

[6] Stair I, 9, 7; Bankt. I, 10, 14; Hume, *Comm.* I, 285; II, 500; *Lect.* III, 128; Kames, *H.L.T.* V, 2; Bell, *Prin.* §2029; More, *Lect.* I, 348; Walker, 66 J.R. 144; cf. *Black* v. *Cadell* (1804) Mor. 13905, 5 Pat. 567; *Greenhorn* v. *Addie* (1855) 17 D. 860, 862; *Eisten* v. *N.B. Ry.* (1870) 8 M. 980, 986; *Horn* v. *N.B. Ry.* (1878) 5 R. 1055; *Black* v. *N.B. Ry.*, 1908 S.C. 444, 452.

[7] See next paragraph. In the nineteenth century some cases do not properly distinguish between assythment and claim for negligent death as the ground of action: see e.g. *Hislop* v. *Durham* (1842) 4 D. 1168; *Morton* v. *Edinburgh & Glasgow Ry.* (1845) 8 D. 288, which also gave rise to criminal proceedings in *H.M.A.* v. *Paton and McNab* (1845) 2 Broun 525; *Maclean* v. *Russell, Macnee & Co.* (1849) 12 D. 1035.

[8] Commonly miscalled an, or the, *actio injuriarum*, but in fact unconnected with that action in Roman law; see *Stewart's Exrx.* v. *L.M.S. Ry.*, 1943 S.C. (H.L.) 19, 39. The

criminal wrong, has caused the death of the pursuers' relative. The action is founded partly on nearness of relationship, giving rise to a claim for solatium for the pain and grief felt at the death of the claimant's relative, and partly on the existence during life as between the claimant and the deceased of a mutual obligation of support in case of necessity, giving rise to a claim for patrimonial loss or the loss of the financial support which was being afforded to the claimant by the deceased and was likely to have continued to be afforded by him, or which at least would have been forthcoming in case of need.[1]

Title to sue in this action

The action was formerly competent only to persons between whom and the deceased there existed a mutual obligation of support in case of need, to a surviving spouse, parent or child,[2] and a question of a person's title to sue had to be determined by whether he could have obtained aliment from the deceased, but the class of entitled persons has been extended by interpretation and legislation. Claims are competent to a widow,[3] or widower,[4] even if separated,[5] but not to a mistress,[6] nor a former wife,[7] for the death of the other spouse. A widow who has remarried may sue. A child, irrespective of age, may claim for the death of either parent,[8] or of any grandparent, provided the intervening parents are dead and also any other grandparents with a prior liability to aliment the pursuer.[9] An illegitimate person may now sue for the

true basis of this action is an extension of the *actio legis Aquiliae*. This action developed in the nineteenth century out of the action of assythment and for a time both were in use and were to some extent confused: see e.g. *Lenaghan* v. *Monkland Iron Co.* (1857) 19 D. 975; *McNaughton* v. *Caledonian Ry.* (1857) 19 D. 271; 21 D. 160.

[1] *Eisten* v. *N.B. Ry.* (1870) 8 M. 980, 984; *Quin* v. *Greenock Tramways Co.*, 1926 S.C. 544, 546; *Hewitt* v. *West's Gas Improvement Co.*, 1955 S.C. 162, 165.

[2] *Eisten* v. *N.B. Ry.* (1870) 8 M. 980, 984; *Darling* v. *Gray* (1892) 19 R. (H.L.) 31.

[3] e.g. *Blaikie* v. *B.T.C.*, 1961 S.C. 44; even if she has remarried or taken up cohabitation with another man: *Donnelly* v. *Glasgow Corpn.*, 1949 S.L.T. 248; though these facts are relevant to damages.

[4] e.g. *McKinlay* v. *Glasgow Corpn.*, 1951 S.C. 495.

[5] cf. *Donnelly* v. *D.*, 1959 S.C. 97; *Jack* v. *J.*, 1961 S.C. 24. If the separated spouse was unwilling to adhere he or she may not have a claim; cf. *Beveridge* v. *B.*, 1963 S.L.T. 248.

[6] cf. *Phipps* v. *Cunard White Star* [1951] 1 T.L.R. 359. But the mistress's children by the deceased now have a claim: Law Reform (Misc. Prov.) (Sc.) Act, 1940, S.2(2).

[7] *Hemmens* v. *B.T.C.*, 1955 S.L.T. (Notes) 48.

[8] *Rankin* v. *Waddell*, 1949 S.C. 555 (father); *McRae* v. *Glasgow Corpn.*, 1915 2 S.L.T. 94 (mother; father insane); *Mill* v. *Dundas*, 1919 2 S.L.T. 65 (mother); *Kelly* v. *Glasgow Corpn.*, 1951 S.C. (H.L.) 15 (mother).

[9] *Hanlin* v. *Melrose & Thomson* (1899) 1 F. 1012; *Cooper* v. *Fife Coal Co.*, 1907 S.C. 564; *Ewart* v. *R. & W. Ferguson*, 1932 S.C. 277; see also *Gay's Tutrix* v. *Gay's Tr.*, 1953 S.L.T. 278.

death of either parent,[1] and a claim may be made on behalf of a posthumous child.[2] Either[3] or both[4] parents may claim for the death of a child, whether legitimate,[5] legitimated,[6] illegitimate[7] or adopted,[8] or of a grandchild if both intervening parents were dead;[9] no claim lies by a step-parent for the death of a stepchild.[10] No claim lies for the death of a brother, sister, or other collateral, there being no mutual obligation of support, not even if in fact grief were felt or loss of support experienced,[11] nor for the death of a step-relative or a relative-in-law.[12] It is not competent to investigate relationship in the reparation action; if marriage or other title to sue is in doubt a separate action must determine it.[13] An executor has no title to sue this form of action, the right of action belonging exclusively to relatives.

Multiple claims

Claims are competent by any combination of persons each of whom has a title to sue, but each concludes for a separate award of damages.[14] Though each relative having title to sue has a separate claim, all entitled relatives must concur in one action to avoid multiplicity of actions and to enable the court to view the claims as interrelated parts of a family claim.[15] If any entitled

1 Law Reform (Misc. Prov.) (Sc.) Act, 1940, S. 2(2).

2 *Moorcraft* v. *Alexander*, 1946 S.C. 466.

3 *Weems* v. *Mathieson* (1861) 4 Macq. 215 (widowed mother); *Fraser* v. *Younger* (1867) 5 M. 861 (widowed mother); *Horn* v. *N.B. Ry.* (1878) 5 R. 1055 (father); *Eisten* v. *N.B. Ry.* (1870) 8 M. 980, 984.

4 Law Reform (Damages and Solatium) (Sc.) Act, 1962, S. 1, overruling *Laidlaw* v. *N.C.B.*, 1957 S.C. 49 and earlier cases cited therein; *Kelly* v. *Nuttall*, 1965 S.C. 427.

5 e.g. *Horn* v. *N.B. Ry.* (1878) 5 R. 1055.

6 *McLean* v. *Glasgow Corpn.*, 1933 S.L.T. 396; see also *McNeill* v. *McGregor* (1901) 4 F. 123.

7 Law Reform (Damages and Solatium) (Sc.) Act, 1962, S. 2, overruling *Weir* v. *Coltness Iron Co.* (1889) 16 R. 614; *Clarke* v. *Carfin Coal Co.*, (1891) 19 R. (H.L.) 63; and *Clement* v. *Bell* (1899) 1 F. 925.

8 Law Reform (Misc. Prov.) (Sc.) Act, 1940, S. 2(1); cf. Adoption Act, 1958, S. 13(1).

9 *Hanlin* v. *Melrose* (1899) 1 F. 1012.

10 *MacDonald* v. *M.* (1846) 8 D. 830.

11 *Greenhorn* v. *Addie* (1855) 17 D. 860 (brothers); *Eisten* v. *N.B. Ry.* (1870) 8 M. 980 (sisters).

12 *Macdonald* v. *M.* (1846) 8 D. 830; *Hoseason* v. *H.* (1870) 9 M. 37; *McAllan* v. *Alexander* (1888) 15 R. 863; *Mackay* v. *M's Trs.* (1904) 6 F. 936; *Hanlin* v. *Melrose* (1899) 1 F. 1012.

13 *Lenaghan* v. *Monkland Iron Co.* (1857) 19 D. 975; *McLean* v. *Glasgow Corpn.*, 1933 S.L.T. 396; cf. *Wallace* v. *Fife Coal Co.*, 1909 S.C. 682; contrast *McDonald* v. *McKenzie* (1891) 18 R. 502; *Johnstone* v. *Spencer*, 1908 S.C. 1015.

14 *Gray* v. *Caledonian Ry.*, 1912 S.C. 339.

15 *Paterson* v. *L.M.S. Ry.*, 1942 S.C. 156; *Kelly* v. *Glasgow Corpn.*, 1951 S.C. (H.L.) 15, 20; *Campbell* v. *West of Scotland Shipbreaking Co.*, 1953 S.C. 173; *Hewitt* v. *West's Gas Improvement Co.*, 1955 S.C. 162.

relative cannot be found or refuses to concur he should be called as a defender for his interest.[1] The court or jury may make no award to one or more pursuers.[2] The mutual obligation of support had to have existed at the date of the death, and had to be one immediately and directly prestable in case of necessity between claimant and deceased.[3] Claims are competent not only where support was actually being afforded at the date of death, or was needed, but where support could legally have been asked for if need had arisen.[4]

Elements of claim

The claim of each entitled pursuer comprises two elements, solatium, a moderate sum given in acknowledgment of grief felt at the relative's death,[5] and patrimonial loss or loss of support, a sum in compensation for the loss of pecuniary support being afforded, and likely to continue to be afforded, to the claimant by the deceased.[6] If a relative has title to sue, the title is to sue for either or both of these elements,[7] as may be appropriate, though they are truly separate claims, and the court or jury may competently make a nil award under either or both heads.[8] In modern practice a sum is claimed to cover both heads and an award usually made without distinguishing how much is applicable to each.[9] In addition a small sum for funeral expenses is customarily given.[10] Injury to the pursuer's health is not a relevant factor in the claim for solatium,[11] though evidence of hurt to feelings by the deceased's suffering between injury and death is relevant.[12] No claim lies for business loss resulting from the death.[13] If, however, loss of support is proved an award must be made, even though the

[1] *Smith* v. *Wilsons & Clyde Coal Co.* (1893) 21 R. 162; *Grant* v. *Wood Bros.* (1902) 10 S.L.T. 296; *Pollok* v. *Workman* (1900) 2 F. 354; *Slorach* v. *Kerr*, 1921 S.C. 285; *Kinnaird* v. *McLean*, 1942 S.C. 448.

[2] e.g. *Wason* v. *B.T.C.*, 1960 S.C. 261.

[3] *Ewart* v. *Ferguson*, 1932 S.C. 277, 285.

[4] *Sagar* v. *N.C.B.*, 1955 S.C. 424; *Dickson* v. *N.C.B.*, 1957 S.C. 157; cf. *Duffy* v. *Kinneil Coal Co.*, 1930 S.C. 596.

[5] e.g. *Kelly* v. *Glasgow Corpn.*, 1951 S.C. (H.L.) 15; *McKinlay* v. *Glasgow Corpn.*, 1951 S.C. 495; *McLeish* v. *Fulton*, 1955 S.C. 46.

[6] *Eisten*, *supra*, 984.

[7] e.g. *Hewitt* v. *West's Gas Improvement Co.*, 1955 S.C. 162; *Love* v. *N.C.B.*, 1956 S.C. 459; *Wason* v. *B.T.C.*, 1960 S.C. 261; *Urquhart* v. *Baxter*, 1961 S.C. 149.

[8] *Rankin* v. *Waddell*, 1949 S.C. 555 (no solatium); *McKinlay*, *supra* (no patrimonial loss); *Cruikshank* v. *Shiels*, 1953 S.C. (H.L.) 1 (possibly no patrimonial loss).

[9] See *Hewitt* v. *West's Gas Improvement Co.*, 1955 S.C. 162, 166.

[10] e.g. *McKinlay*, *supra*; *McLeish* v. *Fulton*, 1955 S.C. 46.

[11] *Kirkpatrick* v. *Anderson*, 1948 S.C. 251; *Nicolson* v. *Cursiter*, 1959 S.C. 350.

[12] *Black* v. *N.B. Ry.*, 1908 S.C. 444, 453.

[13] *Quin* v. *Greenock Tramways Co.*, 1926 S.C. 544.

pursuer has adequate other resources.[1] Any awards made belong to the pursuers absolutely, and are not part of the deceased's estate.

Ground of action

The action is founded on the same facts as would have been a claim by the deceased, had he survived, for reparation for personal injuries done him, i.e. it is founded on breach of a legal duty owed by the defender *to the deceased*.[2] The defender may invoke any defence he could have invoked had the action been brought by the deceased, such as the deceased's voluntary acceptance of risk[3] or contributory negligence[4] or contractual limitation or exclusion of his claim.[5] It is also possible to invoke any defence valid against the pursuer personally, such as that he was *volens* as to a danger which caused his relative's death.[6]

Possible conflicts of actions

Action by the surviving relatives of a person killed for solatium and patrimonial loss to them is independent of and not derived by succession from the deceased;[7] it is distinct from and generally inconsistent with the continuance by the deceased's executor of an action brought by the deceased before his death for solatium to him for his personal injuries, and for past and future patrimonial loss consequent thereon.[8] If the deceased died without bringing an action, his right to claim solatium dies with him,[9] but his surviving relatives may sue; if he died,[10] having brought an action for his injuries, it transmits to his executor, who may continue it for the benefit of the deceased's estate, recovering such damages as the deceased could have done, down to the date

[1] *Cruikshank*, *supra*.

[2] *Horn* v. *N.B. Ry.* (1878) 5 R. 1055, 1061. Accordingly any grounds of action discussed in Ch. 65 may be relied on by an entitled relative, if the victim is not merely injured but killed.

[3] *Steel* v. *Glasgow Iron & Steel Co.*, 1944 S.C. 237; *Baker* v. *Hopkins*, [1958] 3 All E.R. 147.

[4] *McNaughton* v. *Caledonian Ry.* (1858) 21 D. 160; *Lever* v. *Greenock Motors*, 1949 S.C. 88.

[5] *McKay* v. *Scottish Airways*, 1948 S.C. 254.

[6] *Davidson* v. *Sprengel*, 1909 S.C. 566; cf. *Innes* v. *Fife Coal Co.* (1901) 3 F. 335.

[7] *Neilson* v. *Rodger* (1854) 16 D. 325, 330; *Darling* v. *Gray* (1892) 19 R. (H.L.) 31; *Davidson* v. *Sprengel*, 1909 S.C. 566; *McKay* v. *Scottish Airways*, 1948 S.C. 254.

[8] *Darling*, *supra*.

[9] *Bern's Exor.* v. *Montrose Asylum* (1893) 20 R. 859; *Stewart's Exrx.* v. *L.M.S. Ry.*, 1943 S.C. (H.L.) 19, 25; *Smith* v. *Stewart*, 1961 S.C. 91.

[10] *Darling*, *supra*.

of his death only,[1] and this action excludes any action by the relatives;[2] the executor may, however, abandon such an action, which permits the relatives to sue.[3] The executor may, however, bring an action for patrimonial loss caused to the deceased before, and down to the date of, his death,[4] and this action does not exclude an action by entitled relatives for solatium and patrimonial loss to them by reason of, and after, the death.[5] Where an executor has a claim any award falls into the deceased's estate and must be distributed with the rest of that estate.

Transmission of survivor's action

The surviving relative's right of action, once exercised, itself transmits on his death to his executor, who may recover what the relative could have done, but calculated down to the date of his death only.[6]

Claim under Carriage by Air Act

Where a person has been killed in the course of carriage by air, the carrier's liability under the Carriage by Air Act, 1961, is to those entitled by common law, as amended, to sue. The carrier's liability is limited, unless a higher limit is agreed on.

Defamation of deceased relative

Defamation of a deceased relative is actionable by the surviving relatives if it affects their reputations also,[7] and possibly also if it hurts their feelings[8] or if it has caused them pecuniary loss.[9]

[1] *Neilson* v. *Rodger* (1854) 16 D. 325; *Darling, supra*; *Reid* v. *Lanarkshire Traction Co.*, 1933 S.C. 416; see also *Smith* v. *Stewart*, 1960 S.C. 329.

[2] *Darling, supra.*

[3] *Bruce* v. *Stephen*, 1957 S.L.T. 78.

[4] *Smith* v. *Stewart*, 1961 S.C. 91; *Russell's Exrx.* v. *B.R.*, 1965 S.C. 422.

[5] *McGhie* v. *B.T.C.*, 1964 S.L.T. 25; *Gray* v. *N.B. Steel Foundry, Ltd.*, 1968 S.L.T. (Notes) 95.

[6] *Kelly* v. *Glasgow Corpn.*, 1951 S.C. (H.L.) 15; *Nevay* v. *B.T.C.*, 1955 S.L.T. (Notes) 28.

[7] *Broom* v. *Ritchie* (1904) 6 F. 942; cf. *Tullis* v. *Crichton* (1850) 12 D. 867.

[8] *Broom, supra*, 948.

[9] *Broom, supra*, 943, 945.

CHAPTER 67

WRONGS BY INTERFERENCE WITH LIBERTY

Physical detention

INTERFERENCE with an individual's freedom of movement, unless justified, is actionable.[1] It is not unjustifiable interference if the individual wishes, in breach of contract, to leave the place,[2] nor if his liberty of movement is merely hampered but not prevented,[3] nor if he is detained until he satisfies conditions, such as paying a fare. Circumstances may justify detention, such as the safety of the detainee, or of other persons.

A parent, guardian or person *in loco parentis* may detain the child or ward so far as this is reasonable and necessary in the ward's interest. The master of a ship may detain a seaman or passenger if this is necessary for the preservation of order and discipline, or for the safety of the vessel or persons or property on board.[4]

Detention as person of unsound mind

Such detention is actionable[5] unless the person's detention is authorized by the Mental Health (Sc.) Act, 1960, Ss. 24 or 31. A person whose detention is authorized may, if he absents himself without leave, be detained and returned to hospital.[6] All persons concerned in the wrongful detention of a person as a mental patient may be liable, the solicitor who advised,[7] doctors who certified,[8] the sheriff who authorized,[9] and the managers of the mental hospital who detained.[10] The Mental Health (Sc.) Act,

1 *Mackenzie* v. *Young* (1902) 10 S.L.T. 231; *Mackenzie* v. *Cluny Hill Hydro.*, 1908 S.C. 200.

2 *Robinson* v. *Balmain New Ferry Co.* [1910] A.C. 295; *Herd* v. *Weardale Steel Co.* [1915] A.C. 67.

3 *Bird* v. *Jones* (1845) 7 Q.B. 742.

4 *Lundie* v. *MacBrayne* (1894) 21 R. 1085; *Coutts & Park* v. *MacBrayne*, 1910 S.C. 386; *Hook* v. *Cunard S.S. Co.*, [1953] 1 All E.R. 1021.

5 Bell, *Prin.* §2042.

6 1960 Act, S. 36.

7 *Mackintosh* v. *Fraser* (1859) 21 D. 783; 22 D. 421; 1 M. (H.L.) 37.

8 *Strang* v. *S.* (1849) 11 D. 379; *Mackintosh, supra*, 22 D. 422; *Everett* v. *Griffiths* [1921] 1 A.C. 631; *Harnett* v. *Bond* [1925] A.C. 669; *Harnett* v. *Fisher* [1927] A.C. 573; *De Freville* v. *Dill* (1927) 43 T.L.R. 702.

9 *Mackintosh* v. *Arkley* (1866) 8 M. (H.L.) 141.

10 *Strang, supra*; *Mackintosh* v. *Smith and Lowe* (1864) 2 M. 389, 1261; 3 M. (H.L.) 6.

1960, S. 107, protects from liability for an act purporting to be done in pursuance of the Act, unless done in bad faith or without reasonable care.

Wrongful apprehension

Apprehension of a person for alleged crime is actionable unless legally justifiable by warrant,[1] or by circumstances permitting arrest without warrant.[2] A person arrested without warrant must be taken at once to a police station or before a magistrate[3] and be informed of the true ground of his arrest.[4]

Apprehension in good faith is protected, and it is actionable only if done maliciously and without probable cause.[5] These are separate elements, but malice may be inferred from absence of probable cause, recklessness, or unnecessary violence.[6] A conviction negatives absence of probable cause.

Detention after apprehension

A person arrested is normally entitled to be liberated on bail,[7] unless the court thinks it right to refuse.[8] It is actionable to refuse to consider an application for bail, or to fix it at a wholly unreasonable sum.

Wrongful imprisonment

Imprisonment or other deprivation of liberty under judicial authority, if legally unjustifiable, is actionable. Superior court judges are immune from such actions,[9] but magistrates are liable if they act in excess of their jurisdiction and an *ultra vires* sentence is pronounced and executed.[10] But any judicial mistake must be gross to subject to liability, not merely an honest error in statutory

[1] Hume on *Crimes* II, 77; Alison, II, 121; Renton & Brown, 31.

[2] Hume, II, 75; Alison, II, 116; Renton & Brown, 31; cf. *Peggie* v. *Clark* (1868) 7 M. 89; *Beaton* v. *Ivory* (1887) 14 R. 1057; *Leask* v. *Burt* (1893) 21 R. 32; *Jackson* v. *Stevenson* (1897) 24 R. (J.) 38; *Somerville* v. *Sutherland* (1899) 2 F. 185; *Shields* v. *Shearer*, 1914 S.C. (H.L.) 33; *H.M.A.* v. *McGuigan*, 1936 J.C. 16. Various statutes give power to arrest without warrant.

[3] *Lewis* v. *Tims* [1952] A.C. 676.

[4] *Christie* v. *Leachinsky* [1947] A.C. 573.

[5] *Beaton, supra*; *Jackson, supra*; *Young* v. *Glasgow Mags.* (1891) 18 R. 825; *Leask, supra*; *Malcolm* v. *Duncan* (1897) 24 R. 747; *Hill* v. *Campbell* (1905) 8 F. 220.

[6] *Macdonald* v. *Fergusson* (1853) 15 D. 545; *Young, supra*; *Hill* v. *Thomson* (1892) 19 R. 377; *Shields, supra*.

[7] Criminal Procedure (Sc.) Act, 1887, S. 18; Bail (Sc.) Act, 1888, S. 2.

[8] *A.B.* v. *Dickson*, 1907 S.C. (J.) 111; *H.M.A.* v. *Saunders*, 1913 S.C. (J.) 44; *Mackintosh* v. *McGlinchy*, 1921 J.C. 75; *Young* v. *H.M.A.*, 1946 J.C. 5; *Macdonald* v. *Clifford*, 1952 J.C. 22.

[9] *McCreadie* v. *Thomson*, 1907 S.C. 1176, 1182.

[10] *McCreadie, supra*. There is no need to prove malice or lack of probable cause.

interpretation.[1] They are also liable if they act maliciously and without probable cause.[2] The Summary Jurisdiction (Sc.) Act, 1954, S. 75, protects judges and officers of inferior courts unless they have acted maliciously and without probable cause.

Force or fear; Intimidation

A person induced to act by the pressure of force and fear, or intimidation, may claim damages for any loss caused him thereby[3] unless the pressure was legally justifiable in the circumstances.[4] The pressure may be exercised directly on the pursuer, or on a third party who then acts to the pursuer's detriment.[5]

Fraud

Fraud consists in a false representation, made knowingly, or without belief in its truth, or recklessly, with the intention of causing, and actually causing, damage to the pursuer by reliance thereon.[6] The damage may be personal injuries or nervous shock,[7] or possibly submission to sexual intercourse.[8]

Seduction

Seduction consists in obtaining sexual relations with a virgin by fraud, misrepresentations, guile or other means of circumvention, and deflowering her; the wrong is the loss of virginity, consent to intercourse having been obtained by deceit.[9] It therefore differs from fornication and adultery, which are consensual, and from indecent assault and rape, where consent is never given at all.

It is essential that the pursuer aver and establish that she was a virgin,[9] and that her scruples were overcome and that she yielded only to deceit, solicitation or wiles[10] and thereby lost her virginity.

[1] Bell, *Prin.* §2038; *MacPhee* v. *Macfarlane's Exor.*, 1933 S.C. 163.

[2] *Watt* v. *Thomson* (1870) 8 M. (H.L.) 77; *Watt* v. *Ligertwood* (1874) 1 R. (H.L.) 21.

[3] Stair I, 9, 6; Bankt. I, 10, 3; Bell, *Law Dicty.* s.v. Extortion; *Macpherson* v. *Ettles* (1787) Hailes, 1021.

[4] *Brown* v. *Murray* (1874) 1 R. 776.

[5] *Tarleton* v. *McGawley* (1794) Peake 270; *Hewit* v. *Edinburgh Lathsplitters Assoc.* (1906) 14 S.L.T. 489.

[6] Fraud may alternatively cause economic harm: see Ch. 69, *infra*.

[7] *Wilkinson* v. *Downton* [1897] 2 Q.B. 57; *Burrows* v. *Rhodes* [1899] 1 Q.B. 816; *Janvier* v. *Sweeney* [1919] 2 K.B. 316.

[8] cf. *R.* v. *Williams* [1923] 1 K.B. 340.

[9] Fraser, *H. & W.* I, 501. The ground of action of a married or divorced woman or a widow in similar circumstances is not seduction but fraud. Cf. *Shaw* v. *S.* [1954] 2 Q.B. 429.

[10] Hume, *Lect.* III, 132; Fraser, *supra*; *Stewart* v. *Menzies* (1837) 15 S. 1198; affd. 2 Rob. 547; *Murray* v. *Fraser*, 1916 S.C. 623; *Reid* v. *Macfarlane*, 1919 S.C. 518.

The main kinds of wiles have been promise of marriage, not later implemented,[1] courtship with apparent intention to marry,[2] taking advantage of the woman's dependency, as when she is in the man's employment,[3] exercise of dominating influence and fraudulent circumvention.[4] The woman's age, character, and state of knowledge are relevant. Neither intercourse alone,[5] nor pregnancy,[6] is by itself a ground of this action. The fact that the girl is below the age of consent to intercourse does not relieve her of the necessity of proving arts or deceit.[7] The claim may be combined with claims for breach of promise of marriage,[8] for affiliation and aliment.[9] Delay in bringing a claim may raise an inference of condonation, as may the subsequent marriage of the parties.

[1] *McCandy* v. *Turpy* (1826) 4 S. 520; *Walker* v. *McIsaac* (1857) 19 D. 340; *Paton* v. *Brodie* (1858) 20 D. 258; *Forbes* v. *Wilson* (1868) 6 M. 770; *Cathcart* v. *Brown* (1905) 7 F. 951.

[2] *Linning* v. *Hamilton* (1748) Mor. 13909; *Kay* v. *Wilson's Trs.* (1850) 12 D. 845; *Gray* v. *Brown* (1878) 5 R. 971.

[3] *Buchanan* v. *McNab* (1785) Mor. 13918; *Rosses* v. *Bhagvat Sinhjee* (1891) 19 R. 31; *Gray* v. *Miller* (1901) 39 S.L.R. 256; *Brown* v. *Harvey*, 1907 S.C. 558; *Reid* v. *Macfarlane*, 1919 S.C. 518; *MacLeod* v. *MacAskill*, 1920 S.C. 72.

[4] *Murray*, *supra*; *Reid*, *supra*.

[5] *Campbell* v. *Sassen* (1826) 2 W. & S. 309, 333; *Murray*, *supra*.

[6] *Hislop* v. *Ker* (1696) Mor. 13908.

[7] Criminal Law Amdt. Act, 1885, S. 5(1); *Murray*, *supra*.

[8] *Forbes* v. *Wilson* (1868) 6 M. 770.

[9] *Brown*, *supra*; *MacLeod*, *supra*.

CHAPTER 68

WRONGS IN RESPECT OF HONOUR AND REPUTATION

A PERSON has a right of action against another who makes unjustifiable aspersions,[1] hurtful to his honour and self-esteem,[2] or to his reputation and good name in the eyes of others,[3] or to both, by communicating ideas of a derogatory character, usually by words, i.e. *injuria verbis*. The category of verbal injury, *injuria verbis*, as contrasted with real injury, as by assault, comprehends three species of harms, convicium, defamation (or libel or slander[4]), and malicious falsehood, though in some cases verbal injury has been mistakenly considered a category comprehending only cases of convicium and of malicious falsehood, as distinguished from cases of defamation.[5]

Also damaging to a person's reputation are abuses of legal process, comprehending wrongful civil proceedings, wrongful diligence, and wrongful initiation of criminal proceedings.

CONVICIUM

Convicium is the form of verbal injury which consists in insulting, reviling or abusing a person, or holding him up to public hatred, contempt, or ridicule.[6] The requisites of an action on this ground are that the defender has maliciously communicated, of and concerning the pursuer, an idea calculated to bring him into public hatred, contempt or ridicule, and thereby caused him hurt feelings, with or without pecuniary loss. The requisite malice may be inferred from the circumstances and no proof of

[1] Generally Stair I, 9, 4; Bankt. I, 10, 24, and 34; Ersk. I, 5, 30; IV, 4, 80; Hume, *Lect.* III, 133; *Comm.*, I, 340; Bell, *Prin.* §2043; Borthwick, *Libel and Slander*; Cooper on *Defamation and Verbal Injury*; Gatley on *Libel and Slander*.

[2] i.e. an *actio injuriarum*.

[3] i.e. an *actio legis Aquiliae*.

[4] In English law libel and slander are techical terms with distinct legal connotations; in Scots law both terms are used non-technically as synonyms for defamation.

[5] *Paterson* v. *Welch* (1893) 20 R. 744; *Waddell* v. *Roxburgh* (1894) 21 R. 883; *Waugh* v. *Ayrshire Post, Ltd.* (1893) 21 R. 327; *McLaughlan* v. *Orr, Pollock & Co.* (1894) 22 R. 38; *Lever Bros.* v. *Daily Record*, 1909 S.C. 1004; *Andrew* v. *Macara*, 1917 S.C. 247; *Lamond* v. *Daily Record*, 1923 S.L.T. 512; cf. Defamation Act, 1952, S. 14.

[6] Ersk. IV, 4, 80; Hume, *Lect.* III, 139; *Sheriff* v. *Wilson* (1855) 17 D. 528; *Cunningham* v. *Phillips* (1868) 6 M. 926; *Macfarlane* v. *Black* (1887) 14 R. 870, 874; *McLaughlan* v. *Orr, Pollock & Co.* (1894) 22 R. 38, 43.

actual malice, in the shape of malevolence or spite, is necessary.[1] The idea communicated need not be defamatory,[2] but only such as is likely to bring the pursuer into hatred, contempt or ridicule; nor need it be false: *veritas convicii non excusat.*[3] The pursuer must have been hurt in his feelings but need not have suffered any financial or other loss. Convicium has been the ground of action where a newspaper made the pursuer appear addicted to gluttony[4] or made a fool of him,[5] or held him up to public contempt,[6] or attributed unpopular opinions,[7] or made fun of his manners,[8] or attributed to him a desire for bloodshed[9] or an unpopular view about soldiers in wartime,[10] or views about alcohol.[11]

DEFAMATION (OR LIBEL OR SLANDER)

Defamation is the malicious communication to, or to others of and concerning, the pursuer of an idea which is false in fact and derogatory or depreciatory in its nature, to the injury of his feelings or to the damage of his reputation.[12]

Pursuer

The pursuer must establish that the defamation was communicated to him, or to others of and concerning him, and that it referred to him.[13] A reference by mistake to the pursuer, but understood as referring to him, is actionable.[14] The Defamation

[1] Ersk., *supra.*

[2] *Paterson* v. *Welch* (1893) 20 R. 744, 750.

[3] Voet, 47, 10, 9; Ersk., *Prin.* IV, 4, 45; Hume, *Lect.* III, 156; Guthrie Smith, *Damages*, 241; *Cunningham, supra*, 928. In later cases *veritas convicii* has been said to be a defence, but these are cases of defamation, not of convicium proper; e.g. *Friend* v. *Skelton* (1855) 17 D. 548, 553; *Mackellar* v. *Duke of Sutherland* (1859) 21 D. 222, 227.

[4] *Sheriff* v. *Wilson* (1855) 17 D. 528.

[5] *Cunningham* v. *Phillips* (1868) 6 M. 926.

[6] *Macfarlane* v. *Black* (1887) 14 R. 870.

[7] *Paterson* v. *Welch* (1893) 20 R. 744.

[8] *McLaughlan* v. *Orr, Pollock & Co.* (1894) 22 R. 38.

[9] *Waugh* v. *Ayrshire Post* (1893) 21 R. 327; cf. *Lever Bros.* v. *Daily Record*, 1909 S.C. 1004.

[10] *Andrew* v. *Macara*, 1917 S.C. 247.

[11] *Lamond* v. *Daily Record*, 1923 S.L.T. 512.

[12] cf. *Shaw* v. *Morgan* (1888) 15 R. 865, 870; *Waddell* v. *Roxburgh* (1894) 21 R. 883 does not properly distinguish defamation from convicium.

[13] *Jardine* v. *Creech* (1776) Mor. 3438; *Beattie* v. *Mather* (1860) 22 D. 952; *Caldwell* v. *Munro* (1872) 10 M. 717; *Godfrey* v. *Thomsons* (1890) 17 R. 1108; *Waugh* v. *Ayrshire Post* (1894) 21 R. 326; *A.* v. *B. & Co.* (1898) 25 R. 951; *Sadgrove* v. *Hole* [1901] 2 K.B. 1; *Hulton* v. *Jones* [1910] A.C. 20; *Webster* v. *Paterson*, 1910 S.C. 459; *Browne* v. *Thomson*, 1912 S.C. 359, 362.

[14] *Outram* v. *Reid* (1852) 14 D. 577; *Wragg* v. *Thomson*, 1909 2 S.L.T. 409; cf. *Hulton*, *supra*; *Harkness* v. *Daily Record*, 1924 S.L.T. 759; *Cassidy* v. *Daily Mirror* [1929] 2 K.B. 331; *Harper* v. *Provincial Newspapers*, 1937 S.L.T. 462; *Newstead* v. *London Express* [1940] 1 K.B. 377.

Act, 1952, S. 4(5), protects the innocent publisher of defamatory matter if he did not intend to publish it of and concerning the pursuer, did not know of circumstances by virtue of which they might be understood as defamatory of the pursuer, and exercised all reasonable care in relation to the publication. Where a statement is made of a class or group it is actionable by the members individually only if the aspersion applies to each one so as to affect his reputation.[1] If it is made of a large and indeterminate group, such as lawyers or Scotsmen, neither the group nor any member can sue.[2] But if an imputation on a group can be shown truly to point only to particular individuals they may have an action.[3] An incorporated body may sue for aspersions on its corporate business reputation,[4] but not for aspersions on its officers or members, nor can they sue for imputations against the company.[5] Imputations against an unincorporated body are actionable by a partner, particularly when himself named.[6] A trade union may sue for imputations against it.[7]

Defamation by implication

A statement directly defamatory of one may by implication convey an aspersion on another; such is actionable if it be averred what aspersion was conveyed by implication, and the connection between persons directly and impliedly defamed is close and not too remote.[8]

Defamation of a deceased person

In general an executor has no title to sue unless he can establish patrimonial loss,[9] nor have surviving relatives any title, unless the defamation affects their reputations also.[10]

[1] *Macphail* v. *Macleod* (1895) 3 S.L.T. 91; *Wardlaw* v. *Drysdale* (1898) 25 R. 879; *A.* v. *B. & Co.* (1898) 25 R. 951; *Webster* v. *Paterson*, 1910 S.C. 459; *Briggs* v. *Amalgamated Press*, 1910 2 S.L.T. 334; *Browne* v. *Thomson*, 1912 S.C. 359; *Couper* v. *Balfour*, 1914 S.C. 139.

[2] *McFadyen* v. *Spencer* (1892) 19 R. 350; *Wardlaw* v. *Drysdale* (1898) 25 R. 879; *Campbell* v. *Ritchie*, 1907 S.C. 1097; *Campbell* v. *Wilson*, 1934 S.L.T. 249; cf. *Knupffer* v. *London Express* [1944] A.C. 116.

[3] *Le Fanu* v. *Malcolmson* (1848) 1 H.L.C. 637.

[4] *Socy. of Solicitors* v. *Robertson* (1781) Mor. 13935; *Dumfries Fleshers* v. *Rankine*, 10 Dec. 1816, F.C.; *N. of S. Bank* v. *Duncan* (1857) 19 D. 881; *British Legal Life Assce. Co.* v. *Pearl Life Assce. Co.* (1887) 14 R. 818; *D. & L. Caterers* v. *D'Ajou* [1945] K.B. 364.

[5] *Campbell* v. *Wilson*, 1934 S.L.T. 249.

[6] *Hustler* v. *Watson* (1841) 3 D. 366; *Williams* v. *Allan* (1841) 3 D. 600.

[7] *N.U.G.M.W.* v. *Gillian* [1946] K.B. 81; *Willis* v. *Brooks* [1947] 1 All E.R. 191.

[8] *Finburgh* v. *Moss' Empires*, 1908 S.C. 928, 934, 941; cf. *Symmond* v. *Williamson* (1752) Mor. 3435; *N. of S. Banking Co.* v. *Duncan* (1857) 19 D. 881; *Broom* v. *Ritchie* (1904) 6 F. 942, 946; *Chisholm* v. *Grant*, 1914 S.C. 239.

[9] cf. *Smith* v. *Stewart*, 1961 S.C. 91.

[10] *Broom*, *supra*.

Defenders

The pursuer must establish that it was the defender who communicated the statement complained of. An anonymous writer may be identified *comparatione literarum* or otherwise, and evidence of motive may be adduced.[1] The person originating defamation is liable, but each person who repeats or republishes it is also liable,[2] even if he did not know it to be defamatory[3] or honestly believed it to be true.[4] Nor is it a defence that the matter was current rumour, though such a fact may go in mitigation of damages,[5] especially if the repeater discloses the source.[6] The person originating is not liable for an unauthorized publication or repetition by persons to whom it was communicated.[7] Persons who transmit slanderous matter are not liable for repetition unless they could, by taking reasonable care, have become aware of it and refrained from circulating it;[8] nor are clerks or typists[9] or solicitors acting on instructions.[10]

Communication

The idea communicated must be one of fact, not of belief or opinion;[11] it may be communicated in any way in which meaning can be conveyed, not only by words spoken or written,[12] but by photographs,[13] effigies,[14] cartoons,[15] conduct,[16] or in any other way.

[1] *Melville* v. *Crichton* (1820) 2 Mur. 277; *Home* v. *Sandie* (1832) 10 S. 508; *Menzies* v. *Goodlet* (1835) 13 S. 1136; *MacTaggart* v. *MacKillop*, 1938 S.C. 847; *Swan* v. *Bowie*, 1948 S.C. 46.

[2] *Gibson* v. *Cheap* (1823) 1 Sh. App. 459; *Marshall* v. *Renwick* (1834) 13 S. 1127; *Browne* v. *Macfarlane* (1889) 16 R. 368; *Cunningham* v. *Duncan* (1889) 16 R. 383; *Winn* v. *Quillan* (1899) 2 F. 322; *A.B.* v. *Blackwood* (1902) 5 F. 25; *Macdonald* v. *Martin*, 1935 S.C. 621, 641. See also *Jack* v. *Fleming* (1891) 19 R. 1.

[3] *Morrison* v. *Ritchie* (1902) 4 F. 645; cf. *Drew* v. *Mackenzie* (1862) 24 D. 649; *Neilson* v. *Johnston* (1890) 17 R. 442.

[4] *Tidman* v. *Ainslie* (1854) 10 Ex. 63.

[5] *MacCulloch* v. *Litt* (1851) 13 D. 960; *Paul* v. *Jackson* (1884) 11 R. 460.

[6] *Browne* v. *MacFarlane* (1889) 16 R. 368; *Cunningham* v. *Duncan* (1889) 16 R. 383, 390; *Morrison, supra.*

[7] *Weld-Blundell* v. *Stephens* [1920] A.C. 956; cf. *Williamson* v. *Umphray & Robertson* (1890) 17 R. 905.

[8] *Vizetelly* v. *Mudie* [1900] 2 Q.B. 170.

[9] *Evans* v. *Stein* (1904) 7 F. 65.

[10] *Crawford* v. *Adams* (1900) 2 F. 987; cf. *Wilson* v. *Purvis* (1891) 18 R. 72. See also *Watsons* v. *Smeaton* (1805) Hume 624; *Yeo* v. *Wallace* (1868) 5 S.L.R. 253.

[11] *Archer* v. *Ritchie* (1891) 18 R. 719; *Meikle* v. *Wright* (1893) 20 R. 928; *Bruce* v. *Ross* (1901) 4 F. 171; cf. *Neilson* v. *Johnston* (1890) 17 R. 442; *Langlands* v. *Leng*, 1916 S.C. (H.L.) 102.

[12] Broadcasting is equivalent to written defamation: Defamation Act, 1952, S. 1.

[13] *Garbett* v. *Hazell, Watson & Viney* [1943] 2 All E.R. 359.

[14] *Monson* v. *Tussauds* [1894] 1 Q.B. 671.

[15] *Tolley* v. *Fry* [1931] A.C. 333.

[16] *Robertson* v. *Keith*, 1936 S.C. 29.

An expression of opinion as to fact truly stated is not actionable.[1] The words complained of, or all material parts of them or words substantially to the same effect, must be proved to have been used; the defender may escape if he proves that some addition or qualification was added which materially changes their meaning.

Publication to, or of and concerning, the pursuer

The idea complained of may have been communicated only to the pursuer himself, and need not have been published more widely. If it affronts him, he has an action of the nature of an *actio injuriarum* for solatium for affront.[2] Alternatively it may have been communicated to others; if published to others he may also claim for damage to his public reputation and for resultant pecuniary loss.[3] The pursuer must prove that the communication complained of related to him.[4] If he is not clearly identified he must show that the defamatory statement was understood to refer to him.[5] The communication need not have been deliberate, but may have been inadvertent.[6]

Malice

It is necessary to aver that the statement complained of was communicated maliciously or calumniously, but malice sufficient to found the action is imputed to the defender from proof of his communication of defamatory matter. The requisite malice or *animus injuriandi* is inferred from the deliberate communication to the pursuer, or from the communication deliberately, or without taking reasonable care, to other persons of and concerning the pursuer, of a false and defamatory imputation. Further proof of malice is unnecessary. No proof of actual or express malice (i.e. malevolence or spite) is necessary, nor is its absence a defence.[7] Hence it is no defence that the defamation was un-

[1] *Archer, supra.*

[2] *Hutchison* v. *Naismith* (1808) Mor. Appx. Delinquency, 4; *McCandies* v. *McCandie* (1827) 4 Mur. 198; *Bryson* v. *Inglis* (1844) 6 D. 363; *Kennedy* v. *Baillie* (1855) 18 D. 138; *Mackay* v. *McCankie* (1883) 10 R. 537; *Stuart* v. *Moss* (1888) 13 R. 299; cf. *Will* v. *Sneddon, Campbell & Munro*, 1931 S.C. 164.

[3] e.g. *Gordon* v. *Leng*, 1915 S.C. 415.

[4] *Beattie* v. *Mather* (1860) 22 D. 952; *Caldwell* v. *Munro* (1872) 10 M. 717; *A.* v. *B. & Co.* (1898) 25 R. 951.

[5] *Smith* v. *Gentle* (1844) 6 D. 565; *Godfrey* v. *Thomsons* (1890) 17 R. 1108; *Waugh* v. *Ayrshire Post* (1894) 21 R. 326; *Webster* v. *Paterson*, 1910 S.C. 459.

[6] *Outram* v. *Reid* (1852) 14 D. 577; *Gordon* v. *Stubbs* (1895) 3 S.L.T. 10.

[7] Hume, *Lect.*, III, 141, 146, 152; *Tytler* v. *Macintosh* (1823) 2 Mur. 241; *Mackellar* v. *Duke of Sutherland* (1862) 24 D. 1124; *Shaw* v. *Morgan* (1888) 15 R. 865, 870; *Morrison* v. *Ritchie* (1902) 4 F. 645, 650; *Langlands* v. *Leng*, 1916 S.C. (H.L.) 102, 109.

intentional,[1] or that the words were not intended in a defamatory sense,[2] or not intended to harm the pursuer's reputation.[3] Allegations of malice in the past are irrelevant.[4]

In the case of hurt to the pursuer's self-esteem, the claim is an *actio injuriarum* and the requisite malice demands intentional or deliberate communication; in the case of hurt to the pursuer's reputation, the claim is an *actio legis Aquiliae* and the requisite malice may be imputed by deliberate communication, or by communication without having taken reasonable precautions.[5]

Falsity of the idea

The idea communicated must be averred to be in fact false and untrue,[6] but it need not be proved untrue. Falsity is presumed in the pursuer's favour if the words are defamatory in their nature, and the onus is on the defender to prove the truth of his aspersions.[7]

Defamatory quality

The idea must also be of defamatory quality, i.e. such as conveys an imputation on the moral character of the pursuer,[8] or is injurious to his character or credit,[9] or is discreditable to him.[10] Whether words are defamatory is a question of law[11] which has to be determined by an objective standard, the opinion of the fair-minded hearer or reader.[12] Words of censure or sarcasm or abuse are not necessarily defamatory,[13] nor are slang terms of abuse.[14]

[1] *Morrison* v. *Ritchie* (1902) 4 F. 645; *Hulton* v. *Jones* [1910] A.C. 20.

[2] *Nevill* v. *Fine Art Co.* [1895] 2 Q.B. 156.

[3] *Hulton, supra.*

[4] *Stein* v. *Beaverbrook Newspapers, Ltd.*, 1968 S.L.T. 401.

[5] Hume, *Lect.* III, 149; *McLean* v. *Bernstein* (1900) 8 S.L.T. 42; *Morrison* v. *Ritchie* 4 F. 645; *Wood* v. *Edinburgh Evening News*, 1910 S.C. 895.

[6] *Campbell* v. *Ferguson* (1882) 9 R. 467; *Meikle* v. *Wright* (1893) 20 R. 928.

[7] *Scott* v. *McGavin* (1821) 2 Mur. 484; *Mackellar* v. *Duke of Sutherland* (1859) 21 D. 222; *Hunter* v. *Ferguson* (1906) 8 F. 574; cf. *Carson* v. *White*, 1919 2 S.L.T. 215.

[8] *Brownlie* v. *Thomson* (1859) 21 D. 480, 485; *Archer* v. *Ritchie* (1891) 18 R. 719, 727.

[9] *Paterson* v. *Welch* (1893) 20 R. 744, 749; *Waddell* v. *Roxburgh* (1894) 21 R. 883, 886.

[10] *Scott* v. *Sampson* (1883) 8 Q.B.D. 491; *Sim* v. *Stretch* (1936) 52 T.L.R. 669.

[11] *Russell* v. *Stubbs*, 1913 S.C. (H.L.) 14; *Adam* v. *Ward* [1917] A.C. 309.

[12] *Hunter* v. *Ferguson* (1906) 8 F. 574; *Boal* v. *Scottish Catholic Ptg. Co.*, 1907 S.C. 1120; *Leon* v. *Edinburgh Evening News*, 1909 S.C. 1014; *Tolley* v. *Fry* [1930] 1 K.B. 467, 479; *Byrne* v. *Deane* [1937] 1 K.B. 818.

[13] *Watson* v. *Duncan* (1890) 17 R. 404; *Bell* v. *Haldane* (1894) 2 S.L.T. 320; *Christie* v. *Robertson* (1899) 1 F. 1155; *Campbell* v. *Ritchie*, 1907 S.C. 1097; *Rooney* v. *McNairney*, 1909 S.C. 90.

[14] *Mackintosh* v. *Squair* (1868) 5 S.L.R. 635; *Grierson* v. *Harvey* (1871) 43 Sc. Jur. 190; *Jameson* v. *Bonthrone* (1873) 11 M. 703; *Cockburn* v. *Reekie* (1890) 17 R. 568; *Watson* v. *Duncan* (1890) 17 R. 404; *Macdonald* v. *Rupprecht* (1894) 21 R. 389; *Christie* v. *Robertson* (1899) 1 F. 1155; *Mackay* v. *Grant* (1903) 11 S.L.T. 380; *Agnew* v. *British Legal Life Assce. Co.* (1906) 8 F. 422.

Defamatory words

Words must be given their normal and natural meaning, not stretched to make them innocent,[1] and be read as a whole,[2] and in their context.[3]

Innuendo

Words may be *ex facie* defamatory, or *ex facie* innocent or ambiguous but conveying a defamatory meaning only if further facts are established which cast light on the words and indicate that they convey a defamatory imputation. In the latter case the words are actionable only if the pursuer avers an innuendo, explaining what defamatory meaning is the true meaning of the words, in the circumstances in which they were used,[4] and proves that some persons understood the words in that defamatory sense.[5] An innuendo must be supported by averment and proof of circumstances which support the secondary meaning.[6] An innuendo is necessary where the words complained of are in a dialect or a foreign language,[7] are slang, or in any case where the defamatory meaning is not the plain and clear natural meaning of the words. A proper innuendo makes clear the slanderous point of an apparently non-defamatory statement.[8]

Defamatory imputations

It is defamatory falsely to impute guilt of a crime or offence[9] or

1 *Capital and Counties Bank* v. *Henty* (1882) 7 App. Cas. 742; *Hunter* v. *Ferguson* (1906) 8 F. 574; *Duncan* v. *Scottish Newspapers*, 1929 S.C. 14.

2 *Smyth* v. *Mackinnon* (1897) 24 R. 1086; *Wardlaw* v. *Drysdale* (1898) 25 R. 879; *Campbell* v. *Ritchie*, 1907 S.C. 1097; *Grand Theatre (Glasgow)* v. *Outram*, 1908 S.C. 1018; *Leon* v. *Edinburgh Evening News*, 1909 S.C. 1014.

3 *McNeill* v. *Forbes* (1883) 10 R. 867; *Christie* v. *Robertson* (1899) 1 F. 1155; *Morrison* v. *Ritchie* (1902) 4 F. 645.

4 *Broomfield* v. *Greig* (1868) 6 M. 563; *Brydone* v. *Brechin* (1881) 8 R. 697; *Gudgeon* v. *Outram* (1888) 16 R. 183; *Sexton* v. *Ritchie* (1890) 17 R. 680; *Murdison* v. *Sc. Football Union* (1896) 23 R. 449; *Smyth* v. *McKinnon* (1897) 24 R. 1086; *Stewart* v. *Hannah* (1905) 8 F. 107; *Smith* v. *Walker*, 1912 S.C. 224; *Russell* v. *Stubbs*, 1913 S.C. (H.L.) 14; *Cumming* v. *G.N.S. Ry.*, 1916 1 S.L.T. 181; *Duncan* v. *Assoc. Newspapers*, 1929 S.C. 14; *Stein* v. *Beaverbrook Newspapers, Ltd.*, 1968 S.L.T. 401.

5 *McCandies* v. *McCandie* (1827) 4 Mur. 198; *James* v. *Baird*, 1916 S.C. (H.L.) 158.

6 *Caldwell* v. *Munro* (1872) 10 M. 717; *Smith* v. *Walker*, 1912 S.C. 224; *Lloyd* v. *Hickley*, 1967 S.L.T. 225.

7 *Matheson* v. *Mackinnon* (1832) 10 S. 825; *Martin* v. *McLean* (1844) 6 D. 981; *McLaren* v. *Robertson* (1859) 21 D. 183; *Anderson* v. *Hunter* (1891) 18 R. 467; *Bernhardt* v. *Abrahams*, 1912 S.C. 748.

8 *Neilson* v. *Johnston* (1890) 17 R. 442; *Turnbull* v. *Oliver* (1891) 19 R. 154; *Gardner* v. *Robertson*, 1921 S.C. 132.

9 Hume, *Lect.* III, 134; *Paul* v. *Jackson* (1884) 11 R. 460; *Harkness* v. *Daily Record*, 1924 S.L.T. 759 (murder); *Gudgeon* v. *Outram* (1888) 16 R. 183; *Godfrey* v. *Thomson* 1890) 17 R. 1108; *Buchan* v. *N.B. Ry.* (1894) 21 R. 379; *Oliver* v. *Laidlaw* (1895) 3)

criminality generally,[1] or criminal intention,[2] or preparation or attempt to commit crime,[3] or suspicion of crime.[4]

It is also defamatory to impute dishonesty or dishonourable conduct in business;[5] to impute to a person of either sex[6] unchastity or sexual immorality;[7] to impute improper, discreditable or disgraceful conduct, such as immodesty or cowardice;[8] to impute insolvency or financial unsoundness,[9] which is readily inferred from the unjustified publication of a name in a list of persons against whom decrees in absence have passed,[10] or from a bank's refusal to honour a cheque.[11]

S.L.T. 142; *Smyth* v. *Mackinnon* (1897) 24 R. 1086; *Ellis* v. *National Free Labour Assoc.* (1905) 7 F. 629; *Green* v. *Reid* (1905) 7 F. 891; *Stewart* v. *Hannah* (1905) 8 F. 107; *Agnew* v. *British Legal Life Assce. Co.* (1906) 8 F. 422; *Costa* v. *Lumley* (1907) 15 S.L.T. 230; *Boal* v. *Scottish Catholic Printing Co.*, 1907 S.C. 1120; *Webster* v. *Paterson*, 1910 S.C. 549; *Quigley* v. *Brown*, 1913 1 S.L.T. 61; *Cumming* v. *G.N.S. Ry.*, 1916 1 S.L.T. 181; *Jardine* v. *N.B. Ry.*, 1923 S.L.T. 55 (fraud); *Wilson* v. *Purvis* (1890) 18 R. 72; *Reid* v. *Moore* (1893) 20 R. 712; *Kennedy* v. *Henderson* (1903) 11 S.L.T. 156; *Campbell* v. *Ritchie*, 1907 S.C. 1097; *McAdam* v. *City & Suburban Dairies*, 1911 S.C. 430; *Adams* v. *Templeton*, 1913 2 S.L.T. 241; *Neville* v. *C. & A. Modes*, 1945 S.C. 175 (theft); *Mason* v. *Tait* (1851) 13 D. 1347; *Faulks* v. *Park* (1855) 17 D. 247; *Broomfield* v. *Greig* (1868) 6 M. 563; *Logan* v. *Weir* (1872) 10 S.L.R. 22; *Mackay* v. *McCankie* (1883) 10 R. 537; *Campbell* v. *McLachlan* (1896) 4 S.L.T. 143; *A.B.* v. *C.D.* (1904) 7 F. 72; 13 S.L.T. 159; *Rae* v. *S.S.P.C.C.*, 1924 S.C. 102 (other offences).

[1] *Cockburn* v. *Reekie* (1890) 17 R. 568; *Campbell* v. *McLachlan* (1896) 4 S.L.T. 143; *Christie* v. *Robertson* (1899) 1 F. 1155.

[2] *Ogilvie* v. *Scott* (1835) 14 S. 729; cf. *Waugh* v. *Ayrshire Post* (1893) 21 R. 326.

[3] *Oliver* v. *Laidlaw* (1895) 3 S.L.T. 142.

[4] *Lawrie* v. *Campbell* (1800) Hume 606; *Stewart* v. *Hannah* (1905) 8 F. 107; *Boal* v. *Scottish Catholic Ptg. Co.*, 1907 S.C. 1120.

[5] *Johnston* v. *Dilke* (1875) 2 R. 836; *Stuart* v. *Moss* (1885) 13 R. 299; *Macrae* v. *Sutherland* (1889) 16 R. 476; *Cockburn* v. *Reekie* (1890) 17 R. 568; *Turnbull* v. *Oliver* (1891) 19 R. 154; *Webster* v. *Paterson*, 1910 S.C. 459; *Langlands* v. *Leng*, 1916 S.C. (H.L.) 102; *Griffen* v. *Divers*, 1922 S.C. 605.

[6] *Milne* v. *Smiths* (1893) 20 R. 95.

[7] *Rankin* v. *Simpson* (1859) 21 D. 1057; *Brydon* v. *Brechin* (1881) 8 R. 697; *Morrison* v. *Ritchie* (1902) 4 F. 645; *Finburgh* v. *Moss' Empires*, 1908 S.C. 928; *Gilmour* v. *Hansen*, 1920 S.C. 598; *C.* v. *M.*, 1938 S.L.T. 369.

[8] *Mackay* v. *Campbell* (1833) 11 S. 1031; *Graham* v. *Roy* (1851) 13 D. 634; *McLaren* v. *Robertson* (1859) 21 D. 183; *Milne* v. *Walker* (1893) 21 R. 155; *Neill* v. *Henderson* (1901) 3 F. 387; *A.B.* v. *Blackwood* (1902) 5 F. 65; *Gordon* v. *Leng*, 1919 S.C. 415; *Griffen* v. *Divers*, 1922 S.C. 605; *Cuthbert* v. *Linklater*, 1935 S.L.T. 95.

[9] Ersk. IV, 4, 81; Hume, *Lect.* III, 134; *Outram* v. *Reid* (1852) 14 D. 577; *N. of S. Bank* v. *Duncan* (1857) 19 D. 881; *Wright & Greig* v. *Outram* (1889) 16 R. 1004; *A.B.* v. *C.D.* (1904) 7 F. 22; *Russell* v. *Stubbs*, 1913 S.C. (H.L.) 14.

[10] *Andrews* v. *Drummond & Graham* (1887) 14 R. 568; *Taylor* v. *Rutherford* (1888) 15 R. 608; *Rarity* v. *Stubbs* (1893) 1 S.L.T. 74; *Crabbe & Robertson* v. *Stubbs* (1895) 22 R. 860; *McLintock* v. *Stubbs* (1902) 5 F. 1; *Hunter* v. *Stubbs* (1903) 5 F. 920; *Barr* v. *Musselburgh Merchants' Assoc.*, 1912 S.C. 174; *Russell* v. *Stubbs*, 1913 S.C. (H.L.) 14; *Mazure* v. *Stubbs*, 1919 S.C. (H.L.) 112;

[11] *Capital & Counties Bank* v. *Henty* (1882) 7 App. Cas. 741; *King* v. *B.L. Co.* (1899) 1 F. 928; *Fleming* v. *Bank of N.Z.* [1900] A.C. 877; *Wilson* v. *United Counties Bank* [1920] A.C. 102; *Davidson* v. *Barclays Bank* [1940] 1 All E.R. 316; *Gibb* v. *Lombank Scotland*, 1962 S.L.T. 288.

Also defamatory are imputations against a man's character as a public figure in the community,[1] or against his official, professional or commercial honour, reputation or standing,[2] or competency as a skilled tradesman,[3] or any conduct naturally harmful to him in his trade.[4]

It is also defamatory falsely to impute that a person suffers from a contagious or infectious disease,[5] or is of unsound mind[6] or weak in mind.[7]

Loss, injury and damage

Every defamatory communication, even to the pursuer alone, justifies at least an award of solatium for hurt feelings.[8] If it is published more widely and causes damage to reputation, a further award for resultant loss and damage is due.[9] Damages may be aggravated by the circumstances in which the statement was communicated[10] or by repetition.[11] Evidence of the pursuer's good character is incompetent in aggravation of damages. In mitigation of damages there may be proved absence of actual malice,[12] that

[1] Hume, *Lect.* III, 136; *Auld* v. *Shairp* (1875) 2 R. 940; *Coghill* v. *Docherty* (1881) 19 S.L.R. 96; *Macfarlane* v. *Black* (1887) 14 R. 870; *Neilson* v. *Johnston* (1890) 17 R. 442; *Godfrey* v. *Thomson* (1890) 17 R. 1108; *Archer* v. *Ritchie* (1891) 18 R. 719; *Bruce* v. *Leisk* (1892) 19 R. 482; *Falconer* v. *Docherty* (1893) 20 R. 765; *Mitchell* v. *Grierson* (1894) 21 R. 367; *Crawford* v. *Adams* (1900) 2 F. 987; *Hunter* v. *Ferguson* (1906) 8 F. 574; *Browne* v. *Thomson*, 1912 S.C. 359; *Lyal* v. *Henderson*, 1916 S.C. (H.L.) 167; *Gardner* v. *Robertson*, 1921 S.C. 132; *Westwood* v. *Leng*, 1923 S.L.T. 725; *Campbell* v. *Weir*, 1924 S.L.T. 14; *Duncan* v. *Assoc. Scottish Newspapers*, 1929 S.C. 14; *Macdonald* v. *Martin*, 1935 S.C. 621.

[2] Hume, *Lect.* III, 136; *MacRostie* v. *Ironside* (1849) 12 D. 74; *Balfour* v. *Wallace* (1853) 15 D. 913; *Bayne* v. *Macgregor* (1862) 24 D. 1126; *Sharp* v. *Wilson* (1868) 5 S.L.T. 444; *Johnston* v. *Dilke* (1875) 2 R. 836; *Dun* v. *Bain* (1877) 4 R. 317; *McKercher* v. *Cameron* (1892) 19 R. 383; *Oliver* v. *Barnet* (1895) 3 S.L.T. 163; *A.* v. *B.* (1899) 36 S.L.R. 533; *McKeand* v. *Maxwell* (1896) 3 S.L.T. 321; *Simmers* v. *Morton* (1900) 8 S.L.T. 285; *Barclay* v. *Manuel* (1902) 10 S.L.T. 450; *Wright* v. *Steel*, 1909 2 S.L.T. 265; *Tait* v. *Morrison*, 1913 2 S.L.T. 325; *Chisholm* v. *Grant*, 1914 S.C. 239; *Slack* v. *Barr*, 1918 1 S.L.T. 133; *Gordon* v. *Leng*, 1919 S.C. 415.

[3] *Munro* v. *Mudie* (1901) 9 S.L.T. 91; *Vallance* v. *Ford* (1903) 10 S.L.T. 555; *McDonald* v. *McLachlan*, 1907 S.C. 203; *Pybus* v. *Mackinnon* (1908) 15 S.L.T. 1066; *Bryant* v. *Edgar*, 1909 S.C. 1080; *Slack* v. *Barr*, 1918 1 S.L.T. 133.

[4] *Broomfield* v. *Greig* (1868) 6 M. 563; *Macrae* v. *Wicks* (1886) 13 R. 732; *Meikle* v. *Wright* (1893) 20 R. 928; *Menzies* v. *Macdonald* (1899) 1 F. 977; *Lumsden* v. *West Lothian Pub. Co.* (1905) 7 F. 1006; *Adams* v. *Scottish Agricultural Co.*, 1926 S.L.T. 255; *Hamilton* v. *Glasgow Dairy Co.*, 1931 S.C. (H.L.) 67.

[5] *Cunningham* v. *Phillips* (1868) 6 M. 926; *A.* v. *B.*, 1907 S.C. 1154.

[6] *Mackintosh* v. *Weir* (1875) 2 R. 877.

[7] *Henderson* v. *H.*, (1855) 17 D. 348.

[8] *Fletcher* v. *Wilsons* (1885) 12 R. 683; *Cassidy* v. *Connochie*, 1907 S.C. 1112.

[9] *Ritchie* v. *Barton* (1883) 10 R. 813; *Boal* v. *Sc. Catholic Ptg. Co.*, 1908 S.C. 667.

[10] *Cunningham* v. *Duncan* (1889) 16 R. 383, 387; *Morrison* v. *Ritchie* (1902) 4 F. 645.

[11] *Morrison*, *supra*.

[12] *Lowe* v. *Taylor* (1844) 7 D. 117; *White* v. *Clough* (1847) 10 D. 332; *Paul* v. *Jackson* (1884) 11 R. 460; *Cunningham* v. *Duncan* (1889) 16 R. 383.

the defender merely repeated a general report,[1] published it in ignorance of its being inaccurate or defamatory,[2] or published an apology,[3] or that the pursuer was of generally bad character or bad reputation,[4] but not of bad character in respects not in issue,[5] or that he provoked the defamation.[6]

Functions of judge and jury

The court must determine on the pleadings whether the words or actions complained of are capable of bearing a meaning defamatory of the pursuer.[7] If they are not so capable the action falls to be dismissed;[8] if they are so capable, it is for the jury to say whether the words were used, did refer to the pursuer, and were understood in the alleged defamatory sense when they were used.[9] If an innuendo is averred the court must decide whether the words complained of are reasonably susceptible of bearing the innuendo put on them,[10] or whether the meaning sought to be attributed to the words used is a reasonable, natural or necessary interpretation of them.[11] The jury must then say whether the words were used and understood as bearing the defamatory meaning alleged.[12]

DEFENCES TO DEFAMATION CLAIM

It is a defence that the statement was not made by the defender, or that any statement made differed materially from that complained of, or that it was not capable of referring to, nor was it understood as applicable to the pursuer, or that the words were not defamatory. The defender has a defence under the Defamation Act, 1952, Ss. 4 and 14(c), if he published the defamatory statement innocently and tenders amends under that section.

1 *Macculloch* v. *Litt* (1851) 13 D. 960; *Paul, supra.*

2 *Browne* v. *MacFarlane* (1889) 16 R. 368; *Morrison* v. *Ritchie* (1902) 4 F. 645.

3 *Morrison, supra*, 652.

4 *C.* v. *M.*, 1923 S.C. 1; *Plato Films* v. *Speidel* [1961] A.C. 1090.

5 *C.* v. *M., supra.*

6 *Bryson* v. *Inglis* (1844) 6 D. 363; *Paul, supra*; cf. *Tullis* v. *Crichton* (1850) 12 D. 867; *Bertram* v. *Pace* (1885) 12 R. 798.

7 *Capital and Counties Bank* v. *Henty* (1882) 7 App. Cas. 741, 744; *Leon* v. *Edinburgh Evening News*, 1909 S.C. 1014, 1020; *Adam* v. *Ward* [1917] A.C. 309, 329.

8 *Nevill* v. *Fine Art Co.* [1897] A.C. 68; *Russell* v. *Stubbs*, 1913 S.C. (H.L.) 14.

9 *Capital and Counties Bank, supra*; *Russell, supra*; *Adam, supra.*

10 *Fraser* v. *Morris* (1888) 15 R. 454; *Wood* v. *Edinburgh Evening News*, 1910 S.C. 895; *Smith* v. *Walker*, 1912 S.C. 224; *Langlands* v. *Leng*, 1916 S.C. (H.L.) 102, 109; *Duncan* v. *Assoc. Newspapers*, 1929 S.C. 14, 19.

11 *Capital and Counties, supra*; *Russell* v. *Stubbs, Ltd.*, 1913 S.C. (H.L.) 14, 23; *Gollan* v. *Thompson Wyles Co.*, 1930 S.C. 599.

12 *Russell, supra.*

A pursuer cannot complain of words published with his authority or consent,[1] nor of words uttered in the heat of a quarrel (*in rixa*) as an angry retort or abuse,[2] particularly if the words are words commonly used in anger or as abuse, and particularly if an apology be later offered,[3] unless they should appear to have been seriously intended[4] or were subsequently repeated.[5]

Veritas

It is a complete defence, the onus of proof being on the defender,[6] to prove that a statement complained of is true.[7] The defender must specifically aver facts which, if proved on balance of probabilities,[8] will establish the truth of the imputation and justify the statement,[9] and table a counter-issue raising the defence.[10] If the imputation is general, specific instances which justify it must be proved,[11] one or two instances being normally insufficient.[12] *Veritas* may be averred as to only a part of the imputation, if severable[13] but partial proof is useless. It may also be tabled to deny the innuendo.[14] To establish the defence the defender must justify exactly the imputation conveyed, not merely an imputation of the same general kind.[15] Moreover he

[1] *Cook* v. *Ward* (1830) 4 Mor. & P. 99; *Monson* v. *Tussauds* [1894] 1 Q.B. 671, 691, 697; *Chapman* v. *Ellesmere* [1932] 2 K.B. 431.

[2] *Somerville* v. *Buchanan* (1801) Hume 608; *Shand* v. *Finnie* (1802) Hume 612; *McCrae* v. *Stevenson* (1806) Hume 631; *Gibson* v. *Douglas* (1810) Hume 639; *Graham* v. *McKenzie* (1810) Hume 641; *Harper* v. *Fernie* (1810) Hume 643; *Reid* v. *Scott* (1825) 4 S. 5; *Watson* v. *Duncan* (1890) 17 R. 404; *Christie* v. *Robertson* (1899) 1 F. 1155.

[3] *Ewart* v. *Mason* (1806) Hume 633.

[4] *Christie, supra.*

[5] *Mackay* v. *Grant* (1903) 41 S.L.R. 18.

[6] *Gibsons* v. *Marr* (1823) 3 Mur. 261.

[7] *Mitchell* v. *Thomson* (1828) 7 S. 458; *Mackellar* v. *Duke of Sutherland* (1859) 21 D. 222; *Wilson* v. *Weir* (1862) 24 D. 67; *Campbell* v. *Ferguson* (1882) 9 R. 467; *Wallace* v. *Mooney* (1885) 12 R. 710; *Cook* v. *Gray* (1891) 20 S.L.R. 247; *Buchan* v. *N.B. Ry.* (1894) 21 R. 379; *Carson* v. *White*, 1919 2 S.L.T. 215; cf. *R.* v. *S.*, 1914 S.C. 193.

[8] *Andrew* v. *Penny*, 1964 S.L.T. (Notes) 24.

[9] *McNeill* v. *Rorison* (1848) 10 D. 15; *Rankin* v. *Simpson* (1859) 21 D. 1057; *McIver* v. *McNeill* (1873) 11 M. 777; *Fletcher* v. *Wilson* (1885) 12 R. 683; *Macleod* v. *Marshall* (1891) 18 R. 811; *H.* v. *P.* (1905) 8 F. 232.

[10] *McNeill, supra*; *Bertram* v. *Pace* (1885) 12 R. 798; *Blasquez* v. *Lothians* (1889) 16 R. 893; *Browne* v. *McFarlane* (1889) 16 R. 368; *Christie* v. *Crank* (1900) 2 F. 380.

[11] *McRostie* v. *Ironside* (1850) 12 D. 74; *McDonald* v. *Begg* (1862) 24 D. 685; *Hunter* v. *MacNaughton* (1894) 21 R. 850; *Hamilton* v. *Wright* (1895) 3 S.L.T. 10; *Goodall* v. *Forbes*, 1909 S.C. 1300.

[12] *Milne* v. *Walker* (1894) 21 R. 155; *Powell* v. *Long* (1896) 23 R. 534; *Burnet* v. *Gow* (1896) 24 R. 156; cf. *Brownlie* v. *Thomson* (1851) 21 D. 480; *Fletcher, supra.*

[13] *McNeill, supra*; *Mackellar, supra*; *British Workman* v. *Stewart* (1897) 24 R. 624; *O'Callaghan* v. *Thomson*, 1928 S.C. 532.

[14] *Henderson* v. *Russell* (1895) 23 R. 25.

[15] *McKennal* v. *Wilson* (1806) Hume 608; *Burnet* v. *Gow* (1896) 24 R. 156; *Maisel* v. *Financial Times* [1915] 3 K.B. 336; *Sutherland* v. *Stopes* [1925] A.C. 47.

must prove not merely honest and reasonable belief in the truth of the statement, nor suspicion, nor reputation, but its actual truth.[1] At common law the defender had to prove the truth of all material statements, justifying everything in the allegedly defamatory communication, meeting the whole substance of the complaint.[2] By statute,[3] where there are two or more distinct charges, a defence of *veritas* is not to fail if the truth of every charge is not proved, if the words not proved do not materially injure the pursuer's reputation having regard to the truth of the remaining charges.

Absolute privilege

Communications made in certain circumstances are for reasons of public policy absolutely privileged and not actionable, even though defamatory. It is a question of law whether the circumstances confer absolute privilege; if they do the defender is immune from liability whatever his state of mind. The sets of circumstances covered are not necessarily settled, but the courts are reluctant to extend the list.[4] Absolute privilege protects statements made in either House of Parliament[5] and reports thereof in Hansard and fair and accurate reports in the press,[6] but not private reports or reprints of speeches,[6] nor repetition outside the House; statements in petitions to Parliament[7] and to statements by a witness before a select committee;[8] reports and proceedings published by or under authority of either House;[9] official communications between officers of state,[10] or officers of the forces;[11] and notifications in the *Gazette* of acts of state.[12] Absolute privilege protects all statements made in judicial

[1] *Brodie* v. *Blair* (1833) 12 S. 941; *Marshall* v. *Renwicks* (1834) 13 S. 1127; *Peters* v. *Bradlaugh* (1884) 4 T.L.R. 467; *Cookson* v. *Harewood* [1932] 2 K.B. 478.

[2] *Burnaby* v. *Robertson* (1848) 10 D. 855; *Torrance* v. *Weddel* (1868) 7 M. 243; *Bertram* v. *Pace* (1885) 12 R. 798; *Blasquez* v. *Lothians* (1889) 16 R. 893; *Macleod* v. *Marshall* (1891) 18 R. 811; *Milne* v. *Walker* (1893) 21 R. 155; *Christie* v. *Craik* (1900) 2 F. 380; *Andrew* v. *Macara*, 1917 S.C. 247.

[3] Defamation Act, 1952, S. 5.

[4] *Royal Aquarium Socy.* v. *Parkinson* [1892] 1 Q.B. 431, 451.

[5] *Ex p. Wason* (1869) L.R. 4 Q.B. 573; *Dillon* v. *Balfour* (1887) 20 L.R. Ir. 600; *Chenard* v. *Arissol* [1949] A.C. 127.

[6] *Wason* v. *Walter* (1868) L.R. 4 Q.B. 95.

[7] *Kane* v. *Mulvaney* (1866) Ir. R. 2 C.L. 402.

[8] *Goffin* v. *Donnelly* (1881) 50 L.J.Q.B. 303.

[9] Parliamentary Papers Act, 1840, S. 1; *Stockdale* v. *Hansard* (1840) 11 A. & E. 297.

[10] *Chatterton* v. *Secy. of State for India* [1895] 2 Q.B. 189; *Isaacs* v. *Cook* [1925] 2 K.B. 391.

[11] *Dawkins* v. *Paulet* (1869) L.R. 5 Q.B. 94; cf. *Dickson* v. *Wilton* (1859) 1 F. & F. 419; *Dickson* v. *Combermere* (1863) 3 F. & F. 527.

[12] *Grant* v. *Secy. of State for India* (1877) 2 C.P.D. 445.

proceedings, whatever the rank of the court or the position of the person sued,[1] so long as it was not a gratuitous observation. It probably protects also the Lord Advocate as chief public prosecutor, and advocates-depute and procurators-fiscal.[2] Absolute privilege similarly protects persons exercising judicial functions of special jurisdiction, and quasi-judicial functions,[3] but not persons exercising domestic jurisdiction[4] or administrative functions.[5] It may protect church courts.[6] It attaches also to documents used in judicial and quasi-judicial proceedings,[7] though not if published improperly,[8] precognitions,[9] written declarations,[10] the judgment of the court,[11] decrees and extracts,[12] and any document reasonably incidental to the proceedings.[13] Fair and accurate reports of judicial proceedings probably enjoy absolute privilege at common law,[14] as do copies of court decrees and accurate reports of criminal convictions.[15]

Qualified privilege

For reasons of public policy a person may in certain circumstances communicate what is or may be defamatory, without liability in damages unless he is shown to have been motivated by

[1] *Gibb* v. *Scott* (1740) Elchies, Pub. Officer, 9; *Gibsons* v. *Marr* (1823) 3 Mur. 271; *Haggart's Trs.* v. *L.P. Hope* (1824) 2 Sh. App. 125; *Harvey* v. *Dyce* (1876) 4 R. 265; *McMurchy* v. *Campbell* (1887) 14 R. 725, 728; *Royal Aquarium Socy.* v. *Parkinson* [1892] 1 Q.B. 431, 451; *Primrose* v. *Waterston* (1902) 4 F. 783; *Bottomley* v. *Brougham* [1908] 1 K.B. 584; *O'Connor* v. *Waldron* [1935] A.C. 76.

In Scotland a party has only qualified privilege in his pleadings: *Williamson* v. *Umphray* (1890) 17 R. 905, 910; *Gordon* v. *British and Foreign Metaline Co.* (1886) 14 R. 75; *Neill* v. *Henderson* (1901) 3 F. 387; *Slack* v. *Barr*, 1918 1 S.L.T. 133.

[2] *McMurchy, supra*; cf. *Henderson* v. *Robertson* (1853) 15 D. 292; *Craig* v. *Peebles* (1876) 3 R. 441; *Hester* v. *Macdonald*, 1961 S.C. 370.

[3] *Dawkins* v. *Rokeby* (1875) L.R. 7 H.L. 744; *Leeson* v. *G.M.C.* (1889) 43 Ch. D. 366; *Hodson* v. *Pare* [1899] 1 Q.B. 455; *Addis* v. *Crocker* [1961] 1 Q.B. 11; *Lincoln* v. *Daniels* [1961] 3 All E.R. 740.

[4] *Chapman* v. *Ellesmere* [1932] 2 K.B. 431; *Russell* v. *Norfolk* [1949] 1 All E.R. 109.

[5] *Royal Aquarium Socy., supra*; *Attwood* v. *Chapman* [1914] 3 K.B. 275; *Hearts of Oak Assce. Co.* v. *A.G.* [1932] A.C. 392.

[6] *Sturrock* v. *Greig* (1849) 11 D. 1220; *Dunbar* v. *Auchterarder Presbytery* (1849) 12 D. 284; as to dissenting churches see *Thallon* v. *Kinninmont* (1856) 18 D. 27; *Edwards* v. *Begbie* (1850) 12 D. 1134; *McMillan* v. *Free Church of Scotland* (1862) 24 D. 1282.

[7] *Rome* v. *Watson* (1898) 23 R. 733.

[8] *Macleod* v. *Ross* (1892) 20 R. 218; *Richardson* v. *Wilson* (1879) 7 R. 237.

[9] *Watson* v. *McEwan* (1905) 7 F. (H.L.) 109.

[10] *Gompas* v. *White* (1890) 6 T.L.R. 20; *Lilley* v. *Roney* (1892) 61 L.J.Q.B. 725.

[11] *Sturrock, supra*; *Addis, supra*.

[12] *Newton* v. *Fleming* (1848) 6 Bell 175.

[13] *More* v. *Weaver* [1928] 2 K.B. 520.

[14] *Drew* v. *Mackenzie* (1862) 24 D. 649; *Richardson* v. *Wilson* (1880) 7 R. 237; *Wright* v. *Outram* (1889) 16 R. 1004; *Macleod* v. *Ross* (1893) 20 R. 218.

[15] *Buchan* v. *N.B. Ry.* (1894) 21 R. 379.

express or actual malice (malevolence or ill-will) in making the communication.[1] The pursuer need never aver malice and also lack of probable cause.[2] Malice includes animosity, malevolence, and any indirect or improper motive, other than a sense of duty.[3] The defender is presumed to have acted honestly, so that there must be specific averments of facts relevant to infer malice on the defender's part.[4] If the plea of qualified privilege is upheld the defender is wholly free of liability; if the circumstances do not make the occasion privileged, or if the occasion is privileged but the communication were proved made with actual malice, the defender is fully liable. Whether privilege protects or not is determined objectively,[5] independently of whether the defender thought himself privileged, or of his good faith.[6] The sets of circumstances to which qualified privilege applies is not settled nor closed, but, failing precedent, depends on changing conditions.[7] Whether qualified privilege attaches to particular circumstances is a question of law,[8] but this may require investigation of the facts; it is also a question of law whether facts and circumstances are averred from which malice can reasonably be inferred,[9]

[1] *Langlands* v. *Leng*, 1916 S.C. (H.L.) 102; *James* v. *Baird*, 1916 S.C. (H.L.) 158; *Cochrane* v. *Young*, 1922 S.C. 696; *Dunnet* v. *Nelson*, 1926 S.C. 764, 769; *Hayford* v. *Forrester-Paton*, 1927 S.C. 740.

[2] *Webster* v. *Paterson*, 1910 S.C. 459; *Macdonald* v. *Martin*, 1935 S.C. 621; *Notman* v. *Commercial Bank*, 1938 S.C. 522.

[3] *Hamilton* v. *Hope* (1827) 4 Mur. 222, 246; *Adam* v. *Allan* (1841) 3 D. 1058, 1073; *Callendar* v. *Milligan* (1849) 11 D. 1174; *McDonald* v. *Fergusson* (1853) 15 D. 545; *Smith* v. *Green* (1854) 16 D. 549; *Cameron* v. *Hamilton* (1856) 18 D. 423; *Bayne* v. *Macgregor* (1863) 1 M. 615; *Urquhart* v. *Grigor* (1865) 3 M. 283; *Auld* v. *Shairp* (1875) 2 R. 940; *Scott* v. *Turnbull* (1884) 11 R. 1131, 1134; *Suzor* v. *Buckingham*, 1914 S.C. 299, 304, 305; *Suzor* v. *McLachlan*, 1914 S.C. 306, 312; *Hayford* v. *Forrester-Paton*, 1927 S.C. 740, 747.

[4] *Keay* v. *Wilsons* (1843) 5 D. 407; *McIntosh* v. *Flowerdew* (1851) 13 D. 726; *Mackellar* v. *Duke of Sutherland* (1854) 21 D. 222; *Scott* v. *Turnbull* (1884) 11 R. 1131; *Gordon* v. *British & Foreign Metaline Co.* (1886) 14 R. 75; *McMurchy* v. *Campbell* (1887) 14 R. 725; *Innes* v. *Adamson* (1889) 17 R. 11; *Ingram* v. *Russell* (1893) 20 R. 771; *Sheriff* v. *Denholm* (1897) 5 S.L.T. 346; *Macdonald* v. *McColl* (1901) 3 F. 1082; *Lee* v. *Ritchie* (1904) 6 F. 642; *Campbell* v. *Cochrane* (1906) 8 F. 205; *M.* v. *H.*, 1908 S.C. 1130; *Dinnie* v. *Hengler*, 1910 S.C. 4; *Suzor* v. *McLachlan*, *supra*; *Lyal* v. *Henderson*, 1916 S.C. (H.L.) 167; *A.B.* v. *X.Y.*, 1917 S.C. 15; *Mitchell* v. *Smith*, 1919 S.C. 664; *Cochrane* v. *Young*, 1922 S.C. 696; *Elder* v. *Gillespie*, 1923 S.L.T. 32; *Dunnet* v. *Nelson*, 1926 S.C. 764; *Hayford* v. *Forrester-Paton*, 1927 S.C. 740; *Rogers* v. *Orr*, 1938 S.C. 121.

[5] *Hebditch* v. *McIlwaine* [1894] 2 Q.B. 54; *James* v. *Baird*, 1916 S.C. 510, 517; *Cochrane*, *supra*.

[6] *James*, *supra*.

[7] *London Assoc. for Trade* v. *Greenlands* [1916] 2 A.C. 15; *Adam* v. *Ward* [1917] A.C. 309.

[8] *James* v. *Baird*, 1916 S.C. 510; *Hayford*, *supra*. For cases where the court has rejected privilege on the pleadings see *Reid* v. *Coyle* (1892) 19 R. 775; *Ingram* v. *Russell* (1893) 20 R. 771; *Murdison* v. *S.F. Union* (1896) 23 R. 449; *Crawford* v. *Adams* (1900) 2 F. 987; *Morrison* v. *Ritchie* (1902) 4 F. 645.

[9] *Lloyd* v. *Hickley*, 1967 S.L.T. 225.

but the presence or absence of malice, if it has been relevantly averred, is a question of fact.[1] Qualified privilege attaches to occasions, not to persons, nor to particular kinds of communications.[2]

Privileged circumstances

In general a communication enjoys qualified privilege if honestly made by a person in the discharge of a public or private duty, whether legal or moral, or in the conduct of his own affairs, in a matter where his interest is concerned.[3] The duty and interest must be actual, not merely believed.[4]

Statements in discharge of duty

Among statements held privileged as communicated in the discharge of duty, are voluntary statements,[5] information to aid the ends of justice[6] if made to a proper person, not widely or ultroneously repeated,[7] nor wholly unjustifiably or recklessly,[8] statements when taxing a suspect with misconduct[9] unless made in an improper way,[10] or in the course of inquiries,[11] or when threatening prosecution.[12] Also privileged are communications or

[1] *Hayford, supra.*

[2] *James, supra.*

[3] *Toogood* v. *Spyring* (1834) 1 C.M. & R. 181, 193; *Harrison* v. *Bush* (1855) 5 E. & B. 344; *Shaw* v. *Morgan* (1888) 15 R. 865; *Stuart* v. *Bell* [1891] 2 Q.B. 349; *Hebditch* v. *McIlwaine* [1894] 2 Q.B. 60; *Jenoure* v. *Delmège* [1891] A.C. 73; *Macintosh* v. *Dun* [1908] A.C. 390; *Barr* v. *Musselburgh Merchants*, 1912 S.C. 174; *James* v. *Baird*, 1916 S.C. 510; 1916 S.C. (H.L.) 158; *Adam* v. *Ward* [1917] A.C. 309; *A.B.* v. *X.Y.*, 1917 S.C. 15; *Hayford* v. *Forrester-Paton*, 1927 S.C. 740.

[4] *Hebditch, supra; James, supra.*

[5] *Greenlands, Ltd.* v. *Wilmshurst* [1913] 3 K.B. 507; *James, supra.*

[6] *Sheppeard* v. *Fraser* (1849) 11 D. 446; *Macpherson* v. *Cattanach* (1850) 13 D. 287; *Smith* v. *Green* (1853) 15 D. 549; *Ferguson* v. *Colquhoun* (1862) 24 D. 1428; *Rankine* v. *Roberts* (1875) 1 R. 225; *Thomson* v. *Adam* (1875) 4 R. 29; *Green* v. *Chalmers* (1878) 6 R. 318; *Lightbody* v. *Gordon* (1882) 9 R. 934; *Hassan* v. *Paterson* (1885) 12 R. 1164; *Croucher* v. *Inglis* (1889) 16 R. 774; *Buchanan* v. *Glasgow Corpn.* (1906) 13 S.L.T. 203; *Kufner* v. *Berstecher*, 1907 S.C. 797; *West* v. *Mackenzie*, 1917 S.C. 513; *Rae* v. *R.S.S.P.C.C.*, 1924 S.C. 102.

[7] *Walker* v. *Cumming* (1868) 6 M. 318; *Hebditch, supra*; cf. *Hassan, supra*; *Dowgray* v. *Gilmour* (1906) 14 S.L.T. 104.

[8] *Denholm* v. *Thomson* (1880) 8 R. 31; *Douglas* v. *Main* (1893) 20 R. 793; *Currie* v. *Weir* (1900) 2 F. 522; *Brown* v. *Fraser* (1906) 8 F. 1000; *Shaw* v. *Burns*, 1911 S.C. 537.

[9] *Blackett* v. *Lang* (1854) 16 D. 989; *Henderson* v. *Patrick Thomson, Ltd.*, 1911 1 S.L.T. 284; cf. *Chalmers* v. *Barclay Perkins*, 1912 S.C. 521; *Rogers* v. *Orr*, 1939 S.C. 121.

[10] *Hassan, supra*; *Ingram* v. *Russell* (1893) 20 R. 771; *Gray* v. *Maitland* (1896) 4 S.L.T. 38.

[11] *Malcolm* v. *Duncan* (1897) 24 R. 747.

[12] *Wilson* v. *Purvis* (1890) 18 R. 72; *Ramsay* v. *McLay* (1890) 18 R. 130; *Brown* v. *Fraser* (1906) 8 F. 1000; *Handasyde* v. *Hepworth* (1907) 15 S.L.T. 180; *Cumming* v. *G.N.S. Ry.*, 1916 1 S.L.T. 181.

complaints to the proper authority about a matter of public administration,[1] but not complaints to the wrong authority,[2] and criticism of candidates standing for election to public office,[3] so long as not made more widely than necessary.[4]

Statements for the protection of another's interests

Qualified privilege attaches to statements made *bona fide* to another for the protection of that other's interest, such as voluntary statements warning the other against a third party,[5] statements about another in reply to inquiries[6] so long as relevant thereto,[7] answers to inquiries as to business credit,[8] answers to inquiries as to the qualities of a potential employee,[9] including an honest assessment of the employee's qualities, and even voluntary statements to possible employers and other employees.[10]

Communications between persons having a common interest

Qualified privilege attaches to communications between persons having a common interest, the one having an interest to make the statement and the other an interest or duty to receive it,[11] so long as they are made in good faith, and communication

[1] *Warren* v. *Falconer* (1771) Mor. 13933; *Harrison* v. *Bush* (1855) 5 E. & B. 344; *Reid* v. *Moore* (1893) 20 R. 712; *A.* v. *B.* (1895) 22 R. 984; *Barclay* v. *Manuel* (1903) 10 S.L.T. 450; *Cassidy* v. *Connochie*, 1907 S.C. 1112; *Couper* v. *Balfour*, 1913 S.C. 492; *James* v. *Baird*, 1916 S.C. (H.L.) 158.

[2] *Henderson* v. *H.* (1855) 17 D. 348; *Jenoure* v. *Delmège* [1891] A.C. 73; *Hebditch* v. *MacIlwaine* [1894] 2 Q.B. 54; *James, supra.*

[3] *Bruce* v. *Leisk* (1892) 19 R. 482; as to election addresses see Defamation Act, 1952, S. 10, modifying *Braddock* v. *Bevins* [1948] 1 K.B. 580.

[4] *Anderson* v. *Hunter* (1891) 18 R. 467.

[5] *Adams* v. *Coleridge* (1884) 1 T.L.R. 84; *Hunt* v. *G.N. Ry.* [1891] 2 Q.B. 189; *Stuart* v. *Bell* [1891] 2 Q.B. 341; *Milne* v. *Smith* (1892) 20 R. 95; *Nelson* v. *Irving* (1897) 24 R. 1054; *Moffat* v. *Coats* (1906) 14 S.L.T. 392; *A.B.* v. *X.Y.*, 1917 S.C. 15; *Hayford* v. *Forrester-Paton*, 1927 S.C. 740; *Rogers* v. *Orr*, 1939 S.C. 121; cf. *Findlay* v. *Blaylock*, 1937 S.C. 21.

[6] *Waller* v. *Loch* (1881) 7 Q.B.D. 615; *Greenlands, Ltd.* v. *Wilmshurst* [1913] 3 K.B. 507; *London Assoc.* v. *Greenlands* [1916] 2 A.C. 15; *Notman* v. *Commercial Bank*, 1938 S.C. 522.

[7] *Nevill* v. *Fine Art Co.* [1895] 2 Q.B. 156; *Adam* v. *Ward* [1917] A.C. 309.

[8] *Waller, supra*; *Ingram* v. *Russell* (1893) 20 R. 771; *Keith* v. *Lauder* (1905) 8 F. 356; *Macintosh* v. *Dun* [1908] A.C. 390; *Barr* v. *Musselburgh Merchants*, 1912 S.C. 174; *London Assoc., supra*; *Tournier* v. *N.P. Bank* [1924] 1 K.B. 461.

[9] *Watson* v. *Burnet* (1852) 24 D. 494; *Laidlaw* v. *Gunn* (1890) 17 R. 394; *Pullman* v. *Hill* (1891) 1 Q.B. 524; *Sheriff* v. *Denholm* (1898) 5 S.L.T. 234, 346; *Dundas* v. *Livingstone* (1900) 3 F. 37; *Hanton* v. *Hatje* (1907) 15 S.L.T. 531; *A.B.* v. *X.Y., supra*; *Bryant* v. *Edgar*, 1909 S.C. 1080.

[10] *Farquhar* v. *Neish* (1890) 17 R. 716; *Macdonald* v. *McColl* (1901) 3 F. 1082; *A.B.* v. *X.Y., supra*; *Bryant, supra*; *Dundas, supra.*

[11] *Henderson* v. *H.* (1855) 17 D. 348; *Harrison* v. *Bush* (1855) 5 E. & B. 344; *Laughton* v. *Bp. of Sodor and Man* (1872) L.R. 4 C.P. 495; *Hunt* v. *G.N. Ry.* [1891] 2 Q.B. 189;

is not made more widely than necessary.[1] Common interest has been held to exist in many communications between persons as to matters of home and family,[2] as to public officials,[3] as to professional services,[4] as to the character or conduct of an employee,[5] as to business relations of common interest,[6] and as to matters of trade.[7]

Statements in the protection of one's own interests

Qualified privilege also protects statements made in the protection of the defender's own interests, as in reply to attacks or threats,[8] in the pleadings of an action to which the defender is a party (so-called judicial slander),[9] so long as there is no malice

Stuart v. *Bell* (1891] 2 Q.B. 341; *James* v. *Baird*, 1916 S.C. (H.L.) 158; *Adam* v. *Ward* [1917] A.C. 309; *Cochrane* v. *Young*, 1922 S.C. 696; *Watt* v. *Longsdon* [1930] 1 K.B. 130; *Winstanley* v. *Bampton* [1943] 1 K.B. 219.

1 *Dudgeon* v. *Forbes* (1833) 11 S. 1014; *Adam* v. *Allan* (1841) 3 D. 1058; *Leitch* v. *Lyal* (1903) 11 S.L.T. 394.

2 *Adams* v. *Coleridge* (1884) 1 T.L.R. 84; *Moffat* v. *Coats* (1906) 14 S.L.T. 392.

3 *Chiene* v. *Archibald* (1868) 6 S.L.R. 62; *Craig* v. *Jex-Blake* (1871) 9 M. 973; *Rankine* v. *Roberts* (1873) 1 R. 225; *Auld* v. *Shairp* (1875) 2 R. 940; *McMurchy* v. *Campbell* (1887) 14 R. 745; *Shaw* v. *Morgan* (1888) 15 R. 865; *Croucher* v. *Inglis* (1889) 6 R. 774; *Neilson* v. *Johnston* (1890) 17 R. 442; *Jack* v. *Fleming* (1891) 19 R. 1; *Bruce* v. *Leisk* (1892) 19 R. 482; *A.* v. *B.* (1895) 22 R. 984; *Teague* v. *Russell* (1900) 8 S.L.T. 253; *Barclay* v. *Manuel* (1902) 10 S.L.T. 450; *Cassidy* v. *Connochie*, 1907 S.C. 1112; *Murray* v. *Wylie*, 1916 S.C. 365; *Campbell* v. *Weir*, 1924 S.L.T. 14; *Hines* v. *Davidson*, 1935 S.C. 30.

4 *Sadgrove* v. *Hole* [1901] 2 K.B. 1; *Gall* v. *Slessor*, 1907 S.C. 708.

5 *Watson* v. *Burnet* (1862) 24 D. 494; *Milne* v. *Bauchop* (1887) 5 R. 1114; *McMurchy* v. *Campbell* (1887) 14 R. 725; *Innes* v. *Adamson* (1889) 17 R. 11; *Neilson* v. *Johnston* (1890) 17 R. 442; *Farquhar* v. *Neish* (1890) 17 R. 716; *Hunt* v. *G.N. Ry.* [1891] 2 Q.B. 189; *Martin* v. *Cruickshanks* (1896) 23 R. 874; *Newall* v. *Bennett* (1896) 3 S.L.T. 268; *McCallum* v. *McDiarmid* (1900) 2 F. 357; *Dundas* v. *Livingstone* (1900) 3 F. 37; *Teague* v. *Russell* (1900) 8 S.L.T. 253; *Macdonald* v. *McColl* (1901) 3 F. 1082; *Keith* v. *Lauder* (1905) 8 F. 356; *A.* v. *B.*, 1907 S.C. 1154; *Williamson* v. *McCann* (1908) 16 S.L.T. 221; *Bryant* v. *Edgar*, 1909 S.C. 1080; *Couper* v. *Balfour*, 1914 S.C. 139; *A.B.* v. *X.Y.*, 1917 S.C. 15; *Fyvie* v. *Waddell*, 1923 S.L.T. 518; *Dunnet* v. *Nelson*, 1926 S.C. 764.

6 *McCaig* v. *Moscrip* (1872) 10 S.L.R. 140; *Reid* v. *Little* (1894) 2 S.L.T. 244; *Oliver* v. *Barnet* (1895) 3 S.L.T. 163; *Murdison* v. *S.F.U.* (1896) 23 R. 449; *Nelson* v. *Irving* (1897) 24 R. 1054; *Paton* v. *Edine* (1898) 6 S.L.T. 191; *Stewart* v. *Hannah* (1905) 8 F. 107; *Quigley* v. *Brown*, 1913 2 S.L.T. 391; *Cadzow* v. *Edinburgh Distress Committee*, 1914 1 S.L.T. 493; *McGillivray* v. *Davidson*, 1934 S.L.T. 45; *Hines* v. *Davidson*, 1935 S.C. 30.

7 *McLean* v. *Adam* (1888) 16 R. 175; *Barr* v. *Musselburgh Merchants*, 1912 S.C. 174.

8 *Ramsay* v. *Nairne* (1833) 11 S. 1033; *Shaw* v. *Morgan* (1888) 15 R. 865; *Laidlaw* v. *Gunn* (1890) 17 R. 394; *Gray* v. *S.S.P.C.A.* (1890) 17 R. 1185; *Wilson* v. *Purvis* (1890) 18 R. 72; *Milne* v. *Walker* (1893) 21 R. 155; *Sheriff* v. *Denholm* (1898) 5 S.L.T. 346; *Crawford* v. *Dunlop* (1900) 2 F. 987; *Campbell* v. *Cochrane* (1905) 8 F. 205.

9 *McCaig* v. *Moscrip* (1872) 10 S.L.R. 140; *Scott* v. *Turnbull* (1884) 11 R. 1131; *Selbie* v. *Saint* (1890) 18 R. 88; *Williamson* v. *Umphray* (1890) 17 R. 905; *Thomson* v. *Munro & Jamieson* (1900) 8 S.L.T. 327; *Neill* v. *Henderson* (1901) 3 F. 387; *Stevenson* v. *Wilson* (1903) 5 F. 309.

relevantly averred and proved,[1] in challenging a person with misconduct[2] or dismissing an employee for wrongdoing.[3] A statement in reply may be allowed greater latitude than would otherwise be allowed, if it is merely a fair retort to the attack made.[4]

Statements made in seeking redress of grievances

A statement enjoys qualified privilege if made in the course of complaining or seeking redress of some grievance, so long as made to the proper person or body, relevant to the grievance and not motivated by malice.[5] Statements in the pleadings of actions seeking some legal remedy, so long as relevant, are privileged in the same way.[6]

Published reports

Many categories of reports, so long as fair and accurate,[7] and even if summarized,[8] enjoy qualified privilege, in view of the public interest in knowledge of public proceedings. These include fair and accurate reports of the proceedings of Parliament and its committees,[9] extracts from or abstracts of any parliamentary report or paper published by authority of either House[10] or broadcast,[11] a correct[12] copy of or extract from a register

[1] *Gordon* v. *British and Foreign Metaline Co.* (1886) 14 R. 75; *Hay* v. *Cameron* (1898) 6 S.L.T. 48; *Selbie, supra*; *Douglas* v. *Ferguson* (1896) 4 S.L.T. 200; *Stevenson, supra*; *Campbell, supra*; *M.* v. *H.*, 1908 S.C. 1130; *Webster* v. *Paterson*, 1910 S.C. 459; *Mitchell* v. *Smith*, 1919 S.C. 664.

[2] *Finburgh* v. *Moss' Empires*, 1908 S.C. 928; *Gorman* v. *Moss' Empires*, 1913 S.C. 1; *Henderson* v. *Patrick Thomson, Ltd.*, 1911 1 S.L.T. 284; cf. *Neville* v. *C. & A. Modes*, 1945 S.C. 175.

[3] *Cunningham* v. *Petherbridge* (1894) 2 S.L.T. 229; *Hamilton* v. *Wright* (1895) 3 S.L.T. 10; *Suzor* v. *McLachlan*, 1914 S.C. 306; *A.B.* v. *X.Y.*, 1917 S.C. 15; *Dunnet* v. *Nelson*, 1926 S.C. 764.

[4] *Monro* v. *M.* (1803) Hume 616; *Hamilton* v. *Duncan* (1825) 4 S. 414; *Gray* v. *S.S.P.C.A.* (1890) 17 R. 1185; *Milne* v. *Walker* (1893) 21 R. 155; *Brodie* v. *Dowell* (1894) 2 S.L.T. 9; *N.U. Bank Employees* v. *Murray*, 1949 S.L.T. (Notes) 26.

[5] *Hebditch* v. *MacIlwaine* [1894] 2 Q.B. 54; *M.* v. *H.*, 1908 S.C. 1130; *Adam* v. *Ward* [1917] A.C. 309; *Mitchell* v. *Smith*, 1919 S.C. 664; *Rivlin* v. *Bilainkin* [1953] 1 Q.B. 485; *Lincoln* v. *Daniels* [1960] 3 All E.R. 205.

[6] *Scott* v. *Turnbull* (1884) 11 R. 1131; *Mitchell, supra.*

[7] *Crabbe & Robertson* v. *Stubbs* (1895) 22 R. 860; *McLintock* v. *Stubbs* (1902) 5 F. 1; *Hunter* v. *Stubbs* (1903) 5 F. 920; *Hope* v. *Leng* (1907) 23 T.L.R. 243; *Grech* v. *Odhams* [1958] 2 Q.B. 275.

[8] *Duncan* v. *Assoc. Newspapers*, 1929 S.C. 14; *Harper* v. *Provincial Newspapers*, 1937 S.L.T. 462; but see *Wright & Greig* v. *Outram* (1890) 17 R. 596.

[9] *Wason* v. *Walter* (1868) L.R. 4 Q.B. 73.

[10] Parliamentary Papers Act, 1840, S. 3; *Bradlaugh* v. *Gosset* (1884) 12 Q.B.D. 271; *Dingle* v. *Assoc. Newspapers* [1960] 2 Q.B. 405.

[11] Defamation Act, 1952, S. 9.

[12] *Outram* v. *Reid* (1852) 14 D. 577; *Gordon* v. *Stubbs* (1895) 3 S.L.T. 10; *Crabbe* v. *Stubbs* (1895) 22 R. 860; *Hunter* v. *Stubbs* (1903) 5 F. 920.

maintained under statute to which the public has access,[1] fair and accurate reports of the proceedings in a public court of justice,[2] or quasi-judicial body,[3] but not to reports of proceedings behind closed doors,[4] nor reports of prohibited matter,[5] nor probably to reports of foreign judicial proceedings.[6] Privilege attaches also to a report of the proceedings of a public meeting,[7] or of a body or authority in whose proceedings the public has a legitimate interest.[8] By the Defamation Act, 1952, Ss. 7 and 14(d), qualified privilege attaches to publication in newspapers of certain reports scheduled to the Act, some without explanation or contradiction, others only subject to later explanation or contradiction published in the same paper,[9] but always subject to absence of malice, that publication was not prohibited by law, and that it was of public concern and for the public benefit.[10]

Fair comment

A statement is not actionable as defamatory if it is comment, based on facts truly stated, fairly and honestly made, and on a matter of public interest. Such liberty of comment is an aspect of free speech.[11] The statement must be truly comment, i.e. appreciation, evaluation, criticism or opinion, and not really a statement of fact.[12] The facts on which the comment is made must be admitted or proved to be substantially true.[13] The defence does not fail because every allegation of fact is not proved, so long as the

[1] *Fleming* v. *Newton* (1848) 1 H.L. Cas. 363; *Searles* v. *Scarlett* [1892] 2 Q.B. 56; *Russell* v. *Stubbs*, 1913 S.C. (H.L.) 14.

[2] *Richardson* v. *Wilson* (1879) 7 R. 237; *Wright & Greig* v. *Outram* (1890) 17 R. 596; *Buchan* v. *N.B. Ry.* (1894) 21 R. 379; cf. *Macleod* v. *Justices of Lewis* (1892) 20 R. 218; *Kimber* v. *Press Assocn.* [1893] 1 Q.B. 65; *Burnett & Hallamshire Fuel* v. *Sheffield Telegraph* [1960] 2 All E.R. 157.

[3] *Allbutt* v. *G.M.C.* (1889) 23 Q.B.D. 400.

[4] *Wason*, *supra*; *Kimber*, *supra*; *Scott* v. *S.* [1913] A.C. 417.

[5] Judicial Proceedings (Regulation of Reports) Act, 1926; Children and Young Persons (Sc.) Act, 1937, Ss. 45, 52, 54.

[6] *Riddell* v. *Clydesdale Horse Socy.* (1885) 12 R. 976; *Pope* v. *Outram*, 1909 S.C. 230.

[7] See also Public Bodies (Admission to Meetings) Act, 1960, S. 1(5).

[8] *Allbutt* v. *G.M.C.* (1889) 23 Q.B.D. 400; *Adam* v. *Ward* [1917] A.C. 309.

[9] *Khan* v. *Ahmed* [1957] 2 Q.B. 149.

[10] See *Parkhurst* v. *Sowler* (1887) 3 T.L.R. 193; *Ponsford* v. *Financial Times, Ltd.* (1900) 16 T.L.R. 248.

[11] *Merivale* v. *Carson* (1887) 20 Q.B.D. 275; *Godfrey* v. *Thomson* (1890) 17 R. 1108; *Gray* v. *S.S.P.C.A.* (1890) 17 R. 1185; *Langlands* v. *Leng*, 1916 S.C. (H.L.) 102; *Lyon* v. *Daily Telegraph* [1943] 1 K.B. 746.

[12] *Merivale*, *supra*; *Kemsley* v. *Foot* [1952] A.C. 345; *Jones* v. *Skelton* [1963] 3 All E.R. 952; cf. *Adam* v. *Allan* (1841) 3 D. 1058.

[13] *Merivale*, *supra*; *Wheatley* v. *Anderson*, 1927 S.C. 133.

opinion is fair comment having regard to such facts as are proved.[1] The facts must be true, not merely be believed to be true,[2] and must in themselves give foundation for the comment.[3] The comment must be fair, in the sense of being an honest expression of a view *bona fide* held, though it may be harsh, exaggerated, and even perverse or prejudiced; fair does not mean moderate, temperate, or restrained.[4] It ceases to be fair comment if it is really abuse or invective,[5] or if it appears that the comment was motivated by actual malice or other oblique motive.[6] The liberty of comment is restricted to matters of public interest; whether a topic is of public interest is a question of law.[7] Matters of public interest include the conduct of government and of ministers, proceedings in Parliament, reports by departments of State, evidence to and reports from select committees and Royal Commissions; the qualifications of persons seeking public office[8] and the conduct of local government;[9] the administration of justice;[10] the proceedings, decisions, and pronouncements of the churches, their bodies, committees, and leading persons;[11] the conduct of persons holding, or aspiring to, offices of public responsibility;[12] the management of all public institutions, particularly if supported by public funds;[13] works of art and literature put before the public;[14] public entertainments and performances;[15] and generally any matter brought before the public.[16]

[1] Defamation Act, 1952, S. 6.

[2] *Merivale, supra*; *Hunt* v. *Star, Ltd.* [1908] 2 K.B. 309; *Kemsley, supra.*

[3] *Wheatley, supra.*

[4] *Merivale, supra*; *McQuire* v. *Western Morning News* [1903] 3 K.B. 100; *Turner* v. *M.G.M. Pictures* [1950] 1 All E.R. 449; *Silkin v. Beaverbrook Newspapers* [1958] 2 All E.R. 516.

[5] *McQuire, supra.*

[6] *Merivale, supra*; *Thomas* v. *Bradbury, Agnew, Ltd.* [1906] 2 K.B. 627; *Lyle-Samuels* v. *Odhams* [1920] 1 K.B. 135; *Sutherland* v. *Stopes* [1925] A.C. 47; *Kemsley* v. *Foot* [1952] A.C. 345.

[7] *Kelly* v. *Sherlock* (1866) L.R. 1 Q.B. 686.

[8] *Auld* v. *Shairp* (1875) 2 R. 940.

[9] *Langlands* v. *Leng*, 1916 S.C. (H.L.) 102.

[10] *Grech* v. *Odhams* [1958] 2 Q.B. 275; but see *Stirling* v. *Assoc. Newspapers*, 1960 S.L.T. 5.

[11] *Kelly* v. *Tinling* (1865) L.R. 1 Q.B. 699; *Jack* v. *Fleming* (1891) 19 R. 1; *Murray* v. *Wylie*, 1916 S.C. 356.

[12] *Langlands* v. *Leng, supra.*

[13] *Gathercole* v. *Miall* (1846) 16 M. & W. 319; *South Hetton Coal Co.* v. *N.E. News* [1894] 1 Q.B. 133.

[14] *Merivale, supra*; *McQuire, supra*; *Turner* v. *M.G.M.* [1950] 1 All E.R. 461.

[15] *McQuire, supra.*

[16] *Boal* v. *Scottish Catholic Ptg. Co.*, 1907 S.C. 1120.

MALICIOUS FALSEHOOD

This branch of verbal injury deals with injuries to economic interests rather than to reputation and is considered under that head.[1]

WRONGFUL CIVIL PROCEEDINGS

Persons have in general free access to the civil courts to obtain redress of grievances. A vexatious litigant may, however, be required to obtain a judge's concurrence before initiating proceedings.[2] It is not wrongful for a person to pursue any kind of civil claim, merely because the proceedings are held to be incompetent, irrelevant,[3] mistaken, or unfounded in fact,[4] nor to obtain a decree later recalled.[5] The pursuer's only liability is for the expenses of process.[6]

A pursuer is, however, probably liable in damages if he brought the action from express malice,[7] or recklessly harassed a defender with actions when no debt was due.[8] He is certainly liable if he has raised, or persisted in, an action in the full knowledge that he had no ground for action,[9] or has raised an action or taken decree in breach of an agreement not to do so,[10] and probably also if he has taken decree irregularly, i.e. without going through all the necessary procedure, and did so, not innocently or mistakenly or accidentally or negligently,[11] but maliciously,[12] or has maliciously repeated what is substantially

1 Ch. 69, *infra*.

2 Vexatious Actions (Sc.) Act, 1894; *L.A.* v. *Arnold*, 1951 S.C. 256; *L.A.* v. *Rizza*, 1962 S.L.T. (Notes) 8.

3 *Kennedy* v. *Fort William Commrs.* (1877) 5 R. 302, 307.

4 *Ormiston* v. *Redpath, Brown & Co.* (1864) 4 M. 488.

5 *Graham* v. *Dundas* (1829) 7 S. 876; *McGregor* v. *McLaughlin* (1905) 8 F. 70; cf. *Clark* v. *Beattie*, 1909 S.C. 299.

6 *Ormiston, supra*; *Kennedy, supra*; *Harpers* v. *Greenwood* (1896) 4 S.L.T. 116.

7 *Gordon* v. *Royal Bank* (1826) 5 S. 150, 152; *Hallam* v. *Gye* (1835) 14 S. 199, 200; *McGregor* v. *McLaughlin* (1905) 8 F. 70, 76; cf. *Wolthekker* v. *Northern Agricultural Co.* (1862) 1 M. 211.

8 *Ormiston, supra.*

9 *Ormiston, supra*; *Davies* v. *Brown* (1867) 5 M. 842; *Rhind* v. *Kemp* (1893) 21 R. 275; *Pollock* v. *Goodwin's Trs.* (1898) 25 R. 1051.

10 *Sturrock* v. *Welsh* (1890) 18 R. 109; *MacRobbie* v. *MacLellan's Trs.* (1891) 18 R. 470; *Turnbull* v. *Oliver* (1891) 19 R. 154; *Mackersy* v. *Davis* (1895) 22 R. 368; *Gibson* v. *Anderson* (1897) 24 R. 556; *Central Cyclone Co.* v. *Low* (1900) 8 S.L.T. 280; *Gray* v. *Macintosh* (1906) 14 S.L.T. 403. The ground of action in this case is breach of contract.

11 *McGregor, supra*, 76; *Reid* v. *Clark*, 1913 2 S.L.T. 330.

12 *Davies* v. *Brown and Lyell* (1867) 5 M. 842; *MacRobbie, supra*, 475; *Rhind* v. *Kemp* (1894) 21 R. 275; *McGregor, supra*, 76. The decree must first be reduced or set aside: *McGregor, supra*; *Clark* v. *Beattie*, 1909 S.C. 299; if the decree cannot be reduced it must be treated as regularly granted: *Crombie* v. *McEwan* (1861) 23 D. 333; *Gray* v. *Smart* (1892) 19 R. 692; *Jackson* v. *Lillie & Russell* (1902) 10 S.L.T. 448.

the same as a previous claim.[1] A defender should always use due diligence in his own defence and failure to do so may prejudice his subsequent claim for abuse of process.[2]

Wrongful interdict

A person complaining of interdict having been wrongfully granted against him must show that an operative decree of interdict, interim or perpetual, was granted against him,[3] that it has been recalled on some other ground than change of circumstances,[4] that the complainer was thereby prevented from exercising some valid legal rights,[5] and that he sustained some loss in consequence.[6] Interim interdict is obtained *periculo petentis* and deemed wrongfully obtained if not declared perpetual and it caused loss, malice being irrelevant.[7] Interim interdict inverting possession is wrongful if not declared perpetual.[8] Interim interdict seeking to protect possession of land is wrongful only if the possessor is ousted and he acted maliciously and without probable cause.[9] Perpetual interdict is granted only after inquiry, and is therefore wrongful only if recalled on appeal, or set aside on petition, or reduced.

Wrongful sequestration or liquidation

Presenting a petition for sequestration of a person, or liquidation of a company, is wrongful only if the prerequisites for the competency of such a petition are not satisfied,[10] or if presented maliciously and without probable cause.[11]

[1] *Wright* v. *Bennett* [1948] 1 All E.R. 227.

[2] *Ormiston, supra.*

[3] *Buchanan* v. *Douglas* (1853) 15 D. 365; *Wilson* v. *Gilchrist* (1900) 2 F. 391.

[4] *Livingstone* v. *Hamilton Presbytery* (1851) 13 D. 649; *Lovat* v. *Macdonell* (1868) 6 M. 330.

[5] *Jack* v. *Begg* (1875) 3 R. 35; *Aird* v. *Tarbert School Board*, 1907 S.C. 305; *Macdonald* v. *Lord Blythswood*, 1914 S.C. 930.

[6] *Buchanan, supra*; *Arnot* v. *Dowie* (1863) 2 M. 119; *Miller* v. *Hunter* (1864) 3 M. 740.

[7] *Wolthekker* v. *Northern Agricultural Co.* (1862) 1 M. 211; *Abel's Exors.* v. *Edmond* (1863) 1 M. 1061; *Robinson* v. *N.B. Ry.* (1864) 2 M. 84; *Kennedy* v. *Fort William Commrs.* (1877) 5 R. 302; *Fife* v. *Orr* (1895) 23 R. 8; *McGregor* v. *McLaughlin* (1905) 8 F. 70.

[8] *Elibank* v. *Renton* (1833) 11 S. 238; *Wolthekker, supra*; *Kennedy, supra*; *Clippens Oil Co.* v. *Edinburgh & Dist. Water Trs.*, 1907 S.C. (H.L.) 9.

[9] *Moir* v. *Hunter* (1832) 11 S. 30; *Buchanan, supra*; *Kennedy, supra*; *Glasgow City Ry.* v. *Glasgow Coal Co.* (1885) 12 R. 1287.

[10] *Kinnes* v. *Adam* (1882) 9 R. 698, 702; *Smith* v. *Taylor* (1882) 10 R. 291; *Beaumont* v. *Watson* (1895) 2 S.L.T. 454; *Aitchison & Co.* (1903) 10 S.L.T. 501; *Seaspray S.S. Co.* v. *Tenant* (1908) 15 S.L.T. 874; cf. *Quartz Hill Consol. Co.* v. *Eyre* (1883) 11 Q.B.D. 674.

[11] *Kinnes, supra.*

WRONGFUL DILIGENCE

In relation to liability for wrongful use of diligence on a decree, the fundamental distinction is between those kinds of diligence which a party is absolutely entitled to use without need to apply to the court for any authority or special warrant, and those other kinds for which the party must apply to the court for warrant and must make some statement or representation to the court to induce it to grant the necessary authority. In the former class of cases the creditor is liable only if he used the diligence maliciously and without probable cause.[1] In the latter class he is liable if the statement or representation made to the court *periculo petentis* was incorrect in fact, independently of good or bad faith, and warrant were accordingly obtained unjustifiably.[2]

In cases of both classes diligence may be actionable as wrongful if founded on a null decree,[3] or if used unnecessarily,[4] or unjustifiably,[5] or if executed irregularly and without conforming to procedural requirements.[6]

[1] e.g. arrestment on the dependence: *Duff* v. *Bradberry* (1825) 4 S. 23; *Brodie* v. *Young* (1851) 13 D. 737; *Henning* v. *Hewetson* (1852) 14 D. 487; *Baillie* v. *Hume* (1853) 16 D. 161; *Borthwick* v. *Gilkison* (1862) 2 M. 125; *Wolthekker, supra*; *Wilson* v. *Mackie* (1875) 3 R. 18; *Kennedy, supra*; *Gordon* v. *British and Foreign Metaline Co.* (1886) 14 R. 75, 83; *McGregor* v. *McLaughlin* (1905) 8 F. 70, 74; *Kerr* v. *Malcolm* (1906) 14 S.L.T. 191; arrestment in execution: *Taylor* v. *Rutherford* (1888) 15 R. 608; action of furthcoming: *Kinnes* v. *Adam* (1882) 9 R. 698; inhibition; *Macleod* v. *M.* (1836) 15 S. 248; *Wolthekker, supra*; *Beattie* v. *Pratt* (1880) 7 R. 1171; charge for payment: *Wolthekker, supra*; personal poinding: *Wolthekker, supra*; action of poinding of the ground: cf. *Kinnes* v. *Adam, supra*; action of maills and duties: *Kinnes, supra*; action of adjudication: *Kinnes, supra*, 702.

[2] e.g. application for interim interdict: *Wolthekker, supra*; application for *meditatio fugae* warrant: *Battersby* v. *Caldwell* (1828) 6 S. 667; *Swayne* v. *Fife Bank* (1835) 13 S. 1003; *Ford* v. *Muirhead* (1858) 20 D. 949; *Wolthekker, supra*; *Kennedy, supra*; warrant for imprisonment for civil debt: *Cameron* v. *Mortimer* (1872) 10 M. 461; *MacIntosh* v. *Chalmers* (1883) 11 R. 8; warrant for imprisonment for alimentary debt; *Cameron, supra*; warrant for imprisonment on decree *ad factum praestandum*: *Chisholm* v. *Fraser* (1825) 3 S. 442; *Taylor* v. *Macdonald* (1854) 16 D. 378; warrant for imprisonment for process-caption: *Pearson* v. *Anderson* (1833) 11 S. 1008; *Hunter* v. *Kerr* (1842) 4 D. 1175; *Watt* v. *Thomson* (1870) 8 M. (H.L.) 77; arrestment in execution (special cases): *Grant* v. *Airdrie Mags.*, 1939 S.C. 738; sale of poinded effects: *Le Conte* v. *Douglas* (1880) 8 R. 175; sequestration for rent: *Robertson* v. *Galbraith* (1857) 19 D. 1016; *Wolthekker, supra*; *Watson* v. *McCulloch* (1878) 5 R. 843; *Gray* v. *Weir* (1891) 19 R. 25; *Alexander* v. *Campbell* (1903) 5 F. 634.

[3] *MacRobbie* v. *MacLellan's Trs.* (1891) 18 R. 470; *Clark* v. *Beattie*, 1907 S.C. 299, 303.

[4] *Holt* v. *National Bank*, 1927 S.L.T. 484;

[5] *Gibb* v. *Edinburgh Brewery* (1873) 11 M. 705; *Sturrock* v. *Welsh & Forbes* (1890) 18 R. 109; *MacRobbie* v. *MacLellan's Trs.* (1891) 18 R. 470; *Macdougall* v. *McNab* (1893) 21 R. 144; *Mackersy* v. *Davis* (1895) 22 R. 368; *McKinnon* v. *Hamilton* (1866) 4 M. 852; *Nelmes* v. *Gillies* (1883) 10 R. 890; *Kennedy* v. *Creyk* (1887) 15 R. 118.

[6] e.g. *fugae* warrant: *Anderson* v. *Smith*, 26 November, 1814, F.C.; *Milhollam* v. *Bertram* (1826) 5 S. 170; *Strachan* v. *Stoddart* (1828) 7 S. 4; *Cowan* v. *Watt* (1833) 11 S. 999; civil imprisonment: *Strachan, supra*; *Pollock* v. *Clark* (1829) 8 S. 1; *Frame* v. *Campbell.*

WRONGFUL INITIATION OF CRIMINAL PROCEEDINGS

A person who gives information in consequence of which another person is prosecuted is not liable merely because the information was incorrect or the accusation unfounded, but only if his information were given maliciously and without probable cause.[1] These conditions must be specifically averred and proved,[2] and may be inferred from inadequacy of inquiry,[3] prior ill-will,[4] recklessness in complaining,[5] or failure to intimate that a complaint was mistaken.[6] Furthermore action is competent only if no criminal proceedings were taken, or if they failed, or the conviction was quashed on appeal; a conviction negatives lack of probable cause for giving information for prosecution, whether or not there was malice, and the civil court cannot investigate allegations of wrongness of or injustice in the criminal conviction.[7] The Lord Advocate, Crown counsel, and procurators-fiscal acting under solemn procedure have absolute privilege in prosecution and are wholly free from

(1836) 14 S. 914; *Hart* v. *Frame* (1839) McL. & Rob. 595; *Smith* v. *Grant* (1858) 20 D. 1077; decree *ad factum praestandum*: *Stewart* v. *McDougall*, 1908 S.C. 315; process-caption: *Watt* v. *Ligertwood* (1874) 1 R. (H.L.) 21; arrestment: *Meikle* v. *Sneddon* (1862) 24 D. 720; *Borthwick* v. *Gilkison* (1863) 2 M. 125; *Peterson* v. *McLean* (1868) 6 M. 218; *Wilson* v. *Mackie* (1875) 3 R. 18; *Carlberg* v. *Borjesson* (1877) 5 R. (H.L.) 215; *Kennedy*, *supra*; *MacTaggart* v. *MacKillop*, 1939 S.L.T. 65; charge: *Smith* v. *Taylor* (1882) 10 R. 291; *Wilson* v. *Gorman*, 1924 S.L.T. 112; *Parkinson* v. *Bowen*, 1951 S.L.T. 393; See also *Cook* v. *Wallace & Wilson* (1889) 16 R. 565; *McGregor* v. *McLaughlin* (1905) 8 F. 70; personal poinding: *MacKnight* v. *Green* (1835) 13 S. 342; *Struthers* v. *Dykes* (1847) 1437; *McKinnon* v. *Hamilton* (1866) 4 M. 852; *Hamilton* v. *Emslie* (1868) 7 M. 173; 9 D. *Le Conte* v. *Douglas* (1880) 8 R. 175; sequestration for rent: *McLeod* v. *M.* (1829) 7 S. 396; *Cargill* v. *Baxter* (1829) 7 S. 662; *Galloway* v. *Macpherson* (1830) 8 S. 539; *Oswald* v. *Graeme* (1851) 13 D. 1229; *Robertson* v. *Galbraith* (1857) 19 D. 1016; *Watson* v. *McCulloch* (1878) 5 R. 843; *Kennedy* v. *Crayle* (1887) 15 R. 118; *Pollock* v. *Goodwin's Trs.* (1898) 25 R. 1051.

[1] *Arbuckle* v. *Taylor* (1815) 3 Dow 160; *Young* v. *Leven* (1822) 1 Sh. App. 179; *Sheppard* v. *Fraser* (1849) 11 D. 446; *Henderson* v. *Robertson* (1853) 15 D. 292; *Dallas* v. *Mann* (1853) 15 D. 746; *Thomson* v. *Adam* (1865) 4 M. 29; *Rae* v. *Linton* (1875) 2 R. 669; *Green* v. *Chalmers* (1878) 6 R. 318; *Lightbody* v. *Gordon* (1882) 9 R. 934; *Urquhart* v. *McKenzie* (1886) 14 R. 18; *Chalmers* v. *Barclay, Perkins & Co.*, 1912 S.C. 521; *Mills* v. *Kelvin & White*, 1913 S.C. 521.

[2] *Lightbody*, *supra*; *McMurchy* v. *Campbell* (1887) 14 R. 725; *Douglas* v. *Main* (1893) 20 R. 793; *Currie* v. *Weir* (1900) 2 F. 522; *Buchanan* v. *Glasgow Corpn.*, 1910 S.C. 562; cf. *Lewis* v. *Tims* [1952] A.C. 676.

[3] *Lightbody*, *supra*; *Hassan* v. *Paterson* (1885) 12 R. 1164; *Chalmers*, *supra*; *Rae* v. *S.S.P.C.C.*, 1924 S.C. 102.

[4] *Shaw* v. *Burns*, 1911 S.C. 537.

[5] *Macdonald* v. *Fergusson* (1853) 15 D. 545; *Denholm* v. *Thomson* (1880) 8 R. 31; *Brown* v. *Fraser* (1906) 8 F. 1000.

[6] *Richmond* v. *Thomson* (1838) 16 S. 995; *Smith* v. *Green* (1853) 15 D. 549.

[7] *Gilchrist* v. *Anderson* (1838) 1 D. 37; *Kennedy* v. *Wise* (1890) 17 R. 1036; *Hill* v. *Campbell* (1905) 8 F. 220; *Chalmers*, *supra*.

liability.[1] In summary proceedings prosecutors in the public interest are protected both at common law[2] and under statute;[3] in both cases clear proof of malice and lack of probable cause is essential. A private prosecutor is liable only if malice and lack of probable cause be proved.[4] A procurator-fiscal may, however, be liable, independently of malice and lack of probable cause, if he obtains and uses an illegal warrant, such as to search premises for possible evidence of complicity in a crime of which the occupier was not accused.[5] A warrant to search premises is not illegal merely because the occupier has not been charged or apprehended.[6] Search of premises without warrant is justifiable in cases of urgent necessity.[7]

1 *Henderson* v. *Robertson* (1853) 15 D. 292; *McMurchy, supra*; *Hester* v. *Macdonald*, 1961 S.C. 370.

2 *Arbuckle* v. *Taylor* (1815) 3 Dow 160; *Munro* v. *Taylor* (1845) 7 D. 500; *Henderson, supra*; *Craig* v. *Peebles* (1876) 3 R. 441.

3 Summary Jurisdiction (Sc.) Act, 1954, S. 75; see *McCrone* v. *Sawers* (1835) 13 S. 443; *Urquhart* v. *Grigor* (1864) 3 M. 283; *Bell* v. *Black and Morrison* (1865) 3 M. 1026; *Ferguson* v. *McNab* (1885) 12 R. 1083; *Hastings* v. *Henderson* (1890) 17 R. 1130; *Rae* v. *Strathern*, 1924 S.C. 147; *Graham* v. *Strathern*, 1924 S.C. 699.

4 *Bell, supra*, 1029; *Cook* v. *Spence* (1897) 4 S.L.T. 295; *Chalmers* v. *Barclay, Perkins & Co.*, 1912 S.C. 521.

5 *Bell* v. *Black and Morrison* (1865) 3 M. 1026.

6 *Stewart* v. *Roach*, 1950 S.C. 318.

7 *H.M.A.* v. *McGuigan*, 1936 J.C. 16; *H.M.A.* v. *McKay*, 1961 J.C. 47.

CHAPTER 69

WRONGS IN RESPECT OF ECONOMIC RELATIONSHIPS

Fraud

FRAUD consists in making a false representation of fact knowingly, or without belief in its truth, or recklessly, intending that the representee should act in reliance thereon, which act causes him loss in consequence.[1] The act of reliance may be to conclude a disadvantageous contract, in which case damages may be claimed for the loss caused by the fraud whether or not the contract is, or can be, rescinded on account of the fraud which induced it,[2] or conduct resulting in personal injury.[3]

Fraudulent impersonation

A variety of fraudulent misrepresentation is where A represents himself as being B, another person; loss caused thereby is actionable, quite apart from any effect on any contract induced by the impersonation.[4]

Negligent misrepresentation

Where one party is in breach of a duty incumbent on him in the circumstances to exercise reasonable care in representing or communicating information, and causes that other pecuniary loss by his failure, he is liable for the loss caused.[5] The difficulty is in every case to determine whether in the circumstances a duty of care was owed.[6] There is a general duty of common honesty, and a further duty may arise from contract or fiduciary relationship, but no further duty arises merely from a request for information.

[1] *Lees* v. *Tod* (1882) 9 R. 807, 853; *Derry* v. *Peek* (1889) 14 App. Cas. 337, 374; *Boyd and Forrest* v. *G.S.W. Ry.*, 1912 S.C. (H.L.) 93; *Robinson* v. *National Bank*, 1916 S.C. (H.L.) 154.

[2] *Thin & Sinclair* v. *Arrol* (1896) 24 R. 198, 206; *Smart* v. *Wilkinson*, 1928 S.C. 383; *Smith* v. *Sim*, 1954 S.C. 357.

[3] *Langridge* v. *Levy* (1838) 2 M. & W. 519; *Burrows* v. *Rhodes* [1899] 1 Q.B. 816; cf. *Wilkinson* v. *Downton* [1897] 2 Q.B. 57; *Janvier* v. *Sweeney* [1919] 2 K.B. 316.

[4] *Morrisson* v. *Robertson*, 1908 S.C. 332; contrast *Phillips* v. *Brooks* [1919] 2 K.B. 243.

[5] *Hedley Byrne & Co.* v. *Heller and Partners* [1964] A.C. 465.

[6] See *Robinson* v. *National Bank*, 1916 S.C. (H.L.) 154; *Fortune* v. *Young*, 1918 S.C. 11; *Candler* v. *Crane, Christmas & Co.* [1951] 2 K.B. 164.

Innocent misrepresentation

Innocent misrepresentation covers all cases of misrepresentation which, though incorrect, was made neither fraudulently nor in breach of a duty to exercise care in making the representation but inaccurately though honestly. It gives no remedy *ex delicto* even though loss be sustained in consequence.[1]

Malicious falsehood

Malicious or injurious falsehood is a species of verbal injury,[2] sometimes regarded as the only species thereof,[3] and, despite the use of the word 'slander', the kinds of wrongs within the species have little connection with defamation.[4] The wrong consists in communicating maliciously written or oral falsehoods calculated in the ordinary course to produce and in fact producing actual damage. The pursuer must prove communication to persons other than the pursuer,[5] made with actual malice, i.e. *animo injuriandi*, spitefully or malevolently;[6] he must prove the statement to be false;[7] and he must prove actual damage to himself,[8] save that it is not now necessary to aver and prove actual damage if the words on which the action is founded are calculated to cause pecuniary damage to the pursuer.[9] The main cases of malicious falsehood are slander of title, which consists in maliciously making an unfounded imputation on the validity of the pursuer's title to property, heritable or moveable;[10] slander of property, where the defender has maliciously disparaged the

1 *Derry*, *supra*; *Robinson*, *supra*.

2 For the other species see Ch. 68, *supra*.

3 See Defamation Act, 1952, S. 14(b).

4 Slander proper (defamation) and slander of property seem to have been confused in such cases as *Broomfield*, *infra*; *Macrae*, *infra*; and *McLean*, *infra*.

5 *Wilts United Dairies* v. *Robinson* [1958] R.P.C. 94.

6 *White* v. *Mellin* [1895] A.C. 154; *Montgomerie* v. *Paterson* (1894) 11 R.P.C. 221, 237, 633; *Greers* v. *Pearman and Corder* (1922) 39 R.P.C. 406. This is different from defamation cases.

7 *Bruce* v. *Smith* (1898) 1 F. 327, 331; *Royal Baking Powder Co.* v. *Wright, Crossley & Co.* (1901) 18 R.P.C. 95, 99. This is the reverse of the rule in defamation cases.

8 *McLean* v. *Adam* (1888) 16 R. 175; *Ratcliffe* v. *Evans* [1892] 2 Q.B. 524; *Bruce*, *supra*; *Thomson* v. *Fifeshire Advertiser*, 1936 S.N. 56; *Joyce* v. *Motor Surveys* [1948] Ch. 252.

9 Defamation Act, 1952, S. 14(b).

10 *Philp* v. *Morton* (1816) Hume 865; *Yeo* v. *Wallace* (1867) 5 S.L.R. 253; *Montgomerie* v. *Paterson* (1894) 11 R.P.C. 221, 237, 633; *Harpers* v. *Greenwood & Batley* (1896) 4 S.L.T. 116; cf. *Serville* v. *Constance* [1954] 1 All E.R. 662; *Loudon* v. *Ryder* [1953] Ch. 423.

pursuer's property, heritable or moveable, to his loss;[1] slander of goods (or trade libel);[2] and slander of business.[3]

Passing-off

The action for passing-off is intended to protect a trader's commercial goodwill, and gives a right of action where one party has represented his goods or services as being those of the complainer, in a way calculated to deceive the public, to divert custom, and to cause the complainer loss of business.[4] Both parties must normally be engaged in a common field of business.[5] Neither fraudulent intent nor negligence need be established, though the absence of either may mitigate damages for past deception;[6] the question is the likelihood of deception of the public, including the less wary members thereof.[7] Passing-off may be committed in numerous ways, such as marketing goods described as those of another,[8] or another's goods as one's own,[9] imitating the 'get-up' of another's goods,[10] using another's trade-mark,[11] using the

[1] *Hamilton* v. *Arbuthnot* (1750) Mor. 13923; *Western Counties Manure Co.* v. *Chemical Manure Co.* (1874) L.R. 9 Ex. 218; *Ratcliffe* v. *Evans* [1892] 2 Q.B. 524; *White* v. *Mellin* [1895] A.C. 154; *Bruce* v. *Smith* (1898) 1 F. 327; cf. *Broomfield* v. *Greig* (1868) 6 M. 563; *Macrae* v. *Wicks* (1886) 13 R. 732; *Hubbuck* v. *Wilkinson* [1899] 1 Q.B. 86; *Royal Baking Powder Co.* v. *Wright, Crossley & Co.* (1900) 18 R.P.C. 95; *Greers, Ltd.* v. *Pearman and Corder, Ltd.* (1922) 39 R.P.C. 406.

[2] *Hamilton, supra*; *White, supra*; *London Ferro Concrete Co.* v. *Justicz* (1951) 68 R.P.C. 261; *Mentmore Mfg. Co.* v. *Famento* (1955) 72 R.P.C. 157; *Cellactite and British Uralite* v. *Robertson* [1957] C.L.Y. 1989; *Wilts United Dairies* v. *Robinson* [1958] R.P.C. 94.

[3] *Riding* v. *Smith* (1876) 1 Ex. D. 91; *Ratcliffe* v. *Evans* [1892] 2 Q.B. 524; *Baldon* v. *Shorter* [1933] Ch. 427; *Thompson* v. *Fifeshire Advertiser, Ltd.*, 1936 S.N. 56; *Joyce* v. *Motor Surveys, Ltd.* [1948] Ch. 252; cf. *Buchan* v. *Welsh* (1857) 20 D. 222; *Macrae* v. *Wicks* (1886) 13 R. 732.

[4] *Leather Cloth Co.* v. *American Leather Cloth Co.* (1865) 11 H.L.C. 523; *Reddaway* v. *Banham* [1896] A.C. 199; *Cellular Clothing Co.* v. *Maxton & Murray* (1899) 1 F. (H.L.) 29; *Bile Bean Mfg. Co.* v. *Davidson* (1906) 8 F. 1181; *Spalding* v. *Gamage* (1915) 32 R.P.C. 273; *Draper* v. *Trist* [1939] 3 All E.R. 513; *Haig* v. *Forth Blending Co.*, 1954 S.C. 35.

[5] *Dunlop Tyre Co.* v. *Dunlop Motor Co.*, 1907 S.C. (H.L.) 15; *S.U. and Nat. Ins. Co.* v. *Sc. Nat. Ins. Co.*, 1909 S.C. 318.

[6] *Johnston* v. *Orr Ewing* (1882) 7 App. Cas. 219; *Lever* v. *Goodwin* (1887) 36 Ch.D. 1; *G.N.S. Ry.* v. *Mann* (1892) 19 R. 1035; *Cellular Clothing Co., supra*; *Boord* v. *Bagots, Hutton & Co.* [1916] A.C. 382; *Haig, supra.*

[7] *Johnston, supra*; *Spalding, supra*; *Draper, supra.*

[8] *Wilkie* v. *McCulloch* (1823) 2 S. 413; *B.M.A.* v. *Marsh* (1931) 48 R.P.C. 565; *Vokes, Ltd.* v. *Evans* (1931) 49 R.P.C. 140; *Samuelson* v. *Producers' Distributing Co.* [1932] 1 Ch. 201.

[9] *Edinburgh Correspondent Newspaper* (1822) 1 S. 407; *Henderson* v. *Munro* (1905) 13 S.L.T. 57; *Hines* v. *Winnick* [1947] 2 All E.R. 517; *Marengo* v. *Daily Sketch* [1948] 1 All E.R. 406.

[10] *Massam* v. *Thorley's Cattle Food Co.* (1880) 14 Ch. D. 748; *Bayer* v. *Baird* (1898) 25 R. 1142; *Jamieson* v. *J.* (1898) 14 T.L.R. 160; *J. B. Williams Co.* v. *Bromley* (1909) 26 R.P.C. 765; *Haig, supra.*

[11] *Singer Machine Mfrs.* v. *Wilson* (1877) 3 App. Cas. 376; *Melrose-Drover, Ltd.* v. *Heddle* (1901) 4 F. 1120.

complainer's name,[1] using his trade name,[2] selling his sub-standard goods without describing them as such,[3] deceptive advertisements,[4] false attributions of manufacture[5] or of approbation.[6] The use by another of a person's business name is not necessarily passing off but may be so, if apparently intended to deceive.[7] The use by a person of a designation likely to indicate possession of a professional qualification or membership of a professional body may also be interdicted.[8]

Breach of confidence

The disclosure of information which should have been withheld may cause distress and also patrimonial loss.[9] The difficulty is commonly to determine whether a relationship of confidentiality exists, so as to make disclosure wrongful. Such a relationship exists between a professional adviser and his client,[10] and employer and employee,[11] but not between creditor and debtor.[12] A remedy is sometimes available on an alternative ground, such as infringement of copyright.[13] Confidence is important in relation to trade secrets and information, and the communication of knowledge on such matters may be restrained by express restric-

1 *Lee* v. *Haley* (1869) 5 Ch. App. 155; *Boswell* v. *Mathie* (1884) 11 R. 1072; *Dunlop Tyre Co., supra*; contrast *Levy* v. *Walker* (1879) 10 Ch. D. 436; *G.N.S. Ry.* v. *Mann* (1892) 19 R. 1035; *Cowan* v. *Millar* (1895) 22 R. 833; *Bayer, supra*; *Williamson* v. *Meikle*, 1909 S.C. 1272.

2 *Powell* v. *Birmingham Brewery Co.* [1896] 2 Ch. 54; *Reddaway* v. *Banham* [1896] A.C. 199; *Kinnell* v. *Ballantyne*, 1910 S.C. 246; contrast *Cellular Clothing Co.* v. *Maxton and Murray* (1899) 1 F. (H.L.) 29; *British Vacuum Cleaner Co.* v. *New Vacuum Cleaner Co.* [1907] 2 Ch. 312.

3 *Gillette Safety Razor Co.* v. *Franks* (1924) 40 T.L.R. 606; *Spalding* v. *Gamage* (1915) 84 L.J.Ch. 449; *Britains* v. *Morris* [1961] R.P.C. 217.

4 *Masson Seeley & Co., Ltd.* v. *Embossotype Mfg. Co.* (1924) 41 R.P.C. 160.

5 *Bass* v. *Laidlaw* (1886) 13 R. 898; *Thomson* v. *Robertson* (1888) 15 R. 880; *Thomson* v. *Dailly* (1897) 24 R. 1173; *Bass* v. *Laidlaw* (1908) 16 S.L.T. 660.

6 *McCulloch* v. *May* [1947] 2 All E.R. 845; *Sim* v. *Heinz* [1959] 1 All E.R. 547.

7 *Ainsworth* v. *Walmesley* (1866) L.R. 1 Eq. 518; *Williamson* v. *Meikle*, 1909 S.C. 1272; *Office Cleaning Services, Ltd.* v. *Westminster Window and General Cleaners, Ltd.* (1946) 63 R.P.C. 39.

8 *Socy. of Accountants in Edinburgh* v. *Corpn. of Accountants* (1893) 20 R. 750; *Corpn. of Accountants* v. *Socy. of Accountants in Edinburgh* (1903) 11 S.L.T. 424; cf. *Younghusband* v. *Luftig* [1949] 2 K.B. 354.

9 *Mushets* v. *Mackenzie* (1899) 1 F. 756.

10 *Whyte* v. *Smith* (1851) 14 D. 177; *Brown's Trs.* v. *Hay* (1898) 25 R. 1112; *A.B.* v. *C.D.* (1905) 7 F. 72.

11 *Kirchner* v. *Gruban* [1909] 1 Ch. 413; *Bents Brewery Co.* v. *Hogan* [1945] 2 All E.R. 570; cf. *Cameron* v. *Gibb* (1867) 3 S.L.R. 282; *Newman* v. *Kennedy* (1905) 12 S.L.T. 763.

12 *Fulton* v. *Stubbs* (1903) 5 F. 814.

13 Bell, *Comm.* I, 111; *Cadell and Davies* v. *Stewart* (1804) Mor. Appx. Literary Property, 4; *White* v. *Dickson* (1881) 8 R. 896.

tive covenant in a contract, or by principles of copyright, patent or related law, or it may be actionable as breach of confidence.[1]

Wrongful refusal to contract

Refusal to contract is actionable only in the cases of the common carrier and the innkeeper, who each owe a continuing duty to provide their services to any member of the public on demand. A common carrier may refuse goods only if they are not of a class which he professes to carry,[2] or are dangerous or insufficiently packed,[3] or have not been delivered in sufficient time for loading,[4] or are consigned to a place to which he does not ply,[5] or he has no room in his vehicle,[6] or his charges have not been paid or offered;[7] he may refuse a passenger if he is not in a fit state to be carried.[8] An unjustified refusal is actionable.[9] An innkeeper must receive all members of the travelling public and provide accommodation, food and drink unless the traveller gives no security, if requested, to pay his bill, is accompanied by an animal causing alarm to other guests, is not *in itinere*, refuses to pay the charges, or is an undesirable character, or if there is no available accommodation.[10] An unjustifiable refusal justifies damages.[11]

Interference with contract

It is actionable for one person knowingly and unjustifiably to induce breach of a lawful contract between two other persons, thereby causing loss to one of them.[12] The contract may be of any kind. The defender must at the time have known, or the circumstances be such that he reasonably should have known,[13] that in inducing the third party he was inducing him to act in

[1] *Saltman Eng. Co.* v. *Campbell Eng. Co.* (1948) 65 R.P.C. 203; *Stevenson, Jordan & Harrison* v. *Macdonald & Evans* [1952] 1 T.L.R. 101; *Peter Pan Mfg. Corpn.* v. *Corsets Silhouette, Ltd.* [1963] 3 All E.R. 402; *Cranleigh Eng. Co.* v. *Bryant* [1964] 3 All E.R. 289.

[2] *Johnson* v. *Midland Ry.* (1849) 4 Ex. 397.

[3] *Bamfield* v. *Goole* [1910] 2 K.B. 94.

[4] *Batson* v. *Donovan* (1820) 4 B. & Ald. 32.

[5] *Johnson, supra.*

[6] *Riley* v. *Horne* (1828) 5 Bing. 217.

[7] *Wyld* v. *Pickford* (1841) 8 M. & W. 443.

[8] Bell, *Prin.* §159; *Clark* v. *West Ham Corpn.* [1909] 2 K.B. 858.

[9] Bell, *Prin.* §159; *Garton* v. *Bristol and Exeter Ry.* (1861) 1 B. & S. 112.

[10] *Rothfield* v. *N.B. Ry.*, 1920 S.C. 805; cf. *Strathearn Hydropathic Co.* v. *Inland Revenue* (1881) 8 R. 798.

[11] *Ewing* v. *Campbells* (1877) 5 R. 230; *Constantine* v. *Imperial Hotels* [1944] K.B. 693.

[12] *Couper* v. *Macfarlane* (1879) 6 R. 683; *Crofter Co.* v. *Veitch*, 1942 S.C. (H.L.) 1; *Exchange Telegraph Co.* v. *Giulianotti*, 1959 S.C. 19.

[13] cf. *Thomson* v. *Deakin* [1952] Ch. 646, 687; *Cunard S.S. Co.* v. *Stacey* [1955] 1 Lloyd's Rep. 247.

breach of contract with the pursuer,[1] and that knowledge must be of the term of the contract broken by his interference.[2]

The defender will be liable if he intended to, and did, induce breach; he need not have intended to cause loss thereby,[3] nor need he have acted from malicious motive;[4] the breach may be of any term of the contract, and probably be of any importance.[5] The mode of interference is immaterial, and need not be illegal.[6] Some damage must have been caused, but it will readily be inferred.[7]

It is a question of fact whether the inducement of breach is justifiable or not; the contract breaker's self-interest is not justification,[8] but the avoidance of greater evil than mere breach of contract is.[9] A plea of justification may be rebutted by evidence of actual malice.[10] In the case of trade disputes, inducement to break a contract of employment may be protected by the Trade Disputes Act, 1906, S. 3.[11]

Enticement of employees

It is actionable knowingly to entice employees to desert their employment in breach of contract and to the injury of their employer,[12] but not to offer inducements which do not provoke their leaving in breach of contract.[13]

Harbouring another's employee

It is similarly actionable to take into and retain in one's employment a person already contractually bound to another,[14]

[1] *British Industrial Plastics* v. *Ferguson* [1940] 1 All E.R. 479.

[2] *British Homophone, Ltd.* v. *Kunz* [1935] All E.R. Rep. 627.

[3] *B.M.T.A.* v. *Salvadori* [1949] Ch. 556; *Thomson, supra*, 696.

[4] *Quinn* v. *Leathem* [1901] A.C 495, 510; *Glamorgan Coal Co.* v. *S. Wales Miners Fed.* [1905] A.C. 239; *Thompson, supra*, 676.

[5] *Thomson, supra*, 689.

[6] *Thomson, supra*.

[7] *B.M.T.A.* v. *Gray*, 1951 S.C. 586; cf. *Bents Brewery Co.* v. *Hogan* [1945] 2 All E.R. 570; *Jones Bros.* v. *Stevens* [1955] 1 Q.B. 275.

[8] *B.M.T.A.* v. *Gray*, 1951 S.C. 586, 600; cf. *Smithies* v. *N. Assoc. Operative Plasterers* [1909] 1 K.B. 310.

[9] *Glamorgan Coal Co.* v. *S. Wales Miners Fed.* [1905] A.C. 239, 252; *Brimelow* v. *Casson* [1924] 1 Ch. 302; *Findlay* v. *Blaylock*, 1937 S.C. 21; cf. *Muir* v. *Robbie* (1898) 6 S.L.T. 244; *Crofter Co.* v. *Veitch*, 1942 S.C. (H.L.) 1.

[10] *Findlay, supra*, 25.

[11] *Conway* v. *Wade* [1909] A.C. 506; the defence failed in *Rookes* v. *Barnard* [1964] A.C. 1129, and in *Stratford* v. *Lindley* [1965] A.C. 269. See also *Square Grip Reinforcement Co.* v. *MacDonald*, 1968 S.L.T. 65.

[12] *Dickson* v. *Taylor* (1816) 1 Mur. 141; *Kerr* v. *Duke of Roxburgh* (1822) 3 Mur. 126; *McGregor* v. *Mitchell* (1825) 4 S. 52; *Rutherford* v. *Boak* (1836) 14 S. 732; *Roxburgh* v. *McArthur* (1841) 3 D. 556; *Couper* v. *Macfarlane* (1879) 6 R. 683; *Belmont Laundry* v. *Aberdeen Steam Laundry Co.* (1898) 1 F. 45.

[13] *McManus* v. *Bowes* [1938] 1 K.B. 98.

[14] Bell, *Prin.* §2033; *Dickson* v. *Taylor* (1816) 1 Mur. 141; *McGregor* v. *Mitchell* (1825) 4 S. 52; *Rose St. Foundry* v. *Lewis*, 1917 S.C. 341.

whether or not the defender induced the employee to quit the pursuer's employment.[1]

Preventing man from obtaining employment

While it is not wrongful, by report or warning to a prospective employer, to prevent a man from obtaining employment, unless the report is slanderous,[2] it may be so if the report is malicious or there is an actionable conspiracy to frustrate him.[3] Where a 'closed shop' is common or universal a trade union might be liable if it unjustifiably refused to admit a man to membership or expelled him.[4]

Causing consequential loss of services

It is not actionable to cause one person consequential economic loss by injuring or killing another with whom he is in contractual relations and thereby causing him loss of the other's services.[5]

Conspiracy to injure

Conspiracy is the agreement of two or more persons to do an unlawful act, or to do a lawful act by unlawful means.[6] It is actionable only if the predominant motive or purpose of the agreement is to do harm,[7] and harm actually results,[7] or if unlawful means are used, such as to deceive or defraud or do violence or conduct a strike or lockout by means of prohibited conduct.[7] The pursuer must prove all the essential ingredients of the wrong.[8] There must be evidence of collaboration and combined action by two or more defenders.[9] The object of the combined action must have been unlawful in that its predominant purpose or motive was the infliction of injury on the complainer rather than serving the *bona fide* and legitimate interests of the combining parties,[9] or some unlawful means must have been

[1] *Rose St., supra,* 348, 350.

[2] *Keith* v. *Lauder* (1905) 8 F. 356; cf. *Mushets* v. *Mackenzie* (1899) 1 F. 756.

[3] cf. *Mackenzie* v. *Iron Trades Ins. Assoc.*, 1910 S.C. 79; *Rookes* v. *Barnard* [1964] A.C. 1129.

[4] *Bonsor* v. *Musicians' Union* [1956] A.C. 104; cf. *Hewitt* v. *Edinburgh Lathsplitters* (1906) 14 S.L.T. 489.

[5] *Allan* v. *Barclay* (1864) 2 M. 873; *Reavis* v. *Clan Line,* 1925 S.C. 725; *Quinn* v. *Greenock Tramways Co.*, 1926 S.C. 544; *Young* v. *Ormiston,* 1936 S.L.T. 79; *Gibson* v. *Glasgow Corpn.*, 1963 S.L.T. (Notes) 16; cf. *Burgess* v. *Florence Nightingale Hospital* [1955] 1 Q.B. 349.

[6] *Mackenzie* v. *Iron Trades Ins. Assoc.*, 1910 S.C. 79; *Crofter Co.* v. *Veitch,* 1942 S.C. (H.L.) 1, 22.

[7] *Crofter Co., supra.*

[8] *Stratford* v. *Lindley* [1965] A.C. 269.

[9] *Crofter Co., supra.* Malevolence by itself does not make combination actionable.

employed, such as fraud or violence,[1] and actual damage must have resulted by way of loss of business, loss of profit, exclusion from a market or from employment.[2] Thus actions have succeeded where the combination was to hiss an actor off the stage,[3] to compel an employer to dismiss a non-union man,[4] to force a union member to pay a debt to the union,[5] to secure the dismissal of a non-union man,[6] to force an employer to negotiate with a union;[7] they have failed where the combination was to undercut a trade rival,[8] to compel salesmen to refuse to sell to certain customers,[9] to compel an employer to dismiss a non-union man,[10] to compel a retailer to sell at list price,[11] to compel an employee to join the predominant union,[12] to crush a retailer who opposed the wholesalers' policy,[13] and to compel a rival employer to give employees better wages.[14]

Intimidation

It is actionable for one person to cause harm or loss to another by causing him by threats to act to his detriment, or by causing a third party by threats to act to the complainer's detriment. The threats must not be of conduct which is legal, such as to report crime, or to do diligence on a decree. They may be of any unpleasant consequences,[15] and must produce reasonable fear, such as affects even a person of ordinary firmness.[16] The complainer must not only have been threatened but have been coerced and have complied.[17] In many cases the detrimental conduct is a contract or compromise of a dispute;[18] in others it is loss of employment. The Trade Disputes Act, 1906, S. 3, renders it not actionable for

1 *Crofter Co.*, *supra*, 23.
2 *Rookes* v. *Barnard* [1964] A.C. 1129.
3 *Gregory* v. *Duke of Brunswick* (1844) 6 M. & G. 953.
4 *Quinn* v. *Leathem* [1901] A.C. 495.
5 *Gibban* v. *Nat. Amalg. Labourers' Union* [1903] 2 K.B. 600.
6 *Rookes* v. *Barnard* [1964] A.C. 1129.
7 *Stratford* v. *Lindley* [1965] A.C. 269.
8 *Mogul S.S. Co.* v. *McGregor, Gow & Co.* [1892] A.C. 25.
9 *S.C.W.S.* v. *Glasgow Fleshers Assocn.* (1898) 5 S.L.T. 263.
10 *White* v. *Riley* [1921] 1 Ch. 1.
11 *Ware and de Freville* v. *M.T.A.* [1921] 3 K.B. 40.
12 *Reynolds* v. *Shipping Fedn.* [1924] 1 Ch. 28.
13 *Sorrell* v. *Smith* [1925] A.C. 700.
14 *Crofter Co.* v. *Veitch*, 1942 S.C. (H.L.) 1.
15 *Stuart* v. *Whitefoord* (1677) Mor. 16489; *Wiseman* v. *Logie* (1700) Mor. 16505; *Gelot* v. *Stewart* (1871) 9 M. 957; *Gow* v. *Henry* (1899) 2 F. 48; cf. *Dumfriesshire Educ. Authy.* v. *Wright*, 1926 S.L.T. 217.
16 Stair I, 9, 8; cf. *Priestnell* v. *Hutcheson* (1857) 19 D. 495.
17 *Rookes* v. *Barnard* [1964] A.C. 1129; *Stratford* v. *Lindley* [1965] A.C. 269.
18 cf. *McIntosh* v. *Chalmers* (1883) 11 R. 8.

one party, in contemplation or furtherance of a trade dispute, to induce some other person to break his contract of employment, nor to threaten the employer that he will induce some other person to break his contract of employment. But this does not protect a person who breaks or threatens to break his own contract,[1] nor does it apply to disputes between one union and another.[2] The Trade Disputes Act, 1965, provides that an act done in contemplation or furtherance of a trade dispute is not actionable on the ground only that it consists in his threatening (a) that a contract of employment (whether one to which he is a party or not) will be broken, or (b) that he will induce another to break a contract of employment to which that other is a party.

Statutory delicts connected with trade

The Consumer Protection Act, 1961, S. 3 makes it a statutory delict to contravene or fail to comply with any obligation imposed by that Act with regard to safety requirements of goods sold. The Resale Prices Act, 1964, S. 4, makes civilly actionable non-compliance with the provisions of that Act which make it generally unlawful to include in a contract a term or condition providing for minimum resale prices for the goods.

[1] *Rookes, supra,* explained in *Stratford, supra.*
[2] *Stratford, supra.*

CHAPTER 70

WRONGS IN RESPECT OF HERITABLE PROPERTY

Depriving another of title to land

FEW questions arise as actions *ex delicto* from alleged wrongful deprivation of title to land.[1]

Ejection and intrusion

Ejection is the wrong of unwarrantably entering on lands and forcibly casting out the person in actual possession, or of remaining in possession and refusing to remove when any title of occupancy has expired or been withdrawn.[2] Intrusion is entry without violence, *clam vel precario*, when the possessor holds *animo*.[3] In either case the person entitled to possession is entitled to bring an action of summary ejection,[4] and to claim violent profits, and damages for his wrongful ejection;[5] he need aver only possession or title to possess, unless the ejector claims heritable title.[6] Violent profits are penal damages due by an intruder without colour of law.[7] They are double the rent of houses within burghs,[8] and in rural subjects are the greatest profit the pursuer could have made if himself in possession.[9] They include all damage, which the subjects may receive at the defender's hands.[10] Caution for violent profits may be required as a condition of defending the action.[11] They are not due if and so

[1] cf. *Mackie* v. *M.* (1896) 4 S.L.T. 3; *Stobie* v. *Smith*, 1921 S.C. 894; *Rodgers* v. *Fawdry*, 1950 S.C. 483.

[2] cf. *Houldsworth* v. *Brand's Trs.* (1870) 3 R. 304; *Hendry* v. *Walker*, 1926 S.L.T. 678; *Mather* v. *Alexander*, 1926 S.C. 139; *Price* v. *Watson*, 1951 S.C. 359.

[3] Stair I, 9, 25; IV, 28, 1; Bankt. IV, 24, 57; Ersk. IV, 1, 15.

[4] *Hally* v. *Lang* (1867) 5 M. 951, 954.

[5] *Macdonald* v. *Chisholm* (1860) 22 D. 1075.

[6] Ersk. IV, 1, 47; *Ogilvie* v. *Restalrig* (1541) Mor. 14730; *Montgomery* v. *Hamilton* (1548) Mor. 14731; *Gadzeard* v. *Sheriff of Ayr* (1781) Mor. 14732; *Macdonald* v. *Chisholm* (1860) 22 D. 1075.

[7] Ersk. II, 6, 54; *Houldsworth*, *supra*, 310.

[8] Stair I, 9, 27; II, 9, 44; IV, 29, 3; Bankt. I, 10, 133, 147; Ersk. II, 6, 54; Bell, *Prin.* §1268 (c); *Weddell* v. *Buchan* (1611) Mor. 16460.

[9] Stair II, 9, 44; Bankt. I, 10, 133; Ersk. II, 6, 54; *Gardner* v. *Beresford's Trs.* (1877) 4 R. 1091.

[10] *Gardner*, *supra*.

[11] Ejection Caution Act, 1594, c. 217; Stair. IV, 28, 8; *Gardner*, *supra*; cf. *Inglis's Trs.* v. *Macpherson*, 1910 S.C. 46.

long as the defender possessed in good faith,[1] nor so long as a genuine issue of title to possess is being litigated.[2]

Trespass

Trespass is any temporary intrusion into or entry on the lands of another without his permission or legal justification.[3] Under certain statutes[4] trespass is criminal, and criminal proceedings may exclude a civil remedy.[5] It may be committed by entering on another's land on foot, on animal or in a vehicle,[6] by letting a dog into the land,[7] exercising animals on it,[8] pasturing cattle on it,[9] or otherwise. Since an occupier of land possesses it *a caelo usque ad centrum* he can object to any trespass on the air-space above his property, such as overhanging branches of a tree,[10] wires crossing above his land,[11] signs projecting over his land[12] or shooting over his land.[13] The flight of aircraft over land at a reasonable height is neither trespass nor nuisance.[14]

Damages are not recoverable for bare trespass, particularly if innocent, but only if some actual damage is done thereby,[15] or there is also assault on[16] or insult to[17] the landowner. Interdict is competent only if there is apprehension of repeated or continuing trespass,[18] and not if there were no intention to claim a

[1] *Queensberry's Exors.* v. *Symington* (1824) 2 Sh. App. 43, 80; *Carnegie* v. *Scott* (1830) 4 W. & Sh. 431; *Houldsworth, supra.*

[2] *Houldsworth, supra.*

[3] *Geils* v. *Thompson* (1872) 10 M. 327; *Stirling Craufurd* v. *C.N. Trs.* (1881) 8 R. 826; cf. *McAdam* v. *Laurie* (1876) 3 R. (J.) 20.

[4] Trespass (Sc.) Act, 1865, S. 3 (cf. *Paterson* v. *Robertson,* 1944 J.C. 166); Railway Regulation Acts 1840, S. 16; 1868, S. 23; 1871, S. 14; Night Poaching Act, 1828, Ss. 1, 9; Game (Sc.) Act, 1832, Ss. 1, 2; Protection of Birds Act, 1954, S. 15(2); Salmon and Freshwater Fisheries (Protection) (Sc.) Act, 1951.

[5] Game (Sc.) Act, 1832, S. 16.

[6] *Matheson* v. *Stewart* (1872) 10 M. 704; *Perth General Stn. Committee* v. *Ross* (1896) 24 R. (H.L.) 44.

[7] *Stoddart* v. *Stevenson* (1880) 7 R. (J.) 11; *Wood* v. *Collins* (1890) 17 R. (J.) 55.

[8] *Inverurie Mags.* v. *Sorrie,* 1956 S.C. 175.

[9] *Macleod* v. *Davidson* (1886) 14 R. 92; *Robertson* v. *Wright* (1885) 13 R. 174; cf. *Winans* v. *Macrae* (1885) 12 R. 1051.

[10] *Halkerston* v. *Wedderburn* (1781) Mor. 10495.

[11] *Wandsworth Board of Works* v. *United Telephone Co.* (1884) 13 Q.B.D. 904; *Finchley Electric Light Co.* v. *Finchley U.D.C.* [1903] 1 Ch. 437.

[12] *Kelsen* v. *Imperial Tobacco Co.* [1957] 2 Q.B. 334.

[13] *Clifton* v. *Viscount Bury* (1887) 4 T.L.R. 8.

[14] Civil Aviation Act, 1949, S. 10.

[15] *Hill* v. *Merricks* (1813) Hume 397; *Baird* v. *Thomson* (1825) 3 S. 448; *Graham* v. *Duke of Hamilton* (1868) 6 M. 905; *L.A.* v. *Glengarnock Iron Co.,* 1909 1 S.L.T. 15.

[16] *Grahame* v. *Mackenzie* (1810) Hume 641.

[17] *Cook* v. *Neville* (1798) Hume 602.

[18] *Hay's Trs.* v. *Young* (1877) 4 R. 398; *Steuart* v. *Stephen* (1877) 4 R. 893; *Macleod* v. *Davidson* (1886) 14 R. 92; *Merryton Coal Co.* v. *Anderson* (1890) 18 R. 203.

right,[1] if the trespass were done in good faith,[2] or if there is no loss or apprehension of loss.[3]

A trespasser may be conducted off the premises, so long as no greater force is used than is reasonably necessary in the circumstances,[4] as where the trespasser threatens, or offers violence to, or causes reasonable apprehension of violence to, the landowner.[5]

Though animals may graze at the roadside[6] they may not be pastured on another's lands, though interdict against their doing so has been refused where the trespass was trivial[7] or reasonable precautions had not been taken to prevent trespass.[8] A claim for damage done by their trespass is competent, on proof of failure to take reasonable care to keep them in and of damage done; there is probably no liability for bare trespass,[9] particularly by small animals which do no appreciable damage.[10]

Under the Winter Herding Act, 1686, possessors of lands[11] must keep their animals herded the whole year so that they do not eat or destroy their neighbours' ground, wood, hedges, or planting. Contravention infers liability for a penalty of half a mark per beast in addition to damage done[12] to grass[13] or planting. Trespassing animals may be detained until the penalty, damages,[14] and expense of keeping them are paid. The penalty is due though it is not alleged that damage has been done by the trespass.[15] They may not be detained after payment or tender of the penalty and expense of keeping the poinded animals, nor in security of penalties for other cattle previously poinded, which have escaped or been restored.[16]

Trespass is negatived by licence, such as permission to shoot over lands,[17] and may be legally justifiable, as by a warrant to

1 *Steuart* v. *Stephen* (1877) 4 R. 873; *Inverurie Mags.* v. *Sorrie*, 1956 S.C. 175.

2 *Hay's Trs.*, *supra*; *Macleod*, *supra*.

3 *Winans* v. *Macrae* (1885) 12 R. 1051.

4 *Bell* v. *Shand* (1870) 7 S.L.R. 267; *Wood* v. *N.B. Ry.* (1899) 2 F. 1; *MacLure* v. *M.*, 1911 S.C. 200; *Mather* v. *Alexander*, 1926 S.C. 139.

5 *Aitchison* v. *Thorburn* (1870) 7 S.L.R. 347.

6 Stair II, 1, 7.

7 *Winans* v. *Macrae* (1885) 12 R. 1051.

8 *Robertson* v. *Wright* (1885) 13 R. 174.

9 *Robertson* v. *Wright* (1885) 2 Sh. Ct. Rep. 60, sequel to 13 R. 174.

10 *Sanders* v. *Teape* (1885) All E.R. Rep. 1016.

11 As defined therein; see also *Hill* v. *Burnett* (1954) 70 Sh. Ct. Rep. 328.

12 cf. *Shaw and Mackenzie* v. *Ewart*, 2 Mar. 1809, F.C.

13 Including corn: *Govan* v. *Lang* (1794) Mor. 10499; *Loch* v. *Tweedie* (1799) Mor. 10501.

14 Bankt. IV, 41, 16; Ersk. III, 6, 28.

15 *Shaw and Mackenzie*, *supra*; *Leith* v. *Ross* (1896) 11 Sh. Ct. Rep. 110; *Mitchell* v. *McMillan* (1910) 25 Sh. Ct. Rep. 240.

16 *Fraser* v. *Smith* (1899) 1 F. 487.

17 *I.R.C.* v. *Anderson*, 1922 S.C. 284.

search premises,[1] statutory authority to enter premises to see if the law is being complied with,[2] or the common law authority of a constable to enter premises where crime is suspected,[3] or by necessity,[4] such as to effect rescue,[5] recover straying animals,[6] or kill foxes.[7] But trespass is not justified by a wrongful attempt to assert a right.[8]

Encroachment

Encroachment is the permanent usurpation by another of some portion of a man's lands, which gives him a right to seek interdict against the encroachment and to claim damages so far as the other's operations have caused him actual loss or harm.[9]

Withdrawal of or interference with support

Land is entitled to support from adjacent and subjacent land, and a landowner may seek interdict against the operations of another threatening the stability of his land, and damages for loss or harm caused him by interference with the support of his land.[10]

Support of buildings by buildings

Where two buildings have a common gable, each proprietor must maintain and repair his side of the wall as an adequate gable for the other building, and each has a servitude right of support against the other, so that neither owner can demolish without regard to the support of the other's building.[11]

In the case of tenement property the owners of different floors have a common interest in the maintenance of the gables, walls, and other common parts for the benefit of all, and this includes a servitude right of support on the lower flats for the benefit of the upper flats.[12] The duty of support is to take reasonable care, to inspect periodically and to repair in case of necessity.[13]

1 *Stewart* v. *Roach*, 1950 S.C. 318.
2 e.g. factory inspectors (Factories Act, 1961, S. 146).
3 *Shepherd* v. *Menzies* (1900) 2 F. 443; *Southern Bowling Club, Ltd.* v. *Ross* (1902) 4 F. 405.
5 Bell, *Prin.* §956; Hume, *Lect.* III, 206.
5 *Carter* v. *Thomas* [1893] 1 Q.B. 673; *Cope* v. *Sharpe* [1912] 1 K.B. 496.
6 *Morton* v. *McMillan* (1893) 1 S.L.T. 92.
7 *Colquhoun* v. *Buchanan* (1785) Mor. 4997.
8 *Geils* v. *Thompson* (1872) 10 M. 327; *Matheson* v. *Stewart* (1872) 10 M. 704; *Merry & Cuninghame* v. *Aitken* (1895) 22 R. 247; cf. *Merryton Coal Co.* v. *Anderson* (1890) 18 R. 203.
9 See further, Ch. 79, *infra*.
10 See further, Ch. 79, *infra*.
11 Stair II, 7, 6; Ersk. II, 9, 8; Bell, *Prin.* §1003.
12 *Hall* v. *Corbet* (1698) Mor. 12775; *Gray* v. *Greig* (1825) 4 S. 104; *Murray* v. *Gullan* (1825) 3 S. 639; *Brown* v. *Boyd* (1841) 3 D. 1205.
13 *Thomson* v. *St. Cuthbert's Coop. Assocn.*, 1958 S.C. 380.

Nuisance

A nuisance is a use of land conflicting with the maxim *sic utere tuo ut alienum non laedas*, and divisible into three overlapping categories, common law nuisances, statutory nuisances, and conventional nuisances.[1] A nuisance need not be illegal, nor is any unusual use of land necessarily a nuisance; conversely the most ordinary use of land may be a nuisance. Nuisance is a wrong of strict liability, independent both of intention and of negligence.[2] It may be a wrong to a man in his person, affecting his health or safety,[3] or to his property and his enjoyment thereof.[4]

Common law nuisance

Nuisance is an infringement by a neighbour of the natural rights of enjoyment and use of land.[4] Any conduct which occasions serious disturbance or substantial inconvenience to a neighbour or material damage to his property is a nuisance.[5] To amount to nuisance the conduct complained of must be repeated or continuing, not isolated,[6] and must cause material, not trivial or negligible, inconvenience, discomfort or harm.[7] Whether conduct amounts to nuisance is largely a question of neighbourhood, circumstances, and degree.[8] Conduct may be less objectionable if it occurs in a locality suitable for or long appropriated to the kind of use productive of the nuisance.[9] But suitability of locality confers no liberty to perpetrate a nuisance.[10]

A nuisance must be the work of man, by act or neglect,[11] not the creation of nature.[12] It may consist in keeping noisy animals,[13]

[1] cf. Bell, *Prin.* §973, note (a); *Slater* v. *McLellan*, 1924 S.C. 854, 858.

[2] *Hart* v. *Taylor* (1827) 4 Mur. 307, 313; *Duke of Buccleuch* v. *Cowan* (1866) 5 M. 214, 216; *Shotts Iron Co.* v. *Inglis* (1882) 9 R. (H.L.) 78; *Giblin* v. *Lanarkshire C.C.*, 1927 S.L.T. 563.

[3] *Fergusson* v. *Pollok* (1901) 3 F. 1140.

[4] Hume, *Lect.* III, 214; Bell, *Prin.* §974.

[5] *Manson* v. *Forrest* (1887) 14 R. 802; *Fleming* v. *Hislop* (1886) 13 R. (H.L.) 43; *Watt* v. *Jamieson*, 1954 S.C. 56.

[6] *Watt, supra.*

[7] *Watt, supra.*

[8] *Swan* v. *Haliburton* (1830) 8 S. 637; *Donald* v. *Humphrey* (1839) 1 D. 1184; *Robertson* v. *Stewarts* (1872) 11 M. 189; *Inglis* v. *Shotts Iron Co.* (1881) 8 R. 1006; *Manson* v. *Forrest* (1887) 14 R. 802.

[9] *Charity* v. *Riddle*, 5 July 1808, F.C.; *Colville* v. *Middleton*, 28 May 1817, F.C.; *St. Helens Smelting Co.* v. *Tipping* (1865) 11 H.L. Cas. 642; *Cooper and Wood* v. *N.B. Ry.* (1863) 1 M. 499; *Anderson* v. *Aberdeen Hall Co.* (1879) 6 R. 901; *Robertson* v. *Thomas* (1887) 14 R. 822; *Maguire* v. *McNeil*, 1922 S.C. 174, 185.

[10] *St. Helens Co., supra*; *Fraser's Trs.* v. *Cran* (1877) 4 R. 795; *McEwan* v. *Steedman & McAlister*, 1912 S.C. 156; *Maguire, supra.*

[11] *Farrer* v. *Nelson* (1885) 15 Q.B.D. 258.

[12] *Giles* v. *Walker* (1890) 24 Q.B.D. 656; *Davey* v. *Harrow Corpn.* [1957] 2 All E.R. 305; cf. *Stearn* v. *Prentice* [1919] 1 K.B. 394.

[13] *Broder* v. *Saillard* (1876) 2 Ch. D. 692; *Ireland* v. *Smith* (1895) 3 S.L.T. 180; *Spider's Web* v. *Marchant* [1961] C.L.Y. 6359.

or smelly animals,[1] or creatures which prey on a neighbour's crops,[2] or to cause or permit unusual or excessive noise,[3] or vibration,[4] pollution of air by smoke,[5] heat and fumes,[6] smells,[7] sewage[8] or infectious germs,[9] or pollution of running water,[10] or of mill-lades,[11] canals,[12] or dry ditches.[13]

It may be a nuisance to permit to happen on the highway what causes material inconvenience to adjacent property,[14] or to allow to happen adjacent to the highway what interferes with the safe public use thereof,[15] or to do or permit on the highway what endangers other road users in their use thereof.[16] The playing of games may be a nuisance if there is substantial interference with or material danger to passers-by outside the ground.[17] Miscellaneous kinds of conduct amounting to nuisance include using a thatched house as a smithy,[18] keeping a brothel,[19] erecting a

[1] *Rapier* v. *London Tramways Co.* [1893] 2 Ch. 588; *Ireland, supra.*

[2] cf. *Easton* v. *Longlands* (1832) 10 S. 542; *Dumfries Waterworks Commrs.* v. *McCulloch* (1874) 1 R. 975.

[3] *Kinloch* v. *Robertson* (1756) Mor. 13163; *Robertson* v. *Campbell*, 2 Mar. 1802, F.C.; *Maguire, supra*; *Fergusson* v. *McCulloch*, 1953 S.L.T. (Sh. Ct) 113. As to aircraft see Civil Aviation Act, 1949, S. 40.

[4] *Johnston* v. *Constable* (1841) 3 D. 1263; *McEwan* v. *Steedman & McAlister*, 1912 S.C. 156; *Hoare* v. *McAlpine* [1923] 1 Ch. 167; *Maguire, supra.*

[5] *Stewart* v. *Thomson*, 15 Dec. 1807, F.C.; *Laing* v. *Muirhead* (1822) 2 S. 73; See also Clean Air Act, 1956, S. 1.

[6] *Wilson* v. *Brydone* (1877) 14 S.L.R. 667; *Wilson* v. *Gibb* (1903) 10 S.L.T. 293.

[7] *Scott* v. *Leith Commrs.* (1835) 13 S. 646; *Swinton* v. *Pedie* (1839) McL. & R. 1018; *Arnot* v. *Brown* (1852) 15 D. (H.L.) 10; *Robertson* v. *Stewarts* (1872) 11 M. 189; *Chalmers* v. *Dixon* (1876) 3 R. 461; *Harvie* v. *Robertson* (1903) 5 F. 338.

[8] *Mackay* v. *Greenhill* (1858) 20 D. 1251; *Fraser's Trs.* v. *Cran* (1877) 4 R. 794.

[9] *Mutter* v. *Fyfe* (1848) 11 D. 303; *Fleet* v. *Metropolitan Asylum Bd.* (1886) 2 T.L.R. 361.

[10] *Millar* v. *Marshall* (1828) 5 Mur. 28; *Montgomerie* v. *Buchanan's Trs.* (1853) 15 D. 853; *Duke of Buccleuch* v. *Cowan* (1866) 5 M. 214; *Rigby & Beardmore* v. *Downie* (1872) 10 M. 568; *Dodd* v. *Hilson* (1874) 1 R. 527; *Robertson* v. *Stewarts* (1872) 11 M. 189; *Caledonian Ry.* v. *Baird* (1876) 3 R. 839; *McGavin* v. *McIntyre* (1890) 17 R. 818; *Fleming* v. *Gemmill*, 1908 S.C. 340. See also Water (Sc.) Act, 1946, Ss. 61, 64; Rivers (Prevention of Pollution) (Sc.) Act, 1951, S. 22; Border Rivers (Prevention of Pollution) Act, 1951; *Gavin* v. *Ayrshire C.C.*, 1950 S.C. 197.

[11] *Eyre* v. *Earl of Moray* (1827) 5 S. 912.

[12] *Caledonian Ry., supra.*

[13] *Scott* v. *S.* (1881) 8 R. 851.

[14] *Slater* v. *McLellan*, 1924 S.C. 854.

[15] *Fergusson* v. *Pollok* (1901) 3 F. 1140; *Holling* v. *Yorkshire Traction Co.* [1948] 2 All E.R. 662; *Rollingson* v. *Kerr, Stammers & Co.* [1958] C.L.Y. 2427.

[16] *Ogston* v. *Aberdeen Tramways Co.* (1896) 24 R. (H.L.) 8; *Hay* v. *Leslie* (1896) 4 S.L.T. 124; *Parish* v. *Judd* [1960] 3 All E.R. 33; cf. *Reilly* v. *Greenfield Brick Co.*, 1909 S.C. 1328.

[17] *Castle* v. *St. Augustine's Links* (1922) 38 T.L.R. 615; *McLeod* v. *St. Andrews Mags.*, 1924 S.C. 960; *Bolton* v. *Stone* [1951] A.C. 850.

[18] *Vary* v. *Thomson*, 2 July 1805, F.C.

[19] Bell, *Prin.* §974; *Thompson-Schwab* v. *Costaki* [1956] 1 All E.R. 652.

church in the back-green of a house,[1] having a mill-lade adjacent to a public road,[2] and discharging vapour harmful to stonework into a vent.[3]

Plea of coming to the nuisance

It is no defence that the complainer is obliged to put up with a nuisance because he acquired his property after the nuisance had been commenced,[4] even if the nuisance had previously been long continued without objection.

Statutory authority

Conduct is not actionable as nuisance if done under statutory authority, if the statute has authorised the nuisance, or the doing of the thing even if it amounts to a nuisance.[5] But statutory authority does not protect if it merely authorized something which could have been done in a way which does not necessarily cause a nuisance.[6]

Prescription

A complainer's right to object to a nuisance is barred by twenty[7] (formerly forty[8]) years failure to complain, and to that extent a right to continue to commit nuisance may be acquired. The period runs from the date when the complainer might first have taken action; it matters not that complaint has only become worth making by reason of change of use of the premises.[9] Prescription may bar one complainer and not another, and if it applies, it will not bar complaint about an extension or alteration or intensification of the nuisance.[10]

Acquiescence in a nuisance by an adjacent proprietor for less than the prescriptive period gives no right to continue it, unless

1 *Cuming* v. *Stewart* (1850) 12 D. 1258.

2 *Stevenson* v. *Hawick Mags.* (1871) 9 M. 753; *Lang* v. *Bruce* (1873) 11 M. 377.

3 *Watt* v. *Jamieson*, 1954 S.C. 56.

4 *Chalmers* v. *Dixon* (1876) 3 R. 461; *Fleming* v. *Hislop* (1886) 13 R. (H.L.) 43.

5 *Hammersmith Ry.* v. *Brand* (1869) L.R. 4 H.L. 171; *City of Glasgow Union Ry.* v. *Hunter* (1870) 8 M. 156; *L.B. & S.C. Ry.* v. *Truman* (1885) 11 App. Cas. 45; *Quebec Ry.* v. *Vandry* [1920] A.C. 662.

6 *Metropolitan Asylum Bd.* v. *Hill* (1881) 6 App. Cas. 193; *L.A.* v. *N.B. Ry.* (1894) 2 S.L.T. 71; *A.G.* v. *Nottingham Corpn.* [1904] 1 Ch. 673; *Manchester Corpn.* v. *Farnworth* [1930] A.C. 171; *Edgington* v. *Swindon Corpn.* [1939] 1 K.B. 86; *East Suffolk Catchment Bd.* v. *Kent* [1941] A.C. 74; *Marriage* v. *East Norfolk Catchment Bd.* [1950] 1 K.B. 284.

7 Conveyancing (Sc.) Acts, 1924, S. 17 and 1938, S. 4.

8 *Collins* v. *Hamilton* (1837) 15 S. 902; *Robertson* v. *Stewart* (1872) 11 M. 198; *Rigby* v. *Downie* (1872) 10 M. 568; *Fraser's Trs.* v. *Cran* (1877) 4 R. 795; *Midlothian C.C.* v. *Pumpherston Oil Co.* (1904) 6 F. 387.

9 *Harvie* v. *Robertson* (1903) 5 F. 338.

10 *Rigby*, *supra*; *MacIntyre* v. *MacGavin* (1893) 20 R. (H.L.) 49.

there has been some act expressing or implying sanction of it.[1] Acquiescence may bar objection if the potential objector has permitted the other to undertake operations difficult or impossible to undo,[2] or has approbated the operations.[3]

Licence

The licence to use premises in a particular way[4] does not imply permission to create a nuisance thereby.[5]

Public interest

The plea of public interest or public benefit is also no defence to nuisance,[6] but in considering whether to grant or withhold interdict against nuisance, the court may consider the public interest, and suspend the operation of interdict if its immediate operation would cause public inconvenience.[7]

Amelioration

The court may refuse interdict to enable the defender to take remedial action,[8] or if undertakings are given,[9] grant merely interim interdict pending a report.[10]

Statutory nuisances

Numerous statutes provide for the stopping of conduct declared thereby to be a nuisance, frequently making the commission criminally punishable, but not necessarily thereby excluding civil remedies at the suit of aggrieved persons.[11]

[1] *Gowan* v. *Kinnaird* (1865) 4 M. 236; *Duke of Buccleuch* v. *Cowan* (1866) 4 M. 475; *Houldsworth* v. *Wishaw Mags.* (1887) 14 R. 920; cf. Bell, *Prin.* §946; *Bargaddie Coal Co.* v. *Wark* (1859) 3 Macq. 480; *Hill* v. *Dixon* (1850) 12 D. 811.

[2] *Abercorn* v. *Langmuir*, 20 May 1820, F.C.; *Stirling* v. *Haldane* (1829) 8 S. 131; *Bargaddie Coal Co.* v. *Wark* (1859) 3 Macq. 480; *Hill* v. *Wood* (1863) 1 M. 360; *Muirhead* v. *Glasgow Highland Socy.* (1864) 2 M. 420; *Bicket* v. *Morris* (1866) 4 M. (H.L.) 49.

[3] *Aytoun* v. *Douglas* (1800) Mor. Appx. Property, No. 5; *Aytoun* v. *Melville*, ibid., No. 6; *Hart* v. *Taylor* (1827) 4 Mur. 307.

[4] e.g. as public-house or club (Licensing (Sc.) Act, 1959, Ss. 36, 174), or as betting shop (Betting and Gaming Act, 1960, S. 5).

[5] *Pentland* v. *Henderson* (1855) 17 D. 542.

[6] *Duke of Buccleuch* v. *Cowan* (1866) 5 M. 214; *Fraser's Trs.* v. *Cran* (1879) 6 R. 452.

[7] *Inglis* v. *Shotts Iron Co.* (1881) 8 R. 1006, 1021; *Clippens Oil Co.* v. *Edinburgh & District Water Trs.* (1897) 25 R. 370, 383; *Ben Nevis Distillery* v. *British Aluminium Co.*, 1948 S.C. 592.

[8] *Fleming* v. *Gemmill*, 1908 S.C. 340, 349; *McEwan* v. *Steedman & McAlister*, 1912 S.C. 156; 1913 S.C. 761.

[9] *Manson* v. *Forrest* (1887) 14 R. 802.

[10] *Duke of Buccleuch* v. *Brown* (1873) 1 R. 85, 1111; *Fraser's Trs.* v. *Cran* (1877) 4 R. 794; see also *Countess of Seafield* v. *Kemp* (1899) 1 F. 402.

[11] e.g. Public Health (Sc.) Act, 1897, Ss. 16, 17, and 171.

Conventional nuisances

Feu contracts and similar deeds may impose restrictions on the use of lands and declare that certain uses shall be deemed nuisances.[1] Infringement of such a restriction does not necessarily give an aggrieved adjacent proprietor an action, but only if he has a *jus quaesitum tertio* to enforce the restriction.[2]

Escape of danger from land

A person who has created or accumulated on his land something potentially dangerous which was not naturally there is strictly liable to keep it under control, and liable if it escapes and does harm to his neighbour's land, unless he can rely on certain limited defences.[3] Liability is conditional on the creation of a *novum opus* which has innovated on the natural state of things[4] and introduced a new hazard, and on its having escaped and caused resultant harm.

This liability exists in cases of accumulations of water which escape and do harm,[5] the escape of fire from heather burning,[6] escape of smoke and fumes,[7] leaking acid,[8] noise and vibration from explosions.[9] The harm done by the escape may be to heritage,[10] or moveable property,[11] and may possibly consist in personal injuries.[12]

1 Bell, *Prin.* §974; *Porteous* v. *Grieve* (1839) 1 D. 561; *Mutter* v. *Fyfe* (1848) 11 D. 303; *Frame* v. *Cameron* (1864) 3 M. 294; *Anderson* v. *Aberdeen Hall Co.* (1879) 6 R. 907; *Manson* v. *Forrest* (1887) 14 R. 802.

2 *Hislop* v. *MacRitchie's Trs.* (1880) 8 R. (H.L.) 95; *N.B. Ry.* v. *Moore* (1891) 18 R. 1021; *Botanic Gardens Picture House* v. *Adamson*, 1924 S.C. 549.

3 The principle is analogous to, but not identical with, the principle of strict liability laid down for English law in *Rylands* v. *Fletcher* (1868) L.R. 3 H.L. 330, and frequently cited in Scotland.

4 In English cases usually called 'non-natural use of land': see *Rylands, supra*; *Rickards* v. *Lothian* [1913] A.C. 263; *Read* v. *Lyons* [1947] A.C. 156; and cf. *Chalmers* v. *Dixon* (1876) 3 R. 461. Domestic gas, water, and electricity supplies are not 'non-natural' uses of land: *Miller* v. *Addie's Collieries*, 1943 S.C. 150; *McLaughlan* v. *Craig*, 1948 S.C. 599.

5 *Henderson* v. *Stewart* (1818) 15 S. 868, note; *Samuel* v. *Edinburgh and Glasgow Ry.* (1850) 13 D. 312; *Kerr* v. *Earl of Orkney* (1857) 20 D. 298; *Tennent* v. *Earl of Glasgow* (1864) 2 M. (H.L.) 22; *Potter* v. *Hamilton and Strathaven Ry.* (1864) 3 M. 83; *Caledonian Ry.* v. *Greenock Corpn.*, 1917 S.C. (H.L.) 56.

6 *Mackintosh* v. *M.* (1864) 2 M. 1357.

7 *Chalmers* v. *Dixon* (1876) 3 R. 461.

8 *Gemmill's Trs.* v. *Cross* (1906) 14 S.L.T. 576.

9 *Western Silver Fox Ranch* v. *Ross and Cromarty C.C.*, 1940 S.C. 601.

10 e.g. *Kerr, supra.*

11 e.g. *Western Silver Fox Ranch, supra.*

12 *Paterson* v. *Lindsay* (1885) 13 R. 261, 263; *Miles* v. *Forest Rock Granite Co.* [1918] 34 T.L.R. 500; *Shiffman* v. *Order of St. John* [1936] 1 All E.R. 557; *Western Silver Fox Ranch, supra*; but see *Reynolds* v. *Lanarkshire Tramways Co.* (1908) 16 S.L.T. 230; *Read, supra*; *McLaughlan* v. *Craig*, 1948 S.C. 599.

Defences

It is not a relevant defence to show that reasonable care and precautions were taken. It is, however, relevant to prove that there was no escape from the defender's land,[1] that the pursuer was himself in fault,[2] that the *novum opus* was made for the common benefit of both parties,[3] that the pursuer had expressly or impliedly consented to the dangerous operation,[4] that the escape was caused by *damnum fatale*, i.e. circumstances which no human foresight can provide against,[5] that the proximate cause of the escape was the malicious intervention of a third party,[6] or the negligent interference of a kind not foreseeable,[7] that the harm would equally have injured the pursuer even if the defender's works had not been erected,[8] and that the *opus* has been fortified by prescription.[9]

Use of land in aemulationem vicini

A use of land which is lawful may be actionable if the predominant motive is the harm of a neighbour, gratification of spite or other oblique motive, and harm is done thereby,[10] but not if such a motive, if present, is not the predominant one. A legitimate use of land, if not motivated by malice, is unobjectionable merely because it is injurious to the neighbour's interest.[11]

Game damage

A reasonable game population is a normal incident of rural land and an agricultural tenant can complain only if a landlord

[1] *Read, supra.*
[2] *Wilsons* v. *Waddell* (1876) 3 R. 288.
[3] *Prosser* v. *Levy* [1955] 3 All E.R. 577.
[4] *Anderson* v. *Oppenheimer* (1880) 5 Q.B.D. 602.
[5] *Tennent* v. *Earl of Glasgow* (1864) 2 M. (H.L.) 22, 26–7. This defence succeeded in *Nichols* v. *Marsland* (1876) 2 Ex. D. 1; and *Tennent, supra*; it failed in *Caledonian Ry., supra.*
[6] *Rickards, supra.*
[7] *Weston* v. *Tailors of Potterrow* (1839) 1 D. 1218.
[8] *Caledonian Ry., supra*, 61, 65.
[9] *Caledonian Ry., supra*, 65.
[10] Dig. 39, 3, 1; Bankt. I, 10, 40; II, 7, 5; IV, 45, 112; Ersk. II, 1, 2; Kames, *Equity*, 41; Hume, *Lect.* III, 207; Bell, *Prin.* §964, 966; More. *Lect.* I, 608; *Glassford* v. *Astley* (1808) Mor. Appx. Property, No. 7; *Ross* v. *Baird* (1829) 7 S. 361; *Ritchie* v. *Purdie* (1832) 11 S. 771; *Graham* v. *Greig* (1838) 1 D. 171, 177; *Irving* v. *Leadhills Mining Co.* (1856) 18 D. 833; *Young* v. *Bankier Distillery Co.* (1893) 20 R. (H.L.) 76; *Campbell* v. *Muir*, 1908 S.C. 387, 393.

Lord Watson's *obiter* views in *Mayor of Bradford* v. *Pickles* [1895] A.C. 587, 597 cannot be accepted as sound, and that case would have been otherwise decided under Scots law.

[11] *Dunlop* v. *Robertson* (1803) Hume 515; *Glassford* v. *Astley* (1808) Hume 516; cf. *Donald* v. *Esslemont & Macintosh*, 1923 S.C. 122.

permits an unreasonable amount or an unreasonable increase. An agricultural lease is not presumed to carry shooting rights.[1] The tenant cannot prevent the landlord shooting game,[2] nor may he capture them or scare them away himself[3] though at common law he might shoot rabbits without consent[4] unless the landlord had reserved that right[5] or granted it to a shooting tenant. The Ground Game Acts, 1880 and 1906, give the tenant liberty to kill and take hares concurrently with any other person entitled to the game on the same land, subject to certain limitation.[6] A tenant has no claim for damage if he might have prevented it by exercising his rights, as by killing rabbits.[7]

A tenant has a claim for damages if the game population has been materially increased since the lease by the landlord's policy[8] or failure to keep down the game.[9] His claim may be excluded by the lease, but such a clause is strictly construed[10] and may be ineffective.[11] It is doubtful if a tenant has a claim against an adjacent proprietor for keeping an unreasonable stock of game.[12]

Under the Agricultural Holdings (Sc.) Act, 1949, S. 15, a tenant who has sustained damage to his crops from game, the right to take and kill which is vested neither in him nor in anyone claiming under him other than the landlord, and which the tenant has not permission in writing to kill,[13] is entitled on notice given[14] to compensation from his landlord if the damage exceeds one shilling per acre.[15] Failing agreement the amount of compensation is to be settled by arbitration. He cannot claim directly against a shooting tenant.[16]

1 *Copland* v. *Maxwell* (1868) 9 M. (H.L.) 1.
2 *E. Hopetoun* v. *Wight*, 19 Jan. 1810, F.C.
3 *Wemyss* v. *Gulland* (1847) 10 D. 204.
4 *Fraser* v. *Lawson* (1882) 10 R. 396; *Crawshay* v. *Duncan*, 1915 2 S.L.T. 13.
5 *Moncrieff* v. *Arnott* (1828) 6 S. 530.
6 On these see *Stuart* v. *Murray* (1884) 12 R. (J.) 9; *Ferguson* v. *McNab* (1885) 12 R. 1083; *Jack* v. *Nairne* (1887) 14 R. (J.) 20; *Niven* v. *Renton* (1888) 15 R. (J.) 42; *D. Bedford* v. *Kerr* (1893) 20 R. (J.) 65; *Richardson* v. *Maitland* (1897) 24 R. (J.) 32; *Bruce* v. *Prosser* (1898) 25 R. (J.) 54; *McDouall* v. *Cochrane* (1901) 3 F. (J.) 71.
7 *Wood* v. *Paton* (1874) 1 R. 868.
8 *Cameron* v. *Drummond* (1888) 15 R. 489.
9 *Wemyss* v. *Wilson* (1847) 10 D. 194; *Broadwood* v. *Hunter* (1855) 17 D. 340, 1139; *Morton* v. *Graham* (1867) 6 M. 71; *Kidd* v. *Byrne* (1875) 3 R. 255; *Cadzow* v. *Lockhart* (1875) 3 R. 666.
10 *Morton, supra*; *Cadzow, supra.*
11 *Cadzow, supra.*
12 *Thomson* v. *Earl of Galloway*, 1919 S.C. 611.
13 *Ross* v. *Watson*, 1943 S.C. 406.
14 *Morton's Trs.* v. *McDougall*, 1944 S.C. 466.
15 *Roddan* v. *McCowan* (1890) 17 R. 1056.
16 *Inglis* v. *Moirs' Tutors* (1871) 10 M. 204.

Malicious damage to land

Deliberate conduct resulting in actual,[1] or reasonably apprehended,[2] damage to land is actionable. Various statutes[3] give a right of action against local authorities for damages for loss caused by rioting.

Unintentional damage to heritage

Unintentional damage may be caused in numerous ways; the basis of liability may be negligence, nuisance or strict liability for escape of a danger according to the circumstances. Damage caused by road vehicles may import liability for negligence[4] or for nuisance.[5] Damage caused by railway trains imposes similar liabilities. If fire is caused by sparks from a railway engine run under statutory authority, negligence in the construction or use of the engine must be proved[6] and there is no liability if all reasonable precautions have been taken.[7] Under the Railway Fires Acts, 1905 and 1923, the railway authority is liable to a limited extent for damage to agricultural land without proof of negligence.[8]

There is liability if negligence be proved for damage to a harbour by a ship.[9] Under the Harbours, Docks, and Piers Clauses Act, 1847, S. 74, the owner of a vessel is liable to harbour undertakers for damage done, independently of fault,[10] but not if the vessel were beyond control[11] nor in case of inevitable accident.[12] There is also liability if a vessel sinks in a lock or

[1] Ersk. II, 9, 2; Bell, *Prin.* §968; Hume, *Lect.* III, 209.

[2] *Durham* v. *Hood* (1871) 9 M. 474.

[3] Malicious Damage Act, 1812, Ss. 3–4; Malicious Damage (Sc.) Act, 1816, Ss. 2–3; Seditious Meetings Act, 1817, S. 38; Riotous Assemblies (Sc.) Act, 1822, S. 10, all amended by Law Reform (Limitation of Actions) Act, 1954, S. 6(4); see *Scottish Plate Glass Ins. Corpn.* v. *Edinburgh Corpn.*, 1941 S.C. 115; *Capaldi* v. *Greenock Mags.*, 1941 S.C. 310; *Pompa's Trs.* v. *Edinburgh Mags.*, 1942 S.C. 119; *Coia* v. *Robertson*, 1942 S.C. 111.

[4] *Grahamslaw* v. *Veitch's Trs.*, 1923 S.L.T. 162; *Glasgow Corpn.* v. *Barclay Curle & Co.*, 1923 S.C. (H.L.) 78; *Hutchison* v. *Davidson*, 1945 S.C. 395.

[5] *Slater* v. *McLellan*, 1924 S.C. 854.

[6] *Parker* v. *L.N.E. Ry.* (1945) 175 L.T. 137; *Sellwood* v. *L.M.S. Ry.* (1945) 175 L.T. 366; *Campbell* v. *L.M.S. Ry.* [1948] C.L.Y. 4689.

[7] *Vaughan* v. *Taff Vale Ry.* (1860) 5 H. & N. 679; *Murdoch* v. *G.S.W. Ry.* (1870) 8 M. 768; *Port Glasgow and Newark Sailcloth Co.* v. *Caledonian Ry.* (1893) 20 R. (H.L.) 35.

[8] *Groom* v. *G.W. Ry.* (1892) 8 T.L.R. 253; *A.G.* v. *G.W. Ry.* [1924] 2 K.B. 1; *Langlands* v. *B.T.C.* [1956] 2 All E.R. 702.

[9] *C.N.T.* v. *Kelvin Shipping Co.*, 1927 S.C. 622.

[10] *G.W. Ry.* v. *S.S. Mostyn* [1928] A.C. 57; *Workington Harbour Board* v. *Towerfield* [1951] A.C. 112.

[11] *River Wear Commrs.* v. *Adamson* (1877) 2 App. Cas. 743.

[12] *The Boucan* [1909] P. 163.

dock causing obstruction though without damage to the dock.[1] Under the Merchant Shipping (Liability of Shipowners and Others) Acts 1900 and 1958, the right of limiting liability for damages applies also to damage to property on land.[2]

By the Civil Aviation Act, 1949, S. 40(2) damage to property on land by or from an aircraft is actionable without proof of intention, negligence, or otherwise, unless caused or contributed to by the complainer's negligence. There are provisions for limitation of liability and for compulsory insurance.

[1] *The Stonedale No. 1* [1956] A.C. 1; cf. *Greenock Harbour Trs.* v. *B.O.C.M.*, 1944 S.C. 70.

[2] *Mersey Docks and Harbour Bd.* v. *Hay* [1923] A.C. 345; *The Ruapehu* [1927] A.C. 523; [1929] P. 305; *Hamilton* v. *B.T.C.*, 1957 S.C. 300; altering law stated in *Clifton Steam Trawlers* v. *MacIver*, 1953 S.L.T. 230.

CHAPTER 71

WRONGS IN RESPECT OF CORPOREAL MOVEABLE PROPERTY

Spuilzie

SPUILZIE is the taking away of moveables without consent of the owner or order of law, imposing an obligation to restore with all possible profits or to make reparation therefor.[1] The pursuer need only establish lawful possession or custody, not necessarily ownership, and the action lies against any custodier.[2]

Goods spuilzied are tainted by *vitium reale* and may therefore be followed even into the hands of, and be recovered from, a *bona fide* purchaser.[3] The action applies to such cases as unwarranted seizure of goods,[4] use of goods in denial of another's right to possession thereof,[5] keeping found property,[6] failing to return goods borrowed, hired or deposited for custody,[7] selling goods by mistake,[8] and using another's goods by mistake.[9] The action is excluded by good faith,[10] or by any legal or even colourable warrant,[11] or by restitution of the goods.[12] The action prescribes as to the violent profits in three years[13] but an action for recovery still lies thereafter.[14]

[1] Craig, *J.F.* II, 11, 30; Stair I, 9, 16; IV, 26, 2; Bankt. I, 10, 124; Ersk. II, 7, 16; IV. 1, 15; Hume. *Lect.* III, 235; Bell, *Prin.* §527; More, *Lect.* I, 358.

[2] Stair, Ersk., *supra*; *Dalhanna Knitwear Co.* v. *Mohammed Ali*, 1967 S.L.T. (Sh. Ct.) 74.

[3] *Hay* v. *Leonard* (1677) Mor. 10286; cf. *Todd* v. *Armour* (1882) 9 R. 901.

[4] *Paterson* v. *Walker* (1848) 11 D. 167; *Barret* v. *Whyte* (1849) 11 D. 666; *Cleland* v. *Todd* (1849) 11 D. 1039; *Bell* v. *Black and Morrison* (1865) 3 M. 1026; *Walker* v. *Cumming* (1868) 4 M. 318.

[5] cf. *Leitch* v. *Leydon*, 1931 S.C. (H.L.) 1.

[6] cf. *Lawson* v. *Heatly*, 1962 S.L.T. 53.

[7] *Bain* v. *Strang* (1888) 16 R. 186; *Ballingall* v. *Dundee Ice. Co.*, 1924 S.C. 238; *Central Motors* v. *Cessnock Garage Co.*, 1925 S.C. 796.

[8] *Lockhart* v. *Cunninghame* (1871) 8 S.L.R. 151; *MacIntyre* v. *Corson* (1906) 22 Sh. Ct. Rep. 331; *Mackintosh* v. *Galbraith* (1900) 3 F. 66.

[9] *International Banking Corpn.* v. *Ferguson Shaw & Co.*, 1910 S.C. 182; cf. *McLaren* v. *Mann, Byars & Co.* (1935) 57 Sh. Ct. Rep. 57; *McDonald* v. *Provan (of Scotland St.), Ltd.*, 1960 S.L.T. 231.

[10] *A.* v. *B.* (1637) Mor. 14750.

[11] Stair I, 9, 19; *Mackintosh* v. *Galbraith* (1900) 3 F. 66.

[12] Stair, I, 9, 23.

[13] Prescription (Ejections) Act, 1579, c. 81; Ersk. III, 7, 16; *Baillie* v. *Young* (1835) 13 S. 472, 475.

[14] Stair I, 9, 24; Ersk. III, 7, 16; *Hay* v. *Kerr* (1627) Mor. 12131.

Malicious damage to goods

It is actionable for one person, without justification, deliberately to do damage to goods.[1] It is doubtless justifiable to do deliberate damage if necessary to save life, or property of greater value, from serious danger, and in circumstances of emergency. It is justifiable to shoot a dog which is worrying sheep if that is the only way of preventing damage in case of an actual attack, or if there is reason to apprehend a renewal of the attack; there must be actual attack or real and imminent danger, and no other practicable means of protecting the flock, or at least the killer must have acted reasonably in regarding the shooting as necessary.[2]

Unintentional damage to goods

Unintentional damage may be actionable on the ground of negligence, nuisance or one of the heads of strict liability. Thus loss of belongings in a vehicle or ship collision is actionable under negligence,[3] and damage to goods may be actionable under nuisance or strict liability for the escape of danger.[4] Liability for killing animals normally depends on negligence;[5] in case of emergency, if a driver must choose, he should seek to preserve human life even at the cost of killing an animal.[6] By the Dogs Acts, 1906–28, the owner of a dog is liable for injury done by it to any cattle or poultry without proof of previous mischievous propensity in the dog, or the owner's knowledge thereof, or proof that the injury was attributable to neglect on the owner's part.[7]

Liability for damage to a railway[8] or road vehicle depends on

[1] *Graham* v. *Edinburgh Tramways Co.*, 1917 S.C. 7, 10; cf. *Clark* v. *Syme*, 1957 J.C. 1; *Workman* v. *Cowper* [1961] 2 Q.B. 143.

[2] *Cope* v. *Sharpe* [1912] 1 K.B. 496; *Wilson* v. *Buchanan* (1943) 59 Sh. Ct. Rep. 54; *Gott* v. *Measures* [1947] 2 All E.R. 609; *Cresswell* v. *Sirl* [1947] 2 All E.R. 730; *Leven* v. *Mitchell* (1949) 65 Sh. Ct. Rep. 225; *Mitchell* v. *Duncan* (1953) 69 Sh. Ct. Rep. 182; *Farrell* v. *Marshall* (1962) 78 Sh. Ct. Rep. 128.

[3] *Lewis* v. *Laird Line*, 1925 S.L.T. 316; *Reavis* v. *Clan Line*, 1925 S.C. 725; 1926 S.C. 215.

[4] *Weston* v. *Tailors of Potterrow* (1839) 1 D. 1218; *Cleghorn* v. *Taylor* (1856) 18 D. 664; *Campbell* v. *Kennedy* (1864) 3 M. 121; *Reid* v. *Baird* (1876) 4 R. 234; *Moffat* v. *Park* (1877) 5 R. 13; *McIntyre* v. *Gallacher* (1883) 11 R. 64; *Gilmour* v. *Simpson*, 1958 S.C. 477, 487.

[5] *Barclay* v. *G.N.S. Ry.* (1882) 10 R. 144; *Graham* v. *Edinburgh Tramways Co.*, 1917 S.C. 7.

[6] *Parkinson* v. *Liverpool Corpn.* [1950] 1 All E.R. 367; *Sutherland* v. *Glasgow Corpn.*, 1951 S.C. (H.L.) 1.

[7] For criminal liability see also Dogs (Protection of Livestock) Act, 1953.

[8] *Smith* v. *L.M.S. Ry.*, 1948 S.C. 125.

negligence.[1] Thus claims have been brought against road authorities for failing to keep roads in reasonably safe condition,[2] or failing to fence them,[3] or to fence or light an obstruction therein,[4] against manufacturers for defective design or manufacture,[5] and most commonly against the owner of another vehicle for damage sustained in a collision.[6]

Liability for damage to a ship also depends on negligence. This may be by failure to take reasonable care when a ship is being repaired,[7] or that a berth assigned in harbour was safe,[8] or failure to buoy a channel,[9] but most frequently by collision damage caused by negligent navigation.[10] A wrong action in emergency or the agony of danger is not necessarily fault,[11] nor is adoption of the wrong course of action when placed in a dilemma.[12] Negligence may be constituted by failure to obey the Collision Regulations,[13] unless departure from the prescribed course of

[1] In *Hay* v. *Leslie* (1896) 4 S.L.T. 124, in special circumstances, a claim was based on nuisance. In some cases also a claim can be based on breach of an implied term of contract.

[2] *Harris* v. *Leith Mags.* (1881) 8 R. 613; *Johnstone* v. *Glasgow Mags.* (1885) 12 R. 596; *McFee* v. *Broughty Ferry Police Commrs.* (1890) 17 R. 764; *Strachan* v. *Aberdeen Dist. Cttee.* (1894) 21 R. 915; *Blackie* v. *Leith Mags.* (1904) 12 S.L.T. 529; *Costello* v. *Midlothian C.C.*, 1946 S.N. 103; *Alexander* v. *Dundee Corpn.*, 1950 S.C. 123; *Western S.M.T.* v. *Greenock Mags.*, 1958 S.L.T. (Notes) 50.

[3] *Sanderson* v. *Paisley Burgh Commrs.* (1899) 7 S.L.T. 255.

[4] *Nelson* v. *Lanarkshire Lower Ward Cttee.* (1891) 19 R. 311; *Barton* v. *Kinning Park Commrs.* (1892) 29 S.L.R. 329; *Cromar* v. *Haddingtonshire C.C.* (1902) 9 S.L.T. 437; *White* v. *McKean*, 1948 S.L.T. 210.

[5] *Donnelly* v. *Glasgow Corpn.*, 1953 S.C. 107 (on which see *Davie* v. *New Merton Board Mills* [1959] A.C. 604); cf. *Elliot* v. *Young's Bus Service*, 1945 S.C. 445.

[6] *Scott* v. *McIntosh*, 1935 S.C. 199; *Pomphrey* v. *Cuthbertson*, 1951 S.C. 147; *Galbraith's Stores* v. *Glasgow Corpn.* (1958) 74 Sh. Ct. Rep. 126.

[7] *Nautilus S.S. Co.* v. *D. & W. Henderson*, 1919 S.C. 605.

[8] *Mersey Docks Trs.* v. *Gibbs* (1866) L.R. 1 E. & I. App. 93; *Thomson* v. *Greenock Harbour Trs.* (1876) 3 R. 1194; *Renney* v. *Kirkcudbright Mags.* (1892) 19 R. (H.L.) 11; *Parker* v. *N.B. Ry.* (1898) 25 R. 1059; *Mackenzie* v. *Stornoway Pier Commrs.*, 1907 S.C. 435; *S.S. Fulwood* v. *Dumfries Harbour Commrs.*, 1907 S.C. 456; *Mair* v. *Aberdeen Harbour Commrs.*, 1909 S.C. 721; *Walker* v. *Duke of Buccleuch*, 1918 1 S.L.T. 223; *Robertson* v. *Portpatrick and Wigtownshire Jt. Cttee.*, 1919 S.C. 293; *Cormack* v. *Dundee Harbour Trs.*, 1930 S.C. 112; as to private wharf see *Rix* v. *Carlingnose Granite Co.*, 1929 S.N. 62; *Firth Shipping Co.* v. *Morton's Trs.*, 1938 S.C. 177.

[9] *Anchor Line* v. *Dundee Harbour Trs.*, 1922 S.C. (H.L.) 79; cf. *Buchanan* v. *Clyde Lighthouses Trs.* (1884) 11 R. 531; *A/S Forto* v. *Orkney Harbour Commrs.*, 1915 S.C. 743.

[10] *Cayzer, Irvine & Co.* v. *Carron Co.* (1885) 13 R. 114; 9 App. Cas. 873; *S.S. Bogota* v. *S.S. Alconda*, 1924 S.C. (H.L.) 66; *The Heranger* [1939] A.C. 94. See generally Marsden, *Collisions at Sea*.

[11] *The Marpesia* (1872) L.R. 4 P.C. 212; *The Bywell Castle* (1879) 4 P.D. 219; *The Voorwaarts and The Khedive* (1880) 5 App. Cas. 876; *Laird Line* v. *U.S. Shipping Board*, 1924 S.C. (H.L.) 37; *Baron Vernon* v. *Metagama*, 1928 S.C. (H.L.) 21.

[12] *The Highland Loch* [1912] A.C. 312; *The Testbank* (1942) 72 Ll.L.R. 6.

[13] M.S.A., 1894, S. 419(1); Collision Regulations and Signals of Distress Order, 1953 (S.I. 1953, No. 1557). See e.g. *Clan Stuart* v. *Uskhaven*, 1928 S.C. 879; *Grangemouth and*

action can be justified as necessary in order to avoid immediate danger.[1] In addition local rules apply in many areas.[2] A ship and her owners are liable for collision caused by the fault or negligence of a pilot, whether employment were compulsory or not.[3] Damage may also be caused to other vessels negligently but without collision.[4]

Contributory negligence in most ship collision cases is governed by the Maritime Conventions Act, 1911, by which liability is proportionate to the degree in which each vessel was in fault, or if different degrees cannot be established liability is apportioned equally.[5] If it is not established where the fault lies, each ship must bear her own loss.[6]

Under the Merchant Shipping Act, 1894, S. 503, as amended[7] the shipowner's liability is limited, and he is not liable for loss of life or personal injury,[8] or damage or loss to goods on board, or loss of life or personal injury to a person not in the ship by the act or omission of a person in the ship,[9] or in certain other circumstances, beyond 3100 gold francs per ton of the ship's tonnage in respect of loss of life or personal injury, and 1000 gold francs per ton in respect of loss of or damage to goods, so long as the occurrence has taken place without his actual fault or privity.[10] Limitation is obtained by petition to the Court of Session to determine the owner's liability and to distribute it rateably among the claimants.[11]

Damage to aircraft caused by collision depends on negligence,

Forth Towing Co. v. *Wolk*, 1931 S.L.T. 394; *Jolliffe* v. *L.N.E. Ry.*, 1938 S.L.T. 21. As to H.M. ships see *The Truculent* [1952] P. 1; *The Albion* [1953] P. 117.

1 *The Oostvorne* (1921) 6 Ll.L.Rep. 110.

2 e.g. *Bogota* v. *Alconda*, 1924 S.C. (H.L.) 66; *Cameronia* v. *Hauk*, 1927 S.C. 518.

3 Pilotage Act, 1913, S. 15(1); *Thom* v. *J. & P. Hutchison*, 1925 S.C. 386. As to pilot's liability see Pilotage Act, 1913, S. 35; Pilotage Authorities (Limitation of Liability) Act, 1936; see also *Holman* v. *Irvine Harbour Trs.* (1877) 4 R. 406.

4 *The Batavier* (1854) 9 Moo P.C. 286; *The Wheatsheaf* (1866) 13 L.T. 612; *The Industrie* (1871) L.R. 3 A. & E. 303; *The Umona and the Sirius* (1934) 49 Ll. L. Rep. 461; *The Royal Sovereign* (1950) 84 Ll. L. Rep. 549.

5 *Cayzer, Irvine & Co.* v. *Carron Co.* (1884) 9 App. Cas. 873; *The Eurymedon* [1938] P. 51; *Boy Andrew* v. *St. Rognvald*, 1947 S.C. (H.L.) 70; as to time for claiming see *Birkdale S.S. Co.*, 1922 S.L.T. 575; *Reresby* v. *Cobetas*, 1923 S.L.T. 492, 719; *Essien* v. *Clan Line*, 1925 S.N. 75.

6 *The Olympic* v. *H.M.S. Hawke* [1913] P. 214, 247.

7 By M.S. (Liability of Shipowners and Others) Act, 1958.

8 Including injury to crew: *Innes* v. *Ross*, 1957 S.L.T. 121.

9 cf. *The Warkworth* (1884) 9 P.D. 145.

10 *Standard Oil Co.* v. *Clan Line*, 1924 S.C. (H.L.) 1; *The Truculent* [1952] P. 1; *Beauchamp* v. *Turrell* [1952] 2 Q.B. 207; *The Norman* [1960] 1 Lloyd's Rep. 1; *The Lady Gwendolen* [1965] 2 All E.R. 283; cf. *Kidston* v. *McArthur* (1878) 5 R. 936.

11 M.S.A. 1894, S. 504; cf. *Rankine* v. *Raschen* (1877) 4 R. 725.

particularly on the pilot's observance of the Air Navigation Order, 1966 and the Rules of the Air, 1966. Collision between an aircraft taking off, in flight, or landing and one on the ground depends on the Civil Aviation Act, 1949, S. 40.[1]

[1] See also *Blankley* v. *Godley* [1952] 1 All E.R. 436.

CHAPTER 72

WRONGS IN RESPECT OF INCORPOREAL MOVEABLE PROPERTY

Commercial goodwill

In the absence of an enforceable restrictive covenant limiting competition it is not wrongful for a former employee, or seller of the business, to set up in competition and thereby diminish the complainer's goodwill, and even less so for a stranger. Competition may, however, be wrongful if it involves passing off by trading in the same line of business under a name liable to confuse,[1] unless it is the competitor's own name or one under which he has traded for some time, and there is no dishonest intention.[2]

Royal Warrant

The holding of Royal Warrant of Appointment is a quasi-proprietary right and the use of the royal arms or any device or title calculated to deceive may be restrained by interdict.[3]

Trade secrets

There is no right of property in a trade secret, unless it is protected by a patent, and the original discoverer cannot prevent another party who comes to know of it from using it nor even from marketing it under its trade name, unless the trade name carries a connotation of being a particular manufacturer's product rather than goods made to a particular formula.[4]

Infringement of patents, etc.

Infringements of patents, registered trade marks, copyright, registered designs, and plant breeder's right are regulated mainly by the respective statutory rules.[5]

[1] *Tussaud* v. *T.* (1890) 44 Ch. D. 678.

[2] *Brinsmead* v. *Brinsmead & Waddington* (1913) 29 T.L.R. 237, 706; *Jay's, Ltd.* v. *Jacobi* [1933] Ch. 411.

[3] *Royal Warrant Holders Assocn.* v. *Lipman* (1934) 51 R.P.C. 155; see also Trade Marks Act, 1938, S. 61; Patents Act, 1949, S. 92; Trade Descriptions Act, 1968, S. 12.

[4] *Birmingham Vinegar Brewery Co.* v. *Powell* [1897] A.C. 710; *Reddaway* v. *Banham* [1896] A.C. 199.

[5] Ch. 99, *infra*.

CHAPTER 73

MISCELLANEOUS AND UNCERTAIN WRONGS

THE categories of actionable wrongs are not closed or limited to those for which there is precedent and new duties and modes of conduct in breach of duty resulting in harm may be recognized as actionable delicts.

Infringement of privacy

It may be a wrong to bring the name, appearance, characteristics of or facts relating to a person into public notice without his consent or legal justification. Some cases have justified remedies under other principles, such as defamation or infringement of copyright.[1] The difficulty is to draw the line between obnoxious prying and legitimate interest.

Interference with freedom of speech or meeting

It may be actionable to interfere with freedom of speech, as by prohibiting a public meeting when no disturbance was apprehended.[2]

[1] e.g. *White* v. *Dickson* (1881) 8 R. 896; *Pollard* v. *Photographic Co.* (1888) 40 Ch. D. 345; *Monson* v. *Tussaud* [1894] 1 Q.B. 671; *Corelli* v. *Wall* (1906) 22 T.L.R. 532; *Tolley* v. *Fry* [1931] A.C. 333; *Robertson* v. *Keith*, 1936 S.C. 29; *Williams* v. *Settle* [1960] 1 W.L.R. 1072.

[2] cf. *McAra* v. *Edinburgh Mags.*, 1913 S.C. 1059, 1073; see also *Aldred* v. *Langmuir*, 1932 J.C. 22; *Thomas* v. *Sawkins* [1935] 2 K.B. 249; *Duncan* v. *Jones* [1936] 1 K.B. 218.

BOOK V

LAW OF PROPERTY

PART 1

PROPERTY IN GENERAL

CHAPTER 74

NATURE AND CLASSIFICATION OF PROPERTY

THE law of property is concerned with the legal rights which persons have in respect of material things, and of those bodies of rights which are held collectively to amount to immaterial things, and with the relations between persons in respect of such things, material and immaterial. It is concerned with real rights or rights *in rem*, enforceable against persons generally, as contrasted with rights of obligation, which are rights *in personam* and enforceable only against the other party to the obligation.

The things, material and immaterial, in respect of which persons may have proprietary rights are all elements of that person's assets or patrimony. Some are material and have a physical existence, such as land, buildings, vehicles, and animals. Some are immaterial, bodies of rights which collectively amount to a legal thing, such as patent rights and copyrights. Some things, both material and immaterial, are represented and evidenced by documents showing a person's title to them, some are not, but any such document, itself also an object of property, should not be confused with the object of right of property which it evidences.[1]

The word 'property' is also sometimes used for the right of ownership of the property, or the right to that property;[2] and sometimes merely as a synonym for the object of the right of property itself.[3] So too 'possession' is used both of a right in certain property and as a synonym for the objects themselves.

In respect of one object or piece of property various rights may exist, such as ownership, possession, security-holding and so on, and these may be separated so that several persons may

[1] e.g. the title-deeds of land and the rights in land evidenced thereby are separate objects of property.

[2] e.g. Sale of Goods Act, 1893, S. 17—passing of property in goods.

[3] e.g. 'This desirable property' in an advertisement of a house.

simultaneously have rights of different kinds in one object of property, and each right may be dealt with and transferred separately from the others.

Some things are not deemed objects of property; a person does not have a proprietary right in his own person, nor in that of another,[1] nor can anyone acquire a proprietary right in the sea or the air.

CLASSIFICATIONS OF OBJECTS OF PROPERTY

The objects in relation to which persons may have proprietary rights are divided, firstly, into those things deemed heritable, of kinds which formerly descended on the owner's death to his heir-at-law, and those deemed moveable, of kinds which alone formerly descended on his death to his executors.[2] This division corresponds closely but not exactly to that between immoveable and moveable property,[3] and to that of English law between real and personal property.

Secondly, property is cross-divided into those kinds of objects which are corporeal, being physical, material, tangible and visible, such as buildings, and vehicles, and those which are incorporeal, being metaphysical, immaterial, intangible, and invisible, such as claims to money or right of copyright.

The law of property accordingly falls into four divisions: (1) corporeal heritable property, such as land or buildings; (2) incorporeal heritable property, such as titles of honour; (3) corporeal moveable property, such as vehicles and animals; and (4) incorporeal moveable property, such as copyrights and claims of debt. Different rules apply to each of these branches, partly for historical reasons and partly by reason of the natural differences between the kinds of things.

In relation to each division consideration must be given to the kinds of property which fall under that heading, the relations in which persons may stand to that property, the titles by which they hold their rights, and how their titles are created, evidenced, transferred, and extinguished.

A further distinction sometimes drawn is between fungibles, articles which can be valued by weight, measure or number, and replaced by equal amount of the like thing, and non-fungibles,

[1] *Reavis* v. *Clan Line Steamers*, 1925 S.C. 725; cf. *Williams* v. *W.* (1882) 20 Ch. D. 659.

[2] Stair II, 1, 2; Ersk. II, 2, 3; Bell, *Prin.* §636, 1283.

[3] The distinction between immoveables and moveables was drawn in the Roman law, and is still relevant in problems of conflict of laws.

which are unique, have individual qualities and are not exactly replaceable.

Nature of rights

Rights in themselves are always incorporeal as being claims which the courts may recognize and enforce, but they may exist in respect of corporeal or of incorporeal property, e.g. rights to land or vehicles, or to an annuity or a claim of debt or a copyright. A right to or in property deemed heritable is deemed a heritable right, and a right to or in property deemed moveable is deemed a moveable right.[1]

Rights in relation to property

The major distinction of rights is between *jura in re propria*, which an individual may exercise over or in relation to objects of his own property, whether material or immaterial; these are ownership, with the consequential rights of enjoyment, use, selling, giving or bequeathing, and possession;[2] and, on the other hand, *jura in re aliena*, which an individual may exercise over or in relation to objects of another person's property, whether material or immaterial; these include possession and use of another's property under a lease, holding the other's thing in security for debt, and the exercise of a servitude right over the other's property. All these are derogations from and limitations on the other person's more general rights, particularly ownership, in the same subject matter, and co-exist with it. Several persons may accordingly have different kinds of rights simultaneously in one object of property. These kinds of rights must be considered in relation to each of the divisions of property.

Title

The relationship between a person and some object of property is constituted by title. There are various kinds of title, each defining the particular rights which a title-holder, of such a class as owner, temporary possessor or security holder, has in relation to such a kind of object of property, and a considerable part of property law is concerned with the grounds on which and ways in which various kinds of title may be acquired, transferred and extinguished, while the rules of conveyancing are concerned with the methods and deeds necessary to effect transfers of title,

[1] Stair II, 1, 3; Ersk. II, 2, 5.
[2] cf. Bell, *Prin.* §1284.

according to the kind of property and the ground of creation, transfer or extinction of the title.

CLASSIFICATION OF OBJECTS OF PROPERTY

The main classification of objects of property is into those deemed heritable and those deemed moveable, and this division applies both to corporeal or material objects and to incorporeal or immaterial bodies of rights. This classification is important in relation to the proprietary rights which may exist in the particular object, to the modes of acquisition and transfer, to completion of title, to succession on death and to diligence.[1] The date relevant for classification is the date of the event, death, marriage, sale or diligence which raises the question, and later events do not in general alter the character of a thing or right.[2]

The character of a subject may be determined as heritable or moveable by its physical nature, as physically immoveable or moveable, by connection or accession to another subject which is actually immoveable or moveable, or by destination indicated by the owner.[3]

Heritable property

Heritable property includes all subjects naturally immoveable, such as land and minerals, or united to the ground, such as buildings.[4] Trees and annual fruits of the soil are deemed heritable until cut and separated from the soil, when they become moveable;[5] cultivated crops are similarly heritable until harvested, when they become moveable.[6]

Rights connected with heritage

Rights connected with or affecting any heritable subject are also heritable, such as rights of superiority, of fee, of leases,[7] or of servitude, and the former bonds of annual rent.[8] Similarly

1 Stair II, 1, 2; Ersk. II, 2, 3; Bell, *Comm.* II, 1; *Prin.* §1470–71, 1746.

2 Ersk. II, 2, 20.

3 Bell, *Prin.* §1470.

4 Stair II, 1, 40; Ersk. II, 2, 4; Bell, *Prin.* §636, 1471.

5 *Paul* v. *Cuthbertson* (1840) 2 D. 1286; *Nisbet* v. *Mitchell-Innes* (1880) 7 R. 575; *Burns* v. *Fleming* (1880) 8 R. 226; cf. *Breadalbane's Trs.* v. *Pringle* (1854) 16 D. 359; *Allan* v. *Millar*, 1932 S.C. 620; *Munro* v. *Balnagown Estates Co.*, 1949 S.C. 49.

6 *Chalmer's Tr.* v. *Dick's Tr.*, 1909 S.C. 761, correcting Ersk. II, 2, 4; Bell, *Prin.* §1473; see also *Nisbet, supra*; *Morrison* v. *Lockhart*, 1912 S.C. 1017; *McKinlay* v. *Hutchison's Tr.*, 1935 S.L.T. 62.

7 Ersk. II, 2, 6; Bell, *Prin.* §1478.

8 Ersk. II, 2, 5.

rights to feuduties and rents are heritable, though each payment when made is moveable, and unpaid arrears are moveable, being deemed as paid;[1] liability for unpaid arrears falls on the executor and not on the heir of the vassal or tenant. A *jus crediti* in respect of heritable property is heritable,[2] as is a right to demand reconveyance of heritage given subject to condition, on failure of that condition.[3]

Business goodwill is heritable if and so far as the business connection of the undertaking depends on the premises and their situation rather than on any personal qualities;[4] it may be partly heritable and partly moveable.[5]

Rights having a tract of future time

Rights having a tract of future time are heritable, even though unconnected with land; these continue for a period of time, carry a yearly profit to the creditor, but are not related to any particular capital sum, e.g. a yearly premium or annuity.[6] Such debts are burdens on the debtor's heritable succession, though termly payments, when they become due, are moveable.[7] But a legacy of the annual interest for a series of years of a capital sum bequeathed to another has been held moveable.[8]

Titles and honours

Also heritable are titles, coats of arms and honours and dignities if transmissible on the holder's death and not purely personal.[9]

Jura crediti

If the *jus crediti* under a trust entitles the beneficiary to demand delivery or conveyance of heritable subjects, it is heritable, descending to the heirs of the beneficiaries.[10] If, however, it be

[1] Bell, *Prin.* §1505; *Martin* v. *Agnew* (1755) Mor. 5457; 5 B.S. 830; *Logan's Trs.* v. *L.* (1896) 23 R. 848; *Watson's Trs.* v. *Brown*, 1923 S.C. 228.

[2] *Thain* v. *T.* (1891) 18 R. 1196.

[3] *Connell's J.F.* v. *MacWatt*, 1961 S.L.T. 203.

[4] *Bell's Trs.* v. *B.* (1884) 12 R. 85; *Graham* v. *G.* (1898) 5 S.L.T. 319; *Ross* v. *Ross's Trs.* (1901) 9 S.L.T. 340; *Town and County Bank* v. *McBain* (1902) 9 S.L.T. 485; *Graham* v. *G's Trs.* (1904) 6 F. 1015; *Muirhead's Trs.* v. *M.* (1905) 7 F. 496.

[5] *Murray's Tr.* v. *McIntyre* (1904) 6 F. 588.

[6] Stair II, 1, 4; Ersk. II, 2, 6; Bell, *Prin.* §1480; *Crawford's Trs.* v. *C.* (1867) 5 M. 275.

[7] *Hill* v. *H.* (1872) 11 M. 247; *Breadalbane's Trs.* v. *Jamieson* (1873) 11 M. 912; *Reid* v. *McWalter* (1878) 5 R. 630; *de Serra Largo* v. *L's Trs.*, 1933 S.L.T. 391.

[8] *Hill*, *supra*; cf. *Shaw's Trs.* v. *S.* (1870) 8 M. 419.

[9] Ersk. II, 2, 6; Bell, *Comm.* I, 120; *Prin.* §1481; cf. Succession (Sc.) Act, 1964, S. 37 (1)(a).

[10] Bell, *Prin.* §1482; *Durie* v. *Coutts* (1791) Mor. 4624; *Thain* v. *T.* (1891) 18 R. 1196.

merely to demand money, or a share of the trust fund, it is moveable.[1] If the nature of the right is uncertain, it is deemed moveable.[2] The *jura crediti* of rents, and of principal and annual payments of interest on heritable bonds, are heritable, but accruing payments are moveable as soon as they vest in the creditor.[3] An assignee's right to a *spes successionis* to heritable property is a heritable *jus crediti*.[4]

At common law annuities, rents, and payments connected with land did not vest till the term of payment arrived, so that a creditor's executor could claim nothing if the creditor did not survive a term of payment, whereas the interest of money and the profits of daily work vested *de die in diem*. The Apportionment Act, 1870, provides that, unless it is stipulated that no apportionment is to take place,[5] all rents, annuities, dividends, and other periodical payments in the nature of income accrue from day to day and are apportionable accordingly, both as regards liability to make, and the right to receive, the payments.[6]

Things moveable

Things physically moveable are deemed legally moveable, such as money, animals, clothing, books, furniture, machinery, vessels, vehicles, and aircraft,[7] and also the fruits or income of such moveables, such as young animals and the income of money.[8] Debts and undertakings to pay are moveable,[9] as are government stock, shares in companies, claims of damages, though arising in respect of heritable property,[10] a right to a share of the proceeds of heritage,[11] patent rights,[12] and copyrights.[13]

Also moveable are arrears of money due on an annuity, of feuduty or rent, of interest on a bond,[14] and claims to money, such

[1] *Wardlaw's Trs.* v. *W.* (1880) 7 R. 1070; see also *Gilligan, infra*; *Borland's Trs., infra.*

[2] Bell, *supra*; *Somerville's Trs.* v. *Gillespie* (1859) 21 D. 1148; *Learmonts* v. *Shearer* (1866) 4 M. 540; *Auld* v. *Anderson* (1876) 4 R. 211; *Kippen's Trs.* v. *K's Exors.* (1889) 16 R. 668; *Gilligan* v. *G.* (1891) 18 R. 387; *Borland's Trs.* v. *B.*, 1917 S.C. 704.

[3] Bell, *Prin.* §1496.

[4] *Thain* v. *T.* (1891) 18 R. 1196.

[5] *Macpherson's Trs.* v. *M.*, 1907 S.C. 1067.

[6] *Learmonth* v. *Sinclair's Trs.* (1878) 5 R. 548.

[7] Stair, II, 1, 2; Ersk. II, 2, 7; Bell, *Prin.* §1478.

[8] *Adv. Gen.* v. *Oswald* (1848) 10 D. 969; *Hill* v. *H.* (1872) 11 M. 247.

[9] Even where lent on the security of a long lease: *Stroyan* v. *Murray* (1890) 17 R. 1170.

[10] Ersk. II, 2, 7; Bell, *Prin.* §1479; *Gray* v. *Walker* (1859) 21 D. 709; *Muirhead* v. *M's Factor* (1867) 6 M. 95; *Caledonian Ry.* v. *Watt* (1875) 2 R. 917; *Kelvinside Estate Co.* v. *Donaldson's Trs.* (1879) 6 R. 995; *Fairlie's Trs.* v. *F's C.B.*, 1932 S.C. 216.

[11] *Gilligan* v. *G.* (1891) 18 R. 387.

[12] *Adv. Gen.* v. *Oswald, supra.*

[13] Copyright Act, 1956, S. 36(1).

[14] Ersk. II 2, 8; Bell, *Prin.* §1479, 1505; *Martin* v. *Agnew* (1755) Mor. 5457; 5 B.S. 830; *Logan's Trs.* v. *L.* (1896) 23 R. 848; *Watson's Trs.* v. *Brown*, 1923 S.C. 228.

as money sunk in a partnership, or represented by shares in a company,[1] even though the assets of the firm or company consist of or comprise heritable property, and money presently due. A *jus crediti* under a marriage contract to estate which might be heritable or moveable has been held moveable.[2]

Business goodwill is moveable if dependent more on the reputation and connection of the firm than on the situation where it does business;[3] it may be partly heritable and partly moveable.[4]

Things in their nature heritable may be deemed moveable if part of a *universitas* or mixed unity which is regarded as moveable.[5]

The price of land voluntarily sold is moveable, unless payment is heritably secured rather than paid,[6] and even a compulsory sale makes the price moveable in the owner's succession, if he should die before granting a conveyance.[7]

But where land is judicially sold the interest of the heritable creditors therein remains heritable and the shares of the price to which they are entitled continue heritable till their debts are discharged, and fall to their heirs.[8] And sale of a pupil's heritage by his tutor or factor *loco tutoris* leaves the proceeds heritable until the pupil attains minority, when he may dispose of the proceeds as moveable estate.[9]

Obligations bearing interest *ex lege*, independently of stipulation of parties, are moveable for all purposes.[10]

Heritable securities

Bonds to pay money secured by a disposition of heritage in security or by real burden on land were at common law, by reason of their inherent connection with land, deemed heritable in the succession of both debtor and creditor.[11] By statute,[12]

1 *Minto* v. *Kilpatrick* (1832) 11 S. 632; *L.A.* v. *Macfarlane's Trs.* (1893) 31 S.L.R. 357; Partnership Act, 1890, S. 22; Companies Act, 1948, S. 73; cf. *Shaw's Trs.* v. *S.* (1870) 8 M. 419.

2 *Wardlaw's Trs.* v. *W.* (1880) 7 R. 1070; cf. *Gilligan* v. *G.* (1891) 18 R. 387; *Borland's Trs.* v. *B.*, 1917 S.C. 704.

3 *Muirhead's Trs.* v. *M.* (1905) 7 F. 496.

4 *Murray's Tr.* v. *McIntyre* (1904) 6 F. 588.

5 Bell, *Prin.* §1474; *Allan* v. *Millar*, 1932 S.C. 620.

6 Ersk. II, 2, 17; *McLellan* v. *McL.*, 1960 S.C. 348.

7 *Heron* v. *Espie* (1856) 18 D. 917.

8 Ersk. II, 2, 17.

9 *Brown's Tr.* v. *B.* (1897) 24 R. 962.

10 Ersk. II, 2, 13.

11 Ersk. II, 2, 5; Bell, *Prin.* §1485.

12 Titles to Land Consolidation (Sc.) Act, 1868, S. 117; heritable securities affected are defined in S. 3. See also *Stroyan* v. *Murray* (1890) 17 R. 1170 (recorded long lease-moveable); *Peterkin* v. *Harvey* (1902) 9 S.L.T. 434 (decree of Dean of Guild Court declaring holder real creditor-moveable).

however, such securities have been made moveable in the creditor's succession,[1] except *quoad fiscum*, i.e. as to the Crown's right of escheat,[2] and as to the legal rights of children.[3] The change might formerly be defeated by the creditor taking the bond expressly in favour of himself and his heirs, excluding executors, or by executing a minute excluding executors.[4] Such debts remain burdens on the debtor's heirs rather than his executors.[5] The change does not affect the mode of completing title to the bond,[6] nor does it affect the succession to the debtor, in whose succession such a bond is always heritable.[7] The change has been held, where wills destined heritable and moveable portions of the estate differently, to put heritable securities into the moveable portion of the estate.[8]

The common law rule does not hold in respect of the constructive security of a ranking and sale, or in sequestration, nor as to securities taken by a tutor, factor *loco tutoris*, *curator bonis* or father as administrator in law, and such acts of administration do not alter the succession to the pupil.[9]

Personal bonds

Personal bonds, containing a merely personal promise to pay money and not secured over land, were at common law deemed moveable initially, but, by reason of their resemblance to the annual profits of heritage, deemed heritable in the creditor's succession after the due date for repayment of the capital, when interest started to run, and heritable from the start if interest ran at once, or if the term of payment was a distant or uncertain day which evidenced an intention to leave the capital for a period at interest.[10]

1 *Hughes's Trs.* v. *Corsane* (1890) 18 R. 299.

2 1868 Act, S. 117.

3 *Wingate's Trs.* v. *W.*, 1917 1 S.L.T. 75; Succession (Sc.) Act, 1964, S. 34 and Sch. 3, amending 1868 Act, S. 117. Until 1964 such bonds were heritable as regards legal rights of surviving spouses (courtesy and terce) also.

4 Succession (Sc.) Act, 1964, S. 34 and Sch. 3, amending 1868 Act, S. 117.

5 *Bell's Trs.* v. *B.* (1884) 12 R. 85; *Ferrier* v. *Cowan* (1896) 23 R. 703; see also *Brand* v. *Scott's Trs.* (1892) 19 R. 768; *Muir's Trs.* v. *M.*, 1916 1 S.L.T. 372; *Ballantyne's Trs.* v. *B's Trs.*, 1940 S.C. 35.

6 *Hare* (1889) 17 R. 105.

7 *Bell's Trs.*, *supra*.

8 *Guthrie* (1880) 8 R. 34; *Hughes' Trs.* v. *Corsane* (1890) 18 R. 299; but see opinions in *Hare*, *supra*, and *Cunningham* v. *C.* (1889) 17 R. 218, that the section applied only in cases of intestate succession.

9 Bell, *Prin.* §1486; *Lady Graham* v. *E. Hopetoun* (1798) Mor. 5599; *Kennedy* v. *K.* (1843) 6 D. 40; *Heron* v. *Espie* (1853) 18 D. 917.

10 Stair II, 1, 3; Ersk. II, 2, 9; Bell, *Prin.* §1495; *Gray* v. *Walker* (1859) 21 D. 709; *Dawson's Trs.* v. *D.* (1896) 23 R. 1006; *Bennett's Exors.* v. *B's Exors.*, 1907 S.C. 598; *Stark* v. *S.*, 1910 S.C. 397; *Heath* v. *Grant's Trs.*, 1913 S.C. 78.

By the Bonds Act, 1661 (c. 244) all sums contained in contracts and obligations carrying a clause of interest were declared moveable in the creditor's succession,[1] but to remain heritable if containing an express obligation to infeft, *quoad fiscum*, i.e. as respects liability to escheat to the Crown, and in respect of the legal rights of husband and wife, so that neither spouse had a claim, under legal rights to moveables arising on death, to any bond due to the other.[2] Though to remain heritable *quoad* a spouse's legal rights, such bonds are made moveable *quoad* children's legal rights,[3] and statute,[4] by providing that what estate is subject to legitim shall be subject to *jus relictae* or *jus relicti* has repealed the exception dealing with spouses' legal rights. This Act does not affect bonds taken expressly in favour of the creditor and his heirs in heritage, or a specified series of such heirs, or otherwise excluding the creditor's executors.[5] The Act also excepts bonds containing a clause of infeftment and providing for heritable security for the debt, and bonds expressly excluding executors.[6] Such bonds are, however, always moveable in the debtor's succession, unless the heir in heritage is expressly bound.

The statutes regulating the issue of certain securities sometimes also provide expressly that, notwithstanding the running of interest thereon, the bonds shall be moveable in succession.[7]

Things becoming heritable by accession — fixtures

Where a thing by itself moveable is connected with heritage a question may arise whether it remains moveable or has become so annexed to the heritage as to become heritable by accession, to pass with it, and not to be again removeable. While the principle is *accessorium sequitur principale*,[8] it is a question whether accession has taken place or is to be presumed.

In accordance with the maxims *inaedificatum solo, solo cedit*, and *quicquid plantatur solo solo cedit* anything built on or into or affixed to the ground is deemed annexed thereto.[9] Conversely a thing

[1] *Muirhead* v. *M's Factor* (1867) 6 M. 95.

[2] Ersk. II, 2, 10; *Downie* v. *D's Trs.* (1866) 4 M. 1067; *Dawson's Trs., supra*; *Heath, supra.*

[3] *Dawson's Trs., supra.*

[4] Conveyancing (Sc.) Act, 1924, S. 22.

[5] *Duffs* v. *D.* (1745) Mor. 5429.

[6] *Mackay* v. *Robertson* (1725) Mor. 3224; *Kennedy* v. *K.* (1747) Mor. 5499.

[7] *Robertson's Trs.* v. *Maxwell*, 1922 S.C. 267; *McWiggan's Trs.* v. *McW.*, 1922 S.C. 276; cf. *Stewart's Trs.* v. *Battock*, 1914 S.C. 179.

[8] *Brand's Trs.* v. *B's Trs.* (1876) 3 R. (H.L.) 16, 20.

[9] Stair II, 1, 40; *Dowall* v. *Miln* (1874) 1 R. 1180; *Brand's Trs.* v. *B's Trs.* (1876) 3 R. (H.L.) 16, 23; *Nisbet* v. *Mitchell-Innes* (1880) 7 R. 575; *Burns* v. *Fleming* (1880) 8 R. 256; *Miller* v. *Muirhead* (1894) 21 R. 658; *Howie's Trs.* v. *McLay* (1902) 5 F. 214.

merely resting on the ground is not necessarily annexed thereto, though articles annexed only by their own weight may be so adapted to a building or its surroundings as to be deemed fixtures,[1] and moveable things so annexed or adapted that they cannot be removed without destruction of or damage to principal or accessory may be deemed heritable by accession.[2]

Also moveable articles accessory to a principal thing which is heritable may be deemed constructive fixtures, such as a factory bell,[3] or moveable accessories of fixed machinery,[4] though not themselves attached to the heritage.

The cases usually raise two questions, whether the thing has become a fixture, and, if so, whether some person is entitled to sever and remove it.

Degree of fixation

One major point for consideration is the degree or permanence of the affixing, whether the article has been so permanently fixed as to have become part of the heritage, and that it cannot be disjoined without injury to itself or to the heritage, or on the other hand is so lightly attached as to be removable without damage to itself or to the heritage.[5] Things attached to the ground or a building are fixtures.[6] A thing fixed for a substantial period and substantial in itself may be held heritable though in fact it could be, or even had been, removed without damage.[7] Machinery may be a fixture though attached only by its own weight.[8] A lesser degree of fixation renders the article heritable if the article is also essential or material to the use of the heritage,[9] or have special adaptation to the use or improvement of the heritage which it would not have if placed elsewhere,[10] or there be express declaration by the owner that the article should be annexed to the

[1] *Howie's Trs., supra*; *Christie* v. *Smith*, 1949 S.C. 572.

[2] Bell, *Prin.* §1473; *Dowall, supra.*

[3] *Barr* v. *McIlwham* (1821) 1 S. 124.

[4] *Fisher* v. *Dixon* (1845) 4 Bell 286; *Brand's Trs., supra.*

[5] *Fisher* v. *Dixon* (1845) 4 Bell 286; *Dowall, supra*; *Nisbet* v. *Mitchell-Innes* (1880) 7 R. 575; *Marshall* v. *Tannoch Chemical Co.* (1886) 13 R. 1042; *Cochrane* v. *Stevenson* (1891) 18 R. 1208; *Luke* v. *Smith* (1894) 1 S.L.T. 545; *Jamieson* v. *Welsh* (1900) 3 F. 176.

[6] *Tod's Trs.* v. *Finlay* (1872) 10 M. 422; *Graham* v. *Lamont* (1875) 2 R. 438; *Reid's Exors.* v. *R.* (1890) 17 R. 519; *Hobson* v. *Gorringe* [1897] 1 Ch. 182; *Edinburgh Gas Commissioners* v. *Smart*, 1918 1 S.L.T. 80.

[7] *Christie* v. *Smith's Exrx.*, 1949 S.C. 572.

[8] *Brand's Trs.* v. *B's Trs.* (1878) 5 R. 607; *Howie's Trs.* v. *McLay* (1902) 5 F. 214; contrast *Dowall, supra.*

[9] *Fisher, supra*; *Dowall, supra.*

[10] *D'Eyncourt* v. *Gregory* (1866) L.R. 3 Eq. 382; *Dowall, supra.*

heritage.[1] Growing plants are fixtures passing on sale with the land.[2] A slag heap may be a heritable subject though removeable over a period.[3]

The duration of attachment is material and the permanency or quasi-permanency of the fixture is of great significance.[4]

Purpose of attachment

A further question of importance is the object and purpose of the annexation, whether the article was attached for the improvement of the heritage or the better use and enjoyment of the thing annexed. Ornamental shrubs and turf and gravel walks in a garden have been held improvements and not removeable.[5] Tile-hearths have been held heritable, but grates, gas brackets, picture rods, a mirror, ornamental stone lions and fireclay vases to be moveable.[6] Particularly in the case of a tenant fixtures made by him for the better use of heritage for the purposes of his trade are readily held removeable.[7] Such trade fixtures, until removed, are *partes soli* and the property of the landlord and an assignation of them to the landlord in security of advances has been held to amount to renunciation of the right of removal so long as the debt was outstanding.[8] A tenant entitled at the expiry of his lease to remove buildings erected by him cannot do so when he has not implemented his obligations under the lease.[9]

Relationship between parties

The attitude of the court in determining what is fixture and what removable depends also on the relationships of the contending parties. As between heir (or legatee of heritage) and executor of a common ancestor, the court leans in favour of the fixture going with the heritage.[10]

As between seller and purchaser of heritage, failing indication in the contract of sale, the question is mainly one of the degree of

1 *Dowall, supra.*
2 *Nisbet* v. *Mitchell-Innes* (1880) 7 R. 575.
3 *Collective Securities Co.* v. *Ayrshire Assessor*, 1946 S.C. 244.
4 *Christie* v. *Smith's Exrx.*, 1949 S.C. 572, 579.
5 *Burns* v. *Fleming* (1880) 8 R. 226.
6 *Nisbet* v. *Mitchell-Innes* (1880) 7 R. 575.
7 *Dowall* v. *Miln* (1874) 1 R. 1180; *Brand's Trs.* v. *B's Trs.* (1876) 3 R. (H.L.) 16; *Miller* v. *Muirhead* (1894) 21 R. 658; *Edinburgh Gas Commrs.* v. *Smart*, 1918 1 S.L.T. 80.
8 *Miller, supra.*
9 *Smith* v. *Harrison & Co's Tr.* (1893) 21 R. 330.
10 *Elwes* v. *Maw* (1802) 3 East 38; *Dowall, supra*; *Brand's Trs., supra.*

permanence of the fixture[1] and the court leans in favour of the fixture going with the heritage.[2]

As between a heritable creditor and the general creditors or a trustee in bankruptcy, the same principle applies.[3]

As between fiar and a liferenter's representatives, the law is more favourable to the limited owner attaching articles to the heritage with liberty to remove them when his right expires.[4]

Similarly as between landlord and tenant the latter is more readily allowed to remove attachments, particularly those made for the purposes of his business[5] or for the better enjoyment of the articles themselves, so long always as he has implemented his obligations under the lease.[6] The principles applicable as between landlord and tenant apply also to cases of superior and vassal.[7]

The matter may also arise in valuation cases[8] where the principles applicable as between heir and executor apply, and in relation to the diligence which is appropriate.

Modification of position by contract

Parties may by contract modify or exclude the inference which the court might otherwise draw as to fixity or removability, but such a contract will not affect the rights of persons not parties to it, such as a *bona fide* purchaser of the heritage, or the holder of a security over the heritage.[9]

Moveable rights becoming heritable destinatione

Rights originally moveable may become heritable for purposes of succession only, not of diligence, by the creditor or proprietor disclosing the intention that the objects shall fall to himself or his heir.[10] Thus the collection of materials for a building makes them

[1] *Tod's Trs.* v. *Finlay* (1872) 10 M. 422; *Nisbet* v. *Mitchell-Innes* (1880) 7 R. 575; *Cochrane* v. *Stevenson* (1891) 18 R. 1208; *Edinburgh Gas Commrs.* v. *Smart*, 1918 1 S.L.T. 80; *Jamieson* v. *Welsh* (1900) 3 F. 176;

[2] *Graham* v. *Lamont* (1875) 2 R. 438; *Christie* v. *Smith's Exrx.*, 1949 S.C. 572.

[3] *Arkwright* v. *Billinge*, 3 Dec. 1819, F.C.; *Reynolds* v. *Ashby* [1904] A.C. 466; *Howie's Trs.* v. *McLay* (1902) 5 F. 214; see also *Miller* v. *Muirhead* (1894) 21 R. 658; *Luke* v. *Smith* (1894) 1 S.L.T. 545.

[4] *Fisher* v. *Dixon* (1845) 4 Bell 286; *In re Hulse* [1905] 1 Ch. 406.

[5] *Dowall* v. *Miln* (1874) 1 R. 1180; *Brand's Trs.* v. *B's Trs.* (1876) 3 R. (H.L.) 16.

[6] *Smith* v. *Harrison's Tr.* (1893) 21 R. 330.

[7] *Marshall* v. *Tannoch Chemical Co.* (1886) 13 R. 1042.

[8] e.g. *Cowan* v. *Midlothian Assessor* (1894) 21 R. 812; *Dundee Assessor* v. *Carmichael* (1902) 4 F. 525; *Weir* v. *Glasgow Assessor*, 1924 S.C. 670.

[9] *Hobson* v. *Gorringe* [1897] 1 Ch. 182; cf. *Reynolds* v. *Ashby* [1904] A.C. 466; *Ellis* v. *Glover & Hobson* [1908] 1 K.B. 388.

[10] Ersk. II, 2, 14; Bell, *Comm.* II, 2; *Prin.* §1475; *Robertson* v. *Seton* (1637) Mor. 5489; cf. McLaren, I, 198.

heritable *destinatione* as soon as they are assembled at the site or incorporated in the fabric,[1] and funds required to complete a building have been held heritable in succession *destinatione*.[2] Dung made on a farm has been held to belong to the tenant's heir, the tenant being obliged to apply it to the land.[3] Fixed machinery erected by a tenant for working minerals or for farming purposes is also heritable *destinatione* as between the tenant's heir and his executor.[4] Books, silver-plate, jewels, and furniture may by destination be made heritable in succession.[5]

Rights heritable or moveable by destination—conversion and reconversion

The quality of a right in succession as heritable or moveable depends primarily on the quality of the estate as at the date of the owner's death.[6] But this quality may be altered by destination, express or implied, depending on the intention of the creditor or proprietor.[7] Thus the express exclusion of executors in a personal bond will make it heritable.[8] Conversion of a right may also be affected by selling land for money,[9] or laying out money on the purchase of heritage. Under the principle *quod fieri debet infectum valet* land contracted to be sold is accounted already moveable, the price falling to the executor,[10] and conversely.[11] The same rule applies to involuntary sales.[12] A judicial sale also affects conversion,[13] as does sale by a heritable creditor.[14] A trustee or administrator has no implied authority to alter the succession to the estate in his charge and acts of investment or administration do not effect conversion.[15]

[1] *Johnstone* v. *Dobie* (1783) Mor. 5443; *Gordon* v. *G.* (1806) Hume 188; cf. *Stewart* v. *Watson's Hosp.* (1862) 24 D. 256.
[2] *Malloch* v. *McLean* (1867) 5 M. 335; *B. of Scotland* v. *White's Trs.* (1891) 28 S.L.R. 891; but see *Fairlie's Trs.* v. *Fairlie's C.B.*, 1932 S.C. 216.
[3] *Reid's Exors.* v. *R.* (1890) 17 R. 519.
[4] *Brand's Trs.* v. *B's Trs.* (1876) 3 R. (H.L.) 16; *Miller* v. *Muirhead* (1894) 21 R. 658.
[5] Bell, *Prin.* §1475; *Baillie* v. *Grant* (1859) 21 D. 838.
[6] cf. *McLellan* v. *McL.*, 1960 S.C. 348.
[7] Ersk. II, 2, 14; Bell, *Prin.* §1491; *Baird* v. *Watson* (1880) 8 R. 233.
[8] Titles to Land Consolidation (Sc.) Act, 1868, S. 117.
[9] *McAdam's Exor.* v. *Souters* (1904) 7 F. 179.
[10] *Chiesly* v. *C.* (1704) Mor. 5531; *Macfarlane* v. *Greig* (1895) 22 R. 405.
[11] *Malloch* v. *McLean* (1867) 5 M. 335; *Ramsay* v. *R.* (1887) 15 R. 25; *Bank of Scotland* v. *White's Trs.* (1891) 28 S.L.R. 891.
[12] *Heron* v. *Espie* (1856) 18 D. 917; *Macfarlane*, *supra.*
[13] *Macfarlane* v. *Greig* (1895) 22 R. 405; *Royal Bank* v. *Maxwell's Exors.*, 1916 2 S.L.T. 175.
[14] *Howden*, 1910 2 S.L.T. 250; see also *Rossborough's Trs.* v. *R.* (1888) 16 R. 157.
[15] *Macfarlane*, *supra*, 409.

Constructive conversion

Conversion may be deemed effected constructively under the principle *quod fieri debet infectum valet* where trustees are directed to buy or sell heritage, in which case the direction is deemed at once implemented, and the beneficiary's right converted even though the direction has not in fact yet been implemented. The beneficiary's right is then of the kind intended by the truster, though the property held by the trustees may still be in fact of the other kind.[1] A direction to 'pay' beneficiaries normally constructively converts heritage.[2] But if the trustees have merely a power to buy or sell heritage, there is no conversion until or unless the power is exercised, or unless realization is necessary to give effect to the trust purposes and it is effected, or if they have a power exercisable only in certain contingencies or for certain purposes, and the contingency has arisen and the power been exercised.[3] Where conversion operates in consequence of the exercise of a power, it operates only to the extent that is necessary for the execution of the trust purposes and no further.[4] Mere investment by trustees for the preservation of the estate does not effect conversion,[5] nor does the grant by the court of a power of sale, as being necessary for the execution of the trust.[6] In general, where intestacy has resulted, even an express direction to convert

1 Bell, *Prin.* §1492; *Advocate-General* v. *Blackburn's Trs.* (1847) 10 D. 166, 185; *Buchanan's Trs.* v. *Angus* (1862) 4 Macq. 374; *McGilchrist's Trs.* v. *McG.* (1870) 8 M. 689; *McGregor* (1876) 13 S.L.R. 450; *Sheppard's Trs.* v. *S.* (1885) 12 R. 1193; *Watson's Trs.* v. *W.* (1902) 4 F. 798; *Bryson's Trs.* v. *B.*, 1919 2 S.L.T. 303; *Taylor's Trs.* v. *Tailyour*, 1927 S.C. 288.

2 *Cowan* v. *C.* (1887) 14 R. 670; *Kippen's Trs.* (1889) 16 R. 668; *Brown's Trs.* v. *B.* (1890) 18 R. 185; *Playfair's Trs.* v. *P.* (1894) 21 R. 836; *Anderson's Exor.* v. *A's Trs.* (1895) 22 R. 254; *Watson's Trs., supra*; *Steel's Trs.* v. *Steedman* (1902) 5 F. 239; *Bannerman* v. *B's Trs.* (1906) 13 S.L.T. 754.

3 Bell, *Prin.* §1493; *Buchanan* v. *Angus* (1862) 4 Macq. 374; *Duncan's Trs.* v. *Thomas* (1882) 9 R. 731; *Swain* v. *Benzie's Trs.*, 1960 S.C. 357. See also *Auld* v. *Anderson* (1876) 4 R. 211; *Hogg* v. *Hamilton* (1877) 4 R. 845; *Aitken* v. *Munro* (1883) 10 R. 1097; *Sheppard's Tr.* v. *S.* (1885) 12 R. 1193; *Seton's Tr.* v. *S.* (1886) 13 R. 1047; *Bank of Scotland* v. *White's Trs.* (1891) 28 S.L.R. 891; *Anderson's Exrx.* v. *Anderson's Trs.* (1895) 22 R. 254; *Sim* v. *S.* (1895) 22 R. 921; *Peterkin* v. *Harvey* (1902) 9 S.L.T. 434. Conversion was held operated in *Boag* v. *Walkinshaw* (1872) 10 M. 872; *Fotheringham's Trs.* (1873) 11 M. 848; *Nairn's Trs.* v. *Melville* (1877) 5 R. 128; *Baird* v. *Watson* (1880) 8 R. 233; *Galloway's Trs.* v. *G.* (1897) 25 R. 28; *McCall's Trs.* v. *Murray* (1901) 3 F. 380; *Henderson's Trs.* v. *H.* (1907) S.C. 43; *Campbell's Tr.* v. *Dick*, 1915 S.C. 100.

4 *Advocate General* v. *Smith* (1852) 14 D. 585; *Cowan* v. *C.* (1887) 14 R. 670; *Moon's Trs.* v. *M.* (1899) 2 F. 201; *McConochie's Trs.* v. *McC.*, 1912 S.C. 653.

5 *Carfrae* v. *C.* (1842) 4 D. 605; *White* v. *W.* (1860) 22 D. 1335; *Melrose* v. *M's Trs.* (1869) 7 M. 1050; *Baird* v. *Watson* (1880) 8 R. 233; *Cathcart's Trs.* v. *Heneage's Trs.* (1883) 10 R. 1205; *Campbell's Trs.* v. *C's Trs.* (1900) 8 S.L.T. 232; see also *Dundas* v. *D.* (1869) 8 M. 44.

6 *Taylor's Trs.* v. *Tailyour*, 1927 S.C. 288.

will not operate conversion to the prejudice of the heir in heritage.[1] A sale of heritage by a curator bonis under authority of the court has been held to effect conversion where the sale was forced or arose from actual necessity,[2] but does not where it has been merely an act of administration.[3]

Reconversion

If the effect of a direction in a trust deed is constructively to convert heritage to moveables, or vice versa, the beneficiaries, if capable of electing, may, before conversion has actually been effected, elect to take the property destined to them unconverted (since, were conversion effected, the benefit could at once be reconverted).[4] The election to reconvert may be exercised expressly, as by overt act or request, or impliedly, as by such conduct as, together with the lapse of time, indicates a clear intention to accept the property unconverted.[5] Inaction does not evidence intention to reconvert.[6]

[1] *Thomas* v. *Tennent's Trs.* (1868) 7 M. 114; *Smith* v. *Wighton's Trs.* (1874) 1 R. 358; *Cowan* v. *C.* (1887) 14 R. 670; *Brown's Trs.* v. *McIntosh* (1905) 13 S.L.T. 72.

[2] *Macfarlane* v. *Greig* (1895) 22 R. 405; *McAdam's Exor.* v. *Souters* (1904) 7 F. 179; *Dick* v. *D.*, 1925 S.L.T. 337.

[3] *Moncrieff* v. *Miln* (1856) 18 D. 1286; *Brown's Tr.* v. *B.* (1897) 24 R. 962.

[4] *Grindlay* v. *G's Trs.* (1853) 16 D. 27; *Hogg* v. *Hamilton* (1877) 4 R. 845.

[5] McLaren, I, 237; *Hogg* v. *Hamilton* (1877) 4 R. 845; *Peterkin* v. *Harvey* (1902) 9 S.L.T. 434; *Bryson's Tr.* v. *B.*, 1919 2 S.L.T. 303; *Mackintosh's Exor.* v. *M.*, 1925 S.L.T. 674.

[6] *Macgregor* (1876) 12 S.L.R. 450; *Bryson's Tr.*, *supra.*

PART 2
CORPOREAL HERITABLE PROPERTY

CHAPTER 75

LANDHOLDING GENERALLY—THE FEUDAL SYSTEM

THE rights of property in all lands in Scotland are either allodial or udal or feudal.

Allodial land

Lands held allodially are owned outright and absolutely. Only exceptionally is land so held; allodial land includes the Crown's paramount superiority, the sovereign's own property, lands belonging to the sovereign's eldest son as Prince and High Steward of Scotland, superiority rights reserved by the Crown in the lands of subjects, and churches, churchyards, manses, and glebes.[1] Lands acquired compulsorily under statutes are akin to allodial land.[2]

Udal land

In Orkney and Shetland land might formerly be held by possession without any written title, and some land there is still so held, though other land has been feudalized and is held feudally by charter and sasine.[3] Udal land was and is free of all burdens of services or periodical payments.

Feu-holding

The great bulk of the land in Scotland is held by feudal tenure. This mode of landholding was introduced into Scotland in the

[1] Stair II, 3, 4; Ersk. II, 3, 8. Certain churches and manses are now vested in the Church of Scotland General Trustees in free blench holding from the Crown: Church of Scotland (Property and Endowments) Act, 1925, S. 28(3).

[2] Lands Clauses Consolidation (Sc.) Act, 1845, Ss. 80, 126; *Macfarlane* v. *Monkland Ry.* (1864) 2 M. 519; *Elgin Mags.* v. *Highland Ry.* (1884) 11 R. 950; *Inverness Mags.* v. *Highland Ry.* (1893) 20 R. 551; *Heriot's Trust* v. *Caledonian Ry.*, 1915 S.C. (H.L.) 52; *D. Argyll* v. *L.M.S. Ry.*, 1931 S.C. 309; Burgh Police (Sc.) Act, 1892, Ss. 196–200; *Young's Trs.* v. *Grainger* (1904) 7 F. 232.

[3] Stair II, 3, 11; Bankt. II, 3, 10; Ersk. II, 3, 18; Bell, *Prin.* §932; *Sinclair* (1624) Mor. 16393; *Beatton* v. *Gaudie* (1832) 10 S. 286. See also *Bruce* v. *Smith* (1890) 17 R. 1000; *Spence* v. *Union Bank* (1894) 1 S.L.T. 648; *Smith* v. *Lerwick Harbour Trs.* (1903) 5 F. 680; *L.A.* v. *Balfour*, 1907 S.C. 1360; *L.A.* v. *Aberdeen University*, 1963 S.C. 533.

eleventh and twelfth centuries.[1] The main feature was that land was held from a superior in return for certain periodical services or payments; the superior owed the duty of maintaining and protecting his vassal, the vassal owed homage and fealty to his superior, and there was a mutual relation of rights and duties between superior and vassal.

Originally land was granted only for the vassal's lifetime but later it became, subject to certain conditions, a perpetual and heritable grant, but alienable only with the superior's consent.

A collateral element of feudal tenure was that the grant of lands commonly carried rights to superiors to hold courts and do justice and imposed duties on the vassals to attend those courts. Feudal jurisdictions were abolished by the Heritable Jurisdictions Act, 1747.

Essential features of feudal landholding

The essential feature of the feudal system of landholding is that no proprietor owns any piece of land absolutely. The sovereign as paramount superior of all the land in the country, except allodial and udal land, has granted tracts of lands to subjects to hold of and under him for specified returns; these subjects have in turn granted or may grant smaller areas to others, who have in turn granted or may grant smaller pieces and so on.

There is no legal limit to the amount of subfeuing which may be effected[2] nor to the number of subject superiors there may be between the sovereign and the vassal who actually possesses the land.

Feudal landholding thus involves the grant of lands to another on conditions and subject to the performance of services, and a continuing relationship between granter and grantee.

Estates or interests in the land

Accordingly in the feudal system of landholding a number of persons, the Crown, possibly several subject-superiors, and the vassal, all simultaneously have certain interests in any given piece

[1] See generally Ganshof, *Feudalism*; Vinogradoff, 'Origins of Feudalism', 2 Camb. Med. Hist., Ch. 20; 'Feudalism', 3 Camb. Med. Hist., Ch. 18; Barrow, *Feudal Britain, 1066–1314*; Ritchie, *Normans in Scotland*; Innes, *Scotland in the Middle Ages*, ch. 4; Farran, *Principles of Scots and English Land Law*; *Introd. to Scottish Legal History*, ch. 1; Craig, *J.F.* I, 8; Stair II, 3, 1–6; Bankt. II, 3, 1; Ersk. II, 3, 2–10; Bell, *Prin.* §675–9; Ross, *Lect.* II, 23; Bell, *Convg.*, I, 561; Menzies, 502; Wood, 119.

[2] Prior to the Conveyancing (Sc.) Act, 1874, S. 22, subinfeudation could be validly prohibited but only by an express condition in a grant of lands. Scotland has never had the general prohibition of subinfeudation introduced into England by the statute *Quia Emptores*, 1290.

of land; no one of them owns the land outright but each has simultaneously a defined interest or estate in the land conferring rights defined partly by general law and partly by the terms of the grant to him from his superior.[1] The superior retains an interest in land granted and may intervene to prevent it being diminished in value.

The recognized interests which may simultaneously subsist in any piece of land are:

The interest of the King

The interest of the King is that of ultimate and absolute ownership, except in so far as rights in and to a particular tract of land have been granted to his vassal-in-chief. But any and every right not so granted remains to the King.

The interests of superiority or dominium directum

There may be several, or many, interests of superiority, one vested in a vassal-in-chief, who holds directly of the King, and each other vested in a superior who holds of a superior higher in the chain but is himself superior of one or more vassals. The interest which the superior retains to himself in lands is called *dominium directum*, as the highest and most eminent right,[2] and in questions with the over-superior he is the *dominus*.[3] His title bears to be of the whole lands, not only of the superiority.[4]

The interest of fee or dominium utile

The fee of *dominium utile* is vested in the vassal who has nobody below him in the feudal pyramid and enjoys the actual occupation and use of the piece of land.[5] Thus the vassal and not the superior is entitled to possess the lands and draw the rents,[6] and to be deemed the heritor.[7]

Estates may also be distinguished into superiority, which is the residue of rights in land granted to a vassal; fee, which is an estate granted to a person and his heirs generally and accordingly passes in death to whoever may be the heir in heritage of the grantee; tailzied fee or entail, which is an estate granted to a

1 Craig, I, 9, 7; Ersk. II, 3, 1.
2 Ersk. II, 3, 10.
3 Ersk. II, 5, 1.
4 Stair II, 4, 1; Bell, *Prin.* §675; *Hay* v. *Aberdeen Corpn.*, 1909 S.C. 554, 559.
5 Ersk. II, 3, 10.
6 Bell, *Conv.* I, 563.
7 Bell, *Conv.* I, 642; *Dundas* v. *Nicolson* (1778) Mor. 8511.

person and a defined series of his heirs only; and liferent, which is an estate held by the grantee for his own life only.

Tenure

Each person having an estate or feudal interest in any land holds it of and under a superior, who similarly holds it of and under another, up to the superior who holds directly of the Crown, each in turn owing certain prestations to his superior and entitled to certain dues and duties from the vassal who holds of and under him. There is accordingly a relation of tenure between each proprietor and his immediate superior, defining the terms on which he holds the land and what return he owes to his superior, and a chain of tenure between the Crown and the ultimate vassal of lands.

The terms superior and vassal are not absolute but relative to one another, as a superior of lands will himself be vassal of the Crown or an oversuperior, and a vassal may, by subfeuing, make himself superior of a new vassal. So too a person may be simultaneously oversuperior, superior, and vassal of different pieces of land, or be vassal of different superiors in respect of different pieces of land, or superior of different vassals and subvassals in respect of various pieces of land.

The recognized tenures

Various forms of feudal tenure were recognized, according to the conditions under which vassals held their lands. During the military period of feus, if the grant were ambiguous, ward-holding was presumed; after 1746 feu-holding is presumed.[1]

Wardholding

Ward-holding or military service was the most ancient,[2] deriving its name from the fact that during the minority of a vassal the superior was entitled to the guardianship of his person and management of his estate. By this tenure vassals were obliged to serve their superior in war as often as he called for it, or to give other special services.

In addition to the obligation of military service the superior was entitled to certain incidents or casualties exigible where required. These were aids (a) to ransom the lord from imprisonment, (b) for the knighting of his eldest son, and (c) for the

[1] Bell, *Prin.* §684.

[2] Stair II, 3, 32; Ersk. II, 4, 1–4; Bell, *Prin.* §681; see also *D. Argyll* v. *Campbell*, 1912 S.C. 458.

dowry of his eldest daughter on marriage; and the superior was also entitled to certain casualties: these were

(a) Ward: If the heir were under 21, if male, or under 14, if female, the ward or guardianship of the heir belonged to the superior and he had full control of all lands held by military tenure, without at first any liability to account, on the heir's attaining full age, for his stewardship.[1] The right of wardship was often compounded for by a regular annual payment during the heir's minority, known as taxed ward. When the vassal came of age he might sue for his lands from the lord on doing service as heir and paying relief.[2]

(b) Marriage: The lord also had the right to determine the marriage of the heir, originally in the case of heiresses only. If the heir refused the marriage offered he or she was liable for the 'avail' or market value of the match offered. Latterly avail became payable in every case even if the ward married with the superior's consent,[3] or though the lord failed to procure a spouse.[4] Single avail was originally three years' and later two years' free rent of the vassal's lands.[5] In the case of elopement or entry into a nunnery a double avail was payable.[6] By some charters the avail of marriage was a fixed sum, known as taxed avail.

(c) Non-entry was the casualty payable on succession of an heir to a vassal. If by death there was no vassal from whom the superior could exact performance of the services due, he could possess the lands until the vassal's heir did homage to the superior and was accepted by him. Originally if the vassal neglected for a year and a day to enter with the superior he forfeited the holding but later he was allowed to enter with the superior at any time on payment of the casualty of non-entry, measured by the annual value of the lands from the late vassal's death.

(d) Relief was payable on the succession of an heir to a vassal; it was latterly settled at one year's value of the land.[7]

Wrongs inferring forfeiture of the lands

Wrongful acts of the vassal towards his superior were punishable by escheat, recognition, disclamation, and purpresture. Escheat was the forfeiture to the superior of the annual profits of

1 Ersk. II, 5, 5–9.
2 Craig, *J.F.* II, 20, 10.
3 *Campbell* v. *McNaughton* (1677) Mor. 8535; *Arbuthnot* v. *Keith* (1662) Mor. 8528.
4 *Darcie's Case* (1607) 6 Co. Rep. 706.
5 Ersk. II, 5, 20; Bell, *Convg.* I, 565.
6 Ersk. II, 5, 21.
7 Craig *J.F.* II, 20, 30; Stair II, 4, 27; Ersk. II, 5, 47.

land while the vassal was in a state of rebellion against the Crown or his superior. Escheat might be single escheat, whereby the rebel's moveables fell to the Crown as *bona vacantia*, the Crown or a grantee of the escheat having a year in which to exact the moveables and which formed a burden on the superior's right of liferent escheat and was compounded for by a year's rent; the liferent escheat gave the superior the right to possess the feu while the vassal lived and persisted in rebellion but only in liferent, the fee remaining in the rebel. Liferent escheat was burdened with the vassal's debts, if real and attaching to the lands, but not if merely personal, or subsequent to the escheat. It fell by sentence of death and escape, or by denunciation of the vassal for a criminal cause unrelaxed for a year.[1]

Recognition was the penalty for a vassal holding by ward who alienated more than half of the lands held by this tenure of one superior without that superior's consent. If he alienated to a substitute vassal, the deed was void and he forfeited the whole of his interest in the fee.[2] If he alienated to a sub-vassal to hold of and under him, it was alienation if the subfeu were to be held by ward, blench, mortification or for an illusory service, but not if to be held in feu farm for a real return.[3]

Disclamation meant a denial of the superior title, and involved forfeiture of the whole fee.[4] It is now long obsolete.

Purpresture was an encroachment on the superior's lands or rights, and likewise involved forfeiture of the fee.[5] It is now also long obsolete.

The tenure of ward-holding and the casualties of ward, marriage, and recognition were abolished by the Tenures Abolition Act, 1746. Existing tenures by ward were converted into blench holdings if held of the Crown and into feu-holding if held of a subject superior.

Feu-farm

Feu-farm (or soccage) is the perpetual tenure of land in return for a fixed annual farm or rental, in agricultural services, produce of land, or money, and having analogies with the Roman *emphyteusis*. Originally ignoble, it is now the prevailing tenure.[6]

1 Bell, *Prin.* §731.
2 Stair II, 11, 17; Ersk. II, 5, 10–17; *Hay* v. *Muiries' Creditors* (1631) Mor. 6513.
3 Craig III, 3, 8; Stair II, 11, 13.
4 Craig III, 5, 1; Stair II, 11, 29; Ersk. II, 5, 51; Bell, *Prin.* §730.
5 Craig Stair, *supra*; Ersk. II, 5, 52.
6 Stair II, 3, 34; Ersk. II, 4, 5; Bell, *Prin.* §683; Bell, *Convg.* I, 569.

From 1457[1] the king and lords were allowed to make grants of lands in feu, and there was a continuing tendency to substitute feus for ward-holding. Services tended in time to be commuted into money[2] and any not so commuted have now been extinguished.[3]

Feu duty might be in money or in kind down to 1925[4] but all feu duties in kind in feus granted after the 1874 Act must be of fixed amount or quantity,[5] and in all feus granted after 1924 the feu duty must be in sterling money.[6]

The casualties exigible in feu-holding were (a) non-entry, measured by the feu-duty, unless the superior brought an action for declaractor of non-entry; non-entry was abolished in 1874:[7] (b) relief, payable to the superior for granting the heir investiture in the lands, measured by an additional year's feu duty: (c) composition, payable to the superior by a purchaser or other singular successor of the last vassal to obtain recognition as vassal; alienation of a feu was not originally permitted without the superior's consent but after the Tenures Abolition Act, 1746, superiors had to enter purchasers or disponees on payment of a composition; it was measured by a year's rent on the lands as then let: (d) liferent escheat, entitling the superior to a liferent of the fruits of the lands if the vassal were put to the horn and remained so for a year and a day; in 1746 this casualty was abolished where the denunciation for crime was in respect of civil debt only.

Blench holding

Blench holding is the tenure of land in return for services or tributes of various kinds, some valuable and some illusory, and frequently stipulated more in acknowledgment of the superior's rights than as profit to him.[8] In modern cases the tribute in blench holding is usually a penny Scots, *si petatur tantum*.

The casualties were the same as in feu-farm tenure. Lands originally held by ward of the Crown or of the Prince of Scotland were later converted into blench-holding by statute.[9]

[1] Act, 1457, c. 71 (A.P.S. II, 49).
[2] Conveyancing (Sc.) Act, 1874, Ss. 20, 21, and 1924, S. 12.
[3] 1924 Act, S. 12.
[4] 1924 Act, S. 12(1).
[5] 1874 Act, S. 23.
[6] 1924 Act, S. 12.
[7] Conveyancing (Sc.) Act, 1874, S. 4.
[8] Craig I, 11, 5; Stair II, 3, 33; Ersk. II, 4, 7; Bell, *Prin.* §682, 692. But see also *D. Richmond* v. *Countess of Seafield*, 1927 S.C. 833.
[9] Tenures Abolition Act, 1746, S. 2; Admission of Vassals (Sc.) Act, 1751.

Burgage

Burgage was the tenure by which royal burghs, burghs of barony and burghs of regality held lands of the Crown or superior of the burgh; the usual tribute was the duty of watching and warding. The vassal was truly the burghers as a corporation. Burgage tenants normally paid no relief and their lands did not fall into non-entry or ward.[1] For all practical purposes burgage was equated with feu-farm tenure in 1874.[2]

A special case of burgage was the tenure by booking in Paisley. The tenure was from the burgh and transfer was by resignation in presence of the town council, the proceedings being recorded by the Town Clerk and a copy delivered to the new tenant.[3] After 1868 conveyances could be recorded in the Register of Booking and even since 1874 lands held prior thereto by booking must be so recorded.[4]

Mortification

Mortification was the tenure whereby were held feudal subjects given to churches, monasteries or other corporations, ecclesiastical or lay, for religious, charitable or public uses. The only return was *preces et lacrymae*. No services were due and there were no casualties. At the Reformation lands mortified to religious corporations were forfeited and annexed to the Crown.[5]

Since the final abolition of episcopacy in 1690 the only lands remaining mortified to the churches were the manses and glebes of parish ministers.[6] Lands held for religious or charitable purposes may now be held by feu or blench holding.

Kindly tenants

A few cases survive of kindly tenancy, of landholders on former demesne lands of the monarch, who have full proprietorship but yet hold neither feudally or allodially.[7] Rentallers have no charter or feudal title, but are enrolled in the landlord's rent books.

[1] Craig I, 10, 21; Stair II, 3, 38; Ersk. II, 4, 8; Bell, *Prin.* §685, 838.

[2] Conveyancing (Sc.) Act, 1874, S. 25.

[3] See *Chalmers* v. *Paisley Mags.* (1829) 7 S. 718; Conveyancing (Sc.) Act, 1874, S. 26; *McCutcheon* v. *McWilliam* (1876) 3 R. 565.

[4] 1874 Act, S. 25.

[5] See Acts, 1587, c. 29 (A.P.S. III, 431); 1633, c. 10 (A.P.S. V, 27); Stair II, 3, 39–40; Ersk. II, 4, 10, and 11; Bell, *Prin.* §686; Bell, *Convg.* I, 570; Menzies, 521.

[6] Bankt. II, 8, 6; Stair, II, 3, 40 and Ersk. II, 1, 7, tend to treat these lands as *res sacrae*.

[7] See Stair II, 9, 21; III, 9, 15; Ersk. II, 6, 37; Ross, *Lect.* II, 179, 474; Hunter, *L. & T.* I, 423; II, 122; Rankine, *L.*, 152; *Cassilis' Tutor* v. *Lochinvar* (1581) Mor. 15183; 1 Pat. 77; *Craigie Wallace* (1623) Mor. 7191; *Kindly Tenants of Lochmaben* v. *Stormonth*

Later simplification of tenures

Ward holding and the casualties of ward, both simple and taxed ward, marriage, and recognition were abolished in 1746, and lands so held were converted, if held of the Crown, to blench holdings and if held of a subject superior, to feu holdings.[1] The casualties of single and liferent escheat were also abolished.[2]

In 1874[3] blench tenure became virtually a form of feu-farm and the tenure of lands held burgage was assimilated for nearly all purposes to that of feu-farm.

The Conveyancing (Sc.) Act, 1874, prohibited the creation of casualties in new forms and provided for the commutation or redemption of casualties in existing feus, though it remained competent to stipulate for duplications of feu-duty at fixed intervals, commonly every nineteenth year. The Feudal Casualties (Sc.) Act, 1914, made commutation into an extra feu-duty compulsory,[4] and made it incompetent in new feus to stipulate for casualties, duplicands or sums payable at intervals of more than one year, though it is still competent to stipulate for a permanent increase or decrease of feu duty, if certain both as to time and amount.

Crownhold

The Land Commission Act, 1967, established the Land Commission to acquire land suitable for material development and authorized it (S. 17) to dispose of land by way of feu, sale, or lease, the disposition stating that the interest conveyed is to be held by way of crownhold, and containing such conditions restricting development as are necessary to retain for the Crown any element of value which may be or become attributable to the prospect of any development of that land for any other purpose.

(1726) Mor. 15195; *Mounsey* v. *Kennedy*, 30 Nov. 1808, F.C.; *M. Queensberry* v. *Wright* (1838) 16 S. 439; *Royal Four Towns Fishing Assoc.* v. *Dumfriesshire Assessor*, 1956 S.C. 379; Carmont, 'Kindly Tennants' (1910) 21 J.R. 324; Farran, *Scots and English Land Law*, 60–4.

1 Tenures Abolition Act, 1746, Ss. 1–9; see *D. Argyll* v. *Campbell*, 1912 S.C. 458.

2 Ibid., S. 11.

3 Conveyancing (Sc.) Act, 1874, Ss. 3 and 25; cf. *McCutcheon* v. *McWilliam* (1876) 3 R. 565.

4 See *D. Richmond* v. *Seafield*, 1927 S.C. 833; *Macdonald* v. *Small's Trs.*, 1928 S.L.T. 321; *Dowell's, Ltd.* v. *Heriot's Trust*, 1941 S.C. 13; *L.A.* v. *Cummings*, 1942 S.C. 25.

CHAPTER 76

CREATION OF A NEW FEUDAL ESTATE

1 CHARTER

A NEW feudal estate in lands was originally created by the Crown or a subject superior personally, on the lands and in presence of at least two vassals (*pares curiae*) delivering to the grantee a symbolical portion of the lands, earth and stone, as representing the whole, and the grantee thereupon swearing fealty to the superior. It subsequently became the practice to give a written testimony of the grant (*breve testatum*) sealed by granter and witnesses, or a certificate from a notary public, or of two witnesses to the investiture.[1] This constituted proper investiture.

Improper investiture consisted of the granter first executing the *breve testatum* and directing it to his bailie as a warrant to him to give possession to the grantee; the bailie having done so on the lands sealed the *breve testatum*, or sealed a separate declaration of the fact. This became the basis of the later instrument of sasine.

Introduction of charters

Subsequently a charter based on the *breve testatum* was introduced and since then writ has always been recognized as necessary for the constitution and not only for the proof of infeftment or infeudation. At first a separate precept authorizing infeftment accompanied the charter but later the precept of sasine came to be embodied in the charter.[2]

Original charters and charters by progress

An original charter was one by which a feu was first granted, and all subsequent charters are, in case of ambiguity, to be interpreted conformably to the original charter, and, if there be no express alteration, all clauses in the original charter were to be implied in later renewals thereof.[3]

Charters by progress were renewed dispositions of a feu formerly granted, on the vassal's resignation, or confirmation of

[1] Stair II, 3, 12; Ersk. II, 3, 17; Bell, *Prin.* §757, 769; Ross, *Lect.* II, 117; Bell, *Convg.* I, 577; Menzies, 529.

[2] Ersk. II, 3, 33.

[3] Ersk. II, 3, 30; Bell, *Prin.* §757.

his disponee, or the inheritance of his heir, or on apprising and adjudication.[1]

Charter of novodamus

A charter of novodamus is an original grant but replacing a previous grant of the same subjects, and granted to release the grantee from burdens and conditions previously affecting the grant, and to remedy a defect in the former title or modify the conditions on which the subjects are held. A charter of novodamus may be a first grant as well as a renewal of a former grant, and convey subjects to which the grantee was not previously entitled.[2]

2 SASINE

Sasine

Sasine is the taking of legal possession of land, without which physical occupation and possession is of no avail, and which completes the grantee's title to the land independently of actual possession thereof. By taking sasine the vassal becomes infeft in the lands.

Originally possession of the land was delivered to the grantee along with the charter by the superior's bailie sealing the charter in testimony that possession was given, or subscribing a declaration, even in a separate writing, that he had done so.

Precept of Sasine

In the fifteenth century the practice developed of the superior delivering along with the charter a precept of sasine which later, by the Act of 1672, c. 7, was ordered to be engrossed in the charter, before the testing clause. This was a command by the superior to his bailie to give sasine of the subject disponed to the vassal or his attorney by delivery of the appropriate symbols. The person to be infeft had to be identified. Precepts might be general or special (authorizing infeftment only in security, or in liferent, or in fee subject to an entail). Though the name of the bailie to whom the precept was directed was commonly left blank and the precept could be executed by any person giving sasine to the vassal, it had to contain a special mandate to infeft the vassal. Whoever had possession of the precept was presumed to be the vassal's attorney to receive possession in his name.[3]

1 Stair II, 3, 15; Ersk, II, 3, 20; Bell, *Prin.* §775.
2 Stair II, 3, 15; Ersk. II, 3, 23; *Scott* v. *Archbishop of Glasgow* (1680) Mor. 9339.
3 Stair II, 3, 16; Ersk. II, 3, 33; Bell, *Prin.* §876–9.

Instrument of Sasine

Sasine was given on the lands by the superior or his bailie delivering the precept, in the presence of witnesses and of the vassal or his attorney, to a notary who read it, after which the superior or his bailie delivered to the vassal or his attorney the appropriate symbols.[1] Then, the vassal or his attorney put a piece of money in the notary's hand and declared that he took instruments in the hands of the notary, before the witnesses, that he had received sasine of the lands in due form.[2] The notary then extended a written Instrument of Sasine, narrating the precept of sasine and so much of the charter as was necessary for understanding the precept, and subjoined his own attestation, that he, having been specially called for the purpose knew, saw, and heard that these facts were done as are recited in the instrument to which he and the witnesses attached their signatures.[3] Great particularity was required in the instrument and the courts frequently held blunders and omissions fatal to the sasine.[4] An instrument of sasine was the only competent evidence of symbolical delivery of possession.[5]

Where sasine not taken

A charter or disposition not followed by sasine created only a personal right in the grantee and did not vest in him a real or feudal right in the lands, and consequently left the lands subject to the diligence of the granter's creditors, and liable to be defeated by any later disposition of the lands, sasine on which was registered first.[6] An instrument of sasine, evidencing delivery of sasine, and duly recorded in the appropriate Register of Sasines, alone created a real right in the lands in the grantee.

When sasine not required

Exceptionally sasine was not required, in the case of crown lands, royal burghs holding lands burgage,[7] and the former legal liferents of terce and courtesy.

[1] The symbols differed according to the nature of the subjects granted by the superior: the customary ones were earth and stone for lands, clap and happer for mills, net and coble for fishings, a sheaf of corn for parsonage tithes, hasp and staple for houses within burghs, a psalm book and the keys of the church for the patronage of a living, the book of court for a heritable jurisdiction, a penny or a handful of grain for a right of annual rent: Ersk. II, 3, 36; Duff, 100; Bell, *Convg.* I, 655; Menzies, 573.

[2] Bell, *Convg.* I, 650; Menzies, 570.

[3] Stair II, 3, 16–17; Ersk. II, 3, 34–37; Bell, *Convg.* I, 649, Menzies, 569.

[4] Stair II, 3, 18.

[5] Stair II, 3, 16.

[6] Stair II, 3, 16; Ersk. II, 3, 48.

[7] Stair II, 3, 38; Ersk. II, 3, 34; Bell, *Prin.* §839.

Sasine of contiguous or discontiguous subjects

One sasine might suffice for several parcels of land if contiguous, unless held from different superiors, or by different tenures, or where the vassal of one became proprietor of the other by purchase, there being separate titles to each.[1] Discontiguous lands required separate sasine unless they had been united by a crown charter of union, in which case sasine on a place specified or, if none specified, on any of the lands would serve for the whole.[2] Lands held of different superiors, or by different tenures are incapable of union, but subjects of different kinds may be covered by a charter of union and transferred by one sasine.

If lands have been erected by the Crown into a barony, lands spatially separated, and subjects, however different in nature, may be transferred by one sasine as if united by a charter of union.[3]

Sasine of separate heritable subjects

Separate symbolical deliveries were necessary when the charter conveyed other subjects, such as salmon fishings, for which earth and stone were not appropriate symbols.[4]

Warrant for sasine essential

An instrument of sasine is relative to the precept on which it proceeds as its warrant, and was not evidence unless the precept were produced, save in special cases.[5]

3 REGISTRATION

Registration

Publication of sasines was required by several sixteenth century statutes, but these were superseded by the Registration Act, 1617 (c. 16) which established the Register of Sasines and required instruments of sasine and other similar deeds affecting land to be registered within sixty days after their dates, failing which the sasine was ineffectual, save against the granter and his heirs, and successors. Sasine of burgage-lands were included by an Act of 1681.[6]

Sasines have priority according to the date of registration, not according to the date of the sasines themselves.[7]

1 Ersk. II, 3, 44.
2 Stair II, 3, 44; Ersk. II, 3, 45.
3 Stair II, 3, 45; Ersk. II, 3, 46.
4 Ersk. II, 3, 44; Bell, *Convg.* I, 660.
5 Stair II, 3, 19; Mack. II, 3, 15; Ersk. II, 3, 38.
6 Stair II, 3, 20; Ersk. II, 3, 39–41.
7 Act of 1693, c. 13.

An unrecorded sasine is null for all purposes,[1] except against the granter and his heirs,[2] and a recorded sasine with an omission *in essentialibus* is also invalid;[3] such nullities cannot be cured by prescriptive possession.

The instrument was entered in the minute book of the Registers, and subsequently transcribed *ad longum* into the register; any error in essentials, or erasure or other vitiation, was fatal. A certificate of registration was endorsed on the instrument of sasine by the keeper of the register.[4]

Registration in the sasine registers being for publication, the original deed is returned to the grantee after registration, marked as registered, but extracts (now photostat copies) of deeds may be obtained; an extract is as probative as the principal itself, unless there is challenge on the ground of forgery.[5]

Sasine and infeftment after 1845

After 1845[6] symbolical delivery on the lands was unnecessary and infeftment could be obtained by producing to a notary public the warrants of sasine and relative writs and expeding and recording in the Register of Sasines an abbreviated instrument of sasine setting forth that sasine had been given, such sasine to be effectual whether the lands were contiguous or discontiguous, held by the same or different titles, of one or more superiors; the instrument of sasine, if in the revised form permitted by the Act, could be recorded at any time during the grantee's life, and on being recorded had the same effect as if sasine had been taken and an instrument of sasine recorded according to the previous law and practice.

The Lands Transference Act, 1847, permitted short statutory forms of the principal clauses, and the Titles to Land Act, 1858, permitted a short description of the lands in statutory form, rendered the precept of sasine and instrument of sasine unnecessary, and made it competent to record the charter itself, with a warrant of registration thereon, in the Register of Sasines.

The Titles to Land Consolidation (Sc.) Act, 1868 (amended in 1869) and the Conveyancing (Sc.) Act, 1874, established the

[1] *Paterson* v. *Douglas* (1714) Rob. App. 99; *Young* v. *Leith* (1847) 9 D. 932; (1848) 2 Ross. L.C. 103.
[2] *Gray* (1626) Mor. 13540; *Simpson* v. *Blackie* (1678) Mor. 13553.
[3] *Mackintosh* v. *Weir* (1825) 2 Ross L.C. 75; *Davidson* v. *McLeod* (1827) 6 S. 8.
[4] See *Cowper* (1885) 12 R. 415; *Elgin Mags.* (1885) 12 R. 1136; *Hepburn* (1905) 7 F. 484.
[5] Stair II, 3, 24; Ersk. II, 3, 43.
[6] Infeftment Act, 1845.

modern system, which was further developed by the Conveyancing (Sc.) Act, 1924, and the Conveyancing Amendment (Sc.) Act, 1938.

Rights of barony and regality

A royal grant might erect lands *in liberam baroniam*, as one feudal tenement, designated by a general name, though consisting of separate lands, having also extensive rights of jurisdiction within appointed limits and accompanied by pertinents and privileges not attendant on ordinary estates. A charter, or subsequent disposition, of the barony, its name being *nomen universitatis*, conveyed all the lands and separate portions of the barony lands, and all pertinents belonging to it.[1] A royal grant might similarly erect lands *in liberam regalitatem*, where even wider jurisdiction, civil, and criminal, was exercised by the Lord of Regality. Regality jurisdiction has been abolished.[2]

Burghs of barony and regality were erected by the crown to be held of barons or lords of regality.[3]

MODERN CREATION OF NEW FEUDAL ESTATE

The creation may be by a feu-charter, feu-disposition or feu-contract. The former two are identical in form and are unilateral grants giving execution to an intent to give lands in feu. The feu-contract is bilateral, the deed executive of a contract to grant and take land on feu,[4] and appropriate where the parties wish to be able to enforce by personal diligence the obligations undertaken thereby. In addition to the clauses common to all three forms of grant, it contains an express obligation by the vassal to pay and perform the duties undertaken to the superior, and a clause of registration for preservation and execution by virtue of which the superior may use summary diligence to enforce performance of the obligations of the contract. In a feu-charter or feu-disposition the vassal accepts personal liability by acceptance of the deed.[5]

[1] Stair II, 3, 45, and 60; Ersk. I, 4, 25; II, 3, 46; II, 6, 18; Bell, *Prin.* §749–54.

[2] Stair II, 3, 45; Ersk. II, 3, 46; Bell, *Prin.* §749; Heritable Jurisdictions Abolition (Sc.) Act, 1746, Ss. 1, 24.

[3] Bell, *Prin.* §848.

[4] The normal rules of contract apply to the capacity of parties, creation, proof, enforceability and breach of the prior contract to grant a feu: see *L. Clinton* v. *Brown* (1874) 1 R. 1137; *Stodart* v. *Dalzell* (1876) 4 R. 236; *Tayport Land Co.* v. *Dougall's Trs.* (1895) 23 R. 287; *Kerr* v. *Forrest's Tr.* (1902) 10 S.L.T. 67; *Alston* v. *Nellfield Manure Co.*, 1915 S.C. 912; *Mitchell* v. *Stornoway Trs.*, 1936 S.C. (H.C.) 56.

[5] *Hunter* v. *Boog* (1834) 13 S. 205.

Clauses of modern feu-charter, feu-disposition or feu-contract

The clauses and their scope and purposes have been carried on from mediaeval charters and some still bear the names they did in Latin charters. But by statute it is now frequently possible to abbreviate the clauses, though they may bear the same connotations as the older long clauses.

(1) NARRATIVE CLAUSE

The narrative clause sets out the names and designations of the parties, who must be sufficiently identified.[1] The expression 'heritable proprietor' used of the granter implies that he is himself infeft in the lands disponed;[2] if he has no title or only a personal title his grant is validated by accretion if he later obtains infeftment.[3] If not himself infeft he may not deduce his own title from his author in the deed so as to make his deed a warrant for infeftment of the grantee.[4]

An effectual grant may be made by a party having an interest in the lands less than fee, e.g. in liferent, if with the consent of the true owner,[5] or even by a person having no interest if such consent be taken.[6]

The narrative clause also sets out the cause or consideration for the grant, whether gratuitous, as from love, favour and affection, or onerous, for a price or other valuable consideration.[7]

(2) DISPOSITIVE CLAUSE

The dispositive clause is the principal clause; it contains the words of conveyance, the word 'dispone' being no longer essential;[8] the name of the grantee and the destination; a description

[1] *Guthrie* v. *Munro* (1833) 11 S. 465; *Scottish Union Ins. Co.* v. *Calderwood* (1836) 14 S. 667.

[2] Duff 59; Bell, *Convg.* I, 580; Menzies 166.

[3] Stair III, 2, 1; Ersk. II, 7, 2; Bell, *Prin.* §881; *Lockhart* v. *Ferrier* (1837) 16 S. 76; *Innes* v. *Gordon* (1844) 7 D. 141; *McGibbon* v. *McG.* (1852) 14 D. 605; *E. Fife* v. *Duff* (1863) 1 M. (H.L.) 19; *Swans* v. *Western Bank* (1866) 4 M. 663; *Smith* v. *Wallace* (1869) 8 M. 204.

[4] Conveyancing (Sc.) Act, 1924, S. 3, does not apply to original feudal grants.

[5] *Sorley's Trs.* v. *Grahame* (1832) 10 S. 319.

[6] Ersk. II, 3, 21; *Mounsey* v. *Maxwell* (1808) Hume 237; *Stirling* v. *Tenants* (1830) Hume 238.

[7] Ersk. II, 3, 22. This is essential under the Stamp Act, 1891, S. 5.

[8] Prior to the 1868 Act, S. 20, 'dispone' was essential in conveyances of heritage *mortis causa*, and prior to the 1874 Act, S. 27, that word was deemed essential in *inter vivos* deeds. It is still the word normally used. The phrase appropriate to an original grant is: 'sell and in feu-farm dispone'.

of the lands granted; and the reservations, burdens, qualifications and other conditions of the grant.

The dispositive clause is the ruling clause[1] and, unless ambiguous, cannot be modified by the narrative[2] or executive clauses;[3] if ambiguous or deficient other clauses may be invoked to clarify the ambiguity or supply the omission.[4]

Destination

The grant is normally in favour of the grantee and his heirs and assignees whomsoever, but fees being both heritable and transmissible a grant to the grantee alone has the same effect.[5] It may, however, be to the grantee and a special series of heirs, such as his heirs male, or to one person in liferent and another in fee, or to one person, whom failing, to another, or to several persons in common. In the absence of a clause of return, lands granted do not revert to the granter on the failure of heirs.[6] The clause normally concludes with the words 'heritably and irredeemably' but these are redundant.

Description

The lands must be described sufficiently to make them identifiable with certainty and accurately delimitable.[7] A description may be by general name, as by the name of the lands, particularly if an old estate or lands erected into a barony.[8] It may be particular, by boundaries, by measurement, or by reference to a plan,[9] and normally including reference to the parish and county in which the lands lie. Such a description may be general followed by an enumeration of particulars, or a list of particular pieces of land.

1 Ersk. III, 8, 47; Bell, *Prin.* §760.

2 *Chancellor* v. *Mosman* (1872) 10 M. 995; *Brownlie* v. *Miller* (1880) 7 R. (H.L.) 66; *Orr* v. *Mitchell* (1893) 20 R. (H.L.) 27; *Inglis* v. *Gillanders* (1895) 22 R. (H.L.) 51; *D. Sutherland's Trs.* v. *C. Cromarty* (1896) 23 R. (H.L.) 32; *Cooper Scott* v. *Gill Scott*, 1924 S.C. 309.

3 *Forrester* v. *Hutchison* (1826) 4 S. 824.

4 *Kerr* v. *Innes* (1810) 5 Pat. 320, 444; *L.A.* v. *Sinclair* (1865) 5 M. (H.L.) 97; *L.A.* v. *McCulloch* (1874) 2 R. 27; *Orr* v. *Mitchell* (1893) 20 R. (H.L.) 27; *Dick-Lauder* v. *Leather-Cully*, 1920 S.C. 48.

5 Bell, *Convg.* I, 585; *Reid* v. *Young* (1838) 16 S. 383.

6 Ersk. III, 10, 1.

7 Ersk. II, 3, 23; Bell, *Convg.* I, 588; Menzies 541.

8 Bell, *Convg.* I, 589; Menzies 541; cf. *E. Argyle* v. *Campbell* (1668) Mor. 9631. The Keeper of the Registers may reject a deed containing a description too general: *Macdonald* v. *Keeper of Sasine Register*, 1914 S.C. 854.

9 *N.B. Ry. Co.* v. *Hawick Mags.* (1862) 1 M. 200.

Bounding title

The description may or may not constitute a bounding charter or bounding title,[1] i.e. one which sets limits to the lands granted so that even prescriptive possession beyond the limits will not establish ownership thereof,[2] though the grantee may, by prescriptive possession, acquire an incorporeal right, such as a servitude or right to salmon-fishings, beyond his boundaries.[3]

A bounding title may be constituted by specific boundaries, such as a wall or street,[4] or the lands of another,[5] by boundaries and demonstrative measurements,[6] by taxative measurements or measurements which are an essential of the bargain,[7] by measurements and certain boundaries, sufficient to make the area certain,[8] by a general name together with an enumeration of lands possessed by named persons, which enumeration is presumed to be taxative,[9] by a statement that the lands lie within a certain parish or county,[10] by a reference to boundaries on a plan.[11]

If the limits set by a bounding charter are vague or ambiguous, extrinsic evidence may be adduced to fix them.[12]

Where a plan and also a description are used, it is a question of circumstances which will rule.[13] Boundaries, if clearly stated, prevail against plan or measurements,[14] unless measurements are an essential part of the contract.[15]

In general if lands are described as bounded 'by' a feature,

[1] Stair II, 3, 26; Ersk. II, 6, 2; Bell, *Prin.* §738; Duff, 63; Bell, *Convg.* I, 596; Menzies 511.

[2] Stair II, 3, 26; Ersk. II, 6, 3; Bell, *Prin.* §738; *N.B. Ry.* v. *Moon's Trs.* (1879) 6 R. 640; *Reid* v. *McColl* (1879) 7 R. 74.

[3] *Liston* v. *Galloway* (1835) 14 S. 97; *Beaumont* v. *L. Glenlyon* (1843) 5 D. 1337; *E. Zetland* v. *Tennents' Trs.* (1873) 11 M. 469; cf. *E. Dalhousie* v. *McInroy* (1865) 3 M. 1168.

[4] *Kerr* v. *Dickson* (1842) 1 Bell 490; *D. Buccleuch* v. *Edinburgh Mags.* (1864) 2 M. 1114.

[5] *Reid* v. *McColl* (1879) 7 R. 84; but see *Troup* v. *Aberdeen Heritable Soc. Co.*, 1916 S.C. 918.

[6] *Gibson* v. *Bonnington Sugar Co.* (1869) 7 M. 394; *Blyth's Trs.* v. *Shaw Stewart* (1883) 11 R. 99; *Currie* v. *Campbell's Trs.* (1888) 16 R. 237.

[7] *Darroch* v. *Ranken* (1841) 4 D. 219; *Hunter* v. *L. Adv.* (1869) 7 M. 899; cf. *Brown* v. *N.B. Ry. Co.* (1906) 8 F. 534.

[8] *Stewart* v. *Greenock Harbour Trs.* (1866) 4 M. 283.

[9] *Murray* v. *Oliphant's Wife* (1634) Mor. 2262; *Gardner* v. *Scott* (1843) 2 Bell 129; *Critchley* v. *Campbell* (1884) 11 R. 475.

[10] *Gordon* v. *Grant* (1850) 13 D. 1; Bell, *Convg.* I, 597.

[11] *N.B. Ry.* v. *Hawick Mags.* (1862) 1 M. 200.

[12] *Davidson* v. *Anstruther-Easter Mags.* (1843) 7 D. 342; *Dalhousie's Tutors* v. *Minister of Lochlee* (1890) 17 R. 1060.

[13] *Paterson* v. *Carnegie* (1851) 13 D. 997; *N.B. Ry.* v. *Moon's Trs.* (1879) 6 R. 640; *Currie* v. *Campbell's Trs.* (1888) 16 R. 237.

[14] *Ure* v. *Anderson* (1834) 12 S. 494; *Currie, supra.*

[15] *Hepburn & Somerville* v. *Campbell* (1781) Mor. 14168.

that is excluded from the lands,[1] but walls may be common property, the boundary running down the centre line, and if lands are 'enclosed by' walls, the subjects granted include the walls,[2] and where lands are bounded by a non-navigable river they include the *alveus* of the river *ad medium filum*.[3]

Description by reference in statutory forms

The description may be a description by reference in statutory form[4] to a full particular description of the lands (which may be part of a larger description) contained in a prior conveyance recorded in the Register of Sasines to which a reference is given.

Statutory description by general name

It may be a statutory description by general name,[5] which is competent where a previous recorded disposition has specified that lands conveyed and particularly described therein are to be designed and known in future by one general name therein specified. The future deeds must contain the general name, the county, the burgh (if within burgh, a reference to the recorded deed and a statement that that deed prescribed the general name).

Description by reference

It may be a description by reference not in statutory form, such as the lands contained in a deed adequately identified,[6] though not identified in accordance with the requirements of statutory reference.[7] Since 1924[8] reference may be made to a plan, a copy of which is retained in the Register of Sasines. Identification of an earlier recorded deed may be aided by mentioning the Register volume and folio.[9]

Parts and pertinents

A grant of lands carries by implication the parts and pertinents thereof;[10] it conveys not only the surface but the airspace above

[1] *Smyth* v. *Allan* (1813) 5 Pat. 669; *Fleming* v. *Baird* (1841) 3 D. 1015; *St. Monance Mags.* v. *Mackie* (1845) 7 D. 582; *Ewing* v. *York* (1857) 20 D. 351; *D. Buccleuch* v. *Edinburgh Mags.* (1864) 2 M. 1114.

[2] *Wilson* v. *Laing* (1844) 7 D. 113.

[3] *Hamilton Mags.* v. *Bent Colliery Co.*, 1929 S.C. 686.

[4] 1874 Act, S. 61; 1924 Act, S. 8 and Sched. D, amd. 1938 Act, S. 2; cf. *Cattanach's Tr.* v. *Jamieson* (1884) 11 R. 972; *Murray's Tr.* v. *Wood* (1887) 14 R. 856; *Matheson* v. *Gemmell* (1903) 5 F. 448.

[5] 1868 Act, S. 13 and Sched. G.

[6] e.g. 'the house in High Street, Middleburgh, bought by me from XY'.

[7] *Matheson* v. *Gemmell* (1903) 5 F. 448.

[8] Conveyancing (Sc.) Act, 1924, S. 48; see also *Johnston's Trs.* v. *Kinloch*, 1925 S.L.T. 124.

[9] 1924 Act, S. 8.

[10] *Gordon* v. *Grant* (1850) 13 D. 1.

and the earth below, *a caelo usque ad centrum*,[1] buildings on the land,[2] and things annexed actually or constructively to the soil,[3] trees, woods and orchards,[4] mines and minerals,[5] the right of trout-fishing in rivers running through the lands,[6] servitudes attaching to the lands over other lands,[7] seats in the parish church,[8] and parts of the church-yard which have become an adjunct of the lands,[9] and the right to light from the street as laid out or as immemorially existing.[10]

There do not pass as parts and pertinents any rights incapable of alienation, namely, the *regalia majora*, the royal sovereignty and the paramount superiority of the Crown, certain *regalia minora*, namely navigable rivers and highways,[11] and water rights in favour of non-riparian owners where a third party has a title to object.[12]

Nor do there pass as parts and pertinents of lands any of the *regalia minora*,[13] which must be expressly conveyed[14] or may be acquired by prescription on a habile title.[15] In particular rights of salmon-fishing need express grants from the Crown, or Crown grant of lands *cum piscationibus* followed by possession of salmon fishings for the prescriptive period,[16] or prescriptive possession of salmon fishings on a barony title,[17] or a title from a subject-superior *cum piscationibus* followed by prescriptive possession, if the salmon-fishings were originally granted by the Crown.[18] Trout-fishing on the other hand is a pertinent of lands, and may be reserved on a sale or even conveyed to a third party.[19]

[1] Bell, *Prin.* §737.

[2] Ersk. II, 6, 4; Bell, *Prin.* §743; *Rose* v. *Ramsay* (1777) Mor. 9645; *Downie* v. *Wallace* (1777) Mor. Appx. Implied Assignation, 16.

[3] *Graham* v. *Lamont* (1875) 2 R. 438; *Nisbet* v. *Mitchell-Innes* (1880) 7 R. 575.

[4] Stair II, 3, 73; *Bruce* v. *Dalrymple* (1709) Mor. 9638; *Paul* v. *Cuthbertson* (1840) 2 D. 1286.

[5] Ersk. II, 6, 1; Bell, *Prin.* §669; *Addie* v. *Gillies* (1848) 10 D. 836.

[6] *Mackenzie* v. *Rose* (1832) 6 W. & S. 31; see also *Patrick* v. *Napier* (1867) 5 M. 683; *E. Galloway* v. *D. Bedford* (1902) 4 F. 851; *Beckett* v. *Bisset*, 1921 2 S.L.T. 33; *Kilsyth Fish Protn. Assoc.* v. *McFarlane*, 1937 S.C. 757.

[7] Bell, *Prin.* §745; *Borthwick* v. *B.* (1668) Mor. 9632.

[8] *Stephen* v. *Anderson* (1887) 15 R. 72.

[9] Ersk. II, 6, 11; *D. Roxburgh* v. *Miller* (1877) 4 R. (H.L.) 76.

[10] *Donald* v. *Esslemont & Macintosh*, 1923 S.C. 122.

[11] Ersk. II, 6, 17.

[12] *Patrick* v. *Napier* (1867) 5 M. 683.

[13] See Ch. 77, *infra*; Bell, *Prin.* §748.

[14] Ersk. II, 6, 13; Bell, *Prin.* §748; Bell, *Convg.* I, 606.

[15] Bell, *Convg.* I, 606.

[16] *Stuart* v. *McBarnet* (1868) 6 M. (H.L.) 123.

[17] *L.A.* v. *Sinclair* (1867) 5 M. (H.L.) 97; *McDouall* v. *L.A.* (1875) 2 R. (H.L.) 49.

[18] *L.A.* v. *Sinclair*, *supra*; *E. Zetland* v. *Glover Incorpn.* (1870) 8 M. (H.L.) 144; *Smith* v. *Lerwick Harbour Commrs.* (1903) 5 F. 680.

[19] *Don District Board* v. *Burnett*, 1918 S.C. 37.

Nor do obligations and rights of relief against parties other than the granter pass, unless specially assigned or made real burdens.[1]

It is customary, though unnecessary, to conclude the grant of the lands with the phrase 'and my whole right, title and interest in the *dominium utile* of the said subjects'.

The dispositive clause concludes with any reservations, burdens, qualifications and conditions (other than feu-duty) affecting the grant.

Conditions of grant of feu

The dispositive clause contains also the conditions attached by the superior to the grant of the feu. These are distinguished as essential to a feu, without which it cannot exist, such as the reserved superiority, the written charter, and sasine, natural incidents of a feu, which are implied in the grant unless expressly negatived, such as warrandice, and accidentals which must be expressly provided for.[2] These include various kinds of express conditions, some of which may be inherent and others merely personal.

(a) Inherent conditions of grant

Inherent conditions of a feudal grant attach to the lands themselves, not merely to the grantees personally, and transmit with them.[3] Any term which is permanent, inherently connected with the lands, and naturally connected with the grant made, is an inherent condition of the feudal grant.[4] They do not need to be declared real burdens, nor to appear on the Register of Sasines. An example is a clause of relief by the superior in favour of the vassal from minister's stipend and future augmentations, which passes to a disponee from the vassal without special assignation.[5]

Real burdens

Real burdens are conditions which do not only attach to the grantee and his heirs personally, but affect the lands themselves and pass with the lands on their transfer.[6] In the strict sense a

1 *Spottiswoode* v. *Seymer* (1853) 15 D. 458.

2 Ersk. II, 3, 11.

3 Ersk. II, 3, 11; Bell, *Prin.* §861; *Stewart* v. *D. Montrose* (1861) 4 Macq. 499; *Hope* v. *Hope* (1864) 2 M. 670.

4 *Tweeddale's Trs.* v. *E. Haddington* (1880) 7 R. 620; *Robertson* v. *N.B. Ry.* (1874) 1 R. 1213.

5 *Lennox* v. *Hamilton* (1843) 5 D. 1357; *Stewart, supra*; *Hope, supra.*

6 A real burden may also be constituted by separate deed, as by a contract of ground annual.

real burden is a reserved money payment, contained in an original grant or a transmission, due from the lands and enforceable only by real diligence against the lands, unless there is also a personal undertaking enforceable by personal action. A real condition is a condition, such as one regarding the erection of buildings, which is an integral part of an original grant of lands, which can be enforced by personal action and diligence.[1] But the term real burden is applied to both real burdens and conditions.

To constitute a real burden no *voces signatae* or particular words are necessary; it is unnecessary to declare the obligation a real burden or *debitum fundi*, to provide that it shall attach to singular successors or that it shall be inserted in future dispositions of the fee, though all such provisions are common, but it must be clear that the lands are affected and not only the grantee and his heirs. This is more apparent where the obligation is a continuing one than where it is one discharged at once.[2]

The burden must be imposed in the dispositive clause of the constitutive deed[3] and express or imply clearly that not only the grantee and his heirs are to be affected but that the burden is to attach to the lands themselves[4] which must be clearly identified;[5] the condition must appear in full in the grantee's infeftment and the deed constituting the burden must be recorded in the Register of Sasines, unless the burden is an inherent condition of the grant.[6] A real burden, if for payment of money, must be definite in amount,[7] but may be *ad factum praestandum*, even though performance thereof requires outlay of money;[8] the creditor must be identified, though he may be a party to the deed or a third party or unnamed but identifiable.[9] If the burden is not for payment of money the superior, or party in whose favour it is

[1] *Tweeddale's Trs.* v. *E. Haddington* (1880) 7 R. 620. It is questionable whether a right of rod-fishing can be made a real burden: *Harper* v. *Flaws*, 1940 S.L.T. 150.

[2] *Clark* v. *City of Glasgow Life Assce. Co.* (1854) 1 Macq. 668; contrast *Edinburgh Mags.* v. *Begg* (1883) 11 R. 352; *Jolly's Exor.* v. *Viscount Stonehaven*, 1958 S.C. 635.

[3] Bell, *Prin.* §920; *Cowie's Tr.* v. *Muirden* (1893) 20 R. (H.L.) 81, 87; *Kemp* v. *Largs Mags.*, 1939 S.C. (H.L.) 6.

[4] *Tailors of Aberdeen* v. *Coutts* (1840) 1 Rob. 296; *Baird's Trs.* v. *Mitchell* (1846) 8 D. 464; *Arbroath Mags.* v. *Dickson* (1872) 10 M. 630; *Davidson* v. *Dalziel* (1881) 8 R. 990; *Kemp, supra.*

[5] *Cowie's Tr., supra.*

[6] *Tailors of Aberdeen, supra*; *Stewart* v. *D. Montrose* (1861) 4 Macq. 499; *Croall* v. *Edinburgh Mags.* (1870) 9 M. 323; *Liddall* v. *Duncan* (1898) 25 R. 1119.

[7] *Tailors of Aberdeen, supra*; *Erskine* v. *Wright* (1846) 8 D. 863; *Edinburgh Mags.* v. *Begg* (1883) 11 R. 352; *Forbes* v. *Welsh & Forbes* (1894) 21 R. 630.

[8] *Clark* v. *Glasgow Life Assce. Co.* (1854) 17 D. (H.L.) 27; *Edmonstone* v. *Seton* (1888) 16 R. 1.

[9] Bell, *Comm.* I, 730; *Erskine, supra.*

constituted, must have both title and interest to enforce the obligation,[1] and it must be specific,[2] not be contrary to law, inconsistent with the nature of the property disponed, useless or vexatious or contrary to public policy.[3] Whether a co-feuar or other third party has title to enforce a real condition depends on whether he has a *jus quaesitum tertio*,[4] and such a party must prove a real and substantial interest to enforce.[5] A vassal's tenant has no title to challenge enforcement by the superior.[6]

A real condition must be specific and precise;[7] it is construed strictly and *contra proferentem*;[8] an obligation will not readily be held to imply a restriction,[9] nor a restriction on construction to imply a restriction on use.[10]

Since 1874 real burdens and conditions may be validly imposed by reference to a prior writ in which they are set out *ad longum*.[11]

It is common to fence a real burden with irritant and resolutive clauses, designed to rescind the grant if the burden is not implemented: but such clauses are not necessary, and will not make a personal burden into a real burden,[12] but may favour the interpretation that an ambiguous condition is intended to be real. They also provide a powerful sanction for non-implement.

Loss of title or interest to enforce real burden or condition

A superior may lose the right to enforce real conditions against one feuar by long acquiescence in contravention by that

[1] *Tailors of Aberdeen, supra*; *E. Zetland* v. *Hislop* (1882) 9 R. (H.L.) 40; *Waddell* v. *Campbell* (1898) 25 R. 456; *Menzies* v. *Caledonian Canal Commrs.* (1900) 2 F. 953; *Macdonald* v. *Douglas*, 1963 S.C. 374.

[2] *Anderson* v. *Valentine*, 1957 S.L.T. 57.

[3] *Tailors of Aberdeen, supra*; *Orrock* v. *Bennett* (1762) Mor. 15009; *Yeaman* v. *Crawford* (1770) Mor. 14537; *Aberdeen Varieties* v. *Donald*, 1939 S.C. 788; contrast *E. Zetland* v. *Hislop* (1882) 9 R. (H.L.) 40; *Beckett* v. *Bisset*, 1921 2 S.L.T. 33.

[4] *Hislop* v. *MacRitchie's Trs.* (1881) 8 R. (H.L.) 95; *Turner* v. *Hamilton* (1890) 17 R. 494; *Johnston* v. *Walker Trs.* (1897) 24 R. 1061; *Murray's Trs.* v. *St. Margaret's Convent*, 1907 S.C. (H.L.) 8; *Braid Hills Hotel* v. *Manuel*, 1909 S.C. 120; *Nicholson* v. *Glasgow Blind Asylum*, 1911 S.C. 391; *Macdonald, supra*.

[5] *Maguire* v. *Burges*, 1909 S.C. 1283; *Low* v. *Scottish Amicable Bldg. Socy.*, 1940 S.L.T. 295.

[6] *Eagle Lodge, Ltd.* v. *Keir & Cawder Estates, Ltd.*, 1964 S.C. 30.

[7] *Murray's Trs.* v. *St. Margaret's Convent*, 1907 S.C. (H.L.) 8; *Kirkintilloch Kirk Session* v. *Kirkintilloch School Board*, 1911 S.C. 1127; *Anderson* v. *Dickie*, 1915 S.C. (H.L.) 79; *Scottish Temperance Life Assce. Co.* v. *Law Union & Rock Ins. Co.*, 1917 S.C. 175; *Ewing's Trs.* v. *Crum Ewing*, 1923 S.C. 569; *Hunter* v. *Fox*, 1964 S.C. (H.L.) 95.

[8] *Heriot's Hospital* v. *Ferguson* (1773) 3 Paton 674; *Wyllie* v. *Dunnett* (1899) 1 F. 982; *Walker's Trs.* v. *Haldane* (1902) 4 F. 594; *Bainbridge* v. *Campbell*, 1912 S.C. 92.

[9] *Fleming* v. *Ure* (1896) 4 S.L.T. 26; *Kemp* v. *Largs Mags.*, 1939 S.C. (H.L.) 6.

[10] *Mathieson* v. *Allan's Trs.*, 1914 S.C. 464; *Porter* v. *Campbell's Trs.*, 1923 S.C. (H.L.) 94.

[11] 1874 Act, S. 32 and Sched. H, 1924 Act, S. 9 and Sched. E, 1938 Act, S. 2(1).

[12] *Allan* v. *Cameron's Trs.* (1781) 2 Pat. 572.

feuar,[1] or against all in a district by contravention by some of the feuars in the district, but not merely by one.[2] A superior is more readily barred by acquiescence than is a co-feuar with a title to object.[3]

If a superior has undertaken in one feu contract to insert similar conditions in other feu contracts and has not done so the later feuars cannot enforce the conditions in the first case[4] but may claim damages from the superior for breach of contract.[5]

The superior may expressly waive or discharge any conditions, but such does not affect the right of co-feuars to enforce unless they consented to the waiver or discharge.[6]

Effect of alienation of feu by vassal

When a valid real burden or condition has become enforceable by the superior the vassal, even if he alienates the feu, remains liable under his personal obligation for obligations becoming prestable before the change of ownership, while the new vassal incurs liability under the real obligation which transmits with the lands.[7]

Modification or discharge of real burdens and conditions

Such changes may be effected by minute of waiver or charter of novodamus granted by the superior, by his acquiescence in contraventions, or under statute.[8]

(b) Reservation of minerals

A superior in granting lands may and commonly does reserve minerals to himself; general terms such as 'mines' and 'minerals' are open to interpretation, having regard to the circumstances.[9] He may in such a case grant the minerals separately, or convey them with a subsequent disposition of the superiority.[10] A

[1] *Ben Challum, Ltd.* v. *Buchanan*, 1955 S.C. 348.

[2] *Campbell* v. *Clydesdale Bank* (1868) 6 M. 943; contrast *Ewing* v. *Campbell* (1877) 5 R. 230; *Howard de Walden Estates* v. *Bowmaker*, 1965 S.C. 163.

[3] *Liddall* v. *Duncan* (1898) 25 R. 1119; *Mactaggart* v. *Roemmele*, 1907 S.C. 1318.

[4] *Calder* v. *Edinburgh Merchant Co.* (1886) 13 R. 623; *Walker & Dick* v. *Park* (1888) 15 R. 477.

[5] *Dixon's Trs.* v. *Allan's Trs.* (1870) 8 M. (H.L.) 182.

[6] *Dalrymple* v. *Herdman* (1878) 5 R. 847.

[7] *Macrae* v. *Mackenzie's Trs.* (1891) 19 R. 138; *Marshall* v. *Callander Hydro Co.* (1895) 23 R. (H.L.) 55; *Rankine* v. *Logie Den Land Co.* (1902) 4 F. 1074.

[8] e.g. Housing (Sc.) Act, 1966, S. 189.

[9] See further Ch. 78, *infra*.

[10] Bell, *Convg.* I, 611; *Orr* v. *Mitchell* (1893) 20 R. (H.L.) 27.

reservation not made in the original charter but later is ineffective without reinvestiture of the vassal.[1]

Whether a particular substance is or is not a mineral depends on the circumstance of each particular case,[2] but a mineral is something other than the ordinary subsoil of the area and exceptional in character, use or value,[3] and it is material to ascertain what the parties contemplated at the time, which may be determined by reference to whether the substance was or was not called a mineral by mining or commercial persons or by landowners at that time.[4]

If minerals are reserved, there should also be reserved power to enter on the lands, to work the minerals, and other rights necessary for so doing. Reservations of the minerals probably implies right to work only by underground workings, but a right to work probably implies right to the minerals.[5]

(c) *Prohibition of subinfeudation*

A condition forbidding subinfeudation made before the Conveyancing Act, 1874, was valid; if made thereafter it is invalid,[6] and all such provisions are now invalid.[7]

(d) *Prohibition of alienation*

Clauses prohibiting alienation save by leave of the superior were abolished by the Tenure Abolition Act, 1746, S. 10.

(e) *Superior's right of pre-emption*

It is competent to reserve to the granter the right to have the subjects offered to him first if they should be for sale.[8] Such a clause is narrowly construed and must appear on the Register of Sasines if it is to be effectual against singular successors.[9] Intention to exercise the right must be intimated within 40 days,

[1] *Kerse Estates, Ltd.* v. *Welsh*, 1935 S.C. 387.

[2] *Caledonian Ry.* v. *Glenboig Union Fireclay Co.*, 1911 S.C. (H.L.) 72; *Caledonian Ry.* v. *Symington*, 1912 S.C. (H.L.) 9.

[3] *Caledonian Ry., supra*; *Borthwick Norton* v. *Paul*, 1947 S.C. 659.

[4] *Caledonian Ry., supra*; *M. Linlithgow* v. *N.B. Ry.*, 1912 S.C. 1327. See also *D. Hamilton* v. *Bentley* (1841) 3 D. 1121; *N.B. Ry.* v. *Budhill Coal Co.*, 1910 S.C. (H.L.) 1; *Forth Bridge Ry.* v. *Dunfermline*, 1910 S.C. 316.

[5] *D. Hamilton* v. *Dunlop* (1885) 12 R. (H.L.) 65.

[6] 1874 Act, S. 22; Bell, *Prin.* §866; but see *Colquhoun* v. *Walker* (1867) 5 M. 773; *Inglis* v. *Wilson*, 1909 S.C. 1393.

[7] Conveyancing Amdt. Act, 1938, S. 8.

[8] Bell, *Prin.* §861, 865; Bell, *Convg.* I, 612; *E. Mar* v. *Ramsay* (1838) 1 D. 116; *Christie* v. *Jackson* (1898) 6 S.L.T. 245.

[9] *E. Mar, supra*; *Lumsden* v. *Stewart* (1843) 5 D. 501; *McLean* v. *Kennaway* (1904) 12 S.L.T. 117.

or any shorter period prescribed in the grant, after an offer has been made by the vassal.[1]

(f) Superior's right of redemption

The superior may validly reserve right to redeem the feu with buildings, even if the vassal is not anxious to sell.[2]

(g) Superior's reservations of right to divide superiority

At common law a superior cannot interject a mid-superior between himself and his vassal, nor divide the superiority (though this does not prevent a superiority becoming vested in *pro indiviso* owners[3]), but a right to do so may validly be reserved.

(h) Irritancy clause

The Feu-Duty Act, 1597, c. 17, provides, by analogy with *emphyteusis*, that if a vassal fails to pay his feu-duty for two complete years he will forfeit his feu. It is, however, common to include an express irritancy clause *ob non solutum canonem*.[4]

(j) Clause requiring registration within limited period

The superior has an interest that the vassal record his grant quickly so that the superior has an entered vassal and the conditions of the grant are made real burdens on the lands. It is competent to require the grant to be recorded within a limited period on pain of ceasing to be a valid warrant for infeftment thereafter.

(k) Clause conferring monopoly on superior's agents

A clause conferring on an agent chosen by the superior a monopoly of preparing deeds relating to the feu is now void.[5]

(l) Building conditions

The charter commonly includes conditions requiring buildings to be erected, and prescribing the permitted and prohibited uses thereof and of the feu generally. Except so far as qualified by his feu-charter itself,[6] a vassal has liberty in the use of his feu. Any such condition must not be illegal, inconsistent with the nature

[1] Conveyancing Amdt. Act, 1938, S. 9.
[2] *McElroy* v. *D. Argyll* (1902) 4 F. 885.
[3] *Cargill* v. *Muir* (1837) 15 S. 408.
[4] See further Chs. 34, *supra*, and 78, *infra*.
[5] 1874 Act, S. 22.
[6] *Shearer* v. *Peddie* (1899) 1 F. 1201; *Campbell's Trs.* v. *Glasgow Mags.* (1902) 4 F. 752.

of the property, or too vague,[1] or merely vexatious.[2] The superior must have an interest to enforce the condition. Such conditions may be declared real burdens, particularly if there are obligations to pay the cost, in whole or in part, of buildings or works erected or to be erected by the superior.[3] It is a question of fact whether a building satisfies the superior's conditions; if it does not, irritancy of the feu may be granted.[4] Conditions are strictly construed and a restriction on structural changes is not infringed by a change of use.[5]

Reference to conditions stated elsewhere

Real burdens, conditions, provisions or limitations may be imported into a charter by reference therein to another recorded deed in which they are set out at length.[6]

Where there has been in an earlier deed relating to the same subjects a clause directing insertion of conditions in all subsequent deeds, the omission thereof subsequently does not affect the title, unless the direction to refer is fenced with an irritant or resolutive clause. If the lands were possessed for the prescriptive period on a title omitting the conditions these become unenforceable. Even if they are omitted from any deed but the then proprietor's recorded title contains a reference, this now cures any previous omission retrospectively, and if the then proprietor's title omits reference, he may cure the defect by executing a recording deed of acknowledgment.[7]

Alternatively the superior may record in the appropriate register of sasines a unilateral Deed of Declaration of Conditions setting out standard feuing conditions and include a reference thereto in all future charters to individual vassals.[8]

Irritant and resolutive clauses

An irritant clause may be added to annul any act or deed done or made in contravention of the conditions. Such a clause is not essential to make feuing conditions permanently enforceable but may help to show that conditions are so intended.[9] A resolutive

1 *Kirkintilloch Kirk Session* v. *Kirkintilloch School Board*, 1911 S.C. 1127.
2 *Tailors of Aberdeen* v. *Coutts* (1840) 1 Rob. 296.
3 *Edinburgh Mags.* v. *Begg* (1883) 11 R. 352.
4 *Ardgowan Estates* v. *Lawson*, 1948 S.L.T. 186.
5 *Fettes Trust* v. *Anderson*, 1947 S.N. 167.
6 1868 Act, S. 10 and Sched. D.
7 1924 Act, S. 9.
8 1874 Act, S. 32.
9 *Tailors of Aberdeen* v. *Coutts* (1840) 1 Rob. 296.

clause may be added to forfeit the grantee's right and title in the event of contravention, and cause the property to revert to the granter.

It is common to provide that all conditions shall be engrossed *ad longum* in the first infeftment and repeated or validly referred to in all transmissions under pain of irritancy.[1]

(3) TERM OF ENTRY

The date of entry to the lands is expressed, normally in short statutory form.[2] If not expressed it is implied[3] that entry is at the first term of Whitsunday or Martinmas after the last date of the conveyance, unless it appears that another date is intended. Immediate entry means entry as soon as possible.[4]

(4) TENENDAS

This clause[5] sets out the superior of whom the lands are to be held, and the tenure by which they are held.[6] Under a new grant the holding is always *de me*, of and under the granter and his successors.

(5) REDDENDO

This clause[7] specifies the payments due by the vassal to the superior. Since the 1874 Act the annual feu duty must be of fixed amount or quantity.[8] Interest does not run on feu duty *ex lege*, but interest is normally stipulated for, and in any event it runs from a judicial demand for payment.[9] No casualties are now due *ex lege*, but, though no casualty might be stipulated for on the succession of an heir or the transfer to a singular successor, other casualties of a periodical fixed sum or quantity might be stipulated for, provided the sum or quantity was certain and the

[1] cf. *Welsh* v. *Jack* (1882) 10 R. 113.
[2] 1868 Act, S. 5 and Sched. B, No. 1.
[3] 1874 Act, S. 28.
[4] *Heys* v. *Kimball & Morton* (1890) 17 R. 381.
[5] Called from the corresponding clause in the Latin charter: *tenendas praedictas terras de me*.
[6] Bell, *Lect.* I, 632; Menzies 520.
[7] Called from the corresponding clause in the Latin charter: *reddendo inde annuatim*.
[8] 1874 Act, S. 23.
[9] *M. Tweeddale* v. *Aytoun* (1842) 4 D. 862; *M. Tweeddale's Trs.* v. *E. Haddington* (1880) 7 R. 620.

time or times when it should be exigible was also certain and not dependent on any event or occasion except the occurrence of the time at which it was exigible.[1]

Under the Feudal Casualties Act, 1914, it is incompetent now to stipulate for casualties, duplicands or sums payable at intervals of more than one year, and provision was made for the compulsory extinction of existing casualties and duplicands before 1930 on terms of a proportionate increase in the annual feu duty. But it is still permissible to stipulate for a permanent increase or reduction in feu duty, if certain both as to time and amount. The 1924 Act provides that in all prior feus feu duty not expressed in money must be converted to money, and in future feus feu duty must be expressed in sterling money. Rights to carriages and services stipulated for under old feu charters, if not commuted under the 1874 Act, Ss. 20–21, must have been commuted before 1935 or else have been extinguished (S. 12(7)).

(6) ASSIGNATION OF WRITS

This clause assigns the writs constituting the granter's title to the lands to the effect only of maintaining and defending the grantee's right, with an obligation to make them forthcoming to the grantee on all necessary occasions.[2] An inherent condition of the grant needs no assignation but a collateral condition, such as an obligation of relief by a vassal in favour of his disponee, does not transmit in favour of a purchaser from the disponee unless specially assigned.[3]

(7) ASSIGNATION OF RENTS

Apart from express provision, the grantee becomes entitled to the rents of the lands for possession following his term of entry.[4] The short statutory clause 'and I assign the rents', unless qualified, imports an assignation to the rents to become due for the possession following the term of entry, according to the legal and not the conventional terms, unless in the case of forehand rents, in which case it imports an assignation of the rents payable at the

[1] 1874 Act, S. 23.

[2] 1868 Act, Ss. 5, 8 and Sched. B.

[3] *Home* v. *Breadalbane's Trs.* (1842) 1 Bell 1; *Sinclair* v. *M. Breadalbane* (1846) 5 Bell 353; *Spottiswoode* v. *Seymer* (1853) 15 D. 458.

[4] *Lord Glasgow's Trs.* v. *Clark* (1889) 16 R. 545.

conventional terms subsequent to the date of entry.[1] It is unnecessary to intimate to tenants the assignation of rents after the vassal has taken infeftment,[2] but if infeftment is not taken intimation is necessary to preclude the tenants from paying to the assignor.[3]

(8) OBLIGATION OF RELIEF

The clause of relief is an obligation of indemnity which binds the granter to free and relieve the grantee of feu duties and casualties, or money in lieu thereof, payable to the granter's superior now and in all time coming, and of all public, parochial and local burdens exigible prior to the term of entry. Such a clause may, if clearly expressed, give relief from even burdens imposed subsequently to the deed, but this is not presumed from general words;[4] it certainly covers burdens merely later reimposed, the incidence of which is the same as under the former law,[5] but not burdens the incidence or application of which is changed so as to become a new burden.[6] It may cover burdens on buildings subsequently erected if contemplated when the feu was granted.[7] The presumption that relief covers only existing burdens and new burdens similar in character and incidence may, however, be overcome by long contrary usage.[8] The obligation does not extend to any personal tax.[9] The superior's liability may extend to burdens on occupiers as well as on owners.[10] The obligation is probably not available to a vassal who has subfeued and is not himself liable for the burden, nor can he assign it to his sub-vassal

[1] 1868 Act, Ss. 5, 8, Sched. B. For rent purposes farms are arable or pastoral, according to which element predominates in the income thereof: *Mackenzie's Trs.* v. *Somerville* (1900) 2 F. 1278. The legal terms for rent are, if arable, at Whitsunday (after sowing) and Martinmas (after reaping); if pastoral, at Whitsunday, on entry, and Martinmas. The conventional terms are such as the parties may fix; a common arrangement is some postponement. A forehand rent is one payable sooner than law implies, a backhand rent one payable later.

[2] *Webster* v. *Donaldson* (1780) Mor. 2902.

[3] *Flowerdew* v. *Buchan* (1835) 13 S. 615.

[4] *Scott* v. *Edmond* (1850) 12 D. 1077; cf. *Stenhouse's Trs.* v. *St. Andrews Mags.*, 1933 S.C. 373.

[5] *Dunbar's Trs.* v. *British Fisheries Soc.* (1878) 5 R. (H.L.) 221; *Lindsay* v. *Bett* (1898) 25 R. 1155; cf. *Lees* v. *Mackinlay* (1857) 20 D. 6; *Hunter* v. *Chalmers* (1858) 20 D. 1311; *Paterson's Trs.* v. *Hunter* (1863) 2 M. 234; *Wilson* v. *Musselburgh Mags.* (1868) 6 M. 483; *Nisbet* v. *Lees* (1869) 7 M. 881; *Preston* v. *Edinburgh Mags.* (1870) 8 M. 502; *Jopp's Trs.* v. *Edmond* (1888) 15 R. 271; *N.B. Ry. Co.* v. *Edinburgh Mags.*, 1920 S.C. 409.

[6] *Stewart* v. *E. Seafield* (1876) 3 R. 518; *Dunbar's Trs.*, *supra*.

[7] *Preston* v. *Edinburgh Mags.* (1870) 8 M. 502; *Latto* v. *Aberdeen Mags.* (1903) 5 F. 740.

[8] *N.B. Ry.* v. *Edinburgh Mags.*, 1920 S.C. 409.

[9] *Lindsay*, *supra*; *Edinburgh Corpn.* v. *L.A.*, 1923 S.C. 112.

[10] *N.B. Ry.*, *supra*.

because it attaches to his feu.[1] It binds a singular successor in the superiority but not his personal representatives unless the intention to do so is apparent.[2]

A superior has been held liable in damages where he bound himself to take feuars on the opposite side of a road bound to relieve the present feuars of half of the annual liability for upkeep of the road but the opposite side was never in fact feued.[3]

(9) WARRANDICE CLAUSE

By the clause of warrandice[4] the granter binds himself that the subject disponed shall be effectual to the vassal, and that he shall not be evicted therefrom by anyone having a better title thereto. Warrandice is implied in all deeds in a degree varying with the nature of the deed. In donations and gratuitous deeds the obligation is that the granter will not grant any contrary deed, which would render the grant ineffectual, but without prejudice to past deeds granted or to future deeds which the granter may be compelled to grant in fulfilment of a prior undertaking or promise. In deeds granted for consideration less than the true value, warrandice is implied against the granter's past and future deeds. In deeds granted for full and fair consideration, such as on sale, absolute warrandice is implied against the granter's own acts, past or future, and against all defects that may appear to have been in his right to it prior to the grant.[5]

Express warrandice supersedes implied warrandice.

Warrandice was formerly personal or real. Personal warrandice binds the granter personally only, and either generally or specially. By a general clause of warrandice the granter binds himself personally, without specifying by what kind or degree of warrandice, in which case the degree due by implied warrandice attaches. Special warrandice is either simple warrandice, that the granter shall do no act inconsistent with the grant;[6] or warrandice from fact and deed, that the granter has not granted, and will not grant, any contrary deed;[7] and absolute warrandice, by which the granter becomes liable if, through any defect in the right, the grantee be evicted from the subject, in whole or in part, by a

[1] *Latto, supra.*
[2] *McCallum* v. *Stewart* (1870) 8 M. (H.L.) 1.
[3] *Leith School Board* v. *Rattray's Trs.*, 1918 S.C. 94.
[4] Stair II, 3, 46; Ersk. II, 3, 25–32.
[5] Bell, *Prin.* §894.
[6] This is implied in donations.
[7] This is implied in compromises.

third party, even though neither granter nor his authors have done any deed conflicting with the warrandice.[1]

Real warrandice was secured warrandice and existed where some lands were made over to a purchaser and other lands, warrandice-lands, were disponed subsequently in security of the principal lands, enabling the purchaser to have recourse to the warrandice-lands if the principal lands were taken from him; and also where one piece of land was exchanged for another, in which case the purchaser, if evicted from the lands received, had recourse against his lands originally given in exchange, both against the other party, his heirs and singular successors. Real warrandice of the second kind was implied by law in deeds expressly bearing to be excambions. The Conveyancing (Sc.) Act, 1924, S. 14 prohibited future grants of express real warrandice and negatived any implication of real warrandice in future transactions.

Clause of warrandice

The statutory clause 'and I grant warrandice' unless qualified, implies absolute warrandice as regards the lands and writs and evidents, and warrandice from fact and deed as regards the rents.[2] In any event absolute warrandice is implied in a conveyance of heritage for a full price. The clause has effect whether the deed is onerous or gratuitous.[3]

Trustees granting a feu normally grant warrandice from their own facts and deeds only and bind the trust estate and the beneficiaries thereunder in absolute warrandice.[4]

Absolute warrandice guarantees peaceable possession of the subjects conveyed, and warrants the assignation of writs for the purpose of maintaining the grantee in possession of what the grant conveys,[5] but not against disappearance of the property,[6] losses or burdens natural to the right,[7] nor any arising from the nature or legal effects of ownership,[8] nor from servitudes, unless exceptional or very burdensome,[9] nor against losses or burdens caused by supervenient happenings or legislation.[10]

[1] This is implied in sales at a fair price.
[2] 1868 Act, Ss. 5, 8, and Sched. B, No. 1.
[3] *Macalister* v. *M's Exors.* (1866) 4 M. 495.
[4] cf. *Horsburgh's Trs.* v. *Welch* (1886) 14 R. 67.
[5] *Brownlie* v. *Miller* (1880) 7 R. (H.L.) 66.
[6] Bell, *Prin.* §122.
[7] Bell, *Prin.* §895; *MacRitchie's Trs.* v. *Hope* (1836) 14 S. 578.
[8] *Plenderleath* v. *E. Tweeddale* (1800) Mor. 16639; *Brownlie, supra.*
[9] *Urquhart* v. *Halden* (1835) 13 S. 884.
[10] *Muirhead* v. *Lord Colvil* (1715) 5 B.S. 125; *Tay Salmon Fisheries* v. *Speedie*, 1929 S.C. 593; *Mackeson* v. *Boyd*, 1942 S.C. 56.

In the event of eviction a grantee in right of absolute warrandice can recover the full damage thereby sustained.[1] Action founded on the obligation of warrandice is competent when eviction is threatened on an unanswerable ground arising from the granter's fault,[2] or if the granter disputes liability to relieve in the event of eviction,[3] or when eviction has taken place.[4] Threat of eviction should be intimated to the party liable in warrandice. The grantee is not bound to defend, if his right in untenable.[5] If there is partial eviction the grantee may recover indemnity for the actual loss sustained; he cannot claim to reconvey the property and recover its value.[6]

If the grantee successfully defends his right against threatened eviction, he cannot claim his expenses under warrandice;[7] if he defends unsuccessfully, having utilized all competent defences, he is entitled to his expenses as well as compensation for the loss caused by eviction,[8] but not if he omitted a competent defence.[9]

Warrandice is a personal obligation and transmits against the granter's executor, unless granted in terms which bind heirs generally, or heirs of entail.[10]

(10) CLAUSE OF REGISTRATION

A feu-charter or feu-disposition will be registered for preservation only. A feu-contract will be registered for preservation and execution.

The short statutory clause 'and I consent to registration hereof for preservation', unless qualified, imports consent to registration in the Books of Council and Session, or other judges' books, for preservation.[11] If preserved for registration in the Register of Sasines with a warrant specifying that the writ is to be registered for preservation as well as for publication, such registration is

1 *Carmichael* v. *Anstruther* (1821) 1 S. 25; *Galloway* v. *Gardner* (1838) 1 D. 74; *Cairns* v. *Howden* (1870) 9 M. 284.

2 Ersk. II, 3, 30; Bell, *Prin.* §895; *Smith* v. *Ross* (1672) Mor. 16596.

3 *Melville* v. *Erskine's Trs.* (1842) 4 D. 385; *Leith Heritages Co.* v. *Edinburgh and Leith Glass Co.* (1876) 3 R. 789.

4 Bell, *Prin.* §895.

5 *Downie* v. *Campbell*, 31 Jan. 1815, F.C.

6 *Welsh* v. *Russell* (1894) 21 R. 769.

7 Stair II, 3, 46; Ersk. II, 3, 32; Bell, *Convg.* I, 219; *Inglis* v. *Anstruther* (1771) Mor. 16633.

8 Bell, *Convg.* I, 219; *Dougall* v. *Dunfermline Mags.*, 1907 S.C. 151.

9 Bell, *Prin.* §895; *Clerk* v. *Gordon* (1681) Mor. 16605.

10 *D. Montrose* v. *Stuart* (1887) 15 R. (H.L.) 19; *D. Bedford* v. *E. Galloway's Tr.* (1904) 6 F. 971.

11 1868 Act, S. 138, and Sch. B, No. 1. Feu-charters by subject superiors must be recorded in the Books of Council and Session: Bell, *Convg.* I, 645.

equivalent to registration also in the Books of Council and Session for preservation.[1]

(11) TESTING CLAUSE

This clause in ordinary form narrates the authentication of the deed.[2]

COMPLETION OF GRANTEE'S TITLE

The grant of a feu charter, feu disposition or feu contract creates only a personal right in the vassal, but is a warrant for his taking sasine in the lands, formerly by taking sasine on the lands, the expeding of an Instrument of Sasine, and registration of it in the Register of Sasines, and now by registration of the deed in the appropriate division of the General Register of Sasines. To permit registration the grantee must be identified and registration must be effected while he is still alive.

Warrant of registration

If the feucharter contains a general description of the lands, or a particular description of them, or a description by statutory reference, or a description by general name under the 1868 Act, S. 13, the grantee completes title by endorsing at the end of the deed a warrant of registration, signed by the grantee, or his agent, in the form of Schedule F to the Conveyancing Act, 1924, and forwarding the charter to the Keeper of the Registers of Scotland to be recorded in the appropriate division(s) of the General Register of Sasines, and thereafter returned to the grantee for retention, or, formerly, by expeding and sending for recording, with a warrant of registration in his favour, in the form of Schedule H, No. 1, to the 1924 Act, in the appropriate division(s) of the General Register of Sasines, and for later return to the grantee, a notarial instrument in the form of Schedule J of the 1868 Act, and now by expeding a Notice of Title under the Conveyancing Act, 1924, to the same effect and sending it for recording with a warrant of registration in his favour in the form of Schedule F to the 1924 Act thereon.

If, on the other hand, the description of the lands is either in general terms or by reference not in statutory form, the grantee cannot register the deed, but may expede and record in the General Register of Sasines a notarial instrument in the form of

[1] Land Registers (Sc.) Act, 1868, S. 12, amd. Conveyancing (Sc.) Act, 1924, S. 10.
[2] See Ch. 6, *supra*.

Schedule L of the 1868 Act, the feu-charter being used as a midcouple linking the titles of the granter and grantee.

Survivorship and other qualities of the destination are imported into the warrant and a survivor is infeft and needs no further completion of title.

It is still competent for a feu-charter to contain a precept of sasine, and an Instrument of Sasine may be expede and recorded.

Clause of direction

A clause of direction may be inserted before the testing clause, directing registration of specified parts of the deed, or of the deed with specified exceptions.[1] The warrant of registration then bears to request registration in terms of the clause of direction contained in the deed.

Continuity of trust infeftment

If property of a religious or educational body is taken in the name of office-bearers or trustees,[2] or the office of trustee conferred on the holder of an office, or proprietor of an estate, and his successors therein,[3] successors in office are deemed to have a valid and complete title by infeftment as if named in the completed title, without need for conveyance to them.

Notification to Land Commission

On the grant of a feu betterment levy may be chargeable and the grantee must notify the Land Commission of the grant to enable them to assess what, if any, levy is exigible.[4]

LAPSE OF TIME FORTIFYING TITLE: THE POSITIVE PRESCRIPTION

To fortify a grantee's title to lands and obviate challenge after a substantial time the rules of the positive prescription secure a possessor his right against all challenge after the lapse of a stated time, subject to certain conditions.

No amount of possession of heritage can by itself create a title thereto, as the ultimate dominion of all lands is vested in the Crown and any land not covered by the title of a vassal belongs to his superior, and if not covered by the title of a superior belongs to the Crown. Still less can any bare possession avail

[1] 1868 Act, S. 12. [2] 1868 Act, S. 26.
[3] 1874 Act, S. 45; *Mailler's Trs.* v. *Allan* (1904) 6 F. 326.
[4] Land Commission Act, 1967, Ss. 27, 29, 37, and 100.

against a person producing a charter to the lands in question: *nulla sasina, nulla terra*. Possession may, however, fortify a defective title. Thus if a tenant procures a grant of the land *a non domino* and possesses in reliance thereon, without paying rent, for the prescriptive period, he acquires a title good against landlord and third parties.[1] The Prescription Act, 1594, enacted that where a proprietor's charter and sasine were extant and there had been possession for 40 years he should not be required to produce other title. The Prescription Act, 1617 (c. 12), enacted that forty years' peaceable possession without lawful interruption by virtue of heritable infeftment by the Crown or other superior should constitute an unchallengeable title, provided that the possessor could produce a charter with the instrument of sasine following thereon; or where there was no charter extant, one or more instruments of sasine covering forty years, either proceeding upon retours or upon precepts of *clare constat*.[2]

The Conveyancing (Sc.) Act, 1874, S. 34, restated the rule and, as amended and restated by the Conveyancing (Sc.) Act, 1924, S. 16, provides that 'Any *ex facie* valid irredeemable title to an estate in land [defined by the 1874 Act, S. 16, and the 1924 Act, S. 2] recorded in the appropriate Register of Sasines shall be sufficient foundation for prescription [under the Act of 1617] and possession following on such recorded title for the space of twenty years continually and together and that peaceably without any lawful interruption' should be equivalent to possession for forty years under the 1617 Act. No deduction or allowance is now to be made for any period of minority or of legal disability on the part of those against whom prescription is used. The changes made do not affect servitudes, public rights of way or other public rights.[3] Subjects which may be transmitted without sasine, such as leases and servitudes, are within the Act of 1617, and titles thereto might be fortified by prescription.[4]

Title and possession both requisite

The operation of the positive prescription depends on the co-existence of title and possession, and neither will suffice alone

[1] *Grant* v. *G.* (1677) Mor. 10876; *Hilson* v. *Scott* (1895) 23 R. 241; *Fraser* v. *L. Lovat* (1898) 25 R. 603; cf. *Hamilton* v. *Scotland* (1807) Hume 461; *Macdonald* v. *Lockhart* (1853) 1 Macq. 790.

[2] Bell, *Prin.* §2002.

[3] 1924 Act, S. 16.

[4] Bell, *Prin.* §2003. Such subjects are probably not within the category of 'estates in land' as defined by the 1874 and 1924 Acts.

to found prescription.[1] Where both elements co-exist, the lapse of time fortifies the title against all challenge,[2] even by the Crown,[3] save only on the grounds of intrinsic nullity and forgery. Thereafter it is unavailing to inquire whether the title was originally good or bad or whether the granter had or had not right to grant the title.[4]

Requisite title

The title requisite to found prescription was originally a charter of the lands and also the instrument of sasine following thereon,[5] or the sasine of an heir. In modern practice the title requisite is any *ex facie* valid irredeemable title to an estate in land, recorded in the Register of Sasines. This includes a charter or disposition, and a decree of adjudication with infeftment thereon followed by decree of declarator of expiry of the legal,[6] but not a decree of adjudication with infeftment thereon but without declarator of expiry of the legal, which is not *ex facie* irredeemable and requires forty years for prescription to operate,[7] nor any redeemable title, such as a disposition *ex facie* in security only, nor a notarial instrument or notice of title without their warrants.[8]

The deeds founded on must be *ex facie* valid and free from intrinsic nullity, such as absence of subscription,[9] but prescription precludes extrinsic objections,[10] except forgery.[11]

An infeftment with its warrant, such as a charter and sasine or, now, a recorded feucharter or disposition, is a good title for prescriptive purposes though proceeding *a non domino* and though subject to a latent nullity.[12]

1 *Fergusson* v. *Shirreff* (1844) 6 D. 1363; *Lick* v. *Chalmers* (1859) 21 D. 408; *Montgomery* v. *Watson* (1861) 23 D. 635; *Andersons* v. *Lows* (1863) 2 M. 100; *Copland* v. *Maxwell* (1871) 9 M. (H.L.) 1; *Grant* v. *Henry* (1894) 21 R. 358.

2 *Millers* v. *Dickson* (1766) Mor. 10937; *Forbes* v. *Livingstone* (1827) 1 W. & S. 657.

3 *L.A.* v. *Dundas* (1831) 5 W. & S. 723.

4 *L.A.* v. *Graham* (1844) 7 D. 183; *Auld* v. *Hay* (1880) 7 R. 663; *Glen* v. *Scale's Trs.* (1881) 9 R. 317; *Fraser* v. *L.A.* (1898) 25 R. 603; *Ramsay* v. *Spence*, 1909 S.C. 1441.

5 Prescription Act, 1617 (c. 12); *Fraser* v. *Hogg* (1679) Mor. 10784; *Ochterlony* v. *Officers of State* (1825) 1 W. & S. 533; *Glen* v. *Scales's Tr.* (1881) 9 R. 317.

6 *Robertson* v. *D. Atholl* (1815) 3 Dow 108; *McKenzie* v. *Robertson* (1827) 5 S. 694.

7 *Hinton* v. *Connell's Trs.* (1883) 10 R. 1110.

8 *Sutherland* v. *Garrity*, 1941 S.C. 196.

9 *Shepherd* v. *Grant's Trs.* (1847) 6 Bell 153; *Kinloch* v. *Bell* (1867) 5 M. 360; *Glen, supra.*

10 *Fraser* v. *L. Lovat* (1898) 25 R. 603; *Simpson* v. *Marshall* (1900) 2 F. 447; *Troup* v. *Aberdeen Heritable Securities Co.*, 1916 S.C. 918; *Cooper Scott* v. *Gill Scott*, 1924 S.C. 309.

11 *Auld* v. *Hay* (1880) 7 R. 663; *D. Buccleuch* v. *Boyd* (1890) 18 R. 1; *D. Roxburgh* v. *Scott* (1890) 18 R. 8.

12 Stair II, 12, 20; Ersk III, 7, 4; Bell, *Prin.* §2010; *Hilson* v. *Scott* (1895) 23 R. 241; *Tayport Land Co.* v. *Dougall's Trs.* (1895) 23 R. 287; *Fraser* v. *L. Lovat* (1898) 25 R. 603.

The title must be definite[1] and bear to cover the lands in question; if it does not it is not habile to found prescription.[2] Subjects excepted in a disposition describing lands by a bounding title cannot be acquired by prescription.[3] But it is sufficient that the subjects would pass as part and pertinent of lands expressly conveyed.[4]

Requisite possession

The possession relied on must be referable exclusively to the title founded on.[5] It must be specifically and unequivocally related to the subject claimed, as by occupying and using lands. Possession of subjects as part and pertinent of subjects covered by the title suffices, the onus of proof being on the claimant[6] and such possession will prevail even against an express title to the same subjects not followed by possession.[7] In the case of an express grant of minerals possession of the surface is sufficient, but if minerals are claimed as part and pertinent of lands possession of the actual minerals by working them, sufficient to indicate to other parties that the minerals were being claimed, is necessary.[8] The sufficiency of the possession depends on the subject in question; thus fishing by net and coble is the normal mode of possessing salmon fishings, but this is not invariable, and possession by rod and line may suffice.[9]

If two parties have competing titles, their rights must be determined by the state of possession.[10]

The possession must be continuous and uninterrupted. Continuous possession requires regular exercise, though acts of

[1] *Brown* v. *N.B. Ry. Co.* (1906) 8 F. 534; *Hay* v. *Aberdeen Corpn.*, 1909 S.C. 554.

[2] *Education Trust Governors* v. *Macalister* (1893) 30 S.L.R. 818; *Caledonian Ry.* v. *Jamieson* (1899) 2 F. 100.

[3] *N.B. Ry.* v. *Hutton* (1896) 23 R. 522.

[4] Ersk. III, 7, 4; Bell, *Prin.* §2008; *Baird* v. *Fortune* (1861) 4 Macq. 127; *L.A.* v. *Hunt* (1867) 5 M. (H.L.) 1.

[5] *Agnew* v. *Stranraer Mags.* (1822) 2 S. 42; *Officers of State* v. *E. Haddington* (1830) 8 S. 867; *Ross* v. *Milne, Cruden & Co.* (1843) 5 D. 648; *D. Buccleuch* v. *Edinburgh Mags.* (1843) 5 D. 846; *Milne's Trs.* v. *L.A.* (1873) 11 M. 966; *Edmonstone* v. *Jeffrey* (1886) 13 R. 1038; *Houston* v. *Barr*, 1911 S.C. 134; *D. Argyll* v. *Campbell*, 1912 S.C. 458.

[6] *L.A.* v. *Hunt* (1867) 5 M. (H.L.) 1; *Scott* v. *Napier* (1869) 7 M. (H.L.) 35; *D. Argyll, supra.*

[7] *Perth Mags.* v. *E. Wemyss* (1828) 8 S. 82; *E. Fife's Trs.* v. *Cumming* (1830) 8 S. 326.

[8] *Forbes* v. *Livingstone* (1827) 6 S. 167; *L.A.* v. *Wemyss* (1899) 2 F. (H.L.) 1.

[9] *Ramsay* v. *D. Roxburgh* (1848) 10 D. 661; *Stuart* v. *McBarnet* (1868) 6 M. (H.L.) 123; *Warrand's Tr.* v. *Mackintosh* (1890) 17 R. (H.L.) 13.

[10] *Stuart* v. *McBarnet* (1868) 6 M. (H.L.) 123; *L.A.* v. *Lovat* (1880) 7 R. (H.L.) 122; *Heriot's Hosp.* v. *Cormack* (1883) 11 R. 320; *McArly* v. *French's Trs.* (1883) 10 R. 574; *Cooper's Trs.* v. *Stark's Trs.* (1898) 25 R. 1160.

possession may be separated by intervals.[1] Interruption cancels any period of time which has run. It may be effected judicially by citation on a summons under the signet, recorded, if to be valid against singular successors, within 60 days, in the General Register of Sasines and renewed every seven years,[2] or by calling the case in court, when the interruption lasts 40 years,[3] or extra-judicially (*via facti*) by actual dispossession or notarial protest, similarly recorded in the Register of Sasines.[4]

Possession must be exclusive,[5] but does not cease to be so by reason of occasional encroachments by the public, though repetition of such invasions might eventually render possession no longer exclusive.[6]

The possession must also be lawful[7] and peaceable, but need not have been *bona fide*.[8]

The possession may be natural or civil, i.e. enjoyed personally and directly, or mediately, as by vassal[9] or tenant,[10] so long as the latter's possession is ascribed to the superior's or landlord's grant as evidenced by payment of feu-duty or rent.

Possession against title

No kind or amount of possession will establish any right contradictory of or inconsistent with the grant to which it is referred.[11] In particular no possession will confer title to any ground outwith the limits defined in a bounding charter.[12]

Computation of time

The twenty (formerly forty) years run from the end of the day on which infeftment took place[13] and must run to the very end

[1] Stair IV, 40, 20; *Macdonnell* v. *D. Gordon* (1828) 6 S. 600.

[2] Interruptions Act, 1669.

[3] Ersk. III, 7, 43; Bell, *Prin.* §2007; *D. Buccleuch* v. *Edinburgh Mags.* (1843) 5 D. 847.

[4] Ersk. III, 7, 40.

[5] *D. Portland* v. *Gray* (1832) 11 S. 14; *E. Fife's Trs.* v. *Sinclair* (1849) 12 D. 223; *Lindsay* v. *Robertson* (1867) 6 M. 889.

[6] *Young* v. *N.B. Ry.* (1887) 14 R. (H.L.) 53.

[7] *Mackenzie* v. *Renton* (1840) 2 D. 1078; *Ramsay* v. *D. Roxburgh* (1850) 7 Bell 248; *D. Richmond* v. *E. Seafield* (1870) 8 M. 530; *Maxwell* v. *Lamont* (1903) 6 F. 245.

[8] Ersk. III, 7, 15.

[9] *L.A.* v. *McCulloch* (1874) 2 R. 27.

[10] *L.A.* v. *Hall* (1873) 11 M. 967. See also possession by liferenter by constitution: *Shepherd* v. *Grant's Trs.* (1847) 6 Bell 153; liferenter by reservation: *M. Clydesdale* v. *E. Dundonald* (1726) M. 1262.

[11] *Officers of State* v. *E. Haddington* (1831) 5 W. & S. 570; *Fleeming* v. *Howden* (1868) 6 M. 782.

[12] *N.B. Ry.* v. *Hutton* (1896) 23 R. 522.

[13] *Simpson* v. *Marshall* (1900) 2 F. 447; *Buchanan & Gails* v. *L.A.* (1882) 9 R. 1218; *Ogston* v. *Stewart* (1896) 23 R. (H.L.) 16.

of this period. Interruption on even the last day of the period cancels all the prior possession and the period must commence running again. A true owner of lands is not barred by delay from challenging an invalid right to lands not yet fortified by prescription.[1]

Prescriptive progress

To ascertain whether a title granted is unchallengeable by virtue of prescription it is accordingly necessary to find the first *ex facie* valid irredeemable title to the lands in question in favour of the granter, or one from whom he has derived title, which is at least twenty years back from the grant now in question, and to be satisfied as to its validity, and to the unbroken and unchallengeable transmission of the lands from that writ to the present granter.

Connection with granter

Unless the title which is the basis for the operation of prescription is in favour of the present granter himself there must be connecting links between that foundation writ and the granter's own title. *Ex facie* valid irredeemable dispositions by way of gift or on sale are good links. A declarator of irritancy of lands, whereby they came into the granter's ownership, but granted in absence, is not a good connecting link.[2] A decree of adjudication followed by infeftment is good only if followed by declarator of expiry of the legal.[3]

In the case of deaths prior to the Succession (Sc.) Act, 1964, the title of a legatee completed by notice of title proceeding on a valid will, or the title of an heir, established as such by decree of general service, followed by notice of title, form good connecting links.[4]

In the case of deaths since the Succession (Sc.) Act, 1964, confirmation of an executor, if it contains a description of the property, gives him a valid title to the property and he may transmit it to a person entitled by will or under that Act by docket endorsed on the confirmation or certificate of confirmation, and such a docket is a valid link.[5]

1 *Mackie* v. *M.* (1896) 4 S.L.T. 3.
2 *Bruce* v. *Stewart* (1900) 2 F. 948.
3 *Hinton* v. *Connell's Trs.* (1883) 10 R. 1110.
4 *Mackay's Exrx.* v. *Schonbach*, 1933 S.C. 747; *Sibbald's Heirs* v. *Harris*, 1947 S.C. 601.
5 Succession (Sc.) Act, 1964, S. 15 and Sched. 1, amd. Law Reform (Misc. Prov.) (Sc.) Act, 1968, S. 19.

Operation of prescription

The object of the positive prescription is to fortify bad or doubtful titles and place them beyond challenge. It excludes all objections to the title founded on latent nullities or extrinsic objections, but not against intrinsic nullities.[1] A vassal may obtain a fresh title if he fails to pay feuduty and having obtained a charter from another person, possesses thereon for the prescriptive period,[2] or a tenant may acquire a title to the lands good against the landlord if he does not pay rent, obtains a disposition from another party and possesses thereon for the prescriptive period.[3] Good faith is not a requisite for prescription.

Operation of long negative prescription

The operation of the long negative prescription of twenty[4] (formerly forty[5]) years may also operate to fortify a vassal's right, by cutting off claims which challenge his right of property, such as under an alleged will or disposition in favour of the claimant, if not insisted in within twenty years.[6]

1 Ersk. III, 7, 9; Bell, *Prin.* §2015; *Shepherd* v. *Grant's Trs.* (1844) 6 Bell, 153; *Kinloch* v. *Bell* (1867) 5 M. 360.

2 *Hamilton* v. *Scotland* (1807) Hume 461; *Macdonald* v. *Lockhart* (1853) 1 Macq. 790.

3 *Grant* v. *G.* (1677) Mor. 10876.

4 Conveyancing (Sc.) Act, 1924, S. 17.

5 Prescription Acts, 1469, c. 29; 1474, c. 55; and 1617, c. 12.

6 *Pettigrew* v. *Harton*, 1956 S.C. 67.

CHAPTER 77

THE SOVEREIGN'S PARAMOUNT SUPERIORITY

THE rights reserved to the Crown in respect of the feudal lands[1] of the kingdom are the regalia, and no right in lands appropriated by feudal customs to the Crown and *inter regalia* is conveyed by any grant to a subject unless expressed.

The regalia are distinguished into *regalia majora* and *regalia minora*. The former, such as the royal prerogative and the king's paramount superiority over all feudal lands, are inseparable from the royal dignity and cannot be communicated to any subject, or at least cannot be communicated without the consent of parliament, as in the case of annexed estates of the Crown. The latter are communicable to a subject but only by express grant, or grant in terms habile to convey the right, followed by possession thereof for the prescriptive period, and fall into two groups, rights of the nature of *res publicae* deemed by feudal theory to be held by the sovereign in trust for the public, and rights naturally pertinents of land but reserved by feudal custom to the Crown though capable of being granted by it to subjects.[2]

PROPERTY HELD IN TRUST FOR THE PUBLIC

Seas and seashore

While the high-seas are common to all nations and persons, the sovereign has a right of property over the seas within the limits of territorial waters, for the purposes of national defence and the trade of the lieges.[3] This right comprises the rights of free navigation, and of fishing, the right to forbid passage to enemies, the rights of jurisdiction,[4] of search, and of levying tolls or duties.[5]

The shore or foreshore includes all land lying between high and

[1] Salmon fishings in udal lands are not *inter regalia*: *L.A.* v. *Balfour*, 1907 S.C. 1360.

[2] Craig I, 16; Stair II, 3, 60; Ersk. II, 1, 5, and 6; II, 3, 14; II, 6, 13; Bell, *Prin.* §638.

[3] Stair II, 1, 5; Ersk. II, 1, 6; Bell, *Prin.* §639–40; *L.A.* v. *Clyde Nav. Trs.* (1891) 19 R. 174.

[4] *R.* v. *Keyn* (1878) L.R. 2 Ex. D. 63; Territorial Waters Jurisdiction Act, 1878.

[5] Bell *Prin.* §654–5.

low-water mark.[1] Subject to the Crown's rights as trustee for public uses, the foreshore may, however, be alienated by express grant,[2] or acquired by prescriptive possession on a crown title,[3] particularly a barony title, to lands adjoining the seashore, though without express grant or boundary which indicates an intention to convey the seashore.[4]

A right to the shore implies right to rocks and islets occasionally covered by water, seaweed, and the right to prevent persons making any use of the foreshore other than those reserved to the public.[5]

Minerals in the bed of the sea below low-water mark but within territorial waters belong to the Crown,[6] though they may be acquired by prescription on a barony title.[7]

The public have a right, held in trust by the crown, to use the foreshore for purposes of navigation,[8] and, even where the foreshore has been alienated, may have by prescriptive custom a liberty to use the foreshore for recreation.[9] Recreation may include shooting wildfowl.[10] But provision for the creation of a nature reserve may abridge public rights to use the foreshore.[10] A proprietor who, without a grant of harbour, has formed a harbour, may not exclude the public from that part of the shore.[11]

Where lands are bounded by the sea or the seashore the grant includes the shore to the point of lowest ebb,[12] but so far as the

[1] Stair II, 1, 5; Ersk. II, 6, 17; Bell, *Prin.* §641; *Bowie* v. *M. Ailsa* (1887) 14 R. 649; *Musselburgh Real Estate Co.* v. *Musselburgh Mags.* (1905) 7 F. (H.L.) 113; cf. *Officers of State* v. *Smith* (1846) 8 D. 71; 6 Bell, 487; *Agnew* v. *L.A.* (1873) 11 M. 309. As to foreshore in lands held udally, see *Smith* v. *Lerwick Harbour Trs.* (1903) 5 F. 680.

[2] *Agnew, supra.*

[3] *Young* v. *N.B. Ry.* (1887) 14 R. (H.L.) 53; *M. Ailsa* v. *Monteforte*, 1937 S.C. 805.

[4] *Agnew, supra*; *L.A.* v. *Lord Blantyre* (1879) 6 R. (H.L.) 72; *Buchanan* v. *L.A.* (1882) 9 R. 1218; *L.A.* v. *Wemyss* (1899) 2 F. (H.L.) 1. See also *Scrabster Harbour Trs.* v. *Sinclair* (1864) 2 M. 884; *Baillie* v. *Hay* (1866) 4 M. 625; *L.A.* v. *Maclean* (1866) 38 S. Jur. 584; *Officers of State* v. *Smith, supra*; *Gammell* v. *Commrs. of Woods* (1854) 13 D. 854; 3 Macq. 419; *Duchess of Sutherland* v. *Watson* (1868) 6 M. 199; *Keith* v. *Smyth* (1884) 12 R. 66; *Aitken's Trs.* v. *Caledonian Ry.* (1904) 6 F. 465; *Musselburgh Real Estate Co.* v. *Musselburgh Mags.* (1905) 7 F. (H.L.) 113.

[5] Ersk. II, 6, 17; Bell, *Prin.* §644; *Paterson* v. *M. Ailsa* (1846) 8 D. 752; *L. Saltoun* v. *Park* (1857) 20 D. 89; *Nicol* v. *Blaikie* (1859) 22 D. 335; *Colquhoun* v. *Paton* (1859) 21 D. 996; *Baird* v. *Fortune* (1859) 21 D. 848; revd. 4 Macq. 127; *Pirie* v. *Rose* (1884) 11 R. 490.

[6] *Cuninghame* v. *Ayrshire Assessor* (1895) 22 R. 596.

[7] *Wemyss' Trs.* v. *L.A.* (1896) 24 R. 216.

[8] *Agnew* v. *L.A.* (1873) 11 M. 309.

[9] *Scott* v. *Dundee Mags.* (1886) 14 R. 191; cf. *Fergusson* v. *Pollok* (1900) 3 F. 1140; *Hope* v. *Bennewith* (1904) 6 F. 1004; *M. Bute* v. *McKirdy & McMillan*, 1937 S.C. 93.

[10] *Burnet* v. *Barclay*, 1955 J.C. 34.

[11] *E. Stair* v. *Austin* (1880) 8 R. 183.

[12] *Campbell* v. *Brown*, 18 Nov. 1813, F.C.; *Boucher* v. *Crawford*, 30 Nov. 1814, F.C.; *Blyth's Trs.* v. *Shaw Stewart* (1883) 11 R. 99.

shore is covered at high water it is subject to public uses.[1] If the grantee of lands gains by reclamation of lands from the sea he acquires right to the reclaimed land, but subject to public use.[2]

Trust purposes of sea and sea-shore

The public uses for which the sea and seashore are held in trust are navigation and fishing.

Navigation is an alienable right and cannot be encroached on by any grant of ferry, or long exercise of right of ferry, though it must be so exercised as not to interfere with any right of ferry.[3]

Fishing is a secondary use of the sea and shore, and, in the case of salmon fishing, alienable, by an express grant of sea-fishing for salmon, or a grant *cum piscationibus* followed by possession of salmon-fishings.[4] It is questionable whether a grant of white-fishing can be made.[5] Lobster fishing can be granted.[6] A grant of taking oysters, mussels, etc. is competent,[7] but the taking of small shell fish and bait is, if not open to the public, not barred by a general grant of salmon and other fishings without exclusive possession.[8]

Recreation, bathing and other subsidiary uses of the shore are not held in trust but pass with an express or implied grant, so long as the uses for navigation and fishing are not impaired.[9] A

[1] Bell, *Prin.* §643; *Culross Mags.* v. *E. Dundonald* (1769) Mor. 12810; 5 B.S. 556; *Culross Mags.* v. *Geddes* (1809) Hume 554; *Leven* v. *Burntisland Mags.* (1812) Hume 554; *Campbell, supra*; *Cameron* v. *Ainslie* (1848) 10 D. 446; but where the charter is of land bounded by the 'sea-flood' or the 'full sea' it has been held a bounding charter preventing the grantee from acquiring the seashore by prescription: *Berry* v. *Holden* (1840) 3 D. 205; *St. Monance Mags.* v. *Mackie* (1845) 3 D. 852; In this case the superior cannot, if his own lands are so bounded, acquire land from the sea between the vassal's land and high water mark; *Hunter* v. *L.A.* (1869) 7 M. 899; *Montrose Mags.* v. *Commercial Bank* (1886) 13 R. 947.

[2] Bell, *Prin.* §643.

[3] Ersk. II, 1, 6; Bell, *Prin.* §645; *Campbell* v. *C.* (1815) 6 Pat. 417; *Grant* v. *Goodson* (1781) Mor. 12820; 3 Pat. 679; *Colquhoun* v. *D. Montrose* (1804) Mor. 12827, 14283; 4 Pat. 221; *Agnew* v. *L.A.* (1873) 11 M. 309.

[4] Craig I, 16, 38; Stair II, 3, 69; Ersk. II, 6, 15; Bell, *Prin.* §646. *D. Sutherland* v. *Ross* (1836) 14 S. 960. See also *Commrs. of Woods and Forrests* v. *Gammell* (1851) 13 D. 854; 3 Macq. 419; *Anderson* v. *A.* (1867) 6 M. 117.

[5] Stair II, 1, 5; Ersk. II, 6, 17; Bell, *Prin.* §646; *Duchess of Sutherland* v. *Watson* (1868) 6 M. 199; *Nicol* v. *L.A.* (1868) 6 M. 972; *L.A.* v. *McDouall* (1875) 2 R (H.L.) 49, 55; *Gilbertson* v. *Mackenzie* (1878) 6 R. 610, 1322; *Mackenzie* v. *Murray* (1881) 9 R. 186.

[6] *D. Portland* v. *Gray* (1832) 11 S. 14.

[7] *Ramsay* v. *Kellies* (1776) 5 B.S. 445; *Maitland* v. *McClelland* (1860) 23 D. 216; *D. Sutherland* v. *Watson* (1868) 6 M. 199; *Lindsay* v. *Robertson* (1868) 7 M. 239; *St. Andrews Mags.* v. *Wilson* (1869) 7 M. 1105, but see *Parker* v. *L.A.* (1904) 6 F. (H.L.) 37.

[8] *Hall* v. *Whillis* (1852) 14 D. 324.

[9] Bell, *Prin.* §647; *Officers of State* v. *Smith* (1849) 6 Bell 487; *Cameron* v. *Ainslie* (1848) 10 D. 446; *Hagart* v. *Fife* (1870) 9 M. 127; *Keiller* v. *Dundee Mags.* (1886) 14 R. 191.

right to use the foreshore in connection with fishing[1] does not give a right to live there.[2] Fishermen have the use of waste land above high-water mark to dry nets[3] and to use the shore for loading, unloading, drying and pickling white fish.[4]

Navigable rivers

Navigable rivers are vested in the Crown for public use and passage, not merely in tidal reaches but so far upstream as they are fit to transport goods, even though only down-stream.[5] So far as the river is tidal the *alveus* belongs to the Crown, but higher up it belongs to the riparian proprietors though the public has an interest to prevent constructions in the channel which interfere with navigation.[6] The flowing water is public for use of navigation. The banks of public rivers belong to the riparian proprietors and they may exclude the public,[7] save from the use of a tow path, the use of which has been acquired by custom,[8] and so long as the right of navigation is not interfered with.[9] Mooring boats may be done as incidental to navigation, but to keep a raft moored in a public river, or to attach thereto or to the bank pleasure boats, are not incidents of navigation and not permitted.[10]

In some cases the Crown rights of navigation have been granted to statutory trustees to be maintained and improved, as by dredging.[11]

Navigable Lochs

A navigable loch, if wholly within the lands of an adjacent proprietor, is a pertinent of those lands, and if touching the lands of several proprietors belongs to them in common and may be

[1] *McDouall* v. *L.A.* (1875) 2 R. (H.L.) 49.

[2] *McCallum* v. *Patrick* (1868) 7 M. 163.

[3] Fisheries Act, 1705; *McDouall, supra.*

[4] White Herring Fisheries Act, 1771, S. 11; *Scott* v. *Gray* (1887) 15 R. 27; *Campbeltown Shipbuilding Co.* v. *Robertson* (1898) 25 R. 922.

[5] *Grant* v. *D. Gordon* (1776) 3 Pat. 679; *Colquhoun* v. *D. Montrose* (1804) 4 Pat. 221. See also *Bowie* v. *M. Ailsa* (1887) 14 R. 649.

[6] *Colquhoun's Trs.* v. *Orr Ewing* (1877) 4 R. (H.L.) 116; *E. Breadalbane* v. *Colquhoun's Trs.* (1881) 18 S.L.R. 607; cf. *N.B. Ry.* v. *Perth Mags.* (1885) 13 R. (H.L.) 37.

[7] Stair II, 1, 5; *McIntyre's Trs.* v. *Cupar Mags.* (1867) 5 M. 780; *Gibson* v. *Bonnington Sugar Co.* (1869) 7 M. 394; *L.A.* v. *L. Blantyre* (1879) 6 R. (H.L.) 72; cf. *Hagart* v. *Fyfe* (1870) 9 M. 127.

[8] *Carron Co.* v. *Ogilvie* (1806) 5 Pat. 61.

[9] *C.N. Trs.* v. *Greenock Harbour Trs.* (1875) 12 S.L.R. 595; this does not entitle the public to fish for trout: *Grant* v. *Henry* (1894) 21 R. 358.

[10] *Campbell's Trs.* v. *Sweeney*, 1911 S.C. 1319.

[11] *Lord Blantyre* v. *Clyde Nav. Trs.* (1868) 5 S.L.R. 552; (1871) 9 M. (H.L.) 6; (1881) 8 R. (H.L.) 47; *C.N. Trs.* v. *L. Blantyre* (1883) 10 R. 910; *Carswell* v. *Nith Navigation Trs.* (1878) 6 R. 60.

used by all for fishing and boating.[1] The *solum* belongs to each in proportion to and so far as *ex adverso* of his lands,[2] but the water is held in common for boating, fishing, and fowling. The public have a right of navigation, but not to beach or moor boats on private land in connection with a boat-hirer's business, nor can the public by prescription acquire the right to embark and disembark on private ground.[3] Where, however, a navigable loch is a main means of communication, it may be deemed governed by the same rules as a navigable river.[4] The Crown has a right in the water and solum[5] of sea-lochs *intra fauces terrae* below low-water mark which entitles it to prevent anyone from using them for other than recognized public uses.[6]

Port and Harbour

The right of making a safe landing-place into a port or harbour belongs to the Crown, but may be granted by Crown or Parliament to burghs or subjects, expressly,[7] or by charter as a royal burgh followed by prescriptive exercise[8] or even by a barony title followed by prescriptive exercise.[9] Grants of port and harbour are subject to the Crown's rights as trustee for the public, but confer a monopoly within the limits of the grant.[10]

The right implies a further right to exact harbour dues, and a duty to make and maintain the harbour and relative works in a state fit for navigation.[11] The dues are such as are sanctioned by long usage, and are to be used for the repair and maintenance of

[1] Stair II, 3, 73; Bankt. II, 3, 12; Bell, *Prin.* §651.

[2] *Cochrane* v. *E. Minto* (1815) 6 Pat. 159; *MacDonald* v. *Farquharson* (1836) 15 S. 259; *Baird* v. *Robertson* (1839) 1 D. 1051; *Menzies* v. *Macdonald* (1857) 19 D. (H.L.) 1; *Scott* v. *Napier* (1869) 7 M. (H.L.) 35; *Stewart's Trs.* v. *Robertson* (1874) 1 R. 334; *Mackenzie* v. *Bankes* (1878) 4 R. (H.L.) 192.

[3] *Leith-Buchanan* v. *Hogg*, 1931 S.C. 204.

[4] *Macdonell* v. *Caledonian Canal Commrs.* (1830) 8 S. 881; *Swan's Trs.* v. *Muirkirk Iron Co.* (1850) 12 D. 622; *Colquhoun's Trs.* v. *Orr Ewing* (1877) 4 R. 344, 350.

[5] Including subjacent minerals: *Cunninghame* v. *Ayrshire Assessor* (1895) 22 R. 596.

[6] *L.A.* v. *Clyde Nav. Trs.* (1891) 19 R. 174.

[7] Stair II, 3, 61; Ersk. II, 6, 17; Bell, *Prin.* §654; *Dundee Harbour Trs.* v. *Dougall* (1848) 11 D. 6, 1464; 15 D. (H.L.) 3.

[8] *Macpherson* v. *Mackenzie* (1881) 8 R. 706; cf. *Ayr Harbour Trs.* v. *Weir* (1876) 4 R. 79.

[9] Ersk. II, 6, 18; Bell, *Prin.* §755; *E. Stair* v. *Austin* (1880) 8 R. 183.

[10] *Edinburgh Mags.* v. *Scott* (1836) 14 S. 922; *McFarlane* v. *Edinburgh Mags.* (1827) 5 S. 665; 4 W. & S. 76; *Campbeltown Mags.* v. *Galbreath* (1845) 7 D. 220, 255, 482; *Leith Dock Commrs.* v. *Colonial Life Assce. Co.* (1861) 24 D. 64; *Musselburgh Real Estate Co.* v. *Musselburgh Mags.* (1905) 7 F. (H.L.) 113.

[11] Craig I, 15, 15; Ersk. II, 6, 17; *McFarlane*, *supra*; *Bruce* v. *Sandeman* (1827) 5 S. 668; *Campbeltown Mags.* v. *Galbreath* (1845) 7 D. 220, 255, 482; *Bruce* v. *Aiton* (1885) 13 R. 358.

the harbour, any surplus belonging to the grantee.[1] The grantee is not bound to improve the harbour from his own funds, and is not entitled to levy additional dues for this purpose without Parliamentary sanction.[2] A proprietor of a private harbour has been held bound to give fishermen ground for beaching boats for the winter, as the counterpart of a right to levy dues.[3]

Harbours are commonly now regulated by private legislation frequently incorporating the Harbours, Docks and Piers Clauses Act, 1847.[4] The Burgh Harbours Act, 1853, enabled any royal burgh having a harbour to fix a schedule of rates and apply the revenue in extending and improving the harbour. Harbour authorities are liable for negligence, as in buoying the channel or maintaining safe berths.[5]

The Harbours, Piers and Ferries (Sc.) Act, 1937, provides for the voluntary or compulsory acquisition by local authorities of any harbour, pier, ferry or boatslip, their maintenance, and the fixing of dues and their application to the expenses of the undertaking.

Ferry

The right of ferry across public rivers and straits or inlets of the sea belongs to the Crown for the benefit of the public.[6] The right imports the monopoly privilege of carrying travellers, their luggage, and, possibly, vehicles.[7] Its exercise may not interfere with the general liberty of navigation on the same waters, so long as not done to avoid the ferry;[8] nor conversely, may the liberty of navigation be exercised to encroach on the privilege of ferry.[9]

1 *Girdwood* v. *Campbell* (1827) 6 S. 124; (1830) 9 S. 170; *Cowan* v. *Edinburgh Mags.* (1828) 6 S. 586; *Christie* v. *Landale* (1828) 6 S. 813; *Edinburgh Mags.* v. *Leith Shipowners* (1838) 16 S. 1171; *Renfrew Mags.* v. *Hoby* (1854) 16 D. 348; 19 D. (H.L.) 2; *Officers of State* v. *Christie* (1854) 16 D. 454; 18 D. 727.

2 *Christie*, *supra*; *Home* v. *Allan* (1868) 6 M. 189.

3 *Aiton* v. *Stephen* (1876) 3 R. (H.L.) 4.

4 e.g. *Glebe Sugar Refining Co.* v. *Greenock Harbour Trs.*, 1921 S.C. (H.L.) 72.

5 *Buchanan* v. *Clyde Trs.* (1884) 11 R. 531; *Thomson* v. *Greenock Harbour Trs.* (1875) 3 R. 1194; *Renney* v. *Kirkcudbright Mags.* (1892) 19 R. (H.L.) 11; *Parker* v. *N.B. Ry. Co.* (1898) 25 R. 1059; *Niven* v. *Ayr Harbour Trs.* (1898) 25 R. (H.L.) 42; *Walker* v. *D. Buccleuch*, 1918, 1 S.L.T. 223; *Fulwood* v. *Dumfries Harbour Commrs.*, 1907 S.C. 456; *Mackenzie* v. *Stornoway Pier Commission*, 1907 S.C. 435; *Mair* v. *Aberdeen Harbour Commrs.*, 1909 S.C. 721; *A/S Forto* v. *Orkney Harbour Commrs.*, 1915 S.C. 743; *Robertson* v. *Portpatrick Joint Committee*, 1919 S.C. 293; *Anchor Line* v. *Dundee Harbour Trs.*, 1922 S.C. (H.L.) 79.

6 Craig I, 15, 15; Stair II, 3, 60; Ersk. II, 2, 17; Bell, *Prin.* §652.

7 *Ferguson* v. *Dowall*, 18 Jan. 1815, F.C.; 6 Pat. 417; *Baillie* v. *Hay* (1866) 4 M. 625; *Stirling Crawfurd* v. *C.N. Trs.* (1881) 8 R. 826; *L.M.S. Ry.* v. *McDonald*, 1924 S.C. 835.

8 cf. *Mearns* v. *Myers* (1872) 44 S. Jur. 458; 9 S.L.R. 531.

9 *Agnew* v. *L.A.* (1873) 11 M. 309.

A right of private ferry is a monopoly grant by the sovereign to an individual for the public benefit,[1] implying a duty to provide a service and a right to levy fair and reasonable rates,[2] though not excluding neighbouring heritors from transporting themselves in their own boats. It excludes any member of the public from operating a ferry for the public.[3]

The Harbours, Piers and Ferries (Sc.) Act, 1937, authorizes local authorities to acquire, maintain, and operate certain ferries.[4]

Highways

A right of highway is vested in the Crown for the public benefit and confers on members of the public liberty to use the surface of the ground along the defined track for the purpose of passage.[5] The right of property in the soil is vested in the owners of adjacent lands, unless expressly acquired from them.[6] Highways may not be encroached on by individuals or communities.[7]

Under the Roads and Bridges (Sc.) Act, 1878, the management and maintenance of highways and bridges in counties was vested in county road trustees, and in burghs in the town council. The county road trustees were superseded by the county councils in 1889.[8]

Trunk roads, designated by statute, are subject to the Secretary of State for Scotland.[9]

Special roads may be provided by the Secretary of State for Scotland or a local highway authority for special classes of traffic only.[10]

Streets

Streets in burghs are similarly held by the town council under the Crown for the public benefit and public right of passage, and

1 *Campbell* v. *C.*, 18 Jan. 1815, F.C.; *Hunter* v. *Moir* (1830) 9 S. 86; *Moir* v. *Hunter* (1832) 11 S. 32; *D. Montrose* v. *MacIntyre* (1848) 10 D. 896; *Greig* v. *Kirkcaldy Mags.* (1851) 13 D. 975; *Weir* v. *Aiton* (1858) 20 D. 968; *L.M.S. Ry., supra.*

2 *Montrose Mags.* v. *Scott* (1755) Mor. 4167; *Cumming* v. *Smollett* (1852) 14 D. 855.

3 *L.M.S. Ry., supra.*

4 As to rates see *Ross-shire C.C.* v. *Macrae-Gilstrap*, 1930 S.C. 808.

5 Ersk. II, 6, 17; *Waddell* v. *E. Buchan* (1868) 6 M. 690; *Hope Vere* v. *Young* (1887) 14 R. 425.

6 *Galbreath* v. *Armour* (1845) 4 Bell 374; *M. Breadalbane* v. *McGregor* (1848) 7 Bell 43; *Wishart* v. *Wyllie* (1853) 1 Macq. 389; *Thomson* v. *Murdoch* (1862) 24 D. 975; *Campbell* v. *Walker* (1863) 1 M. 825; *Waddell* v. *E. Buchan* (1868) 6 M. 690; *Kelvinside Estate Co.* v. *Donaldson's Trs.* (1879) 6 R. 995.

7 But a landowner may erect an openable gate across a public footpath: *Kirkpatrick* v. *Murray* (1856) 19 D. 91; *Hay* v. *Morton's Trs.* (1861) 24 D. 116; *Sutherland* v. *Thomson* (1876) 3 R. 485.

8 Local Govt. (Sc.) Act, 1889, S. 11.

9 Trunk Roads Acts, 1936 and 1946.

10 Special Roads Act, 1949.

can neither be encroached on by private individuals,[1] nor appropriated for public building or feuing.[2] Only statutory authority permits encroachment on adjacent lands for street improvement.[3]

Fairs and Markets

The right of holding fairs and markets is vested in the Crown for the use of the subject, but is commonly granted to a burgh or an individual for the benefit of the inhabitants of the district. No market or fair can be held without a grant from the Crown, or grant implied in a charter of regality or barony, or inferred from prescriptive exercise or statute.[4] All grants of fair or markets are made subject to any rights already conferred, and these are exempt from interference.[5] Where a right of fair has been granted by royal charter, that grant may be extended by prescriptive usage.[6] Save as authorized by statute or usage, no market dues can be levied.[7]

RIGHTS RESERVED TO THE CROWN

Certain rights in land are deemed *inter regalia*, reserved to the Crown, and impliedly withheld from any grant of lands to subjects.

Gold and silver mines

All mines of gold, and mines yielding silver of specified fineness are *inter regalia*.[8] Though formerly deemed inalienable they were later allowed to be feued to the landowner, or other parties if he refused.[9] The permission has been deemed to give a

[1] *Forbes* v. *Ronaldson* (1783) Mor. 13185; *Gordon* v. *Royal Bank* (1819) 1 Sh. App. 452.

[2] *Miller* v. *Swinton* (1740) Mor. 13527; *Montrose Mags.* v. *Scott* (1762) Mor. 13175; *Young* v. *Dobson*, 2 Feb. 1816, F.C.

[3] *Galashiels Mags.* v. *Schulze* (1894) 21 R. 682.

[4] Bell, *Prin.* §664; *Henderson* v. *E. Minto* (1860) 22 D. 1126; *Blackie* v. *Edinburgh Mags.* (1886) 13 R. (H.L.) 78.

[5] *Falconar* v. *L. Glenbervie* (1642) Mor. 4146; *Farquharson* v. *E. Aboyne* (1619) Mor. 4147; *Stirling Mags.* v. *Murray* (1706) Mor. 4148.

[6] *Central Motors (St. Andrews) Ltd.* v. *St. Andrews Mags.*, 1961 S.L.T. 290.

[7] Bell, *Prin.* §666; *Lochmaben Mags.* v. *Beck* (1841) 4 D. 16; *Boyd & Latta* v. *Haig* (1848) 10 D. 1433; *Linlithgow Mags.* v. *Edinburgh Ry.* (1859) 21 D. 1215; 3 Macq. 691; *Kerr* v. *Linlithgow Mags.* (1865) 3 M. 370; *Maxwell* v. *Dumfries Mags.* (1866) 4 M. 764; *Kilmarnock Mags.* v. *Mather* (1869) 7 M. 548.

[8] Royal Mines Act, 1424, c. 13; Mines and Metals Act, 1592, c. 31.

[9] Stair II, 3 60; Ersk. II, 6, 16; Bell, *Prin.* §669; *E. Hopetoun* v. *Officers of State* (1750) Mor. 13527.

heritable proprietor, as owner of the soil, a *jus quaesitum* to demand such a feu.[1]

This right extends to all proprietors though holding of subject superiors.[2] Such a grant unites the mines with the lands,[3] though if not expressly mentioned in a later conveyance, they do not pass as parts and pertinents.[4]

Petroleum and natural gas

Under the Petroleum (Production) Act, 1934, petroleum and natural gas existing in their natural conditions in strata in Great Britain are vested in the Crown, together with the exclusive rights of searching and boring for and getting them.[5]

Forests

Forests are tracts of land enclosed for the keeping of deer; formerly the privilege of killing deer not privately enclosed was reserved to the Crown, and ground kept for deer hunting was also reserved. A grant of forestry conferred on the grantee the same rights as if his lands had been originally a royal forest and was always deemed oppressive, such that the Session stated that petition should be made to the Crown against such grants for the future. A grant of lands in a royal forest does not carry the right of forest without express words.[6] It was later held[7] that the right of killing deer is not *inter regalia*, so that forestry rights do not now differ from the rights of any proprietor to kill deer on his lands.[8]

Royal fish and fowl

Royal fish belong to the Queen *jure coronae*, not to the taker, nor the owner of the lands on which they are cast.[9] The only royal fish appear to be whales, and not whales taken on the high seas.[10] There is no authority for sturgeon being deemed royal fish in Scotland. Swans may be *inter regalia*.[11]

1 *D. Argyle* v. *Murray* (1739) Mor. 13526. 2 *D. Argyle*, *supra*.

3 *Oughterlony* v. *E. Selkirk* (1755) Mor. 164; *E. Breadalbane* v. *Jameson* (1875) 2 R. 826.

4 *L.A.* v. *Sinclair* (1868) 5 M. (H.L.) 97; *L.A.* v. *McCulloch* (1874) 2 R. 27; *E. Breadalbane*, *supra*.

5 Licences to drill for them are granted by the Crown.

6 Stair II, 2, 68; Ersk. II, 6, 14; Bankt. II, 3, 110; Bell, *Prin.* §670; *M. Athole* v. *L. Faskalie* (1680) Mor. 4653; *Robertson* v. *D. Athole*, 22 May 1810, F.C.

7 *D. Athole* v. *McInroy* (1862) 24 D. 673.

8 See also *Hemming* v. *D. Athole* (1883) 11 R. 93. 9 Stair II, 1, 5; Ersk. II, 1, 10.

10 Bell, *Prin.* §1289; *Suttie* v. *Aberdeen Arctic Co.* (1861) 23 D. 465; (1862) 4 Macq. 355. See also *Bruce* v. *Smith* (1880) 17 R. 1000.

11 Stair II, 3, 60, and 76; *secus*, Ersk. II, 6, 15; see also Bell, *Prin.* §1290; *D. Athole* v. *Macinroy* (1862) 24 D. 673, 682.

Salmon-fishing

The right of salmon-fishing is *jus regale*, vested in the Crown unless granted out. It is a separate interest in lands.[1] It may be granted with lands, or separately, but does not pass by implication with a grant of lands.[2] The grant may be express,[3] or be of lands *cum piscationibus* followed by prescriptive possession of salmon-fishings,[4] or be of a barony title, without mention of fishings, followed by prescriptive possession of salmon-fishings.[5] A specific grant, or lease, of the royal right must include the right to fish by all lawful means, unless specifically limited.[6]

The extent of salmon-fishing so acquired is measured by the possession.[7] A lease of salmon-fishings in the sea does not carry any right to use part of the land for ancillary purposes[8] but a Crown grantee is entitled to access to, and the use of, the foreshore in connection with the fishings.[9]

But the right of salmon-fishing within or *ex adverso* of lands in Orkney or Shetland is not *inter regalia*, this incident of the feudal system being inapplicable to udal lands.[10]

1 *Ogston* v. *Stewart* (1896) 23 R. (H.L.) 16. Contrast trout fishing: *E. Galloway* v. *D. Bedford* (1902) 4 F. 851.

2 Craig I, 16, 38; Stair II, 3, 69; Ersk. II, 6, 11; Bell, *Prin.* §646, 671, 754; *D. Sutherland* v. *Ross* (1836) 14 S. 960; *Commrs. of Woods and Forests* v. *Gammell* (1851) 13 D. 854; 3 Macq. 419; *Anderson* v. *A.* (1867) 6 M. 117; *Ogston* v. *Stewart's Trs.* (1896) 23 R. (H.L.) 16. It is questionable whether sea trout are salmon at common law: *L.A.* v. *Balfour*, 1907 S.C. 1360.

3 Ersk. II, 6, 6, and 15; *L. Gray* v. *Richardson* (1877) 4 R. (H.L.) 76; *D. Argyll* v. *Campbell* (1891) 18 R. 1094.

4 Ersk. II, 6, 15; *Pool* v. *Dirom* (1823) 2 S. 466; *L.A.* v. *Sinclair* (1867) 5 M. (H.L.) 97; *Gordon* v. *Gordon Wolridge* (1868) 6 S.L.R. 156; *Stuart* v. *McBarnet* (1868) 6 M. (H.L.) 123; *E. Zetland* v. *Glover Incorpn. of Perth* (1870) 8 M. (H.L.) 144; *Farquharson* v. *L.A.*, 1932 S.N. 28. The prescriptive period is now 20 years: *Ogston, supra.*

5 Ersk. II, 6, 18; *Nicol* v. *L.A.* (1868) 6 M. 972; *D. Richmond* v. *E. Seafield* (1870) 8 M. 530; *L.A.* v. *Cathcart* (1871) 9 M. 744; *L.A.* v. *N. Lighthouses Commrs.* (1874) 1 R. 950; *L.A.* v. *McCulloch* (1874) 2 R. 26; *L.A.* v. *McDouall* (1875) 2 R. (H.L.) 49; see also *L.A.* v. *Hall* (1873) 11 M. 967.

6 *Johnston* v. *Morrison*, 1962 S.L.T. 322.

7 *L.A.* v. *Cathcart, supra*; *E. Zetland* v. *Tennent's Trs.* (1873) 11 M. 469; *L.A.* v. *L. Lovat* (1880) 7 R. (H.L.) 122; *E. Moray* v. *Forres Mags.* (1886) 23 S.L.R. 279. As to possession see *Milne's Trs.* v. *L.A.* (1869) 11 M. 966; *L.A.* v. *Hall* (1869) 11 M. 967; *D. Richmond* v. *E. Seafield* (1870) 8 M. 530; *L.A.* v. *McCulloch* (1874) 2 R. 27; *McDouall* v. *L.A.* (1875) 2 R. (H.L.) 49; *Richardson* v. *Baroness Gray* (1877) 4 R. (H.L.) 76; *D. Roxburghe* v. *Waldie's Trs.* (1879) 6 R. 663; *L.A.* v. *L. Lovat* (1880) 7 R. (H.L.) 122; *Sinclair* v. *Threipland* (1890) 17 R. 507; *Warrand's Trs.* v. *Mackintosh* (1890) 17 R. (H.L.) 13. As to boundaries between fishings see *E. Zetland* v. *Tennent's Trs.* (1873) 11 M. 469; *E. Zetland* v. *Glover Incorpn. of Perth* (1870) 8 M. (H.L.) 144; *Keith* v. *Smyth* (1884) 12 R. 66; *Stuart Gray* v. *Fleming* (1885) 12 R. 530; *Tain Mags.* v. *Murray* (1887) 14 R. 83; *Campbell* v. *Muir*, 1908 S.C. 387.

8 *Mackinnon* v. *Ellis* (1878) 5 R. 832.

9 *L.A.* v. *Sharp* (1878) 6 R. 108.

10 *L.A.* v. *Balfour*, 1907 S.C. 1360.

Salmon fishing has long been elaborately regulated by statute with provisions for annual and weekly close times, modes of fishing and penalties for illegal fishing.[1]

Wreck

At common law all wrecks became Crown property,[2] unless some living creature were found on board, in which case the owner would claim the wreck within a year and a day.[3] This rule was later obsolete.[4] All unclaimed wreck now belongs to the Crown or its grantee.[5] The local receiver of wreck, must, within 48 hours, give notice to the grantee of any wreck taken into his possession. If it is not claimed by an owner within a year it must be delivered to the grantee, or sold and the proceeds paid to the Crown.

OTHER CROWN RIGHTS

Certain other Crown rights are aspects of the prerogative rather than incidents of its paramount superiority of lands.[6]

Ownerless subjects

Things abandoned by their owners fall to the Crown: *quod nullius est, fit domini regis*.[7] Till such a thing can be deemed abandoned, it must be handed to the police for custody,[8] but if unclaimed after a period may be awarded to the finder, or sold.[8]

Treasure

Treasure hidden in the earth, the proper owner of which cannot be ascertained, belongs to the Crown, under the principle *quod nullius est fit domini regis*, but the right may be granted to a subject expressly.[9] To amount to treasure the articles must be precious, appear to have been concealed in the ground or a

1 Salmon Act, 1696 (c. 35); Salmon Fisheries (Sc.) Acts, 1828–70; Salmon and Freshwater Fisheries (Protection) (Sc.) Act, 1951.

2 Stair III, 3, 27; Ersk. II, 1, 13; Bell, *Prin.* §1292.

3 *Hamilton* v. *Cochran* (1622) Mor. 16791.

4 *Montier* v. *Agnew* (1725) Mor. 16796.

5 Merchant Shipping Act, 1894 Ss. 510–37; see also *Commrs. of Customs* v. *L. Dundas*, 25 May 1810, F.C.; *M. Breadalbane* v. *Smith* (1850) 12 D. 602; *L.A.* v. *Hebden* (1868) 6 M. 489.

6 *L.A.* v. *Aberdeen University*, 1963 S.C. 533.

7 Stair II, 1, 5; III, 3, 27; Ersk. II, 1, 12; Bell, *Prin.* §1288, 1291; *Sands* v. *Bell & Balfour*, 22 May 1810, F.C.; *L.A.* v. *Aberdeen University*, 1963 S.C. 533, 549.

8 Burgh Police (Sc.) Act, 1892, S. 412; Lost Property (Sc.) Act, 1965.

9 Craig I, 16, 40; Stair II, 1, 5; II 1, 5; II, 3, 60; III, 3, 27; Bankt. I, 3, 16; I, 8, 9; II, 1, 8; Ersk. II, 1, 11–12; Bell, *Prin.* §1293; *Cleghorn and Bryce* v. *Baird* (1696) Mor. 13522; *Gentle* v. *Smith* (1788) 1 Bell *Ill.* 375.

building rather than merely abandoned or lost, and the owner be unknown or unascertainable.

Bona Vacantia

Property left by a deceased person, not disposed of by his will, and to whom no heir on intestacy can be found, is *inter regalia minora*, and falls to the Crown as *ultimus haeres*,[1] by way of caduciary right and not by inheritance, under the rule *quod nullius est fit domini regis*. It falls to be delivered to the Queen's and Lord Treasurer's Remembrancer.[2]

By analogy property of unincorporated bodies and juristic persons left undisposed of falls to the Crown.[3]

[1] Stair III, 3, 47; IV, 13, 1; Bankt. III, 3, 91; Ersk. III, 10, 2; Bell, *Prin.* §1294; McLaren, *Wills*, I, 80; Succession (Sc.) Act, 1964, S. 7.

[2] *Rutherford* v. *L.A.*, 1932 S.C. 674.

[3] *Caledonian Employers Benevolent Socy.*, 1928 S.C. 633.

CHAPTER 78

THE ESTATE OF THE SUPERIOR

An estate of superiority is created by any feudal landholder under the Crown when he grants a feu of any part of his lands to be held in fee of and under him. He thereby retains certain rights in the lands, known collectively as the *dominium directum*, which he himself holds of the Crown or of an over-superior, but conveys others to the vassal. All rights in the lands not reserved to the Crown or any over-superior, nor conveyed to the vassal and which do not pass by implication as parts and pertinents of the lands conveyed, are reserved to the superior.[1] He also normally stipulates expressly for feu or blench duty, and formerly for casual payments also, and may impose express conditions on the use of the lands granted.

The estate of superiority is higher and more important than the estate of the vassal.[2] It is also the radical right and the vassal's rights revert to it if they should be suspended or fail.

An estate of superiority can be sold without the vassals' consent, thereby substituting a new superior for the old,[3] but it is indivisible and cannot be split in parts,[4] as such would inconvenience the vassals, though a person's superiority of certain lands can be sold to one and that of other lands to another, the right to feu-duties may be assigned, reserving the other rights of superiority,[5] and a superiority may be divided among creditors or between superior and creditor.[6]

Nor can a superior, unless he has reserved power to do so, or has the vassal's consent, interpose a new mid-superior between himself and his vassals.[7] The right to object is personal to the vassal and may be lost by the lapse of the prescriptive period.[8]

Superior's rights

The superior's rights against the vassal comprise essential or fixed rights, namely the radical right of property in the lands

[1] Bell, *Prin.* §687–8.
[2] Ersk. II, 3, 10.
[3] Bell, *Prin.* §855; *Dreghorn* v. *Hamilton* (1774) Mor. 15015.
[4] Ersk. II, 3, 12; *Montrose* v. *Colquhoun* (1782) 6 Pat. 805.
[5] Stair II, 4, 10; Bell, *Prin.* §688, 703; *Douglas* v. *Vassals* (1671) Mor. 9306.
[6] *Home* v. *Smith* (1794) Mor. 15077.
[7] Bell, *Prin.* §678; *Douglas, supra*; *Argyle* v. *McLeod* (1672) Mor. 15013; *Archbp. of St. Andrews* v. *M. Huntly* (1682) Mor. 15015; *Hotchkis* v. *Walker's Trs.* (1822) 2 S. 70.
[8] Bell, *Prin.* §857; Bell, *Convg.* II, 753; *Hotchkis, supra.*

and the right to some service or payment from the vassal in acknowledgment of the relationship; natural rights, such as arise from the nature of the feudal relationship itself, including formerly, casualties; and accidental rights, such as real burdens, reservations and conditions of the particular grant, depending in every case on the feu-charter or contract.[1]

(1) ESSENTIALS OF A FEU

Radical right of superior

The superior is not divested of any rights in the land, by his grant to the vassal of the *dominium utile*, except in so far as these are thereby conveyed. His infeftment subsists in all other respects, both in questions with his own superior and with third parties. Thus the superior may pursue real actions concerning the lands against any person other than his vassal or persons deriving right from him, such as to eject a squatter.[2]

Right to Feuduty

The feuduty may be any sum agreed by the parties.

The superior has various means for compelling payment of feuduties.

(1) *Personal action*

A personal action for payment is competent against the original vassal *ex contractu*, the vassal by acceptance of the feu making himself personally liable for the feuduties and other obligations of the feu until a purchaser from him has become infeft and notice of change of ownership been given to the superior under the Conveyancing (Sc.) Act, 1874, S. 4.[3] It is also competent against the original vassal and his representatives if he undertook a personal obligation for feu-duties, even after a purchaser from him had entered with the superior.[4] Personal action is also competent against singular successors who enter as vassals, for the feuduties for their period as vassals,[5] against sub-vassals to

1 Ersk. II, 3, 11. 2 *Lagg* (1624) Mor. 13787.

3 Bell, *Prin.* §700; *Tweeddale's Tr.* v. *E. Haddington* (1880) 7 R. 620; *Scottish Drainage Co.* v. *Campbell* (1889) 16 R. (H.L.) 16; *Macrae* v. *Mackenzie's Tr.* (1891) 19 R. 138.

4 *Royal Bank* v. *Gardyne* (1853) 1 Macq. 358; *King's College* v. *Hay* (1854) 1 Macq. 526; *Brown's Trs.* v. *Webster* (1855) 2 Macq. 40; *Dundee Police Commrs.* v. *Straton* (1884) 11 R. 586; *Burns* v. *Martin* (1887) 14 R. (H.L.) 20. See also *Marshall's Tr.* v. *Macneill* (1888) 15 R. 762.

5 *Rollo* v. *Murray* (1629) Mor. 4185.

the extent of their sub-feuduties,[1] possibly against tenants while in possession of the lands,[2] or against intromitters with the profits of the lands during their intromissions.[3]

If there is no continuing personal obligation on the vassal's representatives, his heir may renounce the feu, and the vassal's representatives will be liable only for obligations due at his death.[4] Nor is a disponee in security liable to implementan obligation incumbent only on the vassal.[5]

But the annual feuduty is not only a personal debt, but is a *debitum fundi*, or debt forming a charge on the lands feued and a real right reserved to the superior out of the lands feued.

(2) *Hypothec*

The superior also has a hypothec over the crop and *invecta et illata* on the lands in security of the last or current feuduty, similar but preferable to a landlord's hypothec for his rent,[6] and enforced by sequestration.[7]

(3) *Real security over lands*

The superior, having a real right in the lands, has a preference over purchasers and creditors in voluntary or judicial sales, and in the ranking of creditors in bankruptcy.[8] This extends to the whole lands feued, though divided by sale or sub-feuing, any vassal or sub-feuar who pays having a right of relief against the others for payment in excess of his *pro rata* share.[9]

(4) *Poinding of the ground*

An action for poinding of the ground is a mode of diligence for attaching goods brought on the land by the vassal, and by his

[1] *Hyslop* v. *Shaw* (1863) 1 M. 535; *Tweeddale's Trs., supra*; *Sandeman* v. *Scottish Property Investment Co.* (1881) 8 R. 790.

[2] Bell, *Prin.* §700; but see *Prudential Assce. Co.* v. *Cheyne* (1884) 11 R. 871; *Nelson's Trs.* v. *Tod* (1896) 23 R. 1000.

[3] *Biggar* v. *Scott* (1738) Mor. 4191; *Prudential Assce. Co., supra.*

[4] *Aiton* v. *Russell's Exors.* (1889) 16 R. 625; *Macrae* v. *Mackenzie's Tr.* (1891) 19 R. 139; *Marshall* v. *Callander Hydro Co.* (1896) 23 R. (H.L.) 55.

[5] *Patterson* v. *Robertson*, 1912 2 S.L.T. 494.

[6] Stair II, 4, 7; Mack. II, 6, 12; Ersk. II, 6, 63; Bell, *Comm.* II, 27; *Prin.* §698; Ross II, 392; *Yuille* v. *Lawrie* (1823) 2 S. 155; *Athole Hydropathic Co., Ltd.* (1886) 13 R. 818; *Anderson's Trs.* v. *Donaldson & Co.*, 1908 S.C. 38. It is unaffected by the Hypothec Abolition Act, 1880.

[7] e.g. *Anderson's Trs., supra.*

[8] Bankruptcy (Sc.) Act, 1913, S. 97(2).

[9] Bell, *Prin.* §697; *Wemyss* v. *Thomson* (1836) 14 S. 233; *Little Gilmour* v. *Balfour* (1839) 1 D. 403; *Knight* v. *Cargill* (1846) 8 D. 991; *Nisbet* v. *Smith* (1876) 3 R. 781; *Sandeman* v. *Sc. Property Investment Co.* (1885) 12 R. (H.L.) 67.

tenants, to the extent of their year's unpaid rent.[1] It covers all arrears of feu-duties. The action is not affected by sequestration,[2] though decree taken after sequestration gives preference for one year's arrears and the current term's feuduty only.[3] It may be competent to a divested superior for feuduty due down to the date of his divestiture.[4] A superior cannot bring an action of maills and duties against the tenants or take possession thereunder in view of his vassal's infeftment.[5]

(5) *Adjudication*

Adjudication is competent, as on other *debita fundi*.[6]

(6) *Tinsel of the feu*

The superior may, lastly, seek tinsel of the feu, or declarator of irritancy of the feu *ob non solutum canonem* which infers forfeiture of the vassal's right for breach of the feudal contract by failure to pay feu-duty and returns the land and all on it to the superior.[7] This irritancy exists under statute[8] when two years' feuduties are unpaid, and is frequently also stipulated for conventionally. Declarator is required in all cases that it has been incurred, and the irritancy may be purged by payment before decree is obtained.[9] The superior cannot both claim irritancy of the feu and recover the unpaid arrears of feuduty.[10]

The annulment of the vassal's right does not avoid securities granted by him, but the superior takes the lands free of the security-rights unless the holders thereof purge the irritancy.[11] The annulment, however, avoids all subfeus granted by the

[1] Stair IV, 23, 5, and 10; Ersk. IV, 1, 11; Bell, *Prin.* §699.

[2] Bankruptcy (Sc.) Act, 1913, S. 97(2).

[3] *Campbell* v. *Edinburgh Parish Council*, 1911 S.C. 280; cf. *Aberdeen Corpn.* v. *B. L. Bank*, 1911 S.C. 239.

[4] *Scottish Heritages Co.* v. *N.B. Property Inv. Co.* (1885) 12 R. 550; *Maxwell's Trs.* v. *Bothwell School Board* (1893) 20 R. 958; *Campbell* v. *Edinburgh Parish Council*, 1911 S.C. 280.

[5] *Prudential Assce. Co.* v. *Cheyne* (1884) 11 R. 871.

[6] Bell, *Prin.* §699A; *Sandeman* v. *Scottish Property Investment Co.* (1885) 12 R. (H.L.) 67, 71.

[7] Ersk. II, 5, 26–7; Bell, *Prin.* §701; Bell, *Convg.* II, 754.

[8] Feuduty Act, 1597 (c. 17).

[9] *Lockhart* v. *Shiells* (1770) Mor. 7244; *Rait* v. *Spence* (1848) 11 D. 126; *Hope* v. *Aitken* (1872) 10 M. 347; *Maxwell's Trs.* v. *Bothwell School Board* (1893) 20 R. 958. By the Conveyancing Acts Amdt. Act, 1887, S. 4, no such declarator is deemed final until an extract has been recorded in the appropriate Register of Sasines. See also Conveyancing Amdt. (Sc.) Act, 1938, S. 6.

[10] Bell, *Prin.* §701; *Edinburgh Mags.* v. *Horsburgh* (1834) 12 S. 593.

[11] Ersk. II, 5, 79; *Drummond* v. *Hamilton's Crs.* (1686) Mor. 7235.

vassal, and the lands revert to the superior unaffected by any such rights.[1]

Vassal's right of retention of feuduty

The vassal may withhold payment of feuduty if the superior, acting as such, has failed to perform any essential condition of the feucontract.[2]

Allocation of feuduty

The feuduty attached by a superior to lands feued attaches to every part thereof, notwithstanding that the vassal may have subfeued parts of the lands. The vassal may, however, obtain the superior's consent in his feu-contract to the allocation of a proportion of the total feuduty to each part of the lands in the event of the vassal subfeuing, or the superior may subsequently agree to allocation. Allocation is effected by a memorandum of allocation of feuduty endorsed on the original grant.[3] Alternatively a separate memorandum may be recorded, and this binds heritable creditors and all having interest other than existing heritable creditors who are not parties to it.[4] A vassal may be authorized by his charter to allocate feuduty in certain terms. If a vassal allocates feuduty in a way not authorized it is invalid and each feuar is jointly and severally liable for the cumulo feuduty, though the superior may be barred by acquiescence from objecting.[5] A charter of novodamus may be granted containing an allocation of feuduty.

Superior's sale of feuduties

Without selling his superiority a superior may sell and convey to the purchaser the right, held blench of the superior, to receive the feuduties, and this constitutes a real right to them.[6]

(2) NATURAL RIGHTS

Natural incidents of the feudal relationship differ from essentials in that they may be modified without infringing the feudal

[1] *Cassels* v. *Lamb* (1885) 12 R. 722; *Sandeman* v. *Sc. Property Investment Co.* (1885) 12 R. (H.L.) 67.

[2] Bell, *Prin.* §702; *Gibson* v. *Heriot's Hospital* (1811) Hume 15; *Ainslie* v. *Edinburgh Mags.* (1842) 4 D. 639; *Arnott's Trs.* v. *Forbes* (1881) 9 R. 89; *Thom* v. *Chalmers* (1886) 13 R. 1026.

[3] 1874 Act, S. 8 and Sched. D.

[4] 1924 Act, S. 13.

[5] *Nelson's Trs.* v. *Tod* (1904) 6 F. 475; *Pall Mall Trust* v. *Wilson*, 1948 S.C. 232.

[6] Bell, *Prin.* §703; *Douglas* v. *Vassals* (1671) Mor. 9306.

relationship, if expressly done in the contract itself. They include the implied obligation of warrandice, which may be modified or excluded by the contract, and formerly the superior's right to casualties.[1]

(3) ACCIDENTAL OR CONVENTIONAL RIGHTS

The existence and scope of such rights depends entirely on the agreement of parties; they are never presumed but must be matters of express stipulation,[2] and must appear on the recorded title.

Reservations

The superior's grant may reserve to him certain rights, such as to mines and minerals. The extent of the reservation depends on the interpretation of the particular clause.[3] A reservation of the right to work minerals implies reservation of property in the minerals.[4] Reservation has been held to include the right to form in the reserved mineral strata roads for the underground conveyance of minerals extracted from under other properties,[5] but not the right to mine in strata not expressly reserved nor to use them for conveying coal from other lands.[6]

It is a question of interpretation whether particular mineral substances are covered by the clause of reservation. Whether a substance is covered by a general reservation of 'minerals' depends on whether at the time of the conveyance the substance was called a mineral by landowners and mining engineers in the locality, and whether it was distinct from the ordinary subsoil of the district.[7]

Where the superior has effectively reserved property in the minerals he may work them himself or let the right of extraction to a mineral tenant for a periodical payment or a royalty on the minerals extracted.[8]

It is implied that the mineral working will not remove support from the surface lands,[9] but express provision may be made in

[1] Ersk. II, 3, 11.
[2] Ersk. II, 3, 11.
[3] e.g. *Harvie* v. *Stewart* (1870) 9 M. 129; *Orr* v. *Mitchell* (1893) 20 R. (H.L.) 27; *Cadell* v. *Allan* (1905) 7 F. 606.
[4] *D. Hamilton* v. *Dunlop* (1885) 12 R. (H.L.) 65.
[5] *D. Hamilton* v. *Graham* (1871) 9 M. (H.L.) 98.
[6] *Ramsay* v. *Blair* (1876) 3 R. (H.L.) 41.
[7] *Borthwick-Norton* v. *Gavin Paul*, 1947 S.C. 659.
[8] cf. *Dalgleish* v. *Fife Coal Co.* (1892) 30 S.L.R. 58.
[9] *White* v. *Dixon* (1883) 10 R. (H.L.) 45.

the reservation of minerals for the superior withdrawing support from the lands granted to the vassal,[1] with[2] or without[3] liability to compensate for damage done thereby, and liberty to withdraw support may even be held to have been impliedly reserved.[4]

Under the Coal Industry Nationalisation Act, 1946, S. 64(3) there was vested in the National Coal Board all the rights of superiority, other than that of the Crown, in coal-bearing strata.[5]

Personal burdens

The superior may take the grantee bound by acceptance of the grant to pay money to him or to a third party. Such a burden is binding on the grantee personally and his representatives, but does nor attach to the lands, nor affect a disponee thereof.[6] It is enforceable as an ordinary debt.

Real burdens

A real burden not only binds the grantee, but attaches to and runs with the lands, and affects singular successors of the grantee, but not personal representatives who do not take up the subjects burdened.[7] It may be created by reservation in a grant of lands in favour of the granter, or by express constitution in favour of the granter or a third party, and it requires a payment by the grantee.

To be valid real burden no *voces signatae* are necessary, but it must clearly appear that the lands are to be burdened, and not merely the grantee personally.[8] The creditor must be named or clearly identified,[9] the sum due must be definite in amount,[10] it must appear in the dispositive clause of the feu-charter,[11] and it must appear in the Register of Sasines.[12]

In the absence of a personal obligation for payment a real burden is enforceable only by real diligence against the lands.

[1] *White* v. *Dixon* (1883) 10 R. (H.L.) 45.
[2] *Anderson* v. *McCracken* (1900) 2 F. 780.
[3] *Buchanan* v. *Andrew* (1873) 11 M. (H.L.) 13.
[4] *B. of Scotland* v. *Stewart* (1891) 18 R. 957.
[5] cf. *Wanchope Settlement Trs.* v. *N.C.B.*, 1947 S.N. 185.
[6] *Mackenzie* v. *L. Lovat* (1721) Robertson's App. 607; *Martin* v. *Paterson* (1808) Mor. Personal and Real, No. 5; *Macintyre* v. *Masterton* (1824) 2 S. 664; *Forbes' Trs.* v. *Gordon's Assignees* (1833) 12 S. 219; *Mackenzie* v. *Clark* (1903) 11 S.L.T. 428.
[7] *Macrae* v. *Mackenzie's Trs.* (1891) 19 R. 138.
[8] *Tailors of Aberdeen* v. *Coutts* (1840) 1 Rob. App. 296; *Williamson* v. *Begg* (1887) 14 R. 720.
[9] *Erskine* v. *Wright* (1846) 8 D. 863.
[10] *Edinburgh Mags.* v. *Begg* (1883) 11 R. 352.
[11] Bell, *Prin.* §920; *Cowie's Tr.* v. *Muirden* (1893) 20 R. (H.L.) 81.
[12] *Tailors of Aberdeen, supra*; *Stewart* v. *D. Montrose* (1861) 4 Macq. 499.

The term real burden frequently extends to cover what are strictly real conditions of the grant, which similarly attach to and run with the lands, but do not require payment of money but the performance of some other obligation, such as to build.[1] A real condition can be enforced by personal action against the vassal for the time being.[2] To be a valid real condition it must be expressed or clearly implied that the condition is to affect the lands themselves and not merely the grantee and his heirs.[3] The superior, or party in whose favour the condition is created, must have an interest to enforce it,[3] the condition must not be contrary to law, inconsistent with the nature of the species of property disponed, useless or vexatious, nor contrary to public policy,[3] and the clause constituting the condition must appear in the charter and in the appropriate Register of Sasines.[4]

Obligation to build

In urban feus the superior commonly binds the vassal to build and maintain a dwelling house or other specified premises to a stated value,[5] and this may be declared a real burden and fenced by an irritancy clause. On the vassal's failure the superior may obtain declarator of that fact and obtain an order ordaining the defender to erect the buildings within a specified time. Such an irritancy can be purged at any time before decree of declarator that it has been incurred.[6]

Building restrictions

In respect of building restrictions there is a presumption in favour of freedom of ownership and a restriction not expressed is not readily implied,[7] while a restriction is invalid if vague and affecting merely a question of taste[8] or deemed too vague and indefinite as a restraint on the use of property.[9] *In dubio* a restriction is construed *contra proferentem*,[10] but a restriction clearly

[1] cf. *Edmonstone* v. *Seton* (1888) 16 R. 1.
[2] *Tweeddale's Trs.* v. *E. Haddington* (1880) 7 R. 620.
[3] *Tailors of Aberdeen, supra.*
[4] *Tailors of Aberdeen, supra.*
[5] As to valuation, see *Brechin Mags.* v. *Guthrie, Craig, Peter & Co.*, 1926 S.N. 106.
[6] *Anderson* v. *Valentine*, 1957 S.L.T. 57.
[7] *Middleton* v. *Leslie* (1894) 21 R. 781; *Walker Trs.* v. *Haldane* (1902) 4 F. 594.
[8] *McNeill* v. *Mackenzie* (1870) 8 M. 520.
[9] *Murray's Trs.* v. *St. Margaret's Convent*, 1907 S.C. (H.L.) 8.
[10] *Dennistoun* v. *Thomson* (1872) 11 M. 121; *Banks* v. *Walker* (1874) 1 R. 981; *Moir's Trs.* v. *McEwan* (1880) 7 R. 1141; *Hood* v. *Traill* (1884) 12 R. 362; *Miller* v. *Carmichael* (1888) 15 R. 991; *Middleton* v. *Leslie* (1894) 21 R. 781; *Assets Co.* v. *Lamb & Gibson* (1896) 23 R. 569; *Assets Co.* v. *Ogilvie* (1897) 24 R. 400; *Wylie* v. *Dunnett* (1899) 1 F. 982;

expressed is enforceable in its terms.[1] To be effectual a restriction must be a real burden and not merely a personal right against the grantee.[2]

A restriction validly imposed as a real condition binds singular successors of superior and vassal. In considering whether singular successors are bound the intention of the parties to the original deed is irrelevant, and singular successors are not bound by a clause which admits of doubt in interpretation.[3]

Restrictions may be imported by reference to a plan, provided it is clear that the plan is intended to be a part of the contract,[4] which appears if it is attached to the charter and signed by the superior.[5] The exhibition of a plan before contract does not bind parties to conform thereto,[6] nor is a reference to a feuing-plan for identification of the subjects sufficient to bind grantees to conform thereto.[7] If a feu-contract binds the vassal to build according to a plan and buildings have been erected, but the plan is subsequently lost, the onus is on the vassal to show that alterations proposed are not disconform to the plan.[8]

Objections to restrictions

Restrictions imposed may be open to challenge as being repugnant to the nature of the estate taken by the vassal, contrary to law, too vague,[9] or as being contrary to public policy, being, e.g. in unreasonable restraint of trade.[10] Prohibitions on the use of houses as licensed premises are lawful.[11]

Graham v. *Shiels* (1901) 8 S.L.T. 368; *Walker Trs.* v. *Haldane* (1902) 4 F. 594; *Kerridge* v. *Gray* (1902) 5 F. 283; *Street* v. *Dobbie* (1903) 5 F. 941; *Minister of Prestonpans* v. *The Heritors* (1905) 13 S.L.T. 463; *Shand* v. *Brand* (1907) 14 S.L.T. 704; *Bainbridge* v. *Campbell*, 1912 S.C. 92.

1 *Morrison* v. *McLay* (1874) 1 R. 1117; *Naismith* v. *Cairnduff* (1876) 3 R. 863; *Partick Police Commrs.* v. *G. W. Steam Laundry Co.* (1886) 13 R. 500; *Sandeman's Trs.* v. *Brown* (1892) 20 R. 210; *Millar* v. *Church of Scotland Endowment Cttee. Trs.* (1896) 23 R. 557; *Lawson* v. *Wilkie* (1897) 24 R. 649; *Walker Trs., supra.*

2 *Scottish Temperance Life Assce. Co.* v. *Law Union and Rock Ins. Co.*, 1917 S.C. 175.

3 *Walker* v. *Church of Scotland General Trs.*, 1967 S.L.T. 297.

4 *Sim* v. *Stewart* (1827) 5 S. 841; *Barr* v. *Robertson* (1854) 16 D. 1049; *Free St. Mark's Church Trs.* v. *Taylor's Trs.* (1869) 7 M. 415; *Assets Co.* v. *Lamb & Gibson* (1896) 23 R. 569.

5 *Crawford* v. *Field* (1874) 2 R. 20.

6 *Heriot's Hospital* v. *Gibson* (1814) 2 Dow 301; *Croall* v. *Edinburgh Mags.* (1870) 9 M. 323.

7 *Gordon* v. *Marjoribanks* (1818) 6 Dow 87; *Walker* v. *Renton* (1825) 3 S. 650; *Barr, supra*; *Free St. Mark's Ch. Trs., supra.*

8 *Sutherland* v. *Barbour* (1887) 15 R. 62.

9 *Kirkintilloch Kirk Session* v. *Kirkintilloch Parish Council*, 1911 S.C. 1127.

10 *E. Zetland* v. *Hislop* (1882) 9 R. (H.L.) 40, 47.

11 *Lauder*, 16 June 1815, F.C.; *Ewing* v. *Campbell* (1878) 5 R. 230; *Ewing* v. *Hastie* (1878) 5 R. 439; *E. Zetland, supra*; *Menzies* v. *Caledonian Canal Commrs.* (1900) 2 F. 953; cf. *Gold* v. *Houldsworth* (1870) 8 M. 1006 (long lease).

Enforcement of restrictions

Enforcement is commonly by a clause of irritancy,[1] but failing such provision interdict against contravention is competent.

Title and interest to enforce restrictions

The superior who imposes the restrictions has a clear title to enforce them so long as he has a legitimate interest, and the vassal, in consenting to be bound thereby, *prima facie* concedes the superior's interest to do so.[2] A vassal in seeking release must seek to prove that, by some change of circumstances, any interest which the superior may have had in maintaining the restriction has ceased to exist.[3] What is a sufficient interest depends on the case; it need not be a direct patrimonial interest,[4] nor need it be necessarily beneficial.[5] A contravening vassal may not contend that the superior has no interest in respect of a particular contravention.[6] Only a vassal has a title to sue the superior for declarator that he may do some act which appears to contravene; the vassal's tenant has no such title, not even if the vassal consents.[7]

The onus on a vassal denying the superior's interest is very heavy where the vassal is the original grantee, who is personally bound contractually as well as subject to a real burden, but less so in the case of a singular successor to him.[8]

Enforceability by co-feuars

Prima facie only the superior, who alone is a party to the feu-contract, can seek to enforce the restrictions. But another vassal holding an adjacent feu of the same superior may also have a title to enforce the restrictions, having a *jus quaesitum tertio* under the contract between superior and contravening vassal, but only if there is some mutuality and community of rights and obligations between the feuars, which arises (1) if the superior makes it an express condition of his feu-contract that he will insert the

1 *Carswell* v. *Goldie*, 1967 S.L.T. 339.
2 *Tailors of Aberdeen* v. *Coutts* (1840) 1 Rob. App. 296; *E. Zetland* v. *Hislop* (1882) 9 R. (H.L.) 40, 47; *S.C.W.S.* v. *Finnie*, 1937 S.C. 835.
3 *Campbell* v. *Clydesdale Bank* (1868) 6 M. 943.
4 *Stewart* v. *Bunten* (1878) 5 R. 1108; *Menzies* v. *Caledonian Canal Commrs.* (1900) 2 F. 953; *Forrest* v. *Watson's Hospital* (1905) 8 F. 341; cf. *Beattie* v. *Ure* (1876) 3 R. 634; *Naismith* v. *Cairnduff* (1876) 3 R. 863.
5 *Menzies, supra.*
6 *Waddell* v. *Campbell* (1898) 25 R. 456; *Calder* v. *North Berwick Police Commrs.* (1899) 1 F. 491; *Hill* v. *Millar* (1900) 2 F. 799; *Moyes* v. *McDiarmid* (1900) 2 F. 918.
7 *Eagle Lodge, Ltd.* v. *Keir and Cawder Estates, Ltd.*, 1964 S.C. 30.
8 *Waddell, supra*; *Menzies, supra.*

same general restrictions in all feus granted by him in the same street or locality, or (2) by reasonable implication from a reference in all the feu-contracts to a common plan or scheme of building prepared and adopted by the superior; or (3) by mutual agreement between the feuars themselves. It is not sufficient to confer a title that the other vassal will be prejudiced by the contravention.[1] An adjacent feuar who has no title to object cannot overcome the objection by obtaining the consent and concurrence of the superior.[2] The whole of the titles of the property must be looked at for indication whether conferment of *jus quaesitum tertio* was intended; identity of restriction between one vassal's title and that of the contravener is not in itself sufficient.[3] Restrictions need not be absolutely identical to be mutually enforceable so long as the restrictions which anyone can enforce against any other are clearly ascertainable from his title.[4]

The superiors' failure to impose the restrictions contained in one grant in another granted later destroys the community of interest, and cannot subsequently be cured.[5] Power reserved to the superior to dispense with a restriction also destroys the mutuality requisite for enforcement.[6]

The superior cannot discharge one vassal from the restrictions without the consent of the rest.[7]

The superior's consent to discharge the restriction cannot affect the right to object of a co-feuar, and still less when the co-feuar's renunciation impairs the superior's right to enforce the condition.[8]

The superior may be disentitled to enforce a restriction by his own failure to perform his duties under the feu-contract.[9]

[1] *Hislop* v. *MacRitchie's Trs.* (1881) 8 R. (H.L.) 95; see also *Heriot's Hospital* v. *Cockburn* (1826) 2 W. & S. 302; *Edinburgh Mags.* v. *Macfarlane* (1858) 20 D. 156; *McGibbon* v. *Rankin* (1871) 9 M. 423; *Robertson* v. *N.B. Ry.* (1874) 1 R. 1218; *Maguire* v. *Burges*, 1909 S.C. 1283. A similar right may be conferred on co-disponees as well as on co-feuars: *Braid Hills Hotel* v. *Manuel*, 1909 S.C. 120; *Nicholson* v. *Glasgow Blind Asylum*, 1911 S.C. 391; *Botanic Gardens Picture Ho.* v. *Adamson*, 1924 S.C. 549; *Macdonald* v. *Douglas*, 1963 S.C. 374; *Lawrence* v. *Scott*, 1965 S.C. 403; A vassal's tenant has probably no *ius quaesitum*: see *Eagle Lodge Ltd.* v. *Keir and Cawder Estates Ltd.*, 1964 S.C. 30.

[2] *Hislop*, *supra*.

[3] *Nicholson* v. *Glasgow Blind Asylum*, 1911 S.C. 391.

[4] *Botanic Gardens Picture Ho.* v. *Adamson*, 1924 S.C. 549.

[5] *Walker & Dick* v. *Park* (1888) 15 R. 477; *Botanic Gardens Picture Ho.* v. *Adamson*, 1924 S.C. 549; cf. *Carson* v. *Miller* (1863) 1 M. 604; *Calder* v. *Edinburgh Merchant Co.* (1886) 13 R. 623; *Johnston* v. *MacRitchie* (1893) 20 R. 539; *Bannerman's Trs.* v. *Howard & Wyndham* (1902) 39 S.L.R. 445; *Thomson* v. *Mackie* (1903) 11 S.L.T. 562; *Murray's Trs.* v. *St. Margaret's Convent*, 1907 S.C. (H.L.) 8.

[6] *Turner* v. *Hamilton* (1890) 17 R. 494.

[7] *Dalrymple* v. *Herdman* (1878) 5 R. 847.

[8] *Hislop*, *supra*, 102.

[9] *Stevenson* v. *Steel Co. of Scotland* (1899) 1 F. (H.L.) 91; *Cheyne* v. *Taylor* (1899) 7 S.L.T. 276.

Acquiescence

A superior may be barred from enforcing building restrictions if he has knowingly allowed material breaches to take place and to subsist for some substantial time.[1] To infer acquiescence it must be shown that the superior knew or had full means of knowledge that the restriction was being disregarded.

Silence does not by itself imply consent.

Acquiescence is rather more readily inferred where the contravention involves not merely change of use but structural alterations involving considerable expense.[2]

Acquiescence, if established, extends only to the things acquiesced in, or things *ejusdem generis*, and does not infer abandonment of all the restrictions.[3]

Acquiescence by the superior does not bar a co-feuar, if he has *jus quaesitum tertio*, who can object only if he has a proper interest to do so. Hence a co-feuar is much less readily barred than is a superior from objecting to one breach by failure to object to a prior breach.[4]

Superior's duties to vassals

The superior's main duties to his vassal, on granting the latter a feu, are to warrant his grant, and to relieve from public burdens in terms of his undertaking in the feu-charter. Such obligations run with the lands though not declared real burdens.[5] The superior's duties are the counterpart of the vassal's to him, and he cannot enforce the contract against the vassal if he is unwilling to perform his own part of the contract.[6]

1 *Browns* v. *Burns* (1824) 2 S. 298; *Campbell* v. *Clydesdale Bank* (1868) 6 M. 943; *Ben Challum Ltd.* v. *Buchanan*, 1955 S.C. 348.

2 *Johnston* v. *Walker Trs.* (1897) 24 R. 1061, 1074; *Ben Challum, supra*; *Howard de Walden Estates* v. *Bowmaker*, 1965 S.C. 163.

3 *Stewart* v. *Bunten* (1878) 5 R. 1108, 1116; *Johnston, supra*; *Mactaggart* v. *Roemmele* 1907 S.C. 1318.

4 *Gould* v. *McCorquodale* (1869) 8 M. 165; *Stewart* v. *Bunten* (1878) 5 R. 1108; *Liddall* v. *Duncan* (1898) 25 R. 1119; *Mactaggart* v. *Roemmele*, 1907 S.C. 1318.

5 *Stewart* v. *D. Montrose* (1863) 4 Macq. 499; *Dunbar* v. *British Fisheries Co.* (1878) 5 R. (H.L.) 221; *E. Zetland* v. *Hislop* (1882) 9 R. (H.L.) 40, 48.

6 *Stevenson* v. *Steel Co. of Scotland* (1899) 1 F. (H.L.) 91.

CHAPTER 79

THE ESTATE OF THE VASSAL

THE grant of a feudal charter in favour of a vassal confers on him the *dominium utile* or actual beneficial rights in the whole tract of ground comprehended in the description of the lands conveyed, or held to be carried by the conveyance though not specially mentioned, together with all parts and pertinents of the land on the surface, such as buildings, woods and waters, or under it such as minerals, *a caelo usque ad centrum*,[1] but under exception of *regalia*, unless expressly granted,[2] and of any heritable subjects expressly reserved by the superior.

Barony privileges

The vassal was formerly entitled to additional right, by the erection of his lands into a barony by a general designation. A barony title included all the different rights of which it consisted, though not separately expressed. Thus the conveyance of a barony carries all that belongs to it, or has been possessed as part and pertinent of it, though not specially enumerated; possession of any part of the barony is reputed possession of the whole, and where the baron has a right to any of the *regalia*, a grant of the barony transmits them though not expressly mentioned.[3] A warrant to infeft in a barony has been found sufficient to authorize infeftment in lands described as part of the barony.[4]

But a barony title to lands with parts and pertinents may not be sufficient to give a right to submarine minerals without possession of them.[5]

Parts and pertinents

Among the heritable things rights to which pass as part and pertinent of lands, though not expressly mentioned, are buildings and other things attached to the soil, trees and growing plants, minerals under the surface, water on or under the surface, and such privileges as go with the occupation and use of the lands, or

[1] Stair II, 3, 75; Ersk. 6, 1–5; Bell, *Prin.* §737.
[2] e.g. *Scott* v. *Dundee Mags* (1886) 14 R. 191.
[3] Stair II, 3, 60; Mack. II, 3, 3; Ersk. II, 3, 46; II, 6, 18; see also *L.A.* v. *Hebden* (1868) 6 M. 489.
[4] *Hill* v. *D. Montrose* (1833) 11 S. 958.
[5] *L.A.* v. *Wemyss* (1899) 2 F. (H.L.) 1.

have been enjoyed along with it for the prescriptive period.[1] What are parts and pertinents are defined by possession for the prescriptive period along with, and under the title of, the lands.[2]

Possession of heritage

Possession of heritage is constituted by actual occupation and use of subjects, such occupation and use as is capable of being exercised in relation to the particular subjects, and as evidences the other requisite of possession, an intention to claim and hold the subjects against other claimants.[3] Neither bare occupancy nor intention to claim is sufficient by itself to constitute legal possession.

Possession may be exercised with different intentions according to the capacity in which the possessor claims the right of occupancy and use. A proprietor in possession claims for himself against everyone else (natural possession); if he lets the lands to a tenant he exercises possession mediately through his tenant (civil possession) and claims possession against all, saving the tenant's rights, while the tenant exercises natural possession and claims it against all, saving the landlord's radical right.

Possession as evidence of extent of lands conveyed

Possession of lands may be evidence of the extent of lands conveyed by a charter or disposition.[4] No possession beyond it can avail against a bounding title or boundary adequately described.[5] Thus a general description containing lands possessed by named persons has been held to limit the conveyance to the lands possessed, though other lands were known as part of the lands generally described.[6]

But where lands were described by plan and measurements, neither being strictly accurate, and the boundary was marked by a

1 Stair II, 3, 73; Ersk. II, 6, 4; Bell, *Prin.* §739–48; *Gordon* v. *Grant* (1850) 13 D. 1; *Baird* v. *Fortune* (1861) 4 Macq. 127; *L.A.* v. *Hunt* (1867) 5 M. (H.L.) 1; *N.B. Ry.* v. *Hutton* (1896) 23 R. 522.

2 *Scott* v. *Lord Napier* (1869) 7 M. (H.L.) 35; *Agnew* v. *L.A.* (1873) 11 M. 309; *Stewart's Trs.* v. *Robertson* (1874) 1 R. 334; *Keith* v. *Smyth* (1884) 12 R. 66; *Cooper's Trs.* v. *Stark's Trs.* (1898) 25 R. 1160; *Meacher* v. *Blair-Oliphant*, 1913 S.C. 417.

3 Stair II, 1, 9; Ersk. II, 1, 20; Bell, *Prin.* §1311.

4 *Agnew* v. *L.A.* (1873) 11 M. 309; *Girdwood* v. *Paterson* (1873) 11 M. 647; *Keith* v. *Smyth* (1884) 12 R. 66; *Caledonian Canal Commrs.* v. *Smith* (1900) 8 S.L.T. 124.

5 *N.B. Ry.* v. *Moon's Trs.* (1879) 6 R. 640; *Reid* v. *McColl* (1879) 7 R. 84; *Dalhousie's Tutors* v. *Minister of Lochlee* (1890) 17 R. 1060; 18 R. (H.L.) 72.

6 *Murray* v. *Oliphant* (1634) Mor. 2262; see also *Mansfield* v. *Walker's Trs.* (1835) 1 S. & McL. 203.

line of trees planted by agreement, possession thereunder made the arranged boundary binding on a singular successor.[1]

Bona fide *and* mala fide *possession*

Possession may be *bona fide* or *mala fide*; a *bona fide* possessor is one who, whether rightly or wrongly, honestly believes himself proprietor of the lands on probable grounds and with a good conscience, such as a purchaser in good faith from one who had no title to sell the lands;[2] any other possessor is a *mala fide* possessor. A *bona fide* possessor is put in *mala fide* if another party produces clear and convincing evidence of his right of property and consequent right to possess, or by decree of court, it being a question of circumstances whether a judgment at first instance or only a final judgment on appeal has that effect. In either case he is bound to yield possession, with the whole fruits and profits of the lands during his possession.

Effects of bona fide *possession*

So long as a possessor possesses *in bona fide* he is entitled to keep the fruits that the subjects yielded while he had reason to think his title good, crops produced from seed sown by the *bona fide* possessor, and rents falling legally due during his possession, but not fruits not yet separated from the subject which produced them, such as growing timber.[3]

Possession as basis for prescription

Possession on an *ex facie* valid irredeemable title is essential for the fortification of the title by the positive prescription.[4]

Protection and recovery of possession

The actual possessor of heritage, who has some *prima facie* lawful title to possess the lands,[5] such as infeftment or tenancy,[6] or even a personal title, such as charter without infeftment thereon,[5] or at least a title *prima facie* applicable to the lands, even of servitude,[7] is entitled to protect his possession by interdict against threatened or actual encroachment, or, in case of actual

[1] *Hetherington* v. *Galt* (1905) 7 F. 706.

[2] Ersk. II, 1, 25; *Huntly's Trs.* v. *Hallyburton's Trs.* (1880) 8 R. 50; cf. *Menzies* v. *M.* (1863) 1 M. 1025.

[3] Stair II, 1, 21; Ersk. II, 1, 26.

[4] Ch. 76, *supra*.

[5] *Knox* v. *Brand* (1827) 5 S. 714; *Carson* v. *Miller* (1863) 1 M. 604, 611; see also *Dickson* v. *Dickie* (1863) 1 M. 1157; *Brown's Trs.* v. *Fraser* (1870) 8 M. 820.

[6] *Macdonald* v. *Dempster* (1871) 10 M. 94; *Galloway* v. *Cowden* (1885) 12 R. 578.

[7] *Liston* v. *Galloway* (1835) 14 S. 97; *Carson* v. *Miller* (1863) 1 M. 604; *Drummond* v. *Milligan* (1890) 17 R. 316.

dispossession, by action of ejection.[1] No amount of possession avails if contrary to the title under which the right of possession is claimed.[2] The requisite possession must be *bona fide*,[3] have lasted uninterrupted for at least seven years,[4] have been exercised *nec vi nec clam nec precario*,[5] and have been *prima facie* attributable to some written title, and not merely to contract.[6]

The decision in a possessory action proceeeds on the basis *spoliatus ante omnia restituendus* and the judgment does not decide any issue of heritable title. But standing a possessory judgment the possessor of lands is entitled to hold them as a *bona fide* possessor until ousted by an action in which his title is challenged and found inadequate to justify his possession.[7]

Right of exclusive occupation and use

The proprietor of lands has the exclusive right to occupation and use of the lands *a caelo usque ad centrum*. Thus he may prevent a neighbour from allowing his building[8] to project over the land[9] or from discharging rainwater therefrom on to the land,[10] or allowing his trees to overshadow the land.[11] But he may not object to the flight over his land of aircraft at a height which is reasonable in the circumstances.[12]

Right to exclude trespassers

Trespass is any temporary intrusion or entering upon the lands or heritages of another without his permission or legal justification.[13] Trespass may be committed by an individual, on foot, animal, boat or vehicle, or by allowing his animal to stray on to the proprietor's lands,[14] by picketing on a private road,[15] or entering premises without entitlement.[16]

1 Stair IV, 26, 3; Bankt. II, 1, 33; Ersk. IV, 1, 50.

2 *Haigues* v. *Halyburton* (1705) Mor. 10623; *Lockhart* v. *Sinclair* (1724) Mor. 10625; *Bridges* v. *Elder* (1822) 1 S. 373.

3 *Montgomery* v. *Home* (1664) Mor. 10627; *Dunfermline* v. *Pitmedden* (1698) Mor. 10630.

4 *Colquhoun* v. *Paton* (1859) 21 D. 429.

5 *Calder* v. *Adam* (1870) 8 M. 645; *McKerron* v. *Gordon* (1876) 3 R. 429.

6 *Neilson* v. *Vallance* (1828) 7 S. 182; *Carson, supra*; *Calder* v. *Adam* (1870) 8 M. 645.

7 Stair IV, 17, 2; IV, 45, 17; Bankt. II, 1, 33; IV. 24, 49.

8 Or even a cornice thereof: *Milne* v. *Mudie* (1828) 6 S. 967.

9 *Hazle* v. *Turner* (1840) 2 D. 886; *Urquhart* v. *Melville* (1853) 16 D. 307; *McIntosh* v. *Scott* (1859) 21 D. 363.

10 *Garriochs* v. *Kennedy* (1769) Mor. 13178.

11 *Halkerston* v. *Wedderburn* (1781) Mor. 10495; *Lemmon* v. *Webb* [1895] A.C. 1.

12 Civil Aviation Act, 1949, S. 40.

13 cf. *McAdam* v. *Laurie* (1876) 3 R. (J.) 20.

14 *Robertson* v. *Wright* (1885) 13 R. 174; *McLeod* v. *Davidson* (1886) 14 R. 92; *Thurlow* v. *Tait* (1893) 1 S.L.T. 62; *Arneil* v. *Paterson*, 1931 S.C. (H.L.) 117; cf. *Winans* v. *Macrae* (1885) 12 R. 1051.

15 *Merry* v. *Cuninghame* v. *Aitken* (1895) 22 R. 247.

16 *Merryton Coal Co.* v. *Anderson* (1890) 18 R. 203.

The proprietor may prevent trespass by warning trespassers off his lands[1] but may not eject them forcibly unless the trespasser uses or threatens violence to the proprietor or is doing actual damage to property[2] and even then may use only the force reasonably necessary in the circumstances. An intruder into a private house may more readily be forcibly ejected. He may obtain interdict if there is threat or probability of continuance or repetition of the trespass,[3] unless it were done in good faith[4] or with no intention to claim a right,[5] or no harm was done.[6] Damages may be recovered only if the trespasser has done actual damage.[7] Interdict is not justified by mere assertion of a right without actual trespass.[8]

Trespass is elided if authorized by the proprietor,[9] or justified by the public interest,[10] in case of emergency, to escape from pressing danger or peril apprehended, to recover goods or animals straying on to the lands or being taken there,[11] in pursuit of foxes, which have been preying on sheep or poultry,[12] to investigate or prevent threatened or reasonably suspected crime[13] or in other circumstances of necessity. A person may not, however, enter the lands of another to hunt, save by permission.[14]

Many statutes authorize entry which would otherwise be trespasses,[15] and judicial warrant may authorize entry.[16]

1 *Mather* v. *Alexander*, 1925 S.C. 139.

2 *Bell* v. *Shand* (1870) 7 S.L.R. 267; *Aitchison* v. *Thorburn* (1870) 7 S.L.R. 347; *Wood* v. *N.B. Ry.* (1899) 2 F. 1; cf. *Geils* v. *Thompson* (1872) 10 M. 327. The landowner may be criminally liable for assault: *E. Eglinton* v. *Campbell* (1770) McLaurin 505; *Craw* (1827) Syme 188, 210; *Reid* (1837) 2 Swin. 236; *Kennedy* (1838) 2 Swin. 213.

3 *Baird* v. *Thomson* (1825) 3 S. 448; *Jolly* v. *Brown* (1828) 6 S. 872; *McKerron* v. *Gordon* (1876) 3 R. 429; *Hay's Tr.* v. *Young* (1877) 4 R. 398; *Steuart* v. *Stephen* (1877) 4 R. 873; *Macleod* v. *Davidson* (1886) 14 R. 92; *Merryton Coal Co.* v. *Anderson* (1890) 18 R. 203; *Warrand* v. *Watson* (1905) 8 F. 253; *Inverurie Mags.* v. *Sorrie*, 1956 S.C. 175; see also *Johnson* v. *Grant*, 1923 S.C. 789; *Macleay* v. *Macdonald*, 1928 S.C. 776; 1929 S.C. 371.

4 *Hay's Tr.*, *supra*; *Macleod*, *supra*.

5 *Steuart* v. *Stephen* (1877) 4 R. 873.

6 *Winans*, *supra*.

7 *Graham* v. *D. Hamilton* (1868) 6 M. 965; *Scott's Trs.* v. *Moss* (1889) 17 R. 32; *L.A.* v. *Glengarnock Iron Co.*, 1909 1 S.L.T. 15.

8 *Warrand* v. *Watson* (1905) 8 F. 253; *Inverurie Mags.*, *supra*.

9 cf. *Steuart* v. *Stephen* (1877) 4 R. 873; *Inland Revenue* v. *Anderson*, 1922 S.C. 284.

10 Bell, *Prin.* §956; Hume, *Lect.* III, 206.

11 *E. Morton* v. *McMillan* (1893) 1 S.L.T. 92.

12 *Colquhoun* v. *Buchanan* (1785) Mor. 4997.

13 *Shepherd* v. *Menzies* (1900) 2 F. 443; *Southern Bowling Club* v. *Ross* (1902) 4 F. 405.

14 *Watson* v. *Errol* (1763) Mor. 4991; *M. Tweedale* v. *Dalrymple* (1778) Mor. 4992; *E. Breadalbane* v. *Livingston* (1780) Mor. 4999.

15 See e.g. Burgh Police (Sc.) Act, 1892; Public Health (Sc.) Act, 1897, Ss. 26, 28, 45, 82, 98, 109, 114; Rights of Entry (Gas and Electricity Boards) Act, 1954, S. 1; Mines and Quarries Act, 1954, S. 145; Agriculture (Safety, Health & Welfare Prov.) Act, 1956, Ss. 10(2), 11; Factories Act, 1961, S, 146; Offices, Shops and Railway Premises Act, 1963, S. 53.

16 *Stewart* v. *Roach*, 1950 S.C. 318.

Trespass is a criminal offence only in the case of a person who lodges in any premises, or occupies or encamps on any land which is private property without the consent and permission of the owner or legal occupier[1] and in cases of trespass in quest of fish or game.[2]

Under the Winter Herding Act, 1686, possessors of lands are ordained to have their horses, nolt, sheep, swine and goats herded the whole year and enclosed at night. If they contravene they are liable to a penalty of half a mark per beast as well as for the damage done to the planting.[3] The aggrieved neighbour may detain the straying beasts until paid the penalty and his expenses in keeping them, but not if they had ceased to trespass before being detained.[4] Restitution of a poinded animal must be refused if the statutory penalty has not been rendered.[5] If animals are unlawfully detained, there is liability in damages if they are lost.[6] Interdict against allowing animals to trespass has been refused where it was not proved that the owner had failed to take reasonable precautions to prevent the cattle from trespassing.[7]

A proprietor must take reasonable care for the safety of even trespassers who come on his lands[8] which imports a limited duty to fence and warn of dangers.[9] He may not set man-traps or spring-guns against trespassing persons or animals.[10]

Encroachment

Encroachment is the permanent usurpation by another of some portion of a man's lands,[11] as by trees overhanging his land,[12] a building projecting over it,[13] dumping rubbish on another's lands[14] attaching a flue to the outside of a gable,[15] attaching a

1 Trespass (Sc.) Act, 1865, S. 3; *Paterson* v. *Robertson*, 1944 J.C. 166 (squatters).
2 See further, *infra*.
3 cf. *Shaw & Mackenzie* v. *Ewart*, 2 March 1809, F.C.
4 *McArthur* v. *Jones* (1878) 6 R. 41.
5 *McArthur* v. *Miller* (1873) 1 R. 248.
6 *Fraser* v. *Smith* (1899) 1 F. 487.
7 *Robertson* v. *Wright* (1885) 13 R. 174.
8 Occupiers' Liability (Sc.) Act, 1960, S. 2.
9 *Black* v. *Cadell* (1812) 5 Paton 567; *Hislop* v. *Durham* (1842) 4 D. 1168; *Prentice* v. *Assets Co.* (1889) 17 R. 484; *McGlone* v. *B.R. Board*, 1966 S.C. (H.L.) 1.
10 *H.M.A.* v. *Craw* (1827) Syme 188, 210.
11 Hume, *Lect.* III, 202.
12 *Halkerston* v. *Wedderburn* (1781) Mor. 10495; *Lemmon* v. *Webb* [1895] A.C. 1.
13 Ersk. II, 9, 9; Bell, *Prin.* §941, 967; *Graham* v. *Greig* (1838) 1 D. 171; *McIntosh* v. *Scott* (1859) 21 D. 363; *Leonard* v. *Lindsay* (1886) 13 R. 958; *Wilson* v. *Pottinger*, 1908 S.C. 580.
14 cf. *Whitwham* v. *Westminster Brymbo Coal Co.* [1896] 1 Ch. 894.
15 *Walker* v. *Braidwood* (1797) Hume 512; cf. *Gellatly* v. *Arroll* (1863) 1 M. 592.

sign to another's building,[1] or to a common entrance,[2] erecting a shop signboard above the centre line of the joists between shop and first floor,[3] constructing a road through another's lands,[4] laying a pipe through another's land,[5] letting the roots of trees penetrate another's land,[6] carrying a quarry or mine into a neighbour's lands and extracting the minerals therefrom.

Encroachments underground

The proprietor of lands may object to pipes laid without authority under the surface of his lands,[7] or the roots of trees penetrating through the soil.[8] In so far as he is entitled to the minerals he may interdict another from mining underneath his lands and abstracting the minerals thereunder. Where minerals under his lands have been wrongfully abstracted by another, damages are recoverable for the loss, measured, in the case of inadvertent or mistaken encroachment, by the value of the minerals less the cost of winning and raising them,[9] but in the case of deliberate, fraudulent, furtive or wholly unauthorized encroachment, by the value of the minerals less the cost of raising only.[10] Occasionally other methods of measuring damages have been adopted.[11]

Right to Support

A landowner is entitled as a natural right of property to have his land maintained in its natural state and not affected by operations on adjacent or subjacent land which cause damage by

[1] *Thomson* v. *Crombie* (1776) Mor. 13182; *Drysdale* v. *Lowrie*, 13 May 1812, F.C.

[2] *Mackenzie* v. *Murray* (1812) Hume 520.

[3] *Alexander* v. *Butchart* (1875) 3 R. 156; *McArly* v. *French's Trs.* (1883) 10 R. 574; *Birrell* v. *Lumley* (1905) 12 S.L.T. 719.

[4] *Fergusson Buchanan* v. *Dunbartonshire C.C.*, 1924 S.C. 42.

[5] *Galbreath* v. *Armour* (1845) 4 Bell 374; cf. *Hazle* v. *Turner* (1840) 2 D. 886.

[6] *Lemmon* v. *Webb* [1895] A.C. 1; *McCombe* v. *Reid* [1955] 2 Q.B. 429; *Davey* v. *Harrow Corpn.* [1958] 1 Q.B. 60.

[7] Bell, *Prin.* §942; *Galbreath* v. *Armour* (1845) 4 Bell 374; cf. *Hazle* v. *Turner* (1840) 2 D. 886.

[8] Hume, *Lect.* III, 203; *Butler* v. *Standard Telephones* [1940] 1 All E.R. 121; *Davey* v. *Harrow Corpn.* [1958] 1 Q.B. 60.

[9] *Hilton* v. *Woods* (1867) L.R. 4 Eq. 432; *Jegon* v. *Vivian* (1871) L.R. 6 Ch. 742; *Re United Merthyr Coal Co.* (1872) L.R. 15 Eq. 46; *Ashton* v. *Stock* (1877) 6 Ch. D. 719; *Trotter* v. *Maclean* (1879) 13 Ch. D. 574; *Houldsworth* v. *Brand's Trs.* (1877) 4 R. 369; *Whitwham* v. *Westminster Brymbo Coal Co.* [1896] 2 Ch. 538.

[10] *Durham* v. *Hood* (1871) 9 M. 474; *Ramsay* v. *Blair* (1876) 3 R. (H.L.) 41; *Wilsons* v. *Waddell* (1876) 4 R. (H.L.) 29; *Livingstone* v. *Rawyards Coal Co.* (1880) 7 R. (H.L.) 1; *Llynvi Co.* v. *Brogden* (1870) L.R. 11 Eq. 188; *Phillips* v. *Homfray* (1871) L.R. 6 Ch. 770; *Taylor* v. *Mostyn* (1886) 33 Ch. D. 226; *Bulli Co.* v. *Osborne* [1889] A.C. 351.

[11] *Livingstone, supra*; *Davidson's Trs.* v. *Caledonian Ry.* (1898) 23 R. 45; see also *D. Portland* v. *Wood's Trs.*, 1927 S.C. (H.L.) 1.

withdrawal of support therefrom.[1] The right entitles him to complain of operations, such as mining or quarrying, only if they cause subsidence or otherwise appreciably damage or interfere with the use of the complainer's lands.[2] Each distinct subsidence causing damage is a separate ground of action, even though caused by one mining operation.[3]

The landowner may seek interdict against operations under or alongside his land likely to produce injury or which will necessarily result in subsidence.[4] Alternatively, or additionally, he may recover damages for any actual and appreciable damage caused by subsidence.[5] Negligence need not be proved.[6]

Where the support is afforded in part by underground water or running sand an adjacent proprietor may be entitled, without liability for subsidence, to drain it or appropriate it.[7]

Support to lands already built on

Where buildings had been erected on the surface before the adjacent or subjacent ground was granted to another, the other is *prima facie* bound to continue to afford to the granter's lands the support which they were being afforded at the time of severance. A contractual obligation to pay for damage to buildings may supersede the common law obligation, but may not apply to new buildings on the site of buildings existing at the date of the contract.[8]

Support to lands subsequently built on

Where, however, after the adjacent or subjacent ground had been granted to one person buildings are erected on the surface by the granter or his successors, the latter has no claim for subsidence damage so far as caused by the additional loading on

1 Bell, *Prin.* §970; *Humphries* v. *Brogden* (1848) 12 Q.B. 739; *Caledonian Ry.* v. *Sprot* (1856) 2 Macq. 449; *Bonomi* v. *Backhouse* (1861) 9 H.L. C. 503; *Elliott* v. *N.E. Ry.* (1863) 10 H.L.C. 333; *Buchanan* v. *Andrew* (1873) 11 M. (H.L.) 13; *Livingstone* v. *Rawyards Coal Co.* (1880) 7 R. (H.L.) 1; *Dalton* v. *Angus* (1881) 6 App. Cas. 740; *White* v. *Dixon* (1883) 10 R. (H.L.) 45.

2 *Bonomi, supra*; *Darley Main Colliery Co.* v. *Mitchell* (1886) 11 App. Cas. 127; *Gray* v. *Burns* (1894) 2 S.L.T. 187.

3 *Darley Main, supra*; *Geddes* v. *Haldane* (1906) 13 S.L.T. 707; *D. Abercorn* v. *Merry & Cuninghame*, 1909 1 S.L.T. 321.

4 *Buchanan, supra*; *White* v. *Dixon* (1881) 9 R. 375; *Shawrigg Fireclay Co.* v. *Mitchell Collieries Ltd.* (1903) 5 F. 1131.

5 *Darley Main, supra*; *West Leigh Colliery Co.* v. *Tunnicliffe* [1908] A.C. 27.

6 *Angus* v. *N.C.B.*, 1955 S.C. 175, 181.

7 *Bald* v. *Alloa Coal Co.* (1854) 16 D. 870; *Elliott, supra*; *Popplewell* v. *Hodkinson* (1869) L.R. 4 Ex. 248; *Jordeson* v. *Sutton Gas Co.* [1899] 2 Ch. 217.

8 *Barr* v. *Baird* (1904) 6 F. 524.

the surface, and similarly where the surface is granted, the subjacent strata being reserved.[1]

A contractual obligation to pay for surface damages has been held not restricted to the state of the ground at the date when surface and mineral estates were separated, but to cover damage to a house subsequently built, though opinions were reserved at to the rights of parties if the ground became covered with streets and buildings.[2]

Where the owner of lands grants the surface for a specified purpose which involves loading the surface, the grant, in the absence of evident contrary intention, carries by implication a right to reasonable and necessary support for the works from the granter's adjacent lands and subjacent strata, and this obligation transmits with the lands to a successor of the granter.[3]

The same principles apply in respect of land burdened by railways, roads, pipelines, sewers, or other structures.[4] The Railways Clauses Consolidation (Sc.) Act, 1845, Ss. 70–8, reserves the minerals under a railway line to the landowner, but gives the railway authority power to prevent working within a limited distance on paying compensation.[5]

Variation of right by contract

The right to be supported or to recover compensation for damage caused by withdrawal of support may be modified by contract, particularly when ownership of surface and of subjacent strata are separated, or mineral leases granted. Thus a superior may feu lands, reserving the minerals and excluding liability for damage to the vassal by working the minerals,[6] or reserving right to work in a manner injurious to the surface[7], or right to bring down the surface on payment of damages.[8]

[1] *Hamilton* v. *Turner* (1867) 5 M. 1086; *Dryburgh* v. *Fife Coal Co.* (1905) 7 F. 1083; *Geddes's Trs.* v. *Haldane* (1906) 14 S.L.T. 328.

[2] *Neill's Trs.* v. *Dixon* (1880) 7 R. 741.

[3] *Caledonian Ry.* v. *Sprot* (1856) 2 Macq. 449; *Dalton* v. *Angus* (1881) 6 App. Cas. 740; *N.B. Ry.* v. *Turner* (1904) 6 F. 900.

[4] *Caledonian Ry.* v. *Sprot* (1856) 2 Macq. 449; *Caledonian Ry.* v. *L. Belhaven* (1857) 3 Macq. 56; *Caledonian Ry.* v. *Henderson* (1876) 4 R. 140; *Caledonian Ry.* v. *Dixon* (1880) 7 R. (H.L.) 117; *Aitken's Trs.* v. *Rawyards Coal Co.* (1894) 22 R. 201; *N.B. Ry.* v. *Turners* (1904) 6 F. 900; *Clippens Oil Co.* v. *Edinburgh Water Trs.* (1904) 6 F. (H.L.) 7; *Midlothian C.C.* v. *N.C.B.*, 1960 S.C. 308; see also *Mid and East Calder Gas Light Co.* v. *Oakbank Oil Co.* (1891) 18 R. 788.

[5] *D. Hamilton's Trs.* v. *Caledonian Ry.* (1905) 7 F. 847. See also Harbours, Docks and Piers Clauses Act, 1847.

[6] *Buchanan* v. *Andrew* (1873) 11 M. (H.L.) 13; *White* v. *Dixon* (1883) 10 R. (H.L.) 45.

[7] *Bank of Scotland* v. *Stewart* (1891) 18 R. 957.

[8] *Anderson* v. *McCracken Bros.* (1900) 2 F. 780; *Pringle* v. *Carron Co.* (1905) 7 F. 820; see also *Gray* v. *Burns* (1894) 2 S.L.T. 187.

Many cases turn on the interpretation of particular phrases in the light of their circumstances.[1]

Statutory provisions

The Coal-Mining (Subsidence) Act, 1950, imposed on the National Coal Board the duty to carry out repairs or make payments in respect of subsidence damage after 1st January, 1947, and affecting any dwelling house. There was power also to effect preventive works. The statutory right was alternative to any other rights in respect of the damage.

The Coal-Mining (Subsidence) Act, 1957, applies to subsidence damage caused after its date by the withdrawal of support in connection with the mining of coal. The National Coal Board must execute remedial works or pay the cost of execution of remedial works, and may execute preventive works. It must also pay damages for death or disablement resulting from injury caused by subsidence damage.

The Mines (Working Facilities and Support) Act, 1966, empowers the Court of Session, if satisfied that it is expedient in the national interest and that it is not reasonably practicable to obtain the right by private arrangement, to grant any person a right to search or work any specified minerals, together with certain ancillary rights including a right to let down the surface. Restrictions may be imposed on working minerals required for support.

Rights in buildings

Buildings already on lands are conveyed by feudal grant as part and pertinent of the lands and the proprietor of lands is *prima facie* entitled to erect or demolish buildings on his land, subject to any restrictions in his feu charter and to obtaining planning and other necessary permission.

Buildings must be erected entirely on the proprietor's lands save that where an implied contract can be inferred from a feuing plan or other circumstances the owner of one of several adjoining lots may erect a gable half on the adjacent land without the other proprietor's consent, and reclaim half of the cost when the other proprietor comes to use the common gable.[2]

1 *Galbraith's Tr.* v. *Eglinton Iron Co.* (1868) 7 M. 167; *Hallpenny* v. *Dewar* (1898) 25 R. 889; *Taylor* v. *Auchinlea Coal Co.*, 1912 2 S.L.T. 10; *Dryburgh* v. *Fife Coal Co.* (1905) 7 F. 1083.

2 *Rodger* v. *Russell* (1873) 11 M. 671; *Jack* v. *Begg* (1875) 3 R. 35; *Sinclair* v. *Brown* (1882) 10 R. 45; *Robertson* v. *Scott* (1886) 13 R. 1127; *Berkeley* v. *Baird* (1895) 22 R. 372;

The proprietor of buildings is entitled to have them supported by any adjoining buildings with which he has such common[1] gables or walls and may object to interference with the common gable if likely to harm his building.[2]

A servitude right of support is recognized in two cases. By the servitude *tigni immittendi* the owner of one building has the right to insert a beam or other structural member of his building into the wall of another building, keep it there, and renew it as necessary.[3] By the servitude *oneris ferendi* the owner of the one building has the right to have his building supported by another's building underneath. In this case it implies an obligation on the other to maintain his building.[4]

Rights to Minerals

Save in so far as minerals have been reserved by the Crown or superiors, or been statutorily expropriated,[5] the proprietor has the right to all minerals below the surface of his lands[6] or under highways,[7] lochs[8] and rivers[9] and he may work them, or lease them to another to work.

Timber

Apart from private ownership and development of woodlands the Forestry Commission has the duty of promoting the development of afforestation and the production and supply of timber, including the establishment and maintenance of adequate reserves of growing trees.[10] The Commission may manage, plant and use land put at their disposal by the Secretary of State for Scotland.[11] He may acquire by purchase, lease or exchange,

Fraser v. *Campbell* (1895) 22 R. 558; *Baird* v. *Alexander* (1898) 25 R. (H.L.) 35; *Roberts* v. *Galloway* (1898) 6 S.L.T. 25; *Calder* v. *Pope* (1900) 8 S.L.T. 149; *Stark's Trs.* v. *Cooper's Trs.* (1900) 2 F. 1257; *Wilson* v. *Pottinger*, 1908 S.C. 580.

1 Usually miscalled 'mutual' gables.

2 *Lamont* v. *Cumming* (1875) 2 R. 784; *Leonard* v. *Lindsay & Benzie* (1886) 13 R. 968.

3 Inst. II, 1, 29; Dig. 8, 2, and 3; 50, 16, 62; Forbes, II, 4, 3, 2; Mack. II, 9, 6, 7; Stair II, 7, 6; Bankt. II, 7, 7; Ersk. II, 9, 7; Bell, *Prin.* §1003.

4 Dig. 8, 5, 6–8; *Murray* v. *Brownhill* (1715) Mor. 1452; *Troup* v. *Aberdeen Heritable Securities Co.*, 1916 S.C. 918.

5 Petroleum (Production) Act, 1934, S. 1; Coal Industry Nationalisation Act, 1946, Ss. 5, 64(3), and Sched. 1.

6 *Bruce* v. *Erskine* (1716) Mor. 9642; *Mitchell* v. *York Buildings Co.* (1777) 6 Pat. 795.

7 *Wishart* v. *Wyllie* (1853) 1 Macq. 389.

8 *Baird* v. *Robertson* (1839) 1 D. 1051; *Scott* v. *L. Napier* (1869) 7 M. (H.L.) 35.

9 *Wishart*, *supra*; *Bicket* v. *Morris* (1866) 4 M. (H.L.) 44; *Orr Ewing* v. *Colquhoun's Trs.* (1877) 4 R. (H.L.) 116.

10 Forestry Act, 1967, Ss. 1–2.

11 Ibid., S. 3.

land suitable for afforestation, or acquire it compulsorily; certain categories of land are excepted.[1]

Proprietors of land may make forestry dedication agreements with the Forestry Commissioners, which may be recorded in the Register of Sasines and are then enforceable by the Commissioners against any person having an interest in the land and any person deriving title from him, but not against a *bona fide* purchaser for value of the land prior to the recording of the agreement.[2] If the Commission is satisfied that trees are being damaged by rabbits, hares, or vermin by reason of the occupier of the land's failure to destroy them, it may authorize any competent person to do so, and charge the occupier.[3]

Save in excepted cases a felling licence from the Commission is required for the felling of growing trees[4] and the Commission may give felling directions to the owner of trees requiring him to fell them within a stated period.[5]

Rights in lochs

A sea-loch is an extension of the sea and seashore and no landed proprietor acquires right to the solum or the water thereof.

A loch surrounded entirely by the lands of one proprietor belongs entirely to him, both as to the solum and the water,[6] and he has exclusive rights of fishing.[7] If however a stream runs out of it he may not so use the loch as to infringe the rights of riparian owners in the stream.[8]

If the lands of more than one landowner front on the loch, the titles, or the titles supplemented by evidence of possession, may indicate that one owner has exclusive property in the whole loch,[9] but otherwise each proprietor has an exclusive right in the solum *ex adverso* of his lands out to the middle of the loch[10] and all have a right of property in the water in common, with liberty to sail or fish on the surface and to use it for primary purposes.[11] The

1 Ibid., S. 39–40.
2 Ibid., S. 5.
3 Ibid., S. 7.
4 Ibid., Ss. 9–17.
5 Ibid., Ss. 18–35.
6 Stair II, 3, 7, 3; Bankt. II, 3, 12; Bell, *Prin.* §651; *Macdonell* v. *Caledonian Canal Commrs.* (1830) 8 S. 881.
7 *Montgomerie* v. *Watson* (1861) 23 D. 635.
8 Bell, *Prin.* §1110.
9 *Scott* v. *Lord Napier* (1869) 7 M. (H.L.) 35; *Stewart's Trs.* v. *Robertson* (1874) 1 R. 334; *Meacher* v. *Blair Oliphant*, 1913 S.C. 417.
10 *Cochrane* v. *E. Minto* (1815) 6 Pat. 139.
11 Bell, *Prin.* §1111; *Menzies* v. *MacDonald* (1854) 16 D. 827; 2 Macq. 463; *Mackenzie* v. *Bankes* (1878) 5 R. (H.L.) 192.

Court may regulate or limit the number of boats each proprietor may put on the loch.[1]

If an inland loch is used for navigation, the principles applicable to navigable rivers probably apply.[2]

Rights in surface and percolating water

A landowner is entitled to appropriate and use water which gathers on the surface as in a bog, or percolates through the soil of his land, and to abstract it by a well, even to the detriment of a neighbour's well enjoyed for the prescriptive period.[3] He may drain the water into a stream, but this gives him no greater rights in the water of the stream.[4]

Surface water may be discharged on to an inferior neighbour's land if flowing naturally that way, but surface water may not be drained in a direction other than its natural flow, nor water pumped to the surface or channelled from a stream.[5] An inferior proprietor cannot do anything to prevent the water coming on his land or to cause it to flow back.[6] Nor can he insist on a continuance of a flow of water from higher lands.[7]

Exceptionally, however, a landlord may by necessary operations for agricultural drainage alter the natural flow of water and may then discharge it on to a neighbour's land. The Land Drainage (Sc.) Act, 1930, empowers the Sheriff to regulate such drainage.

Land Drainage

Under the Land Drainage (Sc.) Act, 1958, the owner of any agricultural land may apply to the Secretary of State for Scotland for an improvement order authorizing the execution of such drainage works as will improve the drainage of the land or prevent or mitigate flooding or erosion. The order may provide for an improvement committee of the owners of land affected discharging functions under the order. (Ss. 1–3). The authorized persons must make good damage to land consequential on their

[1] *Mackenzie* v. *Bankes* (1878) 5 R. (H.L.) 192; *Menzies* v. *Wentworth* (1901) 3 F. 941.

[2] *Macdonell* v. *Caledonian Canal Commrs.* (1830) 8 S. 881; *Colquhoun's Trs.* v. *Orr Ewing* (1877) 4 R. 344; *Leith Buchanan* v. *Hogg*, 1931 S.C. 204.

[3] *Linlithgow Mags.* v. *Elphinstone* (1768) Mor. 12805; *Chasemore* v. *Richards* (1859) 7 H.L. Cas. 349; *Mayor of Bradford* v. *Pickles* [1895] A.C. 587; *Milton* v. *Glen Moray Glenlivet Distillery Co.* (1898) 1 F. 135.

[4] *Cowan* v. *L. Kinnaird* (1865) 4 M. 236; *Stevenson* v. *Hogganfield Bleaching Co.* (1892) 30 S.L.R. 86.

[5] Ersk. II, 9, 2; *Campbell* v. *Bryson* (1864) 3 M. 254; *Young* v. *Bankier Distillery* (1893) 20 R. (H.L.) 76.

[6] *Montgomerie* v. *Buchanan's Trs.* (1853) 15 D. 853.

[7] *L. Blantyre* v. *Dunn* (1848) 10 D. 509; *Ardrossan Mags.* v. *Dickie* (1906) 14 S.L.T. 349.

operations, and compensate the owners of non-agricultural land and the occupiers of any land, for damage suffered (Ss. 4–5). An owner may increase the rent of an agricultural holding equal to the increase in rental value attributable to the drainage (S. 6). The Secretary of State may require the execution or maintenance of protective works, and may make grants towards improvement expenditure (Ss. 8–9).

Flood prevention

The Flood Prevention (Sc.) Act, 1961, empowers local authorities, alone or in combination, to carry out works for the prevention or mitigation of flooding of non-agricultural land, on both land within and on land outwith their areas (Ss. 1–3). Flood prevention operations must be carried out under a flood prevention scheme made by the local authority and confirmed by the Secretary of State (S. 4). They may be authorized to acquire compulsorily any land required for the exercise of their powers under the Act (S. 7). Claims are competent for depreciation in the value of any interest in land by the operations (S. 11).

Drainage from mines

In mines a mine-owner may work his minerals to the boundary of his lands, though he may thereby drain water into adjacent workings.[1] The inferior mine-owner must receive the water or leave a barrier of minerals on his side of the boundary.[2] But the superior mine-owner may not pump or otherwise artificially direct water which would not have naturally flowed there into an inferior mine-owner's strata,[3] nor pump it into a stream with the effect of polluting it.[4]

Rights in rivers

Where a river is tidal and navigable[5] it is subject to public rights of navigation and fishing. The *alveus* is vested in the Crown in trust for public purposes[6] and the Crown, or a statutory body in its place, may improve the channel and prevent encroachment.[7]

1 *Baird* v. *Monkland Iron Co.* (1862) 24 D. 1418.

2 *Blair* v. *Hunter Finlay & Co.* (1870) 9 M. 204; *Durham* v. *Hood* (1871) 9 M. 474.

3 *Turner* v. *Ballandene* (1834) 7 W. & S. 163; *Blair, supra*; *Bankier Distillery* v. *Young* (1892) 19 R. 1083; affd. 20 R. (H.L.) 76.

4 *D. Buccleuch* v. *Gilmerton Coal Co.* (1894) 1 S.L.T. 576.

5 This is a question of fact: see *Bowie* v. *M. Ailsa* (1887) 14 R. 649.

6 *L.A.* v. *Clyde Nav. Trs.* (1852) 1 Macq. 46; *Colquhoun's Trs.* v. *Orr Ewing* (1877) 4 R. (H.L.) 116.

7 *Colquhoun's Trs., supra*; see also *L. Blantyre* v. *Clyde Nav. Trs.* (1881) 8 R. (H.L.) 47.

The foreshore is also vested in the Crown.[1] Subject to the public rights the banks belong to the owner of the adjacent lands, and the public have the use of the banks only by custom, grant or use for the prescriptive period.[2]

Where a river is non-tidal but navigable both *alveus* and banks belong to the riparian proprietors but the public have liberty of use of the water for purposes of navigation[3] and probably also the right to moor and anchor.[4] Hence the proprietors cannot alter the *alveus* so as to interfere with the right of navigation.

Rights in private (non-navigable) rivers and streams—the alveus

Where water flows in a definite channel of any size on or under the surface the bed and banks of the stream or river belong to the proprietor of the adjacent lands or, where the stream is the boundary, each owner the bed of the stream, so far as *ex adverso* of his lands, *ad medium filum*.[5] But no proprietor may interfere with the bed of the river, even within his own portion of the *alveus*, so as to interfere with the flowing water or to cause real apprehension of resulting injury,[6] nor obstruct the channels through which the river flows when in spate.[7] Nor may a proprietor erect anything which will hinder the flow of the river higher up,[8] or accelerate it.[9]

He may strengthen the banks on his side to prevent his lands being flooded so long as this does not result in the opposite proprietor's land being further inundated.[10] Nor may he do anything in the bed of the stream which will change the level or direction of the flow, or augment its force.[11]

[1] *L.A.* v. *Lord Blantyre* (1879) 6 R. (H.L.) 72; *Buchanan* v. *L.A.* (1882) 9 R. 1218.

[2] Ersk. II, 1, 5; Bell, *Prin.* §650; *Colquhoun* v. *D. Montrose* (1801) 4 Paton 221; *Carron Co.* v. *Ogilvie* (1806) 5 Paton 61.

[3] *Colquhoun's Trs.* v. *Orr Ewing* (1877) 4 R. 344; 4 R. (H.L.) 116; *E. Breadalbane* v. *Colquhoun's Trs.* (1881) 18 S.L.R. 607; see also *Grant* v. *D. Gordon* (1776) 3 Paton 679; (1782) 2 Paton 582.

[4] *Campbell's Trs.* v. *Sweeney*, 1911 S.C. 1319.

[5] Ersk. II, 1, 5; Bell, *Prin.* §1101; *Wishart* v. *Wylie* (1853) 1 Macq. 389; *McIntyre's Trs.* v. *Cupar Mags.* (1867) 5 M. 780; *Gibson* v. *Bonnington Sugar Co.* (1869) 7 M. 394; *Menzies* v. *M. Breadalbane* (1901) 4 F. 55.

[6] *Morris* v. *Bicket* (1866) 4 M. (H.L.) 44; *Jackson* v. *Marshall* (1872) 10 M. 913; *D. Roxburghe* v. *Waldie's Trs.* (1879) 6 R. 663; *Orr Ewing* v. *Colquhoun's Trs.* (1877) 4 R. (H.L.) 116; *McGavin* v. *McIntyre* (1890) 17 R. 818; 20 R. (H.L.) 49; *Ross* v. *Powrie and Pitcaithley* (1891) 19 R. 314.

[7] *Menzies* v. *E. Breadalbane* (1828) 3 W. & Sh. 235; *Jackson, supra.*

[8] *Morris, supra*; cf. *Hope* v. *Heriot's Hospital* (1878) 15 S.L.R. 400.

[9] *D. Roxburghe* v. *Waldie* (1821) Hume 524.

[10] *Farquharson* v. *F.* (1741) Mor. 12779; *Menzies, supra*; *Morris supra*; *Jackson* v. *Marshall* (1872) 10 M. 913; *Murdoch* v. *Wallace* (1881) 8 R. 855.

[11] *Farquharson, supra*; *Menzies, supra*; *Morris, supra*; *Orr-Ewing, supra.*

Rights in private (non-navigable) rivers and streams—the water

All riparian proprietors have a common interest in the water of a stream but no one has exclusive right of property therein.[1] A proprietor not having lands fronting on the stream has probably no interest in it.[2] Hence no proprietor may use or affect the flow of the water to the prejudice of others. One may, at least in a question with an opposite proprietor, divert part of the stream through a mill-lade, returning the water to the river undiminished,[3] but not divert the flow for agricultural or manufacturing purposes.[4] Still less can water be impounded and stored, save by statutory authority.[5]

Every riparian proprietor is entitled to take water from the stream for primary uses, for drinking by men and animals, and for ordinary domestic purposes, such as cooking, washing and even home brewing,[6] even though this diminishes or even exhausts the supply available for inferior proprietors.[7] The surplus must be returned to the stream within the proprietors' own lands.[8]

But no proprietor may take water for other purposes, such as irrigation or manufacture, if by so doing he infringes the reasonable rights of any inferior proprietor.[9]

A proprietor may also prevent operations by a superior proprietor which result in appreciable change in the quality of the water coming down, such as pollution unfitting the water for primary uses, or for any special use for which an inferior proprietor requires it, such as distilling,[10] but not operations of character of ordinary estate management even if resulting in temporary fouling.[11]

1 *Morris* v. *Bicket* (1864) 2 M. 1082; 4 M. (H.L.) 44.

2 *L. Melville* v. *Denniston* (1842) 4 D. 1231; *Bonthrone* v. *Downie* (1878) 6 R. 324; *M. Breadalbane* v. *West Highland Ry.* (1895) 22 R. 307.

3 *Hamilton* v. *Edington* (1793) Mor. 12824; *Cowan* v. *Kinnaird* (1865) 4 M. 236; *E. Kintore* v. *Pirie* (1903) 5 F. 818.

4 *Bannatyne* v. *Cranston* (1624) Mor. 12769; *M. Abercorn* v. *Jamieson* (1791) Hume 510; *Hamilton, supra*; *Cowan, supra.*

5 *Hunter and Aitkenhead* v. *Aitken* (1880) 7 R. 610; *Willoughby d'Eresby* v. *Wood* (1884) 22 S.L.R. 471.

6 *Johnstone* v. *Ritchie*, 15 Feb. 1822, F.C.; as to water closets see *Bonthrone* v. *Downie* (1878) 6 R. 324.

7 Bell, *Prin.* §1104–5; *Russel* v. *Haig* (1791) Bell's Oct. Cas. 338; *Hood* v. *Williamsons* (1861) 23 D. 496; *D. Buccleuch* v. *Cowan* (1876) 4 R. (H.L.) 14.

8 *Hood* v. *Williamson* (1861) 23 D. 496.

9 *Hamilton* v. *Edington* (1793) Mor. 12824; *Mackenzie* v. *Woddrop* (1854) 16 D. 381; *Young* v. *Bankier Distillery Co.* (1893) 20 R. (H.L.) 76.

10 Bell, *Prin.* §1106; *Rigby and Beardmore* v. *Downie* (1872) 10 M. 568; *Caledonian Ry.* v. *Baird* (1876) 3 R. 839; *Young* v. *Bankier Distillery* (1893) 20 R. (H.L.) 76; *C. Seafield* v. *Kemp* (1899) 1 F. 402; *Fleming* v. *Gemmill*, 1908 S.C. 340.

11 *Armistead* v. *Bowerman* (1888) 15 R. 814.

But in the case of some streams the water has for long been devoted to secondary purposes and a riparian proprietor may have acquired by prescription the right to pollute water.[1]

The Rivers (Prevention of Pollution) (Sc.) Acts, 1951 and 1965, and the Border Rivers (Prevention of Pollution) Act, 1951, seek to prevent pollution and to require preventive measures.

Rights of fishing

The right to fish for salmon is *inter regalia*[2] and does not belong to a proprietor of lands unless expressly granted to him by the Crown with the lands[3] or separately,[4] or there be at least a grant of fishings followed by possession of salmon fishings for the prescriptive period,[5] or a barony title followed by prescriptive possession of salmon fishings.[6] The requisite possession must be for the benefit of the person claiming the right, attributable to the grant and in accordance with it.[7] It must also be exclusive and exercised by a legal method.[8]

The only lawful modes of fishing for salmon are by rod, by net and coble[9] and by cruives.[10] In the sea fixed engines, such as stake nets, are lawful. Unless a proprietor owns both banks he may not fish beyond the *medium filum* of the river,[11] and he may

[1] *Portobello Mags.* v. *Edinburgh Mags.* (1882) 10 R. 130; *McIntyre* v. *McGavin* (1893) 20 R. (H.L.) 49; cf. *Moncreiffe* v. *Perth Police Commrs.* (1886) 13 R. 921.

[2] Stair II, 3, 69; Ersk. II, 6, 15; Bell, *Prin.* §671; *Commrs. of Woods and Forests* v. *Gammell* (1859) 5 Macq. 419; see also *L.A.* v. *Sharp* (1878) 6 R. 108; There is an exception in Orkney and Shetland: *Smith* v. *Lerwick Harbour Trs.* (1903) 5 F. 680; *L.A.* v. *Balfour*, 1907 S.C. 1360.

[3] *Mackenzie* v. *Davidson* (1841) 3 D. 646; *E. Galloway* v. *Birrel* (1868) 5 S.L.R. 113; *Gray* v. *Richardson* (1877) 4 R. (H.L.) 76; *D. Argyll* v. *Campbell* (1891) 18 R. 1094; *Maxwell* v. *Lamont* (1903) 6 F. 245.

[4] *Hogarth* v. *Grant* (1901) 8 S.L.T. 324.

[5] *Sinclair* v. *L.A.* (1867) 5 M. (H.L.) 97; *Stuart* v. *McBarnet* (1868) 6 M. (H.L.) 123; *McCulloch* v. *L.A.* (1874) 2 R. 27; *Sinclair* v. *Threipland* (1890) 17 R. 507; *Ogston* v. *Stewart* (1896) 23 R. (H.L.) 16.

[6] *Nicol* v. *L.A.* (1868) 6 M. 972; *D. Richmond* v. *E. Seafield* (1870) 8 M. 530; *L.A.* v. *Cathcart* (1871) 9 M. 744; *McDouall* v. *L.A.* (1875) 2 R. (H.L.) 49. See also *L.A.* v. *Northern Lighthouses Commrs.* (1874) 1 R. 950.

[7] *Milne's Trs.* v. *L.A.* (1869) 11 M. 966; *D. Argyll, supra*; *Ogston, supra*.

[8] *Ramsay* v. *D. Roxburghe* (1848) 10 D. 661; *Milne* v. *Smith* (1850) 13 D. 112; *Anderson* v. *A.* (1867) 5 M. 499; 6 M. 117; *Maxwell* v. *Lamont* (1913) 6 F. 245.

[9] *Hay* v. *Perth Mags.* (1863) 1 M. (H.L.) 41; *Wedderburn* v. *D. Atholl* (1900) 2 F. (H.L.) 57; *Maxwell* v. *Lamont* (1903) 6 F. 245; *Oswald* v. *McCall*, 1919 S.C. 584.

[10] Stair II, 3, 70; Ersk. II, 6, 15; Bell, *Prin.* §1118; *Halkerston* v. *Scott* (1769) Mor. 14276; *E. Kintore* v. *Forbes* (1828) 3 W. & S. 261; *D. Fife* v. *George* (1897) 24 R. 549.

[11] *Milne, supra*; *Fraser* v. *Grant* (1866) 4 M. 596; *Stuart* v. *McBarnet* (1868) 6 M. (H.L.) 123; *E. Zetland* v. *Tennent's Trs.* (1873) 11 M. 469; *Campbell* v. *Muir*, 1908 S.C. 387.

not interfere with the *alveus*.[1] He may object to pollution of the river[2] or excessive abstraction of water by an inferior riparian proprietor.[3] Salmon fishings may be let on lease.[4] The public have no right to fish in a tidal river within the bounds of an express grant of salmon fishing.[5] The mode of exercising salmon fishing is extensively controlled by statute, penalizing illegal modes. Weekly and annual close times are prescribed.[6] Special legislation applies to the Tweed and the Solway.[7]

The right of fishing for trout in private, i.e., non-tidal and non-navigable, waters is part and pertinent of the lands fronting the loch or river, unless reserved or disponed separately to one other than the proprietor thereof. But it cannot be held separately from property in the loch, stream or adjacent lands.[8] A bare right of access to a private stream or loch does not confer any right of fishing,[9] so that the public cannot acquire a right against a proprietor of the lands or water,[10] nor may an agricultural tenant fish, unless authorized by his lease.[11] Each riparian proprietor may fish *ex adverso* of his own lands[12] and in the case of small streams is not restricted to his own side of the *medium filum*. A proprietor may licence others to fish,[13] or let the fishing rights on lease. The public right to be at or on a non-tidal river for navigation does not imply liberty to fish there, nor can such a right be acquired by prescription.[14] Trout fishing is also regulated by statute.[15]

1 *Mather* v. *Macbraire* (1873) 11 M. 522; *Orr Ewing* v. *Colquhoun's Trs.* (1877) 4 R. (H.L.) 116; *D. Sutherland* v. *Ross* (1878) 5 R. (H.L.) 137; *D. Roxburghe* v. *Waldie's Trs.* (1879) 6 R. 663; *Robertson* v. *Foote* (1879) 6 R. 1290; *Ross* v. *Powrie & Pitcaithley* (1891) 19 R. 314; *Gay* v. *Malloch*, 1959 S.C. 110.

2 *Moncrieff* v. *Perth Police Commrs.* (1886) 13 R. 921; *Armistead* v. *Bowerman* (1888) 15 R. 814; *C. Seafield* v. *Kemp* (1899) 1 F. 402.

3 *D. Roxburghe, supra*; *Pirie* v. *E. Kintore* (1906) 8 F. (H.L.) 16.

4 Stair I, 13, 15; Bankt. I, 17, 10; *Gemmill* v. *Riddell* (1847) 9 D. 727; *E. Fife* v. *Wilson* (1864) 3 M. 323; *Mackintosh* v. *May* (1895) 22 R. 345.

5 *Anderson* v. *A.* (1867) 6 M. 117.

6 See Salmon Act, 1696 (c. 35); Salmon Fisheries (Sc.) Acts, 1828, 1862, 1863, 1864, 1868, and 1870; Salmon and Freshwater Fisheries (Protection) (Sc.) Act, 1951.

7 Solway Act, 1804; Tweed Fisheries Acts 1857 and 1859.

8 *Menzies* v. *Macdonald* (1854) 16 D. 827; *Patrick* v. *Napier* (1867) 5 M. 683; *E. Galloway* v. *D. Bedford* (1902) 4 F. 857.

9 *Ferguson* v. *Shireff* (1844) 6 D. 1363; *Montgomery* v. *Watson* (1861) 23 D. 635.

10 *Montgomery, supra*; *Arthur* v. *Aird*, 1907 S.C. 1170.

11 *Copland* v. *Maxwell* (1871) 9 M. (H.L.) 1.

12 *Menzies* v. *Wentworth* (1901) 3 F. 941; *Arthur, supra.*

13 *E. Galloway, supra.*

14 *Grant* v. *Henry* (1894) 21 R. 358.

15 See Trout (Sc.) Acts, 1902 and 1933; Salmon and Freshwater Fisheries (Protection) (Sc.) Act, 1951.

Rights of game

The right of property in land includes as a pertinent the exclusive right to take or kill game[1] on the lands.[2] A proprietor may accordingly exclude from his lands as trespassers persons entering thereon to kill game.[3] Sporting rights dissociated from any right in the lands themselves are not recognized.[4] Various statutes make poaching, i.e. trespass in pursuit of game, criminal.

A proprietor of lands[5] may grant a lease of shootings, which is a true lease[6] and not merely a personal licence,[7] or the exclusive right of shooting game on the lands, saving the agricultural tenant's rights, and this impliedly imposes on the shooting tenant liability to relieve the proprietor of the agricultural tenant's claims for damage arising from an unduly large stock of game.[8]

An agricultural tenant has no right implied by his lease to kill game,[9] but may kill rabbits to protect his crops[10] and scare game so long as not scaring it from the lands completely.[11] By the Ground Game Act, 1880,[12] every occupier of land has a right, inseparate from his occupancy, to kill and take rabbits and hares on the land. Agricultural tenants have also rights at common law and under statute to compensation for damage by game.[13]

Conservation and control of deer

The Deer (Sc.) Acts, 1959 and 1967, established a Red Deer Commission to advise the Secretary of State for Scotland and landowners as to red deer. It may authorize the killing of marauding deer, and make control schemes for the reduction of deer

[1] There is no complete legal definition of game; many statutes contain their own definitions.

[2] *Welwood* v. *Husband* (1874) 1 R. 507.

[3] *E. Breadalbane* v. *Livingstone* (1791) 3 Pat. 221; *Pollock, Gilmour & Co.* v. *Harvey* (1828) 6 S. 913; *Birkbeck* v. *Ross* (1865) 4 M. 272.

[4] *Johnstone* v. *Gilchrist*, 1934 S.L.T. 271.

[5] cf. *M. Huntly* v. *Nicol* (1896) 23 R. 610.

[6] *Macpherson* v. *M.* (1839) 1 D. 794; *Sinclair* v. *L. Duffus* (1842) 5 D. 174; *Menzies* v. *M.* (1861) 23 D. (H.L.) 16; *Stewart* v. *Bulloch* (1880) 8 R. 381.

[7] *E. Aboyne* v. *Innes*, 22 June 1813, F.C.; *Pollock, Gilmour & Co.* v. *Harvey* (1828) 6 S. 913; *Birkbeck* v. *Ross* (1865) 4 M. 272.

[8] *Byrne* v. *Johnson* (1875) 3 R. 255; *Eliott's Trs.* v. *E.* (1894) 21 R. 858; see also *Inglis* v. *Moir's Tutors* (1871) 10 M. 204; *Kidd* v. *Byrne* (1875) 3 R. 255.

[9] *E. Hopetoun* v. *Wight*, 17 Jan. 1810, F.C.; *Wemyss* v. *Gulland* (1847) 10 D. 204; *Copland* v. *Maxwell* (1868) 9 M. (H.L.) 1; *Welwood, supra.*

[10] *Moncrieff* v. *Arnott* (1828) 6 S. 530; *Inglis* v. *Moir's Tutors* (1871) 10 M. 204; *Brown* v. *Thomson* (1882) 9 R. 1183; *Fraser* v. *Lawson* (1882) 10 R. 396.

[11] *Wemyss, supra.*

[12] Amended by Agriculture (Sc.) Act, 1948, Ss. 48, 50, and Crofters (Sc.) Act, 1955, S. 27.

[13] Ch. 88, *infra.*

where they are damaging agriculture and forestry (Ss. 1–11). The Commission may provide services and equipment for the killing of red deer, and their disposal (Ss. 12–18). The rights of occupiers of land to recover compensation for damages caused by red deer continue unaffected (S. 19). Close seasons are fixed for red deer (S. 21). The poaching of all species of deer is penalized (Ss. 22–5).

LIMITATIONS ON USES OF LAND

Common law and statute both impose material qualifications on a landowner's power to use his lands as he wills. The common law principles apply the maxim *sic utere tuo ut alienum non laedas.*

Use in aemulationem vicini

No proprietor of lands may use them, or act on them, *in aemulationem vicini*, doing what may be legal but with the sole or predominant purpose of inconveniencing or harming his neighbour.[1] The presumption is against such being his purpose,[2] and operations on land cannot be restrained if undertaken for a proprietor's own legitimate purposes or benefit or if only incidentally injuring a neighbour.[3]

Nuisance

At common law nuisance is any use of land which causes substantial inconvenience or injury to an adjacent proprietor in the ordinary use and enjoyment of his property. The conduct complained of need not be illegal, nor any unusual or unnatural use of property. The commoner kinds of nuisance are the emission of noise or fumes, the pollution of air or water. The complainer need not prove intent to harm, nor lack of due care to prevent harm.[4]

Statutory nuisances

Legislation, particularly the Burgh Police (Sc.) Acts and the Public Health (Sc.) Acts, prescribe that large numbers of acts of different kinds, all prejudicial to public health or comfortable

[1] Bankt. IV, 45, 112; Ersk. II, 1, 2; Bell, *Prin.* §964; *Somerville* v. *S.* (1613) Mor. 12769; *Dunlop* v. *Robertson* (1803) Hume 515; *Campbell* v. *Muir*, 1908 S.C. 387; *More* v. *Boyle*, 1967 S.L.T. (Sh. Ct.) 38. The observations of Lord Watson in *Mayor of Bradford* v. *Pickles* [1895] A.C. 587 are obiter and unsound. See also Ch. 70, *supra.*

[2] Bankt., *supra.*

[3] *Somerville*, *supra*; *Dunlop*, *supra.*

[4] Ch. 70, *supra.*

enjoyment of life, shall be statutory nuisances, the commission of which are statutory offences.

Restrictions imposed by Planning Acts

The Town and Country Planning (Sc.) Act, 1947, requires local planning authorities to prepare and revise development plans of their districts, indicating the manner in which they propose land therein should be used. Landowners require permission from the planning authority for any development of land, i.e., building, engineering, mining or other operations in, on, over or under land, or the making of any material change in the use of any buildings or other land,[1] subject to certain exceptions (S. 10). Planning permission may be revoked or modified (S. 19). Under the similar Act of 1954 compensation may be claimed for the refusal of planning permission or its grant subject only to conditions (S. 16), or for revocation or modification of planning permission (S. 40). Under the similar Act of 1959 applications for planning permission must be accompanied by a certificate of notice to other owners of land affected, and stating that the land is not an agricultural holding or that notice has been given to every tenant of an agricultural holding affected by the application (S. 36).

Caravan sites

The Caravan Sites and Control of Development Act, 1960, prohibits the use of land as a caravan site without a local authority licence, subject to certain exemptions (Ss. 1–4). Conditions may be attached to site licences, against which appeal lies to the Sheriff,[2] and altered at any time (Ss. 5–9). A site licence may, with the consent of the local authority, be transferred to a new occupier of the land, and a person acquiring an estate in land by operation of law and thereby becoming occupier is entitled to have the licence endorsed to him (S. 10). Sites in use at the commencement of the Act are exempted from the requirements of a site licence but subject to special provisions (Ss. 13–20). Local authorities may provide caravan sites and for that purpose may acquire land compulsorily (S. 24).

Control of buildings

In burghs the Dean of Guild Court exercises control over buildings in the interests of stability and safety and health by

[1] Discontinuance of an existing use is not a material change of use: *Paul* v. *Ayrshire C.C.*, 1964 S.C. 116.

[2] cf. *Clyde Caravans (Langbank) Ltd.* v. *Renfrew C.C.*, 1962 S.L.T. (Sh. Ct.) 20.

requiring that plans be deposited and authority obtained for building and alteration. In landward areas of counties a committee of the County Council exercises similar control.[1] A proprietor of adjoining property has a title to object to the grant by the Court of a warrant for building or alteration which infringes his property rights.[2]

Pipe-lines

The Pipe Lines Act, 1962, provides that cross-country pipe-lines (as defined in S. 65) may not be constructed without the authority of the Minister of Power, nor a local pipe-line (not over 10 miles) without notice to the Minister (Ss. 1–8). The Minister may prevent an unnecessary multiplicity of pipe-lines (Ss. 9–10). A pipe-line promoter may apply for compulsory purchase powers (Ss. 11–14). Requirements may be imposed as to the construction of pipe-lines (Ss. 20–3) and their safety (Ss. 24–6) and the Minister may require demolition of structures or deposits which imperil pipe-lines (Ss. 27–32).

Public Rights of Way

A public right of way is a right exercisable by any member of the public to pass from one public place to another public place[3] by a definite track.[4] It may be created by grant, but is normally acquired by prescriptive use (forty years) in a way implying assertion of a public right, openly and without interruption.[5] It may be vindicated by any member of the public or by a society formed to vindicate such rights.[6]

It will be lost by disuse for the prescriptive period (forty years), or by unchallenged contrary actings by the proprietor though for a lesser period,[7] or may be extinguished by statute.[8]

Access to the countryside

The Countryside (Scotland) Act, 1967, established the Countryside Commission for Scotland with functions for the

1 Building (Sc.) Act, 1959; and see Building Standards (Sc.) Regs. 1963 (S.I. 1897, 1963).

2 But see *Park* v. *Blair*, 1961 S.L.T. 397.

3 *Campbell* v. *Lang* (1853) 1 Macq. 451; *Young* v. *Cuthbertson* (1854) 1 Macq. 455; *M. Bute* v. *McKirdy & McMillan*, 1937 S.C. 93.

4 *Mackintosh* v. *Moir* (1871) 9 M. 574.

5 *Burt* v. *Barclay* (1861) 24 D. 218; *Mann* v. *Brodie* (1885) 12 R. (H.L.) 52; *Macpherson* v. *Scottish Rights of Way Socy.* (1888) 15 R. (H.L.) 68; *McInroy* v. *D. Atholl* (1891) 18 R. (H.L.) 46.

6 *Potter* v. *Hamilton* (1870) 8 M. 1064.

7 Rankine, *Landownership*, 337.

8 e.g. New Towns (Sc.) Act, 1968, S. 23.

provision, development and improvement of facilities for the enjoyment of the Scottish countryside, and the conservation and enhancement of its natural beauty (Ss. 1–4). The Commission may (S. 5) make proposals for development projects or schemes, and (S. 6) by agreement acquire land, or acquire it compulsorily, hold and manage it, dispose of it, provide equipment and services, and exercise powers to carry out work or provide services or facilities conferred by the Act on local authorities or local planning authorities, on their own or, with consent, on other persons' land, agreements as to which may be recorded in the Register of Sasines.

Access agreements may be made (Ss. 10, 12–13) in respect of open country by the local planning authority with any person having an interest in land and (S. 14) a local planning authority may make an access order in respect of any land. A person interested in land comprised in an access agreement or order may not carry out any work substantially reducing the area to which the public may have access. Access agreements and orders have to be recorded in the Register of Sasines and are enforceable against persons having interest in the land and their successors (S. 16). A person entering on land comprised in the agreement or order for open-air recreation without causing damage is not a trespasser, nor under any liability by reason only of so entering or being on the land (S. 11).

Such agreements or orders may (S. 17–18) make provision for securing safe and sufficient access for the public to the land, for the improvement or repair of means of access, new means of access, safety measures, and the prevention of impediments or dangers. Compensation is payable for access orders (Ss. 20–3). Local authorities may acquire land for open-air recreation (S. 24), as may the Secretary of State (S. 25).

Local planning authorities may by agreement or by compulsory order create public paths over land (Ss. 30–8), and the Commission may make proposals for long-distance routes which, if approved by the Secretary of State, shall be implemented by the local planning and other authorities concerned (Ss. 39–42).

Local planning authorities may provide country parks, camping sites, caravan sites, accommodation, meals and refreshments, and parking places (Ss. 48–51) and improve waterways for recreation (Ss. 61–2), as may local water authorities (S. 63) and electricity boards (S. 64). The Forestry Commission may also (S. 58) provide tourist, recreational or sporting facilities. In exercising their functions relating to land under any enactment every Minister, department, and public body must have regard to the desirability of conserving the natural beauty and amenity of the countryside (S. 66).

Nature conservation

Under the National Parks and Access to the Countryside Act, 1949, the Nature Conservancy may (Ss. 15–20) enter into agreements with the owners, tenants and occupiers of land to secure that it be managed as a nature reserve, or may acquire land compulsorily for nature reserves, and may make by-laws for the protection of the reserve. Local authorities may (S. 21) provide nature reserves on any land in their areas. The Nature Conservancy must (S. 23) inform local planning authorities of areas of special scientific interest.

Ancient Monuments and historic buildings

The Ancient Monuments Acts 1913 to 1953 enable the Ministry of Works to purchase or accept, or accept guardianship of, ancient monuments, and to preserve and protect them and regulate amenities in proximity to them. Interference with a scheduled ancient monument is an offence. Grants may be made for the preservation of historic buildings, their contents and adjoining land.[1]

A local planning authority may make tree preservation orders for the preservation of trees and woodlands, and building preservation orders restricting the demolition, alteration or extension of building of special architectural or historic interest,[2] and the Secretary of State has to compile lists of buildings of such interest.[3]

The Local Authorities (Historic Buildings) Act, 1962, extended to Scotland by the Civic Amenities Act, 1967, enables local authorities to make contributions towards the repair and maintenance of buildings of historic or architectural interest.

Amenities

The Civic Amenities Act, 1967, requires local planning authorities to designate areas of special architectural or historic interest the character or appearance of which it is desirable to

[1] Functions transferred to Secretary of State for Scotland: Transfer of Functions (Scottish Royal Parks and Ancient Monuments) Order, 1969 (S.I. 383, 1969).

[2] Town and Country Planning (Sc.) Act, 1947, S. 26–27; see also Ss. 38, 96; *Tronsite Ltd.* v. *Edinburgh Corpn.*, 1965 S.C. 129.

[3] Ibid., S. 28.

preserve or enhance as conservation areas (S. 1), makes further provision for penalizing unauthorized work on buildings listed as of special architectural or historic interest or acts of wilful damage to a listed building (Ss. 2–3). Local planning authorities may execute works necessary for the preservation of an unoccupied listed building, or compulsorily purchase any such building which is not being properly preserved (Ss. 6–7) or make building preservation orders (Ss. 10–11).

Local planning authorities are empowered to secure the preservation or planting of trees and their replacement (Ss. 12–17). They must provide refuse dumps open to the public (S. 18). Dumping old motor vehicles is an offence (S. 19) and the local authority has the duty of removing and disposing of abandoned vehicles, recovering the expense of so doing (Ss. 20–2) and of disposing of other refuse (S. 23).

Highlands and Islands Development Board

The Highlands and Islands Development (Sc.) Act, 1965, established the Development Board to promote social and economic development in the crofting counties.[1] The Board has power (S. 4) to acquire land by agreement or compulsorily, to hold and manage land and dispose of it (S. 5), to erect buildings and carry out works or other operations on land and provide equipment and services (S. 6), to carry on businesses, and (S. 8) make grants and loans. They also (S. 10) have powers of entry on lands and (S. 11) powers to demand information about land or businesses.

[1] Further powers were conferred by a similar Act of 1968.

CHAPTER 80

JOINT AND COMMON PROPERTY: COMMON INTEREST

EITHER the superiority or the fee of heritage may be vested at any time in more than one person, holding the lands undivided, either as joint owners or owners in common.[1]

Joint Property

In the case of joint ownership, of which the main instances are the ownership by trustees or partners, the land is possessed undivided, and the owners together have one title to one estate in every part of the lands.[2] All joint owners have equal interests therein, and on the death of any one his interest passes by accretion to the survivors until there remains but one who then has the sole title.[3] No joint owner can alienate or dispose by will of his interest in the land, nor burden it, and it does not pass on his intestacy as part of his estate. Decisions affecting the land must be reached by a majority and actions must be brought by all owners jointly.[4] No one joint owner has any claim to have the subjects divided to give him a title to any individual share thereof.[5]

Common Property

In the case of ownership in common,[6] of which an instance is the right of heirs portioners on intestacy,[7] the land is possessed undivided, but each owner has his own separate title to a fraction of the undivided whole. The interests of owners in common are not necessarily equal. On the death of any one his right does not pass to the others by accretion but passes to his own heirs on intestacy.[8] He may alienate his share, or dispose of it by will, or

1 In the older books and cases the terminology is confused and joint property and common property are not clearly distinguished. See *Banff Mags.* v. *Ruthin Castle*, 1944 S.C. 36, 68.

2 *Cargill* v. *Muir* (1837) 15 S. 408; *McNeight* v. *Lockhart* (1843) 6 D. 128; *Schaw* v. *Black* (1889) 16 R. 336, 340.

3 *Banff Mags.*, *supra*, 68–9.

4 *Grozier* v. *Downie* (1871) 8 M. 826; cf. *Schaw* v. *Black* (1889) 16 R. 336.

5 *Banff Mags.*, *supra.*

6 Stair I, 7, 15; I, 16, 4; Bankt. I, 8, 38; Ersk. III, 3, 56; Bell, *Prin.* §1072.

7 *Cargill* v. *Muir* (1837) 15 S. 408; *McNeight* v. *Lockhart* (1843) 6 D. 128.

8 *Schaw* v. *Black* (1889) 16 R. 336; *Banff Mags.* v. *Ruthin Castle*, 1944 S.C. 36, 68.

burden it.[1] So long as the land is possessed in common decisions affecting it must have the agreement of all and actions must be brought by all proprietors in common,[2] while any one may prevent alteration or extraordinary use of the property, but not necessary repairs.[3]

So long as the community of property subsists no one proprietor in common has title to any identifiable parts of the lands, but any one may at any time call for a division of the lands by agreement, or if the others will not agree, bring an action for their division[4] or, if indivisible, or where division would be inequitable to some of the parties,[5] for their sale and division of the realized value: *nemo in communione invitus detineri potest.*[6]

It is probably incompetent for a testator to seek to exclude the right of legatees in common to pursue for division, or division and sale,[7] but one *pro indiviso* proprietor may by contract bar himself from resorting to an action of division or sale.[8] Division is not precluded by the existence of a bond over the subjects,[9] but may be by the existence of a necessarily continuing common interest, such as that of flat-dwellers in the common entrance and stair.

Division and sale where one proprietor disappeared

Where one of two or more *pro indiviso* proprietors has not been heard of for seven years the other or others may petition the court to sell the property by public roup or private bargain. If the petition is granted and sale effected, the title granted by the petitioners is as good and valid to the purchaser as if the absent person had been a party to the sale and conveyance. The share of the price attributable to the absent person is consigned in bank.[10]

[1] *Cargill* v. *Muir* (1837) 15 S. 408; *Johnston* v. *Crawford* (1885) 17 D. 1023.

[2] *Millar* v. *Cathcart* (1861) 23 D. 743; *Lade* v. *Largs Bakery Co.* (1863) 2 M. 17; *Aberdeen Station Cttee.* v. *N.B. Ry.* (1890) 17 R. 975, 984. But any one can take action to check trespass: *Warrand* v. *Watson* (1905) 8 F. 253.

[3] *Deans* v. *Woolfson*, 1922 S.C. 221.

[4] *Morrison* v. *Kirk*, 1912 S.C. 44.

[5] *Thom* v. *Macbeth* (1875) 3 R. 161; *Morrison, supra*, 48.

[6] Bell, *Prin.* §1079; *Milligan* v. *Barnhill* (1782) Mor. 2486; *Bryden* v. *Gibson* (1837) 15 S. 486; *Anderson* v. *A.* (1857) 19 D. 700; *Brock* v. *Hamilton* (1852) 19 D. 701; *Thom* v. *Macbeth* (1875) 3 R. 161; *Grant* v. *Heriot's Trust* (1906) 8 F. 647; *Morrison* v. *Kirk*, 1912 S.C. 44; *Banff Mags., supra.*

[7] *Grant, supra*, 658.

[8] *Morrison, supra*, 47.

[9] *Morrison, supra.*

[10] Presumption of Life Limitation (Sc.) Act, 1891, S. 4.

Common property in common gables and walls

A further instance of common property exists where a common gable, or dividing wall between two plots of land, has been built.[1] Either proprietor may object to operations by the other on the common gable or wall liable to be injurious to it as his gable or wall.[2]

Common interest

A right different from common property exists among the owners of subjects possessed in separate portions, but united by their common interest therein. This right is incorporated with the several rights of individual property. Sale or division cannot resolve any difficulties arising in management, but the exercise of the common interest must, in case of dissension, be regulated by law or equity.[3]

Instances of this arise where a superior feus lands retaining the property of a common square or garden, in which each feuar has no property but a common interest,[4] or where the square or garden is held in common by the feuars, each having a right of property in common and also a common interest in the square, or feuars have a common interest in a passage along the side of their respective feus,[5] or several frontagers in a street have a common interest in the space above the street as an inlet for light and air.[6]

Law of the tenement

The chief instances of common interest arise in flatted buildings, where different storeys and houses therein belong to different proprietors. This combines the individual property of each in his own house with a common interest in the rest of the whole, so far as necessary for his support, stability and cover. Apart from express provision in the titles, custom regulates the relative rights of proprietors.[7] The ownership of the solum, any garden or basement area in front, and the garden or court at the rear belong to the owners of the ground floor houses, subject to a

1 *Walker* v. *Sherar* (1870) 8 M. 494.

2 Bell, *Prin.* §1075, 1078; *Warrens* v. *Marwick* (1835) 13 S. 944; *Dow and Gordon* v. *Harvey* (1869) 8 M. 118; *Lamont* v. *Cumming* (1875) 2 R. 785.

3 Bell, *Prin.* §1086; cf. *Grant* v. *Heriot's Trust* (1906) 8 F. 647, 659.

4 *Watson's Hospital* v. *Cormack* (1883) 11 R. 320; *Grant, supra.*

5 *Mackenzie* v. *Carrick* (1869) 7 M. 419; *Grant, supra.*

6 *Donald* v. *Esslemont & Macintosh*, 1923 S.C. 122.

7 Stair II, 7, 6; Bankt. II, 7, 9; Ersk. II, 9, 11; Bell, *Prin.* §1086; *Smith* v. *Giuliani*, 1925 S.C. (H.L.) 45.

common interest of the other owners to be supported and to prevent damage to their houses, as by depriving them of light.[1] The external walls of each house belong to the owner of that house, but the other owners have common interest therein and may prevent operations liable to endanger the security of their houses.[2] Gable walls are the common property of the owners on either side, so far as bounding their respective houses, but all the other owners in the blocks have common interest therein to prevent damage to the stability of the building.[3] The owner of each storey has an interest that storeys below be maintained to support him, and that storeys above be maintained to afford him cover. The floor and roof of each flat are divided along the mid-line of the joists, but neither superior nor inferior proprietor may so act as to weaken the joists or expose them to unusual danger of fire.[4] Hence a shop on the ground floor may not exhibit a sign-board extending above such mid-line, unless such a sign has been assented to or allowed to remain for the prescriptive period.[4] A common entrance, passages, staircase and liftshaft and the walls thereof are the common property of all the premises to which they give access;[5] the side walls of such entrances are the common property of the proprietors and of the owner of the adjacent house.[6]

The roof belongs to the several owners of the topmost storey, but all proprietors have a common interest that it is maintained in repair for their common benefit and not damaged.[7] The attic space may not be converted into an attic storey without consent,[8] but the topmost proprietors may make rooms in the space.[9] Some parts of a tenement such as the common entrance and stair-case are normally common property; one owner cannot carry a

[1] *Johnson* v. *White* (1877) 4 R. 721; *Boswell* v. *Edinburgh Mags.* (1881) 8 R. 986; *McArly* v. *French's Trs.* (1883) 10 R. 574; *Sutherland* v. *Barbour* (1887) 15 R. 62.

[2] *Ferguson* v. *Marjoribanks*, 12 Nov. 1816, F.C.; *Pirie* v. *McRitchie*, 5 June 1819, F.C.; *McKean* v. *Davidson* (1823) 2 S. 480; *Murray* v. *Gullan* (1825) 3 S. 639; *McNair* v. *McLauchlan* (1826) 4 S. 546; *Brown* v. *Boyd* (1841) 3 D. 1205; *Johnston* v. *White* (1877) 4 R. 721.

[3] *Gellatly* v. *Arrol* (1863) 1 M. 592; see *Morris* v. *Bicket* (1864) 2 M. 1081, 1089 and *Todd* v. *Wilson* (1894) 22 R. 172; see also *Watt* v. *Jamieson*, 1964 S.C. 56.

[4] *Alexander* v. *Butchart* (1875) 3 R. 156; *McArly* v. *French's Trs.* (1883) 10 R. 574.

[5] *Taylor* v. *Dunlop* (1872) 11 M. 25.

[6] *Anderson* v. *Dalrymple* (1799) Mor. 12831; *Reid* v. *Nicol* (1799) Mor. Property, Appx. 1; *Ritchie* v. *Purdie* (1833) 11 S. 771; *Graham* v. *Greig* (1838) 1 D. 171; *Gellatly* v. *Arrol* (1863) 1 M. 592; *Taylor* v. *Dunlop* (1872) 11 M. 25.

[7] *Taylor* v. *Dunlop* (1872) 11 M. 25; *Sanderson's Trs.* v. *Yule* (1897) 25 R. 211; *Duncan* v. *Ch. of Scotland Trs.*, 1941 S.C. 145; *Duncan Smith & MacLaren* v. *Heatly*, 1952 J.C. 61.

[8] *Sharp* v. *Robertson* (1800) Mor. Property, Appx. 3; *Watt* v. *Burgess' Tr.* (1891) 18 R. 766.

[9] *Taylor* v. *Dunlop* (1872) 11 M. 25.

flue to the roof through a staircase owned in common.[1] The solum and roof may also be expressly made common property.[2]

These rights of common interest are of a proprietary and not of a servitude character,[3] but do not entitle any proprietor to invade another's premises or conduct operations thereon.[4] The duty which one proprietor owes to another whose common interest may be infringed is of taking reasonable precautions only, and he is not liable unless he should have foreseen the danger of damage and taken precautions, or should in the circumstances have examined periodically for signs of damage.[5]

Where alterations are contemplated, such as the conversion of the ground floor into shops, the other proprietors in the building can prevent the change if the part to be altered is common property,[6] but not if they have merely a common interest in it unless that interest is being prejudiced by the change.[7]

Similarly in 'terrace' or 'semi-detached' houses both proprietors have common interest in the stability of their common gables.

Common[8] Gables

By custom the builder of a tenement or house, into the gable of which he expects that the owner of the adjacent land will wish to dovetail his building, may erect the gable half on either side of the boundary-line and recover half of the cost of erecting it when the adjacent owner comes to make use of the gable.[9] Till then the builder has the property in the whole gable, or possibly property in one half with the right to use the whole till the adjacent owner uses the other half.[10] When the adjacent owner uses it each has a right of common property in the gable. The second builder may insert the ends of joists therein, and bond in front and rear walls, make fireplaces and vents in the gable and heighten

[1] *Taylor* v. *Dunlop* (1872) 11 M. 25.

[2] *Turner* v. *Hamilton* (1890) 17 R. 494; contrast *Johnston* v. *White* (1877) 4 R. 721.

[3] *Smith* v. *Giuliani*, 1925 S.C. (H.L.) 45, 59.

[4] *Smith*, *supra*, 57; *Duncan Smith & MacLaren*, *supra*, 64.

[5] *Thomson* v. *St. Cuthbert's Coop. Assoc. Ltd.*, 1958 S.C. 380.

[6] *Boswell* v. *Edinburgh Mags.* (1881) 8 R. 986; *Sutherland* v. *Barbour* (1887) 15 R. 62; *Turner* v. *Hamilton* (1890) 17 R. 494; *Taylor's Trs.* v. *McGavigan* (1896) 23 R. 945; see also *Arrol* v. *Inches* (1887) 14 R. 394.

[7] *Johnston* v. *White* (1877) 4 R. 721; *Barclay* v. *McEwan* (1880) 7 R. 792; *Calder* v. *Edinburgh Merchant Co.* (1886) 13 R. 623; *Birrell* v. *Lumley* (1905) 12 S.L.T. 719.

[8] Frequently miscalled 'mutual' gables.

[9] *Glasgow R.I.* v. *Wylie* (1877) 4 R. 894; *Sinclair* v. *Brown* (1882) 10 R. 45; *Robertson* v. *Scott* (1886) 13 R. 1127; *Berkeley* v. *Baird* (1895) 22 R. 372; *Baird* v. *Alexander* (1898) 25 R. (H.L.) 35.

[10] *Robertson*, *supra*, 1130–2; cf. *Berkeley*, *supra*, 376.

it reasonably, so long as he does not injure the other's property thereby.[1] It is questionable whether the adjacent owner may make any use of the gable without settling with the party in right of the gable.[2]

The rule of common gables may also be founded on implied contract inferred from a feuing plan or other circumstances, and there is no such rule where there is no basis for inferring the contract.[3] Where a common gable has been unjustifiably erected half on the complainer's lands, the court may allow it to stand subject to compensation to the complainer for the encroachment.[4]

Common walls and fences: march-fences

A wall or fence merely forming a division between properties, as between back greens, is intended only to enclose. If erected exclusively on one owner's land, it is his property; if erected along the boundary it is doubtless common property.

For one party to alter such a common wall without the other's consent might well be a breach of the implied contract under which the wall was built.[5] A garden or field division wall cannot be converted into a mutual gable without consent.[6]

March-fences

Adjoining proprietors may by agreement erect a fence or dyke at common expense, and such may by agreement or practice be treated as a march-fence, in which event it must be maintained at common expense.[7]

By the March Dykes Act, 1661 (c. 284)[8] one proprietor may compel the owner of adjoining lands to share equally the expense of erecting, repairing, or, where necessary, rebuilding[9] march dykes or fences between their lands. Application is made to the Sheriff Court or the Court of Session,[10] failing which, or failing consent, the adjoining proprietor cannot be compelled to share the cost of the fence.[11] The court may refuse an application if the

[1] *Lamont* v. *Cumming* (1875) 2 R. 784; *Robertson, supra*; *Dow & Gordon* v. *Harvey* (1869) 8 M. 118; *Bryce* v. *Norman* (1895) 2 S.L.T. 471; cf. *Wilson* v. *Pottinger*, 1908 S.C. 580.

[2] *Glasgow R.I., supra*, 897.

[3] *Jack* v. *Begg* (1875) 3 R. 35.

[4] *Sanderson* v. *Geddes* (1874) 1 R. 1198; *Grahame* v. *Kirkcaldy Mags.* (1882) 9 R. (H.L.) 91; *Wilson, supra.*

[5] *Lamont* v. *Cumming* (1875) 2 R. 784, 790.

[6] *Jack* v. *Begg* (1875) 3 R. 35, 42.

[7] *Strang* v. *Steuart* (1864) 2 M. 1015.

[8] Stair II, 3, 75; Bankt. I, 10, 153; Ersk. II, 6, 4.

[9] *Paterson* v. *McDonald* (1880) 7 R. 958.

[10] *Pollock* v. *Ewing* (1869) 7 M. 815.

[11] *Ord* v. *Wright* (1738) Mor. 10479.

pursuer's request is oppressive or unfair.[1] The Act applies only to lands exceeding five or six acres in extent.[2] The fence must be beneficial, though not necessarily equally so, to both proprietors.[3]

The March Dykes Act 1669 (c. 38) empowers the sheriff on the application of a landowner where the marches are crooked and unequal to visit the marches,[4] adjudge parts of one estate to the other and if the exchange is not equal, award compensation to the landowner deprived. Under this Act also the Court will refuse an application which would be oppressive or unfair. The sheriff may fix a longer and less direct march if he considers this more convenient for both parties.[5]

Commonty

A commonty is a species of common property but differing from *pro indiviso* rights in common property, being a right to a share in common grounds for the purpose of pasturage, accessory to the commoner's individual lands, and having no existence save as appendages of individually held lands.[6] Commonty only exists where the respective rights of the commoners have not been defined by feudal grant and are ascertained only by possession. Each commoner may prevent attempts by any other to put the common to other than its ordinary use for pasturing animals.

Statute[7] has empowered the Court of Session[8] to value and divide commonties except property belonging to the King, or held in burgage by burghs,[9] according to the value of the rights and interests of the various parties concerned, estimated according to the valuation of their respective lands or properties,[10] and the divisions to be made of the part of the commonty next adjacent to each person's property. Possession in different proportions does not effect the rule of division in proportion to valuation.[11] The Act does not apply where the right is one of servitude,[12] nor a

[1] *E. Peterborough* v. *Garioch* (1784) Mor. 10497; *Secker* v. *Cameron*, 1914 S.C. 354.

[2] *Penman* v. *Douglas* (1739) Mor. 10481; *Secker, supra*.

[3] *Blackburn* v. *Head* (1904) 11 S.L.T. 521.

[4] *L.A.* v. *Sinclair* (1872) 11 M. 137.

[5] *E. Kintore* v. *E. Kintore's Trs.* (1886) 13 R. 997.

[6] Stair I, 7, 15; More's *Notes*, lii; Bankt. II, 7, 32; Ersk. III, 3, 56; Bell, *Prin.* §1072, 1087; Rankine, *L.O.* 600; *L. Blantyre* v. *Jaffray* (1856) 19 D. 167.

[7] Division of Commonties Act, 1695 (c. 69).

[8] Now competent in the Sheriff Court: Sheriff Courts (Sc.) Act, 1907, replacing 1877 Act, S. 8(3).

[9] *Hunter* v. *Mailler* (1854) 16 D. 641.

[10] *Macandrew* v. *Crerar*, 1929 S.C. 699, see also *Bruce* v. *Bain* (1883) 11 R. 192.

[11] *D. Douglas* v. *Baillie* (1740) Mor. 2474.

[12] *Stewart* v. *Tillicoultry* (1739) Mor. 2469; *Gordon* v. *Grant* (1850) 13 D. 1.

precise and definite share in common grazing,[1] but does where more than one person has title to the property over which the commoners exercised their common interest.[2] Once divided, lots of commonty are held by titles along with other lands.[3]

Common grazing rights

A right of common grazing is not a right of property but a right, of the nature of a servitude, enjoyed by several proprietors or tenants in common, to the pro indiviso use of certain ground for grazing animals.[4] The right may be constituted by grant[5] or by prescription. Where several proprietors have a right of common grazing, none has a right for an indefinite number of animals but their claims are proportioned to the rents of the several lands and to the number of cattle that each can winter on his own lands. The proportions may be fixed by an action of souming and rouming.

Runrig lands

Where lands are divided runrig different proprietors have separate property in adjacent strips or ridges of land.[6] By statute[7] such lands may be redivided into consolidated portions according to the rights of the several proprietors,[8] but lands belonging to burghs and incorporations, and patches over four acres, are excluded.[9]

1 *Macandrew* v. *Crerar*, 1929 S.C. 699.
2 *Stewart* v. *Mackenzie* (1748) Mor. 2476; *Maitland* v. *Lambert* (1769) Mor. 2483.
3 *Walker* v. *Miln* (1871) 9 M. 823; *Edmonstone* v. *Jeffray* (1886) 13 R. 1038.
4 Ersk. II, 9, 14–16.
5 e.g. *Macandrew* v. *Crerar*, 1929 S.C. 699.
6 See Ersk. III, 3, 59; Bell, *Prin.* §1098.
7 Runrig Lands Act, 1695 (c. 36).
8 *Davidson* v. *Kerr* (1748) Elch. Runridge, No. 1; *Davidson* v. *Heddell* (1829) 8 S. 219; *Lady Gray* v. *Richardson* (1876) 3 R. 1031; affd. 4 R. (H.L.) 76.
9 Bell, *supra*; *Burns* v. *Boyle* (1829) 7 S. 415.

CHAPTER 81

ENTAILED ESTATE OR TAILZIED FEE

An entail is a disposition of the superiority or the fee of lands containing an express destination thereof to a prescribed series of heirs of the grantee other than the heirs at law,[1] clauses prohibiting alienation, contracting of debt affecting the estate, and altering of the order of succession,[2] and clauses irritant, annulling any prohibited act if done, and resolutive, annulling the right to the estate of an heir contravening the provisions of the entail.[3] Entailing lands was made competent by the Entail Act, 1685, (c. 22), and was competent only of subjects which could be feudalized.[4] The object was to enable landowners to ensure that their lands passed undivided and unburdened down through the family.

Essentials

Entails might be embodied in any deed which could convey, or include, a conveyance of lands, but commonly in a *mortis causa* settlement. The essentials were the destination, the three cardinal prohibitions, the irritant and resolutive clauses, and registration in the Register of Tailzies.

The destination had to be to a special class of heirs, different from[5] that of the legal order of succession,[6] who must be designed

1 *Moubray's Trs.* v. *M.* (1895) 22 R. 801, 808.

2 Known as the cardinal prohibitions.

3 See generally Stair II, 3, 43; Bankt. II, 3, 133; Ersk. III, 8, 22; Bell, *Comm.* I, 43; *Prin.* §1716–74; Ross, *Lect.* II, 503; Menzies, 719; Sandford, *Entails*, *passim.*

4 *Dalyell* v. *D.*, 17 Jan. 1810, F.C.; *Stirling* v. *Dunn* (1827) 3 W. & S. 462; *Henderson* v. *Drysdale* (1834) 7 W. & S. 441; *Stewart* v. *Nicolson* (1859) 22 D. 72; *Howden* v. *Rocheid* (1869) 7 M. (H.L.) 110; *Brown* v. *Soutar* (1870) 8 M. 702. Heritable rights which cannot be feudalized, such as of leases by assignation: *E. Dalhousie* v. *Ramsey-Maule* (1782) Mor. 10963; *Maule* v. *Maule*, 4 Mar. 1829, F.C.; see also *Chisholm* v. *Chisholm-Batten* (1864) 3 M. 202, 226; or rights of reversion, can be entailed but bind *inter haeredes* only. Moveables cannot be entailed: *Baillie* v. *Grant* (1859) 21 D. 838; *Kinnear* v. *K.* (1877) 4 R. 705; *Sandys* v. *Bain's Trs.* (1897) 25 R. 261; but see *Bute* v. *B's Trs.* (1880) 8 R. 191; *Adam's Trs.* v. *Wilson* (1899) 1 F. 1042.

5 *Leny* v. *L.* (1860) 22 D. 1272; *Moubray's Trs.*, *supra.*

6 For this, see Ch. 111, *infra.* If under the final branch of a destination entailed property descended to the heirs whomsoever of the maker or the last substitute heir, the estate is held in fee by the last substitute: *E. March* v. *Kennedy* (1760) 2 Pat. 49.

so as to be recognizable as a line of heirs,[1] and transmission had to be without division among heirs-portioners.[2]

Cardinal prohibitions and irritant and resolutive clauses

The 1685 Act required these clauses to be expressed. If the entail was defective in one or more of the cardinal prohibitions, the entail was binding in other respects. The Rutherfurd Act, 1848, S. 43 made an entail invalid in one prohibition, or as to irritant or resolutive clause, invalid as regards all,[3] but a relaxation of the cardinal prohibitions *in gremio* of the entail did not make otherwise valid prohibitions ineffectual.[4] After Acts of 1848, 1858, and 1860[5] express inclusion of any of these clauses was unnecessary, provided the entail contained an express clause authorizing registration in the Register of Entails. On a contravention by the heir in possession the next heir was entitled to seek declarator and have himself served heir to the last heir who did not contravene;[6] the contravening heir might purge the irritancy by reducing the contravening deed.[7] The cardinal prohibitions were formerly interpreted very strictly[8] but latterly less so.[9]

Registration

Deeds of entail had to contain a description of the lands adequate for infeftment, not only to convey the lands, but to make it apparent from the Register of Entails what subjects were fettered.[10] The deed of entail required to be recorded in the Register of Entails under the authority of the court. An unrecorded deed of entail was not protected by the 1685 Act and, though binding on the heirs themselves, was ineffective against onerous creditors of the heir in possession;[11] such an heir might sell[12] and was not obliged to reinvest the price.[13] A feudal title

[1] *Leny, supra*; *Gordon* v. *G's Trs.* (1866) 4 M. 501.

[2] Because such inheritance would make the estate liable to subdivision: Bell, *Prin.* §1723; *Farquhar* v. *F.* (1838) 1 D. 121; *MacDonald* v. *Lockhart* (1842) 5 D. 372; *Collow's Trs.* v. *Connell* (1866) 4 M. 465; *Connell* v. *Grierson* (1867) 5 M. 379. See also *Primrose* v. *P.* (1854) 16 D. 498.

[3] *D. Hamilton* v. *L. Hamilton* (1870) 8 M. (H.L.) 48.

[4] *Catton* v. *Mackenzie* (1872) 10 M. (H.L.) 12.

[5] All re-enacted by Titles to Land Consolidation (Sc.) Act, 1868, S. 14.

[6] *Bontine* v. *Graham* (1840) 1 Rob. App. 347.

[7] *Abernethie* v. *Gordon* (1840) 1 Rob. App. 434.

[8] *Lang* v. *L.* (1839) MacL. & Rob. 871; *Lumsden* v. *L.* (1843) 2 Bell 104; *Cathcart* v. *C.* (1863) 1 M. 759; *Fraser* v. *F.* (1879) 7 R. 134.

[9] *Wallace* v. *W's Trs.* (1880) 7 R. 902.

[10] *King* v. *E. Stair* (1846) 5 Bell 82.

[11] *Willison* v. *Callender* (1724) Mor. 15369.

[12] *Graham* v. *G.* (1829) 8 S. 231.

[13] *Montgomerie* v. *E. Eglinton* (1843) 2 Bell 149.

to the lands entailed also required to be duly completed by registration in the Register of Sasines.

Special conditions

The maker of an entail might adject further special conditions, such as provisions for payment of annuities, conditions that heirs of entail should use a particular surname, arms and designation,[1] or clauses of devolution providing that in certain circumstances the lands entailed should descend to another line of heirs.[2]

Reserved powers

Relaxation of the cardinal prohibitions, so long as not contradictory thereof,[3] could competently be included in an entail, in the form of reserved powers to such effect as to sell to pay the entailer's debts,[4] to grant feus within reasonable limits,[5] to sell or to excamb the estate and to re-invest in land to be entailed on the same heirs,[6] to grant provisions to the surviving spouse and younger children,[7] and to nominate heirs.[8]

Contravention

On contravention of an entail by an heir in possession the next heir was entitled by the Act of 1685 to pursue a declarator thereof and have himself served heir to the last non-contravening heir infeft in the fee.[9] A contravening heir is entitled to purge the irritancy by performing the condition or rescinding the *ultra vires* action.[10] Deeds granted after contravention but before irritancy was declared are valid in questions with purchases or *bona fide* onerous creditors.[11]

1 Bell, *Prin.* §1725; Bell, *Convg.* II, 1010; *Moir* v. *Graham* (1794) Mor. 15537; *Munro* v. *M.* (1828) 3 W. & S. 344; *Cumming's Trs.* v. *C.* (1832) 10 S. 804; *Hunter* v. *Weston* (1882) 9 R. 492.

2 Bell, *Prin.* §1726; *M. Hastings* v. *Lady Hastings* (1847) 6 Bell 30; *V. Hawarden* v. *Elphinstone's Trs.* (1866) 4 M. 353; *Campbell* v. *C.* (1868) 6 M. 1035; *Munro* v. *Butler Johnstone* (1868) 7 M. 250; *Home* v. *H.* (1876) 3 R. 591; *Nicolson* v. *Arbuthnott* (1878) 5 R. 872.

3 *Baird* v. *B.* (1844) 6 D. 643, 650.

4 Bell, *Prin.* §1728; *Scot* v. *His Heirs of Tailzie* (1751) Mor. 15394.

5 *Cathcart* v. *Schaw* (1755) 1 Pat. 618; *Innes* v. *Kerr* (1812) 5 Pat. 609, 768.

6 *Baird, supra.*

7 *Dickson* v. *D.* (1854) 1 Macq. 729; *Catton* v. *Mackenzie* (1872) 10 M. (H.L.) 12; *Chancellor's Trs.* v. *Sharples's Trs.* (1896) 23 R. 435; *Balfour-Melville* v. *Mylne* (1901) 3 F. 421.

8 Rankine, *L.O.*, 713. As to reserved power to disentail without judicial authority, see *Abbey* v. *Atholl Properties, Ltd.*, 1936 S.N. 97.

9 Bell, *Prin.* §1761; *Dundas* v. *Murray* (1774) Mor. 15430; *Bontine* v. *Graham* (1840) 1 Rob. 347.

10 *Abernethie* v. *Gordon* (1840) 1 Rob. App. 434.

11 Entail Amdt. Act, 1848, S. 40.

Assignation or attachment of heir's rights

An heir in possession may assign the lands in security, under the qualification that the security shall be *ipso facto* extinguished by the heir's death.[1] The lands may similarly, and under the same qualification, be attached by the heir's creditors.[2] The *spes successionis* of an heir-apparent cannot be attached by creditors.[3]

Prohibition of new entails after 1914

The Entail (Sc.) Act, 1914, S. 2, without prejudice to existing entails, prohibited the making of fresh entails, and provided that where, at its date, any money, land or moveables was held for purchasing land to be entailed but the direction had not been carried into effect, the date when the deed directing such entailing came into operation should be held to be the date of any entail to be made in execution of the direction, whatever its actual date.[4] Attention need now, accordingly, be given only to the powers of heirs of entail in possession under pre-1914 entails, and to the disentail of entailed lands.

Powers of heir of entail in possession at common law

An heir of entail in possession is not a mere liferenter of the lands, but a full fiar, subject, however, to the fetters of the entail.[5] In view of the purpose of entailing lands and of the cardinal prohibitions of a strict entail his common law powers were very restricted.

The cardinal prohibition against alienation prevented an heir in possession from selling or granting feus,[6] granting leases of more than ordinary duration,[7] leasing for a grassum in addition to the rent,[8] or letting the mansion-house beyond his lifetime.[8] But the prohibition might be qualified and power to feu or lease given.[9]

The power to excamb might be contained in an entail[10] but

[1] *Graham* v. *Hunter* (1828) 7 S. 13; *Grahame* v. *Alison* (1833) 6 W. & S. 518; *Ferrier* v. *Gartmore Heritable Creditors* (1835) 13 S. 1121.

[2] *Nairne* v. *Gray*, 15 Feb. 1810, F.C.; *Bontine* v. *Graham* (1840) 1 Rob. 347.

[3] *Beaton* v. *Macdonald* (1821) 1 S. 49.

[4] *Elliott Lockhart's Trs.* v. *E.L.*, 1927 S.C. 614, 620. See also *Lumsden's Trs.* v. *L.*, 1917 S.C. 579.

[5] *E. Galloway* v. *D. Bedford* (1902) 4 F. 851, 867; *Somervell's Tr.* v. *S.*, 1909 S.C. 1125, 1130; see also *E. Breadalbane* v. *Jamieson* (1877) 4 R. 667.

[6] *Cathcart* v. *Schaw* (1756) 1 Pat. 618.

[7] *Eliott* v. *Pott* (1821) 1 Sh. App. 16, 89.

[8] *Eliott, supra.* [9] *Cathcart, supra.*

[9] *Innes* v. *Ker* (1813) 5 Pat. 768; *E. Elgin* v. *Wellwood* (1821) 1 Sh. App. 44.

[10] *Baird* v. *B.* (1847) 6 Bell 7.

could be exercised only to such an extent as is consistent with the subsistence of the entail over the bulk of the estate.[1]

The prohibition against charging with debt disentitled an heir in possession, unless the entail enabled him to do so, from burdening the estate or succeeding heirs with the expense of improvements made by him on the estate.

Unless it were given him by the entail or by private Act an heir in possession had no power at common law to sell for payment of debts which affected or might be made to affect the estate.

An heir in possession could, however, work minerals even to the point of exhausting them,[2] cut wood, if ready for cutting,[3] and the cutting does not interfere with the amenity of the mansion-house;[4] he could not let the mansion-house for longer than his lifetime,[5] nor demolish it and sell the materials,[6] though he may demolish and replace by another house equally good.[7]

Statutory Powers

The powers of heirs of entail in possession have been greatly extended by various statutes, which have empowered them, within the limits set by the several Acts, to do the following:

(a) to grant leases;[8]
(b) to grant building leases;[9]
(c) to feu;[10]

1 *Dalhousie's Trs.* v. *D.* (1878) 6 R. 141.

2 *Muirhead* v. *Young* (1855) 17 D. 875; (1858) 20 D. 592; *Muirhead* v. *M's Trs.* (1899) 7 S.L.T. 2.

3 *Bontine* v. *Graham's Trs.* (1827) 6 S. 74.

4 *Boyd* v. *B.* (1870) 8 M. 637; *Huntley's Trs.* v. *Hallyburton's Trs.* (1880) 8 R. 50; see also *Ker* v. *Graham's Trs.* (1827) 6 S. 73, 270; *Macqueen* v. *Tod* (1899) 1 F. 1069; Entail (Sc.) Act, 1914, S. 7.

5 *Leslie* v. *Orme* (1780) 2 Paton 533; *Montgomerie* v. *Vernon* (1895) 22 R. 465; modified by Entail (Sc.) Act, 1914, S. 6; see also *Hill* (1851) 14 D. 13; *Spiers* (1854) 17 D. 289.

6 *Gordon* v. *G.*, 24 Jan. 1811, F.C.

7 *Moir* v. *Graham* (1826) 4 S. 730; *E. Breadalbane* v. *Jamieson* (1877) 4 R. 667.

8 Entail Improvement Act, 1770, S. 1: *Hamilton* v. *H.* (1846) 9 D. 53; *Campbeltown Coal Co.* v. *D. Argyll*, 1926 S.C. 126; Entail Powers (Sc.) Act, 1836, S. 2, extended by Entail Act, 1838: see *Forbes* v. *Wilson* (1873) 11 M. 454; *Gould* v. *G's Trs.* (1899) 2 F. 130; *E. Galloway* v. *D. Bedford* (1902) 4 F. 851; (1904) 6 F. 971; *L. Abinger's Trs.* v. *Cameron*, 1909 S.C. 1245; Entail Amdt. Act, 1848, S. 4; Entail Amdt. Act, 1853, S. 5; Entail Amdt. (Sc.) Act, 1868, S. 3; Entail (Sc.) Act, 1882, S. 4.

9 Entail Improvement Act, 1770, S. 4: *Carrick* v. *Miller* (1868) 6 M. (H.L.) 101; *Gordon* v. *Rae* (1883) 11 R. 67; *Carter* v. *Lornie* (1890) 18 R. 353; *Montgomery* v. *Vernon* (1895) 22 R. 465; *McDowel* v. *McD.* (1904) 6 F. 575; Entail Sites Act, 1840, S. 1 (and see also New Parishes (Sc.) Act, 1844, S. 10); Entail Amdt. Act, 1848, S. 4; Entail Amdt. Act, 1853, S. 5; Entail Amdt. (Sc.) Act, 1868, S. 3: *Stewart* v. *Murdoch* (1882) 9 R. 458; Entail (Sc.) Act, 1882, S. 4.

10 Entail Sites Act, 1840, S. 1 (and see also New Parishes (Sc.) Act, 1844, S. 10); Entail Amdt. Act, 1848, S. 4: *Farquharson* (1870) 9 M. 66; *D. Portland*, 1909 1 S.L.T. 72;

(d) to excamb;[1]
(e) to sell;[2]
(f) to charge the estate for expenditure;[3]
(g) to grant family provisions;[4]
(h) to erect cottages.[5]

Termination of entail at common law

An entail comes to an end at common law (a) when all the heirs of entail are dead[6] or the estate comes to be held by the last heir called as heir under the deed. If estate comes to be held by the heirs whomsoever or heirs general of an institute, such estate is deemed fee-simple estate without judicial procedure;[7] (b) when heirs-portioners have not been excluded and succeed under the destination;[8] (c) by prescriptive possession of the lands on a fee-simple title or one made up under the entail but in which the

Entail Amdt. Act, 1853, S. 5: *E. Kinnoul* (1862) 24 D. 379; Entail Amdt. (Sc.) Act, 1868, S. 3; Entail (Sc.) Act, 1882, S. 4; Entail (Sc.) Act, 1914, S. 4: *Jolly's Exrx.* v. *V. Stonehaven*, 1958 S.C. 635.

1 Entail Improvement Act, 1770, S. 32; Entail Powers (Sc.) Act, 1836, S. 3, extended by Entail Act, 1838; Entail Amdt. Act. 1848, S. 5; Entail Amdt. (Sc.) Act, 1853, S. 5; Entail Amdt. Act, 1868, S. 14.

2 Tenures Abolition Act, 1746, Ss. 14, 16; Sales to the Crown Act, 1746, Ss. 2–3: *Fleeming* v. *Howden* (1868) 6 M. (H.L.) 113; Land Tax Redemption Act, 1801, S. 61; Entail Powers (Sc.) Act, 1836, S. 7; Lands Clauses Consolidation (Sc.) Act, 1845, Ss. 7, 67: *Whitelaw* v. *W's Curator*, 1931 S.L.T. 99; Entail Amdt. Act, 1848, Ss. 4, 25: *McKenzie* v. *McK.* (1849) 11 D. 1115; *Scott Plummer* (1885) 12 R. 1349; *Laurie* (1898) 25 R. 636; *Callander-Brodie* (1904) 12 S.L.T. 474; *L.A.* v. *E. Moray's Trs.* (1905) 7 F. (H.L.) 116; *Kinloch*, 1920 2 S.L.T. 79; *D. Richmond*, 1929 S.L.T. 441; Entail Amdt. Act, 1853, S 5; Entail Amdt. (Sc.) Act, 1868, S. 9; Entail Amdt. (Sc.) Act, 1875, S. 6; Entail (Sc.) Act, 1882, Ss. 4, 19: *Ballantine* (1883) 10 R. 1061; *Stirling Stuart*, 1915 2 S.L.T. 260; *E. Rothes*, 1918 1 S.L.T. 164; *Hope Vere*, 1921 2 S.L.T. 271; *D. Sutherland*, 1922 S.L.T. 250; *Keck*, 1949 S.C. 462.

3 Entail Improvement Act, 1770, S. 9; Entail Amdt. Act, 1848, Ss. 4, 13: *M. Breadalbane's Trs.* v. *Campbell* (1868) 6 M. (H.L.) 43; Entail Amdt. Act, 1853, S. 5; Entail Amdt. (Sc.) Act, 1868, S. 11; Entail Amdt. (Sc.) Act, 1875, Ss. 7–8; Entail Amdt. (Sc.) Act, 1878: *E. Kinnoul* v. *Haldane*, 1911 S.C. 1279; *Shepherd's Exors.* v. *Mackenzie*, 1913 S.C. 144; *Maxwell-Stuart's Tr.* v. *M.S.*, 1947 S.L.T. 59; Entail Act, 1880; Entail (Sc.) Act, 1882, S. 4; War Damage Act, 1939, Ss. 6, 11; War Damage Act, 1941, S. 7; War Damage Act, 1943, S. 66. As to charging succession duty, see *Blythswood's J.F.* v. *Douglas*, 1935 S.C. 511.

4 Entail Provisions Act, 1824, S. 1: *Callander* v. *C.* (1869) 7 M. 777; see also *Hunter Blair* v. *H.B.* (1899) 1 F. 437; *Somervill's Tr.* v. *S.*, 1909 S.C. 1125; Entail Amdt. Act, 1848, S. 21: *Brodie* v. *B.* (1867) 6 M. 92; *Balfour-Melville* v. *Duncan* (1903) 5 F. 1079; Entail Amdt. Act, 1853, S. 5; Entail Amdt. (Sc.) Act, 1868, S. 6; *E. Haddington*, 1919 S.C. 727; Entail Amdt. (Sc.) Act, 1875, S. 10; Entail Amdt. (Sc.) Act, 1878; Entail (Sc.) Act, 1882, S. 24.

5 Entail Cottages Act, 1860, S. 1; Entail Amdt. (Sc.) Act, 1868, S. 12; Entail Amdt. (Sc.) Act, 1875, S. 3.

6 *Henry* v. *Watt* (1832) 10 S. 644.

7 *E. March* v. *Kennedy* (1760) 2 Paton 49; *Steele* v. *Coupar* (1853) 15 D. 385; *Gordon* v. *G's Trs.* (1882) 9 R. (H.L.) 101; Entail Amdt. Act, 1875, S. 13.

8 Bell, *Convg.* II, 1048; *Collow's Trs.* v. *Connell* (1866) 4 M. 465.

fetters of the entail have not been included expressly or by reference;[1] and (d) by prescriptive possession under an entail of later date, though covering the same lands and under the same conditions.[2] Also at common law an entail defective in one or more of the cardinal prohibitions was to that extent ineffective and so might not prevent alienation to an onerous purchaser.[3]

The Entail Amdt. Act, 1848, S. 43, enacted that an entail defective as to one of the cardinal prohibitions was deemed defective as to all of them, and such an entail might be terminated if challenged by an heir.[4]

Disentail

An heir of entail in possession if of full age, *capax*, and not debarred by marriage-contract[5] may, with the authority of the Court, disentail and acquire the estate in fee-simple (a) without consent if he is the only heir of entail in existence;[6] (b) without consent if he was born after 1 August, 1848, (old entail)[7] or after the date of the entail (new entail)[8] (c) with the consent of the heir-apparent if the heir was born before and the heir apparent born after the date of the entail;[9] (d) with the consents of the three nearest heirs of entail or of the whole heirs of entail, if less than three, in being at the date thereof and the date of the Court's first interlocutor in the application, or the consents of the three nearest heirs who at these dates are entitled next in order to succeed, or the consents of the heir-apparent under the entail and of the heirs, at least two in number, including the heir-apparent, who in order successively would be heirs apparent, provided always that the nearest heir for the time entitled to succeed after the heir in possession is at least 21 and not legally incapacitated.[10]

1 *Cathcart* v. *Maclaine* (1846) 8 D. 970; *Holmes and Campbell* v. *Cuninghame* (1851) 13 D. 689.

2 *E. Eglinton* v. *Montgomerie* (1843) 2 Bell 149; *Stewart* v. *S.* (1846) 5 Bell 139; *Inglis* v *I.* (1851) 14 D. 54.

3 *Carrick* v. *Buchanan* (1844) 3 Bell 342; *Lindsey* v. *Oswald* (1863) 2 M. 249.

4 *D. Hamilton* v. *L. Hamilton* (1870) 8 M. (H.L.) 48.

5 1848 Act, S. 8; 1882 Act, S. 17; Bell, *Prin.* §1774A; *Scott Douglas* (1883) 10 R. 952; *Pringle* v. *P.* (1891) 18 R. 895; *Lockhart*, 1909 1 S.L.T. 36.

6 1848 Act, S. 3; 1875 Act, S. 5(3); 1882 Act, S. 3; *Gorden* v. *Mosse* (1851) 13 D. 954; *Bruce Gardyne* v. *B.G.* (1883) 11 R. 60.

7 1848 Act, S. 2: an 'old' entail is one dated before 1st August 1848.

8 1848 Act, S. 1: a 'new' entail is one dated on or after 1st August 1848.

9 1848 Act, Ss, 1, 2; 1882 Act, S. 3.

10 1848 Act, S. 3; 1853 Act, S. 19; 1882 Act, S. 3; consent may be given at 21: 1875 Act, S. 4; and in the course of an application to the court: 1875 Act, S. 5(1).

The consent of an heir of entail, if under age or *incapax*, may be given by a *curator ad litem*;[1] the court has power to value an heir's expectancy and when the value is paid into bank or secured to the satisfaction of the court, to dispense with his consent;[2] it may authorize a factor *loco absentis* to execute an instrument of disentail,[3] and may even force disentail when the heir in possession has, after the 1882 Act, contracted debt.[4]

Money derived from the sale of part of an entailed estate or invested in trust to purchase lands to be settled on the heirs of entail may be acquired by the heir outright by application to the court.[5] Where money has been invested in trust for the purchase of land to be entailed, the person who would have become institute under the intended entail may acquire the funds free of the entail.[6] An heir who seeks to disentail must produce a schedule showing the debts and family provisions affecting the fee and not secured.[7]

Disentail is effected by applying to the Court of Session for authority to execute, and executing and recording in the Register of Entails, an instrument of disentail in the form provided by the 1848 Act,[8] subscribed by the disentailing heir and a notary before two witnesses. When recorded, it absolutely frees and relieves the entailed estate of all the restrictions imposed thereby. The disentail only removes the fetters of entail and does not evacuate the destination of the lands.[9] A superior who has been heir of entail in possession retains the right to enforce building restrictions after he has become fee simple proprietor.[10] Disentail proceedings can be reduced where the procedure has not taken

[1] 1882 Act, S. 12.

[2] 1875 Act, S. 5(2); 1882 Act, S. 13; *Baird* v. *B.* (1891) 18 R. 1184; *D. Sutherland* v. *M. Stafford* (1892) 19 R. 504; on calculation see *de Virte* v. *Wilson* (1877) 5 R. 328; *E. Kintore*, 1918 S.C. 883. Interest does not run until it is paid or secured: *Pringle* v. *P.* (1892) 19 R. 926.

[3] 1882 Act, S. 14; Presumption of Life Limitation (Sc.) Act, 1891, S. 8.

[4] 1882 Act, S. 18; *L. Napier & Ettrick's Trs.* v. *Napier* (1901) 3 F. 579; *Somervell's Tr.* v. *Dawes* (1903) 5 F. 1065; *Somervell's Tr.* (1906) 13 S.L.T. 718; *Somervell's Tr.* v. *S.*, 1907 S.C. 528; 1909 S.C. 1125.

[5] 1848 Act, S. 26.

[6] 1848 Act, S. 27; *Black* v. *Auld* (1873) 1 R. 133; *Craig* v. *Picken's Trs.* (1886) 13 R. 603; *Tireman*, 1930 S.L.T. 561; *Fletcher* v. *F.'s Trs.*, 1934 S.C. 291.

[7] 1848 Act, Ss. 6, 32; 1875 Act, S. 12(5). Third parties, if not secured, may object to disentail: *Irving* v. *I.* (1871) 9 M. 539; *Baikie* v. *Kirkwall Educ. Trust*, 1914 S.C. 860; *Glasgow Corpn.* v. *L. Blythswood*, 1920 S.C. 398; cf. *L. Stonehaven*, 1926 S.L.T. 64.

[8] 1848 Act, S. 32; by the 1853 Act the disentail may be executed and the authority of the Court later applied for. In such a petition the court will not consider whether an irritancy has been incurred: *Inverclyde*, 1953 S.L.T. (Notes) 70.

[9] 1848 Act, S. 32; *Gray* v. *G's Trs.* (1878) 5 R. 820.

[10] *MacDonald* v. *Douglas*, 1963 S.C. 374.

account of provisions for younger children,[1] but instruments of disentail and deeds granted under authority of the court under the Entail Acts are final if not appealed.[2]

[1] *Nicolson's Trs.* v. *N.*, 1925 S.L.T. 383.

[2] 1882 Act, S. 29; *V. Fincastle* v. *E. Dunmore* (1876) 3 R. 345; *Mackenzie* v. *Catton's Trs.* (1877) 5 R. 313.

CHAPTER 82

THE LIFERENT ESTATE

OLDER authorities regarded liferent as a personal servitude, or burden on the fee of land,[1] but it is better to regard proper liferent of heritage (as distinct from improper or beneficiary liferent, where the liferenter is only a beneficiary, the fee being vested in trustees)[2] as a distinct estate in land, limited both in duration and by the concurrent existence of the estate of fee vested in another, the two estates in the land coexisting and mutually limiting each other.[3] Proper liferent is normally concerned with, possibly even confined to, cases where the liferenter is feudally vested in heritage,[4] whereas improper liferent may be, and frequently is, a right attaching to moveables, or to a mixed estate of heritage and moveables.

Nature of proper liferent

A proper liferent is the right to possess, use, and enjoy heritable subjects during the grantee's life, without destroying or wasting their substance, *salva rei substantia*, corresponding to the *usufructus* of the civil law.[5] Liferent is *prima facie* and normally a right to enjoy the use of heritage for the grantee's lifetime, but it includes also cases where the limited right may terminate before death, on the occurrence of some intervening and uncertain event, such as a daughter's marriage[6] or a widow's second marriage. The fee of the subjects is vested in another person, to whom the rights of actual possession, use and enjoyment revert on the expiry of the liferent. If the fee is not conferred on anyone it remains vested in the granter, and if he has died, in his *haereditas jacens*.[7] A liferent may be made subject to a resolutive condition or to prohibitions on specified uses of the lands, though these may be unenforceable if too vague or otherwise objectionable.[8]

[1] Stair II, 6, 4; Bankt. II, 6; Ersk. II, 9, 39: *Patrick* v. *Napier* (1867) 5 M. 683, 699.

[2] On improper liferent, see Ch. 104, *infra*.

[3] Ersk. II, 9, 41; Bell, *Comm.* I, 52; Bell, *Prin.* §1037.

[4] *Miller* v. *Inland Revenue*, 1930 S.C. (H.L.) 49, 56; *Fogo's J.F.* v. *Fogo's Trs.*, 1929 S.C. 546, is a case of proper liferent of a mixed estate.

[5] Bell, *Prin.* §1037.

[6] cf. *Carruthers* v. *Crawford*, 1945 S.C. 82.

[7] *Cumstie's Trs.* v. *C.* (1876) 3 R. 921; *Carruthers*, *supra*.

[8] *Chaplin's Trs.* v. *Hoile* (1890) 18 R. 27; *Wemyss* v. *W.*, 1921 S.C. 30; *Balfour's Trs.* v. *Johnston*, 1936 S.C. 137; *Veitch's Exor.* v. *V.*, 1947 S.L.T. 17.

Whether grant of fee or of liferent

It is a question of the granter's intention and of interpretation whether a gift or bequest of heritage is one in liferent only or in fee.[1] A liferent with a power of disposal, if unqualified, amounts to a grant of fee.[2] The fact that the fee is not disposed of and will fall into intestacy if the gift be held to be of liferent only is not at all conclusive in favour of its being interpreted as a gift of fee, but is a factor to be weighed in case of doubt.[3]

Initial gift of the fee later qualified

Words in a deed conferring initially a gift of fee to a beneficiary may be later qualified by expressions which may be held either to abridge the gift or merely to attach conditions to its use or enjoyment. The general principle is that unless the later qualifications in terms purport to abridge the gift itself they relate only to the mode of enjoyment.[4] Qualifications in a later separate deed are more readily held to reduce an initial gift than if in the same deed.[5]

Whether gift of restricted right of fee

In some cases a gift has apparently been made of a fee subject to certain restrictions, but the tendency has been to hold such gifts to be gifts of fee, the restrictions being ineffectual,[6] and there is now no recognized kind of right intermediate between fee and liferent.[7]

[1] See e.g. *Henderson's Trs.* v. *H.* (1876) 3 R. 320; *Gibson's Trs.* v. *Ross* (1877) 4 R. 1038; *Anderson* v. *Thomson* (1877) 4 R. 1101; *Houston* v. *Mitchell* (1877) 5 R. 154; *Smith's Trs.* v. *S.* (1883) 10 R. 1144; *Lawson's Trs.* v. *L.* (1890) 17 R. 1167; *Mitchell* v. *Ch. of Scotland* (1895) 2 S.L.T. 629; *Whitehead's Trs.* v. *W.* (1897) 24 R. 1032; *Newall's Trs.* v. *Inglis's Trs.* (1898) 25 R. 1176; *Jamieson's Trs.* v. *J.* (1899) 2 F. 258; *Mackenzie's Trs.* v. *M.* (1899) 2 F. 330; *Sim* v. *Duncan* (1900) 2 F. 434; *Patrick* v. *Fowler* (1900) 2 F. 690; *Crawford's Trs.* v. *Working Boys' Home* (1901) 8 S.L.T. 371; *Brash's Trs.* v. *Phillipson*, 1916 S.C. 271; *Lethem* v. *Evans*, 1918 1 S.L.T. 27; *Smart* v. *S.*, 1926 S.C. 392; *Mearns* v. *Charles*, 1926 S.L.T. 118; *Graham* v. *G's Trs.*, 1927 S.C. 388; *Fogo's Trs.*, 1929 S.C. 546; *Duncan* v. *Edinburgh R.I.*, 1936 S.C. 811.

[2] *Rattray's Trs.* v. *R.* (1899) 1 F. 510; *Mickel's J.F.* v. *Oliphant* (1892) 20 R. 172.

[3] *Smith's Trs.* v. *S.* (1883) 10 R. 1144; *Lawson's Trs.* v. *L.* (1890) 17 R. 1167; *Spink's Exors.* v. *Simpson* (1894) 21 R. 551; *Sim* v. *Duncan* (1900) 2 F. 434; *Gillies' Trs.* v. *Hodge* (1900) 3 F. 238; *Milne's Trs.* v. *Milne's Exor.*, 1937 S.C. 149.

[4] *Tweeddale's Trs.* v. *T.* (1905) 8 F. 264.

[5] *Russell* v. *Bell's Trs.* (1897) 24 R. 666; *Tweeddale's Trs.*, *supra*; *Ford's Trs.* v. *F.*, 1940 S.C. 426.

[6] *Johnston* v. *J.* (1903) 5 F. 1039.

[7] cf. *Cochrane's Exrx.* v. *C.*, 1947 S.C. 134; overruling *Denholm's Trs.* v. *D's Trs.*, 1907 S.C. 61; and *Heavyside* v. *Smith*, 1929 S.C. 68; and qualifying *Ironside's Exor.* v. *I.*, 1933 S.C. 116.

Whether grant of liferent or lesser right

It is a question of interpretation whether a right granted, whatever it be called in the deed granting it, is a proper liferent of heritage or a lesser right such as a bare licence to occupy, or personal right of occupation, corresponding to the Roman *habitatio*, which is not an estate in the land, confers no real right, and is but a mere burden on the fee thereof.[1] A person entitled to occupancy is liable to the burdens incumbent on an occupier such as local rates, but not for feu-duty or landlord's repairs,[2] or interest on a bond over the property.[3]

Subjects of liferent

The subjects of proper liferent of heritage are only such heritable things as are not consumed by use; hence rights to minerals, unless expressly given in liferent, are excluded. But a liferenter may enjoy the revenue of mineral-workings opened or let by the granter of the liferent as much as the rents of farms.[4]

Creation

Liferents of heritage arising by operation of law were formerly recognized, in the legal rights of terce and courtesy,[5] but all proper liferents are now conventional, created by constitution in favour of a third party,[6] or by reservation, when an owner conveys land to another in fee, reserving a liferent to himself.[6] Infeftment by registration in the Register of Sasines, on behalf of the liferenter, is necessary to confer real rights in the lands,[6] except in liferent by reservation, which depends on the granter's existing sasine.[7] The rights and powers of liferenters by reservation have in some cases been treated as greater, and closer to those of a fiar.[8]

[1] *Clark* v. *C.* (1871) 9 M. 435; *Rodger's Trs.* v. *R.* (1875) 2 R. 294; *Kinloch's Trs.* v. *K* (1880) 7 R. 596; *Bayne's Trs.* v. *B.* (1894) 22 R. 26; *Cathcart's Trs.* v. *Allardice* (1899) 2 F. 326; *Johnston* v. *J.* (1904) 6 F. 665; *Smart's Trs.* v. *S's Trs.*, 1912 S.C. 87; *Montgomerie-Fleming's Trs.* v. *Carre*, 1913 S.C. 1018; contrast *Morris* v. *Anderson* (1882) 9 R. 952; *Mackenzie's Trs.* v. *Kilmarnock's Trs.*, 1909 S.C. 472; *Johnstone* v. *Mackenzie's Trs.*, 1912 S.C. (H.L.) 106; *Milne's Trs.* v. *M.*, 1920 S.C. 456; see also *Ctess. of Lauderdale*, 1962 S.C. 302.

[2] *Clark, supra*; *Bayne's Trs., supra*; *Johnstone, supra.*

[3] *Cathcart's Trs., supra.*

[4] *Wardlaw* v. *W's Trs.* (1875) 2 R. 368.

[5] See Ch. 108, *infra.*

[6] Stair II, 6, 6; Bankt. II, 6, 6; Ersk. II, 9, 41; Bell, *Comm.* I, 53; *Prin.* §1040–1; *Hardie* v. *Mags. of Port Glasgow* (1864) 2 M. 746.

[7] Ersk. II, 9, 42; Bell, *Prin.* §1055.

[8] Bell, *Prin.* §1040.

Restrictions on creation of liferents of heritage

By the Entail Amendment (Rutherfurd) Act, 1848, Ss. 47–8, it was competent to grant a liferent interest in lands in favour only of a party in life[1] at the date of the grant, and where any land is, by virtue of a deed dated on or after 1 August, 1848, held in liferent by a party of full age, born after that date, such party is deemed to be fee simple proprietor and may apply to the court for declarator accordingly.[2] By the Entail Act, 1914, S. 8, this principle was extended to deeds dated before the stated date. It is accordingly incompetent to create a perpetual series of liferents of heritage. The *nobile officium* cannot be invoked to confer a right on persons other than those for whom the statutory right is created, such as a pupil or minor,[3] but the provision does not apply to an annuity.[4] The Law Reform (Misc. Prov.) (Sc.) Act, 1968, S. 18, imposes similar restrictions on the duration of liferents created by a deed executed after 25 November, 1968.

Mode of creation of proper liferent of heritage

A liferent interest is created by a feu-charter or disposition or will or marriage contract bearing to be in favour of the grantee in liferent, or for his liferent use, or words to the same effect,[5] and to another in fee. Title is completed by recording the feu-contract or disposition in the Register of Sasines, or by expeding a notice of title following on the will or marriage-contract and recording it similarly.

Destinations to parents and children

If the destination in the deed is to one in liferent and his heirs or children *nascituri* in fee the party called is deemed fiar;[6] if to one in liferent only, or liferent allenarly, or in alimentary liferent, and to his heirs in fee, the party called has only a liferent but has also a fiduciary fee, or holds the fee in trust, till they come into existence, for the persons who may be heirs at the date of his

[1] cf. *Stewart's Trs.* v. *Whitelaw*, 1926 S.C. 701; *Reid's Trs.* v. *Dashwood*, 1929 S.C. 748.

[2] *Middleton*, 1929 S.C. 394; *Earl of Moray*, 1950 S.C. 281; see also *Harvey's Trs.* v. *H.*, 1942 S.C. 582.

[3] *Crichton-Stuart's Tutrix*, 1921 S.C. 840.

[4] *Drybrough's Tr.* v. *D's Tr.*, 1912 S.C. 939.

[5] The destination may be to two or more in liferent and to one of them, or the survivor or the heir of the survivor, in fee, or to two or more in conjunct fee and liferent.

[6] *Frog's Creditors* v. *His Children* (1735) Mor. 4262; *Lillie* v. *Riddell* (1741) Mor. 4267; *Lindsay* v. *Dott* (1807) Mor. Fiar, Appx. 1; *Dewar* v. *McKinnon* (1825) 1 W. & S. 161; *Ferguson's Trs.* v. *Hamilton* (1862) 4 Macq. 397; *McClymont's Exors.* v. *Osborne* (1895) 22 R. 411; *Dalrymple's Trs.* v. *Watson's Trs.*, 1932 S.L.T. 480.

death.[1] The fee in such cases cannot be *in pendente* and if not destined to a named fiar, nor vested in the liferenter under the doctrine of fiduciary fee, remains with the granter and passes to his heirs. Similarly if the liferenter dies without heirs of the destined class the fee reverts to the granter. If the fiar predeceases the liferenter the right of fee passes to the fiar's heirs under the destination, failing whom it falls into the *haereditas jacens* of the fiar and passes to the fiar's heir under the rules of intestacy.[2]

These rules have no application where the fiar is named and in existence, nor where the fee is destined to named children and other children born later, when it vests in the named children for themselves and those subsequently born,[3] nor where the fee is vested in trustees to hold for a parent in liferent and unnamed children in fee,[4] nor where the fiars were other than the children or heirs of the body of the liferenter.[5]

These rules, though applicable originally to heritage, were extended to moveables[6] and to mixed estate,[7] and to cases of improper liferent, with an interposed trust.[8]

The Trusts (Sc.) Act, 1921, S. 8 largely displaces the rule of *Frog's Creditors*;[9] it provides that where in any deed property is conveyed to any person in liferent and in fee to persons who, when the conveyance comes into operation, are unborn or incapable of ascertainment, the person to whom the property is conveyed in liferent is not to be deemed fiar merely because the liferent is not expressed to be a liferent allenarly, but all such conveyances, unless a contrary intention appears, have effect as if it were declared to be a liferent allenarly. This rule, unlike the rule of *Frog's Creditors*,[9] applies whatever the relationship between liferenter and unborn or unascertainable fiars. A fiduciary fiar, at common law or under this provision, may be given by the court the powers of a trustee.[10]

[1] *Newlands* v. *N's Creditors* (1798) 3 Ross L.C. 634; *Miller* v. *M.* (1833) 12 S. 31; *Douglas* v. *Thomson* (1870) 8 M. 374; *Snell* v. *White* (1872) 10 M. 745; *Ferguson* v. *F.* (1875) 2 R. 627; *Cumstie* v. *C's Trs.* (1876) 3 R. 921; *Dawson* (1877) 4 R. 597; *Tristram* v. *McHaffies* (1894) 22 R. 121; *Gifford's Trs.* v. *G.* (1903) 5 F. 723; see also *Studd* v. *Cook* (1883) 10 R. (H.L.) 53, 61; *Lockhart's Trs.* v. *L.*, 1921 S.C. 761.

[2] *Todd* v. *Mackenzie* (1874) 1 R. 1203.

[3] *McGowan* v. *Robb* (1862) 1 M. 141; (1864) 2 M. 943; *Martin's Trs.* v. *Milliken* (1864) 3 M. 326.

[4] *Rait* v. *Arbuthnott* (1892) 19 R. 687; *Gifford's Trs.* v. *G.* (1903) 5 F. 723.

[5] *Ramsay* v. *Beveridge* (1854) 16 D. 764.

[6] *McClymont's Exors.* v. *Osborne* (1895) 22 R. 411.

[7] *Fraser's Trs.* v. *Turner* (1901) 8 S.L.T. 466.

[8] *Lockhart's Trs.* v. *L.*, 1921 S.C. 761.

[9] *Frog's Creditors* v. *His Children* (1735) Mor. 4262; see *Colville's Trs.* v. *Marindin*, 1908 S.C. 911.

[10] 1921 Act, S. 8(2): but see *Cripp's Trs.* v. *C.*, 1926 S.C. 188.

Where the destination is governed by the rule of *Frog's Creditors*[1] infeftment in favour of the parent in liferent and the children in fee gives an unqualified right of fee to the parent, but if the destination is governed by the 1921 Act, S. 8, infeftment gives the parent a fiduciary fee.[2] If infeftment is taken only in favour of the parent in liferent the granter is not divested as fiar.[3]

Where a fiduciary fee is held for children *nascituri*, unless the deed of gift indicates a contrary intention, the fee vests in each child on coming into existence,[4] subject to partial defeasance if other children are born, or if a child does not survive the expiry of the liferent. The fiduciary fee lasts only so long as required to ascertain the fiar.[5]

Destinations to spouses

In this class of cases the main rules of construction are: A destination to spouses in joint or conjunct fee gives an equal right of fee to each, if survivorship be added, the survivor takes the whole fee.[6] A destination in conjunct liferent gives each a liferent of a half and to the survivor liferent of the whole.[7] A destination in conjunct fee and liferent *prima facie* gives the fee to the husband and a liferent to the wife if she survives,[8] but different interpretations are justified if the husband paid a price for the property,[9] or the property came from the wife or her relatives,[10] or the heirs of one spouse are favoured.[11] If the destination includes mention of survivorship, the survivor will have the fee, whoever had it during the marriage.

1 *Frog's Creditors* v. *His Children* (1735) Mor. 4262; see *Colville's Trs.* v. *Marindin*, 1908 S.C. 911.

2 *McLachlan's Trs.* v. *McL.* (1858) 20 D. 612; *Livingstone* v. *Waddell's Trs.* (1899) 1 F. 831.

3 *Stewart* v. *Rae* (1883) 10 R. 463; *Livingstone, supra.*

4 *Beattie's Trs.* v. *Cooper's Trs.* (1862) 24 D. 519; *Robertson* (1869) 7 M. 1114; *Douglas* v. *Thomson* (1870) 8 M. 374; *Turner* v. *Gaw* (1894) 21 R. 563.

5 *Ferguson* v. *F.* (1875) 2 R. 627; *Maule* (1876) 3 R. 831; *Black* v. *Mason* (1881) 8 R. 497.

6 *Walker* v. *Galbraith* (1895) 23 R. 347; *Perrett's Trs.* v. *P.*, 1909 S.C. 522. The older view was that the fee was in one, normally the husband; Stair II, 6, 10; Ersk. III, 8, 36; Bell, *Convg.* II, 834.

7 *Reid's Trs.* v. *R.* (1879) 6 R. 916; *Dick's Trs.* v. *Baird*, 1909 1 S.L.T. 101; *Paull* v. *Forbes*, 1911 1 S.L.T. 29.

8 Stair, Ersk., *supra*; *Millar* v. *M. Lansdowne*, 1910 S.C. 618.

9 *Fisher's Trs.* v. *F.* (1844) 7 D. 129.

10 *Smith Cunninghame* v. *Anstruther's Trs.* (1872) 10 M. (H.L.) 39; *Brough* v. *Adamson* (1887) 14 R. 858.

11 *Smith Cunninghame, supra.*

Destinations to strangers

The main rules of interpretation in this case are:

If there is a destination to two strangers and the heirs of one, the fee goes to the one having heirs, the other having a liferent only.[1] If to two strangers in conjunct fee and liferent each has a share in the liferent, the survivor a liferent of the whole, and the heirs of each take a half share of the fee.[2] If such a destination mentions survivorship, the survivor has the whole fee.[3]

Liferenter's powers

The liferenter is *interim dominus* or proprietor for life.[4] Though infeft he cannot alienate the lands *inter vivos*[5] or *mortis causa*;[6] he cannot grant a feu,[7] nor a lease[8] or servitude for any period longer than his own life. As he is not in general entitled to cut timber, he cannot sell trees, but coppice wood may be sold as well as cut,[9] though the purchaser's rights cease on the liferenter's death.[10] Where minerals had been worked by the granter, a liferenter has been held entitled to concur with the fiars in renewing the leases, provided there was no substantial danger of exhaustion of the minerals.[11]

Subject thereto he has the ordinary powers of administration of a proprietor, subject to the overriding consideration that nothing may be done to depreciate the capital value of the fee of the lands.

Liferenter's rights

The liferenter is entitled to all uses of the subjects and their fruits, subject to not destroying the substance of the subjects;[12] he is entitled to possession, and to appropriate all industrial or natural produce separated from the land during his liferent.[13] He may gather brushwood and windfalls, and timber and extraordinary windfalls necessary for the maintenance and repair of

[1] Ersk. III, 8, 35; Bell, *Prin.* §1709.
[2] Ersk, Bell, *supra*; *Paul* v. *Home* (1872) 10 M. 937.
[3] Craigie, *Herit.*, 558; cf. *Devlin* v. *Lowrie*, 1922 S.C. 255.
[4] Ersk. II, 9, 41.
[5] cf. *Ferguson* v. *F.* (1875) 2 R. 627; *Chaplin's Trs.* v. *Hoile* (1890) 18 R. 27; *Devlin* v. *Lowrie*, 1922 S.C. 255.
[6] *Carruthers* v. *Crawford*, 1945 S.C. 82.
[7] Bell, *Prin.* §1056; *Redfearn* v. *Maxwell*, 7 Mar. 1816, F.C.
[8] Bell, *Prin.* §1057; *Fraser* v. *Croft* (1898) 25 R. 496.
[9] *Tait* v. *Maitland* (1825) 4 S. 247; *Macalister's Trs.* v. *M.* (1851) 13 D. 1239.
[10] Stair II, 3, 74; Ersk. II, 9, 58; Bell, *Prin.* §1058.
[11] *Wardlaw* v. *W's Trs.* (1875) 2 R. 368.
[12] Ersk. II, 9, 56; Bell, *Prin.* §1044; *Rogers* v. *Scott* (1867) 5 M. 1078.
[13] *Nisbett* v. *N's Trs.* (1835) 13 S. 517.

the buildings and fences,[1] but only after intimation to the fiar.[2] The liferenter is also entitled to coppice wood, cut regularly as it ripens,[3] and his rights may be expressly extended.[4]

He may continue to work, and takes the royalties of, any minerals being worked when the liferent opens, but may not open new mines or quarries,[5] and particularly may take minerals necessary for domestic and estate use,[6] and for this purpose may open workings, probably subject to liability to account to the fiar.

He is entitled to feuduties,[7] and rents,[8] according to the legal terms of payment,[9] and if entitled to the liferent interest in a heritable bond, to the termly payment of interest,[10] but not to casualties, grassums or other extraordinary profits of land.[11]

Liferenter's liabilities

The liferenter is liable for all the annual and periodical burdens attaching to the subjects, such as feuduty, stipend and annual rates, but not for burdens attaching to heritors only occasionally.[12]

He is not liable for fair wear and tear or natural deterioration of the subjects, but he is bound to preserve the subjects in as good condition as he got them and to meet the expenses necessary for normal repairs.[13] If the fiar executes repairs the liferenter must pay the interest of the expenditure.[14]

In the event of natural decay or accidental destruction of the subjects liferented, neither fiar nor liferenter is bound to restore.

1 *Macalister's Trs.* v. *M.* (1851) 13 D. 1239.

2 *Dickson* v. *D.* (1823) 2 S. 152; *Tait* v. *Maitland* (1825) 4 S. 247.

3 *Macalister's Trs.* v. *M.* (1851) 13 D. 1239.

4 *Dingwall* v. *Duff* (1833) 12 S. 216.

5 Bankt. II, 6, 6; Ersk. II, 9, 57; Bell, *Comm.* I, 61; *Prin.* §1042, 1070; *Wardlaw* v. *W's Trs.* (1875) 2 R. 368; *Dick's Trs.* v. *Robertson* (1901) 3 F. 1021; cf. *Guild's Trs.* v. *G.* (1872) 10 M. 911; *Baillie's Trs.* v. *B.* (1891) 19 R. 220; *Nugent* v. *N's Trs.* (1899) 2 F. (H.L.) 21.

6 *Lamington* v. *Her Son* (1682) Mor. 8240; *D. Roxburghe* v. *Duchess*, 19 Jan. 1816, F.C.; *Dickson, supra.*

7 Ersk. II, 9, 42; Bell, *Prin.* §1048.

8 Ersk. II, 9, 64; Bell, *Prin.* §1047.

9 *Trotter* v. *Cunninghame* (1837) 2 D. 140; *Campbell* v. *C.* (1849) 11 D. 1426; *Blaikie* v. *Farquharson* (1849) 11 D. 1456.

10 Bell, *Prin.* §1049.

11 *Ewing* v. *E.* (1872) 10 M. 678; *Gibson* v. *Caddall's Trs.* (1895) 22 R. 889; contrast *Montgomerie Fleming's Trs.* v. *M.F.* (1901) 3 F. 591, where held that duplications of feuduties were to be treated as liferenter's income.

12 Ersk. II, 9, 61; Bell, *Prin.* §1061; *Anstruther* v. *A's Tutors* (1823) 2 S. 306; *Clark* v. *C.* (1871) 9 M. 435; *Rodger's Trs.* v. *F.* (1875) 2 R. 294; *Bayne's Trs.* v. *B.* (1895) 22 R. 26; *Cathcart's Trs.* v. *Allardice* (1899) 2 F. 326; *Johnstone* v. *Mackenzie's Trs.*, 1911 S.C. 321; *Smart's Trs.* v. *S's Trs.*, 1912 S.C. 87.

13 Ersk. II, 9, 60; Bell, *Prin.* §1062; *Scott* v. *Haliburton* (1823) 2 S. 435.

14 *Laird* v. *Fenwick* (1807) Mor. Liferenter, Appx. 4.

If the fiar does so, the liferenter must contribute in proportion to his interest; if the liferenter does so, the fiar must compensate him according to his interest, or the fee will be burdened with the capital cost, but not the interest, during the liferent.[1]

If there is danger that the liferenter will dilapidate the estate, he may be required to find caution that he will not do so.[2]

A liferenter is not bound to make improvements and if he does so they are presumed made for his own benefit.[3] Expenditure on additions or improvements is a burden on the fiar.[4]

He is not liable for the granter's debts, which attach to the fee, if sufficient to discharge them,[5] but is liable for interest on heritable bonds due from the land during the liferent.[6]

If the fiar has no other means of subsistence, the liferenter must aliment the fiar, but this burden does not transmit against his heirs[7] nor is it effectual against his creditors.[8]

Assignation of liferent

A proper liferent of heritage is not assignable and no person other than the named liferenter can be infeft in the liferent.[9] But a liferenter may assign the rents and profits arising from the liferent either outright or in security but for the duration of his liferent only, and the assignee has only a personal claim against the liferenter and cannot acquire a real right in the lands.[10]

Termination of liferent

On the expiry of the liferent, or last liferent, by death, or the event which limits the liferent, the estate falls automatically to the fiar.[11] If he has not already done so, he must complete title as fiar by recording the feu-contract or disposition in his favour, or expeding and recording a notice of title on the will or marriage-contract. A liferent may also be discharged or renounced by the liferenter.[12] It also comes to an end by consolidation with the fee, if liferent and fee come to be vested in the same person.[13]

1 Ersk. II, 9, 60; Bell, *Prin.* §1063; *Nelson* v. *Gordon* (1874) 1 R. 1097.
2 Ersk. II, 9, 59; Bell, *Prin.* §1064; *Ralston* v. *Leitch* (1803) Hume 293.
3 *Wallace* v. *Braid* (1900) 2 F. 754. 4 *Shaw's Trs.* v. *Bruce*, 1917 S.C. 169.
5 Bell, *Prin.* §1060; *Stewart* v. *S.* (1792) Bell Oct. Cas. 220.
6 *Forbes* v. *F.* (1765) 2 Pat. 84; see also *Fraser* v. *Croft* (1898) 25 R. 496; *Wallace* v. *Braid* (1900) 2 F. 754.
7 Ersk. II, 9, 62–3. 8 *Blair* v. *Scott's Trs.* (1737) Elch. Aliment 5; Bell, *Prin.* §1065.
9 Stair II, 6, 7; Ersk. II, 9, 41; *Ker's Trs.* v. *Justice* (1868) 6 M. 627, 631.
10 Stair, *supra*; Ersk. II, 9, 41, and 56; cf. *Chaplin's Trs.* v. *Hoile* (1890) 18 R. 26.
11 Ersk. II, 9, 64; Bell, *Prin.* §1066.
12 Ersk. II, 9, 68; Bell, *Prin.* §1066; *Pretty* v. *Newbigging* (1854) 16 D. 667; *Foulis* v. *F.* (1857) 19 D. 362; *Smith* v. *Campbell* (1873) 11 M. 639.
13 *Martin* v. *Bannatyne* (1861) 23 D. 705.

The liferenter's executors are entitled to any rents or other money which fell due before the liferenter's death, but had not been paid. The executors are entitled to rents due according to the legal terms, notwithstanding the conventional terms,[1] and to any crop sown by the liferenter before his death: *messis sementem sequitur*.[2] The profits of fishings, mines, and similar subjects accrue *de die in diem* and must be apportioned down to the date of death.[3] But natural fruits of the soil, such as woods, belong to the fiar.

Fiar's rights

The fiar has the reversionary right to enter into full possession and enjoyment of the lands on the termination of the liferent, and during its continuance the right to interfere, if necessary, to maintain the integrity of the estate, but not to present possession; hence he cannot remove tenants.[4] He may plant trees during the liferenter's possession and insist on their being protected.[5]

He is entitled to timber which falls or is felled on the estate, to normal thinnings, and to windfalls caused by exceptional storms,[6] but not timber necessary for the comfortable enjoyment of the liferenter's dwellinghouse[7] nor is he entitled to denude the estate of timber for ordinary requirements.[8] He may work minerals excepted from the liferent, subject to liability to the liferenter for surface damage, but must leave enough for the liferenter's use. Also he may not hurt the amenity of the liferenter's possession.[9]

1 Ersk. II, 9, 64.

2 Ersk. II, 9, 65; *Macmath* v. *Nisbet* (1621) Mor. 15877; *Guthrie* v. *Mackerston* (1671) Mor. 15891; *Cockburn* v. *Brown* (1748) Mor. 15911; *Keith* v. *Logie's Heirs* (1825) 4 S. 267.

3 Apportionment Act, 1870, S. 2; see also *Campbell* v. *C.* (1849) 11 D. 1426; *Tennent's Exor.* v. *Lawson* (1897) 35 S.L.R. 72; *Balfour's Exors.* v. *Inland Revenue*, 1909 S.C. 619.

4 *Buchanan* v. *Yuille* (1831) 8 S. 843.

5 *Ewing* v. *E.* (1881) 19 S.L.R. 20.

6 Craig II, 8, 17; Dirl. & St. 337; Stair II, 3, 74; Bankt. II, 6, 6; Ersk. II, 9, 58; Bell, *Comm.* I, 61; *Prin.* §1046, 1058; *Macalister's Trs.* v. *M.* (1851) 13 D. 1239.

7 *Fraser* v. *Middleton* (1794) Mor. 7849; *Dickson* v. *D.* (1823) 2 S. 152; *Tait* v. *Maitland* (1825) 4 S. 247.

8 *Stanfield* v. *Wilson* (1680) Mor. 8244.

9 Bell, *Prin.* §1070.

CHAPTER 83

TEINDS, CHURCH, MANSE, AND GLEBE

TEINDS or tithes are the proportion of the profit of lands due for the support and maintenance of the church and clergy.[1] In many cases before the Reformation grants of tithes were made to laymen, and they became secularized and temporal rights. At the Reformation church lands and teinds frequently were granted by the Crown as temporal lordships to laymen, sometimes known as titulars of the teinds or Lords of Erection, who presented ministers to charges, sometimes with the right to a stipend.

All former church lands were with certain exceptions annexed to the Crown in 1587[2] and subsequent erections were voided by statute of 1592.[3] In 1625 the Crown revoked all grants of church lands or of teinds made since 1587 and appointed commissions to value teinds and reach a settlement with the titulars. Differences were settled by the King as arbiter and his decrees-arbitral of 1629 was confirmed by statutes of 1663 and 1690.[4]

Teinds are therefore both an interest in land held by a landowner who has a title as titular of teinds, subject to the burden of providing stipend, and a burden on lands due by a heritor to the titular and providing a fund for affording a stipend to the parochial clergy. They were *debita fructuum*, not *debita fundi*, but are now a real burden on the lands.

Teinds might be drawn teinds, valued teinds or redeemed teinds. Drawn teinds, or teinds drawn in kind, were one-tenth of the annual produce of the lands, the balance being known as the stock. They might be parsonage teinds, due to the incumbent of the living, and due from grain raised by cultivation, or vicarage teinds, due to the vicar, deputed to serve the parish, and due from minor and accidental products, such as cattle, fish, fowls and eggs, and regulated by custom. By custom, they were payable in money, not kind. If there were no vicar, they also were due to the parson.[5]

[1] See generally Stair II, 2 and 8; Ersk. II, 10; Bell, *Prin.* §1146; Buchanan on *Teinds*; Connell on *Teinds and Parishes*; and *Galloway* v. *E. Minto*, 1920 S.C. 354, esp. L. Sands at pp. 358–82; affd. 1922 S.C. (H.L.) 24.

[2] Ersk. II, 10, 19.

[3] Ersk. II, 10, 23.

[4] Ersk. II, 10, 28.

[5] Ersk. II, 10, 13; Bell, *Prin.* §1151; *Scott* v. *Methven* (1851) 13 D. 991. Bishop's teinds were also recognized: *L.A.* v. *E. Galloway* (1873) 11 M. 896.

The heritor notified the titular to teind the former's crops by a certain day, failing which the heritor himself in presence of witnesses stacked the teind sheaves.

Frequently heritor and titular arranged for delivery by the former annually of a fixed number of bolls of corn. The Act 1633, c. 17, ended the practice of titulars drawing teinds, permitting heritors to lead in their own crop after the teind had been valued and the price paid or secured.

In valued teinds, the teinds were valued judicially by the Teinds Commission or latterly by the Court of Session as Commission of Teinds[1] on the basis of one-fifth of the clear rent.[2] This fixed the value for all time. Valued teind could then be surrendered to the minister in perpetuity, which limited the heritor's liability to the amount of his teinds.[3] Teinds in the hands of titulars or parsons were in 1633 made redeemable by heritors at stated rates of purchase.[4]

Increases in stipend, up to the limit of the free teind of the parish, might be obtained by a minister by a process of augmentation before the Court of Teinds. The minimum stipend was five chalders (80 bolls) of victual or 500 marks.[5] The value of a chalder was later fixed at £100 Scots.[6] An augmentation could not be brought before twenty years from the last augmentation. By the Teinds Act, 1808, stipends were to be awarded in grain or victual, unless where it appeared necessary to provide a money stipend, converted into money, according to the fiars prices of the county; the value of a chalder varied from year to year and county to county.

Standardization of stipend

By the Church of Scotland (Property and Endowments) Act, 1925, stipend is to be payable thereafter only in money at a standard value ascertained in manner fixed by the Act, and fixed at the first term of Martinmas at least six months after the benefice becomes vacant (S. 3), or at the election of a minister then in office (S. 4), or on notification by the General Trustees (S. 5). Standardized stipend is payable half-yearly in arrears to the General Trustees of the Church (S. 8). The minister or General Trustees might down to 1936 apply for augmentation of stipend

1 Court of Session (Sc.) Act, 1825, S. 54.
2 Acts, 1633, cc. 15 and 17; Bell, *Prin.* §1160.
3 *McEwan* v. *Watt*, 1922 S.C. 203.
4 See *Galloway* v. *E. Minto*, 1922 S.C. (H.L.) 24.
5 £27:15:6⅔ Stg.
6 £8:6:8 Stg.

(S. 10). The Clerk of Teinds has to prepare (S. 11) for every parish in Scotland a teind roll specifying the total teind of the parish, the amount applicable to each heritor, the value of the whole stipend payable to the minister and the proportion payable by each heritor.[1] The standard value of the stipend exigible from teinds, the 'standard charge', is made a real burden on the whole of the lands subject thereto, unless and until intimation of allocation is made by the General Trustees and a disponer of lands to the Clerk of Teinds, when it is allocated on the portions of the lands disponed (Ss. 12–13). Stipend of small amounts is compulsorily redeemed or extinguished (Ss. 14–15),[2] and surplus teinds may be sold (S. 18). Once the teind roll of a parish has been declared final the values entered are binding on titular and heritors.[3]

Church

The expense of maintaining and repairing the parish church formerly lay on the heritors or heritable proprietors of lands within the parish,[4] excluding titulars of teinds,[5] superiors,[6] liferenters,[7] and tenants.[8] Under the Church of Scotland (Property and Endowments) Act, 1925, Ss. 21–32, all property in all churches, with a few exceptions, is transferred to the Church of Scotland General Trustees and heritors are released from duties of maintenance and repair.

Manse

The minister of a landward or burghal-landward parish was entitled to have a manse provided, maintained, and repaired or rebuilt at the expense of the heritors,[9] but the minister of a burghal parish was not so entitled. He was entitled to have the manse garden walled,[10] to have a water supply[11] and an access

[1] cf. *Glasgow University Court* v. *Colmonell Common Agent*, 1933 S.C. 612.

[2] cf. *Ch. of Scotland General Trs.* v. *Downie*, 1946 S.C. 335.

[3] *Glasgow University Court* v. *Lord Advocate*, 1961 S.C. 246.

[4] Ersk. II, 10, 63; Bell, *Prin.* §1164; *Minister* v. *Heritors of Dunning* (1807) Mor. Kirk. Appx. 4.

[5] *Reid* v. *Commrs. of Woods* (1850) 12 D. 1215.

[6] *Dundas* v. *Nicolson* (1778) Mor. 8511; *Strathblane Heritors* v. *Glasgow Corpn.* (1899) 2 F. (H.L.) 25.

[7] *Lady Anstruther* v. *A.* (1823) 2 S. 306.

[8] *McLaren* v. *Clyde Trs.* (1868) 6 M. (H.L.) 81.

[9] Ersk. II, 10, 57; Bell, *Prin.* §1165; cf. *Elgin Mags.* v. *Gatherer* (1841) 4 D. 25; *Downie* v. *McLean* (1883) 11 R. 47.

[10] *Maxwell* v. *Langholm Presbytery* (1867) 5 S.L.R. 16.

[11] *E. Glasgow* v. *Murray* (1868) 7 M. 6; *Smith* v. *Prestonpans Heritors* (1903) 5 F. 333.

road.[1] He may let the manse furnished in the summer.[2] Under the Church of Scotland (Property and Endowments) Act, 1925, Ss. 21–32, the property in manses and the responsibility for the upkeep thereof was transferred to the Church of Scotland General Trustees. Under S. 40 any manse-maill payable in lieu of a manse had to be redeemed by the heritors.

Glebe

The minister of a country parish is entitled to a glebe of four acres of arable land, or sixteen soums of pasture land,[3] picked from church lands in a particular order. The minister may, without the heritors' consent, excamb the glebe lands,[4] and with the consent of the heritors and the Court of Teinds' authority,[5] feu the glebe. He is also entitled to grass for a horse and two cows from church grass lands, failing which to £20 Scots yearly.[6] The minister of a burghal parish is not entitled to a glebe nor to minister's grass.

The rights of ministers to glebe and grass have been preserved by the Church of Scotland (Property and Endowments) Act, 1925, but statutory procedure (S. 30) provides for implement of the heritors' obligations and transfer of the ownership of glebes to the General Trustees of the Church.

[1] *McPhail* v. *Kilbrandon Heritors*, 1914 S.C. 1015.

[2] *Aberdour Heritors* v. *Roddick* (1871) 10 M. 221; *I.R.C.* v. *Fry* (1895) 22 R. 422.

[3] Stair II, 3, 40; Ersk. II, 10, 59; Bell, *Prin.* §1172, 1176; *Macmillan* v. *Kintyre Presbytery* (1867) 6 M. 36; cf. *Arbroath Mags* v. *Presbytery of Arbroath* (1883) 10 R. 767; *Arbroath Heritors* v. *The Minister* (1883) 20 S.L.R. 781; *Alpine* v. *Dumbarton Heritors* (1907) 15 S.L.T. 489.

[4] *Bain* v. *Lady Seafield* (1887) 14 R. 939; *Dalhousie's Tutors* v. *Minister of Lochlee* (1891) 18 R. (H.L.) 72; *Cadell* v. *Allan* (1905) 7 F. 606; *McEwan's Trs.* v. *Ch. of Scotland General Trs.*, 1940 S.L.T. 357.

[5] Glebe Lands (Sc.) Act, 1886, S. 17; *Boyd* (1882) 19 S.L.R. 828; see also *Minister of Carriden* v. *Heritors*, 1910 S.C. 1131; *Minister of Wilton* v. *Heritors*, 1925 S.C. 372.

[6] cf. *Macmillan* v. *Kintyre Presbytery* (1867) 6 M. 36.

CHAPTER 84

REAL BURDENS AND GROUND ANNUALS

A PERSON seised of an estate in land may create *jura in re aliena* or interests over his land in favour of other persons, constituting burdens on his rights and limitations on his enjoyment of the lands. The recognized categories of burdens are real burdens and ground annuals, redeemable dispositions in security, servitudes, licences, and leases.

Real Burdens

A real burden is a debt payable from and attaching as a burden to lands themselves and not merely binding the owner personally. It is not a feudal estate in land but a burden qualifying the owner's real rights in the land.[1]

It may be created by reservation, as by disposition of lands to a grantee under burden of a money payment to the granter,[2] or by constitution, as by a disposition or bequest of lands under burden of a payment by the grantee to a third party.[3]

No *voces signatae* are necessary to create a real burden, so long as the intention is clearly to make the payment a real burden payable from the lands.[4] The burden must be clearly and precisely stated,[5] be included in the dispositive clause of the deed,[6] be declared to affect the lands,[7] and the sum[8] and the name of the creditor[9] must be clearly specified, and these elements must appear in the disponee's infeftment in the Register of Sasines.[10] A burden cannot be constituted by a general disposition

[1] Bell, *Prin.* §923.
[2] cf. *Davidson* v. *Dalziel* (1881) 8 R. 990; *Ewing's Trs.* v. *Crum Ewing*, 1923 S.C. 569.
[3] e.g. *Storeys* v. *Paxton* (1878) 6 R. 293.
[4] *Tailors of Aberdeen* v. *Coutts* (1840) 1 Rob. 296; *Arbroath Mags.* v. *Dickson* (1872) 10 M. 630; cf. *Davidson* v. *Dalziel* (1881) 8 R. 990; *Wilson's Trs.* v. *Brown's Exors.* (1907) 15 S.L.T. 747; *Buchanan* v. *Eaton*, 1911 S.C. (H.L.) 40.
[5] *Falconer Stewart* v. *Wilkie* (1892) 19 R. 630; *Ewing's Trs.* v. *Crum Ewing*, 1923 S.C. 569.
[6] Bell, *Prin.* §920; *Williamson* v. *Begg* (1887) 14 R. 720; *Cowie* v. *Muirden* (1893) 20 R. (H.L.) 81; *Scott* v. *S's Trs.* (1898) 6 S.L.T. 119; *Kemp* v. *Largs Mags.*, 1939 S.C. (H.L.) 6.
[7] *Tailors of Aberdeen* v. *Coutts* (1840) 1 Rob. App. 296; *Mackenzie* v. *Clark* (1903) 11 S.L.T. 428.
[8] *Tailors of Aberdeen, supra*; *Edmondstone* v. *Seton* (1888) 16 R. 1; *Anderson* v. *Dickie*, 1914 S.C. 706.
[9] *Stenhouse* v. *Innes & Black* (1765) Mor. 10264; *Erskine* v. *Wright* (1846) 8 D. 863.
[10] *Tailors of Aberdeen, supra*; *Mackenzie* v. *Clark* (1903) 11 S.L.T. 428.

of lands,[1] unless by expeding a notice of title on the debtor's lands, specifying the creditor, the burden and the writs imposing it.[2] An obligation *ad factum praestandum* can be made a real burden on lands.[3] A burden originally properly constituted may be continued by reference in later deeds to a recorded deed containing the burden, though reference will not suffice to constitute a burden.[4] An irritancy clause is not necessary nor will it make a burden real, but it may help to indicate the intention to make a burden real, and it provides a sanction against omission of the burden from later deeds. The creditor's title is completed by the disponee's infeftment.[5]

There may be added a personal obligation by the debtor but this will not transmit against any singular successor in the subjects unless he undertakes it,[6] as by agreement in a future disposition signed by the disponee.[7]

Enforcement

The real burden being *debitum fundi*, the creditor may in default of payment bring a personal action for payment, poind the ground, or attach the lands by adjudication, but not bring an action of maills and duties unless preceded by an adjudication, nor enter into possession unless there is an express clause to that effect or a power of sale implying that.[8] A power of sale may be expressly conferred on the creditor in a reserved burden.[9] The disponee is not personally bound by a real burden but a personal bond may be taken by the granter in favour of the creditor in addition. Apart from such personal obligation real burdens do not transmit against heirs who do not take up the subjects.[10] Any personal obligation is enforceable in the same way as a personal bond, and it may be transmitted against singular successors in the lands by an agreement *in gremio* of a subsequent conveyance.[11]

1 *Morrison's Trs.* v. *Webster* (1878) 5 R. 800; *Cowie's Trs.* v. *Cowie* (1891) 18 R. 706; *Cowie* v. *Muirden* (1893) 20 R. (H.L.) 81; *Scott* v. *S.* (1898) 6 S.L.T. 119.

2 Conveyancing (Sc.) Act, 1924, S. 4 and Sched. B1.

3 *Edmondstone, supra*; but see *Beckett* v. *Bisset*, 1921 2 S.L.T. 33.

4 *Allan* v. *Cameron's Trs.* (1780) 2 Pat. 572; *Wylie* v. *Allan* (1830) 8 S. 337; Titles to Land Consolidation (Sc.) Act, 1868, S. 10; Conveyancing (Sc.) Act, 1874, S. 32.

5 *Cowie's Trs.* v. *Muirden* (1893) 20 R. (H.L.) 81.

6 *Gardyne* v. *Royal Bank* (1853) 1 Macq. 358.

7 Conveyancing (Sc.) Act, 1874, S. 47; *Carrick* v. *Rodger, Watt & Paul* (1881) 9 R. 242; *Ritchie & Sturrock* v. *Dullater Feuing Co.* (1881) 9 R. 358. See also Conveyancing (Sc.) Act, 1924, S. 15.

8 Bell, *Comm.* I, 732; *Prin.* §922.

9 *Wilson* v. *Fraser* (1824) 2 Sh. App. 162.

10 *Macrae* v. *Mackenzie's Trs.* (1891) 19 R. 138.

11 1874 Act, S. 47; *Carrick, supra*; *Ritchie & Sturrock, supra.*

Succession

Real burdens are now moveable in the creditor's succession.[1] The creditor's executor completes title by recording a notice of title under the Conveyancing (Sc.) Act, 1924.

Assignation

The creditor may assign the benefit of the real burden and the assignee completes his title by recording the assignation in the Register of Sasines.[2] The creditor's heir completes his title to the burdens in the same way as to a bond and disposition in security.[3]

Extinction

The burden is extinguished in the same way as a bond and disposition in security, by executing and recording a discharge in the appropriate Register of Sasines,[4] but a less formal discharge may suffice.[5]

Contract of Ground Annual

A contract of ground annual, whereby a stipulated annual payment is due perpetually from lands, may be entered into instead of, or in addition to, a feu contract, but is found particularly where lands could not be subfeued (as in lands held burgage before 1874,[6] or lands held subject to a valid prohibition, imposed before 1874, against subinfeudation).[7] The right to the payment may be created by direct grant,[8] but normally by reservation, on lands being disponed by the creditor.

The contract, which must be probative, may be unilateral, disponing the lands in security of, and under the real burden of, the annual payment of a stated sum by way of ground annual, but is normally bilateral, containing a narrative clause, disposition by the granter of the lands, with description of the lands, reservation of the ground annual and declaration of it to be

[1] 1868 Act, S. 117; 1874 Act, S. 30; Succession (Sc.) Act, 1964, Sched. 3; cf. *Hughes' Trs.* v. *Corsane* (1890) 18 R. 299.

[2] Conveyancing Act, 1874, S. 30: formerly the assignation was intimated to the debtor, usually also recorded.

[3] Notice of title; Conveyancing (Sc.) Act, 1924, S. 4.

[4] 1924 Act, Sched. K.

[5] *Cameron* v. *Williamson* (1895) 22 R. 293.

[6] Conveyancing (Sc.) Act, 1874, S. 25; cf. *Arbroath Mags.* v. *Dickson* (1872) 10 M. 630.

[7] cf. Ross, *Lect.* II, 321; *Ch. of Sc. Endowment Cttee.* v. *Provident Assoc. of London*, 1914 S.C. 165, 172.

[8] Bell, *Prin.* §887, 908; *Ch. of Sc., supra.*

a real burden in the dispositive clause,[1] other burdens, such as an obligation to build,[2] possibly provision for its redemption, irritant and resolutive clauses and other clauses appropriate to a disposition, a clause binding the purchaser personally in payment of the ground annual and redisponing the lands in real security thereof to the creditor, a clause of common consent to registration for preservation and execution, and a testing clause. The amount of ground annual must be specific,[3] the creditor clearly ascertainable,[1] it must be clear that the burden is real,[4] and it must enter the Register of Sasines.[5] Registration completes the disponee's title to the lands and also the creditor's real right to the ground annual due from them. The disponee is personally bound independently of registration.[6] The creditor may also become infeft by registration under the disposition in security.

On the analogy of duplicands in feu contracts contracts of ground annual formerly sometimes stipulated for grassums or duplications periodically.[7] The Feudal Casualties (Sc.) Act, 1914, provides for the redemption or extinction of such payments as in the case of feudal casualties.

Notification to Land Commission

On the creation of a ground annual the grantee must notify the Land Commission as betterment levy may be payable.[8]

Incidence of liability

A contract of ground annual does not create a feudal relation between the granter and the disponee of the lands but merely an obligation to pay or act. The personal obligation of the disponee binds him and his successors in perpetuity, despite transfer of the lands,[9] and does not transmit to a singular successor in the lands.[10] The real burden does, however, transmit to singular successors and ceases to bind the disponee on his parting with the lands. Obligations *ad factum praestandum*, such as to build, unless

[1] Bell, *Prin.* §920; *Cowie* v. *Muirden* (1893) 20 R. (H.L.) 81.
[2] *Marshall's Trs.* v. *McNeill* (1888) 15 R. 762.
[3] *Stenhouse* v. *Innes & Black* (1765) Mor. 10264.
[4] *Arbroath Mags.* v. *Dickson* (1872) 10 M. 630.
[5] *McDonald* v. *Place* (1821) Hume 544.
[6] cf. *Inverness Mags.* v. *Bell's Trs.* (1827) 6 S. 160.
[7] e.g. *Murdoch* v. *Caledonian Ry.* (1906) 14 S.L.T. 527; *Murray* v. *Bruce*, 1917 S.C. 623.
[8] Land Commission Act, 1967, Ss. 27, 29, 37, and 100.
[9] *Millar* v. *Small* (1853) 1 Macq. 345; cf. *King's College* v. *Hay* (1854) 1 Macq. 526.
[10] *Gardyne* v. *Royal Bank* (1853) 1 Macq. 358.

made a real burden, do not transmit against singular successors[1] and to be validly made real burdens they must be clear and definite.[2]

A ground annual is postponed to any feuduty payable for the lands burdened, but is preferable to all charges on the lands created subsequently.

Creditor's remedies

The creditor in a ground annual is entitled to poind the ground,[3] or lead an adjudication; if infeft under the grantee's disposition in security, he may bring an action of maills and duties,[4] or utilize any of the other remedies open to a creditor in a bond and disposition in security. He has no power of sale unless by special stipulation.[5] The personal obligation justifies a personal action for payment against the original disponee or his representatives,[6] but this is discharged by the obligant obtaining his discharge in bankruptcy.[7]

If the contract contains a conventional irritancy, declarator may be sought that it has been incurred. If irritancy be declared it bars any claim for arrears due under the contract.[8] By statute[9] a legal irritancy, comparable to the irritancy *ob non solutum canonem* in feu-rights has been introduced, entitling the creditor to bring an action of adjudication against the proprietor of the lands for forfeiture of the lands and their adjudication to the creditor.

On the bankruptcy of the owners of the lands the creditor in a ground annual may by poinding of the ground recover one year's arrears of annual due and the current half-year's payment, in preference to the claims of the trustees in sequestration.[10]

No interest is due on a ground annual,[11] unless expressly provided for.

[1] *Marshall's Trs.* v. *Macneill* (1888) 15 R. 762; *Edmondstone* v. *Seton* (1888) 16 R. 1; contrast similar obligations in feu contract; cf. *Tweeddale's Trs.* v. *E. Haddington* (1880) 7 R. 625.

[2] *Tennant* v. *Napier Smith's Trs.* (1888) 15 R. 671; *Edmondstone* v. *Seton* (1888) 16 R. 1; cf. *Marshall's Trs.*, *supra.*

[3] Bell, *Prin.* §887; cf. *Bell's Trs.* v. *Copland* (1890) 23 R. 651.

[4] *Somerville* v. *Johnstone* (1899) 1 F. 726; see also Conveyancing (Sc.) Act, 1924, s. 23 (4).

[5] *Wilson* v. *Fraser* (1824) 2 Sh. App. 162.

[6] Subject to Conveyancing (Sc.) Act, 1874, S. 12.

[7] Bankruptcy (Sc.) Act, 1913, S. 137.

[8] *Wingate's Trs.* v. *W.* (1892) 29 S.L.R. 406.

[9] 1924 Act, S. 23(5).

[10] Bankruptcy (Sc.) Act, 1913, S. 114; *Bell's Trs.* v. *Copeland* (1896) 23 R. 650.

[11] Bell, *Prin.* §32; *Scott Moncrieff* v. *L. Dundas* (1835) 14 S. 61.

Allocation

Where lands subject to a ground annual are divided, each portion remains liable for the whole sum due, unless the creditor consents[1] or has agreed by a clause in the contract to be bound by any allocation made on division.

Redemption

Provision may be made for the debtor redeeming the annual payments for a lump sum.

Succession

Ground annuals were heritable in the creditor's succession till 1964[2] but are moveable since then,[3] and transmit in the debtor's succession with the lands.

Transfer

Right to a ground annual may be transferred by assignation,[4] completed before 1874 by intimation and since then[5] by assignation recorded in the Register of Sasines. Such an assignation has statutorily implied terms.[6]

Restriction

A ground annual may be restricted as regards any portion of the land out of which it is payable by a deed of restriction in statutory form[7] recorded in the appropriate register of Sasines.

Extinction and discharge

If the burden be omitted from the proprietor's title for the prescriptive period, the ground annual will be extinguished.[8] But a failure to repeat or refer to burdening clauses may be rectified by the proprietor granting and recording a deed of acknowledgement.[9] A ground annual is not extinguished *confusione*, by the creditor acquiring the burdened lands.[10] It may be renounced and

[1] *Thomson* v. *Scott* (1828) 6 S. 526.
[2] cf. *Campbell's Trs.* v. *L.N.E. Ry.*, 1930 S.C. 182.
[3] 1868 Act, Ss. 3, 117; 1874 Act, S. 30; Succession (Sc.) Act, 1964, Sched. 3.
[4] For form see Conveyancing (Sc.) Act, 1924, S. 23, and Sched. K.
[5] 1874 Act, S. 30, now 1924 Act, S. 23.
[6] 1924 Act, S. 23.
[7] 1924 Act, S. 23(3), 43, and Sched. K.
[8] Ersk. III, 4, 6; Bell, *Convg.* II, 1156; *King* v. *Johnston*, 1908 S.C. 684, 687.
[9] 1924 Act, S. 9(4) and Sched. E.
[10] *Murray* v. *Parlane's Trs.* (1890) 18 R. 287; *Healy and Young's Trs.* v. *Mair's Trs.*, 1914 S.C. 893. See also *King*, *supra*.

discharged and the land disburdened in whole or in part by a discharge form, recorded in the appropriate Register of Sasines.[1]

Statutory real burdens

The standard value of the stipend exigible from the teinds of any lands, if exceeding £1, is made a statutory real burden (called the standard charge) on the lands in favour of the Church of Scotland General Trustees preferable to all other securities or burdens not incidents of tenure.[2] It may be allocated on part of the lands when these are disponed.[3]

Statutory charging orders

Where an owner of a house has completed in respect of any house or building any works required to be executed by notice of a local authority he may, subject to certain conditions, obtain from the local authority a charging order burdening the house with an annuity to repay the amount at six per cent for thirty years. The charging order must be recorded in the Register of Sasines and has priority over all existing and future estates, interests, and incumbrances, except feuduties, teinds, ground annuals, stipends, and standard charges in lieu of stipends, and certain statutory charges. Such an annuity is recoverable in the same way as feuduty.[4]

Statutory charge over land

Where money is payable to an agricultural tenant in respect of compensation by his landlord and the latter has failed to pay it, the Secretary of State may, on the landlord's application, create a charge on the holding by a charging order, burdening the holding with an annuity to pay the sum due, and record it in the Register of Sasines.[5]

[1] 1924 Act, S. 23(2) and Sched. K.
[2] Church of Scotland (Property and Endowments) Act, 1925, S. 12.
[3] Ibid., S. 13.
[4] Housing (Sc.) Act, 1966, Ss. 28–30.
[5] Agricultural Holdings (Sc.) Act, 1949, S. 70.

CHAPTER 85

SECURITIES OVER HERITAGE

An owner of lands may use them to support his personal credit by granting redeemable rights in those lands to a lender in security for the repayment of the money borrowed. There are now two main classes of dispositions in security, the bond and disposition in security, which creates a real right qualifying the borrower's rights in the lands, and the ex facie absolute disposition in which the lender is nominally made owner of the lands.

Several modes of creating heritable securities are now obsolete, namely the wadset,[1] infeftment of annualrent,[2] and heritable bond.[3] The first of these has developed into the *ex facie* absolute disposition, and the last into the bond and disposition in security.

Agreement to grant security

The creation of a right in security over heritable property must be effected by agreement solemnly authenticated, holograph or adopted as holograph, followed by disposition of the security subject to the creditor in security, completed by his infeftment thereon. The essentials of the contract are agreement on the amount of the loan, its duration, the rate of interest thereon, the subjects to be conveyed in security, and any special conditions which may be agreed. Statute and common law imply numerous other terms into the contract. *Rei interventus* in the shape of actually lending the money may validate an improbative agreement to borrow and to give security over land. The contract to dispone lands in security by itself confers only a personal right and no real security until the disposition in security has been completed.[4] This must be done while the debtor is solvent, and will be reducible if the disposition is made within 60 days before the debtor's bankruptcy,[5] but not if the creditor has merely delayed formally completing his right till within that time.[6]

1 Stair II, 10; Ersk. II, 8; Bell, *Prin.* §901–7.

2 Stair II, 5; Ersk. II, 8, 31; Bell, *Prin.* §908.

3 Ersk. II, 2, 13; Bell, *Prin.* §909.

4 cf. *Arbroath Mags.* v. *Dickson* (1872) 10 M. 630; *Ch. of Sc. Endowment Cttee.* v. *Provident Assocn.*, 1914 S.C. 165.

5 Bell, *Comm.* II, 211; *Rose* v. *Falconer* (1868) 6 M. 960; *Stiven* v. *Scott & Simson* (1871) 9 M. 923; *Gourlay* v. *Hodge* (1875) 2 R. 738; *Jones' Trs.* v. *Allan* (1901) 4 F. 374.

6 *Guild* v. *Young* (1884) 22 S.L.R. 520; *Sc. Provident Instn.* v. *Cohen* (1888) 17 R. 112.

The validity of the prospective debtor's title to the lands proposed to be disponed in security requires careful consideration[1] and also his power to borrow and grant a disposition in security.[2] Trustees have power to borrow on the security of heritable trust estate.[3]

BOND AND DISPOSITION IN SECURITY

The commonest form of grant of a right in security is by a bond and disposition in security. The owner of the lands grants a probative deed narrating his having borrowed a stated sum of money from the creditor, which he bind himself and his executors to repay, with a fifth part more of liquidate penalty in case of failure, and interest at a stated rate,[4] and dispones designated lands to the creditor, heritably but redeemably, in security of the personal obligation to repay, reserving power of redemption but granting the creditor power of sale on default in payment.[5] The disposition in security of lands carries also pertinents and fixtures.[6] The creditor must be clearly identified, and the sum repayable definite in amount.[7] Notwithstanding this, it is competent to create a security for an obligation *ad factum praestandum*, certainly if performable by expenditure of money.[8]

The provision for a fifth part more of liquidate penalty covers only the expenses to which the bondholder is put in recovery of his debt[9] or the expenses of defending the creditor's preference against a third party.[10]

The bond must be precise as to the rate of interest and starting date if there is to be any security for the interest.[11] It is competent

[1] A granter of a bond and disposition in security must be, or become, himself infeft in the lands since his title thereto may not be deduced in the bond itself under the 1924 Act, S. 3.

[2] cf. *Paterson's Trs.* v. *Liqdr. of Caledonian Heritable Security Co.* (1885) 13 R. 369.

[3] Trusts (Sc.) Act, 1921, S. 4(d).

[4] Down to this point the deed is in the same form as a personal bond undertaking repayment of debt: see Ch. 53, *supra*.

[5] For statutory form see Titles to Land Consolidation (Sc.) Act, 1868, S. 116 and Sched. FF. See also *Cumming* v. *Stewart*, 1928 S.C. 296.

[6] *Yuille* v. *Rushbury* (1888) 15 R. 828; *Howie's Trs.* v. *McLay* (1902) 5 F. 214; *Edinburgh & Leith Gas Commrs.* v. *Smart*, 1918 1 S.L.T. 80; *Richardson's Trs.* v. *Ballachulish Slate Quarries Co.*, 1918 1 S.L.T. 413; see also *Traill's Trs.* v. *Free Church of Scotland*, 1915 S.C. 655.

[7] *Smith Sligo* v. *Dunlop* (1885) 12 R. 907; cf. *Edmonstone* v. *Seton* (1888) 16 R. 1.

[8] *Edmonstone* v. *Seton* (1888) 16 R. 1.

[9] Bell, *Convg.* I, 255; *Allan* v. *Young* (1757) Mor. 10047; *Bruce* v. *Scottish Amicable Life Assce. Socy.*, 1907 S.C. 637; *Mitchell* v. *Allardyce*, 1915 2 S.L.T. 398.

[10] *Orr* v. *Mackenzie* (1839) 1 D. 1046.

[11] *Forbes* v. *Welsh and Forbes* (1894) 21 R. 630; *Alston* v. *Nellfield Co.*, 1915 S.C. 912.

to provide that a lower rate of interest will be accepted if interest is paid punctually, but such a provision is strictly applied.[1] The loan must be made at or before the time of delivery of the bond to the creditor or of his taking infeftment on it, because securities for future debts are null so far as contracted after the infeftment,[2] though this does not apply where the lender was under an absolute obligation to make the advance, though it was not in fact made till after infeftment,[3] nor where the creditor insisted on having infeftment completed before paying the money lent.[4]

The disposition in security contains a description of the lands and their burdens and conditions, such as is required for an absolute disposition, either particularly or by reference. If the security subjects are capable of being feued, power to feu may be reserved to the granter, but must be exercised subject to any conditions affecting the reservation.[5] It is not necessary to repeat or refer to conditions or irritant or resolutive clauses affecting the lands in a deed creating or transmitting a heritable security.[6]

The clause of assignation of rents imports[7] an assignation to the creditor of the rents and other duties (including feuduties and casualties in the case of a superiority, and ground annuals and grassums in the case of a ground annual) payable after the date from which interest is to run, power to the creditor to insure buildings against fire and to recover the premiums from the debtor, on default in payment[8] of interest or principal or on the proprietor's notour bankruptcy or his granting a trust deed for creditors to enter into possession and uplift the rents and other duties, to insure against loss by breakage of glass and claims by tenants and third parties and against such other risks as a prudent proprietor would reasonably insure against, and to make all necessary renewals and repairs on the property, subject to accounting to the debtor for any balance of rents or sums received beyond what is necessary for payment of the principal, interest, and penalty and all expenses incurred in reference to possession, including expenses of factorage, management, insurance, renewals, and repair. The assignation of rents is completed by the

[1] *Alston, supra*; *Gatty* v. *Maclaine*, 1921 S.C. (H.L.) 1; cf. *Don's Trs.* v. *Cameron* (1885) 22 S.L.R. 348.

[2] Bankruptcy Act, 1696, c. 5; *Black* v. *Curror & Cowper* (1885) 12 R. 990; cf. *Bell's Tr.* v. *B.* (1884) 12 R. 85.

[3] *Dempster* v. *Kinloch* (1750) 2 Ross L.C. 632.

[4] *Dunbar* v. *Abercromby* (1789) 2 Ross L.C. 638.

[5] *Cumming* v. *Stewart*, 1928 S.C. 296.

[6] Conveyancing (Sc.) Act, 1924, S. 9.

[7] Conveyancing (Sc.) Act, 1924, S. 25(1)(a).

[8] *McAra* v. *Anderson*, 1913 S.C. 931; *Graham's Tr.* v. *Dow's Tr.*, 1917 2 S.L.T. 154; *Gibson* v. *Mair*, 1918 S.C. 353.

recording of the bond and there is no need to intimate to the tenants, and it is preferable to a mere assignation or arrestment even though intimated or used before infeftment is taken by recording the bond.[1] Tenants must continue to pay their rents to the proprietor until interpelled by the bondholder.

The clause of assignation of writs imports[2] an assignation of writs and evidents with power to the creditor, in the event of sale, subject to the rights of any person holding prior rights to possession of such writs and evidents, to deliver them to the purchaser and to assign to the purchaser any right to have the writs and evidents made forthcoming.[3]

The warrandice clause in statutory form imports absolute warrandice as regards the lands and the title deeds thereof and warrandice from fact and deed as regards the rents.[4]

The clause reserving right of redemption imports[5] a right to redeem the security in manner prescribed by the Act.

The expenses clause imports that any deed necessarily granted by the creditor on the debtor making payment and redeeming his lands shall be at the debtor's expense,[6] and that the debtor is to be liable for the whole expenses of preparing, executing and recording the bond, and all reasonable expenses incurred by the creditor in calling it up, realizing or attempting to realize the security subjects, and exercising the other powers conferred on him.[7]

Position of Bondholder

The bondholder completes his title to the security subjects by recording the bond in the Register of Sasines or, particularly where the bond is embodied in a deed for other purposes, recording a notice of title to the bond.[8] If the granter is a company it must also effect registration in the Register of Charges kept by the Registrar of Companies.[9] The creditor does not normally take

[1] Bell, *Convg.* I, 641; see also *Stevenson* v. *Dawson* (1896) 23 R. 496.

[2] 1924 Act, S. 25(1)(b).

[3] As to the creditor's right to have delivery of the titles to the property see Bell, *Prin.* §914; *Tawse* v. *Rigg* (1904) 6 F. 544, 546; *Boyd* v. *Turnbull & Findlay*, 1911 S.C. 1006, 1010. The creditor cannot retain the titles against the debtor save in security of the debt, but cannot be compelled to redeliver them until his debt has been repaid: *Boyd* v. *Turnbull & Findlay*, *supra*. See also 1924 Act, S. 27.

[4] 1868 Act, S. 119.

[5] 1924 Act, S. 25(1)(c).

[6] 1868 Act, S. 119.

[7] 1924 Act, S. 25(2).

[8] 1868 Act, S. 17; 1924 Act, S. 3.

[9] Companies Act, 1948, Ss. 95 and 106A (added by Companies (Floating Charges) (Sc.) Act, 1961, S. 6).

possession of nor manage the property. Unless he does so he does not become feudal vassal nor become liable for feuduty.

He cannot act to the prejudice of the debtor and forfeits the right to recovery of the debt if he renders himself unable to restore the debtor on repayment to his position when the bond was granted.[1] The Court might interfere, at the instance of the debtor or his other creditors, to prevent an unfair use by the bondholder of his power of sale.[2]

He may enter into possession with the debtor's consent, or in pursuance of any action of maills and duties, and may eject summarily a debtor in personal occupation.[3] A creditor in possession may let the security subjects or part of them for not longer than 7 years, but may with the sheriff's authority grant leases for up to 21 years, or in the case of minerals, 31 years.[4] A creditor in possession has power[5] to make all necessary repairs and charge the cost of management, insurance and repairs to the sum due by the debtor. A creditor in possession is liable for feuduties,[6] and rates,[7] and subject to an occupier's liability to visitors.[8]

Position of debtor

The debtor remains heritable proprietor and while in possession can do all ordinary administration but may not prejudice the creditor's security by contracts outwith ordinary management, without the creditor's consent; such contracts are not enforceable by or against the creditor.[9] Thus the creditor may have set aside leases of unusual length granted by the debtor or granted on unduly favourable terms.[10]

1 *N. Albion Property Inv. Co.* v. *McBean's C.B.* (1893) 21 R. 90; *Mackirdy* v. *Webster's Trs.* (1895) 22 R. 340.

2 *Beveridge* v. *Wilson* (1829) 7 S. 279; *Bell* v. *Gordon* (1838) 16 S. 657.

3 Heritable Securities (Sc.) Act, 1894, S. 5; altering rules stated in *Wylie* v. *Her. Sec. Inv. Assoc.* (1871) 10 M. 253; *Sc. Prop. Inv. Co. Bldg. Soc.* v. *Horne* (1881) 8 R. 737; and *Smith's Trs.* v. *Chalmers* (1890) 17 R. 1088. This power does not give the creditor all the powers of a landlord against a tenant, and he may not demand caution for violent profits: *Inglis's Trs.* v. *Macpherson*, 1910 S.C. 46. This remedy is incompetent against a liferenter by constitution: *Sc. Union and National Ins. Co.* v. *Smeaton* (1904) 7 F. 174.

4 Heritable Securities (Sc.) Act, 1894, Ss. 6, 7.

5 1868 Act, S. 119; *Sc. Amicable Herit. Sec. Assocn.* v. *N. Assce. Co.* (1883) 11 R. 287; *Glasgow Provident Inv. Soc.* v. *Westminster Fire Office* (1888) 15 R. (H.L.) 89.

6 *City of Glasgow Bank Liqr.* v. *Nicolson's Trs.* (1882) 9 R. 689.

7 *Greenock Police Board* v. *Greenock Property Inv. Co. Liqr.* (1885) 12 R. 832; *N.B. Property Inv. Co.* v. *Paterson* (1888) 15 R. 885.

8 *Baillie* v. *Shearer's J.F.* (1894) 21 R. 498.

9 *Heron* v. *Martin* (1893) 20 R. 1001; *Morier* v. *Brownlie & Watson* (1895) 23 R. 67; *Smith* v. *Soeder* (1895) 23 R. 60.

10 *Mitchell* v. *Little* (1820) Hume 661; *Reid* v. *McGill*, 1912 2 S.L.T. 246.

He may sell the lands, but only under burden of the bond, and does not, by so doing, escape liability under his personal obligations to repay. He may, with the creditor's consent, feu parts of the lands.[1] A feu without consent or restriction of the right in security is reducible at the instance of a purchaser from the bond holder if the latter has exercised his power of sale.[2] Until the creditor intimates the assignation of rents to the tenants, they are entitled to pay them to the debtor as landlord.[3]

By the recording of the bond the creditor obtains a right preferable to personal creditors of the debtor,[4] but if the creditor has not taken possession he has no preference over the rents against factors collecting them and given the right by the debtor to retain the rents in satisfaction of their claims.[5]

Assignation

A bond may be assigned in whole or in part by the creditor,[6] and when recorded on behalf of the assignee in the Register of Sasines, the assignation constitutes the assignee creditor in the obligation.[7] An unconditional agreement to take an assignation of a bond is binding though the bond be found to be defective.[8] A creditor is not bound to grant an assignation so long as the debtor's objections to the creditor's claim for interest are outstanding.[9] A debtor who has sold the security subjects under burden of the bond is entitled, if the creditor calls on him to pay under the personal obligation, to have the bond assigned to him.[10] A creditor who is being repaid cannot be compelled to grant an assignation if his rights would be in any way prejudiced.[11] An assignation need contain no description of or reference to the property,[12] nor any reference to burdens or conditions of title.[13]

[1] *Sones* v. *Mill* (1903) 11 S.L.T. 98.
[2] *Cumming* v. *Stewart*, 1927 S.C. 296.
[3] *Forsyth* v. *Aird* (1853) 16 D. 197; *Bridge* v. *Brown's Trs.* (1872) 10 M. 958; *Stevenson, Lauder & Gilchrist* v. *Dawson* (1896) 23 R. 496.
[4] *Neils* v. *Lyle* (1863) 2 M. 168.
[5] *Stevenson, Lauder & Gilchrist* v. *Dawson* (1896) 23 R. 496.
[6] Form in 1924 Act, Sched. K, No. 1, superseding 1868 Act, S. 124 and Sch. GG.
[7] 1924 Act, S. 28.
[8] *Forbes* v. *Welsh & Forbes* (1894) 21 R. 630; cf. *Bennie's Trs.* v. *Couper* (1890) 17 R. 782.
[9] *Bruce* v. *Scottish Amicable Life Assurance Socy.*, 1907 S.C. 637.
[10] *North Albion Property Inv. Co.* v. *MacBean's C.B.* (1893) 21 R. 90; *Mackirdy* v. *Webster's Trs.* (1895) 22 R. 340.
[11] *Guthrie & McConnachy* v. *Smith* (1880) 8 R. 107; *Fleming* v. *Black*, 1913 1 S.L.T. 386.
[12] 1924 Act, S. 31.
[13] 1924 Act, S. 9.

An assignation contains no express warrandice but warrandice *debitum subesse* is implied.[1]

A bond may also be assigned by a general disposition of the creditor's property, title being completed by notice of title.

An assignee may retain a bond in security of other debts due to him by the assignor even though repaid the sum for which he obtained the assignation.[2]

Creditor's succession to bond

Until 1868 securities over heritage were heritable in the creditor's succession. By S. 117 of the 1868 Act, such securities were to be moveable in succession, unless (a) executors were expressly excluded from the destination,[3] and in relation (b) to claims by the fisc and (c) to legal rights of spouses and of children. Executors might also be excluded by a minute recorded in the Register of Sasines,[4] and the exclusion of executors removed also by minute[5] or by assigning, bequeathing or conveying the security to himself or any other person without expressing or repeating such exclusion.[6] By the Succession (Sc.) Act, 1964, S. 34, even if executors are excluded bonds are moveable in succession, but remain heritable quoad fiscum and as regards a child's claim to legitim.[7]

Completion of title

Persons who come in right of bonds on the creditor's death complete title by recording a notice of title to the bond,[8] but may assign, restrict, discharge, or otherwise deal with the security without completing title thereto, by deducing title in the assignation or other deed from the last recorded title to the bond, specifying the unrecorded writs connecting them with that title.[9] The methods competent under earlier Acts are still competent.[10]

1 *Leith Heritages Co.* v. *Edinburgh & Leith Glass Co.* (1876) 3 R. 789; *Reid* v. *Barclay* (1879) 6 R. 1007.

2 *Colquhoun's Trs.* v. *Diack* (1901) 4 F. 358.

3 Such exclusion had to be maintained by repetition in subsequent assignations if it was to remain effective.

4 1868 Act, Sched. DD.

5 1868 Act, Sched. EE.

6 1868 Act, S. 117.

7 Legal rights of spouses in heritage were abolished by the 1964 Act.

8 1924 Act, S. 4(3). It proceeds on production of the last recorded title to the security, any deeds giving the deceased title thereto, and the deceased's will or confirmation.

9 1924 Act, S. 3.

10 Testate succession: bond heritable–notarial instrument: 1868 Act, S. 126, Sched. JJ; bond moveable—writ of acknowledgment, 1868 Act, S. 125, Sched. II; 1874 Act, S. 63; or notarial instrument. Intestate succession: bond heritable—writ of acknowledgement,

Debtor's succession

Liability under a bond transmits heritably even if the bond is recorded after the debtor's death. If the heritage disponed in security was insufficient to meet the debt, the debtor's other heritage was liable for the balance.[1] If several properties were subject to one security, the debt was apportioned among the heirs in proportion to the values of their properties, after deduction of preferable burdens.[2] If property subject to a bond was specifically bequeathed, the legatee took it subject to the burden, notwithstanding a direction to the trustees to pay all debts.[3] In no case, however, was an heir liable beyond the value of the heritage to which he succeeded.[4] In a question with the creditor, however, both the deceased's heritable and his moveable estate were liable for payment of the debt, and the creditor could sue his heirs or his executors but if the executor paid he had a right of relief against the heir to the heritage burdened with the bond.

In the case of deaths after 10 September, 1964, the deceased's whole estate vests in his executor[5] and the executor is liable to the creditor, save that any rules whereby any particular debt of a deceased fell to be paid out of any particular part of his estate remain unaltered.[6] The executor, as a bare administrator of the estate, is not liable beyond the amount of estate falling under his control.

At common law a successor to the debtor was not personally liable under the personal obligation in the bond, unless he granted a bond of corroboration. By the Conveyancing (Sc.) Act, 1874, S. 47, a heritable security and the personal obligation transmit against any person taking the security subjects[7] by succession, gift or bequest,[8] or by conveyance where an agreement to this effect

or notarial instrument: 1868 Act, S. 126, Sched. JJ; or special service; bond moveable—notarial instrument. Writs of acknowledgment have been abolished in the case of creditors' deaths after 10 Sept. 1964: Succession (Sc.) Act, 1964, Sched. 3.

[1] *Douglas' Trs.* v. *D.* (1868) 6 M. 223; *Duncan* (1883) 10 R. 1042; *Bell's Trs.* v. *B.* (1884) 12 R. 85.

[2] *Ferrier* v. *Cowan* (1896) 23 R. 703.

[3] *Brand* v. *Scott's Trs.* (1892) 19 R. 768; *Muir's Trs.* v. *M.*, 1916 1 S.L.T. 372; *Ballantyne's Trs.* v. *B's Trs.*, 1940 S.C. 35.

[4] 1874 Act, S. 12, repealed by Succession (Sc.) Act, 1964, Sched. 3.

[5] Succession (Sc.) Act, 1964, S. 14.

[6] Hence the principles of the cases of *Douglas, Duncan, Bell, Ferrier, Brand, Muir's Trs.*, and *Ballantyne's Trs.* still apply.

[7] *Lamb* v. *Field* (1889) 27 S.L.R. 242; *Fenton Livingstone* v. *Crichton's Trs.*, 1908 S.C. 1208. Not against the debtor's trustees: *Macrae* v. *Gregory* (1903) 11 S.L.T. 102.

[8] e.g. *Welch's Exors.* v. *Edinburgh Life Assce. Co.* (1896) 23 R. 772, where held legatee's liability limited to the value of the estate inherited.

appears *in gremio* of the conveyance.[1] By the Conveyancing (Sc.) Act, 1924, S. 15, the personal obligation transmits in terms of the 1874 Act, S. 47, only if the conveyance is signed by the new proprietor and summary diligence is not competent under S. 47 against any obligant taking by succession, gift or bequest unless there is an agreement to the transmission signed by such obligant.[2]

The seller of lands burdened with a bond remains personally liable unless discharged by the creditor, though he may have a right of relief against a purchaser if the latter has undertaken to do so. There may consequently be several successive proprietors all personally bound.[3] Where the seller of bonded lands took the disponee bound to relieve him of the personal obligation, this obligation of relief was held not to transmit against a subsequent disponee under S. 47,[4] but where the seller did so and became bankrupt and his trustee assigned the obligation of relief to the creditor in the bond, the obligation was held to avail the creditor to recover from the purchaser the whole balance due under the bond.[5]

Creditor's remedies

So long as the debtor who granted the bond lives he is personally liable for repayment, and may be sued personally, even if he has disposed of the security subjects. In the normal form of bond he binds himself, his heirs, executors and representatives whomsoever, without the necessity of discussing them in their order, and the creditor may accordingly claim from heirs in moveables[6] or in heritage[7] or both,[8] though *inter heredes* debts heritably secured are payable by heirs in heritage.[9]

If, as is normal, the granter has consented to registration for execution, the creditor may record the bond and do summary diligence; this remedy may be exercised concurrently with notice calling up the bond, as a preliminary to sale.[10] The creditor may, if the proprietor defaults in payment of principal or interest, becomes notour bankrupt, or grants a trust deed for creditors,

[1] See also *Carrick* v. *Rodger, Watt & Paul* (1881) 9 R. 242; *Ritchie & Sturrock* v. *Dullater Feuing Co.* (1881) 9 R. 358; *Wright's Trs.* v. *McLaren* (1891) 18 R. 841.

[2] Form in 1924 Act, Sched. A, Form 2.

[3] *Glasgow Univ.* v. *Yuill's Tr.* (1882) 9 R. 643.

[4] *Sherry* v. *S's Trs.*, 1918 1 S.L.T. 31.

[5] *Caledonian Heritable Secy. Co.* v. *Stewart* (1889) 27 S.L.R. 690.

[6] *Carnegie* v. *Knowes* (1627) Mor. 3564.

[7] *B.L. Co.* v. *L. Reay* (1850) 12 D. 949.

[8] Bell, *Convg.* I, 251.

[9] *Bell's Tr.*, *supra.*

[10] *McWhirter* v. *McCulloch's Trs.* (1887) 14 R. 918; *McNab* v. *Clarke* (1889) 16 R. 610.

enter into possession of the security subjects,[1] by consent or by bringing an action of maills and duties against the proprietor,[2] and give notice of the raising thereof to the tenants, which notice interpels the tenants from paying rent to the proprietor. Intimation of decree in the action being made to the tenants has the effect of a decree for the rents and a charge thereon, and payment to the creditor is a complete discharge to the tenants. Decree also gives the creditor a title to collect the rents[3] and to use landlord's sequestration if necessary to recover them.[4] Tenants can set off against rents claims against the proprietor arising out of the tenancy only.[5] A creditor who enters into possession becomes liable for feuduty,[6] rates,[7] and may be liable as occupier to the public.[8] A bondholder who takes possession is entitled to delivery of leases and other estate documents[9] and may grant leases.[10]

Whether or not he has entered into possession, the creditor may, by poinding the ground, attach moveables on the ground belonging to the proprietor,[11] or to tenants but only to the extent of rents due and unpaid.[12] But unless carried through by sale of poinded effects sixty days before the proprietor's sequestration it is not available against his trustee in bankruptcy except to the extent of the current half-year's interest and one year's arrears.[13]

A creditor may, after obtaining decree of poinding the ground, attach the security subjects by adjudication,[14] and, under the debtor's personal obligation in the bond, may also attach the debtor's whole heritable estate by adjudication.[14] But adjudication in the latter case only falls within the Diligence Act, 1661, whereby adjudications in security for debt led within a year and a

1 Conveyancing (Sc.) Act, 1924, S. 25(1).
2 Heritable Securities Act, 1894, Ss. 3–7.
3 *Forsyth* v. *Aird* (1853) 16 D. 197; *Chamber's J.F.* v. *Vertue* (1893) 20 R. 257.
4 *Robertson's Trs.* v. *Gardner* (1889) 16 R. 705.
5 *Chamber's J.F.* v. *Vertue* (1893) 20 R. 257; *Marshall's Trs.* v. *Banks*, 1934 S.C. 405.
6 *City of Glasgow Bank Liqdrs.* v. *Nicholson's Trs.* (1882) 9 R. 689.
7 *Greenock Police Board* v. *Liqdr. of Greenock Property Inv. Socy.* (1885) 12 R. 832; but see now Valuation and Rating (Sc.) Act, 1956.
8 *Baillie* v. *Shearer's J.F.* (1894) 21 R. 498.
9 *Macrae* v. *Leith*, 1913 S.C. 901.
10 *Mackenzie* v. *Imlay's Trs.*, 1912 S.C. 685.
11 *N. Albion Property Inv. Co.* v. *McBean's Curator* (1893) 21 R. 90; *Mackirdy* v. *Webster's Trs.* (1895) 22 R. 340.
12 *Brown* v. *Scott* (1859) 22 D. 273.
13 Bankruptcy (Sc.) Act, 1913, S. 114.
14 Ersk. II, 8, 37; Bell, *Comm.* I, 753.

day of that first made effectual rank *pari passu*, and is postponed to sequestration unless completed for a year and a day.[1]

A creditor may also use inhibition against the debtor.[2]

Exercise of creditor's power of sale

The statutory form of bond grants the creditor power of sale on the debtor's default in payment. If the debtor fails to pay the sums due under the personal obligation within three months of a demand for payment made to him in statutory form the creditor may without further intimation or process sell the lands by public roup at Edinburgh or Glasgow or the head burgh of the county in which the main part of the lands are situated or the nearest burgh.[3] Demand once validly made need not be repeated though sale be delayed,[4] but notice ceases to be effective after five years if no exposure to sale has followed, or five years after the date of the last exposure.[5] The debtor may dispense with the whole or part of the period of notice.[6] On expiry of the notice without payment the creditor must advertise the sale.

Advertisement, specifying the property and stating the time and place of sale and upset price, must be made once weekly for at least six weeks (four weeks if the upset price does not exceed £1000) after the expiry of the three months' warning period[7] in a newspaper[8] published in Edinburgh or Glasgow and, save for lands in Midlothian or Lanarkshire, in one published in the county where the lands are situated, failing which in one published in the next county. Alternative provisions as to advertising apply where the upset price does not exceed £1000.[9] Similar provisions apply to advertisement of re-exposure.

Exposure for sale must be not less than 42 days (28 days if less than £1000) from the first insertion of the advertisement, in

1 Gloag and Irvine, *Rights in Security*, 109.

2 *Clarke* v. *McNab* (1888) 15 R. 569.

3 1924 Act, S. 33 and Sched. M. See also *Stuart's Tr.* v. *S.* (1904) 12 S.L.T. 356. Intimation to other security holders over the same subjects is also advisable: *Stewart* v. *Brown* (1882) 10 R. 192; *Leach* v. *Johnstone* (1886) 24 S.L.R. 78. As to cases where the debtor is dead and his heir cannot be found, or his address is unknown, or the address of the person entitled to intimation cannot be ascertained, see Heritable Securities Act, 1894, S. 16.

4 *Howard & Wyndham* v. *Richmond's Trs.* (1890) 17 R. 990.

5 1924 Act, S. 33.

6 1924 Act, S. 35.

7 *Ferguson* v. *Rodger* (1895) 22 R. 643; see also *Glas* v. *Stewart* (1830) 8 S. 843; *Hope* v. *Moncreiff* (1833) 11 S. 324; *Melville and Dundas* (1854) 16 D. 419.

8 A mere advertising paper suffices: *E. Rosslyn* (1830) 8 S. 964; *Dickson* v. *Dumfries Mags.* (1831) 9 S. 282. See also *Walter's Tr.* v. *O'Mara* (1902) 9 S.L.T. 395.

9 1924 Act, Ss. 36–8.

Edinburgh or Glasgow or any burgh in the county where the land lies or nearest to the chief part of it. The sale is invalid if the due time has not elapsed.[1] The lands may be exposed as a whole or in lots, and the creditor may apportion the feuduty or other burdens but not so as to prejudice the rights of any third party.[2]

The selling creditor and the debtor[3] may not bid, but one of several joint creditors selling may bid[4] and a postponed bondholder may also do so.[5]

In selling the creditor acts in a fiduciary capacity for the owner and any postponed bondholders and he must not do anything prejudicial to a sale at the best obtainable price.[6] The proprietor of part of the security subjects not sold may challenge the validity of the sale of the part sold on the ground of inadequacy of price.[7]

On receipt of the price the creditor must count and reckon therefor with the debtor and any postponed creditors and consign any surplus after deduction of the debt secured, with interest, penalties and expenses, and after paying all previous incumbrances and the expenses of discharging them, in bank in the joint names of the seller and purchaser for behalf of the parties having best rights thereto, the bank being named in the articles of roup.[8]

The debtor or a postponed bondholder may be barred from challenging irregularities in the procedure if he knew of them and delayed unreasonably to object.[9]

Protection of purchaser

The bondholder may grant the purchaser a disposition of the lands in the usual form.[10] A sale by a bondholder under the 1924 Act, Ss. 32 to 40, is to be valid and effectual though any person to whom notice requires to be given may be in pupillarity or minority or subject to legal incapacity. Any sale and disposition in implement thereof is to be as valid to the purchaser as if made by a proprietor of land and shall import an assignation to the purchaser of the warrandice contained or implied in the bond and also an obligation by the debtor to ratify, approve, and confirm the sale and disposition.

1 *Ferguson* v. *Rodger* (1895) 22 R. 643; see also *Roscoe* v. *Mackersy* (1905) 7 F. 761.
2 1924 Act, S. 40.
3 *Jamieson* v. *Edinburgh Mutual Inv. & Bldg. Soc.*, 1913 2 S.L.T. 52.
4 *Wright* v. *Buchanan*, 1917 S.C. 73.
5 *Scottish Imperial Ins. Co.* v. *Lamond* (1883) 21 S.L.R. 98.
6 *Park* v. *Alliance Heritable Secy. Co.* (1888) 7 R. 546; *Scott* v. *Davidson*, 1914 S.C. 791.
7 *Davidson* v. *Scott*, 1915 S.C. 924.
8 1868 Act, S. 122.
9 *Stewart* v. *Brown* (1882) 10 R. 192.
10 1868 Act, S. 119.

Where a disposition bears to be granted in exercise of the power of sale contained in a bond the purchaser's title is not challengeable after five years from its recording on the ground that the debt has ceased to exist unless that fact appeared on the Register of Sasines or was known to the purchaser prior to payment of the price, or on the ground of want or defect of notice or advertisement, or that such power was otherwise improperly or irregularly exercised, but without prejudice to any claim of damages competent against the person exercising the power.[1]

Where land is sold and no surplus remains,[2] or any surplus has been consigned in bank,[3] a certificate of no surplus or of consignation and the disposition to the purchaser, when recorded in the Register of Sasines, have the effect of completely disencumbering the land sold of the selling creditor's security and of all securities and diligences posterior to that creditor's security, except when the security and diligences are assigned to the purchaser as further or collateral security.[4]

A *pari passu* bondholder who cannot obtain the consent of the other *pari passu* bondholders may apply for warrant to sell to the sheriff, who may authorize either or both creditors or some other person to sell, and may grant a disposition and disencumber the lands of both bonds, the balance of the price after expenses being paid to the creditors according to their rights and preferences.[5]

A postponed bondholder may sell but cannot disburden the lands of prior bonds unless he can pay them off in full, in which case he can enforce a discharge.[6]

Foreclosure

At common law a creditor could not purchase for himself.[7] By the Heritable Securities Act, 1894, S. 8, a creditor who has called for repayment, and advertised and exposed for sale lands held in security[8] at a price not exceeding the amount due under

1 1868 Act, S. 119; 1924 Act, S. 41.

2 1874 Act, S. 48.

3 Titles to Land Consolidation (Sc.) Act, 1868, S. 122.

4 1924 Act, S. 42.

5 Heritable Securities (Sc.) Act, 1894, S. 11, remedying difficulty found in *Nicholson's Trs.* v. *McLaughlin* (1891) 19 R. 49.

6 *Adair's Trs.* v. *Rankine* (1895) 22 R. 975.

7 *Taylor* v. *Watson* (1846) 8 D. 400; *Stirling's Trs.* (1865) 3 M. 851. But another bondholder may purchase: *Begbie* v. *Boyd* (1837) 16 S. 232.

8 The whole lands must be exposed for sale in one lot: *Webb's Exors.* v. *Reid* (1906) 14 S.L.T. 323.

the security and any prior security and any securities ranking *pari passu* with his security, exclusive of expenses, or at any lower price, may apply to the sheriff for decree forfeiting the right of redemption and declaring that he has right to the lands described in the bond, at the price at which it was last exposed, which the sheriff may grant, after service on the proprietor and other creditors and such intimation and inquiry as he may think fit. On the extract decree, containing a description of the lands, being recorded in the Register of Sasines, the debtor's right of redemption is extinguished and the creditor has right to the lands as if the disposition in security had been an irredeemable disposition at the date of the decree. The recording disencumbers the lands of all securities and diligences posterior to the security of the holder of the decree. Alternatively, the sheriff may order re-exposure at a price fixed by him; the creditor may bid and if he purchases, the sheriff may grant decree to confer title on him, or the creditor may grant a disposition to himself.[1] The decree or disposition must refer to the burdens and conditions of the title.[2]

The surplus price, if any, over the sum due is consigned or a certificate of no surplus executed and recorded,[3] whereupon the creditor's right and title to the lands is absolute and irredeemable and the lands disencumbered of securities and diligences as in the case of sale under the Act. The debtor's personal obligation, so far as not extinguished by the price, remains in force.[4] No purchaser from the creditor or any other successor in title in the lands is under any duty to inquire into the regularity of the proceedings under which such creditor has acquired right to the lands by virtue of the Act, or is affected by any irregularity therein, without prejudice to any competent claim of damages against such creditor.[5]

Pari passu *and postponed bonds*

A proprietor may grant more than one bond and disposition in security of the same lands. Such dispositions have priority according to the dates of their recording in the Register of Sasines.[6] But by agreement, stated in a clause in the later bond or a separate deed, signed by the consenting creditors, one bond

[1] 1894 Act, Ss. 9–10.
[2] 1924 Act, S. 9.
[3] 1874 Act, S. 48.
[4] 1894 Act, S. 9.
[5] 1894 Act, S. 10; *Sutherland* v. *Thomson* (1905) 8 F. (H.L.) 1.
[6] 1868 Act, S. 120.

may be postponed to another, or two or more may be ranked *pari passu*.

A prior bondholder exercising the power of sale may sell at a price leaving nothing for a postponed bondholder,[1] but the court may interdict a sale at an unfavourable time or if the interests of postponed bondholders are being ignored.[2]

A *pari passu* bondholder may take action to sell the security subjects for payment of his own debt without the consent of the other creditors, but their securities are unaffected by the sale.[3] By the Heritable Securities Act, 1894, S. 11, a *pari passu* bondholder desiring to sell, who cannot obtain the consent of another *pari passu* bondholder, may apply to the sheriff for warrant to sell, which the sheriff may order, and on payment or consignation of the price, the sheriff may grant a conveyance and disencumber the lands. The balance of the price, after payment of expenses, is paid to the creditors according to their just rights and preferences.

Restriction, redemption, and discharge

A bond may be restricted to part only of the lands therein contained by a deed of restriction[4] recorded in the Register of Sasines. Where a superiority has been disponed in security the creditor may consent to the grant of feus and to the restriction of his security to the superiority of the lands feued without prejudice to its subsistence over the fee of the remainder of the lands.[5]

A bond may be renounced and discharged, in whole or in part, and the lands redeemed and disburdened, by a discharge in statutory form recorded in the Register of Sasines.[6] Payment to account may be endorsed on the bond.

The debtor may redeem the lands disponed at the time and place of payment, or at any term of Whitsunday or Martinmas thereafter on three months' warning, on payment of principal, interest, and liquidated expenses and termly failures corresponding thereto, if incurred, or failing acceptance, on consignation in

[1] *Wilson* v. *Stirling* (1843) 8 D. 1261.

[2] *Beveridge* v. *Wilson* (1829) 7 S. 279; *Kerr* v. *McArthur's Trs.* (1848) 11 D. 301; *Stewart* v. *Brown* (1882) 10 R. 192, 203.

[3] *Nicholson's Trs.* v. *McLaughlin* (1891) 19 R. 49.

[4] 1868 Act, S. 133, Sched. (OO); 1924 Act, S. 30, Sched. K; this may be combined with a partial discharge.

[5] *Sones* v. *Mill* (1903) 11 S.L.T. 98.

[6] 1868 Act, S. 132 and Sched. (NN); 1924 Act, S. 29, Sched. K. An uninfeft creditor may grant a discharge: *Macrae* v. *Gregory* (1903) 11 S.L.T. 102.

bank.[4] The notice is given in the same way as notice calling up a bond. If the debtor cannot grant a discharge, a certificate of consignation completely disencumbers the land to the extent of the amount consigned.[1] Premonition is necessary even if the creditor is in possession under a decree of maills and duties.[2]

The disposition is security being only an accessory of the personal debt, a bond may be extinguished by payment, proved by writ or oath,[3] a recorded discharge or a narrative of repayment in a recorded deed being necessary only to clear the record,[4] by compensation,[5] or by confusion, as where the creditor succeeds to the lands held by him in security,[6] unless he does so in a different capacity,[7] or by the creditor entering into possession and ingathering the rents, to the extent of his intromissions.[8]

BOND FOR CASH CREDIT AND DISPOSITION IN SECURITY

A disposition of lands in security may be adjected to a bond for cash credit in the same way as to a personal bond, securing repayment of the fluctuating balance on a cash account, up to a stated maximum. The bond must also state the method whereby the outstanding debt at any given time will be ascertained, normally by a stated account and certificate by a stated official of the lending body. Such an account and certificate suffices for the purpose of summary diligence, but does not bar a challenge of the figures. The clause of consent to registration must expressly be made applicable to the stated account and certificate. Such a disposition, once recorded, creates an effectual security for future as well as past advances, but to do so there must be stated *in gremio* of the bond a statutory clause[9] that the principal and interest which may become due upon such cash accounts or credits shall be limited to a definite sum to be specified in the security, not exceeding the amount of the principal sum[10] and

[1] 1868 Act, S. 119; 1874 Act, S. 49; 1924 Act, S. 32 and Sched. L. See also *Bruce* v. *Scottish Amicable Life Assce. Socy.*, 1907 S.C. 637.

[2] *Bruce, supra.*

[3] *Jackson* v. *Nicoll* (1870) 8 M. 408.

[4] *Cameron* v. *Williamson* (1895) 22 R. 293.

[5] *Rankin* v. *Arnot* (1680) Mor. 572; *McDowal* v. *Fullerton* (1714) Mor. 576.

[6] *Hogg* v. *Brack* (1832) 11 S. 198; *Murray* v. *Parlane's Tr.* (1890) 18 R. 287.

[7] *Colville's Trs.* v. *Marindin*, 1908 S.C. 911; see also *Fleming* v. *Imrie* (1868) 6 M. 363; *Crichton's Trs.* v. *Clarke*, 1909 1 S.L.T. 467; *Sherry* v. *S's Trs.*, 1918 1 S.L.T. 31.

[8] *Baillie* v. *Menzies* (1711) 2 Ross L.C. 713.

[9] Debts Securities (Sc.) Act, 1856, S. 7.

[10] Interest accumulated under the agreement as to credit is principal: *Reddie* v. *Williamson* (1863) 1 M. 228.

three years' interest thereon at 5%.[1] If this is done the borrower may draw out and pay in sums as may be agreed, and the infeftment in security is equally valid and effectual as if the whole sums advanced on the cash credit has been paid prior to the date of sasine or infeftment thereon. If the interest limit be overstated in the bond, the security for interest is invalid,[2] and it may be that the whole security is invalid.[3]

In case of default the disposition in security normally contains the same powers of realization as a bond and disposition in security.

It is thought that a bond for cash credit can be assigned only to the extent of the balance due at the date of assignation, and not transferring the creditor's part of a continuing account so as to permit future dealings with the security.

OTHER BONDS AND DISPOSITIONS IN SECURITY

A disposition of lands in security may also be combined with a bond of corroboration, bond of relief or bond of annuity, or with a bond and assignation in security of moveable rights.

EX FACIE ABSOLUTE DISPOSITION

A proprietor of heritage may also grant a right in security over heritage, particularly for the repayment of a future or fluctuating debt, by an absolute disposition of the heritage to the creditor. Though the disposition is in terms and *ex facie* absolute and not redeemable, the common intention is that the disponee (creditor) should hold the subjects in security only. The terms on which he holds can be proved only by writ or oath,[4] and the disponee normally grants a separate writing, a back-letter or back-bond, setting out the conditions on which the subjects have been conveyed to him, and obliging himself to reconvey on getting

[1] cf. *Morton* v. *Hunter* (1828) 7 S. 172; 4 W. & S. 379.

[2] *Alston* v. *Nellfield Co.*, 1915 S.C. 912.

[3] *Anderson* v. *Dickie*, 1914 S.C. 706, 717.

[4] Trusts Act, 1696 (c. 25); Bell, *Prin.* §1995; *Robertson* v. *Duff* (1840) 2 D. 279; *Seth* v. *Hain* (1855) 17 D. 1117; *Walker* v. *Buchanan, Kennedy & Co.* (1857) 20 D. 259; *Marshall* v. *Lyell* (1859) 21 D. 514; *Laird* v. *Laird & Rutherford* (1884) 12 R. 294; *Dunn* v. *Pratt* (1898) 25 R. 461. But proof is not thus limited if the holder of the disposition admits that the documents do not give a true account of the agreement between him and the granter; *Burnett* v. *Morrow* (1864) 2 M. 929; *Murray* v. *Wright* (1870) 8 M. 722; *Grant's Trs.* v. *Morrison* (1875) 2 R. 377; *Grant* v. *G.* (1898) 6 S.L.T. 203. And a third party having an interest may prove the trust qualifying the disposition by any evidence: *Wallace* v. *Sharp* (1885) 12 R. 687; *Hastie* v. *Steel* (1886) 13 R. 843. The writ need not be probative; *Paterson* v. *P.* (1897) 25 R. 144, 175.

repayment of the debt.[1] The back-letter may contain conditions on the use of the subjects as well as relative to repayment.[2] Alternatively, a bilateral minute of agreement states the conditions.[3] The disposition is in the same form as a disposition following on sale, save that the consideration is stated as 'for certain onerous causes and considerations'. The creditor completes title by recording the disposition in the Register of Sasines as would a purchaser.

If the back-letter is recorded the obligation to denude on repayment is a real limitation on the disponee's right and the security may be limited to sums advanced down to that date.[4] Recording publishes the conditions which qualify the disponee's right.[5] If the back-letter is unrecorded the disponee can sell or burden the subjects and generally act as absolute proprietor, though such action may be in conflict with his undertaking in the back letter. The disponer has only a personal right to have the lands reconveyed or the proceeds of their sale paid to him, on his repaying the debt secured by the disposition.[6]

An *ex facie* absolute disposition is a valid security for any debt incurred or to be incurred, before or after the date of infeftment thereunder.[7] If, however, the back-letter bears that the disposition was granted in security of a specific debt only, there is no right to retain the subjects in security of other debts.[8]

Position of creditor (disponee)

If the back-letter is unrecorded the disposition confers on the creditor all the rights of a feudal proprietor[9] so that he can possess and occupy the lands,[10] draw the rents, let on lease,[11] remove

[1] e.g. *Smith* v. *S.* (1879) 6 R. 794.

[2] e.g. *Macintyre* v. *Cleveland Petroleum Co.*, 1967 S.L.T. 95.

[3] e.g. *Stewart* v. *Brown* (1882) 10 R. 192; *Duncan* v. *Mitchell* (1893) 21 R. 37.

[4] Bell, *Prin.* §912; Menzies, 861.

[5] *National Bank* v. *Union Bank* (1885) 13 R. 380, 390; *Edinburgh Entertainments, Ltd.* v. *Stevenson*, 1926 S.L.T. 286.

[6] *Thomson* v. *Douglas, Heron & Co.* (1786) Mor. 10229; *Somervails* v. *Redfearn* (1813) 5 Pat. 707; *National Bank* v. *Union Bank* (1886) 14 R. (H.L.) 1.

[7] *Maitland* v. *Cockerell* (1827) 6 S. 109; *Russell* v. *E. Breadalbane* (1831) 5 W. & S. 256; *Tierney* v. *Court* (1832) 10 S. 664; *James* v. *Downie* (1836) 15 S. 12; *Robertson* v. *Duff* (1840) 2 D. 279, 291.

[8] *Robertson, supra*; cf. *Anderson's Tr.* v. *Somerville* (1899) 36 S.L.R. 833.

[9] *Gardyne* v. *Royal Bank* (1853) 1 Macq. 368; *McLelland* v. *Bank of Scotland* (1857) 19 D. 574; *National Bank* v. *Union Bank* (1886) 14 R. (H.L.) 1.

[10] *Sc. Herit. Security Co.* v. *Allan Campbell & Co.* (1876) 3 R. 333.

[11] But not where the lease is a fictitious device: *Heritable Sec. Inv. Assoc.* v. *Wingate's Tr.* (1880) 7 R. 1094.

tenants, and remove the debtor from possession.[1] He cannot be dispossessed by the trustee in the debtor's sequestration until the sum due has been paid.[2] He may sell the lands without the debtor's consent and give a good title to the purchaser,[3] but if he does so unfairly the debtor, as owner in equity, has an action of damages against him, though he cannot impugn the sale.[4] The purchaser's title is qualified by any trust disclosed in the creditor's title.[5] The debtor may interdict a sale when the balance due by him was neither admitted nor liquidated.[6] The creditor may, however, allow the debtor to remain in possession,[7] in which case he cannot challenge a lease granted by the debtor,[8] nor is he liable as principal for goods bought by the debtor in connection with the lands.[9] He is liable as vassal for feuduty and implement of all the conditions of the feu due to the superior.[10] If while in possession he makes improvements he is entitled to be reimbursed to the extent that the debtor is *lucratus* thereby.[11]

If the creditor goes bankrupt the trustee in his sequestration stands in his place and takes the property subject to the obligation to the debtor as true owner and with no better title than the creditor had,[12] but the trustee may sell and confer a good title, free of the latent trust, on a purchaser who gives full value and is ignorant of the latent qualification.[12]

As between a bondholder and a creditor infeft under a subsequent *ex facie* absolute disposition, the creditor is not, however, deemed proprietor and has been held not entitled to reduce a sale by the bondholder[13] but entitled to be relieved of feuduty by a bondholder who took possession.[14]

1 *Rankin* v. *Russell* (1868) 7 M. 126; *Sc. Property Inv. Co. Bldg. Soc.* v. *Horne* (1881) 8 R. 737.

2 *Lindsay* v. *Davidson* (1853) 15 D. 583.

3 *Aberdeen Trades Council* v. *Shipconstructors Assocn.*, 1948 S.C. 94.

4 *Parks* v. *Alliance Her. Sec. Co.* (1880) 7 R. 546; *Baillie* v. *Drew* (1884) 12 R. 199; *Duncan* v. *Mitchell* (1893) 21 R. 37; *Shrubb* v. *Clark* (1897) 5 S.L.T. 125; *Rimmer* v. *Usher*, 1967 S.L.T. 7.

5 *Livingstone* v. *Allan* (1900) 3 F. 233.

6 *Lucas* v. *Gardner* (1876) 4 R. 194; contrast *Mackintosh* v. *Leslie* (1907) 15 S.L.T. 2.

7 *Leckie* v. *L.* (1854) 17 D. 77.

8 *Abbott* v. *Mitchell* (1870) 8 M. 791.

9 *Newcastle Chemical Co.* v. *Oliphant & Jamieson* (1881) 9 R. 110.

10 *Clark* v. *City of Glasgow Life Assce. and Reversionary Co.* (1850) 12 D. 1047; *City of Glasgow Bank* v. *Nicolson's Trs.* (1882) 9 R. 689.

11 *Nelson* v. *Gordon* (1874) 1 R. 1093.

12 *Heritable Reversionary Co.* v. *Millar* (1892) 19 R. (H.L.) 43.

13 *Stewart* v. *Brown* (1892) 10 R. 192.

14 *City of Glasgow Bank* v. *Nicolson's Trs.* (1880) 9 R. 689.

Position of debtor (disponer)

The debtor has only a personal right to have the lands re-conveyed or the proceeds of their sale paid to him, after satisfying the creditor's claims for principal and interest.[1] A conveyance in security qualified by a back letter does not cease to be a right in security only by reason of the lapse of time[2] but if the back letter is unrecorded possession by the creditor for the prescriptive period will confer an absolute right of property and the rights under the back-letter be cut down.[3] The debtor may also confer an indefeasible title by a discharge, or by destroying an unrecorded back-letter.[4]

The debtor may be left in possession of the lands,[5] in which case he may grant a lease[6] and remove tenants,[7] though an implied mandate from the creditor to grant a lease falls on his bankruptcy.[8] As true owner with the radical right to the lands he may sue for injury to the lands by third parties.[9] If he becomes bankrupt his trustee in bankruptcy cannot recover the lands without making full payment of the debt.[10]

The debtor's reversionary right is assignable[11] outright or in security, and if assigned and intimated, the security of the creditor is limited to advances made prior to the date of intimation to him of the assignation.[12] The appointment of a judicial factor is equivalent to an intimated assignation and the disponee can claim interest on the loan to that date only.[13]

Extent of right in security

The creditor is entitled to hold the subjects until satisfaction has been made of all debts due to him by the debtor.[14] The terms of the back letter may determine whether the security covers

[1] *Thomson* v. *Douglas, Heron & Co.* (1786) Mor. 10229; *Somervails* v. *Redfearn* (1813) 5 Pat. 707; *National Bank* v. *Union Bank* (1886) 14 R. (H.L.) 1.

[2] *Smith* v. *S.* (1879) 6 R. 794; cf. *Scott* v. *Stewart* (1779) 3 Ross L.C. 464; *National Bank* v. *Union Bank* (1885) 13 R. 380, 400.

[3] *Chambers* v. *Law* (1823) 2 S. 366.

[4] *National Bank, supra*, 13 R. 400.

[5] *Leckie* v. *L.* (1854) 17 D. 77.

[6] *Abbott* v. *Mitchell* (1869) 8 M. 268; *Ritchie* v. *Scott* (1899) 1 F. 728.

[7] *Traill* v. *T.* (1873) 1 R. 61.

[8] *Ritchie, supra.*

[9] *McBride* v. *Caledonian Ry.* (1894) 21 R. 620; *Vincent* v. *Wood* (1899) 6 S.L.T. 297; *Scobie* v. *Lind*, 1967 S.L.T. 9.

[10] *Lindsay* v. *Davidson* (1853) 15 D. 583.

[11] *Dundee Calendering Co.* v. *Duff* (1869) 8 M. 289; *National Bank, supra.*

[12] *National Bank, supra.*

[13] *Campbell's J.F.* v. *National Bank*, 1944 S.C. 495.

[14] *Robertson* v. *Duff* (1840) 2 D. 279; *Nelson* v. *Gordon* (1874) 1 R. 1093.

debts incurred after the disposition as well as before or at the time thereof. Even if it bear to be granted in security of a specified existing debt, the creditor may retain in respect of later advances.

Creditor–disponee's remedies

The creditor who holds an *ex facie* absolute disposition is *ex facie* proprietor and cannot poind the ground.[1] He may collect rents without an action of maills and duties. He may have the debtor, if in possession, ejected by declarator and removing,[2] but not by summary ejection. If he realizes the security by sale he will be liable to the debtor if he does so excessively and prejudices the latter's reversionary rights.[3]

If the creditor possesses under the disposition to him for the prescriptive period, the debtor's right of reversion is cut off.[4]

Similarly, the debtor can vest an unqualified title in the creditor by discharging his right of reversion, or by destroying the back letter.[5]

Creditor's succession

Land held under a disposition *ex facie* absolute but truly in security is always heritable in succession,[6] and heirs complete title as to any other heritage. But they take the property subject to the debtor's equitable claim to the reversion.

Debtor's succession

The debtor has merely a conditional reversionary claim under the back letter, which transmits to the debtor's heirs in heritage.

Redemption and reconveyance

The debtor may discharge his liability by payment without obtaining any deed of discharge, but the only competent mode of recovering the lands is by reconveyance by the creditor.[7] The creditor is entitled, before reconveying, to payment of all debts incurred before or after the back bond, and reimbursement of

1 *Sc. Heritable Security Co.* v. *Allan, Campbell & Co.* (1876) 3 R. 333.

2 *Rankin* v. *Russell* (1868) 7 M. 126; *Sc. Property Investment Co. Bldg. Soc.* v. *Horne* (1881) 8 R. 737.

3 *Nelson* v. *National Bank*, 1936 S.C. 570.

4 *Munro* v. *M.*, 19 May 1812, F.C.; *Paul* v. *Reid*, 8 Feb., 1814, F.C.; *Chambers* v. *Law* (1823) 2 S. 366; cf. *Smith* v. *S.* (1879) 6 R. 794.

5 *National Bank* v. *Union Bank* (1885) 13 R. 380, 400.

6 1868 Act, Ss. 3 and 117; Bell, *Prin.* §1478, 1485; cf. *Stroyan* v. *Murray* (1890) 17 R. 1170.

7 *National Bank* v. *Union Bank* (1885) 13 R. 380, 400.

outlays made on the subjects by him, which were really of the nature of meliorations.[1] When the creditor has discharged the debt, he is still entitled to require the debtor to take the lands back.[2] A creditor may grant an undertaking to reconvey on conditions, which amounts to a personal obligation and is assignable.[3]

It is questionable whether a creditor's recording of a back letter, execution of a reconveyance to the debtor, and his obtaining of a decree in absence ordaining him to register it, operates as a feudal divestiture in a question with the superior.[4]

Competition with prior bondholder

If a proprietor has granted a bond and disposition in security and subsequently grants an *ex facie* absolute disposition the disponee under the latter deed is deemed a mere security-holder in a question with a prior bondholder.[5]

FLOATING CHARGE OVER HERITAGE

By the Companies (Floating Charges) (Sc.) Act, 1961, an incorporated company or society registered under the Industrial and Provident Societies Acts, 1965 and 1967, may grant security for any present or future debt by creating a floating charge over all or any of the property, heritable and moveable, which may from time to time be comprised in its property and undertaking. The Schedule to the 1967 Act modifies the 1961 Act in its application to such societies. It attaches to the property then comprised in the company's property on the commencement of winding up, but is subject to the rights of anyone who has effectually executed diligence, or holds a fixed security ranking in priority to the floating charge, or another floating charge ranking in priority.[6] Whether a charge affects particular heritage depends on the terms of the instrument of charge executed.[7] Subject to the Companies Act, 1948, a floating charge has effect in relation to heritage, notwithstanding that it is not recorded in the Register

1 *Nelson* v. *Gordon* (1874) 1 R. 1093.
2 *Clydesdale Bank* v. *McIntyre*, 1909 S.C. 1405.
3 *McCallum's Trs.* v. *McNab* (1877) 4 R. 520.
4 *Marshall's Trs.* v. *Macneill* (1888) 15 R. 762.
5 *Stewart* v. *Brown* (1882) 10 R. 192; cf. *City of Glasgow Bank* v. *Nicolson's Trs.* (1882) 9 R. 689; *King* v. *Johnston*, 1908 S.C. 684.
6 1961 Act, S. 1. As to ranking see also S. 5. 'Fixed security' is defined by S. 8.
7 S. 2.

of Sasines.[1] It is implied that a floating charge is assignable, and it is probably heritable in the creditor's succession, if granted over heritage only, but moveable if granted over a mixed aggregate of heritable and moveable property, or over moveable property only.

The charge thereby created can be enforced only by petition for winding-up the company.[2]

CATHOLIC AND SECONDARY SECURITIES

Where one party has a security over two or more subjects of the debtor and another party has a postponed security over only one of these subjects, the parties are termed catholic and secondary creditors and on grounds of equity rules have been developed to minimize prejudice. If the catholic creditor realizes the security subjects over which the secondary creditor's security also extends he must assign to the latter his security over the other subjects,[3] but if the catholic creditor discharges the bond over the other subject, the secondary creditor cannot object.[4] If both subjects are realized, the debtor being bankrupt, the catholic creditor will be deemed to have exhausted first the other subject, thereby giving the secondary creditor the preferable right, in a question with the unsecured creditors, to the balance realized from both subjects.[5] If the catholic creditor himself holds a second bond over the subjects not covered by the secondary creditor's bond he may first exhaust the subjects covered also by the secondary creditor's bond and leave the maximum surplus towards his own second bond over the other subjects.[6] If there are secondary bondholders over both or all subjects, as between them the burden of the catholic bond has to be apportioned rateably according to the value of each estate.[7]

LAND HELD ON LEASE AS SECURITY

Ordinary leases

A lease of ordinary duration may, unless assignation is prohibited, be assigned in security, but the creditor obtains no

[1] S. 3. But a company must record it in its own register of charges and register it with the Registrar of Companies: Companies Act, 1948, Ss. 106A and 106H, added by 1961 Act, Sched. II. A society must give information to the Assistant Registrar of Friendly Societies for Scotland: 1967 Act, S. 4.

[2] 1961 Act, S. 4.

[3] Kames, *Equity* I, 125; Bell, *Comm.* II, 417; *Kemp's Trs.* v. *Ure* (1822) 1 S. 235.

[4] *Morton* (1871) 10 M. 292.

[5] *Littlejohn* v. *Black* (1855) 18 D. 207; *Nicol's Trs.* v. *Hill* (1889) 16 R. 416.

[6] *Preston* v. *Erskine* (1715) Mor. 3376.

[7] *Ferrier* v. *Cowan* (1896) 23 R. 703.

preferential right unless he actually enters into possession of the subjects,[1] which involves liability for the rent,[2] and for performance of the duties of working the subjects, if agricultural or mineral. Even to make the tenant his creditor's manager would not relieve the latter of liability.[3] Even where the creditor would incur no liability for working, as in the case of an urban lease, he must take possession.[4]

Long leases

A lease for not less than 31 years, registered under the Registration of Leases Act, 1857, may be assigned in security by bond and assignation in security in the form of Schedule B to that Act. Recording of the assignation completes the right in security, and constitutes it a real security over the lease to the extent assigned.[5] A bond and assignation in security is transferable, in whole or in part, by translation in the form of Schedule D to the Act, also recorded.[6]

The creditor is entitled under the bond to exercise power of sale on default in payment.[7] Without prejudice thereto, he is entitled, on default of payment of capital, or of a term's interest or annuity for six months after it has fallen due, to obtain warrant from the Sheriff to enter on possession of the lands leased, uplift the rents from any sub-tenant and to sublet as the tenant might have done. He is not entitled to poind the ground nor to bring an action of maills and duties against subtenants in possession. No such creditor, unless and until he enters into possession, is personally liable to the landlord in any of the obligations of the lease.[7]

On repayment a discharge of the bond and assignation in security is granted in the form of Schedule H to the Act and recorded,[8] which disburdens the lease.

A long lease has the disadvantage that, towards its expiry, it is an asset of diminishing value, and would become valueless if it expired while held in security.

1 Bell, *Prin.* §1212; *Inglis* v. *Paul* (1829) 7 S. 469; *Benton* v. *Craig's Tr.* (1864) 2 M. 1365; *Clark* v. *West Calder Oil Co.* (1882) 9 R. 1017; *Mess* v. *Hay* (1898) 25 R. 298; 1 F. (H.L.) 22.

2 *Ramsay* v. *Commercial Bank* (1842) 4 D. 405; *Moncreiff* v. *Ferguson* (1896) 24 R. 47.

3 *Macphail* v. *McLean's Tr.* (1887) 15 R. 47; *Mess, supra.*

4 *Wright* v. *Walker* (1839) 1 D. 641; *Roberts* v. *Wallace* (1842) 5 D. 6; *Hardie* v. *Cameron* (1879) 19 S.L.R. 83; *Macphail, supra.*

5 1857 Act, S. 4; Bell, *Prin.* §1212A; *Rodger* v. *Crawford* (1867) 6 M. 24; Such a security is moveable in the creditor's succession: *Stroyan* v. *Murray* (1890) 17 R. 1170.

6 S. 6.

7 Sale is carried through under the provisions of the Titles to Land Consolidation Act, 1868, or of the Conveyancing Act, 1924, S. 24.

8 S. 13.

CHAPTER 86

SERVITUDES

A SERVITUDE is a real right conceived in favour of one tenement of land, the dominant tenement, availing against another adjacent tenement, the servient tenement, whereby the owner of the servient tenement is obliged to suffer the other to exercise certain rights over his lands, or is restrained from the unfettered liberty of use of his lands.[1]

Other authorities distinguish personal and praedial servitudes, affecting respectively the rights and the lands of the persons burdened. But the only so-called personal servitude is liferent, which is today better regarded as an interest in land, or a beneficial right under a trust, than as a burden on another's property, and all true servitudes are praedial and affect land.[2]

Servitudes are also classed as natural, legal, and conventional. A natural servitude, or natural burden of land, springs from its natural situation, as where inferior lands are obliged to receive water draining naturally from higher lands. A legal servitude may be created by statute,[3] or by long-standing custom for reasons of public necessity or utility. Conventional servitudes are created by agreement, express or implied.[4]

Servitudes are also classed as urban or rural according as they affect houses and buildings or open ground, and positive or negative, according as they entitle the dominant tenement to exercise rights of use on or over the servient tenement or merely limit the freedom of the proprietor's use of the servient tenement.[5]

Only restrictions legally recognized can be servitudes

Servitudes being conventional may be of as many kinds as the ways in which one owner of land may agree to have his liberty of use of his lands limited in favour of a neighbour,[6] but not every

[1] Generally Craig II, 8, 43; Stair II, 7,; Mack. II, 9; Dirleton, 276; Hope, *Maj. Prac.* III, 24; *Min. Pract.*, 10, 17; Spott., 307; Forbes, II, 4, 1; Bankt. II, 7; Ersk. II, 9; Bell, *Prin.* §979.

[2] Bell, *Prin.* §981; cf. *Patrick* v. *Napier* (1867) 5 M. 683, 699.

[3] e.g. *Caledonian Ry.* v. *Sprot* (1855) 2 Macq. 449; *Caledonian Ry.* v. *Belhaven* (1857) 3 Macq. 56; *McCulloch* v. *Dumfries Water Commrs.* (1863) 1 M. 334.

[4] Bell, *Prin.* §980.

[5] Bell, *Prin.* §982–3.

[6] Stair II, 7, 5, and 9; Ersk. II, 9, 2.

restriction will be recognized as a servitude. Positive servitudes require sasine or possession, and their existence is usually apparent on inspection though they do not necessarily appear *ex facie* of the title of the servient tenement as recorded. Negative servitudes do not admit of possession, however, and only well-recognized categories are accepted; they are, in any event, anomalous and a category not to be enlarged.[1] Even among positive servitudes most cases belong to categories with well-known incidents, and a servitude of another category must be specifically created to receive recognition. But the classes of servitudes are not closed, and new kinds may be accepted.[2] It is questionable whether a restriction hedged with unusual qualifications or exceptions falls within the known category of servitude on which it is founded.[3] Questions may arise whether a right is a personal privilege, or to be ascribed to a right of ownership, or to a right of servitude,[4] or whether a burden is a personal prohibition on a disponee or a servitude.[5]

Servitudes real, not personal

A servitude is a burden on one tenement of land for the benefit of an adjacent tenement, which attaches to the lands independently of ownership, and is distinct from a personal privilege which does not benefit the dominant tenement or the owner thereof as such. Thus rights of golfing,[6] or curling and skating,[7] or walking,[8] or fishing,[9] or shooting,[10] are not servitudes; such privileges may subsist only as personal licences.[11]

Transmission of servitudes

A servitude properly constituted transmits for the benefit of successors in the ownership of the dominant tenement, and

[1] *Sivwright* v. *Wilson* (1828) 7 S. 210.

[2] *Dyce* v. *Hay* (1852) 1 Macq. 305, 312; *Harvey* v. *Lindsay* (1853) 15 D. 768, 775; *Patrick* v. *Napier* (1867) 5 M. 683, 709.

[3] *Braid Hills Hotel Co.* v. *Manuel*, 1909 S.C. 120.

[4] See *Baird* v. *Feuars of Kilsyth* (1878) 6 R. 116; *Murray* v. *Peddie* (1880) 7 R. 804; *Robertson's Trs.* v. *Bruce* (1905) 7 F. 580.

[5] *Anderson* v. *Dickie*, 1914 S.C. 706.

[6] Distinguish a customary right to play golf: *Kelly* v. *Burntisland Mags.* (1812) in 9 D. 293, note; *Earlsferry Mags.* v. *Malcolm* (1829) 7 S. 755; (1832) 11 S. 74; *Dyce* v. *Hay* (1849) 11 D. 1266, 1279; 1 Macq. 311; *Sanderson* v. *Musselburgh Mags.* (1859) 21 D. 1011; 22 D. 240.

[7] *Harvey* v. *Lindsay* (1853) 15 D. 768.

[8] *Cleghorn* v. *Dempster* (1805) Mor. 16141; *Dyce, supra.*

[9] *Patrick* v. *Napier* (1867) 5 M. 683; *Harper* v. *Flaws*, 1940 S.L.T. 150.

[10] *Huntly* v. *Nicol* (1896) 23 R. 610; cf. *Hemming* v. *D. Athole* (1883) 11 R. 93.

[11] Bell, *Prin.* §979.

transmits against successors in the ownership of the servient tenement, if followed by infeftment or by possession and enjoyment by the owner of the dominant tenement.[1] A restriction on the use of land, not being a known servitude, even if constituted by agreement registered in the Register of Sasines is not binding on singular successors if it does not form part of the title.[2] Where a servitude is subject to a condition a successor cannot retain the servitude without implementing the condition.[3]

Praedial servitudes generally

Servitudes exist for the benefit of the dominant tenement of land as such and burden the servient tenement. There must therefore be two tenements, reasonably adjacent, and owned by different persons.[4] They are inseparable from the tenements and cannot be alienated separately, or made into rights independently of the title to the lands in question.[5] The right may be exercised only for the benefit of the dominant tenement, not for that of another.[6]

Any land or building may be a dominant tenement, a royal burgh may be,[7] and any lands in private ownership may be a servient tenement, but lands held for statutory purposes cannot be subject to a servitude which would interfere with those purposes.[8]

The owner of the servient tenement is not generally bound to do anything, but merely to suffer the invasion of his rights required by the fair exercise of the servitude;[9] thus he need not repair a way over which another has a servitude right of way;[10] still less can he be required to provide any services.[11] Nor is he limited save in so far as the servitude requires.

The servitude must be used for the benefit of the dominant

[1] Stair II, 7, 1; Bell, *Prin.* §979; *N.B. Ry. Co.* v. *Park Yard Co.* (1898) 25 R. (H.L.) 47; *Braid Hills Hotel Co.* v. *Manuel*, 1909 S.C. 120, 126; *Hunter* v. *Fox*, 1964 S.C. (H.L.) 95.

[2] *Campbell's Trs.* v. *Glasgow Corpn.* (1902) 4 F. 752; *Murray's Trs.* v. *St. Margaret's Convent* (1906) 8 F. 1109, 1120; 1907 S.C. (H.L.) 8. See also *McTavish's Trs.* v. *Anderson* (1900) 8 S.L.T. 80.

[3] *Tennant* v. *Napier Smith's Trs.* (1888) 15 R. 671.

[4] *Donaldson's Trs.* v. *Forbes* (1839) 1 D. 494; *Grierson* v. *Sandsting School Board* (1882) 9 R. 437, 441; *Harper* v. *Flaws*, 1940 S.L.T. 150.

[5] *Patrick* v. *Napier* (1867) 5 M. 683; *Drummond* v. *Milligan* (1867) 17 R. 316.

[6] *Murray* v. *Peebles Mags.*, 8 Dec. 1808, F.C.; *Scotts* v. *Bogles*, 6 July, 1809, F.C.

[7] *Feuars of Dundee* v. *Hay* (1732) Mor. 1824.

[8] *Ayr Harbour Trs.* v. *Oswald* (1883) 10 R. (H.L.) 85; *Ellice's Trs.* v. *Caledonian Canal Commrs.* (1904) 6 F. 325.

[9] Stair II, 7, 5; Bankt. II, 7, 7, and 14; Ersk. II, 9, 1; Bell, *Prin.* §984; *Sc. Highland Distillery Co.* v. *Reid* (1877) 4 R. 1118, 1122; *Allan* v. *MacLachlan* (1900) 2 F. 699.

[10] *Allan* v. *MacLachlan* (1900) 2 F. 699.

[11] *Tailors of Aberdeen* v. *Coutts* (1840) 1 Rob. App. 296, 310.

tenement only and not for other persons or lands in lieu, or in addition,[1] nor generally for commercial ends.[2]

The owner of the dominant tenement must exercise his rights *civiliter*, in the way least burdensome to the servient tenement,[3] and the owner of the latter may use his lands as he pleases so long as he permits the continued exercise of the servitude right.[4] The burden on the servient tenement may not be increased beyond the right acquired.[5]

A servitude, being a restraint on the free use of property, is strictly construed, in that it may be constituted only in recognized ways, in case of doubt is presumed to be of the degree least burdensome to the servient tenement, and imposes no greater restraint than is necessary for its fair exercise. In particular a negative servitude must be construed strictly.[6]

CREATION OF SERVITUDES

Apart from servitudes created by statute,[7] all have their origin in conventional provisions, though their incidents are determined by law. The constitution may be *in gremio* of a disposition or other deed, in a *mortis causa* settlement, or by separate deed.[8] The deed must be probative, or equivalent thereto.

Questions may arise as to the title of a person to create a servitude; an owner of lands may do so, as may an heir of entail with power of sale,[9] an owner who had disponed the servient tenement in security by *ex facie* absolute disposition,[10] but an estate factor may not[11] nor may one of several *pro indiviso* proprietors.[12]

[1] Bell, *Prin.* §986; *Carstairs* v. *Brown* (1829) 7 S. 607; *Anstruther* v. *Caird* (1861) 24 D. 149; *L. Blantyre* v. *Dumbarton Waterworks Commrs.* (1888) 15 R. (H.L.) 56.

[2] *Agnew* v. *L.A.* (1873) 11 M. 309, 333.

[3] Ersk. II, 9, 34; *Beveridge* v. *Marshall*, 18 Nov. 1808, F.C.; *Rattray* v. *Tayport Patent Slip Co.* (1868) 5 S.L.R. 219; *Sutherland* v. *Thomson* (1876) 3 R. 485; *Orr Ewing* v. *Colquhoun's Trs.* (1877) 4 R. (H.L.) 116, 121.

[4] Ersk. *supra*; Bell, *Prin.* §987; *Oliver* v. *Robertson* (1869) 8 M. 137; *Sutherland* v. *Thomson* (1876) 3 R. 485; *Sc. Highland Distillery Co.* v. *Reid* (1877) 4 R. 1118; *Donaldson* v. *E. Strathmore* (1877) 14 S.L.R. 587.

[5] Ersk. II, 9, 4; Bell, *Prin.* §988; *Dunbar Mags.* v. *Sawers* (1829) 7 S. 672; *Young* v. *Cuddie* (1831) 9 S. 500; *White* v. *W.* (1906) 8 F. (H.L.) 41.

[6] *Hunter* v. *Fox*, 1964 S.C. (H.L.) 95.

[7] e.g. *Caledonian Ry.* v. *Sprot* (1855) 2 Macq. 449; *Caledonian Ry.* v. *Belhaven* (1857) 3 Macq. 56; *McCulloch* v. *Dumfries Water Commrs.* (1863) 1 M. 334.

[8] e.g. *Smith* v. *Stewart* (1884) 11 R. 921.

[9] *Bowman Ballantine* (1883) 10 R. 1061.

[10] *Union Heritable Securities Co.* v. *Mathie* (1886) 13 R. 670.

[11] *Macgregor* v. *Balfour* (1899) 2 F. 345.

[12] *Grant* v. *Heriot's Trust* (1906) 8 F. 647.

A servitude may be created in return for a periodical payment,[1] or without payment expressly therefor.

Express grant

Both positive and negative servitudes may be created by express grant[2] from a person who is, or at least comes later to be, owner of the servient tenement,[3] contained in the titles of the tenements,[4] or in a separate probative writ,[5] or by oral or improbative agreement followed by *rei interventus*,[6] but it need not be recorded in the Register of Sasines.[7] If, however, a positive servitude be not so recorded it is not valid against singular successors of the granter unless it has been followed by possession so as to be discoverable by inspection or reasonable inquiry.[8] A negative servitude, however, is incapable of possession and, if the grant is not recorded, may not come to the notice of a singular successor of the granter. This is the only way in which a negative servitude can be created[9] and the grant must be in terms clearly indicating the intention to create a permanent right.[10]

The intention to grant,[11] and the nature and extent of the right granted,[12] must be clear.

Implied grant

A positive servitude may be held granted by implication only exceptionally, where lands are disponed and certain servitude rights over the granter's other lands are necessary for the use of the disponed lands, as for access to them,[13] not merely where they

1 *Stewart* v. *Steuart* (1877) 4 R. 981.

2 Ersk. II, 9, 35; Bell, *Prin.* §994; *Dundas* v. *Blair* (1886) 13 R. 759; *Inglis* v. *Clark* (1901) 4 F. 288; *Metcalfe* v. *Purdon* (1902) 4 F. 507. As to power to grant, see also *Bowman Ballantine* (1883) 10 R. 1061; *Macgregor* v. *Balfour* (1899) 2 F. 345; *Grant* v. *Heriot's Trust* (1906) 8 F. 647.

3 *Stephen* v. *Brown's Trs.*, 1922 S.C. 136.

4 *Gray* v. *Fergusson* (1792) Mor. 14513, and see 7 S. 212, note; *Argyllshire Commrs.* v. *Campbell* (1885) 12 R. 1255.

5 *Macgregor* v. *Balfour* (1899) 2 F. 345; *Campbell's Trs.* v. *Glasgow Corpn.* (1902) 4 F. 752, 757; *Murray's Trs.* v. *St. Margaret's Convent* (1906) 8 F. 1109, 1120.

6 *Stirling* v. *Haldane* (1829) 8 S. 131; *Macgregor, supra.*

7 Bell, *Prin.* §994; *Cowan* v. *Stewart* (1872) 10 M. 735; *Banks* v. *Walker* (1874) 1 R. 981. See also *Alexander* v. *Butchart* (1875) 3 R. 156.

8 Bell, *Prin.* §990; *N.B. Ry. Co.* v. *Park Yard Co.* (1898) 25 R. (H.L.) 47; *Campbell's Trs.* v. *Glasgow Corpn.* (1902) 4 F. 752.

9 *Dundas* v. *Blair* (1886) 13 R. 759.

10 *Cowan* v. *Stewart* (1872) 10 M. 735.

11 *Sivwright* v. *Wilson* (1828) 7 S. 210; *Cowan* v. *Stewart* (1872) 10 M. 735; *Russell* v. *Cowper* (1882) 9 R. 660; *King* v. *Barnetson* (1896) 24 R. 81.

12 *Ross* v. *Cuthbertson* (1854) 16 D. 732.

13 Stair II, 7, 6, 10; Ersk. II, 6, 9; *Balds* v. *Alloa Coal Co.* (1854) 16 D. 870; *Caledonian Ry.* v. *Sprot* (1856) 2 Macq. 449; *McGavin* v. *McIntyre* (1874) 1 R. 1016; *Walton Bros.* v.

were used in connection with and are required for the convenient and comfortable enjoyment of the lands retained.[1] Negative servitudes, such as of light, cannot be constituted by implied grant.[2]

Express or Implied reservation

If the disponer of a tenement wishes to retain any positive right over lands disponed he may and should reserve it expressly,[3] and the constitution of a servitude by implied reservation is possible but is seldom upheld. Both tenements must have been in the ownership of the same person and later separated.[4]

Reservations may be implied where after separation some right over one tenement is absolutely necessary for the use of the other tenement[5] but not where some use was being made of the one part for the benefit of the other and was necessary for the comfortable or convenient enjoyment of the other,[6] as such would be a derogation from the disponer's own grant.[7]

Prescription

A positive servitude may be held created by actual use of a right for an uninterrupted period of forty years.[8] The claimant must be infeft in the tenement claiming the servitude right.[9] The possession or use of the right claimed must be uninterrupted,[10] open and such as to amount to a clear assertion of the kind of servitude right claimed, must not have been in reliance on any permission or licence, must have been exercised peaceably rather than in face of opposition, and known, or such as reasonably should have been known, to the owner of the servient tenement

Glasgow Mags. (1876) 3 R. 1130; *McLaren* v. *City of Glasgow Union Ry. Co.* (1878) 5 R. 1042; *Rome* v. *Hope Johnstone* (1884) 11 R. 653; *Union Herit. Secy. Co.* v. *Mathie* (1886) 13 R. 670; *Fraser* v. *Cox*, 1938 S.C. 506.

1 *Ewart & Cochrane* (1861) 4 Macq. 117; *Gow's Trs.* v. *Mealls* (1875) 2 R. 729; *Alexander* v. *Butchart* (1875) 3 R. 156; *Campbell* v. *Halkett* (1890) 27 S.L.R. 1000; *Cullens* v. *Cambusbarron Soc.* (1895) 23 R. 209. See also *Argyllshire Commrs. of Supply* v. *Campbell* (1885) 12 R. 1255; *Boyd* v. *Hamilton*, 1907 S.C. 912.

2 *Inglis* v. *Clark* (1901) 4 F. 288; *Metcalfe* v. *Purdon* (1902) 4 F. 507.

3 *Shearer* v. *Peddie* (1899) 1 F. 1201.

4 *Menzies* v. *M. Breadalbane* (1901) 4 F. 59.

5 Bell, *Prin.* §992; *Fergusson* v. *Campbell*, 1913 1 S.L.T. 241.

6 *Ewart* v. *Cochrane* (1861) 4 Macq. 117; See also *Gow's Trs.* v. *Mealls* (1875) 2 R. 729; *McLaren* v. *City of Glasgow Union Ry. Co.* (1878) 5 R. 1048.

7 Bell, *Prin.* §992; *Shearer* v. *Peddie* (1899) 1 F. 1201.

8 Prescription Act, 1617; preserved by Conveyancing (Sc.) Act, 1874, S. 34, and Conveyancing (Sc.) Act, 1924, S. 16 (2); *Scotland* v. *Wallace*, 1964 S.L.T. (Sh. Ct.) 9.

9 Stair II, 3, 73; II, 7, 2; Ersk. II, 9, 3; Bell, *Prin.* §993; *Beaumont* v. *Lord Glenlyon* (1843) 5 D. 1337; *McDonald* v. *Dempster* (1871) 10 M. 94.

10 *Macnab* v. *Ferguson* (1890) 17 R. 397; *McInroy* v. *D. Atholl* (1891) 18 R. (H.L.) 46.

or his agents on the spot.[1] If acquired in this way, the kind and extent of servitude right acquired is determined by the prescriptive possession proved, though it may be extended to include such a development of the use as could reasonably be held involved in the possession,[2] but it may not be increased.[3]

Acquiescence

A servitude may be held established by acquiescence in the exercise of a servitude right, yielding an inference of a grant and personally barring challenge thereof. The right acquiesced in must be obvious and such as to preclude the inference that it was a mere licence.[4]

POSITIVE SERVITUDES

Positive servitudes are those rights which the owner of the dominant tenement of land is entitled to exercise over the servient tenement and which are capable of possession in the form of active exercise. They consist *in patiendo*. An obligation consisting *in faciendo* is not a servitude.[5] Some are urban, appropriate to tenements in towns, other rural, appropriate to country districts.

POSITIVE URBAN SERVITUDES

Support

Two servitudes of support are recognized;[6] the servitude *tigni immittendi*[7] is the right to insert into the wall of the servient tenement a beam or other structural member of the dominant tenement, maintain it there, and renew it when necessary. The servitude *oneris ferendi*[8] is the right to rest the beams of the dominant on the wall of the servient tenement and latterly to have whole rooms resting on another's tenement. In this case alone

1 *McInroy* v. *D. Atholl* (1891) 18 R. (H.L.) 46; *McGregor* v. *Crieff Co-operative Socy.*, 1915 S.C. (H.L.) 93.

2 Ersk. II, 9, 4; Bell, *Prin.* §993; *Carstairs* v. *Spence*, 1924 S.C. 380, 385; *Kerr* v. *Brown*, 1939 S.C. 140; See also *E. Kintore* v. *Pirie* (1906) 8 F. (H.L.) 16; *White* v. *W.* (1906) 8 F. (H.L.) 41.

3 *Dunbar Mags.* v. *Sawers* (1829) 7 S. 672; *Kerr* v. *Brown*, 1939 S.C. 140.

4 Bell, *Prin.* §946; *Macgregor* v. *Balfour* (1899) 2 F. 345, 351.

5 *Nicolson* v. *Melvill* (1708) Mor. 14516.

6 Stair II, 7, 6; Mack. II, 9, 6, 7; Forbes II, 4, 3, 2; Bankt. II, 7, 7; Ersk. II, 9, 7; Bell, *Prin.* §1003.

7 Inst. II, 1, 29; Dig. 50, 16, 62.

8 Dig. 8, 5; *Robertson* v. *Sc. Union and National Ins. Co.*, 1943 S.C. 427.

the servitude implies a duty on the servient owner to maintain the servient tenement.[1]

Stillicide

The servitude of stillicide or eavesdrop[2] entitles the dominant tenement to discharge rainwater from a roof on to the servient tenement.[3] Apart from this servitude there is no right to do so though there is a right to discharge surface water by natural drainage on to the inferior lands.[4]

POSITIVE RURAL SERVITUDES

Way, Access, or Passage

A servitude right of way differs from a public right of way in that the rights of use, and the title to vindicate it, are in the owner of the dominant tenement only, not in the public or any members thereof.[5] The kind of right of way granted, whether for foot passage, horse road, drove road, or carriage road,[6] depends on the grant or the possession exercised. A grant of wider use implies grant of narrower uses.[7] The right may be limited to use for particular purposes[8] in which case the dominant owner may be restricted to that use, and the right lapses if that use is no longer necessary.[9]

The servient owner may erect gates but may not lock them[10] and, with the consent of the dominant owner or the authority of the court, substitute an alternative way equally convenient.[11] The

[1] Stair II, 7, 6; Ersk. II, 9, 8; Bell, *Prin.* §1003; *Murray* v. *Brownhill* (1715) Mor. 14521.

[2] Stair II, 7, 7; Mack. II, 9, 8; Forbes II, 4, 3, 2; Bankt. II, 7, 12; Ersk. II, 9, 9; Bell, *Prin.* §1004.

[3] *Stirling* v. *Finlayson* (1752) Mor. 14526; *Scouller* v. *Pollock* (1832) 10 S. 241; *Mathieson* v. *Gibson* (1874) 12 S.L.R. 124.

[4] Bell, *Prin.* §968; *Campbell* v. *Bryson* (1864) 3 M. 254; *Anderson* v. *Robertson*, 1958 S.C. 367.

[5] *Thomson* v. *Murdoch* (1862) 24 D. 975; cf. also *Paterson* v. *Airdrie Water Co.* (1893) 20 R. 370; *Ayr Burgh Council* v. *B.T.C.*, 1955 S.L.T. 219.

[6] Including motor cars: *Smith* v. *Saxton*, 1928 S.N. 59; but see *Crawford* v. *Lumsden*, 1951 S.L.T. (Notes) 62.

[7] *Swan* v. *Buist* (1834) 12 S. 316; *Malcolm* v. *Lloyd* (1886) 13 R. 512; *Carstairs* v. *Spence*, 1924 S.C. 380. See also *Reid* v. *Haldane's Trs.* (1891) 18 R. 744, 746; *Millar* v. *Christie*, 1961 S.C. 1.

[8] *Bruce* v. *Wardlaw* (1748) Mor. 14525; *Porteous* v. *Allan* (1773) Mor. 14512; *Winans* v. *L. Tweedmouth* (1888) 15 R. 540; *Carstairs* v. *Spence*, 1924 S.C. 380, 385.

[9] *Cronin* v. *Sutherland* (1899) 2 F. 217.

[10] *Oliver* v. *Robertson* (1869) 8 M. 137; *Sutherland* v. *Thomson* (1876) 3 R. 485.

[11] *Bain* v. *Smith* (1871) 8 S.L.R. 539; *Moyes* v. *McDiarmid* (1900) 2 F. 918.

court cannot sanction alteration if the right is clearly defined by grant or possession.[1]

Aqueduct

The servitude of aqueduct[2] is the right to lead water from the servient into the dominant tenement, and implies a right of access to the lade or pipes at reasonable times for repair[3] and a right to prevent buildings interfering with the line of supply.[4] The water may be for natural uses or for water power.[5] The dominant owner must maintain the works.[6] Neither dominant nor servient owner may pollute the water any more than he may pollute a stream.[7] Similar to this is the servitude of dam or dam-head, the right of gathering water on the neighbour's land and of building dykes or dams for containing the water.[8]

Aquaehaustus

This is the right of drawing water at a stream, well or pond on the servient tenement, particularly for cattle but possibly for other purposes also.[9] The servient owner may still take water so long as he does not prejudice the dominant owner's requirements.[10]

Pasturage

The grant is normally of a right of pasturage of stock in common with others of a community.[11] If indefinite in extent the grant is measured by the amount of stock that can be pastured on the servient tenement.[12] Tree planting on servient land is

1 *Hill* v. *McLaren* (1879) 6 R. 1363; *Moyes*, *supra*.

2 Stair II, 7, 8; Mack. II, 9, 4; Forbes II, 4, 3; Bankt. II, 7, 28; Ersk. II, 9, 13, and 35; Bell, *Prin.* §1012.

3 *Weir* v. *Glenny* (1833) 7 W. & S. 244.

4 *Tennant's Trs.* v. *Dennistoun* (1894) 2 S.L.T. 78.

5 *Prestoun* v. *Erskine* (1714) Mor. 10919; *L. Blantyre* v. *Dunn* (1848) 10 D. 509; See also *McIntyre* v. *Orr* (1868) 6 S.L.R. 152.

6 *Scottish Highland Distillery* v. *Reid* (1877) 4 R. 1118; *Smith* v. *Denny Police Commrs.* (1880) 7 R. (H.L.) 28; *Strachan* v. *Aberdeen* (1905) 12 S.L.T. 725.

7 *Ewen* v. *Turnbull's Trs.* (1857) 19 D. 513; *Mackay* v. *Greenhill* (1858) 20 D. 1251; *Caledonian Ry.* v. *Baird* (1876) 3 R. 839.

8 *Sc. Highland Distillery*, *supra*; see also *Robson* v. *Chalmers Property Co.*, 1965 S.L.T. 381.

9 Stair II, 7, 11; Ersk. II, 9, 12; Bell, *Prin.* §1011; *Macnab* v. *Munro Ferguson* (1890) 17 R. 397; as to underground water, see *Harper* v. *Stuart* (1907) 15 S.L.T. 550; *Crichton* v. *Turnbull*, 1946 S.C. 52.

10 *Donaldson* v. *E. Strathmore* (1877) 14 S.L.R. 587; *Crichton* v. *Turnbull* 1946 S.C. 52.

11 Stair II, 7, 14; Ersk. II, 9, 15; Bell, *Prin.* §1013; see e.g. *Dundee Mags.* v. *Hunter* (1843) 6 D. 18; (1858) 20 D. 1067; *Campbell* v. *McKinnon* (1867) 5 M. 636.

12 *L. Breadalbane* v. *Menzies* (1741) 5 B.S. 710.

permissible so long as sufficient pasturage is left to satisfy the servitude.[1]

Fuel, feal, and divot

In these servitudes[2] the right is to dig peat for fuel,[3] or take clods for fencing and roofing. There is implied a right of access to the locality and liberty to stack and dry peats.[4]

Discharge of drainage

A servitude right to discharge waste water has been recognized, but not closet sewage.[5]

Other rural servitudes

Other recognized rural servitudes include taking sea-ware,[6] stone, slate,[7] sand or gravel,[8] for the benefit of the dominant tenement, and of bleaching linen.[9]

A more modern development is the wayleave, or right to run a pipeline through land,[10] or an electricity or telephone line over it. The Pipelines Act, 1962, enables the Minister of Power to control the development of cross-country pipelines, and enables bodies wishing to construct such lines to obtain compulsorily the rights needed therefor.

NEGATIVE SERVITUDES

Negative servitudes consist *in non faciendo*, in rights in the owner of the dominant tenement to prevent or restrain some action by the owner of the servient tenement but which are not capable of possession in the sense of being exercised, and which

[1] *Fraser* v. *Secy. of State for Scotland*, 1959 S.L.T. (Notes) 36.

[2] Stair II, 7, 31; Mack. II, 9, 32; Bankt. II, 7, 31; Ersk. II, 9, 17; Bell, *Prin.* §986, 1014.

[3] cf. *Watson* v. *Sinclair*, 1966 S.L.T. (Sh. Ct.) 77; as to coal, see *Harvie* v. *Stewart* (1870) 9 M. 129.

[4] *Dingwall* v. *Farquharson* (1797) 3 Pat. 564; *Dinwiddie* v. *Corrie* (1821) 1 S. 164; *Grierson* v. *Sandsting School Board* (1882) 9 R. 437.

[5] *Kerr* v. *Brown*, 1939 S.C. 140.

[6] *E. Morton* v. *Covingtree* (1760) Mor. 13528; *Baird* v. *Fortune* (1800) 4 Macq. 127; *Agnew* v. *L.A.* (1873) 11 M. 309, 333; *McTaggart* v. *McDouall* (1867) 5 M. 534, 547.

[7] Bell, *Prin.* §1015; *Murray* v. *Peebles Mags.*, 8 Dec. 1808, F.C.; *Keith* v. *Stonehaven Harbour Commrs.* (1830) 5 W. & S. 234.

[8] *Sharp* v. *D. Hamilton* (1829) 7 S. 679; *Aikman* v. *D. Hamilton* (1830) 8 S. 943; 6 W. & S. 64.

[9] *Sinclair* v. *Dysart Mags.* (1779) Mor. 14159; 2 Pat. 554; *Rattray* v. *Tayport Patent Slip Co.* (1868) 5 S.L.R. 219.

[10] cf. *Mackenzie* v. *Gillanders* (1870) 7 S.L.R. 333; *Bridges* v. *Fraserburgh Police Commrs.* (1889) 25 S.L.R. 151.

therefore require constitution by express grant.[1] Any probative writing will suffice and it need not enter the title.[2] Words purporting to create a negative servitude must be construed strictly, there being a presumption for freedom.[3] Meaningless words must be ignored.[3]

The only recognized negative servitudes are of light and air and of prospect,[4] based on the servitudes *ne luminibus officiatur*, *non aedificandi*, and *altius non tollendi*.

In each case the servitude is a restriction on the liberty of the owner of the servitude tenement to use his property. He may be taken bound not to build, or to plant trees or bushes, so as to cut off the dominant tenement's light or view,[5] or not to build higher than a stated height,[6] or not to open a window in his wall which would overlook the dominant tenement.[7] Servitudes of light cannot be constituted by implied grant.[8] There is no recognized servitude of prospect in favour of an upper proprietor against a lower proprietor in flatted premises.[9]

EXTINCTION OF SERVITUDES

A servitude may be extinguished (1) by express discharge or renunciation in probative writing by the owner of the dominant tenement.[10] (2) It may be lost by conduct on the part of the owner of the dominant tenement evidencing an intention to relinquish it or barring him personally from seeking to enforce it.[11] (3) It

[1] *Dundas* v. *Blair* (1886) 13 R. 759; *King* v. *Barnetson* (1896) 24 R. 81; *Inglis* v. *Clark* (1901) 4 F. 288; *Metcalfe* v. *Purdon* (1902) 4 F. 507.

[2] *Cowan* v. *Stewart* (1872) 10 M. 735; *Banks* v. *Walker* (1874) 1 R. 981; *Campbell's Trs.* v. *Glasgow Corpn.* (1902) 4 F. 752; *Proprs. of Royal Exchange, Glasgow* v. *Cotton*, 1912 S.C. 1151; *Stephen* v. *Brown's Trs.*, 1922 S.C. 136.

[3] *Hunter* v. *Fox*, 1964 S.C. (H.L.) 95.

[4] Stair II, 7, 9; Mack. II, 9, 9; Forbes II, 4, 3, 2; Bankt. II, 7, 5; Ersk. II, 9, 10; Bell, *Prin.* §1005.

[5] *McNeill* v. *Mackenzie* (1870) 8 M. 520; *Malloch* v. *Gray* (1872) 10 M. 774; *Argyllshire Commrs.* v. *Campbell* (1885) 12 R. 1255; *Johnson* v. *MacRitchie* (1893) 20 R. 539; *Clark* v. *Perth School Board* (1898) 25 R. 919; *Hunter* v. *Fox*, 1964 S.C. (H.L.) 95.

[6] Bell, *Prin.* §1007; *Edinburgh Mags.* v. *Brown* (1833) 11 S. 255; *Edinburgh Mags.* v. *Paton & Ritchie* (1858) 20 D. 731; *Malloch* v. *Gray* (1872) 10 M. 774; but see *Banks* v. *Walker* (1874) 1 R. 980.

[7] Bell, *Prin.* §1006; *Forbes* v. *Wilson* (1724) Mor. 14505.

[8] *Inglis* v. *Clark* (1901) 4 F. 288; *Metcalfe* v. *Purdon* (1902) 4 F. 507; cf. *King* v. *Barnetson* (1896) 24 R. 81.

[9] *Birrell* v. *Lumley* (1905) 12 S.L.T. 719.

[10] Stair II, 7, 4; Ersk. II, 9, 37; Bell, *Prin.* §998; see also *Macdonald* v. *Inverness Mags.*, 1918 S.C. 141; *Macdonald* v. *M.* (1959) 48 L.C. 22.

[11] Bell, *Prin.* §999; Rankine, *L.O.* 441; *Muirhead* v. *Glasgow Highland Socy.* (1864) 2 M. 420; *Bridges* v. *L. Saltoun* (1873) 11 M. 588; *Campbell Douglas* v. *Hozier* (1878) 16 S.L.R. 14; *Mags. of Rutherglen* v. *Bainbridge* (1886) 13 R. 745; *Davidson* v. *Thomson*

may be extinguished, as by acquisition of the servient tenement under compulsory powers free of servitudes.[1] (4) It is extinguished if either dominant or servient tenement be destroyed, though only suspended if either tenement be merely temporarily incapacitated, as by requisition.[2] (5) It is extinguished *confusione* if both tenements come into the ownership of the same person.[3] If the tenements are subsequently separated again, the servitude does not revive but must be reconstituted.[4] This does not, however, happen if though the same person comes to own both tenements he does so on different titles and a subsequent separation of the tenements is to be anticipated independently of his volition.[5] (6) It may be extinguished by the running of the negative prescription. A positive servitude will be lost by the complete non-exercise of the rights conferred for forty years, from the last occasion on which the right was exercised.[6] If there is interruption of user by the servient tenement, it must be, and can be intended as, an assertion of adverse right.[7] A negative servitude will be lost by the failure to challenge conduct by the servient owner infringing the servitude restriction for forty years from the date of the first contravention.[8] The negative prescription may apply even though the servitude appears in the titles of the servient tenement.[9] (7) Statutory powers may interfere with or extinguish servitudes.[10]

THIRLAGE

Thirlage is frequently classed with servitudes, though really depends on other principles. Thirlage is the restriction of lands

(1890) 17 R. 287; cf. *Stevenson* v. *Donaldson*, 1935 S.C. 551. Acquiescence in a limitation of a right does not extinguish it: *Millar* v. *Christie*, 1961 S.C. 1.

[1] *Oban Mags.* v. *Callander and Oban Ry. Co.* (1892) 19 R. 912; *Largs Hydropathic, Ltd.* v. *Largs Town Council*, 1967 S.L.T. 23.

[2] Ersk. II, 9, 37; Bell, *Prin.* §995; *Forbes' Trs.* v. *Davidson* (1892) 19 R. 1022; *Porteous* v. *Haig* (1901) 3 F. 347; *Gordon's Trs.* v. *Thompson*, 1910 S.C. 22; cf. *Winans* v. *L. Tweedmouth* (1888) 15 R. 540, 568.

[3] Mack. II, 9, 32; Ersk. II, 9, 16, and 37; Bell, *Prin.* §997; *Donaldson's Trs.* v. *Forbes* (1839) 1 D. 449.

[4] Ersk. II, 9, 37; *Union Bank* v. *Daily Record* (1902) 10 S.L.T. 71.

[5] Bell, *Prin.* §997; *Carnegie* v. *MacTier* (1844) 6 D. 1381, 1407; *Union Bank* v. *Daily Record* (1902) 10 S.L.T. 71.

[6] Conveyancing (Sc.) Act, 1924, S. 17(2); Ersk. II, 9, 37; *Beaton* v. *Ogilvie* (1670) Mor. 10912; *Graham* v. *Douglas* (1735) Mor. 10745; cf. *Brown* v. *Carron Co.*, 1909 S.C. 452.

[7] *Stevenson* v. *Donaldson*, 1935 S.C. 551.

[8] Ersk. II, 9, 37; Bell, *Prin.* §999; *Wilkie* v. *Scott* (1688) Mor. 11189; Conveyancing (Sc.) Act, 1924 S. 17(2).

[9] *Graham* v. *Douglas* (1735) Mor. 10745.

[10] E.g. Lands Clauses Consolidation (Sc.) Act, 1845, Ss. 93–8; Housing (Sc.) Act, 1966, S. 51; New Towns (Sc.) Act, 1968, S. 19.

and their inhabitants to particular mills for the grinding of corn with the burden of paying such duties and services as are expressed or implied in the constitution of the right. Multures are the proportion of grain paid to the miller for the grinding of the rest.[1]

1 Ersk. II, 9, 18 *et seq.*; Bell, *Prin.* §1016 *et seq.*; see also *Stobbs* v. *Caven* (1873) 11 M. 530; *Sutherland* v. *Reid's Trs.* (1881) 8 R. 514; *Forbes' Trs.* v. *Davidson* (1892) 19 R. 1022; *L.A.* v. *E. Home* (1895) 2 S.L.T. 435; *Porteous* v. *Haig* (1901) 3 F. 347; *Sempill* v. *Leith-Hay* (1903) 5 F. 868; *Edinburgh Mags.* v. *Edinburgh United Breweries* (1903) 5 F. 1048; *Brown* v. *Livingstone-Learmonth's Trs.* (1906) 14 S.L.T. 142; *Brown* v. *Carron Co.*, 1909 S.C. 452; *Gordon's Trs.* v. *Thompson*, 1910 S.C. 22.

CHAPTER 87

LICENCES

A LICENCE is an express or implied permission to enter on or do on or in relation to land what would otherwise be a trespass or other wrong, such as to enter on, or occupy, premises[1] or camp on land, or shoot over it,[2] or fish a stream through lands,[3] or post bills on a wall.[4] It is only by licence that persons other than travellers may enter such premises as stations.[5] It may be a gratuitous grant, or onerous, granted in pursuance of contract,[6] such as the contract to admit to a theatre to see a show, and, in either case, conditional[7] or unconditional. A licence to enter is frequently implied, as by the exhibition of goods for sale,[8] or by the opening of a place as a public park.[9]

A licence confers no real right in the land, but is a personal right only, revocable at any time, unless the grant or contract provides to the contrary,[10] and is invalid against singular successors of the landlord. It is not assignable by the licensee. If revoked before the due termination, expressly or by sale of the land or use inconsistently with the licence, the licensee has only a personal claim against the licensor for breach of contract. Thus an employee permitted to occupy a house in connection with his employment

[1] *Johnston* v. *J.* (1904) 6 F. 665; cf. *Clark* v. *C.* (1871) 9 M. 430; *Gibson* v. *Stewar,* (1894) 21 R. 437; *Bayne's Trs.* v. *B.* (1894) 22 R. 26; *Cathcart's Trs.* v. *Allardice* (1899) 2 F. 326.

[2] cf. Night Poaching Act, 1828, S. 1; Game (Sc.) Act, 1832 (Day Trespass Act), S. 1; *Calder* v. *Robertson* (1878) 6 R. (J.) 3; *Jack* v. *Nairne* (1887) 14 R. (J.) 20; *Richardson* v. *Maitland* (1897) 24 R. (J.) 32; *Thurlow* v. *Tait* (1893) 1 S.L.T. 62; *Morrison* v. *Andersont* 1913 S.C. (J.) 114.

[3] *Copland* v. *Maxwell* (1871) 9 M. (H.L.) 1.

[4] *U.K. Advertising Co.* v. *Glasgow Bag Wash Co.*, 1926 S.C. 303; cf. *Popular Amusements, Ltd.* v. *Edinburgh Assessor,* 1909 S.C. 645; see also *Wilson* v. *Kincardineshire Assessor,* 1913 S.C. 704; *L.N.E.Ry.* v. *Glasgow Assessor,* 1937 S.C. 309; *Perth Mags.* v. *Perth Assessor* 1937 S.C. 549, 558.

[5] *Perth General Stn. Office* v. *Ross* (1897) 24 R. (H.L.) 44.

[6] *Johnston, supra*; see also *Inland Revenue* v. *Anderson,* 1922 S.C. 284; *Glasgow Tramway Co.* v. *Glasgow Corpn.* (1898) 25 R. (H.L.) 77.

[7] Thus children may be allowed to enter certain premises only if accompanied.

[8] The distinction formerly drawn between invitees (persons expressly or impliedly invited to enter) and licensees (persons expressly or implicitly permitted to enter) which was relevant to the question of the occupier's liability for harm, is not relevant for the purposes of this chapter.

[9] cf. *Taylor* v. *Glasgow Corpn.*, 1922 S.C. (H.L.) 1; *Plank* v. *Stirling Mags.*, 1956 S.C. 92.

[10] *Johnston, supra*; see also *Inland Revenue* v. *Anderson,* 1922 S.C. 284; *Glasgow Tramway Co.* v. *Glasgow Corpn.* (1898) 25 R. (H.L.) 77.

is not entitled to stay after dismissal and, if he does, may be ejected as a trespasser.[1]

The occupier of premises owes to a person invited or licensed to enter the duty of reasonable care in the circumstances, owed by an occupier to a legitimate visitor.[2]

A person expressly or impliedly licensed to come on premises becomes a trespasser if he stays there after the purpose on which he came has been fulfilled, and may be ejected, if necessary by reasonable force.[3] But a person *prima facie* a trespasser may be deemed a licensee if trespass in such circumstances has been so repeatedly tolerated as to imply acquiescence by the occupier in his presence.[4]

1 *Sinclair* v. *Tod*, 1907 S.C. 1038.
2 Occupiers Liability (Sc.) Act, 1960, Ss. 1–2.
3 *Wood* v. *N.B. Ry.* (1899) 2 F. 1.
4 *Dumbreck* v. *Addie's Collieries*, 1929 S.C. (H.L.) 51; *Breslin* v. *L.N.E. Ry.*, 1936 S.C. 816.

CHAPTER 88

LEASES

A LEASE or tack is the letting on hire of lands or buildings for a determinate period on conditions including a pecuniary return known as rent,[1] or in mineral leases lordship. The return may be in goods rather than money. The grant of occupancy of a house to a servant, if his occupancy is ancillary and necessary to the performance of his duties, is treated as an incident of a service contract rather than a lease,[2] unless there are exceptional provisions.[3] While the same principles are generally applicable modern statutory modifications have made the rules applicable to urban leases for habitation or business and to agricultural leases for farming diverge so that they require separate treatment, while special legislation deals with crofters' holdings. The conveyance of lands for minerals to be mined or quarried therefrom, though in reality a sale of part of the lands, is normally known as a mineral lease and the incidents of such a transaction are treated as within the law of leases,[4] save that a power to grant leases does not, generally, unless minerals have previously been let, import a power to grant mineral leases.[5] The lease of land for a long term for the erection of buildings, and the letting of sporting rights over land are also exceptional classes of leases.

It may sometimes be a narrow question whether an agreement is a lease or, on the other hand, a licence,[6] or a sale,[7] or a disposition in security,[8] or a joint adventure.[9]

[1] Stair II, 9, 1; Mack. II, 6, 5; Bankt. II, 9, 1; Ersk. II, 6, 20; Ross. *Lect.* II, 456; Bell, *Prin.* §1177; Hunter, *Landlord and Tenant*; Rankine, *Leases*; Paton and Cameron, *Landlord and Tenant*.

[2] *Sinclair* v. *Tod*, 1907 S.C. 1038; *M. Bute* v. *Prenderleith*, 1921 S.C. 281; *Pollock* v. *Inverness Assessor*, 1923 S.C. 693; *Cairns* v. *Innes*, 1942 S.C. 164; *MacGregor* v. *Dunnett*, 1949 S.C. 510; *Cargill* v. *Phillips*, 1951 S.C. 67.

[3] *Dunbar's Trs.* v. *Bruce* (1900) 3 F. 137; *Carron Co.* v. *Francis*, 1915 S.C. 872.

[4] *Campbell* v. *Grant* (1827) 6 S. 188; *Gowans* v. *Christie* (1873) 11 M. (H.L.) 1, 12; *Mungall* v. *Bowhill Coal Co.* (1900) 2 F. 1073.

[5] *Campbell* v. *Wardlaw* (1887) 10 R. (H.L.) 65; *Nugent's Trs.* v. *N.* (1898) 25 R. 475.

[6] *Brand* v. *Bell's Trs.* (1872) 11 M. 42; *Glasgow Tramway Co.* v. *Glasgow Corpn.* (1897) 24 R. 628; *Bo'ness Mags.* v. *Linlithgowshire Assessor*, 1907 S.C. 774; *Popular Amusements, Ltd.* v. *Edinburgh Assessor*, 1909 S.C. 645; *Wilson* v. *Kincardineshire Assessor*, 1913 S.C. 704; *I.R.C.* v. *Anderson*, 1922 S.C. 284; *U.K. Advertising Co.* v. *Glasgow Bagwash Co.*,

For notes 7, 8, 9 see next page.

Contract for a lease

The parties to a contract to let and to take lands on lease must respectively have capacity to grant[1] and to take[2] lands on lease. They must have reached agreement[3] on at least the salient elements of the contract, namely the subjects, the duration of the lease, and the rent. Some other terms, if not expressed, will be supplied by legal implication, such as that entry, if not stated, is to be immediate.[4]

Their agreement, if to endure for more than a year, must be constituted by writing probative or holograph or adopted as holograph of both parties, failing which either has *locus poenitentiae*,[5] unless resiling has been barred by actings on the faith of oral or improbative agreement, established by writ or oath, and held to amount to homologation or *rei interventus*.[6] The actings relied on may be proved by parole.[7] An inference of grant of a lease may be drawn from a unilateral obligation to grant followed by *rei interventus* and possession by the tenant.[8]

But a contract to let heritage for not more than a year may be constituted orally and proved *prout de jure*.[9] A verbal lease for

1926 S.C. 303; *Broomhill Motor Co.* v. *Glasgow Assessor*, 1927 S.C. 447; *Perth Mags.* v. *Perth Assessor*, 1937 S.C. 549; *L.M.S. Ry.* v. *Assessor of Public Undertakings*, 1937 S.C. 773; *Chaplin* v. *Perth Assessor*, 1947 S.C. 373; *Mann* v. *Houston*, 1957 S.L.T. 89.

7 *Ferguson* v. *Fyffe* (1868) 6 S.L.R. 68; *Brand* v. *Bell's Trs.* (1872) 11 M. 42; *McCosh* v. *Ayrshire Assessor*, 1945 S.C. 260; *Collective Securities Co.* v. *Ayrshire Assessor*, 1946 S.C. 244.

8 *Heritable Securities Inv. Assoc.* v. *Wingate* (1880) 7 R. 1094; cf. *Paterson's Tr.* v. *P's Trs.* (1891) 19 R. 91.

9 *Beresford's Tr.* v. *Argyllshire Assessor* (1884) 11 R. 818.

1 Only an infeft proprietor can grant a valid lease: Bell, *Prin.* §1181. A liferenter cannot grant a lease for longer than his liferent: *Thomson* v. *Merston* (1628) Mor. 8252. As to trustees' powers, see Trusts (Sc.) Act, 1921, Ss. 4–5. As to bondholder in possession, see Heritable Securities Act, 1894, Ss. 6–7: *Mackenzie* v. *Imlay's Trs.*, 1912 S.C. 685; as to *ex facie* absolute disponee, see *Abbott* v. *Mitchell* (1870) 8 M. 791; *Ritchie* v. *Scott* (1899) 1 F. 728.

2 As to trustees' powers, see Trusts (Sc.) Act, 1921, S. 10.

3 *Dallas* v. *Fraser* (1840) 11 D. 1058; *Erskine* v. *Glendinning* (1871) 9 M. 656; *Buchanan* v. *D. Hamilton* (1878) 5 R. (H.L.) 69; *Christie* v. *Fife Coal Co.* (1899) 2 F. 192; *Wight* v. *Newton*, 1911 S.C. 762; *Gray* v. *Edinburgh University*, 1962 S.C. 157.

4 *Christie, supra.*

5 *Walker & Flint* (1863) 1 M. 417; *Fowlie* v. *McLean* (1868) 6 M. 254; *Gibson* v. *Adams* (1875) 3 R. 144; *Sinclair* v. *Caithness Flagstone Co.* (1880) 7 R. 1117.

6 *Sellar* v. *Aiton* (1875) 2 R. 381; *Gibson* v. *Adams* (1875) 3 R. 144; *Wilson* v. *Mann* (1876) 3 R. 527; *Station Hotel, Nairn* v. *Macpherson* (1905) 13 S.L.T. 456.

7 *Gowan's Trs.* v. *Carstairs* (1862) 24 D. 1382; *Walker* v. *Flint* (1863) 1 M. 417; *Allan* v. *Gilchrist* (1875) 2 R. 587.

8 *Campbeltown Coal Co.* v. *D. Argyll*, 1926 S.C. 126.

9 Bell, *Prin.* §1187; *Monteith* v. *Tenants* (1582) Mor. 8397; *Fraser* v. *Leslie* (1581) Mor. 12405; *Gibson* v. *Adams* (1875) 3 R. 144.

more than a year, if followed by possession, is obligatory for a year.

Duration

A lease may be for any duration, even renewable for ever.[1] If no duration be expressed the lease is treated as one for a year only, renewable by tacit relocation,[2] provided that possession is taken.[3]

The lease in implement of the contract

A contract to let heritage should be implemented by a written lease, which should, if for over a year, be probative or holograph of both parties. If not holograph or probative of both, it is equally binding if followed by possession or other actings implying homologation or *rei interventus*.[4] But written agreement to let for more than a year may equally be completed by possession or other actings unequivocally referable thereto and implying homologation or *rei interventus*.[5] An oral agreement to let for more than one year, if followed by possession thereunder, is binding on both parties for one year, or till the end of any year thereof.[6]

An agreement for a lease for not more than a year does not require to be completed by a written lease. A presumption of the relationship of lease arises from mere occupation of lettable subjects.[7]

A lease is liable to reduction on such a ground as that it was obtained by fraudulent misrepresentation.[8]

A formal lease normally contains a clause of warrandice undertaking to indemnify the lessee if he is evicted from the subjects of let.[9]

[1] *Campbell* v. *McLean* (1870) 8 M. (H.L.) 40; cf. *L.A.* v. *Fraser* (1762) 2 Pat. 66 (1140 years); *Carron Co.* v. *Henderson's Trs.* (1896) 23 R. 1042 (171 years); *Crawford* v. *Livingstone's Trs.*, 1938 S.C. 609 (354 years). Building leases are commonly for 99 or 999 years.

[2] *Dunlop* v. *Steel Co. of Scotland* (1879) 7 R. 283.

[3] *Gray* v. *Edinburgh Univ.*, 1962 S.C. 157.

[4] *Carlyle* v. *Baxter* (1869) 6 S.L.R. 425; *Bathie* v. *L. Wharncliffe* (1873) 11 M. 490; *Ballantine* v. *Stevenson* (1881) 8 R. 959; *Wight* v. *Newton*, 1911 S.C. 762; *Wares* v. *Duff-Dunbar's Trs.*, 1920 S.C. 5; *Danish Dairy Co.* v. *Gillespie*, 1922 S.C. 656; *Pollok* v. *Whiteford*, 1936 S.C. 402.

[5] *Campbell* v. *McLean* (1870) 8 M. (H.L.) 40; *Forbes* v. *Wilson* (1873) 11 M. 454; *Sellar* v. *Aiton* (1875) 2 R. 381; *Gardner* v. *Beresford's Trs.* (1878) 5 R. 638; 5 R. (H.L.) 105; *Bell* v. *Goodall* (1883) 10 R. 905; *Sutherland's Tr.* v. *Miller's Tr.* (1888) 16 R. 10; *Buchanan* v. *Harris & Sheldon* (1900) 2 F. 935.

[6] *Neill* v. *E. Cassilis*, 22 Nov. 1810, F.C.

[7] *Glen* v. *Roy* (1882) 10 R. 239.

[8] *Beresford's Tr.* v. *Gardner* (1877) 4 R. 363.

[9] *Menzies* v. *Whyte* (1888) 15 R. 470; *D. Bedford* v. *E. Galloway's Tr.* (1904) 6 F. 971; *Dougall* v. *Dunfermline Mags.*, 1908 S.C. 151; *Wolfson* v. *Forrester*, 1910 S.C. 675.

A lease does not, in general, require any registration to complete the title of the tenant.

Interpretation

The ordinary principles of construction fall to be applied to a lease. If it relates to lands in Scotland, it *prima facie* falls to be interpreted by Scots law, even if drawn in English form.[1] If the terms are ambiguous, the lease may be construed by the possession which has followed on it,[2] but not by the circumstances in which it was granted.[3] Where certain terms are uncertain, as by describing lands as formerly tenanted by another, extrinsic evidence is admissible to clarify the doubt.[4]

Modification of lease

The usual principle applies that a written lease cannot be qualified or modified save by other probative writing.[5] Alleged collateral agreements made prior to the execution of the lease may be proved by writ or oath.[6] Alleged agreements made subsequent to the lease and modifying it similarly require proof by writ or oath followed by *rei interventus*,[7] or parole evidence of an oral agreement followed by actings in pursuance thereof and implying acquiescence.[8] Apart from agreement, consent to actings in contravention of a lease may be implied from knowledge and acquiescence, which may be proved by parole,[9] and a lease may be altered *rebus ipsis et factis* by acts of the parties necessarily and unequivocally importing an agreement to alter the lease, which acts may be proved by parole.[9]

Real rights under lease

At common law leases were purely contractual and conferred only personal rights on the tenants, binding the landlord and his representatives but not binding on the landlord's singular succes-

[1] *Macintosh* v. *May* (1895) 22 R. 345.

[2] *Mackay* v. *Maclachlan* (1899) 7 S.L.T. 48; *Watters* v. *Hunter*, 1927 S.C. 310.

[3] *Shawrigg Fireclay Co.* v. *Larkhall Collieries* (1903) 5 F. 1131.

[4] *E. Ancaster* v. *Doig*, 1960 S.C. 203.

[5] *Carmichael* v. *Penny* (1874) 11 S.L.R. 634; *Downie* v. *Laird* (1902) 10 S.L.T. 28; *Korner* v. *Shennan*, 1950 S.C. 285.

[6] *Philip* v. *Gordon Cumming's Exors.* (1869) 7 M. 859; *Stewart* v. *Clark* (1871) 9 M. 616; *Perdikou* v. *Pattison*, 1958 S.L.T. 153; see also *Pollok* v. *Whiteford*, 1936 S.C. 402.

[7] *Kirkpatrick* v. *Allanshaw Coal Co.* (1880) 8 R. 327; *Skinner* v. *L. Saltoun* (1886) 13 R. 823; *Turnbull* v. *Oliver* (1891) 19 R. 154; *Page* v. *Strains* (1892) 30 S.L.R. 69; *Garden* v. *E. Aberdeen* (1893) 20 R. 896; *Dickson* v. *Bell* (1899) 36 S.L.R. 343.

[8] *Baillie* v. *Fraser* (1853) 15 D. 747; *Bargaddie Coal Co.* v. *Wark* (1858) 3 Macq. 467; *Kirkpatrick*, *supra*; *Carron Co.* v. *Henderson's Trs.* (1896) 23 R. 1042.

[9] *Bargaddie Coal Co.*, *supra*; *Carron Co.*, *supra*, 1049.

sors such as purchasers of the lands from him. The Leases Act, 1449, as interpreted, in certain circumstances confers on tenants real rights in the lands leased. It has been held applicable to all heritable rights capable of being the subjects of separate lease, farms, houses, minerals, salmon fishings, and shootings.[1] The Act avails against the landlord's singular successors, such as purchasers and adjudging creditors, succeeding heirs of entail, superiors taking the lands by liferent escheat of the vassal, and the Crown.[2]

As interpreted, the Act requires five elements for its application, viz.: (1) that the lease, if for longer than a year, be in writing;[3] (2) that it applies to lands and other heritable subjects, such as houses, minerals or salmon fishings;[4] (3) that the tenant has taken possession under the lease;[5] (4) that there is a defined duration of the lease, and hence a definite ish or expiry.[6] This may not be defined in years but, e.g. for a lifetime;[7] and (5) that there is a specified rent, not necessarily substantial, but at least not illusory.[8] It is immaterial whether or not a grassum or capital payment has been payable at the commencement of the lease as well as an annual rent.[9]

Registration of leases

The Registration of Leases Act, 1857,[10] provides that probative leases for 31 years or more, or with an obligation of renewal so as to endure for that period, of land not exceeding 50 acres (save in mining leases) may be recorded in the Register of Sasines. When

[1] *Farquharson*, (1870) 9 M. 66.

[2] Stair II, 4, 66; II, 9, 25; Bankt. II, 9, 45; Ersk. II, 5, 79.

[3] Stair II, 9, 4,; Mack. II, 6, 5; Bankt. II, 9, 5; Ersk. II, 9, 24; Bell, *Prin.* §1190; Bell, *Leases*, I, 34.

[4] Bankt. II, 9, 1; Ersk. II, 6, 27; Bell, *Comm.* I, 65; *Campbell* v. *McKinnon* (1867) 5 M. 651; also a lease for sporting purposes, and probably even a lease of shootings without the land: *Farquharson* (1870) 9 M. 66; but not game or fishing leases: *Birkbeck* v. *Ross* (1865) 4 M. 272; *E. Galloway* v. *D. Bedford* (1902) 4 F. 851.

[5] Stair II, 9, 7; Mack. II, 6, 5; Bankt. II, 9, 3; Ersk. II, 6, 25; Bell, *Prin.* §1209–11. The possession must be by the tenant, and after the date of entry fixed by the lease: *Johnston* v. *Cullen* (1676) Mor. 15231. Limited acts of occupation before the date of entry will not suffice: *Millar* v. *McRobbie*, 1949 S.C. 1.

[6] Stair II, 9, 16; Mack. II, 6, 5; Bankt. II, 9, 5; Ersk. II, 6, 24; Bell, *Prin.* §1194; Bell, *Leases*, I, 38, 215; Bell, *Convg.* II, 1210; cf. *Wilson* v. *Mann* (1876) 3 R. 527; *Barbour* v. *Chalmers* (1891) 18 R. 610; *Bisset* v. *Aberdeen Mags.* (1898) 1 F. 87.

[7] *Thomson* v. *T.* (1896) 24 R. 269; see also *Campbell* v. *McLean* (1870) 8 M. (H.L.) 40.

[8] Stair II, 9, 29; Mack. II, 6, 5; Bankt. II, 9, 5; Ersk. II, 6, 24; Bell, *Prin.* §1197–1202; Bell, *Convg.* II, 1114; *Keith* v. *Ogilvie* (1629) Mor. 15238; *Mann* v. *Houston*, 1957 S.L.T. 89.

[9] Bell, *Prin.* §1201; *Mann, supra.*

[10] Amended by Conveyancing (Sc.) Act, 1924, S. 24; Long Leases (Sc.) Act, 1954, Ss. 26–7.

recorded, such leases are valid against singular successors though there be no rent, no definite ish, and the lessee has not entered into possession. A lease so recorded may be assigned, absolutely or in security,[1] the assignee's right being completed by registration.

Death of or sale by landlord

When a landlord dies, or sells lands or buildings leased, if the leases come within the Acts of 1449 or 1857, the heirs or purchasers take the lands subject to the burden of all the natural incidents of the leases, but free of any purely personal incidents or conditions which transmit against the landlord's executors only.[2]

Personal conditions in leases

Notwithstanding the Leases Act, 1449, and the Registration of Leases Act, 1857, there may be terms and conditions in a lease deemed purely personal to the parties and not real or among the normal incidents of the relationship of landlord and tenant, and such will not bind a singular successor of the landlord. Among such have been a provision whereby rent is to be attributed towards a prior debt;[3] that an abatement from rent is to be made for services to be rendered by the tenant;[4] that, in a lease for 999 years, the landlord would grant a feu on demand;[5] that, on expiry of the lease, the landlord would grant a renewal for four years;[6] that a tenant could cut peats from another part of the landlord's estate.[7]

But a right of pasturage on commonty has been held an incident of a lease and so to be enforceable against a singular successor of the landlord,[8] and possibly also an obligation to repay tenants' improvement expenditure.[9]

Assignation and subletting

Assignation imports transferring the lessee's rights to another who will stand in his place as tenant of the landlord, assuming his

[1] *Crawford* v. *Campbell*, 1937 S.C. 596.

[2] *Arbuthnot* v. *Colquhoun* (1772) Mor. 10424; *Walker* v. *Masson* (1857) 19 D. 1099; *Gardiner* v. *Stewart's Trs.*, 1908 S.C. 985; *Riddell's Exors.* v. *Milligan's Exors.*, 1909 S.C. 1137.

[3] Bell, *Prin.* §1202.

[4] *Ross* v. *Duchess of Sutherland* (1838) 16 S. 1179; cf. *Montgomery* v. *Carrick* (1848) 10 D. 1387; *Page* v. *Strains* (1892) 30 S.L.R. 69.

[5] *Bissett* v *Aberdeen Mags.* (1898) 1 F. 87.

[6] *Jacobs* v. *Anderson* (1898) 6 S.L.T. 234.

[7] *Duncan* v. *Brooks* (1894) 21 R. 760.

[8] *Findlay* v. *Stuart* (1890) 29 S.L.R. 15.

[9] *Swan* v. *Fairholme* (1894) 2 S.L.T. 74.

rights and liabilities. Subletting imports the letting by the tenant of the whole or part of the subjects let to him to another, himself continuing as tenant of his landlord but becoming landlord of his sub-tenant.[1]

Leases are contracts involving *delectus personae* so that assignation and subletting are incompetent, unless permitted expressly by the lease, or by a recognized exception to this rule.[2] There is no power, unless expressly conferred, to assign or sublet agricultural subjects, or shootings or fishings.[3] This rule does not impliedly exclude a tenant's heir, or the trustee in his sequestration.[4] Express power to assign or sublet is, however, conferred if the destination in the lease is to the tenant, his assignees and subtenants.

Implied power to assign and sublet is recognized, as common law exceptions to the general rule, in the cases of (1) liferent leases;[5] (2) leases for the duration of the tenant's tenure of an office;[6] (3) farm leases of extraordinary endurance;[7] (4) urban leases,[8] though this implied power may be expressly excluded and the exception probably does not extend to furnished lettings;[9] and (5) leases of mines and minerals, unless expressly excluded.

An express exclusion of power may be fenced by a conventional irritancy, which, if incurred, cannot be purged before decree.[10] Where there is an express exclusion, an exclusion of subtenants does not import exclusion of assignees also, and conversely.[11]

Where assignation or subletting is excluded by law, or expressly, the court will set aside transactions or devices designed to evade the prohibition.[12]

[1] Stair II, 9, 22; Bankt. II, 9, 17; Ersk. II, 6, 34; *Skene* v. *Greenhill* (1825) 4 S. 25; *Burns* v. *Martin* (1887) 14 R. (H.L.) 20.

[2] Stair II, 9, 22; III, 1, 16; Mack. II, 6, 7–8; Bankt. II, 9, 11; Ersk. II, 6, 31; Bell, *Comm.* I, 76; *Prin.* §1215; Bell, *Leases* I, 175; *D. Portland* v. *Baird* (1865) 4 M. 10, 22.

[3] Bell, *Prin.* §1214; *Fife* v. *Wilson* (1864) 3 M. 323; *Mackintosh* v. *May* (1895) 22 R. 345.

[4] *Alison* v. *Proudfoot* (1788) Mor. 15290.

[5] Stair II, 9, 26; Mack. II, 6, 7; Bankt. II, 9, 11, and 46; Ersk. II, 6, 32; Bell, *Comm.* I, 77; Bell, *Leases*, I, 186.

[6] *Pringle* v. *McLagan* (1802) Hume 808.

[7] Ersk. II, 6, 32; Bell, *Prin.* §1215; Interpreted to mean leases of 37 or more years: Bell, *Leases*, I, 186; *Pringle*, *supra*; but possibly covering any lease of over 21 years; cf. *Bain* v. *Mackenzie* (1896) 23 R. 528, 533.

[8] Bankt. II, 9, 12; Ersk. II, 6, 31; Bell, *Comm.* I, 76; II, 32; *Prin.* §1274; Bell, *Leases* I, 184; *Hatton* v. *Clay & McLuckie* (1865) 4 M. 263; *Robb* v. *Brearton* (1895) 22 R. 885.

[9] Rankine, *Leases*, 175.

[10] *Porter* v. *Paterson* (1813) Hume 862; *Lyon* v. *Irvine* (1874) 1 R. 512.

[11] Bell, *Comm.* I, 77; *Crawford* v. *Maxwell* (1758) Mor. 15307; *Trotter* v. *Dennis* (1770) Mor. 15282.

[12] *Porter*, *supra*; *Hamilton* v. *Somerville* (1855) 17 D. 344; *Hatton*, *supra*; *Lyon* v. *Irvine* (1874) 1 R. 512.

The lease frequently expressly excludes from the destination assignees and/or subtenants, sometimes qualifying this by providing an exception for such as may be approved by the landlord,[1] or if the landlord consents in writing.[2] Where consent is required the landlord is not bound to give any reason for withholding consent.[3] The fact that a landlord does not object to assignees taking possession does not automatically imply his recognition of them as tenants.[4]

Difficult issues may arise, as to whether a trustee for creditors is in substance as assignee or merely a manager.[5] In many older cases a tenant was held to have forfeited his lease if he left the country permanently and committed the management of a farm to another.[6] An heir-at-law claiming to succeed on death is not excluded by an exclusion of assignees.[7]

Assignation, as between tenant and assignee

The agreement to assign and the terms thereof are a separate contract, liable to reduction for fraud like any other,[8] and normally to be constituted and proved by formal writings.[9] An intending assignee must be presumed to have seen the lease and to be aware of limitations therein on subletting.[10] If the assignee cannot implement his part of the bargain the assignation falls.[11]

Completion of Assignation

Where assignation is competent it is effected by a probative deed of assignation, delivered to the assignee[12] and intimated to the landlord, assignations having priority in competition by date of intimation.[13] Intimation may be formal, evidenced by an instrument of intimation signed by a notary and witnesses,[14] or under the

[1] *Dewar* v. *Ainslie* (1892) 20 R. 203.
[2] *M. Breadalbane* v. *Whitehead* (1893) 21 R. 138.
[3] *Muir* v. *Wilson*, 20 Jan. 1820, F.C.; *Wight* v. *E. Hopetoun* (1855) 17 D. 364.
[4] *Elphinstone* v. *Monkland Iron Co.* (1886) 13 R. (H.L.) 98; contrast *Aglionby* v. *Watson* (1809) Hume 845.
[5] *Young's Trs.* v. *Anderson* (1809) Hume 843; *Dewar, supra*; cf. *M. Breadalbane, supra.*
[6] *E. Dalhousie* v. *Wilson* (1802) Mor. 15311; *Arnot & Bell* (1805) Hume 576; *Monro* v. *Miller*, 11 Dec. 1811, F.C.; *Watson* v. *Douglas*, 13 Dec. 1811, F.C.; *Stirling* v. *Miller*, 29 June 1813, F.C.; *Sydserf* v. *Todd*, 8 Mar. 1814, F.C.
[7] *Murdoch* v. *M's Trs.* (1863) 1 M. 330.
[8] *Duncan* v. *Cowie* (1841) 4 D. 47; *Hay* v. *Rafferty* (1899) 2 F. 302.
[9] *Smith* v. *Riddell* (1886) 14 R. 95. But see *Kinnimont* v. *Paxton* (1892) 20 R. 128.
[10] *Leechman* v. *Sievwright* (1826) 4 S. 683.
[11] *Smith, supra.*
[12] Ersk. III, 5, 3; *Grant* v. *Gray* (1828) 6 S. 489.
[13] *Inglis* v. *Paul* (1829) 7 S. 469.
[14] Stair II, 10, 17; III, 3, 7; Mack. II, 5, 3; Bankt. III, 1, 6; Ersk. III, 5, 3; Bell, *Prin.* §1463; Bell, *Convg.* I, 307.

Transmission of Moveable Property (Sc.) Act, 1862, S. 2,[1] or conduct may be held equivalent thereto.[2] In a question with third parties the assignation must be completed by transfer of possession to the assignee.[3]

Where assignation is competent it may be made absolutely or in security, but in the latter case the creditor must take possession, and he becomes liable to the landlord for all the prestations due under the lease.[4]

Under the Registration of Leases (Sc.) Act, 1857, probative leases for 31 years or more, or containing an obligation to renew so as to endure for that period, and assignations thereof, in the form of Schedule A to the Act, may be recorded in the Register of Sasines to the effect (S. 3) of making the lease effectual to the assignee against any singular successor of the landlord infeft after the recording. Assignations in security in the form of Schedule B when recorded complete the right thereunder and constitute a real security over the lease to the extent assigned (S. 4).[5] The creditor under an assignation in security may (S. 6), on default, apply to the sheriff for warrant to enter on possession, which warrant, if granted, is a title to the creditor to enter into possession, uplift rents and sublet as freely as the tenant might have done, subject to becoming personally liable to the landlord for the obligations of the lease.

Obligations arising out of assignations

A completed and intimated or recorded assignation substitutes the assignee in place of the cedent as tenant. Unless continuing liability be stipulated for,[6] the cedent ceases to be liable and the assignee becomes liable for the rent for the future.[7] The assignee becomes liable, and the cedent continues to be liable, for arrears of rent.[8] In the event of the tenant's bankruptcy an assignation, though completed and intimated, does not give the assignee a complete right against the tenant's trustee in bankruptcy unless

[1] Strictly speaking this Act is inapplicable to a heritable right.

[2] Stair I, 7, 9, and 45; Mack. II, 5, 5; Bankt. III, 1, 12; Ersk. III, 5, 4; Bell, *Comm.* II, 17; *Prin.* §1465; *Tod's Trs.* v. *Wilson* (1869) 7 M. 1100.

[3] Stair II, 1, 6; Bankt. II, 9, 4; Ersk. II, 6, 25; Bell, *Comm.* I, 66, 755; Bell, *Prin.* §1209–12; Bell, *Leases* I, 451; *Brock* v. *Cabbell* (1830) 5 W. & S. 476; *Ramsay* v. *Commercial Bank* (1842) 4 D. 405; *Clark* v. *West Calder Oil Co.* (1882) 9 R. 1017, 1024.

[4] *Brock, supra*; *Inglis* v. *Paul* (1829) 7 S. 469.

[5] *Crawford* v. *Campbell*, 1937 S.C. 596.

[6] *Gray's Trs.* v. *Benhar Coal Co.* (1881) 9 R. 225.

[7] *Skene* v. *Greenhill* (1825) 4 S. 25; *Burns* v. *Martin* (1887) 14 R. (H.L.) 20, 25.

[8] *Bannatine* v. *Scot* (1632) Mor. 15274; *Gemmell* v. *Low* (1823) 2 S. 486; *Ramsay* v. *Commercial Bank* (1842) 4 D. 405.

the assignee has taken possession,[1] or the lease is one registered under the Registration of Leases Act, 1857, when the assignation is completed by registration under that Act.

Sublease

If competent, a sublease must be constituted and proved in the same way as the main lease. If it satisfies the requirements of the Acts of 1449 or 1857 it confers a real right against the main tenant. If he can competently sublet in whole or in part the tenant cannot confer on his subtenant any greater rights in the lands than he himself enjoys under his lease.

The duration of a sublease cannot be greater than that of the main lease and, if silent as to duration, it must expire then. If expressed to endure so long, a claim for damages lies if the main lease be reduced before its due ish.[2] If the main lease be terminated at a break, the subtenant has no claim on being then evicted.[3]

If the sublease were competent, the subtenant's right is valid against the landlord, and if entitled to protection under the Acts of 1449 or 1857, valid also against the landlord's singular successors so that the subtenant cannot be evicted if the tenant deserts his lease or renounces it in favour of the landlord.[4]

If, however, the sub-lease were incompetent, the subtenant may be removed by the landlord as possessing without title,[5] or the landlord may consent to or ratify the sublease or may bar himself from objecting by conduct inferring acquiescence in the sublease.[6]

Obligations arising from sub-leases

All obligations due under the main lease continue in force.[7] As between landlord and subtenant, no obligations arise *ex contractu*[8] but may arise *ex delicto*.[9] The landlord, if the sublease were competent or acquiesced in, may not eject the subtenant as

1 *Ramsay, supra.*

2 *Middleton* v. *Yorstoun* (1826) 5 S. 162; *Middleton* v. *Megget* (1828) 7 S. 76; contrast *Laidlaw* v. *Wilson* (1830) 8 S. 440.

3 *Logan* v. *Weir* (1872) 9 S.L.R. 268.

4 Stair II, 9, 22; Bankt. II, 9, 17; Ersk. II, 6, 34; Bell, *Leases* I, 470; *E. Morton* v. *Tenants* (1625) Mor. 15228.

5 In this case the subtenant has a claim of damages against the tenant.

6 e.g. *Hay* v. *McTier* (1806) Hume 836; *Maule* v. *Robb* (1807) Hume 835; see also *Fraser* v. *F.* (1833) 11 S. 565; *Elgin's Trs.* v. *Walls* (1833) 11 S. 585.

7 Bankt. II, 9, 17; Ersk. II, 6, 34; Bell, *Comm.* I, 76.

8 *Maxwell* v. *Queensberry's Exors.* (1830) 5 W. & S. 771; cf. *Dick* v. *Taylor's Trs.* (1831) 10 S. 19.

9 *Duffy* v. *Mungle* (1871) 8 S.L.R. 537; Occupiers Liability (Sc.) Act, 1960, S. 3.

possessing without title, but only at the termination of the main lease.[1] He may enforce his claim for rent against the tenant by arresting the subrents due by the subtenant to the tenant and, if otherwise competent, under his right of hypothec sequestrate the subtenant's *invecta et illata*, at least so far as the subrents have not been paid to the tenant.[2]

A sublease, in the absence of contrary stipulation, contains an implied warrandice against eviction which gives the subtenant a claim if prematurely evicted as by the landlord's resumption of part of the lands.[3]

Even if the main tenant's possession has come to an end, a subtenant cannot be summarily ejected without warning.[4]

As between tenant and subtenant, the obligations depend on their contract together with such terms as may be implied from the general relationship of landlord and tenant. If the subtenant is in breach of contract the tenant may recover damages.[5] A subtenant may have an option to renew if the tenant himself obtains an extension of the lease from the landlord; this does not transmit further unless expressly assigned.[6] Conditions binding on the tenant under the main lease do not bind the subtenant unless incorporated in the sublease.[7] A subtenant is not a servant of the tenant for the purposes of vicarious liability for his fault.[8]

Succession

A lease is an incorporeal heritable right passing at common law on the tenant's death intestate to his heir.[9] The heir might take up the lease, assuming liability for all future obligations, and liberating the tenant's estate for the future, though not for arrears of rent.[10] If the heir renounced the lease he was liable to the landlord in damages for obligations unfulfilled.[11] The heir might be held by his conduct to have abandoned the lease.[12]

[1] *Robb* v. *Menzies* (1859) 21 D. 277; including termination at a break in the main lease: *Logan* v. *Weir* (1872) 9 S.L.R. 268.

[2] *Edinburgh Mags.* v. *Provan's Creditors* (1665) Mor. 6235; *Blane* v. *Morrison* (1785) Mor. 6232; *Williamson* v. *Forbes* (1830) 8 S. 405.

[3] *Downie* v. *Laird* (1902) 10 S.L.T. 28.

[4] *Robb* v. *Brearton* (1895) 22 R. 885.

[5] *Ebbw Vale Steel Co.* v. *Wood's Tr.* (1898) 25 R. 439.

[6] *Robertson* v. *Player* (1876) 4 R. 218.

[7] *Fergusson* v. *Brown* (1902) 9 S.L.T. 341.

[8] *Phillipps* v. *Hunter* (1904) 6 F. 814.

[9] Ersk. II, 2, 6; II, 6, 3; Bell, *Comm.* I, 76; *Prin.* §1219; Bell, *Leases* I, 146, 508; *Bain* v. *Mackenzie* (1896) 23 R. 528; the heir takes also improvements made by the tenant: *Reid's Exors.* v. *R.* (1890) 17 R. 519.

[10] *Burns* v. *Martin* (1887) 14 R. (H.L.) 20; *Bain* v. *Mackenzie* (1896) 23 R. 528.

[11] *Bethune* v. *Morgan* (1874) 2 R. 186; cf. *Scott's Exors.* v. *Hepburn* (1876) 3 R. 816.

[12] *Watt* v. *Duff* (1852) 14 D. 879; *Gray* v. *Low* (1859) 21 D. 293.

Under the Succession (Sc.) Act, 1964, S. 16, the lease now vests in the tenant's executor, who may assign it to any one of the persons entitled to succeed to the estate, irrespective of prohibitions on assignation, or if unable to dispose of the lease may terminate it.

The tenant cannot bequeath a lease unless it is assignable, or he is empowered to name an heir[1] or bequeath the lease.[2] By the 1964 Act, S. 29, provided there is no express prohibition, a tenant may validly bequeath a lease to any one of the persons who would have been entitled to succeed to it as his intestate heirs. It may be a question of construction whether a bequest includes a lease.[3]

If an heir refuses to take up a lease which has not reached its natural termination, he is liable in damages to the landlord for any obligations undertaken by the tenant remaining unfulfilled at his death.[4]

Tenant's bankruptcy

Whether a lease be assignable voluntarily or not, it will, in the absence of express contrary provision, pass on the tenant's bankruptcy to the trustee in his sequestration.[5] The latter may adopt the lease, in which case he incurs personal liability for arrears[6] and for future rent, or disclaim the lease without incurring any liability. He must elect within a reasonable time and ultimate disclaimer will not be prejudiced by temporary intromissions with the subjects in connection with realization of the bankrupt's effects.[7] The express exclusion of the right of the trustee in bankruptcy is held to give the landlord a right to terminate the lease, but it cannot be founded on by the bankrupt.[8]

Unless there is an express provision the tenant's bankruptcy does not terminate the lease.[9]

Landlord's duties—to give possession

The landlord must cede to the tenant full possession of the subjects let,[10] and the tenant is entitled to call on the landlord to

1 Bell, *Prin.* §1219; *Irvine* v. *Fiddes* (1827) 5 S. 534.

2 *Stewart* v. *Pirie* (1832) 11 S. 139; statutory powers under Agricultural Holdings (Sc.) Act, 1949, S. 20; Crofters (Sc.) Act, 1955, S. 10.

3 e.g. *Hardy's Trs.* v. *H.* (1871) 9 M. 736; *Edmond* v. *E.* (1873) 11 M. 347; *Grant* v. *Morren* (1893) 20 R. 404; *Maclagan's Trs.* v. *L.A.* (1903) 11 S.L.T. 227.

4 *Bethune* v. *Morgan* (1874) 2 R. 186.

5 Bell, *Prin.* §1216. See also *McKinley* v. *Hutchison's Tr.*, 1935 S.L.T. 62.

6 *Dundas* v. *Morrison* (1857) 20 D. 225.

7 *McGavin* v. *Sturrock's Tr.* (1891) 18 R. 576.

8 *Dobie* v. *M. Lothian* (1864) 2 M. 788.

9 *Dobie, supra.*

10 *Tennent's Trs.* v. *Maxwell* (1880) 17 S.L.R. 463.

remove or eject possessors,[1] or to authorise him to do so. Possession must be given timeously, failing which the tenant may rescind the contract.[2] Unless any portion of the subjects is reserved, possession must be given of the whole subjects let.[3] But in a lease of agricultural land minerals,[4] woods,[5] and game and wild animals are reserved by law, and other rights may be reserved by the lease.

Maintenance of tenant's possession

The landlord must also do nothing and, so far as within his power, permit to be done nothing to evict the tenant from the subjects let or any material part of them during the lease, on pain of an action on the warrandice expressed or implied in the lease.[6] The warrandice, if not expressed, always implied in a lease, is absolute warrandice.[7]

Claim under warrandice

A claim under warrandice is competent only when eviction has taken place, or is certain to take place in consequence of the landlord's fault, or is threatened when liability is disputed,[8] or is avoided by the expiry of the lease, leaving a liability for violent profits.[9] A claim lies where the tenant is deprived of the whole or part of the subjects let or loses the full use of the subjects.[10]

Recourse under warrandice against eviction does not lie where the eviction results from change in the law,[11] compulsory purchase or requisition under statute,[12] the actings of a third party for whom the landlord is not liable,[13] the actings of a third party, the risk

[1] Stair I, 15, 6; Bankt. II, 9, 21; Ersk. II, 6, 28.

[2] *Drummond* v. *Hunter* (1869) 7 M. 347.

[3] But cf. *Webster* v. *Lyell* (1860) 22 D. 1423: When letting a house furnished the landlord may lock certain cupboards and wardrobes: *Miller* v. *Wilson*, 1919 1 S.L.T. 223.

[4] Bell, *Prin.* §1226.

[5] Bell, *Prin.* §1226.

[6] Ersk. II, 6, 25, and 39; Bell, *Comm.* I, 644; *Prin.* §894, 1208, 1253; Bell, *Convg.* I, 200.

[7] *Middletons* v. *Yorstoun* (1826) 5 S. 162; *Middleton* v. *Meggat* (1828) 7 S. 76; *Kinloch* v. *Fraser* (1829) 7 S. 819.

[8] Ersk. II, 3, 30; Ross, *Lect.* II, 493; Bell, *Comm.* I, 645; *Lyell* v. *Shepherd* (1894) 2 S.L.T. 440.

[9] *Hyslop* v. *Queensberry's Exors.* (1823) 2 Sh. App. 63; *Bell* v. *Queensberry's Exors.* (1824) 3 S. 416; *Kelloch* v. *Queensberry's Exors.* (1824) 3 S. 418.

[10] *Guthrie* v. *Shearer* (1873) 1 R. 181; *Christie* v. *Wilson*, 1915 S.C. 645.

[11] *Holliday* v. *Scott* (1830) 8 S. 831; *Kirkcaldy Cinema* v. *Kirkcaldy Mags.*, 1915 2 S.L.T. 42.

[12] cf. *Tay Salmon Fisheries* v. *Speedie*, 1929 S.C. 592; *Mackeson* v. *Boyd*, 1924 S.C. 56.

[13] *Gardner* v. *Walker* (1862) 24 D. 1430.

of which both landlord and tenant had taken,[1] or the prohibition of the tenant's business as a nuisance.[2]

Where the eviction is partial and temporary, the appropriate compensation is by way of claim of damages,[3] including indemnification for loss and inconvenience caused and any expenses reasonably incurred by the tenant in seeking to preserve the property;[4] where it is partial but permanent, compensation is normally by way of deduction from the rent.[5]

Where the eviction is total, as where the lease is reduced, a claim for damages lies against the landlord.[6]

Eviction by damnum fatale *or accident*

Where the tenant is evicted in whole or in part by *damnum fatale*, or unforeseeable accident for which neither party was to blame, such as fire, neither party is bound to restore the damaged subjects,[7] and the tenant may abandon the lease and treat the contract as at an end if the eviction is total,[8] or have an abatement of rent if it be partial.[9] Hence tenants have been held entitled to abandon where agricultural lands have been overwhelmed by sand[10] or swept away by water[11] or houses rendered uninhabitable by fire.[12]

In mineral leases abandonment is competent if the mineral seam is exhausted[13] or is unworkably thin,[14] but probably not because of physical difficulties of mining.[15]

Tenants have been held entitled to abatement of rent where premises were damaged by fire, but not beyond repair.[16]

1 *Piers* v. *Black* (1680) Mor. 16605; *Reid* v. *Shaw* (1822) 1 S. 334.

2 *Murray* v. *Buchanan* (1776) Mor. 10636.

3 *Bisset* v. *Whitson* (1842) 5 D. 5; *Menmuir* v. *Airth* (1863) 1 M. 929.

4 *Robertson* v. *Menzies* (1828) 6 S. 452; *Huber* v. *Ross*, 1912 S.C. 898.

5 *Craig* v. *Miller* (1888) 15 R. 1005; *Duncan* v. *Brooks* (1894) 21 R. 760; *Dougall* v. *Dunfermline Mags.*, 1908 S.C. 151.

6 *Hyslop* v. *Queensberry's Exors.* (1823) 2 Sh. App. 63; cf. *Eliott's Trs.* v. *E.* (1894) 21 R. 858.

7 *Walker* v. *Bayne* (1815) 6 Pat. 217; see also *Duff* v. *Fleming* (1870) 8 M. 769; *D. Hamilton's Trs.* v. *Fleming* (1870) 9 M. 329.

8 Stair I, 15, 2; *Duff*, *supra*; *Gowans* v. *Christie* (1873) 11 M. (H.L.) 1.

9 Stair, *supra*; Mack. III, 3, 5; Bankt. II, 9, 24; Ersk. II, 6, 41; *Muir* v. *McIntyre* (1887) 14 R. 470; *Sharp* v. *Thomson*, 1930 S.C. 1092.

10 *Lindsay* v. *Home* (1612) Mor. 10120.

11 *Futt* v. *Ruthven* (1671) 2 B.S. 504.

12 *Drummond* v. *Hunter* (1869) 7 M. 347; *Duff* v. *Fleming* (1870) 8 M. 769; *Allan* v. *Markland* (1882) 10 R. 383.

13 *Wilson* v. *Mader* (1699) Mor. 10125; *Murdoch* v. *Fullerton* (1829) 7 S. 404; *Fleming* v. *Baird* (1871) 9 M. 730; cf. *Gowans*, *supra*.

14 *Gray* v. *Hog* (1706) 4 B.S. 635.

15 *Edmiston* v. *Preston* (1675) Mor. 15172, on which see *Gowans*, *supra*, 5.

16 *Allan* v. *Markland* (1882) 10 R. 383; *Critchley* v. *Campbell* (1884) 11 R. 475.

If, however, the tenant be evicted by foreseeable accident for which either party was to blame, that party is liable to restore the subjects and compensate the other for loss caused by the calamity.[1]

A tenant is not, however, entitled to abandon or to abatement of rent merely because the enterprise carried on in the premises let proves unprofitable, or less profitable than expected,[2] or is made less profitable by some event for which the landlord is not to blame.[3] Nor is the landlord responsible for deterioration of the soil, the effects of wind and weather, nor the condemnation of a farm's water supply.[4]

Tenant's duty to take possession

A tenant is under a duty to take possession at the due date of entry, failing which he is liable in damages.[5] He must further retain possession unless he has lawfully assigned or sublet the premises or has justification for abandoning possession. If he does not, the landlord may claim damages,[6] or rescind the lease.[7] Unless personal possession be expressly stipulated for[8] a tenant may possess by his family or employees.[9]

Tenant's duty not to invert possession

A tenant inverts possession when he uses premises let in a way inconsistent with the purposes of the lease and of any particular qualifications on use imposed by the lease, but not necessarily by isolated illegalities or conduct unconnected with his character as tenant. In every case it is a question of interpretation of the lease, and of circumstances and degree of conduct. Thus it has been held inversion to turn a market garden into an amusement park,[10] to establish an alehouse on a farm,[11] to convert a shop into an exhibition,[12] to use a farm building as a posting station,[13] to use back

[1] *Sutherland* v. *Robertson* (1737) Mor. 13979; *Hardie* v. *Black* (1768) Mor. 10133; *Maclellan* v. *Kerr* (1797) Mor. 10134.
[2] *Dixon* v. *Campbell* (1824) 2 Sh. App. 175.
[3] e.g. road diversion diminishing trade of restaurant.
[4] *Wilkie* v. *Gibson* (1902) 9 S.L.T. 431.
[5] Stair II, 9, 31; Bankt. II, 9, 21; Ersk. II, 6, 39; Bell, *Prin.* §1222; *Mathieson* v. *Nicolson* (1819) 2 Mur. 141.
[6] *Graham* v. *Stevenson* (1792) Hume 781; *Smith* v. *Henderson* (1897) 24 R. 1102.
[7] *Watson* v. *Douglas*, 13 Dec. 1811, F.C.
[8] *Edmund* v. *Reid* (1871) 9 M. 782.
[9] *Gibson* v. *Clark* (1895) 23 R. 295.
[10] *Heriot's Hospital* v. *Heriot's Gardener* (1751) Elch., *Pactum Illicitum*, 20.
[11] *Miln* v. *Mitchell* (1787) Mor. 15254.
[12] *Leechman* v. *Sievwright* (1826) 4 S. 683.
[13] *Bailie* v. *Mackay* (1842) 4 D. 1520.

premises as a stable,[1] to use stables and offices for stage-coach horses,[2] to sublet land to a railway company for use as a siding,[3] or even to turn a grist mill into a flour mill,[4] or into a grist and yarn mill,[5] though it is not inversion to hold auction sales in premises let as a shop.[6]

Inversion is even more wrongful if involving unauthorized building[7] or structural alterations[8] on the subjects let, including even attaching a show-case to the front of a shop,[9] or nuisance.[10]

Inversion is a fundamental breach of contract which entitles the landlord to interdict the offending use, or to declare the lease at an end and to eject the tenant. On the other hand the landlord may expressly ratify the conduct, or act in such a way as to imply acquiescence.[11]

Tenant's duty to pay rent

The tenant is bound to pay the agreed rent at the terms agreed upon, failing which he is liable to various sanctions.[12]

Tenant's duty of care

The tenant is bound to make reasonable use and take reasonable care of the premises and will be liable in damages if by misuse or overloading[13] he causes damage or destruction. The general and recognized practice of tenants and of any trade in question is the criterion of reasonable use.[13]

Notification to Land Commission

Betterment levy may be chargeable on a disposition creating a tenancy for a term of years certain of not less than seven years, or on the assignation on sale of a tenancy granted, renewed or

1 *Hood* v. *Miller* (1855) 17 D. 411.
2 *D. Argyll* v. *McArthur* (1861) 23 D. 1236.
3 *Mercer* v. *Esk Valley Ry.* (1867) 5 M. 1024; cf. *Leck* v. *Merryflats Brick Co.* (1868) 5 S.L.R. 619.
4 *Bayley* v. *Addison* (1901) 8 S.L.T. 379.
5 *Ford* v. *Hillocks* (1808) Mor. Appx. Tack., 17.
6 *Reid* v. *Keith* (1870) 8 M. (H.L.) 110.
7 *Inglis* v. *Balfour* (1778) M. Appx. Tack 34; *Armstrong* v. *Bryceson* (1807) Hume 837; cf. *Kehoe* v. *M. Lansdowne* [1893] A.C. 451.
8 *Muir* v. *Wilson* (1822) 1 S. 406; *Leck* v. *Fulton* (1854) 17 D. 408.
9 *B.L. Co.* v. *Purdie* (1905) 7 F. 923; cf. *Morrison* v. *Forsyth*, 1909 S.C. 329.
10 *Mowbray* v. *Ewbank* (1833) 11 S. 714; cf. *D'Eresby's Trs.* v. *Strathearn Hydropathic Co.* (1873) 1 R. 35.
11 *Young* v. *Ramsay* (1825) 1 W. & S. 560; *Ferguson* v. *Methven* (1857) 19 D. 794; cf. *D. Portland* v. *Samson* (1847) 5 D. 476.
12 See further, *infra*.
13 *Glebe Sugar Refining Co.* v. *Paterson* (1900) 2 F. 615.

extended for a term of years certain of not less than seven years, or on assignation notified in accordance with the Act which is an assignation on sale of a tenancy granted, renewed, or extended for a term of years certain of less than seven years. For this purpose the lessee must notify the Land Commission.[1]

URBAN LEASES

An urban lease is a lease of buildings, with or without land, for residential or business purposes.

Control of letting agencies

By the Accommodation Agencies Act, 1953, it is an offence to demand or take money for registering the requirements of a person seeking the tenancy of a house, for giving particulars of a house to let, or for advertising a house as to let without authority. This does not strike at bona fide advertising or acting as agent for letting.

Constitution and proof of contract

The general principles as to constitution and proof of leases apply. In the case of small dwelling houses regulated by the Houseletting and Rating Act, 1911, no agreement, verbal or written, for the let of a small dwelling house is binding if made more than two months before the commencement of the let.[2] In accordance with the general rule, the landlord is bound to give the tenant possession of the whole subjects let at the due date of entry, failing which the tenant may abandon the lease.[3]

Fitness for habitation or other use

The landlord impliedly warrants that the subjects let are reasonably fit for the purpose of the let.[4] If they are not so, he must put them into tenantable condition at entry.[5] Whether a house is habitable or not is a question of fact.[6] There is, however, no warranty that no defects exist, nor that none will arise during the tenancy. If the landlord has failed to make the premises

[1] Land Commission Act, 1967, Ss. 27, 29, 30, 37, and 100. [2] 1911 Act, S. 2.

[3] *Drummond* v. *Hunter* (1869) 7 M. 347; cf. *Winans* v. *Mackenzie* (1883) 10 R. 941. But in the case of a furnished let the owner may probably lock cupboards, etc.: *Miller* v. *Wilson*, 1919 1 S.L.T. 223. Similarly the tenant may abandon if the premises are requisitioned for an uncertain period: *Mackeson* v. *Boyd*, 1942 S.C. 56.

[4] Ersk. II, 6, 39; Bell, *Prin.* §1253; *Glebe Sugar Refining Co.* v. *Paterson* (1900) 2 F. 615.

[5] Bankt. I, 20, 15; II, 9, 20; Ersk. II, 6, 43; *Dickie* v. *Amicable Property Investment Co.*, 1911 S.C. 1079.

[6] *Mechan* v. *Watson*, 1907 S.C. 25.

tenantable, the tenant should refuse to enter and may claim damages;[1] if he does he may be held barred from resiling[2] unless he entered in reliance on promises to repair.[3] Similarly the tenant may resile if the premises are alleged to possess advantages which they do not.[4]

Maintenance during lease

During the let the landlord must maintain the premises in wind and watertight condition, habitable and tenantable against the ordinary attacks of the elements.[5] This imports tightness against ordinary attacks of the elements, not against exceptional encroachments.[6] He is bound to take due care to put them into wind and watertight condition if by accident they become not so, but this is not a warranty, and he is not in breach of contract till a defect is brought to his notice and he fails to remedy it.[7]

But the landlord is not liable for deterioration or destruction caused by the fault of the tenant[8] or a third party,[9] nor for the consequences of accident or damnum fatale,[9] nor does he contract that due care will be taken by independent contractors whom he employs.[10]

If the premises become unfit the tenant may suspend possession for a time,[11] or if the defect is material, renounce it and give up the lease[12] but may be held barred if he delays substantially, even in reliance on promises of repairs.[13] The tenant may retain or with-

[1] *Kippen* v. *Oppenheim* (1847) 10 D. 242; *Critchley* v. *Campbell* (1884) 11 R. 475; *Anderson* v. *Watson* (1894) 2 S.L.T. 293.

[2] *Whitelaw* v. *Fulton* (1871) 10 M. 27; *Webster* v. *Brown* (1892) 19 R. 765; *Scottish Heritable Security Co.* v. *Granger* (1881) 8 R. 459; *Baikie* v. *Wordie's Trs.* (1897) 24 R. 1098; *McManus* v. *Armour* (1901) 3 F. 1078.

[3] *Hall* v. *Hubner* (1897) 24 R. 875; *Caldwell* v. *McCallum* (1901) 4 F. 371; *Dickie*, *supra*.

[4] *Brodie* v. *McLachlan* (1900) 8 S.L.T. 145.

[5] Ersk. II, 6, 43; this does not extend to damp rising from the foundations: *McGonigal* v. *Pickard*, 1954 S.L.T. (Notes) 62.

[6] *Reid* v. *Baird* (1876) 4 R. 234.

[7] *Wolfson* v. *Forrester*, 1910 S.C. 675; see also *Baikie* v. *Wordie's Trs.* (1897) 24 R. 1098; *Irvine* v. *Caledonian Ry.* (1902) 10 S.L.T. 363.

[8] *Smith* v. *Henderson* (1897) 24 R. 1102; *Mickel* v. *McCoard*, 1913 S.C. 896; cf. *Corrie, Mackie & Co.* v. *Stewart* (1885) 22 S.L.R. 350.

[9] *Allan* v. *Robertson's Trs.* (1891) 18 R. 932; *Sandeman* v. *Duncan's Trs.* (1897) 5 S.L.T. 21; *Hampton* v. *Galloway & Sykes* (1899) 1 F. 501; *N.B. Storage Co.* v. *Steele's Trs.*, 1920 S.C. 194.

[10] *Wolfson*, *supra*; *Dickie*, *supra*.

[11] *Burns* v. *McNeil* (1898) 5 S.L.T. 289; *Souter* v. *Mulhern*, 1907 S.C. 723.

[12] *McKimmie's Trs.* v. *Armour* (1899) 2 F. 156.

[13] *Forbes* v. *Ferguson* (1899) 7 S.L.T. 293; *Dickie* v. *Amicable Property Inv. Co.*, 1911 S.C. 1079; *Mullen* v. *Dunbarton C.C.*, 1933 S.L.T. 185; *Proctor* v. *Cowlairs Co-op. Socy.*, 1961 S.L.T. 434.

hold the rent, or claim damages for loss sustained.[1] The landlord can be held liable in damages only if the defects are his fault.[2] If the tenant fails to claim damages timeously, the court may infer abandonment of the claim in return for acceptance of abandonment of the lease.[3]

If the tenant or his family sustain personal injuries by reason of the state of the premises the landlord may be liable in damages under principles of delictual liability.[4]

Statutory conditions of fitness for habitation

By the Housing (Sc.) Act, 1966, S. 6, in any contract to which the section applies[5] there shall, notwithstanding any stipulation to the contrary, be implied a condition that the house is, at the commencement of the tenancy, and an undertaking that it will be kept by the landlord during the tenancy, in all respects reasonably fit for human habitation,[6] but not when a house is let for not less than 3 years on the terms that it will be put by the lessee into a condition in all respects reasonably fit for human habitation, and the lease is not determinable at the option of either party before the expiration of three years. The landlord, or any person authorized by him may at reasonable times on notice given in writing enter premises affected to view the state and condition thereof. S. 5 lists factors to be considered in determining whether a house is unfit for human habitation if and only if it is so far defective in one or more of the said matters that it is not reasonably suitable for occupation in that condition.[7]

Statutory obligation to repair

In any lease of a house granted on or after 3 July, 1962, for less than 7 years[8] there is implied a provision that the lessor will

[1] *Reid* v. *Baird* (1876) 4 R. 234.

[2] *Hampton* v. *Galloway & Sykes* (1899) 1 F. 501; *Irvine* v. *Caledonian Ry.* (1902) 10 S.L.T. 363; *N.B. Storage Co.* v. *Steele's Trs.*, 1920 S.C. 194.

[3] *Lyons* v. *Anderson* (1886) 13 R. 1020.

[4] *Miller* v. *Addie's Collieries*, 1934 S.C. 150; *McLaughlan* v. *Craig*, 1948 S.C. 599; Occupier's Liability (Sc.) Act, 1960, S. 3. See also *McCormick* v. *Fife Coal Co.*, 1931 S.C. 19.

[5] i.e. to contracts before 31 July 1923 for letting a house at not over £16, or contract thereafter for letting a house at not over £26, but not to contracts for the letting by a local authority of any house purchased or retained by it for housing under Ss. 20 or 40 of the Act.

[6] This implies a duty to report defects to the landlord: *Morgan* v. *Liverpool Corpn.* [1927] 2 K.B. 131. There may be a duty under this section to prevent flood water entering a house: *Duff* v. *Glasgow Corpn.*, 1968 S.L.T. (Sh. Ct.) 6.

[7] cf. *Haggarty* v. *Glasgow Corpn.*, 1964 S.L.T. (Notes) 95.

[8] Housing (Sc.) Act, 1966, S. 9.

(a) keep in repair the structure and exterior of the house (including drains, gutters, and external pipes) and (b) keep in repair and proper working order the installations for the supply of water, gas, and electricity and for sanitation (including basins, sinks, baths and sanitary conveniences) and for space heating or heating water, and any provision that the lessee will repair the premises shall be of no effect in respect of these matters.[1] This implied repairs provision does not require the lessor (a) to carry out any works or repairs for which the lessee is liable by virtue of his duty to use the premises in a proper manner, or would be so liable apart from any express undertaking on his part; (b) to rebuild or reinstate the premises in the case of destruction or damage by fire, or by tempest, flood, or other inevitable accident; or (c) to keep in repair or maintain anything which the lessee is entitled to remove from the house; subsec. (1) does not avoid the part of any provision which imposes on the lessee any of the requirements of (a) or (c).[2] In determining the standard of repair required by the implied repairs provision regard must be had to the age, character, and prospective life of the house and the locality in which it is situated. The lessor has implied power, on written notice, to enter the premises to view their condition.[3]

Section 8 may be excluded or modified by provisions in a lease, authorized by the sheriff on the application of either party with the other's consent, if it is reasonable to do so. Beyond that, contracting-out is void, as is provision for irritancy or penalty on the lessee if he relies on S. 8.[4]

Landlord's duty of care for visitor's safety

The landlord owes *ex contractu* a duty of reasonable care to his tenant to have regard for the latter's safety, but owes no such duty *ex contractu* to the tenant's family or visitors.[5] Under the Occupiers' Liability (Sc.) Act, 1960, S. 3, where premises are occupied or used by virtue of a tenancy[6] under which the landlord is responsible for the maintenance or repair of the premises, he must show towards any persons who or whose property may from time to

[1] Ibid., S. 8(1).
[2] Ibid., S. 8(2).
[3] Ibid., S. 8(3) and (4).
[4] Ibid., S. 10.
[5] *McMartin* v. *Hannay* (1872) 10 M. 411; *Grant* v. *McClafferty*, 1907 S.C. 201; *Cameron* v. *Young*, 1908 S.C. (H.L.) 7; *Mellon* v. *Henderson*, 1917 1 S.L.T. 257; *Grant* v. *Fleming*, 1914 S.C. 228.
[6] Defined as including a subtenancy, a statutory tenancy, and any contract conferring a right of occupation, e.g. a service contract with a right to occupy premises.

time be on the premises[1] the same reasonable care in respect of dangers arising from any failure on his part in carrying out his responsibility as is required under S.2 of the Act to be shown by an occupier of premises to persons entering on them. The standard of reasonable care may be extended, restricted, modified or excluded by agreement,[2] and no obligation is imposed in respect of risks which the visitor has willingly accepted as his,[3] i.e. as to which *volenti non fit injuria* applies.[4] A tenant may be *volens* if he has not complained of a danger or stayed long after it has arisen or not been remedied.

Tenant's remedies

Where the landlord has been in breach of his obligation to maintain the premises in tenantable condition the tenant may have a claim of damages, or may withhold the rent, or may relinquish possession of the premises. Damages are appropriate where inconvenience and loss have been caused,[5] but not for destruction by *damnum fatale*,[6] nor for damage not attributable to any fault on the landlord's part.[7] A tenant who remains in occupation after becoming aware of a defect is not entitled to damages unless he remained in reliance on an assurance that the defect would be cured: *volenti non fit injuria*. If the landlord does not remove the defect the tenant should leave and claim damages for the expense of so doing.[8] Tenants have been held entitled to throw up the lease,[9] or at least to suspend possession,[10] where the landlord's failure has been material and is not readily remediable. The materiality of the defect and the time necessary to make the premises tenantable are questions of fact.[11] Where the landlord has unreasonably delayed or refused to perform some of his

[1] i.e. tenants, their family, guests, and casual visitors.

[2] S. 2(1); but such agreement could affect only a party to it: if contained in the lease it binds the tenant only.

[3] S. 2(3); cf. *Birrell* v. *Anstruther* (1866) 5 M. 20.

[4] cf. *Grant* v. *McClafferty*, 1907 S.C. 201.

[5] *Hamilton* (1667) Mor. 10121; *Deans* v. *Abercrombie* (1681) Mor. 10122; *Bissett* v. *Whitson* (1842) 5 D. 5; *Reid* v. *Baird* (1876) 4 R. 234; *Tennent's Trs.* v. *Maxwell* (1880) 17 S.L.R. 463; *Scott, Croall & Sons* v. *Moir* (1895) 3 S.L.T. 70; *Irvine* v. *Caledonian Ry.* (1902) 10 S.L.T. 363.

[6] *Sandeman* v. *Duncan's Trs.* (1897) 5 S.L.T. 21.

[7] *Allan* v. *Robertson's Trs.* (1891) 18 R. 932.

[8] *Proctor* v. *Cowlairs Co-operative Socy.*, 1961 S.L.T. 434.

[9] *Kippen* v. *Oppenheim* (1847) 10 D. 242; *Anderson* v. *Watson* (1894) 2 S.L.T. 293; *Souter* v. *Mulhern*, 1907 S.C. 723. Contrast *Lowndes* v. *Buchanan* (1854) 17 D. 63.

[10] *Burns* v. *McNeil* (1898) 5 S.L.T. 289; cf. *Sc. Heritable Secy. Co.* v. *Granger* (1881) 8 R. 459.

[11] *McKimmie's Trs.* v. *Armour* (1899) 2 F. 156.

duties, the tenant may retain rent for the period of non-implement,[1] unless he has, in the lease, waived the right to do so.[2]

Tenant's duties

Within a reasonable time of the date of entry the tenant must enter into possession.[3] Failure or refusal, unless justifiable, infers liability in damages.[4] Thereafter, he is bound to occupy the subjects without unreasonable intermission until the end of the lease. Possession may normally be taken and retained by the tenant's family or others on his behalf, but prolonged absence may justify termination of the contract for breach of a material condition.[5]

The tenant must take reasonable care of the premises let;[6] thus a shop tenant must furnish the premises, keep them heated and aired, but need not open nor carry on a business there.[7] It is relevant matter for damages that a tenant has left a house unoccupied, unheated and uncleaned, whereby damage resulted.[8] A tenant is liable if, by not having turned off the water, damage resulted from burst pipes.[9] He will also be liable for damage caused by overloading floors.[10] He must plenish urban subjects, so as to provide security for rent, and may be ordered by the court to do so or to find caution for rent.[11] He must not invert the possession as by carrying on a trade in premises let as a house.

Rates

The tenant as occupier is normally liable for local rates, but the owner is liable for occupier's rates in small houses subject to the House-Letting and Rating Act, 1911.[12]

1 *Buchan* v. *Leith* (1708) 4 B.S. 716; *Gordon* v. *Suttie* (1826) 4 Mur. 86; *Kilmarnock Gas Co.* v. *Smith* (1872) 11 M. 58; *Corrie* v. *Stewart* (1882) 22 S.L.R. 350.

2 *Skene* v. *Cameron*, 1942 S.C. 393; *Glasgow Corpn.* v. *Seniuk*, 1968 S.L.T. (Sh. Ct.) 47.

3 Stair II, 9, 31; Bankt. II, 9, 21; Ersk. II, 6, 39; Bell, *Prin.* §1222; *Robertson* v. *Cockburn* (1875) 3 R. 21.

4 *Mathieson* v. *Nicolson* (1819) 2 Mur. 141; cf. *Bethune* v. *Morgan* (1874) 2 R. 186; *Scott's Exors.* v. *Bethune* (1876) 3 R. 816.

5 *Blair Trust* v. *Gilbert*, 1941 S.N. 2 (tenant imprisoned).

6 Ersk. II, 6, 43.

7 *Whitelaw* v. *Fulton* (1871) 10 M. 27.

8 *Smith* v. *Henderson* (1897) 24 R. 1102.

9 *Mickel* v. *McCoard*, 1913 S.C. 896.

10 *Caledonian Ry.* v. *Greenock Sacking Co.* (1875) 2 R. 671; *Corrie, Mackie & Co.* v. *Stewart* (1885) 22 S.L.R. 350; *Glebe Sugar Refining Co.* v. *Paterson* (1900) 2 F. 615.

11 *Wright* v. *Wightman* (1875) 3 R. 68; *McLelland* v. *Garson* (1883) 10 R. 445.

12 S. 7; the application of the Act is amended by the Rent Restriction Act, 1920, S. 16(1).

Rent

The rent is fixed contractually and is payable at such intervals as may be agreed. If the rent is not fixed nor otherwise ascertainable, a reasonable rent, *quantum valeat*, is implied.[1]

Statutory control and regulation of rents

Since 1915 the rents of certain categories of unfurnished dwellings have been statutorily controlled or regulated by the Rent and Mortgage Interest Restrictions Acts, 1920 to 1939, the Landlord and Tenant (Rent Control) Act, 1949, the Crown Lessees (Protection of Sub-Tenants) Act, 1952, the Housing Repairs and Rents (Sc.) Act, 1954, the Rent Act, 1957, and the Rent Act, 1965.[2]

The Rent Acts 1920 to 1939 apply to a house or part of a house let as a separate dwelling.[3] If let as a separate dwelling the Acts apply even if part of the premises are used for business purposes,[4] but the tenant is not protected unless he uses the dwelling-house as his residence.[5]

The Acts do not apply to (i) Crown property;[6] (ii) houses provided by local authorities, new town development corporations or housing associations or trusts (including the Scottish Special Housing Association or executive councils under the National Health Service (Sc.) Act, 1947[7]); (iii) a house or part of a house let furnished or with board and attendance, i.e. where the rent fairly attributable to furniture or attendance, forms a substantial portion of the whole rent;[8] (iv) a house consisting of or comprising

[1] *Ogilvie* v. *Booth* (1868) 5 S.L.R. 231.

[2] Certain other statutes have incidental effect on matters of rent control or regulation. This body of legislation is quite chaotic and it is extremely difficult to state the principles clearly or concisely. The case-law is voluminous. See generally, Megarry, *The Rent Acts*; Field-Fisher, *Rent Regulation and Control.*

[3] 1920 Act, S. 12(2); *Neale* v. *del Soto* [1945] K.B. 144; *Cowan* v. *Acton*, 1952 S.C. 73; *Goodrich* v. *Paisner* [1957] A.C. 65. Tenants sharing accommodation were accordingly excluded from protection until the 1949 Act, S. 7, which gave tenants sharing with the landlord the protection of a tenant of a furnished house, S. 8, which protected tenants sharing with another tenant, and S. 9, which protected certain sub-tenants.

[4] 1920 Act, S. 12; 1939 Act, S. 3, cf. *Vickery* v. *Martin* [1944] K.B. 679; *Pender* v. *Reid*, 1948 S.C. 381; *Cargill* v. *Phillips*, 1951 S.C. 67; *Cowans* v. *Acton*, 1952 S.C. 73.

[5] cf. *Menzies* v. *Mackay*, 1938 S.C. 74; *Cowan*, *supra*; *Langford Property Co.* v. *Tureman* [1949] 1 K.B. 29.

[6] *T.A. & A.F.A. of London* v. *Nichols* [1949] 1 K.B. 35. But exemption does not extend to subtenants or assignees from the Crown: Crown Lessees (Protection of Sub-tenants) Act, 1952, S. 1.

[7] 1939 Act, S. 3(2) and (8); Housing (Repairs and Rents) (Sc.) Act, 1954, S. 25.

[8] 1920 Act. S. 12(2); 1923 Act, S. 10; 1939 Act, S. 3(2); Rent of Furnished Houses Control (Sc.) Act, 1943, S. 5; *Palser* v. *Grinling*; *Property Holding Co.* v. *Mischeff* [1948] A.C. 291.

licensed premises;[1] (v) a house let with land unless the rateable value of the land let separately would be less than a quarter of that of the house, or, in the case of houses brought under control in 1939, land not exceeding two acres;[2] (vi) premises erected after or converted after the Housing (Repairs and Rents) (Sc.) Act, 1954;[3] (vii) houses let with a substantial quantity of land or other premises;[4] (viii) agricultural holdings occupied by the farmer; (ix) tenancies rent free or at low rent;[5] (x) premises let primarily for business purposes;[6] (xi) houses with a rateable value of over £200.[7]

Old control, new control, decontrol, recontrol and regulation

Old controlled houses are those build before 2 April 1919, which had a standard rent or rateable value not exceeding £90 at 3 August 1914 and were controlled immediately before 2 September 1939 by the Acts of 1920 to 1938. Houses of higher rateable value than £35 were decontrolled by the 1938 Act.

New controlled houses are those which had a rateable value not exceeding £90 at 16 May 1939 and which were brought under control by the 1939 Act for the first time, or had been controlled under old control, decontrolled, and were recontrolled by the 1939 Act.

The Housing (Repairs and Rents) (Sc.) Act, 1954, decontrolled houses erected or converted thereafter, and the Rent Act, 1957, S. 11, decontrolled all houses the rateable value of which exceeded £40, and excluded the operation of the Rent Acts 1920–39 from leases coming into operation after that Act.

The Rent Act, 1965, is declared to regulate the tenancy of all other houses the rateable value of which did not exceed £200, if the houses were not already controlled by reason of the 1957 Act's financial limit, or uncontrolled because of its exclusion of new leases, or if the house is not already controlled only because the 1954 Act, S. 27, had decontrolled it. Hence regulation applies if a fresh lease is granted,[8] or a house is released from control by order of the Secretary of State,[9] or on a second succession to a controlled tenancy.[10]

1 1933 Act, Ss. 1(3) and 15; 1939 Act, S. 3(2); 1965 Act, Sched. 1, para. 2.
2 1920 Act, S. 12(2); 1939 Act, S. 3(3).
3 1954 Act, S. 27.
4 1920 Act, S. 12(2); cf. *Pender* v. *Reid*, 1948 S.C. 381.
5 1920 Act, S. 12(7).
6 1939 Act, S. 3(3); *Cargill* v. *Phillips*, 1951 S.C. 67; *Cowan* v. *Acton*, 1952 S.C. 73.
7 1965 Act, S. 1(1).
8 1957 Act, S. 11(2).
9 1965 Act, S. 12.
10 1965 Act, S. 13.

Permitted increases in rent

The standard rent is the rent at which the house was let, in the case of old controlled houses, on 3 August 1914, or, in the case of new controlled houses, on 1 September 1939, or, if not then let, the rent at which it was last let previously, or the rent at which it was first let after the relevant date. If the rent was less than the rateable value, the rateable value at the relevant date is the standard rent.[1] The landlord must under penalty supply the tenant on request with a written statement of the standard rent.[2]

Old Control

In the case of old controlled houses the landlord may make the following increases on the standard rent: (i) 6% of expenditure on improvement or structural alteration of the house incurred between 4 August 1914 and 2 July 1920, and 12½% of any such expenditure after 2 July 1920; if the tenant thinks such expenditure was unnecessary he may in certain circumstances apply to the sheriff to suspend or reduce the increase;[3] (ii) the excess amount of owner's rates payable on the house for the year to 15 May 1920 over the amount for the year to 15 May 1915;[4] (iii) if the landlord is responsible under the House Letting and Rating (Sc.) Acts, 1911 and 1920, for payment of the occupier's rates, they may be recovered in full in addition to the standard rent;[5] (iv) 15% of the net rent;[6] (v) if the landlord is responsible for all repairs to the house, he may increase the rent by not more than 25% of the net rent;[7] if responsible for only part of the repairs, he may increase the rent by such part of 25% as he and the tenant may agree, or, failing agreement, as the sheriff may fix; if the tenant is entirely responsible for repairs no addition may be made to the rent.[8]

[1] 1920 Act, S. 12(1); 1933 Act, S. 6; 1939 Act, Sched. I.

[2] 1920 Act, S. 11; see also *Di Mascio* v. *Munro*, 1956 S.C. 245.

[3] 1920 Act, S. 2(1) and (5); 1923 Act, S. 18(5); 1933 Act, S. 7; Housing (Sc.) Act, 1962, S. 16.

[4] 1920 Act, Ss. 2(1) and 18(1). Owner's rates on property were abolished by the Valuation and Rating (Sc.) Act, 1956, and all rates are now payable by occupiers.

[5] 1920 Act, Ss. 2(1) and 18(1).

[6] 1920 Act, S. 2(1). The net rent was the standard rent, less the amount of occupier's rates if paid by the landlord; if occupier's rates were paid by the tenant the net rent is the same as the standard rent. This increase in now subject to the procedure of the Housing (Repairs and Rents) (Sc.) Act, 1954, S. 19.

[7] The landlord is deemed responsible for all repairs for which the tenant is under no express liability. This increase is now subject to the procedure of the Housing (Repairs and Rents) (Sc.) Act, 1954, S. 19.

[8] 1920 Act, S. 2(1) and (5); 1923 Act, S. 18(5).

If the tenant considers that the house is not in a reasonable state of repair he may apply to the local authority for a certificate to that effect. If one is granted and a copy served on the landlord, the tenant may withhold any increase under heads (iv) and (v) above until the necessary repairs have been executed.

New control

In the case of new controlled houses the landlord may make the following increases on the standard rent; (i) 8% of any expenditure on improvement or structural alteration of the house since September 1939; if the tenant thinks the expenditure unnecessary he may in certain circumstances apply to the sheriff to suspend or reduce the increase;[1] (ii) if the landlord is responsible under the House Letting and Rating (Sc.) Act, 1911 and 1920, for the occupier's rates on the house, he may recover the full amount of the rates from the tenant.[2]

Notice of increases: overpayments

No increase of rent is recoverable unless the landlord has served on the tenant notice in the prescribed form of his intention to increase the rent.[3] Any increase exceeding those permitted is prohibited and any agreement to pay more is unenforceable.[4] Within two years of payment a tenant may recover from the landlord any sum paid in excess of the amounts permitted under the Acts by deduction from rent payable or by other competent means.[5]

Premiums

It is an offence to make a condition of the grant, renewal or continuance of a tenancy that the tenant pay any fine, premium or other like sum or any pecuniary consideration other than the rent, and any such payment made is recoverable.[6]

Rent books

Where rent is payable weekly the landlord must provide a rent book[7] which must contain a notice in the prescribed terms.[8]

1 1920 Act, S. 2(1); 1933 Act, S. 7; 1939 Act, Sched. I.
2 1920 Act, S. 2(1); 1939 Act, Sched. I.
3 1920 Act, S. 3(2).
4 1920 Act, S. 1; 1939 Act, Sched. I.
5 1920 Act, S. 14(1); 1923 Act, S. 8(2); 1938 Act, S. 7(6); 1939 Act, Sched. I.
6 1923 Act, S. 9(1); 1939 Act, Sched. I; Landlord and Tenant (Rent Control) Act, 1949, S. 2.
7 1938 Act, S. 6.
8 1933 Act, S. 14.

Post-1939 lettings

The Landlord and Tenant (Rent Control) Act, 1949 provides for landlord or tenant applying to the local Rent Tribunal[1] to fix a reasonable rent for houses let after 1 September 1939, which rent, if different from the standard rent, is to become the standard rent.[2] Provision is made for apportionment of standard rent where the subjects let form part of subjects let after that date. The local authority must maintain a register of the tribunal's determinations under the Act.[3] Where a tenant shares accommodation with the landlord, or with other persons but not with the landlord, and the separate accommodation would not be a dwelling-house to which the Rent Acts apply, it is to be deemed a dwelling house to which those Acts apply and provision is made for fixing its standard rent.[4] The Tribunal has power to extend security of tenure.[5]

Repairs increases, 1954

The Housing (Repairs and Rents) (Sc.) Act, 1954, permitted an increase of the rent of a controlled house[6] by 50%,[7] if the landlord were responsible for repairs and (a) (i) the house is in good and tenantable repair; (ii) it is not in any other respect unfit for human habitation, and (b) the landlord has produced satisfactory evidence that work to the value specified in Schedule I has been carried out during the period specified. If the landlord is responsible only partly for repairs, the increase is reduced proportionately.[8] The landlord must first serve a notice of increase,[9] whereupon the tenant may apply to the local authority for a certificate that either or both of the conditions justifying an increase are not fulfilled; if granted this stops any repairs increase.[10]

The 1954 Act also permitted the recovery of the increased cost of services provided for the tenants under a pre-1939 letting, subject to certain conditions.[11]

1957 Act increases

The Rent Act, 1957, provides[12] that, where the landlord is responsible for repairs, so long as the conditions justifying

[1] Established under the Rent of Furnished Houses Control (Sc.) Act, 1943; see *infra*.
[2] As amended by Housing (Repairs and Rents) (Sc.) Act, 1954, S. 28.
[3] S. 5. [4] Ss. 7–8. [5] S. 11.
[6] With exceptions: S. 16(3); and modifications: S. 20.
[7] Raised from 40% to 50% by Rent Act, 1957, S. 9(1).
[8] S. 16. [9] S. 17. [10] S. 81.
[11] S. 31.
[12] S. 7.

increase of rent under the 1954 Act and those stated in Ss. 8–10 of the 1957 Act are satisfied, controlled rents shall be increased by 25% of the pre-1954 rent. A repairs increase under the 1954 Act may be made as well as a 1957 Act increase, but no 1957 Act increase is recoverable for any period in respect of which a repairs increase is recoverable.[1]

The Rent Act, 1957, released from control under the Rent Acts houses with a rateable value exceeding £40 on 7 November 1956,[2] and the Rent Acts were not to apply to tenancies created after the Act.[3] Premiums are not to be charged for decontrolled tenancies, and restrictions were imposed on the exaction of payment of rent in advance under decontrolled tenancies.

Regulated tenancies, 1965

By the Rent Act, 1965, the Rent Acts as thereby amended are applied to every tenancy of a dwelling-house the rateable value of which did not exceed £200, with certain exceptions. A tenancy to which the Rent Acts are thereby applied is called a regulated tenancy.[3]

The rent payable under a regulated tenancy, instead of being controlled by the Rents Acts and the Acts of 1954 and 1957, is to be regulated under the 1965 Act.[4] The Secretary of State for Scotland appoints rent officers for each local authority area[5] to prepare and keep up to date a register of rents of houses. Landlord or tenant or both may apply for the registration of a rent for a dwelling-house;[6] the rent officer may determine a fair rent[7] and register it as the rent for the house, or confirm the rent for the time being registered and note the confirmation in the register. If objection in writing be made the matter is referred to the rent assessment committee. Rent assessment committees are constituted, consisting of a chairman and one or two other members, chosen from a panel drawn up by the Secretary of State for Scotland.[8] The committee may confirm the rent officer's determination, or determine a fair rent for the house. The registration of any rent has effect from the date of application for the registration, unless exceptionally. Once a rent has been registered no

[1] S. 7(3); S. 8(2).
[2] S. 11.
[3] S. 1.
[4] S. 2.
[5] S. 24 (counties (including small burghs) and large burghs).
[6] S. 26 and Sched. 3.
[7] Relevant factors: S. 27. See also *Stewart's J.F.* v. *Gallacher*, 1967 S.C. 59; *Crofton Investment Trust* v. *Greater London Rent Assessment Cttee.* [1967] 2 All E.R. 1103.
[8] S. 25 and Sched. 2.

application by either party alone for the registration of a different rent may be entertained for three years, unless there has been such change in circumstances as to make the registered rent no longer a fair rent.[1]

Persons intending, by erection or conversion, to provide a house, or to make improvements in a house, or to let on a regulated tenancy a house not subject to such a tenancy, may apply to the rent officer for a certificate of fair rent for the premises as erected, converted or improved. Such applications may also be referred to a rent assessment committee.[2]

Controlled tenancies under pre-1965 legislation may by order of the Secretary of State be converted into regulated tenancies[3] and areas may be released from rent regulation.[4]

The registered rent is the maximum recoverable and any excess payable contractually is irrecoverable.[5] Until the rent payable under a regulated tenancy has been registered it is fixed at that payable at 8 December 1965, with only limited possible increases which in case of dispute may be referred to the sheriff.[6]

Payment of rent

The general rules as to discharge of an obligation by payment apply to payments of rent. Discharge may be made expressly or by implication, by the presumption from the production of three discharges for consecutive termly payments that all preceding payments have been made.[7] Rents of urban tenements fall under the triennial prescription;[8] after three years after each term's rent has fallen due the constitution and resting-owing of the debt must be proved by writ or oath[9] or by judicial admission.[10] Rents also prescribe under the quinquennial prescription, unless proved to be due and resting-owing by the writ or oath of the tenant.[11] Furthermore actions for rent prescribe in ten years unless wakened every five years.[11] This prescription is excluded only if rents have been sued for within the period, not if there have been partial payments.[12]

1 Sched. 3, paras. 1–3.
2 Sched. 4.
3 S. 11.
4 S. 12.
5 S. 3.
6 Ss. 3–9.
7 i.e. The *apocha trium annorum*; Stair I, 18, 2; Bankt. I, 24, 13; Ersk. III, 4, 10; Bell, *Prin.* §567, 585.
8 Prescription Act, 1579.
9 *Deans* v. *Steele* (1853) 16 D. 317.
10 *Ritchie* v. *Little* (1836) 14 S. 216.
11 Prescription Act, 1669.
12 *Nisbet* v. *Bailie* (1729) Mor. 11059.

A claim for rent may be extinguished by compensation,[1] as where the tenant has a liquid counter-claim for goods sold to the landlord, but not where the tenant's claim is illiquid, as for damages,[2] unless that claim can be liquidated at once.[3]

Retention of rent

The tenant[4] may retain, and withhold payment of the whole or part of the rent admittedly due if the landlord has failed substantially to perform obligations incumbent on him under the lease, such as failing to put the tenant or maintain him in possession of a material part of the subjects let,[5] or withholding an accessory of the subjects let,[6] or failure to erect buildings promised,[7] or failure to put buildings into tenantable state,[8] or failure to execute necessary repairs, whereby the tenant suffered damage,[9] but not for failure in minor respects, such as temporary failure of water supply to a farm[10] or temporary defects in drainage.[11]

Whether to allow retention or not is in the discretion of the court, and it is rarely allowed where the landlord's failure is in a respect collateral to the giving and maintenance of possession or the main purpose of the lease, or the damage alleged is insubstantial.[12] If retention is refused the tenant must resort to a claim of damages, but a valid claim of retention does not preclude a claim of damages as well.[13]

A tenant who has obtained damages against the landlord cannot also retain his rent,[14] but he may retain in respect of an unsatisfied decree for damages for fundamental breach of the lease.[15]

1 Compensation Act, 1592; Stair I, 18, 6; Bankt. I, 24, 23; Ersk. III, 4, 11; Bell, *Comm.* II, 553; *Prin.* §572.

2 *Humphrey* v. *Mackay* (1883) 10 R. 647; *Sheppherd* v. *McNab* (1896) 3 S.L.T. 240; *Christie* v. *Birrell*, 1910 S.C. 986.

3 *Johnstone* v. *Cleghorn* (1824) 2 S. 688; *Johnston* v. *Inglis* (1832) 10 S. 260; *Davie* v. *Stark* (1876) 3 R. 1114; *Inch* v. *Lee* (1903) 11 S.L.T. 874.

4 Including a statutory tenant holding under the Rent Acts: *Stobbs* v. *Hislop*, 1948 S.C. 216.

5 *Duncan* v. *Brooks* (1894) 21 R. 760.

6 *Kilmarnock Gas Light Co.* v. *Smith* (1872) 11 M. 58.

7 *Campbell* v. *Mundell* (1896) 3 S.L.T. 287.

8 *Munro* v. *McGeochs* (1888) 16 R. 93; *McDonald* v. *Kydd* (1901) 3 F. 923; *E. Galloway* v. *McConnell*, 1911 S.C. 846; *Haig* v. *Boswall-Preston*, 1915 S.C. 339; contrast *Stewart* v. *Campbell* (1889) 16 R. 346.

9 *Fingland & Mitchell* v. *Howie*, 1926 S.C. 319.

10 *Russell* v. *Sime*, 1912 2 S.L.T. 344.

11 *Burns* v. *McNeil* (1898) 5 S.L.T. 289; *Brown* v. *Simpson*, 1910 1 S.L.T. 183.

12 *Johnston* v. *Inglis* (1832) 10 S. 260; *McRae* v. *Macpherson* (1843) 6 D. 302; *Dods* v. *Fortune* (1854) 16 D. 478.

13 *Fingland & Mitchell* v. *Howie*, 1926 S.C. 319.

14 *Christie* v. *Wilson*, 1915 S.C. 645.

15 *Marshall's Trs.* v. *Banks*, 1934 S.C. 405.

A wider right of retention may be exercised in the event of the landlord's bankruptcy, on the principle of balancing accounts in bankruptcy,[1] of arrears due at the date of the first deliverance in the landlord's sequestration.[2]

Where a right of retention is properly exercised the rent may be consigned till the conditions are satisfied which will make it payable.[3]

Abatement of rent

By agreement rent fixed may be abated. A tenant is entitled to an abatement of rent if part of the subjects let have been rendered unusable by *damnum fatale*, as where houses have been burned.[4]

Landlord's remedies for rent

On non-payment of rent the landlord may bring a personal action for payment of the sum due and do any form of diligence thereon. An alleged agreement to allow an abatement from the rent stated in a written lease must be proved by writ or oath.[5]

At common law a legal right of irritancy existed when two years' rent was unpaid.[6] The Act of Sederunt of 14 December 1756 which regulated this remedy applies only to agricultural leases, so that in relation to urban leases irritancy can be enforced only by an extraordinary removing in the Court of Session.

The lease may contain provision for a conventional irritancy for non-payment of rent, which is enforceable according to its terms.[7] Enforcement of an irritancy bars a claim of damages for premature termination of the lease.[8]

Under the Houseletting and Rating Act, 1911, S. 5, if the tenant of a small dwelling-house under that Act is in arrears with rent for not less than 7 days, 48 hours' notice of termination of let may be given, and (S. 6) if the tenant fails to remove a summary application for removing may be brought in the Sheriff or Burgh Police Court. The court may grant not more than 48 hours delay

[1] Bell, *Comm.* II, 124.
[2] Bankruptcy (Sc.) Act, 1913, Ss. 41, 97.
[3] *McDonald* v. *Kydd* (1901) 3 F. 923.
[4] *Duff* v. *Fleming* (1870) 8 M. 769; *Allan* v. *Markland* (1882) 10 R. 383; *Critchley* v. *Campbell* (1884) 11 R. 475; *Sharp* v. *Thomson,* 1930 S.C. 1092.
[5] *Turnbull* v. *Oliver* (1891) 19 R. 154.
[6] Stair II, 9, 32; Bankt. II, 9, 23; Ersk. II, 6, 44; cf. *M. Breadalbane* v. *Stewart* (1904) 6 F. (H.L.) 23.
[7] cf. *McDouall's Tr.* v. *Macleod,* 1949 S.C. 593.
[8] *Buttercase* v. *Geddie* (1897) 24 R. 1128.

unless on cause shown, or on caution for, or consignation of, the rent due being found or made.

Hypothec

The landlord also has at common law a right of hypothec[1] in the case of houses, shops, market gardens, and mines,[2] but not now available over subjects let for agriculture or pasture and exceeding two acres in extent,[3] which confers a right in security, without the need to take possession, over *invecta et illata* in the subjects, such as furniture and plenishing, stock in trade, and equipment, and moveables generally,[4] but not over money, bonds, bills, the tenant's clothes[5] and, probably, his tools of trade.[6] It covers also goods on the premises, held on hire[7] or hire-purchase, or sold but not removed,[8] but not goods, not hired, belonging to a third party such as a member of the family or lodger,[9] nor single articles, hired or not hired, in premises let furnished, where the remainder of the furnishing does not fall within the hypothec.[10] The true owner's remedy in these cases is to appear before the sheriff and claim to have them withdrawn from the sequestration.[11] Hypothec covers a subtenant's goods in respect of his sub-rent, and also of the principal rent.[12]

In the case of lets of small dwellings covered by the House-letting and Rating Act, 1911, it does not (S. 10) cover bedding material, all tools and implements of trade, used or to be used by the occupier or any member of his family as his means of livelihood, which are in the house, and also such further furniture and plenishing as the occupier may select to the value of £10, according to the sheriff-officer's valuation.

The landlord may interdict the tenant from removing the *invecta et illata* and, if they have been removed, may after intimation to the tenant, which may for exceptional reasons stated be

1 Stair I, 13, 14; Bankt. I, 18, 7; Ersk. II, 6, 56; Bell, *Prin.* §1234.

2 *Linlithgow Oil Co.* v. *E. Rosebery* (1903) 6 F. 90.

3 Hypothec Abolition Act, 1880; as to houses and fields let separately see *Clark* v. *Keirs* (1888) 15 R. 458.

4 Including animals: *Lamb* v. *Grant* (1874) 11 S.L.R. 672 (cow and calf).

5 Bell, *Prin.* §1276.

6 *Macpherson* v. *M's Tr.* (1905) 8 F. 191.

7 *Penson* v. *Robertson*, 6 June 1820, F.C.; *Nelmes* v. *Ewing* (1883) 11 R. 193; *McIntosh* v. *Potts* (1905) 7 F. 765.

8 *Ryan* v. *Little*, 1910 S.C. 219; but see *Lippe* v. *Colville* (1894) 1 S.L.T. 616.

9 *Bell* v. *Andrews* (1885) 12 R. 961; *Pulsometer Engineering Co.* v. *Gracie* (1887) 14 R. 316 (agent's samples).

10 *Edinburgh Albert Bldgs. Co.* v. *General Guarantee Corpn.*, 1917 S.C. 239. As to goods under 'sale or return' contract see *Macdonald* v. *Westren* (1888) 15 R. 988.

11 *Lindsay* v. *E. Wemyss* (1872) 10 M. 708.

12 *Steuart* v. *Stables* (1878) 5 R. 1024.

dispensed with,[1] obtain judicial warrant to have them brought back,[2] but these are exceptional measures importing liability in damages if obtained by statements not justified[3] or if there is genuine dispute as to rent and such extreme measures are unnecessary in the circumstances.[4]

If no application is made to enforce the hypothec by landlord's sequestration the *invecta et illata* may be removed or sold, but if sequestration is granted it attaches goods not removed even though sold and the landlord's claim is superior to that of the purchaser.[5]

Extent of security conferred by hypothec

The right of hypothec gives security for one year's rent, but not for prior arrears.[6] If not sought to be enforced within three months of the last term of payment, the right falls.[7]

Sequestration for rent

The landlord enforces his right of hypothec by petition for landlord's sequestration in the sheriff court.[8] It is usual to sequestrate for rent due and in security of that falling due at the next term.[9] Warrant to sequestrate is normally obtained on an *ex parte* statement by the landlord, and under this a sheriff officer inventories and values the *invecta et illata*.[10] They are then deemed *in manibus curiae* and any person removing them, if acting in good faith, must account for their value, or, if in bad faith, incurs liability for the rent.[11] The order for sequestration will be recalled on payment or consignation of the rent.[12] Failing payment, the landlord then obtains warrant from the court to have the sequestrated goods sold by auction. The owner of property

[1] *Johnston* v. *Young* (1890) 18 R. (J.) 6; *McLaughlan* v. *Reilly* (1892) 20 R. 41; *Jack* v. *Black*, 1911 S.C. 691.
[2] *Nelmes* v. *Ewing* (1883) 11 R. 193; *Donald* v. *Leitch* (1886) 13 R. 790.
[3] *Jack*, *supra*; *Shearer* v. *Nicoll*, 1935 S.L.T. 313.
[4] *Gray* v. *Weir* (1891) 19 R. 25.
[5] *Ryan* v. *Little*, 1910 S.C. 219.
[6] *Young* v. *Welsh* (1833) 12 S. 233.
[7] *Thomson* v. *Barclay* (1883) 10 R. 694; *Donald* v. *Leitch* (1886) 13 R. 790.
[8] *Duncan* v. *Lodijinsky* (1904) 6 F. 408. A landlord has been held disentitled to sequestrate where he was himself materially in breach of contract: *Guthrie* v. *Shearer* (1873) 1 R. 181; *Tennent's Trs.* v. *Maxwell* (1880) 17 S.L.R. 463. But it is no defence that the tenant merely has an illiquid claim against the landlord: *Hoggs* v. *Caldwell* (1882) 19 S.L.R. 452.
[9] *Donald* v. *Leitch* (1886) 13 R. 790.
[10] Including effects belonging to unauthorized subtenant: *Lippe* v. *Colville* (1894) 1 S.L.T. 616. As to procedure see *Taylor* v. *MacKnight* (1882) 9 R. 857.
[11] Bell, *Prin.* §1244; *Stewart* v. *Peddie* (1874) 2 R. 94; *Jack* v. *McCaig* (1880) 7 R. 465.
[12] *Tennant's Trs.* v. *Maxwell* (1880) 17 S.L.R. 463.

hired by the tenant should apply to the sheriff or judge of the roup to have the property reserved and the tenant's own property sold first, failing which he has no claim against the landlord.[1]

The landlord is liable in damages if he has used sequestration unjustifiably[2] but not merely because the tenant propounded a counter-claim which is well founded.[3]

The landlord's right to sequestrate for rent is unaffected by the mercantile sequestration of the tenant[4] but claims having preferential ranking in bankruptcy have priority over the landlord's claim for rent out of the proceeds of sale.

Regulation of use of subjects let

Apart from not inverting the possession, common law does not impose restrictions on the use made of subjects let. Express conditions frequently prohibit use of the premises for business,[5] for particular trades,[6] or for any trade likely to be a nuisance.[7]

Extension or renewal of lease

A lease may be extended for a further period on the same terms and conditions, or be renewed on different terms, in any of the modes in which an original lease can be constituted and proved. Neither party is bound by negotiations or proposals not accepted but the continuance of negotiations excludes any inference of agreement, such as extends the lease under the principle of tacit relocation.[8] Hence if the tenant remains in possession after the expiry of the old lease, this may raise an inference of acceptance of the new terms offered.

Termination of lease before ish

An urban lease may be terminated before the date of expiry by renunciation, or where an irritancy has been incurred.

1 *Lindsay* v. *E. Wemyss* (1872) 10 M. 708; *McIntosh* v. *Potts* (1905) 7 F. 765.

2 *Riddle* v. *Mitchell* (1870) 8 S.L.R. 140; *Turnbull* v. *Oliver* (1891) 19 R. 154; *Pollock* v. *Goodwin's Trs.* (1898) 25 R. 1051; *Alexander* v. *Campbell's Trs.* (1903) 5 F. 634; *Gilmour* v. *Craig* (1908) 15 S.L.T. 797; *Gray* v. *Smart* (1892) 19 R. 692; *Shearer* v. *Nicoll*, 1935 S.L.T. 313.

3 *Craig* v. *Harkness* (1894) 2 S.L.T. 307.

4 Bankruptcy (Sc.) Act, 1913, S. 115.

5 e.g. *Ewing* v. *Hastie* (1878) 5 R. 439 (school); cf. *Colville* v. *Carrick* (1883) 10 R. 1241; *Graham* v. *Shiels* (1901) 8 S.L.T. 368 (nursing home).

6 e.g. *Macdonald* v. *Campbell* (1889) 16 R. 540.

7 *Frame* v. *Cameron* (1864) 3 M. 290.

8 *Macfarlane* v. *Mitchell* (1900) 2 F. 901; *Buchanan* v. *Harris & Sheldon* (1900) 2 F. 935. On tacit relocation, see *infra*.

Renunciation

A tenant may renounce his lease where the landlord has been in fundamental breach of contract.

Extraordinary removing

A declarator that an irritancy has been incurred and that a tenant must remove, under pain of ejection, may be brought in the Court of Session, or Sheriff Court.[1] The irritancy may be legal, arising on default in payment of rent for two successive years,[2] or conventional, contained in the lease, to cover such cases as the tenant's bankruptcy[3] or non-payment of rent for a stated period.[4] The declaratory conclusion is not always essential.[4] A legal irritancy may be purged by payment before decree passes, but a conventional irritancy cannot be so purged unless it merely expresses a legal irritancy.[5] A landlord may found on an irritancy provision though on a previous default he has waived his option to terminate the lease.[6]

Termination of lease at ish

The expiry of the contractual duration of a lease terminates it only if either party has given due notice to the other of his intention to terminate it. Failing such notice tacit relocation applies.

Tacit relocation

Where there has been no express agreement for a renewal or extension of a lease, but neither party has given due notice of intention to terminate the lease at the expiry of its term, an extension of the lease is implied by law for the same period as the expiring lease, if for less than a year, and, if for a term of years, for a further year, on the same terms and conditions.[7] It may continue thereafter for further periods in the same way. Tacit relocation may be inferred also where a landlord has given notice to quit but has taken no further action and allowed the tenant to

[1] Sheriff Courts (Sc.) Act, 1907, Ss. 5(3)(4), 7.

[2] Stair II, 9, 32; Bankt. II, 9, 23; Ersk. II, 6, 44; In the case of urban subjects (not affected by the Act of Sederunt, 14 Dec. 1756) the extraordinary removing must be in the Court of Session: *Cormack* v. *Copland* (1754) 5 B.S. 820; *Nisbet* v. *Aikman* (1866) 4 M. 284.

[3] *Bidoulac* v. *Sinclair's Tr.* (1889) 17 R. 144.

[4] *D. Argyll* v. *Campbeltown Coal Co.*, 1924 S.C. 844.

[5] *Duncanson* v. *Giffen* (1878) 15 S.L.R. 356; *McDouall's Trs.* v. *Macleod*, 1949 S.C. 593.

[6] *Lurie* v. *Demarco*, 1967 S.L.T. (Notes) 110.

[7] Stair II, 9, 23; Bankt. II, 9, 32; Ersk. II, 6, 35; Bell, *Prin.* §1265; cf. *Neilson* v. *Mossend Iron Co.* (1887) 13 R. (H.L.) 50, 54; *Douglas* v. *Cassillis & Culzean Estates*, 1944 S.C. 355.

remain in possession.[1] It is founded on the implied consent of all parties to the lease; accordingly notice by one of joint tenants is enough to exclude tacit relocation.[2] Tacit relocation is excluded by agreement for a new lease, even if improbative, but on which possession had continued,[3] or by the tenant's continuance in circumstances implying his acquiescence in new conditions intimated,[4] or by even verbal notice of intention to terminate,[5] but not by an ineffectual notice to quit.[6] If a tenant has given notice but then refuses to leave he cannot rely on tacit relocation, and is liable to be ejected as a squatter and liable for violent profits, i.e. for the greatest sum for which the subjects could have been let.[7]

The principle of tacit relocation is probably inapplicable to leases which are, by common understanding, seasonal only, such as of furnished houses, grass parks, fishings and shootings.[8] It does not apply to rights of occupancy of a house as an incident of a contract of service.[9] An option to renew a lease is not a term continued by tacit relocation after its expiry.[10]

Ordinary removings

A lease accordingly terminates at the ish only if either party has given to the other, before the date of expiry of the lease, due notice of termination.

Where houses, with or without land attached not exceeding two acres, lands not exceeding two acres let without houses, mills, fishings and shootings, and other heritable subjects (except land exceeding two acres in extent) are let for a year or more, notice of termination must be given in writing by or on behalf of one party to the other at least 40 days before the termination of the tenancy (Whitsunday or Martinmas as the case may be).[11]

1 *Taylor* v. *E. Moray* (1892) 19 R. 399; *Milner's C.B.* v. *Mason*, 1965 S.L.T. (Sh. Ct.) 56.
2 *Smith* v. *Grayton Estates, Ltd.*, 1960 S.C. 349.
3 *Buchanan* v. *Harris & Sheldon* (1900) 2 F. 935.
4 *Macfarlane* v. *Mitchell* (1900) 2 F. 901.
5 *Craighall Cast-Stone Co.* v. *Wood*, 1931 S.C. 66.
6 *Gates* v. *Blair*, 1923 S.C. 430.
7 *Tod* v. *Fraser* (1889) 17 R. 226.
8 *Macharg* (1805) Mor. Removing, Appx. 4.
9 *Dunbar's Trs.* v. *Bruce* (1900) 3 F. 137; *Sinclair* v. *Tod*, 1907 S.C. 1038; *Cairns* v. *Innes*, 1942 S.C. 164.
10 *Commercial Union Assce. Co.*, 1964 S.C. 85.
11 Sheriff Courts (Sc.) Act, 1907, S. 37; see also Sched. I, Rules 110–14, and Form V. The notice must specify the subjects: *Scott* v. *Livingstone*, 1919 S.C. 1. The common law form of action applies also to controlled tenancies: *Purves* v. *Graham*, 1924 S.C. 477. The requirement of written notice applies only when procedure for summary ejection is being followed and informal notice, at least by the tenant, suffices for an ordinary removing.

The normal term dates are Whitsunday (15 May) and Martinmas (11 November) but, in the absence of express stipulation, a tenant shall enter or remove from a house at noon on 28 May or 28 November, as the case may be, or if that date be a Sunday, on the next day.[1] Despite this, where warning to remove is given 40 days before, it must be 40 days before 15 May or 11 November.[2] Notice does not warrant summary ejection from the subjects let, but entitles the proprietor to apply to the sheriff for a warrant for summary ejection[3] in common form against the tenant and everyone deriving right from him.[4] Informal notice by the tenant of intention to quit suffices, the requirement of written notice applying only where the procedure for summary ejection is being followed out.[5]

Summary application for removing

Where houses or other heritable subjects are let for less than a year, any authorized person may present to the sheriff a summary application for removing, decree in which has the effect of a decree of removing and warrant of ejection. In the absence of express stipulation notice to remove[6] must be, in the case of a let for not more than four months, one-third of the period of let,[7] and where the let exceeds four months, at least forty days.[8]

Summary removing from small dwelling-houses

In small dwellings, regulated by the House Letting and Rating Act, 1911, lets, except for a shorter period than a month, terminate and are terminable only at noon on the 28th of a month or, if that date be a Sunday, on the next Monday, and lets for a shorter period than a month terminate and are terminable at noon on a Monday.[9] Notice of termination on the day on which the

[1] Removal Terms (Sc.) Act, 1886, S. 4. Notice to remove 'at Whitsunday' is good: *Campbell's Trs.* v. *O'Neill*, 1911 S.C. 188.

[2] 1907 Act, S. 37; cf. *Dunlop* v. *Meiklem* (1876) 4 R. 11; *Fraser's Trs.* v. *Maule* (1904) 6 F. 819.

[3] This is a misnomer for 'summary removing': *Campbell's Trs.* v. *O'Neill*, 1911 S.C. 188.

[4] 1907 Act, S. 37; cf. *Robb* v. *Brearton* (1895) 22 R. 885.

[5] *Craighall Cast Stone Co.* v. *Wood Bros.*, 1931 S.C. 66.

[6] Sheriff Courts (Sc.) Act, 1907, S. 38, and Sched. Form K.

[7] Subject to a minimum of 28 days: Rent Act, 1957, S. 16 and Sched. 6, para. 29.

[8] Sheriff Courts (Sc.) Act, 1907, S. 38, and Sheriff Court Rules, 115–22, Action for summary removing are dealt with summarily as under the Small Debt Acts, and are not subject to review: Rule 119; but the decree may be suspended if the proceedings are fundamentally null: *Robertson* v. *Thorburn*, 1927 S.L.T. 562; see also *Mackay* v. *Menzies*, 1937 S.C. 691. No appeal lies to the High Court of Justiciary: *Lovell* v. *Macfarlane*, 1949 J.C. 123.

[9] 1911 Act, S. 3.

next payment of rent falls due may be given by either party in accordance with the provisions of the 1907 Act but expire only at noon on the day on which a payment of rent falls due or, if that is not a lawful date for the termination of a let under the Act, at noon on the next lawful day. If the let is for more than three months, 40 days notice must be given; if for less, the notice is one-third of the period of let[1] with a minimum of 28 days.[2] If, however, the occupier of a small dwellinghouse is in arrear with the rent for not less than 7 days, the landlord may give notice to terminate the let 28 days later.[3]

If the occupier fails to remove, the owner may make to the sheriff a summary application for removing, decree in which has the effect of a decree of removing and warrant of ejection. The sheriff or magistrate may not grant a delay of more than 48 hours unless on cause shown, or on caution found for or consignation of the rent due.[4]

Statutory powers to terminate leases

If an executor in whom a deceased intestate's interest under a lease has vested, is satisfied that the interest cannot be disposed of according to law and so informs the landlord, or the interest is not so disposed of within a year or such longer period as may be agreed or fixed by the sheriff, either party may, on giving six months' notice, terminate the lease.[5]

Where premises, in respect of which a closing order, demolition order, clearance order or resolution declaring a building an obstruction has become operative, is the subject of a lease or sublease, either party may apply to the sheriff for an order determining the lease which he may order, conditionally or unconditionally.[6]

Ejection

An action of ejection,[7] craving warrant summarily to eject the defender from certain premises, is appropriate where the occupier

1 S. 4, as amd. by Rent Act, 1957, Sched. 6, para. 30.
2 Rent Act, 1957, S. 16, and Sched. 6, para. 30.
3 S. 5, as amd. by Rent Act, 1957, Sched. 6, para. 30.
4 1911 Act, S. 6.
5 Succession (Sc.) Act, 1904, S. 16(3); see also S. 16(7).
6 Housing (Sc.) Act, 1966, S. 187.
7 A warrant of ejection is the executory part of the decree in an action for removing or summary removing. As to the substantive action of ejection see *Price* v. *Watson*, 1951 S.C. 359. An ejection is not incompetent merely because a question of law is involved: *Cairns* v. *Innes*, 1942 S.C. 164; *Asher* v. *Macleod*, 194 S.C. 558.

has never had legal title to occupy the premises,[1] such as a squatter, or intruder encroaching on property, or a tenant whose tenancy has been terminated by notice but who, though not entitled to remain as a statutory tenant, refuses to remove,[2] or a person whose title to occupy has terminated, such as a servant entitled to occupy a house as part of his remuneration and now dismissed.[3] It is incompetent where the person in possession founds on a title to possess,[4] or had a title which is said to have terminated.[5]

An owner is not entitled at his own hand to eject a person in possession on an *ex facie* valid title, even on allegation that the person obtained the let by fraud.[6]

Statutory restrictions on removing tenants

In houses controlled under the Rent and Mortgage Interest Restriction Acts, 1920–1939, the landlord may, save by agreement, recover possession of the controlled house only under a decree of court. Decree of removal may be granted only where the court considers it reasonable to grant it, and is satisfied that suitable alternative accommodation is available for the tenant or will be available when the decree takes effect,[7] or has power to do so in the excepted cases.[8]

A certificate of the local housing authority certifying that they will provide suitable alternative accommodation for the tenant by the date specified in the certificate is conclusive evidence that such accommodation will be available.[9] Where no certificate is produced to the court accommodation is considered suitable if it consists of a controlled house or of premises which will in the opinion of the court afford to the tenant security of tenure reasonably equivalent to the security afforded by a controlled house,[10] and is, in the opinion of the court, reasonably suitable to the needs of the tenant and his family, as regards proximity to place of work and either similar as regards rental[11] and extent to

[1] *Colquhoun's Trs.* v. *Purdie*, 1946 S.N. 3; cf. *Paterson* v. *Robertson*, 1944 J.C. 166. As to ejection of spouse see *Millar* v. *M.*, 1940 S.C. 56; *Labno* v. *L.*, 1949 S.L.T. (Notes) 18.

[2] e.g. *Cowan* v. *Acton*, 1952 S.C. 73.

[3] cf. *Dunbar's Trs.* v. *Bruce* (1900) 3 F. 137; *Sinclair* v. *Tod*, 1907 S.C. 1038; *Cairns*, *supra*; contrast *MacGregor* v. *Dunnet*, 1949 S.C. 510.

[4] *Wallace* v. *Kerr*, 1917 S.C. 102; *Lowe* v. *Gardiner*, 1921 S.C. 211; *Scottish Supply Assocn.* v. *Mackie*, 1921 S.C. 882.

[5] *Hally* v. *Lang* (1867) 5 M. 951; *Scottish Property Inv. Co. Bldg. Soc.* v. *Horne* (1881) 8 R. 737; *Lowe*, *supra*; *Cook* v. *Wylie*, 1963 S.L.T. (Sh. Ct.) 29.

[6] *Brash* v. *Munro & Hall* (1903) 5 F. 1102.

[7] 1933 Act, S. 3.

[8] See *infra*.

[9] cf. *Burgh of Paisley* v. *Bamford*, 1950 S.L.T. 200.

[10] 1933 Act, Ss. 3(2), 15(a), and 16(1).

[11] *Turner* v. *Keiller*, 1950 S.C. 43.

the accommodation afforded by dwelling-houses provided in the neighbourhood by any housing authority for persons whose needs as regards extent are, in the opinion of the court, similar to those of the tenant and his family,[1] or otherwise reasonably suitable to the means of the tenant and to the needs of the tenant and his family as regards extent and character.[2] The alternative accommodation must be a house in which the occupier and his family can live without causing it to be overcrowded under the Housing (Sc.) Act, 1935.[3]

Exceptionally, decree of removal may be granted without proof of suitable alternative accommodation being available if:[4]

(a) The tenant has not paid any rent lawfully due[5] or has broken the conditions of his tenancy;[6]

(b) The tenant or someone living with him or his subtenant is a nuisance to adjoining occupiers or has been convicted of using the house for an immoral or illegal purpose or is causing the house to deteriorate;[7]

(c) That the tenant has given notice to quit and the landlord has in consequence sold or let the house and would be seriously prejudiced if he could not obtain possession;[8]

(d) That the tenant has after 31st July 1923, in the case of an old controlled house, and after 1 September 1939, in the case of a new controlled house, without the consent of the landlord, assigned or sublet the whole house or sublet part of the house, the remainder being already sub-let;[9]

(e) That the house consists of or includes premises with an off-licence and the tenant has been convicted of a licensing offence or renewal of the licence has been refused;[10]

(f) That the house is so overcrowded as to be dangerous or injurious to the health of the inmates and the tenant has not taken all reasonable steps to remove any lodger or subtenant contributing to the overcrowding;

(g) That the house is reasonably required by the landlord for occupation by some person in the whole-time employment of the

[1] 1933 Act, S. 3(3) and (4).
[2] *Stewart* v. *Mackay*, 1947 S.C. 287.
[3] 1938 Act, Ss. 7(3), 8(3); see also *Glasgow Corpn.* v. *Bruce*, 1942 S.C. 81.
[4] 1933 Act, Sched. I.
[5] *Bird* v. *Hildage* [1948] 1 K.B. 91; *Dallanty* v. *Pellow* [1951] 2 K.B. 858.
[6] *Chapman* v. *Hughes* (1923) 129 L.T. 223.
[7] *Schneiders* v. *Abrahams* [1925] 1 K.B. 301; *Hodson* v. *Jones* [1951] W.N. 127.
[8] *Barton* v. *Fincham* [1921] 2 K.B. 291.
[9] *Dalrymple's Trs.* v. *Brown*, 1945 S.C. 190; *Baker* v. *Turner* [1950] A.C. 401; *Regional Properties* v. *Frankenschwerth* [1951] 1 All E.R. 178.
[10] On-licence premises are decontrolled by 1933 Act, S. 1(3).

landlord or of some tenant of the landlord and either (1) the tenant was previously in the employment of the landlord and the house was let to him in consequence of that employment,[1] or (2) the court is satisfied by a certificate granted by the Department of Agriculture for Scotland that the house is required for an agricultural worker;[2]

(h) That the house is reasonably required by the landlord (unless he became landlord by purchasing the house after 7 November 1956) for occupation as a residence for himself, or any son or daughter over 18 years of age, or his father or mother;[3]

(i) that the rent charged by the tenant to a subtenant of part of the house is in excess of the maximum rent which the Acts permit him to recover in respect of the sublet part.[4]

If a landlord obtains decree of removal on ground (g) or (h) by misrepresentation or concealment of material facts, the court may order him to pay compensation to the tenant for damage or loss sustained as the result of the decree.[5]

The court has also a general power to suspend or stay the execution of a decree of removing or to postpone the date of repossession or to adjourn the application for such periods and on such terms as he thinks fit.[6]

Statutory tenancy

If the contractual letting of a controlled tenancy is terminated by notice but the landlord is not entitled to recover possession, the tenant retains possession as a statutory tenant, provided that he occupies the house as his residence or, if temporarily absent, intends to return to reside in the house within a reasonable period.[7] A deserted wife's occupation is not equivalent to retention of possession by the tenant.[8]

Death of tenant—statutory tenancy

In the case of dwellings controlled by the Rent and Mortgage Increase Restrictions Act, 1920–39, the term 'tenant' includes

[1] *Read* v. *Gordon* [1941] 1 K.B. 495; *Royal Crown Derby Co.* v. *Russell* [1949] 2 K.B. 417; *Grimond* v. *Duncan*, 1949 S.C. 195; *Railway Executive* v. *Macdonald*, 1950 S.C. 308.

[2] *Kemp* v. *Ballachulish Estate Co.*, 1933 S.C. 478; *Barclay* v. *Hannah*, 1947 S.C. 245.

[3] New paragraph substituted by Rent Act, 1957, Sched. 6, para. 21; see also *Maxwell* v. *Mulhern*, 1968 S.L.T. (Sh. Ct.) 43.

[4] 1933 Act, S. 4(1).

[5] 1920 Act, S. 5(6) and (7); 1923 Act, S. 4; 1933 Act, Sched. 2; 1939 Act, Sched. I.

[6] 1920 Act, S. 5(2).

[7] 1920 Act, S. 15(1); *Skinner* v. *Geary* [1931] 2 K.B. 546; *Menzies* v. *Mackay*, 1938 S.C. 74.

[8] *Temple* v. *Mitchell*, 1956 S.C. 267.

the widow of a tenant who was residing with him at the time of his death, or where the tenant leaves no widow or is a woman, such member of the tenant's family so residing for not less than six months before the death as may be decided in default of agreement by the sheriff.[1] On the death of the tenant of a controlled dwelling such a surviving member of the family becomes statutory tenant and continues to be protected from eviction. No further transmission of protected tenancy, however, takes place on the death of a statutory tenant, and on his death the tenancy is terminable by the landlord;[2] a statutory tenancy is not assignable nor capable of bequest, nor does it pass to an executor.[3] If a tenancy is bequeathed the beneficiary must intimate it to the landlord if he wishes to continue the contractual tenancy rather than be merely a statutory tenant.[4]

Under the Rent Act, 1965, S. 13, if the first successor leaves a widow residing with him or is a woman or leaves no widow but a member of his family was residing with him for not less than six months immediately before his death, the widow or such member of the first successor's family as may in default of agreement be decided by the sheriff is to be second successor and the right to retain possession passes to him, as a regulated tenancy under the 1965 Act, not as a statutory tenancy.

A statutory tenancy terminates if the tenant voluntarily surrenders possession, or fails to use the house as his residence, or it ceases to exist, or he accepts a new contractual tenancy, or the court grants decree of removal, or the statutory protection ceases to apply.[5]

Recovery of possession of regulated dwellings

An owner-occupier of a dwelling who has let it on a regulated tenancy under the Rent Act, 1965, may (S. 14) recover possession if, apart from the Rent Acts, the landlord would be entitled to recover possession of the dwelling-house, and the court is satisfied that the dwelling-house is required as a residence for the owner-occupier or any member of his family who resided with the owner-occupier when he last occupied the dwelling-house as a residence, provided that not later than the commencement of the

1 1920 Act, S. 12(1)(g); 1933 Act, S. 13; 1935 Act, S. 1; Housing (Repairs and Rents) (Sc.) Act, 1954, S. 33.

2 *Joint Properties, Ltd.* v. *Williamson*, 1945 S.C. 68; *Campbell* v. *Wright*, 1952 S.C. 240; *Grant's Trs.* v. *Arrol*, 1954 S.C. 306.

3 *Lovibond* v. *Vincent* [1929] 1 K.B. 687.

4 *Grant's Trs.*, *supra.*

5 1965 Act, S. 12.

tenancy or 8 May 1966 the landlord has given notice in writing to the tenant that possession may be recovered under S. 14, and that the dwelling house has not since the commencement of that Act been let on a regulated tenancy with respect to which the previous proviso was not satisfied.[1] The tenant must be warned in writing at the outset of the lease that the landlord may invoke the relevant provisions of the 1965 Act.

Other conditions of lease

A lease may contain other conditions such as an option to the tenant to buy, if the landlord should decide to sell,[2] or an option to purchase on notice given,[3] or permitting the erection and removal of greenhouses or temporary buildings.[4]

LEASES OF FURNISHED HOUSES

The lease of a house, or part thereof, furnished, is governed by the same principles as unfurnished houses. In the absence of express stipulation the landlord must relieve the tenant of the liability for occupier's rates.[5]

The landlord may lock cupboards and other receptacles.[6] The tenant may remove pictures and store them in one of the rooms, even against the landlord's wishes.[7]

Furnished premises

The Rent of Furnished Houses Control (Sc.) Act, 1943[8] created in areas to which the Act was applied tribunals to which the lessor or lessee of houses or parts of houses within the same limits of rateable value as the Rent Acts let with furniture or services, or the local authority for the area, might refer the contract. The tribunal may after enquiry approve the rent payable or reduce it to such sum as they thought reasonable. Particulars of the contract and the rent have to be registered by the tribunal.

[1] Ss. 15 and 16 deal with recovery of possession of houses held for occupation by ministers of religion, and by persons employed in agriculture.

[2] *Pickett* v. *Lindsay's Trs.* (1905) 13 S.L.T. 440; cf. *Fraser* v. *Denny, Mott & Dickson*, 1944 S.C. (H.L.) 35.

[3] *Penman* v. *Mackay*, 1922 S.C. 385.

[4] *Murray* v. *Campbell* (1879) 6 R. 1163; *Ferguson* v. *Paul* (1885) 12 R. 1222; see also *Burns* v. *Fleming* (1880) 8 R. 226.

[5] *Macome* v. *Dickson* (1868) 6 M. 898; *Sturrock* v. *Murray*, 1952 S.C. 454.

[6] *Miller* v. *Wilson*, 1919 1 S.L.T. 223.

[7] *Miller* v. *Stewart* (1899) 2 F. 309.

[8] Amended, Landlord and Tenant (Rent Control) Act, 1949, S. 17 and Sched. 2, and 1965 Act, S. 39(1) and (12).

After registration the case might be referred for reconsideration on the ground of change of circumstances, and the tribunal might then approve, increase or reduce the rent. Rents in excess of registered rents, and fines or premiums for the grant, renewal or continuance of a letting are offences and illegal and recoverable. This Act also applies[1] where a tenant shares part of the accommodation rented with the landlord so that it is not a 'separate dwelling' within the meaning of the Rent Acts, even though there is no payment for furniture or services. The Act does not apply to lettings where a substantial element of rent is attributable to board[2] nor to holiday lettings.[3]

Where the house is the subject of a regulated tenancy the 1943 Act is excluded.[4]

Security of tenure

Under the 1949 Act, Ss. 11 and 17, if application has been made to fix or reconsider rent, a subsequent notice to quit will not have effect before the expiry of six months from the tribunal's decision, unless it shortens the period, and an application after service of the notice has the same effect.[5] Thereafter further extensions may be granted of not more than six months at a time.

LEASES FOR BUSINESS PURPOSES

The principles applicable to urban leases apply generally also to leases for business premises. Thus the implied undertaking of fitness for the purpose of let applies,[6] the right to abandon if the premises are destroyed,[7] the obligation to keep the premises wind and water tight,[8] and the landlord's liability for damage caused by fault.[9]

The lease is not terminated by failure of the purpose for which the premises were let, such as the loss of a licence,[10] nor does it imply any obligation on the landlord not to establish a rival business.[11]

1 By Landlord and Tenant (Rent Control) Act, 1949, Ss. 7 and 17.
2 1943 Act, S. 9(3). 3 1965 Act, S. 39(11). 4 1965 Act, S. 39(5).
5 1949 Act, S. 17; 1965 Act, S. 39(6).
6 *Sandeman* v. *Duncan's Trs.* (1897) 5 S.L.T. 21.
7 *Drummond* v. *Hunter* (1869) 7 M. 347; *Duff* v. *Fleming* (1870) 8 M. 769.
8 *Wolfson* v. *Forrester*, 1910 S.C. 675.
9 *Hampton* v. *Galloway & Sykes* (1899) 1 F. 501; *N.B. Storage Co.* v. *Steele's Trs.*, 1920 S.C. 194.
10 *Donald* v. *Leitch* (1886) 13 R. 790; *Hart's Trs.* v. *Arrol* (1903) 6 F. 36.
11 *Craig* v. *Millar* (1888) 15 R. 1005; see also *Randall* v. *Summers*, 1919 S.C. 396.

The tenant is liable for harm caused by overloading the premises.[1]

The tenant has been held bound to furnish and air premises, but not to open and carry on business therein.[2] The tenant of a shop, unless expressly prohibited, may use it for auction sales.[3] A tenant's loss of his licence does not entitle the landlord to damages.[4] In the absence of general custom, the tenant may not attach showcases outside the shop,[5] but this does not prevent temporary signs on special occasions.[6]

The landlord is liable for detriment of the tenant's business by operations *in suo* only so far as they amount to derogation from his grant.[7]

The landlord may object to a tenant converting part of the premises for living, but may be barred by delay from objection.[8]

Shops—prolongation of tenancies

The Tenancy of Shops (Sc.) Act, 1949,[9] entitles the tenant of a shop, as defined by the Shops Act, 1950, whose lease has ended and who is unable to obtain a renewal on terms satisfactory to him, to apply to the sheriff within 21 days of the notice and before it takes effect for a renewal of his tenancy. The sheriff, whose decision is final, may determine that the tenancy be renewed for not longer than a year at such rent and terms as he thinks reasonable, or may dismiss the application, and shall not determine that the tenancy be renewed, if satisfied of one of stated conditions.[10] Further renewals may be made.[11] If renewal is granted a new lease is deemed to arise.[12] This Act does not protect subtenants,[13] and a tenant protected by this Act cannot claim protection under the Rent Acts as a regulated tenant.[14]

1 *Caledonian Ry. Co.* v. *Greenock Sacking Co.* (1875) 2 R. 671; *Corrie, Mackie & Co.* v. *Stewart* (1885) 22 S.L.R. 350; *Glebe Sugar Refining Co.* v. *Paterson* (1900) 2 F. 615.

2 *Whitelaw* v. *Fulton* (1871) 10 M. 27.

3 *Keith* v. *Reid* (1870) 8 M. (H.L.) 110.

4 *Hart's Trs.* v. *Arrol* (1903) 10 S.L.T. 733.

5 *B.L. Co.* v. *Purdie* (1905) 7 F. 923.

6 *Morrison* v. *Forsyth*, 1909 S.C. 329.

7 *Huber* v. *Ross*, 1912 S.C. 898.

8 *Moore* v. *Munro* (1896) 4 S.L.T. 172.

9 Made permanent by the Tenancy of Shops (Sc.) Act, 1964.

10 S. 1(1)–(3) and (7); cf. *Craig* v. *Saunders & Connor*, 1962 S.L.T. (Sh. Ct.) 85.

11 S. 1(4).

12 *Scottish Gas Board* v. *Kerr's Trs.*, 1956 S.L.T. (Sh. Ct.) 69.

13 *Ashley Wallpaper Co.* v. *Morrisons Assoc. Cos.*, 1952 S.L.T. (Sh. Ct.) 25.

14 1965 Act, S. 1(3).

BUILDING LEASE

The grant of plots of ground at an annual rental on long leases, of 99 or 999 years, on which the tenant is obliged to build a house of specified size and value, in uncommon in Scotland, but competent as an alternative to granting a feu,[1] and indeed necessary where the vassal was prohibited from granting feus, as he would be if holding under an entail. Where such a lease is granted it is assignable by the tenant, *inter vivos* or by will, and passes as heritage on his death intestate. On the expiry of the lease the land and buildings revert to the landlord.

Conditions are commonly imposed as to the use of premises to be built.[2]

Such leases, if for over 31 years and not exceeding 50 acres, are registrable in the Register of Sasines under the Registration of Leases Act, 1857. If registered the lease is valid against singular successors of the landlord even without possession. The lease is assignable under the Act, absolutely or in security.[3]

The Long Leases (Scotland) Act, 1954[4] enabled certain lessees and sub-lessees of property let under a lease for not less than 50 years granted before 10 August 1914 and occupied as a private dwelling-house forming his usual residence, to require the landlord before 1959 and subject to certain conditions to grant a feu right of the property (S. 1). An occupying lessee who acquired his interest otherwise than by inheritance, on or after 10 May 1951, is not so entitled (S. 3). A grant of a feu might be refused in certain cases on the ground of public interest (S. 4). Leases and sub-leases expiring within five years of the Act may be continued to Whitsunday, 1960 (Ss. 15–16).

AGRICULTURAL LEASES

Common law principles regulate the capacity of parties, and the modes of constitution and proof of leases of land for agricultural purposes.[5] The Leases Act, 1449 and the Registration of Leases Act, 1857, apply to agricultural leases.

[1] e.g. *Bisset* v. *Aberdeen Mags.* (1898) 1 F. 87.

[2] e.g. *Gold* v. *Houldsworth* (1870) 8 M. 1006; *L. Macdonald* v. *Campbell* (1889) 16 R. 540; *Ferguson* v. *Brown* (1902) 9 S.L.T. 341.

[3] *Crawford* v. *Campbell*, 1937 S.C. 596.

[4] Superseding Leasehold Property (Temporary Provisions) Act, 1951, and Long Leases (Temporary Provisions) (Sc.) Act, 1951, extended by Leasehold Property Act and Long Leases (Sc.) Act Extension Act, 1953.

[5] cf. *Gray* v. *Edinburgh University*, 1962 S.C. 157.

Numerous statutory provisions, however, apply to agricultural holdings.[1] Save as expressly provided in the Agricultural Holdings (Sc.) Act, 1949, any question or difference of any kind whatsoever between the landlord and the tenant of an agricultural holding arising out of the tenancy or in connection with the holding (not being a question or difference as to liability for rent) is to be determined by arbitration[2] or by the Land Court.[3] The arbiter may, and shall if so directed by the sheriff, state a case for the opinion of the sheriff, whose opinion is final unless within a limited time either party appeals to the Court of Session.[4]

Minimum duration

Unless a letting for less than a year was approved by the Secretary of State before the lease was entered into, a lease of land for use as agricultural land for a shorter period than from year to year takes effect as a lease from year to year, unless leased only for grazing or mowing during some specified period of the year,[5] or leased by a tenant under a lease for less than from year to year.[6]

Written leases, and terms therein

Where there is not in force a lease in writing[7] embodying the terms of the tenancy, or, there is such a lease (i) entered into on or after 1 November 1948, or (ii) entered into before then, the period of which has expired and is being continued in force by tacit relocation, and the lease contains no provision for one or more of the matters specified in Schedule V to the 1949 Act, or a provision inconsistent therewith or with S. 5 of the Act, either party may call on the other to enter into such a lease; if no lease has been concluded within six months, the terms of the

[1] 'Agricultural holding' means the aggregate of land comprised in a lease, not being land let during the tenant's continuance in any office, appointment or employment held under the landlord, which is used for agriculture (including horticulture, fruit growing, seed growing, meadow land, osier land, market gardens, dairy farming and livestock breeding and keeping, grazing land and nursery grounds, and the use of land for woodlands when that is ancillary to the farming of land) for the purpose of a trade or business: Agricultural Holdings (Sc.) Act, 1949, Ss. 1, 93(1); *Stirrat* v. *Whyte*, 1968 S.L.T. 157. No extent is prescribed. Land may be designated as agricultural land by the Secretary of State: Agriculture (Sc.) Act, 1948, S. 86(1). The only lands apparently excluded are lands let e.g. for a rifle range, or for grazing and exercising racehorses, or for a golf course.

[2] 1949 Act, S. 74; *Houison-Crawford's Trs.* v. *Davies*, 1951 S.C. 1; *Brodie* v. *Ker*, 1952 S.C. 216.

[3] 1949 Act, S. 78; as to Crown land, see Ss. 86–7.

[4] 1949 Act, S. 75; *MacNab of MacNab* v. *Willison*, 1960 S.C. 83; *Forsyth Grant* v. *Salmon*, 1961 S.C. 54.

[5] *Mackenzie* v. *Laird*, 1959 S.C. 266.

[6] Agricultural Holdings (Sc.) Act, 1949, S. 2; cf. *Mackenzie* v. *Laird*, 1959 S.C. 266.

[7] Not limited to probative leases: *Grieve* v. *Barr*, 1954 S.C. 414.

tenancy stand referred to arbitration.[1] The arbiter may make provision for Schedule V matters not covered by the lease, and further provisions which may be agreed.[2] Where liability for the maintenance or repair of any fixed equipment is transferred from one party to the other thereunder consequential adjustments may be made.[3]

Record of Holding

Where a lease has been entered into, a record of the condition of the fixed equipment on the holding must be made forthwith, and is then deemed to form part of the lease.[4]

Landlord's duties

The landlord must yield vacant possession of the subjects let.[5] If it is not given timeously, or not at all, the tenant may rescind the lease and claim damages.[6]

If there is material discrepancy between the subjects let and the subjects to which entry is given, the tenant may reduce the lease and claim damages,[7] or claim a deduction from the rent for the past period of possession,[8] or withhold rent till the deficiency is remedied.[9]

The landlord must also allow the use of such roads on his estate or adjoining farms as are reasonably incidental to the lands let.[10]

Reservations

In agricultural leases there are impliedly reserved to the landlord the minerals, with liberty to prospect for them, of access thereto and working them, on payment of damages for surface damage,[11] woods, with liberty of access thereto,[12] and game, and wild animals.[13]

1 1949 Act, S. 4(1).
2 S. 4(2) and (3).
3 S. 6.
4 1949 Act, S. 5(1).
5 cf. *Winans* v. *Mackenzie* (1883) 10 R. 941.
6 *Smith* v. *Robertson* (1832) 10 S. 829; *Tennant's Trs.* v. *Maxwell* (1880) 17 S.L.R. 463.
7 *Oliver* v. *Suttie* (1840) 2 D. 514.
8 *Riddell* v. *Grosset* (1791) 3 Pat. 203; *Yeaman* v. *Gilruth* (1792) Hume 783.
9 *Kilmarnock Gas Co.* v. *Smith* (1872) 11 M. 58; *Guthrie* v. *Shearer* (1873) 1 R. 181.
10 *Duncan* v. *Scott* (1876) 3 R. (H.L.) 69; *Galloway* v. *Cowden* (1885) 12 R. 578; *Addison* v. *Brown* (1907) 15 S.L.T. 674.
11 Stair II, 9, 31; Bankt. II, 9, 21; Ersk. II, 6, 22; Bell, *Prin.* §1226; *Colquhoun* v. *Watson* (1668) Mor. 15233.
12 Bankt. II, 9, 21; Ersk. II, 6, 22; Bell, *Prin.* §1226.
13 *Maxwell* v. *Copland* (1870) 9 M. (H.L.) 1; cf. *Wemyss* v. *Gulland* (1847) 10 D. 204.

Conventional reservations may be included to any effect agreed on, but common reservations include power to resume parts of the subjects let for mining, roads, planting, feuing or excambing.[1] The extent of resumption permitted depends on the fair interpretation of the reserved power.[2] Whether the purpose for which resumption is intended falls within the power is again a matter of interpretation.[3] Power of resumption implies liability to compensate the tenant, normally by reduction of rent,[4] but sometimes in other ways.[5] The claim to compensation may be held departed from by express or implied renunciation.[6]

Power to enter on holding

The landlord or anyone authorized by him may at all reasonable times enter on the holding to view the state of the holding, to fulfil the landlord's responsibilities to manage the holding in accordance with the rules of good estate management,[7] or to provide, improve, replace or renew fixed equipment otherwise than in fulfilment of these responsibilities.[8]

Implied duties

The landlord is impliedly bound at common law to furnish the buildings necessary to enable the tenant to cultivate the land in the mode contemplated,[9] and to put the houses, offices, water supply,[10] and fences, but not drains,[11] on a farm into tenantable repair at the time of entry,[12] such as to render them capable of lasting, with ordinary care, to the ish.[13] If the tenant sustains loss by reason of the insufficiency of any of these items, he may claim damages, but must make timeous intimation of the defect and of his claim.[14] If the landlord fails to give possession of buildings in

1 *Menmuir* v. *Airth* (1863) 1 M. 929; *Caledonian Ry.* v. *Smith* (1877) 14 S.L.R. 510.
2 *Stewart* v. *Lead* (1825) 1 W. & S. 68; *Trotter* v. *Torrance* (1891) 18 R. 848.
3 *Admiralty* v. *Burns*, 1910 S.C. 531; *Turner* v. *Wilson*, 1954 S.C. 296; *Pigott* v. *Robson*, 1958 S.L.T. 49; *Secy. of State for Scotland* v. *Campbell* (1959) 47 L.C. 49.
4 *Menmuir*, *supra*; claim lies against the landlord only: *Lanark Middle Ward Dist. Cttee.* v. *Marshall* (1896) 24 R. 139.
5 *Bertram* v. *Guild* (1880) 7 R. 1122; see also *Kininmonth* v. *British Aluminium Co.*, 1915 S.C. 271.
6 *Belshes* v. *Fraser* (1839) 1 D. 1071.
7 See Agriculture (Sc.) Act, 1948, Sched. V.
8 1949 Act, S. 18.
9 *Barclay* v. *Neilson* (1878) 5 R. 909.
10 *Christie* v. *Wilson*, 1915 S.C. 645.
11 *Wight* v. *Newton*, 1911 S.C. 762.
12 Bankt. I, 20, 10; II, 11, 21; Ersk. II, 6, 39; Bell, *Prin.* §1253.
13 *Davidson* v. *Logan*, 1908 S.C. 350; cf. *Mossman* v. *Brocket* (1810) Hume 850.
14 *Ferrier* v. *Readman* (1898) 6 S.L.T. 109; *Hamilton* v. *D. Montrose* (1906) 8 F. 1026; *Christie* v. *Wilson*, 1915 S.C. 645.

tenantable order, the tenant is entitled to an abatement of rent,[1] or to retain the rent.[2]

Statutorily implied terms

There is deemed incorporated in every lease of an agricultural holding (a) an undertaking by the landlord that, at the commencement of the tenancy or as soon as is reasonably possible thereafter, he will put the fixed equipment on the holding into a thorough state of repair, and will provide such buildings and other fixed equipment as will enable an occupier reasonably skilled in husbandry to maintain efficient production as respects both the kind of produce specified in the lease, or in use to be produced on the holding, and the quality and quantity thereof, and will during the tenancy effect such replacement or renewal of the buildings or other fixed equipment as may be rendered necessary by natural decay or by fair wear and tear; and (b) a provision that the liability of the tenant in relation to the maintenance of fixed equipment shall extend only to a liability to maintain the fixed equipment on the holding in as good a state of repair (natural decay and fair wear and tear excepted) as it was in immediately after it was put in repair or, in the case of equipment provided, improved, replaced or renewed during the tenancy, as it was in immediately after it was so provided, improved, replaced or renewed. Nevertheless, either party may by agreement undertake work legally incumbent on the other. The tenant cannot be required to pay the whole or part of the premium due under a fire insurance policy over any fixed equipment.[3] The landlord cannot contract out of his statutory liability to put the fixed equipment into order and to provide buildings.[4]

Tenant's rights and duties

The tenant is entitled to be given vacant possession of the subjects let at the date of entry.

The tenant must maintain the buildings, fences, and gates on the farm, unless they have decayed to the extent where renewal is necessary.[5] He is not liable for damage caused by *damnum fatale*[6]

[1] *Munro* v. *McGeoghs* (1888) 16 R. 93; *Stewart* v. *Campbell* (1889) 16 R. 346.

[2] *McDonald* v. *Kydd* (1901) 4 F. 923; *E. Galloway* v. *McConnell*, 1911 S.C. 846; *Haig* v. *Boswall-Preston*, 1915 S.C. 339.

[3] 1949 Act, S. 5(2)–(4).

[4] *Secretary of State for Scotland* v. *Sinclair* (1959) 48 L.C. 10.

[5] Bell, *Prin.* §1254; *Johnstone* v. *Hughan* (1894) 21 R. 777.

[6] *York Buildings Co.* v. *Adams* (1741) Mor. 10127; *Clerk* v. *Baird* (1741) Mor. 10128.

or by sheer accident. Damages may be recovered for the loss of use of premises by reason of decay.[1]

If the tenant is bound to reside on the subjects let, he is in breach if he does not, even by reason of imprisonment.[2]

A lease is deemed to include a provision that the liability of the tenant in relation to fixed equipment extends only to a liability to maintain the fixed equipment in as good a state of repair (natural decay and fair wear and tear excepted) as it was in immediately after it was put in repair as aforesaid or, in the case of equipment provided, improved, replaced or renewed during the tenancy, as it was in immediately after it was so provided.[3]

Good husbandry

The lease frequently contains an express, and always an implied, obligation on the tenant to conform to the rules of good husbandry.[4] These depend in part on the practice of the district and deviation, if alleged, must be determined by the opinion of men of experience in the district.[5]

Permanent pasture

Either party may demand a reference to arbitration of whether the amount of land required by the lease to be maintained as permanent pasture should be reduced.[6]

Compensation to outgoing tenants

Certain agreements by incoming tenants to compensate outgoing tenants or refund compensation to the landlord are declared void.[7]

Freedom of cropping and of disposal of produce

Notwithstanding any custom or the terms of the lease or of any agreement, a tenant is entitled, subject to certain provisos, without incurring any penalty, forfeiture or liability, to dispose of the produce of the holding other than manure produced thereon and to practise any system of cropping of the arable land.[8]

1 *Johnstone, supra*; *Hamilton* v. *D. Montrose* (1906) 8 F. 1026.
2 *Blair Trust Co.* v. *Gilbert*, 1940 S.L.T. 322.
3 1949 Act, S. 5(2)(b).
4 *Maxwell* v. *McMurray* (1776) 5 B.S. 515; *Thomson's Reps.* v. *Oliphant* (1824) 3 S. 275; *Hunter* v. *Miller* (1863) 1 M. (H.L.) 49; cf. *Hendry* v. *Marshall* (1878) 5 R. 687; *Countess of Stair* v. *Willison* (1883) 20 S.L.R. 315.
5 *M. Tweeddale* v. *Brown* (1821) 2 Mur. 563.
6 1949 Act, S. 9, as amd. by Agriculture Act, 1958, Sched. I.
7 S. 11.
8 cf. *Carron Co.* v. *Donaldson* (1858) 20 D. 681; *Hunter* v. *Miller* (1862) 24 D. 1011.

But if the tenant exercises his rights in such a manner as to injure or deteriorate the holding, or to be likely to do so, the landlord may interdict him or recover damages for deterioration, on his quitting the holding.[1]

Record of condition of holding

Either party may at any time during the tenancy require the making of a record of the condition of the fixed equipment on, and of the cultivation of, the holding and the tenant may require the making of a record of existing improvements carried out by him or in respect of which he has, with the landlord's consent, paid compensation to an outgoing tenant, and of any fixtures or buildings which under the Act he is entitled to remove.[2]

Compensation for game damage[3]

Where the tenant of an agricultural holding has sustained damage to his crops from game,[4] the right to kill and take which is vested neither in him nor in anyone claiming under him other than the landlord and which the tenant has not permission in writing to kill, he is entitled to compensation from his landlord for the damage if it exceeds in amount one shilling per acre of the area over which it extends.[5] Notice must be given when the damage is first observed and a reasonable opportunity given to inspect the damage, and written notice of the claim must be given within a month after the end of the calendar year, or other period of twelve months agreed upon, in respect of which it is made.[6] The amount of compensation, in default of agreement, is to be determined by arbitration. Where the right to kill and take game is vested in some person other than the landlord, the landlord is entitled to be indemnified by him against claims for compensation.[7] Where a tenant had permission to kill deer, it was held that the permission excluded a claim for compensation for

[1] 1949 Act, S. 12. See *Mackenzie's Trs.* v. *Somerville* (1900) 2 F. 1278; *Taylor* v. *Steel-Maitland*, 1913 S.C. 502. Damages are measured by the diminution in rent obtainable on reletting: *Williams* v. *Lewis* [1915] 3 K.B. 493.

[2] 1949 Act, S. 17.

[3] 1949 Act, S. 15.

[4] Defined, S. 15(4) as deer, pheasant, partridges, grouse, and black game. Ground game is excluded, because a tenant can protect himself against ground game at common law and under the Ground Game Acts.

[5] Even if damage is done partly by game coming from an adjacent estate: *Thomson* v. *E. Galloway*, 1919 S.C. 611.

[6] See *E. Morton's Trs.* v. *MacDougall*, 1944 S.C. 410.

[7] cf. *Kidd* v. *Byrne* (1875) 3 R. 255. The agricultural tenant cannot claim direct against the sporting tenant: *Inglis* v. *Moir's Tutors* (1871) 10 M. 204.

damage caused by that kind of game.[1] The statutory right to kill deer[2] does not take away the right to compensation where the tenant had no written permission to kill deer.[3]

Rent

The amount of rent, and the terms for payment thereof, are determined by the lease. As between landlord's executor and his heir-at-law, and between landlord and purchaser from him, however, a difference may arise between the terms when the rent is legally due and those when it is due according to the lease. In principle rent is not due legally, though it may be conventionally, until the tenant has had the benefit of the crop. Hence in arable farms, with entry at Martinmas, the legal terms are the following Whitsunday and Martinmas. In pastoral farms, with entry at Whitsunday, the legal terms are the Whitsunday of entry, and the following Martinmas. Rents payable conventionally before the legal terms are designated forehand rents; if payable later, backhand rents. As between landlord's executor and his heir-at-law, the legal terms apply, except in the case of forehand rents, when the conventional terms apply.

As between selling landlord and purchasing landlord, the purchaser is entitled to the rents falling due for possession following his term of entry according to the legal terms, but in the case of forehand rents he is entitled to rents payable at the conventional terms following the term of his entry.[4]

Abatement of rent

If the tenant is deprived of the beneficial use of a substantial part of the subjects let more than temporarily he is entitled to an abatement of rent.[5]

Variation of rent

Either party may demand a reference to arbitration of what rent should be payable as from the next date when the tenancy could have been terminated by notice to quit.[6]

1 *Ross* v. *Watson*, 1943 S.C. 406.
2 Agriculture (Sc.) Act, 1948, S. 43.
3 *L. Auckland* v. *Dowie*, 1965 S.C. 37.
4 Titles to Land Consolidation (Sc.) Act, 1868, S. 8; *Baillie* v. *Fletcher*, 1915 S.C. 677.
5 *Sharp* v. *Thomson*, 1930 S.C. 1092.
6 1949 Act, S. 7, as amd. Agriculture Act, 1958, S. 2; *Guthe* v. *Broatch*, 1956 S.C. 132; *Secy. of State* v. *Young* (1960) 48 L.C. 31; *Secy. of State* v. *Sinclair* (1961) 50 L.C. 6; *Anderson* v. *Bennie* (1962) 50 L.C. 38; *Graham* v. *Gardner*, 1966 S.L.T. (Land Ct.) 12.

Where the landlord has carried out one or more stated improvements to the holding he may increase the rent to the extent of the increase in rateable value.[1]

Restriction of penal rent or liquidated damages

Notwithstanding anything in the lease making the tenant of an agricultural holding liable to pay a high rent or other liquidated damages in the event of breach or non-fulfilment of any of the terms or conditions of the lease, the landlord is not entitled to recover any sum in such cases in excess of the damage actually suffered by him in consequence of the breach or non-fulfilment.[2]

Remedies for non-payment of rent

If rent is not duly paid, the landlord may bring a personal action for payment and do diligence thereon.[3] A formal lease frequently contains a clause of consent to registration on which summary diligence may proceed.

The landlord's hypothec over *invecta et illata* has been abolished in the case of land exceeding two acres in extent let for agriculture or pasture.[4]

The legal irritancy *ob non solutum canonem* exists in case of non-payment of rent for two successive years.[5] The Act of Sederunt of 14 December 1756 authorizes caution to be required on one year's rent being in arrear, and a declarator of irritancy and summary removing to be brought in the sheriff court on the rent being two years in arrears.

A conventional irritancy to any effect, including non-payment of rent, may be inserted in the lease, and is enforceable according to its terms.[6]

When six months' rent is due and unpaid, the landlord may raise an action for removing in the Sheriff Court against the tenant, concluding for his removal at the next term of Whitsunday or Martinmas, and, unless the arrears are paid or caution found for them and for one year's rent further, the sheriff may decern the tenant to remove and eject him at the term.[7] Removal in this way does not prejudice the tenant's outgoing claims.[8]

1 1949 Act, S. 8.

2 1949 Act, S. 16.

3 A tenant's claim for damages is not a relevant defence: *Christie* v. *Birrell*, 1910 S.C. 986.

4 Hypothec Abolition (Sc.) Act, 1881, S. 1; but see *Clark* v. *Keirs* (1888) 15 R. 458.

5 Stair II, 9, 32; Bankt. II, 9, 23; Ersk. II, 6, 44.

6 *McDouall's Trs.* v. *Macleod*, 1949 S.C. 593.

7 1949 Act, S. 19; cf. *Ballantyne* v. *Brechin* (1893) 1 S.L.T. 306; *Fletcher* v. *F.*, 1932 S.L.T. (Sh. Ct.) 10. If there is a dispute as to liability for rent it is for the court though other disputes have to be determined by arbitration: S. 74; *Brodie* v. *Ker*, 1952 S.C. 216.

8 S. 19(2).

Retention of rent

The right to retain rent on the landlord's breach exists in agricultural leases.[1] A tenant may not retain on account of temporary failure of the water supply[2] or defect in the drains,[3] nor in addition to an award of damages.[4] But he may retain until the amount of compensation due to him for improvements is paid or accounted for.[5]

The right to retain rent may be excluded by the lease.[6]

Assignation

At common law agricultural leases of ordinary duration, and also leases of shootings and fishings, are not assignable without express power to do so.[7]

Tenant's death testate—Bequest of lease

The tenant may, unless his legatee is expressly excluded,[8] by will or other testamentary writing, bequeath his lease to his son-in-law or daughter-in-law or anyone of the persons who would be, or would in any circumstances, have been, entitled to succeed to his estate on intestacy.[9] The landlord cannot by the lease deprive the tenant of his right of bequest.[10] A legatee accepting must give notice within 21 days, or as soon as possible;[11] the landlord may give a counter-notice objecting to the legatee as tenant, whereupon the legatee may apply to the Land Court to be declared tenant.[12] If any reasonable ground of objection by the landlord is established the Land Court shall declare the bequest null.[13] If the legatee does not accept, or the bequest is declared null, the lease devolves as intestate estate.[14] The acquirer of the lease must give notice to the landlord and unless the landlord gives a

[1] e.g. *E. Galloway* v. *McConnell*, 1911 S.C. 846; *Haig* v. *Boswall-Preston*, 1915 S.C. 339.
[2] *Russell* v. *Sime*, 1912 2 S.L.T. 344.
[3] *Brown* v. *Simpson*, 1910 1 S.L.T. 183.
[4] *Christie* v. *Wilson*, 1915 S.C. 645.
[5] *D. Argyll* (1935) 23 L.C. 58.
[6] *Skene* v. *Cameron*, 1942 S.C. 393.
[7] Bell, *Prin.* §1214; *Mackintosh* v. *May* (1895) 22 R. 345.
[8] *Kennedy* v. *Johnstone*, 1956 S.C. 39.
[9] Succession (Sc.) Act, 1964, Sched. 2, para. 19, replacing 1949 Act, S. 20(1).
[10] *Howie* v. *Lowe* (1952) 40 L.C. 14.
[11] cf. *Wight* v. *M. Lothian's Trs.* (1952) 40 L.C. 25.
[12] cf. *Kennedy*, *supra*.
[13] See *Sloss* v. *Agnew*, 1923 S.L.T. (Sh. Ct.) 33; *Service* v. *D. Argyll*, 1951 S.L.T. (Sh. Ct.) 2; *Howie* v. *Lowe*, 1952 S.L.C.R. 14; *Fraser* v. *Murray's Trs.*, 1954 S.L.C.R. 10; *Reid* v. *Duffus Estate, Ltd.*, 1955 S.L.C.R. 13. The validity of the bequest falls to be determined by an ordinary court: *Mackenzie* v. *Cameron* (1894) 21 R. 427.
[14] Succession (Sc.) Act, 1964, Sched. 2, para. 21, replacing 1949 Act, S. 20(7).

counter-notice, the lease binds the landlord and the acquirer from the date of acquisition. The landlord may object before the Land Court to the person thus acquiring the lease.[1] The Land Court must declare the acquirer tenant unless the landlord established a reasonable ground of objection.[2] A testator's trustees, if authorized by the will to carry on the farm, may claim to be accepted as tenants.[3] The fact that, on the tenant's death, his interest vests in his executor[4] does not prevent the operation, in relation to the legatee, of the Crofters Holdings (Sc.) Act, 1886, S. 16(a) to (h), or the 1949 Act, S. 20(2) to (7).[5]

Tenant's death intestate

On a tenant's death intestate his interest in the lease vests, formerly in his heir, and now in his executor.[6]

If the tenant's interest is not the subject of bequest[7] or is the subject of bequest but it has not been accepted, or has been rendered void by the Crofters Holdings (Sc.) Act, 1886, S. 16 or the Agricultural Holdings (Sc.) Act, 1949, S. 20, and a condition of the lease prohibits assignation, the executor may nevertheless transfer the interest to any one of the persons entitled to succeed to the deceased's intestate estate, or to claim legal rights or the prior rights of a surviving spouse, in or towards satisfaction of that person's claim. But he may not transfer the interest to any other person without the landlord's consent.[8]

If the executor is satisfied that the interest cannot be disposed of according to law and so informs the landlord, or if it has not been disposed of within a year or such longer period as, failing agreement, may be fixed by the sheriff, landlord or executor may, on giving notice of such length as may be agreed, failing which, notice of not less than one year nor more than two years ending with such term of Whitsunday of Martinmas as may be specified, terminate the lease, notwithstanding any contrary rule of law or provision therein, without prejudice to any claim for compensation or damages in respect of the termination of the lease.[9]

[1] Ibid., para. 22, replacing 1949 Act, S. 21.
[2] 1949 Act, S. 20(4); *Reid* v. *Duffus Estate, Ltd.*, 1955 S.L.C.R. 13.
[3] *Dalgety's Trs.* v. *Drummond*, 1938 S.C. 709.
[4] Succession (Sc.) Act, 1964, S. 14.
[5] Ibid., S. 16(8).
[6] Ibid., S. 14.
[7] As in the case of intestacy *quoad* the lease, whether or not there is total intestacy.
[8] S. 16(1) and (2).
[9] 1964 Act, S. 16(3)–(5); see also S. 16(6).

Further protection of tenants who are near relatives of a deceased tenant and who have acquired right on his death is conferred by the Agriculture (Misc. Prov.) Act, 1968, S. 18.

Tenant's insolvency

At common law neither the tenant's insolvency, nor granting a trust deed, nor notour bankruptcy, nor sequestration, annuls the lease but it is customary to provide for a conventional irritancy arising in such cases.[1]

Tacit relocation

Notwithstanding any agreement or contrary provision in the lease, the tenancy of an agricultural holding, instead of terminating at the stipulated date, continues by tacit relocation and then from year to year unless and until notice of termination is given.[2] Tacit relocation is based on implied consent of all parties and a notice of removing by one of joint tenants excludes it and ends the lease.[3]

Termination of lease at break

Agricultural leases commonly contain provision for either party to terminate the lease at a break, or term short of the full duration of the lease, on due notice given.[4]

Termination of lease of agricultural holding

Notwithstanding the expiry of the stipulated endurance of a lease of an agricultural holding, the tenancy, including tenancies continued by tacit relocation, does not terminate unless either party[5] has given the other written notice, not less than one nor more than two years before the termination, of intention to end the tenancy.[6] Notice has to be given in the manner of notice of removal under the Removal Terms (Sc.) Act, 1886, S. 6,[7] or in

[1] *Lindsay* v. *Hogg* (1855) 17 D. 788; *Chalmer's Tr.* v. *Dick's Tr.*, 1909 S.C. 761.

[2] 1949 Act, S. 3; cf. *Macfarlane* v. *Mitchell* (1900) 2 F. 901.

[3] *Smith* v. *Grayton Estates*, 1960 S.C. 349.

[4] On notice, see *Strachan* v. *Hunter*, 1916 S.C. 901.

[5] As to joint tenants see *Graham* v. *Stirling*, 1922 S.C. 90; *Smith* v. *Grayton Estates, Ltd.* 1960 S.C. 349.

[6] 1949 Act, S. 24(1) and (2). The notice must be clear and explicit: Bell, *Prin.* §1271; *Strachan* v. *Hunter*, 1922 S.C. 901. It is incompetent to contract out of this provision: *Duguid* v. *Muirhead*, 1926 S.C. 1078.

[7] The 1886 Act, S. 6, deals only with the manner of sending the notice: the form of notice must conform to the 1907 Act, Sched. I and relative forms: *Dept. of Agriculture* v. *Goodfellow*, 1931 S.C. 556; *Rae* v. *Davidson*, 1954 S.C. 361.

the manner prescribed by the Sheriff Courts (Sc.) Act, 1907,[1] and such notice comes in place of that required by the 1907 Act.[2] The provisions as to notice do not affect the right to remove a tenant whose estate has been sequestrated under the Bankruptcy (Sc.) Act, 1913, or who has incurred an irritancy or other liability to remove, not to a notice in performance of a stipulation entitling the landlord to resume land for building or other non-agricultural purposes.[3] A question whether the ground stated for the removal is justified falls to be decided by arbitration.[4]

Consent of Land Court

Where notice to quit is given to the tenant of an agricultural holding and within one month the tenant serves a counter-notice, the notice to quit is not effective unless the Land Court consents to the operation thereof. Certain cases are excepted from this restriction; if one is relied on the notice to quit must state that it is given by reason of one of the excepted grounds.[5] The Land Court may consent to the operation of a notice to quit only if satisfied as to one or more of specified matters, stated by the landlord in his application for their consent,[6] and even if satisfied, the Land Court may withhold consent if in all the circumstances it appears that a fair and reasonable landlord would not insist on possession. If the Land Court consents it may impose such conditions as appear requisite for securing that the land will be used for the purpose for which the landlord proposes to terminate the tenancy, and may vary or revoke any such conditions.[6]

Removings from other lands over two acres.

Where lands exceeding two acres are held under a probative lease specifying a term of endurance, and written notice to

[1] Ss. 34–6; See *Scott* v. *Livingstone*, 1919 S.C. 1; *Watters* v. *Hunter*, 1927 S.C. 310.

[2] S. 24(4). By S. 24(3) the provisions of the 1907 Act relative to removings have effect subject, in the case of agricultural holdings, to S. 24.

[3] S. 24(6).

[4] *Houison-Craufurd's Trs.* v. *Davies*, 1951 S.C. 1; see also *McCallum* v. *Macnair*, 1952 S.C. 216.

[5] S. 25; and see also S. 28, amd. Agriculture Act, 1958, Sched. I, para. 38; cf. *McCallum* v. *Buchanan-Smith*, 1951 S.C. 73; *Edinburgh University* v. *Craik*, 1954 S.C. 190; *Macnabb* v. *Anderson*, 1957 S.C. 213; *Halliday* v. *Fergusson*, 1961 S.C. 24; *Carnegie* v. *Davidson*, 1966 S.L.T. (Land Ct.) 3; *Glencruitten Trs.* v. *Love*, 1966 S.L.T. (Land Ct.) 5; *Pentland* v. *Hart*, 1967 S.L.T. (Land Ct.) 2; *Murray* v. *Nisbet*, 1967 S.L.T. (Land Ct.) 14.

[6] Ss. 26–7, amd. by Agriculture Act, 1958, Sched. 2, Part II. See *Grant* v. *Murray*, 1950 S.L.C.R. 3; *Burnett* v. *Gordon*, 1950 S.L.C.R. 9; *Cooper* v. *Muirden*, 1950 S.L.C.R. 45; *Mackenzie* v. *Tait*, 1951 S.L.C.R. 3; *Macnabb* v. *Anderson*, 1955 S.C. 38; *McCallum* v. *Arthur*, 1955 S.C. 188; *Shaw Mackenzie* v. *Forbes* (1957) 45 L.C. 34; *E. Angus Properties*,

remove is given (a) when the lease is for three years and upwards not less than one nor more than two years before the termination of the lease, and (b) when the lease is from year to year (including lands occupied by tacit relocation) or for any other period less than three years, not less than six months before the termination, the lease or an extract thereof has the same effect as an extract decree of removing and, along with written authority from the lessor of his agent, is sufficient warrant to eject the party in possession. Ejection under this provision is not competent after six weeks from the ish.[1]

Letter of removal—lands over two acres

Where a tenant in possession of lands exceeding two acres, with or without a written lease, has granted a letter of removal, holograph or attested by one witness, it has the same force and effect as an extract decree of removing and is a sufficient warrant for ejection after the same notice as is required under S. 34, unless the letter is dated and signed within 12 months before the date of removal or first ish, in which case no notice of any kind is necessary.[2]

Removal—lands over two acres held without written lease

Where lands exceeding two acres in extent are occupied by a tenant without a written lease and the tenant has given no letter of removal the lease terminates on written notice to either party by or on behalf of the other, not less than six months before the termination of the tenancy; if the tenant fails to remove the notice entitles the landlord to apply for and obtain a summary warrant of ejection against the tenant and everyone deriving right from him.[3]

Extraordinary removing

Where an irritancy has been incurred, the landlord may bring a declarator and removing, seeking warrant to eject the tenant.[4]

A declaratory conclusion is unnecessary if the fact on which the irritancy depends is admitted or instantly verifiable,[5] or if the

Ltd. v. *Chivers*, 1960 S.L.C.R. 1. The Land Court may, by S. 30, as amd. by Agriculture Act, 1958, Sched. 1, Part II, impose a penalty on the landlord for breach of such a condition.

[1] Sheriff Courts (Sc.) Act, 1907, S. 34, and Sched. I, rules 110–14.

[2] Sheriff Courts (Sc.) Act, 1907, S. 35, and Sched. I, rules 110–14.

[3] Sheriff Courts (Sc.) Act, 1907, S. 36, and Sched. I, rules 110–14; see e.g. *Scott* v. *Livingstone*, 1919 S.C. 1; *Watters* v. *Hunter*, 1927 S.C. 310.

[4] e.g. *Macnab* v. *Nelson*, 1909 S.C. 1102.

[5] e.g. *Lyon* v. *Irvine* (1874) 1 R. 512.

lease provides that declarator is unnecessary,[1] or if there is provision for nullity at the landlord's option.[2] A dispute whether rent is being not paid, so as to incur an irritancy, or retained, falls to be determined by arbitration.[3]

Other provisions as to notices to quit

Special provisions are made for notices to quit where the holding has been agreed to be sold.[4] Notices to quit part of holdings are not to be invalid in certain special cases.[5] A tenant may treat a notice to quit part as a notice to quit the entire holding.[6] Where the tenant is dispossessed of part of the holding, the tenant is entitled to a reduction of rent.[7]

Ejection

Ejection is competent where a person without title is in possession and declines to remove.[8]

Removal of manure

After notice to terminate the tenancy has been given by either party the tenant may not, subject to any contrary agreement, sell or remove from the holding manure or compost, or hay or straw or roots grown in the last year of the tenancy, unless he has given the landlord or incoming tenant a reasonable opportunity of purchasing any of these at their fair market value or value provided by the lease.[9]

Removal of fixtures and buildings

A tenant may, during his tenancy or within six months, or longer if agreed, from the end thereof, remove any engine, machinery, fencing or other fixture[10] affixed to an agricultural holding by the tenant, and any building erected by him on the holding, other than one for which he is entitled to compensation under the Act or otherwise, not being affixed or built in pursuance of some obligation or instead of something belonging to the

1 As in *Waugh* v. *More Nisbett* (1882) 19 S.L.R. 427.

2 As in *Stewart* v. *Warnocks* (1883) 20 S.L.R. 863; see also *Bidoulac* v. *Sinclair's Tr.* (1889) 17 R. 144; *Buttercase & Geddie's Trs.* v. *Geddie* (1897) 24 R. 1128.

3 *Brodie* v. *Ker*, 1952 S.C. 216.

4 1949 Act, S. 31.

5 1949 Act, S. 32.

6 1949 Act, S. 33.

7 1949 Act, S. 34.

8 *Colquhoun's Trs.* v. *Purdie*, 1946 S.N. 3.

9 1949 Act, S. 13.

10 The common law principles determine whether a thing is or is not a fixture.

landlord, provided he has paid all rent owed by him and performed or satisfied all his other obligations to the landlord in respect of the holding and given written notice of his intention to remove them. The landlord may give a counter-notice electing to purchase a fixture or building.[1]

Compensation to tenant for disturbance

Where the tenancy of an agricultural holding terminates by reason of a notice to quit or counter-notice under S. 33,[2] but not where a tenant's counter-notice under S. 25 is excluded, the landlord must compensate the tenant for disturbance to the extent of the loss or expense directly attributable to the quitting of the holding[3] which is unavoidably incurred by the tenant,[4] to the amount of at least one year's and not more than two years' rent[5] of the holding.[6] Even where the minimum statutory compensation is claimed particulars of the claim must be furnished.[7]

Compensation to tenant for improvements

Tenants are entitled also, on quitting the holding at the termination of the tenancy, to compensation for certain old improvements made under the Agricultural Holdings Acts of 1923 and 1931, subject in some cases to conditions,[8] and to compensation for new improvements begun after 1 November 1948.[9]

Compensation for special standard of farming

If the value of the holding to an incoming tenant has been increased during the tenancy by the continuous adoption of a special standard of farming, the tenant is entitled on notice given to compensation from the landlord in respect of the value thereof to an incoming tenant.[10]

[1] 1949 Act, S. 14.

[2] cf. *Johnston* v. *Malcolm*, 1923 S.L.T. (Sh. Ct.) 81; *Hendry* v. *Walker*, 1927 S.L.T. 333.

[3] cf. *Keswick* v. *Wright*, 1924 S.C. 766; *Macgregor* v. *Board of Agriculture*, 1925 S.C. 613.

[4] *Barbour* v. *McDouall*, 1914 S.C. 844.

[5] As to what is 'rent' see *Bennie* v. *Mack* (1832) 10 S. 255; *D. Hamilton's Trs.* v. *Fleming* (1870) 9 M. 329; *Callander* v. *Smith* (1900) 8 S.L.T. 109; *Clark* v. *Hume* (1902) 5 F. 252; *M. Breadalbane* v. *Robertson*, 1914 S.C. 215.

[6] 1949 Act, S. 35; cf. *McHarg* v. *Speirs*, 1924 S.C. 272.

[7] *McLaren* v. *Turnbull*, 1942 S.C. 179; see also *Simpson* v. *Henderson*, 1944 S.C. 365; *Edinburgh Corpn.* v. *Gray*, 1948 S.C. 538.

[8] Ss. 37–46; as to pre-1909 improvements, see S. 96; see also *Gibson* v. *Sherret*, 1928 S.C. 493; *Turnbull* v. *Millar*, 1942 S.C. 521.

[9] Ss. 47–55.

[10] S. 56.

Payment to assist in reorganization of tenant's affairs

In cases where compensation for disturbance is payable, a landlord must also in certain cases pay the tenant a sum to assist in the reorganization of the tenant's affairs, amounting to four times the annual rent of the holding.[1] Where land is acquired compulsorily these provisions apply as if the acquiring authority were the landlord.[2]

Compensation to landlord for deterioration of holding

The landlord may, on the tenant quitting the holding on the termination of the tenancy, claim compensation for any dilapidation or deterioration of or damage to any part of the holding by non-fulfilment by the tenant of his responsibilities to farm in accordance with the rules of good husbandry,[3] and also for the diminished value of the holding generally.[4]

Contracts as to compensation

Save as provided in the Act, either party is entitled to compensation in accordance with the 1949 Act and not otherwise, and is so entitled notwithstanding any agreement to the contrary.[5]

Settlement of claims between landlord and tenant

Any claim of whatever nature by the tenant or the landlord of an agricultural holding against the other arising under the Act or any custom or agreement, and on or out of the termination of the tenancy, falls to be determined by arbitration.[6] An award or agreement under the Act as to compensation, expenses or otherwise, may, if not paid within a month, be recorded for execution in the Books of Council and Session or Sheriff Court books and is enforceable like a recorded decree arbital.[7] A sum payable to a tenant as compensation may be created by the Secretary of State a charge on the holding by a charging order, burdening the holding with an annuity to pay the sum due, recorded in the Register of Sasines.[8]

The Act also[9] refers to arbitration any question or difference

[1] Agriculture (Misc. Prov.) Act, 1968, Ss. 9 and 11.

[2] Ibid., Ss. 12 and 14–15.

[3] Ss. 57, 59–64. See also *Douglas* v. *Cassillis and Culzean Estates*, 1944 S.C. 355.

[4] Ss. 58, 59–64. As to claim see *Adam* v. *Smyth*, 1948 S.C. 455.

[5] cf. *Young* v. *Oswald*, 1949 S.C. 412.

[6] S. 68; see also Ss. 74–8; *Chalmers Property Inv. Co.* v. *McColl*, 1951 S.C. 24.

[7] S. 69.

[8] S. 70; as to charge in favour of a landlord not himself absolute owner of the holding, see S. 82.

[9] S. 74; *Brodie* v. *Ker*, 1952 S.C. 216.

of any kind between the parties, except a question or difference as to liability for rent. An arbiter acting under the Act may at any stage in the arbitration *ex proprio motu* state a case on a question of law for the opinion of the sheriff, and either party may apply to the sheriff to direct the arbiter to do so. The sheriff's opinion is final and binding on the arbiter,[1] unless either party appeals to the Court of Session whose decision is final.[2]

Settlement of differences

Any question or difference which by the 1949 Act or under the lease is required to be determined by arbitration may be determined by the Land Court on joint application.[3]

SMALL LANDHOLDERS AND CROFTERS

The Crofters Holdings (Sc.) Act, 1886 to 1908, made special provision for the holding of lands in the crofting counties[4] and established the Crofters Commission. The Small Landholders Act, 1911, substituted the expression 'landholder', extended the special provisions to holdings throughout the whole country,[5] and established the Scottish Land Court, which superseded the Crofters Commission.[6] The Crofters Acts, 1955 and 1961, recreated the category of crofters in the crofting counties only, applied portions of the earlier legislation as amended thereto, and established a new Crofters Commission for administration purposes, leaving the Land Court with its judicial functions.

SMALL LANDHOLDERS

The Small Landholders (Scotland) Acts 1886 to 1931[7] made the Crofters Acts 1886 to 1908, applicable throughout Scotland[8] to then existing crofter holdings under the 1886 Act,[9] to holdings

[1] *Mitchell-Gill* v. *Buchan*, 1921 S.C. 390. [2] 1949 Act, Sched. 6, paras. 19–20.

[3] 1949 Act, S. 78; *Rattray and Kennedy* (1950) 40 L.C. 36.

[4] Argyll, Caithness, Inverness, Orkney, Ross and Cromarty, Sutherland and Zetland.

[5] This was amended by the Land Settlement Act, 1919, and the Small Landholders and Agricultural Holdings (Sc.) Act, 1931.

[6] 1911 Act, Ss. 3, 25. As to the relation of the Land Court to the Court of Session see *Kennedy* v. *Johnstone*, 1956 S.L.T. 73.

[7] I.e. the Crofters Holdings (Scotland) Acts, 1886 and 1887; the Crofters Common Grazings Regulation Acts, 1891 and 1908; and the Small Landholders (Scotland) Acts, 1911, 1919, and 1931. Parts of these Acts do not now, under the Crofters Act, 1955, Sched. 6, apply in the crofting counties.

[8] 1911 Act, S. 1.

[9] *Yool* v. *Shepherd*, 1914 S.C. 689; *Stormonth-Darling* v. *Young*, 1915 S.C. 44; *Taylor* v. *Fordyce*, 1918 S.C. 824.

held by a tenant from year to year who resides on or within two miles from the holding and cultivates it by himself or his family, and, with effect from the end of the lease, to every holding held on lease at the date of the Act for longer than a year by such a tenant, subject to certain provisos, and to holdings constituted by the registration of an applicant under the 1912 Act.[1] There were excluded land rented at more than £50 per annum, unless not exceeding 50 acres, garden ground or any land to which the Land Court determined the Acts should not apply, land within burghs, market gardens,[2] glebes, small holdings, allotments, woodlands, permanent grass parks, land held and used for public recreation, or land acquired for any public undertaking.[3]

Conditions of tenure

Such a landholder may be removed only for breach of one or more of the statutory conditions[4] or for non-payment of rent.[5] Holdings may be resumed by the landlord for reasonable purposes.[6]

The rent may be altered by agreement or fixed by the Land Court,[7] which may also cancel arrears.[8] The tenancy may be renounced,[9] but not assigned[10] but if the landholder is by age or infirmity unable to work the holding he may obtain power from the Land Court to assign it to his son-in-law or to any person who would succeed him on intestacy.[11] Without the landlord's consent the landholder has no power to subdivide the holding, or sublet, except to holiday visitors, or for less than a year.[12] He may not erect a new house on the holding, except in substitution for one already there, unless he is a new holder established by the Department of Agriculture when he may do so with the consent

[1] 1911 Act, S. 2. See also *Kidd* v. *Morison*, 1916 S.C. 759.

[2] *Grewar* v. *Moncur's C.B.*, 1916 S.C. 764.

[3] 1911 Act, S. 26(3); see also *McNeill* v. *D. Hamilton's Trs.*, 1918 S.C. 221.

[4] 1886 Act, S. 1, amd. 1911 Act, S. 10. This includes bankruptcy: *Secy. of State for Scotland* v. *Black*, 1965 S.L.T. (Land Ct.) 2.

[5] Ibid., S. 3.

[6] Ibid., S. 2, amd. 1911 Act, S. 19; *Whyte* v. *Stewart*, 1914 S.C. 675.

[7] Ibid., Ss. 5–6; see also 1911 Act, S. 13; *McNeil* v. *D. Hamilton's Trs.*, 1918 S.C. 221; *McKelvie* v. *D. Hamilton's Trs.*, 1918 S.C. 301; *Dept. of Agriculture* v. *Burnett*, 1937 S.L.T. 292.

[8] Ibid., S. 6.

[9] Ibid., S. 7, amd. 1911 Act, S. 18.

[10] Ibid., S. 1, amd. 1911 Act, S. 21.

[11] 1911 Act, S. 21 amd. Succession (Sc.) Act, 1964, Sched. 2, para. 15; Land Settlement Act, 1919, S. 13.

[12] 1886 Act, S. 1; 1911 Act, S. 10; *McNeil*, *supra*; *Little* v. *McEwan*, 1965 S.L.T. (Land Ct.) 3.

of the Department and the landlord.[1] There is provision for compensation for improvements[2] and holdings may be enlarged.[3] A holding may be bequeathed,[4] new holdings may be created,[5] and there is provision for vacant holdings,[6] the regulation of common grazings[7] and the making by the Land Court of a record of the holding.[8]

COTTARS

A cottar is the occupier of a dwelling-house with or without land who pays no rent, or the tenant from year to year of a dwelling-house situated in a crofting parish who resides therein and who pays an annual rent, not exceeding £6 in money, with or without garden ground, but without arable or pasture land.[9] Cottars, if removed, or if paying rent and renouncing their tenancy or being removed, are entitled to compensation for permanent improvements, and may receive loans or assistance from the Secretary of State like crofters.[10]

STATUTORY SMALL TENANTS

The Small Landholders Acts apply also, only so far as expressly applied, to statutory small tenants, who are tenants from year to year, or leaseholders, not otherwise disqualified in terms of the 1911 Act, in regard to whom the 1911 Act, S. 2, provides that they shall not be held existing yearly tenants or qualified leaseholders, and the successors of such tenants or leaseholders, being their heirs, legatees, or assignees.[11] Certain other provisions apply only to statutory small tenants.[12] They may, notwithstanding contrary agreement, obtain from the Land Court renewal of tenancies at the expiry of leases, unless the landlord can satisfy

[1] 1886 Act, S. 1; 1911 Act, S. 10(2).
[2] 1886 Act, Ss. 11–15, amd. 1911 Act, S. 16.
[3] Ibid., Ss. 8–10; see also Agriculture (Misc. Prov.) Act, 1968, S. 16.
[4] Ibid., S. 16, amd. 1911 Act, Ss. 20, 22 and Succession (Sc.) Act, 1964, Sched. 2, paras. 9, 15.
[5] 1911 Act, S. 7.
[6] 1911 Act, S. 17.
[7] 1911 Act, S. 24.
[8] Small Landholders Act, 1931, S. 10.
[9] 1886 Act, S. 34; Crofters (Sc.) Act, 1955, S. 28(4).
[10] 1955 Act, S. 28(1); 1961 Act, Sched. 1, para. 7; *White* v. *Cameron*, 1966 S.L.T. (Land Ct.) 7.
[11] 1911 Act, Ss. 2(iii)(b), 32(1), and (2).
[12] 1911 Act, S. 32(3) to (15).

the Land Court of a reasonable objection.[1] The Agricultural Holdings (Scotland) Acts apply as if the tenancy were a lease.[2] Either party may apply to the Land Court to fix an equitable rent, or the period for which the tenancy is to be renewed.[3] Such a tenant has no power to assign his lease[4] but may bequeath it, and it transmits on intestacy.[5] A statutory small tenant has the option, on giving notice to the landlord, to convert his tenure into that of a landholder and acquire the privileges thereof.[6]

CROFTERS' HOLDINGS

Special provision is now made for the tenure of lands by crofters by parts of the Crofters Holdings (Scotland) Acts, 1886, parts of the Small Landholders (Scotland) Acts 1911, 1919, and 1931,[7] and the Crofters (Scotland) Acts, 1955 and 1961. A new Crofters Commission was established in 1955.[8] The Land Court has power, with stated exceptions, to determine any question of fact or law arising under the Acts of 1955 or 1961.[9]

A croft is a holding situated in the crofting counties[10] to which before the 1955 Act, any of the provisions of the Landholders Acts 1886 to 1931 relating to landholders, or to statutory small tenants, applied,[11] or a holding in the crofting counties constituted a croft by the registration of the tenant thereof as a crofter under S. 4 of that Act,[12] or a holding which the Secretary of State has directed that it be a croft.[13] Any right in pastoral or grazing land held by the tenant of a croft, alone or in common, is deemed part of the croft.[14]

1 Ibid., S. 32(4).
2 Ibid., S. 32(5).
3 Ibid., S. 32(6) to (8).
4 Ibid., S. 32(1).
5 Ibid., S. 32(1).
6 Ibid., S. 32(11); Small Landholders (Sc.) Act, 1931, S. 14.
7 Parts of these Acts have, by the 1955 Act, Sched. 6, ceased to have effect in the crofting counties, and parts of the 1911 Act are modified in their application to the crofting counties.
8 1955 Act, s. 1, and Sched. 1. The Commission may (S. 15) obtain information about crofts.
9 1961 Act, S. 4.
10 Argyll, Caithness, Inverness, Orkney, Ross and Cromarty, Sutherland, and Zetland.
11 See 1886 Act, S. 34; 1911 Act, S. 1.
12 1955 Act, S. 3, amd. 1961 Act, Sched. I, para. 9; *Fea Mortification Trs.* v. *Cursiter*, 1967 S.L.T. (Land Ct.) 10.
13 1961 Act, S. 2.
14 1955 Act, S. 3(5). But see *Campbell* v. *Secretary of State for Scotland* (1960) 48 L.C. 41; *Ross* v. *Graesser*, 1962 S.C. 66.

The Crofters Commission maintains a Register of Crofts containing specified particulars.[1]

Enlargement of holdings

Crofters may apply to the Land Court for enlargement of their holdings and that court, if satisfied that there is land available may subject to certain limitations order the lease of the land or part thereof by the landlord to the applicants at a fair rent and on such terms and conditions as the court considers just.[2]

Security of tenure

A crofter is not subject to be removed from his croft except where one year's rent is unpaid, or in consequence of a breach of one or more of the statutory conditions of tenure[3] other than payment of rent, or in pursuance of any statute.[4] Contracts to the contrary are void unless approved by the Land Court.

Rent

The rent is that payable in 1955 or at the date of first letting, if thereafter, unless and until altered under the 1955 Act.[5] It may be altered by agreement in writing.[6] The Land Court may, on the application of either party, determine a fair rent, which is not, save by agreement, alterable for seven years.[7]

Record of croft

The Land Court must, on the application of either party make a record of the condition of the cultivation of a croft and of the buildings and other permanent improvements thereon, and by whom they have been executed and paid for. In the absence of contrary agreement a crofter is entirely responsible for the maintenance of buildings whether provided by himself or by his landlord.[8]

Renunciation; assignation; subdivision; subletting

A crofter may renounce his tenancy at any term of Whitsunday or Martinmas on one year's written notice to the landlord.[9] He may not, save with the written consent of the Crofters'

[1] 1961 Act, S. 3.
[2] 1886 Act, Ss. 11–15 and 21, as amd. 1911 Act, S. 16.
[3] 1955 Act, Sched. 2. These include prohibitions on purporting to assign the tenancy, dilapidation, subletting, or subdividing the croft. See, e.g., *Culfargie Estates* v. *Leslie* (1957) 45 L.C. 38.
[4] 1955 Act, S. 3.
[5] 1955 Act, S. 5(1).
[6] 1955 Act, S. 5(2).
[7] 1955 Act, S. 5(3).
[8] *Holman* v. *Henderson*, 1965 S.L.T. (Land Ct.) 13.
[9] 1955 Act, S. 7, amended 1961 Act, Sched. 1, para. 1.

Commission, assign his croft[1] nor, save with written consent of the landlord and the Commission, subdivide his croft.[2]

After 1961 a crofter may sublet his croft without the landlord's consent,[3] but requires the written consent of the Commission.[4] Subleases existing in 1961 are validated by intimation to the Commission.[5] The Commission may require crofts inadequately used to be sublet.[6] A subtenant, save exceptionally, is not a crofter nor the tenant of an agricultural holding.[7]

Succession

A crofter may, by testamentary writing,[8] bequeath his tenancy to any one person, but a bequest to a person not one of the crofter's family is void unless the Commission determines otherwise. The landlord may object, and if the Commission upholds the objection, the right to the croft devolves on the deceased crofter's heir-at-law.[9] If the right devolves on the heir-at-law the landlord shall, subject to the determination of any dispute by the Commission, accept as successor any heir who would be entitled to succeed failing nearer heirs and who applies within three months.[10] If thereafter no person has been accepted as successor the Commission must nominate the person who appears to be the nearer heir and who has intimated a desire to succeed to the tenancy, failing which it must declare the croft vacant.[11]

Resumption of croft

The Land Court may authorize the resumption of a croft or part thereof by the landlord, for some reasonable purpose[12] having relation to the good of the croft or of the estate or to the public

[1] 1955 Act, S. 8; *Vestey* v. *Holmes*, 1967 S.L.T. (Land Ct.) 7.
[2] 1955 Act, S. 9.
[3] 1961 Act, S. 11(2).
[4] 1961 Act, S. 11(3)–(6).
[5] 1961 Act, S. 11(1).
[6] 1961 Act, S. 12.
[7] 1961 Act, S. 13.
[8] Cf. *Cameron* v. *Holman* (1951) 39 L.C. 14; *McKillop* v. *Secretary of State for Scotland* (1951) 39 L.C. 17.
[9] 1955 Act, S. 10. Questions as to the validity or effect of the bequest fall to be determined by any court having jurisdiction to determine the validity and effect of the deceased's whole testamentary writings.
[10] cf. *MacDonald* v. *Doxford Estates Co.* (1952) 40 L.C. 39.
[11] 1955 Act, S. 11, 1961 Act, Sched. 1, para. 2. The provisions of the Succession (Sc.) Act, 1964, did not apply to crofts: 1964 Act, S. 37(1)(b), until made applicable by the Law Reform (Misc. Prov.) (Sc.) Act, 1968, S. 8.
[12] Defined, S. 12(2); See *Andrew* v. *Mackay* (1938) 47 L.C. 30; *Mackay's Trs.* v. *Colthart* (1958) 47 L.C. 43; *Murray's Trs.* v. *Ross*, 1964 S.L.T. (Land Ct.) 9; *Lochiel Estates* v. *Campbell*, 1968 S.L.T. (Land Ct.) 2.

interest, on terms and on the landlord making adequate compensation in money or by letting other land of equivalent value in the neighbourhood or otherwise.[1]

Removal of crofter

The Land Court may make an order for the removal of a crofter when one year's rent of a croft is unpaid, or a crofter has broken one or more of the statutory conditions, other than that as to payment of rent.[2] That Court may on the application of the Secretary of State make an order for the removal of a crofter whose right to compensation for permanent improvements has been transferred to the Secretary of State[3] if the crofter has abandoned his croft, or broken any of the other statutory conditions or broken any of the conditions of repayment of a loan contained in the agreement therefor.[4]

Compensation for improvements and for deterioration

If a crofter renounces his tenancy or is removed, he is entitled to compensation for permanent improvements made on the croft[5] if suitable thereto, executed and paid for by him or any of his predecessors and executed otherwise than in pursuance of a specific agreement or, if so executed, not recompensed.[6] The landlord is entitled to compensation for any deterioration of, or damage to, fixed equipment.[7] The amount of compensation is fixed, failing agreement, by the Land Court.[8]

Vacant crofts

When a croft becomes vacant the landlord must notify the Crofters' Commission and may not let the croft save with the consent of the Commission or of the Secretary of State. The Commission may require the landlord to submit his proposals for reletting the croft, failing which the Commission may themselves let the croft, in which case the landlord may apply to the Land Court for variation of the terms and conditions of letting.[9]

[1] 1955 Act, S. 12, amd. 1961 Act, Sched. 1; *M. Bute* v. *Baxter*, 1966 S.L.T. (Land Ct.) 6.

[2] 1955 Act, S. 13(1); *Culfargie Estates* v. *Leslie* (1957) 45 L.C. 38. This includes bankruptcy: *Secy. of State for Scotland* v. *Black*, 1965 S.L.T. (Land Ct.) 2.

[3] Under S. 23(3), where the Secretary of State has given financial assistance to the crofter by way of loan under S. 22.

[4] 1955 Act, S. 13(2).

[5] *Mackenzie* v. *Roger*, 1964 S.L.T. (Land Ct.) 8.

[6] 1955 Act, S. 14(1)–(3), and (10); see also 1961 Act, S. 6; *Church of Scotland General Trs.* v. *Thomson* (1958) 47 L.C. 17; *Davidson's Exrx.* v. *Stewart*, 1964 S.L.T. (Land Ct.) 6.

[7] 1955 Act, S. 14(6)–(7) amended 1961 Act, Sched. 1, para. 4.

[8] 1955 Act, S. 14(8)–(9).

[9] 1955 Act, S. 16 amd. 1961 Act, Sched. 1, para. 5.

Absentee crofters

If a crofter is not ordinarily resident on, or within ten miles of, the croft, and it is in the general interest of the crofting community in the district that the tenancy be terminated and the croft let to some other person, the Commission may terminate the tenancy and require the crofter to relinquish occupation.[1] In certain circumstances the crofter may obtain a feu of the dwellinghouse and garden ground.[2]

Aged crofters

If a crofter is unable through illness or old age or infirmity properly to work his croft and is willing to renounce the tenancy on retaining the dwellinghouse, and it is in the general interest of the crofting community that he be authorized to do so, the Commission may authorize him to renounce his tenancy. In such a case the crofter may obtain a feu of the dwellinghouse and garden.[3]

Improvements

Crofters may erect buildings or other structures or execute works on the croft reasonably required to enable them to make use of the croft for any subsidiary or auxiliary occupation which will not interfere substantially with the use of the croft as an agricultural subject, and such are permanent improvements of the croft.[4]

Reorganization schemes

The Commission may promote schemes for the reorganization of crofting townships, providing, subject to safeguards, for the reallocation of the land in such amounts as is most conducive to the efficient use of that land and the general benefit of the township.[5]

Financial assistance

The Secretary of State may make schemes for providing grants and loans to crofters.[6]

[1] 1955 Act, S. 17(1)–(3), amd. 1961 Act, S. 7.
[2] 1955 Act, S. 17(4)–(10), amd. 1961 Act, S. 7 and Sched. 1, para. 6.
[3] 1955 Act, S. 18; *McLean* v. *Roger*, 1964 S.L.T. (Land Ct.) 11; *MacKenzie* v. *Crofters' Commission*, 1966 S.L.T. (Land Ct.) 13.
[4] 1961 Act, S. 5.
[5] 1961 Act, Ss. 8–9, replacing 1955 Act, Ss. 19–20.
[6] 1955 Act, Ss. 22–23; 1961 Act, S. 14.

New crofts

The landlord and tenant of certain kinds of holdings, not being crofts, may apply jointly to the Secretary of State to have such holding declared a croft. Provision is made for enlarging crofts, and land may be added to common grazings.[1]

Common grazings

Crofters sharing in a common grazing may appoint a grazings committee whose duty is to maintain the common grazings and fixed equipment, to carry out works for their improvement and to make and administer common grazings regulations, which require the Commission's confirmation, for management and use of the common grazings.[2] Common grazings may be enlarged.[3] Rights in a common grazing imply rights to water thereon for stock.[4] The common grazings committee may be made responsible for the dyke or fence separating the grazings from the individual holdings,[5] but has no power in relation to a township access road.[6] The Commission may apportion part of common grazing for the exclusive use of a crofter who applies.[7]

SPORTING LEASE

A sporting lease, or lease of shooting, is normally the grant for a term of years of the personal privilege of entering on lands and there shooting certain kinds of game, and removing them thence.[8] Assignation or subletting is incompetent.[9] The terms of the lease may exclude the right of the landlord and his agricultural tenants.[10] Such is a proper lease binding on singular successors.[11]

[1] 1961 Act, S. 2; see also 1911 Act, S. 7.

[2] 1955 Act, Ss. 24–7, amd. 1961 Act, S. 15; *Neish* v. *North Talisker Grazing Cttee.*, 1968 S.L.T. (Land Ct.) 4.

[3] 1961 Act, S. 2.

[4] *MacColl* v. *Downie's Trs.* (1961) 50 L.C. 28.

[5] *Crofters Commission* v. *Cameron of Garth*, 1964 S.C. 229.

[6] *MacDonald* v. *Greig*, 1964 S.L.T. (Land Ct.) 5.

[7] *Crofters Commission* v. *South Scorrybreck Grazings Cttee.*, 1968 S.L.T. (Land Ct.) 8.

[8] cf. *Fraser* v. *Patrick* (1879) 6 R. 581; *Critchley* v. *Campbell* (1884) 11 R. 475; *Elliott's Tr.* v. *E.* (1894) 21 R. 858, 863; *Butter* v. *Foster*, 1912 S.C. 1218. The lease may take the form of a lease of the lands, the anticipated use being only the harbouring of game, which the tenant has liberty to shoot: e.g. *Farquharson* (1870) 9 M. 66; cf. *Patrick* v. *Harris's Trs.* (1904) 6 F. 985.

[9] *E. Fife* v. *Wilson* (1864) 3 M. 323; *Mackintosh* v. *May* (1895) 22 R. 345.

[10] *North* v. *Cumming* (1864) 3 M. 173. By the Ground Game Act, 1880, S. 1, the occupier of lands has an inalienable right to kill and take ground game thereon so that a landlord cannot now by a game lease exclude the agricultural tenant's rights to kill ground game.

[11] *Farquharson* (1870) 9 M. 66. As to damages for not getting full possession see *Critchley* v. *Campbell* (1884) 11 R. 475.

It is an implied condition that the game tenant shall not allow the stock of game to be increased to an extravagant extent;[1] if he does allow the game to increase to an excessive and unreasonable extent, whereby injury is done to the estate, he is liable in damages. The landlord commonly makes the game tenant bound to free and relieve him of any claims made on him by agricultural tenants for game damage to his crops, and to keep the game population down to a reasonable extent,[2] with liberty, if this be not done, himself to enter and protect himself by reducing the number of game.

A landlord who believes his estate is being detrimentally affected by an unreasonable stock of game, and wishes to claim damages therefor, must give notice thereof timeously, so that the shooting tenant may rectify his default or at least obtain evidence that the game is not excessive, failing which he may be barred by delay.[3]

An agricultural tenant may claim damages from his landlord if the latter has increased the game on the farm beyond a fair average stock.[4] The agricultural tenant has no direct right of action against the game tenant, unless there be some contractual relation between them.[5]

A lease of fishings is of the same general character.[6]

MINERAL LEASES

A so-called mineral lease is truly a sale of the minerals coupled with a licence for a period to enter on the lands and extract and remove the minerals, on payment of a lordship or royalty.[7] The rights of parties are almost always regulated by a written lease[8] and most of the cases concern the interpretation of particular deeds. A tenant is not, unless the lease provides therefor,[9] entitled to have the lease reduced merely on the ground that the minerals cannot be worked at a profit, even if no rent be payable,[10] but only if there proves to be none of the mineral sought,

1 *Kidd* v. *Byrne* (1875) 3 R. 255; *Elliott's Trs., supra.*

2 *Kidd, supra*; see also *Inglis* v. *Moir's Tutors* (1871) 10 M. 204.

3 *Elliott's Trs., supra.*

4 *Drysdale* v. *Jamieson* (1832) 11 S. 147; *Wemyss* v. *Wilson* (1847) 10 D. 194; *Morton* v. *Graham* (1876) 6 M. 71; cf. *Broadwood* v. *Hunter* (1855) 17 D. 340. As to interdicting landlord see *Wemyss* v. *Gulland* (1847) 10 D. 204.

5 *Inglis* v. *Moir's Tutors* (1871) 10 M. 204; *Kidd, supra.*

6 *Gemmill* v. *Riddell* (1847) 9 D. 727.

7 *Gowans* v. *Christie* (1873) 11 M. (H.L.) 1, 12; *Campbell* v. *Wardlaw* (1883) 10 R. (H.L.) 65, 68.

8 The common law regulates constitution and proof of such a lease.

9 *Wylie & Hill* v. *Belch* (1867) 4 S.L.R. 29; *Fleming* v. *Baird* (1871) 9 M. 730.

10 *Gowans, supra.*

or it becomes exhausted, or the working of it becomes impracticable.[1]

Landlord's duties

The landlord is bound to cede possession to the tenant of so much of the surface of his lands as is necessary for working the minerals, to permit access thereto, and to cede possession of the mineral field or strata comprised in the lease, with liberty to make the necessary shafts and access roads.[2]

Assignation is normally excluded.[3]

Landlord's rights—rent or royalty

The payment due by the tenant may be an annual rent or a lordship or royalty based on the quantity or value of the minerals extracted.[4] The landlord has the usual remedies for the recovery of his lordship or royalties; landlord's hypothec extends to royalties.[5] He is not prevented from claiming arrears by having for years accepted a fixed rent by reason of the tenant's inaccurate returns of output.[6]

Tenant's rights

The tenant is entitled to be given possession of the mineral strata.

Assignation and subletting are not competent at common law unless expressly permitted.[7]

Tenant's duties and liabilities

The mode of working is normally provided for by the lease, and the tenant may incur liability in damages for contravention of those provisions.[8]

The tenant is normally taken bound to fence the ground

[1] Stair I, 15, 2; Bankt. I, 2, 14; Bell, *Prin.* §1208; *Gowans, supra*; cf. *Murdoch* v. *Fullerton* (1829) 7 S. 404; *Dixon* v. *Campbell* (1829) 8 S. 970; *Sinclair* v. *Mossend Iron Co.* (1854) 17 D. 258; *Bargaddie Coal Co.* v. *Wark* (1860) 23 D. 44; *Thomson* v. *Gordon* (1869) 7 M. 687.

[2] See *Harrowar's Trs.* v. *Erskine* (1827) 5 S. 307; *Galbraith's Tr.* v. *Eglinton Iron Co.* (1868) 7 M. 167.

[3] *M. Breadalbane* v. *Whitehead* (1893) 21 R. 138; see also *Elphinstone* v. *Monkland Iron Co.* (1886) 13 R. (H.L.) 98; *Ebbw Vale Steel Co.* v. *Woods' Tr.* (1898) 25 R. 439.

[4] cf. *Adam* v. *Napier* (1843) 5 D. 736; *Guthrie* v. *Cochran* (1846) 19 S. Jur. 69; *Waugh* v. *Russel* (1870) 7 S.L.R. 222; *Dalgleish* v. *Fife Coal Co.* (1892) 30 S.L.R. 58.

[5] *Linlithgow Oil Co.* v. *E. Rosebery* (1903) 6 F. 90.

[6] *Simpson's Trs.* v. *Gower* (1874) 11 S.L.R. 309.

[7] cf. *D. Portland* v. *Baird* (1865) 4 M. 10; *Clark* v. *West Calder Oil Co.* (1882) 9 R. 1017.

[8] *Carron Co.* v. *Henderson's Trs.* (1896) 23 R. 1042; *Jackson's Tr.* v. *Dixon* (1901) 3 F. 782; *Shawsrigg Fireclay Co.* v. *Larkhall Collieries* (1903) 5 F. 1131.

occupied and all workings and access roads[1] and as occupier of the lands leased he must take reasonable care for the safety of persons coming in the vicinity of the premises.[2]

He may incur liability to adjacent mineral tenants if by abnormal operations he causes flooding or other damage to their workings.[3]

Duty to support superincumbent land

Unless permitted by his lease to do so, with or without provision for compensation, a mineral tenant is not entitled to work the minerals in such a way as to bring down the surface or damage buildings thereon. If he does so the mineral tenant may accordingly incur liability to his landlord, or to the latter's feuars[4] or surface tenants.[5]

The mineral tenant is frequently taken bound to relieve his landlord of all claims made against the latter for damage by subsidence.[6]

A clause binding the tenant to pay for damage to the surface has been held not to cover damage done by smoke or vapour emitted in the process.[7]

Obligation not to encroach beyond boundary

The tenant must confine his operations to the parts of underground strata underlying the landlord's land. If he goes beyond the boundary he encroaches on another's minerals and becomes liable in damages for wrongful abstraction of minerals.[8] Nor may he discharge water which accumulates in the workings into another's workings.[9] An inferior mineowner may carry out operations to prevent the influx of water from the upper mine,[10]

[1] *Ferrier* v. *Readman* (1898) 6 S.L.T. 109; cf. *Hislop* v. *Durham* (1842) 4 D. 1168; *McFeat* v. *Rankin's Trs.* (1879) 6 R. 1043; *McLean* v. *Warnock* (1883) 10 R. 1052; *Gavin* v. *Arrol* (1889) 16 R. 509; *Prentice* v. *Assets Co.* (1890) 17 R. 484.

[2] Occupiers Liability (Scotland) Act, 1960, Ss. 1, 2.

[3] *Durham* v. *Hood* (1871) 9 M. 474; contrast *Wilson* v. *Waddell* (1876) 4 R. (H.L.) 29; cf. *Rankin* v. *Dixon* (1847) 9 D. 1048.

[4] *Dryburgh* v. *Fife Coal Co.* (1905) 7 F. 1083; cf. *Highgate* v. *Paisley Mags.* (1896) 23 R. 992.

[5] cf. *Hamilton* v. *Turner* (1867) 5 M. 1086; *Stewart's Hospital* v. *Waddell* (1890) 17 R. 1077.

[6] e.g. *Mid & E. Calder Gas Light Co.* v. *Oakbank Oil Co.* (1891) 18 R. 788.

[7] *Galbraith's* v. *Eglinton Iron Co.* (1868) 7 M. 167.

[8] cf. *Houldsworth* v. *Brand's Trs.* (1876) 3 R. 304; (1877) 4 R. 369; *Livingstone* v. *Rawyards Coal Co.* (1880) 7 R. (H.L.) 1; *Davidson's Trs.* v. *Caledonian Ry.* (1895) 23 R. 45.

[9] *Baird* v. *Monklands Iron Co.* (1862) 24 D. 1418; cf. *Irving* v. *Leadhills Mining Co.* (1856) 18 D. 833.

[10] *Wauchope* v. *E. Abercorn* (1780) 2 Pat. 519.

but the upper mineral tenant is not obliged to leave a barrier of unworked mineral as a protection to neighbouring workings against being inundated with water.[1] An encroaching mineral tenant may also incur liability for surface damage.[2]

Termination

On the termination of the lease the tenant is bound to leave the workings in good order and may be liable in damages for breach of an express condition of the lease on that matter.[3] He is normally taken bound to restore the surface when mining or quarrying is completed. If he fails to remove in terms of his lease the tenant is liable for damages for breach of contract.[4] A customary provision allows the tenant to remove buildings and machinery erected by him, if they are not taken over by the landlord at valuation.[5]

SMALL HOLDINGS

The Small Holdings Act, 1892, empowers county councils to acquire land for the provision of small holdings, i.e. holdings exceeding one acre and not exceeding fifty acres or with an annual value for income tax purposes not exceeding £50, which they may sell or let to persons desiring themselves to cultivate the holdings.[6] Such a holding is to be held subject to statutory conditions.[7] Such holdings are not small landholdings under the Small Landholders (Sc.) Act, 1911.[8]

ALLOTMENTS

The Allotments (Sc.) Act, 1892, empowers local authorities to acquire land for letting in allotments to persons resident in their areas. An allotment may not exceed one acre, and no building other than a shed or greenhouse may be erected. Such holdings are not small landholdings under the Small Landholders (Sc.) Act, 1911.[8]

1 *Harvey* v. *Wardrop* (1824) 3 S. 322.
2 *Allan* v. *Robertson's Trs.* (1891) 18 R. 932.
3 *Elphinstone* v. *Monkland Iron Co.* (1886) 13 R. (H.L.) 98; *Duke of Portland* v. *Wood's Trs.*, 1927 S.C. (H.L.) 1.
4 *Houldsworth* v. *Brand's Trs.* (1876) 3 R. 304.
5 *Wilson* v. *Douglas* (1868) 7 M. 112.
6 1892 Act, Ss. 1–4.
7 Ibid., S. 9.
8 1911 Act, S. 26(3)(e).

CHAPTER 89

VOLUNTARY TRANSFER OF LAND

VOLUNTARY transfer of land may be effected in pursuance of an enforceable contract of sale or of excambion, or of an intention to gift. Transfer of possession does not transfer title, which is effected only, formerly by the purchaser taking sasine under a precept of sasine granted by the disponer and recording an instrument of sasine, and now by the seller granting a disposition in the purchaser's favour and the purchaser becoming infeft by recording the disposition in the Register of Sasines.

SALE OF HERITAGE

The contract of sale of heritage[1] is regulated by common law;[2] the parties must have power to sell and buy, and the contract must be constituted in writing probative, or holograph,[3] or adopted as holograph,[4] of both parties,[5] or their agents,[6] or by informal agreement established by writ or oath and perfected by *rei interventus* or homologation.[7] The deeds are usually known as missives of sale, but the contract is sometimes contained in a minute of sale,[8] or where land is sold by public auction, in Articles of Roup containing the conditions of sale, to which a document is appended narrating the offers and the preference of the highest

[1] Including land and buildings, whether held feudally or on leasehold, and other rights heritable by nature, such as feu-duties and ground annuals.

[2] If moveables, e.g. furniture or stock-in-trade, are sold by the same contract, the Sale of Goods Act, 1893, applies to the contract *quoad* the moveables: see e.g. *Allan* v. *Gilchrist* (1875) 2 R. 857; see also *Allan* v. *Millar*, 1932 S.C. 620.

[3] *Scottish Lands and Buildings Co.* v. *Shaw* (1880) 7 R. 756; *Caithness Flagstone Co.* v. *Sinclair* (1880) 7 R. 1117. See also *Weir* v. *Robertson* (1872) 10 M. 438; *Littlejohn* v. *Hadwen* (1882) 20 S.L.R. 5.

[4] *Gavine's Trs.* v. *Lee* (1883) 10 R. 448; *Harvey* v. *Smith* (1904) 6 F. 511; *Brown's Trs.* v. *McDonald*, 1922 S.L.T. 7.

[5] Stair I, 10, 9; Ersk. III, 2, 2; *Goldston* v. *Young* (1868) 7 M. 188; *McLaren* v. *Law* (1871) 44 S. Jur. 17; *Littlejohn* v. *Hadwen* (1882) 20 S.L.R. 5; *Gavine's Trs.* v. *Lee* (1883) 10 R. 448; *Malcolm* v. *Campbell* (1891) 19 R. 278; *McGinn* v. *Shearer*, 1947 S.C. 334.

[6] *Whyte* v. *Lee* (1879) 6 R. 699; *Scottish Land Co.* v. *Shaw* (1880) 7 R. 756; cf. *Caithness Flagstone Co.* v. *Sinclair* (1880) 7 R. 1117; see also *Mitchell* v. *Scott's Trs.* (1874) 2 R. 162.

[7] *Gowan's Trs.* v. *Carstairs* (1862) 24 D. 1382, 1388; *Stewart* v. *Burns* (1877) 4 R. 427; *Heiton* v. *Waverley Hydropathic Co.* (1877) 4 R. 830; *Mowat* v. *Caledonian Bank* (1895) 23 R. 270; *McLean* v. *Scott* (1902) 10 S.L.T. 447; *Kinnear* v. *Young*, 1936 S.L.T. 574; But see *Errol* v. *Walker*, 1966 S.C. 93.

[8] Bell, *Lect.* II, 698; *Menzies*, 889.

offer.[1] Such must be executed by or on behalf of both parties.[1] The creation, and the exercise of, an option to purchase heritage must be similarly created and exercised.[2] A contract to build and to sell the site and building must doubtless be similarly constituted, but a contract to build for a person on his land does not require formal constitution.

Power of sale or purchase

Parties must have the requisite legal power; if the authority of the court is necessary it should be obtained first,[3] rather than a contract be concluded conditional on the power being obtained.[4] A sale is void if vitiated by illegality.[5]

Advertisements

Statements in advertisements about the property are not normally held obligatory[6] but may be, as where an offer referred to the property 'as advertised' and thereby imported into the offer the advertisement and the conditions of the title deeds therein referred to.[7]

Consensus in idem

It may be a narrow question in some cases whether *consensus* has been reached, where in the negotiations new conditions and qualifications are introduced.[8] In many cases the question has arisen whether *consensus* was precluded by error, as to the seller's title,[9] or the holding,[10] the identification[11] or extent of the sub-

[1] *Shiell* v. *Guthrie's Trs.* (1874) 1 R. 1083; *Moncrieff* v. *Lawrie* (1896) 23 R. 577.

[2] cf. *Hamilton* v. *Lochrane* (1899) 1 F. 478; *Burns* v. *Garscadden* (1901) 8 S.L.T. 321. See also *Anderson* v. *A.*, 1961 S.C. 59.

[3] cf. *Clyne, Petr.* (1894) 21 R. 849; *Hodge, Petr.* (1904) 11 S.L.T. 709; *Campbell Wyndham Long's Trs.*, 1951 S.C. 685; 1962 S.C. 132.

[4] cf. *Dow's Trs.*, 1947 S.C. 524; *Horne's Trs.* 1952 S.C. 70.

[5] *McPherson's Trs.* v. *Watt* (1877) 5 R. (H.L.) 9; contrast *Noble* v. *Campbell* (1876) 4 R. 77; *Shiell* v. *Guthrie's Trs.* (1874) 1 R. 1083.

[6] *Hamilton* v. *Western Bank* (1861) 23 D. 1033.

[7] *Nisbet* v. *Smith* (1876) 3 R. 781 explained in *Bremner* v. *Dick*, 1911 S.C. 887; see also *Mossend Theatre Co.* v. *Livingstone*, 1930 S.C. 90.

[8] e.g. Consensus: *Colquhoun* v. *Wilson's Trs.* (1860) 22 D. 1035; *Westren* v. *Millar* (1879) 7 R. 173; *Charles* v. *Shearer* (1900) 8 S.L.T. 273; *Freeman* v. *Maxwell*, 1928 S.C. 682. No consensus: *Milne* v. *Marjoribank's Trs.* (1836) 14 S. 533; *Johnston* v. *Clark* (1855) 18 D. 70; *Bate* v. *Corstorphine* (1869) 6 S.L.R. 401; *Dickson* v. *Blair* (1871) 10 M. 41; *Heiton* v. *Waverley Hydro Co.* (1877) 4 R. 830; *Westren* v. *Millar* (1879) 7 R. 173; *Nelson* v. *Assets Co.* (1889) 16 R. 898; *Hay* v. *Aberdeen Mags.*, 1909 S.C. 554; *Harvey* v. *Smith* (1904) 6 F. 511; *E. Kilbride Development Corpn.* v. *Pollok*, 1953 S.C. 370.

[9] *McConnell* v. *Chassels* (1903) 10 S.L.T. 790.

[10] e.g. *McConnell* v. *Chassels* (1903) 10 S.L.T. 790.

[11] e.g. *Macdonald* v. *Newall* (1898) 1 F. 68; *Houldsworth* v. *Gordon Cumming*, 1910 S.C. (H.L.) 49.

jects,[1] or the ground burdens,[2] or by misrepresentation.[3] Consensus may be deemed suspended by conditions in offer or acceptance[4] or may be subject to a resolutive condition.[5] The missives embody the contract until a disposition in implement is signed and delivered, and till then dissensus may be found.[6] *Rei interventus* cannot supply lack of consensus.[7]

Essentials of contract

The essentials of the contract, apart from formalities of constitution and *consensus*, are identification of the property and agreement on the price. Identification depends largely on the description employed, which may be in any form which adequately designates the lands.[8] An error in extent, if substantial, may justify rescission of the contract.[9] The price may be fixed by the contract, or means for fixing it, such as valuation or arbitration,[10] be settled thereby. Interest runs on the price from the date of settlement.

Any qualifications on the *prima facie* rule that a selling proprietor has right to the whole subjects *a caelo usque ad centrum*, other than those imposed by general law or actually known to the other party, should be made the subject of express statement in the contract. Thus the absence of any provision that the minerals, if reserved to the superior, are so reserved entitles the other party to resile.[11]

Other usual conditions

Other usual provisions of the contract include the date of entry, the date for payment of the price, an undertaking to give vacant

[1] e.g. *Hamilton* v. *Western Bank* (1861) 23 D. 1033; *Morton* v. *Smith* (1877) 5 R. 83; *Woods* v. *Tulloch* (1893) 20 R. 477; and see Ch. 33, *supra*; cf. *Anderson* v. *Lambie*, 1954 S.C. (H.L.) 43.

[2] e.g. *Clason* v. *Steuart* (1844) 6 D. 1201; *Johnston* v. *Clark* (1855) 18 D. 70; *Steuart's Trs.* v. *Hart* (1875) 3 R. 192; *Welsh* v. *Russell* (1894) 21 R. 769; *Bremner* v. *Dick*, 1911 S.C. 887.

[3] *Brownlie* v. *Miller* (1880) 7 R. (H.L.) 66.

[4] *Stobo* v. *Morrisons (Gowns), Ltd.*, 1949 S.C. 184; contrast *Erskine* v. *Glendinning* (1871) 9 M. 656. See also *Campbell* v. *Douglas* (1676) Mor. 8470; *Broomfield* v. *Young* (1757) Mor. 9446; *Fulton* v. *Johnston* (1761) Mor. 8446.

[5] *Hardy* v. *Sime*, 1938 S.L.T. 18.

[6] *Morrison* v. *Gray*, 1932 S.C. 712.

[7] *E. Kilbride Development Corpn.* v. *Pollok*, 1953 S.C. 370.

[8] For cases of error on this account see *Macdonald* v. *Newall* (1898) 1 F. 68; *Houldsworth* v. *Gordon Cumming*, 1910 S.C. (H.L.) 49; cf. *Anderson* v. *Lambie*, 1954 S.C. (H.L.) 43.

[9] *Hamilton* v. *Western Bank* (1861) 23 D. 1033; *Morton* v. *Smith* (1877) 5 R. 83; *Woods* v. *Tulloch* (1893) 20 R. 477.

[10] e.g. *E. Selkirk* v. *Nasmyth* (1778) Mor. 627.

[11] *Whyte* v. *Lee* (1879) 6 R. 699; *Crofts* v. *Stewart's Trs.*, 1927 S.C. (H.L.) 65; *Mossend Theatre Co.* v. *Livingstone*, 1930 S.C. 90; *Campbell* v. *McCutcheon*, 1963 S.C. 505.

possession, provisions as to fittings and fixtures, the amount of any feuduty, ground annual, or stipend payable, the incidence of liability for common parts of properties, such as a roof, the apportionment of local rates and rents, and arrangements as to any existing securities. A stipulation for immediate entry means only to give entry as early as is practicable.[1] If a date for entry be specified and the seller cannot meet it, the purchaser may resile.[2] If no date of entry be specified, an immediate entry is probably implied.[3] Settlement[4] is implied as the date or term of entry, unless otherwise agreed. The contract may be rescinded if the feuduty is materially different from that stated in the contract.[5] Nor is a purchaser bound to accept a title subject to liability for a cumulo unallocated feuduty. Many stipulations are, however, implied into such contracts by long standing custom. Thus it is implied that the title is feudal.[6]

The purchaser is not affected by any agreement between the seller and another relative to the lands if it is not, or is not capable of being made, a real burden or condition affecting the lands.[7]

Risk

The contract being a common law sale, the risk passes to the purchaser immediately on conclusion of the contract: *periculum rei venditae nondum traditae est emptoris*;[8] the purchaser should insure at once.

SELLER'S OBLIGATIONS

The seller's main obligations are to execute a disposition conveying the property sold, to give a good marketable title, vacant possession of the property, clear searches, and warrandice. The seller is entitled to a reasonable time to produce a good title or to clear defects from it.

A contract for the sale of heritage constitutes only a personal obligation to demand implement or the price. To convey a real

[1] *Heys* v. *Kimball & Morton* (1890) 17 R. 381.
[2] *Kelman* v. *Barr's Tr.* (1878) 5 R. 816.
[3] As to disposition see Conveyancing (Sc.) Act, 1874, S. 28.
[4] i.e. exchange of the price against executed disposition.
[5] *Clason* v. *Steuart* (1844) 6 D. 1201; *Steuart's Trs.* v. *Hart* (1875) 3 R. 192; *Welsh* v. *Russell* (1894) 21 R. 769; *Bremner* v. *Dick*, 1911 S.C. 887; As to the phrase 'nominal feuduty' see *Johnston* v. *Clark* (1855) 18 D. 70. As to allocation of feuduty see *Robertson* v. *Douglas* (1886) 13 R. 1133.
[6] cf. *McConnell* v. *Chassels* (1903) 10 S.L.T. 790.
[7] *Morier* v. *Brownlie & Watson* (1896) 23 R. 67; *Wallace* v. *Simmers*, 1960 S.C. 255.
[8] cf. Ersk. III, 3, 7; Bell, *Comm.* I, 472; R. Brown, *Sale*, 355.

right to the heritage contracted for requires the execution by the seller of a disposition of the heritage in implement of the contract and its recording in the appropriate Register of Sasines.

Good title

A purchaser is entitled to a good or at least marketable title, such as to protect him from eviction or even the risk of reasonable challenge, and to be an acceptable subject of future sale or disposition in security.[1] This may be waived by a contract whereby the seller has undertaken only to put the seller in this place,[2] but not by a condition that the seller will give no search,[3] nor by an offer of absolute warrandice.[4] In articles of roup there is commonly a clause that the buyer will take the title as it stands. If the title tendered is not good the purchaser may resile, or, even after settlement, have the disposition reduced and the price repaid.[5]

What is good title

A good title is constituted by an *ex facie* valid charter of the lands now sold in favour of the seller, or one from whom the seller has derived title, recorded in the appropriate Register of Sasines and followed by possession thereon, peaceably and without interruption for at least twenty years continuously.[6] If the estate now sold was created less than twenty years ago the title of the creator of the fee must be examined to ensure that he had capacity and power to create the fee. If created substantially more than twenty years ago the latest *ex facie* valid irredeemable title to the estate in land more than twenty years old will suffice as the basis for prescription[6] but reference will almost certainly be made therein back to the founding charter, and possibly to other deeds outwith the prescriptive period, as containing burdens and conditions.

The running of the positive prescription fortifies any challengeable title but the buyer must inquire whether within the prescriptive period there is any intrinsic defect, such as a conveyance *a non domino*. Examination of the titles will not, however, disclose any extrinsic defect, such as that an earlier proprietor conveying the lands by will was not of sound disposing mind. But the obligation to transfer a good title is not concerned with such extrinsic objections.[7]

1 *Liqdr. of Style & Mantle, Ltd.* v. *Prices Tailors, Ltd.*, 1934 S.C. 548.
2 *Leith Heritage Co.* v. *Edinburgh & Leith Glass Co.* (1876) 3 R. 789.
3 *Mackenzie* v. *Clark* (1895) 3 S.L.T. 128.
4 *Nairne* v. *Scrymgeour* (1676) Mor. 14169.
5 *Crofts* v. *Stewart's Trs.*, 1927 S.C. (H.L.) 65.
6 Conveyancing (Sc.) Act, 1924, S. 16.
7 *Sutherland* v. *Garrity*, 1941 S.C. 196, 201.

Where the title contains a number of transfers or transmissions within the prescriptive period, each link must validly connect the new with the previous proprietor. Each deed constituting a link must have been granted by a person having legal capacity and power to grant it; it must have been properly executed and stamped; the destination must connect with the next proprietor; the description of the property must be such as can support the possession enjoyed in reliance thereon;[1] there must be no burdens or qualifications other than those known and agreed to be assumed by the purchaser; and there must be no claims for death duties outstanding exigible from the property. A notarial instrument or notice of title is not a valid link in title without the warrants, e.g. trust disposition, on which it proceeds.[2] A decree of service of an heir is reducible within the prescriptive period,[3] but is a valid link in title.[4] An extract decree of reduction of a deed, decree or instrument recorded or forming a link in a title recorded in the Register of Sasines must be recorded in the Register of Sasines[5] but this provision protects only persons acquiring rights in the lands between the obtaining and the recording of the decree of reduction.[6]

A title tendered is good notwithstanding the existence of a reasonable feuduty, which is a natural element of a feu, or servitudes of an ordinary character,[7] or leases usual in such a property,[8] or that the seller was only a heritable creditor when he sold with the consent of the party entitled to the reversion,[9] or that one link in the title is a decree of general service,[10] or the confirmation of an executor.[11] It is not good if the superior has a right of redemption of the feu,[12] or there are restrictions[13] or a prohibition[14] on building, or prohibitions on use,[15] or the subjacent minerals are reserved to the

[1] *Auld* v. *Hay* (1880) 7 R. 663; *Troup* v. *Aberdeen Heritable Securities Co.*, 1916 S.C. 918.
[2] *Sutherland* v. *Garrity*, 1941 S.C. 196.
[3] *Stobie* v. *Smith*, 1921 S.C. 894.
[4] *Sibbald's Heirs* v. *Harris*, 1947 S.C. 601.
[5] Conveyancing (Sc.) Act, 1924, S. 46.
[6] *Mulhearn* v. *Dunlop*, 1929 S.L.T. 59.
[7] *Gordonston* v. *Paton* (1682) Mor. 16606; *Welsh* v. *Russell* (1894) 21 R. 769.
[8] cf. *Lothian and Border Farmers* v. *McCutchion*, 1952 S.L.T. 450.
[9] *Dundee Calendering Co.* v. *Duff* (1869) 8 M. 289.
[10] *Mackay's Exrs.* v. *Schonbach*, 1933 S.C. 747; *Sibbald's Heirs* v. *Harris*, 1947 S.C. 601.
[11] Succession (Sc.) Act, 1964, S. 17 (where the death occurred after 9 Sept. 1964 only).
[12] *McElroy* v. *D. Argyll* (1901) 4 F. 885.
[13] *Louttit's Trs.* v. *Highland Ry.* (1892) 19 R. 791; *Smith* v. *Soeder* (1895) 23 R. 60.
[14] *Urquhart* v. *Halden* (1835) 13 S. 844; *Robertson* v. *Rutherford* (1841) 4 D. 121.
[15] *Ewing* v. *Hastie* (1878) 5 R. 439; *Graham* v. *Shiels* (1901) 8 S.L.T. 368; *McConnell* v. *Chassels* (1903) 10 S.L.T. 790.

superior, particularly if with power to work them[1] (unless parties knew that the minerals were reserved to a third party), or the title is to a long lease only and not a feu,[2] or the lands were possibly still affected by a creditor's debts,[3] or the titles include a declarator of irritancy under a contract of ground annual, pronounced in absence,[4] or the only description of the lands was by reference to a missing plan,[5] or the titles included an excambion, the parties to which had no power to excamb.[6]

Time for furnishing title

The seller must furnish a satisfactory title within a reasonable time,[7] though not necessarily by the date of entry. If he cannot or will not do so the purchaser may resile.[8] Timeous furnishing of title may be expressly stipulated for,[9] or the purchaser may call on the seller to furnish a title within a specified but reasonable time.[10] If the purchaser has objections to the title tendered he must make them within a reasonable time.[11] The seller is entitled to a reasonable time, on any objection being made, in which to furnish a good title, and for this purpose a date may be fixed. The buyer must either accept the title offered, or rescind the contract; he is not entitled to accept but insist on a deduction from the price.[12] It may be expressly agreed that the buyer take the title as it stands, or that he be held to have examined the titles and satisfied himself, in which case, unless the seller has absolutely no title to the lands or is wholly unable to give a title, warrandice only can be asked unless there be an actual challenge.

Curing defective title

When a seller tenders a defective title but asserts his ability and willingness to cure the defect, he must be given a reasonable

1 *Whyte* v. *Lee* (1879) 6 R. 699; *Todd* v. *McCarroll* (1917) 55 S.L.R. 17; *Crofts* v. *Stewart's Trs.*, 1927 S.C. (H.L.) 65; *Mossend Theatre Co.* v. *Livingstone*, 1930 S.C. 90; *Campbell* v. *McCutcheon*, 1963 S.C. 505. See also *Macdonald* v. *Newall* (1898) 1 F. 68; *Bremner* v. *Dick*, 1911 S.C. 887.

2 *Carter* v. *Lornie* (1890) 18 R. 353.

3 *D. Devonshire* v. *Fletcher* (1874) 1 R. 1056.

4 *Bruce* v. *Stewart* (1900) 2 F. 948.

5 *Maclachlan* v. *Bowie* (1887) 25 S.L.R. 734.

6 *Bruce* v. *Stewart* (1900) 2 F. 948.

7 *Raeburn* v. *Baird* (1832) 10 S. 761.

8 Allowed in *Fleming* v. *Harley's Trs.* (1823) 2 S. 373 (3 yrs.); *Hutchinson* v. *Scott* (1830) 8 S. 377 (14 mos.); *Kelman* v. *Barr's Trs.* (1878) 5 R. 816 (6 mos.). Refused in *Dick* v. *Cuthbertson* (1831) 5 W. & S. 712 (11 years); *Raeburn* v. *Baird* (1832) 10 S. 761 (6 mos.); *Carter* v. *Lornie* (1890) 18 R. 353 (18 mos.).

9 *Kelman, supra*; *Gilfillan* v. *Cadell & Grant* (1893) 21 R. 269.

10 cf. *Burns* v. *Garscadden* (1901) 8 S.L.T. 321; *Stickney* v. *Keeble* [1915] A.C. 386.

11 *Macdonald* v. *Newall* (1898) 1 F. 68.

12 *Earl of Morton* (1738) Mor. 14176; *Aikman* (1772) Mor. 14179; 2 Paton 326.

opportunity to do so, especially where possession is immediately given or does not fall to be given till a later date.[1]

A seller is not entitled to tender a valid title after the purchaser has rescinded the contract on the ground of the tender of an admittedly unmarketable title,[2] or has rescinded for delay in tendering a title,[3] but may do so after the court has held that a title previously tendered was not acceptable.[4] Conversely a buyer has been held barred from taking an objection to the title after the seller had remedied the only defect and the buyer had taken possession and paid the price.[5]

Undertaking to 'take the title as it stands'

A provision to this effect is common in articles of roup.[6] Such a provision will not avail the seller if there is mistake as to the identity or extent of the property professedly sold,[7] unless the discrepancy is really insubstantial,[8] or the title is radically bad, or at least very questionable,[9] but avails where there is curable defect in the title[10] or doubt as to a burden.[11] If there is curable defect the purchaser must implement the contract and cure the defect in title at his own expense.[10]

Extent of subjects sold

The seller is bound to yield possession of and convey title to the whole subjects sold, everything included in but to nothing excluded from the description. If he cannot do so, e.g. where the minerals had not been excepted from the sale but were in fact reserved to the superior, the buyer may reside.[12] The seller is not entitled to time in which to try to acquire the part of the subjects sold to which he had no title.[12]

Identity of subjects sold

The seller must convey, and the buyer is bound to take, only the precise subjects sold, and not any equivalent or adjacent land.[13]

1 *Kinnear* v. *Young*, 1936 S.L.T. 574.
2 *Gilfillan* v. *Cadell & Grant* (1893) 21 R. 269.
3 *McNeill* v. *Cameron* (1830) 8 S. 362. 4 *Carter* v. *Lornie* (1890) 18 R. 353.
5 *Macdonald* v. *Newall* (1898) 1 F. 68.
6 See generally *Morton* v. *Smith* (1877) 5 R. 83.
7 *Waddell* v. *Pollock* (1828) 6 S. 999; *Wood* v. *Edinburgh Mags.* (1886) 13 R. 1006; *Young* v. *McKellar*, 1909 S.C. 1340.
8 *Morton* v. *Smith* (1877) 5 R. 83. 9 *Carter* v. *Lornie* (1890) 18 R. 353.
10 *Sorley's Trs.* v. *Grahame* (1832) 10 S. 319; *Carter* v. *Lornie* (1890) 18 R. 353.
11 *Davidson* v. *Dalziel* (1881) 8 R. 990. 12 *Campbell* v. *McCutcheon*, 1963 S.C. 505.
13 *E. Moray* v. *Pearson* (1842) 4 D. 1411; cf. *Scottish Temperance Assce. Co.* v. *Law Union and Rock Assce. Co.*, 1917 S.C. 175.

Possession

The seller must give the purchaser entry and, unless excluded, actual possession of the whole subjects of sale.[1] The seller cannot enforce the contract if the time of entry is material and he is unable to give entry at the time specified.[2] But if the giving of entry is not essential the seller is not in breach merely because his title is not complete so long as he can complete it within a reasonable time.[3] The purchaser is not bound by any merely personal agreement between the seller and a third party to allow the latter to occupy any part of the lands.[4]

Clearing burdens

The seller is bound, unless there be contrary agreement, to discharge all burdens secured over the lands, and the buyer is entitled to the lands free of conditions, reservations or burdens not stipulated for, or, at least, not reasonable in the circumstances or known to the purchaser.[5] But a servitude is not a burden required to be cleared,[6] nor an ordinary lease, normal for that kind of property.[7]

Exhibition and delivery of titles

The seller must exhibit for the buyer's examination and, so far as possible, deliver with the disposition of the lands sold, a progress of titles for at least the prescriptive period evidencing a clear title to the buyer.[8] So far as the titles relate also to other subjects he cannot deliver them but binds himself to make them available to the buyer on necessary occasions.[9]

Clear search

The seller must also obtain, and normally deliver with the titles, a search, i.e. a record, made by a professional searcher, of all entries in relevant public Registers relating to the property sold or to the seller within certain time limits. If any incumbrances

1 *Heys* v. *Kimball and Morton* (1890) 17 R. 381.
2 *Kelman* v. *Barr's Tr.* (1878) 5 R. 816; *Hunter* v. *Carsewell* (1822) 1 S. 248.
3 *Kelman, supra.*
4 *Mann* v. *Houston,* 1957 S.L.T. 89; *Wallace* v. *Simmers,* 1960 S.C. 255.
5 *Robertson* v. *Rutherford* (1841) 4 D. 121; *Whyte* v. *Lee* (1879) 6 R. 699; *Robertson* v. *Douglas* (1886) 13 R. 1133. As to redemption instalments of stipend see *Church of Scotland Trustees* v. *Dowie,* 1946 S.C. 335.
6 Bell, *Prin.* §895: see also *Gordonston* v. *Paton* (1682) Mor. 16606; *Welsh* v. *Russell* (1894) 21 R. 769.
7 Bell, *Convg.* I, 644.
8 cf. *Porteous* v. *Henderson* (1898) 25 R. 563.
9 cf. *Bald* v. *Scott* (1841) 3 D. 564.

or diligences are revealed thereby the seller is bound to clear them.[1]

Search must be made in the appropriate division of the General Register of Sasines[2] for any writs transferring title to, or burdening the title to, or otherwise affecting, the land in question, for not less than twenty years back[3] from the close of the transaction now effected, to ensure that the seller has a good title and that there are no unextinguished bonds or burdens affecting the land.

Search must also be made in the Register of Inhibitions and Adjudications for any legal bars to voluntary transactions in heritage affecting the seller, or any of his predecessors in title within the 20 years of the positive prescription, for not less than five years back[4] from the close of the transaction now effected.

Searches do not reveal liability for feuduty,[5] real burdens,[5] building conditions or restrictions,[5] servitudes, leases,[6] whether a conveyance was in favour of a conjunct or confident person under the Bankruptcy Act, 1621, heritable securities created before the period of search but still valid, rights of terce or courtesy arising from a death before the Succession (Sc.) Act, 1964,[7] estate duty liabilities, floating charges granted by a company,[8] and certain other unimportant burdens.

The onus is on the seller to instruct the requisite searches and to deliver, or at least exhibit, at settlement of the transaction, a search showing the records clear of incumbrances and diligences, other than any known to and accepted by the parties.[9]

If the purchaser dispenses with the seller's producing a search, that does not bar him from objecting if a clear marketable title

[1] *Dryburgh* v. *Gordon* (1896) 24 R. 1; *Christie* v. *Cameron* (1898) 25 R. 824.

[2] And also in the Burgh Register of Sasines in the case of land in burghs whose burgh register has been discontinued within the period of search.

[3] From the Prescription Act, 1617, to the Conveyancing (Sc.) Act, 1874, the period for prescription fortifying title, and hence for search, was 40 years. See now Conveyancing (Sc.) Act, 1924, S. 16.

[4] Prior to the Titles to Land Consolidation (Sc.) Act, 1868, Ss. 155, 157 and 159, inhibitions, interdictions, adjudications and sequestrations prescribed only after 40 years, and search had accordingly to be carried back 40 years from the close of the present transaction against each proprietor within that period so long as he was proprietor. See now Conveyancing (Sc.) Acts, 1874, Ss. 34, 42, and 1924, S. 44.

[5] These burdens are disclosed by the deeds, but not by the mere entry in the Register.

[6] Except leases recorded under the Registration of Leases Act, 1857.

[7] See *Macnaughton* v. *M.*, 1940 S.C. 441.

[8] Companies (Floating Charges) (Sc.) Act, 1961, S. 3.

[9] *Graham* v. *Hunter's Trs.* (1831) 9 S. 543; *Campbell* v. *Clason* (1838) 1 D. 270; *Fea* v. *Macfarlane* (1887) 24 S.L.R. 628; *Christie* v. *Cameron* (1898) 25 R. 824. As to liability of solicitor for loss arising from burdens which a search would have revealed, see *Fea*, *supra*; *Fearn* v. *Gordon & Craig* (1893) 20 R. 352.

is not disclosed,[1] nor does it absolve the seller from his obligation to clear the record of incumbrances.[2]

Warrandice

Warrandice is the undertaking by the granter of the conveyance that the right granted shall be good and effectual to the grantee, and that if the grantee is evicted by reason of defect in the granter's title, or any fact or deed on his part, the granter will make reparation to him for the loss.[3]

Warrandice may be simple, which gives recourse only against loss resulting from the granter's subsequent deeds, or from fact and deed, which infers recourse against loss arising from the granter's acts, past or future, but not against eviction following on reduction of the granter's title on grounds not personal to himself,[4] or absolute warrandice, which infers recourse on eviction due to any lack of right or default of title of the granter to convey the subjects, whether due to his own act or deed or to defect in his own title, though not against burdens inherent in the grant[5] nor against eviction by supervening legislation.[5]

Warrandice may be expressed in any terms agreed by the parties. Failing that, simple warrandice is implied in donations, warrandice from fact and deed in assignations of debt,[6] and absolute warrandice in sales, leases and other onerous transactions.

Warrandice may, however, be expressly granted in any terms the parties may agree.[7] Warrandice in limited terms excludes any wider warrandice which the law might otherwise imply,[8] and even a grant of absolute warrandice may be limited by the terms of the disposition, as where it conveyed only whatever title the seller could claim to certain subjects.[9]

A purchaser has been held entitled to insist on absolute warrandice from sellers who were, *ex facie* of the records, absolute proprietors, though they alleged that they were only trustees.[10]

1 *Mackenzie* v. *Clark* (1895) 3 S.L.T. 128.

2 *D. Devonshire* v. *Fletcher* (1874) 1 R. 1056.

3 Bell, *Convg.* I, 214. Real warrandice was also formerly recognised: see Ersk. II, 3, 28; but cannot be created, save in the case of securities, since 1924: Conveyancing (Sc.) Act, 1924, S. 14.

4 *MacRitchie's Trs.* v. *Hope* (1836) 14 S. 578.

5 Bell, *Prin.* §915; *Tay Salmon Fisheries* v. *Speedie*, 1929 S.C. 593.

6 There is also implied in this case warrandice *debitum subesse*, i.e. that the debt is valid and subsisting, but not that the debtor is solvent: see also *Reid* v. *Barclay* (1879) 6 R. 1007.

7 e.g. *Coventry* v. *C.* (1834) 12 S. 895; *Strang* v. *S.* (1851) 13 D. 548.

8 *Craig* v. *Hopkins* (1732) Mor. 16623; cf. *Hay* v. *Aberdeen Mags.*, 1909 S.C. 554.

9 *Leith Heritages Co.* v. *Edinburgh & Leith Glass Co.* (1876) 3 R. 789.

10 *Mackenzie* v. *Neill* (1899) 37 S.L.R. 666.

The obligation constituted by granting warrandice affects the granter and his heirs until the possibility of adverse claims is extinguished by the long prescription.[1]

Effects of warrandice

If a grantee is evicted from possession on a ground covered by the warrandice he is entitled by virtue thereof to full compensation for loss caused thereby.[2] The claim also arises where the grantee's title is found to be burdened with a liability which diminishes the value of his right.[3]

No claim is competent till eviction, unless the ground for eviction arises from the act of the granter[4] or the granter disputes his liability to relieve.[5] Hence the grantee is not entitled to recover the expenses of a successful defence of his title, but may normally recover the expenses of an unsuccessful defence.[6]

The claim is only for indemnification against eviction and gives no right to recover the price on offering a reconveyance.[7] If the eviction is total, the claim is for the whole value of the subjects lost, if partial, as where another is held to have a right of servitude over the lands, the claim is for compensation for the loss.

BUYER'S OBLIGATIONS

The buyer's primary obligation is to pay the price on the date fixed or at the term of entry, or in exchange for the disposition. If there is express provision voiding the sale for non-payment by a fixed date, the seller may, if payment be not then made, rescind the contract.[8] Failing such provision, failure to pay by a stipulated date is not generally a ground for rescission[9] and only an unnecessary or unjustifiable delay will justify the imposition of a time for payment and, failing payment, rescission.[9]

If entry has been given the seller has a personal action for the price and, even though he has signed but not delivered a disposition, the seller has a preference for the price over other creditors.[10]

[1] *Welsh* v. *Russell* (1894) 21 R. 709, 773.

[2] Ersk. II, 3, 30; *Cairns* v. *Howden* (1870) 9 M. 284; *Welsh* v. *Russell* (1894) 21 R. 769; cf. *Middleton* v. *Megget* (1828) 7 S. 76.

[3] *Dewar* v. *Aitken* (1780) Mor. 16637; *Briggs' Trs.* v. *Dalyell* (1851) 14 D. 173.

[4] Bell, *Prin.* §895.

[5] *L. Melville* v. *Wemyss* (1842) 4 D. 385; *Leith Heritages Co.* v. *Edinburgh & Leith Glass Co.* (1876) 3 R. 789.

[6] *Dougall* v. *Dunfermline Mags.*, 1908 S.C. 151.

[7] *Welsh* v. *Russell* (1894) 21 R. 769.

[8] *Young* v. *Dunn* (1785) Mor. 14191.

[9] *Rodger (Builders), Ltd.* v. *Fawdry*, 1950 S.C. 483.

[10] *Baird* v. *Jap* (1758) Mor. 14156.

The seller is not entitled to the price if he is still litigating to clear the title, or possibly in some cases so long as it remains subject to appeal.[1]

If settlement is delayed after the purchaser has been given entry, interest runs *ex lege* on the price[2] until or unless it is consigned on deposit receipt in joint names, the purchaser receiving the deposit receipt interest at settlement.[3] If a disposition has been granted but the price has not been fixed or paid and the parties cannot agree, the sale is void and the purchaser must relinquish possession.[4]

If the buyer delays unreasonably to pay the price the seller may rescind the contract, but premature rescission is a breach of contract.[5]

Buyer's duty to become infeft

The buyer is probably also bound to become, or to secure that another becomes, infeft within a reasonable time, so as to relieve the seller of his liabilities to the superior for feuduty and any other obligations incumbent on him.

BREACH OF CONTRACT AND REMEDIES

Seller's default

If the seller is able to, but refuses or delays unreasonably to convey the property sold, or refuses or delays unreasonably to produce a title, so that it is uncertain whether he can or cannot give a good title, the remedies appropriate are specific implement with a conclusion for adjudication in implement[6] or, alternatively, damages, if the buyer does not wish to insist on the purchase, or the court deems it highly inconvenient or unjust to enforce performance.[7] If the seller is no longer able to convey the property, e.g. having sold and conveyed it to another in circumstances

[1] *Traill* v. *Connon* (1877) 5 R. 25.

[2] *Speirs* v. *Ardrossan Canal Co.* (1827) 5 S. 764; *Grandison's Trs.* v. *Jardine* (1895) 22 R. 925. As to rate of interest see *Traill* v. *Connon* (1877) 5 R. 25; *Greenock Harbour* v. *G.S.W. Ry.*, 1909 S.C. (H.L.) 49.

[3] *Prestwick Cinema Co.* v. *Gardiner*, 1951 S.C. 98. As to partial consignation see *Dickson* v. *Munro* (1855) 17 D. 524.

[4] *Stirling* v. *Honyman* (1824) 2 S. 765.

[5] *Burns* v. *Garscadden* (1901) 8 S.L.T. 321.

[6] *McKellar* v. *Dallas's, Ltd.*, 1928 S.C. 503. It is competent to seek implement in relation to heritage only of a composite contract for the sale of heritage and moveables: *Mackay* v. *Campbell*, 1966 S.C. 237.

[7] *Moore* v. *Paterson* (1881) 9 R. 337; *Stewart* v. *Kennedy* (1890) 17 R. (H.L.) 1, 10; *Harvey* v. *Smith* (1904) 6 F. 511; *Plato* v. *Newman*, 1950 S.L.T. (Notes) 30; *Mackay* v. *Campbell*, 1967 S.C. (H.L.) 53.

where that sale cannot be impugned,[1] only damages are competent. If the seller produces a title which is not a valid and marketable title to the subjects sold the buyer is probably not entitled to take or retain the subjects purchased subject to an abatement from the price (the *actio quanti minoris*),[2] but must rescind the entire contract and claim damages for loss of the bargain.[3] It is incompetent for the court to reform a contract; it can only reduce it, but may do so on conditions.[4]

Buyer's default

If the buyer has refused or delayed unreasonably to pay the price the seller may sue him therefor, with interest, offering to deliver a valid disposition, or, if the missives so provide, claim under a provision therein for liquidate damages.[5]

If the buyer has absolutely refused or is manifestly unable to complete his purchase, the seller may rescind the contract and claim damages for the loss of the bargain, or, if the contract so provides, claim forfeiture of any deposit paid or payment under a provision for liquidate damages.

If the buyer justifiably objects to the title tendered and, no other being tendered, repudiates the contract, he is not liable for breach,[6] even though the seller later tenders a valid title,[7] nor is he if the seller has not been able to give entry or a good title at the stipulated date.[8] He is, however, in breach if he takes an objection to the title tendered which is held unjustifiable and has sought to repudiate in reliance thereon.

DISPOSITION

An enforceable contract for the sale of lands is given effect to, and title to the lands transferred, by a disposition. It transmits a fee already constituted to a singular successor of the vassal disponing to be held in his place of the same superior. Prior to 1874 the participation of the superior was essential, and a disposition

[1] cf. *Burns* v. *Garscadden* (1901) 8 S.L.T. 321; *Rodger (Builders), Ltd.* v. *Fawdry*, 1950 S.C. 483.

[2] *Louttit's Trs.* v. *Highland Ry.* (1892) 19 R. 791; see also *Wood* v. *Edinburgh Mags.* (1886) 13 R. 1006; *Brownlie* v. *Miller* (1880) 7 R. (H.L.) 66; *McKillop* v. *Mutual Securities, Ltd.*, 1945 S.C. 166.

[3] As to sale induced by fraud, see *Dobbie* v. *Duncanson* (1872) 10 M. 810.

[4] *Steuart's Trs.* v. *Hart* (1875) 3 R. 192.

[5] *Commercial Bank* v. *Beal* (1890) 18 R. 80.

[6] *Campbell* v. *McCutcheon*, 1963 S.C. 505.

[7] *Gilfillan* v. *Caddell & Grant* (1893) 21 R. 269.

[8] *Kelman* v. *Barr's Tr.* (1878) 5 R. 816.

required infeftment followed by charter or writ of confirmation by the superior, or infeftment following on a charter or writ of resignation by the superior.

Effect of disposition

A disposition in implement of a sale, once delivered to and accepted by the purchaser, becomes the sole measure of the contracting parties' rights, and supersedes all previous communings and contracts, however formal.[1] The parties may agree to exclude this rule,[2] or the disposition may bear to be, or be shown to be, in only part performance of the contract,[3] and a collateral obligation contained in the same contract is not discharged by acceptance of a disposition and taking possession thereon.[4] Where a disposition follows on a decree arbitral it may be permissible to refer to the decree.[5]

A disposition does not, however, exclude reference to the missives where it is averred that it does not in a material respect truly express the agreement contained in the missives.[6]

A disponee is not bound by any merely personal claim against the disponer even if he were aware of it, such as a third party's reserved right of occupancy of part of the premises.[7]

Modern form of disposition

The modern form of disposition[8] is in the main regulated by the Titles to Land Consolidation (Sc.) Act, 1868, as amended, and contains the following clauses.

Narrative Clause

This clause names and designs the granter of the deed, who must have power to sell and convey the lands, normally as heritable proprietor of the subjects hereinafter disponed, and states the price or other consideration for the grant of the lands and acknowledges receipt thereof. If the seller is not himself infeft but

[1] *Lee* v. *Alexander* (1883) 10 R. (H.L.) 91; *Orr* v. *Mitchell* (1893) 20 R. (H.L.) 27; cf. *Norval* v. *Abbey*, 1939 S.C. 724; but see *E. Glasgow's Trs.* v. *Clark* (1889) 16 R. 545; *Baird* v. *Alexander* (1898) 25 R. (H.L.) 35; *Wigan* v. *Cripps*, 1908 S.C. 394; *Butter* v. *Foster*, 1912 S.C. 1218; *Wann* v. *Gray*, 1935 S.N. 8.

[2] *Young* v. *McKellar*, 1909 S.C. 1340; *France* v. *Cox*, 1938 S.C. 506.

[3] *Jamieson* v. *Welsh* (1900) 3 F. 176.

[4] *McKillop* v. *Mutual Securities, Ltd.*, 1945 S.C. 166.

[5] *G.N.S. Ry.* v. *D. Fife* (1901) 3 F. (H.L.) 2; cf. *Young* v. *McKellar*, 1909 S.C. 1340.

[6] *Anderson* v. *Lambie*, 1954 S.C. (H.L.) 43.

[7] *Wallace* v. *Simmers*, 1960 S.C. 255.

[8] Titles to Land Consolidation (Sc.) Act, 1868, Sched. B, No. 1, modified by Conveyancing (Sc.) Act, 1874.

has right to land by a title, e.g. as trustee or judicial factor[1] or executor,[2] a clause is inserted after the clause of entry naming and designing the person last infeft, specifying his infeftment, and deducing the seller's title from him by specifying the writs between the last infeftment and the present seller.[3]

Dispositive clause

No particular words of conveyance are essential so long as present intention to transfer title to the lands is clear.[4] The dispositive clause cannot be denied effect on the ground that other parts of the deed show a different intention, unless its terms are ambiguous, when other parts of the deed may be referred to in aid of its construction.[5]

The dispositive clause contains the destination, i.e. the identification of the person or persons in whose favour the title is being taken. Reference to the disponee's 'heirs and assignees whomsoever' is usual but is implied. This clause may be, and formerly commonly was, complicated by references to survivorship, conjunct fee and liferent, or other special destination,[6] which may raise questions such as of the survivor's power to alter the destination.[7] The seller may be requested to dispone to another than the buyer from him, e.g. to a subpurchaser or donee, in which case the buyer's request is narrated and his consent taken and evidenced by his signature to the disposition.[7]

The lands are described, and the description may be in any way competent in the case of a feucharter.[8] Any exceptions from the property conveyed must be mentioned. The dispositive clause must also contain all reservations, burdens, conditions, limitations and qualifications of the grant, new or old, expressed *ad longum*, or, if old, incorporated by reference to the deed creating them.

The dispositive clause may also contain any allocation of feuduty or other common burdens agreed upon, as where the proprietor of a tenement is selling one of the flats therein.

[1] Conveyancing Act, 1938, S. 1.
[2] Succession (Sc.) Act, 1964, Ss. 14, 15 and 17.
[3] Conveyancing Act, 1924, S. 3.
[4] 1874 Act, S. 27. Formerly the word 'dispone' was essential.
[5] *Orr* v. *Mitchell* (1893) 20 R. (H.L.) 27.
[6] cf. *Brown's Tr.* v. *B.*, 1943 S.C. 488; *Hay's Tr.* v. *Hay's Trs.*, 1951 S.C. 329.
[7] cf. *Anderson* v. *Dick* (1901) 8 S.L.T. 482; *McDougal's Trs.* v. *L.A.*, 1952 S.C. 260. The clause of warrandice is also modified in the case of a disposition direct to a sub-purchaser: cf. *Mackenzie* v. *Neill* (1899) 37 S.L.R. 666.
[8] cf. *Murray's Tr.* v. *Wood* (1887) 14 R. 856; *Matheson* v. *Gemmell* (1903) 5 F. 448.

Term of Entry

The term of the purchaser's entry is normally expressed, but, if not, it is deemed to be the first term of Whitsunday or Martinmas after the last date of the disposition, unless it appears that another date was intended.[1] Postponed entry does not prevent or postpone infeftment.[2]

Obligation to infeft and manner of holding

Originally a vassal might sub-feu, but might not substitute another as vassal in his stead without the superior's consent. Hence the practice arose of a disponer granting two deeds, one bearing that the lands were to be held *de me*, of and under the disponer, the other that the lands were to be held *a me* (*de superiore meo*). The buyer expede and recorded an instrument of sasine referable either to the holding *de me* or to that *a me*, and infeftment thereon completed his real right to the lands, and being ascribed to the *de me* holding constituted him a vassal of the disponer and a subvassal of the superior. When confirmed by the superior the disposition divested the seller and infeftment thereon was ascribed to the *a me* holding, the seller then dropping out as mid-superior. Subsequently the two charters, *de me* and *a me*, were superseded by a disposition with an alternative holding, *a me vel de me*, and a precept of sasine applicable to either holding.[3] Till confirmed this infeftment gave the disponee a title as vassal of the disponer but when confirmed, it substituted him as vassal in place of the disponer. After confirmation the disponee could not impute his infeftment to the *de me* holding.[4] The 1868 Act, repeating earlier provisions, made it unnecessary to insert an obligation to infeft and gave the statutory clause, 'to be holden the said lands *a me* (or *a me vel de me*),' with stated effect.[5] Since 1874 no holding need be mentioned in a disposition, a holding *a me* being implied.[6] The 1868 Act rendered the precept of sasine unnecessary, direct recording of the disposition coming in place of infeftment and the instrument of sasine recording that fact. This clause accordingly does not appear in modern dispositions.

1 1874 Act, S. 28.

2 *Burgh-Smeaton* v. *Whitson* (1907) 14 S.L.T. 839; *Anderson* v. *Dickie*, 1913 S.L.T. 198.

3 An alternative holding was not intended to create a permanent base fee and was not deemed a contravention of a prohibition against subinfeudation: *Colquhoun* v. *Walker* (1867) 5 M. 773; *Inglis* v. *Wilson*, 1909 S.C. 1393.

4 *Chancellor* v. *Brown* (1688) Mor. 3012.

5 1868 Act, S. 6.

6 1874 Act, S. 2.

Procuratory or clause of resignation in favorem

The procuratory (later clause) of resignation *in favorem*[1] was a mandate by the disponer authorising the relinquishment of the lands to the superior for new infeftment, that he might reconvey them to the disponee to be held under the superior as the disponer had himself held them. The 1868 Act, S. 81, replacing earlier legislation, provided a statutory form of clause, 'And I resign the said lands and others for new infeftment or investiture', but the clause was impliedly abolished by the 1874 Act which rendered incompetent the granting of charters or writs of resignation. Under the 1874 Act, the procuratory became unnecessary and, even if inserted, could not be used. It does not appear in modern dispositions.

Assignation of writs

The statutory clause 'And I assign the writs' imports, in the absence of qualification, an absolute and unconditional assignation to such writs and evidents, and to all open procuratories, clauses and precepts, if any, and, as the case may be, therein contained, and to all unrecorded conveyances to which the disponer has right.[2] But the seller, if he needs to retain the writs in respect of other subjects, may bind himself only to make the writs forthcoming on necessary occasions, or if he does not himself possess all the writs, he may assign to his disponee the writs in his possession and any right he has to make the others forthcoming.

Assignation of rents

The statutory form of clause, 'And I assign the rents', unless modified, imports an assignation of the rents to become due for the possession following the term of entry according to the legal and not the conventional terms, unless in the case of forehand rents, in which case it imports an assignation to the rents payable at the conventional terms subsequent to the date of entry.[3]

Obligation of relief

The statutory form of clause, 'And I bind myself to free and relieve my said disponee and his foresaids of all feuduties, casualties and public burdens', imports an obligation to relieve of all feuduties and other duties, or casualties or services due to the

[1] A procuratory of resignation *ad remanentiam* authorised the surrender of the feu by the vassal to the superior.

[2] 1868 Act, S. 8; cf. *Porteous* v. *Henderson* (1898) 25 R. 563.

[3] 1868 Act, S. 8; cf. *Butter* v. *Foster*, 1912 S.C. 1218.

superior, and all public, parochial or local burdens due from or on account of the lands conveyed prior to the date of the disponee's entry.[1] Even if unqualified this clause does not preclude apportionment of feuduty, ground annual and public burdens between the parties by reference to their respective periods of possession.[2] An obligation in wider terms may saddle the disponer with liability even for rates imposed by subsequent legislation.[3] Liability for work done, e.g. on roads, by local authorities, arises only when the authority has allocated the cost to proprietors and requested payment.[4]

Clause of warrandice

The statutory clause, 'And I grant warrandice', imports absolute warrandice as regards the lands and writs and evidents, and warrandice from fact and deed as regards the rents.[5] In dispositions by trustees or judicial factors the granters customarily grant warrandice from their own facts and deeds only, and bind the estate under their charge in absolute warrandice. Even if the disponee knows of it any right excepted from warrandice, such as a bond, should be excepted expressly.[6] A grant of warrandice in statutory form has been held to warrant only what was conveyed by the dispositive clause, and warranted the assignation of writs only for the purpose for which they were assigned, and not that any writ should have any specific effect in law or be valid beyond challenge.[7] The existence of an ordinary urban lease is not a breach of warrandice.[8]

Clause of consent to registration

A disposition can be recorded for preservation in the Books of Council and Session or any other competent record and the granter normally expressly consents thereto. It is not customary to record a disposition for execution, unless the disponee undertakes liability therein for some future payment, in which case, if the disposition contains the disponee's consent to registration and is signed by him, it may be recorded for execution and the disponee may subsequently be charged for payment thereunder.

1 1868 Act, S. 8.
2 cf. *E. Glasgow's Trs.* v. *Clark* (1889) 16 R. 545.
3 *Dunbar Mags.* v. *Mackersy*, 1931 S.C. 180.
4 *McIntosh* v. *Mitchell Thomson* (1900) 8 S.L.T. 48.
5 1868 Act, S. 8.
6 *Horsburgh's Trs.* v. *Welsh* (1886) 14 R. 67.
7 *Brownlie* v. *Miller* (1880) 7 R. (H.L.) 66.
8 *Lothian and Border Farmers* v. *McCutchion*, 1952 S.L.T. 450.

Precept of Sasine

The precept of sasine was a mandate by the disponer to his bailie, and later, to any notary public, to give his disponee sasine of the lands. Since 1858 it has been unnecessary (though competent) to expede and record any instrument of sasine, but necessary only to record the conveyance itself, with a warrant of registration, in the Register of Sasines, and it is accordingly now unnecessary to insert a precept of sasine in any conveyance.[1]

Clause of direction

It is competent to insert a clause of direction specifying which parts of the disposition the granter desires to be recorded in the Register of Sasines. If the warrant of registration bears reference to the clause of direction the disponee may have the disposition recorded in part only, but even though there is such a clause in the disposition the disponee may record the whole deed, or a notarial instrument thereon.

Testing clause

The disposition is attested in customary form. If a granter, such as one joint proprietor, cannot be found or refuses to sign, the parties may, on petition to the *nobile officium*, have the deputy clerk of session authorised to sign the disposition in place of the recalcitrant proprietor.[2]

COMPLETION OF TITLE

Completion of disponee's title

Completion of title makes the disponee infeft in the lands or vests the disponee with a real right to the lands to which he acquired only a personal right by the contract and the disposition in implement thereof. Formerly he became infeft by taking sasine and recording the instrument of sasine in the Register of Sasines.[3] Since 1847 registration has had the effect of taking sasine.[4] But in some cases, such as real burdens,[5] registration completes the creditor's right though there is no infeftment. If there is no infeftment the disponer is not divested and the disponee not invested.[6] It is essential for fortification of title by positive prescription.

[1] 1868 Act, S. 15.

[2] *Lennox*, 1950 S.C. 546; *Boag*, 1967 S.L.T. 275; cf. *Wallace's C.B.* v. *W.*, 1924 S.C. 212; *Pennell's Tr.*, 1928 S.C. 605.

[3] An unrecorded sasine was null: *Young* v. *Gordon's Trs.* (1847) 9 D. 932.

[4] Now 1868 Act, S. 15. [5] 1874 Act, S. 30. [6] Bell, *Prin.* §802.

Completion of disponee's title—older form, by resignation or confirmation

Prior to 1874 the disponee required the superior's intervention to complete his title and establish him as a vassal. By virtue of the disponer's mandate, the procuratory of resignation in the disposition, the disponer resigned the lands to the superior for new infeftment, and the superior granted a charter of resignation in favour of the disponee, similar to an original charter but narrating the deduction of the disponee's title from the disponer and describing the ceremony of resignation (which, latterly, was in most cases imaginary). This contained a precept of sasine on which the disponee could expede an instrument of sasine and complete title by recording it in the Register of Sasines.

Alternatively the disponee under a disposition with a holding *a me vel de me* might take sasine under the *de me* holding and apply to the superior for a charter of confirmation. When granted the disponee's sasine was attributed to the *a me* holding and the holding *de me* (under the disponer as mid-superior) dropped out of the titles.

A combined charter of resignation and confirmation was necessary in certain cases.

The 1868 Act, Ss. 97 and 99, re-enacting provisions from 1847 onwards, permitted direct recording of the disposition, with writ of resignation or of confirmation endorsed thereon, in the Register of Sasines.

The 1874 Act, S. 4, provided that infeftment should imply entry with the superior, so that resignation for new infeftment and confirmation were both unnecessary.

Completion of title in modern practices

The disponee now completes his feudal title to the subjects, if the subjects are described generally, or particularly, or by statutory reference, or by general name under the 1868 Act, S. 13, by endorsing on the disposition a warrant of registration in his favour and recording the deed in the appropriate division of the General Register of Sasines,[1] or by expeding a notarial instrument or notice of title and recording it with a warrant of registration.[2] If the description of the lands is in statutory terms, he completes title by notice of title with warrant of registration, recorded in the Register of Sasines.[3]

[1] 1868 Act, S. 15.
[2] 1868 Act, S. 17; 1924 Act, S. 6.
[3] 1868 Act, S. 19; 1924 Act, S. 6.

A disposition once recorded may still be reduced if the purchaser when he accepted the disposition was aware of a prior contract between seller and a third party and did not inquire whether that contract was still binding or not,[1] or if the disposition contains an inaccurate description of the lands sold, so that it has not correctly given effect to the parties' intentions.[2]

Notice of change of ownership

To free the seller from liability for feuduty the disponee must not only become infeft but the seller must give notice to the superior of change of ownership of the lands.

Notification of sale to Land Commission

Betterment levy may be charged where the development value of land is realised on the conveyance on sale of an interest of *dominium utile*[3] or the assignation on sale of a tenancy for not less than seven years, and for that purpose the grantee must notify the disposition to the Land Commission.[4]

There are exemptions for local authorities and certain other public bodies.[5]

Assignation of unrecorded dispositions

The disponee under a disposition, delivered but not recorded, or any person in right thereof, may assign the disposition to an assignee by assignation endorsed on the disposition, or separately. The assignee may further assign the disposition. The assignee must deduce his title from the latest prior endorsed assignation. The last assignee may complete his title by recording the disposition and the assignation, or the disposition with a notarial instrument or notice of title, or a notarial instrument or notice of title narrating the transmissions since the last infeftment.[6]

Assignation of personal right to land

A personal right to an estate in land descendible to heirs vested formerly in the heir by survivance and was transmissible in the same manner as an unfeudalised conveyance.[7] Heritage now vests in the deceased's executor, by virtue of his confirmation, for the

[1] *Rodger (Builders), Ltd.* v. *Fawdry*, 1950 S.C. 483.
[2] *Anderson* v. *Lambie*, 1954 S.C. (H.L.) 43.
[3] Land Commission Act, 1967, Ss. 27, 29, 37 and 100.
[4] Ibid., S. 37.
[5] Ibid., S. 56.
[6] 1868 Act, S. 22; Conveyancing (Sc.) Act, 1924, S. 7.
[7] 1874 Act, S. 9.

purposes of administration,[1] and a personal right vests in a person entitled to the land under the deceased's will or intestacy to have the land transferred to him by the executor.[2] This personal right is probably assignable and if intimation is made to the executor, the assignee will be entitled to transfer of the land to him.

Assignation of jus crediti *to land.*

A person has a *jus crediti* to land where it is vested in another who is under an obligation, by trust or contract, to convey it to him. Such *jura crediti* are transferable by assignation intimated to the person subject to the obligation, but such an assignation does not confer a feudal title but only entitles the assignee to obtain a conveyance or to lead an adjudication of the lands.

DISPOSITION OF SUPERIORITY

The superiority of lands can be conveyed only if the vassal's estate has already been separated from the superiority by charter and infeftment. It is incompetent to seek in one deed to convey the superiority to one disponee and the fee to another, or to dispone lands reserving the superiority.[3] Nor can a superior, unless he reserved liberty to do so, without his vassal's consent, divide a superiority,[4] though he may dispone it to two or more persons jointly[5] and may dispone separately the superiorities of two parcels of lands held by the one vassal.[6] The right to object may be waived, or a division acquiesced in. Similarly a superior cannot, unless by reserved right or with the vassal's consent, interpose a mid-superior between himself and his vassal.[7]

Form of deed

The form of a disposition of the superiority of lands is the same as that of the fee of the lands, save that the disponer assigns the feurents, duties and casualties instead of the rents, and that the feu-rights of the lands are excepted from the warrandice clauses.[8]

[1] Succession (Sc.) Act, 1964, S. 14. [2] Under S. 15.

[3] *Norton* v. *Anderson*, 6 July 1813, F.C.; *Williams and James* v. *Maclaine's Trs.* (1872) 10 M. 362.

[4] *D. Montrose* v. *Colquhoun* (1780) 6 Pat. 805; *Graham* v. *Westenra* (1826) 4 S. 615. The vassal's right to object may be lost by consent or acquiescence or the lapse of the long prescriptive period; Bell, *Convg.* II, 754.

[5] *Cargill* v. *Muir* (1837) 15 S. 408. [6] *Dreghorn* v. *Hamilton* (1774) Mor. 15015.

[7] *Douglas of Kelhead* v. *Torthorall* (1670) Mor. 15012; *Archbishop of St. Andrews* v. *M. Huntly* (1682) Mor. 15015; *Hotchkis* v. *Walker's Trs.* (1822) 2 S. 70.

[8] *Ceres School Board* v. *Macfarlane* (1893) 23 R. 279.

The superiority can be disponed without conveyance of the lands themselves.[1] Disposition of the superiority carries right to the minerals, if reserved to the superior, unless they are excluded.[2]

If the disposition of the superiority is to the vassal, its grant implies a discharge of past unpaid feu-duties,[3] and the destination in the disposition of the superiority will regulate the succession to the united fee, if superiority and fee are later consolidated.

CONTRACT OF EXCAMBION

The contract of excambion is that for the barter or mutual exchange of lands by heritable proprietors, possibly with a monetary payment to equalise the considerations. The contract to excamb is subject to the same requirements of formalities as the contract to sell.[4] A power to sell heritage does not imply a power to excamb.[5]

EXCAMBION

A contract to excamb lands is given effect by a deed of excambion, which narrates the agreement to excamb and any consideration which was passed to equalise the counterpart transactions, contains clauses dispositive of the one's lands to the other and of the other's lands to the one, as in a disposition, clauses of entry, of assignation by each respectively of writs and of rents, of obligations of relief, of the grant of warrandice, and of consents to registration, and a testing clause. Prior to 1925[6] mutual grants of real warrandice were expressed or implied in excambions. The deed is recorded with two warrants of registration, one on behalf of each party, for preservation and for publication. Alternatively, excambion can be effected by separate dispositions. Title is completed as under a disposition.

DONATION

An intention to donate land is enforceable only if there is a promise or unilateral undertaking embodied in writing, probative or privileged, and delivered, or otherwise constituted but followed

[1] *Gardner* v. *Leith Trinity House* (1841) 3 D. 534; *Williams and James* v. *Maclaine's Trs.* (1872) 10 M. 362.

[2] *Orr* v. *Moir's Trs.* (1893) 20 R. (H.L.) 27.

[3] *E. Argyle* v. *L. McDonald* (1676) Mor. 6323.

[4] *Melville* v. *Wilson* (1829) 7 S. 889; (1830) 8 S. 841.

[5] *Bruce* v. *Stewart* (1900) 2 F. 948. See also Trusts (Sc.) Act, 1921, S. 4(e).

[6] Conveyancing (Sc.) Act, 1924, S. 14.

by actings amounting to *rei interventus* or homologation.[1] The gift may be conditional, in which case the donor retains the right to demand a reconveyance on failure of the condition, which right is an incorporeal heritable right transmissible by will or on intestacy.[2]

A disposition of land in pursuance of an intention to gift is effected in the same form as a disposition on sale, save that the consideration is stated as for love, favour and affection, or words to the same effect. The donee completes title in the same way as an onerous disponee. Questions may arise whether taking the title of heritage in the names of particular persons, who had not given the consideration for the heritage, amounts to gift of the heritage to them. *Prima facie* it does,[3] though as between husband and wife, such a donation was revocable prior to the Married Women's Property (Sc.) Act, 1920, S. 5.[4] A husband has been held entitled to prove that the price of heritage taken in the wife's name had been paid by him, though the disposition bore that it had been paid by her.[5]

1 Stair I, 10, 3; Ersk. III, 3, 88; Bell, *Prin.* §889; *Barron* v. *Rose* (1794) Mor. 8444; *Goldston* v. *Young* (1868) 7 M. 188; see also *Malcolm* v. *Campbell* (1891) 19 R. 278; *Mowat* v. *Thain*, 1947 S.N. 180.

2 *Connell's J.F.* v. *McWatt*, 1961 S.L.T. 203.

3 *Gilpin* v. *Martin* (1869) 7 M. 807.

4 *Johnstone's Trs.* v. *J.* (1896) 23 R. 538.

5 *Smith* v. *S.*, 1917 2 S.L.T. 219.

CHAPTER 90

INVOLUNTARY TRANSFER OF LAND

INVOLUNTARY transfer of land takes place on compulsory purchase of the land, by judicial sale, on the owner's death, or his sequestration, or by operation of legal diligence.

COMPULSORY PURCHASE

Powers to acquire lands compulsorily from the owners thereof is conferred by many statutes, both public-general and local statutes. Statutory codes have been provided to regulate the modes of acquisition, and to provide for compensation.

The main code of procedure is contained in the Lands Clauses Consolidation (Sc.) Act, 1845, amended in 1860, which (S. 1) applies to every undertaking authorized by a subsequent Act which authorized the taking of lands, and is incorporated with that Act, but a subsequent Act may incorporate only parts of the 1845 Act. Other 'Clauses Acts' must also be considered in the case of acquisition for the specific purposes regulated by the relevant Clauses Act, e.g. for waterworks.

Compulsory powers are strictly construed,[1] especially in the case of a trading body.[2] They must be exercised *bona fide*[3] and within the prescribed time or, if none be specified, within three years of the authorizing Act (S. 116).

Purchases by agreement

The undertaking empowered to utilize the 1845 Act may (S. 6) purchase the lands desired by agreement for a lump sum, or for a feuduty or ground annual secured on the revenues of the undertaking (S. 10). This power is confined to lands authorized by the Special Act to be taken,[4] though it may also give power to purchase other lands for extraordinary purposes.[5] It is a question of interpretation whether an agreement to acquire lands is

[1] *Moncreiffe* v. *Perth Harbour Commrs.* (1843) 5 D. 879.

[2] *Galloway* v. *London Corpn.* (1866) L.R. 1 H.L. 34.

[3] *Michael* v. *Edinburgh Corpn.* (1895) 3 S.L.T. 109; *Sydney Corpn.* v. *Campbell* [1925] A.C. 338; cf. *Boswell* v. *G.S.W. Ry.* (1851) 13 D. 1157.

[4] *N.B. Ry. Co.* v. *Tod* (1846) 5 Bell, 184; *Maule* v. *Moncrieffe* (1846) 5 Bell, 333; *Edinburgh Tramways* v. *Black* (1873) 11 M. (H.L.) 57.

[5] Ss. 12, 13; *City of Glasgow Union Ry. Co.* v. *Caledonian Ry.* (1871) 9 M. (H.L.) 115.

conditional on the carrying out of the undertaking, or absolute, rendering the undertaking liable to damages if they abandon the undertaking without having completed the purchase.[1]

Purchase otherwise than by agreement—notice to treat

The promoters of the authorized undertaking must first (S. 17) give notice to all parties interested in the lands they propose to take of their intention to do so, that they are willing to treat, and as to the compensation to be made.[2] If parties fail to treat or do not agree on the compensation, it may be determined by the sheriff (S. 21), or referred to arbitration (Ss. 19–34).[3] If the matter is not referred to arbitration, or an award is not made within the time set by the Act, the party claiming compensation may require a jury to be summoned by the sheriff (Ss. 35–39).[4] Thirteen jurors are to be empanelled, with the sheriff presiding, and they have to assess separately sums payable for the purchase of the land and for damage for injury to it (Ss. 40–48).[5] Compensation to absent parties is to be determined by a valuator appointed by the sheriff (Ss. 56–60). Provision is made for the application of the compensation money (Ss. 61–73). On deposit in bank of the purchase money or compensation awarded, the owners of the lands are to convey the lands to the promoters of the undertaking, failing which the promoters may expede a notarial instrument narrating the compulsory purchase, whereupon the interest of the owners vests absolutely in the promoters of the undertaking who become entitled to immediate possession (Ss. 74–76).[6] Feus and conveyances of lands may be in the form of Schedules A and B to the Act and if registered within 60 days constitute a good and undoubted right and complete and valid feudal title to the promoters for all time (S. 80).[7] The statutory conveyance duly registered appears to create a statutory tenure and to extinguish

[1] *Edinburgh, etc. Ry. Co.* v. *Philip* (1857) 2 Macq. 514; *Scottish N.E. Ry. Co.* v. *Stewart* (1859) 3 Macq. 382; *N.B. Ry. Co.* v. *Benhar Coal Co.* (1886) 14 R. 141.

[2] Notice once given cannot be withdrawn without the owners' consent, and compensation is due; *Lockerby* v. *City of Glasgow Improvement Trs.* (1872) 10 M. 971.

[3] cf. *Smith* v. *Lanarkshire and Ayrshire Ry.* (1905) 12 S.L.T. 783.

[4] Where a special Act incorporates the 1845 Act, it may permit alternative procedure; *Davie* v. *Edinburgh Mags.*, 1951 S.C. 720; cf. *Alexander* v. *N. of Sc. Hydro-Electric Board*, 1952 S.C. 367 where 1845 Act procedure held inapplicable as there was no acquisition of land, but only entry for other purposes but causing damage.

[5] cf. *City of Glasgow Union Ry.* v. *Hunter* (1870) 8 M. (H.L.) 156.

[6] *Alexander* v. *Bridge of Allan Water Co.* (1868) 6 M. 324.

[7] cf. *Campbell* v. *Ayr C.C.* (1904) 11 S.L.T. 587; *Heriot's Trust* v. *Caledonian Ry.*, 1915 S.C. (H.L.) 52; *D. Argyll* v. *L.M.S. Ry.*, 1931 S.C. 309.

the superior-vassal relationship.[1] The promoters may not, in general, without liability to penalty, enter on the lands until the price has been paid, or consigned in bank (Ss. 83–89).[2] Provision is made for intersected land and common land (Ss. 90–98),[3] lands subject to security-rights (Ss. 99–106) or feuduty or ground annual (Ss. 107–111)[4] or to leases (Ss. 112–116),[5] interests omitted to be purchased (Ss. 117–119),[6] and the sale of superfluous land (Ss. 120–127).[7]

The Acquisition of Land (Authorization Procedure) (Sc.) Act, 1947, regulates the compulsory purchase of land by local authorities, where authorized by any Act prior to that Act, with certain exceptions, by certain ministries under certain powers, and in future cases where the 1947 Act is incorporated.[8] The procedure is embodied in Schedule I of the Act. There must be a compulsory purchase order by the acquiring authority, advertised, and copies served on owners, lessees and occupiers.[9] If no objection is made, the confirming authority may confirm it; if objections are made the confirming authority must cause a public inquiry to be held, in accordance with Schedule IV, or afford any objector an opportunity of appearing before and being heard by a person appointed by the confirming authority for the purpose, and the acquiring authority an opportunity of being heard also. The confirming authority may then consider the objections and the report of the person who held the inquiry and confirm the order with or without modifications. After confirmation, the acquiring authority must publish the fact of confirmation and serve a notice thereof on the owners, lessees and occupiers. Similar provision is made for

[1] *Macfarlane* v. *Monklands Ry. Co.* (1864) 2 M. 519, 529; *Elgin Mags.* v. *Highland Ry.* (1884) 11 R. 950; *Inverness Mags.* v. *Highland Ry.* (1893) 20 R. 551; *Inverness Mags.* v. *Highland Ry.*, 1909 S.C. 943; *Fraser* v. *Caledonian Ry.*, 1911 S.C. 145; *Heriot's Trust, supra.*

[2] *Glasgow District Subway Co.* v. *Johnstone* (1892) 20 R. (J.) 28.

[3] cf. *Glasgow City and District Ry. Co.* v. *Mackenzie* (1883) 10 R. 894; *Glasgow Coal Exchange Co.* v. *Glasgow City and District Ry. Co.* (1883) 10 R. 1283; *Glasgow, Yoker & Clydebank Ry. Co.* v. *Moore* (1894) 1 S.L.T. 498; *Bryson & McIntosh* v. *Caledonian Ry.* (1894) 2 S.L.T. 90; *Caledonian Ry.* v. *Turcan* (1898) 25 R. (H.L.) 7.

[4] cf. *Campbell's Trs.* v. *L.N.E. Ry.*, 1930 S.C. 182.

[5] cf. *Hunter* v. *N.B. Ry.* (1849) 12 D. 37.

[6] *Davidson's Trs.* v. *Caledonian Ry.* (1894) 21 R. 1060.

[7] cf. *Glover's Trs.* v. *City of Glasgow Union Ry.* (1869) 7 M. 338; *Caledonian Ry.* v. *City of Glasgow Union Ry.* (1871) 9 M. (H.L.) 115; *N.B. Ry.* v. *Moon's Trs.* (1879) 6 R. 640; *Stewart* v. *Highland Ry.* (1889) 16 R. 580; *Macfie* v. *Callander and Oban Ry.* (1898) 25 R. (H.L.) 19; *Brown* v. *N.B. Ry.* (1906) 8 F. 534; *N.B. Ry.* v. *Birrell's Trs.*, 1918 S.C. (H.L.) 33.

[8] e.g. Housing (Sc.) Act, 1966, Ss. 14, 20, 23, 81, 135, 143, 175, 176; cf. *Scottish Aviation* v. *Lord Advocate*, 1951 S.C. 33; *Peter Holmes & Son* v. *Secretary of State for Scotland*, 1965 S.C. 1.

[9] cf. *McMillan* v. *Inverness C.C.*, 1949 S.C. 77.

compulsory purchase by Ministers (Sched. I, Part II). Special provision is made for certain descriptions of land (Sched. I, Part III). A person aggrieved by a compulsory purchase order may appeal to the Court of Session within six weeks from the notice of confirmation on specified and limited grounds only (Sched. I, Part IV).[1] Where land is acquired compulsorily certain public rights of way over the land may be extinguished. The Lands Clauses Acts are deemed incorporated with the enactment under which compulsory purchase under Schedule I is authorized, with certain modifications (Sched. II).

Compensation is governed by the Land Compensation (Sc.) Act, 1963.[2] Under that Act any question of disputed compensation falls to be determined by one of a panel of official arbiters (S. 2). Once it is established such questions will be referred to the Lands Tribunal for Scotland (S. 8). Rules are provided for the assessment of compensation (Ss. 12–24).[3] The official arbiter's decision on any question of fact is final and binding but he may, and shall, if the Court of Session directs, state a special case for the opinion of that court on any question of law (S. 3). The parties may refer any question of disputed compensation to the Commissioners of Inland Revenue or to an arbiter chosen by the parties (S. 6).

Acquisition by the Land Commission

The Land Commission has power to acquire by agreement or, on being authorized to do so under the Land Commission Act, 1967, compulsorily,[4] any land which in their opinion is land suitable for material development, and any land contiguous or adjacent to that land which in their opinion is required for the purpose of executing works for facilitating the development or use of the first land.[5] The Acquisition of Land (Authorization Procedure) (Sc.) Act, 1947, applies to any such acquisition, with modifications.[6] A special simplified procedure applies for a limited period after the commencement of the Commission's operations.[7]

[1] e.g. *Watson* v. *Lord Advocate*, 1956 S.C. 302.

[2] Consolidating the Acquisition of Land (Assessment of Compensation) Act, 1919, and certain other enactments.

[3] cf. *Venables* v. *Dept. of Agriculture*, 1932 S.C. 573; *McEwing* v. *Renfrewshire C.C.*, 1960 S.C. 53; *Robertson's Trs.* v. *Glasgow Corpn.*, 1967 S.C. 124.

[4] Land Commission Act, 1967, S. 6(3)–(7).

[5] Ibid., S. 6(1) and (2).

[6] Ibid., S. 7.

[7] Ibid., S. 8 and Sched. 2.

When a compulsory purchase order authorizing the Commission to acquire land has come into operation, the Commission may execute a general vesting declaration vesting the land in themselves, containing a particular description of the lands affected or a description by reference under the Conveyancing (Sc.) Act, 1874, S. 61, and serve on occupiers and others who have given information to the Commission with respect to any of the land a notice specifying the land and stating the effect of the declaration. At the end of the period specified therein, the provisions of the Lands Clauses Acts, the Railways Clauses Consolidation (Sc.) Act, 1845, S. 6 (both as incorporated by Sched. 2 to the Acquisition of Land (Authorization Procedure) (Sc.) Act, 1947, and the Land Compensation (Sc.) Act, 1963) apply. The declaration has to be recorded in the General Register of Sasines.[1] A compulsory purchase order must be similarly recorded.[2]

JUDICIAL SALE OR FORECLOSURE

Involuntary transfer also takes place where land is sold in the creditor's exercise of his power of sale under a bond and disposition in security, or if he forecloses under such a bond.[3]

DEATH

On the death of an owner of lands his interest in the lands vests, if he died intestate quoad the land, in his executor, to be held and disposed of in accordance with the law of intestate succession,[4] and if he died testate quoad the land, in the executor or trustee appointed by his will, whom failing in the person deemed entitled to the office of executor, to be held and disposed of in accordance with the directions of the deceased's will. This subject is more appropriately considered in the context of succession.[5]

SEQUESTRATION

If an owner of land is sequestrated, the Act and Warrant of the trustee transfers to and vests in him, as at the date of the first deliverance, the whole heritable estate belonging to the bankrupt in Scotland, subject always to such preferable securities as

[1] Ibid., Ss. 9, 10 and Sched. 3.
[2] Ibid., S. 11(2).
[3] Ch. 85, *supra*.
[4] Succession (Sc.) Act, 1964, Ss. 1(1), 14(1).
[5] Ch. 111–12, *infra*.

existed over the land at that date and are not reducible.[1] This is more fully considered in relation to sequestration.[2]

DILIGENCE

Adjudication

Adjudication is the mode of attaching land in security of or in satisfaction of debt, and also the mode whereby the creditor in an obligation to convey lands may judicially obtain title thereto.

Adjudication for debt

Adjudication proceeds by an action in the Court of Session.[3] Adjudgeable subjects include heritage and heritable rights, liferents, reversions, leases, mines, fishings, heritable securities,[4] a personal right to a conveyance of land,[5] and beneficial rights in heritage generally,[6] but not titles of honour, a hereditary office,[7] arrears of rent or interest,[8] lands taken by a railway and being used for their undertaking,[9] moveables and moveable rights, and some other classes of rights. It is available against the debtor's estate whether he be alive or dead, but in the latter case the heir must be called as defender. It proceeds only on a liquid document of debt, or a debt constituted by decree; the debt must be subsisting and not contingent or prescribed, due and payable, and vested in the adjudger. If the debt is not liquid, or there is no written document of debt, or it is conditional the action must be for constitution of the debt and for adjudication. Constitution is not necessary if the debt has been made real by real burden or heritable bond, but in such a case the adjudication must be preceded by an action of poinding the ground, which makes the arrears of interest a real debt and the accumulated principal and interest itself bear interest and become a real burden.[10]

Litigiosity

A notice of a signeted summons of adjudication or of constitution and adjudication may be registered in the Register of

[1] Bankruptcy (Sc.) Act, 1913, S. 97(2). [2] Ch. 108, *infra*.

[3] Adjudications Act, 1672 (c. 45), and Titles to Land (Consolidation) (Sc.) Act, 1868, S. 59.

[4] 1868 Act, S. 117; *Hare* (1889) 17 R. 105.

[5] *Watson* v. *Wilson* (1868) 6 M. 258. [6] *Stewart* v. *Forbes* (1888) 15 R. 383.

[7] *E. Lauderdale* v. *Scrymgeour Wedderburn*, 1910 S.C. (H.L.) 35.

[8] *Broughton* v. *Fraser* (1832) 10 S. 418.

[9] *Glover's Trs.* v. *Glasgow Union Ry. Co.* (1869) 7 M. 328.

[10] Mackay, *Manual*, 518.

Inhibitions and Adjudications, whereby the lands concerned are rendered litigious,[1] so that the debtor cannot alienate the lands to the prejudice of the creditor, but neither action nor decree has this effect unless the decree of adjudication is recorded in the appropriate Register of Sasines.[2] Notices of litigiosity prescribe in five years[3] and it cannot be founded on after six months from the final decree in the action creating it.[3] Even when completed litigiosity strikes only at voluntary deeds and does not affect those granted in implement of prior obligations.

Competition among adjudgers

All adjudications prior to that first made effectual, and all led subsequently, within a year and a day, rank *pari passu*.[4] Sequestration is statutorily equivalent to a decree of adjudication as at the date of the first deliverance, and consequently other adjudications not made effectual within a year and a day before that date confer no preferential right.[5]

Completion of title

Heritable property not requiring sasine is vested in the adjudger by the decree alone. Where the property is feudal, a decree of adjudication is, except in the case of heritable securities, equivalent to a disposition of the lands in favour of the adjudger, and he may complete title by recording the decree, or expeding a notarial instrument or notice of title thereon, and recording it in the Register of Sasines.[6] Title to heritable securities adjudged is completed by recording the abbreviate of adjudication or the extract decree in the Register of Sasines,[7] and title to long leases by recording the extract decree.[8]

Redemption; expiry of the legal

The right acquired by an adjudger is a judicial security, not a right of property[9] and the debtor retains a right of redemption for ten years, called 'the legal' (i.e. legal period of redemption).[10] On the expiry of the legal the adjudging creditor may foreclose by

[1] Titles to Land Consolidation (Sc.) Act, 1868, S. 159, and Sched. RR.
[2] Conveyancing (Sc.) Act, 1924, S. 44(2).
[3] 1924 Act, S. 44(3).
[4] Bankruptcy Act, 1661 (c. 62); Bell, *Comm.* I, 721.
[5] Bankruptcy (Sc.) Act, 1913, S. 103.
[6] Conveyancing (Sc.) Acts, 1874, S. 62; 1924, S. 4.
[7] 1874 Act, S. 65; 1924 Act, S. 4(3).
[8] Registration of Leases (Sc.) Act, 1857, S. 10, amd. 1924 Act, S. 27.
[9] *Hill* v. *Hill* (1871) 10 M. 3.
[10] *Grindley* v. *Drysdale* (1833) 11 S. 896; *Cochrane* v. *Bogle* (1850) 7 Bell, 65.

obtaining decree in an action of declarator of expiry of the legal, decree in which excludes redemption by the debtor.[1] Decree of expiry of the legal may be reopened, e.g. if the debtor has been a minor during part of the legal and was abroad,[2] or reduced.[3] If no such action be raised the lands remain redeemable though the legal has expired.[4] Alternatively decree of adjudication followed by charter and sasine, or their modern equivalent, recording in the Register of Sasines, and possession thereunder for 40 years after expiry of the legal excludes redemption.[5] But a decree of adjudication, infeftment thereon, charter of confirmation and decree of expiry of the legal do not constitute as '*ex facie* valid irredeemable title to an estate in land' sufficient to found a title by twenty years' prescription.[6]

Payment and Extinction

If the debtor pays off all sums due to the creditor, the adjudication may be extinguished automatically and the debtor's infeftment revive,[7] but he may obtain decree of declarator of extinction and payment, or of reduction and extinction.

Adjudication in security

Adjudication in security is competent if the term of payment of a debt constituted by writing has not arrived,[8] or where the debt is future or contingent.[9] In this form of adjudication there is no legal limit of time for redemption.

Adjudication on debita fundi

Adjudication is competent on such *debita fundi* as heritable bonds, ground annuals, feuduties, and debts constituted real burdens on land, but attaches only to the lands affected by the burden. Such adjudications need not be intimated,[10] nor do they rank *pari passu* under the Bankruptcy Act, 1661. In a competition of adjudgers adjudications on *debita fundi* are preferable to all adjudications on personal debts; *inter se* they have preference according to priority of infeftment. An adjudger may secure preference for arrears of interest by obtaining decree in an action of

1 *Govan* v. *G.* (1758) 2 Paton 27.
2 *Aitken* v. *Aitken* (1809) Bell, *Comm.* I, 744.
3 *Paul* v. *Reid*, 8 Feb. 1814, F.C.
4 *Govan, supra.*
5 *Spence* v. *Bruce*, 21 Jan. 1807, F.C.
6 *Hinton* v. *Connell's Trs.* (1883) 10 R. 1110.
7 Ersk. II, 12, 37.
8 Ersk. II, 12, 42.
9 *Queensberry's Exors.* v. *Tait*, 11 June 1817, F.C.
10 *Young* v. *Scott* (1893) 1 S.L.T. 15.

poinding of the ground, subsequently accumulating principal and interest and adjudging for the total, with interest.

Adjudication in implement

This form of diligence is appropriate where a party has contracted to sell or dispone land in security but refuses voluntarily to convey the lands.[1] The procedure is by action of adjudication in implement. Decree declares the lands to belong to the purchaser, or to be conveyed as security for a loan, as the case may be.[2] This action also lay against the heir of the obligee, the appropriate form being by action of constitution and adjudication,[3] but these provisions have been repealed[4] without making any special provision for such an action being brought against the executor of a deceased obligee. It is also appropriate where no person can be traced who could give a title.[5] This has been held to be the proper way of making up the title of a general disponee of the purchaser of a house where the disponer had died and his heirs could not be found and the disponee had died.[6] The effect of decree is equivalent to a conveyance in ordinary form of the lands contained therein granted in favour of the adjudger. The adjudger completes his title by infeftment on the decree as on a conveyance.[7] In this form of action there is no question of ranking of adjudgers, nor of redemption, the transference effected by decree being absolute and irredeemable.

1 Bell, *Comm.* I, 783; Menzies, 778.

2 *Macgregor* v. *Macdonald* (1843) 5 D. 888.

3 Titles to Land Consolidation (Sc.) Act, 1868, S. 60.

4 Succession (Sc.) Act, 1964, Sched. 3.

5 e.g. *Stewart* v. *Tennant* (1868) 5 S.L.R. 684.

6 *Cunningham's Exor.* v. *Millar's Heirs* (1902) 10 S.L.T. 109.

7 1868 Act, S. 62, as amd. 1869, S. 4, replaced by Conveyancing (Sc.) Acts, 1874, S. 62; 1924 Act, S. 4.

CHAPTER 91

EXTINCTION OF INTERESTS IN LAND

Consolidation

A SUPERIORITY of lands is extinguished by sale to or inheritance by the over-superior and consolidation with the over-superiority. The vassal's estate is extinguished if the superior purchases or inherits the fee, or the vassal purchases or inherits the superiority. The purchaser or successor in each case completes his title to each feudal estate in the usual way and records a minute of consolidation in the Register of Sasines,[1] or appends a minute of consolidation to the disposition to him of the interest later acquired and records it with that disposition.[2] Consolidation is not effected *ipso jure* when both estates come to be vested in one person,[3] nor can two estates not in immediate proximity in the chain of tenure be consolidated, e.g. over-superiority and fee.

Consolidation is also effected by prescription, if the superiority contains the lands in question and it and the lands are possessed on infeftment for the prescriptive period.[4]

Consolidation does not extinguish the fee of the property, but merely unites superiority and fee.[5] The destination of the superiority rules the fee also.[6]

Forfeiture of superiority

Prior to 1847 heirs of a vassal desiring entry could charge a superior who had not completed his own title to the *dominium directum* to do so under penalty of forfeiture of casualties. If the superior did not make up a title, the vassal's heir could obtain

1 Conveyancing Act, 1874, S. 6. Methods of consolidation competent prior to that Act are still competent, viz. resignation *ad remanentiam* and possession of both estates for the prescriptive period: see Bell, *Prin.* §787–91, 821; Bell, *Convg.* II, 781; Menzies, 619; *Walker* v. *Grieve* (1827) 5 S. 469; *Wilson* v. *Pollok* (1839) 2 D. 159.

2 Conveyancing (Sc.) Act, 1924, S. 11, and Sched. G.

3 *Morton* (1668) Mor. 6917; *Bald* v. *Buchanan* (1786) Mor. 15084, 15089; 2 Ross L.C. 210, 230; see also *Park's Curator* v. *Black* (1870) 8 M. 671; *E. Zetland* v. *Glover Incorpn. of Perth* (1870) 8 M. (H.L.) 144.

4 *L. Elibank* v. *Campbell* (1833) 12 S. 74; 3 Ross L.C. 534; *Bontine* v. *Graham* (1840) 1 Rob. 347; *Wilson* v. *Pollock* (1839) 2 D. 159; *Gordon's Trs.* (1849) 21 S. Jur. 174.

5 *E. Zetland* v. *Glover Incorporation of Perth* (1870) 8 M. (H.L.) 144.

6 *Pattison* v. *Dunn's Trs.* (1868) 6 M. (H.L.) 147; *Park's Curator* v. *Black* (1870) 8 M. 671.

decree of tinsel of the superiority, and then charge the over-superior to enter him, and so up to the Crown, who would always enter him.[1] The Titles to Land Consolidation (Sc.) Act, 1868, S. 104, re-enacting an Act of 1847, provides that where a superior had not completed his feudal title, it is competent for a party entitled to obtain an entry to the lands to petition the court to have the superior ordained to complete his title and grant an entry and if he will not, to obtain decree declaring that the superior has forfeited all right to the superiority. The Conveyancing Act, 1874, S. 4, superseded these provisions by making infeftment imply entry with the superior whether the latter's title had been completed or not.

Relinquishment of superiority

A superior may also relinquish his right of superiority in favour of his immediate vassal by a deed of relinquishment which, when accepted by the vassal, recorded in the Register of Sasines, and followed by a writ of investiture by the over-superior, extinguishes the superiority and brings the vassal into an immediate relation of tenure with the next over-superior, subject to no greater duties and casualties than if the superior had remained vassal of the over-superior.[2]

Tinsel of the feu

The feu may be forfeited to the superior if the latter is entitled to involve the statutory irritancy *ob non solutum canonem* or a conventional irritancy contained in the feu-charter.[3] Decree of declarator of irritancy annuls the vassal's rights and all that has followed thereon, including the rights of subvassals.[4]

Statutory expropriation

An expropriating statute may acquire not only the *dominium utile* of land but any rights of superiority therein other than of the Crown, and accordingly extinguish all other feudal interests in that land.[5] But in an acquisition under the Lands Clauses Consolidation (Sc.) Act, 1845, the titles granted, unless specially provided for, do not affect the right of superiority.[6]

[1] Bell, *Convg.* II, 788; Menzies, 834; *Dickson* v. *L. Elphinstone* (1802) Mor. 15024; *Rossmore's Trs.* v. *Brownlie* (1877) 5 R. 201.

[2] Titles to Land Consolidation (Sc.) Act, 1868, Ss. 110–112.

[3] Ch. 78, *supra*.

[4] *Cassels* v. *Lamb* (1885) 12 R. 722; *Sandeman* v. *Scottish Property Investment Co.* (1885) 12 R. (H.L.) 67.

[5] Coal Industry Nationalization Act, 1946, Ss. 5, 64(3), and Sched. 1: *Wanchope Settlement Trs.* v. *N.C.B.*, 1947 S.N. 185.

[6] 1845 Act, S. 126.

PART 3

INCORPOREAL HERITABLE PROPERTY

CHAPTER 92

INCORPOREAL HERITABLE PROPERTY

THE class of incorporeal heritable property includes those rights deemed heritable, and which accordingly formerly devolved on heirs rather than on next of kin by reason of their actual or supposed connection with land, but which are incapable of actual possession and can be vindicated only by action. Among heritable rights which, though in themselves incorporeal, are necessarily connected with particular parcels of corporeal land are all real rights in land, rights of superiority, ownership of land in fee, title to teinds, rights to leases, servitudes, some heritable securities, and claims to feuduties, and rents.[1] Among those not so connected but consisting in legal right only are *jura crediti* to heritage, annuities and similar rights having a tract of future time. Other incorporeal rights deemed heritable are some cases of commercial goodwill, heritable offices, titles of honour, and armorial bearings.

Succession

Formerly all incorporeal heritable rights passed to the heir-at-law on the holder's death, but they now pass to his executor for purposes of administration,[2] except for titles, coats of arms, honours or dignities transmissible on the death of the holder, which still devolve on the heir-at-law.[3]

Jus crediti

A *jus crediti* is a personal right enforceable by action to have payment or delivery of something; it need not be presently exigible but must be effectual in competition with the granter's creditors. It may be heritable or moveable according to the nature

1 Bell, *Comm.* II, 4; but arrears of interest on heritable securities, of feuduties and of rents are moveable: Ersk. II, 9, 64; Bell, *Prin.* §1479.

2 Succession (Sc.) Act, 1964, S. 14.

3 Ibid., S. 37(1).

and quality of the thing or fund against which the claim lies.[1] It will be heritable accordingly if it is a right to transfer of some heritable subject. Among such heritable *jura crediti* have been an obligation to infeft an heir at a determinate date or age,[2] a claim to heritage held under trust[3] and a claim to improvement expenditure not charged on the estate by the maker but bequeathed by him.[4]

Annuities

An annuity is a right continuing for a period of time, carrying a stated yearly profit to the creditor unrelated to any capital sum or stock.[5] It may be payable for any period, according to the gift or contract creating it, but commonly for the granter's, or grantee's, or a third party's, life. An annuity may be unsecured or secured over heritage (by bond of annuity and disposition in security), or made a real burden by reservation.[6] It may be declared alimentary,[7] in which case it cannot be attached by creditors save for alimentary debts,[8] unless in so far as it exceeds a reasonable sum[9] and as regards arrears.[10] Annuities are by nature heritable in the creditor's succession,[11] but if secured over heritage or by real burden they are moveable in the cases affected by the Titles to Land Consolidation (Sc.) Act, 1868, S. 117, as amended. As they become due the termly payments are always moveable.[12] They burden the debtor's heritable succession[13] and, though payable primarily out of income, must in case of deficiency be paid from capital.[14]

[1] Bell, *Comm.* I, 36; II, 4; *Prin.* §1482; *Buchanan* v. *Angus* (1862) 4 Macq. 374; *Young* v. *Martin* (1868) 5 S.L.R. 230.

[2] *Douglas* v. *Douglas and Drummond* (1724) Mor. 12910.

[3] *Durie* v. *Coutts* (1791) Mor. 4624; *Thain* v. *T.* (1891) 18 R. 1196; contrast *Wardlaw's Trs.* v. *W.* (1880) 7 R. 1070; *Gilligan* v. *G.* (1891) 18 R. 387; *Borland's Trs.* v. *B.*, 1917 S.C. 704.

[4] *E. Kintore* v. *Ctss. of Kintore* (1885) 12 R. 1213.

[5] Ersk. II, 2, 6; Bell, *Comm.* II, 4; *Prin.* §1480.

[6] *Buchanan* v. *Eaton*, 1911 S.C. (H.L.) 40.

[7] See *Elliott* v. *Purdom* (1895) 22 R. (H.L.) 26; *Douglas Gardiner & Mill* v. *Mackintosh's Trs.*, 1916 S.C. 125.

[8] *Harvey* v. *Calder* (1840) 2 D. 1095; *Lewis* v. *Anstruther* (1853) 15 D. 263.

[9] *Livingstone* v. *L.* (1886) 14 R. 43.

[10] Bell, *Comm.* I, 127.

[11] Bell, *Prin.* §1480; *Reid* v. *McWalter* (1878) 5 R. 630.

[12] *Hill* v. *H.* (1872) 11 M. 247; *M. Breadalbane's Trs.* v. *Jamieson* (1873) 11 M. 912; *Reid*, *supra*.

[13] *Mackintosh* v. *M's Trs.* (1873) 11 M. (H.L.) 28; *Breadalbane's Trs.*, *supra*; *Moon's Trs.* v. *M.* (1899) 2 F. 201.

[14] *Knox's Trs.* v. *K.* (1869) 7 M. 873; *Kinmond's Trs.* v. *K.* (1873) 11 M. 381; *Adamson's Trs.* v. *A's Exors.* (1891) 18 R. 1133; *Colquhoun's Trs.* v. *C.*, 1922 S.C. 32.

Goodwill

Commercial goodwill is the advantage of the connection or reputation of a business, which attaches customers to it and leads them to continue to patronize that business.[1] It may attach to a business in whole or in part by reason of the locality or premises in which the business is carried on, or in whole or in part by reason of the personality of those conducting the business, their reputation, service or other personal factors. Accordingly, goodwill may be heritable or moveable or partly both; it depends on the circumstances of the case.[2] If goodwill is heritable, it can be sold and assigned only along with the heritable property to which it attaches.

Heritable offices

Certain of the great Offices of State of Scotland are heritable, being held *jure sanguinis*, and the right thereto is not personal but an incorporeal heritable right.[3] Though heritable, such an office is not, in general, alienable or adjudgeable, or otherwise *in commercio*.[4]

Titles of honour

The dignities of grades of peerage are created by the Crown and are heritable,[5] being presumed destined to the grantee and the heirs male of his body,[6] though a special destination may be provided in the patent of ennoblement,[7] and peerages may now be

[1] *Trego* v. *Hunt* [1896] A.C. 7.

[2] *Hughes* v. *Assessor for Stirling* (1892) 19 R. 840; *Philp's Exor.* v. *Philp's Exor.* (1894) 21 R. 482; *Leishman* v. *Glen & Henderson* (1899) 6 S.L.T. 328; *Ross* v. *R's Trs.* (1901) 9 S.L.T. 340; *Town and County Bank* v. *McBain* (1902) 9 S.L.T. 485; *Murray's Tr.* v. *McIntyre* (1904) 6 F. 588; *Graham* v. *G's Trs.* (1904) 6 F. 1015; *Muirhead's Trs.* v. *M.* (1905) 7 F. 496; see also *Barr* v. *Lions, Ltd.*, 1956 S.C. 59.

[3] e.g. High Constable of Scotland: Countess of Erroll; Hereditary Standard Bearer for Scotland: Earl of Dundee; see also *E. Lauderdale* v. *Scrymgeour Wedderburn*, 1910 S.C. (H.L.) 35; Hereditary Keeper of Palace of Holyroodhouse: Duke of Hamilton; of Falkland: Major Michael Crichton-Stuart; of Dunstraffnage: Duke of Argyll; of Stirling: Earl of Mar and Kellie; Hereditary Master of the Queen's Household in Scotland: Duke of Argyll; Principle Usher to the Crown in Scotland: see *Walker Trs.* v. *Lord Advocate*, 1912 S.C. (H.L.) 12; Earl Marshal: see *Bower* v. *Earl Mareschal* (1682) 2 B.S. 18; 3 B.S. 420; Lord Clerk Register: Duke of Buccleuch and Queensberry; see also Act of Union, 1707, S. 20. Other great Offices of State (Lord Justice General, Lord Advocate, Lord Justice Clerk, Solicitor General) are personal and not heritable.

[4] See further *Walker Trs., supra*; *E. Lauderdale, supra.*

[5] Ersk. II, 2, 6; Bell, *Comm.* I, 120; *Prin.* §1481.

[6] *Kennedy* v. *E. of Ruglen and March* (1762) 2 Pat. 55; *Glencairn Peerage* (1797) 1 Macq. 444.

[7] *Herries Peerage Claim* (1858) 3 Macq. 588.

created for the grantee's lifetime only,[1] or a hereditary peerage renounced for the lifetime of the renouncing heir.[2] Hereditary peerages descend *jure sanguinis* according to the destination in the grant, and vest without service or possession.[3] The dignity of peerage is indivisible and incapable of sale or assignation.

The dignity of baronet is similarly heritable, normally destined to the heir male of the first grantee, and vests without service, though service has been the normal mode of establishing a right of succession.

Knighthood is the lowest dignity or title of honour but is personal and not heritable.

Armorial bearings

The grant of arms is part of the royal prerogative[4] but the grant, differencing and registration of arms has long been exercised by the Lord Lyon King of Arms.[5] Arms are a recognised form of incorporeal heritable property held of the Crown and legally protected against infringement.[6] The Public Register of All Arms and Bearings in Scotland is to armorial bearings what the Register of Sasines is to corporeal heritable property. A grant of arms confers on the grantee a right to bear the full undifferenced arms of the grant, and a similar right in perpetuity to the person who is at the time the heir of the grantee according to the grant.

A grant is deemed to be destined to the grantee and his male heirs-at-law.[7] Grants are normally to the grantee and his descendants, or to a series of heirs of entail. Arms, once granted and registered, vest in the heir *jure sanguinis* and without service or sasine, though service or rematriculation may be the best evidence that it has vested.

Clauses are sometimes included in settlements requiring the heir under the deed to assume the name and arms of the granter. In such a case the grantee must constructively resign the arms to the Crown for new grant, by petitioning Lyon, who may give effect to the settler's desires in such mode as he deems right. The

[1] Life Peerages Act, 1958.
[2] Peerage Act, 1963.
[3] Ersk. III, 8, 77.
[4] *McDonell* v. *Macdonald* (1846) 4 Sh. App. 371.
[5] Lyon King of Arms Acts, 1592 (c. 29), 1669 (c. 95), 1672 (c. 47). See also *Cuninghame* v. *Cunyngham* (1849) 11 D. 1139; *Stewart-Mackenzie* v. *Fraser-Mackenzie*, 1922 S.C. (H.L.) 39.
[6] *Cuninghame, supra.*
[7] Stevenson, *Heraldry in Scotland*, 335.

extent and manner of implementing the conditions of the deed depend on its terms.[1] An heir is deemed to have satisfied an arms condition if he has made an unsuccessful application to Lyon for authority to bear the prescribed arms.[2]

Armorial bearings cannot be sold, assigned or transferred *inter vivos*.

[1] *Hunter* v. *Weston* (1882) 9 R. 492; *Munro's Trs.* v. *Spencer*, 1912 S.C. 933; *Munro-Lucas-Tooth*, 1965 S.L.T. (Lyon Ct.) 2; *Munro's Trs.* v. *Monson*, 1962 S.C. 414; 1965 S.C. 84.

[2] cf. *Moir of Leckie* (1794) Mor. 15537.

PART 4

CORPOREAL MOVEABLE PROPERTY

CHAPTER 93

CORPOREAL MOVEABLE PROPERTY—TITLE THERETO AND RIGHTS THEREIN

CORPOREAL moveable property comprises all things having a physical corpus capable of actual possession and which alone formerly transmitted to next of kin on death.[1] It includes animals, clothing, books, pictures, furniture, implements, raw materials, manufactured goods, ships, vehicles and aircraft, banknotes and coin, and in general all things which are physically moveable.[2] Some things legally heritable may become moveable, e.g. trees, on being felled, or conversely things moveable may cease to be moveable, e.g. by fixtures being attached to heritage.[3]

Two legal interests are recognised in corporeal moveables, property or ownership, and possession.

OWNERSHIP

As contrasted with land, where several proprietary estates and interests may co-exist at one time in the one piece of land, there is only one interest of a proprietary nature in moveables, viz. dominion or absolute ownership, which implies, at least at common law, absolute and exclusive liberty of dealing with the object in any way possible, using, consuming, enjoying, letting, selling, bequeathing, giving away or otherwise dealing with it.[4] Ownership is the totality of powers of use and disposal allowed by law. The owner may relinquish for a time some of the bundle of rights which collectively amount to ownership without sacrificing ownership altogether, as by lending or letting the goods on hire to another, retaining the radical right.

[1] Since the Succession (Sc.) Act, 1964, all property, both heritable, with limited exceptions, and moveable, now vests in the owner's executor on the owner's death.

[2] Bell, *Comm.* I, 100, 176; cf. Sale of Goods Act, 1893, S. 62(1) defining 'goods' as 'all corporeal moveables except money'.

[3] cf. Bell, *Prin.* §1283, 1285, 1470.

[4] Bell, *Prin.* §1284.

The acquisition of ownership may be original, by first appropriation of something hitherto unowned, or by creation of a new subject of property,[1] or derivative, by acquisition or transference from another of something hitherto owned by him.[2] Ownership may be lost by transfer to another, by consumption or use, or by dereliction.[3]

Title to corporeal moveables

In general a person's title to the ownership of corporeal moveables is not evidenced by any kind of written title.[4] To this there are certain exceptions.

Every British ship,[5] except river boats or coasters not exceeding 15 tons burthen, must be registered with the Registrar of Shipping and the register is the evidence of title to the ship;[6] possession does not prove title to it.[7] The register discloses the ownership of the 64 shares into which the property in a ship may be divided.[8] The register does not record trusts.[9] A registered owner of a ship or share thereof has an absolute power of disposal of his share, but interests arising under contract or other equitable interests may be enforced against owners or mortgagees of ships in respect of their interest therein in the same way as in respect of other moveable property.[10]

Aircraft must be registered with the Ministry of Aviation, the register showing the person or persons appearing to the Minister to be owners for the time being of that aircraft, who must be persons qualified to be owners of an aircraft so registered.[11]

Motor vehicles must, on being first licensed, be registered with the local authority for the area in which the vehicle is ordinarily kept, and a registration book is issued to the registered owner.[12]

[1] Bell, *Prin.* §1286; Ch. 94, *infra.*

[2] Bell, *Prin.* §1286; Ch. 95, *infra.*

[3] Ch. 96, *infra.*

[4] Some evidence of ownership may, however, be provided by, e.g., a receipt for purchase of goods, if identified with the goods in dispute and good evidence is provided by, e.g., a name or library stamp on a book, or a medallion on a dog's collar.

[5] Defined, Merchant Shipping Act, 1894, S. 1.

[6] 1894 Act, S. 5.

[7] *Hooper* v. *Gumm* (1867) L.R. 2 Ch. 282.

[8] A corporate body, or not more than five persons jointly, may be registered as owning a share: S. 5. Under the Sea Fishing Boats (Sc.) Act, 1886, sea fishing boats are owned in 16 shares by not more than 16 individuals.

[9] 1894 Act, S. 56.

[10] 1894 Act, S. 57.

[11] Air Navigation Order, 1960, art. 2.

[12] Road Vehicles (Registration and Licensing) Regulations, 1955.

The registration book is issued to the person by whom the vehicle is kept and used and the name appearing therein may not be the legal owner of the vehicle. The registration book is not a document of title,[1] but it is evidence of title.[2]

Documents of title to goods

In the case of goods which are the subjects of commercial dealings, documents of title thereto, such as bills of lading under which they are shipped, dock warrants or warehouse warrants under which goods are stored, or delivery orders on a warehouse keeper, are customarily treated as equivalent to the goods themselves, and may be pledged or transferred on sale as if they were the goods themselves.[3] But such are not permanent title-deeds of moveable property in the way the title deeds of heritage are.

Joint and common property in moveables

Moveable property is vested in parties jointly if not only is it possessed *pro indiviso* but they have but one title to the whole property which on the death of one joint owner accresces to the survivors. The ownership of trustees is joint. It is vested in parties in common if, though enjoyed in common, each has a separate title to a determinate share, which transmits separately, and if each can call on the others to divide the property, or sell their shares, or sell the property and divide the proceeds. Where persons have collaborated in producing a new thing by each contributing labour or materials or both, the thing belongs to them as common property in shares proportional to the value of their respective contributions.[4] Whether moveable property belongs to persons jointly or in common may depend on the means of acquisition of the property, or on the terms of any gift or bequest of it to them. A gift or bequest to several persons is joint, but if there are words of severance such as 'equally' or 'in equal shares' the donees are owners in common.

Ownership by husband and wife

While husband and wife may each own moveables individually, other moveables may belong to them jointly, or in common,

[1] i.e. within the Factors Act, 1889, S. 1(4), applied to Scotland by Factors Act, 1890; see *Joblin* v. *Watkins and Roseneave (Motors), Ltd.* [1949] 1 All E.R. 47.

[2] *Central Newbury Car Auctions, Ltd.* v. *Unity Finance, Ltd.* [1957] 1 Q.B. 371.

[3] Ch. 95, *infra*. 'Documents of title' are statutorily defined in the Factors Act, 1889, S. 1(4), applied to Scotland by Factors (Sc.) Act, 1890.

[4] *Wylie & Lochhead* v. *Mitchell* (1870) 8 M. 552. In this and some other cases no proper distinction is drawn between joint and common property.

depending on the source and mode of acquisition of the property.[1]

The Married Women's Property Act, 1964, provides that money derived from any housekeeping allowance or similar provision made by the husband and any property acquired out of such money shall, in the absence of contrary agreement, be treated as belonging to the spouses in equal shares.[2] It is uncertain whether the right in any property acquired is joint or in common.

Ownership of moveables in liferent and fee

It is competent to grant a proper liferent of moveables, such as those in a house granted in liferent;[3] but a proper liferent cannot be constituted over fungibles, which perish by use, but only over such moveables as wear out only so gradually that they will normally continue fit for use beyond the normal duration of a liferent.[4] A liferent of moveables is normally achieved through the intervention of a trust, in which case the liferenter's obligation is to maintain the stock of moveables and replace it as it becomes worn out[5] though the liferenter may consume fungibles.[6]

POSSESSION

Possession is a factual relationship between a person and a corporeal moveable, the holding of the object as against other persons. It is distinguishable into natural possession, or actual possession by the owner himself, and civil possession, which is possession through an intermediary such as an employee.[7] Two elements are relevant to possession, *animus possidendi*, or the mental claim to hold the thing as against others or to retrieve it from them, and *corpus possessionis*, or the actual control of the thing.[8] To acquire legal possession of moveables requires both elements; once possession has been acquired it may be retained though either element be lacking, at least temporarily;[9] and possession can be lost only when both elements are permanently

[1] See *Re Roger's Question* [1948] 1 All E.R. 328; *Rimmer* v. *R.* [1953] 1 Q.B. 63.

[2] cf. *Pyatt* v. *P.*, 1966 S.L.T. (Notes) 73.

[3] cf. *Fraser* v. *Croft* (1898) 25 R. 496; but see Lord Dunedin's dictum in *Miller* v. *Inland Revenue*, 1930 S.C. (H.L.) 49, 56.

[4] Ersk. II, 9, 40; *Rogers* v. *Scott* (1867) 5 M. 1078; *Miller's Trs.* v. *M.*, 1907 S.C. 833.

[5] *Rogers, supra.*

[6] *Miller's Trs., supra.*

[7] Ersk. II, 1, 22; Bell, *Prin.* §1312; *Union Bank* v. *Mackenzie* (1865) 3 M. 765; *Moore* v. *Gledden* (1869) 7 M. 1016; *Mitchell's Trs.* v. *Gladstone* (1894) 21 R. 586.

[8] Stair II, 1, 17; Bankt. II, 1, 26; Ersk. II, 1, 20.

[9] e.g. a person absent from home possesses goods therein *animo* but not *facto*; a forgetful person possesses his goods *facto* but not *animo*.

withdrawn, as where one, having 'lost' a thing, gives up the attempt to find it, or puts it out with intent to get rid of it. More than one person can possess concurrently on different rights which do not mutually conflict; thus an owner of moveables and a pledgee thereof both simultaneously possess for their respective rights and interests.[1]

Distinct from possession is mere custody; the custodier has physical control but his *animus* is only to hold it for the lawful possessor; thus an employee normally has control only for behoof of his employer (who has civil possession through him) and not possession.[2]

Possession is of great importance; it is to moveables what sasine is to heritage, the badge of real right,[3] and generally an essential for the existence of a right in security over moveables.

Lawful possession, possession held vi, clam, aut precario

Possession may also be distinguished into that obtained lawfully, and that obtained *vi*, *clam*, *aut precario*.[4] One who possesses *vi*, such as a thief, acquires possession good against all except the true owner, but his possession is not lawful and can never ripen into legal ownership. A possessor *clam*, such as one to whom goods are sent by mistake, acquires possession defeasible by a claim to possession by the true owner or anyone having a title from the owner to possess.[5] A possessor *precario*, such as a gratuitous borrower, may have his right of possession withdrawn at any time at the will of the true owner.

Temporary transfer of possession

Possession of moveable property may be transferred for temporary purposes under the contracts of *commodatum*, deposit, pledge and *locatio* (other than *locatio operarum*). In each case possession only is transferred, for the purposes and subject to the limitations of the contract in question, and not ownership.[6]

Possession in different characters

Persons may have possession of corporeal moveables in many different characters, their rights against the owners and third

[1] Ersk. II, 1, 22–23.

[2] Stair, Bankt, Ersk., *supra*, Bell, *Prin.* §1311; *Dickson* v. *Nicholson* (1855) 17 D. 1011; *Gladstone* v. *McCallum* (1896) 23 R. 782; *Barnton Hotel Co.* v. *Cook* (1899) 1 F. 1190; with which contrast *Meikle & Wilson* v. *Pollard* (1880) 8 R. 69; and *Robertson* v. *Ross* (1887) 15 R. 67; cf. *Sim* v. *Grant* (1862) 24 D. 1033.

[3] *Moore* v. *Gledden* (1869) 7 M. 1076, 1022.

[4] Ersk. II, 1, 23.

[5] cf. *Louson* v. *Craik* (1842) 4 D. 1452.

[6] Chs. 38, 42, 45, *supra*.

parties varying somewhat according to the character in which possession is held. Thus goods may be possessed as owner, as seller who has not delivered,[1] as seller or buyer in possession after sale,[2] as buyer on sale or return,[3] as pledgee, hirer, hire-purchaser, borrower, depositary, in the exercise of a lien, as carrier, poinding creditor, or finder.

Possession presumes ownership

Older authorities lay down that, in a question with a wrongdoer, or a person asserting an adverse title, a possessor of corporeal moveables is presumed to be owner thereof and that one claiming moveables against a possessor must prove not only that he had once been owner, but how he came to lose possession.[4] This is a mere *prima facie* presumption and is today of lesser weight in view of the common practices of holding goods on hire or hire-purchase,[5] but it still applies to the extent that a possessor is entitled to have his possession protected, and to have it restored, if he has been forcibly dispossessed,[6] and he may be required to surrender possession only by proof that the claimant has a continuing title of ownership. Even a thief is entitled to have his possession protected against anyone except the true owner.

Reputed ownership

The doctrine of reputed ownership was to the effect that a person in possession of moveables was reputed their owner and thus deemed entitled to dispose of the moveables and confer a good title. The object of the doctrine was to protect creditors who were misled by the credit acquired by the debtor, by his having been permitted to possess as apparent owner moveables truly belonging to another. Its effect was to bar the true owner from asserting his right of ownership against the creditors.[7] Hence the plea requires some fraud or gross fault on the true owner's part

[1] Sale of Goods Act, 1893, S. 17.

[2] Ibid., S. 25.

[3] Ibid., S. 18, R. 4.

[4] Stair II, 1, 42; III, 2, 7; IV, 30, 9; Ersk. II, 1, 20, 24; Bell, *Prin.* §1313; *Scot* v. *Elliot* (1672) Mor. 12727; *Macdougall* v. *Whitelaw* (1840) 2 D. 500; *Anderson* v. *Buchanan* (1848) 11 D. 270; *Orr's Tr.* v. *Tullis* (1870) 8 M. 936.

[5] *Hopkinson* v. *Napier*, 1953 S.C. 139.

[6] *Spoliatus ante omnia restituendus.*

[7] Ersk. II, 1, 24; III, 5, 5; Bell, *Comm.* I, 269; *Prin.* §1315; *Cargill* v. *Somerville* (1820) Hume 223; *Shearer* v. *Christie* (1842) 5 D. 132, 141; *Edmond* v. *Mowat* (1868) 7 M. 59; *Marston* v. *Kerr's Tr.* (1879) 6 R. 898, 901; *Hewat's Tr.* v. *Smith* (1892) 19 R. 403; *Mitchell's Trs.* v. *Gladstone* (1894) 21 R. 586.

whereby false credit has been given.[1] In modern practice the doctrine is not important because ownership and possession are now so frequently separated that persons dealing with a possessor are not warranted merely by his possession in believing that he is the owner thereof,[2] and there must be other factors present before the owner will be held barred from vindicating his property from a creditor of the possessor.[3] Mere possession does not confer even apparent authority to dispose of the property, and does not preclude the owner from vindicating his property from one who has dealt with the possessor.[4]

Recovery of possession when lost

An owner who loses possession may follow and recover his property without judicial authority so long as he does so *ex incontinenti*, but not *ex intervallo*.[5] He may by action seek redelivery or restitution of his property, or damages in lieu if it be not returned.[6] In the case of illegal dispossession he may seek recovery by action, proving his ownership, and how he lost possession, as by fraud, theft, or deposit, to counter the presumption of property arising from possession. The action lies against the possessor or one who has fraudulently put away the goods to avoid action.[7] It lies against one who, even in good faith, acquired *in bona fide* from one obtaining the goods by fraud,[8] and against anyone who has bought goods stolen,[9] but not against the innocent transferee from a thief of money or negotiable instruments.[10]

[1] *McBain* v. *Wallace* (1881) 8 R. (H.L.) 106; *Bell, Rannie & Co.* v. *Smith* (1885) 22 S.L.R. 597; *Liqdr. of Brechin Auction Co.* v. *Reid* (1895) 22 R. 711; *Glen* v. *Cameron* (1896) 3 S.L.T. 231.

[2] *Bryce* v. *Ehrmann* (1904) 7 F. 5.

[3] *Hopkinson* v. *Napier*, 1953 S.C. 139; cf. *Marston, supra*; *Duncanson* v. *Jefferis' Tr.* (1881) 8 R. 563; *Thomson* v. *Scoular* (1882) 9 R. 430; *Robertson* v. *McIntyre* (1882) 9 R. 772; *Hogarth* v. *Smart's Tr.* (1882) 9 R. 964; *Scott* v. *S's Tr.* (1889) 16 R. 504.

[4] *Robertson* v. *McIntyre* (1882) 9 R. 772; *Mitchell* v. *Heys* (1894) 21 R. 600; *Lamonby* v. *Foulds*, 1928 S.C. 89.

[5] Ersk. II, 1, 23; Bell, *Prin.* §1319.

[6] Bell, *Prin.* §1318; *Gorebridge Co-operative Socy.* v. *Turnbull*, 1952 S.L.T. (Sh. Ct.) 91; *Dalhanna Knitwear Co.* v. *Mohammed Ali*, 1967 S.L.T. (Sh. Ct.) 74. As to recovery of possession of goods let on hire purchase, see Hire Purchase (Sc.) Act, 1965, Ss. 33–48.

[7] Bell, *Prin.* §1320–21.

[8] *Morrisson* v. *Robertson*, 1908 S.C. 322, where intermediate party's title void: *Secus* if intermediate party's title voidable only: *Macleod* v. *Kerr*, 1965 S.C. 253.

[9] Bell, *Comm.*, I, 307; Bell, *Prin.* §1320; *Bp. of Caithness* v. *Edinburgh Fleshers* (1629) Mor. 4145; *Forsyth* v. *Kilpatrick* (1680) Mor. 9120; *Mackay* v. *Forsyth* (1758) Mor. 4944; *Henderson* v. *Gibson* (1806) Mor. Moveables, Appx. 1; *E. Fife's Trs.* v. *Snare* (1849) 11 D. 1119; cf. *Todd* v. *Armour* (1882) 9 R. 901.

[10] *Walker & Watson* v. *Sturrock* (1897) 35 S.L.R. 26; *Gorebridge Co-operative Socy.* v. *Turnbull*, 1952 S.L.T. (Sh. Ct.) 91.

Possession cannot ripen into ownership

No lapse of time converts mere possession of moveables into ownership. But if possession has been initially transferred, as by loan, the owner's claim to recovery will be excluded by the lapse of the long negative prescription.[1]

1 *Parishioners of Aberscherder* v. *Parishioners of Gemrie* (1633) Mor. 10972.

CHAPTER 94

ORIGINAL ACQUISITION OF PROPERTY IN CORPOREAL MOVEABLES

ORIGINAL acquisition of property is acquisition of property in a moveable subject not previously owned by another, as distinct from derivative acquisition from a previous owner. It may be effected in many ways, depending to some extent on the nature of the thing in question.

Occupation

Occupation is the taking possession of a thing not hitherto owned with the intention of acquiring ownership of it.[1] The rule is: *quod nullius est, fit occupantis*. This mode covers taking shells, pearls, pebbles or precious stones on the seashore, wild birds, animals or fish,[2] even though the taking may be penalized or involve trespass on lands or some other contravention of law.[3] Appropriation confers a right of property only when complete, or proceeding towards full accomplishment, as when pursuing a wounded animal.[4] Once appropriated a wild creature cannot be appropriated by another so long as the first holder's possession continues. If a wild creature, reduced to possession, escapes, the owner loses his ownership as soon as he ceases to pursue and the creature reverts to its ownerless state, and it may be validly acquired by any other person who subsequently reduces it to possession.[5]

Creatures which have been domesticated, or carry a mark of ownership, or are confined in a cage or pen or fishpond, or which, though allowed to roam freely, have a homing instinct (*animus revertendi*) such as cats or pigeons or bees, cannot be acquired by anyone who seizes them.[6]

[1] Stair II, 1, 33; Ersk. II, 1, 10; Bell, *Prin.* §1287–94.

[2] *Wilson* v. *Dykes* (1872) 10 M. 444. Royal fish, however, belong to the Crown: Stair, Ersk., *supra*.

[3] *Scott* v. *Everitt* (1853) 15 D. 288; cf. *Livingstone* v. *E. Breadalbane* (1791) 3 Paton 221; *Leith* v. *L.* (1862) 24 D. 1059, 1062.

[4] Stair, *supra*; Bell, *Prin.* §1289. As to whale-fishing, see also *Hutcheson* v. *Dundee Whale-fishing Co.* (1830) 5 Mur. 164; *Sutter* v. *Aberdeen Arctic Co.* (1862) 4 Macq. 355.

[5] Stair, *supra*; Bell, *Prin.* §1290.

[6] Ersk., *supra*; Bell, *Prin.* §1290.

Finding

Things found in a public place, having been lost, forgotten or dropped, are still deemed constructively in the possession of the true owner, so long as he retains *animus possidendi*, and the finder should make restitution to him, if he knows or can reasonably find the true owner. If he cannot do so, the rule is: *quod nullius est, fit domini regis*.[1] The finder acquires no title by finding and commits theft if he appropriates the thing found.[2] But the finder is entitled to possession against anyone other than the true owner.[3]

Under the Burgh Police (Sc.) Act, 1892, S. 412, goods, articles or money found in burghs must under penalty be deposited with the police within 48 hours. If not claimed within six months they may be awarded to the finder; if claimed by the owner they fall to be returned to him under deduction of expenses and a reward to the finder. Under the Lost Property (Sc.) Act, 1965 the same provision is applied to landward areas of counties. These provisions are probably wide enough to cover also things found in public vehicles within burghs or counties. Under the Winter Herding Act, 1686, cattle which stray may be detained by the finder until the statutory penalty is paid.

Things found in other moveables, as in a vehicle or in the drawer of a desk which has been bought, continue to belong constructively to the former owner thereof and property in them is not acquired with the container.[4]

Things found in or on the heritage of another are constructively in the possession of the proprietor of that heritage and the finder acquires no right of property, but has a possessory right good against all but the true owner,[5] unless the latter has abandoned *animus possidendi*, in which case the finder has a possessory right good against all but the heritable proprietor.[6]

Things found buried in or attached to the lands of another belong not to the finder nor to the owner of the lands but to the Crown: *quod nullius est, fit domini regis*.[7]

[1] Stair II, 1, 33; Ersk. II, 1, 10; Bell, *Prin.* §1291; cf. *Sands* v. *Bell & Balfour*, 22 May 1810, F.C.

[2] *Lawson* v. *Heatly*, 1962 S.L.T. 53; cf. Dogs Act, 1906, S. 4 and Dogs Act, 1925, S. 2.

[3] cf. *Bridges* v. *Hawkesworth* (1851) 21 L.J.Q.B. 75.

[4] cf. *Cartwright* v. *Green* (1803) 8 Ves. 405; *Merry* v. *Green* (1841) 7 M. & W. 623.

[5] *Cleghorn and Bryce* v. *Baird* (1696) Mor. 13523.

[6] cf. *South Staffs Water Co.* v. *Sharman* [1896] 2 Q.B. 44 (rings found in pond); *Hannah* v. *Peel* [1945] K.B. 509 (brooch found in requisitioned house); *Hibbert* v. *McKiernan* [1948] 2 K.B. 142 (golf balls found in rough); *Re Cohen* [1953] Ch. 88 (money found in house).

[7] *Lord Advocate* v. *Aberdeen University*, 1963 S.C. 533.

Treasure Trove

Treasure consists of precious articles, found concealed in the ground or in the fabric of a building,[1] there being no proof of their property or reasonable presumption of their former ownership.[2] Such are among the *regalia minora* and fall to the Crown under the rule: *quod nullius est, fit domini regis.*[3] Treasure concealed in the earth or a secret place of hiding is presumed hidden, and a claimant must overcome this presumption.[4]

Goods forgotten

Goods deposited, forgotten and not reclaimed probably continue recoverable for forty years at common law,[5] but in the case of goods accepted for repair or other treatment but not redelivered or paid for the depositary has power to sell them under the Disposal of Uncollected Goods Act, 1952.

Stray animals

Stray animals belong to the Crown if not claimed by the true owner.[6]

Under the Dogs Act, 1906, the police may seize and detain a dog believed to be a stray. Notice is served on the owner, if known, and after seven days, if he has not claimed it and paid all expenses, the dog may be destroyed.[7] A person taking possession of a stray dog must return it to the owner or take the dog to the police. If the finder desires to keep the dog he may, after taking it to the police station, remove it on giving his name and address, and must keep it for one month, whereupon ownership vests in the finder.[8]

Wrecks

Maritime wreck is governed by statute.[9] If the owner of wreck takes possession of it he must notify the receiver of wreck, and if not the possessor must deliver to it the receiver.[10] The Crown

[1] *Cleghorn* v. *Bryce & Baird* (1696) Mor. 13522.

[2] *Lord Advocate* v. *Aberdeen University*, 1963 S.C. 533, 548.

[3] Craig, *J.F.* I, 16, 40; Stair II, 1, 5; III, 3, 27; Bankt. I, 3, 14–16; I, 8, 9; II, 1, 8; Ersk. II, 1, 11–12; II, 6, 13; Bell, *Prin.* §1293; *Lord Advocate, supra.*

[4] *A.G.* v. *British Museum* [1903] 2 Ch. 598.

[5] *Sands* v. *Bell & Balfour*, 22 May 1810, F.C.

[6] Ersk. II, 1, 12; Bell, *Prin.* §1294.

[7] Dogs Act, 1906, S. 3.

[8] Ibid., S. 4; Dogs (Amdt.) Act, 1928, S. 2.

[9] Merchant Shipping Act, 1894, Ss. 510–537; for older law see Stair III, 3, 27; Ersk. II, 1, 13; Bell, *Prin.* §1292.

[10] 1894 Act, S. 518.

is entitled to all unclaimed wreck, except where the Crown has granted the right to wreck to anyone else.[1]

Creation

A person who makes a thing from materials which he owns owns the completed thing.[2]

Severance

Trees and crops while growing and minerals while in the ground are heritable but become moveable when felled or gathered or extracted and ownership is acquired by the severance, so long as lawful.

Accessio

On the principle *accessorium sequitur principale* a person who owns a principal subject becomes owner of what is accessory thereto; thus the owner of an animal thereby owns its young from their birth.[3] Similarly the owner of money owns the interest produced by that money.[4] By artificial or industrial accession, where a new thing is produced or the value of an old one augmented by the application of skill or art, the owner of the principal subject owns the new form of it or the enhanced value of it, but it is frequently difficult to decide to whom the property in the finished article should belong.[5]

Adjunction

Adjunction takes place where one thing is added to another so as to form a new thing or to alter the character of each, as where embroidery is applied to cloth, or paint to canvas. The property belongs to the owner of the major element, subject to liability to compensate the other for the value of his materials or skill.[6] Bell lays down[7] that, for determining which is principal, that of two substances, one of which can exist separately, the other not, the former is the principal; where both can exist separately, the principal is that which the other is taken to adorn or complete: in the absence of these indications, bulk prevails; next value. And

1 1894 Act, S. 523. cf. *M. Breadalbane* v. *Smith* (1850) 12 D. 602; *L.A.* v. *Hebden* (1868) 6 M. 489.

2 Bell, *Prin.* §1296.

3 Ersk. II, 1, 14–15; Bell, *Prin.* §1297; *Lamb* v. *Grant* (1874) 11 S.L.R. 672.

4 *Brown* v. *Inland Revenue*, 1964 S.C. (H.L.) 180.

5 Bell, *Prin.* §1297–98.

6 Inst. II, 1, 33; Dig. 41, 1, 9, 1; Stair II, 1, 39; Bankt. II, 1, 18; Ersk. II, 1, 15; *Cochrane* v. *Stevenson* (1891) 18 R. 1208.

7 *Prin.* §1298.

in all such cases where there can be no separation, the property is with the owner of the principal, leaving to the other a claim for indemnification.

Specificatio

Where a person in *bona fide*, as by mistake, makes a new thing from materials wholly belonging to another, if the materials are thereby wholly destroyed, the property in the new thing is with the maker, subject to a claim by the owner of the materials for return of an equivalent quantity and quality or for the value of the materials used, but if the materials can be restored to their original state the property in the new thing is in the owner thereof, subject to a claim by the workman for the work done, measured *quantum lucratus*.[1] If the new thing be made from materials belonging partly to two or more persons, it belongs to them in common in proportion to the value of the contribution of each.[2]

Where, however, the new thing is made *in mala fida*, as where the whole or part of the materials have been stolen, no title to the new thing vests in the maker, the doctrine of *specificatio* being an equitable one and applicable only where there is complete good faith on the part of the manufacturer.[3]

Confusion of liquids: commixtion of solids

In the cases of solids and liquids, if the things mixed are of the same kind and the result is inseparable the owners of the quantities mixed have common property in the mixture, sharing it in proportion to the quantity and value each has contributed. If the mixture is again separable into its constituents, each owner continues to own his elements of the mixture. If the things mixed are of different kinds so that the resultant mixture is *tertium quid* the property is with the manufacturer if the mixture be inseparable, and with the owners of the materials inmixed if separable, as in the case of *specificatio*.[4]

[1] Stair II, 1, 41; Ersk. II, 1, 16; Bell, *Prin.* §1298; *International Banking Corpn.* v. *Ferguson Shaw & Son*, 1910 S.C. 182; cf. *Inst.* II, 1, 25.

[2] *Wylie & Lochhead* v. *Mitchell* (1870) 8 M. 552.

[3] *McDonald* v. *Provan (of Scotland St.), Ltd.*, 1960 S.L.T. 231.

[4] Stair II, 1, 34, 36, 41; Ersk. II, 1, 14–17; Bell, *Comm.* I, 276; Bell, *Prin.* §1298(2).

CHAPTER 95

DERIVATIVE ACQUISITION OF PROPERTY IN CORPOREAL MOVEABLES

DERIVATIVE acquisition of moveable property is the acquisition of a proprietary right to moveables which have hitherto been in the ownership of another. It implies the surrender of his proprietary right by the person hitherto the owner. A distinction falls to be drawn between the title for the transfer, and the mode of effecting it, both of which are essential for an effectual transfer of ownership.[1]

Titulus transferendi dominii

The legal title for transfer of ownership is either a voluntary act of will, such as intention to gift, or a contract, or the involuntary operation of law, such as decree of court, legal diligence, or succession on death.

Modus transferendi dominii

The leading principle on mode is that embodied in the maxim *traditionibus non nudis pactis dominia rerum transferuntur.*[2] In general ownership of moveables passes only when possession is transferred or delivered with the intention of transferring the right of property, and neither intention nor agreement will pass the property in moveables without delivery.[3] Only exceptionally, under the Sale of Goods Act 1893, can ownership pass without delivery.[4]

A right of property in moveables cannot be transferred by assignation or other deed without transfer of possession; such a deed at most confers a right to demand delivery.[5]

Delivery may be actual, constructive or symbolical.

Actual delivery

Actual delivery is effected by voluntarily transferring physical possession to the transferee, or an agent for him, together with the

1 Voet, 41, 1, 35; Bell, *Prin.* §1299.

2 cf. *Mathison* v. *Alison* (1854) 17 D. 274; *McArthur* v. *Brown* (1858) 20 D. 1232; *Moore* v. *Gledden* (1869) 7 M. 1016; *Orr's Tr.* v. *Tullis* (1870) 8 M. 936.

3 Stair II, 1, 11; Ersk. II, 1, 19; Bell, *Prin.* §1300; Brown, *Sale*, 390; *Milne* v. *Grant's Exors.* (1884) 11 R. 887, 890; *Brownlee's Exrx.* v. *B.*, 1908 S.C. 232, 240.

4 1893 Act, Ss. 17–18.

5 cf. *Clark* v. *West Calder Oil Co.* (1882) 9 R. 1017.

relinquishment on the transferor's side of any further *animus possidendi* and the acquisition on the transferee's side of *animus possidendi*.[1] But in the case of sale actual delivery to a carrier leaves the goods liable to stoppage *in transitu* if the buyer has become bankrupt or insolvent before the buyer or his agent has taken delivery from the carrier.[2]

Constructive delivery

Constructive delivery is effected by the transfer of some thing essential for the actual delivery of the goods, which transfer puts them beyond the control of the transferor and under the control of the transferee as effectively as actual transfer of them. It may be effected by handing over the key of the premises where the goods are stored,[3] but probably not by merely setting aside the goods within the transferor's premises;[4] or, where goods are in the store of an independent third party, and are adequately ascertained and distinguishable from others of the same kind in the store,[5] by giving the transferee a delivery order addressed to the storekeeper, or by endorsation and delivery of the storekeeper's warrant for the goods, and in either case, making intimation to the storekeeper,[6] who then holds the goods for the transferee, not the transferor.[7] In the case of sale of goods delivery is not effected until the custodier acknowledges to the buyer that he holds the goods on the buyer's behalf.[8]

Symbolical delivery

Symbolical delivery is effected by the transfer of a document recognized by mercantile custom as a symbol of, and equivalent to, the goods themselves. The main recognized case is the endorsation and transfer of a bill of lading received for goods

[1] Ersk. II, 1, 18; III, 3, 8; Bell, *Comm.* I, 183; *Prin.* §1302. cf. Sale of Goods Act, 1893, S. 62, wherein 'delivery' is defined as 'Voluntary transfer of possession from one person to another'. See also *Robertson and Aitken* (1801) Mor. Appx. Sale, 15; *Baxter* v. *Pearson* (1807) Hume 688; *Dunlop* v. *Lambert* (1839) MacL. & R. 663.

[2] Sale of Goods Act, 1893, S. 45.

[3] Ersk. II, 1, 19; III, 3, 8; Bell, *Comm.* I, 186; *Prin.* §1302; *Maxwell & Co.* v. *Stevenson* (1831) 5 W. & S. 269; *W. Lothian Oil Co.* v. *Mair* (1892) 20 R. 64; cf. *Pattison's Trs.* v. *Liston* (1893) 20 R. 806.

[4] *Gibson* v. *Forbes* (1833) 11 S. 916; *Boak* v. *Megget* (1844) 6 D. 662.

[5] It does not suffice to give an order to one's own storekeeper, even though other goods are also in that store: *Anderson* v. *McCall* (1866) 4 M. 765; *Pochin* v. *Robinow* (1869) 7 M. 622, 628.

[6] *Black* v. *Incorporation of Bakers* (1867) 6 M. 136; *Hayman* v. *McLintock*, 1907 S.C. 936; *Price & Pierce* v. *Bank of Scotland*, 1912 S.C. (H.L.) 19.

[7] *Inglis* v. *Robertson & Baxter* (1898) 25 R. (H.L.) 70.

[8] Sale of Goods Act, 1893, S. 29(3).

shipped and in transit, which has the same effect as actual transfer of the goods themselves and enables a transferee to take delivery as owner or holder in security on their being unloaded.[1]

Apart from the bill of lading no kind of document has been held effective as symbolical delivery.[2]

VOLUNTARY TRANSFER OF TITLE TO MOVEABLES

Particular grounds of voluntary transfer—Donation inter vivos[3]

The intention to donate or transfer gratuitously, *animus donandi*, is frequently evidenced only by the fact of delivery or by the donor's manner or expressions uttered at the time of actual transfer.[4] It may be proved by parole evidence, which must be clear and convincing.[5] Proof is easier where there existed circumstances inferring a natural obligation to support or assist the donee.[6] If evidence by the writ or admission on oath of the donor his announced intention or promise constitutes an enforceable unilateral gratuitous obligation.[7] A *pactum donationis*, however, confers on the donee merely a right to claim delivery, and no right in the thing itself passes without delivery. If the intention is not proveable in the ways prescribed the donee has not even a right to claim delivery.[8] If the donor has orally promised a thing to one and gives it to another the latter becomes the owner.[9]

The *animus donandi* must be completed by delivery of the thing gifted, to dispossess the donor and invest the donee with the property in the thing gifted.[10]

A donation is not now revocable, whether on the ground of the donee's ingratitude[11] nor as being *inter virum et uxorem*.[12]

1 Bell, *Prin.* §417, 1305; *Bogle* v. *Dunmore* (1787) Mor. 14216; *Young* v. *Stein's Crs.* (1789) Mor. 1448; *Lickbarrow* v. *Mason* (1793) 6 East 21.

2 e.g. *Paul* v. *Cuthbertson* (1840) 2 D. 1286; *Stiven* v. *Cowan* (1878) 15 S.L.R. 422.

3 For donation *mortis causa*, see Ch. 112, *infra*.

4 cf. *Little* v. *L.* (1856) 18 D. 701.

5 *Sharp* v. *Paton* (1883) 10 R. 1000.

6 *Wilson* v. *Paterson* (1826) 4 S. 817; *Macalister's Trs.* v. *M.* (1827) 5 S. 219; *Farquhar's Trs.* v. *Stewart* (1841) 3 D. 658; *Nisbet's Trs.* v. *N.* (1868) 6 M. 567; *Forbes* v. *F.* (1869) 8 M. 85; *Malcolm* v. *Campbell* (1889) 17 R. 255; cf. *Fairgrieves* v. *Hendersons* (1885) 13 R. 98.

7 Ersk. III, 3, 88. cf. *Balfour* v. *Simpson* (1873) 11 M. 604.

8 Ersk. III, 3, 90.

9 Ersk. III, 3, 90.

10 *Crosbie's Trs.* v. *Wright* (1880) 7 R. 823; *Milne* v. *Scott* (1880) 8 R. 83; *Thompson* v. *Dunlop* (1884) 11 R. 453; *L.A.* v. *Galloway* (1884) 11 R. 541; *Milne* v. *Grant's Exors.* (1884) 11 R. 887; *McNicol* v. *McDougall* (1889) 17 R. 25; *Brownlee's Exor.* v. *B.*, 1908 S.C. 232; *Hubbard* v. *Dunlop's Trs.*, 1933 S.N. 62; cf. *Newton* v. *N.*, 1923 S.C. 15.

11 Bankt. I, 9, 4; Ersk. III, 3, 90; Bell, *Prin.* §64.

12 Married Women's Property (Sc.) Act, 1920, S. 5, altering Stair I, 4, 16; Ersk. I, 6, 29.

In dubio there is a presumption against donation, and actual transfer of goods is to be ascribed to another legal category such as loan, unless the evidence of *animus donandi* is clear.[1] If A's property is in B's hands the onus is on B to prove donation, not on A to prove deposit or agency or other reason for the property being in B's possession.[2] As a consequence of this, *debitor non praesumitur donare*, so that where a debtor gives money or goods to his creditor, the natural presumption is that he intends to reduce or extinguish his debt. This presumption may be overcome by stronger contrary presumption or evidence.[3]

Barter

In barter the agreement to exchange perfects the contract but there is no passing of the property in either thing being exchanged until mutual delivery of both things has been made,[4] or at least the items to be exchanged have been identified and separated and delivery orders in respect thereof transmitted and intimated to the custodiers.[5]

Sale

At common law, sale was a contract only and no right of property in the subject sold was transferred without, nor until, *traditio* was effected.[6] But by the Sale of Goods Act, 1893, Ss. 17–18, the right of property in goods sold passes when the parties intend it to pass, which is normally (S. 18, Rule 1) when the contract is made, even though payment or delivery or both be postponed. Where the right of disposal is reserved until certain conditions are fulfilled (S. 19) the right of property does not pass till then, notwithstanding the delivery of the goods to the buyer, or to a carrier or custodier for transmission to him. Accordingly

[1] Stair I, 8, 2; IV, 45, 17(14); Ersk. III, 3, 92; *Garthland's Trs.* v. *McDowall*, 26 May 1820, F.C.; *Drummond* v. *Swayne* (1834) 12 S. 342; *Farquhar's Trs.* v. *Stewart* (1841) 3 D. 658; *Murray* v. *M.* (1843) 6 D. 176; *B.L. Co.* v. *Martin* (1849) 11 D. 1004; *Robertson* v. *R.* (1858) 20 D. 371; *Heron* v. *McGeoch* (1851) 14 D. 25; *Forbes* v. *F.* (1869) 8 M. 85; *Sharp* v. *Paton* (1883) 10 R. 1000; *Dawson* v. *McKenzie* (1892) 19 R. 261; *Brownlee's Exrx.* v. *B.*, 1908 S.C. 232.

[2] *Malcolm* v. *Campbell* (1889) 17 R. 255; *Penman* v. *White*, 1957 S.C. 338; *McVea* v. *Reid*, 1958 S.L.T. (Sh. Ct.) 60.

[3] Ersk. III, 3, 93; *Edgar* v. *Hamilton's Trs.* (1828) 6 S. 963; *Black* v. *Booth* (1835) 14 S. 113; *Johnstone* v. *Haviland* (1896) 23 R. (H.L.) 6.

[4] Stair I, 14, 1

[5] cf. *Widenmeyer* v. *Burn Stewart & Co.*, 1967 S.L.T. 129.

[6] For some of the consequences of this rule see *McEwan* v. *Smith* (1849) 6 Bell 340; *Melrose* v. *Hastie* (1851) 13 D. 880; *Mathison* v. *Alison* (1854) 17 D. 274; *Wyper* v. *Harvey* (1861) 23 D. 606.

under the 1893 Act a sale is a contract and may also be a conveyance of the right of property, independently of when *traditio* of the actual goods is effected.

Hire-purchase

The completion of the contract normally transfers the right of property to the finance company as owner by sale, though delivery of possession by the seller to the hirer is necessary to complete the hiring relationship between him and the finance company which now owns the goods. The property in the goods hired does not pass to the hirer until he has completed the payments and has exercised the option to purchase.[1]

Credit sale

In credit sale agreement, which is a variety of sale, the property *prima facie* passes when the contract is made, whether or not possession is then transferred.[2]

Conditional sale

Under a conditional sale agreement the property in the goods remains in the seller, notwithstanding that the buyer is given possession of the goods, until the conditions as to payment by instalments or otherwise specified in the agreement are fulfilled.[3]

Other contracts

The only other contract involving transfer of ownership is *mutuum* or improper loan, whereby the borrower on delivery becomes proprietor of the thing lent, subject to an obligation to restore an equal quantity of the same kind and quality.[4]

Who can transfer title of ownership of goods

It is clear that any person who has an unqualified right of property in any corporeal moveable can confer a good title thereto on a donee or purchaser from him, and that a person not having such a right cannot, in general, confer any title.

The fundamental principle is that no one can transfer a better title to goods than he himself has: *nemo dat quod non habet*.[5] Hence a mere custodier or other non-owner in possession cannot transfer

1 Common law, and under Hire-Purchase (Sc.) Act, 1965.

2 Hire-Purchase (Sc.) Act, 1965, S. 1.

3 Ibid.

4 Stair I, 11, 5; Ersk. III, 1, 18; Bell, *Prin.* §200–2; Ch. 38, *supra*.

5 *Whistler* v. *Forster* (1863) 14 C.B.N.S. 248; *Cole* v. *N.W. Bank* (1875) L.R. 10 C.P. 354; *Banque Belge* v. *Hambrouck* [1921] 1 K.B. 321.

a title of ownership by transferring goods, or otherwise. But to this principle various exceptions have, for reasons of commercial convenience, been accepted, both at common law and under statute, under which a person who has no title, or less than a full title of ownership, may give a transferee a full title of ownership, and under which a transferee who takes in good faith, for value and without notice of the transferor's defect in title, himself acquires a good title of ownership. These exceptions are (a) money and negotiable instruments; (b) sales by a non-owner; (c) sales under a voidable title; (d) sales by sellers or buyers having possession of the goods or of documents of title thereto; (d) dispositions by factors; (f) sales of motor vehicles by hire-purchasers; and (g) sales under statutory and other powers of sale.[1]

Hence under the general principle one who has no title at all, e.g., having obtained the goods by fraud which caused essential error, can pass no title at all to a purchaser from him;[2] but in the exceptional cases the transferor can pass a good title, so long as the transferee takes in good faith, for value, and without notice of the seller's defective title.

Theft

It follows also from the general principle of *nemo dat quod non habet* that a thief or embezzler, who has *ex hypothesi* no title of ownership to the goods in question at all[3] cannot pass any title to even an honest transferee who takes in good faith, for value and without knowledge of the theft, still less to a resetter. Stolen property, except money and negotiable instruments, is tainted by a *vitium reale* which is not purged by any transmissions.[4] The goods are recoverable from the thief if he still has possession or he is liable to compensate for their value.[5] They are recoverable from any party into whose hands they have come and he is liable for the value of any not recovered.[6] An intermediate party who has in

[1] In English law a further exception is the sale in market overt (Sale of Goods Act, 1893, S. 22).

[2] cf. *Morrisson* v. *Robertson*, 1908 S.C. 332; *Ingram* v. *Little* [1961] 1 Q.B. 31. See also *Henderson* v. *Gibson*, 17 June 1806, F.C.; *Todd* v. *Armour* (1882) 9 R. 901. But if the fraud gave the taker a title, though a voidable one, he can pass a title to a purchaser from him so long as his own title has not been avoided: *Brown* v. *Marr, Barclay* (1880) 7 R. 472; *Macleod* v. *Kerr*, 1965 S.C. 253.

[3] He may have a right of custody: *O'Brien* v. *Strathern*, 1922 J.C. 55.

[4] *Bp. of Caithness* v. *Fleshers of Edinburgh* (1629) Mor. 9112; *Ferguson* v. *Forrest* (1639) Mor. 9112; *Henderson* v. *Gibson* (1806) Mor. Moveables, Appx. 1; *Todd* v. *Armour* (1882) 9 R. 901.

[5] *Gorebridge Co-operative Socy.* v. *Turnbull*, 1952 S.L.T. (Sh. Ct.) 91.

[6] *Oliver and Boyd* v. *Marr Typefounding Co.* (1901) 9 S.L.T. 170; *Dalhanna Knitwear Co.* v. *Mohammed Ali*, 1967 S.L.T. (Sh. Ct.) 74.

good faith parted with stolen property is not liable to the true owner for restitution or for reparation, but only to recompense the dispossessed ultimate possessor.[1] He is liable to the true owner only for any profit made by selling the goods[2] or for their value if he sold them in bad faith.[3]

EXCEPTIONS

(a) MONEY, AND NEGOTIABLE INSTRUMENTS

Money, both notes and coin, is incapable of being earmarked or identified with any former owner and its circulation and transfer in satisfaction of a pecuniary obligation destroys the title of the previous owner and vests a new title in the person receiving the money so long as he has taken it in good faith, for value and without notice of any defect in the transferor's title.[4] Thus stolen money is recoverable from a thief or a resetter,[5] but not from an honest transferee who has given the thief value for it, e.g., taking it in payment for goods. Money regarded not as currency but as goods, or curios, falls under the ordinary rule applicable to moveables, and not under this exception.[6]

Similarly a holder in due course of a negotiable instrument[7] acquires a good title thereto notwithstanding defect in the title of the transferor. The category of negotiable instruments includes bills of exchange, cheques and promissory notes (including banknotes), Treasury bills, scrip certificates issued to bearer,[8] share warrants issued to bearer,[9] debentures payable to bearer,[10] dividend warrants, banker's drafts and circular notes, but not share certificates or transfers thereof,[11] postal orders,[12] or pension

[1] Sale of Goods Act, 1893, S. 12.

[2] Ersk. III, 1, 10; *Scot* v. *Low* (1704) Mor. 9123; *Walker* v. *Spence & Carfrae* (1765) Mor. 12802.

[3] *Si dolo desiit possidere, dolus pro possessione habetur*; cf. *Kinniburgh* v. *Dickson* (1830) 9 S. 153; *Lockhart* v. *Cunningham* (1870) 8 S.L.R. 151.

[4] Bell, *Prin.* §527–9; 1333; *Hotchkis* v. *Royal Bank* (1797) Mor. 2673; *Swinton* v. *Beveridge* (1799) Mor. 10105; *Crawfurd* v. *Royal Bank* (1749) (Mor) 875; *Lambton* v. *Marshall* (1799) Mor. Bill, Appx. 8; *Scott* v. *Kilmarnock Bank*, 27 Feb. 1812, F.C.

[5] *Gorebridge Co-operative Socy.* v. *Turnbull*, 1952 S.L.T. (Sh. Ct.) 91.

[6] cf. *Moss* v. *Hancock* [1899] 2 Q.B. 111.

[7] As defined by Bills of Exchange Act, 1882, S. 29(1).

[8] *Rumball* v. *Metropolitan Bank* (1877) 2 Q.B.D. 194; *Edelstein* v. *Schuler* [1902] 2 K.B. 144.

[9] Companies Act, 1948, S. 83.

[10] *Bechuanaland Exploration Co.* v. *London Trading Bank, Ltd.* (1898) 2 Q.B. 658; see also Companies Act, 1948, S. 93.

[11] *Colonial Bank* v. *Cady and Williams* (1890) 15 App. Cas. 267; *Longman* v. *Bath Electric Tramways* [1905] 1 Ch. 646.

[12] *Fine Arts Socy.* v. *Union Bank of London* (1886) 17 Q.B.D. 705.

receipts.[1] Bills of lading, dock warrants and similar documents of title to goods, though transferable, are not negotiable instruments.

(b) SALES BY A NON-OWNER

The Sale of Goods Act, 1893, S. 21, provides that, subject to Ss. 23 and 25 of the Act, where goods are sold by a person who is not the owner thereof, and who does not sell them under the authority of or with the consent of the owner, the buyer acquires no better title to the goods than the seller had, unless the owner of the goods is by his conduct precluded from denying the seller's authority to sell. But nothing in the 1893 Act affects the provisions of the Factors Acts,[2] or any enactment enabling the apparent owner of goods to dispose of them as if he were the true owner thereof,[3] or the validity of any contract of sale under any special common law or statutory power of sale or under the order of a court.[4] This section restates the general principle but excepts cases where the owner is precluded from denying the seller's authority. The owner will be so precluded if the seller had ostensible authority to act as his agent,[5] or if the true owner, in allowing the seller the opportunity to sell, had failed to take reasonable care to prevent the buyer being deceived.[6]

(c) SALE UNDER A VOIDABLE TITLE

Where the seller of goods has only a voidable title to those goods, as where he obtained the goods himself under a contract voidable as having been induced by misrepresentation, but his title has not been avoided at the time of the sale, the buyer from him acquires a good title to the goods, provided he buys them in good faith and without notice of the seller's defect of title.[7] If the seller has no title, such as a thief, or a title under a contract wholly void, he can pass no title, even though the buyer takes in good

[1] *Jones* v. *Coventry* [1909] 2 K.B. 1029.

[2] On these see *infra*.

[3] e.g. sale of motor vehicles by a hire-purchase: exception (f), *infra*.

[4] See *infra*.

[5] *Eastern Distributors, Ltd.* v. *Goldring* [1957] 2 Q.B. 600; contrast *Mercantile Credit Co.* v. *Hamblin* [1964] 3 All E.R. 592.

[6] *Mercantile Credit Co., supra*.

[7] Sale of Goods Act, 1893, S. 23; *Phillips* v. *Brooks* [1912] 2 K.B. 243; *Lake* v. *Simmons* [1927] A.C. 487; *Butterworth* v. *Kingsway Motors* [1954] 2 All E.R. 694; *Macleod* v. *Kerr* 1965 S.C. 253.

faith, for value and without notice.[1] It may be sufficient to avoid a contract voidable within the meaning of the Sale of Goods Act, 1893, S. 23, and so prevent property passing, if the seller takes all possible steps to regain the goods even though he does not communicate to the seller his decision to rescind the contract of sale to him.[2]

(d) DISPOSITIONS BY SELLERS AND BUYERS IN POSSESSION

(i) *Seller in possession*

Where a person having sold goods continues or is in possession of the goods, or of the documents of title to the goods, the delivery or transfer by that person, or by a mercantile agent acting for him, of the goods or documents of title under any sale, pledge or other disposition thereof, to any person receiving the same in good faith and without notice of the previous sale, has the same effect as if the person making the delivery or transfer were expressly authorized by the owner of the goods to make the sale.[3] Hence a purchaser or pledgee from such a person obtains a good title provided he takes delivery, receives the goods in good faith, and has no notice of the previous sale. The possession which the seller had must be possession continuing despite the sale and not be possession otherwise re-acquired as, e.g., where a garage sells a car and has it left with them for repainting.[4] It may be possession by an agent.[5] It is not essential that the seller has continued in possession with the buyer's consent.

(ii) *Buyer in possession*

Where a person, having bought or agreed to buy goods,[6] obtains, with the consent of the seller, possession of the goods or the documents of title to the goods, the delivery or transfer by

1 *Cundy* v. *Lindsay* (1878) 3 App. Cas. 459; *Morrisson* v. *Robertson*, 1908 S.C. 332; *Ingram* v. *Little* [1961] 1 Q.B. 31.

2 But see *Macleod, supra.*

3 Sale of Goods Act, 1893, S. 25(1), reproducing almost exactly Factors Act, 1889, S. 8, applied to Scotland by Factors (Sc.) Act, 1890.

4 *Staffs Motor Guarantees, Ltd.* v. *British Wagon Co., Ltd.* [1934] 2 K.B. 305, distinguished in *Union Tpt. Finance* v. *Ballardie* [1937] 1 K.B. 570; *Olds Discount Co.* v. *Krett and Krett* [1940] 2 K.B. 117. See also *Pacific Motor Auctions Pty., Ltd.* v. *Motor Credits (Hire Finance), Ltd.* [1965] A.C. 867.

5 *City Fur Mfg. Co.* v. *Fureenbond (Brokers), Ltd.* [1937] 1 All E.R. 799.

6 A person who obtains possession under a hire-purchase contract has not 'bought or agreed to buy': *Helby* v. *Matthews* [1895] A.C. 471; *Belsize Motor Supply Co.* v. *Cox* [1914] 1 K.B. 244; but a person has, though his contract to buy is conditional, or for purchase with payment by instalments: *Lee* v. *Butler* [1893] 2 K.B. 318.

that person, or by a mercantile agent acting for him, of the goods or documents of title, under any sale, pledge or other disposition thereof, to any person receiving them in good faith and without notice of any lien or other right of the original seller in respect of goods, has the same effect as if the person making the delivery or transfer were a mercantile agent in possession of the goods or documents of title with the consent of the owner.[1] This provision deals with the unauthorized sale by a buyer in possession with the seller's consent, before ownership has vested in him, as where he has not yet paid the price or the whole of it, or he has merely agreed to buy under a conditional contract.[2] The possession must have been obtained with the seller's consent, though that consent may be afterwards withdrawn.[3] A buyer is not in possession with the seller's consent if he stole the goods, but he is if he obtained them by fraudulent misrepresentation or false pretences,[4] unless inducing error so essential as to render the transaction of obtaining void,[5] or on approval, or on sale or return.[6]

(e) TRANSFERS BY FACTORS IN POSSESSION

A factor in possession has power to sell or pledge his principal's property. Where a mercantile agent[7] is, with the consent of the owner, in possession of goods or of the documents of title to goods,[8] any sale, pledge[9] or other disposition of the goods, made by him when acting in the ordinary course of business of a mercantile agent, is, subject to the Factors Acts, 1889 and 1890, as valid as if he were expressly authorized by the owner of the goods to make that disposition, provided that the person taking under the disposition acts in good faith and has not at the time of the disposition notice that the person making the disposition has not authority to make it.[10]

[1] Sale of Goods Act, 1893, S. 25(2) reproducing almost exactly Factors Act, 1889, S. 9, applied to Scotland by Factors Act, 1890; cf. *Browne* v. *Ainslie* (1893) 21 R. 173; *Inglis* v. *Robertson & Baxter* (1898) 25 R. (H.L.) 70; *Graham* v. *Glenrothes Development Corpn.*, 1968 S.L.T. 2.

[2] *Marten* v. *Whale* [1917] 2 K.B. 480; *Wilkes* v. *Livingstone*, 1955 S.L.T. (Notes) 20.

[3] *Cahn* v. *Pockett's Bristol Channel S.P. Co.* [1899] 1 Q.B. 643.

[4] *London Jewellers* v. *Attenborough* [1934] 2 K.B. 206; *Du Jardin* v. *Beadman Bros., Ltd.* [1952] 2 Q.B. 712.

[5] *Morrisson* v. *Robertson*, 1908 S.C. 332.

[6] Sale of Goods Act, 1893, S. 18, R. 4. Making a sale, pledge or other disposition is an act adopting the transaction within Rule 4: *London Jewellers, supra.*

[7] Defined, Factors Act, 1889, S. 1(1).

[8] Defined, S. 1(2)–(4); cf. *Vickers* v. *Hertz* (1871) 9 M. (H.L.) 65.

[9] Defined, S. 1(5).

[10] Factors Act, 1889, S. 2, applied to Scotland by Factors (Sc.) Act, 1890.

The provision applies only to mercantile agents, not, e.g., to servants or carriers or brokers,[1] nor to commercial travellers.[2] Whether a person is a mercantile agent is a question of fact.[3] He must, moreover, have been a mercantile agent when entrusted with the possession of the goods, and not merely have become one later.[4]

He must have been entrusted with possession of the goods or documents and not obtained them by theft, though he may have obtained possession by misrepresentation, so long as not inducing error so essential as to render the obtaining void.[5]

He must have obtained possession as factor, and not in any other capacity or for another purpose.[6]

The sale or other disposition must be in the ordinary course of business; thus a sale, pledge or other disposition is not valid unless made for valuable consideration;[7] it must be effected at a proper place of business, during business hours, and in other respects be such as is normal in that business.[8]

A disposition by a mercantile agent, which would have been valid if the owner's consent to his possession of the goods or documents had continued, is valid notwithstanding the determination of the consent, provided that the person taking under the disposition had not notice at the time that the consent had been determined.[9] Hence if authority terminates by revocation or lapse of time but possession continues the factor can give a good title to an innocent purchaser or pledgee.[10]

A mercantile agent's possession of documents of title, as being or having been, with the consent of the owner in possession of the goods represented thereby or of any other documents of title thereto, is for the purposes of the Factors Act, deemed to be with the consent of the owner.[11] The owner's consent is to be presumed in the absence of evidence to the contrary.[12]

1 *Heyman* v. *Flewker* (1863) 13 C.B. (N.S.) 519.

2 *International Sponge Importers* v. *Watt*, 1909 2 S.L.T. 24.

3 *Weiner* v. *Harris* [1910] 1 K.B. 285; *Lowther* v. *Harris* [1927] 1 K.B. 393.

4 *Heap* v. *Motorists Advisory Agency, Ltd.* [1923] 1 K.B. 577.

5 *Vickers* v. *Hertz* (1871) 9 M. (H.L.) 65; *Folkes* v. *King* [1923] 1 K.B. 282; *Pearson* v. *Rose and Young, Ltd.* [1951] K.B. 275 (where sale not 'in the ordinary course of business').

6 *Brown & Co.* v. *Bedford Pantechnicon Co.* (1889) 5 T.L.R. 449; *Staffs Motor Guarantee, Ltd.* v. *British Wagon Co.* [1934] 2 K.B. 305.

7 Factors (Sc.) Act, 1890, S. 1(2); as to consideration see 1889 Act, S. 5.

8 See *Oppenheimer* v. *Attenborough* [1908] 1 K.B. 221; *Heap, supra*; *Pearson, supra*.

9 Factors Act, 1889, S. 2(2), overruling *Fuentes* v. *Monti* (1868) L.R. 4 C.P. 93.

10 *Moody* v. *Pall Mall Deposit Co.* (1917) 33 T.L.R. 306.

11 1889 Act, S. 2(3).

12 1889 Act, S. 2(4).

(f) SALES OF MOTOR VEHICLES SUBJECT TO HIRE-PURCHASE AGREEMENTS

Where a motor vehicle has been let under a hire-purchase agreement or been agreed to be sold under a conditional sale agreement, and, before the property in the vehicle has become vested in the hirer or buyer, he disposes of it[1] to another person, the disposition has effect as if the title of the owner or seller had been vested in the hirer or buyer immediately before the disposition, provided the disposition is to a private purchaser and he is a purchaser of the motor vehicle in good faith and without notice of the hire-purchase or conditional sale agreement.[2] Where a disposition is made to a trade or finance purchaser,[3] then if the first private purchaser after that disposition is a purchaser in good faith and without notice of the hire-purchase or conditional sale agreement, the disposition to the first private purchaser has effect as if the title of the owner or seller had been vested in the hirer or purchaser immediately before he disposed of it to the trade or finance purchaser.[4] Where the disposition to the first private purchaser in good faith and without notice is a letting under a hire-purchase agreement and the owner disposes of the vehicle by way of transferring to him the property in the vehicle in pursuance of a provision in the hire-purchase agreement in that behalf, the latter disposition (whether the person to whom it is made is then a purchaser in good faith and without a notice of the original agreement or not) shall, as well as the former disposition, have effect as mentioned in S. 27(3).[5]

These provisions have effect notwithstanding the Sale of Goods Act, 1893, S. 21, but without prejudice to the Factors Acts, 1889 and 1890, or of any other enactment enabling the apparent owner of goods to dispose of them as if he were the owner, and they do not exonerate the hirer or buyer from any liability to which he would otherwise be subject.[6]

Certain presumptions in relation to dealings with motor vehicles are also created.[7]

[1] 'Dispose of' is defined in S. 29(1).

[2] Hire-Purchase Act, 1964, S. 27(1)–(2). Ss. 27–29 are not repealed by the Hire-Purchase Act, 1965 or the Hire-Purchase (Sc.) Act, 1965. These provisions apply to all hire-purchase transactions relating to vehicles, without limitation of value or restriction to transactions by private persons.

[3] Defined S. 29(2).

[4] Ibid., S. 27(3).

[5] Ibid., S. 27(4).

[6] Ibid., S. 27(5)–(6).

[7] Ibid., S. 28.

(g) COMMON LAW AND STATUTORY POWERS OF SALE

At common law non-owners have powers of sale to the effect of giving a good title to a purchaser in certain cases:

Common law powers

(i) *Negotiorum gestor*: a *negotiorum gestor* may sell or pledge moveables of which he has taken possession in the exercise of his *gestio* to the effect of conferring a good title on the purchaser. But if the sale were unjustifiable in the circumstances the gestor will be liable in damages to the owner.[1]

(ii) Agent of necessity: an agent of necessity, whose action is justified by necessity and who is unable to communicate with the owners, may validly sell or pledge the goods.[2] If there is no emergency, or the goods are not perishable, the sale is unjustifiable and wrongful.[3]

(iii) Pledgee of goods: a pledgee of goods or of the documents of title to goods may sell, if the time fixed for repayment has expired, but only if he has been given express power to sell, or obtains warrant from the sheriff to do so.[4]

(iv) Superior or landlord exercising hypothec: a superior or landlord who in the exercise of his right of hypothec (where it exists) has sequestrated *invecta et illata* for feuduty or rent unpaid may sell the sequestrated goods under warrant from the sheriff.

(v) Creditor in exercise of diligence: a creditor holding a decree may have the debtor charged to pay and, failing payment, poind his goods and sell them under judicial warrant.

Statutory powers

(i) Pawnbrokers have power to sell by auction unredeemed pledges above 40/- in value.[5]

(ii) Innkeepers have power, subject to formalities, to sell goods brought to the inn by a guest indebted for his entertainment.[6]

(iii) An unpaid seller of goods has a right of resale notwithstanding that the property in the goods has passed to the buyer.[7]

(iv) Warehousemen may sell imported goods in respect of which they have incurred expense.[8]

1 *Kolbin* v. *United Shipping Co.*, 1931 S.C. (H.L.) 128, 138.

2 *Sims* v. *Midland Ry.* [1913] 1 K.B. 103; cf. *Prager* v. *Blatspiel, Stamp and Heacock* [1924] 1 K.B. 566; *Jebara* v. *Ottoman Bank* [1927] 2 K.B. 254.

3 cf. *Sachs* v. *Miklos* [1948] 2 K.B. 23; *Munro* v. *Willmott* [1949] 1 K.B. 295.

4 Bell, *Prin.* §207; see also *Duncan* v. *Mitchell* (1893) 21 R. 37.

5 Pawnbrokers Act, 1872, S. 19, amd. Pawnbrokers Act, 1960, S. 3.

6 Innkeepers Act, 1878, S. 1.

7 Sale of Goods Act, 1893, Ss. 39, 48(2).

8 Merchant Shipping Act, 1894, Ss. 497–8.

(v) Trustees in bankruptcy may sell the bankrupt's property.[1]

(vi) Liquidators of companies can sell the company's property.[2]

(vii) A holder of goods accepted in the course of business for repair or other treatment may sell them if the owner fails to pay and take re-delivery.[3]

Court authority

In many cases sale is competent on warrant obtained from the sheriff on summary application; such cases include sale following sequestration for rent, sale of rejected goods, sale of strayed cattle, sale of perishable goods, and it is thought that all such sales confer a good title on the purchaser.

INVOLUNTARY TRANSFER OF TITLE TO MOVEABLES

Transfer of title to moveables may also be made without or even against the will of the owner by decree of court, by the operation of legal diligence, by mercantile sequestration, or on the owner's death.

Decree of court

Decree of a competent court in a multiple-poinding or action for declarator and delivery may transfer the title to moveables from one party to another and require delivery to the new owner.

Diligence

Moveable property attached by arrestment may be transferred outright to a creditor by decree in an action of furthcoming, or may be ordained to be sold and the price applied in satisfaction of the creditor's claim.[4] Decree establishes judicially in the purchaser a title to the subject arrested.[5]

Moveables attached by poinding or by poinding of the ground may be sold under warrant of the sheriff[6] and a purchaser acquires a good title on making payment and taking delivery of the goods.

[1] Bankruptcy (Sc.) Act, 1913, Ss. 78, 133; see also *Robertson* v. *Adam* (1857) 19 D. 502; *Stewart* v. *Crookston*, 1910 S.C. 609.

[2] Companies Act, 1948, Ss. 245, 303.

[3] Disposal of Uncollected Goods Act, 1952, Ss. 1, 6.

[4] See generally Bell, *Prin.* §2272–83; Graham Stewart, 239; cf. *Lucas's Trs.* v. *Campbell* (1894) 21 R. 1096.

[5] Bell, *Prin.* §2283; *Muirhead* v. *Corrie* (1735) Mor. 687; *Stevenson* v. *Paul* (1680) Mor. 5405; *Stevenson* v. *Grant* (1767) Mor. 2762.

[6] See generally Bell, *Prin.* §2284–90; Graham Stewart, 274, 491.

Sequestration

The Act and Warrant issued to the trustee in bankruptcy *ipso jure* vests in the trustee, *inter alia*, the moveable estate of the bankrupt, wherever situated, so far as attachable for debt to the same effect as if actual delivery or possession had been obtained, subject always to such preferable securities as existed at the date of the sequestration and are not null or reducible.[1] He may sell moveables by public roup or by private bargain and, having by statute[1] an absolute title to the moveable property, can pass an absolute title by sale.

Succession on death

This is dealt with hereafter.[2]

[1] Bankruptcy (Sc.) Act, 1913, S. 97(1).
[2] Chs. 111–114, *infra*.

CHAPTER 96

RIGHTS IN SECURITY OVER CORPOREAL MOVEABLE PROPERTY

One person may acquire rights over corporeal moveable property belonging to another in security of the performance by that other of some obligation, such as payment of money, either by express contract or by operation of law.

The general principle of Scots law is that no security right conferring any real right over the moveables themselves can be created without transfer to the security-holder of possession, actual, constructive or symbolical, of the property over which the right exists,[1] but there are important exceptions where a right in security may exist without possession.

SECURITY RIGHTS REQUIRING POSSESSION

Pledge

A pledge of goods is constituted by agreement completed by transfer of goods to the creditor, by making actual, constructive or symbolical delivery to him,[2] to be held by him in security. The right of property remains with the owner, despite the civil possession of the pledgee. A bare undertaking to pledge not completed by transfer of possession confers no real right over the goods. Pledge may also be effected by the delivery of documents of title to goods, as representing the goods.[3]

The pledgee has no power to use the subject pledged, nor to sell it, unless he has been given authority, or obtains a judicial warrant to do so for non-payment of his debt.[4]

Pledge is a security for the whole debt or any part thereof, and

[1] e.g. *MacKinnon* v. *Nanson* (1868) 6 M. 974; *Stiven* v. *Scott* (1871) 9 M. 923; *Watson's Tr.* v. *Cowan* (1878) 15 S.L.R. 422; *Heritable Securities Investment Assocn.* v. *Wingate's Tr.* (1880) 7 R. 1094; *Robertson* v. *McIntyre* (1882) 9 R. 772; *Clark* v. *West Calder Oil Co.* (1882) 9 R. 1017; *Ewart* v. *Hogg* (1893) 1 S.L.T. 63; *Jones & Co.'s Tr.* v. *Allan* (1901) 4 F. 374; See also *Newbigging* v. *Ritchie's Tr.*, 1930 S.C. 273.

[2] *Moore* v. *Gledden* (1869) 7 M. 1016; *Orr's Tr.* v. *Tullis* (1870) 8 M. 936; *Stiven* v. *Cowan* (1878) 15 S.L.R. 422; *Heritable Securities Inv. Assoc.* v. *Wingate's Tr.* (1880) 7 R. 1094; *Rhind's Tr.* v. *Robertson & Baxter* (1891) 18 R. 623; *Dobell, Beckett & Co.* v. *Neilson* (1904) 7 F. 281; *Price & Pierce* v. *Bank of Scotland*, 1912 S.C. (H.L.) 19.

[3] *Stiven* v. *Watson* (1874) 1 R. 412; Factors Act, 1889, S. 3; *Inglis* v. *Robertson & Baxter* (1898) 25 R. (H.L.) 70.

[4] Stair I, 13, 11; Ersk., III, 1, 33; Bell, *Prin.* §203–8; 1363–64.

is unaffected by payments to account.[1] If deemed of adequate value it is good security for advances made subsequently to the original pledging.[2]

On full payment, or other full performance of the obligation, the pledgee must restore possession to the pledger and relinquish his claims to the goods.

(a) LIENS (OR RETENTION)

A lien[3] is the right of a creditor to retain moveable property, belonging to the debtor but entrusted to the creditor's possession for some purpose, until the creditor's claims against the debtor are satisfied. It may be created by express contract, in any form, in which case it is hardly distinguishable from pledge, or by implication of law, as an implied term of various kinds of contracts of employment.

A lien may be general or special. A general lien is the right of the creditor to withhold the debtor's goods until the balance due to him under a course of dealing is discharged; a special lien is the right of the creditor to withhold the debtor's goods until the balance due to him under the transaction in the course of which he obtained possession of those goods is discharged.[4] Only exceptionally is a general right of lien recognized in Scots law, and normally only a special lien is admitted.[5]

Requisite possession

Actual possession, note merely constructive or fictional, is essential for lien.[6] The possession must be lawful, not acquired by fraud, under a void contract, by informal diligence, nor by mere accident or mistake.[7] Mere custody, as by an employee, will not

1 Ersk. II, 12, 67.

2 *Hamilton* v. *Western Bank* (1856) 19 D. 152; *National Bank* v. *Forbes* (1858) 21 D. 79.

3 The terms retention and lien are confused. Properly speaking the Scottish term is retention (of which there are three varieties: (a) special and general retention (or lien), (b) retention on a property title, and (c) retention of debt), but the English term lien is commonly now used for the right of withholding property and the term retention for the right of withholding money payable to the other party in security of a claim against him. In *Gladstone* v. *McCallum* (1896) 23 R. 783, Lord McLaren distinguishes retention (b) from lien (or retention (a)).

4 Stair I, 18, 7; Ersk. III, 4, 20; Bell, *Comm.* II, 91; *Prin.* 1411.

5 *Harper* v. *Faulds* (1791) Bell's Oct. Cas. 440; *Anderson's Tr.* v. *Fleming* (1871) 9 M. 718.

6 Bell, *Prin.* §1412; *Young* v. *Stein's Trs.* (1789) Mor. 14218; *Paton's Tr.* v. *Finlayson*, 1923 S.C. 872.

7 Bell, *Prin.* §1413; *Glendenning's Crs.* v. *Montgomery* (1745) Elch. Arrest. 24; *MacKenzie* v. *Newall* (1824) 3 S. 206; *Lawson* v. *Craik* (1842) 4 D. 1452; *Dickson* v. *Nicholson* (1855) 17 D. 1011; *Martinez y Gomez* v. *Allison* (1890) 17 R. 332; *Mitchell* v. *Heys* (1894) 21 R. 600; *Shepherd's Trs.* v. *Macdonald, Fraser & Co.* (1898) 5 S.L.T. 296.

suffice to confer a lien.[1] Nor can lien be claimed if there is possession but with specific appropriation inconsistent with the claims of lien.[2]

The right of lien terminates with the loss of possession, unless possession has been surrendered by error, or lost by fraud,[3] or has been relinquished under reservation of the creditor's claim.[4] To avoid depreciation the court may order sale of the subject of lien under reservation of the holder's preference.[5]

If it has once terminated, it does not revive on possession being recovered.[6]

Special lien

A special lien is a right, implied in contracts under which the owner of goods entrusts possession of the goods to another that he may do some work on or in relation to the goods, to retain possession of those goods until his claim for remuneration for the work done on those goods under the contract is satisfied.[7] It is essential that the person claiming the lien have possession of the goods; bare custody, as an employee, will not suffice.[8] The right of lien is lost if possession be surrendered, though part of the goods may be surrendered without prejudicing the lien over the remainder.[9] The right may also be refused if the apparent owner of the goods had only a limited title thereto which excluded the right to create any lien over the goods.[10]

Lien over ship for repairs

A lien is competent for repairs to a ship, but not for the furnishing of necessaries.[11]

[1] *Dickson, supra*; *Gladstone* v. *McCallum* (1896) 23 R. 783; *Barnton Hotel Co.* v. *Cook* (1899) 1 F. 1190; contrast *Meikle & Wilson* v. *Pollard* (1880) 8 R. 69; *Robertson* v. *Ross* (1887) 15 R. 67; *Findlay* v. *Waddell*, 1910 S.C. 670; where parties had possession, not merely custody.

[2] Bell, *Prin.* §1414; *Brown* v. *Somerville* (1844) 6 D. 1267; *Laurie* v. *Denny's Tr.* (1853) 15 D. 404; *Gray's Tr.* v. *Royal Bank* (1895) 23 R. 199.

[3] Bell, *Prin.* §1415.

[4] *Reid* v. *Galbraith* (1893) 1 S.L.T. 273.

[5] *Parker* v. *Brown* (1878) 5 R. 979.

[6] Bell, *Prin.* §1416.

[7] Bell, *Comm.* II, 92; *Prin.* §1419; *Harper* v. *Faulds* (1791) Mor. 2666; Bell's Oct. Cas. 432; *Miller* v. *Hutcheson* (1881) 8 R. 489; *Robertson* v. *Ross* (1887) 15 R. 67.

[8] *Barnton Hotel Co.* v. *Cook* (1899) 1 F. 1190; contrast *Findlay* v. *Waddell*, 1910 S.C. 670.

[9] *Gray* v. *Graham* (1855) 2 Macq. 435.

[10] *Lamonby* v. *Foulds*, 1928 S.C. 89.

[11] Bell, *Prin.* §1420; *Barr & Shearer* v. *Cooper* (1875) 2 R. (H.L.) 14; *Ross & Duncan* v. *Baxter* (1885) 13 R. 186; *Garscadden* v. *Ardrossan Dry Dock Co.*, 1910 S.C. 178.

Lien for freight

In carriage by land, and by sea, a carrier under a contract *locatio operis mercium vehendarum* has a lien on goods carried for the freight but, in the case of carriage by sea, not for dead freight or wharfage dues.[1] It extends over the whole of the goods carried under that contract;[2] if cargo is loaded by a sub-freighter it extends over it to the extent of the sub-freight.[3]

Lien for average loss

In carriage by sea the shipowners have a lien over the cargo for contributions due in respect of general average losses.[4]

Lien for salvage reward

Salvors who have taken possession of a ship or cargo as salvage, have a lien over the saved property for their salvage reward.[5]

Innkeeper's lien

An innkeeper or hotel proprietor has a lien over the guest's property, such as clothing and luggage, brought to the inn, for the expenses of his keep.[6] It is not lost by the guest's temporary absences *animo revertendi*, nor by allowing the guest to depart if his luggage remains at the hotel. By the Innkeepers Act, 1878, the innkeeper has power, subject to certain conditions, to sell goods left at his inn.[7]

Lien of person bestowing skill and labour

In general any person having possession of goods that he may bestow skill and labour on them, has a lien on the goods for the price of his work thereon.[8] A trustee under a trust deed for creditors has been held entitled to a lien over the trust estate in respect of his possession of the trust deed.[9]

[1] Bell, *Prin.* §1423; *Malcolm* v. *Bannatyne*, 15 Nov. 1814, F.C.; *Maclean & Hope* v. *Fleming* (1871) 9 M. (H.L.) 38; As to carriage by rail see *Sc. Central Ry. Co.* v. *Ferguson* (1864) 2 M. 781; *N.B. Ry.* v. *Carter* (1870) 8 M. 998; *Peebles* v. *Caledonian Ry.* (1875) 2 R. 346.

[2] *Lamb* v. *Kaselack, Alsen & Co.* (1882) 9 R. 482.

[3] *Youle* v. *Cochrane* (1868) 6 M. 427.

[4] Bell, *Prin.* §1426.

[5] Bell, *Prin.* §1427.

[6] But see Hotel Proprietors Act, 1956, S. 2(2).

[7] Bell, *Prin.* §1428.

[8] Bell, *Prin.* §1430; *Meikle & Wilson* v. *Pollard* (1880) 8 R. 69; *Robertson* v. *Ross* (1887) 15 R. 67; *Morrison* v. *Fulwell's Tr.* (1901) 9 S.L.T. 34; *Findlay* v. *Waddell*, 1910 S.C. 670; *Train & McIntyre, Ltd.* v. *Wm. Forbes, Ltd.*, 1925 S.L.T. 286; *Lamonby* v. *Foulds*, 1928 S.C. 89.

[9] *Miln's J.F.* v. *Spence's Trs.*, 1927 S.L.T. 425.

Seller's lien

An unpaid seller of goods has, *inter alia*, a lien or right to retain the goods for the price while he is in possession of them, notwithstanding that the property therein may have passed to the buyer.[1] He may exercise this right until payment or tender of the price in cases where (a) the goods have been sold without any stipulation as to credit; (b) where the goods have been sold on credit, but the term of credit has expired; and (c) where the buyer becomes insolvent.[2] The seller may exercise his right of lien notwithstanding that he is in possession of the goods as agent or custodier for the buyer.[3] It may be exercised even after partial delivery has been made.[4] The unpaid seller loses his lien (a) when he delivers the goods to a carrier or other custodier for transmission to the buyer without reserving the right of disposal of the goods; (b) when the buyer or his agent lawfully obtains possession of the goods; and (c) by waiver thereof,[5] but not by reason only that he has obtained decree for the price of the goods.[6] Exercise of the right of lien does not automatically effect rescission of the contract of sale.[7]

General lien

Exceptionally, by agreement express or implied in certain relationships, by the custom of particular professions and trades, a general right of lien is recognised whereby a person, given possession of goods under a contract to do work on or in relation to those goods is entitled to withhold redelivery of them in security of the whole balance due to him under the employment.[8] It may be created by notice imported into a contract to do work, but must be construed consistently with the usages of the trade in question.[9] If founded on usage of trade, the usage must be general, well-known and accepted as the rule. The precise range of the general lien depends in such a case on the usage of the particular profession or trade in question.[10]

[1] Sale of Goods Act, 1893, S. 39(1).
[2] Ibid., S. 41(1).
[3] Ibid., S. 41(2).
[4] Ibid., S. 42.
[5] Ibid., S. 43(1); cf. *Paton's Trs.* v. *Finlayson*, 1923 S.C. 872.
[6] Ibid., S. 43(2).
[7] Ibid., S. 48(1).
[8] Bell, *Comm.* II, 101; *Prin.* §1431–32; *Harper* v. *Faulds* (1791) Bell's Oct. Cas. 440; *Sibbald* v. *Gibson* (1852) 15 D. 217; *Hamilton* v. *Western Bank* (1856) 19 D. 152; *Borthwick* v. *Scottish Widows Fund* (1864) 2 M. 595; *Paul and Thain* v. *Royal Bank* (1869) 7 M. 361.
[9] *Anderson's Trs.* v. *Fleming* (1871) 9 M. 718.
[10] See e.g. *Strong* v. *Phillips* (1878) 5 R. 770.

Lien of mercantile agent or similar agent

A mercantile agent or factor has a general lien over all goods, documents, bills or money belonging to his principal which have come into his possession in the course of the employment as such agent.[1]

It covers the factor's claim for salary or commission,[2] any advances made to the principal, and any liabilities incurred on behalf of the principal[3] but not sums due to the factor arising on a separate account.[4]

A lien similar in extent to that of the mercantile agent has been held to attach in the cases of an auctioneer[5] and a stockbroker.[6]

Solicitor's lien

A solicitor has by custom a general right of lien over all papers entrusted to him by a client,[7] including title deeds, share certificates and the client's will,[8] but not the register of shareholders of a company,[9] nor papers entrusted for a special purpose, inconsistent with the lien,[10] nor the papers in a case which he has been employed to conduct,[11] nor the money received in such a process,[12] nor papers obtained after the client's notour bankruptcy,[13] nor papers acquired while acting for third parties.[14] The right is to retain the papers only, not to dispose of them.[15]

It covers his business account with the client, and also outlays made in the ordinary course of that business such as counsel's fees or the expenses of witnesses,[16] but not a salary as agent[17] nor cash advanced to the client[18] nor the account of the solicitor's Edinburgh agent in Court of Session business,[19] nor the account of the

[1] Bell, *Prin.* §1445: not for debts arising from other transactions: *Brown* v. *Smith* (1893) 1 S.L.T. 158.

[2] *Mackenzie* v. *Cormack*, 1950 S.C. 183.

[3] *Sibbald* v. *Gibson* (1852) 15 D. 217; *Glendinning* v. *Hope*, 1911 S.C. (H.L.) 73.

[4] *Miller* v. *McNair* (1852) 14 D. 955.

[5] *Miller* v. *Hutcheson & Dixon* (1881) 8 R. 489.

[6] *Glendinning*, *supra*.

[7] Bell, *Prin.* §1438.

[8] *Paul* v. *Meikle* (1868) 7 M. 235; *Drummond* v. *Muirhead & Guthrie Smith* (1900) 2 F. 585; cf. *McIntosh* v. *Chalmers* (1883) 11 R. 8; *Tawse* v. *Rigg* (1904) 6 F. 544.

[9] cf. *Gaepel Haematite Co.* v. *Andrew* (1866) 4 M. 617; cf. Companies Act, 1948, S. 110.

[10] *Chisholm* v. *Fraser* (1825) 3 S. 442.

[11] *Callman* v. *Bell* (1793) Mor. 6255.

[12] *Cullen* v. *Smith* (1845) 8 D. 77.

[13] *Jackson* v. *Fenwick's Tr.* (1899) 6 S.L.T. 319.

[14] *National Bank* v. *Thomas White & Park*, 1909 S.C. 1308.

[15] *Ferguson* v. *Grant* (1856) 18 D. 536, 538.

[16] Ersk. III, 4, 21; *Murdoch* (1841) 4 D. 257; *Richardson* v. *Merry* (1863) 1 M. 940, 946; *Palmer* v. *Lee* (1880) 7 R. 651.

[17] *Christie* v. *Ruxton* (1862) 24 D. 1182.

[18] *Christie* v. *Ruxton* (1862) 24 D. 1182; *Wylie's Exor.* v. *McJannet* (1901) 4 F. 195.

[19] *Largue* v. *Urquhart* (1883) 10 R. 1229.

solicitor's English correspondent, at least unless that account has been paid or the Scottish solicitor has accepted liability therefor.[1] The existence of a lien does not prevent the running of the triennial prescription of the account.[2]

The lien cannot be claimed against a trustee in bankruptcy, or the liquidator of a company, either of whom can require the surrender of all papers in the solicitor's charge relating to the estate being administered.[3] Such a surrender, made under reservation of the lien, entitles the solicitor to rank as a preferred creditor for his account,[4] but not to claim against the trustee or liquidator personally.[5] The lien need not be expressly reserved since it is automatically preserved by statute.[6]

In some cases a solicitor may exercise his right of lien not only against the client but against a third party deriving right from the client, such as a purchaser of heritage from, or a lender on heritable security to, the client.[7] No lien can now be acquired as against a heritable creditor by obtaining possession of title deeds after the heritable security has been recorded.[8] Nor can the right be claimed if the solicitor is acting for both parties in connection with the sale or loan, unless he has intimated to the purchaser or lender that he holds the title-deeds and claims a lien over them.[9]

It expires with the loss of possession, but that does not cover lodging the papers in process[10] nor transmitting them to his town agent.[11] Its exercise is subject to the equitable control of the court.[12] It may be waived, but not merely by taking a bill at short date for the money due.[13]

Lien of banker

A banker has a general lien over all bills, notes and negotiable securities in his hands in security of any balance due him by his

[1] *Grand Empire Theatre Liqr.* v. *Snodgrass*, 1932 S.C. (H.L.) 73.

[2] Bell, *Prin.* §1441; *Foggs* v. *McAdam* (1780) Mor. 6252.

[3] Bankruptcy (Sc.) Act, 1913, Ss. 76 and 97; Companies Act, 1948, S. 243; *Liqdr. of Weir & Wilson* v. *Turnbull & Findlay*, 1911 S.C. 1006; *Rorie* v. *Stevenson*, 1908 S.C. 559; *Train* v. *McIntyre's J.F.*, 1925 S.L.T. 286.

[4] *Skinner* v. *Henderson* (1865) 3 M. 867; *Liqdr. of Donaldsons & Co.* v. *White & Park*, 1908 S.C. 309; see also *Miln's J.F.* v. *Spence's Trs.*, 1927 S.C. 425.

[5] *Adam & Winchester* v. *White's Tr.* (1884) 11 R. 863; *Lochee Sawmills Co.* v. *Stevenson*, 1908 S.C. 559; see also *Garden, Haig-Scott & Wallace*, *infra*.

[6] *Garden, Haig-Scott & Wallace* v. *White*, 1962 S.C. 51.

[7] Bell, *Prin.* §1442.

[8] Conveyancing (Sc.) Act, 1924, S. 27, overruling *Provenhall's Crs.* (1781) Mor. 6253.

[9] *Gray* v. *Graham* (1855) 2 Macq. 435; *Drummond* v. *Muirhead & Guthrie Smith* (1900) 2 F. 585.

[10] Bell, *Prin.* §1440.

[11] Bell, *Comm.* II, 112.

[12] *Ferguson & Stuart* v. *Grant* (1856) 18 D. 536.

[13] *Palmer* v. *Lee* (1880) 7 R. 651.

customer,[1] but not over non-negotiable securities, nor non-negotiable securities deposited solely for safe-keeping,[2] unless in special circumstances where the banker had made an advance in reliance on a right of lien,[3] nor securities known to belong to the customer's principal.[4] His right is to retain the securities only, not to realise them,[5] and the right may be excluded by agreement, express or implied.[5]

If a stockbroker lodges negotiable securities with a banker, the latter is entitled to assume that they are the stockbroker's own property, and to claim a lien over them, in the stockbroker's bankruptcy, as against the real owners. But if the banker has notice, either actual, or implied by his knowledge of the usual course of business, that the securities belong to the stockbroker's client, he is not entitled to assume that the stockbroker had any authority to subject his client's securities to a lien for his own general debit balance with the banker, though if the securities are expressly pledged for a specific advance he is entitled to assume that the stockbroker had his client's authority to pledge them, and may accordingly retain them in security of an advance made.[6]

Other cases

A general lien has also been recognised in the cases of bleachers[7] and of calenderers and packers.[8]

Enforcement of lien

A claim of lien merely deprives the owner of his moveables until the claimant's claim be satisfied or the counterpart of the contract be performed. The holder is not entitled to sell unless the court authorises it which it can do possibly only in the case of marketable commodities.

(b) RETENTION ON PROPERTY TITLE

Where one party has a title of property to some subject, heritable or moveable, but is under a personal obligation to transfer or

1 Bell, *Prin.* §1451; *Paul & Thain* v. *Royal Bank* (1869) 7 M. 361; *Alston's Tr.* v. *Royal Bank* (1893) 20 R. 887.

2 *Brandao* v. *Barnett* (1846) 12 Cl. & F. 787.

3 *Robertson's Tr.* v. *Royal Bank* (1890) 18 R. 12.

4 *National Bank* v. *Dickie's Tr.* (1895) 22 R. 740; cf. *Gray's Tr.* v. *Royal Bank* (1895) 23 R. 199.

5 *Robertson's Tr., supra.*

6 *National Bank* v. *Dickie's Tr.* (1895) 22 R. 740.

7 *Anderson's Trs.* v. *Fleming* (1871) 9 M. 718.

8 *Strong* v. *Philips* (1878) 5 R. 770.

convey it to another, he is entitled to retain it in security of the payment of any debt, or the performance of any obligation, due to him by the party to whom he is bound to convey.[1] This right depends on property rather than on possession, and may be exercised over a subject to which the claimant has a title of property, though it be not in his actual possession,[2] and even against the good faith of the contract between the parties.[3]

This right was recognised in cases of sale of goods at common law, when goods sold remained the seller's property till delivered.[4] By the Sale of Goods Act, 1893, the seller's right of retention was in most cases abrogated by the provisions for the passing of the property independently of delivery (Ss. 17, 18) though the unpaid seller was given (S. 39) a lien on the goods, or right to retain them, if still in possession of them, but in security only for the price. The right still exists, however, where the passing of the property in the goods is postponed, and is ratified by S. 39(2).

The principle also applies where property is transferred *ex facie* outright but truly in security only and subject to an obligation to reconvey, as in cases of heritage conveyed in security by *ex facie* absolute disposition qualified by back bond, or of an incorporeal right assigned without qualification,[5] or of corporeal moveables transferred in security by giving the creditor a delivery order for the goods in the hands of a warehouse-keeper, completed by intimation of the order to and alteration of the custodier's books,[6] or transferred by outright sale subject to an obligation to sell back.[7] In such cases, if there is no back bond, or if it does not limit the right of retention, the creditor having *ex facie* a title of property, may retain the subjects until all debts due to him by the granter are paid.[8]

[1] Bell, *Comm.* I, 724; Gloag, *Contract*, 639–44; *Mein* v. *Bogle* (1828) 6 S. 360; *Robertson* v. *Duff* (1840) 2 D. 279; *Melrose* v. *Hastie* (1850) 12 D. 655; (1851) 13 D. 880; *Hamilton* v. *Western Bank* (1856) 19 D. 152; *National Bank* v. *Forbes* (1858) 21 D. 79; *Nelson* v. *Gordon* (1874) 1 R. 1093; *Distillers Co.* v. *Russell's Tr.* (1889) 16 R. 479; *Colquhoun's Tr.* v. *Diack* (1901) 4 F. 358.

[2] *Nelson, supra*, 1099.

[3] *Hamilton, supra*, 162.

[4] *Mein, supra*; *McEwan* v. *Smith* (1847) 9 D. 434; (1849) 6 Bell 340; *Melrose, supra*; *Robertson's Tr.* v. *Baird* (1852) 14 D. 1010; *Wyper* v. *Harveys* (1861) 23 D. 606; *Black* v. *Incorpn. of Bakers* (1867) 6 M. 136; *Distillers Co., supra*; *Robertson & Baxter* v. *McPherson* (1893) 1 S.L.T. 159.

[5] *Russell* v. *E. Breadalbane* (1831) 5 W. & S. 256; *Colquhoun's Tr.* v. *Diack* (1901) 4 F. 358; *Robertson's Tr.* v. *Riddell*, 1911 S.C. 14.

[6] *Hamilton* v. *Western Bank* (1856) 19 D. 152; see also *Hayman* v. *McLintock*, 1907 S.C. 936.

[7] *McBain* v. *Wallace* (1881) 8 R. (H.L.) 106; *Darling* v. *Wilson's Tr.* (1887) 15 R. 180; *Robertson* v. *Hall's Tr.* (1896) 24 R. 120; *Gavin's Tr.* v. *Fraser*, 1920 S.C. 674.

[8] *Hamilton, supra*; *Nelson* v. *Gordon* (1874) 1 R. 1093; *National Bank* v. *Union Bank* (1886) 14 R. (H.L.) 1 (heritage).

The creditor cannot, however, retain against parties deriving right from the debtor, such as the latter's trustee in bankruptcy,[1] or an assignee of the debtor's reversionary right[2] in respect of advances made after the date of the sequestration or intimation of the assignation.

The principle applies also to other cases of absolute right qualified by contract, such as a mandate to buy lands in the mandatary's own name,[3] a trust constituted by *ex facie* absolute conveyance,[4] a lease of premises to which were attached trade fixtures removeable by the tenant,[5] and ownership of a heritable security.[6]

The party having the right of property may not, however, in exercising his right of retention, disregard the express conditions of the contract under which he held that title so as to make the subjects a security for any debt owed to him by the other contracting party.[7]

(c) RETENTION OF DEBT

In the exercise of a right of retention a party to a mutual contract may withhold payment due to the other in security of performance by the other of the obligations due by him.[8] The mutual obligations must arise out of one and the same contract[9] and the right of retention may be asserted in respect both of a demand for a specific thing and of a claim of damages. Thus a buyer may retain the price in security of his claim of damages for failure to deliver within the specified time,[10] or a reasonable time,[11] a consignee for damage in transit,[12] an owner for damage to goods stored,[13] an employer for non-performance of duty,[14]

1 *Callum* v. *Goldie* (1885) 12 R. 1137; *Morton's Tr.* v. *Kirkhope* (1907) 15 S.L.T. 203.

2 *National Bank, supra.*

3 *Brough's Crs.* v. *Jollie* (1793) Mor. 2385.

4 *Robertson* v. *Duff* (1840) 2 D. 279.

5 *Smith* v. *Harrison & Co.'s Tr.* (1893) 21 R. 330; *Jaffrey's Trs.* v. *Milne* (1897) 24 R. 602.

6 *Colquhoun's Tr.* v. *Diack* (1901) 4 F. 358.

7 *Stewart* v. *Bisset* (1770) Mor. Compensation, Appx. 2; *Anderson's Tr.* v. *Somerville* (1899) 36 S.L.R. 833.

8 Bell, *Comm.* II, 118; Gloag, *Contract*, 626; *Johnston* v. *Robertson* (1861) 23 D. 646, 652, 656.

9 *Fulton Clyde, Ltd.* v. *McCallum*, 1960 S.L.T. 253.

10 *Johnston, supra*; *MacBride* v. *Hamilton* (1875) 2 R. 775.

11 *British Motor Body Co.* v. *Shaw*, 1914 S.C. 922.

12 *Taylor* v. *Forbes* (1830) 9 S. 113.

13 *Gibson & Stewart* v. *Brown* (1876) 3 R. 328.

14 *Tait* v. *McIntosh* (1841) 13 S. Jur. 280; *Scottish N.E. Ry.* v. *Napier* (1859) 21 D. 700; *Gibson* v. *McNaughton* (1861) 23 D. 358; *Sharp* v. *Rettie* (1884) 11 R. 745; *Moore's Carving Machine Co.* v. *Austin* (1896) 4 S.L.T. 38.

and a tenant may withhold payment of rent if the landlord has failed to a material extent to execute repairs.[1]

The claim to retain may not apply to a building contract with provision for instalment payment where the employer has unliquidated claims against the builder.[2]

In all cases the claim to retain is not an absolute right but a plea to which the court may refuse effect where the result would be inequitable, or if it is being used merely to delay,[3] or where money has been deposited specifically appropriated to some purpose.[4]

But a right of retention of a sum of money or thing due to the other cannot be exercised by virtue of an illiquid and unascertained claim against the other party not arising out of the mutual obligations of one and the same contract.[5]

Extended right of retention

On equitable grounds, however, an extended right of retention may be recognised in cases where an illiquid claim not arising out of the same contract can be readily verified and quantified,[6] where in the view of the court it would be inequitable to reject the plea of retention,[7] and where the creditor in the liquid claim (against whom the illiquid claim is made) is bankrupt, as that would require the debtor to pay in full and obtain only a ranking in bankruptcy for his illiquid claim if ultimately constituted.[8] In such a case, on the principle of balancing accounts in bankruptcy, a sum admittedly payable may be retained by virtue of an illiquid or disputed or contingent claim, unless the contingency is so remote that it cannot be evaluated.[9]

[1] *Macdonald* v. *Kydd* (1901) 3 F. 923; *E. Galloway* v. *McConnell*, 1911 S.C. 846; *Haig* v. *Boswall-Preston*, 1915 S.C. 339; *Fingland & Mitchell* v. *Howie*, 1926 S.C. 319.

[2] *Field & Allan* v. *Gordon* (1872) 11 M. 132.

[3] *Graham* v. *Gordon* (1843) 5 D. 1207; *Ferguson & Stewart* v. *Grant* (1865) 18 D. 536; *Garscadden* v. *Ardrossan Dry Dock Co.*, 1910 S.C. 178; *E. Galloway, supra*.

[4] *Field, supra*; *McGregor* v. *Alley & McLellan* (1887) 14 R. 535; *Middlemas* v. *Gibson*, 1910 S.C. 577.

[5] Ersk. III, 4, 15; Bell, *Prin.* §573; *National Exchange Co.* v. *Drew* (1855) 2 Macq. 103, 122; *Smith* v. *S.* (1866) 4 M. 279; *Mackie* v. *Riddell* (1874) 2 R. 115; *Sutherland* v. *Urquhart* (1895) 23 R. 284; *Asphaltic Limestone Co.* v. *Glasgow Corpn.*, 1907 S.C. 463; *Christie* v. *Birrells*, 1910 S.C. 986; *Smart* v. *Wilkinson*, 1928 S.C. 383.

[6] *Ross* v. *R.* (1895) 22 R. 461.

[7] *Munro* v. *Macdonald's Exors.* (1866) 4 M. 87; 6*Ross, supra*; *Lovie* v. *Baird's Trs.* (1895) 23 R. 1 (expld. *Sutherland* v. *Urquhart* (1895) 23 R. 284).

[8] Bell, *Comm.* II, 122; *Ross, supra*.

[9] *Mill* v. *Paul* (1825) 4 S. 219; *Borthwick* v. *Scottish Widows Fund* (1864) 2 M. 595; *Hannay & Son's Trs.* v. *Armstrong Bros.* (1877) 4 R. (H.L.) 43; *Scott's Trs.* v. *S.* (1887) 14 R. 1043; *Taylor's Tr.* v. *Paul* (1888) 15 R. 313.

Operation of retention

Where retention is justifiably exercised the party retaining must qualify his claim as quickly as practicable, whereupon compensation will operate between the parties to the effect of extinguishing the lesser claim and diminishing the greater *pro tanto*.[1]

Security by use of sale or hire-purchase transactions

The Sale of Goods Act, 1893, by S. 61(4) does not apply to any transaction in the form of a contract of sale which is intended to operate by way of pledge, charge or other security. A sale with such an object is regulated by common law and must be completed by *traditio*. The rule that no security can be created over moveables without delivery of possession cannot be defeated by such a simulate transaction as a sale of property to another party who immediately lets the property back to the sellers on hire or hire-purchase terms, reserving the right to retake possession if there is default in payments of hire.[2] In each case the reality of the transaction must be examined,[3] and a genuine outright sale, followed by hire or hire-purchase back, seems unobjectionable.

Any *bona fide* hire-purchase contract does, however, in substance provide for security over moveables without possession in that ownership does not pass to the hirer until all the payments of rental have been made and the option to purchase exercised and during that time the owner can on default, subject to the Hire-Purchase (Sc.) Act, 1965, repossess the goods. The owner in substance has lent the hirer the unpaid balance of the purchase price at interest,[4] as provided in the hire-purchase agreement.

SECURITY RIGHTS WITHOUT POSSESSION

In certain limited circumstances rights in security over moveables are recognised though the creditor has not been given possession of the security subjects.[5] These are hypothecs, which are recognised legally or tacitly in certain cases by settled custom, and may be created conventionally in certain other cases.

1 Compensation Act, 1592.

2 *Rennet* v. *Mathieson* (1903) 5 F. 591; *Hepburn* v. *Law*, 1914 S.C. 918; *Gavin's Tr.* v. *Fraser*, 1920 S.C. 674; *Newbigging* v. *Ritchie's Tr.*, 1930 S.C. 273; *Scottish Transit Trust* v. *Scottish Land Cultivators*, 1955 S.C. 254; *G. & C. Finance Corpn., Ltd.* v. *Brown*, 1961 S.L.T. 408.

3 *Robertson* v. *Hall's Tr.* (1897) 24 R. 120; *Scottish Transit Trust, supra.*

4 The decision in *Maclean* v. *McCord*, 1965 S.L.T. (Sh. Ct.) 69 is insupportable.

5 Stair I, 13, 14; Ersk. III, 1, 34; Bell, *Comm.* II, 24; *Prin.* §1385.

LEGAL OR TACIT HYPOTHECS[1]

Feudal superior's hypothec

A feudal superior of lands has a right of hypothec[2] over the fruits of the feu in security of his feuduty, preferable to the landlord's hypothec. It extends also to *invecta et illata*.[3]

Landlord's hypothec

A landlord similarly has a right of hypothec over the tenant's *invecta et illata* in security of his claim for rent.[4] Landlord's hypothec has been abolished in respect of all subjects let for agriculture or pasture and exceeding two acres in extent,[5] and, in the case of lets regulated by the Houseletting and Rating Act, 1911, there are excepted all bedding materials, all tools and implements of trade used or to be used by the occupier or any member of his family as a means of livelihood, which are in the house, and also such further furniture and plenishing as the occupier may select to the value of £10 according to the sheriff-officer's inventory.[6] In cases where it applies, such as houses, shops, market gardens, and mines and quarries, hypothec covers all the *invecta et illata*, including goods obtained on hire or hire-purchase,[7] though not to goods held on hire in premises let furnished.[8]

Hypothec does not cover goods not belonging to the tenant, such as those of one of his family, or of a lodger,[9] or in the tenant's possession for a limited purpose, such as repair.[10] The goods of a sub-tenant, however, may be attached for the sub-rent and also for the principal tenant's rent.[11]

The landlord may obtain interdict against removal of *invecta et illata* to preserve his security and, if they have been removed, may after intimation to the tenant, unless the judgment states an exceptional reason to the contrary,[12] obtain warrant to have them brought back. Such remedies are, however, exceptional and the

[1] Bell, *Comm.* II, 26.
[2] Bell, *Comm.* II, 260.
[3] *Yuille* v. *Lawrie* (1823) 2 S. 155.
[4] Ersk. II, 6, 56; Bell, *Comm.* II, 27; *Prin.* §1234, 1275, 1887.
[5] Hypothec Abolition Act, 1880; as to effect see *McGavin* v. *Sturrock's Tr.* (1891) 18 R. 576.
[6] 1911 Act, S. 10.
[7] *Nelmes* v. *Ewing* (1883) 11 R. 193; *McIntosh* v. *Potts* (1905) 7 F. 765.
[8] *Edinburgh Albert Bldg. Co.* v. *General Guarantee Corpn.*, 1917 S.C. 239.
[9] *Bell* v. *Andrews* (1885) 12 R. 961.
[10] *Pulsometer Co.* v. *Gracie* (1887) 14 R. 316.
[11] *Stewart* v. *Stables* (1878) 5 R. 1024.
[12] *Johnston* v. *Young* (1890) 18 R. (J.) 6; *Jack* v. *Black*, 1911 S.C. 691.

landlord will be liable in damages if interdict is obtained on unfounded statements,[1] or if there is a dispute as to the rent and such extreme steps are unnecessary.[2]

Enforcement

Enforcement of hypothec is by petitioning the sheriff court[3] for warrant to sequestrate the tenant's goods which are then inventoried and valued by a sheriff officer and, failing payment, warrant is sought from the court to have them sold by auction to satisfy the landlord's claim for rent. Once inventoried the goods are deemed to be in the court's custody and any party intromitting with them must account for their value and, if he acts in bad faith, is liable for the rent.[4]

Hypothec secures only one year's rent, and falls if not enforced within three months of the last term of payment. Prior arrears can be recovered only by action.[5]

Solicitor's hypothec

A solicitor who has advanced money on outlays and expenses for a litigation has at common law a claim of hypothec over any expenses awarded to his client, which entitles him to move for decree for expenses in his own favour as agent-disburser, in which case he obtains a right thereto preferable to any ordinary creditor of the client. He may obtain decree therefor even after the client has been sequestrated.[6] His claim is preferable to a claim by the other party under a plea of compensation, unless cross awards of expenses are made in the same action or in two actions arising from the same matters, in which case the claim of compensation is preferable to the solicitor's claim under hypothec.[7] This qualification, it has been said, will not be extended[8] and does not apply where decree in one action has been extracted before the other action has been raised.[9]

The solicitor may even move that he be sisted as a party to the action to make his hypothec over expenses effectual; he is entitled to be sisted where decree for expenses has been actually pronounced, or where an interlocutor has been pronounced on

[1] *Jack, supra*; *Shearer* v. *Nicoll*, 1935 S.L.T. 313.

[2] *Gray* v. *Weir* (1891) 19 R. 25.

[3] *Duncan* v. *Lodijensky* (1904) 6 F. 408.

[4] Bell, *Prin.* §1244.

[5] *Young* v. *Welsh* (1833) 12 S. 233.

[6] Bell, *Comm.* II, 34, *Prin.* §1388; *Hunter* v. *Pearson* (1835) 13 S. 495; *Cullen* v. *Smith* (1845) 8 D. 771; *Peddie* v. *Davidson* (1856) 18 D. 1306.

[7] *Lochgelly Iron Co.* v. *Sinclair*, 1907 S.C. 442; *Fine* v. *Edinburgh Life Assce. Co.*, 1909 S.C. 636; *Byrne* v. *Baird*, 1929 S.C. 624.

[8] *Jack* v. *Laing*, 1929 S.C. 426

[9] *Baird* v. *Campbell*, 1928 S.C. 487.

which decree for expenses necessarily follows, or where the action has been settled in the knowledge that the client was insolvent, and with the intention of defeating the solicitor's right.[1]

If decree for expenses is granted in the client's favour, the solicitor's hypothec is unaffected and, if his claim is intimated to the party liable in expenses, is preferable to that of the trustee in his client's sequestration;[2] but it may be excluded by a prior arrestment of the expenses,[3] or by a duly intimated assignation,[4] and is liable to a plea of compensation by the party liable in expenses.[5]

Statutory charge over property recovered

By statute[6] the court may in any action declare the solicitor entitled to a charge on and a right to payment out of, property of any kind or tenure, which has been recovered or preserved on behalf of the client, for his expenses; if such a declaration be granted, the court may make an order for raising and payment of such expenses as may seem proper, and acts or deeds by the client thereafter, unless in favour of a *bona fide* purchaser or lender, are void as against the solicitor's right. Such a declaration is probably precluded by the client's sequestration,[7] but not by a prior arrestment,[8] or by the client company's liquidation.[9] It is competent though the fund sought to be charged is outwith Scotland.[9] The court has a general discretion to make or refuse a declaration[10] and the Court of Session may grant one in favour of a country agent,[11] or of an agent for a litigant on the poor's roll,[12] but a charge cannot be granted to the prejudice of a counter-claim for expenses by the other party to the action.[13]

Maritime hypothec or liens

Maritime hypothecs (commonly called maritime liens) are rights in security over a ship without possession, recognised only

[1] *Macgregor & Barclay* v. *Martin* (1867) 5 M. 583; *Cornwall* v. *Walker* (1871) 8 S.L.R. 442; *Crawford* v. *Smith* (1900) 8 S.L.T. 249; *Ammon* v. *Tod*, 1912 S.C. 306; *Peek* v. *P.*, 1926 S.C. 565.

[2] *McTavish* v. *Pedie* (1828) 6 S. 593.

[3] *Stephen* v. *Smith* (1830) 8 S. 847.

[4] *Fleeming* v. *Love* (1839) 1 D. 1097.

[5] *Fleeming, supra.*

[6] Solicitors (Sc.) Act, 1933, S. 43, replacing Law Agents (Sc.) Act, 1891, S. 6.

[7] *Tait* v. *Wallace* (1894) 2 S.L.T. 252.

[8] *Automobile Syndicate* v. *Caledonian Ry.*, 1909 1 S.L.T. 499.

[9] *Philip* v. *Willson*, 1911 S.C. 1203.

[10] *Carruthers' Tr.* v. *Finlay & Wilson* (1897) 24 R. 363; *Stenhouse* v. *S's Tr.* (1903) 10 S.L.T. 684; *Smart* v. *Stewart*, 1911 2 S.L.T. 340.

[11] *Bannatyne, Kirkwood, France & Co.*, 1907 S.C. 705.

[12] *Cameron* v. *McDonald*, 1935 S.N. 25.

[13] *O'Keefe* v. *Grieve's Trs.*, 1917 1 S.L.T. 305.

in definite and known cases of necessity,[1] and preferable to the rights of mortgagees.[2]

The ship's master has a lien for his wages and for disbursements properly made by him on account of the ship.[3] Members of the crew similarly have a lien for their wages, which they cannot exclude by contract.[4] A third party who pays the seaman's wages is subrogated to their lien, without written assignation, unless he is shown to have paid in reliance on the owner's personal credit, when he ranks only as an ordinary creditor and postponed to a mortgagee.[5]

A salvor has a lien over the ship for his salvage reward.[6]

Another vessel, damaged in collision, has a lien for its claim of damages against the vessel in fault.[7]

Persons who supply goods to, or execute repairs on, the vessel in a foreign port have no lien for their charges;[8] and there is no such right in a home port unless the vessel be arrested.[9]

The owners of goods shipped may have a lien for loss caused by improper interruption of the voyage, or damage done by improper stowage,[10] or for average loss.[11]

Enforcement of a maritime lien is by petition to the court to declare the lien and to order judicial sale of the ship in satisfaction thereof.[12]

CONVENTIONAL HYPOTHECS[13]

Bond of bottomry

The only conventional hypothecs recognised in Scots law are bonds of bottomry and of respondentia. A bond of bottomry is a

1 Bell, *Prin.* §1397.
2 *Harmer* v. *Bell* (1851) 7 Moo. P.C. 267.
3 Ersk. III, 2, 34; Bell, *Comm.* I, 562; *Prin.* §1400; *Seamen of the Golden Star* v. *Miln* (1682) Mor. 6259; *Sands* v. *Scott* (1708) Mor. 6261; M.S.A., 1894, S. 167(2); *Morgan* v. *Castlegate S.S. Co.* [1893] A.C. 38; *The Orienta* [1895] P. 49.
4 M.S.A., 1894, S. 156.
5 *Clark* v. *Bowring*, 1908 S.C. 1168 (but doubted in *Clydesdale Bank, infra*).
6 *Duncan* v. *Dundee, Perth & London Shipping Co.* (1878) 5 R. 742; *Hatton* v. *A/S Durban Hansen*, 1919 S.C. 154.
7 *Currie* v. *McKnight* (1896) 24 R. (H.L.) 1; *Clan Line* v. *E. Douglas Steamship Co.*, 1913 S.C. 967; *McConnachie*, 1914 S.C. 853. Not so where damage is done not by the other vessel, but by its master or crew, without collision.
8 *Constant* v. *Christensen*, 1912 S.C. 371.
9 *Wood* v. *Hamilton* (1789) 3 Paton 148; *Northgate* v. *Henrich Bjorn (Owners)* (1886) 11 App. Cas. 270; *Clydesdale Bank* v. *Walker and Bain*, 1926 S.C. 72.
10 Bell, *Comm.* II, 38; *Prin.* §1399.
11 Bell, *Comm.* II, 39; *Prin.* §1401.
12 *McConnachie*, 1914 S.C. 853.
13 Bell, *Comm.* II, 24.

bond granted by the owner, or master of a ship, creating security over the ship itself without possession or entry on the ship's register. A bond by an owner is now unknown. The master has implied power to grant a bottomry bond if his ship is in a foreign port, is unable to proceed on its voyage for lack of money, no money is procurable on the owner's personal credit, and communication with the owner is impracticable.[1] If communication were practicable, it must be made and authority obtained.

The essentials of the bond are that it specify the ship, the voyage, the risk, and the event on which it becomes exigible, failing which, if not authorised by the owner, it is unenforceable.[2]

The lender has no claim if communication with the owner were not made, if practicable, if the circumstances did not justify the master's action, or if the ship fail to arrive at her destination. Bottomry bonds are preferred in reverse order of dates, as it is presumed that the latest was that which secured the ship's completion of her voyage.[3]

If the bond is valid the lender may enforce it by arresting the ship and insisting on judicial sale.[4] His claim ranks before any mortgagee of the ship or any ordinary creditor, but is postponed to the maritime lien of the master and seamen.[5]

Bond of respondentia

A respondentia bond may be granted by the owner or master, creating security over the ship's cargo, without possession thereof, or endorsation or delivery of a bill of lading. The ship's master has implied power to grant such a bond if there is no other means of raising money to enable him to prosecute his voyage.[6]

If communication with the cargo owner is practicable, it must be made.

Even if the ship does not arrive at her destination, but the cargo does, the bond is enforceable.[7] Enforcement is by the holders of the bond attaching the cargo and, if not repaid, selling it by judicial authority.

The grant of such a bond renders the shipowners liable to indemnify the cargo owners if the cargo is attached or sold under the bond.[8]

[1] Bell, *Comm.* I, 578; Bell, *Prin.* 452, 1386; *Kleinworth, Cohen & Co.* v. *Cassa Maritima* (1877) 2 App. Cas. 156.

[2] *Miller* v. *Potter, Wilson & Co.* (1875) 3 R. 105.

[3] Bell, *Prin.* §456.

[4] *Lucovitch, Petr.* (1885) 12 R. 1090.

[5] *The Daring* (1868) L.R. 2 Adm. & Ecc. 260.

[6] *Anderson Foundry Co.* v. *Law* (1869) 7 M. 836; *Dymond* v. *Scott* (1877) 5 R. 196.

[7] Bell, *Comm.* I, 584; *Anderson Foundry Co., supra.*

[8] *Anderson Foundry Co., supra.*

Floating charge

At common law the competency of a floating charge, i.e. a charge or security attaching without possession to whatever property and assets belonged for the time being to the debtor, was not recognised by Scots law, even in respect of assets situated in England where a floating charge was competent.[1] By the Companies (Floating Charges) (Sc.) Act, 1961, it was made competent for an incorporated company, for the purpose of securing any debt incurred or to be incurred, to create a floating charge over all or any of the property, heritable or moveable, which might from time to time be comprised in its property and undertaking.[2] It may be created only by the execution under the seal of the company of an instrument of charge as nearly as practicable in the form set out in Sched. I to the Act, or of a bond or written acknowledgement of debt incorporating words to the like effect. It may except certain property from its application.[3] On the commencement of winding up it attaches to the property then comprised in the company's property and undertaking, apart from any excepted property, subject to the rights of any person who (a) has effectually executed diligence on any of the property (b) holds a fixed security over any of the property ranking in priority to the floating charge; or (c) holds over any of the property another floating charge so ranking.[4]

A floating charge affects heritable property though not recorded in the Register of Sasines.[5]

Charges (including floating charges) created by companies registered in Scotland are void against the liquidator and any creditor of the company unless the prescribed particulars and a copy of the instrument of charge are delivered to the registrar of companies for registration within 21 days.[6]

A fixed security arising by operation of law has priority over a floating charge, and any other fixed security has priority unless the contract creating the fixed security was made after the 1961 Act, and the floating charge was registered before the fixed security was made a real right, and the instrument creating the floating charge prohibited the company from subsequently creating any fixed security having priority over, or ranking equally with, the floating charge. *Inter se* floating charges rank accordingly to the time of their registration, unless provided to rank *pari passu*.[7]

[1] *Carse* v. *Coppen*, 1951 S.C. 233. [2] 1961 Act, S. 1(1). [3] 1961 Act, S. 2.
[4] 1961 Act, S. 1(2). 'Fixed security' is defined by S. 8(1)(c). [5] 1961 Act, S. 3.
[6] Companies Act, 1948, S. 106A, added by 1961 Act, Sched. II. [7] 1961 Act, S. 5.

The Industrial and Provident Societies Act, 1967, enables a society registered under the Industrial and Provident Societies Acts, 1965 to 1967, to create such a floating charge. The 1961 Act applies with modifications to such a charge.

Special statutory provisions for securities—Ships

By the Merchant Shipping Act, 1894, S. 31, a ship or a share therein may be mortgaged in security by an instrument in the form of Sched. I, Form B, which must be recorded by the registrar of the ship's port of registry, in the order in which they are produced for registration.[1] On production of a mortgage with a receipt enclosed thereon, the registrar must record that the mortgage has been discharged (S. 32).[2] Mortgagees have priority *inter se* according to the dates when each mortgage is recorded in the register (S. 33).[3] A mortgagee is not deemed owner of the ship, save so far as necessary to make it available as a security for the mortgage debt (S. 34).[4] A mortgagee has power of sale (S. 35), and a mortgage is not affected by the mortgagor's bankruptcy and is preferred to any claim of the other creditors or the trustee in bankruptcy (S. 36). But a bottomry bond and a maritime lien (hypothec) both take priority over a mortgage.[5]

A mortgage may be transferred by instrument (Sched. I, Form G) recorded by the registrar (S. 37) and on transmission by marriage, death or bankruptcy or other lawful means. The transmission has to be authenticated by a declaration of the transferee and recorded by the registrar (S. 38).

If a registered owner wishes to mortgage the ship outwith the country of the port of registry he may, subject to certain conditions, obtain from the registrar a certificate of mortgage (Ss. 39–42). The power of mortgage thereby conferred must be exercised in conformity with the directions in the certificate, and every mortgage made thereunder must be registered by endorsement of a record thereof on the certificate by a registrar or British consular officer. The discharge may be redelivered to the registrar and cancelled (S 43). The owner may authorise the registrar to give notice that a certificate is revoked (S. 46).

[1] The stipulations of the mortgage agreement may be in a separate deed: *The Benwell Tower* (1895) 8 Asp. M.L.C. 13.

[2] cf. *Duthie* v. *Aitken* (1893) 20 R. 214. [3] *Black* v. *Williams* [1895] 1 Ch. 408.

[4] cf. *Laming* v. *Seater* (1889) 16 R. 828.

[5] *The Royal Arch* (1857) Swab. 269; *The Staffordshire* (1872) L.R. 4 P.C. 194; *The Arbonne* (1925) 33 Ll.L.R. 141.

CHAPTER 97

EXTINCTION OF RIGHTS IN CORPOREAL MOVEABLE PROPERTY

THE extinction of ownership of corporeal moveables may take place by voluntary divestiture of title, as by gift, barter, or sale,[1] or by involuntary divestiture of title by operation of law, as by legal diligence, or judicial sequestration, or judicial sale,[2] or by the consumption, destruction, perishing, or loss of the moveable property. In the case of loss property mislaid or forgotten is deemed still to belong to the owner so long as he has *animus possidendi*, and any finder who retains the property for himself commits theft. If, however, the property has been abandoned and *animus possidendi* relinquished the principle *quod nullius est fit domini regis* applies.[3]

Dereliction

Where property has been left with the apparent object of abandoning it, the owner may be criminally liable for abandoning it;[4] if he is not discoverable the property vests in the Crown under the *quod nullius* principle.[5] Property may be left, however, with the intention that another take it away as rubbish, for salvage or destruction. Till collected it remains in the former owner's ownership and possession.[6] Possession and ownership pass constructively when the intended person removes the articles, and any third party who takes the articles for his own purposes commits theft.[6]

Succession

An owner's title to moveables also terminates on his death, when it devolves under the terms of his will or the rules of intestacy.[7]

1 Ch. 95, *supra*.
2 Ch. 95, *supra*.
3 Ersk. II, 1, 12; Bell, *Prin.* §1291.
4 Litter Act, 1958; as to stray dogs, see Dogs Act, 1906, Ss. 3–4; as to abandoned vehicles and other rubbish, see Civic Amenities Act, 1967, Part III.
5 Stair II, 1, 5; III, 3, 27; Mack. II, 1; Bankt. I, 3, 16; I, 8, 4; Ersk. II, 1, 11; Bell, *Prin.* §1294; *Sands* v. *Bell and Balfour*, 22 May 1810, F.C.
6 cf. *Ellermann Wilson Line* v. *Webster* [1952] 1 Lloyd's Rep. 179; *Digby* v. *Heelan* [1952] C.L.Y. 790; R. v. *Samuel* (1956) 40 Cr. A.R. 8; *Williams* v. *Phillips* (1957) 41 Cr. A.R. 5.
7 Chs. 112–3, *infra*.

Loss of possession

Possession is wholly lost when a person, having abandoned or lost physical control, also abandons *animus possidendi*, but not merely by transferring control and custody to another, nor by mere forgetfulness.

PART 5
INCORPOREAL MOVEABLE PROPERTY

CHAPTER 98

INCORPOREAL MOVEABLE PROPERTY AND RIGHTS THERETO

INCORPOREAL moveable property comprises certain kinds of immaterial or incorporeal abstractions, which exist only as bodies of legal claims and rights but have no physical existence which can be actually possessed and which, moreover, are deemed not connected with or like land and are accordingly moveable rather than heritable in succession.[1] The objects of incorporeal moveable property sometimes consist of a single right, such as to payment, but sometimes of groups of various interrelated rights and interests, which can be dealt with separately, such as the various rights which collectively amount to the copyright of a book. Some of these groups of rights exist in relation to a corporeal subject, but are distinct from rights in and to that corporeal subject,[2] while others exist only in the contemplation of the law, unrelated to any corporeal subject.

Title to some kinds of incorporeal moveable property is evidenced by deeds of various kinds, but these writs are merely the evidents of title and do not themselves constitute the property. In other cases the owner has no documentary proof of his title, and the question of ownership may be disputed.

Kinds of incorporeal moveable property

Incorporeal moveable property includes a wide variety of particular rights or groups of rights; the main kinds are decrees of court, claims of debt, claims of damages, rights of relief, rights under contract, negotiable instruments, bills of lading, other documents of title to goods, personal bonds, pension rights, *jura*

1 Ersk. II, 2, 7; Bell, *Comm.* I, 100; *Prin.* §1476–89; cf. Inst. II, 2.

2 Thus the rights which comprise an author's copyright are quite distinct from his rights in and to the manuscript which contains the words which are the subject of his copyright.

crediti under wills and trusts, some rights in security over corporeal property, reversionary rights, policies of insurance, British government and public corporation stock, interests in partnerships and companies, business rights, rights to registered trade marks, to patents, of copyright, in registered designs, and in plant breeders' rights.

Whether a right or group of rights can be described as an object of incorporeal moveable property depends on whether the right or group of rights is assignable *inter vivos*, transmits to executors on death and passes to the trustee in bankruptcy on the holder's sequestration. If it is not assignable or transmissible it is personal and not an object of property.[1]

Interests in incorporeal moveable property

As property of this class consists only in legal rights and claims, capable of legal enforcement, the only interest which can subsist in any object of this class of property is ownership, in the sense of being the person entitled to enforce some or all of the legal rights amounting to such property. Property of this class cannot be possessed separately from ownership. To own something within one of these categories means to have the legal rights and claims which attach by law to the person entitled to such a group of rights; what rights and claims do attach to each kind of incorporeal property are defined by common law or statute, and differ from one category to another. The ownership may, however, be burdened by a disposition in security of some or all of the rights, or it may in some cases be divided, some rights being vested in one person, others in another.

In respect of each kind of incorporeal moveable property the relevant questions are how such property is created, how it is evidenced, what rights and claims against other people are conferred by ownership of it, how the rights may be enforced or protected, whether and, if so, how they may be transferred outright or in security, and how they are extinguished or terminated.

[1] *Tawse's Trs.* v. *L.A.*, 1943 S.C. 124.

CHAPTER 99

ACQUISITION OF INCORPOREAL MOVEABLE RIGHTS

Creation of incorporeal moveable property

THE modes of creation and of a person's acquisition of incorporeal moveable property are various; in some cases it comes into being *ipso jure*, sometimes by registration, by decree of court, by contract, by disposition or bequest of another.

DECREES AND RIGHTS OF ACTION

Decrees

A decree of court for payment or *ad factum praestandum*, pronounced in due course by a court of competent jurisdiction, imposes on the defender against whom it has passed an obligation to obtemper it and vests the party in right of the decree with a *jus exigendi* enforceable by diligence. Hence a decree for the payment of money can be assigned by the party in right[1] and passes on death to and is exigible by the entitled party's executor.[2] Where a third party relieves the debtor by paying his debt, he is entitled to an assignation of the decree from the creditor,[3] and where one joint wrongdoer satisfies a joint and several decree held by a pursuer he is entitled to an assignation of the decree to enable him to recover relief *pro tanto* from the other joint wrongdoers.[4]

Claims of debt

A claim of debt arises from the non-performance of the pecuniary obligation under a contract, as by non-payment at the due date of a liquidated sum due under the contract. Such a claim is an asset of the creditor's estate which may be assigned[5] or

1 *Stewart* v. *Kidd* (1852) 14 D. 527; *Rose* v. *Stevenson* (1888) 15 R. 336; *Purnell* v. *Shannon* (1894) 22 R. 74; *Steven* v. *Broady Norman & Co.*, 1928 S.C. 351.

2 *Morrison* v. *M's Exrx.*, 1912 S.C. 892.

3 *Smith* v. *Gentle* (1844) 6 D. 1164.

4 *Palmer* v. *Wick and Pulteneytown S.S. Co.* (1894) 21 R. (H.L.) 39; see also Law Reform (Misc. Prov.) (Sc.) Act, 1940, S. 3(2); *Central S.M.T. Co.* v. *Lanarkshire C.C.*, 1949 S.C. 450; *N.C.B.* v. *Thomson*, 1959 S.C. 353.

5 Stair III, 1, 3; Ersk. III, 5, 2; Bell, *Prin.* §1341, 1459; *Fraser* v. *Duguid* (1838) 16 S. 1130.

bequeathed and is exigible by his executor[1] or trustee in bankruptcy.[2] A provision that a debt is not to be assigned may bar a claim by a gratuitous assignee,[3] but of doubtful validity against an onerous assignee.

Claims of damages

A claim of damages arising from a breach of obligation, whether *ex contractu* or *ex delicto*, is an incorporeal right capable of vindication by action.[4] It arises *ex lege* on the occurrence of a breach of a valid and enforceable contract, or on the breach of a duty of care not to cause unjustifiable harm owed in the circumstances to the injured person.

A claim arising *ex contractu* transmits as moveable property on the claimant's death, is enforceable by his executor and assignable to a third party.[5]

A claim arising *ex delicto*, if of a personal character, as for injuries to the claimant's person, or character, is purely personal, and though assignable *inter vivos*,[6] if not pursued by him does not pass to his trustee in bankruptcy,[7] and lapses on his death.[8] If, however, action has been initiated during the claimant's lifetime, the claim passes to his executor and may be enforced by the executor for behoof of the estate,[9] and probably assigned by him.

If, on the other hand, the claim is of a proprietary character, for patrimonial loss, such as for loss of earnings or damage to property, the claim, if not pursued by the injured person, is assignable *inter vivos*[10] and, on his death, transmits to his executor and is enforceable for the benefit of the estate.[11] It passes on his bankruptcy to the trustee.[12] Even a claim for damages for loss of or

[1] *Walker* v. *Orr's Trs.*, 1958 S.L.T. 63; cf. *Morrison* v. *M's Exrx.*, 1912 S.C. 893.

[2] Bankruptcy (Sc.) Act, 1913, Ss. 70, 97; *Gallie* v. *Lockhart* (1840) 2 D. 445; *Hallowell* v. *Niven* (1843) 5 D. 655.

[3] *Boswall* v. *Arnott* (1759) Mor. 12578; see also *Strachan* v. *Barclay* (1683) Mor. 4310.

[4] Ersk. II, 2, 17; *Milne* v. *Gauld's Trs.* (1841) 3 D. 345, 350; *Caledonian Ry.* v. *Watt* (1875) 2 R. 917, 921.

[5] *Levett* v. *L.N.W. Ry.* (1866) 2 S.L.R. 207; *Riley* v. *Ellis*, 1910 S.C. 934.

[6] *Traill* v. *Dalbeattie* (1904) 6 F. 798; *Cole-Hamilton* v. *Boyd*, 1963 S.C. (H.L.) 1.

[7] *Muir's Tr.* v. *Braidwood*, 1958 S.C. 169.

[8] *Bern's Exor.* v. *Montrose Asylum* (1893) 20 R. 859; *Stewart* v. *L.M.S. Ry.*, 1943 S.C. (H.L.) 19; *Smith* v. *Stewart*, 1960 S.C. 329.

[9] Bell, *Prin.* §546; *Milne* v. *Gauld's Trs.* (1841) 3 D. 345; *Neilson* v. *Rodger* (1853) 16 D. 325; *Darling* v. *Gray* (1892) 19 R. (H.L.) 31; *Borthwick* v. *B.* (1896) 24 R. 211; *Reid* v. *Lanarkshire Traction Co.*, 1934 S.C. 79; *Stewart, supra*; *Smith, supra.*

[10] cf. *Liqdr. of Larkhall Collieries* v. *Hamilton* (1906) 14 S.L.T. 202.

[11] *Mein* v. *Call* (1844) 6 D. 1112; *Davidson* v. *Tulloch* (1863) 3 Macq. 783; *Garden* v. *Davidson* (1864) 2 M. 758; *Auld* v. *Shairp* (1875) 2 R. 191; *Fraser* v. *Livermore Bros.* (1900) 7 S.L.T. 450; *Riley* v. *Ellis*, 1910 S.C. 934; *Smith* v. *Stewart*, 1961 S.C. 91; *McGhie* v. *B.T.C.*, 1964 S.L.T. 25.

[12] *Muir's Tr., supra.*

injury to heritable property is incorporeal moveable property.[1]

The claim competent to certain close relatives of a person killed by the fault of another, for solatium and damages for the patrimonial loss caused to the claimant by the death,[2] if initiated by the claimant, transmits to the claimant's executor,[3] and is probably assignable *inter vivos*. If action is not initiated by the entitled claimant, the right to do so probably lapses on his death.

Rights of relief

The right of relief possessed by a party who has satisfied a claim of damages for which another party is allegedly truly liable[4] is also a proprietary right.[5] It may exist by contract,[6] or *ex lege*,[7] but arises under statute in the case of joint delinquents[8] and where one of possible joint delinquents has been sued and had the claim of damages judicially constituted against him, though not where he has compromised the claim against him.[9]

JURA CREDITI UNDER CONTRACTS

A right under contract to performance of an obligation is personal and not proprietary if the contract involves an element of *delectus personae*,[10] but if it does not, so that it is a matter of indifference to the debtor to or for whom he must tender performance, the creditor's right is proprietary in nature, assignable,[11] and the *jus exigendi* passes to the creditor's executors.

1 *Heron* v. *Espie* (1856) 18 D. 917, 951; *Caledonian Ry.* v. *Watt* (1875) 2 R. 917; *Kelvinside Estate Co.* v. *Donaldson's Trs.* (1879) 6 R. 995.

2 Under the principle of *Eisten* v. *N.B. Ry.* (1870) 8 M. 980.

3 *Kelly* v. *Glasgow Corpn.*, 1951 S.C. (H.L.) 15; cf. *Hendry* v. *United Collieries*, 1909 S.C. (H.L.) 19, but see *Fraser* v. *Livermore* (1900) 7 S.L.T. 450.

4 *Caledonian Ry.* v. *Colt* (1860) 3 Macq. 833; *Ovington* v. *McVicar* (1864) 2 M. 1066; *McIntyre* v. *Gallacher* (1883) 11 R. 64; *Duncan's Trs.* v. *Steven* (1897) 24 R. 880; *Glasgow Corpn.* v. *Turnbull*, 1932 S.L.T. 457; *Buchanan and Carswell* v. *Eugene*, 1930 S.C. 160.

5 cf. *Harvey* v. *O'Dell* [1958] 2 Q.B. 78.

6 *Binnie* v. *Parlane* (1825) 4 S. 122; *Hamilton* v. *Anderson*, 1953 S.C. 129.

7 e.g. right of person held vicariously liable to relief from person actually in fault: *Semtex* v. *Gladstone* [1954] 2 All E.R. 206; *Lister* v. *Romford Ice Co.* [1957] A.C. 555; or agent's relief from principal: *Eastern Shipping Co.* v. *Quah Beng Kee* [1924] A.C. 177.

8 Law Reform (Misc. Prov.) (Sc.) Act, 1940, S. 3(1); e.g. *Drew* v. *Western S.M.T. Co.*, 1947 S.C. 222.

9 Law Reform (Misc. Prov.) (Sc.) Act, 1940, S. 3(2); *N.C.B.* v. *Thomson*, 1959 S.C. 353; see also *Wimpey* v. *B.O.A.C.* [1955] A.C. 169; *Central S.M.T. Co.* v. *Lanarkshire C.C.*, 1949 S.C. 450.

10 *Hoey* v. *McEwan & Auld* (1867) 5 M. 814; *International Fibre Syndicate* v. *Dawson* (1901) 3 F. (H.L.) 32; *Berlitz School* v. *Duchene* (1903) 6 F. 181; *Cole* v. *Handasyde*, 1910 S.C. 68.

11 Stair III, 1, 2; Ersk. III, 5, 2; Bell, *Prin.* §1459; *Aurdal* v. *Estrella*, 1916 S.C. 882; *Westville Shipping Co.* v. *Abram Steamship Co.*, 1923 S.C. (H.L.) 68.

A right constituted by contract restrictive of the liberty of one party to carry on a business or profession may be assignable by the party in right thereof along with the business protected thereby.[1]

A restrictive condition relative to moveable property does not, in general, transmit with those moveables so as to bind a party subsequently acquiring those goods.[2] An exception exists in the case of goods sold by a supplier subject to a condition as to the price at which they may be resold.[3]

Price of land

The sale of land, whether voluntary or compulsory, operates conversion and the price thereof is moveable, falling to the seller's executor,[4] unless it has been constructively reconverted by a direction to lay it out on the purchase of other heritage.

Arrears of feuduties and interest on heritable bonds

Though the superior's right to recover feuduties is heritable and the creditor's right in heritable bonds sometimes heritable, arrears of payments due are deemed moveable, though secured over land.[5]

Arrears of rent

Accruing payments of rent become moveable once they have vested.[6]

NEGOTIABLE INSTRUMENTS

Negotiable instruments are a special class of incorporeal moveable rights. Negotiability is the quality which attaches by law, following mercantile usage, to certain kinds of documents evidencing indebtedness and conferring a right to obtain payment of money. This quality cannot be conferred by private

[1] *Fraser* v. *Renwick* (1906) 14 S.L.T. 443; *Methven Simpson, Ltd.* v. *Jones*, 1910 2 S.L.T. 14; contrast *Berlitz School* v. *Duchene* (1903) 6 F. 181; *Rodger* v. *Herbertson*, 1909 S.C. 256, where held personal.

[2] *Morton* v. *Muir Bros.*, 1907 S.C. 1211, is an exceptional, and rather doubtful, case.

[3] Restrictive Trade Practices Act, 1956, S. 25(1); modified by Resale Prices Act, 1964, Ss. 1 and 5; *County Laboratories* v. *Mindel* [1957] Ch. 295; *Goodyear Tyre Co.* v. *Lancashire Batteries, Ltd.* [1958] 1 W.L.R. 857.

[4] Bell, *Prin.* §1479; *Heron* v. *Espie* (1856) 18 D. 917.

[5] Ersk. II, 9, 64; Bell, *Prin.* §1479, 1505; *Martin* v. *Agnew* (1755) Mor. 5457; 5 B.S. 830; *Spalding* v. *S.* (1792) Mor. 5257; *Johnston* v. *Cochran* (1829) 7 S. 226; *Hughes' Trs.* v. *Corsane* (1890) 18 R. 299; *Logan's Trs.* v. *L.* (1896) 23 R. 848; *Watson's Trs.* v. *Brown*, 1923 S.C. 228.

[6] Bell, *Prin.* §1496–1504.

agreement to the effect of affecting the rights of third parties to the agreement, though such a stipulation may be good as between the parties to it.[1]

The quality of negotiability imports that (a) the document is transferable by delivery alone, if payable to bearer, or by endorsement and delivery if payable to order, and needs no assignation or intimation thereof; and (b) it confers a good title, notwithstanding lack of, or defect in, the title of the transferor, to a transferee who takes in good faith, for value, and without notice of any defect in the title of the transferor. Both characteristics must attach to any document before it can be regarded as a negotiable instrument.[2]

Negotiability attaches to bills of exchange, promissory notes (including banknotes[3]) and cheques, Treasury bills, share warrants issued to bearer,[4] scrip certificates issued to bearer,[5] debentures payable to bearer,[6] bankers' drafts and circular notes, and dividend warrants. It does not attach to postal orders,[7] share certificates and transfers,[8] pension receipts,[9] nor to deposit receipts.[10]

A bill of lading is not a negotiable instrument as the transferee acquires no better title than the transferor,[11] nor are documents of title under the Factors Acts.

The recognised categories of negotiable instruments are not finally closed, and if the Court finds that a category of documents have, by the general usage and custom of business and trade, been treated as negotiable, it will recognise such a category as entitled to the privileges of negotiability.[12]

The protection of the taker of a negotiable instrument extends only to one who takes in good faith, for value and without knowledge of any defect in the title of the transferor. A transferee may

1 *Bovill* v. *Dixon* (1856) 3 Macq. 1; *Crouch* v. *Credit Foncier* (1873) L.R. 8 Q.B. 374.

2 *London Joint Stock Bank* v. *Simmons* [1891] 1 Ch. 270, 294; [1892] A.C. 201; *Walker* v. *Watson & Sturrock* (1897) 35 S.L.R. 26.

3 cf. Bell, *Prin.* §1340.

4 Companies Act, 1948, S. 83.

5 *Rumball* v. *Metropolitan Bank* (1877) 2 Q.B.D. 194; *Edelstein* v. *Schuler* [1902] 2 K.B. 144.

6 *Bechuanaland Exploration Co.* v. *London Trading Bank* [1898] 2 Q.B. 658.

7 *Fine Arts Socy.* v. *Union Bank of London* (1886) 17 Q.B.D. 705.

8 *Colonial Bank* v. *Cady & Williams* (1890) 15 App. Cas. 267; *Longman* v. *Bath Electric Tramways, Ltd.* [1905] 1 Ch. 646.

9 *Jones* v. *Coventry* [1909] 2 K.B. 1029.

10 *Barstow* v. *Inglis* (1857) 20 D. 230; *Wood* v. *Clydesdale Bank*, 1914 S.C. 397; cf. *Dickson* v. *National Bank*, 1917 S.C. (H.L.) 50.

11 *Lickbarrow* v. *Mason* (1794) 5 T.R. 683; *Gunn* v. *Bolckow, Vaughan & Co.* (1875) 10 Ch. D. 491.

12 *Goodwin* v. *Robarts* (1875) L.R. 11 Ex. 337; (1876) 1 App. Cas. 476; *Bechuanaland Exploration Co.* v. *London Trading Bank* [1898] 2 Q.B. 658.

take in good faith notwithstanding negligence or folly in not suspecting from the circumstances that there is defect in the transferor's title, but not if the circumstances raise actual suspicion or doubt and the instrument is accepted without further inquiry.[1]

In the hands of a *bona fide* holder for value and without notice of any defect in the title of the transferor to him, a negotiable instrument is property, transferable *inter vivos* by delivery, or endorsement and delivery, which passes on death to his executor, and confers a right to payment from the drawee.

BILLS OF LADING

A bill of lading for goods shipped is not only a receipt for goods shipped and evidence of the contract of carriage, but it is also by mercantile custom deemed a symbol of the goods. Possession of it is equivalent to possession of the goods and it is capable of transfer outright or in security by indorsement and delivery in the same way as the goods themselves.[2] The goods need not be specifically ascertained or identified.[3] It is not, however, a negotiable instrument as the transferee never acquires any better title to the goods than the transferor himself had.[4]

Bills of lading are usually drawn in sets of three and if more than one is indorsed to different indorsees the goods belong to the one who first takes an indorsed bill.[5] The shipowner may, however, in the absence of notice of a prior claim, deliver the goods to the person who first presents one of a set of bills.[6] If he has notice of conflicting claims he should warehouse the goods and have the claims determined in a multiplepoinding.

On transfer of the bill, the property in the goods represented thereby passes, and the right of the original consignor to stop the goods *in transitu* is wholly defeated (in the case of transfer outright) or becomes subject to the security (in the case of transfer in security).[7]

If the holders of a bill in security nevertheless allow actual delivery to be made to an onerous third party, such as purchase

[1] *Jones* v. *Gordon* (1877) 2 App. Cas. 616; *London Joint Stock Bank* v. *Simmons* [1892] A.C. 201.

[2] Bell, *Prin.* §417; *Sewell* v. *Burdick* (1884) 10 App. Cas. 74; *Sanders* v. *Maclean* (1883) 11 Q.B.D. 327; *Hayman* v. *McLintock*, 1907 S.C. 936.

[3] *Hayman, supra.*

[4] *Lickbarrow* v. *Mason* (1794) 5 Term Rep. 683.

[5] *Barber* v. *Meyerstein* (1870) L.R. 4 H.L. 317; *Sanders, supra.*

[6] *Glynn* v. *E. & W. India Docks Co.* (1882) 7 App. Cas. 591.

[7] *Lickbarrow, supra*; *Leask* v. *Scott* (1877) 2 Q.B.D. 376; *Kemp* v. *Falk* (1882) 7 App. Cas. 573.

from the party who delivered the bill in security, the holders lose their security.[1]

Other documents of title to goods

Dock warrants, delivery orders, warehouse keepers' certificates and similar documents granted by the custodiers of goods and used as proof of the possession or control of goods,[2] do not, like a bill of lading, represent the goods themselves but, if endorsed and delivered, authorise the possessor to receive the goods referred to in the documents.[3] Endorsation and delivery of such a document and intimation thereof to the custodier accordingly entitles the endorsee to take possession of the goods from the custodier and is accordingly the mode in which the goods may be constructively delivered on sale or in security.[4]

For the transfer of the documents to be effective as constructive delivery of the goods themselves, the custodier must be an independent third party and neither a servant of the granter[5] nor a party having control but with no claim to custody, such as an exciseman.[6] The goods must be sufficiently identified and appropriated to the holder of the documents of title.[7]

The holder of a delivery order obtained in good faith and for value, has a preferable title to that of the original seller of goods as against the purchaser who granted the delivery orders so long as the goods concerned have been sufficiently identified and appropriated to the transferees of the order.[8]

OBLIGATIONS OF DEBT

I.O.U.

An I.O.U. is an acknowledgment of debt and imports an obligation to pay, but is not a promissory note or other form of

[1] *Tod* v. *Merchant Banking Co. of London* (1883) 10 R. 1009.

[2] cf. Factors Act, 1889, S. 1(4) applied by Factors (Sc.) Act, 1890, S. 1, and Sale of Goods Act, 1893, S. 62(1).

[3] *Farina* v. *Home* (1846) 16 M. & W. 119; *McEwan* v. *Smith* (1849) 2 H.L. Cas. 309; *Gunn* v. *Bolckow, Vaughan & Co.* (1875) 10 Ch. App. 491.

[4] *Hamilton* v. *Western Bank* (1856) 19 D. 152; *Fleming* v. *Smith* (1881) 8 R. 548.

[5] *Dobell, Beckett & Co.* v. *Neilson* (1904) 7 F. 281; cf. *Roy's Tr.* v. *Colville & Drysdale* (1908) 5 F. 769.

[6] *Rhind's Tr.* v. *Robertson & Baxter* (1891) 18 R. 623; cf. *Distillers Co.* v. *Russell's Tr.* (1889) 16 R. 479; *Browne* v. *Ainslie* (1893) 21 R. 173. See also *Pochin* v. *Robinow & Marjoribanks* (1869) 7 M. 622.

[7] *Price & Pierce, infra.*

[8] *Price & Pierce* v. *Bank of Scotland*, 1912 S.C. (H.L.) 19; cf. *Connal & Co.* v. *Loder* (1868) 6 M. 1095.

negotiable instrument. It may doubtless be assigned, but only by assignation, not by mere delivery or endorsement and delivery, and will pass to the creditor's executor on his death.[1]

Personal bonds

A personal bond confers on the holder a right to payment from the granter in accordance with the terms of the bond. Such a bond is assignable[2] and transmits to the creditor's executor. If once extinguished by payments it cannot be assigned to a new creditor in security of another debt of the same debtor.[3]

Debentures

A debenture is an instrument of debt granted by a company providing for repayment, with interest so long as the principal is unpaid, and usually creating a security by way of floating charge over the company's property. It is commonly issued as a series of debentures ranking *pari passu*. Debentures may be issued payable to bearer,[4] in which case they are negotiable instruments. A debenture may equally be created in favour of a trustee for debenture holders to whom debenture stock is issued evidencing title to a fractional share of the debenture. In all cases the interest of the debenture-holder is moveable and he may transfer it in the same way as a personal bond or as stock in the company.[5]

British Government stock

The interest of a stockholder in any stock issued by the Government is moveable,[6] and is transferable by instrument in writing, as provided by Treasury regulations.[7]

Local authority securities

Local authorities may create mortgages or stock[8] as securities for money lent them. Mortgages are in statutory form, and may be renewed, transferred or discharged by endorsement thereon,[9] and their issue, transfer, renewal or discharge is recorded in a register of mortgages maintained by the authority.[10] Redeemable

[1] *Thiem's Trs.* v. *Collie* (1899) 1 F. 764.
[2] Bell, *Prin.* §1459.
[3] *Jackson* v. *Nicoll* (1870) 8 M. 408.
[4] Companies Act, 1948, S. 93.
[5] Companies Act, 1948, Ss. 73–82, 86–94.
[6] National Debt Act, 1870, S. 23; *Hog* v. *Hog* (1791) Mor. 5479; 3 Pat. 247.
[7] Finance Act, 1942, S. 47.
[8] County councils and town councils only: Local Govt. (Sc.) Act, 1947, S. 260(1).
[9] 1947 Act, S. 267 and Sched. 7; see also Stock Transfer Act, 1963, S. 1.
[10] 1947 Act, S. 268.

stock may be created in accordance with regulations made by the Secretary of State, which provide for stock certificates, and the transfer of stock.[1]

RIGHTS IN SECURITY OVER PROPERTY

A right in security over heritage constituted by bond and disposition in security is now[2] moveable in the creditor's succession. The bond, however, remains heritable, as at common law, for the purposes of the Crown right to escheat and as regards legal right of children. A bond made moveable by the statute is assignable[3] and passes on the creditor's death to his executors and next-of-kin.[4]

A right in security over corporeal moveables constituted by pledge and delivery of possession, or by lien over goods possessed, is assignable[5] and passes to the creditor's executor on his death.

A right in security over incorporeal moveable rights constituted by assignation in security is itself an incorporeal right capable of assignation, and transmits to the assignee's executor.

REVERSIONARY RIGHTS

Where a person conveys heritable property to another in security by disposition *ex facie* absolute he retains a right of reversion therein, which can be exercised by paying off the sum due with interest and claiming a reconveyance of the security. This reversionary right, though not exercised, is, so long as it may be exercised, a right capable of assignation outright or in security.[6] Where subjects were disponed *ex facie* absolutely to a bank, but truly in security, the back letter not being recorded, and the true owner subsequently assigned the right of reversion to another bank, which assignation was intimated to the first bank, after which both banks made further advances, it was held that the first bank's security was limited to advances made prior to the

[1] 1957 Act, S. 271; S.I. 1952, No. 4219. By S. 270 certain other statutory authorities have similar powers. See e.g. *Downie* v. *D's Trs.* (1866) 4 M. 1067.

[2] Titles to Land Consolidation (Sc.) Act, 1868, S. 117 amd. Succession (Sc.) Act, 1964, Sched. 3; cf. *Hughes' Trs.* v. *Corsane* (1890) 18 R. 299.

[3] *McCutcheon* v. *McWilliam* (1876) 3 R. 565; *Bruce* v. *Sc. Amicable Life Assce. Soc.*, 1907 S.C. 637.

[4] 1868 Act, S. 117, as amd. 1964 Act.

[5] *Moore* v. *Gledden* (1869) 7 M. 1016.

[6] *Forbes* v. *Welsh & Forbes* (1894) 21 R. 630; cf. *McCallum's Trs.* v. *McNab* (1877) 4 R. 520. Where a heritable proprietor grants security by bond and disposition in security he retains the radical right subject to the incumbrance, and can sell his property, subject to the bond.

intimation of the assignation of the reversionary right.[1] The appointment of a judicial factor has the same effect as an intimated assignation.[2]

The reversionary right gives the true owner a title to sue for the protection of the land against the encroachment of a stranger[3] or for damages for injury to the property by a third party.[4]

In the case of security over moveables the reversionary right of the debtor is not generally assignable in security, as a right in security without possession generally avails nought, and pledged subjects cannot be sold outright and the right to recover possession assigned outright to the buyer, possession being exigible when the first security-holder surrenders possession.[5]

Similarly a fiar, during the subsistence of a liferent, has a reversionary right capable of assignation, transmissible and subject to diligence.[6]

POLICIES OF LIFE ASSURANCE

A policy of life assurance has an increasing value as time passes towards its maturity and its surrender value increases. A policy by a husband on his wife's life is part of his moveable estate on his death, survived by her, and legitim is due from it.[7] The sums in policies on the husband's life fall under *jus relictae*.[8] A policy is assignable outright or in security[9] but bare custody without assignation confers no security right on the custodier,[10] nor does payment of premiums by a third party confer any right on the payer.[11] The assignation may be by endorsement on the policy or by separate instrument, must be in writing and must be intimated to the insurance company.[12] The company must acknowledge

[1] *Union Bank* v. *National Bank* (1886) 14 R. (H.L.) 1.
[2] *Campbell's J.F.* v. *National Bank*, 1944 S.C. 495.
[3] *Vincent* v. *Wood* (1899) 6 S.L.T. 297.
[4] *McBride* v. *Caledonian Ry.* (1894) 21 R. 620.
[5] Such a transaction being a sale 'intended to operate by way of security' the Sale of Goods Act, 1893, particularly Ss. 17–18, whereby the subjects could be sold without delivery of possession, does not apply, by S. 61(4) thereof, but the common law applies and requires delivery.
[6] *Brower's Exor.* v. *Ramsay's Trs.*, 1912 S.C. 1374.
[7] *Pringle's Trs.* v. *Hamilton* (1872) 10 M. 621.
[8] *Muirhead* v. *M's J.F.* (1867) 6 M. 95.
[9] Policies of Assurance Act, 1867; *Crossley* v. *City of Glasgow Life Assce. Co.* (1876) 4 Ch. D. 421.
[10] *United Kingdom Life Assce. Co.* v. *Dixon* (1838) 16 S. 1277.
[11] *Wylie's Exrx.* v. *McJannet* (1901) 4 F. 195.
[12] 1867 Act, S. 3; notice prescribed by the Transmission of Moveable Property (Sc.) Act, 1862, is adequate. See also *Brownlee* v. *Robb*, 1907 S.C. 1302.

notice of an assignation.[1] It may be assigned even though when the assured effected the policy he had the intention to assign it.[2] But a policy effected by a man on his own life for the benefit of his wife under the Married Women's Policies of Assurance (Sc.) Act, 1880, cannot be assigned by the spouses to the husband's creditors.[3]

A life policy passes on bankruptcy to the trustee; even if its existence is not disclosed to him and it is kept up by the bankrupt till his death, the trustee is entitled to it.[4] Similarly if an undischarged bankrupt effects a life policy and pays premiums after he has obtained his discharge, it still vests in the trustee who can recover the proceeds for the benefit of the creditors.[5] Discharge in bankruptcy does not revest in the bankrupt a life policy owned by him or acquired before discharge, even though it then has little or no surrender value, but a retrocession of the policy is necessary.

If the policy is void or voidable as against the assured, it is equally so against even an onerous assignee.[6]

SALARY AND PENSION RIGHTS

Entitlement to a salary is a personal claim, which is probably assignable, but is not transmissible on death.

The entitlement to a pension, whether under a contract of employment or under statute, is personal rather than proprietary and, though moveable, the right is not generally assignable nor transmissible.

Certain kinds of rights to salaries or pensions are, on grounds of public policy, not assignable. These include salaries and pensions of public officers and members of the civil and armed services of the crown,[7] national insurance benefits, industrial injury benefits,

[1] 1867 Act, S. 6.

[2] *McFarlane* v. *Royal London Friendly Socy.* (1886) 2 T.L.R. 755.

[3] *Scottish Life Assce. Socy.* v. *Donald* (1901) 9 S.L.T. 200; *Edinburgh Life Assce. Co.* v. *Balderston*, 1909 2 S.L.T. 323; cf. *Pender* v. *Commercial Bank*, 1940 S.L.T. 306; contrast surrender: *Schumann* v. *Scottish Widows' Fund* (1886) 13 R. 678.

[4] *Tapster* v. *Ward* (1909) 101 L.T. 503.

[5] *Re Bennett, ex p. Official Receiver* [1907] 1 K.B. 149; *Re Phillips* [1914] 2 K.B. 689; *Re Stokes, ex p. Mellish* [1919] 2 K.B. 256.

[6] *Scottish Widows' Fund* v. *Buist* (1876) 3 R. 1078.

[7] *Grenfell* v. *Dean and Canons of Windsor* (1840) 2 Beav. 544; *Arbuthnot* v. *Norton* (1846) 5 Moo. P.C. 219; *Willcock* v. *Terrell* (1878) 3 Ex. D. 323; *Apthorpe* v. *A.* (1887) 12 P.D. 192; *Mulvenna* v. *The Admiralty*, 1926 S.C. 842. Cf. *Hollinshead* v. *Hazelton* [1916] 1 A.C. 428. See also Naval and Marine Pay and Pensions Act, 1865, S. 4; Army Act, 1955, S. 203; Air Force Act, 1955, S. 3; Police Pensions Act, 1948, S. 7; Fire Services Acts, 1947, S. 26; 1951, S. 1.

family allowances and supplementary benefits.[1] The same principle applies to payments of aliment to a wife,[2] and alimentary provisions generally,[3] and a liferent if declared alimentary.[4]

JURA CREDITI ON INTESTACY OR UNDER WILLS OR TRUSTS

Spouses' prior rights on intestacy

A surviving spouse's prior rights on intestacy to a dwelling-house or the value thereof,[5] furniture and plenishing[6] and financial provision from the estate[7] are *jura crediti* exigible from the estate, rather than rights of property in, or of succession to, portions of the deceased's estate, but postponed to the claims of creditors. Once vested the rights are probably proprietary, assignable, and transmit to executors.

Legal rights

Legal rights are *jura crediti* for payment of a certain portion of a deceased's estate at the date of death.[8] They are similarly proprietary, once they have vested.

Rights on intestacy

The rights of persons entitled, on a deceased's intestacy, to shares in the free estate,[9] once vested in them by relationship and survivance, are proprietary rights, assignable[10] and transmissible.

Liferent

A right of improper liferent is an incorporeal claim to the whole or part of the income of an estate in trust for the period of

[1] National Insurance Act, 1965, S. 53; National Insurance (Industrial Injuries) Act, 1965, S. 28; Ministry of Social Security Act, 1966, S. 20; Family Allowances Act, 1965, S. 10.

[2] *Re Robinson* (1884) 27 Ch. D. 160.

[3] Ersk. III, 5, 2.

[4] *White's Trs.* v. *Whyte* (1877) 4 R. 786; *Duthie's Trs.* v. *Kinloch* (1878) 5 R. 858; *Hughes* v. *Edwardes* (1892) 19 R. (H.L.) 33; *Cuthbert* v. *Cuthbert's Trs.*, 1908 S.C. 967.

[5] Succession (Sc.) Act, 1964, S. 8(1), (2) and (4).

[6] Ibid., S. 8(3).

[7] Ibid., S. 9.

[8] *Wight* v. *Brown* (1849) 11 D. 459; *Muirhead* v. *M's J.F.* (1867) 6 M. 95; *Inglis* v. *I.* (1869) 7 M. 435; *Cameron's Trs.* v. *Maclean*, 1917 S.C. 416 (*jus relictae*); *Fisher* v. *Dixon* (1843) 2 Bell 63; *McMurray* v. *McM's Trs.* (1852) 14 D. 1048; *Dalhousie* v. *Crokat* (1868) 6 M. 659; *Ross* v. *R.* (1896) 23 R. 802; *Gams* v. *Russell's Trs.* (1899) 7 S.L.T. 289 (*legitim*).

[9] 1964 Act, S. 2.

[10] *Secus, Stevenson's Trs.* v. *Macnaughton*, 1932 S.N. 46, *sed quaere.*

one's life, or a shorter determinate period. Unless declared alimentary, the right is assignable outright or in security, but only for the duration of its continuance.[1]

Alimentary provisions

A provision enjoyed by a person, as under a liferent, which is declared alimentary or for his alimentary use allenarly is *prima facie* not a proprietary right capable of assignation, outright or in security,[2] nor attachable by creditors. In so far, however, as the provision exceeds what the court considers a reasonable provision, it is attachable by creditors,[3] and assignable to them[4] or to third parties.[5] Each term's payment, when paid, is at the beneficiary's absolute disposal, and the protection as alimentary may be ended by the beneficiary in certain circumstances.[6]

The court has, however, declined to sanction the assignation of part of an alimentary provision in order to raise a capital sum, as such a sanction would not be *res judicata* in any future question between the beneficiary and possible alimentary creditors.[5]

Rights of beneficiary

A designated beneficiary, having a vested right under a will or trust settlement, has a *jus crediti* against the executor or trustee for delivery or payment of the property or rights destined to him under the will or trust. This right is heritable or moveable according to the nature of the subject held for his behalf, and may be affected by the testator's or trustee's directions for constructive conversion of parts of the estate. In so far as the estate on which the beneficiary has a claim is, or is constructively deemed to be, moveable or is general or uncertain his *jus crediti* is moveable.[7]

Such a right may, before it is reduced to possession, be assigned

[1] *Bailey's Trs.* v. *B.*, 1954 S.L.T. 282; cf. *Fraser* v. *Carruthers* (1875) 2 R. 595. There is no right to a conveyance of the trust estate in liferent: *Ker's Trs.* v. *Justice* (1868) 6 M. 627.

[2] Ersk. III, 5, 2; *Mackenzie* v. *Morison* (1791) Mor. 10413; *McDonell* v. *Clark*, 25 Mar. 1819, F.C.; *Rennie* v. *Ritchie* (1845) 4 Bell, 221; *Hewats* v. *Robertson* (1881) 9 R. 175.

[3] *Lewis* v. *Anstruther* (1852) 15 D. 260; *Livingstone* v. *L.* (1886) 14 R. 43; *Haydon* v. *Forrest's Trs.* (1895) 3 S.L.T. 182.

[4] *E. Buchan* v. *His Creditors* (1835) 13 S. 1112; *Harvey* v. *Calder* (1840) 2 D. 1095; *Lewis* v. *Anstruther* (1852) 14 D. 857; 15 D. 260.

[5] *Claremont's Trs.* v. *C.* (1896) 4 S.L.T. 144; *Craig* v. *Pearson's Trs.*, 1915 2 S.L.T. 183. See also *Cuthbert* v. *C's Trs.*, 1908 S.C. 967.

[6] *Dempster's Trs.* v. *D.*, 1949 S.C. 92; *Sturgis's Tr.* v. *S.*, 1951 S.C. 637; contrast *Kennedy* v. *K's Trs.*, 1953 S.C. 60; cf. *Hewats* v. *Roberton* (1881) 9 R. 175.

[7] *Buchanan* v. *Angus* (1862) 4 Macq. 374; *Wardlaw's Trs.* v. *W.* (1880) 7 R. 1070.

inter vivos,[1] attached by creditors,[2] and passes to executors under the beneficiary's will or intestacy.

Jura crediti *under marriage contract trusts*

To be a *jus crediti* a provision under a marriage contract trust must confer a present right on the claimant, availing in competition with outside creditors, though not giving a preference. Under an ante-nuptial marriage contract provisions in favour of the wife are of this class.[3] Under a post-nuptial contract a provision for the wife confers a *jus crediti* only so far as reasonable and provided that the husband was solvent at the time of making the provision.[4]

The right conferred on children under a marriage contract may be a *jus crediti*,[5] but the presumption is against conferment of any such right, and such a right will normally be a *spes successionis* only.[4] Children have a *jus crediti* secured against other creditors only if it secured against the father himself.[6] Provisions for children in post-nuptial contracts are accounted gratuitous and are reducible in a competition with creditors if the granter were not solvent at the time of granting.

A *jus crediti* renders the party entitled a creditor of the trust, having a right which is assignable and transmissible.[7]

Spes successionis

A *spes successionis* is a contingent or defeasible right in succession, either on intestacy or under a testamentary deed. *Spes successionis* may mean that A hopes to benefit by the will of B who is still alive, or that A has a right under the said will of B, who is dead, subject to a certain contingency.[8] Among such are a legal right of legitim, so long as the parent is alive,[9] or the right of children under a destination of heritage to a husband or wife in liferent and the children of the marriage in fee,[10] or the right of

[1] *Ker's Trs.* v. *Justice* (1868) 6 M. 627; *Rothwell* v. *Stuart's Trs.* (1898) 1 F. 81; *Macpherson's J.F.* v. *Mackay*, 1915 S.C. 1011. See also *Macknight* (1875) 2 R. 667; *Brigg's Trs.* v. *B.*, 1923 S.L.T. 755; *Robinson* v. *R's Trs.*, 1934 S.L.T. 183; as to intimation of assignation see *Jameson* v. *Sharp* (1887) 14 R. 643; *Browne's Tr.* v. *Anderson* (1901) 4 F. 305.

[2] *Brower's Exor.* v. *Ramsay's Trs.*, 1912 S.C. 1374.

[3] Ersk. III, 9, 22; III, 8, 36; *Wilson's Trs.* v. *W.* (1856) 18 D. 1096; *Carphin* v. *Clapperton* (1867) 5 M. 797.

[4] *Craig* v. *Galloway* (1861) 4 Macq. 267; *Walkinshaw's Trs.* v. *W.* (1872) 10 M. 763.

[5] *Goddard* v. *Stewart's Children* (1844) 6 D. 1018; *Cruikshank's Trs.* v. *C.* (1853) 16 D. 7.

[6] *Fotheringham* v. *F.* (1734) Mor. 12941; *Gordon* v. *Sutherland* (1748) Mor. 12915; *Herries, Farquhar & Co.* v. *Brown* (1838) 16 S. 948; *Mackinnon's Trs.* v. *Dunlop*, 1913 S.C. 232.

[7] *Harvey* v. *Ligertwood* (1872) 10 M. (H.L.) 33.

[8] *Salaman* v. *Tod*, 1911 S.C. 1214, 1223. [9] *Coats* v. *Bannochie's Trs.*, 1912 S.C. 329.

[10] *E. Wemyss* v. *E. Haddington* (1818) 6 Pat. 390; *Macdonald* v. *Hall* (1893) 20 R. (H.L.) 88.

children under a destination in a marriage contract to the children of the marriage, the father having in such a case full power of administration, subject to the obligation to leave the estate to the children at his death,[1] or the right of a beneficiary, subject to a liferent and with a gift-over if the beneficiary should predecease the liferentrix,[2] or the right of any substitute under a destination, whose right may be defeated by the institute.

It differs from a *jus crediti* in that in the latter case the right has vested and is indefeasible though it may not be yet exigible. A person may have a *jus crediti* as against certain claimants and only a *spes successionis* against others.[3]

A *spes successionis* has a present value, depending on the likelihood of its realisation and the value of the hoped for benefit. It is assignable, absolutely or in security, to the effect of giving the assignee a good title against the assignor to the succession, though the assignation can become effective only if and when the right vests.[4] It will not be assigned by a general conveyance by a person of his property.[5]

It is now[6] carried to the trustee in sequestration on the entitled party's sequestration.[7]

An assignee of a contingent interest in a trust has been held entitled to inspect the trust accounts.[8]

INTERESTS IN PARTNERSHIPS AND COMPANIES

Interest in partnership

The interest of a partner in a partnership is a proprietary right, and moveable, even though the partnership assets or business are mainly heritable.[9]

1 *Arthur & Seymour* v. *Lamb* (1870) 8 M. 928.

2 *Rothwell* v. *Stuart's Tr.* (1898) 1 F. 81.

3 *Goddard* v. *Stewart's Children* (1844) 6 D. 1018; *Murray* v. *Macfarlane's Trs.* (1895) 22 R. 927.

4 *Wood* v. *Begbie* (1850) 12 D. 963; *Trappes* v. *Meredith* (1871) 10 M. 38; *Rothwell* v. *Stuart's Tr.* (1898) 1 F. 81; see also *Reid* v. *Morison* (1893) 20 R. 510; *Browne's Tr.* v. *Anderson* (1901) 4 F. 305; *Salaman* v. *Tod*, 1911 S.C. 1214; *Coats* v. *Bannochie's Trs.*, 1912 S.C. 329.

5 *McEwan's Trs.* v. *Macdonald*, 1909 S.C. 57.

6 For former law, see *Beaton and McAndrew* v. *McDonald* (1821) 1 S. 49; *Kirkland* v. *K's Trs.* (1886) 13 R. 798; *Trappes, supra*; *Reid, supra*. See also *Obers* v. *Paton's Trs.* (1897) 24 R. 719.

7 Bankruptcy (Sc.) Act, 1913, S. 97.

8 *Salamon* v. *Morrison's Trs.*, 1912 2 S.L.T. 499.

9 Partnership Act, 1890, S. 22; *Murray* v. *M.* (1805) Mor. Heritable and Moveable, Appx. 4; *Minto* v. *Kirkpatrick* (1833) 11 S. 632; *L.A.* v. *Macfarlane's Trs.* (1893) 31 S.L.R. 357; see also *Irvine* v. *I.* (1851) 13 D. 1367.

The right to claim an accounting and payment of the partner's entitlement passes to his executor.[1]

Though a partner's interest is assignable, the assignee is not entitled to participate in the management of the partnership business or otherwise to act as a partner, but only to receive the share of profits which the assignee would otherwise have been entitled to receive, as agreed by the partners.[2]

Shares in companies

A share in a company limited by shares is a right to a fractional part of the ownership of the company, comprising rights to participate in and vote at meetings, and to receive a proportional part of the dividends declared and of the assets on a winding-up, subject to the liability to pay the full nominal value of the share.[3] The precise rights attaching to classes of shares are determined by the Memorandum and Articles of Association of the particular company. The shares or other interest of a member of a company are moveable property, even if the company's sole objects relate to land or all its property is land.[4]

Shares in a public company are *prima facie* freely transferable, but those of a private company must be,[5] and shares in a public company may be,[6] subject to restriction on transfer imposed by the company's Articles of Association. Subject thereto shares may be transferred outright or in security, attached by creditors, and pass under the owner's will or on intestacy.

Dividends

A dividend, once declared by a company, is a debt owed by the company to each shareholder entitled by virtue of the ownership of shares at the date of closure of the company's transfer books.[7]

BUSINESS RIGHTS

Goodwill

Goodwill is the identity attaching to a professional, industrial or commercial undertaking rendering it probable that it will

[1] *Morrison* v. *M's Exrx.*, 1912 S.C. 892. [2] Partnership Act, 1890, S. 31.
[3] *Colonial Bank* v. *Whinney* (1886) 11 App. Cas. 426; *Re Paulin* [1935] 1 K.B. 26, 57.
[4] Companies Act, 1948, S. 73; *Hog* v. *H.* (1791) Mor. 5457.
[5] Companies Act, 1948, S. 28(1)(a). [6] e.g. *I.R.C.* v. *Crossman* [1937] A.C. 26.
[7] *Wallace, Hamilton & Co.* v. *Campbell* (1824) 2 Shaw's App. 467; *Re Irving, ex p. Brett* (1877) 7 Ch. D. 419; *Re Severn and Wye and Severn Bridge Rail Co.* [1896] 1 Ch. 559; *Bond* v. *Barrow Haematite Co.* [1902] 1 Ch. 353. As to payment, see *Thailwall* v. *G.N. Ry.* [1910] 2 K.B. 509.

continue to do substantial business, to a greater extent than a new, though otherwise similar, undertaking.[1] Goodwill may arise from the personal capacities and qualities of the person conducting the business,[2] or may be associated with the site and premises in which the undertaking is carried on,[3] or from the name, reputation and business connections of the undertaking,[4] or may arise from more than one of these elements. There may be a business goodwill though there are neither premises nor staff.[5] In some circumstances goodwill may be of no value.[6] Whether a particular business has a goodwill or not is a question of fact.[7]

Goodwill is distinguishable as an asset from both the premises in which an existing business is conducted and from its business name,[8] its trade-marks, trade names and stock-in-trade.[9] It may be sold,[10] attached for debt, bequeathed, or pass on intestacy.[11] It may be heritable,[12] moveable,[13] or partly both;[14] which it is is a question of fact in each case.[15] It may be protected by an action for passing off.[16]

A transfer of a practice or business carries the exclusive right to carry on the old business and represent the new as a continuation of the old business,[17] and includes rights to the sole use of the trade name,[18] to the exclusive use of trade marks,[19] to the delivery

1 cf. *Cruttwell* v. *Lye* (1810) 17 Ves. 335; *Churton* v. *Douglas* (1859) John. 174; *Trego* v. *Hunt* [1896] A.C. 7.

2 cf. *Bain* v. *Munro* (1878) 5 R. 416; *Drummond* v. *Leith Assessor* (1886) 13 R. 540; *Thatcher* v. *T.* (1904) 11 S.L.T. 605; *Rodger* v. *Herbertson*, 1909 S.C. 256; *Corbin* v. *Stewart* (1911) 28 T.L.R. 99.

3 cf. *Bain* v. *Munro* (1878) 5 R. 416; *Bell's Tr.* v. *B.* (1884) 12 R. 85; *Philp's Exor.* v. *P's Exor.* (1894) 21 R. 482; *Brown* v. *Robertson* (1896) 4 S.L.T. 17.

4 *Morrison* v. *M.* (1900) 2 F. 382; see also *Hughes* v. *Stirling Assessor* (1892) 19 R. 840.

5 *Donald* v. *Hodgart's Trs.* (1893) 21 R. 246.

6 *Bell's Tr.* v. *B.* (1884) 12 R. 85; *Graham* v. *G's Trs.* (1904) 6 F. 1015; *Mackenzie* v. *Macfarlane*, 1934 S.N. 16.

7 *Reid* v. *R.*, 1938 S.L.T. 415.

8 *Barr* v. *Lions, Ltd.*, 1956 S.C. 59.

9 *Guest's Exor.* v. *I.R.C.*, 1921 S.C. 440.

10 cf. *Donald* v. *Hodgart's Trs.* (1893) 21 R. 246.

11 *Brown* v. *Robertson* (1896) 4 S.L.T. 17; *Morrison's Tr.* v. *M.*, 1915 2 S.L.T. 296; contrast *Philp's Exor.*, *supra*.

12 *Ross* v. *Ross's Trs.* (1901) 9 S.L.T. 340; *Town and County Bank* v. *McBain* (1902) 9 S.L.T. 485; *Muirhead's Tr.* v. *M.* (1905) 7 F. 496.

13 cf. *Bain* v. *Munro* (1878) 5 R. 416.

14 *Murray's Tr.* v. *McIntyre* (1904) 6 F. 588.

15 *Leishman* v. *Glen & Henderson* (1899) 6 S.L.T. 328.

16 *Haig* v. *Forth Blending Co.*, 1954 S.C. 35.

17 *Churton*, *supra*; *Walker* v. *Mottram* (1882) 19 Ch. D. 355.

18 *Churton*, *supra*; *Bradbury* v. *Dickens* (1859) 27 Beav. 53; *Levy* v. *Walker* (1879) 10 Ch. D. 436; *Smith* v. *McBride* (1888) 16 R. 36.

19 Trade Marks Act, 1938; cf. *Cotton* v. *Gillwood* (1875) 44 L.J. Ch. 90; *Ex p. Lawrence* (1881) 44 L.T. (N.S.) 98.

of business books and records,[1] and to the benefit of any existing contracts in restraint of trade.[2] But, unless there is an express restriction, it does not prevent the transferor commencing a new business of the same kind and even in adjacent premises.[3] A voluntary transferor may not solicit the business of former customers,[4] though he may deal with them if they come voluntarily to him,[5] and an involuntary transferor is not thus restricted.[6]

In other cases the transfer of a business identified with certain premises is hardly separable from the premises; the person acquiring the premises acquires the goodwill of the business,[7] and a person acquiring the goodwill acquires the transferor's interest to obtain a renewal of the lease.[8]

Goodwill, unless purely personal, passes on sequestration to the trustee in bankruptcy.[9]

Trade names

One person may not carry on business or trade under a name likely to mislead the public into thinking that it is the business of another,[10] but a person has a *prima facie* right to trade under his own name and the court is reluctant to prevent him doing so.[11] But he may be prevented from doing so if the consequence is the probability of deceiving the public into thinking that his business or goods are those of another.[12] Intent to deceive need not be proved.[13]

[1] *Morrison* v. *M.* (1900) 2 F. 382.

[2] *Townsend* v. *Jarman* [1900] 2 Ch. 698; *Automobile Carriage Builders* v. *Sayers* (1909) 101 L.T. 419.

[3] *Cruttwell, supra*; *Churton, supra*; *Trego, supra.*

[4] *Trego, supra*; *Dumbarton Steamboat Co.* v. *MacFarlane* (1899) 1 F. 993.

[5] *Curl Bros.* v. *Webster* [1904] 1 Ch. 685.

[6] *Ginesi* v. *Cooper* (1880) 14 Ch. D. 596; *Walker* v. *Mottram* (1882) 19 Ch. D. 355; *Dawson* v. *Benson* (1882) 22 Ch. D. 504.

[7] *Bain* v. *Munro* (1878) 5 R. 416; *Bell's Tr.* v. *B.* (1884) 12 R. 85; *Brown* v. *Robertson* (1896) 33 S.L.R. 570; *Leishman* v. *Glen & Henderson* (1899) 6 S.L.T. 328.

[8] *Brown, supra.*

[9] Bankruptcy (Sc.) Act, 1913, S. 97; *Coupland's Tr.* v. *C.* (1886) 23 S.L.R. 456; *Stewart's Tr.* v. *Stewart's Exrx.* (1896) 23 R. 739; *Melrose-Drover, Ltd.* v. *Heddle* (1902) 4 F. 1120.

[10] *Cowan* v. *Millar* (1895) 22 R. 833; *Resartus Co.* v. *Sartor Resartus Co.* (1908) 16 S.L.T. 210; *Williamson* v. *Meikle*, 1909 S.C. 1272; *Rodgers* v. *Rodgers* (1924) 41 R.P.C. 277; *Office Cleaning Services, Ltd.* v. *Westminster Window and General Cleaners, Ltd.* (1946) 63 R.P.C. 39; cf. *Baird & Tatlock (London), Ltd.* v. *Baird & Tatlock, Ltd.*, 1917 1 S.L.T. 46.

[11] *Turton* v. *T.* (1889) 42 Ch. D. 128; *Wright, Layman and Umney, Ltd.* v. *Wright* (1949) 66 R.P.C. 149.

[12] *Smith* v. *McBride and Smith* (1888) 16 R. 36; *Bayer* v. *Baird* (1898) 25 R. 1142; *Cooper & McLeod* v. *McLachlan* (1901) 9 S.L.T. 41; *Williamson, supra*; *Rodgers, supra*; *Marengo* v. *Daily Sketch* (1948) 65 R.P.C. 242; *Baume* v. *Moore* [1958] Ch. 907; *John Haig & Co.* v. *John D. D. Haig, Ltd.*, 1957 S.L.T. (Notes) 36; cf. *Boswell* v. *Mathie* (1884) 11 R. 1072.

[13] *G.N.S. Ry.* v. *Mann* (1892) 19 R. 1035; *Rolls Razor, Ltd.* v. *Rolls Lighter, Ltd.* (1949) 66 R.P.C. 299; *Baume, supra.*

A trade name passes with the goodwill of the business and, in view of the greater risk of confusion, the court is more ready to limit the seller's liberty to carry on business thereafter under the same, or a deceptively similar, name.[1]

The court will readily restrict the use as a trade name of a fancy name if it has become associated with the pursuer's goods and there is material risk of confusion,[2] but will less readily restrict the use of a descriptive name.[3]

The court may restrain the use as a trade name of a place of business if likely to confuse,[4] or of a local name.[5]

Similarly a person or body may not adopt a professional designation, or abbreviation thereof, liable to lead the public to believe that he or they belong to an existing, recognised, body using that designation or abbreviation.[6]

Trade name of goods

Independently of registered trade marks, no trader has any right of property in a trade name or mark, but he may by interdict prevent another trader representing his goods to be those of the complainer,[7] or of a different quality or class,[8] and this right is a proprietary one.[9] No fraudulent representation need be proved,[10] but only the likelihood of deception of a substantial section of the trade or of the public.[11]

1 *Melrose-Drover* v. *Heddle* (1901) 4 F. 1120; *Townsend* v. *Jarman* [1900] 2 Ch. 698; cf. *Barr* v. *Lions, Ltd.*, 1956 S.C. 59.

2 *Premier Cycle Co.* v. *Premier Tube Co.* (1896) 12 T.L.R. 481; *Crystalate Gramophone Record Mfg. Co.* v. *British Crystalite Co., Ltd.* (1934) 51 R.P.C. 315.

3 *General Radio Co.* v. *General Radio Co. (Westminster), Ltd.* [1957] R.P.C. 471; cf. *Bile Bean Mfg. Co.* v. *Davidson* (1906) 8 F. 1181; *Scottish Union and National Ins. Co.* v. *Sc. National Ins. Co.*, 1909 S.C. 318.

4 *G.N.S. Ry.* v. *Mann* (1892) 19 R. 1035; *Cowan* v. *Millar* (1895) 22 R. 833; *Cooper & McLeod* v. *Maclachlan* (1901) 18 R.P.C. 380; *Boussod, Valadon & Co.* v. *Marchant* (1907) 25 R.P.C. 42; cf. *Charleson* v. *Campbell* (1876) 4 R. 149; *Crawford's Trs.* v. *Lennox* (1896) 23 R. 747.

5 *Montgomerie* v. *Donald* (1884) 11 R. 506; *Rugby Portland Cement Co.* v. *Rugby and Newbold Portland Cement Co., Ltd.* (1891) 9 R.P.C. 46; *Grand Hotel Co. of Caledonia Springs, Ltd.* v. *Wilson* [1904] A.C. 103; cf. *Lochgelly Iron Co.* v. *Lumphinnans Iron Co.* (1879) 6 R. 482; *Dunnachie* v. *Young* (1883) 10 R. 874.

6 *Socy. of Accountants in Edinburgh* v. *Corporation of Accountants* (1893) 20 R. 750; *Corporation of Accountants* v. *Society of Accountants in Edinburgh* (1903) 11 S.L.T. 424.

7 *Reddaway* v. *Banham* [1896] A.C. 199; *Birmingham Brewery Co.* v. *Powell* [1897] A.C. 710; *Bass, Ratcliff & Gretton* v. *Laidlaw* (1908) 16 S.L.T. 660; *Oertli* v. *Bowman* [1959] R.P.C. 1.

8 *Spalding* v. *Gamage* (1915) 32 R.P.C. 273; *Britains* v. *Morris* [1961] R.P.C. 217.

9 *Reddaway, supra*; *Spalding, supra*; *Bollinger* v. *Costa Brava Wine Co.* [1960] Ch. 262.

10 *Spalding, supra*; *Baume* v. *Moore* [1958] Ch. 907.

11 *Cellular Clothing Co.* v. *Maxton & Murray* (1899) 1 F. (H.L.) 29; *Office Cleaning Services, supra*; *Haig* v. *Forth Blending Co.*, 1954 S.C. 35.

The pursuer must prove that the name, mark or other get-up has become regarded as indicative of his goods,[1] and that its use was calculated or likely to deceive and to cause confusion and damage to the goodwill of his business.

Trade secrets

Trade secrets are bodies of knowledge, whether relating to customers, markets, sources of supply or methods of manufacture or otherwise, which a person in business or trade regards as and seeks to preserve as peculiarly his own. No exclusive or proprietary right is, however, legally recognised in trade secrets as such, except in so far as they are the subject of trade marks, patents, registered designs, copyright, or plant breeders' rights, and there is no appropriation of property by discovering or annexing or publishing another's trade secrets.[2]

The disclosure of trade secrets may be restricted by restrictive conditions in the contracts of employment of certain employees, in which case they are enforceable if reasonable,[3] and may be actionable as in breach of confidentiality.[4] Apart from these cases an employer cannot prevent or restrain an employee from using, after the employment has ended, any knowledge or skill gained during the employment.[5]

Trade secrets may be sold or shared but no form of assignation is required.

TRADE MARKS

A trade mark means a mark used in relation to goods for the purpose of indicating or so as to indicate a connection in the course of trade between the goods and some person having the right either as proprietor or as registered user to use the mark,

[1] *Singer Mfg. Co.* v. *Kimball & Morton* (1873) 11 M. 267; *Birmingham Brewery Co.* v. *Powell* [1897] A.C. 710; *Bayer* v. *Baird* (1898) 25 R. 1142; *Cellular Clothing Co.* v. *Maxton & Murray* (1899) 1 F. (H.L.) 29; *Kinnell* v. *Ballantyne*, 1910 S.C. 246. See also *John Dewar* v. *Dewar* (1900) 7 S.L.T. 462; *Woolley* v. *Morrison* (1904) 6 F. 451; *Dunlop Tyre Co.* v. *Dunlop Motor Co.*, 1907 S.C. (H.L.) 15.

[2] cf. *Massam* v. *Thorley's Cattle Food Co.* (1877) 6 Ch. D. 574; *United Indigo Co.* v. *Robinson* (1932) 49 R.P.C. 178.

[3] It probably may be reasonable even if unlimited in space or time; see *Leather Cloth Co.* v. *Lorsont* (1869) L.R. 9 Eq. 345; *Davies* v. *D.* (1887) 36 Ch. D. 359; *Forster* v. *Suggett* (1918) 35 T.L.R. 87; *Vandervell Products* v. *McLeod* [1957] R.P.C. 185.

[4] *Neuman* v. *Kennedy* (1905) 12 S.L.T. 763; *Mustad* v. *Allcock* (1928) in [1963] 3 All E.R. 416; *Saltman Eng. Co.* v. *Campbell Eng. Co.* (1948) 65 R.P.C. 203; *Peter Pan Mfg. Corpn.* v. *Corsets Silhouette, Ltd.* [1963] 3 All E.R. 402; cf. *Brown's Trs.* v. *Hay* (1898) 25 R. 1112.

[5] *Morris* v. *Saxelby* [1916] 1 A.C. 688; *Attwood* v. *Lamont* [1920] 3 K.B. 571.

whether with or without any indication of the identity of that person.[1] A mark includes a device, brand, heading, label, ticket, name, signature, word, letter, numeral, or any combination thereof.[1]

At common law a trader who attached a distinctive name or mark to his goods could prevent others copying it in a way misleading to the public on proof that the name had become so associated with his goods as to connote in the market that they were his manufacture or supply.[2]

Since 1875 trade marks may be registered whereby the proprietor obtains a statutory title and need not prove long association to establish his title to the mark.[3] No person may institute any proceeding to prevent or recover damages for the infringement of an unregistered trade mark, without prejudice to the right of action for passing-off goods as those of another.[4]

Registration

There is maintained at the Patent Office, a register of trade marks, divided into Part A and Part B, wherein are entered all registered trade marks with the names, addresses and descriptions of their proprietors, notifications of assignations and transmissions, the names, addresses and descriptions of all registered users, disclaimers, conditions, limitations and such other matters as may be prescribed.[5] A trade mark must be registered in respect of particular goods or classes of goods.[6]

The register may be rectified,[7] or a registration varied or expunged for breach of a condition,[8] or it may be corrected,[9] or the trade mark altered in any manner not substantially affecting its identity.[10]

The registrar may give preliminary advice as to distinctiveness to a person proposing to apply for the registration of a trade mark.[11]

[1] Trade Marks Act, 1938, S. 68(1).

[2] *Singer Mfg. Co.* v. *Loog* (1880) 18 Ch. D. 395; *Reddaway* v. *Banham* [1896] A.C. 199; *Kinnell* v. *Ballantine*, 1910 S.C. 246.

[3] *Boord* v. *Thom & Cameron*, 1907 S.C. 1326, 1342; *Champagne Heidsieck* v. *Buxton* [1930] 1 Ch. 330.

[4] 1938 Act, S. 2.

[5] 1938 Act, S. 1; Trade Marks Rules, 1938; Marks may also be registered at Sheffield in respect of cutlery, and at Manchester for textiles: Ss. 38–39.

[6] 1938 Act, S. 3.

[7] 1938 Act, S. 32.

[8] 1938 Act, S. 33.

[9] 1938 Act, S. 34.

[10] 1938 Act, S. 35.

[11] 1938 Act, S. 42.

REGISTRABILITY—PART A

To be registrable in Part A a trade mark must contain or consist of at least one of the essentials: (a) the name of a company, individual, or firm, represented in a special or particular manner; (b) the signature of the applicant for registration or some predecessor in his business; (c) an invented word or words; (d) a word or words having no direct reference to the character or quality of the goods, and not being according to its ordinary signification a geographical name or surname, (e) any other distinctive mark, but a name or a surname, signature or word or words, other than under the foregoing heads, is not registrable except upon evidence of its distinctiveness.[1]

In all legal proceedings relating to registration the original registration in Part A is to be taken, after 7 years, as valid in all respects, unless it were obtained by fraud, or the trade mark is likely to deceive or cause confusion, or is contrary to law or morality, or scandalous.[2]

The mark must always be distinctive;[3] it need satisfy only one of the five essentials.[4]

(a) *Name*

If a name is used, it must be that of a real, not an imaginary person,[5] unless used in the possessive case,[6] or a surname used alone,[7] or a name printed in the ordinary manner.[8]

(c) *Invented word*

An invented word must have been substantially new when first used by the applicant or at the date of registration, but need not have required great ingenuity to invent.[9] The use of an old word in a new sense is not invention, and the addition of an affix to a known word may not make it an invented word.[10] The combination of ordinary words,[11] a variant spelling,[12] a common descriptive

[1] 1938 Act, S. 9(1); 'distinctive' is defined: S. 9(2).
[2] 1938 Act, S. 13.
[3] *Re Fanfold, Ltd.'s appln.* (1928) 45 R.P.C. 325.
[4] *Re Diamond T. Motor Co.* [1921] 2 Ch. 583.
[5] *Re Holt & Co.'s T.M.* [1896] 1 Ch. 711.
[6] *Pirie's T.M.* [1892] 1 Ch. 35.
[7] *Re Teofani & Co.'s T.M.* (1913) 30 R.P.C. 446.
[8] *Re Fanfold, Ltd.'s appln., supra*; *Staines* v. *La Rosa* (1953) 70 R.P.C. 62.
[9] *Re Eastman Co., Ltd.'s Appln.* [1898] A.C. 571; *Re Kodak, Ltd.'s T.M.* (1903) 20 R.P.C. 337.
[10] *Re Eastman Co., supra*; *Re T. M. Haematogen* (1904) 20 T.L.R. 585.
[11] *Re Eastman Co., supra*; *Re Minnesota Co.'s Appln.* (1924) 41 R.P.C. 237.
[12] *Re Eastman Co., supra*; cf. *Stuart & Co.* v. *Scottish Val de Travers Co.* (1885) 13 R. 1.

foreign word,[4] a foreign place name[1] and an American slang term[2] will not normally be accepted as invented words.

(d) *No direct reference to character or quality*

A word 'having no direct reference to the character or quality of the goods' permits the registration of words though they may suggest some object or quality of such goods.[3]

A word 'not being . . . a geographical name' excludes well known place names, but not necessarily every name attaching to some place in the world.[4]

(e) *Any other distinctive mark*

A surname is not registrable under the fourth head, but may be under the fifth, if distinctiveness is established.[5] In determining distinctiveness the court may consider the inherent qualities of the mark and how far other circumstances have rendered it adapted to distinguish.[6]

REGISTRABILITY—PART B

To be registrable in Part B a trade mark must be capable, in relation to the goods in respect of which it is registered or proposed to be registered, of distinguishing goods with which the proprietor of the trade mark is or may be connected in trade from goods in the case of which no such connection subsists either generally, or, where the trade mark is registered or proposed to be registered subject to limitations, in relation to use within the extent of the registration.[7] A trade mark may be registered in Part B notwithstanding any registration in Part A in the name of the same proprietor of the same trade mark. A Part B mark does not acquire any presumed validity after seven years.

Registrations prohibited

It is not lawful to register as a trade mark or part thereof any matter the use of which would, by reason of its being likely to

1 *Re Boots Drug Co.'s T.M.* [1938] Ch. 54.

2 *Re La Marquise Footwear's Appln.* (1946) 64 R.P.C. 27.

3 e.g. *Re Compagnie Industrielle des Petroles' Appln.* [1907] 2 Ch. 435; *Re J. & P. Coats, Ltd.'s Appln.* [1936] 2 All E.R. 975.

4 *Boots Pure Drug Co.* [1938] Ch. 540.

5 *Re Teofani & Co.'s T.M.* [1913] 2 Ch. 545; *Re Barford & Co., Ltd.'s Appln.* [1919] 2 Ch. 28.

6 *Yorkshire Copper Works, Ltd.* v. *T.M. Registrar* [1954] 1 All E.R. 570.

7 1938 Act, S. 10; see *H. Quennell, Ltd.'s Appln.* (1955) 72 R.P.C. 36; *Goodyear Tyre and Rubber Co.'s Appln.* [1957] R.P.C. 173.

deceive or cause confusion or otherwise, be disentitled to protection in a court of justice, or contrary to law or morality, or any scandalous design.[1] The registration of identical and resembling trade marks, save exceptionally, is prohibited.[2]

Registration may be allowed only subject to disclaimer by the proprietor of any right to the exclusive use of the mark.[3]

The use of the Royal Arms without authority may be restrained.[4] The use of the Red Cross and associated emblems is also restricted.[5]

A registration does not become invalid by reason of the use, subsequent to the registration, of words in the trade mark as the name or description of an article or substance.[6]

Application for registration

Registration is obtained by application in writing to the registrar by a person claiming to be the proprietor of a trade mark used or proposed to be used by him. The person who first designed or used a trade mark is entitled to claim to be proprietor.[7] For the purposes of registration goods are classified in 34 classes.[8] The registrar may, instead of refusing it, treat an application for Part A as one for Part B. The Registrar's decision may be appealed to the Board of Trade or to the Court of Session.[9]

Once accepted an application must be advertised and any person may give notice of opposition to the registration, whereupon the registrar must decide whether and subject to what conditions, if any, the registration is to be permitted. His decision may be appealed to the Court.[10] Thereafter the Registrar registers the trade mark as of the date of the application, and issues the applicant a certificate in the prescribed form.[11] Notice of a trust will not be entered in the register.[12]

[1] 1938 Act, S. 11.
[2] 1938 Act, S. 12; cf. *Electrolux, Ltd.* v. *Electrix, Ltd.* (1954) 71 R.P.C. 23; *Kidax (Shirts), Ltd.'s Appln.* [1960] R.P.C. 117.
[3] 1938 Act, S. 14.
[4] 1938 Act, S. 61; see *Royal Warrant Holder's Assoc.* v. *Deane & Beal* [1912] 1 Ch. 10; *Re Imperial Tobacco Co.'s Appln.* [1915] 2 Ch. 27; *Royal Warrant Holders' Assocn.* v. *Robb*, 1935 S.N. 32.
[5] Geneva Conventions Act, 1957, S. 6.
[6] 1938 Act, S. 15.
[7] *Gynomin T.M.* [1961] R.P.C. 408.
[8] Trade Mark Rules, 1938, Sched. IV.
[9] 1938 Act, S. 17.
[10] 1938 Act, S. 18.
[11] 1938 Act, S. 19.
[12] 1938 Act, S. 64.

In all legal proceedings registration is *prima facie* evidence of the validity of the original registration and of all subsequent assignations and transmissions.[1] If the validity of registration is challenged in any case and decided in favour of the proprietor the court may give a certificate of validity.[2]

Duration of Registration

Registration endures for seven years and may be renewed for 14 years at a time.[3] If renewal be not requested at the due time the registrar may remove the mark from the register, but may later, if satisfied that it is just to do so, restore it.[3]

False representation of registration

It is an offence falsely to represent that a mark is a registered trade mark and in various other respects.[4]

Rights on registration: infringement

Registration in Part A as proprietor of a trade mark, if valid, gives that person the exclusive right to the use of the trade mark in relation to those goods, and that right is infringed by any person who, not being the proprietor or a registered user using by way of the permitted use, uses a mark identical with it or so nearly resembling it as to be likely to deceive or cause confusion, in the course of trade, in relation to any goods in respect of which it is registered, and in such manner as to render the use of the mark likely to be taken either as being used as a trade mark, or as importing a reference to some person having the right either as proprietor or as registered user to use the trade mark or to goods with which such a person as aforesaid is connected in the course of trade. The right to the use of a trade mark is subject to any conditions or limitations entered on the register.[5]

Registration in Part B as proprietor of a trade mark in respect of any goods, if valid, gives that person the same rights as if the registration had been in Part A. In an action for infringement of the right to the use of a trade mark given by registration in Part B, otherwise than by infringements under S. 6, no interdict or other remedy shall be granted to the pursuer if the defender satisfies the court that the use of which the pursuer complains is not likely to deceive or cause confusion or to be taken as indicating a connec-

[1] 1938 Act, S. 46.
[2] 1938 Act, S. 47.
[3] 1938 Act, S. 20.
[4] 1938 Act, S. 60.
[5] 1938 Act, S. 4; *Coca-Cola Co.* v. *Struthers*, 1968 S.L.T. 353. The right to use is not deemed infringed by certain uses, specified in S. 4(3) and (4).

tion in the course of trade between the goods and some person having the right as proprietor or as registered user to use the trade mark.[1]

The use complained of as infringing must be in the course of trade,[2] and the likelihood of deception must be considered in relation to the place of sale of the goods.[3] Use in an advertisement is infringement.[4] Use of the essential features of a trade mark, though added to or modified, is infringement.[5]

Exceptions

Exclusive right to the use of a registered trade mark is not, however, infringed if the goods are to be sold or traded in a place to which the registration does not extend, or where the proprietor has applied the mark or impliedly consented to its use for the goods, or the use of the mark is reasonably necessary to describe parts for articles which bear or might bear the mark,[6] or the use is by a person who can prove continuous use by himself or his predecessors prior to the registration and use by the proprietor or his predecessors,[7] or there is *bona fide* use by a person of the name, or the name of the place of business, of himself or any of his predecessors in business,[8] or use by any person of a *bona fide* description of the character or quality of his goods, provided that this does not import a prohibited reference,[9] or by reason of concurrent use the defender is entitled to be registered for the mark used.[10]

Assignation and transmission

A registered trade mark is assignable and transmissible in connection with the goodwill of a business or separately, in respect of some or all of the goods in respect of which it is registered, except where the result would be that more than one person would enjoy exclusive rights to use identical or similar

[1] 1938 Act, S. 5.

[2] *Aristoc, Ltd.* v. *Rysta, Ltd.* [1945] A.C. 68; *Ravok* v. *National Trade Press, Ltd.* [1955] 1 Q.B. 554.

[3] *Ballantine* v. *Ballantyne Stewart & Co.* [1959] R.P.C. 273; cf. *Cowie Bros.* v. *Herbert* (1897) 24 R. 353.

[4] *Hindhaugh* v. *Inch*, 1923 S.L.T. 667; *Reuter* v. *Mulhens* [1954] Ch. 50.

[5] *Saville Perfumery Co.* v. *Perfect* (1941) 58 R.P.C. 147; cf. *Board* v. *Thom & Cameron*, 1907 S.C. 1326.

[6] 1938 Act, S. 4(2) and (3).

[7] 1938 Act, S. 7.

[8] 1938 Act, S. 8(a): *Baume* v. *Moore* [1958] Ch. 907.

[9] 1938 Act, S. 8(b).

[10] 1938 Act, S. 12(2).

trade marks the use of which is likely to deceive. The Registrar may certify to a proprietor proposing to assign whether his proposed assignment would be invalid.[1]

Associated trade marks, registered by the same proprietor in respect of the same description of goods or nearly resembling each other, are assignable and transmissible as a whole only, unless the registrar dissolves the association.[2]

The registered proprietor may assign and give receipts for any consideration.[3] Assignees or beneficiaries by transmission must apply to the Registrar for registration as proprietors of the trade mark.[4]

Registered users

A person other than the proprietor of a trade mark may be registered as a registered user in respect of any or all of the goods in respect of which it is registered. A registered user may call on the proprietor to take proceedings to prevent infringement and, if the latter fails to do so, may do so himself. He may not assign or transmit the right to the use of the trade mark.[5]

Removal from register

A registered trade mark may be removed from the register, on the application of a person aggrieved, on the ground of non-use.[6]

Defensive registration

If a trade mark consisting of an invented word or words has become so well known in respect of certain goods that its use in relation to other goods would be likely to be taken as indicating a connection between them and the proprietor of the trade mark, he may register it in respect of the other goods as a defensive trade mark.[7]

PATENTS

A patent is a Crown grant, formerly under letters patent sealed with the Great Seal, now in a form authorised by statutory rules and sealed with the seal of the Patent Office but having the same effect,[8] of monopoly rights in respect of an invention. The issue of

[1] 1938 Act, S. 22.
[2] 1938 Act, S. 23.
[3] 1938 Act, S. 24.
[4] 1938 Act, S. 25.
[5] 1938 Act, S. 28.
[6] 1938 Act, S. 26; cf. *John Dewar & Sons* v. *Dewar* (1900) 7 S.L.T. 461.
[7] 1938 Act, S. 27.
[8] Patents Act, 1949, S. 21(1). For form see Patents Rules, 1958, Sched. III.

patents is regulated on behalf of the Crown by the Comptroller General of Patents, Designs and Trade Marks, subject to the supervision of the Board of Trade,[1] and the Patents Appeal Tribunal,[2] subject to appeal to the Court of Session,[3] but nothing in the Act abridges or prejudices the Crown prerogative in relation to letters patent.[4]

There is maintained at the Patent Office a register of patents in which are entered particulars of patents in force, assignations and transmissions of patents and notice of all matters required by the Act to be entered in the register and of all other matters affecting the validity or proprietorship of patents as the comptroller thinks fit. It is open to the public. No notice of any trust is entered therein and the Comptroller is not affected by notice thereof.[5] The court may order rectification of the register[6] and the Comptroller may correct clerical errors therein.[7]

The Comptroller must on request furnish information as to any patent or application for a patent.[8]

The false representation that any article sold is a patented article is an offence[9] and the grant of a patent does not authorize the use of the royal arms or placing them on any article.[10]

The monopoly right prevents any person from making or using the patented article or process; it does not confer on the patentee any right to manufacture the invention, for that he has without any patent.[11]

Patentable inventions

An invention is any manner of new manufacture the subject of letters patent and grant of privilege within S. 6 of the Statute of Monopolies[12] and any new method or process of testing applicable to the improvement or control of manufacture, and includes an alleged invention.[13] Manner of new manufactures includes

[1] The legislation is the Patents Act, 1949. See generally Terrell on *Patents*.

[2] In Scotland, a judge of the Court of Session nominated by the Lord President: 1949 Act, S. 86.

[3] 1949 Act, S. 87.

[4] 1949 Act, S. 102.

[5] 1949 Act, S. 73.

[6] 1949 Act, S. 75.

[7] 1949 Act, S. 76.

[8] 1949 Act, S. 78.

[9] 1949 Act, S. 91(1).

[10] 1949 Act, S. 91(2).

[11] *Steers* v. *Rodger* (1893) 10 R.P.C. 245.

[12] (1623) 21 Jas. I, c. 3; intended to be declaratory of English common law; see *Australian Gold Co.* v. *Lake View Consols, Ltd.* (1901) 18 R.P.C. 105, 114.

[13] 1949 Act, S. 101(1).

improvements in manufactures and methods.[1] A discovery is not patentable,[2] nor is an abstract principle.[3]

A patent may claim a new substance and the claim is to be construed as not extending to that substance when found in nature.[4]

A patent may not be claimed for a substance capable of use as food or medicine if it is a mixture of known ingredients possessing only the aggregate of the known properties thereof, or for a process producing such a substance by mere admixture.[5]

Application

Application may be made by any person claiming to be the true and first inventor of an invention, or by any person who is the assignee of the true and first inventor in respect of the right to make such an application, or the personal representative of an entitled person.[6] True and first inventors include those who discover a mode of manufacture and those who first import a discovery into the realm.[7]

An employee may patent his invention for his own benefit unless he is bound by express or implied contract to communicate the benefit to his employers.[8] But if the idea were suggested by the employer and merely worked out by the employee the employer may be the true and first inventor.[9]

Application is made in a prescribed form and filed at the Patent Office, stating that the applicant is in possession of the invention and naming the person claiming to be the true and first inventor.[10]

Specification

An application must be accompanied by a complete specification describing the invention, or by a provisional specification

[1] *Commercial Solvents Corpn.* v. *Synthetic Products Co.* (1926) 43 R.P.C. 185. See also *Mellor* v. *Beardmore*, 1926 S.N. 133; *G.E.C.'s Appln.* (1943) 60 R.P.C. 1; *Cementation Co., Ltd.'s Appln.* (1945) 62 R.P.C. 151.

[2] *Reynolds* v. *Smith* (1903) 20 R.P.C. 123; *B.T.H.* v. *Charlesworth Peebles & Co.* (1925) 42 R.P.C. 180.

[3] *Neilson* v. *Househill Coal Co.* (1842) 4 D. 1187, 1201; (sequel 5 D. 86, 1180).

[4] 1949 Act, S. 4(7).

[5] 1949 Act, S. 10(1).

[6] Patents Act, 1949, S. 1.

[7] cf. *Plimpton* v. *Malcolmson* (1876) 3 Ch. D. 531, 555; *Avery's Patent* (1887) 36 Ch. D. 307; *Moser* v. *Marsden* (1893) 10 R.P.C. 350.

[8] *Mellor* v. *Beardmore*, 1927 S.C. 597.

[9] *Allen* v. *Rawson* (1845) 1 C.B. 551. See also 1949 Act, S. 56.

[10] 1949 Act, S. 2; Patents Rules, 1958.

followed within twelve months (or, exceptionally, fifteen months) by a complete specification.[1]

A specification must begin with a title indicating the subject to which the invention relates and describe the invention; drawings may be supplied and shall be deemed part of the specification. A complete specification must (a) particularly describe the invention and the method by which it is to be performed;[2] (b) disclose the best method of performing the invention which is known to the applicant and for which he is entitled to claim protection;[3] and (c) end with a claim or claims defining the scope of the invention claimed. The claim or claims must relate to a single invention, be clear and succinct, and be fairly based on the matter disclosed in the specification.[4] A complete specification filed after a provisional specification may include claims in respect of developments of or additions to the invention which would have themselves justified a separate application for a patent.[5] The complete specification may subsequently be amended.[6]

The scope of every claim in the complete specification must be sufficiently and clearly defined[7] so as to delimit the ambit of the monopoly claimed. If the claim is wider than the invention described warrants the patent is invalid.[8]

Construction of specification

A specification is addressed to persons skilled in the branch of technology involved, and the court must be instructed as to the background of the science in question and the meaning of technical terms. It must be read as a whole, including any relevant drawings. A claim should be construed consistently with the specification.

[1] 1949 Act, S. 3. As to the function of the provisional specification see *Newall* v. *Elliott* (1858) 4 C.B. (N.S.) 269; *Stoner* v. *Todd* (1876) 4 Ch. D. 58; As to discrepancy between provisional and complete specification see *Dudgeon* v. *Thomson* (1873) 11 M. 863; *Gillies* v. *Dunbar* (1877) 5 R. 337; *Bailey* v. *Robertson* (1878) 5 R. (H.L.) 179; *Hutchison, Main & Co.* v. *Pattullo* (1888) 15 R. 644.

[2] *British Shoe Machinery Co.* v. *Fussell* (1908) 25 R.P.C. 631.

[3] cf. *British Dynamite Co.* v. *Krebs* (1896) 13 R.P.C. 190.

[4] cf. *Re Bancroft's Appln.* (1905) 23 R.P.C. 89; *Mullard Radio Valve Co.* v. *Philco Radio Corpn.* (1936) 53 R.P.C. 323.

[5] 1949 Act, S. 4.

[6] 1949 Act, Ss. 29–31.

[7] 1949 Act, S. 32(1)(i); cf. *Gillies* v. *Dunbar* (1877) 5 R. 337; *White* v. *Bertram's, Ltd.* (1897) 5 S.L.T. 59; *British Ore Concentration Syndicate* v. *Minerals Separation, Ltd.* (1910) 27 R.P.C. 33; *Natural Colour Kinematograph Co.* v. *Bioschemes, Ltd.* (1915) 32 R.P.C. 256.

[8] *Lord Kelvin* v. *Whyte, Thomson & Co.* (1907) 15 S.L.T. 760.

Priority

Every claim of a complete specification has effect from the priority date prescribed by the Act, and a patent is not invalidated by reason only of the publication or use of the invention on or after the priority date, or by the grant of another patent on a specification claiming the same invention in a claim of the same or later priority date. The priority date is the date of the application, where the complete specification is filed in pursuance of a single application, or the date of filing the application accompanied by the complete specification.[1]

Examination

When the complete specification has been filed application and specification are referred to an examiner. On his report the comptroller may refuse the application or require amendment of application or specification.[2] The examiner must investigate to ascertain whether the invention has been previously published in the U.K., and, if so, the comptroller may refuse the application unless the applicant satisfies him that the priority date is not later than the publication of the invention, or amends his complete specification.[3] The examiner must also investigate to ascertain whether the invention is claimed in any claim or other complete specification published on or after the date of filing the applicant's complete specification and in pursuance of an application dated before that date. If so, the comptroller may require a reference thereto to be made in the applicant's complete specification.[4] If in consequence of the investigations it appears that the invention cannot be performed without substantial risk of infringement of a claim of any other patent, the comptroller may require a reference thereto in the applicant's complete specification.[5]

Refusal of application

The comptroller may refuse an application if it appears frivolous, or that use of the invention may be contrary to law or morality, or claims as an invention a substance usable as food or medicine which is a mixture of known ingredients possessing only the aggregate of the known properties of the ingredients. An invention capable of use contrary to law may be refused a patent unless such use is disclaimed.[6]

[1] 1949 Act, S. 5. [2] 1949 Act, S. 6. [3] 1949 Act, S. 7.
[4] 1949 Act, S. 8, see also S. 11. [5] 1949 Act, S. 9; see also S. 11.
[6] 1949 Act, S. 10; cf. *A. & H.'s Appln.* (1927) 44 R.P.C. 298; *Carpmael's Appln.* (1928) 45 R.P.C. 411; *Riddlesbarger's Appln.* (1936) 53 R.P.C. 57.

Completion of application

An application is void unless within a limited time, not exceeding 15 months, the applicant has complied with all the requirements of the Act.[1] Thereafter the complete specification may be at any time accepted by the comptroller whereupon the comptroller advertises in the Journal the fact that the specification has been accepted and the date on which the application and specification will be open to public inspection.[2] The applicant has the same rights and privileges as if a patent had been sealed save that he cannot institute proceedings for infringement.[3]

Opposition

Within three months of publication of a complete specification any person interested[4] may give the comptroller notice of opposition on any of the grounds that:

(a) the applicant obtained the invention from him;[5]
(b) the invention has been previously published in the U.K.;[6]
(c) the invention is claimed in a complete specification with a priority date earlier than the applicant's;
(d) the invention was used in the U.K. before its priority date;
(e) the invention is obvious and clearly does not involve any inventive step;
(f) the subject of any claim is not an invention;
(g) the complete specification does not sufficiently and fairly describe the invention or the method by which it is to be performed;
(h) in the case of a convention application, the application was not made timeously.

The comptroller must give the applicant notice of the opposition and give both parties an opportunity to be heard before deciding the case.[7]

If it comes to the comptroller's notice, otherwise than by opposition, that the invention has been prohibited in the U.K. before the priority date of the claim, the comptroller may refuse to grant the patent unless the complete specification is amended.[8]

[1] 1949 Act, S. 12.
[2] 1949 Act, S. 13.
[3] 1949 Act, Ss. 13(4), 22(1).
[4] Questions of *locus standi* may arise: see e.g. *Merron's Appln.* (1944) 61 R.P.C. 91.
[5] cf. *Stuart's Appln.* (1892) 9 R.P.C. 452.
[6] cf. *Lowndes' Patent* (1928) 45 R.P.C. 48.
[7] 1949 Act, S. 14.
[8] 1949 Act, S. 15.

Request for grant

Not later than four months (save in special cases) from the publication of the complete specification the applicant may request the grant and sealing of a patent.[1]

Form and effect of patent

A patent sealed with the seal of the Patent Office has effect throughout the U.K. and the Isle of Man, and has the same effect as if sealed with the Great Seal of the U.K.[2]

A patent avails against the Crown. It is in the form prescribed by rules made under the 1949 Act, and may be granted for one invention only.[1]

A patent is dated with the date of filing of the complete specification, and the date is entered in the register of patents.[3]

Duration

A patent endures for sixteen years from its date.[4] It ceases to have effect on the expiry of the period prescribed for the payment of any renewal fee if that fee is not paid timeously.[5] It may be extended, subject for conditions, for five or, exceptionally, ten years on application on the ground that the applicant has not been adequately remunerated by the patent,[6] or for not longer than ten years on the ground of war losses or damage.[7]

Patents of addition

A patent of addition may be granted to a patentee for the improvement or modification of the main invention. If granted it subsists for the period of the main patent.[8]

Revocation of patent by court—grounds of invalidity of patent

A patent may, on the petition of any person interested, be revoked by the court on any of the stated grounds, viz.: (a) that the invention was claimed in a claim of earlier priority date; (b) that the applicant was not entitled to apply; (c) that the patent contravened the petitioner's rights; (d) that the subject of any claim is

[1] 1949 Act, S. 19.
[2] 1949 Act, S. 21.
[3] 1949 Act, S. 22.
[4] 1949 Act, S. 22(3).
[5] 1949 Act, S. 22(4)–(5).
[6] 1949 Act, S. 23; cf. *McCulloch* v. *Comptroller-General of Patents* (1908) 16 S.L.T. 377; *McIlwaine* v. *Comptroller-General*, 1934 S.N. 35.
[7] 1949 Act, S. 24; *Murray* v. *Comptroller-General of Patents*, 1932 S.N. 36.
[8] 1949 Act, S. 26.

not an invention; (e) that the invention is not new, having regard to what was known or used before its priority date, in the U.K.; (f) that the invention is obvious and does not involve any inventive step; (g) that the invention is not useful; (h) that the complete specification does not fairly describe the invention and the method by which it is to be performed; (i) that the scope of any claim of the complete specification is not sufficiently and clearly defined or that any claim is not fairly based on the matter disclosed in the specification; (j) that the patent was obtained on a false suggestion or representation; (k) that the priority or intended use or exercise of the invention is contrary to law; (l) that the invention was secretly used in the U.K. before the priority date of the claim: no account is to be taken of any use for reasonable trial or experiment only or by a Government department or by any other person to whom the applicant had communicated the invention but without the applicant's consent.[1]

A patent may be partly invalid, in that one or more claims are open to objection, and partly valid; invalidity may be curable by amendment of the complete specification.

PARTICULAR GROUNDS OF INVALIDITY

(a) *Prior claim*

To be invalidated by a prior claim the later claim must be in substance identical therewith;[2] the prior claim may be by the same patentee.[3] Overlapping may be avoided by disclaimer in either prior or later specification. But a combination is not prior claimed because the components have previously been claimed separately.[4]

The objection of prior claim may be rebutted by showing the invalidity of the prior claim.[5]

(b) *Obtaining*

It is necessary to prove that the invention was obtained from the petitioner, but fraud need not be proved[6] and voluntary communication suffices.[7]

[1] 1949 Act, S. 32(1) and (2).
[2] *Re Babcock & Wilcox, Ltd.'s Appln.* (1952) 69 R.P.C. 224.
[3] *Martin and Miles Martin Pen Co.* v. *Selsdon Pen Co.* (1949) 66 R.P.C. 193.
[4] *Re Ross's Patent* (1891) 8 R.P.C. 477.
[5] *Robertson* v. *Purdey* (1907) 24 R.P.C. 273.
[6] *Re Thwaites' Appln.* (1892) 9 R.P.C. 515; *Comptroller-General's ruling*, 27 R.P.C. Appx. i.
[7] *Re Dicker's Appln.* (1934) 51 R.P.C. 392; *H's Appln.* [1956] R.P.C. 197.

At least one of the applicants for a patent must be qualified,[1] i.e. the person claiming to be the true and first inventor, including an importer from abroad, a person who has applied to protect the invention in a convention country, the assignee of the right to make application, or the personal representative of a person either of the first two classes or of his personal representative.

(c) *Contravention of petitioner's rights*

The contravention may be by obtaining fraudulently[2] but may take other forms.

(d) *Subject of claim not an invention*

The subject of claim must be an invention within the Act,[3] i.e. it must be a manner of new manufacture or method of testing, and also new and inventive. Manufacture normally connotes the production of a vendible product.[4] New and inventive requires that there be some material difference in the substance or apparatus used, the process or method of use, or the final product.[5]

(e) *Lack of novelty—anticipation*

The test of novelty is whether a prior activity or publication has contained the whole of the invention impugned.[6] A claim to a combination does not lack novelty because part is old,[7] or part is in one prior document and part in another.[8]

(f) *Obviousness*

An invention is bad for obviousness and lack of inventive step if to a skilled person in the field concerned the application or extension of knowledge claimed would have been readily apparent.[9]

With regard both to novelty and obviousness regard must be had to which was known or used in the U.K. before the priority date of the claim concerned. Any fact or idea once published is

1 *Re Carter's Appln.* (1932) 49 R.P.C. 403.
2 *Re Avery's Patent* (1887) 36 Ch. D. 307; *Re Ralston's Patent* (1909) 26 R.P.C. 313.
3 1949 Act, S. 101(1).
4 *Re G.E.C.'s Appln.* (1942) 60 R.P.C. 1; *Virginia-Carolina Chemical Corpn.'s Appln.* [1958] R.P.C. 35.
5 *Reitzman* v. *Grahame-Chapman and Derustit, Ltd.* (1950) 68 R.P.C. 25.
6 *Molins* v. *Industrial Machinery Co.* [1937] 4 All E.R. 295; *Allmanna Svenska Elektriska A/B* v. *Burntisland Shipbuilding Co.* (1952) 69 R.P.C. 63; *Lyle & Scott, Ltd.* v. *Wolsey*, 1955 S.L.T. 322.
7 *Martin and Biro Swan, Ltd.* v. *Millwood* [1956] R.P.C. 125.
8 *Allmanna Svenska, supra.*
9 *Killick* v. *Pye* [1958] R.P.C. 366; see also *Allmanna Svenska, supra*; *Lyle & Scott, Ltd.* v. *Wolsey*, 1955 S.L.T. 322.

known and public knowledge, though not necessarily part of the fund of common knowledge possessed by persons skilled in the relevant industry.

(g) *Not useful*

Inutility means that the invention will not operate or will not produce the promised result.[1] The practical usefulness is not relevant, nor its benefit to the public.[2] All variants of the invention described must have utility, and it should work under all ordinary conditions. What is claimed in each claim must be useful for the purposes for which it is proposed.[3]

(h) *Insufficiency*

The complete specification must describe an embodiment of the invention claimed with sufficient detail to enable it to be understood and put into effect by persons of skill in the field concerned.[4] The description must also be fair and not be unnecessarily complicated, or misleading.[5]

(i) *Ambiguity*

Ambiguity covers lack of definition of the scope of any claim and obscurity.[6]

(j) *Obtained by false representation*

The false representation may be in the application or in the specification. The falsity must be material and have led to the obtaining of the patent.[7]

(k) *Use contrary to law*

The possibility of use of the invention in a way contrary to law will not suffice; the illegal use must be the primary or intended use.[8]

1 *Re Alsop's Patent* (1907) 24 R.P.C. 733; *Edison and Swan Electric Lighting Co.* (1889) 6 R.P.C. 243.

2 *Young and Neilson* v. *Rosenthal* (1884) 1 R.P.C. 29; *Badische Anilin und Soda Fabrik* v. *Levinstein* (1887) 12 App. Cas. 710; *Re Alsop's Patent, supra.*

3 *Leggatt* v. *Hood's Original Darts Accessories, Ltd.* (1950) 68 R.P.C. 3.

4 *Re Shepherd's Applns.* (1938) 56 R.P.C. 100.

5 *Raleigh Cycle Co.* v. *Miller* (1948) 65 R.P.C. 141.

6 *Raleigh Cycle Co.* v. *Miller* (1946) 63 R.P.C. 113; *Rose St. Foundry Co.* v. *India Rubber Co.* (1929) 46 R.P.C. 294; *British Celanese, Ltd.* v. *Courtaulds* (1935) 52 R.P.C. 171.

7 *Raleigh Cycle Co.* v. *Miller* (1948) 65 R.P.C. 141.

8 *Pessers and Moody* v. *Haydon* (1908) 26 R.P.C. 58; *Walton* v. *Ahrens* (1939) 56 R.P.C. 195.

(l) *Prior secret use*

Prior secret use, save in excepted cases,[1] destroys the novelty requisite for validity. The test of lack of novelty is as in other cases.

Revocation by comptroller and surrender of patents

A patent may, within 12 months after sealing, be revoked by the comptroller, on the application of any person interested who did not oppose the grant, on any one or more of the grounds on which the grant of the patent could have been opposed.[2] A patentee may offer to, and, after advertisement and disposal of any objections, be permitted to surrender his patent.[3]

Licences

A patentee has power to grant licences under his patent and to give effectual receipts for any consideration for such licence, subject to the rights of any other person registered in the register of patents.[4] It requires to be registered in the register of patents.[5] It is binding on the successors in title of the patentee who granted it.[6]

No form is required for a licence which may be created by deed, orally,[7] or by implication from conduct.[8]

A licence permits the doing of what would otherwise be an infringement. Failing contrary indication, a licence is personal and not assignable,[9] nor can sub-licences be granted.[10] It may be limited as to time, place, persons, manufacture, use or sale, in which case it is infringement to do anything beyond the terms of the licence. A sole licence imports that the patentee will grant no other licence, an exclusive licence that he will not himself exercise the rights conferred by the licence.[11] Grantees of an exclusive licence may bring an action for infringement in their own name.[12]

[1] 1949 Act, S. 32(2).
[2] 1949 Act, S. 33.
[3] 1949 Act, S. 34.
[4] 1949 Act, S. 74(4).
[5] 1949 Act, S. 74(1).
[6] *National Carbonising Co.* v. *British Coal Distillation, Ltd.* (1936) 54 R.P.C. 41.
[7] *Crossley* v. *Dixon* (1863) 10 H.L. Cas. 293.
[8] *Tweedale* v. *Bullough, Ltd.* (1896) 13 R.P.C. 522.
[9] *Gonville* v. *Howard & Hay* (1903) 21 R.P.C. 49; *National Carbonising Co.* v. *British Coal Distillation, Ltd.* (1936) 54 R.P.C. 41.
[10] *Howard and Bullough, Ltd.* v. *Tweedales and Smelley* (1895) 12 R.P.C. 519.
[11] 1949 Act, S. 101(1).
[12] *Sc. Vacuum Cleaner Co.* v. *Provincial Cinematograph Theatres*, 1915 1 S.L.T. 389.

A licensee, so long as acting under the licence, is barred from disputing the validity of the patent in an action under the licence.[1]

Voluntary endorsement of patent

The patentee may apply to the comptroller for the patent to be endorsed 'licences of right', whereupon any person is thereafter entitled as of right to a licence under the patent on such terms as may, failing agreement, be settled by the comptroller.[2] Such an endorsement may be later cancelled.[3]

Compulsory licences

After three years from sealing any person interested may apply to the comptroller on stated grounds for a licence under the patent or for its endorsement 'licences of right'.[4] The comptroller may order the grant of licences under the patent to such customers of the applicant as he thinks fit as well as to the applicant.[5] A government department may apply for the endorsement of 'licences of right'.[6] Special provisions exist as to inventions relating to food or medicine.[7] Where an order for 'licences of right' has been made under S. 37, any person interested may, after two years apply to the comptroller for the revocation of the patent on any of the grounds in S. 37, and the comptroller may revoke the patent if satisfied.[8]

Crown use

Provision is made whereby a government department and any person authorised in writing by it may make, use and exercise any patented invention for the services of the Crown.[9]

Infringement

Infringement is constituted by the doing after the publication of the complete specification by any person other than the patentee or a licensee from him, of any of the acts the exclusive

[1] *Young & Beilby* v. *Hermand Oil Co.* (1891) 9 R.P.C. 373; sequel 19 R. 867; *Fuel Economy Co.* v. *Murray* [1930] 2 Ch. 93.
[2] 1949 Act, S. 35.
[3] 1949 Act, S. 36.
[4] 1949 Act, S. 37. This provision is intended to obviate abuses of monopoly.
[5] 1947 Act, Ss. 38–9.
[6] 1949 Act, S. 40.
[7] 1949 Act, S. 41.
[8] 1949 Act, S. 42. As to procedure under Ss. 37–42, see Ss. 43–4.
[9] 1949 Act, Ss. 46–9; cf. *Pfizer Corpn.* v. *Ministry of Health* [1965] A.C. 512.

right to do which is vested in the patentee. A person may seek declarator that the use of any process or the sale of any article does not or would not constitute an infringement.[1] Ignorance that conduct infringed the complainer's patent is no defence.[2] The making of an article with the word 'patent' or 'patented' is not sufficient notice to make an infringement liable in damages unless the number of the patent is stated.[3]

To determine whether there has been infringement the specification must be construed and the scope of the monopoly determined by regard to the claims made, and it must be ascertained whether the defender has done anything the monopoly of which belongs to the patentee.[4]

Infringement is constituted by making, using, exercising or selling the patented invention, but not by granting a licence to manufacture under a subsequent patent,[5] nor by merely purchasing, owning or possessing the invention,[6] nor by lending it.[7] The substitution of a mechanical equivalent for a portion of the patent process does not protect from infringement,[8] nor does a merely colourable difference.[9]

Every ground on which a patent may be revoked by the court is available as a defence in proceedings for infringement of a patent.[10] The defender may also deny the pursuer's title to the patent, deny infringement, or plead the licence of the pursuer.

Remedies for infringement

An infringement is remediable by claim of damages,[11] or, alternatively, an accounting and payment of profits,[12] and interdict.[13] Damages may not be awarded against a defender who proves

[1] 1949 Act, S. 66.
[2] *Proctor* v. *Bennie* (1887) 4 R.P.C. 333; but see 1949 Act, S. 59(1).
[3] 1949 Act, S. 59(1); *Wilderman* v. *Berk* (1925) 42 R.P.C. 79.
[4] *Birmingham Sound Reproducers, Ltd.* v. *Collars* [1956] R.P.C. 232.
[5] *Montgomerie* v. *Paterson* (1894) 11 R.P.C. 633.
[6] *Neilson* v. *Betts* (1871) L.R. 5 H.L. 1; *British Shoe Machinery Co.* v. *Collier* (1910) 26 T.L.R. 587.
[7] *United Telephone Co.* v. *Henry* (1884) 2 R.P.C. 11.
[8] *Dubs* v. *Thomson* (1873) 10 S.L.R. 332; *Marchland* v. *Nicholson* (1893) 20 R. 1006; *Van Berkel* v. *Simpson*, 1907 S.C. 165.
[9] *Dudgeon* v. *Thomson* (1897) 4 R. (H.L.) 88; *B.T.H. Co.* v. *Metropolitan-Vickers Electrical Co.* (1928) 45 R.P.C. 1.
[10] 1949 Act, S. 32(4).
[11] As to measure of damages see *United Horse Shoe Co.* v. *Stewart* (1888) 15 R. (H.L.) 45; *Watson Laidlaw & Co.* v. *Pott Cassels & Williamson*, 1914 S.C. (H.L.) 18; *B.T.H. Co.* v. *Charlesworth, Peebles & Co.*, 1923 S.C. 599.
[12] 1949 Act, S. 60; *United Horse Shoe Co., supra.*
[13] 1949 Act, S. 59(4).

that at the date of the infringement he was not aware, and had no reasonable ground for supposing, that the patent existed.[1] Interdict may be granted against the export of infringing goods.[2] A successful pursuer is also entitled to an order for delivery up or destruction of all infringing articles in the defender's possession and control.[3]

Counterclaim for revocation

In an action for infringement the defender may counterclaim for revocation of the patent.[4]

Certificate of contested validity

Where the validity of any claim of a specification has been contested and the claim is found valid, the court may certify that its validity was contested in those proceedings.[5]

Remedy for groundless threats

Where a person by circulars, advertisements or otherwise not merely notifies the existence of a patent but threatens any person with proceedings for infringement of a patent,[6] any person aggrieved may bring an action against him, and is entitled to declarator that the threats are unjustifiable, interdict against the continuance of the threats and such damages, if any, as he has sustained thereby, unless the defender proves that the acts in respect of which proceedings were threatened constitute or, if done, would constitute, an infringement of a patent or of rights arising from the publication of a complete specification in respect of a claim not shown to be invalid.[7] In the case of malicious threats an action for slander of title might lie.[8] That the threat was made in good faith is no defence.[9] The mode of threatening is immaterial[10] and a threat may be made by implication.[11]

[1] 1949 Act, S. 59(1).

[2] *B.T.H. Co.* v. *Charlesworth Peebles & Co.*, 1922 S.C. 680.

[3] *United Telephone Co.* v. *Walker and Oliver* (1886) 5 R.P.C. 63.

[4] 1949 Act, S. 61.

[5] 1949 Act, S. 64(1); *V.D., Ltd.* v. *Boston Deep Sea Fishing Co.* (1934) 52 R.P.C. 1; *Martin* v. *C.B. Protection (Eng.), Ltd.* (1948) 65 R.P.C. 361.

[6] *C. & P. Developments Co. (London), Ltd.* v. *Sisabro Novelty Co.* (1953) 70 R.P.C. 277; *Rosedale Assoc. Mfrs.* v. *Airfix Products, Ltd.* [1956] R.P.C. 360.

[7] 1949 Act, S. 65.

[8] *Montgomerie* v. *Paterson* (1894) 11 R.P.C. 633; cf. *Cars* v. *Bland Light Syndicate* (1911) 28 R.P.C. 33.

[9] *Skinner* v. *Perry* (1893) 10 R.P.C. 1.

[10] *Kurtz* v. *Spence* (1888) 5 R.P.C. 161; *Ellis* v. *Pogson* (1923) 40 R.P.C. 62; *Luna Advertising Co.* v. *Burnham* (1928) 45 R.P.C. 258.

[11] *Luna Co.*, *supra*.

Assignation and transmission

A patent is moveable property[1] and is assignable outright or in security and transmits on death or bankruptcy. An assignation should be by probative deed. It may be of the whole patent rights or of a share therein or of so much of the patent as applies to particular rights or as to any place in or part of the U.K. or Isle of Man.[2] A person becoming entitled by assignation, transmission or operation of law to a patent or share therein, or entitled as mortgagee, licensee or otherwise to any interest in a patent must apply to the comptroller for registration of his title or notice of his interest in the register of patents.[3] Save by bankruptcy a patent is not subject to diligence.[4]

Restrictions on agreements relating to patents

Certain conditions in various agreements connected with patents are avoided by statute,[5] while others, such as patent licence agreements, might amount to restrictions statutorily registrable,[6] or be void at common law as in unreasonable restraint of trade.

REGISTERED DESIGNS

A design means[7] features of shape, configuration, pattern or ornament[8] applied to an article by any industrial process or means, being features which in the finished article appeal to and are judged solely by the eye, but does not include a method or principle of construction or features of shape or configuration which are dictated solely by the function which the article to be made in that shape or configuration has to perform.

Registration

Under the Registered Designs Acts, 1949 to 1961, there is maintained at the Patent Office[9] a register of designs, in which are

[1] *A.G.* v. *Oswald* (1848) 10 D. 969, 979.

[2] 1949 Act, S. 21(1); *Anderson* v. *Patent Oxonite Co.* (1886) 3 R.P.C. 279; *Reitzman* v. *Graham-Chapman and Derustit, Ltd.* (1950) 67 R.P.C. 178.

[3] 1949 Act, S. 74.

[4] *A.G.* v. *Oswald* (1848) 10 D. 969, 979; cf. *Edwards* v. *Picard* [1909] 2 K.B. 903.

[5] 1949 Act, S. 57; *Tool Metal Mfg. Co.* v. *Tungsten Electric Co.* (1955) 72 R.P.C. 209.

[6] Restrictive Trade Practices Act, 1956.

[7] Registered Designs Act, 1949, S. 1(3); cf. *Harvey* v. *Secure Fittings, Ltd.*, 1966 S.L.T. 121.

[8] It has been said that shape and configuration apply to three dimensions and pattern or ornament to two: *Re Kestos, Ltd., regd. design* (1935) 53 R.P.C. 139, 152; see also *Hunter, Walker & Co.* v. *Falkirk Iron Co.* (1887) 14 R. 1072; *Hecla Foundry Co.* v. *Walker, Hunter & Co.* (1889) 16 R. (H.L.) 27.

[9] Another register of limited scope is maintained at Manchester: Designs Rules, 1949, R. 72.

recorded the names and addresses of the proprietors of registered designs, notices of assignations and transmissions of designs and such other matters as may be prescribed or as the registrar may think fit. The register is in general open to the public and certified copies of any entry in the register must be given to anyone requiring them.[1] The register is *prima facie* evidence of any matters required or authorised to be entered therein, but no notice of any trust may be entered therein.[1] The court may order rectification of the register[2] and the registrar may correct any error in an application or the representation of a design or any error in the register.[3]

On application by the person claiming to be the proprietor, a design may be registered in respect of any article or set of articles specified in the application. A design shall not be registered unless it is new or original, and shall not be registered if it is the same as a design previously registered or differs only in immaterial details or in features which are variants commonly used in the trade.[4] The registrar grants a certificate of registration.[5] Thereafter the representation or specimen of the design registered is generally open to inspection at the Patent Office.[6] On request the registrar will inform an enquirer whether a design is registered, in respect of what articles, whether any extension has been granted, the date of registration and the name and address of the proprietor.[7]

Registrar's powers and duties

The Acts do not authorise or require the registrar to register a design the use of which would, in his opinion, be contrary to law or morality.[8] On the request of a proprietor, the registrar may cancel the registration of a design, and any person interested may apply for its cancellation on the ground that it was not new or original, or on any other ground on which the registrar could have refused to register the design.[9]

The registrar must give an applicant for registration an opportunity to be heard before exercising adversely to him any discretion he has under the Act.[10]

[1] 1949 Act, S. 17. [2] 1949 Act, S. 20. [3] 1949 Act, S. 21.
[4] 1949 Act, S. 1(1) and (2). As to proceedings for registration, see S. 3.
[5] 1949 Act, S. 18.
[6] 1949 Act, S. 22. The Board of Trade may delay the inspection of certain designs for time.
[7] 1949 Act, S. 23.
[8] 1949 Act, S. 43.
[9] 1949 Act, S. 11.
[10] 1949 Act, S. 29. As to expenses, evidence and representation, see Ss. 30–32.

Appeals

Appeals from the registrar lie to the Court of Session.[1]

The design

A design may be registered in respect of any article or set of articles of manufacture, including any part made and sold separately, but it must perform some function other than merely carry the design.[2] Articles primarily literary or artistic in character are excluded from registration.[3]

The eye is the sole standard of judgment and a design must show some new effect distinguishable by the eye from previous designs.[4] But it need not possess artistic merit.[5] If the difference in design does not have artistic merit the court requires a more marked difference discernible by the eye.[6]

A design is not registrable for a method or principle of construction by itself, though it may do so incidentally,[7] nor in respect of features of shape and configuration dictated solely by the intended function of the article so shaped.[8]

The design must be new or original,[9] whether the purpose of this be beauty or utility or both, but a registration may be valid in respect of the application of an old pattern to a new kind of article.[10] It may be new or original though composed of constituents which are old[11] provided the whole is in some way an improvement on the parts alone.[12] Applications for registration must be accompanied by a statement saying for what features novelty is claimed.[13]

A design registered in respect of one article may be registered in respect of another or other articles later and is not invalidated by the prior registration.[14]

1 1949 Act, Ss. 28, 45.

2 1949 Act, Ss. 1, 44; *Re Littlewoods Pools, Ltd.'s Appln.* (1949) 66 R.P.C. 309. A fixed building is not, a portable building is, registrable: *Portable Concrete Buildings, Ltd.* v. *Bathcrete* [1962] R.P.C. 49.

3 1949 Act, S. 1(4); Design Rules, 1949, R. 26. Many such articles would come within the Copyright Act, 1956.

4 *Re Smith's Regd. Design* (1889) 6 R.P.C. 200.

5 *Hecla Foundry Co.* v. v. *Walker, Hunter & Co.* (1889) 16 R. (H.L.) 27.

6 *Re Smith's Regd. Design, supra.*

7 *Re Bayer's Design* (1907) 25 R.P.C. 56.

8 1949 Act, S. 1(3); *Stenor, Ltd.* v. *Whitesides* [1948] A.C. 107.

9 1949 Act, S. 1(2).

10 *Saunders* v. *Wiel* [1893] 1 Q.B. 470.

11 *Heath* v. *Rollason* [1898] A.C. 499.

12 *Phillips* v. *Harbro Rubber Co.* (1919) 36 R.P.C. 79.

13 Designs Rules, 1949, R. 14(2); cf. *Hunter, Walker & Co.* v. *Falkirk Iron Co.* (1887) 14 R. 1072.

14 1949 Act, S. 4(1).

Effect of registration

Registration gives the registered proprietor the copyright in the registered design, i.e. the exclusive right in the U.K. and Isle of Man to make or import for sale or for use for the purposes of any trade or business, or to sell, hire or offer for sale or hire, any article in respect of which the design is registered, being an article to which the registered design has been applied, and to make anything for enabling any such article to be made as aforesaid in the U.K. or elsewhere.[1] It is an offence falsely to represent that a design applied to an article sold is registered in respect of that article.[2]

Duration of copyright

Subject to the Act, copyright in a registered design subsists for five years from the date of registration. On application before the expiry the registrar extends the copyright for a second and a third period of five years.[3]

Proprietorship of design

The author of a design is the proprietor, unless it is executed for another person for payment, in which case that other is the proprietor.[4]

Assignation and transmission

The right of property in a design is assignable and transmits as moveable property on intestacy or under a will[5] or to a trustee in bankruptcy. On assignation or transmission the assignee or beneficiary becomes proprietor.[6] A person who becomes entitled to a design or a share therein by assignation, transmission, or operation of law or as mortgagee of an interest in a design, must apply to the registrar for registration of his title or of notice of his interest.

Licences

The registered proprietor of a design may grant a licence to do any of the acts restricted to him by the copyright in the design. A person becoming entitled as licensee to an interest in a registered design must have his interest noted in the register of designs.[7] No

[1] 1949 Act, S. 7; cf. *Haddon* v. *Bannerman* [1912] 2 Ch. 602; *Dorling* v. *Honnor Marine* [1965] Ch. 1.

[2] 1949 Act, S. 35.

[3] 1949 Act, S. 8.

[4] 1949 Act, S. 2.

[5] 1949 Act, S. 19(4).

[6] 1949 Act, S. 2.

[7] 1949 Act, S. 19.

special form is provided but it must be clear that permission is being granted to apply the design.

Compulsory licences

After a design has been registered any person interested may apply to the registrar for the grant of a compulsory licence on the ground that the design is being applied in the U.K. by any industrial process to such an extent as is reasonable in the circumstances.[1] The registrar may allow a reasonable time to begin manufacture in the U.K. If made, an order for compulsory licence has the same effect as a grant of a licence by the proprietor.[1]

Infringement of design

Infringement consists in doing any act the exclusive right to do which is vested in the proprietor by the registration of his design. The question is frequently whether one design differs sufficiently from a registered design to be distinct from it; this must be determined by the eye alone[2] and depends only on shape or configuration, not on identity of function.[3] There is no infringement if the eye would not confuse the two designs under normal conditions.[4]

Defences other than non-infringement are that the registration is invalid or has expired, or the licence of the registered proprietor. The defender may claim that the registration should be cancelled.

Infringement claims may be brought only by the registered proprietor[5] and justify damages, interdict, an order for delivery of infringing goods,[6] or a count, reckoning and payment of profits.

Damages will not be awarded against a defender who proves that at the date of infringement he was not aware and had no reasonable grounds for supposing that the design was registered.[7]

Where the validity of the design is upheld, a certificate of contested validity may be given.[8]

[1] 1949 Act, S. 10.

[2] *Holdsworth* v. *McCrea* (1867) L.R. 2 H.L. 380; *Hecla Foundry Co.* v. *Walker, Hunter & Co.* (1889) 16 R. (H.L.) 27; *Re Kestos, Ltd., Regd. Design* (1935) 53 R.P.C. 139.

[3] *Hecla Foundry Co., supra.*

[4] *Hutchison Main & Co.* v. *St. Mungo Mfg. Co.* (1907) 24 R.P.C. 265.

[5] 1949 Act, S. 7(1).

[6] cf. *Knowles* v. *Bennett* (1895) 12 R.P.C. 137.

[7] 1949 Act, S. 9(1). The marking 'Registered' without the number does not affect him with knowledge.

[8] 1949 Act, S. 25(1); *Harvey* v. *Secure Fittings, Ltd.*, 1966 S.L.T. 121.

Action for threats

Where any person by circulars, advertisements or otherwise threatens[1] any other person with proceedings for infringement of a registered design, any person aggrieved thereby may claim declarator that the threats are unjustified, interdict against the continuance of the threats, and damages sustained by reason of the threats. A mere notification that a design is registered is not a a threat of proceedings.[2] A claim for threats may be adduced as a counterclaim in an action for infringement.[3] A malicious statement that another's products infringe a registered design may ground an action for injurious falsehood.

Unregistered designs

A design never registered, or one the registration of which has expired, confers no proprietary rights on the user and he has no ground for objection if another uses the same or a similar design, though he may have a right of action if the circumstances amount to passing-off.

COPYRIGHT

Copyright is the exclusive right to exercise, and to authorize other persons to exercise, certain rights in literary or artistic material. The right is distinct from the property in the manuscript embodying the words.[4] It subsists not in the ideas but in the execution, presentation and order of words.[5] Copyright existed at common law[6] but now exists only under the Copyright Act, 1956.[7] Work no longer copyright is the common property of all, and anyone may republish at his will.

Copyright subsists, subject to the Act, in every original literary, dramatic or musical work which is unpublished and of which the author was a qualified person when the work was made.[8]

[1] cf. *Paul Trading Co., Ltd.* v. *Marksmith* (1952) 69 R.P.C. 301; *Rosedale Assoc. Mfrs.* v. *Airfix Products, Ltd.* [1956] R.P.C. 360.

[2] 1949 Act, S. 26.

[3] e.g. *Kleeman* v. *Rosedale Assoc. Mfrs.* (1953) 71 R.P.C. 78.

[4] *Re Dickens* [1935] Ch. 267.

[5] *Donoghue* v. *Allied Newspapers, Ltd.* [1938] Ch. 106; see generally Bell, *Comm.* I, 110–5; Copinger and Skone James on *Copyright*. Copyright legislation dates from 1709; the 1956 Act takes account of the International Copyright Convention of Berne, 1885, later revised, and the Universal Copyright Convention of Geneva, 1952.

[6] cf. *Tennyson* v. *Forrester* (1871) 43 S. Jur. 278.

[7] 1956 Act, S. 46(5).

[8] 1956 Act, S. 2(1). 'Qualified person' is defined: S. 1(5).

Copyright also subsists in an original literary, dramatic, or musical work which has been published if the first publication took place in the United Kingdom or in another country to which the section extends, or the author was a qualified person when the work was first published, or the author had died before that time, but was a qualified person immediately before his death.[1]

Originality

Originality relates not to idea or substance but to words, to original skill or labour employed in collection, preparation or execution, not necessarily to originality of idea.[2] Hence collections,[3] compilations and formulae are protected. Skill and labour may be exercised by change of medium,[4] compiling works of information,[5] making selections,[6] adaptations,[7] or abridgements,[8] new arrangements of music.[9] A new edition may be so materially different from a former edition to be entitled to independent copyright.[10]

The title of a work can rarely be the subject of copyright, on the ground of lack of originality,[11] but the identity or similarity of one title to another may give rise to an action for passing off.[12] An author may also be able to protect his pen name by a passing-off action.[13]

[1] 1956 Act, S. 2(2).

[2] *Harpers* v. *Barry, Henry & Co.* (1892) 20 R. 133.

[3] *Bailey & Taylor* (1830) 1 Russ. & My. 73 (mathematical tables); *Alexander* v. *Mackenzie* (1846) 9 R. 748 (collection of conveyancing styles); *Univ. of London Press* v. *Univ. Tutorial Press* [1916] 2 Ch. 601 (examination questions).

[4] e.g. translating: *Byrne* v. *Statist Co.* [1914] 1 K.B. 622; reporting: *Walker* v. *Lane* [1900] A.C. 539.

[5] *Exchange Telegraph Co.* v. *Gregory* [1896] 1 Q.B. 147; *B.B.C.* v. *Wireless League Gazette Pub. Co.* [1926] Ch. 433; *Football League, Ltd.* v. *Littlewoods Pools, Ltd.* [1959] Ch. 637; contrast *Cramp* v. *Smythson* [1944] A.C. 329.

[6] *Macmillan* v. *Suresh Chunder Deb.* (1890) 17 Ind. L.R. (Calcutta) 951.

[7] *Hatton* v. *Keane* (1859) 7 C.B. 268.

[8] *Macmillan* v. *Cooper* (1923) 40 T.L.R. 186; cf. *Sweet* v. *Benning* (1855) 16 C.B. 459.

[9] *Wood* v. *Boosey* (1867) L.R. 3 Q.B. 223; *Boosey* v. *Fairlie* (1877) 7 Ch. D. 301.

[10] cf. *Black* v. *Murray* (1870) 9 M. 341; *Blacklock* v. *Pearson* [1915] 2 Ch. 376.

[11] *Dicks* v. *Yates* (1881) 18 Ch. D. 76; *Ladbroke* v. *William Hill (Football), Ltd.* [1964]; 1 All E.R. 465; cf. *Broemel* v. *Meyer* (1912) 29 T.L.R. 148; *Francis Day & Hunter* v. *Twentieth Century Fox Corpn.* [1940] A.C. 112.

[12] e.g. *Primrose Press Agency Co.* v. *Knowles* (1885) 2 T.L.R. 404; contrast *Outram* v. *London Evening Newspapers Co.* (1910) 27 T.L.R. 231; *Ridgway Co.* v. *Hutchinson* (1923) 40 R.P.C. 335; *Cooper* v. *Richmond Hill Press, Ltd.* [1957] R.P.C. 363; *Kark* v. *Odhams Press, Ltd.* [1962] 1 All E.R. 636; cf. *Constable* v. *Brewster* (1824) 3 S. 215; *Edinburgh Correspondent* (1822) 1 S. 407 n.

[13] *Hines* v. *Winnick* [1947] Ch. 708; *Forbes* v. *Kemsley Newspapers, Ltd.* [1951] 2 T.L.R. 656.

Publication

A work is published when reproductions have been issued to the public,[1] not by exhibiting a manuscript, allowing persons to read it, sending the text as a letter to a correspondent, delivering the text as lectures,[2] performing a musical or dramatic work in public, exhibiting an artistic work, or constructing an architectural work of art. Public performance of a dramatic or musical work is not publication.[3] Presentation of copies to friends is not 'issue to the public'.[4]

Unauthorised publication does not amount to publication for copyright purposes.[5]

Publication which is merely colourable and not intended to satisfy the reasonable requirements of the public has to be disregarded.[6]

Letters remain unpublished though sent,[7] but letters to the editor of a newspaper imply a licence to the latter to publish and even to abbreviate or alter.[8]

Acquisition of statutory rights of copyright

Under the Copyright Act, 1842, no action could be brought for infringement of copyright in a book, unless it was duly registered at Stationers' Hall.[9] Since the 1911 Act, and under the 1956 Act, no registration or other procedure is necessary to acquire copyright. Copyright in an unpublished work attaches *ipso jure* when it is created, and in a published work when it is published.

Where public policy precludes acquisition of copyright

On grounds of public policy a claim to copyright in an immoral, obscene, libellous or scandalous work will not be enforced.[10] Nor

[1] 1956 Act, S. 49(2); cf. Ss. 12(9), 13(10). [2] *Caird* v. *Sime* (1887) 14 R. (H.L.) 37.

[3] 1956 Act, S. 49(2).

[4] *Prince Albert* v. *Strange* (1849) 1 M. & G. 25.

[5] 1956 Act, S. 49(3); cf. *Webb* v. *Rose* (1732) in (1766) 4 Burr. 2330; *Macklin* v. *Richardson* (1770) 2 Amb. 694.

[6] 1956 Act, S. 49(2)(b); *Francis, Day & Hunter* v. *Feldman* [1914] 2 Ch. 728.

[7] The recipient acquires the property in the letter as an object, but not the copyright; cf. *Philip* v. *Pennell* [1907] 2 Ch. 577.

[8] *Walter* v. *Lane* [1900] A.C. 539; *Springfield* v. *Thame* (1903) 89 L.T. 242, but see *Davis* v. *Miller* (1855) 17 D. 1166.

[9] 1842 Act, S. 24; cf. *Black* v. *Murray* (1870) 9 M. 341; *Thomas* v. *Turner* (1886) 33 Ch. D. 292.

[10] *Clementi* v. *Golding* (1809) 2 Camp. 25; *Hine* v. *Dale* (1809) 2 Camp. 27n.; *Lawrence* v. *Smith* (1822) Jac. 471; *Murray* v. *Benbow* (1822) Jac. 474n; *Stockdale* v. *Onwhyn* (1826) 5 B. & C. 173; *Baschet* v. *London Illustrated Standard Co.* [1900] 1 Ch. 73; *Glynn* v. *Western Feature Film Co.* [1916] 1 Ch. 261; *Pasickniak* v. *Dojacek* (1928) 42 T.L.R. 545.

can copyright be recognised in works purporting to be what they are not.[1]

Subjects of copyright—literary work

Literary work includes any written table or compilation;[2] i.e. expressed in any form of symbols or characters. It need not be 'literature',[3] nor have any quality of style, nor need the written words be meaningful.[4] There must, however, be skill and labour in the arrangement of words: hence there is generally no copyright in the title of a book or article, nor in advertisement slogans or laudatory statements.[5]

Literary work does not cover a cardboard sleeve pattern,[6] a photograph album,[7] or a cricket scoring sheet.[8]

Subject of copyright—dramatic and musical works

In dramatic[9] and musical works[10] there may be copyright in the text or score, and separate rights to prevent public performance without consent, and to prevent broadcasting or reproduction on records or film without consent.

Duration of copyright

Copyright subsists till 50 years from the end of the calendar year in which the author died, and then expires.[11]

If before the death of the author the work had neither been published, nor performed in public, nor records thereof offered for sale to the public, nor been broadcast, copyright subsists till 50 years from the end of the calendar year in which one of these acts was first done.[11]

[1] *Wright* v. *Tallis* (1845) 1 C.B. 893; *Slingsby* v. *Bradford Patent Truck Co.* [1906] W.N. 51.

[2] 1956 Act, S. 48(1); cf. *Leslie* v. *Young* (1893) 21 R. (H.L.) 57 (timetables); *McNeil* v. *Rolled Steel Forge Co.*, 1930 S.N. 145 (catalogue). Maps and plans are 'drawings' and protected under S. 3(1).

[3] *Maple* v. *Junior Army and Navy Stores* (1882) 21 Ch. D. 369; *Harpers* v. *Barry, Henry & Co.* (1892) 20 R. 133; *Univ. of London Press* v. *Univ. Tutorial Press* [1916] 2 Ch. 601, 608; *Purefoy Eng. Co.* v. *Sykes, Boxwell & Co.* (1955) 72 R.P.C. 89.

[4] *Anderson* v. *Lieber Code Co.* [1917] 2 K.B. 469 (telegraph code); *Pitman* v. *Hine* (1884) 1 T.L.R. 39 (shorthand); *Ladbroke* v. *William Hill (Football), Ltd.* [1964] 1 All E.R. 465.

[5] *Sinanide* v. *La Maison Kosmes* (1928) 139 L.T. 365.

[6] *Hollinrake* v. *Truswell* [1894] 3 Ch. 420.

[7] *Schove* v. *Schminske* (1886) 33 Ch. D. 546.

[8] *Page* v. *Wisden* (1869) 20 L.T. 435.

[9] Defined, 1956 Act, S. 48(1); see also *Tate* v. *Fullbrook* [1908] 1 K.B. 821.

[10] Not defined by 1956 Act, but see definition in (repealed) Musical (Summary Proceedings) Copyright Act, 1902, S. 3.

[11] 1956 Act, S. 2(3).

Acts restricted by copyright

The acts restricted by the copyright in a literary, dramatic or musical work are[1] (a) reproducing[2] the work in any material form; (b) publishing[3] the work; (c) performing[4] the work in public; (d) broadcasting the work; (e) causing the work to be transmitted to subscribers to a diffusion service; (f) making any adaptation[5] of the work; (g) doing, in relation to an adaptation of the work, any of acts (a) to (e).

Publication of unpublished manuscripts

Copyright is not infringed by the reproduction or publication of a copyright unpublished work, the manuscript or a copy of which is kept in a library or museum, if the author has been dead for 50 years and 100 years have elapsed since the work was made.[6]

Publication in breach of confidence

Apart from infringement of copyright unauthorised reproduction or publication, as of letters received, may be actionable as a breach of confidence or of trust.[7] Action for breach of confidence may also protect where copyright does not, e.g. against the publication of ideas or information communicated in confidence.[8]

Copyright in published editions of works

Subject to the Act, copyright subsists in every published edition of any one or more literary, dramatic or musical works if the first publication took place in the U.K., or in another country to which the section extends, or the publisher of the edition was a qualified person. Such copyright vests in the publisher and subsists for 25 years; it restricts the making of a reproduction of the typographical arrangement of the edition, with an exception for libraries of particular classes.[9]

[1] 1956 Act, S. 2(5).

[2] 1956 Act, S. 48(1).

[3] 1956 Act, S. 49.

[4] 1956 Act, S. 48.

[5] 1956 Act, S. 2(6).

[6] 1956 Act, S. 7(6) and (7).

[7] 1956 Act, S. 46(4); *Pope* v. *Curl* (1741) 2 Atk. 341; *Gee* v. *Pritchard* (1818) 2 Swans. 402; *Prince Albert* v. *Strange* (1849) 1 M. & G. 25; See also *White* v. *Dickson* (1881) 8 R. 896; *McCosh* v. *Crow* (1903) 5 F. 670.

[8] cf. *Exchange Telegraph* v. *Gregory* [1896] 1 Q.B. 147; see also *Chilton* v. *Progress Printing Co.* [1895] 2 Ch. 29; *Exchange Telegraph* v. *Howard* (1906) 22 T.L.R. 375; *Philip* v. *Pennell* [1907] 2 Ch. 577.

[9] 1956 Act, S. 15; See also S. 16. This protects reprints of works out of copyright. Thus the Stair Society acquired copyright in its photo-reprint (1962–64) of Balfour's *Practicks* (pub. 1754), the copyright of which had expired; cf. *Black* v. *Murray* (1870) 9 M. 341.

Copyright in artistic works

Copyright subsists in artistic work[1] which is unpublished and of which the author was a qualified person when he made it or for a substantial part of the period of making. If original artistic work has been published copyright subsists in it only if the first publication took place in the U.K. or in another country to which the section extends, or the author was a qualified person at the time when the work was first published, or the author had died before that time but was a qualified person immediately before his death.[2] As in literary, dramatic and musical works the expression, not the idea, is protected.[3]

Copyright under S. 3 subsists till the end of 50 years from the end of the calendar year in which the author died, and then expires, but in the case of an engraving, unpublished at the author's death, it subsists for 50 years from the year in which it is first published, and the copyright in a photograph subsists till 50 years from the end of the calendar year in which it is first published, and then expires.[4]

The acts restricted by copyright in an artistic work are (a) reproducing the work in any material form; (b) publishing the work; (c) including the work in a television broadcast; (d) causing a television programme which includes the work to be transmitted to subscribers to a diffusion service.

Copyright in sound recordings

Copyright subsists in every sound recording[5] of which the maker was a qualified person when it was made, if published and if the first publication of the recording took place in the United Kingdom or another country to which the section extends. It subsists till 50 years from the end of the year in which the recording is first published and then expires; it vests in the maker of the sound recording, or, in the absence of contrary agreement, in the person who commissions the making of a sound recording and pays or agrees to pay for it, if the recording is made in pursuance of that copyright.[6]

1 Defined (S. 3(1)) as paintings, sculptures, drawings, engravings and photographs, buildings or models for buildings, and works of artistic craftsmanship: artistic quality is irrelevant. By S. 48(1) sculpture includes any cast or model made for the purpose of sculpture, drawings include any diagram, map, chart or plan, and engravings any etching, lithograph, wood-cut, print or similar work, not being a photograph.

2 1956 Act, S. 3(2) and (3).

3 *Kenrick* v. *Lawrence* (1890) 25 Q.B.D. 99.

4 1956 Act, S. 3(4).

5 Defined, 1956 Act, S. 12(9).

6 1956 Act, S. 12(1)–(4).

The acts restricted by the copyright in a sound recording are (a) making a record embodying the recording; (b) causing the recording to be heard in public; and (c) broadcasting the recording; but certain acts are deemed not to be infringements.[1]

Copyright in cinematograph films

Subject to the Act copyright subsists in cinematograph films of which the maker was a qualified person, and in every such film which has been published, if the first publication took place in the U.K. or another country to which the section extends. Such copyright lasts for 50 years, vests in the maker of the film, and, with certain qualifications, restricts the rights to make a copy of the film, cause the film to be seen or heard in public, broadcast the film, or cause it to be transmitted to subscribers to a diffusion service.[2]

Copyright in television broadcasts and sound broadcasts

Subject to the Act, copyright subsists in every television broadcast made by the B.B.C. or I.T.A. from a place in the U.K. or another country to which the section extends, and in every sound broadcast made by either authority from such a place. It vests in the B.B.C. or I.T.A., subsists for 50 years, and restricts the making, otherwise than for private purposes, of a film or copy of a film of a television broadcast, the making, otherwise than for private purposes, of a sound recording or a record embodying such a recording of a sound broadcast or the sounds of a television broadcast, the causing of a broadcast to be seen or heard in public by a paying audience, or re-broadcasting a sound or television broadcast.[3]

Ownership of copyright

Copyright in a literary, dramatic, musical or artistic work attaches to the author thereof.[4] Subject to any contrary agreement, where a literary or dramatic or artistic work is made by an author in the course of his employment by a newspaper or periodical

[1] 1956 Act, S. 12(5)–(8); see also S. 16, and *Harms* v. *Martans Club, Ltd.* [1927] 1 Ch. 526; *P.R.S.* v. *Hawthorn Hotel, Ltd.* [1933] Ch. 855; *Jennings* v. *Stephens* [1936] Ch. 469.

[2] 1956 Act, S. 13; See also S. 16; cf. *Milligan* v. *Broadway Cinema Productions*, 1923 S.L.T. 35.

[3] 1956 Act, S. 14; see also S. 16.

[4] 1956 Act, S. 4(1). 'Author' is not defined: as to who is author see *Tate* v. *Thomas* [1921] 1 Ch. 503; *Donoghue* v. *Allied Newspapers* [1938] Ch. 106. In relation to a photograph the 'author' is the owner of the material on which it is taken: S. 48(1).

under a contract of service or apprenticeship and made for publication in a newspaper or periodical, the copyright is in the newspaper proprietor in so far as it relates to publication in a newspaper or periodical, but no further, and where a person commissions a photograph, portrait or engraving and pays or agrees to pay for it, the person commissioning is entitled to any copyright therein;[1] and where in any other case a work is made in the course of the author's employment by another under a contract of service or apprenticeship, the employer is entitled to the copyright.[2]

Prospective ownership of copyright

Copyright which will or may come into existence in respect of future work may be assigned by the prospective owner, and it then vests in the assignee on coming into being.[3]

Transfer and transmission

Copyright is transferable by assignation or by will, or transmissible by operation of law, as moveable property.[4] It is a distinct subject of property from the material objects which embody the expressions which are the subject of copyright, such as a manuscript, score or painting.[5] The copyright is deemed, failing contrary indication in the will, conveyed by a bequest of the manuscript of an unpublished literary, dramatic or musical work, or of an unpublished artistic work, in so far as the testator was owner of the copyright immediately before his death.[6]

An assignation of copyright may be total or limited as to classes of acts vested in the owner, or as to the countries in relation to which the owner has exclusive right, or as to the period for which it is to subsist, or in more than one of these ways.[7]

[1] cf. *Crooke* v. *Scots Pictorial Publishing Co.* (1906) 14 S.L.T. 127.

[2] 1956 Act, S. 4(2)–(5). As to works published anonymously or pseudonymously, see 1956 Act, S. 11 and Sched. II. As to works of joint authorship, see 1956 Act, S. 11 and Sched. III.

[3] 1956 Act, S. 37; cf. *Ward Lock & Co.* v. *Long* [1906] 2 Ch. 550; *Macdonald* v. *Eyles* [1921] 1 Ch. 631.

[4] 1956 Act, S. 36(1); cf. *Re Grant Richards* [1907] 2 K.B. 33 (bankruptcy). It is not clear what diligence, if any, is appropriate for attaching copyright, though royalties can be arrested.

[5] cf. *Cooper* v. *Stephens* [1895] 1 Ch. 567; but see *Caddell & Davies* v. *Stewart* (1804) Mor., Literary Property, Appx. 4; *Clark* v. *Adam* (1832) 6 W. & S. 141; *London Ptg. Alliance* v. *Cox* [1891] 3 Ch. 291.

[6] 1956 Act, S. 38.

[7] 1956 Act, S. 36(2).

An assignation must be in writing signed by or on behalf of the assignor.[1]

Once it has been assigned the author may not claim to exercise any of the rights protected by copyright.[2]

Licences in respect of copyright

A licence or permission may be granted in respect of any copyright, thereby legalising something which would otherwise have been unlawful.[3] Any such licence granted by the owner of the relevant copyright binds every successor in title to his interest in the copyright except a purchaser in good faith for value without notice of the licence or a person deriving title from such a purchaser.[4] A licence may be oral, or implied by conduct, but an exclusive licence must be in writing. It authorises the licensee, to the exclusion of all others, to exercise a right which would otherwise be exercisable solely by the owner of the copyright.[5] A licence is probably assignable, unless there is *delectus personae*.[6]

Infringement

Infringement is constituted by the doing of any act the exclusive right to do which[7] is vested in the owner of the copyright. Infringement is also constituted by certain importations, sales and other dealings with infringing articles.[8]

Certain dealings with literary, dramatic and musical works[9] and with artistic works[10] are however not deemed infringements.

Infringement by reproduction involves making a substantial use of the form of expression, not the idea, plot or principle, of the copyright work,[11] taken from that work. It is frequently a question

[1] 1956 Act, S. 36(3). No particular form is necessary, and a receipt for money may be held to imply an assignation: *Jeffreys* v. *Kyle* (1855) 18 D. 906; *Levy* v. *Rutley* (1871) L.R. 6 C.P. 523; *London Ptg. Alliance* v. *Cox* [1891] 3 Ch. 291; *Savory* v. *World of Golf, Ltd.* [1914] 2 Ch. 566; *Ornamin (U.K.)* v. *Bacsa* [1964] R.P.C. 293.

[2] *Educ. Co. of Ireland* v. *Fallon Bros.* [1919] 1 I.R. 62.

[3] cf. 1956 Act, Ss. 1(2), 5(2). The commonest case is an agreement with a publisher to print and publish a book, the author retaining the copyright. cf. *Cunningham* v. *Maclachlan & Stewart's Tr.* (1891) 18 R. 460.

[4] 1956 Act, S. 36(4).

[5] 1956 Act, S. 19.

[6] cf. *Griffith* v. *Tower Publishing Co.* [1897] 1 Ch. 21; *Re Jude's Musical Compositions, Ltd.* [1907] 1 Ch. 651.

[7] i.e. the acts listed in Ss. 2(5) and 3(5).

[8] S. 5.

[9] Ss. 6–8.

[10] Ss. 9–10. See also Design Copyright Act, 1968.

[11] *Lennie* v. *Pillans* (1843) 5 D. 416; *Alexander* v. *Mackenzie* (1847) 9 D. 748; *Hollinrake* v. *Truswell* [1894] 3 Ch. 420.

of degree whether the amount reproduced is so substantial as to amount to infringement.[1] Not only the quantity, but the value and importance of the matter reproduced matters.[2] The words or other mode of expression need not be copied exactly.

There is no infringement merely by reason of similarity of statement, particularly where both works in question necessarily draw on the same sources.[3]

Infringement in other ways includes an unauthorised reprint, performing the work in public, broadcasting the work, adapting or translating it.

Indirect infringement is effected by anyone who without the licence of the copyright owner sells or exposes for sale an infringing work, imports it, unless for private or domestic use.

Infringement is actionable at the instance of the copyright owner by way of claims for damages, interdict, count, reckoning and payment of profits, or otherwise. In certain circumstances particular remedies are excluded.[4] The copyright owner has also rights in respect of the intromission by a person with an infringing copy.[5] Provision is also made for cases where an exclusive licence has been granted in respect of the copyright,[6] for the proof of certain facts in copyright actions, and for penalties and summary proceedings in respect of dealings which infringe copyright.[7]

False attribution of authorship

The 1956 Act,[8] without prejudice to other civil or criminal remedies, imposes restrictions, the contravention of which is actionable as a breach of statutory duty, on falsely attributing literary, dramatic, musical or artistic work to a person not the author thereof, without the latter's permission, during his life or within twenty years of his death.

[1] *White* v. *Briggs* (1890) 18 R. 223.

[2] *Bramwell* v. *Helcomb* (1836) 3 M. & Cr. 737; *Saunders* v. *Smith* (1838) 3 M. & Cr. 711; *Neale* v. *Harmer* (1897) 13 T.L.R. 209; *Ladbroke* v. *William Hill (Football), Ltd.* [1964] 1 All E.R. 465.

[3] cf. *Kelly* v. *Morris* (1866) L.R. 1 Eq. 697; *Scott* v. *Stanford* (1867) L.R. 3 Eq. 718; *Cox* v. *Land and Water Journal Co.* (1869) L.R. 9 Eq. 324; *Pike* v. *Nicholas* (1870) L.R. 5 Ch. 251.

[4] S. 17. As to measure of damages see *Sutherland Publishing Co.* v. *Caxton Publishing Co.* [1936] Ch. 323; as to injunction see *Borthwick* v. *Evening Post* (1888) 37 Ch. D. 449.

[5] S. 18. Damages under S. 18 are cumulative with those under S. 17; *Caxton Pub. Co.* v. *Sutherland Pub. Co.* [1939] A.C. 178. As to measure of damages see also *Birn* v. *Keene* [1918] 2 Ch. 281.

[6] S. 19.

[7] Ss. 20–21.

[8] S. 43; see also *Carlton Illustrators* v. *Coleman* [1911] 1 K.B. 771; *Preston* v. *Raphael Tuck, Ltd.* [1926] Ch. 667.

Use of copyright in education

Copyright is not infringed by reason only of the reproduction, or adaptation, of the work for educational purposes.[1]

Crown copyright

The Crown is entitled to copyright in literary, dramatic, musical or artistic work made by or under the direction or control of Her Majesty or a government department, and in work first published in the U.K. if by or under the direction or control of Her Majesty or a government department. Such copyrights subsist so long as the work is unpublished, or till 50 years after publication.[2] Special provisions are made as to the public records.[3] In Scotland the right of printing Bibles belongs to the Crown and is exercised by publishers under licence.[4]

Performing rights: the Performing Right Tribunal

The owner of copyright in a literary, dramatic or musical work, sound recording or television broadcast, may grant a licence to perform his work or to do another act restricted by copyright. Societies exist with the main object of negotiating the granting of such licences, as owner or as agent for the owner of the copyright, to persons wishing to perform the work in question. Such societies may make licence schemes setting out the classes of cases in which they are willing to grant licences, and on what terms and conditions.[5]

The Act establishes a Performing Right Tribunal to determine disputes between licensing bodies and persons requiring licences.[6] Licence schemes may be referred to the tribunal,[7] and persons claiming to have been refused a licence may apply to it for a licence.[8]

PLANT BREEDERS' RIGHTS

The Controller of the Plant Variety Rights Office may on application grant plant breeders' rights to a person who has

[1] 1956 Act, S. 41.
[2] 1956 Act, S. 39.
[3] 1956 Act, S. 42.
[4] *King's Printers* v. *Manners & Miller* (1828) 3 W. & S. 268. As to England see *Oxford and Cambridge Universities* v. *Eyre and Spottiswoode* [1963] 3 All E.R. 289.
[5] 1956 Act, S. 24.
[6] 1956 Act, S. 23; see also Ss. 29–30.
[7] 1956 Act, Ss. 25–6.
[8] 1956 Act, S. 27.

bred or discovered a variety of plant, or his successor in title.[1] Provision is made for the protection of an applicant pending the decision of his application.[2] An appeal lies from the Controller to the Plant Variety Rights Tribunal.[3]

Rights are exercisable for a period prescribed by a scheme under the Act, but for not less than 15 or 18 and not exceeding 25 years, with possible extension by the Controller. Rights may be surrendered or terminated.[4]

The holder of plant breeders' rights in a plant variety has the exclusive right himself, and to authorise others, to sell the reproductive material of the plant variety, to produce the reproductive material in Great Britain for sale, and to exercise certain other rights.[5] Infringement is actionable for damages, interdict, count and reckoning for profits, as in the cases of other proprietary rights.[5] There is no right to damages for an innocent infringement.[6] A holder must be able to maintain reproductive material capable of producing the variety to which the rights relate.[7]

The Controller may grant an applicant, by way of compulsory licence, any rights as respects a plant variety which the holder might have granted.[8]

Plant breeders' rights may be assigned outright or in security,[9] attached by diligence and pass on intestacy or under a will like other proprietary rights.

1 Plant Varieties and Seeds Act, 1964, Ss. 1–2, and Sched. 2.
2 1964 Act, S. 1(3) and Sched. 1.
3 1964 Act, S. 1(4) and 10.
4 1964 Act, S. 3.
5 1964 Act, S. 4 and Sched. 3.
6 1964 Act, S. 4(3).
7 1964 Act, S. 6.
8 1964 Act, S. 7.
9 cf. 1964 Act, S. 8.

CHAPTER 100

OUTRIGHT TRANSFER OF INCORPOREAL MOVEABLE PROPERTY

INCORPOREAL moveable property, unless non-assignable, may freely be transferred outright to another party, thereby substituting him in the granter's place to the same force and effect as if he had been the original owner of that property.

Titulus et modus transferendi dominii

For valid transfer of an assignable right there must be both *titulus et modus transferendi dominii*. The *tituli* in question in outright transfer are the intention to gift[1] and the contracts of barter and sale.

Gift

The intention to make a donation, whether *inter vivos* or *mortis causa*, of a right must be clearly evidenced. *In dubio* there is a presumption against gift, and intention to donate must be clearly proved;[2] if not proved, loan or other redeemable transfer will be inferred. To be effectual a unilateral deed of gift must generally be delivered.[3] Parole proof of intention to donate is competent only where there has been delivery to the donee or someone on his behalf of the document evidencing the right alleged to be donated.[4]

Donation inter vivos

A donation *inter vivos* requires evidence of the requisite *animus donandi* and execution and delivery of the assignation or

[1] cf. *Macfarlane's Exor.* v. *Miller* (1898) 25 R. 1201; *Scott's Trs.* v. *Macmillan* (1905) 8 F. 214; *Carmichael* v. *C's Exor.*, 1920 S.C. (H.L.) 195, 203; *Macpherson's Exor.* v. *Mackay*, 1932 S.C. 565 (donations *mortis causa*); *Brownlee* v. *Robb*, 1907 S.C. 1302 (donation *inter vivos*).

[2] *Ross* v. *Mellis* (1871) 10 M. 197; *Jamieson* v. *McLeod* (1880) 7 R. 1131; *Thomson's Exor.* v. *T.* (1882) 9 R. 911; *Sharp* v. *Paton* (1883) 10 R. 1000, 1056; *Milne* v. *Grant's Exors.* (1884) 11 R. 887; *Connell's Trs.* v. *C's Trs.* (1886) 13 R. 1175; *Dawson* v. *McKenzie* (1892) 19 R. 261, 271; *Penman's Trs.* v. *P.* (1896) 4 S.L.T. 66; *Brownlee* v. *Robb*, 1907 S.C. 1302; *Brownlee's Exrx.* v. *B.*, 1908 S.C. 232, 242.

[3] *Jarvie's Tr.* v. *J's Trs.* (1887) 14 R. 411; *Connell's Trs.* v. *C's Tr.*, 1955 S.L.T. 125. cf. *Tennent* v. *T's Trs.* (1869) 7 M. 936; *Cameron's Trs.* v. *C.*, 1907 S.C. 407.

[4] *Anderson's Trs.* v. *Webster* (1883) 11 R. 35; *Drummond* v. *Mathieson*, 1912 1 S.L.T. 455.

transfer requisite to transfer title to the right donated from donor to donee if registered or intimated by the donee. Delivery of a writ evidencing the right, such as a share certificate, will not suffice by itself. A negotiable instrument can be donated by delivery, or endorsement and delivery,[1] and the goods represented by a document of title by delivery, or endorsement and delivery thereof. Money in the form of notes or coin can be donated by bare delivery *animo donandi*.[2] Paying a debt due by another may be a donation to the real debtor.[3] It is essential that the transaction takes immediate effect; an intention to gift is unenforceable,[4] though a promise to give may be enforceable.

The gift may be conditional, but any condition may be invalid on the ground of illegality or contrariety to public policy.[5] Gifts to charitable funds may be conditional so that if the charitable purpose fails the gift is returnable,[6] or they may be held absolute in which case, if the charitable purpose fails, the moneys will fall to be applied *cy près*.[7]

Donation mortis causa

An incorporeal moveable right may be donated *mortis causa*, in contemplation of though not necessarily in immediate apprehension of death. Such a donation is revocable if the donor recovers,[8] but becomes a perfected gift if he dies. It must be effected by such act or deed as is required to complete a transfer of title to the kind of property in question and, at least normally, completed by delivery to, or on behalf of, the donee.[9] The normal cases are of claims to money, particularly deposit receipts.[10]

Contract of barter or of sale

A contract of barter or of sale of incorporeal moveable rights is regulated entirely by common law. The essentials are agreement on the subject-matter of contract, precisely which rights are to be transferred, and the thing to be taken in exchange or the price.

1 cf. *Swan's Exors.* v. *McDougall* (1868) 5 S.L.R. 675.

2 *Malcolm* v. *Campbell* (1889) 17 R. 255; cf. opening account in donee's name: *Boucher's Trs.* v. *B's Trs.* (1907) 15 S.L.T. 157.

3 *Douglas's Trs.* v. *D.* (1868) 6 M. 223.

4 *Allison* v. *Anderson* (1907) 15 S.L.T. 529.

5 cf. *Parkinson* v. *College of Ambulance* [1925] 2 K.B. 1.

6 cf. *Re Gillingham Bus Disaster Fund* [1959] Ch. 62.

7 cf. *Re North Devon Relief Fund Trust* [1953] 2 All E.R. 1032; *Re Hillier* [1954] 2 All E.R. 59.

8 *Macfarquhar* v. *McKay* (1869) 7 M. 766.

9 *Morris* v. *Riddick* (1867) 5 M. 1036.

10 See *infra*, Ch. 112.

Other matters may be specifically dealt with. There are no general requirements as to formalities of contract.[1] A person having notice of vice affecting his title to rights cannot validly assign them.[2]

Completion of contract

A completely constituted contract of sale of incorporeal rights, however, vests only an equitable claim in the buyer and requires to be completed by conveyance of the right, normally by assignation in writing, normally followed by intimation of the assignation to the debtor in the obligation or registration of the new owner in a public register.

Decrees of court, claims of debt or of damages

The sale of such a right is frequently part of a compromise whereby a defender settles the pursuer's claim and acquires his right, to aid him in working out relief against another defender,[3] but it may be to an independent third party,[4] or may be as part of a transaction whereby the corporeal subject, in respect of which the claim arises, was sold.[5]

Negotiable instruments

A bill of exchange or other negotiable instrument may be transferred by negotiation pursuant to an agreement to transfer the claim therein. But it may also be agreed to be sold[6] or assigned,[7] particularly as part of a sale of economic assets, and be transferred in pursuance thereof by assignation in the same way as other incorporeal rights. But until or unless the bill is actually transferred under the contract by assignation, the holder may negotiate it to any innocent third party who, if he gives value, acquires a good title by negotiation, leaving the disappointed buyer or assignee to a claim of damages for breach of contract.

Bills of lading

As a symbol of the goods described therein as shipped, a bill of lading may be agreed to be sold, unless its terms preclude

[1] But see Banking Companies (Shares) Act, 1867, S. 1 (repealed, Statute Law Revision Act, 1966); see *Mitchell* v. *City of Glasgow Bank* (1878) 6 R. 420; 6 R. (H.L.) 66; *Neilson* v. *James* (1882) 9 Q.B.D. 546.

[2] *Moff* v. *Smith's Trs.*, 1930 S.N. 162.

[3] e.g. *Gardiner* v. *Main* (1895) 22 R. 100; *Traill* v. *A/S Dalbeattie* (1904) 6 F. 798; *Cole-Hamilton* v. *Boyd*, 1963 S.C. (H.L.) 1.

[4] *Bentley* v. *Macfarlane*, 1963 S.C. 279.

[5] *Symington* v. *Campbell* (1894) 21 R. 434.

[6] *Embiricos* v. *Anglo-Austrian Bank* [1905] 1 K.B. 677.

[7] *Dawson* v. *Isle* [1906] 1 Ch. 633.

transfer.[1] The contract must be completed by delivery or endorsement and delivery of the bill.[2] The whole property in the goods passes if the transfer of the bill was intended to have that effect. But a transfer passes no property in the goods where the transfer has been made without consideration,[3] where the transferor himself had no property in the goods and no authority to deal with the property in them, as where he had already sold the goods apart from the bill of lading,[4] or where the transfer is made to a transferee who does not take *in bona fide*, being aware of facts which make the transfer inoperative, such as the buyer's insolvency.[5]

Documents of title to goods

A warrant granted by a storekeeper or warehousekeeper acknowledging holding certain goods to the order of a named person is a species of property which may be sold or assigned in security. To complete the contract the warrants must be endorsed and transmitted to the purchaser, and intimation made to the storekeeper.[6]

Liferent

A liferent, whether proper or improper, may be assigned unless declared not assignable,[7] or, if improper, unless declared alimentary[8] and then only so far as excessive. If assignable, the right assigned subsists only for the duration of the cedent's, and not of the assignee's, life.[9]

Rights under marriage contracts

A right under a marriage contract, if vested, may be sold and assigned, but probably not if not yet vested.[10]

Beneficial interests under trusts

Excepting interests declared alimentary,[11] and even then only so far as excessive,[12] a beneficial interest under a trust may be

1 *Henderson* v. *Comptoir d'Escompte de Paris* (1873) L.R. 5 P.C. 253.
2 *Sewell* v. *Burdick* (1884) 10 App. Cas. 74. 3 *Sewell*, *supra*, 80.
4 *Gurney* v. *Behrend* (1854) 3 E. & B. 622; *London Joint Stock Bank* v. *British Amsterdam Maritime Agency* (1910) 11 Asp. M.L.C. 571.
5 *Cuming* v. *Brown* (1808) 9 East 506; *Pease* v. *Gloahec* (1866) L.R. 1 P.C. 219.
6 *Connal* v. *Loder* (1868) 6 M. 1095; *Inglis* v. *Robertson & Baxter* (1898) 25 R. (H.L.) 70.
7 *Chaplin's Trs.* v. *Hoile* (1890) 18 R. 27; *Scottish Union and National Ins. Co.* v. *Smeaton* (1904) 7 F. 174.
8 *Claremont's Trs.* v. *C.* (1896) 4 S.L.T. 144; *Craig* v. *Pearson's Trs.*, 1915 2 S.L.T. 183. See also *Cuthbert* v. *C's Trs.*, 1908 S.C. 967.
9 Ersk. II, 9, 41. 10 *McDonald* v. *McGrigor* (1874) 1 R. 817.
11 *Rothwell* v. *Stuart's Trs.* (1898) 1 F. 81.
12 *Claremont's Trs.* v. *C.* (1896) 4 S.L.T. 144; *Cuthbert* v. *C's Trs.*, 1908 S.C. 967.

assigned by contract followed by assignation, intimated to the trustees.[1]

Beneficial interests in succession

A *spes successionis*, or non-vested contingent right of succession, is assignable, unless such a transaction with the right is prohibited by the deed under which the *spes* arises,[2] to the effect of giving the buyer a good title in a question with the seller to the right, estate or succession when it comes to be vested in the seller.[3] If the contingency whereby the right transmits to the seller never happens, *contractus perit emptori*. A legacy given, subject to postponed vesting, has been held to confer an assignable prospective interest between the testator's death and the date of vesting.[4]

A provision such as an annuity, made in succession, unless declared alimentary or non-assignable, is assignable onerously or gratuitously.[5]

Policies of life assurance

The right under a policy of life assurance to receive an agreed sum on the happening of an agreed event is a right of property[6] which may be sold outright before that event happens. The contract to sell or assign may be constituted in any form.[7] The contract is void if the life assured has died before the contract was made.[8] A policy effected under the Married Women's Policies of Assurance (Sc.) Act, 1880, S. 2, cannot be validly assigned by husband and wife to the former's creditors,[9] but may be surrendered by the trustee with the wife's concurrence.[10]

The contract must be completed by a deed of assignation[11] intimated by the assignee to the insurers, and to entitle the buyer

1 *Macpherson's J.F.* v. *Mackay*, 1915 S.C. 1011.

2 cf. *Kirkland* v. *K's Tr.* (1886) 13 R. 798.

3 *Trappes* v. *Meredith* (1871) 10 M. 38; see also *Reid* v. *Morison* (1893) 20 R. 510; *Salaman* v. *Todd*, 1911 S.C. 1214; *Coats* v. *Bannochie's Trs.*, 1912 S.C. 329.

4 *Rothwell* v. *Stuart's Trs.* (1898) 1 F. 81.

5 *White's Trs.* v. *Whyte* (1877) 4 R. 786.

6 *Re Moore* (1878) 8 Ch. D. 519; *Hadden* v. *Bryden* (1899) 1 F. 710.

7 For a special case see *Ballantyne's Trs.* v. *Scottish Amicable Life Assce. Socy.*, 1921 2 S.L.T. 75.

8 *Scott* v. *Coulson* [1903] 2 Ch. 249.

9 *Scottish Life Assce. Co.* v. *Donald* (1901) 9 S.L.T. 200; *Edinburgh Life Assce. Co.* v. *Balderston*, 1909 2 S.L.T. 323.

10 *Schumann* v. *Scottish Widows' Fund Socy.* (1886) 13 R. 678.

11 Statutory form in Policies of Assurance Act, 1867, Sched. But a deed of assignation in common form suffices, as does any equivalent deed: *Caledonian Ins. Co.* v. *Beattie* (1898) 5 S.L.T. 349; *Brownlee* v. *Robb*, 1907 S.C. 1302.

to receive the sum due under the policy he must continue to pay the premiums and prove the death of the life assured.[1]

Sale of shares or marketable securities

A sale of shares or marketable securities may be concluded direct with the purchaser or through the agency of brokers on the Stock Exchange. A contract for the sale of shares or securities may be made orally. Any person who buys or sells any stock or marketable security of the value of £5 or upwards as a broker or agent must forthwith make, execute and transmit a stamped contract note to his principal, or his vendor or purchaser.[2]

The purchaser may repudiate the contract if the seller delivers share warrants rather than registered shares,[3] but not if lots of the shares bought are tendered from several different sellers.[4]

The seller is under a duty to deliver the share or stock certificate and to execute an instrument of transfer,[5] and must do nothing to prevent the purchaser having himself registered as proprietor of the shares.[6] It is the duty of the buyer to prepare and tender a transfer,[7] but in stock exchange transactions the transferor frequently tenders the transfer. The buyer may refuse payment for a transfer unaccompanied by the share certificate unless it is certified that the certificate is at the company's office. The seller does not guarantee the purchaser's registration.[8]

Time is of the essence of the contract.[9]

In the event of breach the injured party may claim specific implement, damages, or an indemnity, depending on the circumstances. Specific implement will not normally be granted of a contract to transfer government stock,[10] nor of a contract to sell shares readily available in the market, though it may if the market in the shares is restricted.[11] A purchaser may be ordained to execute a transfer.[12]

[1] The Presumption of Life Limitation Act, 1891, does not apply (S. 11). See also *N.B. and Mercantile Ins. Co.* v. *Stewart* (1871) 9 M. 534.

[2] Finance (1909–10) Act, 1910, S. 78.

[3] *Iredell* v. *General Securities Corpn., Ltd.* (1916) 33 T.L.R. 67.

[4] *Benjamin* v. *Barnett* (1903) 8 Com. Cas. 244; cf. *Lamont, Macquisten* v. *Inglis* (1903) 11 S.L.T. 10.

[5] *Neilson* v. *James* (1882) 9 Q.B.D. 546; *London Founders Assocn.* v. *Clarke* (1888) 20 Q.B.D. 576.

[6] *London Founders Assocn., supra*; *Hooper* v. *Herts* [1906] 1 Ch. 549.

[7] *Lyle and Scott, Ltd.* v. *Scott's Trs.*, 1959 S.C. (H.L.) 64.

[8] *Marr* v. *Buchanan Younger & Co.* (1852) 14 D. 467.

[9] *Rothschild* v. *Hennings* (1829) 9 B. & C. 470; *Black* v. *Cullen* (1853) 15 D. 646.

[10] *Nutbrown* v. *Thornton* (1804) 10 Ves. 159.

[11] *Cheale* v. *Kenward* (1858) 3 De G. & J. 27.

[12] *Shaw* v. *Fisher* (1848) 2 De G. & Sm. 11.

In other cases damages are recoverable, as where a purchaser declines to accept stock or to pay therefor.[1]

The seller is entitled to an indemnity from the buyer in respect of a call, though made after the contract but before the date of completion,[2] and in respect of any liability as a contributory if the company has commenced winding-up.[3]

Contract to sell goodwill

The goodwill of a business may in some cases be deemed so connected in whole or in part with the premises in which it has been carried on[4] as to require a contract for its sale to be constituted in writing, but in other cases the goodwill is quite separate from sale of the premises and business name,[5] and accordingly, in general, writing, though common,[6] is unnecessary. The sale of a going business implies sale of its goodwill.

Goodwill partakes of so many elements that it is desirable to specify what rights are contracted to be sold: *prima facie* a sale will pass the right to carry on the old business and use the old trade name,[7] and to the business books.[8] It will be a breach of contract for the seller subsequently to take advantage of the connection formed by him in the old business,[9] but, unless there is a restrictive clause in the sale, he may set up a new business in competition.

Contracts to assign trademarks, patents, copyright, registered designs and plant breeders' rights

Each of these statutory forms of incorporeal property may be assigned, outright or in security, in accordance with the conditions in the relevant statute. The contract to assign need not be constituted in writing, but must be given effect to by assignation in writing.[10]

1 *Dorriens* v. *Hutchinson* (1804) 1 Smith 420;
2 *Hawkins* v. *Maltby* (1867) L.R. 3 Ch. App. 188; 4 Ch. App. 200.
3 *Rudge* v. *Bowman* (1868) L.R. 3 Q.B. 689; *Neilson* v. *James* (1882) 9 Q.B.D. 546.
4 cf. *Hughes* v. *Stirling Assessor* (1892) 19 R. 840; *Murray's Tr.* v. *McIntyre* (1904) 6 F. 588; *Graham* v. *G's Trs.* (1904) 6 F. 1015; *Muirhead's Trs.* v. *M.* (1905) 7 F. 496; *Edinburgh Assessor* v. *Caira and Crolla*, 1928 S.C. 398.
5 cf. *Barr* v. *Lions, Ltd.*, 1956 S.C. 59.
6 cf. *Smith* v. *McBride & Smith* (1888) 16 R. 36; *Smart* v. *Wilkinson*, 1928 S.C. 383.
7 *Churton* v. *Douglas* (1858) John. 174; *Walker* v. *Mottram* (1881) 19 Ch. D. 355; *Smith*, *supra*.
8 *Morrison* v. *M.* (1900) 2 F. 382.
9 *Trego* v. *Hunt* [1896] A.C. 7.
10 e.g. *Mackay* v. *M.*, 1914 S.C. 200.

Mode of transfer

The former mode of effecting the transfer of a right was by making the third party the creditor's mandatory for the exaction and discharge of the debt, but without imposing any obligation to account to the mandant.[1] While this is still competent, the modern practice is to transfer the claim by assignation. No particular form or words are in general essential and any words clearly indicating transference will operate an assignation.[2] Prior to 1862 two forms of assignation were in use; in one the cedent directly assigned the debt as well as the bond itself; in the other the cedent constituted the assignee the assignee to both sum and deed and surrogated the assignee in place of the cedent. The Transmission of Moveable Property (Scotland) Act, 1862, applicable primarily to personal bonds or conveyances[3] of moveable estate,[3] provides forms appropriate generally to moveable rights, which may be written on the deed assigned, or form a separate deed. They contain only a narrative clause, clause of assignation, and require to be attested in the usual way, or, presumably, be holograph or adopted as holograph. In an assignation of a bond warrandice is implied; if the transfer is gratuitous simple warrandice is implied; if onerous there are implied warrandice from fact and deed and *debitum subesse*, i.e. that the debt is subsisting and due by the debtor to the cedent.[4] He does not warrant that the debtor is solvent.[5] The assignation impliedly covers all writs relating exclusively to the debt assigned.[6] The 1862 Act, S. 1, declares an assignation registrable in the books of any court in terms of any clause of registration contained in the bond or conveyance assigned.

Interpretation

An assignation is open to interpretation to determine such questions as whether it is an assignation outright or in security,[7] and precisely what rights the assignation was intended to cover.[8]

[1] cf. *Ritchie* v. *McLachlan* (1870) 8 M. 815.

[2] *Carter* v. *McIntosh* (1862) 24 D. 925; *Caledonian Ins. Co.* v. *Beattie* (1898) 5 S.L.T. 349; *Brownlee* v. *Robb*, 1907 S.C. 1302; cf. *McCutcheon* v. *McWilliam* (1876) 3 R. 565.

[3] Defined in S. 4.

[4] *Ferrier* v. *Graham's Trs.* (1828) 6 S. 818; *Sinclair* v. *Wilson and Maclellan* (1829) 7 S. 401; *Reid* v. *Barclay* (1879) 6 R. 1007.

[5] Ersk. II, 3, 25; *Barclay* v. *Liddel* (1671) Mor. 16591.

[6] *Finlaw* v. *E. Northesk* (1670) Mor. 6544; *Lyell* v. *Christie* (1823) 2 S. 288; *Webster* v. *Reid's Trs.* (1859) 20 D. 83.

[7] *Eaglesham* v. *Grant* (1875) 2 R. 960; *Purnell* v. *Shannon* (1894) 22 R. 74.

[8] *Robertson* v. *Wright* (1873) 1 R. 237; *McCutcheon* v. *McWilliam* (1876) 3 R. 565; *Greenock Harbour Trs.* (1888) 15 R. 343; *Liqdr. of Larkhall Collieries* v. *Hamilton* (1906) 14 S.L.T. 202.

Implications of assignation

A cedent impliedly confers on the assignee all powers necessary to make the assignation effectual, by intimation or otherwise.[1]

Intimation

While a delivered assignation is effective as between the cedent and the assignee[2] intimation of the assignation to the debtor or holder of the fund is necessary to acquaint him with the transfer, to interpel him from paying to the original creditor or any other assignee,[3] to divest the cedent,[4] and to complete the assignee's right and make it effectual against all parties.[5] It also renders it incompetent to prove any exception against the debt unless the subject had been rendered litigious before intimation or the assignee admits on oath that the assignation was gratuitous or in trust for the cedent.[6] The assignation is effective from the date of intimation in a question with other assignees or third parties.[7] It may be made after the death of the cedent.[8]

The debtor's actual knowledge of an assignation is sufficient to interpel him from paying the cedent,[9] but does not effect a transfer to the assignee in a competition with creditors.[10] An assignation delivered but not intimated to the debtor is good against the cedent and his executors but defeasible by a later assignation intimated first,[11] by payment by debtor to cedent,[12] by diligence by the cedent's creditors, confirmation of an executor-creditor to his estate,[13] or confirmation of a trustee on his sequestrated estates. An unintimated assignation does not prevent the subject assigned from passing to the trustee in the event of the assignor's sequestration.[14]

1 *Miller* v. *Muirhead* (1894) 21 R. 658.
2 Stair III, 1, 15; *Thome* v. *T.* (1683) 2 B. S. 49; *Grant* v. *Gray* (1828) 6 S. 489.
3 *McGill* v. *Laurestoun* (1558) Mor. 843; *McDowal* v. *Fullerton* (1714) Mor. 840; *Allan* v. *Urquhart* (1887) 15 R. 56.
4 *Drummond* v. *Muschet* (1492) Mor. 843; *L. Rollo* v. *Niddrie* (1665) 1 B.S. 510.
5 Stair III, 1, 6; Ersk. III, 5, 3; Bell, *Comm.* II, 16; *Liquidator of Union Club* v. *Edinburgh Life Assce. Co.* (1906) 8 F. 1143.
6 *Lang* v. *Hislop* (1854) 16 D. 908.
7 *Wallace* v. *Edgar* (1663) Mor. 837; *Shiells* v. *Ferguson, Davidson & Co.* (1876) 4 R. 250; *Chambers' J.F.* v. *Vertue* (1893) 20 R. 257; *Macpherson's J.F.* v. *Mackay*, 1915 S.C. 1011.
8 *Brownlee* v. *Robb*, 1907 S.C. 1302.
9 *Leith* v. *Garden* (1703) Mor. 865.
10 *L. Rollo, supra*; *Dickson* v. *Trotter* (1776) Mor. 873.
11 *L. Rollo, supra*; *Newlands* v. *Miller* (1882) 9 R. 1104; *Campbell's Trs.* v. *Whyte* (1884) 11 R. 1078.
12 *Drummond, supra.*
13 *Sinclair* v. *S.* (1726) Mor. 2793.
14 *Moncrieff's Trs.* v. *Balfour*, 1928 S.N. 64, 139.

Mode of intimation

At common law the regular mode of intimation was for a procurator for the assignee to deliver to the debtor, in the presence of a notary and two witnesses, a copy of the assignation and a schedule of intimation, and to have the notary expede an instrument of intimation signed by the notary and the witnesses. Alternatively the assignee might produce the assignation to the debtor, deliver a copy of it, and obtain an attested or holograph acknowledgment of intimation.[1] These modes are still competent. Under the Transmission of Moveable Property (Scotland) Act, 1862, S. 2, intimation may be validly made by a notary public delivering a certified copy of the assignation to the debtor, and certifying intimation in the form set out in the Act, Sched. C, or by the assignee or his agent transmitting a certified copy of the assignation by post and obtaining the debtor's written acknowledgment of receipt by him of the copy. The copy need contain only such part of the deed containing the assignation as concerns the subject matter of the assignation. Where an interest in a testamentary trust has been assigned intimation to the solicitors of the trust is probably sufficient intimation to the trustees.[2] Though intimation should be made to each of joint and several debtors,[3] intimation to one trustee has been held sufficient.[4] An assignation of the uncalled capital of a company must be intimated to all the shareholders.[5] Intimation to an absent person may be made in the statutory modes, or by edictal citation, to a firm by intimation to all the partners,[6] and to a company at its registered office.

Equivalents of intimation

Various kinds of conduct are deemed equivalent to intimation of the assignation to the debtor. These include the assignee's taking possession of the right by entering into enjoyment of the rents or interest, which implies the debtor's knowledge of and compliance with the assignation;[7] action or diligence against the debtor, at the instance of the assignee and founded on the assignation;[8] actual payment by the debtor to the assignee of part of the

[1] Bell, *Convg.* I, 312.

[2] *Browne's Tr.* v. *Anderson* (1901) 4 F. 305.

[3] Ersk. III, 5, 5.

[4] *Jameson* v. *Sharp* (1887) 14 R. 643.

[5] *Liqdr. of Union Club* v. *Edinburgh Life Assce. Co.* (1906) 8 F. 1143; *Ballachulish Slate Quarries* v. *Malcolm* (1908) 15 S.L.T. 963; *Ballachulish Slate Quarries* v. *Menzies* (1908) 16 S.L.T. 48.

[6] *Hill* v. *Lindsay* (1846) 8 D. 472.

[7] Ersk. III, 5, 3.

[8] Ersk. III, 5, 4; *Whyte* v. *Neish* (1622) Mor. 854; *Dougall* v. *Gordon* (1795) Mor. 851.

principal, or of interest;[1] a written promise by the debtor to pay the assignee;[2] participation by the debtor as a party to the assignation,[3] but not merely as witness;[4] production of the assignation by the assignee in an action to which the debtor is a party;[5] intimation by the assignee by letter to the debtor and the latter's answers thereto;[6] attendance and voting by an assignee of a share in a firm at a meeting of the partners;[7] and intimation to the debtor's factor and entry by him in the debtor's books.[8]

The registration of assignations of bonds or contracts in the Books of Council and Session or Sheriff Court books for preservation, or for preservation and execution, does not effect publication and is not equivalent to intimation,[9] but registration of the deed in the Register of Sasines is.[10] The debtor's actual knowledge is not equivalent to intimation[11] particularly in a case of competition between an unintimated assignation and other claims.[12]

Where intimation unnecessary

If the assignation is granted by one who is the debtor himself,[13] or to the person to whom intimation would otherwise have to be made, such as the trustee of the debtor fund,[14] intimation is unnecessary. It is also unnecessary in the case of the statutory assignation effected by the Act and Warrant of a trustee on a sequestrated estate.[15] A bill of exchange accepted payable at a

[1] *Livingston* v. *Lindsay* (1626) Mor. 860.

[2] *Home* v. *Murray* (1674) Mor. 863.

[3] *L. Ballenden's Crs.* (1707) Mor. 865; *Turnbull* v. *Stewart* (1751) Mor. 868.

[4] *Murray* v. *Durham* (1622) Mor. 855.

[5] *Dougal* v. *Gordon* (1795) Mor. 851; cf. *Faculty of Advocates* v. *Dickson* (1718) Mor. 866.

[6] *Gray* v. *D. Hamilton* (1708) Rob. App. 1; *Wallace* v. *Davies* (1853) 15 D. 688.

[7] *Hill* v. *Lindsay* (1857) 10 D. 78.

[8] *E. Aberdeen* v. *E. March* (1730) 1 Pat. 44; but see Bell, *Convg.* I, 318.

[9] *Tod's Trs.* v. *Wilson* (1869) 7 M. 1100; *Cameron's Trs.* v. *C.*, 1907 S.C. 407.

[10] *Paul* v. *Boyd's Trs.* (1835) 13 S. 818; *Edmond* v. *Aberdeen Mags.* (1858) 3 Macq. 116; *Rodger* v. *Crawfords* (1867) 6 M. 24.

[11] Stair II, 1, 24; More, *Notes*, cclxxi; Ersk. III, 5, 5; Bell, *Comm.* II, 18; *Adamson* v. *McMitchell* (1624) Mor. 859; *L. Westraw* v. *Williamson & Carmichael* (1626) Mor. 859; *Dickson* v. *Trotter* (1776) Mor. 873; *Fac. of Advocates* v. *Dickson* (1718) Mor. 866; cf. *Leith* v. *Garden* (1703) Mor. 865.

[12] *L. Rollo* v. *Laird of Niddrie* (1665) 1 B.S. 510.

[13] *Browne's Tr.* v. *Anderson* (1901) 4 F. 305.

[14] *E. Argyle* v. *Macdonald* (1676) Mor. 842; *Russell* v. *Breadalbane* (1831) 5 W. & S. 256; *Miller* v. *Learmonth* (1870) 42 S. Jur. 418; *Mounsey* (1896) 4 S.L.T. 46; *Ayton* v. *Romanes* (1893) 3 S.L.T. 203.

[15] Bankruptcy (Sc.) Act, 1913, S. 97(1); *Tod's Tr.* v. *Wilson* (1869) 7 M. 1100; *Watson* v. *Duncan* (1879) 6 R. 1247; *Kirkland* v. *K's Tr.* (1886) 13 R. 798; *Greenock Harbour Trs.* (1888) 15 R. 343.

banker's operates on presentment as an intimated assignation of the acceptor's funds in the banker's hands.[1]

Effect of Assignation

The effect of an intimated assignation is to divest the cedent completely and to put the assignee in his place, entitled to sue for the enforcement of the assigned right, and do diligence thereon,[2] to receive payment and grant a good discharge therefor: *Assignatus utitur jure auctoris.*

Quality of assignee's right

By virtue of the maxim *nemo plus juris ad alium transferre potest quam ipse habet* the assignee obtains no better right than the cedent himself possessed. If the right was terminable or defeasible against the cedent, it remains so against the assignee.[3] The debtor may utilise against the assignee all pleas, rights of action, and defences which would have been competent against the cedent, even though the assignee took in good faith and for value.[4] But pleas emerging subsequently to the assignation cannot competently be pleaded against the assignee.[5] The debtor may, however, expressly undertake that pleas competent between the original parties shall not be pleadable in a question with an assignee,[6] or may bar himself by his conduct from challenging the assignee's rights.[7]

Where cedent's right subject to latent trusts or claims

But an assignee who takes in good faith, for value, and without notice of any latent trusts or claims affecting the cedent's right,[8] obtains the assigned right free of any such claim, and accordingly

1 *B.L. Co.* v. *Rainey's Tr.* (1885) 12 R. 825; *Sutherland* v. *Commercial Bank* (1882) 20 S.L.R. 139.

2 *Grier* v. *Maxwell* (1621) Mor. 828.

3 *Johnstone-Beattie* v. *Dalziel* (1868) 6 M. 333; *Chambers' Trs.* v. *Smiths* (1878) 5 R. (H.L.) 151; *Train* v. *Clapperton*, 1908 S.C. (H.L.) 26.

4 Stair I, 10, 16; III, 1, 20; IV, 40, 21; Ersk. III, 5, 10; Bell, *Prin.* §1468; *McDowells* v. *Bell & Rannie* (1772) Mor. 4974; *Shiells* v. *Ferguson, Davidson & Co.* (1876) 4 R. 250; *Scottish Widows' Fund* v. *Buist* (1878) 5 R. (H.L.) 64; *Arnott's Trs.* v. *Forbes* (1881) 9 R. 89; cf. *Duncan* v. *Brooks* (1894) 21 R. 760.

5 *Shiells, supra*; *Macpherson's J.F.* v. *Mackay*, 1915 S.C. 1011.

6 *Bovill* v. *Dixon* (1854) 16 D. 619; 3 Macq. 1.

7 *Bovill, supra*; *Scottish Equitable Life Assce. Socy.* v. *Buist* (1877) 4 R. 1076.

8 It is noteworthy that in many cases where ownership of a right is registered the register may not notice any trust or similar equitable claim; see e.g. register of shares if company registered in England (Companies Act, 1948, S. 117); register of trademarks (Trade Marks Act, 1938, S. 64); register of patents (Patents Act, 1949, S. 73); register of designs (Registered Designs Act, 1949, S. 17).

obtains a better title than his cedent had. Thus where a shareholder assigned his share, which *ex facie* he held absolutely, to a creditor in security of a private loan, the assignee was held entitled to it in preference to and free of the claim to the share by a partnership for which the cedent had held the share as trustee.[1]

This principle does not apply if the assignee did not take in complete good faith and in the belief that the cedent was entitled to assign absolutely, nor if the assignation were gratuitous, nor if the assignee had knowledge of the claim qualifying the cedent's right. Nor does it apply to the general assignation effected by sequestration to the trustee for the body of creditors in a sequestration, for they take the bankrupt's rights *tantum et tale* as vested in him, and are affected by even latent trusts and claims affecting his rights, having given no value for the assignation effected by the sequestration.[2]

Special cases

In various cases a formal assignation followed by intimation is unnecessary. A negotiable instrument is transferred by delivery, or by endorsement and delivery;[3] bills of lading by delivery or endorsement and delivery;[4] policies of marine insurance by indorsement thereon so long as the assured still has an interest in the subject-matter insured or had, before or at the time of losing his interest, expressly or impliedly agreed to assign the policy;[5] bottomry and respondentia bonds probably by assignation in common form;[6] and share warrants to bearer by delivery of the warrant.[7]

Special forms of assignation

In other cases a special form of assignation is utilised: life insurance policies are assigned either in one of the forms authorised by the Transmission of Moveable Property (Sc.) Act, 1862, or in the form authorised by the Policies of Assurance Act, 1867; interests in Government stock may be transferred in the same mode as shares or stock in limited companies;[8] local authority

[1] *Somervails* v. *Redfearn* (1813) 1 Dow 50; cf. *Burns* v. *Laurie's Trs.* (1840) 2 D. 1348.

[2] *Gordon* v. *Cheyne* (1824) 2 S. 675; *Heritable Reversionary Co.* v. *Millar* (1892) 19 R. (H.L.) 43; *Bank of Scotland* v. *Liquidators of Hutchison Main & Co.*, 1914 S.C. (H.L.) 1.

[3] Bills of Exchange Act, 1882.

[4] Bills of Lading Act, 1855, S. 1.

[5] Marine Insurance Act, 1906, Ss. 50–51.

[6] But see *The Petone* [1917] P. 198.

[7] Companies Act, 1948, S. 83.

[8] cf. National Debt Act, 1870, S. 23; Finance Act, 1942, S. 47 and Sched. 11; Government Stock Regulations, 1943 (S.R. & O. 1943, No. 1). See also now Stock Transfer Act, 1963.

mortgages by transfer endorsed thereon in the form in the Local Government (Scotland) Act, 1947, Sched. 7, and attested, without prejudice to other mode of assignation, the transfer being registered in the register of mortgages maintained by the authority;[1] shares or stock or debentures of companies incorporated under the Companies Acts in the manner provided by the Articles of the company, which is normally a common form instrument of transfer signed by both transferor and transferee, each before one witness, and sent to the company's office for registration;[2] fully paid securities (including shares, stock, debenture stock, etc.) issued by any company within the Companies Act, 1948, except a company limited by guarantee or an unlimited company, or by any body incorporated in Great Britain by or under any enactment or by Royal Charter except a building society or a society registered under the Industrial and Provident Societies Act, 1893, or by the Government of the United Kingdom (with certain exceptions), or by any local authority, and units of an approved unit trust scheme may be transferred by an instrument in the form set out in the Stock Transfer Act, 1963, Sched. 1, executed by the transferor only without need for any witness,[3] and specifying the consideration, the description of the securities, the transferor's and transferee's names and addresses. The consideration may be inserted in the transfer or supplied by separate brokers' transfers in the form set out in Sched. 2.[4]

Trade Marks: Patents: Designs: Copyright: Plant Breeder's rights

A registered trade mark is assignable, in connection with the goodwill of a business or separately, and in respect of some or all of the goods in respect of which it is registered, the assignee being bound to apply to the Register of Trade Marks to register his title thereto.[5]

A patent may be assigned and notice of the assignation must be recorded in the Register of Patents.[6]

An assignee of a registered design or to a share therein must apply to the Register of Designs for the registration of his title as proprietor thereof.[7]

1 Local Government (Sc.) Act, 1947, §267–68.

2 Companies Act, 1948, §73–82.

3 Except, by Stock Transfer Act, 1963, S. 2(4), a transfer executed under the Conveyancing (Sc.) Act, 1924, S. 18, on behalf of a person who is blind or unable to write.

4 Stock Transfer Act, 1963.

5 Trade Marks Act, 1938, Ss. 22–25.

6 Patents Act, 1949, Ss. 73–74.

7 Registered Designs Act, 1949, S. 19.

An assignation of copyright, total or partial, is effective only if in writing signed by or on behalf of the assignor.[1]

Plant breeder's rights are assignable like other kinds of proprietary rights.[2]

Assignation of funds by bill or cheque

A bill of exchange accepted payable at a banker operates on presentment as an intimated assignation of the acceptor's funds in the banker's hands,[3] and a cheque drawn for value also operates assignation of the drawer's funds.[4]

Universal assignation

A universal assignation of incorporeal rights, except such as are deemed purely personal to the holder and not proprietary, is effected by death or bankruptcy. On death they pass to the deceased's executor. On the appointment of a trustee in bankruptcy they pass to him under his Act and Warrant.

1 Copyright Act, 1956, S. 36.
2 Plant Varieties and Seeds Act, 1964, S. 4(4).
3 *B.L. Co.* v. *Rainey's Tr.* (1885) 12 R. 825.
4 *Sutherland* v. *Commercial Bank* (1882) 20 S.L.R. 139.

CHAPTER 101

TRANSFER OF INCORPOREAL MOVEABLE RIGHTS IN SECURITY

ANY incorporeal moveable right capable of being assigned outright may equally be assigned in security of the payment of money or the performance of some similar obligation. Assignation of incorporeal moveable rights may be conjoined with a personal obligation to repay in a bond and assignation in security. Assignation in security is effected by the same means as outright assignation,[1] but is subject to an obligation expressed in the assignation, or (where the assignation is *ex facie* absolute) contained in a separate backbond or agreement, to retrocess or reassign to the cedent or assignor the rights assigned, on repayment or due performance of the obligations secured by the assignation. The equitable assignment recognised in English law, created by the deposit of the title deeds of property, or share certificates, or insurance policies, is ineffective in Scotland.[2]

In the case of mortgaging company shares the delivery to the assignee of an executed instrument of transfer with the relative share certificate enables the transferee to have himself registered as owner with the company,[3] without disclosure of his obligation to reconvey on being repaid, but such a security is defeasible by a subsequent transfer by the debtor registered earlier[4] or by arrestments by another creditor. To deposit the share certificates with the creditor together with transfers executed by the owner as transferor but blank as to the transferee is valid in England[5] but questionable in Scotland since the Blank Bonds and Trusts Act, 1696 (c. 25) declares void instruments delivered blank as to the creditor's name.[6]

[1] *Caledonian Ins. Co.* v. *Beattie* (1898) 5 S.L.T. 349.

[2] *Christie* v. *Ruxton* (1862) 24 D. 1182 (title deeds); *Gourlay* v. *Mackie* (1887) 14 R. 403 (share certificates); *Strachan* v. *McDougle* (1835) 13 S. 954; *Wylie's Exrx.* v. *McJannet* (1901) 4 F. 195 (insurance policies); contrast *Sc. Provident Inst.* v. *Cohen* (1888) 16 R. 112, where deposit of insurance policy in England held valid.

[3] *Guild* v. *Young* (1884) 22 S.L.R. 520; *Morrison* v. *Harrison* (1876) 3 R. 406.

[4] *Rainford* v. *Keith* [1905] 1 Ch. 296.

[5] *Colonial Bank* v. *Cody* (1890) 15 App. Cas. 267.

[6] cf. *Shaw* v. *Caledonian Ry.* (1890) 17 R. 466, 478.

Security-holder's rights

An assignee in security takes the assigned right *tantum et tale* as vested in the cedent, and subject to all defects and objections thereto.[1] If the right was defeasible or terminable in the hands of the cedent it remains so in the hands of the assignee.[2] But he takes it free from latent trusts and claims prestable against the cedent, provided that he took the assignation in good faith, for value, and without notice of the trust or claim in question.[3]

Extent of security

Where rights, such as company shares, are assigned in security by *ex facie* absolute transfer, the assignee is entitled to hold them as security both for advances made at the date of the transfer and for subsequent advances,[4] but if the transfer bears to be in security of a specific advance[5] or a limitation of the assignee's title appears in a collateral agreement a further assignation must be executed if it is desired to make the subjects available as security for further advances.[6]

True owner's reversionary right

Despite the assignation the true owner retains a reversionary right in the rights assigned entitling him on implementing his obligation to the assignee to call for a retrocession. The reversionary right may itself be of sufficient value to be assignable in security. If it is so assigned and the assignation intimated to the assignee in security of the right itself, the assignee of the right has no security for advances made subsequently to the intimation that the reversionary right was no longer vested in the true owner.[7]

An assignee in security must, so long as he holds the rights in security, have regard to the true owner's reversionary right, and must not, e.g., ignore a rights issue of shares made to existing shareholders; he should communicate such an offer to the true owners, and is liable in damages if they lose by his failure to do so.[8]

[1] cf. *National Bank* v. *Dickie's Tr.* (1895) 22 R. 740, 754.

[2] *Johnstone-Beattie* v. *Dalziel* (1868) 6 M. 333; *Chambers's Trs.* v. *Smiths* (1878) 5 R. (H.L.) 151; *Train* v. *Clapperton*, 1907 S.C. 517.

[3] *Somervails* v. *Redfearn* (1813) 1 Dow 50; cf. *Burns* v. *Lawrie's Trs.* (1840) 2 D. 1348; contrast *Heritable Reversionary Co.* v. *Millar* (1892) 19 R. (H.L.) 43.

[4] *Hamilton* v. *Western Bank* (1856) 19 D. 152; *National Bank* v. *Union Bank* (1886) 14 R. (H.L.) 1; *National Bank* v. *Dickie's Tr.* (1895) 22 R. 740.

[5] *Anderson's Tr.* v. *Somerville* (1899) 36 S.L.R. 833.

[6] *National Bank*, *supra*, 753.

[7] *National Bank* v. *Union Bank* (1886) 14 R. (H.L.) 1.

[8] *Waddell* v. *Hutton*, 1911 S.C. 575.

Retrocession

On due performance of the obligation secured the assignee may be called on and, if need be, ordained by the court, to execute a retrocession of the assigned rights to the cedent, or to account to the borrower for his transactions with the assigned rights. In the case of the transfer of numbered company shares in security, the assignee is probably bound, failing express or implied authority to act otherwise, to retain and account for and reconvey the specific shares transferred, since the title to these shares is known to be good, whereas the title to other shares might depend on a forged transfer.[1]

Retention or realisation

If the cedent fails to implement his obligation, whether and when the assignee is entitled to retain the rights assigned in security free from the cedent's reversionary right, or to realise them, depends primarily on the terms of the contract under which the rights were assigned. If the assignation is *ex facie* absolute, qualified by a separate obligation to reconvey, the creditor probably has a power of realisation,[2] but not if the assignation bears to be in security, in which case the reversionary right exists till cut off by the long negative prescription or till power of sale is obtained from the court and exercised.[3]

1 *Crerar* v. *Bank of Scotland*, 1921 S.C. 736; affd. 1922 S.C. (H.L.) 137 (where owner had acquiesced in receiving back other shares of the same denomination).

2 cf. *Baillie* v. *Drew* (1884) 12 R. 199; *Duncan* v. *Mitchell* (1893) 21 R. 37 (both *ex facie* absolute dispositions of heritage).

3 cf. Bell, *Prin.* §207; *Murray* v. *Smith* (1899) 6 S.L.T. 357.

CHAPTER 102

EXTINCTION OF INCORPOREAL MOVEABLE RIGHTS

INCORPOREAL moveable rights are extinguished in various ways, many being peculiar to particular kinds of rights.

They may all be lost completely, though the rights are not thereby extinguished, by outright assignation in pursuance of intention to gift, or of contract of barter or of sale, or by assignation in security and retention or realisation by the creditor (assignee) on the cedent's failure to implement his obligation.

Decrees of court are extinguished by satisfaction of the decree.

Claims of debt, or kindred pecuniary claims, are extinguished by full payment, evidenced by a receipt[1] or by facts and circumstances[2] or by cancellation and return to the debtor of any bill of exchange or bond which had evidenced the debt,[3] or by a discharge.[4]

Claims of damages are extinguished by full payment or by discharge proceeding on a compromise or settlement.[5]

A right of action for damages for personal injuries must be brought within three years,[6] unless circumstances exist justifying an extension of that time.[7]

Policies of insurance are extinguished by payment in terms thereof.

Shares in companies are extinguished only by liquidation of the company, or by a reduction of capital which involves paying out the shareholders of that class.[8]

Claims to legal rights, to legacies, to shares in trust estates or intestate estates are extinguished by payment or transfer and discharge.

[1] *McLaren* v. *Howie* (1869) 8 M. 106.

[2] *Chrystal* v. *C.* (1900) 2 F. 373.

[3] *Niven* v. *Burgh of Ayr* (1899) 1 F. 400.

[4] *Kippen* v. *K's Trs.* (1874) 1 R. 1171 (claim under marriage contract); *Neish's Trs.* v. *N.* (1897) 24 R. 306 (rights under marriage contract); *Obers* v. *Paton's Trs.* (1897) 24 R. 719 (legitim).

[5] *McLean* v. *Hassard* (1903) 10 S.L.T. 593 (seduction); *McDonagh* v. *MacLellan* (1886) 13 R. 1000; *N.B. Ry.* v. *Wood* (1891) 13 R. 1000 (personal injuries).

[6] Law Reform (Limitation of Actions, etc.) Act, 1954, S. 6.

[7] Limitation Act, 1963, Ss. 8–13.

[8] e.g. *Wilson and Clyde Coal Co.* v. *Scottish Ins. Corpn.*, 1949 S.C. (H.L.) 90.

Indefinite continuance

Such rights as copyright in unpublished literary work, or a trade name acquired by long use, may continue indefinitely.

Lapse of time

The rights conferred by registration of a trade mark, grant of a patent, registration of a design, creation and publication of a work the subject of copyright, and the grant of plant breeder's rights, all lapse automatically after the expiry of the time for which the law grants the respective rights, except in so far as the right may be, and is, extended.[1]

Short prescriptions

Rights belonging to one of the classes affected by the triennial, quinquennial, or sexennial prescriptions are not completely extinguished by the lapse of the requisite period, but the mode and onus of proof is altered. In the case of bills of exchange[2] and cheques,[3] after the lapse of six years, the bill cannot be founded on but the holder may still prove the debt evidenced by the bill, and that it remains resting-owing, but only by the writ or oath of the alleged debtor.[4] If the bill were taken for a pre-existing debt, that debt may be proved, and that it is resting-owing, *prout de jure*.[5]

Prescription

Incorporeal moveable rights may be completely extinguished[6] by the long negative prescription, formerly of forty, now of twenty, years.[7] Thus the running of the prescriptive period cuts off such claims as a claim of debt[8] or to a *condictio indebiti*,[9] a claim of damages,[10] a claim of legitim[11] or of *jus relictae*,[12] a claim to a

1 Ch. 99, *supra*.
2 Bills of Exchange Act, 1772, S. 40.
3 *McCraw* v. *McCraw's Trs.* (1906) 13 S.L.T. 757.
4 *Darnley* v. *Kirkwood* (1845) 7 D. 595.
5 *Hunter* v. *Thomson* (1843) 5 D. 1285; *Blake* v. *Turner* (1860) 23 D. 15; *Fullerton's Trs.* v. *Macdowall* (1897) 5 S.L.T. 248; cf. *Milne's Trs.* v. *Ormiston's Trs.* (1893) 20 R. 523.
6 Ersk. III, 7, 8; *Kermack* v. *K.* (1874) 2 R. 156.
7 Prescription Acts, 1469, 1474 and 1617; Conveyancing Act, 1924, S. 17; *Sutherland C.C.* v. *Macdonald*, 1935 S.C. 915; *Marr's Exrx.* v. *Marr's Trs.*, 1936 S.C. 64.
8 *Dundas* v. *D.* (1827) 5 S. 790; *Buchanan* v. *Bogle* (1847) 9 D. 686; *Murray* v. *Mackenzie* (1897) 4 S.L.T. 231.
9 *Edinburgh Mags.* v. *Heriot's Trust* (1900) 7 S.L.T. 371.
10 *Cooke* v. *Falconer's Reps.* (1850) 13 D. 157.
11 *Sanderson* v. *Lockhart-Mure*, 1946 S.C. 298.
12 *Campbell's Trs.* v. *C's Trs.*, 1950 S.C. 48.

legacy[1] or under a trust deed,[2] arrears of an annuity,[3] a balance allegedly due on current account with a bank,[4] the right to levy harbour-dues,[5] but does not extinguish the liability of a trustee to account for his intromissions.[6]

The prescriptive period runs from day to day commencing with the day when the property right vested and could first have been claimed by action and was not claimed, or when it was last claimed.[7]

Non valens agere

The prescriptive period does not run so long as the creditor is *non valens agere*, i.e. not in a legal position to make his claim effectual. Under the old Acts years of minority were excluded from deduction, but under the 1924 Act[8] no deduction is made for any period of minority or legal disability. A fiar is *valens* though the liferenter take no action to enforce his claim.[9]

Interruption

A period of prescription which has run is cancelled by interruption and it must start to run afresh. Interruption may take place down to the last moment of the period[10] but the longer the period has run the clearer must be the interruption.

Interruption may take place judicially by citation in an action (but citation itself prescribes in seven years unless the parties be minors), or calling a summons in court, which operates an interruption of twenty (formerly forty) years.[11] The action must claim the debt or other right in question.[12] If the defender is assoilzied the action does not effect interruption.[13] Or interruption may be effected by diligence, provided it distinctly intimates to the debtor that the creditor is prosecuting his claim.[14]

[1] *Briggs* v. *Swan's Exors.* (1854) 16 D. 385; *Jamieson* v. *Clark* (1872) 10 M. 399; *Pettigrew* v. *Harton*, 1956 S.C. 67.

[2] *Pollock* v. *Porterfield* (1779) 2 Pat. 495.

[3] *Henderson* v. *Burt* (1858) 20 D. 402.

[4] *Macdonald* v. *N. of S. Bank*, 1942 S.C. 369.

[5] *Renfrew Mags.* v. *Hoby* (1854) 16 D. 348; cf. *Dundee Harbour Trs.* v. *Dougall* (1852) 24 S. Jur. 385.

[6] *Bertram Gardner & Co.'s Tr.* v. *King's Remembrancer*, 1920 S.C. 555; *Hastie's J.F.* v. *Morham's Exors.*, 1951 S.C. 668.

[7] *Campbell's Trs.* v. *C's Trs.*, 1950 S.C. 48.

[8] *Campbells Trs.*, *supra*; see also *Harvie* v. *Robertson* (1903) 5 F. 338.

[9] *Pettigrew* v. *Harton*, 1956 S.C. 67.

[10] *Simpson* v. *Marshall* (1900) 2 F. 447.

[11] *Wallace* v. *E. Eglinton* (1830) 8 S. 1018.

[12] Ersk. III, 7, 41.

[13] *Montgomery* v. *Fowles* (1795) Bell, Fol. Cas. 203.

[14] *E. Hopetoun* v. *York Bldgs. Co.* (1784) Mor. 11285.

Interruption may also be effected extra-judicially by actually assuming possession, or by a notarial protest, or by any act by the debtor implying acknowledgment of his obligation, such as granting a bond of corroboration with a letter asking for indulgence as to payment,[1] submitting the particular claim to arbitration,[2] admitting that a legacy is due,[3] paying interest on a bond,[4] or agreeing to a temporary adjustment of the dispute between the parties.[5]

Interruption is not affected by discussion about a claim,[6] nor by a general submission to arbitration of all claims.[7]

1 *Aitken* v. *Malcolm* (1766) Hailes 148.
2 *Vans* v. *Murray*, 14 June 1816, F.C.
3 *Briggs* v. *Swan's Exor.* (1854) 16 D. 385.
4 *Kermack* v. *K.* (1874) 2 R. 156.
5 *Simpson* v. *Marshall* (1900) 2 F. 447.
6 *Pitmedden* v. *Munro* (1705) Mor. 11261.
7 *Garden* v. *Rigg* (1743) Mor. 11274.

BOOK VI

LAW OF TRUSTS

CHAPTER 103

THE TRUST CONCEPT

THE principle of the trust is that the ownership of certain property is legally vested in one or more persons, but though nominal owners, they are not absolute or beneficial owners and are obliged, by the terms of the trust under which they have acquired ownership, to hold the property for certain purposes defined by the trust and to administer it for the benefit of others, the beneficiaries designated by the trust, which purposes are a qualification of the nominal owners' rights and constitute a burden on the property preferable to all claims by and through them, and subject also to a reversionary right remaining with the truster, his heirs and assignees, so far as the estate is not exhausted by the purposes.[1]

The older Scottish authorities treat trust as a branch of mandate[2] or of deposit[3] or a combination of these.[4] But in mandate and deposit full ownership does not vest in the mandatory or depositary, whereas it does so vest in a trustee; nor can mandate arise posthumously; nor are these contracts appropriate to heritage or incorporeal moveables. Nor can trust accurately be regarded as a contract *sui generis*,[5] or a quasi-contract.[6] Despite a superficial similarity the trust appears not to be derived from the *fideicommissum*, which was a qualification on a legacy binding the legatee to transmit a benefit to another.[7]

In England the trust concept has been developed to a high degree over a long period in the Court of Chancery and the Chancery Division. The concept is of concurrent ownership, the trustee having nominal and formal ownership recognised at law, but the beneficiary having a concurrent ownership recognised and

[1] cf. *Camille and Henry Dreyfus Foundation* v. *I.R.C.* [1956] A.C. 39, 47.

[2] Stair I, 12, 17.

[3] Stair I, 13, 7; Bankt. I, 15, 14; Ersk. III, 1, 32; Bell, *Comm.* I, 29; I, 37; II, 174; II, 387; *Prin.* §1482, 1991–2.

[4] Bell, *Comm.* I, 30; *Liqdrs. of Western Bank* v. *Douglas* (1860) 22 D. 447; *Cunningham* v. *Montgomerie* (1879) 6 R. 1333, 1337; *Croskery* v. *Gilmour's Trs.* (1890) 17 R. 697, 700; criticized *Allen* v. *McCombie's Trs.*, 1908 S.C. 710, 717.

[5] As proposed by Menzies, *Trustees*, S. 21.

[6] McLaren, *Wills*, §1508.

[7] cf. Craig, *J.F.* II, 5, 9; Bankt. I, 18, 12. For the distinction between English trust and Roman-Dutch *fideicommissum* see *Abdul Hameed Sitti Kadija* v. *De Saram* [1946] A.C. 208.

enforceable only in equity. Scottish trust law, though an indigenous development, has borrowed much from English principles,[1] but it does not regard the trust as an instance of concurrent legal and equitable ownership, but rather of legal ownership qualified by the rights of parties having *jura crediti* against the subjects owned.[2]

Essentials of trust

The essentials of a trust are that an owner of property, the truster, makes over the legal ownership of property, *inter vivos* or *mortis causa*, to another or others, the trustees; a full legal right of property vests in the trustees and may be held by them against all parties; they are not, however, entitled to the benefit or enjoyment of the property transferred but hold it for the trust purposes; these purposes are declared when the property is transferred or when a subsequent declaration is made in terms of a reserved power to do so; the trust purposes limit the trustees' rights in the property and impose a burden on it preferable to all claims against their property; but the radical right to the trust property, if the trust purposes fail or do not exhaust the property, remains with the truster and the property reverts to him.[3]

Parties and relations

Three parties are necessary to a trust relationship, truster, trustee, and beneficiary, but they need not always be distinct, and one person may participate in any two or all three roles, save that a sole trustee cannot be sole beneficiary.

The relationship of truster to trustee is that of donor to donee; of trustee to beneficiary that of legal owner of property to holder of a *jus crediti* against that property; and of truster to beneficiary that of benevolent donor to party benefited. These relationships give rise to mutual rights and duties, in some ways similar to, but distinct from, those arising *ex contractu* or *ex delicto*.[4] In particular the right of the beneficiary is sometimes *ad rem*, to have conveyed to him specific property, but is normally only *in personam*, to have the trustees account for their administration and pay over what is due therefrom.[5]

[1] See criticism of dictum in *Fleeming* v. *Howden* (1868) 6 M. (H.L.) 113, 121, in *Heritable Reversionary Co.* v. *Millar* (1892) 19 R. (H.L.) 43, 49; *Wink's Exors.* v. *Tallent*, 1947 S.C. 470; and *Camille & Henry Dreyfus Foundation* v. *I.R.C.* [1956] A.C. 39, 47.

[2] *I.R.C.* v. *Clark's Trs.*, 1939 S.C. 11, 26.

[3] Stair I, 13, 7; see also I, 12, 17; IV, 45, 22; Bell, *Prin.* §1991.

[4] *Allen* v. *McCombie's Trs.*, 1909 S.C. 710, 716.

[5] *I.R.C.* v. *Clark's Trs.*, 1939 S.C. 11, 26; *Parker* v. *L.A.*, 1958 S.C. 426; 1960 S.C. (H.L.) 29.

Categories of trusts

The major classification of trusts is into private and public trusts. In the former the beneficial interests are vested only in private individuals. In the latter the trust is for the benefit of the public or some substantial and determinable portion of it, and the trust may continue for a substantial time, or even indefinitely. The same general principles apply to both kinds of trusts, and the statutes apply equally.

Trusts are also distinguishable into simple and special trusts. In the former property is vested in one as trustee and no specific trust purposes are prescribed by the truster, who may call on the trustee to convey the trust estate as he directs.[1] In the latter the purpose of the trust is set out and the trustee must execute the truster's directions.[2]

Trusts may also be express or implied, express where the intention of the truster to create a trust is declared expressly, implied where that intention is held to be implied in his directions.

Among trusts implied by law are resulting trusts, where property is held by a trustee for purposes not declared or which have failed, when he is then deemed to hold on a resulting trust for the truster, and constructive trusts, raised by operation of law independently of the will of the trustee, as where a trustee obtains trust property for his own benefit but is deemed by law to hold it in trust.

The administration of all classes of trusts is supervised by the court, utilising both common law powers and powers it has by virtue of the *nobile officium*, but common law powers do not apply to matters made the subject of specific regulation by statute.[3]

Extensions of trust concept

Apart from trusts strictly so-called the trust concept, in the broad sense of persons administering property for the benefit of others, has been extended to cover the cases of tutors and curators, of judicial factors, trustees in bankruptcy and executors, to all of whom is applied in different ways the idea of fiduciary duty, while many other categories of persons, such as company promoters, in

[1] e.g. the nominee holder of shares in a company: e.g. *Crerar* v. *Bank of Scotland*, 1922 S.C. (H.L.) 137; cf. *I.R.C.* v. *Silverts, Ltd.* [1951] Ch. 521.

[2] e.g. disposition to trustees to hold property for a widow in liferent and thereafter to pay the fee to the children.

[3] *Tennent's J.F.* v. *T.*, 1954 S.C. 215.

some cases company directors, and others have been held subject to fiduciary duties. In modern times the trust concept has also been applied to commercial purposes in such contexts as the investment trust, the unit trust, the trustee savings bank and the trustee for debenture holders.

CHAPTER 104

PRIVATE TRUSTS

CONSTITUTION AND PROOF OF TRUST

Capacity to create trust

ANY person legally capable of disposing of his own property may constitute a trust in respect thereof to the extent of his rights therein. Hence pupils and mentally disordered persons cannot create a trust, but all other persons, including corporations, can. Partnerships cannot hold feudal land in the firm name, but may create a trust whereby it is held by some or all of the partners as trustees for the firm. Persons having a limited interest in property, such as liferenters, may create a trust to exercise the rights enjoyed in such a limited capacity. A bankrupt can create a trust in respect of the reversion of his estate.

Subjects of a trust

Any property, heritable or moveable, corporeal or incorporeal, capable of transfer or assignation may be the subject of a trust. Rights purely personal, such as a peerage,[1] and rights not assignable, such as an alimentary right, cannot be made the subject of a trust. A trust of immoveable property furth of Scotland is competent only to the extent that the *lex loci* permits land there to be held in trust.[2]

The trust fails from uncertainty if the subjects of the trust are not adequately defined so as to be unascertainable,[3] but the uncertainty may be resolved by the terms of the trust deed as a whole in the circumstances.[4] A direction to the trustees to apply a lesser sum for stated purposes does not make the trust uncertain.[5]

Creation—express trust

An express trust is created by a conveyance of property by a person having power to do so to another, and bearing to be in trust for purposes declared therein or to be separately declared, or

[1] *Buckhurst Peerage Case* (1876) 2 App. Cas. 1.
[2] *Brown's Trs.* v. *Gregson*, 1920 S.C. (H.L.) 89.
[3] *Ewen* v. *E's Trs.* (1830) 4 W. & S. 346, criticized in *Dundee Mags.* v. *Morris* (1858) 3 Macq. 134, 154.
[4] *Stewart* v. *S.*, 26 Nov. 1813, F.C.; *Barr's Trs.* v. *Ardrossan Castle Curling Club* (1901) 3 F. 903.
[5] *Macduff* v. *Spence's Trs.*, 1909 S.C. 178.

by a conveyance *ex facie* absolute qualified by a back-bond or acknowledgement, granted by the recipient, of the fact of the trust and the purposes for which he receives the property.[1] The former mode of creation burdens the truster's radical right, whereas the latter divests him, leaving him only the trustee's obligation to reconvey if the trust purposes fail, or when they have been served.[2] The conveyance may be made *inter vivos*, or *mortis causa*, becoming effective on the truster's death. No particular or technical words are necessary, so long as the intention to create a trust is apparent.[3] The word 'trust' is neither necessary nor conclusive, and whether a conveyance is absolute or in trust is a question of interpretation.[4] The trust may not come into being immediately the conveyance becomes effective, as where lands were conveyed on death to one in liferent and to trustees in fee.[5]

Writing, though normal, is not essential to the creation of a trust, except in so far as the transfer of the property to the trustee requires writing. The Trusts Acts, 1921 and 1961, apply to 'trusts' which term means and includes any trust created by any deed or other writing, or by private or local Act of Parliament, or by Royal Charter, or by resolution of any corporation or public or ecclesiastical body.[6]

Creation—implied trust

A trust may be held created by implication where a conveyance is made of a right in terms which do not expressly create a trust but indicate a desire or wish or request which is held to imply the creation of a trust, usually called a precatory trust. Such an intention will be held implied only if the request can be construed as imperative in effect;[7] if not the donee takes the property free from any trust limitation.[8] Into which category a particular case

1 cf. *Keanie* v. *K.*, 1940 S.C. 549.

2 *Robertson* v. *Duff* (1840) 2 D. 279, 291; cf. *McLelland* v. *Bank of Scotland* (1857) 19 D. 574; *Gilmour* v. *G.* (1873) 11 M. 853; *City of Glasgow Bank* v. *Nicolson's Trs.* (1882) 9 R. 689.

3 *Gillespie* v. *City of Glasgow Bank* (1879) 6 R. (H.L.) 104; *Macpherson* v. *M's C.B.* (1894) 21 R. 386; *Leitch* v. *L.*, 1927 S.C. 823.

4 *Bannatyne* v. *Dunlop* (1894) 1 S.L.T. 484; *Urquhart's Exors.* v. *Abbott* (1899) 1 F. 1149; contrast *Gow's Trs.* v. *G.*, 1912 2 S.L.T. 256; *Johnston* v. *J.* (1903) 5 F. 1039.

5 *Edmond* v. *Lord Provost of Aberdeen* (1898) 1 F. 154.

6 Trusts Act, 1921, S. 2. The Act accordingly cannot be invoked by a body holding endowments but established by public general statute: *Edinburgh R.I. Management Board*, 1959 S.C. 393; cf. *Leven Penny Savings Bank*, 1948 S.C. 147.

7 e.g. *Reddie's Trs.* v. *Lindsay* (1890) 17 R. 558; *Reid's Trs.* v. *Dawson*, 1915 S.C. (H.L.) 47.

8 e.g. *Wilson* v. *Lindsay* (1878) 5 R. 539; *Barclay's Exor.* v. *McLeod* (1880) 7 R. 477; *Hamilton's Trs.* v. *H.* (1901) 4 F. 266; *Denholm's Trs.* v. *D.'s Trs.*, 1908 S.C. 255; *Garden's Exor.* v. *More*, 1913 S.C. 285; *Campbell's Trs.* v. *Kinsey-Morgan's Trs.*, 1915 S.C. 298; *Smart* v. *S.*, 1926 S.C. 392.

falls is a question of interpretation, there being no presumptions.[1] A relevant factor is whether what the recipient may have to hold in trust is certain or uncertain.[2]

An implied trust may also be held created by a gift subject to conditions in favour of third parties, such as to bequeath any balance of the gift to named beneficiaries.[3] If the qualification of the gift is not made a condition thereof the donee is not bound and the named beneficiaries are mere substitutes of the donee.[4] A liferent may be deemed a burden on the fee but a fee cannot be deemed a condition of or burden on a liferent to the effect of making a gift subject to condition equivalent to a mere liferent.[5]

Again an implied trust may be held created by a gift, such as one for the purpose of maintaining the donor's family. This may be a statement of motive or hope, or on the other hand as in effect obligatory.[6] In the latter case only have the beneficiaries an enforceable claim against the donee.[7] In such cases the trust obligation is frequently rather indefinite.[8]

The conferment on a donee of a power to dispose of or apportion certain property may be held to imply a duty to exercise the power so as to benefit potential beneficiaries; the power, that is, may be deemed of the nature of a trust.[9]

The truster's radical right

Where the conveyance bears to be for trust purposes, but the ultimate purpose is reconveyance of the reversion of the property to the truster after satisfaction of the primary purpose, such as the payment of debts, the radical right to the property remains in the truster.[10] But if the ultimate purpose is to convey the reversion to a third party, the granter is wholly divested of radical right, even though he has reserved a liferent interest, and the radical right passes to the third party.[11]

[1] *Re Williams* [1897] 2 Ch. 12; *Re Oldfield* [1904] 1 Ch. 549.

[2] *Reddie's Trs., supra.*

[3] *Falconer Stewart* v. *Wilkie* (1892) 19 R. 630; *Murray* v. *Macfarlane's Trs.* (1895) 22 R. 927; *Heavyside* v. *Smith*, 1929 S.C. 68.

[4] *Reid* v. *Dobie*, 1921 S.C. 662; *Robertson* v. *Hay-Boyd*, 1928 S.C. (H.L.) 8.

[5] cf. *Gibson's Trs.* v. *Ross* (1877) 4 R. 1038; *Fogo's J.F.* v. *Fogo's Trs.*, 1929 S.C. 546.

[6] *Jack* v. *Marshall* (1879) 6 R. 543; *Urquhart's Exors.* v. *Abbott* (1899) 1 F. 1149; *Rigg* (1905) 13 S.L.T. 144; *Michie's Exor.* v. *M.* (1905) 7 F. 509; *Gow's Trs.* v. *G.*, 1912 2 S.L.T. 256.

[7] e.g. *Leitch* v. *L.*, 1927 S.C. 823.

[8] *Barry's Trs.* v. *B.* (1888) 15 R. 496; *Leitch, supra*; *Chalmers's J.F.* v. *C.* (1903) 5 F. 1154.

[9] *McDonald* v. *McGrigor* (1874) 1 R. 817; *Miller* v. *M.* (1906) 13 S.L.T. 770.

[10] *Gilmour* v. *G.* (1873) 11 M. 853. See also *Lindsay* v. *Giles* (1844) 6 D. 771; *Globe Ins. Co.* v. *Murray* (1854) 17 D. 216; *Williams* v. *Maclaine's Trs.* (1872) 10 M. 362; *Drysdale's Trs.* v. *D.*, 1940 S.C. 85.

[11] *Turnbulls* v. *Tawse* (1825) 1 W. & S. 80; *Smitton* v. *Martin* (1839) 2 D. 225.

Where on the other hand the conveyance is *ex facie* absolute, it vests the legal estate in the trustee, subject to a personal obligation to use it for the trust purposes and to reconvey if they fail or when they are satisfied.[1]

Appointment of trustees

Appointment may be in the principal trust deed or in a codicil thereto.[2]

Each person designated as a trustee must be adequately identified, by name[3] or by description.[4] The designation of nominate trustees 'and their heirs' only entitles the heir of the last survivor to complete title for the purpose of transmitting the trust estate, but does not make him a trustee, and is no more than law implies.[5] But a clearly expressed intention that a trustee's heir shall become a full trustee is valid.[6]

The truster may delegate to a trustee the power to appoint trustees to succeed him; such a power must be exercised in strict accordance with the power conferred.[7]

A truster may also give to beneficiaries, not being themselves trustees, power to appoint new trustees or to add to the trustees.[8]

Nomination of a person as executor or judicial factor may amount to appointment as trustee if the duties are those of a trustee and it appears that the person nominated is to perform them.[9]

Capacity to be a trustee

Anyone who has legal capacity to hold and deal with property for himself may be a trustee thereof for another; a minor may, but enjoys the privileges of a minor[10] and, if he has curators, they must consent to his assuming office, but cannot thereafter control his actings as trustee. Bankruptcy is not an automatic disqualification.[11] An alien may be a trustee but not so as to qualify him to be

1 *Robertson* v. *Duff* (1840) 2 D. 279, 291; *Higginbotham's Trs.* v. *H.* (1886) 13 R. 1016; *Smith* v. *Stuart* (1894) 22 R. 130; *Montgomery's Trs.* v. *M.* (1895) 22 R. 824.

2 *Mackilligan* v. *M.* (1855) 18 D. 83; *Edinburgh R.I.* v. *L.A.* (1861) 23 D. 1213.

3 This is the normal case.

4 e.g. *Martin* v. *Ferguson's Trs.* (1892) 19 R. 474 (another's trustees); *Brown* v. *Hastie*, 1912 S.C. 304 (X's heir-male).

5 Conveyancing (Sc.) Act, 1874, S. 43; Executors (Sc.) Act, 1900, S. 6.

6 *Brown*, *supra*; *Glasgow W.I.* v. *Cairns*, 1944 S.C. 488.

7 *Bowman* v. *B.*, 1910 1 S.L.T. 381.

8 *Payne* v. *Stamford* [1896] 1 Ch. 288; *McGrady's M.C. Trs.* v. *Hamilton*, 1932 S.C. 191.

9 *Ainslie* v. *A.* (1886) 14 R. 209; *Bannatyne* v. *Dunlop* (1894) 1 S.L.T. 484; *Urquhart's Exors.* v. *Abbott* (1899) 1 F. 1149; *Reid's Exors.* v. *R.*, 1954 S.L.T. (Notes) 20.

10 *Hill* v. *City of Glasgow Bank* (1879) 7 R. 68, 74.

11 *Neilson* (1865) 3 M. 559.

owner of a British ship.[1] A corporation may be a trustee,[2] subject, in the case of companies, to this being *intra vires* of the company's objects.[3] A local authority may be trustee of a public trust.[4] It is not a disqualification that a trustee has a beneficial interest in the trust estate, but if a sole trustee becomes sole beneficiary the trust is extinguished *confusione*.

Trustees ex officiis

Trustees may be nominated as being the holders of specified offices;[5] which offices are intended may require interpretation.[6] If the office, or body in which the office exists, has been changed, the nomination is valid if the body or office continues identifiable.[7] An *ex officio* trustee cannot be compelled to act unless it is a condition of his being appointed to the office,[8] and he may resign.[9] Persons nominated as executors have the powers of trustees[10] and act as such if the testamentary purposes require the estate to be held rather than distributed at once.

Number of trustees

Any number of persons may be appointed trustees. If any one accepts office the trust is duly constituted,[11] unless the appointment be expressly made jointly, in which case all named must accept and act, and the trust fails if one declines or dies.[12] One or more may be stated to be *sine quo (vel quibus) non*, in which case such a trustee is not bound to accept office, but if he does, has a veto on the acts of the other trustees.[13] A particular number may be specified to be a quorum, in which case the trust may be duly constituted if only one trustee accepts, he being then able, unless precluded by the trust deed, to assume new trustees to complete

[1] British Nationality and Status of Aliens Act, 1914, S. 17.
[2] cf. Universities (Sc.) Act, 1889, S. 5(3).
[3] cf. *Leith's Exor.*, 1937 S.L.T. 208.
[4] *Robertson*, 1938 S.C. 276.
[5] e.g. *Edinburgh Mags.* v. *McLaren* (1881) 8 R. (H.L.) 140; *Edmond* v. *Lord Provost of Aberdeen* (1898) 1 F. 154.
[6] *Murdoch* v. *Glasgow Mags.* (1827) 6 S. 186; *Bruce* v. *Presbytery of Deer* (1867) 5 M. (H.L.) 20; *Buchanan's Trs.* v. *Buchanan Bequest Trs.* (1886) 14 R. 284; *Boe* v. *Anderson* (1857) 20 D. 11; *Scottish American Investment Co.* v. *Morgan* (1903) 11 S.L.T. 362.
[7] *Mailler's Trs.* v. *Allan* (1904) 7 F. 326; *St. Silas Church Vestry* v. *St. Silas Church Trs.*, 1945 S.C. 110; contrast *Kilmarnock Parish Council* v. *Ossington's Trs.* (1896) 23 R. 833.
[8] *Shepherd* v. *Hutton's Trs.* (1855) 17 D. 516.
[9] Trusts (Sc.) Act, 1921, S. 2; see also *McGrouther's Trs.*, 1911 S.C. 315.
[10] Ibid. cf. *Ainslie* v. *A.* (1886) 14 R. 208; *Tod* (1890) 18 R. 152.
[11] *Findlay* (1855) 17 D. 1014.
[12] *Dawson* v. *Stirton* (1863) 2 M. 196.
[13] *Forbes* v. *Honyman* (1808) 5 Pat. 226.

the quorum.[1] Less than the specified quorum cannot represent the trust,[2] save that any trustee may act to prevent breach of trust,[3] or to protect himself from individual liability.[4] Statute[5] now provides that unless the contrary be expressed it is implied in every trust deed that a majority of the trustees accepting and surviving shall be a quorum.

Accepting trustees are joint owners of the trust property; when one dies it passes to the survivors or survivor.[6]

Acceptance or declinature

No person designated as trustee, whether nominate or *ex officio*, need accept office,[7] nor does he incur any responsibility unless he accepts office. A promise to the truster during his life to act as his trustee is not binding.[8] Trustees should accept or decline expressly, but acceptance may be inferred from knowingly acting as trustee.[9] Acceptance merely to assume new trustees does not impose liability for further administration.[10] Delay in acceptance does not necessarily imply declinature.[11]

Failure of trustees

In an *inter vivos* private trust, the truster has an implied power to appoint new trustees if those originally appointed have died or declined.[12] But in a public trust, unless the truster reserved power to appoint, an application to the *nobile officium* of the court is necessary.[13] In a *mortis causa* private trust, if all the nominated trustees have predeceased, or have declined office or become unable to act, the court has power at common law[14] and under

1 McLaren on *Wills*, S. 1655.
2 *Morison* v. *Gowans* (1873) 1 R. 116; *Neilson* v. *Mossend Iron Co.* (1885) 12 R. 499.
3 *Neilson, supra*; *Mackenzie* v. *M.* (1886) 13 R. 507; *Birnie* v. *Christie* (1891) 19 R. 334; *Caldwell's Trs.* v. *C.*, 1923 S.L.T. 694.
4 *Taylor* v. *Noble* (1836) 14 S. 817.
5 Trusts (Sc.) Act, 1921, S. 3(b).
6 *Gordon's Trs.* v. *Eglinton* (1851) 13 D. 1381; *Findlay* (1855) 17 D. 1014; *Oswald's Trs.* v. *City of Glasgow Bank* (1879) 6 R. 461.
7 *Shepherd* v. *Hutton's Trs.* (1855) 17 D. 520.
8 *Adam* v. *Grieve* (1867) 5 M. 284, 288.
9 *Mitchell* v. *Davidson* (1855) 18 D. 284; *Ker* v. *City of Glasgow Bank* (1879) 6 R. (H.L.) 52; *Gillespie* v. *City of Glasgow Bank* (1879) 6 R. 813.
10 *Blain* v. *Paterson* (1836) 14 S. 361; *Millar* v. *Black's Trs.* (1837) 2 S. & McL. 866.
11 *Darling* v. *Watson* (1825) 1 W. & S. 188.
12 *Lindsay* v. *L.* (1847) 9 D. 1297; *Tovey* v. *Tennent* (1854) 16 D. 866; *Newlands* v. *Miller* (1882) 9 R. 1104.
13 *Lindsay* v. *L.* (1847) 9 D. 1297; *Anderson's Trs.* v. *Scott*, 1914 S.C. 942; *Glentanar* v. *Sc. Industrial Musical Assoc.*, 1925 S.C. 226.
14 *Campbell* v. *C.* (1752) Mor. 16203; *Grant* (1790) Mor. 7454.

statute[1] to appoint a new trustee or trustees, or may appoint a judicial factor to administer the trust.[2]

If the last surviving trustee has died without assuming a new trustee, the title in the trust property passes to the heir of the last surviving trustee for the purpose only of assuming new trustees and transmitting the property to them.[3]

Proof of trust

A trust need not be constituted in writing, save in so far as writing is necessary for the transfer of title of particular items of property to the trustee, and even such transfers need not bear to be in trust. But, if denied, that fact that property is held in trust and not absolutely must, as between truster and trustee,[4] be proved by the alleged trustee's writ or oath.

By the Blank Bonds and Trusts Act 1696 (c. 25) it is provided that no declarator that property is held in trust will be granted 'except upon a declaration or backbond of trust lawfully subscribed by the person alleged to be the trustee, and against whom or his heirs or assignees the declarator shall be intended, or unless the same be referred to the oath of the party simpliciter'. Parole evidence that property is held not absolutely but in trust is thus incompetent. The Act has uniformly been applied both to cases of dispositions *ex facie* in security and dispositions *ex facie* absolute but alleged to have been granted in trust.[5] It need not be invoked where the conveyance bears *in gremio* to be in trust. It applies only to declarators of trust, by the truster or his representatives against the trustee or his representatives. There is some uncertainty as to the limits of application of the Act.[6] It has been held applicable to an allegation that an assignation of a decree was in security only and not absolute.[7]

It applies to conveyances of land,[8] and also to moveable property for which a written title is necessary[9] but not where title

[1] 1921 Act, S. 22.

[2] *Smart* (1854) 16 D. 1004; *Russell* (1855) 17 D. 1005; *Graham* (1868) 6 M. 958; *Blackwood* (1894) 1 S.L.T. 601.

[3] Conveyancing (Sc.) Act, 1874, S. 43; Executors (Sc.) Act, 1900, S. 6.

[4] Third parties may prove trust *prout de jure*: *Murdoch* v. *Wyllie* (1832) 10 S. 445; *Wink* v. *Speirs* (1867) 6 M. 77; *City of Glasgow Bank* v. *Nicolson's Tr.* (1882) 9 R. 689; *Anderson* v. *Yorston* (1906) 14 S.L.T. 54.

[5] *Leckie* v. *L.* (1854) 17 D. 77.

[6] *Newton* v. *N.*, 1923 S.C. 15; *Galloway* v. *G.*, 1929 S.C. 160.

[7] *Purnell* v. *Shannon* (1894) 22 R. 74.

[8] e.g. *Robertson* v. *R.*, 1929 S.L.T. 510.

[9] *Laird* v. *Laird & Rutherford* (1884) 12 R. 294 (patent); cf. *McNair's Exrx.* v. *Litster*, 1939 S.C. 72.

thereto need not be constituted in writing, even if in fact it has been so constituted.[1]

It applies only against the truster, and the holder of an *ex facie* absolute title to property may prove *prout de jure* that he holds it in trust.[2]

The Act does not apply to cases founded on mandate,[3] or partnership,[4] or *negotiorum gestio*[5] and it has not always been held applicable between spouses.[6] Nor does it apply where the holder's title is alleged to be held by fraud[7] or in breach of mandate.[8] It does not apply to questions arising with creditors.[9] Where the alleged trustee states that an absolute disposition does not truly represent the relation between him and the alleged truster, but that it is subject to qualifications, parole proof has been admitted.[10]

It does not apply where there is no 'deed of trust' within the meaning of the Act;[11] a deposit receipt is not such a deed of trust, not being evidence of ownership,[12] but entries in business books may be.[13]

Where the Act applies the declaration or back-bond need not be probative, but any writing under the alleged trustee's hand, or signed by him, will suffice.[14] But the writ cannot be explained or

1 *McConnachie* v. *Geddes*, 1918 S.C. 391.

2 *Murdoch* v. *Wylie* (1832) 10 S. 445; cf. *Hastie* v. *Steel* (1886) 13 R. 843.

3 *Horne* v. *Morrison* (1877) 4 R. 977; *Pant-Mawr Quarry Co.* v. *Fleming* (1883) 10 R. 457; *Dunn* v. *Pratt* (1898) 25 R. 461; *Anderson* v. *Yorston* (1906) 14 S.L.T. 54; *McConnachie* v. *Geddes*, 1918 S.C. 391; *Beveridge* v. *B.*, 1925 S.L.T. 234; *Galloway* v. *G.*, 1929 S.C. 160.

4 *Forrester* v. *Robson's Trs.* (1875) 2 R. 755; *Horne, supra*; *Laird* v. *Laird & Rutherford* (1884) 12 R. 294. But see *Adam* v. *A.*, 1962 S.L.T. 332.

5 *Spreul* v. *Crawford* (1741) Mor. 16201; *Marshall* v. *Lyell* (1859) 21 D. 521.

6 *Anderson* v. *A's Trs.* (1898) 6 S.L.T. 204; *Newton* v. *N.*, 1923 S.C. 15; *Galloway* v. *G.*, 1929 S.C. 160. Contrast *Inglis* v. *Smith's Exrx.*, 1959 S.L.T. (Notes) 78; *Weissenbruch* v. *W.*, 1961 S.C. 340.

7 *Wink* v. *Speirs* (1867) 6 M. 77; *Marshall* v. *Lyell* (1859) 21 D. 521; *Tennent* v. *T's Trs.* (1870) 8 M. (H.L.) 10.

8 *Pant Mawr Quarry Co., supra*; *McConnachie* v. *Geddes*, 1918 S.C. 391.

9 *Wink* v. *Speirs* (1867) 6 M. 77; *City of Glasgow Bank* v. *Nicolson's Tr.* (1882) 9 R. 689; *Anderson, supra.*

10 *Walker* v. *Buchanan, Kennedy & Co.* (1857) 20 D. 259; *Murray* v. *Wright* (1870) 8 M. 722; *Grant's Trs.* v. *Morison* (1875) 2 R. 377; *Grant* v. *Mackenzie* (1899) 1 F. 889.

11 *Gardiner* v. *Cowie* (1897) 4 S.L.T. 256; missives of sale of land constitute a 'deed of trust' within the Act: *Dunn* v. *Pratt* (1898) 25 R. 461. See also *Govan New Bowling Green Club* v. *Geddes* (1898) 25 R. 485, where trust not relevantly averred.

12 *Anderson* v. *N. of S. Bank* (1901) 4 F. 49; *Cairns* v. *Davidson*, 1913 S.C. 1054; *Dickson* v. *National Bank*, 1917 S.C. (H.L.) 50; *McConnachie, supra*; *Newton, supra*; *Royal Bank* v. *Perpetual Tr. Co.*, 1954 S.L.T. (Notes) 48.

13 *Knox* v. *Martin* (1850) 12 D. 719; *Seth* v. *Hain* (1855) 17 D. 1117; *Walker* v. *Buchanan, Kennedy & Co.* (1857) 20 D. 259; *Thomson* v. *Lindsay* (1873) 1 R. 65.

14 *Mackay* v. *Ambrose* (1829) 7 S. 699; *Taylor* v. *Crawford* (1833) 12 S. 39; *Macfarlane* v. *Fisher* (1837) 15 S. 978.

qualified by parole evidence of the parties' understandings or intentions.[1]

Proof of trust purposes

The Trusts Act, 1696, applies only to proving the existence of trust; if it is admitted or proved that the title to property is not absolute but in trust, the purposes and conditions of the trust may be proved *prout de jure*.[2]

Revocation of trust

An *inter vivos* trust, if created solely for the administration of his own affairs, is revocable at any time by the truster,[3] but if, as by delivery of the deed, or by its registration, rights have been conferred on other parties, it is, unless a power of revocation has been reserved,[4] not revocable without the consent of all the beneficiaries.[5]

A testamentary trust is revocable, until it takes effect, notwithstanding a declaration of irrevocability,[6] or delivery to or for behoof of the beneficiaries,[7] unless there has been a definite express prior contract, proveable only by writ or oath,[8] not to revoke.[9] It may, however, be made irrevocable, if the truster has divested himself of his property in favour of third party beneficiaries with the intention that such divestiture be irrevocable. The presumption is against irrevocable divestiture, but the question is one of intention.[10] Considerations which tend to give an irrevocable character to a disposition in trust are: (1) delivery of the deed;[11] (2) *de praesenti* conveyance of the property; (3) declaration

[1] *Pickard* v. *P.*, 1963 S.C. 604.

[2] *Livingstone* v. *Allan* (1900) 3 F. 233; *National Bank* v. *Mackie's Trs.* (1905) 13 S.L.T. 383.

[3] *Murison* v. *Dick* (1854) 16 D. 529; *Mackenzie* v. *M's Trs.* (1878) 5 R. 1027; *Byres' Trs.* v. *Gemmell* (1895) 23 R. 332, 337; *Watt* v. *Watson* (1897) 24 R. 330; *Torrance* v. *T's Trs.*, 1950 S.C. 78; *Ross* v. *Ross's Trs.*, 1967 S.L.T. 12.

[4] *Robertson* v. *R's Trs.* (1892) 19 R. 849.

[5] *Tennent* v. *T's Trs.* (1869) 7 M. 936; *Spalding* v. *S's Trs.* (1874) 2 R. 237; *Robertson*, *supra*; *Shedden* v. *S's Trs.* (1895) 23 R. 228; *Lyon* v. *L's Trs.* (1901) 3 F. 653; *Walker* v. *Amey* (1906) 8 F. 376; *Scott* v. *S.*, 1930 S.C. 903; *Lawson's Trs.* v. *L.*, 1938 S.C. 632; *Campbell* v. *C's Trs.*, 1967 S.L.T. (Notes) 30.

[6] *Byres' Trs.*, *supra*, 339.

[7] *Mackenzie* v. *M's Trs.* (1878) 5 R. 1027.

[8] *Mackenzie's Trs.* v. *Kilmarnock's Trs.*, 1909 S.C. 472; *Smith* v. *Oliver*, 1911 S.C. 103.

[9] *Paterson* v. *P.* (1893) 20 R. 484; *Murray* v. *Macfarlane's Trs.* (1895) 22 R. 927; *Mackenzie's Trs.* v. *Kilmarnock's Trs.*, 1909 S.C. 472; *Smith* v. *Oliver*, 1911 S.C. 103.

[10] *Turnbulls* v. *Tawse* (1825) 1 W. & S. 80; *Walker* v. *Amey* (1906) 8 F. 376; *Bertram's Trs.* v. *B.*, 1909 S.C. 1238.

[11] cf. *Connell's Trs.* v. *C's Tr.*, 1955 S.L.T. 125.

of irrevocability; (4) the fact that what is conveyed is not the whole estate of the granter; (5) the beneficiaries being persons in existence; (6) the beneficiaries being the granter's children as a class; (7) immediate enjoyment, or power to the trustees to give immediate enjoyment; (8) discretion to the trustees to make certain advances to the granter without any right of the granter to demand them.[1]

Where revocation is competent it may be effected expressly, by deed, or impliedly, as in the case of a testamentary trust deed by the execution of a later trust deed, or a codicil to the original deed, inconsistent therewith, or by the operation of the rule of the *conditio si testator sine liberis decesserit*.

Alimentary trusts

If one of the purposes of a trust is to hold property for the alimentary use of a beneficiary, the trust is irrevocable.[2] The beneficial interest need not be expressly declared 'alimentary' so long as the intention is that the trustees are to hold and administer the estate for the maintenance of the beneficiary.[3]

Trusts arising by implication of law

A trust may also be deemed created by legal implication, independently of the truster's expressed intention. This class includes constructive and resulting trusts and the trust created by the doctrine of the fiduciary fee.

Constructive trusts

A constructive trust arises where a person holding a fiduciary position obtains some personal benefit from that position; he is then deemed by construction of law to hold the benefit as trustee for the beneficiaries.[4] This arises, e.g. where a partner, unknown to his co-partners, obtains a lease of the premises in which the firm had carried on business,[5] or a trustee secretly purchases trust property for his own behoof.[6]

[1] *Nelson* v. *N's Trs.*, 1921 1 S.L.T. 82.

[2] *White's Trs.* v. *Whyte* (1877) 4 R. 786; *Hughes* v. *Edwards* (1892) 19 R. (H.L.) 33; *Eliott's Tr.* v. *E.* (1894) 21 R. 975; *Main's Trs.* v. *M.*, 1917 S.C. 660.

[3] *Arnold's Trs.* v. *Graham*, 1927 S.C. 353.

[4] e.g. *Laird* v. *L.* (1858) 20 D. 972; *Fleeming* v. *Howden* (1868) 6 M. (H.L.) 121; *Aberdeen Mags.* v. *Aberdeen University* (1876) 4 R. (H.L.) 48; *Huntingdon Copper Co.* v. *Henderson* (1877) 4 R. 294; 5 R. (H.L.) 1; *Stewart* v. *Chalmers* (1904) 7 F. 163; *Stevenson* v. *Wilson*, 1907 S.C. 445.

[5] *McNiven* v. *Peffers* (1868) 7 M. 181; cf. *Wilson* v. *W.* (1789) Mor. 16376; *Marshall* v. *M.*, 23 Feb. 1816, F.C.

[6] *York Buildings Co.* v. *Mackenzie* (1795) 3 Pat. 378; *Hamilton* v. *Wright* (1842) 1 Bell 574.

Resulting trusts

A resulting trust arises where a beneficial interest under a trust has not been disposed of, or has lapsed, in which case the property must be held on a resulting trust for the truster or his representatives by virtue of his radical right in the trust property.[1]

This applies, e.g., where property has been conveyed in trust but trust purposes have not been declared; or the trust purposes do not exhaust the trust estate, or fail in part from uncertainty or illegality; or a trustee has been given discretionary powers but has declined office or not exercised them.[2] Trustees are not entitled to avoid a resulting trust by applying trust funds to purposes similar to those directed,[3] nor is a resulting trust avoided by the truster merely disinheriting his next of kin but conferring no right on anyone else.[4]

Doctrine of fiduciary fee

Where property is destined, without a trust, to one in liferent and the heirs of his body *nascituri* in fee, the parent has an unqualified right of fee.[5]

Where, however, property is destined to a person in liferent allenarly and to other persons, not yet born or not yet ascertained, in fee, the liferenter is deemed fiduciary fiar until the ultimate fiars are born or otherwise ascertained, when they become fiars and the fiduciary fiar becomes merely liferenter.[6] In such a case the person is virtually a trustee for himself in liferent and his children in fee.[7]

By the 1921 Act, S. 8, where property is conveyed to one in liferent and in fee to persons unborn or incapable of ascertainment all such conveyances have effect as if the liferent were declared to be a liferent allenarly. The liferenter or any person to whom the fee or part thereof is presumptively destined, or who may have an interest, even prospective or contingent, under such conveyance, or the Accountant of Court, may apply to the court for authority

[1] *Boyle* v. *E. Glasgow's Trs.* (1858) 20 D. 943.

[2] e.g. *Sinclair* v. *Traill* (1840) 2 D. 694; *McLeish's Trs.* v. *McL.* (1841) 3 D. 914; *Anderson* v. *Smoke* (1898) 25 R. 493; *Sutherland's Trs.* v. *S's Tr.* (1893) 20 R. 925; *Edmond* v. *Lord Provost of Aberdeen* (1898) 1 F. 154; *McCaig* v. *Glasgow University*, 1907 S.C. 231; *Hedderwick's Trs.* v. *H's Exor.*, 1910 S.C. 333; contrast *Templeton* v. *Burgh of Ayr*, 1910 2 S.L.T. 12.

[3] *Ness* v. *Mill's Trs.*, 1923 S.C. 344.

[4] *Sinclair* v. *Trail* (1840) 2 D. 694; *Gardner* v. *Ogilvie* (1857) 20 D. 105; *Neilson* v. *Stewart* (1860) 22 D. 646; *Cowan* v. *C.* (1887) 14 R. 670; *Edmond*, *supra*.

[5] *Frog's Creditors* v. *His Children* (1735) Mor. 4262.

[6] *Newland's* v. *N's Creditors* (1794) Mor. 4289; (1798) 4 Pat. 43. The justification is that he fee cannot be *in pendente*: see Ersk. II, 1, 4.

[7] *Snell* v. *White* (1872) 10 M. 745.

to exercise all or such of the powers, or to do all or such of the acts, competent to a trustee at common law or under the 1921 Act as may seem fit to the court, or to appoint a trustee or trustees, with all the powers of trustees at common law and under the Act, or a judicial factor to hold the property in trust in place of the liferenter or fiduciary fiar.[1]

THE OBJECTS AND PURPOSES OF TRUSTS

The objects of a trust are the beneficiaries who have interests under the trust. Every trust must have one or more objects in whose favour the court can enforce performance, though the object's interest may be contingent or remote. The objects may not be directly designated, but the trustees may have discretionary power to benefit certain objects which they may select.

Any legal person, natural or juristic, may be the object of a trust and benefit thereunder. Animals may not be made trust objects,[2] but trusts for preventing cruelty to animals,[3] or for benefiting animals useful to man,[4] are valid as indirectly beneficial to humanity. Trust funds may, if directed, be spent on objects who are not legal persons if next of kin do not object, but such spending is unenforceable.[2]

The erection or maintenance of tombs or memorials is a valid object if it involves benefit to some living person or persons, as by repairing a church,[5] or beautifying it,[6] or maintaining a churchyard,[7] and trustees, if directed to do so, may, but cannot be compelled to, make a reasonable provision for a tomb or memorial to a truster.[8] An extravagant provision for a tomb may be invalid.[9]

Trusts for objects not entitled to enforce performance may be made effective by making a legal person the object, attaching a condition of implementing the truster's wishes, and with a gift-over in the event of non-implement.[10]

1 *Webb*, 1934 S.N. 115.

2 *Re Dean* (1889) 41 Ch. D. 532; *Re Grove-Grady* [1929] 1 Ch. 557; [1931] W.N. 89.

3 *Re Foveaux* [1895] 2 Ch. 501; *Re Wedgwood* [1915] 1 Ch. 113; *Glasgow S.P.C.A.* v. *National Anti-Vivisection Socy.*, 1915 S.C. 757; contrast *Lewis* v. *Fermor* (1887) 18 Q.B.D. 532.

4 *Re Vaughan* (1886) 33 Ch. D. 187; *Re Douglas* (1887) 35 Ch. D. 472.

5 *Re Vaughan* (1886) 33 Ch. D. 187; *Re Douglas* (1887) 35 Ch. D. 472.

6 *Re King* [1923] 1 Ch. 243.

7 *Re Pardoe* [1906] 2 Ch. 265.

8 *McCaig* v. *Glasgow University*, 1907 S.C. 231, 244; *MacKintosh's J.F.* v. *L.A.*, 1935 S.C. 406.

9 *McCaig, supra*; *McCaig's Trs.* v. *Lismore Kirk-Session*, 1915 S.C. 426; *Aitken's Trs.* v. *A.*, 1927 S.C. 374; *MacKintosh's J.F., supra.*

10 *Re Tyler* [1891] 3 Ch. 252; *Re Davies* [1915] 1 Ch. 543; *Robson's J.F.* v. *Wilson*, 1922 S.L.T. 640.

Uncertainty as to objects

The trust must fail, in whole or in part, if there is uncertainty as to the object the truster wished to benefit,[1] as where the disposal of part of the trust funds is left to the absolute discretion of the trustees.[2] It is not, however, void, even though the trustees have discretion, if the objects are defined, even generally, or to be selected from a defined class.[3] Scots law does not recognise any doctrine of secret trusts, so that in a testamentary trust the classes from which the trustee may select objects of benevolence must be declared in writing.[4]

Trust purposes

The trust purposes are the truster's intentions for the application of the trust funds to achieve his desired ends. They must be sufficiently declared to enable the trustees to give effect to them,[5] failing which the trustees hold on a resulting trust for the truster and his representatives. The purposes may be set out in the deed constituting the trust, or be subsequently declared, or stated by reference to another trust,[6] and may possibly even be delegated to another to state.[7] In the case of testamentary trusts the purposes must be in writing.[8]

Trust purposes may be, but will not readily be, inferred from the selection as trustee of a person of particular qualifications and giving the administration of the trust to him without further specification of purposes.[9]

There are no trust purposes where the disposal of the trust estate is left entirely to the discretion of the trustees,[10] or where the

[1] *Dundas* v. *D.* (1837) 15 S. 427; *Hamilton's Trs.* v. *H.* (1901) 4 F. 266; cf. *Anderson* v. *Smoke* (1898) 25 R. 493.

[2] *Sutherland's Trs.* v. *S's Tr.* (1893) 20 R. 925; *Shaw's Trs.* (1893) 1 S.L.T. 308; *Wilson's Trs.* v. *W's Trs.* (1894) 1 S.L.T. 548; *McGregor's Trs.* v. *Bosomworth* (1896) 3 S.L.T. 231; *Playfair's Trs.* v. *P.* (1900) 2 F. 686.

[3] *Warrender* v. *Anderson* (1893) 1 S.L.T. 304; *Smellie's Trs.* v. *Glasgow R.I.* (1905) 13 S.L.T. 450; *Mitchell's Trs.* v. *Fraser*, 1915 S.C. 350; *Bannerman's Trs.* v. *B.*, 1915 S.C. 398.

[4] *Shaw's Trs.* v. *Greenock Medical Aid Socy.*, 1930 S.L.T. 39.

[5] e.g. *Sutherland's Trs.* v. *S's Tr.* (1893) 20 R. 925; *Re Barron* (1932) 48 T.L.R. 205; *Dodds* v. *Bain*, 1933 S.N. 16.

[6] *Murray* (1898) 6 S.L.T. 149; *Re Gooch* [1929] 1 Ch. 740.

[7] *Edmond* v. *Lord Provost of Aberdeen* (1898) 1 F. 154, 164.

[8] *Wilson* v. *Lindsay* (1878) 5 R. 539; *Shaw's Trs.* v. *Greenock Medical Aid Socy.*, 1930 S.L.T. 39.

[9] *Dunne* v. *Byrne* [1912] A.C. 407, 410; contrast *Re Garrard* [1907] 1 Ch. 382; *Re Barclay* [1929] 2 Ch. 173; *Re Bain* [1930] 1 Ch. 224.

[10] *Sutherland's Trs.* v. *S's Tr.* (1893) 20 R. 925; *Allan* (1893) 1 S.L.T. 308; *Wilson's Trs.* v. *W's Trs.* (1894) 1 S.L.T. 548; *McGregor's Trs.* v. *Bosomworth* (1896) 3 S.L.T. 231; *Anderson* v. *Smoke* (1898) 25 R. 493; *Playfair's Trs.* v. *P.* (1900) 2 F. 686.

purposes are stated simply as 'charities' and no person is appointed to select which charities.[1]

Trust purposes illegal

A trust is void if its purposes are criminal, prohibited, or otherwise illegal. But the promotion of a society contrary to Christianity is not illegal,[2] nor is the furtherance of religions or denominations other than the established church.[3]

Trust purposes contra bonos mores

The trust is void in so far as a purpose is deemed *contra bonos mores*, such as the furtherance of immorality,[4] but not compensation for past immorality[5] nor provision for illegitimate children,[6] or where a condition might have prompted the beneficiary to resort to corruption.[7] A trust provision has been held *pro non scripto* as being *contra bonos mores* when subject to a condition that a daughter should not reside with her mother.[8]

Trust purposes contrary to public policy

Trust purposes are void in so far as they are deemed contrary to what the court considers is public policy. It is impossible to define comprehensively what may be held contrary to public policy. The category, however, includes any purposes wholly lacking in benefit to any living person,[9] and probably any purpose contrary to the safety of the realm, or to peace and good order therein, or to honesty in public life.[10] It also covers any trust the purpose of which is the withdrawal of the truster's estate from the hands of his creditors.[11]

Trust purposes not void though ineffective

Trust purposes are not necessarily wholly void if requiring the trustees to apply the trust funds in a manner legally impossible;

1 *Angus's Exrx.* v. *Batchan's Trs.*, 1949 S.C. 335.

2 *Bowman* v. *Secular Society* [1917] A.C. 406.

3 *Hardie* v. *Morrison* (1899) 7 S.L.T. 42 (R.C. church).

4 *Johnstone* v. *Mackenzie's Exors.* (1835) 14 S. 106; *Young* v. *Johnston* (1880) 7 R. 760; *Troussier* v. *Matthew*, 1922 S.L.T. 670.

5 *Webster* v. *W's Trs.* (1886) 14 R. 90. Unless granted in pursuance of a contractual undertaking to do so, in consideration of immoral relations.

6 *Hyde* [1932] 1 Ch. 95.

7 *Egerton* v. *E. Brownlow* (1853) 4 H.L. Cas. 1; *Barker*, 1919 S.C. 109.

8 *Fraser* v. *Rose* (1849) 11 D. 1466.

9 *McCaig* v. *University of Glasgow*, 1907 S.C. 231; *McCaig's Trs.* v. *Kirk Session of Lismore*, 1915 S.C. 426; *Aitken's Trs.* v. *A.*, 1927 S.C. 374; *Lindsay's Exor.* v. *Forsyth*, 1940 S.C. 568; cf. *Brown* v. *Burdett* (1882) 21 Ch. D. 667.

10 cf. *Parkinson* v. *College of Ambulance* [1925] K.B. 1.

11 *E. Rosebery* v. *Cowie* (1823) 2 S. 443; *Wright* v. *Harley* (1847) 9 D. 1151.

the trustees must give effect to the trust purposes so far as possible,[1] and *quoad ultra* hold the funds on a resulting trust.

STATUTORY RESTRICTIONS ON TRUST PURPOSES

Various statutes have imposed restrictions on possible trust purposes.

(a) *Perpetual series of fees*

It is incompetent, with or without a trust, to create a perpetual series of fees of land, the holders of which are debarred from disposing of their lands *inter vivos* or *mortis causa*. By the (Rutherfurd) Entail Amendment (Sc.) Act, 1848, S. 47, amended by the Entail (Sc.) Act, 1914, S. 8, where land or estate, held under a deed of trust, is in the lawful possession of a party of full age born after the date of the trust deed, such party is not affected by any conditions therein and is deemed the fee-simple proprietor of the lands and may apply to the Court of Session for declarator accordingly.[2] The provisions apply not only to entails but also to trust deeds containing simple destinations.[3]

(b) *Series of liferents*

The creation of a series of liferents is restricted, as to heritage, by the (Rutherfurd) Entail Amendment (Sc.) Act, 1848, S. 48 amended by the Entail (Sc.) Act, 1914, S. 8, by which any liferenter of full age born after the date of the deed constituting the liferents may have his right enlarged to a fee.[4]

The creation is restricted as to moveables by the Trusts (Sc.) Act, 1921, S. 9, re-enacting the Entail Amendment (Sc.) Act, 1868, and extended by the Conveyancing (Sc.) Act, 1924, S. 45. Section 9 permits the constitution[5] or reservation by a trust or otherwise of a liferent interest in moveable and personal estate in Scotland in favour only of a person in life at the date of the deed constituting or reserving such liferent, and provides that where any such estate in Scotland is, by virtue of any deed dated after 31st July 1868,[6] to be held in liferent by or for behoof of a

[1] *Kinnear* v. *K's Trs.* (1875) 2 R. 765 (entail of moveables); *Gibson's Trs.* v. *Ross* (1877) 4 R. 1038; *Sandys* v. *Bain's Trs.* (1897) 25 R. 261; *Baillie's Tr.* v. *Whiting*, 1910 S.C. 887; *Lumsden's Trs.* v. *L.*, 1917 S.C. 579 (direction to entail: entails prohibited).

[2] *Harvey's Trs.* v. *H.*, 1942 S.C. 582; *E. Moray*, 1950 S.C. 281.

[3] *L. Middleton*, 1929 S.C. 394.

[4] *Crichton-Stuart's Tutrix*, 1921 S.C. 840.

[5] As to date of constitution under power of appointment see *Muir's Trs.* v. *Williams*, 1943 S.C. (H.L.) 47; *Malcolm's Trs.* v. *M.*, 1950 S.C. (H.L.) 17.

[6] The date of a testamentary or *mortis causa* deed is to be taken as the death of the granter, and the date of any marriage contract as the date of the dissolution of the marriage.

person of full age born[1] after the date of such deed, such estate shall belong absolutely to such person, and the trustees are bound to convey the estates to such person.[2] The 1924 Act extends the provision to deeds dated on or prior to 31 July 1868. A liferent in favour of a person unborn at the date of the deed is unaffected during the liferenter's minority.[3] A liferenter *in utero* at the testator's death is not 'in life' at the date of the deed and is entitled to the fee of the estate.[4] The section probably applies where the liferenter has a power of appointment within a certain group and uses it to create a liferent in favour of one not in life when the first liferent was created, but not if the power of appointment is a general power, the creation of a liferent being in this case the act of the donee of the power.[5]

The court has declined to apply the section to annuities,[6] or where the liferenter gets more than a liferent,[7] such as a liferent plus a contingent fee,[8] and doubts have been expressed as to the applicability of the section where the conversion of liferent to fee would prejudice parties other than subsequent liferenters or designated fiars.[9]

These restrictions are in substance restated by the Law Reform (Misc. Prov.) (Sc.) Act, 1968, S. 18, in relation to liferents created by deeds dated after the passsing of that Act.

(c) *Accumulation of income*

There is no objection to a trust continuing in perpetuity, the trustees disbursing the income periodically or as directed by the truster.[10] But accumulation of trust income for long periods, unobjectionable at common law so long as for a rational purpose and some definite period being fixed for its termination, is limited now by the Trusts (Sc.) Act, 1961,[11] S. 5.[12] That section provides:

[1] Including posthumous children: *Reid's Trs., infra.*
[2] *Reid's Trs.* v. *Dashwood*, 1929 S.C. 748.
[3] *Stuart's Trs.* v. *Whitelaw*, 1926 S.C. 701, 718.
[4] *Reid's Trs., supra.*
[5] *Stewart's Trs., supra.*
[6] *Drybrough's Tr.* v. *D's Tr.*, 1912 S.C. 939.
[7] *Baxter* v. *B.*, 1909 S.C. 1027; *Mackenzie's Trs.* v. *M.*, 1922 S.C. 404.
[8] *Macculloch* v. *McCulloch's Trs.* (1903) 6 F. (H.L.) 3; *Shiell's Trs.* v. *S's Trs.* (1906) 8 F. 848.
[9] *Shiell's Trs., Baxter, Mackenzie's Trs., supra.*
[10] *Suttie* v. *S's Trs.* (1846) 18 Sc. Jur. 442; cf. *Stewart's Trs.* v. *Whitelaw*, 1926 S.C. 701.
[11] Formerly by the Accumulations Act, 1800, commonly known as the Thellusson Act, extended to Scotland by later Acts, and partly repealed by Entail (Sc.) Act, 1914, S. 9.
[12] The restrictions apply (S. 5(5)) to wills, settlements and other dispositions made on or after 28 July 1800, but in the case of wills only where the testator was living and of testamentary capacity after one year from that date.

'(2) No person may by any will, settlement or other disposition dispose of any property in such manner that the income thereof shall be wholly or partially accumulated for any longer period than one of (a) the life of the grantor;[1] or (b) twenty-one years from the death of the grantor;[2] or (c) the minority or respective minorities of any person or persons living or *in utero* at the death of the grantor;[3] or (d) the minority or respective minorities of any person or persons who, under the terms of the will, settlement or other disposition directing the accumulation would for the time being, if of full age, be entitled to the income directed to be accumulated;[4] or (e) a term of twenty-one years from the date of the making of the settlement or other disposition;[5] or (f) the duration of the minority or respective minorities of any person or persons living or *in utero* at that date,[5] and a direction to accumulate income during a period specified in (e) or (f) shall not be void, nor the accumulation contrary to S. 5, solely by reason of the fact that the period begins during the life of the grantor and ends after his death.

(3) Where accumulation is directed otherwise than as aforesaid, the direction is void, and the income directed to be accumulated shall, so long as directed to be accumulated contrary to the section, go to and be received by the person or persons who would have been entitled thereto if such accumulation had not been directed.'[6]

The restrictions are imperative and cannot be overcome by consent.[7] The accumulation may be directed expressly,[8] or impliedly, or arise from the execution of the settlement in the circumstances which have happened.[9]

[1] cf. *Stewart's Trs.* v. *S.*, 1927 S.C. 350; *Union Bank* v. *Campbell*, 1929 S.C. 143.

[2] *Campbell's Trs.* v. *C.* (1891) 18 R. 992; *Barbour* v. *Budge*, 1947 S.N. 100.

[3] cf. *Campbell's Trs.*, *supra.*

[4] cf. *Re Cattell* [1907] 1 Ch. 567; [1914] 1 Ch. 177. S. 5(4) declares that a direction to accumulate income during a period under (d) is not to be void, nor the accumulation contrary to the section, solely by reason of the fact that the period begins during the life of the grantor and ends after his death.

[5] Added by Law Reform (Misc. Prov.) (Sc.) Act, 1966, S. 6. By S. 6(3) these additional periods apply only in relation to instruments taking effect after 3 August 1966, and in the case of an instrument made in the exercise of a special power of appointment only when the instrument creating the power takes effect after that date.

[6] On disposal of surplus income see *Dowden's Trs.*, 1965 S.C. 56.

[7] *Maxwell's Tr.* v. *M.* (1877) 5 R. 249.

[8] *Smith* v. *Glasgow R.I.*, 1909 S.C. 1231.

[9] *Lord* v. *Colvin* (1860) 23 D. 111; *Mackenzie* v. *M's Trs.* (1877) 4 R. 962; *Maxwell's Trs.*, *supra*; *Campbell's Trs.* v. *C.* (1891) 18 R. 992; *Logan's Trs.* v. *L.* (1896) 23 R. 849; *Moon's Trs.* v. *M.* (1899) 2 F. 201; *Hutchison* v. *Grant's Trs.*, 1913 S.C. 1211; *Mitchell's Trs.* v. *Fraser*, 1915 S.C. 350; *Innes' Trs.* v. *Bowen*, 1920 S.C. 133; *Watson's Trs.* v. *Brown*, 1923 S.C. 228; *Stewart's Trs.* v. *Whitelaw*, 1926 S.C. 701.

The restrictions do not apply to capital accumulations, such as rent or royalties of mines,[1] nor to premiums of a life insurance policy,[2] nor to accumulations which do not arise directly or indirectly from the will or settlement, such as the inability to make payments to a beneficiary by reason of his insanity,[3] savings out of income,[4] or the retention of income for an absent beneficiary.[5]

The restrictions imposed by S. 5 apply in relation to a power to accumulate income whether or not there is a duty to exercise that power, and whether or not the power to accumulate extends to income produced by the investment of income previously accumulated.[6]

Disposal of income which otherwise would have been accumulated

Where the section applies to stop accumulation or further accumulation the income directed to be accumulated, so long as directed to be accumulated contrary to the 1961 Act, goes to the person who would have been entitled thereto if accumulation had not been directed.

Where the income of a bequest was to be accumulated till it reached a stated total and further accumulation was cut off before then, the bequest was held fixed at that sum, subsequent income not being addable to the capital.[7]

VARIATION OF TRUST PURPOSES

The court may,[8] on the petition of the trustees or any of the beneficiaries[9] under a trust under any will, settlement or other disposition, approve on behalf of (a) any of the beneficiaries who by reason of nonage or other incapacity is incapable of assenting, or (b) any person (whether ascertained or not) who may become one of the beneficiaries as being at a future date[10] or on the happening of a future event a person of any specified description or a member of any specified class of persons, but not including any person who is capable of assenting and would be of that

[1] *Campbell* v. *C's Trs.* (1882) 10 R. (H.L.) 65; *Ranken's Trs.* v. *R.*, 1908 S.C. 3.

[2] *Cathcart's Trs.* v. *Heneage's Trs.* (1883) 10 R. 1205. [3] *Lord, supra.*

[4] *Lindsay's Trs.*, 1911 S.C. 584. [5] *Mitchell's Trs., supra.*

[6] Law Reform (Misc. Prov.) (Sc.) Act, 1966, S. 6(2).

[7] *Donaldson's Trs.* v. *L.A.*, 1938 S.L.T. 106.

[8] Trusts (Sc.) Act, 1961, S. 1(1). As to jurisdiction see *Clarke's Trs.*, 1966 S.L.T. 249. The court may authorise variation notwithstanding a declaration of irrevocability in an *inter vivos* deed: *Ommanney*, 1966 S.L.T. (Notes) 13.

[9] Defined, S. 1(6); *Countess of Lauderdale*, 1962 S.C. 302; see also *Trs. of G. B. Thomson Trust*, 1963 S.C. 141.

[10] See *Buchan*, 1964 S.L.T. 51.

description, or a member of that class if the said date had fallen or the said event had happened at the date of the petition to the court, or (c) any person unborn, any arrangement varying or revoking all or any of the trust purposes,[1] or enlarging the powers of the trustees of managing or administering the trust estate. But the court must not approve an arrangement on behalf of any person unless of opinion that the carrying out thereof would not be prejudicial to that person.[2] Such an approved arrangement is not reducible by a minor beneficiary on the ground of minority and lesion.[3] Where a trust purpose is an alimentary liferent[4] or income the court may authorise any arrangement varying or revoking that trust purpose and making new provision in lieu thereof, including new provision for the disposal of the fee or capital of the trust estate or of such part thereof as was burdened with the liferent or income, but not unless (a) the arrangement would be reasonable, having regard to the income of the beneficiary from all sources, and to such other factors, if any, as the court considers material,[5] and (b) the arrangement is approved by the alimentary beneficiary, or by the court on his behalf.[6]

ESTABLISHMENT AND OPERATION OF THE TRUST

An *inter vivos* trust is established only when the trust settlement, or conveyance in appropriate form of the subjects of trust,

[1] As in *Baroness Lloyd*, 1963 S.C. 37, where arrangement involved taking the funds out of the jurisdiction.

[2] The interest of a person may be protected by insurance: *Robertson*, 1962 S.C. 196; *Young's Trs.*, 1962 S.C. 293. See also *Aikman*, 1968 S.L.T. 137.

[3] Ibid., S. 1(3).

[4] Not merely a right of occupancy: *Countess of Lauderdale*, 1962 S.C. 302.

[5] In relation to this the court will have regard to the effect of the arrangement on the fiars of the liferented funds: *Colville*, 1962 S.C. 185.

[6] Ibid., S. 1(4). For examples of variations approved see *Colville*, 1962 S.C. 185; *Robertson*, 1962 S.C. 196; *Gibson's Tr.*, 1962 S.C. 204; *Findlays*, 1962 S.C. 210; *Dunlop*, 1962 S.C. 245; *Countess of Lauderdale*, 1962 S.C. 302; *Robinson*, 1962 S.L.T. 304; *Law*, 1962 S.C. 500; *Pelham Burn*, 1964 S.C. 3; *Phillips*, 1964 S.C. 141; *Wyndham*, 1964 S.L.T. 290; *Sutherland*, 1968 S.L.T. 252. Variation was refused as prejudicial to parties unborn in *Young's Trs.*, 1962 S.C. 293, and where it was impossible to say if the removal of the alimentary character would be reasonable: *Bergius' Trs.*, 1963 S.C. 194. It is unnecessary for the court to authorise variation in respect of a contingent alimentary liferent which the beneficiary could himself renounce: *Findlay*, *supra*; *Smillie*, 1966 S.L.T. 41; or of the revocation of an alimentary liferent which had ceased to be protected: *Cargill*, 1965 S.L.T. 193; or of a liferent which had ceased to be alimentary: *Strange*, 1966 S.L.T. 59; cf. *Law*, 1962 S.C. 500. Remote contingencies need not be insured against: *Buchanan*, 1964 S.C. 26. Approval was held unnecessary in the circumstances in *Dick*, 1963 S.C. 598.

If there is to be an immediate distribution of capital but the alimentary liferenter is not to take the full actuarial value of his interest insurance against estate duty liability in the event of the liferenter's early decease may be necessary: *Colville*, *supra*; *Gibson's Tr.*, *supra*.

has been executed and delivered to the trustees or beneficiaries, or to some person on behalf of either, not merely for safe-keeping, but with the intention of transferring right to the subjects of trust, that they be held against the granter and for behoof of the beneficiaries.[1]

A testamentary trust is established by the death of the truster, which makes the settlement irrevocable and is equivalent to delivery.

If there is no delivery there must be an equivalent which takes the subjects out of the truster's control and puts them in the control of the trustees or beneficiaries. This may be done by recording the deed in the Books of Council and Session,[2] or, with lesser presumption of intention, in the General Register of Sasines,[3] but not by merely taking the title to property in the name of another, or in one's own name as trustee for that other, which has the effect only of a testamentary destination.[4]

Intimation to the beneficiaries of the existence of a trust in their favour, does not make a revocable trust irrevocable,[5] nor complete a trust where there has been no divestiture,[6] and, if the truster had divested himself by delivery, is unnecessary.[7]

Acceptance of office

A person nominated as trustee is not compellable and may decline office. It is questionable whether any prior agreement between truster and trustee that the latter will act is legally enforceable.[8] An office holder nominated as trustee *ex officio* is not compellable unless acceptance is an express or implied condition of his holding the office.[9]

Declinature or disclaimer may be, and preferably should be, express but may be inferred from conduct such as refusal to allow his name to be used in trust documents. Delay by itself is not declinature,[10] but if prolonged may justify an inference of declinature. A clear declinature is final. An *ex officio* trustee may decline without prejudice to the right of his successors in office to

[1] *Cameron's Trs.* v. *C.*, 1907 S.C. 407.
[2] *Cameron's Trs.*, *supra*; see also *Tennent* v. *T's Trs.* (1869) 7 M. 936; *Obers* v. *Paton's Trs.* (1897) 24 R. 719.
[3] *Cameron's Trs.*, *supra*; *Carmichael* v. *C's Exors.*, 1920 S.C. (H.L.) 195, 202.
[4] *Dennis* v. *Aitchison*, 1923 S.C. 819, 825; 1924 S.C. (H.L.) 122.
[5] *Buyers* v. *Gemmell* (1895) 23 R. 332.
[6] *Cameron's Trs.*, *supra*.
[7] *Linton* v. *I.R.C.*, 1928 S.C. 209.
[8] Bell, *Comm.* I, 30; *Prin.* §1993.
[9] *Shepherd* v. *Hutton's Trs.* (1855) 17 D. 576.
[10] *Darling* v. *Watson* (1823) 2 S. 607.

act.[1] A trustee cannot accept in part and decline in part[2] though he may accept office as trustee but decline other offices, such as curator to children, associated with it.

A trustee nominate may accept expressly, and written acceptance is advisable,[3] or acceptance may be inferred from actings such as performing the duties of a trustee[4] or allowing his name to be used in trust documents[5] or so acting as to lead third parties to act in reliance on his being a trustee.[6] But intromissions with trust property may be explicable otherwise.

Duty to ascertain extent and purposes of trust estate

Trustees who accept must ascertain the nature and extent of the trust estate, and any circumstances relating to it, such as securities over parts of it, and ascertain the trust purposes.[7] Discovery of the nature and extent of the estate may involve some investigation, and the trustees must make reasonable inquiries to discover the trust assets and liabilities.

If any of the purposes are not clear, they should obtain expert advice thereon.

Vesting of property in trustees

The trustees who accept must take steps to complete title to the trust subjects in the modes appropriate to the different subjects, by taking possession of corporeal moveables, and having them kept in safe custody, by completing title, as trustees, to heritage, and by completing title in their own names, as trustees where competent,[8] to incorporeal moveable rights. The trustees will be personally liable if they allow trust estate to be lost by not reducing it to possession.[9]

In so far as the trust estate consists of debts owed to the trust estate by, or claims of damages against, other parties, the trustees

[1] *Edinburgh Mags.* v. *McLaren* (1881) 8 R. (H.L.) 140.
[2] *Cumming* v. *Hay* (1834) 12 S. 508; *Re Lord and Fullerton's Contract* [1896] 1 Ch. 228.
[3] *Millar* v. *Brodie's Trs.* (1902) 4 F. 846.
[4] *Blain* v. *Paterson* (1836) 14 S. 361; *Seton* v. *Dawson* (1841) 4 D. 310; *Watson* v. *Crawcour* (1843) 5 D. 1182.
[5] *Ker* v. *City of Glasgow Bank* (1879) 6 R. (H.L.) 52; *Cameron's Trs.* v. *C.*, 1907 S.C. 407.
[6] *Gillespie* v. *City of Glasgow Bank* (1879) 6 R. 813.
[7] cf. *Edmond* v. *L.P. of Aberdeen* (1898) 1 F. 154.
[8] No notice of any trust may be entered on the register of members of a company registered in England (Companies Act, 1948, S. 117) nor on the register of trade marks (Trade Marks Act, 1938, S. 64), register of patents (Patents Act, 1949, S. 73(3)) or register of designs (Registered Designs Act, 1949, S. 17(4)).
[9] *Millar's Trs.* v. *Polson* (1897) 24 R. 1038; *Mustard* v. *Mortimer's Trs.* (1899) 7 S.L.T 71.

must ingather sums due, without regard to the debtor's interest,[1] if necessary giving serious consideration to the necessity for litigation, but being entitled, if it is reasonable in the circumstances, to allow delay[2] or take a security[3] or payment by instalments, and in the case of claims of damages being bound to press them unless advised that the chance of recovering is small.[4]

Trustees have power to compromise,[5] or to submit and refer to arbitration all claims connected with the trust estate,[6] and such action is valid if the trustees use reasonable care and prudence and have taken competent advice, even though it later appears that the compromise was a bad bargain.[7] A compromise is not invalid though founded on a mistake in law if the trustees acted with reasonable care and genuinely considered the problem.[8] In making a reference trustees must act with reasonable prudence in the circumstances.[9]

The trustees must also ascertain the liabilities of the trust estate and pay outstanding debts. In the case of testamentary trusts the trustees cannot be compelled to pay debts until six months after the truster's death. They may then, if they believe after reasonable inquiry and on reasonable grounds, that the estate is solvent, pay *primo venienti* and without requiring the creditors to constitute their debts, if satisfied that they are proper charges on the estate,[10] but if the estate is small and the validity or amount of the claims doubtful, the trustees may require them to be formally constituted by decree.[11] The trustees must act impartially among the creditors and if the claims raise doubts as to the solvency of the estate, they should pay all rateably only and not prefer an unsecured creditor to one secured.[12]

Debts may be paid despite the existence of a future contingent claim against the estate.[13]

Trustees act as a body

In administering a trust in being the trustees act as a body and not by a majority. The trust deed may provide for administration

[1] *Lee's Trs.* v. *Dun*, 1913 S.C. (H.L.) 12.
[2] *Re Hurst* (1892) 67 L.T. 96.
[3] *Henderson* v. *H's Trs.* (1900) 3 F. 17.
[4] cf. *More's Exors.* v. *Malcolm* (1835) 13 S. 313; *Forman* v. *Burns* (1853) 15 D. 362; *Brown's Trs.* v. *B.* (1888) 15 R. 581.
[5] Bell, *Prin.* §1998.
[6] Bell, *Prin.* §1998; Trusts (Sc.) Act, 1921, S. 4(i).
[7] *Buchanan* v. *Eaton*, 1911 S.C. (H.L.) 40.
[8] *Hadden* v. *Bryden* (1899) 1 F. 710.
[9] *Thomson's Trs.* v. *Muir* (1867) 6 M. 145.
[10] *Laird* v. *Hamilton*, 1911 1 S.L.T. 27; 1921 Act, S. 4(1)(m).
[11] *McGaan* v. *McG's Trs.* (1883) 11 R. 249.
[12] *Laird, supra*; *Taylor & Ferguson* v. *Glass's Trs.*, 1912 S.C. 165.
[13] *Taylor, supra.*

by a prescribed quorum of trustees, in which case the prescribed number must both attend meetings and consent to acts of administration, and, by statute,[1] failing express contrary provision, every trust shall be held to include a provision that a majority of the trustees accepting and surviving shall be a quorum. While a quorum or majority may administer the estate, they should do nothing without consulting their co-trustees, giving them an opportunity to attend meetings, and information as to the business to be transacted.[2] Intimation of meetings and business thereat is unnecessary if the trustee had actual knowledge thereof and an opportunity to attend and state his views.[3] Where a deed bears to be granted by a quorum of trustees in favour of any person other than a beneficiary or co-trustee and it is in fact executed by a quorum and the grantee has dealt onerously and in good faith with the trustees, the deed is not void or challengeable on the ground that (1) any trustee or trustees under the trust was not consulted in the matter; or (2) that he did not concur in, or consent to the granting of the deed; or (3) that there has been any other omission or irregularity of procedure on the part of the trustees or any of them in relation to the granting of the deed.[4]

Position of minority trustees

An act of the majority binds the trust, but the minority trustees are not personally liable for any consequences of the act unless they authorised, acquiesced in or adopted the act of the majority.[5] Where the act is, however, the carrying into effect by a majority of a course of action agreed to by the minority, their acquiescence will be inferred.[6]

A minority cannot, in general, take independent action in the administration of the trust, but, as it is the duty of every trustee to protect the trust estate and to prevent breaches of trust by co-trustees, a minority may take action against the majority for improper alienation of trust property,[7] or to prevent action detrimental to the trust,[8] or to resolve a deadlock in trust

[1] 1921 Act, S. 3.

[2] *Malcolm* v. *Goldie* (1895) 22 R. 968; see also *Reid* v. *Maxwell* (1852) 14 D. 449; *Wyse* v. *Abbott* (1881) 8 R. 983; *Darling* v. *D.* (1898) 25 R. 747; *Stewart* v. *Dobie's Trs.*, 1914 2 S.L.T. 292; *Slimon* v. *S's Trs.*, 1915 2 S.L.T. 19.

[3] *Darling*, *supra*.

[4] 1921 Act, S. 7.

[5] *Higgins* v. *Livingstone* (1816) 2 Pat. 243; *Lumsden* v. *Buchanan* (1865) 3 M. (H.L.) 89.

[6] *Lumsden* v. *Buchanan* (1864) 2 M. 695, 743; *Cunninghame* v. *City of Glasgow Bank* (1879) 6 R. (H.L.) 98.

[7] *Ross* v. *Allan's Trs.* (1850) 13 D. 44.

[8] *Reid* v. *Maxwell* (1852) 14 D. 449.

administration,[1] or the minority may act alone against detriment to the trust estate when the consents of the others cannot be obtained,[2] or for their own protection.[3]

Personal liability of trustees to third parties

Where trustees contract with third parties, they are *prima facie* personally liable under their contract, unless there is express or implied agreement that the trust estate only is to be held bound.[4] In some cases the inference may be excluded by contracting expressly 'as trustees only',[5] but in cases of obligations constituted by bills of exchange the inference must be excluded by the clearest expression.[6] But the trustees' solicitor is presumed to contract with them as representatives only.[7]

Where trustees sell heritage they are bound only to grant warrandice from their own facts and deeds, but to bind the trust estate in absolute warrandice.[8] If they adopt the truster's contracts they may become personally liable for their implement.[9]

Resignation of trustees

At common law a trustee had probably no implied power to resign office.[10] Under the Trusts (Sc.) Act, 1921, S. 3(a) every trust is held, unless the contrary be expressed,[11] to include power to a trustee to resign.[12] Good grounds for doing so are ill-health,[13] or residence outwith the jurisdiction,[14] or conflict between personal

[1] *Dick* (1899) 2 F. 316.

[2] *McCulloch* v. *Wallace* (1846) 9 D. 32; *Stewart* v. *Dobie's Trs.* (1890) 1 F. 1183, 1187; *Duncan* v. *D.* (1892) 20 R. 200.

[3] *Taylor* v. *Noble* (1836) 14 S. 817.

[4] *Jeffrey* v. *Brown* (1824) 2 Sh. App. 102; *Cullen* v. *Baillie* (1846) 8 D. 511; *Lumsden* v. *Buchanan* (1865) 3 M. (H.L.) 89; *Brown* v. *Sutherland* (1875) 2 R. 615; cf. *Brebner* v. *Henderson*, 1925 S.C. 643.

[5] *Muir* v. *City of Glasgow Bank* (1879) 6 R. (H.L.) 21; *Mulholland* v. *Macfarlane's Trs.*, 1928 S.L.T. 251.

[6] *Brown* v. *Sutherland* (1875) 2 R. 615; cf. *Brebner, supra*; *Scottish & Newcastle Breweries, Ltd.* v. *Blair*, 1967 S.L.T. 72.

[7] *Cullen, supra*; *Ferme, Ferme & Williamson* v. *Stephenson's Trs.* (1905) 7 F. 902.

[8] *Forbes' Trs.* v. *Mackintosh* (1822) 1 S. 497; *Hill* v. *Kinloch* (1856) 18 D. 722; *Horsburgh* v. *Welch* (1886) 14 R. 67.

[9] *Laing* v. *Duff* (1845) 7 D. 556; *Dundas* v. *Morrison* (1857) 20 D. 225; *Mackessack* v. *Molleson* (1886) 13 R. 445. See also *Sturrock* v. *Robertson's Tr.*, 1913 S.C. 582.

[10] But see *Maclean* (1895) 22 R. 872.

[11] cf. *Maxwell's Trs.* v. *M.* (1874) 2 R. 71; *Thomson* v. *Miller's Trs.* (1883) 11 R. 401; *Anderson's Trs.*, 1932 S.C. 226.

[12] As to form of resignation, see S. 19(1).

[13] *Dick's Trs.* v. *Pridie* (1855) 17 D. 835.

[14] *Watson* v. *Crawcour* (1844) 6 D. 687; *Gordon* (1854) 16 D. 884; *Alison* (1886) 23 S.L.R. 362.

interests and those of the trust.[1] But a sole trustee is not entitled to resign unless he has assumed new trustees and they have accepted office, or the court has appointed new trustees or a judicial factor.[2] If trustees all wish to resign they must first assume new trustees or apply for appointment of new trustees or a judicial factor.[3]

A trustee who has accepted any legacy or bequest or annuity expressly given on condition of his accepting the office of trustee may not resign under the Act, unless otherwise expressly declared in the trust deed,[4] nor may a trustee appointed on the footing of receiving remuneration for his services resign in the absence of express power to do so; but the court may authorise such a trustee to resign on such conditions, if any, as to repayment or otherwise of his legacy as the court may think just.[5] In granting authority to resign the court has regard to the interests of the trust,[6] but cannot refuse it merely because it might prejudice beneficiaries or cause expense to the trust.[7] A trustee who resigns though not entitled to do so probably remains liable as a trustee, and transactions with the trust estate may be challengeable as not having his consent.[8]

A trustee entitled to resign may do so by minute entered in the trust sederunt book and signed by him and the other trustees. It take immediate effect. Or he may sign a minute of resignation in the form of Schedule A to the Act, register it in the Books of Council and Session, and intimate it to the remaining trustees or, if the residence of any cannot be found, to the Keeper of Edictal Citations. Such a resignation takes effect on the receipt of the last intimation.[9] Resignation once completed cannot be withdrawn.[10]

When resignation is completed the trustee is divested of the whole property and estate of the trust, which devolves on the remaining trustees without conveyance or transfer, though a conveyance may be demanded.[11]

[1] *Guthrie* (1895) 22 R. 879; *Johnston*, 1932 S.N. 38.
[2] 1921 Act, S. 3, proviso (1), and S. 19(2); *Walker* v. *Downie*, 1933 S.L.T. 30.
[3] *Maxwell's Trs., supra*; *Erentz's Trs.* v. *E's J.F.* (1897) 25 R. 53; *McConnell's Trs.* (1897) 25 R. 330.
[4] See *Bunten* v. *Muir* (1894) 21 R. 370; *Assets Co.* v. *Shirress* (1896) 4 S.L.T. 120.
[5] 1921 Act, S. 3, proviso (2); *Johnston*, 1932 S.L.T. 261; *Collie*, 1933 S.L.T. 46.
[6] *Dick's Trs.* v. *Pridie* (1855) 17 D. 835; *Alison* (1886) 23 S.L.R. 362; *Scott* v. *Muir* (1894) 22 R. 78; *Guthrie* (1895) 22 R. 879; *Tod* v. *Marshall* (1895) 23 R. 36; *Orphoot* (1897) 24 R. 871; *Johnston*, 1932 S.L.T. 261.
[7] *McConnell's Trs.* (1897) 25 R. 330.
[8] *Hill* v. *Mitchell* (1846) 9 D. 239; *Maclean* (1895) 22 R. 872.
[9] 1921 Act, S. 19(1).
[10] *Fullerton's Trs.* v. *James* (1895) 23 R. 105.
[11] 1921 Act, S. 20.

The resignation of a trustee also appointed an executor implies resignation also as executor, unless the contrary is expressly declared.[1]

After resignation a trustee is not responsible for anything done by his successors in administering the trust. He is entitled for his own protection to obtain a discharge from the other trustees[2] or from the beneficiaries, if of full age and not incapacitated, failing which he may petition the court for discharge.[3] A discharge by co-trustees probably does not exonerate from liability for acts done while a trustee, but only for acts done after his resignation,[4] and such a discharge is reducible if obtained fraudulently or in breach of trust.[5]

Assumption of new trustees

Unless the contrary is expressed, all trusts are held to include power to the trustee or trustees, or to a quorum of the trustees,[6] to assume new trustees.[7] This power will not be excluded by implication,[8] and is additional to any power conferred by the trust deed,[9] but may be excluded where the power is a matter of contract, as in a marriage-contract trust.[10]

Whether and when to exercise the power is in the discretion of the trustees, unless the trust deed requires that there be a prescribed number of trustees. If a majority or quorum is exercising the power notice must be given to all the trustees[11] who are available to act.[12] The minority may object only on allegations of impropriety or corruption or similar matters of bad faith.[13]

If any trustee is insane or incapable of acting by reason of physical and mental disability or by continuous absence from the U.K. for six months or more, the remaining trustee or trustees may assume new trustees, but when the signatures of a quorum of

1 1921 Act, S. 28.

2 Ibid., S. 4(g).

3 Ibid., S. 18; see *Mackenzie's Trs.* v. *Sutherland* (1895) 22 R. 233; *Matthew's Tr.* (1894) 2 S.L.T. 122.

4 *Duncan* (1882) 20 S.L.R. 8.

5 *Hastie's J.F.* v. *Morham's Exors.*, 1951 S.C. 668.

6 Including assumed trustees and trustees appointed by the Court: 1921 Act, S. 2; but not a judicial factor: 1921 Act, S. 5(3).

7 1921 Act, S. 3(b).

8 *Allan's Trs.* v. *Hairstens* (1878) 5 R. 576.

9 *Maxwell's Trs.* v. *M.* (1874) 2 R. 71; *Allan's Trs., supra*; but see *Anderson's Trs.* v. *A.*, 1932 S.C. 226, 231; *Thomson* v. *Miller's Trs.* (1883) 11 R. 401.

10 *Munro's Trs.* v. *Young* (1887) 14 R. 574.

11 *Wyse* v. *Abbot* (1881) 8 R. 983.

12 *Malcolm* v. *Goldie* (1895) 22 R. 968.

13 *Neilson* v. *N's Trs.* (1885) 12 R. 670.

trustees cannot be obtained, it is necessary to obtain the consent of the court on application by the acting trustee or trustees or any one or more of the beneficiaries.[1]

In exercising the power a trustee should take reasonable care that the new trustees are fit persons for the office.

If a trustee is assuming others to enable him to resign he owes a special duty to the beneficiaries to take care in the selection of the new trustees and, despite his retiral, he might be held liable for any breach of trust which was an object of his retiral,[2] but not merely if his retiral had permitted or facilitated a breach of trust.[3]

Where there is a deadlock as to the assumption of a trustee the Court may intervene *nobili officio* to make an appointment,[4] and it may in special circumstances interdict the assumption of new trustees.[5]

Assumption is effected by deed of assumption in the form of Sched. B to the 1921 Act, executed by the assuming trustees; it contains a general conveyance to the whole trustees, existing and assumed, of the trust estate, and may contain a special conveyance of heritable property, and is effectual as an assignation in favour of the whole trustees of the trust moveable property.[6]

Assumed trustees have the same powers as nominated trustees, unless the trust deed provides otherwise,[7] and they may in turn assume further trustees.[8] They are not personally liable for their predecessors' administration, unless they have homologated it or acquiesced in it, but they are bound to account for their predecessors' intromissions, so far as these have not been examined and discharged.[9]

Appointment of new trustees by truster

If the trustees appointed fail the truster, if still alive, may appoint new trustees.[10] In private *inter vivos* trusts, such as marriage contract trusts, there is implied a power to appoint new

[1] 1921 Act, S. 21.
[2] *Head* v. *Gould* [1898] 2 Ch. 250.
[3] *Clark* v. *Hoskins* (1868) 37 L.J. Ch. 561.
[4] *Aikman* (1881) 9 R. 213; *Dick* (1899) 2 F. 316; *Taylor*, 1932 S.C. 1.
[5] *Neilson* v. *N's Trs.* (1885) 12 R. 670; *Neilson* v. *Mossend Iron Co.* (1885) 12 R. 499; *Foggo* (1893) 20 R. 273.
[6] 1921 Act, S. 21.
[7] e.g. *Wilson's Tr.* v. *W.*, 1909 1 S.L.T. 124; *Waddell's Trs.* v. *Crawford*, 1926 S.C. 654.
[8] A judicial factor has no such power of assumption: 1921 Act, S. 26.
[9] *Somerville's Trs.* v. *Wemyss* (1854) 17 D. 151.
[10] *Glentanar* v. *Scottish Industrial Musical Assocn.*, 1925 S.C. 226.

trustees.[1] In a public trust new trustees must be appointed by the court under the *nobile officium*.[2] If the truster is dead, the power to appoint new trustees may have been conferred on the trustees nominated or on a third party.

Appointment of new trustees by the court

When trustees cannot be assumed under any trust deed[3] or when any person who is the sole trustee appointed in or acting under any trust deed is or has become insane or is or has become incapable of acting by reason of physical or mental disability, or by being absent continuously from the United Kingdom for a period of at least six months, or by having disappeared for a like period, the court may, on the application of any party having interest in the trust estate,[4] appoint a trustee or trustees with all the powers incident to the office, in which case the trustee who has become insane or incapable of acting ceases to be a trustee. The Court may grant warrant to complete title to heritable property, specifying or referring to it, and specification therein of moveable or personal property is effectual as an assignation in favour of the trustees so appointed.[5] The court will generally appoint only persons subject to Scottish jurisdiction,[6] and will act only where there is no trustee who can assume new trustees.

Under the *nobile officium* the Court may appoint new trustees whenever that is necessary for the administration of the trust.[7]

The court will not, however, appoint new trustees under an English trust, even though it holds Scottish heritage.[8]

Removal of trustees

The Court may at common law, for the protection of the beneficiaries, and the proper administration of the trust, remove a trustee from office.[9] This is clearly justified if the trustee is

1 *Wilson* (1864) 2 M. 1304; *Newlands* v. *Miller* (1882) 9 R. 1104. But see *Welsh's Trs.* v. *W.* (1871) 10 M. 16; *Malcolm* v. *Goldie* (1895) 22 R. 968.

2 *Glentanar, supra.*

3 e.g. where no trustees have been appointed: *Pattullo* (1908) 16 S.L.T. 637; *Auld*, 1925 S.L.T. 83; or those appointed have failed: *Zoller* (1868) 6 M. 577; *Graham* (1868) 6 M. 958; this provision does not cover the case of a deadlock among trustees: *Aikman* (1881) 9 R. 213; *Dick* (1899) 2 F. 316; *Taylor*, 1932 S.C. 1.

4 Including beneficiaries.

5 1921 Act, S. 22; *Boazman*, 1938 S.L.T. 582.

6 *Simpson's Trs.*, 1907 S.C. 87; *Stewart's Trs.*, 1913 S.C. 647; see also *Coats's Trs.*, 1925 S.C. 104.

7 *Lamont* v. *L.*, 1908 S.C. 1033; *Taylor*, 1932 S.C. 1.

8 *Hall* (1869) 7 M. 667; *Brockie* (1875) 2 R. 923; *Cripp's Trs.* v. *C.*, 1926 S.C. 188.

9 *Taylor* v. *Adams's Trs.* (1876) 13 S.L.R. 268; *Gilchrist's Trs.* v. *Dick* (1883) 11 R. 22; *Orr Ewing's Trs.* v. *O.E.* (1885) 13 R. (H.L.) 1; *Harris* v. *Howie's Trs.* (1893) 21 R. 16; *Stewart* v. *Chalmers* (1904) 7 F. 163; *Wishart*, 1910 2 S.L.T. 229.

sacrificing the interest of the trust, or acting dishonestly,[1] but may be justified even by deliberate interference with trust purposes,[2] but is not normally justified by mere negligent management of the trust[3] or disharmony among the trustees.[4] It may be justified if the trustee is unable to act impartially as trustee consistently with his position in some other capacity,[5] or where some of the trustees were furth of Scotland and made no attempt to participate in trust business.[6] A trustee's sequestration is sometimes a good ground for removing him.[7]

By statute[8] when any person who is sole trustee is or has become insane or incapable of acting by reason of physical or mental disability or by being absent continuously from the United Kingdom for a period of at least six months or by having disappeared for a like period, the Court may appoint new trustees, superseding the person insane, incapable or absent thereby.[9]

Further,[10] if any trustee is insane or incapable of acting by reason of physical or mental disability or absent from the United Kingdom continuously for at least six months or has disappeared for a like period, such trustee shall, in the cases of insanity or incapacity,[11] and may, in the other cases, on application by any co-trustee or beneficiary or other person interested in the trust estate, be removed from office by the court.[12]

Superseding trustees by judicial factor

The Court may sequestrate the trust estate and appoint a judicial factor to administer it, thereby superseding the trustees in their administration but not removing them. The appointment is

[1] *Birnie* v. *Christie* (1891) 19 R. 334; *Whyte* (1891) 28 S.L.R. 901; *Wishart, supra*; *Gilchrist's Trs.* v. *Dick* (1883) 11 R. 22. See also *Dryburgh* v. *Walker's Trs.* (1873) 1 R. 31.

[2] *Jackson* v. *Welch* (1865) 4 M. 177; *McWhirter* v. *Latta* (1889) 17 R. 68; *Whyte* (1891) 28 S.L.R. 901.

[3] *Taylor* v. *Adam's Trs.* (1876) 13 S.L.R. 268; *Gilchrist's Trs., supra*; *Harris* v. *Howie's Trs.* (1893) 21 R. 16.

[4] *Hope* v. *H.* (1884) 12 R. 27; *Stewart* v. *Chalmers* (1904) 7 F. 163; *MacGilchrist's Trs.* v. *MacG.*, 1930 S.C. 635.

[5] *Thomson* v. *Dalrymple* (1865) 3 M. 336; *Cherry* v. *Patrick*, 1910 S.C. 32.

[6] *Walker* (1869) 6 M. 973.

[7] *Soutar's Trs.* v. *Brown* (1852) 15 D. 89; *Neilson* (1865) 3 M. 559; *Jackson* v. *Welch* (1865) 4 M. 177; *Walker, supra*; *Whittle* v. *Carruthers* (1896) 23 R. 775; *Stewart* v. *Chalmers* (1904) 7 F. 163; *Wishart, supra.*

[8] 1921 Act, S. 22.

[9] cf. *Walker* (1868) 6 M. 973; *Lees* (1893) 1 S.L.T. 42.

[10] 1921 Act, S. 23.

[11] *Tod* v. *Marshall* (1895) 23 R. 36.

[12] cf. *Waugh's Tr.* (1892) 20 R. 57; *Dickson's Trs.* (1894) 2 S.L.T. 61.

sought by petition at the instance of the trustees or some of them or of the beneficiaries. A ground less than would justify removal of the trustees may justify their supersession by a judicial factor, such as a deadlock in administration;[1] a ground which would justify removal will probably always justify their supersession by a judicial factor. Sequestration is also appropriate where the trustees' conduct seems to make it dangerous to leave the trust in their hands,[2] or where the trustee interferes with the rights of parties.[3]

Such sequestration is a temporary expedient and the factor's appointment may be recalled at any time on cause shown.[4]

ADMINISTRATION OF THE TRUST

During the period of the trustees' administration of the trust their major duty is to conserve the trust estate.

Duty to ingather estate

Trustees' first duty is to reduce to possession, ingather and, where appropriate, realise the trust estate committed to them. Thus they must sell the goodwill of the truster's business[5] and recover debts due to the trust,[6] and may be liable in damages for undue delay in realisation of assets,[7] or loss suffered by the trust by reason of their lack of diligence.

Duty to pay debts

Debts must be paid before anything is distributed to beneficiaries. Testamentary trustees are entitled after six months from the truster's death, unless the estate may be insolvent, to pay creditors *primo venienti*.[8] They must make provision for secured or other preferential debts,[9] but need not make provision for contingent claims against the estate.[10] Creditors must, if required,

1 *Morris* v. *Bain* (1858) 20 D. 716; *Wyse* v. *Abbot* (1881) 8 R. 983; *Stewart* v. *Morrison* (1892) 19 R. 1009; *Henderson* v. *H.* (1893) 20 R. 536; contrast *Scott* (1905) 13 S.L.T. 589; *Young's Trs.*, 1930 S.L.T. 731.

2 *Morris* v. *Bain* (1858) 20 D. 716; *Henderson* (1901) 9 S.L.T. 16; *Young* (1901) 9 S.L.T. 20.

3 *McWhirter* v. *Latta* (1889) 17 R. 68.

4 *Sawers* v. *S's Tr.* (1891) 19 S.L.R. 258.

5 *Donald* v. *Hodgart's Trs.* (1893) 21 R. 246.

6 *Carruthers* v. *Cairns* (1890) 17 R. 769.

7 *Murray's Trs.* v. *M.* (1905) 13 S.L.T. 274.

8 *Stewart's Trs.* v. *Evans* (1871) 9 M. 810; *Taylor & Ferguson* v. *Glass's Trs.*, 1912 S.C. 165.

9 *Lamond's Trs.* v. *Croom* (1871) 9 M. 662; *Beith & Mackenzie* (1875) 3 R. 185.

10 *Taylor & Ferguson*, *supra*.

prove their claims by competent evidence.[1] Trustees are personally liable to creditors who have made claims, or whose claims are known, if they distribute the estate without meeting the creditors' claims. After six months creditors must, if the estate has been distributed, claim against the beneficiaries.[2]

Duty to pay expenses of the trust

The trustees are bound to pay out of the trust estate the testator's death-bed and funeral expenses, the dues for confirmation, the charges of solicitors, valuators, stockbrokers, and others reasonably employed,[3] the expense of petitioning the court, where necessary, and similar necessary outlays. In the case of a continuing trust, the initial expenses of realising and ingathering the estate and all extraordinary expenses are chargeable against capital, but the ordinary and continuing expenses of administration are chargeable against revenue.[4]

Duty of distribution or administration

Once the trustees have ingathered all the trust assets and paid all debts and obligations immediately due, together with the necessary expenses of these transactions, they must distribute the estate to the beneficiaries entitled thereto, or hold and administer the trust assets for the trust purposes, as the trust purposes may require.

Directions which are self-contradictory,[5] illegal, *contra bonos mores* or contrary to public policy cannot be implemented, and directions to do what could immediately be undone by the beneficiary need not be followed.[6]

Duty of care

A trustee is under a duty in administering the trust to exercise the care of a reasonably prudent man,[7] which is judged

[1] cf. *Farquhar* v. *F.* (1886) 13 R. 596; *Dunn's Tr.* v. *Hardy* (1896) 23 R. 621.

[2] *Beith* v. *Mackenzie* (1875) 3 R. 185.

[3] 1921 Act, S. 4(f); *Thomson* v. *Douglas* (1856) 18 D. 1240; *Baxter & Mitchell* v. *Wood* (1864) 2 M. 915.

[4] *Pearson* v. *Casamajor* (1840) 2 D. 1020; *Thomson* v. *Douglas* (1856) 18 D. 1240; *Baxter & Mitchell* v. *Wood* (1864) 2 M. 915; *Smith* v. *Bennie* (1890) 18 R. 44; *Howden* v. *Simson* (1895) 23 R. 113.

[5] *Murray* v. *Matheson's Trs.* (1896) 6 S.L.T. 149; *Leask* v. *Fourth Edinburgh Property Investment Co.* (1898) 6 S.L.T. 161.

[6] *Spens* v. *Monypenny's Trs.* (1875) 3 R. 50; *Dow* v. *Kilgour's Trs.* (1877) 4 R. 403; *Kennedy's Trs.* v. *Warren* (1901) 3 F. 1087; *Turner's Trs.* v. *Fernie*, 1908 S.C. 883.

[7] *Speight* v. *Gaunt* (1883) 9 App. Cas. 1, 20; *Learoyd* v. *Whiteley* (1887) 12 App. Cas. 727, 733; *Knox* v. *Mackinnon* (1888) 15 R. (H.L.) 83; *Raes* v. *Meek* (1889) 16 R. (H.L.) 31, 33; *Buchanan* v. *Eaton*, 1911 S.C. (H.L.) 40, 45.

objectively.[1] It is immaterial that the office of trustee is not gratuitous,[2] though a remunerated trustee may be liable if he does not have the business skill which he professes when accepting the duty of trust.[3]

While a high standard is set by the court there is not absolute liability for error or loss, nor for mere error of judgment, but good faith, honesty and conduct adequate by the trustee's own judgment do not necessarily amount to care reasonable in the view of the court. Whether a trustee has taken reasonable care or been negligent depends on the circumstances as they were known at the time, including reasonably foreseeable future possibilities, but conduct is not to be judged by hindsight.[4]

Duty not to delegate

A trustee must retain the control and administration of the trust and not delegate or surrender it to fellow-trustees or agents.[5] But a trustee may, and should, employ persons of knowledge and skill to advise on technical matters, and to carry out technical operations, within the spheres of their respective technical competences, in circumstances where a reasonably prudent man would do so in managing his own affairs.[6] He must not, however, subordinate his judgment to their advice, but must seek to evaluate it and himself take the decisions. Such persons must be properly qualified,[7] employed only within the sphere of their professional competence and function,[8] supervised so far as is reasonable in the circumstances,[9] and questions of policy must be reserved to the trustee.[10]

Provided the trustee employs properly qualified and competent advisers, he is not liable for dishonesty or malperformance of duties properly entrusted to them.[11]

[1] *Learoyd*; *Knox*; *Raes*; *supra*. [2] *Jobson* v. *Palmer* [1893] 1 Ch. 71.

[3] *Speight*, *supra*; *National Trs. Co. of Australasia* v. *General Finance Co. of Australasia* [1905] A.C. 373.

[4] *Gillespie* v. *Gardner*, 1909 S.C. 1053.

[5] *Wyman* v. *Paterson* (1900) 2 F. (H.L.) 37; cf. *Wolfe* v. *Richardson*, 1927 S.L.T. 490.

[6] *Wilson's Tr.* v. *Wilson's Crs.* (1863) 2 M. 9; *Leith* v. *East Coast S.S. Co.*, 1909 1 S.L.T. 53; e.g. accountant: *Peddie* v. *Beveridge* (1860) 22 D. 707; solicitor: *Taylor* v. *Adam's Trs.* (1876) 13 S.L.R. 268; stockbroker: *Speight* v. *Gaunt* (1883) 9 App. Cas. 1, 10. There is power at common law: *Hay* v. *Binny* (1861) 23 D. 594, and under the Trusts (Sc.) Act, 1921, S. 4(f), to appoint factors and law agents and to pay them suitable remuneration. See also *Cormack* v. *Keith & Murray* (1893) 20 R. 977.

[7] *Speight*, *supra*; *Robinson* v. *Harkin* [1896] 2 Ch. 415.

[8] *Speight*, *supra*; *Johnstone* v. *Thorburn* (1901) 3 F. 497.

[9] *Speight*, *supra*; *Wyman*, *supra*.

[10] *Learoyd* v. *Whiteley* (1887) 12 App. Cas. 727.

[11] *Speight*, *supra*.

Duty not to be auctor in rem suam

A trustee must not permit a conflict between his own interests and those of the trust wherein the former does or may benefit at the expense of the latter. Any benefit or profit arising from the office of trust or the management of the trust property cannot accordingly be taken by the trustee but must be attributed to the trust estate.[1]

A trustee accordingly must act gratuitously and take no fee for work done or time spent on trust business even in a professional capacity, unless the truster authorised him to do so or all the beneficiaries have expressly or impliedly agreed to a charge being made,[2] and not even if it is beneficial to the trust that a trustee should do work for the trust personally.[3] Nor may the trustee's firm or professional partner act for remuneration.[4] If a trustee acts in a professional capacity for the trust he may recover only his outlays.[5]

But a trustee may receive payment from the trust for services rendered in another capacity under a pre-existing agreement, such as a contract of employment with the deceased truster.[6]

Duty not to make profit from the trust

A trustee must also make no personal profit from the trust, unless the truster has authorised it or all the beneficiaries consent, and any benefit accruing to him from the use or possession of trust property is held to belong to the trust.[7] Thus if goods are sold by a trustee to the trust estate the profit falls to be paid to the trust.[8] Trustees who converted the truster's business into a company were held not entitled to apply for shares therein.[9] An assignation of a lease by trustees of an insolvent deceased has been reduced at the instance of creditors on the estate.[10] A trustee has

[1] *Huntington Copper Co.* v. *Henderson* (1877) 4 R. 294; 5 R. (H.L.) 1; *Caldwell's Trs.* v. *C.*, 1923 S.L.T. 694; *Lister* v. *Marshall's Tr.*, 1927 S.N. 55.

[2] *Home* v. *Pringle* (1841) 2 Rob. 384; *Robertson* v. *Morison* (1849) 6 Bell 422; *Lord Gray and Others* (1856) 19 D. 1; *Lauder* v. *Millars* (1859) 21 D. 1353; *Lewis's Trs.* v. *Pirie*, 1912 S.C. 574; *Henderson* v. *Watson*, 1939 S.C. 711.

[3] *Mackie's Trs.* v. *M.* (1875) 2 R. 312.

[4] *Lord Gray, supra*; *Mitchell* v. *Burness* (1878) 5 R. 1124; *Henderson, supra.*

[5] *Aitken* v. *Hunter* (1871) 9 M. 756; *Munro's Trs.* v. *Murray & Ferrier* (1871) 9 S.L.R. 174. Contrast *Lewis's Trs.* v. *Pirie*, 1912 S.C. 574.

[6] *Lawrie* v. *L's Trs.* (1892) 19 R. 675.

[7] *Laird* v. *L.* (1858) 20 D. 972; *Aberdeen Mags.* v. *Aberdeen Univ.* (1877) 4 R. (H.L.) 48; *Henderson* v. *Watson*, 1939 S.C. 711; *Wilson* v. *Smith's Trs.*, 1939 S.L.T. 120.

[8] *Henderson* v. *Huntington Copper Co.* (1877) 5 R. (H.L.) 1; *Cherry's Trs.* v. *Patrick*, 1911 2 S.L.T. 313.

[9] *Taylor* v. *Hillhouse's Trs.* (1901) 9 S.L.T. 31.

[10] *Meff* v. *Smith's Trs.*, 1930 S.N. 162.

been permitted, however, to bid at an auction of trust property at upset prices fixed by an independent valuation.[1]

Trustee transacting with trust estate

The trustee must also refrain from transacting as an individual with the trust estate, and any such purported transaction is voidable even though there be no evidence of unfairness or prejudice to the trust.[2] This principle strikes at direct,[3] indirect[4] and collusive[5] transactions equally. It does not prohibit a transaction between the trust estate and a relative of a trustee, so long as the latter is acting independently and not collusively for the trustee,[6] nor between a trustee under one trust and himself as trustee under another trust,[7] nor between a trustee and a third party who purchased trust estate unconditionally.[8]

A trustee is not entitled to evade this principle by resigning office and thereby obtaining a contract which the trustees could not have obtained.[9]

This principle suffers exception in the case of a trust deed for creditors, where the trustee is customarily held entitled to a commission on the money he has to handle.[10]

So, too, trustees may not lend trust money to one of themselves, even if he gives proper security for repayment.[11]

A trustee may, however, transact with a beneficiary in relation to the latter's interest in the trust estate, but in view of the fiduciary relationship it must be shown that the trustee acted fairly and honestly, gave full information and full value and did not take advantage of the beneficiary.[12]

1 *Coats's Trs.*, 1914 S.C. 723. A beneficiary may lawfully bid: *Shiell* v. *Guthrie's Trs.* (1874) 1 R. 1083.

2 *York Buildings Co.* v. *Mackenzie* (1795) 3 Pat. 378; *Aberdeen Ry. Co.* v. *Blaikie Bros.* (1854) 1 Macq. 461; *Hall's Trs.* v. *McArthur*, 1918 S.C. 646.

3 *Perston* v. *P's Trs.* (1863) 1 M. 245.

4 *Keech* v. *Sandford* (1726) Cha. Cas. 61; *Wilson's Trs.* v. *W.* (1789) Mor. 16376; *McNiven* v. *Peffers* (1868) 7 M. 181; *Ritchie* v. *R's Trs.* (1888) 15 R. 1086; *Halley's Trs.* v. *H.*, 1920 2 S.L.T. 343.

5 *Gillies* v. *Maclachlan's Reps.* (1846) 8 D. 487; *Aberdeen Mags.* v. *Aberdeen Univ.* (1877) 4 R. (H.L.) 48; *Dunn* v. *Chambers* (1897) 25 R. 247; *Taylor* v. *Hillhouse's Trs.* (1901) 9 S.L.T. 31.

6 *Burrell* v. *B's Trs.*, 1915 S.C. 333.

7 *Templeton* v. *Burgh of Ayr*, 1912 1 S.L.T. 421.

8 *Wright* v. *Morgan* [1926] A.C. 788.

9 *Halley's Trs.* v. *H.*, 1920 2 S.L.T. 343.

10 *Dall* v. *Drummond* (1870) 8 M. 1006.

11 *Perston* v. *P's Trs.* (1863) 1 M. 245; *Ritchie* v. *R's Trs.* (1888) 15 R. 1086; *Croskery* v. *Gilmour's Trs.* (1890) 17 R. 700.

12 *Grieve* v. *Cunningham* (1869) 8 M. 317; *Thomson* v. *Eastwood* (1877) 2 App. Cas. 215; *Buckner* v. *Jopp's Trs.* (1887) 14 R. 1006; *Dougan* v. *Macpherson* (1902) 4 F. (H.L.) 7; *Aitken* v. *Campbell's Trs.*, 1909 S.C. 1217; *Stewart* v. *MacLaren*, 1920 S.C. (H.L.) 148.

Challenge

Making charges, taking benefits, or transacting with the trust estate are acts not void but voidable. They may be authorised or ratified. Normally only a trust beneficiary has title to challenge any such transaction[1] and he must also have an interest to do so,[2] though if the trust estate is insolvent the creditors may challenge any payments to a trustee for professional services,[3] and the truster or his representatives may challenge a trustee's transaction if prejudicial to their reversionary rights.[4]

Authority to trustee to charge

Failing contrary provision in the trust deed, a trustee must act gratuitously. But the truster may authorise a trustee to charge for his services, benefit from the trust, or transact with it. The extent of authority conferred depends on the interpretation of the grant.[5] Authority to trustees to appoint one of themselves to do work normally remunerated, such as to act as trust solicitor, implies authority to pay him ordinary professional fees,[6] but not to pay for work as trustee and not in a professional capacity.[7] Failing such authority a trustee who acts in a professional capacity is entitled to his outlays only, but to no fees, and this rule disqualifies his firm also.[8]

The beneficiaries may expressly or impliedly allow a trustee to charge for his services, benefit from the trust or transact with it, so long as they have full knowledge of their rights in the matter, and preferably also have independent legal advice,[9] or they may bar themselves from objecting to charges made for work done for the trust.[10]

1 *Aberdeen* v. *Stratton's Trs.* (1867) 5 M. 726; *Fleming* v. *Imrie* (1868) 6 M. 363; *Brown's Trs.* v. *Horne* (1905) 12 S.L.T. 614; 15 S.L.T. 205n.

2 *Ashburton* v. *Escombe* (1892) 20 R. 187.

3 *Bonaccord Marine Ass. Co.* v. *Souter's Trs.* (1850) 12 D. 1010.

4 *Hamilton* v. *Wright* (1842) 1 Bell 574.

5 *Mills* v. *Brown's Trs.* (1900) 2 F. 1035.

6 *Goodsir* v. *Carruthers* (1858) 20 D. 1141; *Lewis's Trs.* v. *Pirie*, 1912 S.C. 577; cf. *Cameron's Trs.* v. *C.* (1864) 3 M. 200.

7 *Re Chalinder and Herington* [1906] 1 Ch. 58.

8 *Seton* v. *Dawson* (1841) 4 D. 310; *Fegan* v. *Thomson* (1855) 17 D. 1146; *Manson* v. *Baillie* (1855) 2 Macq. 80; *Lord Gray* (1856) 19 D. 1; *Turner* v. *Fraser's Trs.* (1897) 24 R. 673.

9 *Munro's Trs.* v. *Murray* (1871) 9 S.L.R. 174.

10 *Ommanney* v. *Smith* (1854) 16 D. 721; *Dixon* v. *Rutherford* (1863) 2 M. 61; *Scott* v. *Handyside's Trs.* (1868) 6 M. 753.

Benefits to or transactions with former or subsequent trustees

It is clear that a trustee cannot evade the principle that he must not benefit from or transact with the trust merely by resigning,[1] but it is uncertain whether the prohibition prevents any former trustee from benefiting or transacting with the trust, and, if so, for how long.[2] Probably if the trustees had resigned office before the transaction was ever mooted, it would be valid, unless challengeable on other grounds.[3]

A benefit to or transaction with a person is not challengeable merely because that person later becomes a trustee,[4] though it may be doubtful in the case of a prospective trustee, or one having the power to become a trustee.[5]

Power and duty to appoint solicitors and factors

Trustees have power, unless it is at variance with the terms or purposes of the trust, to appoint factors and law agents and to pay them suitable remuneration.[6] Unless they are men of business they probably have a duty to appoint a solicitor. A solicitor nominated in the trust deed has no permanent right to the post and cannot prevent the trustees superseding him.[7] Even a trustee so nominated may be superseded, unless the legal functions are made part of his duties as trustee.[8]

If trustees are authorised to appoint one of themselves as solicitor to the trust they should do so by resolution, duly minuted, but even if appointed informally such a person may claim remuneration for his services.[9] Trustees appointed by the court may appoint and remunerate one of themselves as solicitor and factor.[10]

A trustee who acts as solicitor is not entitled to professional remuneration but only to reimbursement of outlays, unless the trust deed authorises the payment of remuneration.[11]

1 *Ex parte James* (1803) 8 Ves. 353; *Wright* v. *Morgan* [1926] A.C. 788.

2 See *Brown* v. *Burt* (1848) 11 D. 338; *Aberdeen Ry. Co.* v. *Blaikie Bros.* (1854) 1 Macq. 461; *Dunn* v. *Chambers* (1897) 25 R. 247; *Re Boles and British Land Co.'s Contract* [1902] 1 Ch. 244.

3 But see *Hamilton* v. *Wright* (1842) 1 Bell 574, 591.

4 *Fleming* v. *Irvine* (1868) 6 M. 363.

5 *Clark* v. *C.* (1884) 9 App. Cas. 733.

6 Trusts (Sc.) Act, 1961, S. 4(f).

7 *Cormack* v. *Keith & Murray* (1893) 20 R. 977.

8 *Nairn's Trs.* v. *Stewart*, 1910 2 S.L.T. 432.

9 *Lewis's Trs.* v. *Pirie*, 1912 S.C. 574.

10 *Allan's Tr.* v. *McDougall* (1899) 7 S.L.T. 26.

11 *Scott* v. *Handyside's Trs.* (1868) 6 M. 753; *Munro's Trs.* v. *Murray & Ferrier* (1871) 9 S.L.R. 174.

Duties of trust solicitor

His duties are to give legal advice on legal matters referred to him, to frame legal documents, negotiate tax matters, conduct correspondence and receive and pay money on behalf of the trust.

It is no part of a trust solicitor's duty to volunteer advice as to investments,[1] or make enquiries as to the financial sufficiency of investments.[2]

Liability of trustees for their solicitor or factor

Trustees must supervise their solicitor or factor and are liable for losses caused by their failure, as by allowing trust funds to remain in his control and be embezzled.[3]

Duty and powers of investment

If the trust is a continuing one the trustees must invest all funds in their care in investments authorised by statute or the trust deed, realising any not so authorised and reinvesting the proceeds. The balance of uninvested cash should be kept as low as is reasonably practicable, and trustees are personally liable for loss of interest on funds which could and should have been invested.[4] There should be no unreasonable delay in doing so though circumstances may justify some delay.[5]

Trustees have been held liable for the loss sustained by leaving money an unreasonable time on deposit receipt.[6]

At common law a trustee could be said to be exercising his duty of care in relation to investments only if he invested in fixed interest securities of H.M. Government and of public and local authorities in the United Kingdom, or on heritable security.

Powers conferred by trust deed

A trust deed may confer wider powers of investment, or limit the permissible investments, or specify the classes of investments in which the trust estate is to be invested. But special powers

[1] *Curror* v. *Walker's Trs.* (1889) 16 R. 355.

[2] *Johnstone* v. *Thorburn* (1901) 3 F. 497.

[3] *Gordon's Trs.* v. *Scott* (1882) 19 S.L.R. 549; *Carruthers* v. *C.* (1896) 23 R. (H.L.) 55; *Mustard* v. *Mortimer's Trs.* (1899) 7 S.L.T. 71; *Ferguson* v. *Paterson* (1900) 2 F. (H.L.) 37; *Buchanan* v. *Eaton*, 1911 S.C. (H.L.) 40.

[4] *Melville* v. *Noble's Trs.* (1896) 24 R. 243; *Clarke* v. *C's Trs.*, 1925 S.C. 693.

[5] *Acct. of Court* v. *Baird* (1858) 20 D. 1176; *Gordon* v. *City of Glasgow Bank* (1879) 7 R. 55; *Browning's Factor* (1905) 7 F. 1037; *Dunbar's Trs.*, 1915 S.C. 860.

[6] *Melville*, *supra*; cf. *Manners* v. *Strong's J.F.* (1902) 4 F. 829.

wider than those conferred by statute are strictly construed[1] and even express general powers only authorize investment in a way a prudent man might deem reasonable.[2] In investing within the authorised classes of investments, trustees must consider the propriety of the particular investments and may be liable for loss from inadequate investigation.[3] Power limited to specified investments is strictly construed.[4]

A direction to retain the truster's own investments is binding unless the preservation of the estate, which is the overriding consideration, renders it prudent to realise and reinvest;[5] a mere power to retain the truster's own investments must be exercised in the way a prudent business man would exercise it.[6] Similarly power to continue the truster's business is strictly construed and must be exercised prudently.[7] Power to lend to the truster's firm does not authorize continuance of the loan to the firm after its composition has changed.[8] Trustees may collectively be a partner in a firm carrying on the truster's business.[9]

Personal securities

Power to lend on personal security may be given, and includes lending on personal credit, without security, but trustees who lend on this basis and incur loss must justify their action by showing that no safer investment was open to them.[10] A loan to a trustee is utterly *ultra vires*, even with security.[11]

1 *Ritchie's* v. *R's Trs.* (1888) 15 R. 1086; *Roy* v. *R's Trs.* (1895) 3 S.L.T. 209; *Henderson* v. *H's Trs.* (1900) 2 F. 1295.

2 *Cunningham* v. *Montgomerie* (1879) 6 R. 1333; *Knox* v. *Mackinnon* (1888) 15 R. (H.L.) 83; *Thomson's Trs.* v. *Henderson* (1890) 18 R. 24; *Re Smith* [1896] 1 Ch. 71; cf. *Merchant Company's Widows' Fund Trs.*, 1948 S.L.T. (Notes) 70.

3 *Alexander* v. *Johnstone* (1899) 1 F. 639.

4 *Sanders* v. *S's Trs.* (1879) 7 R. 157; *Scott's Hospital Trs.*, 1913 S.C. 289.

5 *Alexander* v. *Lowson's Trs.* (1890) 17 R. 571; *Galloway* v. *Campbell's Trs.* (1905) 7 F. 931; *Stevenson's Trs.*, 1924 S.L.T. 792; *Thomson's Trs.* v. *Davidson*, 1947 S.C. 654.

6 *Brownlie* v. *B's Trs.* (1879) 6 R. 1233; *Robinson* v. *Fraser's Tr.* (1881) 8 R. (H.L.) 127; *Thomson's Trs.* v. *T.* (1889) 16 R. 517; *Thomson's Trs.* v. *Henderson* (1890) 18 R. 24; *Boyd's Tr.* v. *B.*, 1908 S.C. 1147; *Clarke* v. *C's Trs.*, 1925 S.C. 693.

7 *Alexander* v. *Lowson's Trs.* (1890) 17 R. 571; *Smith* v. *Patrick* (1901) 3 F. (H.L.) 14; *MacKechnie's Trs.* v. *Macadam*, 1912 S.C. 1059; see also *Murray's Trs.* v. *M.* (1905) 13 S.L.T. 274; *Dalgety's Trs.* v. *Drummond*, 1938 S.C. 709.

8 *Smith* v. *Patrick* (1901) 3 F. (H.L.) 14; contrast *Alexander*, *supra*; *MacKechnie's Trs.*, *supra*.

9 *Beveridge* v. *B.* (1872) 10 M. (H.L.) 1; contrast *Paterson's Tr.* v. *Learmont* (1870) 8 M. 500.

10 *Knox* v. *Mackinnon* (1888) 15 R. (H.L.) 83; but see *Cathcart* v. *Baxter's Trs.*, 1921 1 S.L.T. 150.

11 *Ritchies* v. *R's Trs.* (1888) 15 R. 1086; *Croskery* v. *Gilmour's Trs.* (1890) 17 R. 697.

Heritable securities

In investing in heritable securities trustees must act prudently and consider the value and suitability of the security subjects.[1] Some loans on heritable securities may be unsuitable.[2] A trustee is not chargeable with breach of trust by reason only of the proportion borne by the amount of the loan to the value of the property at the time when the loan was made if in making the loan the trustee acted on a report by a person reasonably believed to be an able practical valuator, instructed and employed independently of any owner of the property,[3] and the amount of the loan by itself or in combination with any other loan or loans ranking prior to or pari passu with it does not exceed two thirds of the value stated in such report.[4] Where a trustee has improperly advanced on a heritable security which would at the time of the investment have been a proper investment for a lesser sum, the security is to be deemed an authorized investment for the less sum, and the trustee is liable only to make good the sum advanced in excess thereof, with interest.[5]

Statutory powers of investment

In addition to any powers of investment conferred by the trust deed[6] trustees may invest trust funds in the ways authorized by the Trustee Investments Act, 1961.[7] A trustee may[8] invest any property[9] in any manner specified in Part I[10] or II[11] of Schedule I of the Act. He may also[12] divide the trust funds into two parts, equal in value at the time of the division, no transfer being made from one part to the other unless authorized by the Act or unless

[1] *Maclean* v. *Soady's Tr.* (1888) 15 R. 966; *Raes* v. *Meek* (1889) 16 R. (H.L.) 31; *Crabbe* v. *Whyte* (1891) 18 R. 1065.

[2] *Maclean* v. *Soady's Tr.* (1888) 15 R. 966; *Boyd* v. *Greig*, 1913 1 S.L.T. 398; A postponed bond, though not prohibited, is generally unsuitable: *Alexander* v. *Johnstone* (1899) 1 F. 639. See also *Guild* v. *Glasgow Educ. Endowment Board* (1887) 14 R. 944; *Crabbe* v. *Whyte* (1891) 18 R. 1065; *Cowan's Trs.* v. *Ferrie's C.B.* (1897) 24 R. 590; *Hutton* v. *Annan* (1898) 25 R. (H.L.) 23; *Johnstone* v. *Thorburn* (1901) 3 F. 497.

[3] cf. *Manners* v. *Strong's J.F.* (1902) 4 F. 829.

[4] 1921 Act, S. 30; see also *Raes, supra*; *Crabbe, supra*.

[5] 1921 Act, S. 29.

[6] Trustee Investments Act, 1961, S. 3(1).

[7] This Act supersedes Trusts (Sc.) Act, 1921, Ss. 10, 11, 12(3) and (4).

[8] S. 1(1).

[9] Defined S. 4(4).

[10] Known as 'narrower-range investments not requiring advice' and including Defence Bonds, National Savings Certificates and deposits in the P.O.S.B., trustee savings bank or bank deposits.

[11] Known as 'narrower-range investments requiring advice' and including fixed-interest securities of H.M. Government, nationalised undertakings and local authorities, debentures of U.K. companies, building society deposits, and loans on heritable security.

[12] S. 2.

a compensating transfer of property of equal value is made in the appropriate direction. The former part must be invested in narrower-range investments;[1] the latter part may be invested in any manner specified in Part III of Schedule I of the Act.[2]

Investments may be varied from time to time.[3]

Property accruing to a trust after it has been divided, if accruing to the trustee as owner or former owner of property comprised in either part of the fund, falls to be treated as belonging to that part of the fund, but in other cases must be apportioned between the two parts of the fund, or a compensating transfer be made, so that the value of each part of the fund is increased by the same amount. Property acquired for money is to be treated as investment and not as accrual to the trust fund, and accrual does not include the case of a dividend or interest becoming part of a trust fund.[4]

Where property falls to be taken out of the trust fund, the trustee has a discretion as to the choice of property to be taken out.[5]

A valuation in writing of any property by a person reasonably believed by the trustee to be qualified to make it is conclusive in determining whether the division of the trust fund under S. 2(1) or any transfer or apportionment of property has been duly made.[6]

The powers of investment conferred by the 1961 Act, S. 1, may be extended by Order in Council,[7] and the Treasury may by statutory instrument alter the proportions of the parts of a divided trust fund to the limit of the wider-range part being three-fourths of the whole. While such an order is in force a divided trust fund may be again divided, once only.[8]

The Court of Session no longer has power to approve extra-statutory investments for trust funds,[9] but the extension of investment powers does not lessen the power of any court to confer wider powers of investment on trustees, nor affect the extent to which any such power may be exercised.[10] But the Court will not normally widen trustees' powers beyond those given in the trust deed and by statute.[11]

1 i.e. Sched. I, Parts I and II.

2 Known as 'wider-range investments' and including securities issued by companies incorporated in the U.K., shares in building societies, and units of a unit trust scheme, subject to the qualifications in Sched. I, Part IV.

3 S. 1(1). 4 S. 2(3). 5 S. 2(4). 6 S. 5.

7 1961 Act, S. 12. 8 1961 Act, S. 13.

9 1961 Act, S. 14, amending 1921 Act, S. 27.

10 1961 Act, S. 15; cf. *Gibson's Trs.*, 1933 S.C. 190.

11 *Mitchell Bequest Trs.*, 1959 S.C. 395; *Inglis*, 1965 S.L.T. 326.

Relation of special powers and statutory powers

The statutory powers to invest in narrower range investments[1] are additional to any power conferred otherwise, e.g. by a trust deed.[2] Any special power to invest in investments authorized by law has effect as a power to invest under Ss. 1 or 2 of the 1961 Act.[3] Where a trustee is authorized to hold property including wider-range investments apart from the 1921 Act or S. 1 of the 1961 Act, or which become part of a trust fund under the 1921 Act, S. 4(o) or (p),[4] S. 2 is modified by Sched. 2, and applies only to what is not special-range property, which property is carried to a separate part of the fund.[5]

Property which belongs to the narrower-range or wider-range and is converted into special-range property, or is special-range property and accrues to the trust fund after its division under S. 2, shall be carried to such a separate part of the fund. Where property carried to such a separate part is converted into other than special-range property, it must be transferred to the narrower-range part or the wider-range part or apportioned between them, and any transfer from one of these parts to the other must be made which is necessary to secure that the value of each of these parts is increased by the same amount.[6]

Care and advice in choosing investments

In exercising his investment powers a trustee must have regard to the need for diversification of investments, so far as is appropriate to the circumstances of the trust, and to the suitability to the trust of investments of the description proposed and of the investment proposed as one of that description.[7]

Before exercising any power to invest in a manner specified in Part II or III of Sched. I of the 1961 Act, or before investing in the exercise of a special power a trustee must obtain and consider proper advice on whether the investment is satisfactory having regard to the foregoing considerations. A trustee retaining any investment made in the exercise of such a power and in such a manner must determine at what intervals the circumstances, and in particular the nature of the investment, make it desirable to obtain such advice, and must obtain and consider such advice accordingly.[8]

[1] i.e. S. 1. [2] S. 3(1). [3] S. 3(2).
[4] Added to 1921 Act, by 1961 Act, S. 10.
[5] S. 3(3); not applicable to cases listed in S. 3(4). [6] Sched. 2.
[7] 1961 Act, S. 6(1).
[8] 1961 Act, S. 6(2) and (3).

For these purposes proper advice is the advice of a person who is reasonably believed by the trustee to be qualified by his ability in and practical experience of financial matters; he may give the advice in the course of his employment as an officer or servant. The advice must be given or be subsequently confirmed in writing. One trustee may, if otherwise qualified, give advice to a co-trustee, and the need for advice does not apply where the powers of trustee are being lawfully exercised by an officer or servant competent to give proper advice.[1]

In respect of lending money on the security of property a trustee is not chargeable with breach of trust by reason only of the proportion borne by the amount of the loan to the value of the property at the time when the loan was made, if it appears to the court that in making such a loan the trustee was acting on a report as to the value of the property made by a person whom the trustee reasonably believed to be an able practical valuator instructed and employed independently of any owner of the property and the amount of the loan by itself or in combination with any other loan or loans upon the property ranking prior to or *pari passu* with the loan in question does not exceed two-thirds of the value of the property as stated in such report.[2] The advice required by the 1961 Act shall not include advice on the suitability of the particular loan.[3]

Application of statutory investment powers to other persons

Persons, not trustees, such as local authorities and public bodies, who have a statutory power of making investments which is, or includes, power to make the investments trustees may make, or those authorized by the Trusts (Sc.) Act, 1921, S. 10, now have the investment powers of Ss. 1–6 of the 1961 Act.[4]

Appropriation of investments

In general trustees have no power to appropriate particular investments towards particular prospective claims on the trust fund,[5] but may have this power where parts of the trust fund have to be paid at different times.[6] Where severance is effected any appreciation in investments set apart belongs to the beneficiaries thereof.[7]

1 1961 Act, S. 6(4), (5) and (6).

2 1921 Act, S. 30.

3 Trustee Investments Act, 1961, S. 6(7)

4 1961 Act, S. 7; see also S. 11.

5 *Colville's Trs.* v. *C.*, 1914 S.C. 255; *Duncan's Trs.*, 1951 S.C. 557.

6 *Robertson* v. *Fraser's Tr.* (1881) 8 R. (H.L.) 127; *Manners* v. *Strong's J.F.* (1902) 4 F. 829; *Henderson's Tr.* v. *H.* (1900) 3 F. 17.

7 *Vans Dunlop's Trs.* v. *Pollok*, 1912 S.C. 10.

Duty to keep accounts

A trustee is bound to keep proper trust accounts,[1] and it is prudent to have them audited periodically.[2] Many questions have arisen as to allocation of expenditure between capital and income. In the accounts the trustees must account for all property expressly committed to the trust, and for anything which is constructively deemed trust property, such as anything acquired by a trustee while acting as *auctor in rem suam*.

General powers conferred by trust deed

To enable the trustees to carry out the administration of the trust the truster may confer powers on them expressly, or may merely confer all the powers attaching at common law or by statute to trustees. At common law a trustee had power to alienate the trust estate absolutely or in security if that were the truster's intention as disclosed in the trust deed: in case of doubt the trustee might seek the court's authority. Trustees also have power at common law and without the court's authority to do acts of ordinary administration, such as themselves to manage a farm.[3] Powers conferred may be permissive and discretionary, which the trustees may exercise if they think proper, or be mandatory, which they must exercise, and in effect directory.

Acts authorized or prohibited

Acts expressly authorized are clearly within the powers of the trustees, and other powers may be implied by the terms of the trust deed.[4] Certain acts may be prohibited expressly[5] or impliedly[6] and there is clearly no power to do them, and a direction to do something else has the same effect as an express prohibition.[7]

There is also no power to do what, even though not prohibited, is at variance with the terms or purposes of the trust.[8] The grant of a limited power does not necessarily make a more extensive statutory power at variance with the trust purposes.[9]

1 *Ross* v. *R.* (1896) 23 R. (H.L.) 67; *Polland* v. *Sturrock's Exors.*, 1955 S.L.T. (Notes) 77.

2 *Wyman* v. *Paterson* (1900) 2 F. (H.L.) 37; cf. [English] Trustee Act, 1925, S. 22(4) (nor more often than every three years unless exceptionally).

3 *Dunbar's Trs.*, 1915 S.C. 860.

4 *Brotchie* v. *Stewart* (1869) 7 M. 1031.

5 *Hay's Trs.* v. *Hay Miln* (1873) 11 M. 694; *Oliver's Trs.* (1876) 3 R. 639; *Marshall's Trs.* (1897) 24 R. 478.

6 e.g. *Petrie's Trs.* v. *Ramsay* (1868) 7 M. 64; *Anderson* (1876) 3 R. 639; *Whyte's Factor* v. *W.* (1891) 18 R. 376.

7 *Thomson* v. *Miller's Trs.* (1883) 11 R. 401.

8 e.g. *Naismith's Trs.* v. *N.*, 1909 S.C. 1380.

9 *Kerr's Trs.* v. *Kerr's Curator*, 1907 S.C. 678; *Anderson's Trs.*, 1932 S.C. 226.

Discretionary powers

Where a power conferred involves an element of discretion the discretion may be exercised only in the respect as to which it has been conferred.[1] It must be exercised with care and *bona fide*;[2] the court will intervene only if there is bad faith or abuse of power,[3] or if there has been gross misjudgment in the exercise of the discretion.[4] If an element of discretion is necessary and has not been given to the trustees, the court will itself, on petition to the *nobile officium*, exercise the necessary discretion.[5]

The exercise of discretionary powers may be limited to named trustees or original trustees.[6] If there are no contrary indications in the trust deed, they may be exercised even by assumed trustees or by a judicial factor.[7] They may be exercised by a majority of the trustees, on notice to the remainder of their proposed action.[8] The court will not advise trustees on how to exercise a discretionary power.[9]

General statutory powers of trustees

In all trusts the trustees have by statute[10] power to do the following, where such acts are not at variance with the terms or purposes of the trust,[11] and such acts when done are as effectual as if such powers had been contained in the trust deed, viz.:

(a) to sell the trust estate or any part thereof, heritable as well as moveable;[12]

(b) to grant feus of the heritable estate or any part thereof;[13]

1 *Kinmond's Trs.* v. *Mess* (1898) 25 R. 819; *Potter's Trs.* v. *Allan*, 1918 S.C. 173.

2 *Train* v. *Buchanan's Trs.*, 1908 S.C. (H.L.) 26; *Caldwell's Trs.* v. *C.*, 1923 S.L.T. 694.

3 *Douglas* v. *D's Trs.* (1872) 10 M. 943; *MacTavish* v. *Reid's Trs.* (1904) 12 S.L.T. 404; *Brown* v. *Elder's Trs.* (1906) 13 S.L.T. 837; *Chivers' Trs.* v. *Stewart*, 1907 S.C. 701; *Train* v. *Buchanan's Trs.*, 1908 S.C. (H.L.) 26.

4 *Thomson* v. *Davidson's Trs.* (1888) 15 R. 719; *Ritchie* v. *Davidson's Trs.* (1890) 17 R. 673; cf. *Sinclair's Trs.* v. *S.*, 1913 S.C. 178.

5 *Baird* v. *B's Trs.* (1872) 10 M. 482; *MacTavish*, *supra*.

6 e.g. *Laurie* v. *Brown*, 1911 1 S.L.T. 84; *Paterson's Trs.* v. *Findlay*, 1918 S.C. 713; *Lansdale's Trs.* v. *Nicol*, 1918 2 S.L.T. 10.

7 *Woodwards' J.F.*, 1926 S.C. 534; *Maclachlan's Trs.* v. *Gingold*, 1928 S.L.T. 408; *Shorter*, 1930 S.L.T. 535.

8 *Slimon* v. *S's Trs.*, 1915 2 S.L.T. 19.

9 *Stair's Trs.* (1896) 23 R. 1070; *Scott's Hospital Trs.*, 1913 S.C. 289.

10 1921 Act, S. 4.

11 See *Chalmer's Hospital Trs.*, 1923 S.C. 220; *Darwin's Trs.*, 1924 S.L.T. 778; *Leslie's J.F.*, 1925 S.C. 464; *Lothian's C.B.*, 1927 S.C. 579.

12 As to mode of sale, see 1921 Act, S. 6; *Binnie* v. *B's Trs.* (1889) 16 R. (H.L.) 23. The purchaser is concerned with whether the trustees have power of sale but not with whether their sale is expedient or not; *Kidd* v. *Paton's Tr.*, 1912 2 S.L.T. 363.

13 cf. *Anderson* (1876) 3 R. 639; *Elgin Mags.* v. *Morrison* (1882) 10 R. 342.

(c) to grant leases of any duration (including mineral leases) of the heritable estate or any part thereof[1] and to remove tenants;

(d) to borrow money on the security of the trust estate or any part thereof, heritable as well as moveable;[2]

(e) to excamb any part of the trust estate which is heritable;[3]

(ee)[4] to acquire with funds of the trust estate any interest in residential accommodation (whether in Scotland or elsewhere) reasonably required to enable the trustees to provide a suitable residence for occupation by any of the beneficiaries;[5]

(f) to appoint factors and law agents and to pay them suitable remuneration;

(g) to discharge trustees who have resigned and the representatives of trustees who have died;

(h) to uplift, discharge or assign debts due to the trust estate;

(i) to compromise or to submit and refer all claims connected with the trust estate;[6]

(j) to refrain from doing diligence for the recovery of any debt due to the truster which the trustees may reasonably deem irrecoverable;

(k) to grant all deeds necessary for carrying into effect the powers vested in the trustees;

(l) to pay debts due by the truster or by the trust estate without requiring the creditors to constitute such debts where the trustees are satisfied that the debts are proper debts of the trust;[7]

(m) to make abatement or reduction, either temporary or permanent, of the rent, lordship, royalty, or other consideration stipulated in any lease of land, houses, tenements, minerals, metals or other subjects, and to accept renunciations of leases of any such subjects;

(n) to apply the whole or any part of trust funds which the

[1] cf. *Birkmyre* (1881) 8 R. 477 (999 years).

[2] This seems to imply power to make the security effective: *Paterson* v. *Caledonian Her. Sec. Co.* (1885) 13 R. 369. The lender is concerned with the power to borrow and any limitation thereon, but not with the way the trustees apply the money: *Buchanan* v. *Glasgow University*, 1909 S.C. 47.

[3] *Bruce* v. *Stewart* (1900) 2 F. 948.

[4] Added by Trusts (Sc.) Act, 1961, S. 4.

[5] Save for this limited purpose, trustees, unless given it expressly, have no power to purchase heritage; they may, exceptionally, obtain it from the Court under the *nobile officium*: *Hall's Trs.* v. *McArthur's Trs.*, 1918 S.C. 646; *Anderson's Trs.*, 1921 S.C. 315; *Fletcher's Trs.*, 1949 S.C. 330. Absence of power to buy heritage does not prevent rebuilding: *Armstrong* v. *Wilson's Trs.* (1904) 7 F. 353.

[6] cf. *City of Glasgow Bank* v. *Geddes' Trs.* (1880) 7 R. 731; *Hadden* v. *Bryden* (1899) 1 F. 710; *Tennent's J.F.* v. *T.*, 1954 S.C. 215.

[7] cf. *McGaan* v. *McG's Trs.* (1883) 11 R. 249.

trustees are empowered or directed by the trust deed to invest in the purchase of heritable property in the payment or redemption of any debt or burden affecting heritable property which may be destined to the same series of heirs and subject to the same conditions as are by the trust deed made applicable to heritable property directed to be purchased;

(o)[1] to concur, in respect of any securities of a company (being securities comprised in the trust estate) in any scheme or arrangement—

(i) for the reconstruction of the company;
(ii) for the sale of all or any part of the property and undertaking of the company to another company;
(iii) for the acquisition of the securities of the company, or of control thereof, by another company;
(iv) for the amalgamation of the company with another company; or
(v) for the release, modification, or variation of any rights, privileges or liabilities attached to the securities or any of them;

in like manner as if the trustees were entitled to such securities beneficially; to accept any securities of any denomination or description of the reconstructed or purchasing or new company in lieu of, or in exchange for, all or any of the first-mentioned securities; and to retain any securities so accepted as aforesaid for any period for which the trustees could have properly retained the original securities;

(p)[2] to exercise, to such extent as the trustees think fit, any conditional or preferential right to subscribe for any securities in a company (being a right offered to them in respect of any holding in the company) to apply capital money of the trust estate in payment of the consideration, and to retain any such securities for which they have subscribed for any period for which they have power to retain the holding in respect of which the right to subscribe for the securities was offered (but subject to any conditions subject to which they have that power); to renounce, to such extent as they think fit, any such right; or to assign, to such extent as they think fit and for the best consideration that can reasonably be obtained, the benefit of any such right or the title thereto to any person, including any beneficiary under the trust.

1 Added by Trustee Investments Act, 1961, S. 10.
2 Added by Trustee Investments Act, 1961, S. 10.

Furthermore the 1921 Act is to have effect as if the powers conferred by S. 4 included a power to enter into forestry dedication agreements under the Forestry Act, 1967, S. 5, relating to the trust estate or any part thereof,[1] and a power to enter into access agreements under the Countryside (Sc.) Act, 1967, S. 10(1), relating to the trust estate or any part thereof.[2]

Validity of transactions in questions with third parties

Where, after 27 August, 1961, trustees enter into a transaction with any person under which they purport to do so in relation to the trust estate an act of any of the descriptions specified in paras. (a) to (ee) above, the validity of the transaction and of any title acquired by that person is not challengeable by him or any other person on the ground that the act in question is at variance with the terms or purposes of the trust: if the transaction were entered into by trustees acting under the supervision of the Accountant of Court this section shall have effect only if he consents thereto.[3]

Powers granted by the Court

The Court may[4] grant authority to trustees (but not trustees under any trust constituted by private or local Act[5]) to do any of the acts mentioned in the statutory list of general powers of trustees, notwithstanding that such act is at variance with the terms or purposes of the trust, on being satisfied that such act is in all the circumstances expedient for the execution of the trust. Where there is reasonable doubt whether a proposed act is at variance with the trust purposes trustees should apply to the court to have the power granted, or their petition refused as unnecessary.[6] Whether a grant of powers is expedient or not depends on the circumstances of the case.[7] The court will not extend trustees' powers of investment nor their immunities beyond what is stipulated in the trust deed and the Trustee Investments Act, 1961.[8]

[1] Forestry Act, 1967, Sched. 2, para. 4(2).
[2] Countryside (Sc.) Act, 1967, S. 13(5).
[3] Trusts (Sc.) Act, 1961, S. 2.
[4] 1921 Act, S. 5.
[5] S. 5; *Church of Scotland General Trustees*, 1931 S.C. 704.
[6] *Hamilton's Trs.*, 1919 2 S.L.T. 81; *Leslie's J.F.*, 1925 S.C. 464; *Lothian's C.B.* 1927 S.C. 579; *Christie's Trs.*, 1946 S.L.T. 309; *Cunningham's Tutrix*, 1949 S.C. 275.
[7] See *Downie* (1879) 6 R. 1013; *Gunn* (1892) 29 S.L.R. 903; *Simpson* v. *Moffat Working Men's Inst. Trs.* (1892) 19 R. 389; *Old Meldrum U.F. Church* (1908) 15 S.L.T. 913; *Chalmers' Hospital (Banff) Trs.*, 1923 S.C. 220; *Stranraer Original Secession Congregation*, 1923 S.C. 722; *Darwin's Trs.*, 1924 S.L.T. 778; *McCrie's Trs.*, 1927 S.C. 556; *Gibson's Trs.*, 1933 S.C. 190.
[8] *Inglis*, 1965 S.L.T. 326.

Trustees must consider the terms and purposes of their trust before exercising a statutory power.[1] While the scope of 'at variance with the terms and purposes of the trust' is uncertain it is wider than prohibited acts, and requires consideration of the express trust purposes and also the general purpose underlying the trust.[1]

Whether to exercise a power or not is a matter of policy and discretion requiring individual consideration in each case.[2]

Powers granted by Court under nobile officium

While the Court will not by the exercise of the *nobile officium* override the truster's intention or extend trustees' powers merely because that would be beneficial, the Court may exceptionally grant further powers if the truster's conditions are making the trust unworkable, or endangering the trust estate, or rendering the purposes fruitless.[3]

Statutory powers cannot be extended by the *nobile officium* though it may supply a *casus omissionis* or provide machinery to make powers more effective.[4]

Nor will the Court under the *nobile officium* readily ratify a purported exercise by trustees of a power not possessed, or an unauthorised act.[5]

Power to make advances of capital

Trustees may be empowered expressly to make advances of capital to beneficiaries,[6] and by the 1921 Act, S. 16, the court may, under such conditions as it sees fit, authorize trustees to advance any part of the capital of a fund destined, absolutely or contingently, to beneficiaries who, at the date of application to the Court, are not of full age, if it appears that the income of the fund is insufficient or not applicable to, and that such advance is necessary for, the maintenance or education of such beneficiaries, or any of them, that it is not expressly prohibited by the trust

1 *Leslie's J.F.*, 1925 S.C. 464; *Lothian's C.B.*, 1927 S.C. 579.

2 *Binnie* v. *B's Trs.* (1889) 16 R. (H.L.) 23; *Caldwell's Trs.* v. *C.*, 1923 S.L.T. 694.

3 *Kinloch* (1859) 22 D. 174; *Berwick* (1874) 2 R. 90; *Noble's Trs.*, 1912 S.C. 1230; *Scott's Hospital Trs.*, 1913 S.C. 289; *Glasgow Y.M.C.A.*, 1934 S.C. 452.

4 *Tod* v. *Anderson* (1869) 7 M. 412, 413; *Crichton-Stuart's Tutrix*, 1921 S.C. 840; *Campbell-Wyndham-Long's Trs.*, 1951 S.C. 685; *Campbell*, 1958 S.C. 275; *Campbell-Wyndham-Long's Trs.*, 1962 S.C. 132.

5 *Campbell* (1890) 18 R. 149; *Clyne* (1894) 21 R. 849; *Drummond's J.F.* (1894) 21 R. 932; *Hall's Trs.* v. *McArthur*, 1918 S.C. 646; *Ferrier's Tutrix*, 1925 S.C. 571; *Christie's Trs.*, 1932 S.L.T. 35; *Dow's Trs.*, 1947 S.C. 524; *Horne's Trs.*, 1952 S.C. 70.

6 cf. *Baird's Trs.* v. *Duncanson* (1892) 19 R. 1045; *Maclachlan's Trs.* v. *Gingold*, 1928 S.L.T. 409; *Moss's Trs.* v. *King*, 1952 S.C. 523.

deed, and that the rights of such beneficiaries, if contingent, are contingent only on their survivance.[1] Section 16 permits advances to be authorized before majority and to continue thereafter.[2] Advances already made cannot be ratified under the section,[3] but can by the *nobile officium*.[4] In cases not covered by the trust deed or by S. 16 the Court, in the exercise of the *nobile officium*, may authorize an advance, e.g. to a beneficiary who has attained majority,[5] or to a beneficiary without a vested interest.[6]

Power to make allowances from income

Where trustees hold funds for behoof of children who have a vested right, though the date for payment is postponed, they are entitled to pay from the income sums necessary for the maintenance and education of the children.[7] The Court will not interfere with the trustees' exercise of discretion as to the amount unless there is a gross misconception of duty,[8] but may intervene at the instance of a beneficiary to settle the amount payable.[9]

Superintendence order

Under the 1921 Act, S. 17, trustees or any of them may apply for an order on the Accountant of Court to supervise their administration, so far as relates to investment and distribution of the funds among the creditors and beneficiaries. If an order is made the Accountant will annually examine and audit the trust accounts and may at any time report to the court on any matter arising in the administration of the trust and obtain the directions of the court thereupon.[10]

Petition for directions

Under the Administration of Justice (Sc.) Act, 1933, S. 17, trustees, or a majority and quorum of them, may apply to the

[1] cf. *Websters* v. *Miller's Trs.* (1887) 14 R. 501; *Ross's Trs.* (1894) 21 R. 995; *Robertson's Trs.*, 1909 S.C. 236; *Bett's Trs.*, 1922 S.C. 21; *Macfarlane* v. *M's Trs.*, 1931 S.C. 95; *Paton's Trs.*, 1953 S.L.T. 276; *Anderson's Trs.*, 1957 S.L.T. (Notes) 5.

[2] *Macfarlane's Trs.*, *supra*; *Anderson's Trs.*, 1936 S.C. 460.

[3] *Young's Trs.* (1895) 3 S.L.T. 192.

[4] *Christie's Trs.*, 1932 S.C. 189; see also *Cockburn's Trs.*, 1935 S.C. 670.

[5] *Robertson's Trs.*, 1909 S.C. 236; *Sinclair's Trs.*, 1921 S.C. 484; *Frew's Trs.*, 1932 S.C. 501.

[6] *Craig's Trs.*, 1934 S.C. 34; *Stewart* v. *Brown's Trs.*, 1941 S.C. 300.

[7] *Edmiston* v. *Miller's Trs.* (1871) 9 M. 987; *Stewart's Trs.* v. *S.* (1871) 8 S.L.R. 367; *Mackintosh* v. *Wood* (1872) 10 M. 933; *Christie* v. *C's Trs.* (1877) 4 R. 620; *Seddon* (1893) 20 R. 675; *Atherstone's Trs.* (1896) 24 R. 39.

[8] *Douglas* v. *D's Trs.* (1872) 10 M. 943; *Spears's Trs.* v. *S.* (1873) 11 M. 731.

[9] *Baird* v. *B's Trs.* (1872) 10 M. 482; *Muir* v. *M's Trs.* (1887) 15 R. 170.

[10] *Stevenson's Trs.*, 1924 S.L.T. 792; *Donaldson's Trs.* v. *D.*, 1932 S.L.T. 463; 1933 S.N. 93. See also *Liddell's Trs.* v. *L.*, 1929 S.L.T. 169.

court for direction on questions relating to the investment, distribution, management or administration of the trust estate under their charge, or as to the exercise of any power vested in, or as to the performance of any duty imposed on, them, even though it may affect contingent interests in the trust estate, whether of persons born or unborn. Such petitions may appropriately be presented to aid trustees faced with a practical difficulty but not where the question is not related to any matter on which the trustees require immediate guidance, nor where the question can be dealt with conveniently in a special case.[1] A petition is generally incompetent in the absence of an interested party.[2] Where in such a case an interested party, by excusable error, had not been represented, the court may later give him an opportunity of doing so.[3]

INTERESTS ARISING UNDER TRUSTS

The interest of the beneficiary

The interest of the beneficiary under a trust deed is a *jus crediti*, enforceable by action against the trustees[4] but not against any debtor to the trust estate.[5] The *jus crediti* is heritable if the beneficiary is entitled to a specific conveyance of heritage, but in other cases is moveable.

INTERESTS ARISING UNDER TRUSTS
ANNUITIES

If a trust purpose is the payment of an annuity provision for this must be made before any residue can be paid away. An annuity is *prima facie* chargeable against heritage,[6] and if the income is inadequate it must be paid out of capital.[7] Unless the annuity is declared alimentary, the trust need not be kept in being merely to pay an annuity. If all parties consent, the trustees may purchase an annuity from an insurance company, or the annuitant may take the actuarial capital value of an annuity, or the annuitant may take

1 *MacKintosh's J.F.* v. *L.A.*, 1935 S.C. 406; *Andrew's Trs.* v. *Maddeford*, 1935 S.C. 857; *Peel's Trs.* v. *Drummond*, 1936 S.C. 786; *Henderson's Trs.* v. *H.*, 1938 S.C. 461; *Grant's Trs.* v. *Hunter*, 1938 S.C. 501; cf. *Tait's J.F.* v. *Lillie*, 1940 S.C. 534.

2 *Henderson's Trs.*, *supra.*

3 *Milne's Tr.*, 1936 S.C. 487.

4 Ersk. III, 9, 11; Bell, *Comm.* I, 35.

5 *Hinton* v. *Connell's Trs.* (1883) 10 R. 1110.

6 *Breadalbane's Trs.* v. *Jamieson* (1873) 11 M. 912; *Mackintosh* v. *M's Trs.* (1873) 11 M. (H.L.) 28; *Moon's Trs.* v. *M.* (1899) 2 F. 201.

7 *Knox's Trs.* v. *K.* (1869) 7 M. 873; *Kinmond's Trs.* v. *K.* (1873) 11 M. 381.

a bond of annuity from a residuary legatee, and the trust can be terminated.

But if the annuity has been declared alimentary the trust cannot be ended, even if all parties consent.[1]

INTERESTS ARISING UNDER TRUSTS
INTERESTS IN LIFERENT AND IN FEE

A common trust purpose is to hold property for certain persons in liferent, and for others in fee. Such a liferent is an improper liferent, where a property is vested in the trustees, the liferenter having merely a *jus crediti* against the trustees, as contrasted with proper liferent where he has the title to the liferented property in his own name and is virtually proprietor but subject to the condition *salva rerum substantia*[2] and the reversionary right of the fiar. Save in so far as expressly or impliedly modified by the trust deed, the rights of liferenter and of fiar under a trust are the same as those which would have been enjoyed under proper liferent and fee respectively.[3]

In an improper liferent under a trust the trustees must administer the trust estate and hold the balance between liferenter(s) and fiar(s) and possibly also between liferenters of heritable and of moveable estate and between fiars of heritable and of moveable estate. The liferenter is not entitled to challenge the exercise by the trustees of discretionary powers vested in them.[4]

Whether gift of liferent or of fee

Questions of interpretations may arise, whether trustees have to hold certain property for one in liferent and another in fee, or have to transfer the fee outright. Gifts of 'income',[5] 'interest',[6] 'rents',[7] or of property 'during their lifetime'[8] have been held to

[1] *Smith and Campbell* (1873) 11 M. 639; *Cosens* v. *Stevenson* (1873) 11 M. 761; *Whyte's Trs.* v. *W.* (1877) 4 R. 786; *Montgomery's Trs.* v. *M.* (1888) 15 R. 369; *Hughes* v. *Edwardes* (1892) 19 R. (H.L.) 33.

[2] *Miller* v. *I.R.C.*, 1928 S.C. 819, 837.

[3] *Rogers* v. *Scott* (1867) 5 M. 1078; *Campbell* v. *Wardlaw* (1883) 10 R. (H.L.) 65; *Johnstone* v. *Mackenzie's Trs.*, 1912 S.C. (H.L.) 106.

[4] *Caithness' Trs.* v. *C.* (1877) 4 R. 937.

[5] *Crawford's Trs.* v. *Working Boys' Home* (1901) 8 S.L.T. 371.

[6] *Patrick* v. *Fowler* (1900) 2 F. 690.

[7] *Mackenzie's Trs.* v. *M.* (1899) 2 F. 330; *Sim* v. *Duncan* (1900) 2 F. 434; *Sinclair* v. *S's Exors.* (1901) 8 S.L.T. 485.

[8] *Smith's Trs.* v. *S.* (1883) 10 R. 1144; *Spink's Exors.* v. *Simpson* (1894) 21 R. 551; *Dunlop* v. *McCrorie*, 1909 1 S.L.T. 544; *Brash's Trs.* v. *Phillipson*, 1916 S.C. 271; *Lethem* v. *Evans*, 1918 1 S.L.T. 27; *Duncan* v. *Edinburgh R.I.*, 1936 S.C. 811.

be liferents though in one case an instruction to hold and distribute annually was held a bequest of the fee.[1]

A gift of income only will not be interpreted as a gift of fee merely because the fee is undisposed of,[2] but where a bequest is ambiguous the avoidance of intestacy as to the fee may be an element to be considered.[3]

A gift to one with a gift of the same subjects to another after, or on the death of, the first beneficiary, does not necessarily make the first gift one of liferent only.[4]

Discretions to 'hold for' or 'invest for' a beneficiary are equivocal and depend on their context for their interpretation,[5] but a direction to divide normally connotes a gift of fee.[6]

Initial gift later qualified

If the words used in an earlier part of a settlement are habile to transfer a right of fee, the question has frequently arisen whether words in a later part cut down or qualify the initial gift. The whole deed, or deeds, must be read as a whole, but if their provisions are irreconcilable the court may rely on the principle that the later of two inconsistent provisions must prevail.[7] A gift of fee is, however, exigible despite directions to trustees to hold the capital or pay the income periodically,[8] unless there are other trust purposes which necessitate the holding of the capital by the trustees.[9]

Unless qualifications adjected to the initial gift clearly purport

[1] *Anderson* v. *Thomson* (1877) 4 R. 1101.

[2] *Henderson's Trs.* (1892) 29 S.L.R. 356; *Spink's Exors., supra*; *Sim, supra*; *Crawford's Trs., supra.*

[3] *Henderson's Trs.* v. *H.* (1876) 3 R. 320; *Smith's Trs.* v. *S.* (1883) 10 R. 1144; *Lawson's Trs.* v. *L.* (1890) 17 R. 1167; *Gillies' Trs.* v. *Hodge* (1900) 3 F. 238; *Lethem* v. *Evans*, 1918 1 S.L.T. 27; *Milne's Trs.* v. *M's Exor.*, 1937 S.C. 149.

[4] *Rae's Tr.* v. *R.* (1893) 20 R. 826; *Mitchell* v. *Ch. of Scotland* (1895) 2 S.L.T. 629; *Davis* v. *D.* (1898) 6 S.L.T. 24; *Young's Trs.* v. *Y.* (1899) 7 S.L.T. 266; *Reid* v. *Dobie*, 1921 S.C. 662; *Smart* v. *S.*, 1926 S.C. 392; *Ironside's Exor.* v. *I's Exor.*, 1933 S.C. 116.

[5] e.g. *Muir's Trs.* v. *M's Trs.* (1895) 22 R. 553; *Whitehead's Trs.* v. *W.* (1897) 24 R. 1032; *White* v. *Gow* (1900) 2 F. 1170; *Peden's Trs.* v. *P.* (1903) 5 F. 1014; *Macfarlane's Trs.* v. *M.* (1903) 6 F. 201; *Forrest's Trs.* v. *Reid* (1904) 7 F. 142; *Anderson's Trs.* v. *A.* (1904) 7 F. 224; *Nicol's Trs.* v. *Farquhar*, 1918 S.C. 358; *Murray's Trs.* v. *M.*, 1919 S.C. 552; *Smith's Trs.* v. *Clark*, 1920 S.C. 161; *Milne's Trs.* v. *Milne's Exor.*, 1937 S.C. 149.

[6] *Brown* v. *B's Trs.* (1890) 17 R. 517; *Fyfe's Trs.* v. *Duthie*, 1908 S.C. 520; *Cowan's Trs.* v. *Jardine*, 1913 S.C. 927; *Watson's Trs.* v. *W.*, 1913 S.C. 1133; *Livingston's Trs.* v. *L's Trs.*, 1939 S.C. (H.L.) 17.

[7] *Livingston's Trs.* v. *L's Trs.*, 1939 S.C. (H.L.) 17, 37.

[8] *Miller's Trs.* v. *M.* (1890) 18 R. 301; *Hargrave's Trs.* v. *Schofield* (1900) 3 F. 14; *Forsyth* v. *F.* (1901) 3 F. 929; *Yuill's Trs.* v. *Thomson* (1902) 4 F. 815; *Bate's Trs.* v. *B.* (1906) 8 F. 861; *Veitch's Trs.* v. *Rutherford*, 1914 S.C. 182; *Graham* v. *G's Trs.*, 1927 S.C. 388.

[9] *Graham's Trs.* v. *G.* (1899) 2 F. 232; *White* v. *W's Trs.*, 1916 S.C. 435.

to enlarge or restrict the gift,[1] they will be held to qualify only the manner of enjoyment.[2] Trustees may be expressly empowered to cut down a beneficiary's right to a liferent.[3]

Rights intermediate between liferent and fee

In some cases the courts recognised anomalous rights intermediate between a liferent and a full fee, such as a fee restricted to the rights of administration, consumption and sale, or a liferent with power of sale and consumption,[4] but these cases have now been overruled.[5]

Implied gifts of liferent or of fee

Apart from express gifts, the courts have held in many cases that a gift of liferent[6] or of fee[7] has been made by necessary implication from the terms of the settlement. Where a family provision is made to persons by a parent or one *in loco parentis* and payment is postponed but income is neither disposed of nor to be accumulated a liferent is implied.[8]

Rights of beneficiaries

Both liferenters and ultimate fiars acquire vested rights in their respective interests from the commencement of the trust and these interests may be dealt with by them as part of their estates. Thus a liferenter may assign outright or in security his liferent claims on the trust, so long as his liferent is not declared alimentary.[9]

[1] *Scott's Trs.* v. *Dunbar* (1900) 2 F. 516; *Anderson's Trs.* v. *A.* (1904) 7 F. 224; *Ford's Trs.* v. *F.*, 1940 S.C. 426.

[2] *Christie's Trs.* v. *Murray's Trs.* (1889) 16 R. 913; *Clouston's Trs.* v. *Bulloch* (1889) 16 R. 937; *Campbell's Trs.* v. *C.* (1889) 16 R. 1007; *Brown* v. *B's Trs.* (1890) 17 R. 517; *Lawson's Trs.* v. *L.* (1890) 17 R. 1167; *Mickel's J.F.* v. *Oliphant* (1892) 20 R. 172; *Wilkie's Trs.* v. *Wight's Trs.* (1893) 21 R. 199; *Greenlees' Trs.* v. *G.* (1894) 22 R. 136; *Mackay's Trs.* v. *M's Trs.* (1897) 24 R. 904; *Newall's Tr.* v. *Inglis' Trs.* (1898) 25 R. 1176; *Watson's Trs.* v. *W.*, 1913 S.C. 1133; *Crumpton's J.F.* v. *Barnardo's Homes*, 1917 S.C. 713; *Graham* v. *G's Trs.*, 1927 S.C. 388.

[3] *Chambers' Trs.* v. *Smith* (1878) 5 R. (H.L.) 151; *White's Trs.* v. *W.* (1896) 23 R. 836; *Turnbull's Trs.* v. *T's Trs.* (1900) 2 F. 1183.

[4] *Denholm's Trs.* v. *D.*, 1908 S.C. 255; *Heavyside* v. *Smith*, 1929 S.C. 68; doubted in *Ironside's Exor.* v. *I's Exor.*, 1933 S.C. 116; *Duncan* v. *Edinburgh R.I.*, 1936 S.C. 811.

[5] *Cochrane's Exrx.* v. *C.*, 1947 S.C. 134.

[6] *Duncan's Trs.* (1877) 4 R. 1093; *Miller's Trs.* v. *McLellan*, 1911 1 S.L.T. 444; *Bate's Trs.* v. *B.* (1906) 8 F. 861; *Mactaggart's Trs.* v. *Hare*, 1935 S.C. 543.

[7] *Douglas* v. *D.* (1843) 6 D. 318; *Campbell* v. *Eckford* (1852) 15 D. 173; *Burgh-Smeaton* v. *B.S.'s J.F.*, 1907 S.C. 1009.

[8] *Duncan's Trs.*, *supra*; *Mactaggart's Trs.*, *supra*.

[9] See Stair II, 6, 7; Ersk. II, 9, 41; Bell, *Convg.* I, 332; *Ker's Trs.* v. *Justice* (1868) 6 M. 627; *Chaplin's Trs.* v. *Hoile* (1890) 18 R. 27; *Scottish Union and National Ins. Co.* v. *Smeaton* (1904) 7 F. 174.

The fiar may assign outright or in security his claim to the fee or a share thereof, or bequeath it, and it passes on his death intestate as part of his estate.

Conversion

The character and extent of the beneficial interest, as heritable or moveable, depends on the character of the fund or estate to which the beneficiary has a claim, whether in liferent or in fee. But that character may be affected by the provisions of the trust deed, as well as by the truster's actings before the trust becomes effective. If he has sold heritage, the price goes to those having a claim to the moveables and conversely. If he has directed his trustees to sell his heritage, or part of it, then his intention is deemed to have been to give the beneficiaries the proceeds, and the right is, by the doctrine of constructive conversion, held moveable, even before the direction has been carried out. But if he has merely empowered his trustees to sell his heritage or part of it, then the right is not converted until or unless the power is exercised. If the power to sell exists only for particular purposes, i.e. case of necessity or is otherwise conditioned, no conversion takes place until or unless the power is exercised.

Conversion is not effected by a sale of heritage authorized by the Court on the grounds of expediency, if such was not the truster's intention.[1]

Duties of trustees

The trustees have the sole, and whole, duties of conserving and administering the trust estate and the whole powers vested in trustees. But in administering the trust and exercising the powers they must hold the scales fairly between the capital and income, long-term and short-term benefits and the interests of fiar and liferenter. The allocation of income, or the incidence of burdens, may be modified by the trust deed[2] or left to the trustees' discretion,[3] but is otherwise determined by the following general principles:—

Allocation of benefits

The general principle is that recurring income and profits belong to the liferenter, but accretions to capital belong to the

[1] *Taylor's Trs.* v. *Tailyour*, 1927 S.C. 288.
[2] e.g. *Lord Hamilton's Trs.*, 1935 S.C. 705.
[3] *Low's Trs.* (1871) 8 S.L.R. 638; *Warrack's Trs.* v. *W.*, 1919 S.C. 522.

fiar. Thus feuduties,[1] rents, the interest of money, dividends on company shares,[2] cash distributions,[3] the rents or royalties of minerals worked, or at least let if not worked, in the truster's lifetime,[4] wayleaves,[5] the profits from mineral leases held by the truster and which the trustees were authorized to continue to work,[6] payments for surface damage,[7] the proceeds of thinnings of timber, copse-wood and normal windfalls,[8] have been held to fall to the liferenter. There have been held to fall to the fiar capital repayments or distributions from accumulated profits or issues of bonus shares by companies,[9] the profits from mines opened by the trustees after the truster's death, unless the trustees had been directed to work the minerals,[10] the profits from mineral leases held by the truster, till they ran out,[11] profits of timber sold,[12] a share for several years after the truster's death in the profits of a firm in which he had been a partner.[13]

Royalties on literary work published before the truster's death have been held income, but on works published posthumously to be capital.[14]

In the special cases of wasting assets the liferenter has generally been held entitled to the profits earned, though the capital assets were depreciating.[15]

Where company shares are sold between the dates of two dividends the liferenter is entitled to the proportion of the price which

[1] As to former casualties, duplicands and grassums, see *Lamont-Campbell* v. *Carter-Campbell* (1895) 22 R. 260; *Montgomerie-Fleming's Trs.* v. *M.F.* (1901) 3 F. 591; *Ross's Trs.* v. *Nicoll* (1902) 5 F. 146; *Dunlop's Trs.* v. *D.* (1903) 6 F. 12; *Macdougall's Factor* v. *Watson*, 1909 S.C. 215.

[2] *Re Marjoribanks* [1923] 2 Ch. 307.

[3] *Blyth's Trs.* v. *Milne* (1905) 7 F. 799.

[4] *Waddell* v. *W.*, 21 Jan. 1812, F.C.; *Guild's Trs.* v. *G.* (1872) 10 M. 911; *Wardlaw* v. *W's Trs.* (1875) 2 R. 368; *Campbell* v. *Wardlaw* (1883) 10 R. (H.L.) 65.

[5] *Naismith's Trs.* v. *N.*, 1909 S.C. 1380.

[6] *Strain's Trs.* v. *S.* (1893) 20 R. 1025; *Main's Trs.* v. *M.* (1901) 3 F. 994.

[7] *Gould* v. *G's Trs.* (1899) 2 F. 130.

[8] *Breadalbane's Trs.* v. *D. Buckingham* (1854) 16 D. 359.

[9] *Cunliff's Trs.* v. *C.* (1900) 3 F. 202; *Gunnis's Trs.* v. *G.* (1903) 6 F. 104; *Blyth's Trs.* v. *Milne* (1905) 7 F. 799; *Howard's Trs.* v. *H.*, 1907 S.C. 1274.

[10] *Campbell* v. *Wardlaw* (1883) 10 R. (H.L.) 65; *Ranken's Trs.* v. *R.*, 1908 S.C. 3; *Naismith's Trs.* v. *N.*, 1909 S.C. 1380.

[11] *Ferguson* v. *F's Trs.* (1877) 4 R. 532; *sed quaere*.

[12] Bell, *Prin.* §1046; *Macalister's Trs.* v. *M.* (1851) 13 D. 1239.

[13] *Freer's Trs.* v. *F.* (1897) 24 R. 437; *Dykes's Trs.* v. *D.* (1903) 6 F. 133; cf. *Wilson's Trs.* v. *W.* (1871) 8 S.L.R. 437.

[14] *Davidson's Trs.* v. *Ogilvie*, 1910 S.C. 294; cf. *Earl Haig's Trs.* v. *I.R.C.*, 1939 S.C. 676.

[15] *Hay's Trs.* v. *H.* (1903) 11 S.L.T. 306; *McLeod's Trs.* v. *McL.*, 1916 S.C. 604; *Warrack's Trs.* v. *W.*, 1919 S.C. 552.

represents the dividend accrued to date, having regard to the dividend expected and not that ultimately paid.[1]

Incidence of burdens

The general rule is that annual or other regular and ordinary outgoings fall on the liferenter, and capital outlays on the fiar.[2] Thus the liferenter must bear feuduty, local rates, fire insurance premiums,[3] interest on bonds secured over the property held in liferent,[4] and ordinary repairs,[5] but is entitled to the gratuitous use of minerals and timber on the estate, so far as necessary for repairs.[6]

But the fiar is chargeable with the repayment of bonds over the property liferented, extraordinary repairs, renewals, rebuilding, or other permanent improvements which will benefit the fee ultimately.[7] Neither party is liable for accidental destruction of the subjects by a cause for which neither is responsible[8] and restoration must be apportioned.

Payments such as in extinction of building society advances, made up of elements of principal and of interest, must be apportioned.

Incidental expenditure such as house factor's commission, solicitor's fees and outlays must also be divided between liferenter and fiar, though all expenses incurred on behalf of the estate and the beneficiaries as a whole are chargeable against capital.[9]

Apportionment at close of liferent

At common law a liferenter had no right to any part of payments due after the liferent terminated[10] but certain payments were deemed to accrue *de die in diem* and thus fell to be apportioned

[1] *Donaldson* v. *D's Trs.* (1851) 14 D. 165; *Cameron's Factor* v. *C.* (1873) 1 R. 21; *McLeod's Trs.* v. *McL.*, 1916 S.C. 604; See also *Gardiner Baird* (1907) 15 S.L.T. 25.

[2] Stair, More's Note, ccxv; Bankt. II, 6, 30; Ersk. II, 9, 61; Bell, *Prin.* §1061; *Ross's Tr.* v. *Nicoll* (1902) 5 F. 146; cf. *Vallombrosa Rubber Co.* v. *Farmer*, 1910 S.C. 579.

[3] *Brown* v. *Soutar & Meacher* (1870) 8 M. 702; *Glover's Trs.* v. *G.*, 1913 S.C. 115; *Milne's Trs.* v. *M.*, 1920 S.C. 456.

[4] *Glover's Trs.*, *supra.*

[5] Stair II, 6, 4; Ersk. II, 9, 61; Bell, *Prin.* §1061; *Johnstone* v. *Mackenzie's Trs.*, 1912 S.C. (H.L.) 106.

[6] *Dickson* v. *D.* (1823) 2 S. 152; *Macalister's Trs.* v. *M.* (1851) 13 D. 1239.

[7] *Preston* v. *P's Trs.* (1853) 15 D. 271; *Mackenzie* (1896) 4 S.L.T. 24; *Pottie* (1902) 4 F. 876; *Templeton* v. *Ayr Mags.*, 1912 1 S.L.T. 421; *Noble's Trs.*, 1912 S.C. 1230; *Shaw's Trs.* v. *Bruce*, 1917 S.C. 169.

[8] Ersk. II, 9, 60; Bell, *Prin.* §1063; *Scot* v. *Forbes* (1755) Mor. 8278.

[9] *Baxter & Mitchell* v. *Wood* (1864) 2 M. 915; *Paton* v. *P's Trs.* (1903) 5 F. 528.

[10] Bell, *Prin.* §1047.

according to the time during which they had accrued. These included interest on personal bonds,[1] profits of fishings, collieries and the rents of industrial subjects,[2] and the income of a *universitas*, such as of the residue of an estate.[3]

The Apportionment Act, 1870, provides that all rents, annuities, dividends and other periodical payments of the nature of income are to be considered as accruing from day to day and apportionable accordingly. Annual sums payable under policies of assurance are excluded (S. 6), and the Act has been held inapplicable to the profits of a partnership or business[4] and directors' fees, fixed at a rate per annum.[5]

The Act may be excluded by earlier statute,[6] or clear indication of the truster's intention.[7]

It is the practice to apportion outlays on the same basis.

Termination of liferent

A liferent normally terminates on the liferenter's death or any earlier event which is provided to have that effect, such as marriage,[8] or purported assignation of his right,[9] or on the expiry of any period, short of life, for which it has been created,[10] or by consolidation, if liferent and fee become vested in the same person. Exceptionally a gift of the annual profits of a sum may be held to continue beyond the beneficiary's lifetime.[11]

If not declared alimentary, the liferent may be renounced and the trustees called on to denude in favour of the fiar.[12]

It may doubtless be lost by the long negative prescription.[13]

Accretion in joint liferent

Where a liferent is conferred on several persons, the question whether, on the death of one, his interest in the trust accresces to the others, or falls to the fiar, is one of the intention disclosed by

[1] Ersk. II, 9, 66.
[2] Ersk., *supra*; Rankine, *Landownership*, 737.
[3] *Wood* v. *Menzies* (1871) 9 M. 775; *Fergusson* v. *F's Trs.* (1877) 4 R. 532; *Andrew's Trs.* v. *Hallett*, 1926 S.C. 1087.
[4] *Re Cox's Trusts* [1878] 9 Ch. D. 159.
[5] *Liqdr. of Fife Linoleum Co.* v. *Lornie* (1906) 13 S.L.T. 670.
[6] *Latta* v. *Edinburgh Ecclesiastical Commrs.* (1877) 5 R. 266.
[7] *Low's Trs.* (1871) 8 S.L.R. 638; *Macpherson's Trs.* v. *M.*, 1907 S.C. 1067.
[8] e.g. *Glover's Trs.* v. *G.*, 1913 S.C. 115; *McLeod's Trs.* v. *M.*, 1916 S.C. 604.
[9] e.g. *Chaplin's Trs.* v. *Hoile* (1891) 19 R. 231.
[10] cf. *Campbell* v. *Wardlaw* (1883) 10 R. (H.L.) 65.
[11] *McDonald's Trs.* v. *McD's Exrx.*, 1940 S.C. 433.
[12] *Martin* v. *Bannatyne* (1861) 23 D. 705, 708; *McMurdo's Trs.* v. *McM.* (1897) 24 R. 458; *Dunsmure's Trs.* v. *D.*, 1920 S.C. 147.
[13] Bell, *Prin.* §609; *Stuart* v. *Cuming* (1711) Mor. 10722.

the trust instrument. Accretion applies where the right is joint,[1] but not if there are words of severance, such as 'equally', 'in equal shares', or 'share and share alike',[2] though these inferences may be overruled by other evidence of contrary intention.[3] Where the gift is to a class there is normally accretion even though words of severance are used.[4] If one liferenter forfeits his interest, as by claiming legal rights, that interest does not necessarily accresce to the others.[5] A gift in liferent to persons and the survivors must result in accretion, whether the decease happens before or after the liferent opens.[6]

Right of occupancy

A right of occupancy is akin to a liferent but the beneficiary is not responsible for the burdens which a liferenter has to bear, and is not entitled to let the subjects but must occupy them personally.[7] Whether the beneficiary has a liferent or only a right of occupancy is a question of interpretation and circumstances.[8]

Alimentary liferent

Where the interest of a liferenter under a trust is declared to be alimentary, or for his alimentary use allenarly, or for his maintenance and support, or in similar words,[9] the interest is protected from the diligence of creditors so far as the amount of the liferent is not excessive for his maintenance and support, but *quoad ultra* may be attached.[10] Nor may it be assigned *ab ante* in

[1] Stair III, 8, 27; Bell, *Prin.* §1882; *Richardson* v. *Macdougall* (1868) 6 M. (H.L.) 18; *Buchanan's Trs.* (1883) 20 S.L.R. 666; *Napier's Trs.* v. *N.*, 1908 S.C. 1160; *Andrew's Exors.* v. *Andrew's Trs.*, 1925 S.C. 844.

[2] *Paxton's Trs.* v. *Cowie* (1886) 13 R. 1191; *Wilson's Trs.* v. *W's Trs.* (1894) 22 R. 62; *Bowman* v. *Richter* (1900) 2 F. 624; *Farquharson* v. *Kelly* (1900) 2 F. 863; *Young's Trs.* v. *Y.*, 1927 S.C. (H.L.) 6.

[3] *Ritchie's Trs.* v. *McDonald,* 1915 S.C. 501.

[4] *Bartholomew's Trs.* v. *B.* (1904) 6 F. 322.

[5] *M. Breadalbane's Trs.* v. *Pringle* (1841) 3 D. 357; *Rose's Trs.* v. *R.*, 1916 S.C. 827.

[6] *Fergus and Others* (1872) 10 M. 968.

[7] *Clark* (1871) 9 M. 435; *Johnston* v. *J.* (1904) 6 F. 665; *Milne's Trs.* v. *M.*, 1920 S.C. 456.

[8] cf. *Bayne's Trs.* v. *B.* (1894) 22 R. 26; *Cathcart's Trs.* v. *Allardice* (1899) 2 F. 326; *Smart's Tr.* v. *S's Trs.*, 1912 S.C. 87; all doubted in *Johnstone* v. *Mackenzie's Trs.*, 1912 S.C. (H.L.) 106; *Glover's Trs.* v. *G.*, 1913 S.C. 115; *Montgomerie-Fleming's Trs.* v. *M.F.'s J.F.*, 1913 S.C. 1018; *Milne's Tr.*, *supra*; see also *Miller* v. *I.R.C.*, 1928 S.C. 819; 1930 S.C. (H.L.) 49.

[9] *Chambers' Trs.* v. *Smith* (1878) 5 R. (H.L.) 51; *Reliance, etc. Socy.* v. *Halkett's Factor* (1891) 18 R. 615; *Dewar's Trs.* v. *D.*, 1910 S.C. 730; *Arnold's Trs.* v. *Graham,* 1927 S.C. 353; contrast *Douglas, Gardiner & Mill* v. *Mackintosh's Trs.*, 1916 S.C. 125.

[10] *Hamilton's Trs.* v. *H.* (1879) 6 R. 1216; *Livingstone* v. *L.* (1886) 14 R. 43; *Claremont's Trs.* v. *C.* (1896) 4 S.L.T. 144; *Inglis' Tr.* v. *I.*, 1924 S.C. 226.

whole or in part,[1] save possibly *quoad excessum*,[2] or under sequestration in bankruptcy.[3] It may be declined before acceptance.[4]

A person cannot validly create an alimentary liferent in his own favour[5] save that a woman may do so when settling her own property by ante-nuptial marriage contract,[6] though in this case the protection does not continue after she has become a widow.[7]

An alimentary fee is impossible.[8]

An alimentary liferent once created cannot be cancelled, even by consent of all parties,[9] nor can the liferenter discharge the provision and entitle the trustees to denude,[10] save that an alimentary liferent to a woman ceases to enjoy alimentary protection when she becomes a widow and may then be renounced and, unless there is any further trust purpose to be served, the trustees required to denude.[11]

Modification of alimentary liferent

At common law, even if an alimentary liferenter and all interested parties were *sui juris* and consented, a liferent declared alimentary could not be discharged or terminated in whole or in part,[12] not even if the alimentary liferenter had also become fiar.[13]

By statute,[14] however, where a trust purpose entitles a beneficiary to an alimentary liferent, or alimentary income, from the trust estate or any part thereof, the court may if it thinks fit, on the petition of the trustees or any of the beneficiaries, authorize any arrangement varying or revoking that trust purpose and making new provision in lieu thereof, including, if the court thinks fit, new provision for the disposal of the fee or capital of the trust estate or, as the case may be, of such part thereof as was burdened

[1] *Hewats* v. *Robertson* (1881) 9 R. 175.
[2] *Claremont's Trs.*, *supra*; *Craig* v. *Pearson's Trs.*, 1915 2 S.L.T. 183.
[3] *Claremont's Trs.*, *supra*; *Cuthbert* v. *C's Trs.*, 1908 S.C. 967.
[4] *Ford* v. *F's Trs.*, 1961 S.C. 122; cf. *Douglas-Hamilton* v. *Hamilton's Trs.*, 1961 S.C. 205.
[5] *Primrose's Crs.* v. *Heirs* (1744) Mor. 15501; *Ker's Trs.* v. *Justice* (1866) 5 M. 4; *White's Trs.* v. *Whyte* (1877) 4 R. 786; *Robertson* v. *R's Tr.* (1878) 16 S.L.R. 13; *Hamilton's Trs.* v. *H.* (1879) 6 R. 1216.
[6] *Burn-Murdoch's Trs.* v. *Tinney*, 1937 S.C. 743.
[7] *Martin* v. *Bannatyne* (1861) 23 D. 705; *Dempster's Trs.* v. *D.*, 1949 S.C. 92; *Sturgis's Tr.* v. *S.*, 1951 S.C. 637.
[8] *Wilkie's Trs.* v. *Wight's Trs.* (1893) 21 R. 199; *Watson's Trs.* v. *W.*, 1913 S.C. 1133; *Dempster's Trs.*, *supra.*
[9] *Hughes* v. *Edwardes* (1892) 19 R. (H.L.) 33.
[10] *Smith* v. *Campbell* (1873) 11 M. 639; *Cosens* v. *Stevenson* (1873) 11 M. 761; *White's Trs.* v. *Whyte* (1877) 4 R. 786; *Montgomery's Trs.* v. *M.* (1888) 15 R. 369.
[11] *Martin*, *supra*; *Dempster's Trs.*, *supra*; *Sturgis's Tr.*, *supra.*
[12] *Hughes* v. *Edwards* (1892) 19 R. (H.L.) 33; *Forbes* v. *F.*, 1957 S.L.T. 346.
[13] *Miller's Trs.*, 1953 S.L.T. 225.
[14] Trusts (Sc.) Act, 1961, S. 1(4).

with the liferent or the payment of the income; but it shall not authorize such an arrangement unless (a) it considers that the carrying out of the arrangement could be reasonable, having regard to the income of the alimentary beneficiary from all sources, and to such other factors, if any, as the court considers material, and (b) the arrangement is approved by the alimentary beneficiary, or, where the alimentary beneficiary is a person on whose behalf the court is empowered by S. 1(1) or (2) to approve the arrangement, the arrangement is so approved by the court under that subsection.

Powers under nobile officium

The court has power, under the *nobile officium*, to sanction the variation of a trust as to capital and assets to beneficiaries,[1] but the court has rarely exercised this power and it seems confined to cases for which there is precedent.[2] This power is not, however, limited or restricted by the 1961 Act.[3]

INTERESTS ARISING UNDER TRUSTS
MARRIAGE CONTRACT TRUSTS

The purposes of an *inter vivos* marriage-contract trust, whether ante-nuptial or post-nuptial, are normally the protection of the interests of the surviving spouse, particularly if the wife survive, and of the children of the marriage, from the other spouse and his creditors. The funds may be contributed by either, or both, spouses, or their parents, and the trust purposes normally include provisions for the disposal of the income *stante matrimonio*, and provisions, frequently by alimentary liferent, for the surviving spouse and for the children, frequently by gift of the fee. A wife may validly create in her own favour an alimentary liferent over property contributed by her or her father in her ante-nuptial marriage-contract,[4] but cannot do so by post-nuptial marriage-contract.[5]

A marriage contract is not revocable, even if both spouses consent, because the children of the marriage, even though not

[1] *Christie's Trs.*, 1932 S.L.T. 35.
[2] *Coles*, 1951 S.C. 608.
[3] 1961 Act, S. 1(5).
[4] *Martin* v. *Bannatyne* (1861) 23 D. 705; *Dempster's Trs.* v. *D.*, 1949 S.C. 92; *Sturgis's Tr.* v. *S.*, 1951 S.C. 637; see also *Neame* v. *N's Trs.*, 1956 S.L.T. 57; *Strange*, 1966 S.L.T. 59.
[5] *Cargill*, 1965 S.L.T. 193.

yet conceived, are deemed parties to it and no direct act of the spouses can impair the interests prospectively created in the children's favour.[1]

Marriage-contract provisions in favour of the surviving spouse or children are commonly expressed to be in full satisfaction of claims competent to the spouse or children, as the case may be, by way of legal rights or otherwise, on the death of the first-deceasing spouse. But provisions in antenuptial marriage contracts executed after 10 September 1964 cannot discharge the right of any child of the marriage, or more remote descendant, to legitim unless such child or issue elects to accept the provisions made in his favour under the contract in lieu of legitim.[2]

A wife cannot, *stante matrimonio*, discharge an annuity provided by ante-nuptial marriage-contract in the event of her survivance, even though it be not declared alimentary.[3] She may renounce an alimentary liferent before entering into enjoyment of it, provided her right is contingent and she is not seeking to convert it into any other kind of right.[4]

An alimentary liferent in the wife's favour will cease to be alimentary when her husband dies, whether or not there are surviving issue of the marriage, unless it is clearly and explicitly provided that the alimentary character of the liferent is to continue.[5] Accordingly in the normal case authority to remove the alimentary restriction is unnecessary.[6]

Where marriage terminated by nullity or divorce

Difficulties may arise where a *casus improvisus* arises, such as the termination of the marriage by decree of nullity or of divorce. In such a case the interpretation of the marriage-contract, in the unforeseen circumstances, may give rise to results probably unintended.[7] An obligation in terms prestable on the death of one spouse, whether by that spouse's personal obligation, or in succession to him, becomes enforceable if that spouse is divorced, the guilty spouse being fictionally treated as having died and forfeited provisions in his or her favour at the date of the decree of

[1] *Adv.-Gen.* v. *Trotter* (1847) 10 D. 56, 70; *Harvey's J.F.* v. *Spittal's Curator* (1893) 20 R. 1016, 1021.
[2] Succession (Sc.) Act, 1964, S. 12.
[3] *Menzies* v. *Murray* (1875) 2 R. 507; *Ker's Trs.* v. *K.* (1895) 23 R. 317.
[4] *Douglas-Hamilton* v. *Hamilton's Trs.*, 1961 S.C. 205.
[5] *Dempster's Trs.* v. *D.*, 1949 S.C. 92; *Sturgis's Tr.* v. *S.*, 1951 S.C. 637.
[6] *Strange*, 1966 S.L.T. 59.
[7] e.g. *Fortington* v. *Kinnaird*, 1942 S.C. 239.

divorce,[1] and this rule applies even where the obligant bound is not the divorced spouse but a third party, such as that spouse's parent.[2] But the fiction that the divorced spouse is dead, though it has the effect of accelerating payment of the contractual provisions to the innocent spouse, does not accelerate provisions in favour of the children or other third parties.[3]

Where the estate of a divorced spouse included a liferent interest, the innocent spouse was held entitled to her legal rights out of the liferent interest, notwithstanding the fiction that the divorced spouse had died.[4]

A spouse who has forfeited pecuniary provisions in her favour in the marriage-contract is not necessarily thereby debarred from exercising powers conferred on her by the deed, such as to fix the period of division.[5]

LIABILITIES OF TRUSTEES

Liability to beneficiaries

The liability to beneficiaries is to account for intromissions and to make over to them, at the time directed by the trust deed, the property to which they are entitled thereunder on the basis that the trust has been prudently administered.

Liability to third parties

The trustees are liable to creditors of the truster to the value of the trust estate only,[6] but must show care and diligence towards them in realising the estate, and a clause of protection will not protect trustees from liability for lack of diligence in a question with creditors.[7]

Where trustees incur liability to third parties, the liability may or may not be limited to the value of the trust estate, even though incurred on behalf of the trust. Unless liability is expressly limited,[8] or it is clear that the creditor accepted the trust as his

[1] Stair I, 4, 20; More's Note, xxvii; Bankt. I, 5, 34; Ersk. I, 6, 46; Hume, *Lect.* I, 172; Bell, *Prin.* §1622; Fraser, *H. & W.* II, 1217; *Fortington, supra*; *Coat's Trs.* v. *I.R.C.*, 1965 S.C. (H.L.) 45.

[2] *Johnstone-Beattie* v. *J.* (1867) 5 M. 340; *Fortington, supra*, disapproving *Drummond* v. *Bell-Irving*, 1930 S.C. 704.

[3] *Harvey's J.F.* v. *Spittall's Curator* (1893) 20 R. 1016; *Dawson* v. *Smart* (1903) 5 F. (H.L.) 24.

[4] *Scott* v. *S.*, 1930 S.C. 903; *Selsdon* v. *S.*, 1934 S.C. (H.L.) 24.

[5] *McGrady's Trs.* v. *McG.*, 1932 S.C. 191.

[6] *Cullen* v. *Baillie* (1846) 8 D. 511; *Stewart's Trs.* v. *S's Exor.* (1896) 23 R. 739.

[7] *Cowan* v. *Crawford* (1836) 14 S. 744.

[8] *Gordon* v. *Campbell* (1842) 1 Bell 428.

debtor,[1] the presumption is that the creditor relies on the credit of the trustees as individuals.[2] Trustees who take shares in a company are personally liable for calls on the shares and, if the company is unlimited, for its liabilities, and their liability is not limited to the extent of the trust estate.[3] They are entitled to relief from the trust estate *quantum valeat* if the investment was authorized.[4] In cases of liability to third parties the liability of trustees is joint and several.[5]

BREACH OF TRUST

Breach of trust includes not only any dishonest dealing with the trust property but any inability or failure to account, or any failure, intentional or unintentional, to implement obligatory provisions of the trust deed,[6] or to take the care or show the diligence required of a prudent trustee.[7] All trustees are jointly and severally liable for breach of trust.[8] Where a trustee has diverted funds into his own pockets he must repay the trust, with interest; if he has employed trust assets for his own purposes, he must account for the capital and, at the beneficiaries' option, for the profit made thereon, or pay interest at a rate fixed by the court.[9] If he has mixed trust funds with his own money, he must pay interest at such rate as the court may fix[10] and restore the trust assets to the trust.[11] Where he has made an unauthorized investment the beneficiaries may adopt it or require the restoration of the capital invested, with interest from the date thereof; if they do not adopt it the trustee must keep it[12] or sell it and in either case

[1] *Cullen, supra.*

[2] *Cullen, supra*; *Maclean's Tr.* v. *M.* (1850) 13 D. 90; *Lumsden* v. *Buchanan* (1865) 3 M. (H.L.) 89; *Brebner* v. *Henderson*, 1925 S.C. 643; *Johnston* v. *Waddell*, 1928 S.N. 81.

[3] *Lumsden, supra*; *Lumsden* v. *Peddie* (1866) 5 M. 34; *Muir* v. *City of Glasgow Bank* (1879) 6 R. (H.L.) 21.

[4] *Cunningham* v. *Montgomerie* (1879) 6 R. 1333; *Robinson* v. *Fraser's Tr.* (1881) 8 R. (H.L.) 127. Contrast *Brownlie* v. *B's Trs.* (1879) 6 R. 1233; *Sanders* v. *S's Trs.* (1879) 7 R. 157; *City of Glasgow Bank* v. *Parkhurst* (1880) 7 R. 749.

[5] *Oswald's Trs.* v. *City of Glasgow Bank* (1879) 6 R. 461; *Croskery* v. *Gilmour's Trs.* (1890) 17 R. 697; *Allen* v. *McCombie's Trs.*, 1909 S.C. 710; *Johnston, supra.*

[6] *Hood* v. *Macdonald's Tr.*, 1949 S.C. 24.

[7] *Town and County Bank, Ltd.* v. *Walker* (1904) 12 S.L.T. 411, 412; *Clarke* v. *C's Trs.*, 1925 S.C. 693.

[8] *Allen* v. *McCombie's Trs.*, 1909 S.C. 710.

[9] *Cochrane* v. *Black* (1855) 17 D. 321; *Laird* v. *L.* (1855) 17 D. 984; (1858) 20 D. 972; *Douglas* v. *D's Trs.* (1864) 2 M. 1379.

[10] *Malcolm's Exors.* v. *M.* (1869) 8 M. 272.

[11] *Macadam* v. *Martin's Tr.* (1872) 11 M. 33; *Jopp* v. *Johnston's Tr.* (1904) 6 F. 1028.

[12] *Henderson* v. *H's Trs.* (1900) 2 F. 1295.

account to the trust for the capital and interest it would have earned as a trustee investment.[1]

Damages for breach of trust

Where trustees' actings in breach of trust have resulted in loss to the trust estate, they are liable in damages, measured by the deficiency in the trust estate caused by the breach of duty.[2] There is no liability merely for the breach if it has not caused pecuniary loss.[3] If the breach has been merely by failure to invest, the damages will be the difference between the interest which could have been earned on proper investments and that actually earned.[4]

A trustee who has been in breach of duty may escape liability in damages if the loss would have occurred independently of his breach of trust,[5] or if due diligence and performance of duty would have recovered nothing.[6]

If the breach consists merely in unreasonable delay in paying beneficiaries, the damages will be interest from the date when payment should have been made, and that whether or not the trust estate was yielding income.[7] If the breach is merely leaving trust funds on deposit receipt or deposit account when they could have been more profitably invested, the damages will be the difference between the interest earned and that which could have been earned on trustee investments.[8]

If the breach is by investment in an unauthorized investment, he is liable for any loss of capital or income actually sustained[9] and must take over the investment as his own,[10] but the beneficiaries may adopt the investment and accept it as trust property. A trustee cannot set off a gain on one transaction in breach of trust against a loss on another, nor general beneficial administration against a loss by a particular breach of trust.[11]

[1] *Douglas* v. *D's Trs.* (1864) 2 M. 1379; *Beveridge's Tr.* v. *B.*, 1908 S.C. 791; *Wright* v. *Morgan* [1926] A.C. 788.

[2] *Town and County Bank* v. *Walker* (1904) 12 S.L.T. 411.

[3] *Buchanan* v. *Eaton*, 1911 S.C. (H.L.) 40; *McKnight's Trs.* v. *Free Church of Sc.*, 1916 S.C. 349; cf. *In re Brogden* (1888) 38 Ch. D. 546.

[4] *Melville* v. *Noble's Trs.* (1896) 24 R. 293; *Clarke* v. *C's Trs.*, 1925 S.C. 693.

[5] *Carruthers* v. *C.* (1896) 23 R. (H.L.) 55.

[6] *Millar's Trs.* v. *Polson* (1897) 24 R. 1038.

[7] *Lees's Trs.* v. *Dun*, 1912 S.C. 50; *Clarke* v. *C's Trs.*, 1925 S.C. 693; *Waddell's Trs.* v. *Crawford*, 1926 A.C. 654.

[8] *Melville* v. *Noble's Trs.* (1896) 24 R. 293; *Clarke*, *supra*.

[9] *Learoyd* v. *Whiteley* (1887) 12 App. Cas. 727; *Crabbe* v. *Whyte* (1891) 18 R. 1065; *Beveridge's Tr.* v. *B.*, 1908 S.C. 791; *Cross* v. *C's Trs.*, 1919 1 S.L.T. 166.

[10] *Henderson* v. *H's Trs.* (1900) 2 F. 1295.

[11] *Clarke*, *supra*.

If a trustee has inmixed trust funds with his own, he is liable to credit the trust with such rate of interest as seems proper to the court, possibly even to interest at the highest legal rate, the interest being compounded,[1] always provided that the trust funds could have been invested to profit.

Liability for co-trustees

At common law a trustee is not liable for the acts of his co-trustees unless he authorized them, or acquiesced in them, or negligently failed to interfere. Section 3(d) of the 1921 Act implies a provision that each trustee shall not be liable for the acts and intromissions of co-trustees, but this is no wider than the common law provision. Hence beneficiaries may sue one trustee only for breach of trust.[2] A trustee may not leave the active administration to a co-trustee.[3] If a trustee doubts the judgment or integrity of a co-trustee he should intervene. He will be liable if he suspects misappropriation and takes no steps to recover the money and to prevent further money getting into the suspect trustee's hands.[4]

Liability for solicitors, factors, and others

Trustees are bound, in appointing solicitors, factors, and other advisers, to take reasonable care to choose persons properly qualified and in good business repute, and they must exercise reasonable supervision,[5] but are not responsible if such an agent acts incapably or dishonestly if they had no reasonable grounds for suspecting him.[6] They will be responsible if they leave funds in an agent's hands and he misappropriates them, but not if he does so with funds entrusted to him for a particular purpose.[7]

Liability for accidental loss

Trustees are not liable for loss caused accidentally to the trust estate, unless there has been serious negligence on their part, as by leaving heritage uninsured against fire.

[1] *Malcolm's Exors.* v. *M.* (1869) 8 M. 272, 277.

[2] *Aitkenhead* v. *Oliver,* 1933 S.N. 18.

[3] *Carruthers* v. *Cairns* (1890) 17 R. 769; *Adair's Factor* v. *Connell's Trs.* (1894) 22 R. 116; cf. *Seton* v. *Dawson* (1841) 4 D. 310; *Edmond* v. *Dingwall's Trs.* (1866) 4 M. 1011. Contrast *Kennedy* v. *K.* (1884) 12 R. 275.

[4] *Millar's Trs.* v. *Polson* (1897) 24 R. 1038.

[5] *Wyman* v. *Paterson* (1900) 2 F. (H.L.) 37.

[6] *Home* v. *Pringle* (1841) 2 Rob. App. 384.

[7] *Speight* v. *Gaunt* (1883) 9 App. Cas. 1; *Buchanan* v. *Eaton,* 1911 S.C. (H.L.) 40.

Relief against beneficiary or co-trustee instigating breach

If a trustee has committed a breach of trust at the instigation, or request, or with the consent in writing,[1] of a beneficiary, the court may, if it thinks fit, make such order as to the court seems just to apply all or any part of the interest of the beneficiary in the trust estate by way of indemnity to the trustee or person claiming through him.[2]

The section does not give the trustee any personal right of action against the beneficiary but only a liberty to ask the court to exercise a discretion in his favour.[3] The instigation, request, or consent must be to do something which is a breach of trust *per se*, not something permissible which becomes breach of trust by the way in which the trustee does it,[4] and it must be to do something which the beneficiary knows or should have known to be a breach of trust.[5]

Express protective clause in trust deed

It is common to insert in trust deeds clauses purporting to confer on trustees protection, or even immunity, from liability for breach of trust, but the cases suggest that such clauses confer no greater protection than trustees have at common law, and probably no clause would protect against the consequences of gross negligence or conduct not in good faith.[6] Even protection from liability on specified grounds will be denied effect if conflicting with the fundamental duty of a trustee to exercise due care in the administration of the trust.[7]

Statutory protection

The 1921 Act, S. 3(d) provides that all trusts shall be held to include, unless the contrary be expressed, a provision that each trustee is to be held liable only for his own acts and intromissions and not for the acts and intromissions of co-trustees and is not to be liable for omissions. This extends to all trustees whether gratuitous or not.[8] The section is declaratory of common law

1 'In writing' applies to 'consent' only: *Griffith* v. *Hughes* [1892] 3 Ch. 105.
2 1921 Act, Ss. 31, 32(2).
3 *Henderson's Trs.* v. *H.* (1900) 2 F. 1295.
4 *Cathcart's Trs.* v. *C.* (1907) 15 S.L.T. 646.
5 *Henderson's Trs., supra*; *Cathcart's Trs., supra.*
6 *Seton* v. *Dawson* (1842) 4 D. 318; *Thomson* v. *Christie* (1852) 1 Macq. 236; *Knox* v. *Mackinnon* (1888) 15 R. (H.L.) 83, 86; *Raes* v. *Meek* (1889) 16 R. (H.L.) 31; *Clarke* v. *C's Trs.*, 1925 S.C. 693, 707.
7 *Raes, supra*; *Clarke, supra.*
8 1921 Act, S. 2.

rather than extensive of it. Non-liability for omissions does not cover the omission to perform the main duties of a trustee, nor the omission to take ordinary precautions and reasonable care, nor the failure to do something required by the trust deed, nor conduct so neglectful as to be a positive breach of duty.[1]

It does not exclude liability for matters improperly delegated to agents.[2]

The trustee, as at common law, is liable for the actings of co-trustees only so far as he has expressly or impliedly authorized them.[3]

Relief by the Court

If it appears to the court that a trustee is or may be personally liable for any breach of trust, but has acted honestly and reasonably, and ought fairly to be excused for the breach of trust, the court may relieve the trustee either wholly or partly from personal liability for it.[4]

To qualify for relief the trustee's conduct must have been both honest and reasonable; honest but negligent conduct is not reasonable,[5] nor is failure to comply with a statutory requirement,[6] nor unauthorized investment.[7]

Breach resulting from honest and reasonable misconstruction of the trust deed may be excused[8] though if the trustee was in substantial doubt he should have taken advice rather than risked his interpretation.[9]

The court always has a discretion and must always deem the circumstances such that the trustee ought fairly to be excused.

Prescription

A claim against trustees in respect of a particular transaction or alleged misapplication of the funds may be barred by the long negative prescription.[10] But no lapse of time entitles a trustee to continue doing what is a breach of trust,[11] nor does it elide the

[1] *Raes* v. *Meek* (1889) 16 R. (H.L.) 31; *Melville* v. *Noble's Trs.* (1896) 24 R. 243; *Clarke* v. *C's Trs.*, 1925 S.C. 636.

[2] *Wyman* v. *Paterson* (1900) 2 F. (H.L.) 37.

[3] Ersk. III, 3, 36; Bell, *Prin.* §2000.

[4] Trusts (Sc.) Act, 1921, S. 32.

[5] *Clarke* v. *C's Trs.*, 1925 S.C. 693.

[6] *Re Stuart* [1897] 2 Ch. 583.

[7] *Chapman* v. *Browne* [1902] 1 Ch. 785.

[8] *Re Grindey* [1898] 2 Ch. 593; *Re Mackay* [1911] 1 Ch. 300.

[9] *Clarke, supra.*

[10] *Barns* v. *B's Trs.* (1857) 19 D. 626; *Cooper Scott* v. *Gill Scott*, 1924 S.C. 309, 331.

[11] *Aberdeen University* v. *Irvine* (1866) 4 M. 392; 6 M. (H.L.) 29; *Thain* v. *T.* (1891) 18 R. 1196.

liability of trustees to account for their intromissions, nor protect the representatives of former trustees from liability.[1]

DENUDING AND TERMINATION OF TRUST

Right of beneficiaries to end the trust

If all beneficiaries are legally capable of consenting, and concur in asking the trustees to do so, the trustees must terminate the trust and are entitled to be exonered and discharged.[2] This may be impossible if unborn issue have contingent rights. Though there is no age at which a person is deemed incapable of begetting or bearing children, if the possibility of issue seems very remote the court may authorize the trustees to denude on the beneficiaries finding caution to repay in the event of children being born.[3] A beneficiary may also accelerate the termination of the trust by paying off debts which delay termination.[4]

Where the truster has conferred an unqualified and indefeasible fee on a beneficiary and that provision has vested, the beneficiary may claim the provision free of restrictions imposed by the trust deed which would otherwise fetter and restrict the fee.[5]

Where the whole provisions of an antenuptial marriage contract applicable to the intended marriage have been fulfilled the truster can call for repayment of the trust funds.[6]

Termination is not generally possible if one of the interests under the trust is an alimentary right of liferent or annuity, in which case the trust must be maintained even though all parties wish to terminate the trust,[7] unless the liferent has ceased to enjoy alimentary protection, there are no ulterior interests requiring the protection of the trust, and all interested parties concur,[8] or unless the trust is varied by the Court under the Trusts (Sc.) Act, 1961, or unless the Court under the *nobile officium* authorizes the trustees to denude.[9]

1 *Hastie's J.F.* v. *Morham's Trs.*, 1951 S.C. 668.
2 *E. Lindsay* v. *Shaw*, 1959 S.L.T. (Notes) 13.
3 *Cameron* v. *Young* (1873) 45 Sc. Jur. 272; *Munro* v. *Macarthur* (1878) 16 S.L.R. 126; *De la Chaumette's Trs.* v. *De la C.* (1902) 4 F. 745; *McPherson's Trs.* v. *Hill* (1902) 4 F. 921; *Turnbull's Trs.* v. *T.* (1907) 15 S.L.T. 229; *Snodgrass*, 1922 S.C. 491.
4 *White's Trs.* v. *Nicol*, 1923 S.C. 859.
5 *Miller's Trs.* v. *M.* (1890) 18 R. 301; *Yuill's Trs.* v. *Thomson* (1902) 4 F. 815; *Macculloch* v. *McCulloch's Trs.* (1903) 6 F. (H.L.) 3.
6 *Steel's Trs.* v. *Cassels*, 1939 S.C. 502.
7 *Eliott's Trs.* v. *E.* (1894) 21 R. 975; *Main's Trs.* v. *M.*, 1917 S.C. 660; *Howat's Trs.* v. *H.*, 1922 S.C. 506; *Smith's Trs.* v. *Dinwoodie*, 1958 S.L.T. 305.
8 *Dempster's Trs.* v. *D.*, 1949 S.C. 92; *Sturgis's Trs.* v. *S.*, 1951 S.C. 637.
9 *Gray* v. *G's Trs.* (1877) 4 R. 378; *Stillie's Trs.* v. *S's Trs.* (1901) 3 F. 1054.

Nor is denuding at the instance of the beneficiaries competent if it will prejudice the trustees in their administration of the trust.[1]

Termination in accordance with trust deed

The trustees are bound to bring the trust to an end at the time or in the circumstances provided for by the trust deed. Only exceptionally may payment be deferred.[2] Trustees are not entitled to defer distribution because an adopted child has a claim for aliment.[3]

The trustees are bound to account to the beneficiaries for the trust estate received from the truster and their whole intromissions with it, making good deficiencies and accounting for everything constructively deemed part of the trust estate. The present trustees must account not only for their own, but for former trustees' intromissions also.[4] Former trustees and their representatives are not discharged from liability to account by the long negative prescription.[5]

If the trustees have a discretion whether, or how much, to pay a beneficiary,[6] their discretion is not challengeable unless manifestly unreasonable, or possibly even only if reached *in mala fide* or *ultra vires*.[7]

Duty to pay proper beneficiary

A trustee must take care to pay only to the proper beneficiary;[8] he is entitled to be discharged only if he has done so.[9]

If the trustee pays to the wrong beneficiary he remains absolutely liable to the right one and is bound to account to him for capital and interest from the date when it was payable, notwithstanding good faith or honesty of mistake or even advice which proves incorrect.[10] The only safe course, if there is any doubt, is to raise a multiplepoinding and pay only as authorized

1 *De Robeck* v. *I.R.C.*, 1928 S.C. (H.L.) 34.

2 e.g. *De Robeck* v. *I.R.C.*, 1928 S.C. (H.L.) 34; *Campbell* v. *Borthwick's Trs.*, 1930 S.N. 156 (debts still outstanding).

3 *Beaton* v. *B's Trs.*, 1935 S.C. 187; *Hutchison* v. *H's Trs.*, 1951 S.C. 108 (but see now Succession (Sc.) Act, 1964, S. 23).

4 *Lees's Trs.* v. *Dun*, 1913 S.C. (H.L.) 12; *Hastie's J.F.* v. *Morham's Exor.*, 1951 S.C. 668.

5 *Hastie's J.F.*, *supra*.

6 As to whether trustees had a discretion or not, see *Galloway* v. *Elgin Mags.*, 1946 S.C. 353.

7 *Dundee General Hospitals* v. *Bell's Trs.*, 1952 S.C. (H.L.) 78.

8 As to the duty of finding beneficiaries where the trustees have a discretion see *Caldwell's Trs.* v. *C.*, 1923 S.L.T. 694.

9 *Lamond's Trs.* v. *Croom* (1871) 9 M. 681.

10 *Nat. Trs. of Australasia* v. *General Finance Co. of Australasia* [1905] A.C. 373.

by the court.[1] If there is doubt as to the identity or qualifications of a purported beneficiary it may suffice to have taken reasonable precautions and made reasonable enquiries before payment.[2] Where the right of beneficiaries depends on a decree presuming the death of an absent person, payment may be made, subject to an obligation to repay if the presumption of death turns out to be incorrect.[3]

The trustee is not, however, liable for paying the wrong beneficiary if he did so through mistake of foreign law, so long as he had taken reasonable steps to ascertain that law,[4] or if the true beneficiary's actings led to the wrong payment,[5] or the true beneficiary's title is derived from the wrong beneficiary and the trustee is in ignorance of this, as where an assignation has not been intimated to him.[6]

Recovery of mis-payment

Money paid to the wrong beneficiary is recoverable by the trustees if the mistake be one of fact,[7] or of the interpretation of the trust deed,[8] but probably not if the mistake was as to general law.[9] The wrong beneficiary must repay if he still has the payment intact, or mixed with his general funds, but need not if it was specifically appropriated to a purpose and has already been spent on that purpose.[10]

The true beneficiaries may sue the wrong beneficiary direct, provided the trustees are also called.[11] They are not necessarily barred by having granted a discharge wide enough to cover the payment made by the trustees.[11] The beneficiaries may follow the trust property, to the effect of reclaiming it, or the property into which it has been converted, if the trustee has parted with it in breach of trust,[12] unless the taker from him has taken the

[1] cf. *McLevy's Trs.*, 1947 S.N. 119.
[2] *Flett* v. *Brown's Exor.*, 1915 2 S.L.T. 261.
[3] *Barr* v. *Campbell*, 1925 S.C. 317.
[4] *Leslie* v. *Baillie* (1847) 2 Y. & C. Ch. 91.
[5] *E. Strathmore* v. *Rescobie Heritors* (1888) 15 R. 364.
[6] *Phipps* v. *Lovegrove* (1873) L.R. 16 Eq. 80; contrast *Hallows* v. *Lloyd* (1888) 39 Ch. D. 686.
[7] *Tainsh* v. *Rollo* (1824) 3 S. 47; *Credit Lyonnais* v. *Stevenson* (1901) 9 S.L.T. 93.
[8] cf. *Chichester Diocesan Fund* v. *Simpson* [1944] A.C. 341; *British Hydro-Carbon Chemicals, Ltd. and B.T.C.*, 1961 S.L.T. 280.
[9] *Rowan's Trs.* v. *R.*, 1940 S.C. 30; cf. *Glasgow Corpn.* v. *Lord Advocate*, 1959 S.C. 203.
[10] cf. *Re Diplock* [1948] Ch. 465, 521.
[11] *Armour* v. *Glasgow R.I.*, 1909 S.C. 916.
[12] *Taylor* v. *Forbes* (1830) 4 W. & S. 444; *Airdrie Mags.* v. *Smith* (1850) 12 D. 1222; *Re Hallett's Estate* (1879) 13 Ch. D. 696; *Sinclair* v. *Brougham* [1914] A.C. 398; *Banque Belge* v. *Hambrouck* [1921] 1 K.B. 321.

property in good faith, for value, and without notice of the trust affecting it.[1]

Trustee's right to reimbursement

A trustee is impliedly entitled to be reimbursed for all expenses and outlays properly incurred by him in the administration of the trust, but he loses that right if guilty of culpable neglect of his duty as trustee.[2] The claim is preferable to that of creditors and beneficiaries.[3]

Exoneration and discharge

Trustees who resign office, or die, are entitled to a discharge from the continuing trustees or the beneficiaries,[4] or, if that is impossible, from the court.[5]

At the ending of the trust the trustees are entitled, unless they have been guilty of breach of trust, to exoneration from their intromissions,[6] to be relieved of any contingent liabilities arising under the trust deed, and to a formal unconditional discharge on denuding.[7] The trust deed may provide for exoneration in a particular way, as by audit of accounts,[8] or that a simple receipt shall be a sufficient discharge.[9]

A discharge must be granted by the correct person, or by a duly authorized agent of such a person.[10] Court authority cannot supply the lack of a discharge in respect of moveables where the beneficiary cannot by the law of his domicile grant one.[11] The sufficiency of a discharge in respect of heritage depends on the *lex loci rei sitae*.[12] Trustees are entitled to discharge in respect of their own intromissions only, and not in respect of those of their predecessors.[13]

[1] *Somervails* v. *Redfearn* (1813) 1 Dow 50; cf. *Thomson* v. *Clydesdale Bank* (1893) 20 R. (H.L.) 59; *Bertram Gardner & Co.* v. *King's Remembrancer*, 1920 S.C. 555.

[2] *Johnstone* v. *Beattie* (1856) 18 D. 343; *Goodsir* v. *Carruthers* (1858) 20 D. 1141; *Cunningham* v. *Montgomerie* (1879) 6 R. 1333; *Robertson* v. *Fraser's Tr.* (1881) 8 R. (H.L.) 127; *Anderson* v. *A's Tr.* (1901) 4 F. 96; *Jackson* v. *J's Trs.*, 1918 1 S.L.T. 119.

[3] *Thomson* v. *Tough* (1880) 7 R. 1035; *MacGregor* v. *MacLennan's Trs.* (1898) 25 R. 482; *More* v. *Kirkhope & Gilmour* (1907) 15 S.L.T. 203.

[4] Trusts (Sc.) Act, 1921, S. 4(g); see also *Bunten* v. *Muir* (1894) 21 R. 370.

[5] *Matthew's Trs.* (1894) 2 S.L.T. 122.

[6] *Edmond* v. *Dingwall's Trs.* (1860) 23 D. 21.

[7] *Fleming* v. *Brown* (1861) 23 D. 443.

[8] *Tod* v. *T's Trs.* (1842) 4 D. 1275.

[9] *Lumsden's Trs.* v. *L.*, 1921 1 S.L.T. 155.

[10] *Cameron* v. *Panton's Trs.* (1891) 18 R. 728.

[11] *Sawyer* v. *Sloan* (1875) 3 R. 271; *Atherstone's Trs.* (1896) 24 R. 39; *Sawry-Cookson* v. *S.C.'s Trs.* (1905) 8 F. 157.

[12] *Ogilvy* v. *O's Trs.*, 1927 S.L.T. 83.

[13] *Mackenzie's Exor.* v. *Thomson's Trs.*, 1965 S.L.T. 410.

Beneficiaries will be barred from subsequent claims on the trustees by a discharge, provided it was granted with full knowledge of the affairs of the trust, and discharge may be implied by their actings.

A discharge, even if general, covers only items in the contemplation of parties at the time the discharge was granted, and does not preclude a claim on a surplus which emerges after division had been made,[1] or a claim for reimbursement of money mistakenly paid to the beneficiary,[2] or a claim for money paid by mistake to the wrong beneficiary.[3]

A discharge is reducible if granted under fraud or essential error.[4]

Discharge by Court

If trustees cannot otherwise obtain a discharge, as when the beneficiaries are absent or incapable, or delay or refuse unreasonably, they may petition the court for discharge.[5]

Effect of exoneration and discharge

Once trustees have been exonered and discharged by formal discharge or judicial decree they cannot be called to account unless the discharge is first reduced, on the ground of fraud, misrepresentation, or that the beneficiaries were ignorant of their rights.

Completion of title by beneficiary on lapsed trust

If a trustee has died or become incapable of acting before transferring the estate to the beneficiary entitled to the possession thereof for his own absolute use, the latter may apply to the court for authority to complete title in his own name to the property.[6]

1 *Burns* v. *B's Trs.*, 1911 2 S.L.T. 392; cf. *Symmer's Trs.* v. *S.*, 1918 S.C. 337; *Dickson's Trs.* v. *D's Trs.*, 1930 S.L.T. 226.

2 *Johnstone* v. *Mackenzie*, 1912 S.C. (H.L.) 106.

3 *Armour* v. *Glagow R.I.*, 1909 S.C. 916.

4 *Dickson* v. *Halbert* (1854) 16 D. 586; *Scott* v. *Craig's Reps.* (1897) 24 R. 462; *Straker* v. *Campbell*, 1926 S.L.T. 262.

5 1921 Act, S. 18; see *Fotheringham* v. *Salton* (1852) 14 D. 427; *Davidson* v. *Ewen* (1895) 3 S.L.T. 162; *Mackenzie's Trs.* v. *Sutherland* (1895) 22 R. 233; *Paterson's Trs.* v. *P.* (1899) 7 S.L.T. 134; *Glen's Trs.* v. *Miller*, 1911 S.C. 1178; *Greenshield's Trs.* v. *G.*, 1915 2 S.L.T. 189.

6 1921 Act, S. 24; cf. *Macknight* (1875) 2 R. 667; *Cowper* (1897) 5 S.L.T. 85; *Paisley Cemetery Co.*, 1933 S.L.T. 415; *Scott's Trs.*, 1957 S.L.T. (Notes) 45.

CHAPTER 105

PUBLIC TRUSTS

PUBLIC trusts are those which are intended for the benefit of a section of the public and which may be enforced by *popularis actio*.[1] The class includes trusts for religious, educational, philanthropic, and charitable purposes.

The general principles of trust administration, and the provisions of the Trusts (Sc.) Acts, apply to public as much as to private trusts. The court may also exercise its *nobile officium*, as to appoint new *ex officio* trustees when the offices, the holders of which had been trustees, were abolished,[2] or to appoint a judicial factor.[3]

In some cases it may be difficult to distinguish between a public trust and a voluntary association or benefit society having charitable or other public purposes.[4] The court will, in general, not supplement any deficiency in the constitution of a voluntary association, which it will do in the case of a charitable trust. If a voluntary association has charitable purposes its funds are held by the committee in trust for those purposes, and the purposes cannot, unless otherwise provided in the rules, be altered without the consent of all the subscribers.[5]

Certainty of subjects

The subjects to be held in trust must be adequately defined, otherwise the trust may fail *ab initio*. It may be uncertain whether the subjects are capital or only income,[6] and when the subjects fall to be held for the trust purposes.[7]

[1] McLaren, *Wills*, II, 917, approved in *Anderson's Trs.* v. *Scott*, 1914 S.C. 942, 955. See also *Wink's Exors.* v. *Tallent*, 1947 S.C. 470, 476.

[2] *Mackay*, 1955 S.C. 361; *Coal Industry Social Welfare Organization*, 1959 S.L.T. (Notes) 3. As to powers of investment see *Mitchell Bequest Trs.*, 1959 S.C. 395; as to retrospective sanction of disposal of funds see *E. Kilbride Nursing Assocn.*, 1951 S.C. 64; *Armadale Nursing Assocn.*, 1954 S.L.T. (Notes) 37.

[3] *Vollar's J.F.* v. *Boyd*, 1952 S.L.T. (Notes) 84.

[4] *Mitchell* v. *Burness* (1878) 5 R. 954; *Edinburgh Y.W.C.A.* (1893) 20 R. 894; *Smith* v. *L.A.* (1899) 1 F. 741; *Gibson* (1900) 2 F. 1195; *Edinburgh Lord Provost*, 1956 S.L.T. (Notes) 31.

[5] *McCaskill* v. *Cameron* (1840) 2 D. 537; *Steedman* v. *Malcolm* (1842) 4 D. 1441.

[6] *Crawford's Trs.* v. *Working Boys Home* (1901) 8 S.L.T. 371.

[7] *Elder's Trs.* v. *Free Church* (1892) 20 R. 2.

Conditions

The truster's benevolence may be subject to suspensive or resolutive condition. If the conditions are not satisfied the gift will fail[1] or lapse.[2]

Appointment of trustees

As in a private trust, trustees must be nominated or adequately identified, but from the favour to public and particularly charitable purposes the court will not allow a trust to fail because of failure to appoint trustees,[3] or slight error or ambiguity in the nomination of trustees.[4] Resignation, assumption of new trustees, and removal are subject to the same rules as in private trusts, and the powers and duties of trustees are the same in either class of trusts. Persons are frequently nominated *ex officiis* as trustees.[5] If the body in which the office exists is abolished or materially altered, it is a question of circumstances whether that trusteeship lapses or transfers to any corresponding office in the replacement body.[6] *Ex officio* trustees are not debarred from acting by neglect of their predecessors to act in the trust.[7] The court may appoint new *ex officio* trustees.[8]

If no trustees are nominated, or the trustees fail or decline, a judicial factor will be appointed.[9]

Trust objects and purposes

The trust objects and purposes must be declared in the trust deed, or a deed incorporated therein by reference. They cannot be privately communicated to the trustees, the English doctrine of secret trusts having no place in Scots law.[10]

The court is not concerned with the desirability or feasibility

1 *Bute's Trs.* v. *M. Bute* (1904) 7 F. 49.

2 *Young's Trs.* v. *Perth Trades* (1893) 20 R. 778; *Bannerman* v. *B's Trs.* (1896) 23 R. 959.

3 *Dundee Mags.* v. *Morris* (1858) 3 Macq. 134; *Presbytery of Deer* v. *Bruce* (1867) 5 M. (H.L.) 20; *Murray* (1891) 29 S.L.R. 173; *Lindsay's Trs.* v. *L.*, 1938 S.C. 44.

4 *Murdoch* v. *Glasgow Mags.* (1827) 6 S. 186; *Gordon's Hospital* v. *Aberdeen Ministers* (1831) 9 S. 909; *Aberdeen Synod* v. *Milne's Trs.* (1847) 9 D. 745; *Trinity Chapel Trs.* (1893) 1 S.L.T. 87.

5 *Buchanan's Trs.* v. *Buchanan Bequest Trs.* (1886) 14 R. 284. As to local authority as trustees see *Robertson*, 1938 S.C. 276.

6 *Kilmarnock Parish Council* v. *Ossington's Trs.* (1896) 23 R. 833; *Mailler's Trs.* v. *Allan* (1904) 7 F. 326; *St. Silas Church Vestry* v. *St. Giles Church Trs.*, 1945 S.C. 110.

7 *Edinburgh Mags.* v. *McLaren* (1879) 8 R. (H.L.) 140.

8 *Mackay*, 1955 S.C. 361; *Coal Industry Social Welfare Organization*, 1959 S.L.T. (Notes) 3.

9 e.g. *Robbie's J.F.* v. *Macrae* (1893) 20 R. 358.

10 *Shaw's Trs.* v. *Greenock Medical Aid Socy.*, 1930 S.L.T. 39.

of the truster's scheme,[1] though it would hold void any purposes illegal, immoral, *contra bonos mores* or contrary to public policy, or wholly lacking in public benefit,[2] but only with whether the objects and purposes are stated with sufficient certainty. If the truster's scheme is impossible of performance, as by reason of inadequacy of funds, the gift may be held to fail, or a *cy près* scheme may have to be settled.[3]

While the law will not permit a testator to let another make his will for him, in public bequests a testator may define the classes of persons or objects whom he wishes to benefit, leaving it to the trustees to select the precise objects of benefit.[4]

Certainty of objects

The institution or body or class of persons to be benefited must be defined with reasonable certainty so that the trustees know who are to benefit. Thus bequests to 'the deserving working people in the parish of A'[5], 'such of my children as the trustees may think most deserving'[6] 'to and among such charitable and philanthropic societies, institutions and objects in or connected with G'[7] and 'among such charitable institutions, persons, or objects',[8] have all been held adequately certain, but 'charities in G',[9] 'public, benevolent or charitable purposes in connection with the parish of L',[10] 'to be disposed of by my trustees in such manner as they may think proper',[11] 'religious or charitable purposes in connection with R',[12] 'charitable or other institutions or societies',[13] 'religious, charitable or educational institutions in E. G. and A',[14] 'any poor relations, friends or acquaintances',[15] have all been held void from uncertainty.

[1] e.g. *McLean* v. *Henderson's Trs.* (1880) 7 R. 601 (promotion of phrenology); cf. *Hardie* v. *Morison* (1899) S.L.T. 42 (promotion of free thought held void from uncertainty).

[2] cf. *McCaig* v. *Glasgow University*, 1907 S.C. 231; *McCaig's Trs.* v. *Kirk Session of Lismore*, 1915 S.C. 426; *Aitken's Trs.* v. *A.*, 1927 S.C. 374; *Lindsay's Exor.* v. *Forsyth*, 1940 S.C. 568.

[3] *Ness* v. *Mills's Trs.*, 1928 S.C. 344.

[4] *Crichton* v. *Grierson* (1828) 3 W. & S. 329; cf. *Blair* v. *Duncan* (1901) 4 F. (H.L.) 1; *Cleland's Trs.* v. *C.*, 1907 S.C. 591; *Dick's Trs.* v. *D.*, 1908 S.C. (H.L.) 27; *Allan's Exor.* v. *A.*, 1908 S.C. 807.

[5] *Laurie* v. *Brown*, 1911 1 S.L.T. 84.

[6] *Mitchell's Trs.* v. *Fraser*, 1915 S.C. 350.

[7] *Shedden's Tr.* v. *Dykes*, 1914 S.C. 106.

[8] *Cameron's Trs.* v. *Mackenzie*, 1915 S.C. 313.

[9] *Low's Exors.* (1873) 11 M. 744.

[10] *Turnbull's Trs.* v. *L.A.*, 1918 S.C. (H.L.) 88.

[11] *Sutherland's Trs.* v. *S's Tr.* (1893) 20 R. 925.

[12] *McGrouther's Trs.* v. *L.A.* (1907) 15 S.L.T. 652.

[13] *Jaffrey's Trs.* v. *L.A.* (1903) 11 S.L.T. 119.

[14] *Brown's Trs.* v. *McIntosh* (1905) 13 S.L.T. 72.

[15] *Salvesen's Trs.* v. *Wye*, 1954 S.C. 440.

In judging certainty, specification of a limited locality is a favourable factor, but not conclusive.[1] A bequest for named 'purposes' is much wider and vaguer than to similar 'institutions'.[2] If the object designated has changed its name or combined with another similar body, the gift does not fail if the object in substance continues and is identifiable despite change of name or amalgamation.[3]

If there is adequate indication of the class of objects to be benefited the power to select the precise objects, if not expressly conferred,[4] will be implied from the truster's appointment of a trustee or executor.[5]

The power of selection may be exercised by anyone who holds the office of trustee, even assumed, unless there are indications that the truster restricted the power of choice to the original trustees,[6] but not by a judicial factor.[7]

Where the precise objects are to be selected by the trustees, or another designated person, uncertainty may arise if the selectors fail or refuse to act.[8]

Objects undefined and purposes only stated

In many cases trusters do not specify the precise objects to be benefited nor even the class of objects but define their benevolence only by reference to the furtherance of stated general purposes. Questions frequently arise as to the certainty or otherwise of the purposes stated.

Certainty of purposes

'Public' ends or purposes without further definition are too uncertain to receive effect,[9] and are wider than charitable

1 *Low's Exors., supra*; *Turnbull's Trs., supra*; *Edgar's Trs.* v. *Cassels*, 1922 S.C. 395.

2 *McConochie's Trs.* v. *McC.*, 1909 S.C. 1046.

3 *Pringle* v. *Tweeddale* (1823) 2 S. 588; *McGrouther's Trs.* v. *L.A.* (1908) 15 S.L.T. 652; *Paterson's Trs.* v. *Christie* (1899) 1 F. 508; contrast *Free Church* v. *Overtoun* (1904) 7 F. (H.L.) 1; *Colvill's Trs.* v. *Marindin*, 1908 S.C. 911.

4 *Crichton* v. *Grierson* (1828) 3 W. & S. 329; *Dick's Trs.* v. *D.*, 1907 S.C. 953; *McPhee's Trs.* v. *McP.*, 1912 S.C. 75.

5 *Dundas* v. *D.* (1836) 15 S. 427; *Allan's Exor.* v. *A.*, 1908 S.C. 807; *Wordie's Trs.* v. *W.*, 1916 S.C. (H.L.) 126.

6 *Shedden's Tr., supra*; *Shorter*, 1930 S.L.T. 535; *Angus's Exor.* v. *Batchan's Trs.*, 1949 S.C. 335, overruling *Woodard's J.F.*, 1926 S.C. 534.

7 *Robbie's J.F., supra*; *Bruce's Factor* v. *Forbes* (1904) 12 S.L.T. 377; *Angus's Exor., supra*; *Vollar's J.F.* v. *Boyd*, 1952 S.L.T. (Notes) 84; see also, exceptionally, *Macfarlane's J.F.*, 1910 1 S.L.T. 29.

8 e.g. *Hill's Tr.* v. *Thomson* (1874) 2 R. 68; *Simson* (1883) 10 R. 540; *Robbie's J.F.* v. *Macrae* (1893) 20 R. 358; *Laurie* v. *Brown*, 1911 1 S.L.T. 84; *Shedden's Tr.* v. *Dykes*, 1914 S.C. 106; *Landale's Tr.* v. *Nicol*, 1918 2 S.L.T. 10.

9 *Blair* v. *Duncan* (1901) 4 F. (H.L.) 1; *Turnbull's Trs.* v. *L.A.*, 1918 S.C. (H.L.) 88; *Reid's Trs.* v. *Cattanach's Trs.*, 1929 S.C. 727.

purposes.[1] 'Public' could cover a gift to an election fund or a Yeomanry regiment.[2] So too a bequest for the advancement of art, science, or literature has been held too vague.[3]

'Educational' purposes are uncertain without further specification; but bequests for the promotion of phrenology,[4] to a University bursary fund,[5] for a bursary for Gaelic speaking persons,[6] for an educational scheme for the poor,[7] for a school in a defined locality,[8] for the maintenance of a school in connection with a named church,[9] have all been upheld.

'Religious' purposes alone are too vague and uncertain,[10] but gifts for home missions,[11] missionary purposes especially in Africa,[12] missionary associations, one being named,[13] foreign missions in named areas,[14] native missionaries to preach the gospel,[15] religious institutions conducted according to Protestant principles,[16] Christian purposes,[17] have all been upheld. A bequest for masses for the benefit of particular individuals has been held valid, as substantially the endowment of worship in a particular church.[18]

'Charitable' is, however, deemed a sufficiently certain term in Scots law, and one entitled to a benignant construction;[19] though not as wide as 'public' it does not have any precise or clearly defined meaning; still less does it have a narrow or technical

[1] *Blair, supra*; *Turnbull's Trs., supra*, 92.
[2] *Blair, supra.*
[3] *Harper's Trs.* v. *Jacobs*, 1929 S.C. 345.
[4] *McLean* v. *Henderson's Trs.* (1880) 7 R. 601.
[5] *Milne's Exors.* v. *Aberdeen University Court* (1905) 7 F. 642.
[6] *Macdonell's Trs.* v. *M's Trs.*, 1911 2 S.L.T. 170.
[7] *Chalmers' Trs.* v. *Turriff School Board*, 1917 S.C. 676.
[8] *Ferguson* v. *Marjoribanks* (1853) 15 D. 637.
[9] *Kelland* v. *Douglas* (1863) 2 M. 150.
[10] *Macintyre* v. *Grimond's Trs.* (1905) 7 F. (H.L.) 90; *Shaw's Trs.* v. *Esson's Trs.* (1905) 8 F. 52; *McConochie's Trs.* v. *McC.*, 1909 S.C. 1046.
[11] *Miller's Trs.* v. *Kirkcaldy* (1905) 13 S.L.T. 454.
[12] *Adam's Trs.* v. *A.* (1908) 16 S.L.T. 144.
[13] *Miln's Trs.* v. *Drachenhauer*, 1921 1 S.L.T. 152.
[14] *Allan's Exors.* v. *A.*, 1908 S.C. 807.
[15] *Renouf's Trs.* v. *Haining*, 1919 S.C. 497.
[16] *Bannerman's Trs.* v. *B.*, 1915 S.C. 398.
[17] *Macray* v. *M.*, 1910 2 S.L.T. 74.
[18] *Lindsay's Exor.* v. *Forsyth*, 1940 S.C. 568.
[19] *Crichton* v. *Grierson* (1828) 3 W. & S. 329; *Dundee Mags.* v. *Morris* (1858) 3 Macq. 134; *Cleland's Trs.* v. *C.*, 1907 S.C. 591; *Weir* v. *Crum Brown*, 1908 S.C. (H.L.) 3; *Dick* v. *Audsley*, 1908 S.C. (H.L.) 27; *Hay's Trs.* v. *Baillie*, 1908 S.C. 1224; *Macduff* v. *Spence's Trs.*, 1909 S.C. 178; *Paterson's Trs.* v. *P.*, 1909 S.C. 485; *Mackinnon's Trs.* v. *M.*, 1909 S.C. 1041; *Wordie's Trs.* v. *W.*, 1916 S.C. (H.L.) 126; *Turnbull's Trs.* v. *L.A.*, 1918 S.C. (H.L.) 88; *Wink's Exors., supra*; *Pomphrey's Trs.* v. *Royal Naval Benevolent Trust*, 1967 S.L.T. 61.

meaning.[1] It is a relative term, taking colour from the objects to which it is applied; it includes the relief of poverty,[2] but also social or ethical amelioration of the people of K,[3] hospitals,[4] the prevention of cruelty to animals,[5] a clergy salary fund,[6] the erection of a free school,[7] the maintenance, education and upbringing of destitute children,[8] homes for war-disabled men,[9] the National Trust for Scotland.[10]

But a bequest to 'relations, friends or acquaintances' does not become public and charitable merely because the adjective 'poor' is prefixed, and it remains a private trust.[11]

Synonyms of 'charitable' such as 'beneficent',[12] 'philanthropic',[13] 'benevolent',[14] 'deserving',[15] and even 'useful'[16] have equally been deemed sufficiently certain to be enforceable.

For the purpose of taxing statutes, however, which should be interpreted similarly in Scotland and England, 'charitable' bears the very wide meaning attached to it by numerous English Chancery decisions, interpreting the [English] Charitable Gifts Act, 1601, of being generally beneficial to the public,[17] and this includes many purposes not 'charitable' in the more limited use of the term in Scots law, other than in the context of taxation.[18]

Other words such as 'beneficial', 'patriotic', 'for behoof of

1 *Income Tax Commrs.* v. *Pemsel* [1891] A.C. 531, 557; *Wink's Exors.* v. *Tallent*, 1947 S.C. 470, 477; *Baird's Trs.* v. *L.A.* (1888) 15 R. 682, where charitable was limited to the relief of poverty, is too narrow a view.

2 *Baird's Trs.* v. *L.A.* (1888) 15 R. 682; *Blair* v. *Duncan* (1901) 4 F. (H.L.) 1; *Weir*, *supra*; *Cameron's Trs.* v. *Mackenzie*, 1915 S.C. 313.

3 *L.A.* v. *Anton*, 1909 2 S.L.T. 326.

4 *Smellie's Trs.* v. *Glasgow R.I.* (1905) 13 S.L.T. 450.

5 *Smellie's Trs.*, *supra.*

6 *Roberts* v. *Smith's J.F.*, 1929 S.L.T. 71.

7 *Ferguson* v. *Marjoribanks* (1853) 15 D. 637.

8 *Forrest's Trs.* v. *Alexander*, 1925 S.N. 80.

9 *Jowett's Trs.* v. *Jowett's Heirs*, 1952 S.L.T. 131.

10 *Highgate's Trs.* v. *N.T.S.*, 1957 S.L.T. (Notes) 37.

11 *Salvesen's Trs.* v. *Wye*, 1954 S.C. 440.

12 *Paterson's Trs.*, *supra.*

13 *Mackinnon's Trs.*, *supra.*

14 *Hay's Trs.*, *supra.*

15 *Laurie* v. *Brown*, 1911 S.L.T. 84; *Weir*, *supra*; *Mitchell's Trs.* v. *Fraser*, 1915 S.C. 350.

16 *Cobb* v. *C's Trs.* (1874) 21 R. 638.

17 *I.T. Commrs.* v. *Pemsel* [1891] A.C. 531; *Wink's Exors.* v. *Tallent*, 1947 S.C. 470, 477; *I.R.C.* v. *Glasgow Police Athletic Assoc.*, 1953 S.C. (H.L.) 13; *Camille and Henry Dreyfus Foundation* v. *I.R.C.*, 1955 S.L.T. 335; [1956] A.C. 39. For English cases see Tudor on *Charities*; Snell, *Equity*. In *Pemsel* it was said that in English law charity comprises four classes, trusts for the relief of poverty, for the advancement of education, for the advancement of religion, and for other purposes beneficial to the community not falling under any of the preceding heads.

18 *Blair* v. *Duncan* (1901) 4 F. (H.L.) 1.

children' are probably too vague. 'Benevolent' probably means no more than 'charitable'.[1]

The court regards charitable purposes favourably and will, if need be, appoint trustees to receive the bequest and administer it.[2] But a bequest to 'charities' without appointment of trustees or power to anyone to select particular charities is void for uncertainty.[3]

The War Charities Act, 1940, provides for the registration[4] with the county or town council of every war charity[5] and for regulations governing such bodies being made by the Secretary of State for Scotland.[6]

Conjoined and alternative expressions

Purposes stated conjunctively, such as 'charitable and benevolent', are normally held valid, any purposes selected having to satisfy both tests.[7] So too where several classes of objects are stated the bequest is valid if all are valid and sufficiently specific.[8]

Purposes stated disjunctively or alternatively, such as 'benevolent or charitable' may be void for uncertainty if truly alternative, as such a direction would permit the trustee to favour one class to the exclusion of the other,[9] but are not void if the adjectives are

1 *Wink's Exors.* v. *Tallent*, 1947 S.C. 470, 484.

2 *Lindsay's Trs.* v. *L.*, 1938 S.C. 44.

3 *Angus's Exrx.* v. *Batchan's Trs.*, 1949 S.C. 335.

4 S. 2; see also *Clydeside Air Raid Distress Fund Assocn.* v. *Clydeside, etc., Cttee.*, 1948 S.L.T. (Notes) 28.

5 Defined, S. 11.

6 Ss. 4, 5, and 12.

7 *Hill* v. *Burns* (1826) 2 W. & S. 80; cf. *Miller* v. *Black's Trs.* (1837) 2 S. & McL. 866 ('benevolent and charitable'); *Cobb* v. *C's Trs.* (1894) 21 R. 638: ('useful, benevolent and charitable institutions'); *Caldwell's Trs.* v. *C.*, 1921 S.C. (H.L.) 82: ('charitable and benevolent institutions'); *Edgar's Trs.* v. *Cassels*, 1922 S.C. 35: ('benevolent, charitable and religious institutions'); *Macrae's J.F.* v. *Martin*, 1937 S.L.T. 209: ('religious and charitable purposes'); contrast *McConochie's Trs.* v. *McC.*, 1909 S.C. 1046.

8 *Brough* v. *B's Trs.*, 1950 S.L.T 117.

9 'charitable or other': *Jeffrey's Trs.* v. *L.A.* (1903) 1 S.L.T. 119; 'charitable or religious': *Macintyre* v. *Grimond's Trs.* (1905) 7 F. (H.L.) 90; *Shaw's Trs.* v. *Weir*, 1927 S.L.T. 641; 'charitable or public': *Blair* v. *Duncan* (1901) 4 F. (H.L.) 1; 'charitable, benevolent or religious objects': *Shaw's Trs.* v. *Esson's Trs.* (1905) 8 F. 52; *Shaw's Trs.* v. *Greenock Medical Aid Socy.*, 1930 S.L.T. 39; 'charitable institutions or deserving agencies': *Symmer's Trs.* v. *S.*, 1918 S.C. 337; 'public, benevolent or charitable purposes': *Turnbull's Trs.* v. *L.A.*, 1918 S.C. (H.L.) 88; 'charitable or other deserving institutions in G': *Campbell's Trs.* v. *C.*, 1921 S.C. (H.L.) 12; 'charitable, educational or benevolent societies or public institutions in Scotland': *Reid's Trs.* v. *Cattanach's Trs.*, 1929 S.C. 727; 'religion, education or the poor': *Shaw's Trs.* v. *Weir*, 1927 S.L.T. 641; 'religious or benevolent institutions': *Shaw's Trs.* v. *Greenock Medical Aid Socy.*, 1930 S.L.T. 39; 'charitable or social institutions': *Rintoul's Trs.* v. *R.*, 1949 S.C. 297.

held to be used exegetically of each other, or synonymously.[1] So too a direction to pay residue for charitable or religious purposes or for other objects of a similar nature has been held void as not defining the objects sufficiently.[2]

Interpretation of purposes

Trustees are frequently faced with problems of the interpretation of the trust purposes in view of changes which have taken place since the trust was created and of deciding whether particular claimants for benefit are eligible. In every case the question is of the truster's intention as disclosed by the words used in the gift. Thus a university bursary fund was held open to women students, but only to the colleges of the University as at the time of the bequest;[3] and a trust for the Universities of Scotland to be open to universities founded long after the gift.[4]

Trustees' powers

The trustees' powers are those conferred by common law,[5] the Trusts (Sc.) Acts, 1921 to 1961, and the trust deed. The court will not interfere with the exercise of powers within the discretion of the trustees[6] unless exceptionally[7] and may grant further powers where necessary and not at variance with the trust purposes.[8]

1 'benevolent or charitable': *Hay's Trs.* v. *Baillie*, 1908 S.C. 1224; *Wink's Exors.* v. *Tallent*, 1947 S.C. 470; 'charities or benevolent or beneficent institutions': *Paterson's Trs.* v. *P.*, 1909 S.C. 485; 'charitable or philanthropic institutions': *Mackinnon's Trs.* v. *M.*, 1909 S.C. 1041; 'charitable or educational': *Dick* v. *Audsley*, 1908 S.C. (H.L.) 27; *Chalmers' Trs.* v. *Turriff School Board*, 1917 S.C. 676; 'religious or charitable institutions': *Bannerman's Trs.* v. *B.*, 1915 S.C. 398; 'charitable or benevolent schemes': *Brough's Trs.* v. *B.*, 1950 S.L.T. 117.

2 *Campbell's Trs.* v. *Edinburgh R.I.*, 1932 S.N. 10.

3 *Blyth Scholarship Fund Trs.* v. *St. Andrews University Court* (1905) 7 F. 855.

4 *Strathclyde Univ.* v. *Carnegie Trs.*, 1968 S.L.T. 317. See also *Allan* v. *Stiell's Trs.* (1876) 4 R. 162; *Bogie's Trs.* v. *Swanston* (1878) 5 R. 634; *Irvine Mags.* v. *Muir* (1888) 15 R. 396; *Anderson's Bursary Trs.* v. *Sutherland* (1889) 16 R. 574; *Paterson's Trs.* v. *Christie* (1899) 1 F. 508; *Ferguson Bequest Fund* (1899) 1 F. 1224; *Gerard Trs.* v. *Monifieth Mags.* (1901) 3 F. 800; *Lyon's Trs.* v. *Aitken* (1904) 6 F. 608; *Mailler's Trs.* v. *Allan* (1904) 7 F. 326; *Playfair* v. *Kelso Ragged Industrial School* (1905) 7 F. 751; *Kinloss Parish Council* v. *Morgan*, 1908 S.C. 192.

5 e.g. to feu lands: *Elgin Mags.* v. *Morrison* (1882) 10 R. 342; *Jameison* (1884) 21 S.L.R. 541.

6 *McCulloch* v. *Dalry Kirk Session* (1876) 3 R. 1182; *Ferguson Bequest Fund* v. *Educational Endowments Commrs.* (1887) 14 R. 624; *Robertson's Trs.*, 1948 S.C. 1.

7 *Thomson* v. *Davidson's Trs.* (1888) 15 R. 719; *Ritchie* v. *Davidson's Trs.* (1890) 17 R. 673.

8 *Downie* (1879) 6 R. 1013; *Philp's Trs.* (1893) 20 R. 900; see also *Mailler's Trs.* v. *Allan* (1904) 7 F. 326; *McCrie's Trs.*, 1927 S.C. 556; *Gibson's Trs.*, 1933 S.C. 190; *Glasgow Y.M.C.A.*, 1934 S.C. 452.

Trustees' liabilities

The trustees of public and charitable trusts owe the same duties, in general, as do trustees of private trusts, but they have been treated with greater favour by the courts than trustees of private trusts. If the administration has been honest, the court will not punish merely mistaken conduct.[1]

Title to enforce trust purposes

The executor,[2] and formerly also the heir-at-law,[3] of the founder of a charity, has an interest to see that the trust is properly administered. Any person who has an actual or contingent interest in the proper administration of the trust, as being an actual or possible beneficiary, has a title to pursue actions necessary for ascertaining and declaring the powers and duties of the trustees and enforcing their execution.[4]

Failure of trust purposes

By reason of change in, or unforeseen, circumstances, trustees of a public trust may find it impracticable to give effect, or further effect, to the purpose of the trust. The trust does not on that account necessarily fail altogether. If the gift has been for a definite charitable purpose, which has failed during the truster's lifetime, or has failed after his death but before the funds become available for the trust purposes, the court will not substitute another charitable purpose.[5]

The cy près *principle*

Where the intention of the truster cannot be effected in the precise manner directed by him, the court, from the favour it shows to public and charitable bequests, if it can find expressed or implied a general or overriding charitable purpose, will not allow the trust to fail but will *ex nobili officio* settle a scheme to enable the funds to be applied *cy près*, as nearly as possible to the

1 *Andrews* v. *Ewart's Trs.* (1886) 13 R. (H.L.) 69, 73. See also *Edinburgh Mags.* v. *McLaren* (1881) 8 R. (H.L.) 140; *Buchanan Bequest Trs.* v. *Dunnett* (1895) 22 R. 602; *Morrison* v. *St. Andrews School Board*, 1918 S.C. 51.

2 *Campbell* v. *McIntyres* (1824) 3 S. 126.

3 *McLeish's Trs.* v. *McL.* (1841) 3 D. 914.

4 *Ross* v. *Heriot's Hospital* (1843) 5 D. 589; *Edinburgh Mags.* v. *Edinburgh Professors* (1851) 13 D. 1187; *Liddle* v. *Bathgate Kirk Session* (1854) 16 D. 1075; *Carmont* v. *Mitchell's Trs.* (1883) 10 R. 829; *Mackie* v. *Edinburgh Presbytery* (1896) 33 S.L.R. 479.

5 *Burgess's Trs.* v. *Crawford*, 1912 S.C. 387.

intended purpose.[1] The principle does not apply to private trusts, even if of a charitable nature,[2] or to benevolent funds.[3]

The settlement of a *cy près* scheme is an exercise of the *nobile officium* and exercisable only by the Inner House of the Court of Session. The trustees must petition the court, putting forward a draft scheme embodying their proposals. The facts are normally ascertained by remit to a reporter who also reports on the suitability of the proposed scheme. The Court may require revision or amendment of the proposed scheme.

The *cy près* principle is applicable where there is a charitable bequest without adequate indication of the means whereby it is to be effected,[4] or a charitable bequest to an institution or body which does not and has never existed,[5] or a charitable bequest is inadequate to achieve the purpose in the way directed,[6] or by reason of change of circumstances the purpose cannot be effected in the particular way intended by the truster,[7] or there is a practical deadlock in the trust administration,[8] or the trust has become unworkable,[9] or the trust purposes have failed.[10]

The *cy près* principle has been applied to the effect of varying the means of administration of the bequest,[11] or of extending the benefits to further categories of persons,[12] though the court

[1] *Clephane* v. *Edinburgh Mags.* (1869) 7 M. (H.L.) 7; *Hay's J.F.* v. *Hay's Trs.*, 1952 S.C. (H.L.) 29. See also *Glasgow Magdalene Inst.*, 1964 S.C. 227.

[2] *Anderson's Trs.* v. *Scott*, 1914 S.C. 942.

[3] *Lord Provost of Edinburgh*, 1956 S.L.T. (Notes) 31.

[4] *Burgess's Trs.* v. *Crawford*, 1912 S.C. 387, 396, following *Rymer* v. *Stanfield* [1895] 1 Ch. 19; *Tod's Trs.* v. *Sailors', etc., Socy.*, 1953 S.L.T. (Notes) 72; contrast *Laing's Trs.* v. *Perth Model Lodging House*, 1954 S.L.T. (Notes) 13.

[5] *Tait's J.F.* v. *Lillie*, 1940 S.C. 534; cf. *Robertson's Trs.*, 1948 S.C. 1.

[6] *Aberdeen Univ.* v. *Irvine* (1869) 7 M. 1087; *Governors of John Watt's Hospital* (1893) 20 R. 729; *Portobello Female School Trs.* (1900) 2 F. 418; *Gibson* (1900) 2 F. 1195; *Governors of Mitchell's Hospital* (1902) 4 F. 582; *Clyde Industrial Training Ship Assocn.*, 1925 S.C. 676; cf. *Davidson's Trs.* v. *Arnott*, 1951 S.C. 42; *Macrae's Trs.*, 1955 S.L.T. (Notes) 33.

[7] *Thomson's Trs.*, 1930 S.C. 767.

[8] *Rosyth Canadian Fund Trs.*, 1924 S.C. 352.

[9] *Scotstown Moor Children's Camp*, 1948 S.C. 630; *Cuthbert's Trs.* v. *C.*, 1958 S.C. 629. As to experimental operation of a charity see *Edinburgh Corpn.* v. *Cranston's Trs.*, 1960 S.C. 244.

[10] *Glasgow Royal Infirmary* v. *Glasgow Mags.* (1888) 15 R. 264; *Gibson* (1900) 2 F. 1195.

[11] *Clephane* v. *Edinburgh Mags.* (1869) 7 M. (H.L.) 7; *Burnett's Trs.* (1876) 4 R. 127; *Downie* (1879) 6 R. 1013; *Glasgow Infirmary* (1887) 14 R. 680; *Simpson* v. *Moffat Working Men's Institute* (1892) 19 R. 389; *John Watt's Hospital Governors* (1893) 20 R. 729; *Falkirk Certified Industrial School* v. *Ferguson Bequest Fund* (1899) 1 F. 1175; *Portobello Female School Trs.* (1900) 2 F. 418; *Thomson's Mortification*, 1908 S.C. 1078; *Glasgow S.P.C.A.* v. *National Anti-Vivisection Socy.*, 1915 S.C. 757; *Stranraer Original Secession Congregation*, 1923 S.C. 722; *Rosyth Canadian Fund Trs.*, 1924 S.C. 352; *Clyde Industrial Training Ship Assocn.*, 1925 S.C. 676; *Thomson's Trs.*, 1930 S.C. 767; *Clutterbuck*, 1961 S.L.T. 427.

[12] *Carnegie Park Orphanage Trs.* (1892) 19 R. 605; *John Reid Prize Trs.* (1893) 20 R. 938; *Gibson* (1900) 2 F. 1195; *Mitchell's Hospital Governors* (1902) 4 F. 582; *Clark*

cannot take the latter course if that is at variance with the donor's apparent intention,[1] or otherwise varying the method of attaining the truster's objective,[2] or transferring the funds to another trust or body with similar objects.[3]

Difficulty of administration does not by itself justify application for a scheme,[4] nor does inadequacy of funds,[5] but difficulty may become impossibility and the court has occasionally acted in cases of strong expediency for varying the means of applying the trust funds.[6]

In considering whether or not to approve a proposed scheme the Court will not normally agree to the trust funds being removed from Scotland,[7] and will normally require the scheme to relate to the same district and to benefit the same kind of persons as the failed scheme.[8]

But the principle is inapplicable where the gift is to a particular institution and no other and that has ceased to be, or the gift is to be applied in a particular way, which is no longer practicable, and no other. In these cases the gift fails.[9] Unless there be an absolute dedication of the fund to the purposes of charity generally, or unless it can be affirmed that the truster has preferred the general object of charity to his residuary legatees there is no room for the principle of *cy près* or approximation.[10]

If a gift or bequest has taken effect in favour of a charity, it must be accepted that there is a general charitable intention, and even if the institution fails after the trust has come into operation, the bequest falls to be applied *cy près*[11] unless there is shown to be a

Bursary Fund Trs. (1903) 5 F. 433; *Dunbar Kirk Session*, 1908 S.C. 852; *Chalmers Hospital (Banff) Trs.*, 1923 S.C. 220; *Holt*, 1952 S.L.T. (Notes) 23.

[1] *Grigor Medical Bursary Fund Trs.* (1903) 5 F. 1143; *Mailler's Trs.* v. *Allan* (1904) 7 F. 326; *Duart Bursary Fund Trs.*, 1911 S.C. 9.

[2] *Campbell Endowment Trust*, 1928 S.C. 171.

[3] *Scotstown Moor Children's Camp*, 1948 S.C. 630; *Tod's Trs.* v. *Sailors', etc., Socy.*, 1953 S.L.T. (Notes) 72; *Cumming's Exors.* v. *C.*, 1967 S.L.T. 68.

[4] *Glasgow Domestic Training School*, 1923 S.C. 892; cf. *Gerard's Trs.* v. *Monifieth Mags.* (1901) 3 F. 800, 804; *Scotstown Moor Children's Camp*, 1948 S.C. 630.

[5] *Ness* v. *Mill's Trs.*, 1923 S.C. 344.

[6] *Gibson's Trs.*, 1933 S.C. 190; *Glasgow Y.M.C.A.*, 1934 S.C. 458; *Clutterbuck*, 1961 S.L.T. 427.

[7] *Goodman*, 1958 S.C. 377.

[8] *Milngavie District Nursing Assocn.*, 1950 S.L.T. (Notes) 45; *Pencaitland, etc., Nursing Assocn.*, 1954 S.L.T. (Notes) 28.

[9] *Burgess's Trs.* v. *Crawford*, 1912 S.C. 387, 395, following *Clark* v. *Taylor* (1853) 1 Drew. 642; *Pennie's Trs.* v. *R.N.L.I.*, 1924 S.L.T. 520; *Laing's Trs.* v. *Perth Model Lodging House*, 1954 S.L.T. (Notes) 13; cf. *Forrest's Trs.* v. *Alexander*, 1925 S.N. 80.

[10] *Young's Tr.* v. *Deacons of Trades of Perth* (1893) 20 R. 778; *Tait's J.F.* v. *Lillie*, 1940 S.C. 534; *Hay's J.F.* v. *Hay's Trs.*, 1952 S.C. (H.L.) 29; *Paterson* v. *Aberdeen Sailors' Mission Institute*, 1953 S.L.T. (Notes) 34.

[11] *Anderson's Trs.* v. *Scott*, 1914 S.C. 942; *Davidson's Trs.* v. *Arnott*, 1951 S.C. 42.

resulting trust for the truster or donor.[1] Similarly if a charitable bequest has taken effect but is not realizing its purpose a *cy près* modification to enable it to do better is proper.[2] Under an application for a *cy près* scheme the court will not normally ratify a transfer of funds already made without authority.[3]

Failure of trust purposes—voluntary fund

Where money is raised or collected from the public for a public purpose, such as a disaster relief fund, and cannot be expended, application may be made for a *cy près* scheme if there is a discoverable general charitable intention,[4] but if not, the money falls to be repaid to the donors, if discoverable,[5] unless it can be held to be outright gift, in which case it falls to the Crown on the failure of the trust purposes.[6]

1 *Young's Trs.* v. *Perth Trades* (1892) 20 R. 778.

2 *Carnegie Park Orphanage Trs.* (1892) 19 R. 605; cf. *Edinburgh Mags.* v. *McLaren* (1881) 8 R. (H.L.) 140.

3 *E. Kilbride Nursing Assocn.*, 1951 S.C. 64; *Armadale Nursing Assocn.*, 1954 S.L.T. (Notes) 37.

4 *Gibson* (1900) 2 F. 1195.

5 *Bain* v. *Black* (1849) 11 D. 1287; 6 Bell 317; *Connell* v. *Ferguson* (1857) 19 D. 482; *Mitchell* v. *Burness* (1878) 5 R. 954; cf. *Re North Devon Relief Fund* [1953] 2 All E.R. 1032; *Re Ulverston New Hospital* [1956] Ch. 622.

6 *Maltmen of Stirling*, 1912 S.C. 887; *Anderson's Trs.* v. *Scott*, 1914 S.C. 942; *Caledonian Employees' Benevolent Socy.*, 1928 S.C. 633.

CHAPTER 106

OTHER USES OF THE TRUST CONCEPT

THE trust concept, whereby property is held by persons under a duty to hold it for, and account for it to, beneficial owners has various other legal applications. Trusteeship is utilized in connection with savings and investments; various classes of persons have attributed to them some of the characteristics and fiduciary duties of trustees; and a debtor may transfer his assets to a trustee for behoof of creditors as an alternative to being sequestrated.[1]

TRUSTEE SAVINGS BANKS

A trustee savings bank is an unincorporated body which receives deposits of money and pays interest thereon, enabling small investors to have their money kept in safety, yet readily withdrawable and earning interest. Such Savings Banks are regulated by Statute;[2] the formation of a bank must be approved by the National Debt Commissioners, which body, together with an Inspection Committee, supervises the functioning of such banks. The bank itself takes no benefit from the money deposited, apart from deducting management expenses. It does not carry on the full range of business of a commercial bank, such as making advances or discounting bills, but may now maintain current accounts on which customers may operate by drawing cheques.[3] It must publish a half-yearly financial statement.[4]

No person may make deposits with more than one savings bank[5] and the maximum deposit of each customer is limited.[6] The property of a trustee savings bank is vested in four custodian trustees, appointed from the general trustees who are the managers of the bank,[7] and they may sue and be sued in their representative capacity.

It may be wound up as an unregistered company[8] at the

[1] Ch. 108, *infra*.
[2] Trustee Savings Banks Act, 1954 to 1968.
[3] Trustee Savings Bank Act, 1964.
[4] Companies Act, 1948, S. 433; Sched. 13.
[5] Trustee Savings Bank Act, 1954, S. 17.
[6] Ibid., Ss. 12, 15.
[7] Ibid., S. 9.
[8] Companies Act, 1948, Ss. 398 *et seq*.

instance of a creditor, the National Debt Commissioners, or a commissioner appointed to investigate the affairs of the bank.[1] The Post Office Savings Bank provides generally similar facilities but is regulated by separate Act.[2]

INVESTMENT TRUSTS

An investment 'trust' is a company which, instead of using its capital in productive or commutative business, invests it in a range of shares in other companies and other investments and distributes the total dividends received to its own members as dividends on their shares. The advantages are that a single investment by a shareholder gives indirectly a wide spread of investments in a large number of companies, minimizing the danger of the decline or failure of a particular company or industry. The investment trust is subject to the ordinary rules of company law.

UNIT TRUSTS

The unit trust[3] is also an application of the trust concept to widen the spread of a person's investments and minimize risks. It is created by a trust deed between managers and a trustee, usually a bank or financial house, but separate from the management company or group. The duration of the trust is normally limited but may be renewed. The managers of the unit trust scheme acquire blocks of a range of stock exchange securities, transferring them to be held by the trustee named in the trust deed. The managers offer to the public 'units' which each represent fractional shares of the whole trust portfolio, at prices related to the Stock Exchange value of the underlying blocks of shares.[4] The investors are the beneficiaries under the trust deed and periodically receive distributions representing their *pro rata* shares of the dividends and interest received by the trustee from the underlying securities.

There are two main types of unit trusts, fixed and flexible. In the former the managers are authorized by the trust deed to invest only in defined securities; in the latter they have much greater discretion.

1 Trustee Savings Bank Act, 1954, S. 50.

2 Post Office Savings Bank Act, 1954.

3 Statutory definition in Prevention of Fraud (Investments) Act, 1958, S. 26.

4 The precise formula is stated in the trust deed and makes an allowance for management expenses.

The conditions under which a unit may be authorized by the Board of Trade are contained in the Prevention of Fraud (Investments) Act, 1958, S. 17 and Sched. 1.[1] The Board of Trade has power to order an investigation into the affairs of a unit trust scheme.

Unlike a company's share capital the number of units in a scheme is not fixed and the managers may issue as many as they can persuade investors to buy, thus giving them more money to invest. Also units have no par or nominal value and their quoted value varies by reference to the values of the shares and other securities held by the trustee. The advantages are to give the investor an interest in a large number of companies, spreading the risk very widely, giving him the benefits of extra investment management, and relieving him of much of the trouble connected with managing investments. There is nothing comparable to the meetings of shareholders in a company and meetings of unit-holders are called only when necessary.

An investor who wishes to dispose of his investment may sell his units back to the managers, who may create fresh units and sell them to other investors, the difference between the two prices representing the manager's commission.[2]

The Board of Trade may appoint inspectors to investigate the administration of any unit trust scheme,[3] generally as in the case of a company. Both trustees and managers are required to keep various records.[4]

COMPANY PROMOTERS AS TRUSTEES

A promoter of a company stands in a fiduciary relation to the nascent company[5] and accordingly must not make any direct or indirect profit at the expense of the company, and is accountable for any secret profit.[6] If he sells his own property to the company, he must disclose his interest and let the purchase be considered by an independent body of directors.[7]

[1] cf. *Allied Investors Trust, Ltd.* v. *B.O.T.* [1956] 1 Ch. 232.

[2] The manager's buying and selling prices are quoted in the daily press.

[3] Prevention of Fraud (Investments) Act, 1958, S. 12.

[4] Unit Trust Record Regulations, 1946.

[5] *Erlanger* v. *New Sombrero Phosphate Co.* (1878) 3 App. Cas. 1236.

[6] *Emma Silver Mining Co.* v. *Grant* (1879) 11 Ch. D. 918; *Whalley Bridge Co.* v. *Green* (1879) 5 Q.B.D. 103; *Mann* v. *Edinburgh Northern Tramways* (1892) 20 R. (H.L.) 7; *Gluckstein* v. *Barnes* [1900] A.C. 240; *Re Leeds and Hanley Theatre of Varieties* [1902] 2 Ch. 809.

[7] *Erlanger, supra; Lagunas Nitrate Co.* v. *Lagunas Syndicate* [1899] 2 Ch. 392.

DIRECTORS AS TRUSTEES

Directors of a company, though not strictly trustees, also stand in a fiduciary position to the company,[1] though not for individual shareholders.[2] They are therefore liable to make good monies they have misapplied, are disabled from contracting personally with the company, and must account to the company for any profit made as a result of their fiduciary position.[3] The company's funds are like a trust fund in that they may be reclaimed from a third party who has taken them in the knowledge of their *ultra vires* payment.[4]

TRUSTEES OF FRIENDLY SOCIETIES AND TRADE UNIONS

Friendly societies and trade unions are not incorporated and their property must accordingly be vested in trustees for behoof of the society[5] or union[6].

TUTORS AS TRUSTEES

Under the Guardianship of Infants Act, 1925, S. 10, a father or mother holding the legal office of tutor to his or pupil child is deemed to be and always to have been a trustee within the meaning of the Trusts (Sc.) Act, 1921. The 1921 Act, S. 2, provides that 'trustee' includes any tutor, and 'trust deed' any decree, deed, or other writing appointing a tutor, curator or judicial factor. These provisions, however, do not make a parent a trustee in the full sense or give him the power to hold property as full owner, in trust, but merely gives him the powers of a trustee in dealing with the pupil's estate.[7] The 1925 Act, S. 10, does not apply to a tutor-at-law.[8]

1 *York and N. Midland Ry.* v. *Hudson* (1853) 16 Beav. 485; *G. E. Ry.* v. *Turner* (1872) L.R. 8 Ch. App. 149; *Re Forest of Dean Co.* (1878) 10 Ch. D. 450.

2 *Percival* v. *Wright* [1902] 2 Ch. 421.

3 *Regal (Hastings), Ltd.* v. *Gulliver* [1942] 1 All E.R. 378.

4 *Moxham* v. *Grant* [1900] 1 Q.B. 88.

5 Friendly Societies Act, 1896, S. 49.

6 Trade Union Act, 1871, S. 8.

7 *Dempster*, 1926 S.L.T. 158; cf. *Hamilton's Tutors*, 1924 S.C. 364; see also *Linton* v. *I.R.C.*, 1928 S.C. 209.

8 *Shearer*, 1924 S.C. 445, disapproving *Forbes*, 1922 S.L.T. 294; cf. *Ferrier's Tutrix*, 1925 S.C. 571.

CURATORS AS TRUSTEES

By the Trusts (Sc.) Act, 1921, S. 2, 'trust deed' includes any decree, deed, or other writing appointing a curator, and 'trustee' includes any curator. A curator, however, does not have the legal title to the ward's property in his name, and the effect of the provision is merely to give the curator the powers of a trustee.

CHAPTER 107

JUDICIAL FACTORS

THE Court of Session has long, by virtue of its *nobile officium*, exercised the power to appoint persons as judicial factors to manage and administer property where this is necessary to avoid danger of loss or resolve a deadlock in administration.[1] Since 1857 appointment is made by a Lord Ordinary on petition, without prejudice to the Inner House's exercise of the *nobile officium*. The Sheriff Court may also now appoint a factor where the annual value of the estate does not exceed £100,[2] but not a factor *loco absentis*.[3] Any appointment is temporary in that it may be recalled when the necessity for the appointment has ended.[4]

Appointment

An appointment is sought by petition to the Court of Session or Sheriff Court,[5] by anyone having an interest in the property being preserved, but in cases where it is desired to safeguard an award of damages made to pupils and/or minors a factor may be appointed *de plano* by the Court if the natural guardian is absent, or unfit and consents to the appointment.[6] An appointment may be made *ad interim*, in which case the appointee must report monthly to the Accountant of Court.[7]

A petition may be presented by any person having an interest in the person or estate requiring protection, including a person desiring a *curator bonis* for himself,[8] and the Accountant of Court.[9] The petition usually proposes the name of a person, who may be the, or a, petitioner, as being suitable to be appointed.

Any person interested may lodge answers to the petition and oppose the appointment, or object to the petitioner's nominee

1 See A.S. 13 February 1730; Judicial Factors (Sc.) Acts, 1849, Ss. 4–6, and 10; 1889, S. 14; and generally Irons on *Judicial Factors*.

2 Judicial Factors (Sc.) Act, 1880, S. 4; *Penny* v. *Scott* (1894) 22 R. 5.

3 Ibid., S. 3.

4 *Turnbull* v. *Ross's J.F.*, 1916 2 S.L.T. 249; *Gowans*, 1917 2 S.L.T. 61.

5 Estate not exceeding £100 only; Judicial Factors (Sc.) Act, 1880, S. 4; *Penny* v. *Scott* (1894) 22 R. 5.

6 *Collins* v. *Eglinton Iron Co.* (1882) 9 R. 500; *McAvoy* v. *Young's Paraffin Light Co.* (1882) 19 S.L.R. 441; *Boylan* v. *Hunter*, 1922 S.C. 80.

7 *McCulloch* v. *McC.*, 1953 S.C. 189.

8 *Mark* (1845) 7 D. 882; *Perry* (1903) 10 S.L.T. 536; *A.B.* (1909) 16 S.L.T. 557.

9 1889 Act, S. 10.

for the post. If a minor or *incapax* can express views about the proposed factor, the court will consider those views.[1]

Who may be appointed

The person appointed may be any person of full age and legal capacity whom the Court is willing to trust.[2] It will normally appoint the person proposed by the petitioner.[3] He acts as an officer of the Court and under the supervision of the Accountant of Court, and the court will therefore only exceptionally appoint a person resident outwith the jurisdiction of the court.[4] His powers and duties are largely determined by statutes and Acts of Sederunt. He should have no interest in the estate adverse to that of his ward.[5]

Only exceptionally will the court appoint more than one person as factor[6] and it will not appoint one person, whom failing, another.[7]

Caution

The factor must find caution for his intromissions,[8] of a kind and to an amount fixed by the court;[9] the cautioner may be a person[10] or an insurance company or guarantee association.[11] The cautioner is liable for the factor's defalcations, even prior to the date of the bond of caution.[12]

Sequestration of estate

The court may, as well as appointing a judicial factor, sequestrate the estate, which takes it out of the control of the possessor and vests it in the court, to be managed by an independent person accountable to the court.[13] This is generally done

[1] *Macdonald* (1896) 4 S.L.T. 4; *Dick* (1901) 9 S.L.T. 177.

[2] *Pool* (1896) 4 S.L.T. 216 (clergyman); a woman may be appointed: *Chalmers' Trs.* v. *Sinclair* (1897) 24 R. 1047; *Duff*, 1910 2 S.L.T. 202; *Smith Sligo*, 1914 1 S.L.T. 287.

[3] *Brown* v. *Edinburgh Northern Tramways Co.* (1888) 15 R. 615.

[4] *Sim* v. *Robertson* (1901) 3 F. 1027; *Napier* (1902) 9 S.L.T. 439; *Duff*, 1910 2 S.L.T. 202; *Collins*, 1921 2 S.L.T. 36; *Forsyth*, 1932 S.L.T. 462; contrast *Harper*, 1932 S.L.T. 496.

[5] *Hagart* (1893) 1 S.L.T. 62; *Leslie* (1904) 12 S.L.T. 359; *Johnston* v. *Barbé*, 1928 S.N. 86.

[6] *Sloan* (1844) 7 D. 227.

[7] *Dow* (1847) 9 D. 616; *Thomson* (1851) 14 D. 311.

[8] 1849 Act, S. 2.

[9] *McKinnon* (1884) 12 R. 184; *C. and Others*, 1939 S.C. 736. As to sufficiency of bond of caution see *Anderson's Factor* (1869) 6 S.L.R. 675.

[10] *Fraser's J.F.* (1892) 19 R. 500.

[11] *McKinnon* (1884) 11 R. 676; *Harley* (1888) 25 S.L.R. 445; *Harris* (1901) 8 S.L.T. 415.

[12] *Wallace's Factor* v. *McKissock* (1898) 25 R. 642.

[13] Bell, *Comm.* II, 244.

where the legal right is in a person whom it is necessary to supersede,[1] and must be sought in cases of partnership estates and trust estates where the trust is not latent.[2] It is resorted to only to suspend during the period of the factory the right of any person to intromit with the estate.[3]

Cases where appointments made

The usual cases of the appointment of a judicial factor are the appointment of a factor *loco tutoris* on the estate of a pupil without a tutor,[4] of a *curator bonis* on the estate of a minor,[5] or on the estate of a person physically or mentally incapax and thereby unable to manage or instruct the management of his affairs,[6] of a judicial factor on a trust estate where the trust has become unworkable because of differences of opinion among the trustees,[7] or the whole trustees desire to resign,[8] or the trustees have come

[1] *Courage* v. *Ballantine*, 1946 S.C. 351.

[2] *Booth* v. *Mackinnon* (1908) 15 S.L.T. 848.

[3] *Ferguson* v. *Murray* (1853) 15 D. 682; *Booth, supra.*

[4] *Macintyre* (1850) 13 D. 951; *Davidson* (1855) 17 D. 629; *Ross* (1857) 19 D. 699; *Lamb* (1858) 20 D. 1323; *Collins* v. *Eglinton Iron Co.* (1882) 9 R. 500; *McAvoy* v. *Young's Paraffin Oil Co.* (1882) 19 S.L.R. 441; *Anderson* v. *Muirhead* (1884) 11 R. 870; *Connolly* v. *Bent Colliery Co.* (1897) 24 R. 1172; *Balfour Melville* (1903) 5 F. 347; *Hutcheon* v. *Alexander*, 1909 1 S.L.T. 71; *Boylan* v. *Hunter*, 1922 S.C. 80; *Fairley* v. *Allan*, 1948 S.L.T. (Notes) 81; *Falconer* v. *Robertson*, 1949 S.L.T. (Notes) 57. An appointment may be made if there is a conflict of interest between parent and pupil child: *Allan* (1895) 3 S.L.T. 87; contrast *Wardrop* v. *Gossling* (1869) 7 M. 532; *Cochrane* (1891) 18 R. 456. A mother cannot be appointed, as she is tutor under the Guardianship of Infants Acts, 1886 and 1925: *Willison* (1890) 18 R. 228; cf. *Jack* v. *N.B. Ry.* (1886) 14 R. 263. Nor can a factor act as guardian jointly with the mother as tutor: *Speirs*, 1946 S.L.T. 203. A factor *loco tutoris* becomes *curator bonis* when the ward becomes minor: *Reid* (1882) 19 S.L.R. 546; Judicial Factors (Sc.) Act, 1889, S. 11; *Stiven* v. *Masterton* (1892) 30 S.L.R. 50; *Balfour Melville, supra.*

[5] *McNab* v. *McN.* (1871) 10 M. 248 (superseding father); *Hutchison* (1881) 18 S.L.R. 725; *Thomson* (1881) 19 S.L.R. 105; *Anderson* v. *Muirhead* (1884) 11 R. 870.

[6] Bell, *Prin.* §2121; *Mark* (1845) 7 D. 882; *Acct. of Court* v. *Morrison* (1857) 19 D. 504; *Irving* v. *Swan* (1868) 7 M. 86; *Anderson's Trs.* v. *Skinner* (1871) 8 S.L.R. 325; *Sawyer* v. *Sloan* (1875) 3 R. 271; *C.B.* v. *A.B.* (1891) 18 R. (H.L.) 40; *Simpson* v. *S.* (1891) 18 R. 1207; *A.B.* (1908) 16 S.L.T. 557; *Smith Sligo*, 1914 1 S.L.T. 287; *Duncan*, 1915 2 S.L.T. 50; see also *Dowie* v. *Hagart* (1894) 21 R. 1052, where total inability not alleged. Medical certificates will only exceptionally be dispensed with: *Leslie* (1895) 3 S.L.T. 128; *Calderwood* v. *Duncan* (1907) 14 S.L.T. 777; and one at least must be independent of any hospital where the ward is confined: *Knox* (1894) 2 S.L.T. 388; *Kennedy* (1901) 8 S.L.T. 426. The court may remit where necessary to independent experts: *Greig*, 1923 S.L.T. 434; *Davies* v. *D.*, 1928 S.L.T. 142; *Shand* v. *S.*, 1950 S.L.T. (Notes) 32; *Brown* v. *Hackston*, 1960 S.C. 27. As to the office generally see *Bryce* v. *Graham* (1828) 6 S. 425; 3 W. & S. 323; *I.R.C.* v. *McMillan's C.B.*, 1956 S.C. 142.

[7] Trusts (Sc.) Act, 1921, S. 3(1); *Hope* v. *H.* (1884) 12 R. 27; *Stewart* v. *Morrison* (1892) 19 R. 1009; *Yuill* v. *Ross* (1900) 3 F. 96; *Scott* (1905) 13 S.L.T. 589; *Pott* v. *Stevenson*, 1935 S.L.T. 106; contrast *Bannerman* (1895) 3 S.L.T. 209; *Young's Trs.*, 1930 S.L.T. 731.

[8] *Maxwell's Trs.* v. *M.* (1874) 2 R. 71; *McMath* (1896) 4 S.L.T. 19.

to have an interest adverse to the beneficiaries,[1] or the trustees have failed to keep proper accounts,[2] or otherwise acted in breach of trust,[3] or the trust estate might be removed from Scotland,[4] of a judicial factor on a partnership estate,[5] of a judicial factor on the bankrupt estate of a deceased person,[6] or on the estate of a person sequestrated or threatened with sequestration, pending the appointment of a trustee,[7] of a judicial factor *loco absentis*,[8] on the estate of a deceased to whom no executor had confirmed,[9] or where there was a conflict between executor and the estate,[10] and in various other miscellaneous cases.[11] An

1 *Foggo* (1893) 20 R. 273; *Henderson* v. *H.* (1893) 20 R. 536; *Young* (1901) 9 S.L.T. 20; *Henderson* (1901) 9 S.L.T. 16; cf. *Maitland's Trs.* (1903) 11 S.L.T. 78; *Sawers* v. *S's Tr.* (1891) 19 S.L.R. 258.

2 *Henderson* (1901) 9 S.L.T. 16.

3 *McWhirter* v. *Latta* (1889) 17 R. 68; contrast *Gilchrist's Trs.* v. *Dick* (1883) 11 R. 22; *Harris* v. *Howie's Tr.* (1893) 21 R. 16; see also *Dryburgh* v. *Walker's Trs.* (1873) 1 R. 31; *Gibson Smith* v. *G.S.*, 1930 S.N. 35.

4 *Orr Ewing's Trs.* v. *O.E.* (1885) 13 R. (H.L.) 1; *Bowman* v. *Russell's Trs.* (1891) 19 R. 205.

5 *Young* v. *Collins & Feely* (1853) 15 D. (H.L.) 35; *Macpherson* (1869) 6 S.L.R. 348; *Dickie* v. *Mitchell* (1874) 1 R. 1030; *Eadie* v. *MacBean's C.B.* (1885) 12 R. 660; *Allan* v. *Gronmeyer* (1891) 18 R. 784; *Booth* v. *Mackinnon* (1908) 15 S.L.T. 848; see also *Mackenzie* v. *Macfarlane*, 1934 S.N. 16; *Anderson* v. *Blair*, 1935 S.L.T. 377; *Carabine* v. *C.*, 1949 S.C. 521; see also *Simeone* 1950 S.L.T. 399.

6 Bankruptcy (Sc.) Act, 1913, S. 163; cf. *Masterton* v. *Erskine's Trs.* (1887) 14 R. 712; *Begg & Co.* (1893) 1 S.L.T. 274; *Moncrieff's Trs.* v. *Halley* (1899) 1 F. 696; *Lowe's J.F.*, 1925 S.C. 11; *Bathgate* v. *Kelly*, 1926 S.L.T. 155; see also *Dunn* v. *Britannic Assce. Co.*, 1932 S.L.T. 244.

7 Bankruptcy (Sc.) Act, 1913, S. 14; cf. *Innes, Chambers & Co.* v. *McNeill*, 1917 1 S.L.T. 89; *Stewart* v. *Waldie*, 1926 S.L.T. 526.

8 Stair IV, 50, 28; Bell, *Prin.* §2120; *Kennedy* v. *Maclean* (1851) 13 D. 705; *Peterson* (1851) 13 D. 951; *Gibson* (1882) 19 S.L.R. 605; *Dobson* (1903) 11 S.L.T. 44; *Lunan* v. *Macdonald*, 1927 S.L.T. 661; contrast *Steel* (1874) 11 S.L.R. 160.

9 *London and Brazilian Bank* v. *Lumsden's Trs.*, 1913 1 S.L.T. 262.

10 *Thomson* v. *McNicol* (1871) 8 S.L.R. 623; *Birnie* v. *Christie* (1891) 19 R. 334; *Campbell* v. *Barbour* (1895) 23 R. 90.

11 To protect contingent interests under trust: *Carmont* v. *Mitchell's Trs.* (1883) 10 R. 829; *Raes* v. *Meek* (1889) 16 R. (H.L.) 31; or the interest of untraceable beneficiaries: *Doig* (1882) 20 S.L.R. 210; pending litigation: *Speirs* v. *S.* (1877) 5 R. 75; *Pattison's C.B.* (1898) 5 S.L.T. 400; *Blackwood* v. *Reith* (1905) 13 S.L.T. 629; *Simpson's Exor.* v. *Simpson's Trs.*, 1912 S.C. 418; *Tegner* v. *Henderson*, 1930 S.L.T. 23; to enforce jurisdiction: *Ross* v. *R.* (1885) 12 R. 1351; *Edgar* v. *Fisher's Trs.* (1893) 21 R. 59, 1076; on *haereditas jacens*: *Handyside* v. *L.A.*, 1909 1 S.L.T. 268; *Murray* v. *L.A.*, 1916 1 S.L.T. 369; *Rutherford* v. *L.A.*, *Cook* v. *L.A.*, 1932 S.C. 674; on estates held *pro indiviso* where there is dispute as to management: *Bailey* v. *Scott* (1860) 22 D. 1105; *Allan* (1898) 6 S.L.T. 152; to preserve a sequestrated estate until a trustee in bankruptcy has been elected: *Cuthbertson* v. *Gibson* (1887) 14 R. 736; *Youngson*, 1911 2 S.L.T. 448; Bankruptcy (Sc.) Act, 1913, S. 14; to hold an estate where the fee is vested in persons unascertained or unknown: Trusts (Sc.) Act, 1921, S. 8; *Napier* v. *N.*, 1963 S.L.T. 143; cf. *Gibson*, 1967 S.L.T. 150; on public companies at common law: *Glasgow & Barrhead Ry. Co.* (1850) 12 D. 1014; or under statute: Companies Clauses Consolidation Act, 1845, Ss. 56–7 (See *Broad* v. *Edinburgh Northern Tramways* (1888) 15 R. 615; *Cotton* v. *Beattie* (1889) 17 R. 262; Companies Clauses Act, 1863, Ss. 25–6; Railway Companies (Sc.) Act, 1867, S. 4;

appointment may be made though much of the estate is in England.[1]

A curator *ad litem* is not a judicial factor but merely a person appointed by the court to safeguard the interests of a person, legally or in fact *incapax*, who is a party to a litigation.

Supervision

A judicial factor is subject to the supervision of the Accountant of Court[2] who audits the factory accounts annually and fixes the factor's commission. His audit and report are conclusive against the factor, if not objected to,[3] and he must report the factor's failure in duty to the Court.[4]

A factor who has failed to lodge accounts annually is liable to a minimum penalty of half-a-year's salary for each year in which he has so failed[5] though exceptionally the Court has exercised a discretion not to impose such a penalty.[6]

Even though the Accountant at his audit passes investments made by a judicial factor, that does not relieve him of liability for improper investments.[7]

But if a factor has annually presented his accounts for audit and no complaint been made, a beneficiary cannot challenge his management by an action of court, reckoning, and payment.[8]

Duties

The factor, having found caution, must extract his appointment, take possession of the estate, and lodge within six months a rental of the lands and an inventory of the moveables forming the estate under his charge.[9]

The factor must recover all writs and documents belonging to the estate and, if necessary, complete title to property in name of the ward.[10] He must pay debts and ingather sums due to the

Haldane v. *Girvan and Portpatrick Ry.* (1881) 8 R. 669; see also *Greenock Harbour Trs.* v. *Greenock Harbour Trust J.F.*, 1910 S.C. (H.L.) 32; on long-quiescent sequestration: *Cheyne's Trs.*, 1933 S.L.T. 184.

1 *Watson*, 1932 S.L.T. 434.

2 Judicial Factors (Sc.) Acts, 1849, Ss. 10–23; 1889, Ss. 1–6; Bell, *Prin.* §2114; *Aitken* (1893) 21 R. 62; *Accountant of Court*, 1907 S.C. 909.

3 1849 Act, S. 15.

4 1849 Act, S. 20.

5 A. S. 13 Feb. 1730, S. 4; *Lowe* v. *Simpson* (1872) 11 M. 17; *Roxburgh* (1882) 19 S.L.R. 545.

6 *Morrison* v. *Dryden* (1890) 17 R. 704.

7 *Hutton* v. *Annan* (1898) 25 R. (H.L.) 23.

8 *Cormack* v. *Simpson's J.F.*, 1960 S.L.T. 197.

9 Bell, *Prin.* §2118; Pupils Protection Act, 1849, Ss. 3, 12.

10 A factor *loco absentis* does not make up title to the absentee's property: *McCaig* (1902) 10 S.L.T. 195.

estate[1] and revenue accruing, and invest the estate funds in trustee securities. The Accountant has to consider the sufficiency of the investments but the factor is responsible for them though the Accountant has approved in the past.[2] He must watch legal proceedings relating to the factory estate,[3] but avoid unnecessary litigation.[4]

He must close his accounts annually and lodge them within a month with the Accountant with relative vouchers.[5] He must bank the estate money and is chargeable with heavy interest on monies kept overlong in his hands.[6]

He must act with the same honesty as a trustee and not, e.g., sell shares belonging to his ward to a company of which he is managing director.[7] In case of conflict of interest he should resign.[8]

If managing the ward's property he must preserve the estate and not alter it, as by felling timber, unless that is necessary.[9]

General duty of care

As in the case of a trustee, a factor may not delegate his duties, though he may obtain legal or other necessary professional advice,[10] nor speculate with the trust estate,[11] but must exercise care, diligence and thought in administering the estate.

Title to heritable property

A judicial factor has no right to heritable property and, if the *dominium* is vested in the ward, he need take no action; if not, he should complete title in the ward's name. But if appointed on a trust estate, on which there is no dominus, he must complete title in his own name if it is necessary to sell or burden the lands, and must obtain power from the court to do so.[12] Bonds over heritage are taken in name of the ward, if any, or of the factor as such factor.

1 Including recovering trust money wrongly paid away: *Henderson* v. *Watson*, 1939 S.C. 711.

2 *Hutton* v. *Annan* (1898) 25 R. (H.L.) 23.

3 *Thyne's C.B.* (1882) 19 S.L.R. 724; *Tait* v. *Gray* (1908) 15 S.L.T. 1068.

4 *Ross* v. *Devine* (1878) 5 R. 1015.

5 1849 Act, Ss. 4, 11–14.

6 1849 Act, S. 5.

7 *Dunn* v. *Chambers* (1897) 25 R. 247; *A.B.'s C.B.*, 1927 S.C. 902.

8 *Perston's Trs.* v. *P.* (1863) 1 M. 245; *Dunn*, *supra*.

9 *Morrison's C.B.* v. *M's Trs.* (1880) 8 R. 205; *Macqueen* v. *Tod* (1899) 1 F. 1069, 1075.

10 *Barlas* v. *Moncrieff* (1859) 21 D. 725.

11 *Kirkland* (1848) 10 D. 1232.

12 *Maconochie* (1857) 19 D. 366; *Leslie's J.F.*, 1925 S.C. 464; see Titles to Land Consolidation (Sc.) Act, 1868, S. 24; Conveyancing (Sc.) Acts, 1874, S. 44, and 1924, S. 5(3).

Title to moveable property

The official extract of a factor's appointment has the effect of an assignation or transfer of moveable property.[1] Investments should be taken in the factor's name as such factor.[2]

Powers

Though he has generally no power over his ward's person,[3] a factor *loco tutoris* has been authorized to detain the ward in Scotland despite the ward's father,[4] and a *curator bonis* to have delivery of the person of an incapax for transfer to an asylum.[5] He has a right to the writs and documents of the estate and may obtain authority to take possession of them.[6]

A judicial factor, i.e. any person holding a judicial appointment as a factor or curator on another person's estate,[7] is a trustee within the meaning of the Trusts (Scotland) Acts, and has all a trustee's powers.[8]

He has all ordinary powers of administration such as to complete title to heritage in the ward's name,[9] grant leases, with the approval of the Accountant,[10] grant abatements of rent,[11] rearrange debts,[12] discharge a bond,[13] enforce payment of a bond,[14] pay accounts,[15] compromise claims,[16] take legal advice,[17] sell moveable property,[18] to distribute the estate,[19] at least in ordinary cases to compromise an action,[20] to remit income to the receiver

[1] 1889 Act, S. 13.

[2] *Acct. of Court* v. *Crumpton's C.B.* (1886) 14 R. 55; *Brodie* v. *L.N.W. Ry.*, 1912 2 S.L.T. 447.

[3] cf. *Dick* v. *Douglas*, 1924 S.C. 787.

[4] *Moncreiff* (1891) 18 R. 1029.

[5] *Christie's Curator* (1869) 7 M. 1130.

[6] *Orr Ewing's J.F.* (1884) 11 R. 682; *McLachlan* v. *Bell* (1895) 23 R. 126; *McAlley's J.F.* (1900) 2 F. 1198; *Ferguson's C.B.*, (1905) 7 F. 898.

[7] Trusts (Sc.) Act, 1961, S. 3; replacing definition in Trusts (Sc.) Act, 1921, S. 2, and superseding *Leslie's J.F.*, 1925 S.C. 464.

[8] 1921 Act, S. 2; as to investment in his own name where the Bank of England or an English company refuses to recognize trusts, see *Acct. of Court* v. *Crumpton's C.B.* (1886) 14 R. 55; *Brodie* v. *L.N.W. Ry.*, 1912 2 S.L.T. 447.

[9] *Melville's C.B.*, 1924 S.L.T. 110; *Waring*, 1933 S.L.T. 190.

[10] *Pattison's C.B.* (1890) 17 R. 303; *Tosh's J.F.*, 1913 S.C. 242.

[11] *Pattison's C.B.*, *supra*.

[12] *Moncreiff* (1894) 1 S.L.T. 528.

[13] *Wills* (1879) 6 R. 1096; *Keith's C.B.* (1893) 1 S.L.T. 13.

[14] *Yule* v. *Alexander* (1891) 19 R. 167.

[15] *Brown's Factor* (1902) 9 S.L.T. 490.

[16] *Scott* v. *Craig's Reps.* (1897) 24 R. 462.

[17] *Thyne's C.B.* (1882) 19 S.L.R. 724.

[18] *Morison* (1901) 4 F. 144.

[19] *Wharrie's J.F.*, 1916 1 S.L.T. 345.

[20] *Anderson* (1855) 17 D. 596; *Tennent's J.F.* v. *T.*, 1954 S.C. 215.

of an English incapax,[1] to sue for injuries sustained by the ward,[2] but not without special powers to rebuild a mansion-house.[3]

A factor's actings in the course of administration do not, if voluntary, alter the rights of succession to the estate, but otherwise if the act were necessary.[4]

On behalf of his ward he may elect between legal and testamentary provisions,[5] but not normally exercise discretionary powers entrusted to trustees whom he replaces.[6]

Special powers

If he requires special powers he reports to the Accountant and if there is doubt or special circumstances applies to the Court for necessary powers.[7] Acts done under special powers are not unchallengeable nor is the factor relieved of responsibility therefor.[8]

Thus judicial factors have been granted powers to complete title to heritage,[9] to sell heritage,[10] to lease heritage,[11] to grant tenants abatement of rent,[12] to cut ripe timber,[13] to realize heritable bonds and purchase heritage,[14] to repay heritable bonds,[15] to grant

1 *Gilchrist*, 1950 S.L.T. (Notes) 42.
2 *Cole-Hamilton* v. *Boyd*, 1963 S.C. (H.L.) 1.
3 *Semple* v. *Tennent* (1888) 15 R. 810.
4 *Stuart* (1855) 17 D. 378, 380; *Moncreiff* v. *Miln* (1856) 18 D. 1286; *Macfarlane* v. *Greig* (1895) 22 R. 405; *Macqueen* v. *Tod* (1899) 1 F. 1069; *McAdam's Exor.* v. *Souters* (1904) 7 F. 179; *Macfarlane's Trs.* v. *M.*, 1910 S.C. 325; *Taylor's Trs.* v. *Shepherd*, 1927 S.L.T. 226.
5 *McCall's Trs.* v. *McCall's C.B.* (1901) 3 F. 1065; *Skinner's C.B.* (1903) 5 F. 914.
6 *Robbie's J.F.* v. *Macrae* (1893) 20 R. 358; *Bruce's Factor* v. *Forbes* (1904) 12 S.L.T. 377; *Macdonald's Factor* v. *M.*, 1925 S.L.T. 426; *Vollar's J.F.* v. *Boyd*, 1952 S.L.T. (Notes) 84. Discretionary powers were held not personal but exercisable by a factor in *Woodward's J.F.* v. *W's Exrx.*, 1926 S.C. 534; *Shorter*, 1930 S.L.T. 535; *Macrae's J.F.* v. *Martin*, 1937 S.L.T. 209, but see *Angus's Exrx.* v. *Batchan's Tr.*, 1949 S.C. 335.
7 Judicial Factors (Sc.) Act, 1849, Ss. 7–8; *Tosh's J.F.*, 1913 S.C. 242; *Lowe's J.F.*, 1925 S.C. 11; *Lothian's C.B.* 1927 S.C. 579. The court may disagree with the Accountant as to granting powers: *Young* (1905) 43 S.L.R. 648.
8 *Milne* (1837) 15 S. 1104; *Wood* (1855) 17 D. 580.
9 *Paterson's J.F.* v. *Lindsay*, 1916 2 S.L.T. 244; *Leslie's J.F.*, 1925 S.C. 464; *McMurtrie*, 1939 S.N. 48. As to moveables see *Brower's Exor.*, 1938 S.C. 451.
10 *Jamieson* v. *Allardice* (1872) 10 M. 755; *Wood* (1896) 3 S.L.T. 277; *Young* (1905) 43 S.L.R. 648; contrast *Stirling's J.F.*, 1917 1 S.L.T. 165; *McLeay*, 1921 1 S.L.T. 340; this power is now nominally given by Trusts (Sc.) Act, 1921, Ss. 2, 4: *Lowe's J.F.*, 1925 S.C. 11; *Lothian's C.B.*, 1927 S.C. 579; *McBain*, 1928 S.N. 103; *Cooper & Son's J.F.*, 1931 S.L.T. 26; power was refused in *Molleson* v. *Hope* (1888) 15 R. 665; *Gilligan's Factor* v. *Fraser* (1898) 25 R. 876; the need to seek power to sell is not elided by the Trusts (Sc.) Act, 1961, S. 2: *Barclay*, 1962 S.L.T. 137; it depends on circumstances whether power to purchase heritage (Trusts (Sc.) Act, 1961, S. 4) need be sought: *Bristow*, 1965 S.L.T. 225.
11 *Carnochan* (1894) 2 S.L.T. 79.
12 *Grant's Curator* (1880) 7 R. 1014.
13 *Horsburgh's C.B.* (1901) 9 S.L.T. 216; contrast *Macqueen* v. *Tod* (1899) 1 F. 1069.
14 *Steven's J.F.* (1907) 15 S.L.T. 17.
15 *Macbean's C.B.* (1890) 28 S.L.R. 8.

entail provisions,[1] to consent on the ward's behalf to a sale,[2] to accept personal instead of real security for an annuity,[3] or concur on the ward's behalf with his partners in selling the firm business,[4] to retain shares with an uncalled liability,[5] to make allowances to the ward's dependants,[6] to exhume the testator and rebury him, erecting a mausoleum at the place,[7] to resign the ward's offices of trustee,[8] and to make charitable donations,[9] to grant transfers of stock,[10] to carry on a farm and to borrow money for that purpose,[11] to apply to the English court to complete title to an English mortgage,[12] to realize capital to supplement a liferent,[13] to compromise an action.[14]

Though the court has a residuum of common law powers in dealing with factories these do not apply to matters specifically regulated by statute.[15]

Ultra vires *actings*

If a factor acts *ultra vires* the court will not normally subsequently ratify his actings[16] but may do so.[17] In such a case the factor is personally liable for the *ultra vires* expenditure, but may have a claim for any benefit to the estate,[18] and where possible must effect restitution *in integrum*.[19]

Factor's commission

The factor's remuneration is fixed by the Accountant at each annual audit and debited in the following account.[20] His commission is in full of all services, save that he is entitled to legal

1 *Gordon's C.B.* (1902) 4 F. 577.
2 *Cowan's C.B.* (1902) 5 F. 19.
3 *Saunders* (1882) 19 S.L.R. 544.
4 *Bontine's Curator* (1870) 8 M. 976.
5 *Browning's Factor* (1905) 7 F. 1037.
6 *Allan* v. *Mackay & Ewing* (1869) 8 M. 139; *Paterson's Curator* (1876) 3 R. 554; *Latta* (1880) 7 R. 881; *Gardner* (1882) 20 S.L.R. 165; *Simson* (1883) 10 R. 540; *Balfour* (1889) 26 S.L.R. 268; *Blackwood* (1890) 17 R. 1093; *Bowers* v. *Pringle Pattison's C.B.* (1892) 19 R. 941; *A.B.* (1894) 2 S.L.T. 311; *Howden* v. *Simson* (1895) 23 R. 113; *Rutherford's J.F.*, 1931 S.L.T. 587.
7 *Kilpatrick* (1881) 8 R. 592.
8 *Laidlaw* (1882) 10 R. 130.
9 *M's C.B.* (1904) 12 S.L.T. 30.
10 *Pennycuick*, 1925 S.L.T. 362.
11 *Rutherford's J.F.*, 1931 S.L.T. 587; contrast *Drew*, 1938 S.L.T. 435.
12 *Ayton's J.F.*, 1937 S.L.T. 86.
13 *Leith's J.F.* v. *L.*, 1957 S.C. 307.
14 *McDougall* (1853) 15 D. 776; *Anderson* (1857) 19 D. 329; *Tennent's J.F.* v. *T.*, 1954 S.C. 215.
15 *Tennent's J.F.*, *supra*.
16 *Clyne* (1894) 21 R. 849; *Drummond's J.F.* (1894) 21 R. 932; *Hodge* (1904) 11 S.L.T. 709.
17 *Robertson's Curator* (1876) 3 R. 619; *Drummond's J.F.*, *supra*; *Blair's C.B.*, 1921 1 S.L.T. 248.
18 *Semple* v. *Tennent* (1888) 15 R. 810.
19 *Campbell* v. *Grant* (1869) 8 M. 227.
20 1849 Act, S. 13.

advice. He may recover actual outlays,[1] but neither he nor his firm may charge fees for services rendered.[2]

Recall of appointment

The court which has made an appointment may recall it if circumstances justify that course,[3] but recall will not be made automatically on request.[4] One appointment may be recalled and another made instead.[5]

Resignation of factor

A factor may resign, by petition to the court to discharge and replace him.[6]

Death of factor

On a factor's death a petition must be brought for discharge of the deceased factor's representatives and appointment of a new factor in his stead.[7]

Removal of factor

A factor is liable to suspension or removal from office for misconduct or failure to perform his duties, to forfeiture of commission, payment of expenses and fine, and where the estate has sustained damage, is liable in reparation.[8] Where necessary, on a factor's removal, a new factor may be appointed.[9] In such a case the new factor alone has title to object to the old factor's accounts.[10]

Denuding and discharge

When the necessity for his administration has passed[11] the factor petitions the Court for his discharge, which the Court,

[1] *Mitchell* v. *Burness* (1878) 5 R. 1124.

[2] *Lord Gray* (1856) 19 D. 1; *Mitchell, supra.*

[3] *Milne* v. *Wills* (1868) 5 S.L.R. 189; *Sawyer* v. *Sloan* (1875) 3 R. 271; *Tweedie* (1886) 14 R. 212; *Fisher* v. *Edgar* (1894) 21 R. 1076; *Fraser* (1901) 9 S.L.T. 271; *A.B.* v. *A.B.'s C.B.* (1908) 16 S.L.T. 583; *Turnbull* v. *Ross's J.F.*, 1916 2 S.L.T. 249; *Gowans*, 1917 2 S.L.T. 61; *Inglis* v. *I.*, 1927 S.N. 181; *A.B.* v. *C.D.*, 1929 S.L.T. 517.

[4] *Masterton* v. *Erskine's Trs.* (1887) 14 R. 712; *Balfour Melville* (1903) 5 F. 347; *Macalister* v. *Crawford's Trs.*, 1909 1 S.L.T. 232.

[5] *Souter* v. *Finlay* (1890) 18 R. 86.

[6] *Halliday's C.B.*, 1912 S.C. 509.

[7] cf. *Dalziel* (1898) 5 S.L.T. 255.

[8] 1849 Act, S. 6; see also Ss. 19–21; *Walker* v. *Buchanan* (1888) 15 R. 1102; *Marshall* v. *Chisholm* (1901) 3 F. 642; a factor appointed in the sheriff court may be removed by the Court of Session: *Forrest* v. *F's J.F.* (1898) 6 S.L.T. 68.

[9] *Walker, supra*; *Port's C.B.* (1901) 9 S.L.T. 271.

[10] *Port's C.B., supra.*

[11] Discharge and exoneration *ad interim* may be granted: *Smith* (1882) 19 S.L.R. 435.

after receiving the Accountant's report, hearing any parties who appear, and making any further inquiry which may be necessary, may grant. On production of the extract discharge the Accountant delivers up the bond of caution.[1] The court will not normally grant a discharge if there has been no judicial audit, even where the accounts have been examined on the beneficiary's behalf.[2]

[1] 1849 Act, S. 34; *Campbell* v. *Grant* (1870) 8 M. 908.

[2] *Aiton's Factor* (1875) 13 S.L.R. 175; *Nicol's Curator* (1884) 11 R. 867; *Aitken* (1893) 21 R. 62.

BOOK VII

BANKRUPTCY

CHAPTER 108

INSOLVENCY, NOTOUR BANKRUPTCY, AND SEQUESTRATION

THE general term bankruptcy comprises three states or stages of inability to implement one's financial obligations, simple insolvency, notour bankruptcy when the insolvency becomes public, and finally mercantile sequestration,[1] when the debtor's property is taken out of his hands and put under official control for realization and equitable distribution among creditors under judicial authority.[2]

INSOLVENCY

A person is insolvent for practical purposes if he is unable, or refuses without adequate cause, to meet current obligations as they become due even though his total assets, if realized, would have enabled him to do so.[3] He is absolutely insolvent if, even though able to meet present demands, his total assets would not meet his total liabilities. Insolvency is a state of fact, not fixed by any public or legal criteria. As between debtor and creditor practical insolvency is relevant; as between competing creditors challenging alienations or preferences, however, absolute insolvency at the material time is necessary. Where a deed prescribes that consequences follow if a person is 'bankrupt', mere insolvency is not sufficient.[4] The expiry of a charge on a decree for payment is *prima facie* proof of insolvency, and it is irrelevant that failure to pay is alleged to be wilful and not due to lack of means.[5]

Insolvency by itself does not prevent a debtor from contracting,

[1] Distinguishable from the sequestration by the court of a trust estate or a partnership estate, and from landlord's sequestration to enforce his hypothec for rent.

[2] See generally Bell, *Comm.*, II, 152 *et seq.*; Goudy, *Bankruptcy*; Wallace, *Bankruptcy*.

[3] *Watt* v. *Findlay* (1846) 8 D. 529; *Knowles* v. *Crooks* (1865) 3 M. 457; *Clendinnen* v. *Rodger* (1875) 3 R. (J.) 3; *Shaw* v. *City of Glasgow Bank* (1878) 6 R. 332; *Mitchell* v. *City of Glasgow Bank* (1878) 6 R. (H.L.) 66; *Hannan* v. *Henderson* (1879) 7 R. 380; *Fleming* v. *Smith* (1881) 8 R. 548; *Teenan's Tr.* v. *T.* (1886) 13 R. 833; *McNab* v. *Clarke* (1889) 16 R. 610; *Aitken* v. *Kyd* (1890) 28 S.L.R. 115; *Mackenzie* v. *Tod*, 1912 1 S.L.T. 464; *Sc. Milk Marketing Board* v. *Wood*, 1936 S.C. 604; cf. Sale of Goods Act, 1893, S. 62(3).

[4] Bell, *Comm.* II, 153; *Munro* v. *Cowan*, 8 June 1813, F.C.; *Furness* v. *Liqdr. of Cynthiana S.S. Co.* (1893) 21 R. 239.

[5] *Scottish Milk Marketing Board* v. *Wood*, 1936 S.C. 604.

nor from litigating, though the court may require him to find caution for expenses,[1] but a seller may stop goods *in transitu* to an insolvent buyer,[2] and an insolvent buyer should refuse to take delivery of goods.[3] A creditor may also use diligence, by arrestment, inhibition or adjudication, in security against an insolvent debtor though the debt be not yet due.

Effects of insolvency: reduction of gratuitous alienations at common law

A person who is absolutely insolvent is deemed to administer his estate for behoof of his creditors generally.[4] Accordingly at common law every gratuitous alienation of property or rights, direct or indirect, by an insolvent is reducible at the instance of an onerous creditor, being presumed to be effected in fraud of the whole creditors.[5] Any onerous creditor may challenge,[6] either by way of action or by exception.[7] He must prove that the transaction was gratuitous[8] or the consideration grossly inadequate,[9] that the debtor was then and still is insolvent[10] or that the transaction attacked made him insolvent,[11] though the circumstances may yield an inference of fraud,[12] but need not prove that the disponee had any fraudulent intent.[13] The satisfaction of a prior legal obligation is an answer to the plea that a transfer was gratuitous.[14]

A provision by an insolvent under an ante-nuptial marriage contract is good to the extent of a reasonable provision for the wife or children only.[15] Provisions under a post-nuptial marriage

1 *Bell* v. *Anderson* (1862) 24 D. 603; *Weir* v. *Buchanan* (1876) 4 R. 8; *Ritchie* v. *McIntosh* (1881) 8 R. 747; *Stevenson* v. *Lee* (1886) 13 R. 913; *Lawrie* v. *Pearson* (1888) 16 R. 62; *Johnstone* v. *Dryden* (1890) 18 R. 191.

2 Sale of Goods Act, 1893, S. 44.

3 Ibid., S. 45(4); Bell, *Comm*, I, 253.

4 Bell, *Comm.* II, 170, 184; *Dobie* v. *Macfarlane* (1854) 17 D. 97; *Main* v. *Galbraith* (1881) 8 R. 880.

5 *McCowan* v. *Wright* (1853) 15 D. 494; *Main, supra*; *Obers* v. *Paton's Trs.* (1897) 24 R. 719.

6 *McCowan, supra*; *Edmond* v. *Grant* (1853) 15 D. 703; *Wink* v. *Speirs* (1867) 6 M. 77.

7 Bankruptcy (Sc.) Act, 1913, S. 8; *Dickson* v. *Murray* (1866) 4 M. 797; *Cook* v. *Sinclair* (1896) 23 R. 925.

8 *Morrison* v. *Carron Co.* (1854) 16 D. 1125; *Forsyth* v. *Duncan* (1863) 1 M. 1054.

9 *Lindsay* v. *Shield* (1862) 24 D. 821; *Watson* v. *Grant's Trs.* (1874) 1 R. 882; *Abram S.S. Co.* v. *Abram*, 1925 S.L.T. 243; *Ritchie* v. *Scottish Automobile Ins. Co.*, 1931 S.N. 83.

10 *McCowan, supra*; *Abram, supra.*

11 *McKenzie* v. *Fletcher* (1712) Mor. 924.

12 *McCowan, supra.*

13 *McCowan, supra*; *Main, supra.*

14 *McCowan, supra*; *Taylor* v. *Jones* (1888) 15 R. 328.

15 Bell, *Comm.* I, 683; *Carphin* v. *Clapperton* (1867) 5 M. 797; *Watson* v. *Grant's Trs.* (1874) 1 R. 882; *Hall's Trs.* v. *Macdonald* (1892) 20 R. (H.L.) 88; *McKinnon's Trs.* v. *Dunlop*, 1913 S.C. 232.

contract to take effect on the insolvent's death are probably reducible.[1] A policy of assurance under the Married Women's Policies of Assurance (Sc.) Act, 1880 is not reducible on the ground of insolvency but if it is proved that the policy was effected and the premiums paid to defraud creditors, or if the life assured be made bankrupt within two years, the creditors may claim repayment of the premiums from the trustee out of the proceeds of the policy.[2]

Reduction of fraudulent preferences at common law

Any transaction whereby the insolvent, in the knowledge thereof, directly or indirectly confers a preference on one creditor to the prejudice of the others is reducible at common law.[3] Fraudulent intent is presumed[4] and the preferred creditor's knowledge is irrelevant,[5] but the granter must be aware of his insolvency at the date of granting[6] and have granted the preference intentionally and in contemplation of bankruptcy.[7] Thus a disposition of heritage, when insolvent, to the lender of the money to build it, has been reduced,[8] as has a consent to decree for redelivery of goods sold and delivered,[9] and an agreement with certain creditors to set aside a part of his income to pay their debts, they undertaking not to enforce their claims.[10] Giving security, or undertaking to do so, is challengeable[11] but merely giving an acknowledgment of debt is not.[12]

Transactions exempt from challenge

Cash payments for debts actually due,[13] transactions in the ordinary course of trade,[14] and *nova debita*, such as mutual

[1] *Guthrie* v. *Cowan* (1846) 9 D. 124.
[2] 1880 Act, S. 2.
[3] Bell, *Comm.* II, 226; *McCowan* v. *Wright* (1853) 15 D. 594; *Wilson* v. *Drummond* (1856) 16 D. 275; *B. of Scotland* v. *Faulds* (1870) 7 S.L.R. 619; *Lamond* v. *Stewart & Bissett* (1887) 15 R. 32.
[4] *McCowan, supra*; *Wilson, supra*; *Taylor* v. *Jones* (1888) 15 R. 328.
[5] *McCowan, supra*; *Wilson, supra.*
[6] *McCowan supra*; *Macdonald* v. *Logan* (1903) 11 S.L.T. 369; *MacDougall's Trs.* v. *Ironside*, 1914 S.C. 186.
[7] *Ehrenbacher* v. *Kennedy* (1874) 1 R. 1131; *Macdonald* v. *Logan* (1903) 11 S.L.T. 369.
[8] *Wylie, Stewart & Marshall* v. *Jervis*, 1913 1 S.L.T. 465.
[9] *Laurie's Tr.* v. *Beveridge* (1867) 6 M. 85.
[10] *Munro* v. *Rothfield*, 1920 S.C. (H.L.) 165.
[11] *McCowan* v. *Wright* (1853) 15 D. 494; *Thomas* v. *Thomson* (1866) 5 M. 198; see also *Renton & Gray's Tr.* v. *Dickison* (1880) 7 R. 951.
[12] *Williamson* v. *Allan* (1882) 9 R. 859.
[13] *Thomas, supra*; *Coutts' Tr.* v. *Webster* (1886) 13 R. 1112; see also *Lamond* v. *Stewart & Bisset* (1887) 15 R. 32; *Pringle's Tr.* v. *Wright* (1903) 5 F. 522.
[14] Bell, *Comm.* II, 228; *Thomas, supra.*

obligations incurred,[1] are not reducible without proof of actual fraud.

A security granted by an insolvent, who ultimately becomes bankrupt, in consideration of advances to be made, does not make it an illegal preference.[2] Successive indorsations of a bill of lading are not struck at unless fraudulently indorsed and received.[3] An assignation of a lease to a creditor who advanced money to enable a debtor to pay a composition to other creditors has been held not illegal.[4]

Reduction of gratuitous alienations under statute

Under the Bankruptcy Act, 1621 (c. 18) alienations by a debtor of any of his property 'to any conjunct and confident person without true, just, and necessary cause and without a just price really paid' are null if challenged by creditors prejudiced, by action of reduction.[5] The Act has been held to apply to every kind of deed by which property or an obligation is transferred,[6] but probably not to the payment of money or the delivery of goods.[7] Conjunct persons are close relatives by blood[8] or affinity;[9] confident persons are those in whom the granter is presumed to place unusual trust,[10] such as senior employees, confidential clerks,[11] but not trustees,[12] nor a debtor.[13]

The onus of proving the transaction onerous is on the grantee.[14]

[1] *Taylor* v. *Farrie* (1855) 17 D. 639; *Miller's Tr.* v. *Shields* (1862) 24 D. 821; *Stiven* v. *Scott & Simson* (1871) 9 M. 923; cf. *Clark* v. *West Calder Oil Co.* (1882) 9 R. 1017.

[2] *McInnes* v. *McCallum* (1901) 9 S.L.T. 215; see also *Renton & Gray's Tr.* v. *Dickison* (1880) 7 R. 951.

[3] *Adamson, Howie & Co.* v. *Guild* (1867) 6 M. 347.

[4] *Hay* v. *Rafferty* (1899) 2 F. 302.

[5] See generally Bell, *Comm.* II, 171.

[6] *Laing* v. *Cheyne* (1832) 10 S. 200; *Buchanan* v. *Carrick* (1838) 16 S. 358; *Thomas* v. *Thomson* (1865) 3 M. 1160; *Gorrie's Tr.* v. *Gorrie* (1890) 17 R. 1051; *Obers* v. *Paton's Trs.* (1897) 24 R. 719.

[7] *Dobie* v. *Macfarlane* (1854) 17 D. 97; *Thomas, supra*; *N.B. Ry.* v. *White* (1882) 20 S.L.R. 129; *Main* v. *Galbraith* (1891) 8 R. 880; *Thomson* v. *Spence*, 1961 S.L.T. 395.

[8] *Brown* v. *Murray* (1754) Mor. 886; *Hodge* v. *Morrisons* (1883) 21 S.L.R. 40; *Dawson* v. *Thorburn* (1888) 15 R. 891 (daughter); *Gorrie's Tr.* v. *G.* (1890) 17 R. 105 (son); *Tennant* v. *Miller* (1897) 4 S.L.T. 318 (wife); *McLay* v. *McQueen* (1899) 1 F. 804 (intended spouse).

[9] *Hume* v. *Smith* (1673) Mor. 899; *Mercer* v. *Dalgardno* (1695) Mor. 12563.

[10] Ersk. IV, 1, 31; Bell, *Comm.* II, 175.

[11] *Edmond* v. *Grant* (1853) 15 D. 703; *Bank of Scotland* v. *Gardiner* (1907) 15 S.L.T. 229.

[12] *McLay* v. *McQueen* (1899) 1 F. 804.

[13] *Todd* v. *Anglian Ins. Co.*, 1933 S.L.T. 274; see also *Ritchie* v. *Scottish Automobile Ins. Co.*, 1931 S.N. 83.

[14] Bell, *Comm.* II, 172, 179; *Buccleuch* v. *B's Crs.* (1757) Mor. 12575; *Horne* v. *Hay* (1847) 9 D. 651; *Matthew's Tr.* v. *M.* (1867) 5 M. 975; *N.B. Ry.* v. *White* (1882) 20 S.L.R. 129; *Hodge* v. *Morrisons* (1883) 21 S.L.R. 40; *Taylor* v. *Jones* (1888) 15 R. 328; *Dawson* v. *Thorburn* (1888) 15 R. 891; *Kyd* v. *Gorrie* (1890) 17 R. 1051.

The requirement of true, just and necessary cause is satisfied by a legal obligation incurred prior to insolvency, and that whether the deed is granted in satisfaction of the obligation,[1] or in security therefor.[2] Provisions in ante-nuptial marriage-contracts are not affected so long as the debtor's insolvency was unknown,[3] and so long as the provisions are not excessive.[4] It is doubtful whether provisions in a post-nuptial marriage contract are protected.[5] A post-nuptial provision has been held unaffected so far as moderate, though made after the husband's insolvency.[6] Reasonable provisions for bastard children[7] and policies of life insurance by the debtor for the benefit of his wife or children[8] are protected.

A 'just price' is a price reasonably adequate for the transfer, such as to indicate a *bona fide* transaction.[9] It must have been actually paid.[10]

If the granter is insolvent at the date of challenge insolvency at the date of granting is presumed, but this presumption can be rebutted.[11]

A successful challenge makes the alienated property part of the debtor's general estate, but does not give the challenger any right to the property himself.[12]

Third parties who in good faith, for value, and in ignorance of the debtor's insolvency, acquired the subject alienated are protected.[13]

Alienations during insolvency in defraud of diligence

The Bankruptcy Act, 1621, c. 18, also provides that if there is any voluntary payment or right to any person in defraud of the lawful and more timely diligence of another creditor the debtor

[1] *Horne* v. *Hay* (1847) 9 D. 651; *Williamson* v. *Allan* (1882) 9 R. 859; contrast *Dawson* v. *Thorburn* (1888) 15 R. 891; *Kyd* v. *Gorrie* (1890) 17 R. 1051.

[2] *Thomas* v. *Thomson* (1866) 5 M. 198.

[3] Ersk. IV, 1, 33; *Garden* v. *Stirling* (1822) 2 S. 39; *Scott* v. *Ross* (1822) 1 S. 519; *McLay* v. *McQueen* (1899) 1 F. 804; cf. *Watson* v. *Grant's Trs.* (1874) 1 R. 882.

[4] *Corbidge* v. *Somervell's Trs.*, 1911 S.C. 1326.

[5] *Sharp* v. *Christie* (1839) 1 D. 396; *Guthrie* v. *Cowan* (1846) 9 D. 124; *Watson* v. *Grant's Trs.* (1874) 1 R. 882; *Robertson's Trs.* v. *R.* (1901) 3 F. 359.

[6] *McBain* v. *Robertson* (1900) 8 S.L.T. 101; contrast *Robertson's Tr.* v. *R.* (1901) 3 F. 359, where conveyance was of whole estate and rendered husband insolvent.

[7] *Downs* v. *Wilson's Tr.* (1886) 13 R. 1101; *Valentine* v. *Reimers* (1892) 19 R. 519.

[8] Married Women's Policies of Assurance (Sc.) Act, 1880, S. 2.

[9] cf. *Tennant* v. *Miller* (1847) 4 S.L.T. 318.

[10] Bell, *Comm.* II, 177–80; *N.B. Ry.* v. *White* (1893) 20 S.L.R. 129; *Hodge* v. *Morrisons* (1883) 21 S.L.R. 40.

[11] Bell, *Comm.* II, 172; *Bolden* v. *Ferguson* (1863) 1 M. 522.

[12] Bell, *Comm.* II, 183; *Bell* v. *Gow* (1862) 1 M. 183; *Cook* v. *Sinclair* (1896) 23 R. 925.

[13] 1621 Act; *Williamson* v. *Sharp* (1851) 14 D. 127.

must make the same forthcoming to the creditor having used the first lawful diligence. Challenge is competent by any creditor who had begun to use diligence which would have attached the subject alienated. The debtor must have been insolvent and the challenge will fail if this is unknown to the grantee[1] though there need not have been any collusion.[2] The voluntary payment may be made in any form, direct or indirect, and may be in favour of a stranger, and may be a disposition in trust for behoof of all the granter's creditors.[3] It must have been granted voluntarily, and alienations under pressure of diligence are not voluntary.[4] Payments in cash of debts presently due are not challengeable,[5] nor are *nova debita*,[6] but deeds granted in implement of a prior legal obligation may be challengeable.[7] A successful challenge protects the diligence of the challenging creditor and has the same effect in relation to third parties as a challenge under the earlier branch of the statute.[8]

NOTOUR BANKRUPTCY

Notour[9] bankruptcy is now constituted:[10]

1. by sequestration, or by the issuing of an adjudication of bankruptcy or the granting of a receiving order in England or Ireland; or

2. by insolvency,[11] concurring—

A. (1) with a duly executed charge for payment, where a charge is necessary, followed by the expiry of the days of charge without payment;[12]

[1] Bell, *Comm.* II, 186; *Royal Bank* v. *Kennedy* (1708) Mor. 1057; *Tweedie* v. *Din* (1715) Mor. 1037.

[2] *Grant* v. *McEdward's Trs.* (1835) 13 S. 424; *Mackenzie* v. *Calder* (1868) 6 M. 833.

[3] *Grant*, *supra*; *Mackenzie*, *supra*.

[4] *Gordon* v. *Bogle* (1724) Mor. 1041.

[5] *Forbes* v. *Brebner* (1751) Mor. 1042.

[6] Bell, *Comm.* II, 188.

[7] *Mansfield* v. *Walker's Trs.* (1833) 11 S. 813.

[8] Bell, *Comm.* II, 190.

[9] i.e. notorious. For history of the concept see Bell, *Comm.* II, 192. It was introduced by the Bankruptcy Act, 1696, c. 5.

[10] Bankruptcy (Sc.) Act, 1913, Ss. 5, 6.

[11] i.e. practical insolvency, whether or not absolute insolvency; *Teenan's Tr.* v. *T.* (1886) 13 R. 833; *McNab* v. *Clarke* (1889) 16 R. 610; *Aitken* v. *Kyd* (1890) 28 S.L.R. 115.

[12] Unless, probably, there is adequate excuse for the nonpayment: cf. *McBean* v. *Wright* (1868) 7 M. 23. Notour bankruptcy is not suspended by intimating an appeal during the currency of the charge: *Fleming* v. *Yeaman* (1884) 21 S.L.R. 722 (H.L.). The charge must be regular: *Beattie* v. *McLellan* (1844) 6 D. 1088; *Graham* v. *Bell* (1875) 2 R. 972; and must have expired: *Baillie* (1899) 6 S.L.T. 324; *Arrol* v. *Christie* (1901) 4 F. 262; *Laird* v. *Scott*, 1913 2 S.L.T. 409.

(2) where a charge is not necessary,[1] with the lapse without payment of the days which must elapse before poinding or imprisonment[2] can follow on a decree or warrant for payment of a sum of money;

(3) with a poinding or seizure of any of the debtor's moveables for non-payment of rates or taxes;

(4) with a decree of adjudication of any part of his heritable estate for payment or in security; or

B. with sale of any effects belonging to the debtor under a sequestration for rent.

Notour bankruptcy of a company[3] is constituted in any of the foregoing ways or by any of the partners being rendered notour bankrupt for a company debt.[4]

Any person who can be liable for debt may be made notour bankrupt.

Notour bankruptcy commences when its several requisites concur and then continues until the debtor, if sequestrated, obtains his discharge, and in other cases till insolvency ceases, but it may be constituted anew within that period or after it ceases.[5] Proof that it has ceased may be by payment of debts,[6] or that the creditors have acceded to a trust deed or accepted a composition. But it does not cease by an arrangement to pay debts by instalments.[7]

Reduction under statute of fraudulent preferences granted by notour bankrupt

Fraudulent preferences are also reducible under the Bankruptcy (Sc.) Act, 1696 (c. 5)[8] at the instance of creditors prior to the date of the preference, or of the trustee in sequestration,

[1] On a Small Debt decree granted when the debtor is personally present: *Shiell* v. *Mossman* (1871) 10 M. 58.

[2] For cases where imprisonment is competent see Debtors (Sc.) Act, 1880, S. 4, and Crown Proceedings Act, 1947, S. 49. See also *Black* v. *Watson* (1881) 9 R. 167; *Harvie* v. *Smith*, 1908 S.C. 474.

[3] Defined, 1913 Act, S. 2: it includes bodies corporate, politic or collegiate, and partnerships (e.g. *Mullen* v. *Campbell*, 1923 S.L.T. 497) or unlimited companies. An unincorporated association cannot be made notour bankrupt: *Pitreavie Golf Club* v. *Penman*, 1934 S.N. 15.

[4] 1913 Act, S. 6. A limited company may also be made notour bankrupt to the effect of equalizing diligences: *Clark* v. *Hinde, Milne & Co.* (1884) 12 R. 347; cf. *Wotherspoon* v. *Linlithgow Mags.* (1863) 2 M. 348.

[5] 1913 Act, S. 7; cf. *Blair* v. *N.B. Mercantile Ins. Co.* (1889) 16 R. 947; 17 R. (H.L.) 76; *Wood* v. *Cranston & Elliot* (1891) 18 R. 382; *Arrol* v. *Christie* (1901) 4 F. 262.

[6] *Drybrough* v. *Walker*, 1909 2 S.L.T. 239.

[7] *Neil's Trs.* v. *B.L. Bank* (1898) 36 S.L.R. 139.

[8] See generally Bell, *Comm.* II, 192.

whether representing prior creditors or not,[1] on proof that the debtor is notour bankrupt, that the deed was voluntary and in satisfaction or further security[2] of a prior debt, that it was granted at, or after, or within six months before,[3] notour bankruptcy, and that the challenge is made by or on behalf of prior creditors, or by the trustee in sequestration.

Fraudulent preferences include any alienation outright or in security,[4] and such transactions as favour the creditor, such as renouncing a claim,[5] paying in advance,[6] discharging a debt,[7] granting a lease,[8] mortgaging a ship,[9] giving property to a third party who undertook to pay the creditor,[10] endorsing a bill or cheque,[11] conveying property under a promise to give security for a past loan,[12] granting further security for a prior debt,[13] making an advance on security to be granted later on request,[14] promising to pay a particular creditor,[15] promising to give goods later for money paid,[16] sending goods to be sold with permission to keep the price,[17] getting a debtor to pay a creditor direct,[18] abandoning a defence to an action,[19] granting a disposition in security of heritage, the bankrupt to sell the subjects.[20]

To be challengeable the preference must be in favour of the

1 *Galbraith* v. *B.L. Co.* (1898) 36 S.L.R. 139.

2 *Moore* v. *Gledden* (1869) 7 M. 1016.

3 1696 Act (sixty days before) as amended by Companies Act, 1947, S. 115(3). The date of a deed is the date of its registration or delivery or intimation or such other proceeding as is requisite in the particular case: Bankruptcy (Sc.) Act, 1913, S. 4. As to computing time see *Greig* v. *Anderson* (1883) 20 S.L.R. 421.

4 *Stiven* v. *Scott & Simson* (1871) 9 M. 923; *Renton & Gray's Tr.* v. *Dickison* (1880) 7 R. 951; *Paterson's Tr.* v. *P's Tr.* (1891) 19 R. 91; see also *Torrance* v. *Traill's Trs.* (1897) 24 R. 837.

5 Bell, *Comm.* II, 197; *Keith* v. *Maxwell* (1795) Mor. 1163.

6 *Speir* v. *Dunlop* (1825) 4 S. 92; *Blincow's Tr.* v. *Allan* (1828) 7 S. 124, 753; 7 W. & S. 26; *McFarlane* v. *Robb* (1870) 9 M. 370; *Rose* v. *Falconer* (1868) 6 M. 960.

7 *Renton & Gray's Trs., supra.*

8 *Morrison* v. *Carron Co.* (1854) 16 D. 1125; *Kyd* v. *Gorrie* (1890) 17 R. 1051.

9 *Anderson* v. *Western Bank* (1859) 21 D. 230.

10 *Tait* v. *Mowat* (1893) 1 S.L.T. 75; cf. *Craig's Tr.* v. *C.* (1903) 10 S.L.T. 556.

11 *Nicol* v. *McIntyre* (1882) 9 R. 1097; *Horsburgh* v. *Ramsay* (1885) 12 R. 1171; *Carter* v. *Johnstone* (1886) 13 R. 698; *Anderson's Tr.* v. *Somerville* (1899) 1 F. 90.

12 *Hill's Trs.* v. *MacGregor* (1901) 8 S.L.T. 387.

13 *Price & Pierce* v. *Bank of Scotland*, 1912 S.C. (H.L.) 19.

14 *Gourlay* v. *Mackie* (1887) 14 R. 403.

15 *Dods* v. *Welsh* (1904) 12 S.L.T. 110.

16 *Wright* v. *Mitchell* (1871) 9 M. 516; *Gourlay* v. *Hodge* (1875) 2 R. 738; *Rhind's Tr.* v. *Robertson & Baxter* (1891) 18 R. 623.

17 *Craig's Tr.* v. *Macdonald, Fraser & Co.* (1902) 4 F. 1132.

18 *Newton & Sons' Trs.* v. *Finlayson*, 1928 S.C. 637.

19 *Wilson* v. *Drummond's Reps.* (1853) 16 D. 275; *Laurie's Tr.* v. *Beveridge* (1867) 6 M. 85.

20 *Neil's Tr.* v. *B.L. Bank* (1898) 36 S.L.R. 139.

creditor in an existing debt,[1] though a transaction is not taken outwith the Act by the intervention of a third party to conceal the true transaction.[2]

The mere granting of an acknowledgment of an existing debt is not struck at,[3] nor is implement of obligations as they fall due.[4]

Security validly created before the pre-notour bankruptcy period is not challengeable,[5] nor is a landlord's resumption of possession of a servant's farm on his death,[6] nor is security within the period but in substitution for an equivalent security granted before the period.[7] Nor is a sale to a third party, not a creditor, avoided because or if the intention was to use the price to pay a creditor.[8]

Exceptions from liability to reduction

There are three classes of transactions recognized as excepted from reduction under the statute.[9]

(a) payments of obligations presently due,[10] in cash,[11] or by cheque or bill, or by consignation in court,[12] but not by indorsation of a cheque received from another,[13] nor by bills in the debtor's favour,[14] nor by payment by the debtor's debtor at his request to his creditor,[15] nor by payment to marriage contract trustees who had not accepted office,[16] nor by selling bonded property and paying the price to creditors.[17]

(b) transactions in the ordinary course of trade, such as a sale in the market at a fair price,[18] delivery of goods in implement

[1] *Ferguson* v. *Welsh* (1869) 7 M. 592; *McDougall's Trs.* v. *Gibbon* (1889) 16 R. 740; *Wilson's Tr.* v. *Raeburn* (1901) 38 S.L.R. 288.

[2] *Barbour* v. *Johnstone* (1823) 2 S. 351; *Ramsay* v. *Scales' Reps.* (1829) 7 S. 749.

[3] *Matthews' Trs.* v. *M.* (1867) 5 M. 957; *Williamson* v. *Allan* (1882) 9 R. 859.

[4] *Taylor* v. *Farrie* (1855) 17 D. 639; *Stiven* v. *Scott & Simson* (1871) 9 M. 923.

[5] *Moore* v. *Gledden* (1869) 7 M. 1016; *Guild* v. *Young* (1884) 22 S.L.R. 520.

[6] *Torrance* v. *Traill's Trs.* (1897) 24 R. 837.

[7] *Roy's Tr.* v. *Colville & Drysdale* (1903) 5 F. 769; contrast *Dobell, Beckett & Co.* v. *Neilson* (1904) 7 F. 281; *Price* v. *Peirce, supra.*

[8] *Wilson's Tr.* v. *Raeburn* (1901) 38 S.L.R. 288.

[9] Bell, *Comm.* II, 200–16.

[10] *Coutt's Tr.* v. *Doe & Webster* (1886) 13 R. 1112; *Commercial Bank* v. *Angus's Trs.* (1901) 4 F. 181; *Pringle's Trs.* v. *Wright* (1903) 5 F. 522.

[11] *Craig* v. *Hunter* (1905) 13 S.L.T. 525; *Whatmough's Tr.* v. *B.L. Bank*, 1934 S.C. (H.L.) 51.

[12] *Stiven* v. *Reynolds* (1891) 18 R. 422.

[13] *Carter* v. *Johnstone* (1886) 13 R. 698; *Anderson's Tr.* v. *Somerville* (1899) 7 S.L.T. 75; contrast *Richmond* v. *United Collieries* (1905) 13 S.L.T. 458.

[14] *Nicol* v. *McIntyre* (1882) 9 R. 1097.

[15] *Miller* v. *Philip* (1883) 20 S.L.R. 862.

[16] *Angus's Tr.* v. *A.* (1901) 4 F. 181.

[17] *Neil's Tr.* v. *B.L. Co.* (1898) 6 S.L.T. 227.

[18] Bell, *Comm.* II, 205; *Bruce* v. *Hamilton* (1832) 10 S. 250.

of contract,[1] return of an article bought but not paid for,[2] an auctioneer conducting a sale and retaining the proceeds under a clause of lien,[3] retiring an accommodation bill before its maturity,[4] but the exception has not covered such transactions as requiring return of goods sold, for re-sale,[5] or payment by indorsation of bills still current,[6] or payment in advance.[7] Transactions which bear evidence of collusion are not within the exception.[8]

(c) *nova debita*, namely transactions where the debtor and creditor incur mutual obligations simultaneously or *unico contextu*,[9] including selling for a fair price paid,[10] lending money but taking security therefor,[11] undertaking a cautionary obligation as a condition of the renewal of a bill,[12] granting an assignation in security of new advances and the continuation of old advances,[13] renewing a heritable loan,[14] assigning debts for an immediate advance,[15] but not paying the price of heritage and taking an assignation of the unrecorded conveyance in security.[16]

Title to, and mode of, challenge

Title to challenge is conferred only on those creditors whose debts were in existence when the alleged preference was granted,[17] on the trustee in sequestration[18] or the liquidator of a company if representing prior creditors.[19] A trustee under a trust deed for

[1] *Gibson* v. *Forbes* (1833) 11 S. 916; *Taylor* v. *Farrie* (1855) 17 D. 639; *Miller's Tr.* v. *Shield* (1862) 24 D. 821.

[2] *Loudon Bros.* v. *Reid & Lauder's Tr.* (1877) 5 R. 293.

[3] *Crockart's Tr.* v. *Hay*, 1913 S.C. 509; contrast *Craig's Tr.* v. *Macdonald, Fraser & Co.* (1904) 4 F. 1132.

[4] *McLaren's Tr.* v. *National Bank of Sc.* (1897) 24 R. 920.

[5] *Morton's Tr.* v. *Fifeshire Auction Co.*, 1911 1 S.L.T. 405.

[6] *Horsburgh* v. *Ramsay* (1885) 12 R. 1171; *Carter* v. *Johnstone* (1886) 13 R. 698.

[7] *McFarlane* v. *Robb* (1870) 9 M. 370.

[8] Bell, *Comm.* II, 204; *Scougall* v. *White* (1828) 6 S. 494; *Stewart* v. *Scott* (1832) 11 S. 171; *White* v. *Briggs* (1843) 5 D. 1148.

[9] *Cowdenbeath Coal Co.* v. *Clydesdale Bank* (1895) 22 R. 682.

[10] *Cranston* v. *Bontine* (1830) 8 S. 425; *Gibson* v. *Forbes* (1833) 11 S. 916; *Taylor* v. *Farrie* (1855) 17 D. 639; *Miller's Tr.* v. *Shield* (1862) 24 D. 821.

[11] *Cowdenbeath Coal Co., supra*; *Taylor* v. *Farrie* (1855) 17 D. 639; *Price & Pierce* v. *Bk. of Scotland*, 1912 S.C. (H.L.) 19; *Robertson's Tr.* v. *Union Bank*, 1917 S.C. 549.

[12] *Ferguson* v. *Welsh* (1869) 7 M. 592; cf. *Weir's Tr.* v. *Mackenzie* (1868) 6 S.L.R. 107; *McDougall's Tr.* v. *Gibbon* (1889) 16 R. 740.

[13] *Browne's Trs.* v. *B.* (1902) 10 S.L.T. 97.

[14] *Renton & Gray's Tr.* v. *Dickison* (1880) 7 R. 951.

[15] *Smith* v. *Smyth* (1887) 16 R. 392.

[16] *MacArthur* v. *Campbell's Tr.*, 1953 S.L.T. (Notes) 81.

[17] Bell, *Comm.* II, 194; *Brown* v. *McCallum* (1890) 18 R. 311; *Cook* v. *Sinclair* (1896) 23 R. 925.

[18] 1913 Act, S. 9.

[19] *Clarke* v. *West Calder Oil Co.* (1882) 9 R. 1017.

creditors may challenge only if the deed empowers him and the creditors have acceded thereto.[1]

The challenge may be by action[2] or exception.[3] If successful it lays the subject open to the diligence of creditors or, if sequestration has been granted, takes it into the estate falling to the trustee.[4]

Effect of notour bankruptcy on diligence used

Arrestments and poindings used within sixty days before or four months after the constitution of notour bankruptcy are ranked *pari passu* as if they had all been used of the same date. Any creditor judicially producing in a process relative to an arrestment or poinding liquid grounds of debt or decree of payment within such period is entitled to rank as if he had executed an arrestment or a poinding.[5] If the first or any subsequent arrester obtains in the meantime a decree of furthcoming and preference and thereupon recovers payment, or a poinding creditor carries through a sale, he is accountable for the sum recovered to those who under the Act may be found to have a right to a ranking *pari passu* thereon. If any arrestments have been used for attaching the same effects after four months after the bankruptcy, such shall not compete with those used within the stated periods or subsequent thereto, but may rank with each other on any reversion of the fund attached.[6] Sequestration is equivalent to an arrestment on behalf of all the creditors, and if arrestment occurs within the stated dates, the creditors and any arrester within that period rank *pari passu*.[7]

A creditor who, by completing his diligence within the statutory period, recovers payment is accountable for the sum recovered to those who, under the Act, may be eventually found entitled to *pari passu* ranking thereon.[8]

Notour bankruptcy, furthermore, makes the debtor liable to sequestration without his consent if he has resided or had a place of business in Scotland within the year prior to the petition.[9]

[1] *Fleming's Trs.* v. *McHardy* (1892) 19 R. 542; *McLaren's Tr.* v. *National Bank* (1897) 24 R. 920.

[2] *Cook* v. *Sinclair* (1896) 23 R. 925.

[3] 1913 Act, S. 8.

[4] *Cook, supra.*

[5] *Clark* v. *Hinde Milne & Co.* (1884) 12 R. 347.

[6] 1913 Act, S. 10.

[7] *Nicolson* v. *Johnstone & Wright* (1872) 11 M. 179; *Mitchell* v. *Scott* (1881) 8 R. 875; *Galbraith* v. *Campbell's Trs.* (1885) 22 S.L.R. 602; *Stewart* v. *Jarvie*, 1938 S.C. 309.

[8] 1913 Act, S. 10; *Dobbie* v. *Nisbet* (1854) 16 D. 881; *Wood* v. *Cranston & Elliot* (1891) 18 R. 382.

[9] 1913 Act, S. 11; *Gairdner* v. *Macarthur*, 1918 2 S.L.T. 123.

SEQUESTRATION

Courts which may award sequestration

Sequestration, i.e. the setting apart of property in neutral custody,[1] may be awarded by the Court of Session or the sheriff court of a county where the debtor resided or carried on business for the year preceding the petition, or, in the case of a deceased debtor, for the year preceding his death.[2] But no sequestration may be awarded by any court after production of evidence that sequestration has already been awarded by another court and is still undischarged, and where a prior petition is in dependence before any court, the court to which a subsequent petition is presented may remit it to the other court.[3] The later of two or more awards of sequestration is to be remitted to the first in date,[4] but each sheriff may take proceedings for the preservation of the estate.[5] Sequestration may be transferred from one sheriff court to another.[6] A person already adjudicated bankrupt in England cannot be sequestrated in Scotland.[7] An unincorporated association cannot be sequestrated,[8] nor can a company incorporated under the Companies Acts.[9]

When sequestration competent

Sequestration may be awarded of the estate of any person[10]—

1: in the case of a living debtor[11] subject to the jurisdiction of the Supreme Courts of Scotland:[12]

(a) on his own petition, with the concurrence of a creditor or creditors whose debt or debts amount to not less than £50, whether liquid or illiquid, so long as not contingent;[13]

[1] *Sinclair* v. *Edinburgh Parish Council*, 1909 S.C. 1353.

[2] 1913 Act, S. 11; *Strickland*, 1911 1 S.L.T. 212; *Gairdner* v. *Macarthur*, 1918 2 S.L.T. 123.

[3] 1913 Act, S. 16; but see *Mellor* v. *Drummond*, 1919 2 S.L.T. 68.

[4] 1913 Act, S. 17. [5] 1913 Act, S. 18. [6] 1913 Act, S. 19.

[7] *Bank of Scotland* v. *Youde* (1908) 15 S.L.T. 847.

[8] *Pitreavie Golf Club* v. *Penman*, 1934 S.L.T. 247.

[9] *Standard Property Inv. Co.* v. *Dunblane Hydropathic Co.* (1884) 12 R. 328.

[10] 1913 Act, Ss. 11–12; cf. *Gairdner* v. *Macarthur*, 1918 2 S.L.T. 123.

[11] Executors may be sequestrated as such: *Bain* (1901) 9 S.L.T. 14, 15; a firm may be sequestrated: *Commercial Bank* v. *Tod's Tr.* (1896) 33 S.L.R. 161; an incorporated company may not: *Standard Property Inv. Co.* v. *Dunblane Hydropathic Co.* (1884) 12 R. 328.

[12] The grounds of jurisdiction are: domicile (i.e. residence: *Strickland*, 1911 1 S.L.T. 212); ownership of heritage; forty days' continuous residence in one locality: *Joel* v. *Gill* (1859) 21 D. 929; *Gairdner*, *supra*.

[13] *Knowles* v. *Crooks* (1865) 3 M. 457; *Forbes* v. *Whyte* (1890) 18 R. 182; *Stuart & Stuart* v. *Macleod* (1891) 19 R. 223. As to claim of damages for delict, see *Miller* v. *McIntosh* (1884) 11 R. 729.

(b) on the petition of such a creditor or creditors, provided the debtor be notour bankrupt[1] and within the previous year resided or had a dwelling-house or place of business in Scotland; or in the case of a company if it be notour bankrupt and within the year had carried on business in Scotland, and any partner so resided or had a dwelling house or if the company have had a place of business in Scotland.

2: in the case of a deceased debtor[2] who at the date of his death was subject to the said jurisdiction:

(a) on the petition of a mandatary to whom he had granted a mandate to apply for sequestration;

(b) on the petition of a creditor or creditors qualified as above.[3] A deceased debtor need not be insolvent or notour bankrupt, but must have resided or had a house or carried on business in Scotland.[4]

Petitions without the living debtor's consent are competent only within four months of his notour bankruptcy; creditor's petitions for sequestration of a deceased debtor are competent at any time but no sequestration may be awarded till six months from his death, unless he was then notour bankrupt or his successor concurs[5] or renounces the succession, in which case it shall be awarded forthwith; in all other cases a petition is competent at any time and sequestration may follow as the Act directs.[6]

To be a creditor qualified to petition or concur a person must have a claim on which he is entitled to sue.[7] If a creditor withdraws or becomes bankrupt or dies, another creditor may be sisted in his place.[8] The debt founded on may be liquid, or illiquid, such as a claim for damages for breach of contract,[9] but must not be contingent.[10]

Petition and productions

A petition for sequestration must be accompanied[11] by the creditor's oath or affidavit as to the verity of the debt claimed

[1] *Walter Baillie & Son* (1899) 6 S.L.T. 324; *Arrol* v. *Christie* (1901) 4 F. 262; *Laird* v. *Scott*, 1913 2 S.L.T. 409.

[2] Not including a dissolved company: *Stewart & McDonald* v. *Brown* (1898) 25 R. 1042.

[3] *Wryghte* v. *Lindsay* (1860) 3 Macq. 772; *McLatchie* v. *Angus* (1899) 1 F. 946; alternatively creditors may apply under S. 163 for appointment of a judicial factor to wind up the estate: *Stewart* v. *Waldie*, 1926 S.L.T. 526.

[4] 1913 Act, S. 23. [5] *Hope* (1850) 12 D. 913. [6] 1913 Act, S. 13.

[7] *Bonar* v. *Liddell* (1841) 3 D. 830; *Fleming* v. *Yeaman* (1884) 21 S.L.R. 722.

[8] 1913 Act, S. 33; *Forsyth* (1883) 10 R. 1061; *Stewart* v. *Wetherdair*, 1928 S.C. 577.

[9] *Anderson* v. *Monteith* (1847) 9 D. 1432; *Knowles* v. *Crooks* (1865) 3 M. 457; *Simpson* v. *Myles* (1881) 9 R. 104; see also *Millar* v. *McIntosh* (1884) 11 R. 729 (damages for delict).

[10] 1913 Act, S. 12; *Forbes* v. *Whyte* (1890) 18 R. 182. [11] 1913 Act, Ss. 20–4.

and specifying any security held therefor,[1] by an unambiguous account and vouchers of the debt,[2] and by written evidence of notour bankruptcy.[3] If the debtor is not a party to the petition he is cited to appear and show cause why sequestration should not be granted.[4] If the debtor dies during the proceedings the petition may proceed against his successors.[5]

If a petitioning creditor's oath does not conform to statutory requirements he cannot amend it, and the petition must be dismissed.[6] Where there are competing petitions in different courts the courts must refuse or recall one, having in view the course most convenient in the interests of creditors.[7] A petitioning creditor may withdraw and another creditor be sisted in his place.[8] A debtor tendering payment to avoid sequestration must offer the sum due with interest.[9]

Preservation of estate

Before sequestration the court may, if necessary, take immediate measures for the preservation of the estate, by appointing a judicial factor or otherwise.[10] He cannot interfere with the diligence of creditors.[11] Where there are conflicting awards of sequestration, and during the dependence of petitions or appeals, the court may make orders for interim administration of the estate.[12]

[1] *Learmonth* v. *Patton* (1845) 7 D. 1094; *Aitken* v. *Woodside* (1852) 14 D. 572; *Gordon* v. *Paul* (1855) 17 D. 779; *Knowles* v. *Crooks* (1865) 3 M. 457; *Dow* v. *Union Bank* (1875) 2 R. 459; *Blair* v. *N.B. and Mercantile Ins. Co.* (1889) 16 R. 325, 947; 17 R. (H.L.) 76.

[2] *Scott* v. *S.* (1847) 9 D. 1347; *Turnbull* v. *McNaughton* (1850) 12 D. 1097; *Knowles* v. *Crooks* (1865) 3 M. 457; *Ballantyne* v. *Barr* (1867) 5 M. 330; *Simpson* v. *Myles* (1881) 9 R. 104; *Clark* v. *Thom* (1884) 11 R. 469; *Aitken* v. *Kyd* (1890) 28 S.L.R. 115; *Geddes* v. *Reid* (1894) 2 S.L.T. 244; *Riddell* v. *Galbraith* (1896) 24 R. 51.

[3] *Macnab's Trs.* v. *Clarke* (1889) 16 R. 610; *Aitken* v. *Kyd* (1890) 28 S.L.R. 115; *Baillie* (1899) 6 S.L.T. 398; *Arrol* v. *Christie* (1901) 4 F. 262.

[4] cf. *Train* v. *Steven* (1904) 7 F. 47; *Central Motor Engineering Co.* v. *Galbraith*, 1918 S.C. 755.

[5] *B.L. Co.* (1893) 1 S.L.T. 385; *Younger* (1902) 40 S.L.R. 102.

[6] *Younger* v. *Cronin*, 1926 S.L.T. 238.

[7] *Kellock* v. *Anderson* (1875) 3 R. 239; *Tennent* v. *Martin & Dunlop* (1879) 6 R. 786; *Fletcher* v. *Anderson* (1883) 10 R. 835; *Govan* (1901) 8 S.L.T. 415; *Barns Graham* v. *Bowie* (1903) 5 F. 1230; *Calder* (1904) 12 S.L.T. 398; *Duncan* v. *Trotter*, 1936 S.L.T. 162.

[8] 1913 Act, S. 33; *Forsyth* (1883) 10 R. 1061; *Stewart* v. *Wetherdair, Ltd.*, 1928 S.C. 577.

[9] *McCumiskey Bros.* v. *MacLaine*. 1922 S.L.T. 104.

[10] 1913 Act, S. 14; *Partridge* v. *Baillie* (1873) 1 R. 253; *McCreadie* v. *Douglas* (1882) 10 R. 108; *Cuthbertson* v. *Gibson* (1887) 14 R. 736; *Stewart* v. *Waldie*, 1926 S.L.T. 526.

[11] *Urquhart* v. *Macleod's Tr.* (1883) 10 R. 991.

[12] 1913 Act, Ss. 18, 168.

Award of sequestration

If the petition is by, or with the concurrence of, the debtor the court awards sequestration forthwith. Otherwise, if the debtor does not appear, or appears but does not pay the debt or produce evidence that it was paid, the court awards sequestration.[1] If the statutory conditions are satisfied the court has no discretion but is bound to award sequestration.[2] The debtor may oppose a creditor's petition;[3] so may another creditor.[4] The award may, on petition within 40 days, be recalled, on any grounds stated, or which could have been stated, for opposing the award of sequestration, or which have since emerged,[5] or as being an abuse of process.[6] Sequestration may be recalled if in the circumstances the petition was an abuse of process,[7] or notour bankruptcy had not been established,[8] or it had already been granted in a competing process,[9] or there was defect in the petitioner's oath[10] or the account was unspecific,[11] or because the bankruptcy was essentially a foreign one.[12] If objection appears *ex facie* of the proceedings, or nine-tenths of the creditors petition, the sequestration must be recalled, unless cause be shown to the contrary.[13] It is not a ground for recall that if given an opportunity to realize assets the debtor could settle his debts;[14] nor because there was inadequate evidence of insolvency.[15] If the defect in the oath is latent the court has a discretion to recall or not.[16]

1 1913 Act, Ss. 28–30.

2 *Stuart & Stuart* v. *Macleod* (1891) 19 R. 223; *Arthur* (1903) 10 S.L.T. 550.

3 *Riddell* v. *Galbraith* (1896) 24 R. 51; *Purves* v. *Grant* (1900) 2 F. 1174.

4 *Blair* v. *Mackenzie* (1899) 1 F. 854.

5 *Muir* v. *Stevenson* (1850) 12 D. 512; *Elder* v. *Thomson* (1850) 12 D. 994; *Campbell* v. *Myles* (1853) 15 D. 685; *Ure* v. *McCubbin* (1857) 19 D. 758; *Aitken* v. *Kyd* (1890) 28 S.L.R. 115; *Riddell, supra*; *Drummond* v. *Clunas Tiles*, 1909 S.C. 1049; *Menzies* v. *Poutz*, 1916 S.C. 143; *Livingstone's Crs.* v. *L's Tr.*, 1937 S.L.T. 391; *Pert* v. *Bruce*, 1937 S.L.T. 475.

6 *Bain* (1901) 9 S.L.T. 15; *Smith* v. *Pirie's Tr.* (1907) 14 S.L.T. 705.

7 *Bain* (1901) 9 S.L.T. 15; *Smith* v. *Pirie's Trs.* (1907) 14 S.L.T. 705.

8 *Drummond* v. *Clunas Tiles*, 1909 S.C. 1049.

9 *Jarvie* v. *Robertson* (1865) 4 M. 79; *Kellock* v. *Anderson* (1875) 3 R. 239; *Tennent* v. *Martin & Dunlop* (1879) 6 R. 786; *Fletcher* v. *Anderson* (1883) 10 R. 835; *Giles* (1898) 5 S.L.T. 311; *Barns Graham* v. *Bowie* (1903) 5 F. 1230; *Lochrie* v. *McGregor*, 1911 S.C. 21; *Welsh* v. *Hourston*, 1914 2 S.L.T. 333.

10 *Blair* v. *N.B. and Mercantile Ins. Co.* (1889) 16 R. 325, 947; 17 R. (H.L.) 76.

11 *Riddell* v. *Galbraith* (1896) 24 R. 51; contrast *Gillon* v. *Caesar* (1882) 10 R. 59.

12 *Cooper* v. *Baillie* (1878) 5 R. 564.

13 1913 Act, S. 31; *Tennent* v. *Martin* (1879) 6 R. 786; *Mitchell* v. *Motherwell* (1888) 16 R. 122; *Blair* v. *N.B. & Merc. Ins. Co.* (1889) 16 R. 325; *Riddell* v. *Galbraith* (1896) 24 R. 51.

14 *Mackenzie* v. *Tod*, 1912 1 S.L.T. 464.

15 *Aitken* v. *Kyd* (1890) 28 S.L.R. 115.

16 *Nakeski-Cumming* v. *Gordon*, 1924 S.C. 217.

Where sequestration cannot be recalled it may be annulled by the court under the *nobile officium*.[1]

Reduction of a sequestration is also competent but requires clear averments for its relevancy,[2] but if possible should be resorted to rather than an application to the *nobile officium*.[3]

The effect of sequestration

On being sequestrated a debtor's contractual capacity becomes limited; an offer made to contract is revoked[4] and he probably has no power to conclude any contract, unless possibly of a kind to be performed personally. A mandate granted to an agent falls[5] and, failing contrary agreement, a partnership is dissolved.[6] Contracts in progress are not automatically terminated,[7] and if the contract includes an element of *delectus personae* the bankrupt may perform.[8] Otherwise they pass to the trustee as assets in the sequestration. Some contracts, such as leases, may contain provision for their termination on the tenant's bankruptcy,[9] and an employee may treat the bankruptcy as a breach of contract.[10]

The bankrupt's title to sue for personal wrongs is unimpaired, though any damages recovered will pass to the trustee,[11] but any title to sue for patrimonial loss passes to the trustee.[12] If a defender is sequestrated the action may be allowed to proceed against him.[13]

Property held by the bankrupt as agent or trustee and distinguishable from his general assets belongs to the principal or beneficiaries in preference to the creditors,[14] but not if it has become

[1] *A.B.* (1842) 5 D. 74; *Anderson* (1866) 4 M. 577; *Cooper* v. *Baillie* (1878) 5 R. 564; *Macleish's Trs.* (1896) 24 R. 151; *Ballantyne* (1900) 2 F. 1077; *Craig & Co.*, 1946 S.C. 19.

[2] *Whitlie* v. *Gibb* (1898) 25 R. 412; *Tough's Tr.* v. *Edinburgh Parish Council*, 1918 S.C. 107; *Central Motor Eng. Co.* v. *Galbraith*, 1918 S.C. 755.

[3] *Central Motor Eng. Co.* v. *Gibbs*, 1917 S.C. 490.

[4] Bell, *Prin.* §74.

[5] *McKenzie* v. *Campbell* (1894) 21 R. 904.

[6] Partnership Act, 1890, Ss. 33, 47.

[7] *Greenlees* v. *Port of Manchester Ins. Co.*, 1933 S.C. 383. As to sale of goods, see Sale of Goods Act, 1893, Ss. 41–8.

[8] *Anderson* v. *Hamilton* (1875) 2 R. 355.

[9] Bell, *Comm.* I, 76; *Fraser* v. *Robertson* (1881) 8 R. 347; *Ebbw Vale Steel Co.* v. *Wood's Tr.* (1898) 25 R. 439.

[10] *Hoey* v. *McEwan & Auld* (1867) 5 M. 814, 817; *Day* v. *Tait* (1900) 8 S.L.T. 40; *Laing* v. *Gowans* (1902) 10 S.L.T. 461.

[11] *Jackson* v. *McKechnie* (1875) 3 R. 130; *Clarke* v. *Muller* (1884) 11 R. 418.

[12] *Scott* v. *Johnston* (1885) 12 R. 1022; *Muir's Tr.* v. *Braidwood*, 1958 S.C. 169.

[13] *Anderson* v. *Stevenson* (1895) 2 S.L.T. 503.

[14] *Macadam* v. *Martin's Tr.* (1872) 11 M. 33; *Dixon & Wilson* v. *McIntyre* (1898) 6 S.L.T. 188; *Jopp* v. *Johnston's Tr.* (1904) 6 F. 1028.

mixed with his other assets.[1] Sequestration also infers certain public disabilities.[2]

Notwithstanding sequestration a bankrupt retains a radical right in the property transferred judicially to the trustee.[3]

Registration of sequestration

The party applying for sequestration must present or transmit, before the expiration of the second lawful day after the court's first deliverance, an abbreviate of the petition and deliverance to the Keeper of the Register of Inhibitions and Adjudications for recording. On being recorded the abbreviate has from the date of the deliverance the effect of an inhibition and of a citation in an adjudication of the estate of the debtor at the instance of the creditors afterwards ranked.[4] This effect expires after five years, but may, and unless the trustee has been discharged must, be renewed for periods of five years.[5] Within four days from the deliverance the petitioner must also insert a notice in the Edinburgh Gazette and one within six days in the London Gazette.[6]

Protective measures

At any time after sequestration the sheriff may cause to be sealed up and put in safe custody the bankrupt's books and papers and have his premises locked up. He may grant warrant to take possession of money or other moveable property, and regulate interim possession and administration of the estate.[7] He may appoint a judicial factor to manage the estate between sequestration and the appointment of a trustee.[8]

[1] *Hofford* v. *Gowans*, 1909 1 S.L.T. 153.

[2] cf. *Thom* v. *Aberdeen Mags.* (1885) 12 R. 701.

[3] *White* v. *Stevenson*, 1956 S.C. 84.

[4] 1913 Act, S. 44 and Sched. A; Bell, *Comm.* II, 134, 144; *Jarvie* v. *Robertson* (1865) 4 M. 79. Failure, delay or error may be rectified by petition to the *nobile officium* for authority to record correctly: see *Stark* v. *Hogg* (1886) 23 S.L.R. 507; *Train* v. *McIntyre, Ltd.*, 1923 S.C. 291.

[5] Conveyancing (Sc.) Act, 1924, S. 44(4).

[6] 1913 Act, S. 44 and Sched. B. Adherence to the statutory form is essential: *Gray* v. *Cockburn* (1844) 6 D. 569; *Von Rotberg* (1876) 4 R. 263. As to delay or error in inserting the notice see *Robertson* v. *Wilson* (1885) 12 R. 1361; *McCosh* (1898) 25 R. 1019; *Taylor* (1900) 3 F. 1139; *Murray* (1906) 8 F. 957; *Robertson*, 1909 S.C. 444; *Morgan*, 1922 S.C. 589; *Train & McIntyre, Ltd.*, 1923 S.C. 291; *Car Mart, Ltd.*, 1924 S.C. 269; *White Cross Ins. Assocn.*, 1924 S.C. 372.

[7] 1913 Act, Ss. 15, 168; see also *Bannatyne* v. *Thomson* (1902) 5 F. 221; *Neilson's Factor*, 1927 S.C. 595.

[8] *Partridge* v. *Baillie* (1873) 1 R. 253; *McCreadies* v. *Douglas* (1882) 10 R. 108; *Cuthbertson* v. *Gibson* (1887) 14 R. 736; *Brown* v. *Bayley's Trs.*, 1910 S.C. 76.

Effect of sequestration on diligence

Sequestration operates from the date of the first deliverance in the petition as a full and complete diligence over the debtor's estate in favour of the whole body of creditors, makes incompetent any diligence by a creditor, and excludes ordinary rights of action by any creditor against the debtor.[1] But the Act does not restrict an action of maills and duties[2] nor a landlord's right of hypothec.[3] In the case of a deceased debtor the same provisions apply though sequestration be more than seven months after death. If awarded within seven months of the death, any preference acquired after sixty days before death is ineffective against the trustee.[4]

Meeting for election of trustee

The court, in the deliverance awarding sequestration, appoints a meeting of the creditors to be held between six and twelve days after the appearance in the Gazette of the notice of sequestration to elect a trustee.[5] At the meeting the creditors attend.

Voting and ranking of creditors

To vote and rank for a dividend, a creditor must produce at the meeting for electing the trustee or thereafter, an oath as to his debt and the account and vouchers necessary to prove it.[6] A creditor may vote and rank for the accumulated sum of principal and interest to the date of sequestration: if the debt is not payable till later he may rank for it under deduction of interest from that date and of any discount due.[7] If the claim depends on a contingency he may apply to the trustee, or the court, to value the contingent debt.[8] A creditor for an annuity may vote only if the annuity is valued.[9] An acknowledgement of debt by the bankrupt granted after his sequestration does not establish a loan so as to

[1] 1913 Act, Ss. 103–4; cf. *Dow* v. *Union Bank* (1875) 2 R. 459; *Stiven* v. *Reynolds* (1891) 18 R. 422; *McKenzie* v. *Campbell* (1894) 21 R. 904.

[2] *Dick's Tr.* v. *Whyte's Tr.* (1879) 6 R. 596; *Thomson* v. *Scoular* (1882) 9 R. 430.

[3] 1913 Act, S. 115.

[4] 1913 Act, S. 106; see also *Rough's Tr.* v. *Miller* (1857) 19 D. 305.

[5] 1913 Act, S. 63; *Wilson* (1891) 19 R. 219; as to wrong date see *Watt, Philp & Co.* (1877) 4 R. 641; error in notice: *Foubister* (1869) 8 M. 31; *Von Rotberg* (1876) 4 R. 263; no notice: *Somerville & Co.* (1905) 7 F. 651; inadequate notice: *Car Mart, Ltd.*, 1924 S.C. 269.

[6] 1913 Act, Ss. 45–7; *Woodside* v. *Esplin* (1847) 9 D. 1486; *Galloway* v. *Henderson* (1849) 12 D. 394; *Stewart* v. *Struthers* (1865) 3 M. 1031; as to lost voucher see *Robertson* v. *Tough's Tr.*, 1925 S.C. 234; *Coull's Tr.*, 1934 S.C. 415.

[7] 1913 Act. S. 48.

[8] 1913 Act, S. 49.

[9] 1913 Act, S. 50.

entitle to a ranking.[1] The trustee cannot reject a decree of court when he could have, but did not, opposed its grant.[2]

The court, on appeal, may sustain as adequately vouched a claim rejected by the trustee.[3]

Valuation and deduction of securities

For the purpose of voting, a creditor holding a security[4] must value the security and vote in respect of the balance only, but in questions as to the disposal of the estate, he may vote as a creditor for the full amount of the debt.[5] Similarly he must value the obligation of a co-obligant with the bankrupt,[6] and in a company's sequestration the value he is entitled to draw from the estates of the partners.[7] The trustee or a majority of creditors may require from a creditor a conveyance of the security at his valuation plus twenty per cent, which he is bound to grant.[8]

For the purpose of ranking for dividends he must value his security and deduct it from the debt. The trustee is entitled to a conveyance of the security on payment of its value, or to reserve to the creditor the full benefit of such security, the creditor in either case to rank for the balance.[9] If the trustee so elects, the creditor cannot withdraw his claim.[10] The trustee must claim conveyance without delay[11] and offer payment at once.[12] A security may be revalued for a second dividend.[13]

A creditor is not bound to value and deduct a security not belonging to the bankrupt estate,[14] nor a mere personal security.[15]

[1] *Carmichael's Tr.* v. *C.*, 1929 S.C. 265.

[2] *Dow* v. *Pennell's Tr.*, 1929 S.L.T. 674.

[3] *Inglis* v. *I's Tr.*, 1925 S.L.T. 686.

[4] Defined, 1913 Act, S. 2; cf. *Hay* v. *Durham* (1850) 12 D. 676; *Gibson* v. *Greig* (1853) 16 D. 233; *Borthwick* v. *Scottish Widows Fund* (1864) 2 M. 595; *Mitchell* v. *Motherwell* (1888) 16 R. 122; see also *Mackinnon's Tr.* v. *Bank of Scotland*, 1915 S.C. 411.

[5] 1913 Act, S. 55.

[6] 1913 Act, S. 56; *Forrest* v. *Borthwick* (1848) 11 D. 308; *Wink* v. *Mortimer* (1849) 11 D. 995.

[7] 1913 Act, S. 57.

[8] 1913 Act, S. 58; cf. *Greig* v. *Crichton* (1853) 15 D. 742; *Russell* v. *Daniel & Green* (1868) 6 M. 648.

[9] 1913 Act, S. 61; cf. *Glasgow University* v. *Yuill's Tr.* (1882) 9 R. 643; *Royal Bank* v. *Millar & Co.'s Tr.* (1882) 9 R. 679; *Brickman's Tr.* v. *Commercial Bank* (1901) 9 S.L.T. 145; *Wood* v. *Mackay's Tr.*, 1936 S.C. 93; valuation is to be made at the date of claim: *Commercial Bank* v. *Muirhead's Tr.*, 1918 1 S.L.T. 132.

[10] *Macdougall's Tr.* v. *Lockhart* (1903) 5 F. 905.

[11] *Henderson's Tr.* v. *Auld & Guild* (1872) 10 M. 946.

[12] *Maclachlan* v. *Maxwell*, 1910 S.C. 87.

[13] *Commercial Bank* v. *Speedie's Tr.* (1885) 13 R. 257; *Union Bank* v. *Calder's Tr.*, 1937 S.C. 850.

[14] *B.L. Co.* v. *Gourlay* (1877) 4 R. 651; *Royal Bank* v. *Purdom* (1877) 15 S.L.R. 13.

[15] *Assets Co.* v. *Jackson* (1889) 26 S.L.R. 592.

If he values and deducts his security, his right remains a security right against the debtor and he must account to the debtor for any surplus on realization or may require the debtor to accept a reconveyance.[1]

Election of trustee

If two or more creditors give notice to the sheriff,[2] he attends and presides,[3] as does the sheriff clerk who initials the oaths and productions, and takes minutes recording the names and designations of the creditors present and the amount for which they claim. If the sheriff is not present the creditors elect a preses and clerk.[4] The creditors present or their mandataries elect a fit person to be trustee, or two or more trustees to act in succession.[5]

No qualification is prescribed for the office of trustee. It is not lawful to elect as trustee the bankrupt, any person conjunct or confident with him, one who holds an interest opposed to the general interest of the creditors, or whose residence is not within the jurisdiction of the Court of Session.[6] If the sheriff be present and there be no competition for the office, by deliverance on the minutes he declares the chosen person to be trustee. If there be objection stated, the sheriff may decide, or hear parties within four days and declare elected the person whom he finds duly elected.[7] If the sheriff be not present, the preses forthwith reports the proceedings to the sheriff, and if there has been no objection or competition the sheriff declares the person or persons elected; if there has been competition or objection, the parties lodge notes of objections, the sheriff hears them, and decides.[8] The sheriff's judgment must be given with the least possible delay and is not subject to review.[9] At the meeting the creditors fix a sum for which the trustee shall find security for his intromissions, and

[1] *Kinmond, Luke & Co.* v. *Finlay* (1904) 6 F. 564; *Clydesdale Bank* v. *McIntyre*, 1909 S.C. 1405.

[2] Including an honorary sheriff-substitute: *Mann* v. *Tait* (1892) 20 R. 13.

[3] He may attend and preside though not summoned: *Mann* v. *Tait* (1892) 20 R. 13.

[4] 1913 Act, S. 64.

[5] 1913 Act, S. 64; *Farquharson* v. *Sutherlands* (1888) 15 R. 759; the bankrupt's wife may not vote: 1913 Act, S. 60; *MacNaught* v. *Sievwright*, 1927 S.C. 285; 1928 S.C. 687.

[6] 1913 Act, S. 64; on adverse interest see *McFarlane* v. *Grieve* (1848) 10 D. 551; *Forrest* v. *Borthwick* (1848) 11 D. 308; *Colville* v. *Ledingham* (1850) 13 D. 415; *Philip Woolfson, Ltd.*, 1962 S.L.T. 252.

[7] 1913 Act, S. 65.

[8] 1913 Act, S. 66; cf. *Brown* v. *Lindsay* (1869) 7 M. 595; *Wiseman* v. *Skene* (1870) 8 M. 661; *Moncur* v. *Macdonald* (1887) 14 R. 305; *Muirhead* v. *Meikle*, 1917 S.C. 554.

[9] 1913 Act, S. 67; *Rankine* v. *Douglas* (1871) 9 M. 1053; *Farquharson* v. *Sutherlands* (1888) 15 R. 759; *Smith* v. *Wilson* (1892) 19 R. 428; *Yeaman* v. *Little* (1906) 8 F. 702.

decide on the sufficiency of the caution offered. Within seven days of the deliverance declaring his election, the trustee must lodge with the sheriff clerk a bond of caution or the bond of a guarantee society.[1] If no creditors attend, the debtor may petition the *nobile officium* of the court to call a fresh meeting of creditors.[2]

Election and removal of commissioners

At the meeting for election of a trustee the creditors also elect three commissioners, who must be creditors or mandataries of creditors. A person cannot be a commissioner if disqualified from being trustee. They need not find caution, and a majority is a quorum. If a commissioner declines to act, dies, resigns, or becomes incapacitated a new one falls to be elected. A majority of creditors may remove a commissioner and elect another.[3] The commissioners' duties are to superintend the trustee, concur with him in submissions and transactions, give advice and assistance relative to the management of the estate and decide as to paying or postponing a dividend. A commissioner may not be entitled to purchase part of the bankrupt's estate.[4] The court will not interfere with the exercise of their discretion in their duties, unless abuse of their office is alleged.[5]

Agent in sequestration

The trustee normally appoints a solicitor to act as agent in the sequestration. He is not barred from purchasing part of the bankrupt's assets.[6]

Creditors' meetings

Statute requires two general meetings of creditors, the first, at which the trustee and commissioners are elected, and the second, after the bankrupt's public examination, to receive the trustee's report, but special meetings may be called for particular purposes, e.g. to decide on an offer of composition.[7] Failure to convene a statutory meeting as required may be rectified by petition to the *nobile officium*.[8]

[1] 1913 Act, S. 69, and Sched. C. [2] *Robb & Co.*, 1925 S.N. 31.
[3] 1913 Act, Ss. 72–3.
[4] *Whyte* v. *Forbes* (1890) 17 R. 895; *Haddow* v. *Watson* (1894) 2 S.L.T. 376; *Wishart* v. *Howatson* (1897) 5 S.L.T. 84.
[5] *Weldon* v. *Ferrier* (1879) 7 R. 235.
[6] *Noble* v. *Campbell* (1876) 4 R. 77; *Rutherford* v. *MacGregor* (1891) 18 R. 1061.
[7] 1913 Act, Ss. 134, 136.
[8] *Wilson* (1891) 19 R. 219.

Trustee's caution

At the meeting for election of the trustee the creditors fix the sum for which the trustee must find security for his intromissions. The trustee elected must within seven days lodge with the sheriff-clerk a bond of caution.[1] The cautioner is liable for the trustee's intromissions, notwithstanding any negligence by creditors or commissioners in supervising the trustee's actings.[2]

Winding up under Deed of Arrangement

At the meeting for the election of a trustee or any subsequent meeting called for the purpose, a majority in number and three-fourths in value of the creditors present or represented may resolve that the estate ought to be wound up under a Deed of Arrangement, and that an application should be presented to the court to sist procedure for not more than two months. If such a resolution is carried it is not necessary to elect a trustee.[3]

The bankrupt, or any person appointed by the meeting, may report such a resolution to the court within four days and apply for a sist of the sequestration.[4] If it is granted the court may make any arrangements necessary for the interim management of the estate.[5]

The creditors may at any time within the period of sist produce to the court a Deed of Arrangement subscribed by, or by authority of, a majority in number and three-fourths in value of the creditors. The court after consideration, intimation, and any inquiry thought necessary, may approve it and declare the sequestration at an end; such a Deed is thereafter as binding on all the creditors as if they had all acceded thereto, though the sequestration remains in effect if necessary for preventing, challenging or setting aside preferences.[6] If the sequestration be declared at an end, the judgment is recorded.[7] It is competent for a creditor in a debt incurred subsequent to the deed of arrangement to petition for sequestration anew.[8]

[1] 1913 Act, S. 69 and Sched. C; *Rankine* v. *Douglas* (1871) 9 M. 1053.

[2] 1913 Act, Ss. 69, 139; *Creighton* v. *Rankin* (1838) 1 Rob. App. 131; *Biggar* v. *Wright* (1846) 9 D. 78.

[3] 1913 Act, S. 34; see also *N. of S. Banking Co.* v. *Ireland* (1880) 8 R. 117. The bankrupt's wife may vote on such a resolution: 1913 Act, S. 60; *MacNaught* v. *Sievwright*, 1927 S.C. 285.

[4] 1913 Act, S. 35.

[5] 1913 Act, S. 36.

[6] 1913 Act, S. 37; if the Deed is produced within the two months judicial approval may be granted outwith that period: *Williamson's Crs.*, 1923 S.L.T. 122. As to the court's duty in judging of the reasonableness of the Deed, see *Stone* v. *Woodhouse Hambly & Co.*, 1937 S.C. 824.

[7] 1913 Act, S. 39.

[8] *A.* v. *B.*, 1912 2 S.L.T. 498.

The deed may provide for the realization and distribution of the estate by the creditors or by a trustee, or for reinvestiture of the bankrupt on payment of a fixed sum. If an instalment due under a deed of arrangement be not paid, the debt revives, less any sums paid.[1] The deed may provide for the bankrupt's discharge.

If the resolution be not reported, or a sist be refused, or the Deed of Arrangement be not produced, or not approved of, the sequestration proceeds.[2]

Discharge of bankrupt on composition

At the meeting for the election of a trustee the bankrupt or his friends may offer a composition to the creditors on the whole debts, at so much per pound, with security for payment thereof. If a majority in number and three-fourths in value present resolve that the offer and security be entertained for consideration, the trustee advertises in the Gazette a notice that an offer has been made and entertained, and will be decided upon at the meeting to be held after the bankrupt's examination, and notifies each of the creditors of the resolution, the meeting, and the offer and security proposed with an abstract of the state of affairs and the valuation of the estate.[3]

If at the meeting after the bankrupt's examination a majority in number and three-fourths in value of the creditors accept the offer and security, a bond of caution for payment of the composition must be lodged with the trustee, who reports the resolution and transmits the bond to the court for approval. If the court finds that the offer with security has been duly made and is reasonable and assented to by the requisite majority it approves thereof.[4]

An offer of composition may also be made at the meeting after the bankrupt's examination, or at any subsequent meeting called for the purpose by the trustee.[5] If the composition is approved the bankrupt makes a declaration that he has made a full surrender of his estate and not granted any preference; the court, if satisfied, discharges the bankrupt of his debts, declares the sequestration at an end and the bankrupt reinvested in his estates.[6] If an offer of composition is rejected or has become

[1] *Alexander & Austin* v. *Yuille* (1873) 1 R. 185.

[2] 1913 Act, S. 38; cf. *Coutts* v. *Jones* (1900) 2 F. 1066.

[3] 1913 Act, S. 134.

[4] 1913 Act, S. 135.

[5] 1913 Act, S. 136.

[6] 1913 Act, S. 137; except on cause shown no party may withdraw even prior to the court's approval: *Lee* v. *Stevenson's Tr.* (1883) 11 R. 26; *Annan* v. *Marshall* (1887) 25 S.L.R. 94.

ineffectual, no other offer may be entertained unless nine-tenths in number and value assent in writing.[1]

The composition offered must be reasonable in the circumstances.[2]

A creditor who holds a security must, as in a sequestration, value his security and deduct that amount before claiming.[3] The subject of security does not belong to the creditor but is realizable by him;[4] if it does not realize the balance of the creditor's claim he may demand a composition on the shortfall.[5]

If the offer of composition is accepted a bond of caution for payment of the composition, executed by the bankrupt and the cautioner, is lodged with the trustee. This agreement cannot be resiled from.[6] The sequestration proceedings continue notwithstanding the composition negotiations until the Court discharges the bankrupt.[7] On receipt of the bond of caution the trustee reports the resolution to accept the composition to the court which may approve it.[8] Approval may be opposed, on such grounds as fraud,[9] inadequacy of composition,[10] or insufficiency of caution, or procedural irregularity. If the court approves the offer, the bankrupt makes a declaration that he has made a full and fair surrender of his estate, and has not granted any preference or security or entered into any secret or collusive agreement.[11] The requirements that a composition of at least 5/- per pound be paid or secured[12] apply. If satisfied the court discharges the bankrupt of all debts and obligations for which he was liable at the date of sequestration, and ends the sequestration and reinvests the bankrupt in his estates, reserving the claims of the creditors against him and the cautioner for payment of the composition.[13]

Position, duties and powers of trustee

The trustee on a sequestrated estate represents the general creditors only, not any special class of them separately, such as

1 1913 Act, S. 142.
2 *Bradshaw* v. *Kirkwood* (1904) 7 F. 249.
3 *Macbride* v. *Stevenson* (1884) 11 R. 702.
4 *Craig* v. *Somerville* (1894) 2 S.L.T. 139, 243, explained in *Clydesdale Bank* v. *McIntyre*, 1909 S.C. 1405.
5 *Bryson* v. *Lawrie* (1895) 2 S.L.T. 535.
6 *Ironside* v. *Gray* (1841) 4 D. 629; *Lee* v. *Stevenson's Tr.* (1883) 11 R. 26.
7 1913 Act, Ss. 137, 139; *Neilson* v. *Russell* (1843) 5 D. 475; *Latta* v. *Bell* (1862) 24 D. 1247.
8 1913 Act, S. 138; *Lee, supra.*
9 e.g. *Hay* v. *Rafferty* (1899) 2 F. 302.
10 e.g. *Bradshaw* v. *Kirkwood* (1904) 7 F. 249.
11 1913 Act, S. 137.
12 1913 Act, S. 146(1).
13 1913 Act, S. 137; *Shiells* v. *Reid* (1829) 7 S. 535; *Fleming* v. *Walker's Trs.* (1876) 4 R. 112.

creditors in an alimentary debt.[1] He may seek to reduce illegal preferences and need not aver that he represents prior creditors.[2]

He takes the bankrupt's property *tantum et tale* as vested in the bankrupt, subject to all the rights and equities affecting it at the time of the bankruptcy.[3] Hence property vested in the bankrupt in trust only does not vest in the trustee in bankruptcy.[4] The title to property is transferred to him as trustee, whereas the liquidator of a company is an administrator only and has no title in his own name.[5]

He may adopt and perform any contract in which the bankrupt was engaged,[6] or repudiate the contract, thereby rendering the estate liable in damages for breach of contract.[7]

With the consent of the commissioners he may compromise any question arising in the sequestration.[8]

The trustee may not take benefit from the bankrupt's fraud in obtaining a discharge of a security by concealing the fact of his bankruptcy,[9] and is barred by the bankrupt's failure to intimate an assignation.[10]

He has a title to sue for loss or harm caused to the bankrupt's estate, but not for solatium for injuries to the bankrupt personally.[11] He may sist himself as a party to an action in which the bankrupt is engaged, and settle it, but the settlement may be challenged as granted for a grossly inadequate consideration.[12] When a trustee sists himself as defender he becomes liable to the whole conclusions of the action.[13] If he litigates he becomes personally liable in expenses.[14]

[1] *Corbet* v. *Waddell* (1879) 7 R. 200.

[2] *Neil's Tr.* v. *B.L. Bank* (1896) 6 S.L.T. 227; *Hill's Tr.* v. *H.* (1901) 8 S.L.T. 467.

[3] *Fleeming* v. *Howden* (1868) 6 M. (H.L.) 113; cf. *Molleson* v. *Challis* (1873) 11 M. 510; *N.B. Ry.* v. *Lindsay* (1875) 3 R. 168; *Graeme's Tr.* v. *Giersberg* (1888) 15 R. 691; *Colquhoun's Tr.* v. *Campbell's Trs.* (1902) 4 F. 739.

[4] *Heritable Reversionary Co.* v. *Millar* (1892) 19 R. (H.L.) 43.

[5] *Gray's Trs.* v. *Benhar Coal Co.* (1881) 9 R. 225; *Clark* v. *West Calder Oil Co.* (1882) 9 R. 1017.

[6] *Mackessack* v. *Molleson* (1886) 13 R. 445; *McGavin* v. *Sturrock's Tr.* (1891) 18 R. 576; *Imrie's Tr.* v. *Calder* (1897) 25 R. 15; *Sturrock* v. *Robertson's Tr.*, 1913 S.C. 582; cf. *Edinburgh Heritable Security Co.* v. *Stevenson's Tr.* (1886) 13 R. 427.

[7] *Kirkland* v. *Cadell* (1878) 16 S. 860; *Kerr* v. *Dundee Gas Co.* (1861) 23 D. 343; *Anderson* v. *Hamilton* (1875) 2 R. 355.

[8] 1913 Act, S. 172; *Graham's Tr.* v. *Morton*, 1945 S.L.T. 48.

[9] *Molleson* v. *Challis* (1873) 11 M. 510; *Colquhoun's Tr.* v. *Campbell's Trs.* (1902) 4 F. 739.

[10] *Graeme's Tr.* v. *Giersberg* (1888) 15 R. 691; *Dunn's Tr.* (1896) 4 S.L.T. 45; cf. *Paul's Tr.* v. *P.*, 1912 2 S.L.T. 61.

[11] *Muir's Tr.* v. *Braidwood*, 1958 S.C. 169.

[12] *Clarke* v. *Cumming* (1891) 28 S.L.R. 343.

[13] *Watson* v. *Duncan* (1896) 4 S.L.T. 75.

[14] *Ellis* v. *E.* (1870) 8 M. 805; *Cowie* v. *Muirden* (1893) 20 R. (H.L.) 81; *Scott* v. *Thurso River Harbour Trs.* (1895) 23 R. 268.

The trustee is entitled to commission or fee as settled by the commissioners, with an appeal to the Accountant of Court.[1]

Removal of trustee

A majority in number and value of the creditors at a meeting called for the purpose may remove the trustee or accept his resignation;[2] one-fourth of the creditors in value may petition the court for removal of the trustee, which the court may do if sufficient reason appears; if the trustee has been discharged, died, resigned, been removed or remain at any one time for three months furth of Scotland, any commissioner or creditor may apply to the court to hold a meeting to devolve the estate on the next trustee, or to elect a new trustee.[3]

If the trustee has retained excessive funds uninvested the court must dismiss him,[4] and may remove him on a report by the Accountant of Court without petition by the creditors.[5] It is questionable whether the bankrupt can petition for his removal.[6] A petition and complaint by a creditor against a trustee's conduct has been held incompetent.[7]

Duties of trustee and commissioners

The trustee, within ten days of the confirmation of his election, must present an abbreviate of the fact for recording in the Register of Inhibitions and Adjudications.[8] He must, as soon as possible, take possession of the bankrupt's estate and effects, title deeds, papers and documents and make up an inventory of his estate and effects and a valuation showing the estimated value and annual revenue thereof, and send copies to the Accountant.[9]

The bankrupt must make up and deliver to the clerk of the meeting for election of the trustee, a state of his affairs, specifying his property including property in expectancy or to which he may have an eventual right, the names of his creditors and debtors, debts due by and to him, and a rental of his heritage. He must

[1] 1913 Act, S. 121–2; *Assets Co.* v. *Guild* (1885) 13 R. 281; *McLaren's Tr.* (1895) 2 S.L.T. 583; *Paul's Tr.* v. *Milne*, 1912 2 S.L.T. 304; *McGregor's Sequestration*, 1955 S.L.T. 270.

[2] cf. *McFadyean* v. *Campbell* (1884) 21 S.L.R. 479; the bankrupt's wife, though a creditor, may not vote: *MacNaught* v. *Sievwright*, 1928 S.C. 687.

[3] 1913 Act, S. 71; *McFadyean* v. *Campbell* (1884) 21 S.L.R. 479.

[4] 1913 Act, S. 79; *Acct. in Bankruptcy* v. *Peacock's Tr.* (1867) 8 M. 158.

[5] *Acct. in Bankruptcy, supra*; *Laing* v. *Hally* (1871) 8 M. 753; *Acct. in Bankruptcy* v. *Davie* (1884) 11 R. 1013.

[6] *Robertson* v. *Mitchell* (1871) 9 M. 741.

[7] *Paterson* v. *Robson* (1872) 11 M. 76.

[8] 1913 Act, S. 75.

[9] 1913 Act, S. 76.

give every information and assistance necessary to enable the trustee to execute his duty, under pain of imprisonment and forfeiture of the benefit of the Act.[1]

The trustee has to manage, recover and realize the bankrupt's estate and convert it into money according to the direction of the creditors or with the advice of the commissioners, and lodge the money in bank.[2] He is liable in penal interest for retaining money unbanked too long, and liable to dismissal without claim to remuneration.[3]

He must keep a sederunt book, recording all proceedings necessary to give a correct view of the management of the estate, and regular accounts.[4]

The commissioners superintend the trustee's actings, advising and assisting in the management of the estate, decide as to paying or postponing a dividend, may assemble to ascertain the situation of the bankrupt estate, and any one may report to a general meeting of the creditors.[5]

The trustee's Act and Warrant

On the trustee's bond of caution being duly lodged, the sheriff confirms his election as trustee and the sheriff clerk issues an Act and Warrant in his favour, with a copy to the Accountant of Court. This is an effectual title to the trustee to perform his statutory duties and evidence of his right and title to the sequestrated estate.[6]

The Act and Warrant[7] *ipso jure* transfers to and vests in the trustee or any succeeding trustee, for behoof of the creditors, absolutely and irredeemably, as at the date of the sequestration, with all right, title, and interest, the whole property of the debtor, namely (1) the moveable estates of the bankrupt, wherever situated, so far as attachable for debt or capable of voluntary alienation by the bankrupt, to the same effect as if actual delivery or possession had been obtained, or intimation made at that date, subject always to such preferable securities as existed at the date of the sequestration, and are not null or reducible;[8] (2) the whole

[1] 1913 Act, S. 77. The trustee must, if necessary, compel the bankrupt to lodge his state of affairs: *Scobie* v. *Hill's Tr.* (1869) 8 M. 161.

[2] 1913 Act, S. 78. [3] 1913 Act, S. 79. [4] 1913 Act, S. 80.

[5] 1913 Act, S. 81. [6] 1913 Act, S. 70.

[7] 1913 Act, S. 97 and Sched. D.

[8] There are excepted the wearing apparel of the bankrupt, his wife and family and his tools of trade; a dentist's instruments are tools of trade: *Macpherson* v. *M's Tr.* (1905) 8 F. 191; but not a solicitor's library: *Pennell* v. *Elgin*, 1926 S.C. 9. No delivery or intimation is necessary to complete the trustee's title: *Hill* v. *Lindsay* (1846) 8 D. 472; *Tods's Trs.* v. *Wilson* (1869) 7 M. 1100.

heritable estate belonging to the bankrupt in Scotland to the same effect as if a decree of adjudication in implement of sale, as well as a decree of adjudication for payment and in security of debt, subject to no legal reversion, had been pronounced in favour of the trustee, and recorded at the date of the sequestration, and as if a poinding of the ground had then been executed, subject always to such preferable securities as existed at the date of the sequestration, and are not null and reducible,[1] and the creditors' right to poind the ground.[2] But this transfer does not affect the rights of the superior, any question between the heir and a creditor's executor, nor the rights of the ancestor's creditor; if part of the bankrupt's heritage be held under entail or a limited title, the trustee's right is limited to the extent of the interest which the bankrupt might legally convey or his creditors attach; (3) all real estate in England, Ireland,[3] or any of H.M. dominions belonging to the bankrupt and all interest which he held therein to the same effect as if he had been adjudicated bankrupt there, provided the Act and Warrant is registered in the chief court of bankruptcy for the country; (4) any non-vested contingent right of succession or interest in property conceived in favour of the bankrupt under the will or settlement of any party deceased or under marriage-contract, or under any other deed, instrument or writing of an irrevocable nature, to the same effect as if an assignation of such right or interest had been executed by the bankrupt and intimation thereof made at the date of the sequestration, subject always to such preferable securities as existed at that date and are not null or reducible.[4]

A person claiming right to any estate included in the sequestration may petition to have it taken out of the sequestrated estate.[5] This includes property acquired by the bankrupt by fraud,[6] property held in trust by him,[7] or held as factor, agent, or executor,[8] and funds belonging to a third party but wrongly inmixed with those of the bankrupt, so long as identifiable.[9]

[1] *Garden, Haig-Scott & Wallace* v. *White*, 1962 S.C. 51.

[2] Hence a bankrupt occupying a house owned by him becomes, by virtue of S. 97, only a precarious occupier: *White* v. *Stevenson*, 1956 S.C. 84.

[3] As to Republic of Ireland, see *Murphy's Tr.*, 1933 S.L.T. 632.

[4] 1913 Act, S. 97; *Obers* v. *Paton's Trs.* (1897) 24 R. 719; *Salaman* v. *Tod's Trs.*, 1911 S.C. 1214.

[5] 1913 Act, S. 99.

[6] *Fleeming* v. *Howden* (1868) 6 M. (H.L.) 113; *Molleson* v. *Challis* (1873) 11 M. 510; *Heritable Reversionary Co.* v. *Millar* (1892) 19 R. (H.L.) 42; *Colquhoun's Tr.* v. *Campbell's Trs.* (1902) 4 F. 739; *Gamage* v. *Charlesworth's Tr.*, 1910 S.C. 257.

[7] *Leck* v. *Gairdner* (1855) 17 D. 1075; *Cochrane* v. *Black* (1867) 19 D. 1019; *Heritable Reversionary Co., supra.*

[8] *Macadam* v. *Martin's Tr.* (1872) 11 M. 33.

[9] *Macadam, supra.*

If the bankrupt is in right of an alimentary provision, the court may determine whether it exceeds a suitable aliment and order the excess to be paid to the trustee. Such order may later be varied in the event of change of circumstances.[1]

Even the discharge of the bankrupt, if without composition or consent of creditors, does not annul the sequestration with respect to property then vested in him, though not payable till after the discharge.[2]

The Act and Warrant does not operate infeftment and the bankrupt must grant all deeds necessary for recovering his property and feudally vesting his heritage in the trustee.[3] The trustee may complete title in his own name by notarial instrument[4] or notice of title,[5] or in the case of long leases, by registration.[6] If the bankrupt's title to any estate has not been completed, the trustee may complete title in his own person for behoof of the creditors, or in the person of the bankrupt.[7] The trustee may, without making up a feudal title and without the bankrupt's conveyance, grant such conveyance of heritage as the bankrupt might have granted.[8]

Where the heir of a deceased bankrupt has made up title the trustee may have the estate transferred to him.[9]

After-acquired property

Any property acquired by, or descending, reverting or otherwise coming to the bankrupt after sequestration and before the bankrupt has obtained his discharge falls under the sequestration. On application to the court it may be declared vested in the trustee.[10] Such a vesting order is necessary to make the trustee's right effectual against the diligence of creditors whose debts have

[1] 1913 Act, S. 98; cf. *Blaikie* v. *Peddie* (1871) 10 M. 140; *Learmonth* v. *Miller* (1875) 2 R. (H.L.) 62; *Corbet* v. *Waddell* (1879) 7 R. 200; *Scott's Tr.* v. *S.* (1884) 12 R. 182; *Heydon* v. *Forrest's Tr.* (1895) 3 S.L.T. 182; *Inglis's Tr.* v. *I.*, 1924 S.C. 226; *Macdonald's Tr.* v. *M.*, 1938 S.C. 536.

[2] *Trappes* v. *Meredith* (1871) 10 M. 38.

[3] 1913 Act, S. 100; cf. *Pennell's Tr.*, 1928 S.C. 605.

[4] Titles to Land Consolidation (Sc.) Act, 1868, S. 25.

[5] Conveyancing (Sc.) Act, 1924, Ss. 4 and 24.

[6] Registration of Leases (Sc.) Act, 1857, S. 11.

[7] 1913 Act, S. 100.

[8] *Munro* v. *Fraser's Trs.* (1851) 13 D. 1209.

[9] 1913 Act, S. 101.

[10] 1913 Act, S. 98; *Jackson* v. *McKechnie* (1875) 3 R. 130; *Taylor* v. *Charteris & Andrew* (1879) 7 R. 128; *Garland's Tr.* (1898) 6 S.L.T. 122; *Napier's Tr.* v. *de Saumarez* (1899) 1 F. 614; cf. *Barron* v. *Mitchell* (1881) 8 R. 933. Acquirenda does not cover professional earnings after sequestration: *Mason* v. *Paterson* (1904) 12 S.L.T. 511; but does cover a salary under a contract of service so far as exceeding a sufficiency: *Caldwell* v. *Hamilton*, 1919 S.C. (H.L.) 100; *Young* v. *Turnbull*, 1928 S.N. 46.

been incurred after sequestration.[1] If when a succession opens a beneficiary is under sequestration, the right to elect between legal rights and conventional provisions is in the trustee.[2] A *spes successionis* does not fall under sequestration and the bankrupt cannot be required to assign it, though an assignation might be made a condition of the bankrupt's discharge.[3] The bankrupt may not do anything in relation to a *spes successionis* to the prejudice of his creditors, such as to discharge legitim gratuitously.[4]

Bankrupt's spouse's property

Property genuinely belonging to the bankrupt's spouse is not affected by the sequestration. A life policy effected by a married man on his own life for the benefit of his wife or children is protected,[5] but if the policy was effected with intent to defraud creditors or if the life insured is made bankrupt within two years, the creditors may claim repayment of the premiums out of the proceeds.[6] A donation completed within a year and a day before the donor's sequestration is revocable at the instance of the donor's creditors.[7]

The bankrupt's state of affairs

At the meeting for the election of the trustee the bankrupt must deliver to the clerk a state of his affairs and rental of his heritage.[8] In the case of a firm separate states are required for the firm and for each partner.

Examination of bankrupt

Within eight days of the Act and Warrant the trustee must apply to the sheriff to name a day for the public examination of the bankrupt. The sheriff issues a warrant for the bankrupt to attend, and the trustee advertises in the Gazette and intimates by post to all creditors his name and designation, election as trustee, the time of the bankrupt's examination, and the time of a second

[1] *Grant* v. *Green's Tr.* (1901) 3 F. 1016.

[2] *Wishart* v. *Morrison* (1895) 3 S.L.T. 29; see also *Bell's Tr.* v. *B's Tr.*, 1907 S.C. 872.

[3] *Trappes* v. *Meredith* (1871) 10 M. 38; *Reid* v. *Morrison* (1893) 20 R. 510; see also *Kirkland* v. *K's Tr.* (1886) 13 R. 798; *Browne's Tr.* v. *Anderson* (1901) 4 F. 305.

[4] *Obers* v. *Paton's Trs.* (1897) 24 R. 719.

[5] Married Women's Policies of Assurance (Sc.) Act, 1880.

[6] *Schumann* v. *Scottish Widows' Fund Socy.* (1886) 13 R. 678; *Kennedy's Trs.* v. *Sharpe* (1895) 23 R. 146; *Barras* v. *Scottish Widows' Fund Socy.* (1900) 2 F. 1094; *Chrystal's Tr.* v. *C.*, 1912 S.C. 1003.

[7] Married Women's Property (Sc.) Act, 1920, S. 5(b).

[8] 1913 Act, S. 77; see also *York* v. *Gossman* (1861) 23 D. 1245; *Scobie* v. *Hill's Tr.* (1869) 8 M. 161.

meeting of creditors.[1] The sheriff may have the bankrupt apprehended and brought for examination.[2]

On the trustee's application the sheriff may order an examination of the bankrupt's wife and family, and others who can give information relative to his estate.[3] All must answer lawful questions relating to the affairs of the bankrupt. The examination is on oath, before the sheriff. There are penalties for refusal to answer.[4] The trustee may call on third parties to produce documents relevant to the bankrupt's affairs.[5]

Before the close of his examination the bankrupt may correct his state of affairs, and takes a statutory oath, which is engrossed in the sederunt book and signed by him and the sheriff.[6]

Second meeting of creditors

The trustee prepares a report for the second meeting of creditors, setting out the state of the bankrupt's affairs and an estimate of what the estate may produce. The creditors may receive an offer of composition, and may give indications for the recovery, management, and disposal of the estate.[7]

Realization of the bankrupt's heritable estate

A creditor holding security over the bankrupt's heritage preferable to the right of the trustee, may sell it, notwithstanding the sequestration,[8] but he and the purchaser may be required to account for any reversion of the price. The trustee may sell with the concurrence of a heritable creditor, or the trustee may sell alone, without interference from any heritable creditor.[9] With the concurrence of a majority of creditors, of the heritable creditors, and of the Accountant, the trustee may sell heritage by private bargain.[10] The trustee must make up a scheme of ranking and division of the price and report it to the court, whose approval

[1] 1913 Act, S. 83.
[2] 1913 Act, S. 84; *McKellar* v. *Livingston* (1861) 23 D. 1269; if he is out of Scotland see S. 85; cf. *Sinclair* v. *Bremner's Tr.* (1897) 5 S.L.T. 136.
[3] 1913 Act, S. 86; cf. *Burnet* v. *Calder* (1855) 17 D. 933; *Park* v. *Robson* (1871) 10 M. 10; *Jack's Tr.* v. *Jack's Trs.*, 1910 S.C. 34.
[4] 1913 Act, Ss. 87–90; questions as to the merits of a particular creditor's claim have been held incompetent: *Delvoitte* v. *Baillie's Tr.* (1877) 5 R. 143.
[5] *Selkirk* v. *Service* (1880) 8 R. 29.
[6] 1913 Act, S. 91; *Somerville* v. *Darlington* (1859) 21 D. 467; *Unger* v. *Blogg* (1867) 5 M. 1049.
[7] 1913 Act, S. 92.
[8] 1913 Act, Ss. 108, 110; cf. *Somervell's Tr.* v. *S.*, 1909 S.C. 1125.
[9] 1913 Act, S. 110; cf. *Callum* v. *Goldie* (1885) 12 R. 1137.
[10] *Dobie* v. *Lothian* (1864) 2 M. 788.

is warrant against the purchaser for payment of the price.[1] Poinding of the ground not carried into execution by sale 60 days before sequestration is invalid in any question with the trustee.[2] At a public sale any creditor may purchase, but not the trustee, a commissioner, the solicitor or any partner of his.[3]

Realization of moveable property

The trustee may realize the bankrupt's moveable property in the most convenient manner, according to the directions given by the creditors at any meeting, or with the advice of the commissioners.[4] Sale of book debts is not thereby authorized, unless twelve months have elapsed from sequestration, when they may be sold.[5] A *jus crediti* under a trust may be sold.[6]

Where the trustee sells the goodwill of the bankrupt's business he is entitled to delivery of ancillaries, such as of a public house licence, from the bankrupt, to have it transferred.[7]

Abandonment of claims

A claim to an asset alleged to fall within the sequestration may be abandoned, but only if the claim was considered at a meeting of the creditors.[8] Abandonment is not to be inferred by permitting heritable creditors to enter into possession of heritage while both trustee and bankrupt were discharged and no composition had been paid.[9]

Even the discharge of the trustee on the footing that all available funds have been ingathered and distributed does not prevent the sequestration subsisting.[10]

Creditor's claims

To participate in the distribution of assets a creditor must produce an oath as to his claim with account and vouchers,

[1] 1913 Act, S. 112; *McMillan* v. *Smyth* (1879) 6 R. 601; *Callum, supra.*

[2] 1913 Act, S. 114.

[3] 1913 Act, S. 116.

[4] 1913 Act, S. 78.

[5] *Robertson* v. *Adamson* (1857) 19 D. 502; *Stewart* v. *Crookston*, 1910 S.C. 609; 1913 Act, Ss. 78, 133.

[6] *McDonald* v. *McGrigor* (1874) 1 R. 817.

[7] *Selkirk* v. *Coupland* (1886) 23 S.L.R. 456; *Fraser's Tr.* v. *F.* (1896) 23 R. 978; as to limitation on power of sale of copyright, see 1913 Act, S. 102.

[8] *Fleming* v. *Walker's Trs.* (1876) 4 R. 112; *Northern Heritable Securities Investment Co.* v. *Whyte* (1888) 16 R. 100; affd. 18 R. (H.L.) 37; *Macdonald* v. *Mackintosh* (1905) 7 F. 771; *Scottish Equitable Life Assce. Socy.* v. *Hunter*, 1910 2 S.L.T. 296.

[9] *National Bank* v. *Carter* (1894) 2 S.L.T. 59.

[10] *Whyte* v. *Northern Heritable Securities Investment Co.* (1891) 18 R. (H.L.) 37.

which must, however, be scrutinized more carefully than in the case of claims to vote.[1] The evidence required to support a claim to rank depends on the rules of evidence.[2] A debt cannot be referred to the oath of bankrupt or trustee.[3]

Ranking of creditors

The trustee must classify and rank the creditors' claims as (a) privileged or preferential claims; (b) ordinary claims, and contingent claims when valued; if not valued the claim entitles the creditor to have a dividend set aside till the contingency has been purified; and (c) postponed claims, which rank only on any surplus. A creditor holding security must value it and is entitled to be ranked for the balance only.[4] The trustee may take over the security at the creditor's valuation.[5] If not taken over it may be realized by the creditor, but if he realizes less than the valuation, the sum realized is substituted for the valuation.[6] Obligations by co-obligants and collateral securities do not need to be valued and deducted for purposes of ranking.[7]

Preferential claims

In the division of a bankrupt's estate the following claims have priority over all other debts:

(1) the trustee's commission and his solicitor's account;

(2) in the case of a deceased debtor, deathbed and funeral expenses;[8] and

(3) the following, ranking equally *inter se* and payable in full, unless the assets are insufficient, when they abate in equal proportions:[9]

(a) all poor or other local rates due by the bankrupt at the prescribed date,[10] having become due and payable within

[1] 1913 Act, S. 54.

[2] *Forbes* v. *Manson* (1851) 13 D. 1272; *Purvis* v. *Dowie* (1869) 7 M. 765.

[3] *Jackson* v. *McIver* (1875) 2 R. 882; *Carmichael's Tr.* v. *C.*, 1929 S.C. 265.

[4] 1913 Act, S. 61.

[5] Ibid., *Hunter* v. *Slack* (1860) 22 D. 1166; see also *Ross* v. *Equitable Loan Co. of Scotland* (1826) 5 S. 178; *Henderson's Tr.* v. *Auld & Guild* (1872) 10 M. 946.

[6] *Henderson's Tr., supra*; *McDougall's Tr.* v. *Lockhart* (1903) 5 F. 905; *Kinmond, Luke & Co.* v. *Finlay* (1904) 6 F. 564; *Clydesdale Bank* v. *McIntyre*, 1909 S.C. 1405; *Maclachlan* v. *Maxwell*, 1910 S.C. 87.

[7] 1913 Act, Ss. 21, 45; *Black* v. *Melrose* (1840) 2 D. 706; *Ewart* v. *Latta* (1865) 3 M. (H.L.) 36; *Glasgow University* v. *Yuill's Trs.* (1882) 9 R. 643.

[8] 1912 Act, S. 118(5).

[9] 1913 Act, S. 118, amd. Companies Act, 1947, Ss. 91, 115.

[10] Date of the award of sequestration, or the date of the deceased debtor's death, or, if sequestration not awarded, the date of the concourse of diligence for distribution of the estate of a party notour bankrupt: S. 118(4).

12 months before that date,[1] and all assessed taxes, land tax, property or income tax assessed on him up to the fifth of April before that date, not exceeding one year's assessment;

(b) all wages or salary of any clerk or servant,[2] in respect of service rendered to the bankrupt during four months before that date, not exceeding £200 to any one;

(c) all wages of any workman or labourer not exceeding £200 to any one, whether for time or for piece work in respect of services to the bankrupt during four months before that date; but where any labourer in husbandry has contracted for payment to him of a portion of his wages in a lump sum, the priority extends to the whole of such sum or a part thereof as the court may decide to be due under the contract proportionate to the time of service to the said date;

(d) and (e): repealed.

(f)[3] all sums due in respect of contributions payable during 12 months before the said date by the bankrupt as employer of any persons under the National Insurance (Industrial Injuries) Act, 1965, or, either as the employer of any person or as a self-employed or non-employed person under the National Insurance Act, 1965.

Preference also attaches to any sum not exceeding £50 ordered to be paid by way of compensation for failure to reinstate in civil employment,[4] to any sum not exceeding £50 ordered to be paid by way of compensation for non-reinstatement in employment,[5] to any sum due from the bankrupt on account of tax deductions for the twelve months next before the date mentioned in S. 118(4).[6]

Crown debts do not, as such, enjoy any preference,[7] but the bankrupt's discharge does not extinguish any debt due to the Crown.[8]

[1] cf. *N.B. Property Investment Co.* v. *Paterson* (1888) 15 R. 885; *Campbell* v. *Edinburgh Parish Council*, 1909 S.C. 1353.

[2] Not including the manager and secretary of a company: *Scottish Poultry Journal Co.* (1896) 4 S.L.T. 167; *Clyde Football Club* (1900) 8 S.L.T. 328.

[3] Added by National Insurance (Industrial Injuries) Act, 1946 (now 1965).

[4] Reinstatement in Civil Employment Act, 1944, S. 21.

[5] National Service Act, 1948, S. 56(6).

[6] Finance Act, 1952, S. 30(6).

[7] *L.A.* v. *Walker's Tr.*, 1910 1 S.L.T. 128; *Admiralty* v. *Blair's Tr.*, 1916 S.C. 247.

[8] *L.A., supra.*

A creditor cannot claim any preference by obtaining a decree against the trustee personally.[1]

Ordinary creditors

Ordinary creditors are those not entitled to preferential ranking, including preferential creditors' claims for amounts in excess of those for which they are entitled to preference. All such ordinary claims rank equally *inter se*, and abate in the same proportion.

Ordinary claims include the contingent claim of a woman for the aliment of her bastard by the bankrupt till it should attain thirteen,[2] calls not made on shares held by the bankrupt,[3] the expenses of an action pending at the date of sequestration in which the trustee declined to sist himself,[4] a claim by a tenant for compensation for land resumed,[5] but not a wife's claim for future aliment decerned for in a separation and aliment, this being incapable of valuation,[6] nor for an alimentary annuity.[7]

Postponed creditors

Creditors postponed to all ordinary creditors are the bankrupt's wife, in respect of property which she has lent or entrusted to her husband or allowed to be mixed with his funds,[8] and persons who have lent money to a firm on terms of repayment out of the profits thereof, or have purchased the goodwill of a business in consideration of a share in the profits thereof.[9]

Prohibition on double ranking

It is a fundamental rule that there must be no double ranking for any claim. Thus a creditor may not rank for the full amount of bills in the acceptor's sequestration and also in the sequestration of the debtor for whose accommodation the bills had been accepted,[10] nor for the full debt, when before sequestration a cautioner had paid part of the debt,[11] nor may a creditor rank for

[1] *Thomson* v. *Friese-Greene's Tr.*, 1944 S.C. 336.
[2] *Downs* v. *Wilson's Tr.* (1886) 13 R. 1101.
[3] *Cresswell Ranche & Cattle Co.* v. *Balfour Melville* (1902) 9 S.L.T. 356.
[4] *Miller* v. *McIntosh* (1884) 11 R. 729.
[5] *Bertram* v. *Guild* (1880) 7 R. 1122.
[6] *Matthew* v. *M's Tr.* (1907) 15 S.L.T. 326.
[7] *Muirhead* v. *Miller* (1877) 4 R. 1139.
[8] Married Women's Property (Sc.) Act. 1881, S. 1(4); *Cochrane* v. *Lamont's Tr.* (1891) 18 R. 451; *Hodge* v. *Mitchell* (1908) 16 S.L.T. 289.
[9] Partnership Act, 1890, S.3
[10] *Anderson* v. *Mackinnon* (1876) 3 R. 608.
[11] *Mackinnon's Tr.* v. *Bank of Scotland*, 1915 S.C. 411.

the full debt and the cautioner also for the sum he has had to pay on the debtor's behalf,[1] nor for the full debt against both a firm and a partner thereof.[2]

The rule does not apply where a debtor has compounded with his creditors without being made bankrupt or divested of his estate.[3]

Dividends

The whole estate, when reduced to money, after expenses, is to be divided among the creditors at the date of sequestration.[4] To entitle a creditor to participate he must have produced his oath and grounds of debt, such as would be necessary to prove the debt in an action of constitution, two months before the time for the first dividend, or one month if payment has been accelerated.[5] A creditor may revise his claim.[6] A creditor too late for the first dividend is entitled to have it made up at a subsequent dividend.[7] Creditors abroad may lodge oaths at a later period.[8] A creditor claiming a preferential ranking should claim it expressly, or be allowed to amend his claim so to claim.[9] The trustee must not admit a claim on a basis he believes to be incorrect[10]

If the trustee thinks that evidence is required in support of a claim he should allow it to be led.[11] He must act only on legal evidence that debts are truly resting-owing.[12]

After four months from the award of the sequestration the trustee makes up a state of funds; the commissioners, after examining it, declare whether any dividend be declared.[13] The

[1] *Jamieson* v. *Forrest* (1875) 2 R. 701; *Harvie's Trs.* v. *Bank of Scotland* (1885) 12 R. 1141; *Veitch* v. *National Bank*, 1907 S.C. 554.

[2] 1913 Act, S. 62; *McClelland* v. *McCowan* (1849) 11 D. 1168.

[3] *Mackinnon* v. *Monkhouse* (1881) 9 R. 393.

[4] 1913 Act, S. 117.

[5] As to claim not timeously lodged, see *Scobie* v. *Hill's Tr.* (1869) 8 M. 161; *Hodge* v. *Wishart*, 1912 S.C. 1012.

[6] *Beattie's Trs.* v. *Story's Tr.* (1901) 9 S.L.T. 10; *Ritchie's Trs.* v. *McColl's Tr.* (1904) 6 F. 883.

[7] *Commercial Bank* v. *Muirhead's Tr.*, 1918 1 S.L.T. 132.

[8] 1913 Act, Ss. 119–20.

[9] *Crerar* v. *Clement's Tr.* (1905) 7 F. 939.

[10] *Ritchie's Trs.* v. *McCall's Tr.* (1904) 6 F. 883.

[11] *Oliver* v. *Wallace* (1869) 7 M. 407; *Purvis* v. *Dowie* (1869) 7 M. 764; *Ritchie* v. *Balgarnie* (1875) 2 R. 297.

[12] *Marshall* v. *Smith* (1871) 9 S.L.R. 42; *Williamson* v. *Allan* (1882) 9 R. 859.

[13] 1913 Act, Ss. 121–2. The trustee should not issue any deliverance regarding claims until he is in a position to declare a dividend: *Monkhouse* v. *Mackinnon* (1880) 8 R. 454.

trustee examines the claims and rejects or admits them or requires further evidence, completes a list of creditors entitled to a dividend, and intimates in the Gazette and to the creditors the proposed dividend.[1] He makes up a scheme of division and pays the dividends six months from the award of sequestration. The dividends attaching to claims under appeal, contingent creditors and other claimants not entitled to uplift them, are lodged in bank.[2]

Subsequent dividends

Eight months after sequestration a further state of funds is prepared, and after ten months a further dividend paid. Subsequent dividends are paid every three months from the previous one. In certain circumstances dividends may be accelerated or postponed.[3]

Unclaimed dividends are transmitted to the Queen's and Lord Treasurer's Remembrancer and may be recovered from him by the creditor on petition.[4]

Discharge of bankrupt

The bankrupt may be discharged of his debts if his creditors accept an offer of composition.[5] Apart from that he may, at any time after the second meeting of creditors, petition the court for discharge, but requires the consent of all his creditors. He may petition six months after the award of sequestration with the consent of a majority in number and four-fifths in value,[6] after 12 months with the consent of a majority in number and two-thirds in value,[6] after 18 months with the consent of a majority in number and value,[6] and after two years without any consents.[7] The trustee must prepare a report on the bankrupt's conduct, how far he has complied with the Act and, particularly, whether the bankrupt has made a fair discovery and surrender of his estate, attended the diet of examination, was guilty of any collusion, and whether his bankruptcy arose from innocent misfortune or losses

[1] 1913 Act, S. 123–4; cf. *Ritchie* v. *Balgarnie* (1875) 2 R. 297; *Lipman & Co.'s Tr.* (1893) 20 R. 818.

[2] 1913 Act, Ss. 125–6.

[3] 1913 Act, Ss. 127–33.

[4] *Stark's Trs.*, 1932 S.C. 653.

[5] *Supra.*

[6] i.e. of the creditors who have produced oaths in the sequestration: *Buchanan* v. *Wallace* (1882) 9 R. 621.

[7] 1913 Act, S. 143. As to mode of consent see *Wylie & Lochhead* v. *Young* (1859) 21 D. 577.

in business, or from culpable or undue conduct.[1] The court in each case orders intimation and may grant or refuse discharge, or defer consideration or annex conditions.[2]

Despite the lapse of two years and absence of opposition the court may refuse discharge if it appears from the trustee's report that the bankrupt fraudulently concealed any part of his estate or effects, or wilfully failed to comply with any of the provisions of the Act.[3]

If found entitled to his discharge, the bankrupt must make a declaration or oath that he has made a full and fair surrender of his estate, and has not granted or promised any payment, nor entered into any secret or collusive agreement or transaction to obtain the concurrence of any creditor to his discharge.[4] If the court is satisfied it discharges him of all debts and obligations contracted by him or for which he was liable at the date of sequestration.[5] An abbreviate of the discharge must be recorded in the Register of Inhibitions and Adjudications.[6]

A bankrupt is not entitled to discharge unless a dividend or composition of not less than 5/- in the pound has been paid, or security for payment thereof found, or that the failure to pay so much has in the opinion of the court arisen from circumstances for which the bankrupt cannot justly be held responsible.[7]

[1] The bankrupt may claim a report without any fee: *White* v. *W's Tr.* (1879) 6 R. 854. The trustee may not withhold a report requested at a proper time: *Mather* v. *McKittrick* (1881) 8 R. 952. If a report is not obtainable the court may request one from the Accountant of Court: *White* (1893) 20 R. 600; *Mackay* (1896) 24 R. 210; see also *Cruikshank* v. *Gowans* (1899) 1 F. 692. The minute of the creditors' consent must refer to the trustee's report: *Scott & Campbell* v. *Couper* (1872) 10 M. 626. A creditor who had not claimed: *Cant* v. *Bayne* (1868) 6 M. 368; and a contingent creditor: *Brown* (1899) 7 S.L.T. 10; may object to discharge.

[2] 1913 Act, S. 143. The court may impose a condition delaying discharge: *Buchanan* v. *Wallace* (1882) 9 R. 621; *Shand* (1882) 19 S.L.R. 562; or defer considering it: *Neill* v. *N's Tr.* (1873) 1 R. 320; a condition may also be imposed of assigning part of future income for the creditors: *Hamilton* v. *Caldwell*, 1916 S.C. 809; *Leslie* v. *Cumming & Spence* (1900) 2 F. 643; *Hurst* v. *Beveridge* (1900) 2 F. 702; *Reid* v. *Morrison* (1893) 20 R. 510; see also *Kirkland* v. *K's Tr.* (1886) 13 R. 798. Discharge is not precluded by a refusal to assign part of an alimentary provision to the creditors: *Blaikie* v. *Peddie* (1871) 10 M. 140.

[3] 1913 Act, S. 149; *Millar* (1877) 5 R. 144.

[4] As to case where bankrupt has become insane, see *Roberts* (1901) 3 F. 779.

[5] 1913 Act, S. 144.

[6] 1913 Act, S. 145.

[7] 1913 Act, S. 146; *Alison* v. *Robertson's Trs.* (1890) 18 R. 212; cf. *Bain* v. *Milne* (1870) 8 M. 784; *Wilson & Co.* (1882) 20 S.L.R. 17; *Clarke* v. *Crockatt* (1883) 11 R. 246; *Boyle* (1885) 12 R. 1147; *Phillips* (1885) 13 R. 91; *White* (1893) 1 S.L.T. 42; *McCarter* v. *Aikman* (1893) 20 R. 1090; *Bremner* (1900) 2 F. 1114; *Neilson* (1910) 3 F. 446; *Gemmell* (1902) 4 F. 441; *Bell* v. *B's Tr.*, 1908 S.C. 853; *Inglis* v. *Lyle*, 1928 S.N. 58; *Sinclair*, 1932 S.N. 53; *Inglis*, 1937 S.L.T. 619. It is doubtful whether S. 146 applies to discharge under deed of arrangement: *Stone* v. *Woodhouse, Hambly & Co.*, 1937 S.C. 824.

Refusal of discharge under this proviso does not prejudice a subsequent application if the requisite dividend be later paid.[1] Even though 5/- has been paid it may be made a condition of discharge that the bankrupt assign part of his future income for behoof of the creditors.[2] The court may grant discharge though no dividend has been paid,[3] or may suspend the operation of the discharge.[4]

All preferences, payments, and collusive agreements for obtaining the bankrupt's discharge are null and void; creditors participating forfeit their dividend and may be ordered to pay double the payment given. If the bankrupt had been personally concerned in or cognisant of such preference, he forfeits all right to discharge.[5]

A discharge may be reduced on the ground of failure to disclose assets, but fraudulent intent must be proved.[6]

In exceptional circumstances the bankrupt may petition the court *ex nobili officio* to discharge him and reinvest him in his estates,[7] and the court has similarly discharged a deceased bankrupt who had made full payment.[8]

Effect of discharge

Once discharged the bankrupt is freed from all debts and obligations for which he was liable at the date of sequestration, but is not reinvested in his estate which remains vested in the trustee for distribution among creditors,[9] nor is he freed from any debt due to the Crown.[10] All rights arising subsequent to discharge vest in the bankrupt and he is liable to the diligence of creditors whose claims have arisen since the date of sequestration. A liability for aliment continues, though arrears are wiped out by the discharge.[11]

[1] 1913 Act, S. 146.

[2] *Kirkland* v. *K's Tr.* (1886) 13 R. 798; *Leslie* v. *Cumming & Spence* (1900) 2 F. 643; *Hurst* v. *Beveridge* (1900) 2 F. 702. Contrast *Blaikie* v. *Peddie* (1871) 10 M. 140.

[3] *Bain, supra.*

[4] *Bell* v. *B's Tr.*, 1908 S.C. 853.

[5] 1913 Act, S. 150–1; see *Thomas* v. *Waddell* (1869) 7 M. 558; *Pendreigh's Tr.* v. *McLaren* (1871) 9 M. (H.L.) 49; *Thomas* v. *Sandeman* (1872) 1 M. 81; *Pendreigh* (1875) 2 R. 769; *Brand* v. *Gillon* (1894) 2 S.L.T. 405; *McCulloch* v. *Gillon* (1897) 34 S.L.R. 753.

[6] *City of Glasgow Bank and Liqdrs.* v. *Palmer* (1882) 19 S.L.R. 809.

[7] *Aitken* v. *Robson*, 1914 S.C. 224; *Sinclair*, 1932 S.N. 53; *Laing*, 1962 S.C. 168; *Black*, 1964 S.C. 276; *Fraser*, 1967 S.L.T. 178.

[8] *Gray's Exces.*, 1928 S.L.T. 558.

[9] 1913 Act, S. 144; cf. *Trappes* v. *Meredith* (1871) 10 M. 38.

[10] Ibid., S. 147.

[11] *Tulloch* v. *Pollock* (1847) 9 D. 582; *Downs* v. *Gourlay* (1886) 13 R. 1101.

Discharge of the trustee

After final division of the funds the trustee calls a meeting of creditors to consider an application for his discharge. He may then apply to the court, which may discharge him, in which case his bond of caution will be delivered up.[1]

Unclaimed dividends and any unapplied balances are lodged in bank, the deposit receipts being transmitted to the Accountant of Court. After the trustee's discharge any entitled creditor may apply to the Accountant to receive his dividend if deposited not more than seven years before. After seven years the deposit receipts are passed to the Queen's and Lord Treasurer's Remembrancer who uplifts the sums therein.[2]

When each dividend is to be paid, the commissioners audit the trustee's accounts and fix his commission or fee, subject to an appeal to the Accountant of Court.[3] The proper basis for this is a percentage of the assets ingathered.[4]

Even after trustee and bankrupt have been discharged a new trustee may be appointed on estate later acquired by petition to the *nobile officium*.[5]

Powers under nobile officium

The court frequently has to invoke the *nobile officium* to permit the rectification of procedural mistakes in sequestration, and also to deal with *casus improvisus*, such as to authorize a third trustee to proceed in a sequestration commenced over forty years earlier,[6] and to appoint a judicial factor where there had been no proceedings in the sequestration for over seventy years, the trustee had died, and the records of the sequestration had been lost.[7]

SUMMARY SEQUESTRATION

Where a debtor's assets do not exceed £300 his estate may be wound up by the process of summary sequestration, which proceeds in the same way as ordinary sequestration as modified by the 1913 Act, Ss. 175 and 176.[8] Summary sequestration is inapplicable to deceased debtors.[9]

[1] 1913 Act, S. 152.
[2] 1913 Act, S. 153.
[3] 1913 Act, Ss. 121–2.
[4] *McGregor's Seqn.*, 1955 S.L.T. 270.
[5] *Cockburn's Trs.*, 1941 S.C. 187.
[6] *Coull's Tr.*, 1934 S.C. 415.
[7] *Cheyne's Trs.*, 1933 S.L.T. 184.
[8] 1913 Act, S. 174.
[9] Ibid.

PUNISHMENT OF FRAUDULENT DEBTORS

At common law it is criminal to conceal funds for the purpose of defrauding creditors.[1]

The debtor in a process of sequestration is punishable criminally for various acts and omissions, in some cases unless he proves to the satisfaction of the court that he had no intention to defraud.[2] The trustee, if he has reasonable grounds to suspect that the bankrupt has been guilty of any offence under the Act, must report the fact to the Lord Advocate.[3]

If an undischarged bankrupt obtains credit to the extent of ten pounds or upwards from any person without informing him that he is an undischarged bankrupt, he is also guilty of crime.[4] This provision applies only to one who is an undischarged bankrupt by Scots law.[5]

It is a crime for any creditor wilfully and with intent to defraud to make any false claims or tender any proof, affidavit, declaration or statement of account which is untrue in any material particular.[6]

A person guilty of wilful falsehood in any oath made in pursuance of this Act is liable to prosecution at the instance of the Lord Advocate or of the trustee with the concurrence of the Lord Advocate.[7]

EXTRA JUDICIAL SETTLEMENTS

Without resort to judicial sequestration the estate of an insolvent may be realized and distributed among his creditors under a trust deed for creditors or a composition contract. Either process avoids much of the publicity of sequestration and can frequently be achieved more cheaply and expeditiously. But one recalcitrant creditor may frustrate the process.

TRUST DEED FOR CREDITORS

Under this procedure the insolvent dispones his whole estate to a named person as trustee for behoof of his creditors, for realization thereof and distribution among them according to their

[1] *H.M.A.* v. *Neill* (1873) 2 Coup. 395; *H.M.A.* v. *Cornelius* (1884) 5 Coup. 443; *Howman* v. *Mackie* (1891) 18 R. (J.) 30.

[2] 1913 Act, S. 178; *Adair* v. *Isaacs*, 1946 J.C. 84.

[3] 1913 Act, S. 180.

[4] 1913 Act, S. 182; *H.M.A.* v. *Macleods* (1886) 16 R. (J.) 1; *Maclean* v. *McCord*, 1965 S.L.T. (Sh. Ct.) 69, *sed quaere*.

[5] *Kaye* v. *H.M.A.*, 1957 J.C. 55.

[6] 1913 Act, S. 179.

[7] 1913 Act, S. 186.

various claims and preferences. Unlike a private trust for family or testamentary purposes, where the trustee represents the truster, the trustee in this case represents the creditors and holds for them. The creditors' claims lie against the trustee whereas in an *inter vivos* family trust their claims are against the truster, irrespective of the existence of the trust.[1] Such a trust deed is irrevocable if intimated to creditors, if the trustee takes possession of the estate, and if the debtor is not rendered notour bankrupt within 60 days thereafter.[2] It is reducible at common law if it gives an undue preference to any creditor and, if granted within 60 days of notour bankruptcy, it is reducible under the Act of 1696. If thus challengeable a non-acceding creditor may do diligence against the estate.[3] It is invalid against a creditor doing diligence if the trustee does not obtain delivery of the insolvent's assets.[4]

The granting of a trust deed does not prevent an application for sequestration which, if granted, supersedes the private trust.[5] In this event the trustee under the trust deed must account to the trustee in the sequestration for his intromissions,[6] but is not obliged to denude until reimbursed for outlays and expenses.[7]

It is normally a condition that all creditors who accede or receive a dividend are held to have discharged their claims in full, and that on realization and distribution the truster will be discharged. A non-acceding creditor may at any time petition for sequestration, which supersedes the trust deed.[8] An acceding creditor may petition only if the object of the trust is being defeated by non-acceding creditors.[9] The debtor himself may apply for sequestration, which supersedes the trust deed.[10] Accession may be established by oral approval and such circumstances as purchasing at a sale of the debtor's effects.[11] A bare

[1] If it is merely a trust for family purposes, the trustees are not liable to creditors: *Lucas's Trs.* v. *Beresford's Trs.* (1892) 19 R. 943.

[2] *Synnot* v. *Simpson* (1854) 5 H.L. Cas. 121; *Carmichael* v. *C's Exor.*, 1920 S.C. (H.L.) 195, 201.

[3] *Nicolson* v. *Johnstone* (1872) 11 M. 179.

[4] *Doughty* v. *Wells* (1906) 14 S.L.T. 299.

[5] Bell, *Comm.* II, 391; *McAlister* v. *Swinburne* (1874) 1 R. 958; see also *Thomson* v. *Tough's Tr.* (1880) 7 R. 1035; *Salaman* v. *Rosslyn's Trs.* (1900) 3 F. 298.

[6] *Craig* v. *Pollard* (1896) 3 S.L.T. 267; *Salaman, supra.*

[7] Bell, *Prin.* §1453, 1998; but see *Mess* v. *Sime's Tr.* (1898) 1 F. (H.L.) 22.

[8] Bell, *Comm.* II, 391; *Campbell* v. *Macfarlane* (1862) 24 D. 1097; *Nicolson* v. *Johnstone* (1872) 11 M. 179; *Kyd* v. *Waterson* (1880) 7 R. 884; *Salaman* v. *Rosslyn's Trs.* (1900) 3 F. 298.

[9] *Jopp* v. *Hay* (1844) 7 D. 260; *Campbell, supra.*

[10] *McAlister* v. *Swinburne* (1874) 1 R. 958; *Thomson* v. *Tough's Tr.* (1880) 7 R. 1035.

[11] *Marianski* v. *Wiseman* (1871) 9 M. 673.

claim for a dividend does not imply accession.[1] If the trustee is himself a creditor he is not prevented from doing diligence on his debt.[2]

The deed sometimes enumerates the creditors; this interrupts prescription of their debts[3] and bars the debtor from subsequently objecting to the debts, save on grounds of fraud or essential error.[4]

Accession of creditors

A creditor may or may not accede to the distribution of the debtor's estate under the trust deed, and that accession may be proved by writ[5] or oath or even by circumstances.[6] In accession it is implied that all creditors shall be bound, or none; hence if the estate is distributed under the trust deed an acceding creditor is bound by all of the deed.[7] But accession may not continue binding in the event of supervening change of circumstances[8] and an acceding creditor may apply for sequestration, if that is necessary to prevent non-acceding creditors from obtaining a preference.[9] The acceding creditors may appoint a committee to assist the trustee in winding up the estate.

A non-acceding creditor may, equally with acceding creditors, claim a dividend, and may sue the trustee therefor.[10] He is not barred from subsequently suing the debtor for his debt.[11] He may challenge the trust deed under the Bankruptcy Act, 1621, if diligence had been initiated before the trust deed,[12] and may reduce it under the Blank Bonds and Trusts Act, 1696, if notour bankruptcy was constituted prior to the trust deed or within the next six months.[13] He may by diligence secure an effectual preference.[14] He may petition for sequestration of the debtor.[15]

[1] *Athya* v. *Clydesdale Bank* (1881) 18 S.L.R. 287; *Davidson* v. *Union Bank* (1881) 19 S.L.R. 15; *Heritable Securities Investment Assocn.* v. *Wingate* (1891) 29 S.L.R. 904.

[2] *Paterson* v. *Barclay* (1868) 5 S.L.R. 503.

[3] Bell, *Prin.* §598; *Blair* v. *Horn* (1858) 21 D. 1004.

[4] *Cruickshank* v. *Thomas* (1893) 21 R. 257.

[5] A letter will suffice: *Henry* v. *Strachan & Spence* (1897) 24 R. 1045.

[6] *Renton* v. *Scott* (1854) 16 D. 1030; *Marianski* v. *Wiseman* (1871) 9 M. 673.

[7] *Gibson* v. *Macdonald* (1824) 3 S. 374; *Ogilvie* v. *Taylor* (1887) 14 R. 257.

[8] *Lockie* v. *Mason* (1837) 15 S. 547.

[9] *Jopp* v. *Hay* (1844) 7 D. 260; *Campbell & Beck* v. *Macfarlane* (1862) 24 D. 1097.

[10] *Ogilvie, supra.*

[11] *Thew* v. *Sinclair* (1881) 8 R. 467; *Athya* v. *Clydesdale Bank* (1881) 18 S.L.R. 287; *Davidson* v. *Union Bank* (1881) 19 S.L.R. 15; *Heritable Securities Inv. Assoc.* v .*Wingate* (1891) 29 S.L.R. 904.

[12] *Grant* v. *McEdward's Trs.* (1835) 13 S. 424.

[13] *Mackenzie* v. *Calder* (1868) 6 M. 833; *Nicolson* v. *Johnstone and Wright* (1872) 11 M. 179.

[14] *Nicolson, supra.*

[15] *Kyd* v. *Waterson* (1880) 7 R. 884.

The trustee must complete title to each item of property in the appropriate manner,[1] but the debtor, though he has no immediate powers of management,[2] retains the radical right and is entitled to any reversion after the trust purposes have been satisfied;[3] he may accordingly bequeath his property,[4] prevent the trustee misapplying it,[5] and require an accounting from the trustee.[6]

The survivor of trustees may act[7] and the court will appoint a new trustee if necessary,[8] and an interim trustee pending a new appointment.[9]

Trustee's duties and powers

The trustee has the right to take action necessary for administration and realization of the estate; apart from express powers he has the powers of a trustee under the Trusts (Scotland) Acts, 1921 to 1961.[10] The trust deed commonly confers on him the powers of a trustee in sequestration. He cannot, however, challenge preferences granted by the debtor, from whom he himself holds his title.[11] In claiming disputed property he has no better right than the debtor,[12] but may recover any of the debtor's property unwarrantably removed by a creditor, or its value.[13] He must exercise care, and conform to any rules set out in the trust deed for the management of the estate.[14] If he carries on the debtor's business he is personally liable for its debts.[15]

[1] Bell, *Comm.* II, 386; *Doughty* v. *Wells* (1906) 14 S.L.T. 299; *Mess* v. *Sime's Tr.* (1898) 1 F. (H.L.) 22; cf. *Lamb's Trs.* v. *Reid* (1883) 11 R. 76.

[2] *Ritchie* v. *Scott* (1899) 1 F. 728.

[3] *Gilmour* v. *Gilmours* (1873) 11 M. 853.

[4] *Herries, Farquhar & Co.* v. *Brown* (1838) 16 S. 948; *Gilmour* v. *Gilmours* (1873) 11 M. 853.

[5] *Buttercase & Geddie's Tr.* v. *Geddie* (1887) 24 R. 1128.

[6] Bell, *Comm.* II, 392; *Ritchie* v. *McIntosh* (1881) 8 R. 747; *Buttercase & Geddie's Tr.*, *supra*; *Campbell* v. *Cullen*, 1911 1 S.L.T. 258.

[7] *Clark's Trs.* v. *McRostie*, 1908 S.C. 196.

[8] *Royal Bank of Scotland* (1893) 20 R. 731.

[9] *Mitchell*, 1937 S.L.T. 474.

[10] Trusts (Sc.) Act, 1921, Ss. 2–4; *Gardner* v. *Scott's Tr.* (1889) 26 S.L.R. 535; *Royal Bank of Scotland* (1893) 20 R. 741; cf. *Maddaford* v. *Duncan* (1893) 20 R. 789; *Clark's Trs.*, *supra*.

[11] *Fleming's Trs.* v. *McHardy* (1892) 19 R. 542; *Cook* v. *Sinclair* (1896) 23 R. 925; *McLaren's Tr.* v. *National Bank* (1897) 24 R. 920.

[12] *Hogarth* v. *Smart's Tr.* (1882) 9 R. 964.

[13] *Murray* v. *Macdonald, Fraser & Co.* (1898) 5 S.L.T. 296.

[14] Bell, *Comm.* II, 392; *Cruickshank* v. *Thomas* (1893) 21 R. 257; *Buttercase & Geddie's Tr.* v. *Geddie* (1897) 24 R. 1128.

[15] *Miller* v. *Downie* (1876) 3 R. 548; *Macphail* v. *Maclean's Tr.* (1887) 15 R. 47; *Ford* v. *Stephenson* (1888) 16 R. 24; cf. *Moncrieff* v. *Ferguson* (1896) 24 R. 47; as to whether he is an 'assignee' under a lease, see *Dewar* v. *Ainslie* (1892) 20 R. 203.

Having realized the estate, he must adjudicate on creditors' claims and pay dividends thereon.[1] If the trust deed so provides the rules of ranking applicable in sequestration apply, failing which the common law rules, under which creditors holding securities rank without deducting the value of their securities.[2] A non-acceding creditor is entitled to his share unconditionally, and may sue the trustee therefor.[3]

The trustee, and members of any advisory committee, are in a fiduciary position to the debtor and to the creditors and must not act unfairly or collusively.[4]

He is personally liable for contracts entered into in the course of administering the trust estate[5] with a right of relief against the estate and any creditors who have authorized his actings.[6]

He is personally liable to a creditor if he divests himself in favour of the truster without satisfying that creditor's claim.[7] He should not allow one creditor to intromit with the trust estate, but any such creditor who does is liable to restore to the trust estate the value of anything taken out of it.[8] He may be liable in damages to the truster for negligent administration causing loss to the trust estate.[9]

The trustee must account to the truster and the creditors for his intromissions. The trust deed frequently provides for audit of his accounts and fixing of his remuneration by a committee of creditors. If no such provision be made he must submit his accounts to the Accountant of Court who audits them and fixes his remuneration.[10] He has a lien over the estate for his outlays, expenses, and remuneration.[11]

If the disposition in trust is superseded by sequestration, he is entitled to commission down to the date of confirmation of the trustee in the sequestration, but not thereafter to retain the estate in satisfaction of his claim.[12] In such a case the trustee must also

[1] As to appropriation of payments see *Wilson's Trs.* v. *Watson* (1900) 2 F. 761.

[2] *Kirkcaldy* v. *Middleton* (1841) 4 D. 202; *Glasgow University* v. *Yuill's Tr.* (1882) 9 R. 643.

[3] *Ogilvie* v. *Taylor* (1887) 14 R. 399.

[4] *L. Ashburton* v. *Escombe* (1892) 20 R. 187; *Campbell* v. *Cullen*, 1911 1 S.L.T. 258; cf. *Farmers Mart* v. *Milne*, 1814 S.C. (H.L.) 84.

[5] *Ellis* v. *E.* (1870) 8 M. 805; *Macphail* v. *Maclean's Tr.* (1887) 15 R. 47; *Ford* v. *Stephenson* (1888) 16 R. 24; see also *Moncrieffe* v. *Ferguson* (1896) 24 R. 47.

[6] *Mercer* v. *Orr* (1823) 2 S. 574; *Cleghorn* v. *Gordon* (1827) 5 S. 203; *Carswell* v. *Munn's Trs.* (1832) 10 S. 677.

[7] *Cruickshank* v. *Thomas* (1893) 21 R. 257.

[8] *Smart* v. *Stewart*, 1910 S.C. 18; 1911 S.C. 668.

[9] *Houston* v. *Sale* (1909) 25 Sh. Ct. Rep. 25.

[10] 1913 Act, S. 185.

[11] *Thomson* v. *Tough's Tr.* (1880) 7 R. 1035.

[12] *Dall* v. *Drummond* (1870) 8 M. 1006; see also *Moss* v. *Sime's Tr.* (1898) 1 F. (H.L.) 22.

count and reckon with the trustee in the sequestration for his intromissions.[1]

The creditors may abandon any asset to the debtor, and the trustee may be authorized on their behalf to discharge the debtor at any stage.[2]

Discharge of truster

The trust deed normally provides for discharge of the debtor by creditors acceding or drawing dividends. This does not bind non-acceding creditors[3] but does not invalidate the trust so as to permit creditors to do separate diligence against the estate.[4]

Discharge of trustee

After distribution of the estate the trustee is entitled to his discharge; if necessary he should do so by action of multiple-poinding.

EXTRA-JUDICIAL COMPOSITION CONTRACT

If creditors are agreeable to let a debtor continue in business as if solvent they may agree to accept a composition on their debts in full discharge of the debtor's obligations to them. Such an arrangement is effected by a bilateral contract,[5] which need not be probative.[6] It is implied in any such contract that all the creditors concur in the arrangement,[7] that all will be treated equally,[8] and that the debtor has made a full disclosure of his estate and the extent of his insolvency.[9] It is usually expressly provided that the concurrence of all creditors be obtained within a stated time, and the contract may provide for security for payment of the composition.[10] It normally also provides for the debtor's discharge on payment of the agreed composition.

The accession of creditors may be proved by writing, probative

[1] *Craig* v. *Pollard* (1896) 3 S.L.T. 267; *Salaman* v. *E. Rosslyn's Trs.* (1900) 3 F. 298.
[2] *Flett* v. *Mustard*, 1936 S.C. 269.
[3] *Ogilvie* v. *Taylor* (1887) 14 R. 257.
[4] *Nicolson* v. *Johnstone* (1872) 11 M. 179; *Henderson* v. *H's Trs.* (1882) 10 R. 185; *Lamb's Tr.* v. *Reid* (1883) 11 R. 76.
[5] Bell, *Comm.* II, 398.
[6] Bell, *supra*; cf. *Thew* v. *Sinclair* (1881) 8 R. 467.
[7] Bell, *Comm.* II, 400.
[8] *Macfarlane* v. *Nicoll* (1864) 3 M. 237; *Bank of Scotland* v. *Faulds* (1870) 42 Sc. Jur. 557; *Ironside* v. *Wilson* (1871) 9 S.L.R. 73.
[9] *Baillie* v. *Young* (1837) 15 S. 893.
[10] *Eaglesham* v. *Grant* (1875) 2 R. 960; *Miller* v. *Downie* (1876) 3 R. 548, 553; see also *Allan, Buckley Allan & Milne* v. *Pattison* (1893) 21 R. 195.

or improbative,[1] or by the minutes of a meeting of creditors, or by writ of an agent,[2] but is not merely established by delay in rejecting an inadequate composition.[3]

The creditors may resile and insist on their full claims if the debtor fails to implement any essential conditions of the contract.[4]

Any preference shown by the debtor to any creditor, as an inducement to agree to the composition-contract, or as a personal favour, is unenforceable.[5] Any such preference may be challenged by the debtor, his cautioner, any other creditor, or the trustee in a supervening sequestration. But in the absence of express stipulation a creditor is entitled at common law to a composition on the full amount of his debt without deduction for any security held.[6]

Position of debtor

The debtor retains possession of his estate unless he has agreed to hand it over to another for administration, or to administer it subject to supervision.[7]

Debtor's failure

If the debtor fails to pay the full composition undertaken or any instalment due a creditor may do diligence for the whole balance of the full debt, or proceed against the cautioner.

Discharge of debtor

If the debtor implements all his undertakings under the contract he is entitled to discharge in terms thereof and delivery up of the documents of debt.[8]

Discharge of cautioner

The cautioner is discharged by any material alteration of the contract without his consent,[9] but not by the debtor's sequestration for non-payment of an instalment,[10] by the creditors ranking

[1] Bell, *Comm.* II, 398; *Kilpatrick* v. *Miller* (1825) 4 S. 80.

[2] *Henry* v. *Strachan & Spence* (1897) 24 R. 1045.

[3] *Thew* v. *Sinclair* (1881) 8 R. 467.

[4] *Brown* v. *McIntyre* (1830) 8 S. 847; *Caillon* v. *Shanks* (1851) 14 D. 41; *Woods, Parker & Co.* v. *Ainslie* (1860) 22 D. 723; *Alexander* v. *Yuille* (1873) 1 R. 185; *Neil's Trs.* v. *B.L. Co.* (1898) 36 S.L.R. 139.

[5] Bell, *Comm.* II, 399; *Macfarlane* v. *Nicoll* (1864) 3 M. 237; *Bank of Scotland* v. *Faulds* (1870) 42 Sc. Jur. 557; contrast *Hay* v. *Rafferty* (1899) 2 F. 302.

[6] *MacBride* v. *Stevenson* (1884) 11 R. 702.

[7] cf. *Scott* v. *Campbell* (1834) 12 S. 447.

[8] Bell, *Comm.* II, 400.

[9] Bell, *Prin.* §263; *Scott* v. *Campbell* (1834) 12 S. 447; cf. *Allan, Buckley Allan & Milne* v. *Pattison* (1893) 21 R. 195.

[10] *Thomson & Craig* v. *Latta* (1863) 1 M. 913.

therein,[1] or consenting to the debtor's discharge therein.[2] Discharge of the debtor on full implement of the composition contract discharges the cautioner also.[3] A cautioner, if he has to pay, has a right of relief against the debtor, and a right to an assignation from the creditors of their claims.[4]

JUDICIAL FACTOR WINDING UP ESTATES OF DECEASED PERSONS

Any creditor of a deceased person, or person having an interest in the succession to a deceased, if the deceased left no settlement appointing trustees or other parties having power to manage his estate or part thereof, or in the event of their not accepting or acting, may apply to the Court of Session or, where the assets are estimated not to exceed £500, to the sheriff, for the appointment of a judicial factor, whom the court may appoint to administer the estate subject to the supervision of the Accountant of Court in accordance with the Judicial Factors Acts, and in the case of an insolvent estate shall divide it among the creditors in accordance with the rules as to ranking obtaining in sequestrations.[5]

This provision does not require the deceased to have been insolvent, or intestate, but only that no trustees or executors are acting. If a creditor subsequently petitions for sequestration, it must be granted.[6] A judicial factor has been appointed when the trustee died and procedure to appoint a new trustee proved abortive.[7] The appointment may be recalled if a person is decerned executor-dative.[8]

After payment of a dividend and the discharge of a factor another factor may be appointed on a prima facie case being made for the existence of further assets.[9]

The appointment of a judicial factor is equivalent to the intimated assignation of the debtor's reversionary rights in subjects disponed in security.[10]

[1] *Thomson & Craig, supra.*
[2] 1913 Act, S. 52.
[3] Bell, *Comm.* I, 376; *Fleming* v. *Wilson* (1823) 2 S. 336; cf. *Calder* v. *Borthwick* (1829) 7 S. 840; *Morton Trs.* v. *Robertson's J.F.* (1892) 20 R. 72.
[4] Bell, *Prin.* §255.
[5] 1913 Act, Ss. 163–4; see generally *Masterton* v. *Erskine's Trs.* (1887) 14 R. 712; *Lamb* (1902) 9 S.L.T. 438; *Youngson*, 1911 2 S.L.T. 448; *Stewart* v. *Waldie*, 1926 S.L.T. 526; *Dunn* v. *Britannic Assce. Co.*, 1932 S.L.T. 244; *Macdonald, Fraser & Co.* v. *Cairns' Exrx.*, 1932 S.C. 699.
[6] *Arthur* (1903) 10 S.L.T. 550.
[7] *Moncreiff's Trs.* v. *Halley* (1899) 1 F. 696; cf. *Cheyne's Trs.*, 1933 S.L.T. 184.
[8] *Masterton* v. *Erskine's Trs.* (1887) 14 R. 712.
[9] *Wright* (1901) 9 S.L.T. 278.
[10] *Campbell's J.F.* v. *National Bank*, 1944 S.C. 495.

A judicial factor has no title to sue for behoof of the whole body of creditors for the reduction of a gratuitous alienation granted by the debtor.[1]

In winding up the estate the factor must, if the estate was insolvent, rank creditors as in a sequestration.[2]

[1] *Reid's J.F.* v. *Reid*, 1959 S.L.T. 120.
[2] *Newton's Exrx.* v. *Meiklejohn's J.F.*, 1959 S.L.T. 71.

BOOK VIII

SUCCESSION

CHAPTER 109

RIGHTS IN SUCCESSION

THE rules of succession regulate the way in which property descends on the death of the owner to those who succeed in his place. Succession or universal succession deals with the disposal of the whole estates and assets of the deceased as distinct from singular succession to particular subjects of persons who have rights to those subjects by virtue of a conveyance *inter vivos*, as on gift or sale.[1]

The law of succession falls into three major divisions. The first concerns those legal rights conferred on certain survivors by law independently of the wishes of the deceased; the second concerns legal or intestate succession, the rules for the distribution of the remainder of the deceased's property if he has left no effective directions for its distribution; and the third concerns testate succession, the rules applicable where the deceased has left a written expression of his wishes for its distribution, in the form of a will or testament. In each division heritable and moveable property have to be considered separately. An appendage to the law of succession is the rules regulating the duties and power of the executor whose function is to ingather and distribute the estate in accordance with the rules of succession.

All rights of succession are postponed to the claims of creditors against the deceased's estate.

Death

For rules as to succession to property to operate, the owner must have died. The fact and date of death of the deceased can normally be ascertained with certainty. In case of doubt, as where a person has disappeared, action must be brought at common law, or under the Presumption of Life Limitation (Sc.) Act, 1891, to have him presumed dead. In petitions at common law there must be evidence deemed adequate to rebut the presumption that a person continues in life for a substantial period.[2] Under the 1891

[1] Ersk. III, 8, 1.

[2] Dickson, *Evidence*, §116. The period has been stated as 80 or 100 years: Stair IV, 45, 17(19); or 100 years: Bankt. II, 6, 31. For factors weighing with the court see *Fairholme* v. *F's Trs.* (1858) 20 D. 813; *Bruce* v. *Smith* (1871) 10 M. 130; *Rhind's Trs.* v. *Bell* (1878) 5 R. 527; *Williamson* v. *W.* (1886) 14 R. 226; *Greig* v. *Edinburgh Merchant Co.*, 1921 S.C. 76.

Act a person entitled to succeed to any estate on the death of the absentee, or to any estate the transmission of which to the petitioner depends on the death of the absentee, or who is the fiar of estate burdened with a liferent in favour of the absentee, may petition. If the absentee has disappeared and not been heard of for seven years or more, the court may find the fact of disappearance, the date at which he was last known to be alive, and that he died at a specified date, or, failing sufficient evidence that he died at any definite date, that he is presumed to have died seven years after the date on which he was last known to be alive.

Even after decree the absentee may recover the estate from the person who obtains it under the Act, or his gratuitous alienee, or its price, if it has been sold, for thirteen years from the date at which the title to the estate, if registrable in a public register, was so registered, or, in other cases, the date on which possession was taken of it, but thereafter recovery is excluded. The Act does not apply to the rights of parties having a right preferable to that of the absentee or his representatives, nor does it apply to claims under policies of insurance.

The common law presumption of life continuing for a substantial time is not altered by the provision of the Divorce (Sc.) Act, 1939, S. 5, whereby a dissolution of marriage may be decreed on the ground of presumed death.[1]

Survivance

Rights vest by succession only in persons who survive the deceased. In the ordinary case survivance is easily established but there may be narrow cases, particularly where the time of death of the deceased is not certainly fixed.[2] Survivance must be proved and is not presumed from juniority in age.[3] Unless a will requires survivance to a stated time, or by a stated period, survivance of the deceased by a person claiming in succession by even the slightest discernible time will suffice.[4] If a person has survived rights of succession vest in him or her and transmit as part of his or her estate.

Deaths in a common calamity

Where relatives die in a common calamity there was no presumption at common law as to survivorship of any one rather

[1] *Secretary of State for Scotland* v. *Sutherland*, 1944 S.C. 79.

[2] cf. *Wing* v. *Angrave* (1860) 8 H.L. Cas. 183.

[3] *Drummond's J.F.* v. *H.M.A.*, 1944 S.C. 298; contrast Dig. 34, 5, 10; *Hickman* v. *Peacey* [1945] A.C. 304.

[4] cf. *Morgan* v. *Scoulding* [1938] 1 K.B. 786.

than another.[1] By the Succession (Sc.) Act, 1964, S. 31, where two persons have died in circumstances indicating that they died simultaneously or rendering it uncertain which, if either, of them survived the other, then, for all purposes affecting title to property or claims to legal rights or the prior rights of a surviving spouse, (a) where the persons were husband and wife, it shall be presumed that neither survived the other;[2] and (b) in any other case, it shall be presumed that the younger person survived the elder, unless the elder has left a testamentary disposition containing a provision, however expressed in favour of the younger if he survives the elder and, failing the younger, in favour of a third person, and the younger person has died intestate,[3] then it shall be presumed for the purposes of that provision that the elder survived the younger.[4]

The deceased's estate

Rights of succession affect only the deceased's estate, his property or assets after deduction of or provision for all debts and liabilities. His assets comprise all things and rights capable of being valued in or converted into money, or exacted from others. Hence coats of arms and some titles of honour, though descendible to heirs, are not assets in the succession having value, while other titles of honour are purely personal and do not transmit to heirs at all.

Accordingly funds conveyed *inter vivos* to trustees but in which the deceased had retained a radical right were assets subject to legal rights,[5] and a liferent provision by a wife's father to her husband and forfeited by him when she divorced him was subject to legitim on her death.[6] Other subjects held to be *in bonis* of the deceased at death have included policies of insurance held by a deceased on his own life,[7] or on the life of his wife, who survived him,[8] or of his surviving son.[9]

Claims deemed not to be assets of the deceased's estate include

[1] *Drummond's J.F.* v. *H.M.A.*, 1944 S.C. 298; *Mitchell's Exrx.* v. *Gordon's Factor*, 1953 S.C. 176; *Ross's J.F.* v. *Martin*, 1955 S.L.T. 117.

[2] Hence the result in *Ross's J.F.*, *supra*, would still apply.

[3] Defined by S. 36(1) as wholly or partly intestate.

[4] The reason for, and application of, case (b) is obscure.

[5] *Montgomery's Trs.* v. *M.* (1895) 22 R. 842; *Drysdale's Trs.* v. *D.*, 1940 S.C. 85, distinguishing *Wright* v. *Bryson*, 1935 S.C. (H.L.) 49.

[6] *Gavin's Trs.* v. *Walker's Trs.* (1907) 15 S.L.T. 681.

[7] *Muirhead* v. *M's Factor* (1867) 6 M. 95.

[8] *Pringle's Trs.* v. *Hamilton* (1872) 10 M. 621.

[9] *Chalmers' Trs.* (1882) 9 R. 743.

a posthumous share of partnership profits, payable to the executor,[1] a donation made by husband to wife before his death,[2] accumulations of income which fell into intestacy,[3] a right of action for damages for personal wrong not pressed by the deceased before his death.[4]

Whether assets are heritable or moveable

Questions may also arise whether particular funds or assets of the deceased's estate are deemed heritable or moveable.[5] Heritable securities are deemed moveable estate in the creditor's succession, but are excluded from account in computing legitim,[6] and probably also in computing *jus relictae vel relicti*.[7]

Among moveable assets have been held policies of insurance on the deceased's own life payable to his executors,[8] a policy on the life of the deceased's surviving wife,[9] a policy on a surviving son's life payable to the surviving spouse, but intended as a provision for the son's widow and children,[10] and a widow's receipt from her late husaband's estate for the price of his heritage, sold on his behalf and passing to her on his death.[11]

For the purposes of legal rights the valuation of the deceased's estate is at the date of death.[12]

Debts and death duties

All rights of succession are exigible only after payment of the deceased's debts and settlement of his outstanding obligations, and settlement of sums due on his death by way of death duties and capital gains tax.

Debts fall to be paid out of heritage or moveables according

[1] *Adamson's Trs.* v. *A's Exors.* (1891) 18 R. 1133.

[2] *Hutton's Trs.* v. *H's Trs.*, 1916 S.C. 860; overruling *Fann* v. *McDonald*, 1913 S.C. 937; by the Married Women's Property (Sc.) Act, 1920, S. 5, such a gift would now be irrevocable.

[3] *Wilson's Trs.* v. *Glasgow R.I.*, 1917 S.C. 527; but see also *Moon's Trs.* v. *M.* (1899) 2 F. 201; *McGregor's Trs.* v. *Kimbell*, 1911 S.C. 1196.

[4] *Smith* v. *Stewart*, 1960 S.C. 329.

[5] See generally Ch. 74, *supra*.

[6] Titles to Land Consolidation (Sc.) Act, 1868, S. 117, amd. Succession (Sc.) Act, 1964, Sched. 3.

[7] This matter is not clear from the way the 1868 Act was amended in 1964.

[8] *Muirhead* v. *M's Factor* (1867) 6 M. 95.

[9] *Pringle's Trs.* v. *Hamilton* (1872) 10 M. 621.

[10] *Chalmer's Trs.* (1882) 9 R. 743.

[11] *McLellan* v. *McL.*, 1960 S.C. 348.

[12] *E. Dalhousie* v. *Crokat* (1868) 6 M. 659; *Gilchrist* v. *G's Trs.* (1889) 16 R. 1118; *Maben* v. *M's Exors.* (1901) 8 S.L.T. 486; *Moss' Trs.* v. *M.*, 1916 1 S.L.T. 321; *Russell* v. *A.G.*, 1917 S.C. 28.

as they relate to or are charged on heritage or moveables,[1] but as since 1964[2] the whole estate vests in the deceased's executor all claims may competently be made against him.

The executor is accountable for all estate duty leviable or payable in respect of both heritage and moveables.[3]

[1] *Ross* v. *R's Trs.* (1901) 9 S.L.T. 340; *Smith's Trs.* v. *S.*, 1912 1 S.L.T. 484; *Heath* v. *Grant's Trs.*, 1913 S.C. 78.

[2] Succession (Sc.) Act, 1964, S. 14.

[3] Ibid., S. 19(1).

CHAPTER 110

STATUTORY PRIOR RIGHTS AND LEGAL RIGHTS

STATUTORY PRIOR RIGHTS

THE Intestate Husband's Estate (Sc.) Acts, 1911 and 1919, gave a widow, where her husband died wholly[1] intestate and without leaving lawful issue,[2] a right to his whole estate, heritable and moveable, if not exceeding £500, and if exceeding that value, to £500 drawn rateably from heritage and moveables in addition to, and in priority to, legal rights in the balance of the estate. This prior right was extended to widowers,[3] and to cases of partial intestacy,[4] and raised to £5000,[5] thereby having the effect in many cases of excluding the application of the rules of legal rights and of intestate succession altogether. Despite the Legitimacy Act 1926, a surviving spouse was entitled to this sum in competition with an illegitimate child.[6]

This statutory claim, where applicable, was postponed to the claims of creditors but ranked in priority to common law legal rights and to all rights of succession on intestacy. Unlike claims to legal rights, statutory prior rights did not, and do not, apply where there is a will disposing of the whole estate, or avail against it, but only where there was, or is, a total or partial intestacy.

This statutory claim has now been replaced, in the case of deaths after 10th September 1964, by the statutory prior rights of the surviving spouse of an intestate under the Succession (Sc.) Act, 1964, Ss. 8 and 9,[7] which by S. 10(2) rank in priority to all legal rights.

LEGAL RIGHTS

At common law it has long been settled in Scotland that certain surviving relatives of a deceased have legal claims against his

[1] *Taylor's Exors.* v. *T.*, 1918 S.C. 207.
[2] *Grant* v. *Munro*, 1916 1 S.L.T. 338.
[3] Law Reform (Misc. Prov.) (Sc.) Act, 1940, S. 5(1).
[4] Ibid., S. 5(2).
[5] Intestate Husband's Estate (Sc.) Act, 1959.
[6] *Osman* v. *Campbell*, 1946 S.C. 204.
[7] For these see Ch. 111, *infra*.

estate, preferred to the claims of those who take his estate on intestacy, and, with certain qualifications, not defeasible by any will left by the deceased. Such claims are deemed of the nature of debts due from the deceased's estate rather than rights of succession, and therefore, though postponed to outside creditors, and, in the case of total or partial intestacy, to claims to statutory prior rights, are preferred to all rights of succession.[1] The rules of intestate succession, or the dispositions of a deceased's will can therefore operate on the part of the deceased's estate, sometimes called dead's part, not required to satisfy prior statutory rights (in cases of total and partial intestacy only) and legal rights. Some amendments as to entitlement to legal rights have been made by the Succession (Sc.) Act, 1964, and other statutes. By the Succession (Sc.) Act, 1964, S. 33(1) any reference in a deed taking effect after the commencement of the 1964 Act to *jus relicti*, *jus relictae*, or to legitim, is to the relevant legal right as modified by the 1964 Act.

Claims to legal rights cannot be made in respect of property which did not form part of the deceased's estate at the date of his death but accrued subsequently.[2] In general the estate must be valued at the date of death and legal rights are not affected by subsequent appreciation or depreciation, but exceptionally depreciation or losses on realization have been taken into account.[3]

A claim to legal rights, like another claim of debt, is excluded if not claimed within the period of the long negative prescription.[4]

Legal rights exigible at common law from heritage-terce

At common law a surviving widow had a right of terce, to a liferent of one-third of the income of her husband's heritage. It attached to all heritage, whether acquired by succession, or otherwise, including shootings,[5] and the income of heritable bonds,[6] but not to rights of superiority,[7] of patronage, of reversion, profits from minerals,[8] and the mansion house.[9] At common law,

[1] *Naismyth* v. *Boyes* (1899) 1 F. (H.L.) 69, 81; *Russell* v. *A.G.*, 1917 S.C. 28; *Cameron's Trs.* v. *McLean*, 1917 S.C. 416.

[2] *Lindsay's Trs.* v. *L.*, 1931 S.C. 586; *Findlay's Trs.* v. *F's Trs.*, 1941 S.C. 492.

[3] *Warrack* v. *W's Trs.*, 1934 S.L.T. 302; *Milne* v. *M's Trs.*, 1931 S.L.T. 336; *Alexander* v. *A's Trs.*, 1954 S.C. 436.

[4] *Sanderson* v. *Lockhart-Mure*, 1946 S.C. 298; *Campbell's Trs.* v. *C's Trs.*, 1950 S.C. 48.

[5] *Taylor* v. *Ovenstone's Trs.*, 1939 S.C. 786.

[6] Fraser, *H. & W.* II, 1086; *Rossborough's Trs.* v. *R.* (1888) 16 R. 157.

[7] *Nisbett* v. *N's Trs.* (1835) 13 S. 517.

[8] *Constable's Trs.* v. *C.* (1904) 6 F. 826; *Grosset* v. *G.*, 1959 S.L.T. 334.

[9] Ersk. II, 9, 44, 49; *Constable's Trs.* v. *C.* (1904) 6 F. 826.

the marriage must have subsisted for a year and a day, or a child been born of it.[1]

It formerly extended only to heritage in which the husband was infeft, and ranked before any of the husband's personal creditors,[2] but after 1924 it extended also to land held on a personal title capable of being completed by registration in the Register of Sasines, and to heritage held in trust for his behoof, but was postponed to the claim of any personal creditor.[3] It extended also to heritable securities.[4]

Terce vested without infeftment but the widow required to complete her title by service, and by kenning to the terce, a process which alloted a particular portion of the heritage for her exclusive possession. These were superseded by actions of declarator of right to terce, or of the annual value of the terce.[5] The terce might be redeemed at the instance of persons entitled to the fee of the heritage for a capital sum.[6] A right to terce might be held abandoned if no steps were taken to claim it.[7]

At common law terce was also exigible when the wife divorced the husband, just as if he were dead,[8] but this is no longer exigible.[9]

Lesser terce

Land already burdened by subsisting terce might be further charged, with lesser terce in favour of the fiar's widow. It amounted to a liferent of one-third of the profits of the lands under deduction of the main terce. When the prior widow died, lesser terce enlarged to the full terce.[10]

Exclusion of terce

A widow might have her claim to terce excluded by express discharge or renunciation, by acceptance of a conventional

[1] Ersk. II, 9, 51. Some authorities (Fraser, *H. & W.*, II, 1083; McLaren, *Wills*, §158) thought that this requisite was removed by the Intestate Moveable Succession Act, 1855, S. 7, but this view seems unwarranted: see Bell, *Conv.* II, 847.

[2] *Rossborough's Trs.* v. *R.* (1888) 16 R. 157; *Black's Trs.* v. *Scott* (1895) 3 S.L.T. 8.

[3] Conveyancing (Sc.) Act, 1924, S. 21(4), amd. Conveyancing Amdt. (Sc.) Act, 1938, S. 5.

[4] Titles to Land Consolidation (Sc.) Act, 1868, S. 117.

[5] Conveyancing (Sc.) Act, 1924, S. 21(1); cf. *de Serra Largo* v. *de S.L.'s Trs.*, 1933 S.L.T. 301.

[6] Conveyancing (Sc.) Act, 1924, S. 21(1) and (3); *Dickson* v. *D.*, 1931 S.L.T. 75; *Thomson's Trs.* v. *T.*, 1942 S.L.T. 22; *Russell* v. *Louden*, 1950 S.L.T. (Notes) 39.

[7] *Pringle's Exces.*, (1870) 8 M. 622.

[8] *Harvey* v. *Farquhar* (1872) 10 M. (H.L.) 26.

[9] Succession (Sc.) Act, 1964, S. 25.

[10] Ersk. II, 9, 47; Conveyancing (Sc.) Act, 1924, S. 21(3).

provision, as in a marriage contract, unless it appeared that the husband intended the widow to have her terce as well as the conventional provision,[1] and by the husband's complete alienation of terceable subjects.

Abolition of terce

Terce is not exigible from the estate of any person dying after 10th September, 1964,[2] and references in any deed taking effect thereafter to terce are of no effect.[3]

Legal rights exigible at common law from heritage-courtesy

At common law a surviving husband had a right of liferent of the whole of his late wife's heritable estate, provided that a child, who had been born alive, and heard to cry,[4] had been born of their marriage, who was, or would have been, if he had survived, the mother's heir.[5] Formerly it extended only to the wife's heritage acquired by succession but not to heritage acquired by singular title;[6] after 1874 it attached to all her heritage.[7] It attached to entailed lands, superiorities and lands held burgage, and after 1924 to lands held by trustees for behoof of the wife and to lands held on a personal title capable of completion by recording in the Register of Sasines,[8] and to the wife's heritable bonds.[9]

The child need not have survived to inherit but must have been born alive;[10] legitimation *per subsequens matrimonium* also sufficed.[11] A surviving child born to the wife by a previous marriage defeated the husband's right, because the right belonged to the widower as father of her heir rather than as husband.[12]

The right vested *ipso jure* and no service or other procedure was necessary to make up title. It might be redeemed at the option of persons entitled to the fee of the heritage on payment of a

[1] Act, 1681, c. 10; *Craik* v. *Penny* (1891) 19 R. 339; *Douglas* v. *D's Trs.* (1906) 13 S.L.T. 749; *Moss's Trs.* v. *M.*, 1916 2 S.L.T. 31.

[2] Succession (Sc.) Act, 1964, S. 10(1).

[3] Ibid., S. 33(1).

[4] *Roberton* v. *Moderator of General Assembly* (1833) 11 S. 297.

[5] Stair II, 6, 19; Ersk. II, 9, 52–4; Bell, *Comm.* I, 60; *Prin.* §1606; Fraser, *H. & W.*, II, 1118.

[6] Ersk. II, 9, 54; *Watt* v. *Wilkin* (1855) 13 R. 218.

[7] Conveyancing (Sc.) Act, 1874, S. 37; *Walker* v. *W's Trs.*, 1917 S.C. 46.

[8] *Lord Clinton* v. *Trefusis* (1869) 8 M. 370; Conveyancing (Sc.) Act, 1924, S. 21(4), amd. Conveyancing Amendment (Sc.) Act, 1938, S. 5.

[9] Titles to Land Consolidation (Sc.) Act, 1868, S. 117.

[10] *Roberton* v. *Moderator of General Assembly* (1833) 11 S. 297.

[11] *Crawfurd's Trs.* v. *Hart* (1802) Mor. 12698.

[12] Ersk. II, 9, 53.

capital sum.[1] As well as on death it was exigible if the husband divorced his wife, but it is no longer exigible.[2]

The right might be excluded by the husband's express discharge, but not by a conventional provision not declared to be in lieu of courtesy,[3] and it could be defeated by the wife's alienation of subjects from which courtesy was exigible.

Courtesy not now exigible

By the Succession (Sc.) Act, 1964, S. 10(1), the legal right of courtesy is not exigible out of the estate of a person dying after the commencement of that Act. By S. 33(1) references in any deed taking effect after that date to courtesy are of no effect.

Legal rights in moveable estate—jus relictae

At common law a surviving widow has a claim of *jus relictae*, to one-third of her husband's moveable estate if there are surviving children of the marriage or of a former marriage by him, or issue of predeceased children,[4] or to one-half if there are no surviving children or if all surviving children have discharged their claims to legitim. A former wife has no claim. The claim vests on his death, but is postponed to all claims of debt against the hsuband, to deathbed and funeral expenses and executry expenses. It is not a right of property in any particular part of the *ipsa corpora* of the deceased's estate, but merely a *jus crediti* for payment of a certain fraction of the value of the estate at the date of death.[5]

The fund against which the claim lies is the free moveable estate after deduction of claims of debt and expenses and, in cases of total or partial intestacy, of statutory prior rights.[6] It does not include funds which become part of the executry estate only after the deceased's death.[7] Personal bonds having a clause of interest are excluded from the estate liable, as also are heritable securities.[8] The fund is ascertained at the date of death and the claim is not affected by later appreciation or depreciation.[9] No

[1] Conveyancing (Sc.) Act, 1924, S. 21(3) and (9).

[2] Succession (Sc.) Act, 1964, S. 25.

[3] *Hamilton* v. *Boswell* (1720) Rob. 192, 346.

[4] Succession (Sc.) Act, 1964, S. 11(4).

[5] *Stewart* v. *Keiller* (1902) 4 F. 657; *Cameron's Trs.* v. *Maclean*, 1917 S.C. 416; see, however, *Millar* v. *M's Trs.*, 1914 1 S.L.T. 414.

[6] Succession (Sc.) Act, 1964, S. 10(2).

[7] *Findlay's Trs.* v. *F's Trs.*, 1941 S.C. 492.

[8] Titles to Land Consolidation (Sc.) Act, 1868, S. 117, amd. Succession (Sc.) Act, 1964, Sched. 3.

[9] *Gilchrist* v. *G's Trs.* (1889) 16 R. 1118; *Maben* v. *M's Exors.* (1901) 8 S.L.T. 486; *Moss' Trs.* v. *M.*, 1916 1 S.L.T. 321; cf. *Russell* v. *A.G.*, 1917 S.C. 28; *Alexander* v. *A's Trs.*, 1954 S.C. 436.

claim can be made in respect of any asset not passing to the executor.[1] Income falling into intestacy by reason of the statutory prohibitions on accumulations is excluded.[2] Personal bonds bearing interest were heritable *quoad jus relictae vel relicti* but are now moveable for these purposes.[3] Heritable bonds still heritable for these purposes.[4]

The widow is also entitled to the interest earned by her share from the date of death till payment, subject to income tax.[5]

If the widow is maintained by one of the children the expenditure on aliment may be set-off against her claim to *jus relictae*.[6]

If not claimed within the period of the long negative prescription the right is excluded by prescription.[7]

Legal rights in moveable estate—jus relicti

By statute,[8] a husband is entitled on the death of his wife to the same share and interest in her moveable estate as is taken by a widow in her husband's estate.[8] It also is of the nature of a debt, a certain share of the wife's estate fixed in value at the date of her death. No claim can be sustained where it would affect the spouse's ante-nuptial or post-nuptial marriage contract.[9]

The Conjugal Rights (Sc.) Act, 1861, S. 6, provides that after a decree of separation *a mensa et thoro* at the instance of a wife, her property on her decease intestate, passes to her heirs and representatives as if her husband had been then dead. In such a case the husband, being notionally dead, has no claim to *jus relicti*.

Similarly, former husbands have probably no claim.

It is exigible from the moveable estate after deduction of claims of debt and expenses and, in the case of total or partial intestacy, of statutory prior rights.[10] The claim may be discharged, or satisfied by conventional provision, as in a marriage contract.[11]

[1] *Ventisei* v. *V's Exors.*, 1966 S.C. 21; constrast *Beveridge* v. *B's Exrx.*, 1938 S.C. 160 (discretionary death gratuity included).

[2] *Lindsay's Trs.* v. *L.*, 1931 S.C. 586.

[3] Conveyancing (Sc.) Act, 1924, S. 22.

[4] Titles to Land Consolidation (Sc.) Act, 1868, S. 117, amd. Succession (Sc.) Act, 1964, Sched. 3.

[5] cf. *Summers* v. *S's Trs.* (1893) 1 S.L.T. 77.

[6] *Mackenzie* v. *M's Trs.* (1873) 11 M. 681; *Wick* v. *W.* (1898) 1 F. 199.

[7] *Campbell's Trs.* v. *C's Trs.*, 1950 S.C. 48; *Pettigrew* v. *Harton*, 1956 S.C. 67; cf. *Mill's Trs.* v. *M's Exors.*, 1965 S.L.T. 375.

[8] Married Women's Property (Sc.) Act, 1881, S. 6; *Simon's Tr.* v. *Neilson* (1890) 18 R. 135; *Russel* v. *A.G.*, 1917 S.C. 28.

[9] 1881 Act, S. 8.

[10] Succession (Sc.) Act, 1964, S. 10(2).

[11] *Buntine* v. *B's Trs.* (1894) 21 R. 714.

Legal rights in moveable estate—legitim

Legitim (*legitima portio*) or bairn's part is the legal right of children and more remote issue to a share in a deceased parent's moveable estate.[1] It is exigible from the estate of each parent in turn and it matters not which parent predeceases the other.[2] The claim is to one-third of the net moveable estate of the deceased if there is also a surviving spouse claiming *jus relictae vel relicti*, or to one-half if there is no surviving spouse or if the surviving spouse has discharged his or her right of *jus relictae vel relicti*.[3] Where one spouse had divorced the other the division on the death of either spouse is still tripartite.[4]

The claim is a debt due by the entire free moveables and not a burden on any part thereof more than on any other,[5] but is postponed to the deceased parent's debts, to deathbed and funeral, and executry, expenses and, in the case of total or partial intestacy, to the claim of a surviving spouse to statutory prior rights.[6] A party entitled to legitim is not entitled to demand any particular part of the deceased's moveables in satisfaction of his claim.[7]

The legitim fund

The legitim fund consists of the whole free moveable estate of which the deceased parent was possessed at the time of death,[8] but not heritable securities[9] or real burdens on land.[10] The fund may be diminished by conversion of moveables into heritage, or by the deceased's alienation of his moveables *inter vivos*[11] so long as it was not a simulate transaction designed merely to defeat the children's rights.[12]

The value of the fund has to be ascertained at the date of

1 Ersk. III, 9, 22.

2 Prior to the Married Women's Property (Sc.) Act, 1881, S. 7, legitim was due only from a father's estate.

3 Ersk. III, 9, 19–20.

4 *Gavin's Trs.* v. *Walker's Trs.* (1907) 15 S.L.T. 681.

5 *Macdougal* v. *Wilson* (1858) 20 D. 658; *Snody's Trs.* v. *Gibson's Trs.* (1883) 10 R. 599.

6 Succession (Sc.) Act, 1964, S. 10(2).

7 *Cameron's Trs.* v. *Maclean*, 1917 S.C. 416.

8 *Snody's Trs.* v. *Gibson's Trs.* (1883) 10 R. 599; cf. *Chalmers' Trs.* v. *C.* (1882) 9 R. 743; *Monteith* v. *M's Trs.* (1882) 9 R. 982.

9 Titles to Land Consolidation (Sc.) Act, 1868, S. 117.

10 Conveyancing (Sc.) Act, 1874, S. 30.

11 *Skinner* v. *Beveridge* (1872) 10 S.L.R. 12; *Boustead* v. *Gardner* (1879) 7 R. 139; *Hutton's Trs.* v. *H's Trs.*, 1917 S.C. 860.

12 *Nicolson's Assignee* v. *Macalister's Trs.* (1841) 3 D. 675; *Buchanan* v. *B.* (1876) 3 R. 556, 559.

death,[1] and no account can be taken of losses incurred after realization of the estate,[2] nor of subsequent appreciation.[3]

Who are entitled to claim legitim

Claims on the legitim fund are competent to the children of the deceased,[4] by whichever of his or her marriages they were born,[5] including posthumous children.[6] At common law claims were limited to legitimate children[7] but illegitimate children now have an equal claim.[8] At common law children only could claim,[9] but by statute[10] if a child who would have been entitled to legitim has predeceased his issue take the share their parent would have done if he had survived the deceased. If all those entitled to legitim are related to the deceased in the same degree the division is *per capita*, but if they are related in different degrees the division is *per stirpes*. Adopted children now fall to be treated for all purposes of succession as children of the adopter[11] and hence may claim legitim. Stepchildren have no claim.[12]

But a child succeeding to heritage as heir-at-law of the deceased was not entitled at common law to share in legitim unless he collated the heritage.[13] If on the other hand an heir-at-law was the only surviving child unforisfamiliated, or the heritage devolved on heirs-portioners who were the only surviving children unforisfamiliated, he or they were entitled to the whole legitim fund as well as to the heritage.[14] An heir-at-law who had been disinherited was entitled to claim legitim.[15]

Shares in the legitim fund vest on the parent's death in all the children surviving, and now in them and in the issue of predeceased children, but excluding any children who have renounced or discharged legitim. The parent can neither deprive

[1] *McMurray* v. *McM's Trs.* (1852) 14 D. 1048. But see *Alexander* v. *A.*, 1954 S.C. 436.
[2] *E. Dalhousie* v. *Crokat* (1868) 6 M. 659; *Russel* v. *A.G.*, 1917 S.C. 28.
[3] *Ross* v. *Masson* (1843) 5 D. 483; *McMurray, supra*; *Gilchrist* v. *G's Trs.* (1889) 16 R. 1118.
[4] cf. *Cairns* v. *C's Trs.*, 1916 1 S.L.T. 42 (child disinherited by will).
[5] *Chapman* v. *Gibson* (1631) Mor. 8163; *Henderson* v. *Sanders* (1634) Mor. 8164; *Bishop's Trs.* v. *B.* (1894) 21 R. 728; *Elliot's Exrx.* v. *E.*, 1953 S.C. 43.
[6] *Jervey* v. *Watt* (1762) Mor. 8170.
[7] As to legitimated child see *Blair* v. *Kay's Trs.*, 1940 S.L.T. 464.
[8] Law Reform (Misc. Prov.) (Sc.) Act, 1968, S. 2.
[9] cf. *Macnab* v. *M's Exor.* (1894) 2 S.L.T. 350.
[10] Succession (Sc.) Act, 1964, S. 11.
[11] Ibid., S. 23(1). See also Law Reform (Misc. Prov.) (Sc.) Act, 1966, S. 5.
[12] *Henderson* v. *Sanders* (1634) Mor. 8164.
[13] *Gilmour's Trs.* v. *G.*, 1922 S.C. 753.
[14] *Countess Dowager of Kintore* v. *E. Kintore* (1886) 13 R. (H.L.) 93; *Cairns* v. *C.'s Trs.*, 1916 1 S.L.T. 42.
[15] *Cairns* v. *C's Trs.*, 1916 1 S.L.T. 42.

issue of their right to legitim nor apportion it unequally among them.[1]

If any child entitled to legitim does not claim it the amount released does not accresce to those claiming but falls into the part of the estate disposable by will or the rules of intestacy.[2]

Interest is due on a claim for legitim which the executor has unduly delayed to pay.[3] A claim not made within the period of the long negative prescription is thereafter barred.[4]

If legitim is insufficient for children's aliment and education they are entitled to have the inadequacy supplied from the free estate.[5]

Collation inter haeredes *at common law*

At common law if a child of the deceased was heir-at-law and succeeded to the deceased's heritable property, he might participate in legitim, or dead's part, only on condition of collating the heritage, i.e. of throwing the heritage into a common fund with the legitim fund and sharing it equally with those entitled to the moveables.[6] There was no right to collate with the surviving spouse who claimed *jus relictae vel relicti*, nor where the heir-at-law was not one of the heirs in moveables.[7]

The obligation to collate extended also to whatever the heirs-at-law had received by gift, or deed *inter vivos* or testamentary, provided he would otherwise have succeeded to it as heir,[8] but a person who was not the heir-at-law did not have to collate heritage bequeathed to him.[9] It probably sufficed to collate the value in the division of the estate, and it was not necessary to convey the heritage to himself and the heirs in moveables *pro indiviso*.[9] But collation was excluded if the heir had sold the heritage.[10] If the

1 *Monteith* v. *M's Trs.* (1882) 9 R. 982, 994.

2 *Fisher* v. *Dixon* (1840) 2 D. 1121; (1843) 2 Bell 63; *Stewart* v. *S's Trs.*, 1909 1 S.L.T. 340; *Smith's Trs.* v. *S.*, 1912 1 S.L.T. 484.

3 *Gilchrist* v. *G's Trs.* (1889) 16 R. 1118; *Bishop's Trs.* v. *B.* (1894) 21 R. 728; *Ross* v. *R.* (1896) 23 R. 802; but see *Grant* v. *G.* (1898) 25 R. 948; *Wick* v. *W.* (1898) 1 F. 199; *Kearon* v. *Thomson's Trs.*, 1949 S.C. 287.

4 *Sanderson* v. *Lockhart-Mure*, 1946 S.C. 298; *Campbell's Trs.* v. *C's Trs.*, 1950 S.C. 4.

5 *Urquhart's Exors.* v. *Abbott* (1899) 1 F. 1149.

6 *McCaw* v. *McC.* (1787) Mor. 2383; *Anstruther* v. *A.* (1836) 14 S. 272; 2 S. & McL. 369; *Gilmour* v. *G's Trs.*, 1920 2 S.L.T. 369; *Colville's J.F.* v. *Nicoll*, 1914 S.C. 62.

7 *Jamieson* v. *Walker* (1896) 23 R. 547; *Robertson* v. *R.* (1907) 15 S.L.T. 249; *Colville's J.F.*, *supra*.

8 *Murray* v. *M.* (1678) Mor. 2374, 4807; *Balmain* v. *Glenfarquhar* (1719) Mor. 2378; *Dawson's Trs.* v. *D.*, 1913 2 S.L.T. 210; *Gilmour* v. *G's Trs.*, 1920 2 S.L.T. 369.

9 *Fisher's Trs.* v. *F.* (1850) 13 D. 245; *McCall's Tr.* v. *McCall's C.B.* (1901) 3 F. 1065; *Waddell's J.F.* v. *W.*, 1924 S.C. 877.

10 *McCall's Tr.* v. *McCall's C.B.* (1901) 3 F. 1065.

heir died without having elected to collate or not, his representatives might do so in his place.[1]

There was no need for collation where the heir-at-law was also the sole heir in moveables.[2]

Under the Succession (Sc.) Act, 1964, S. 1, the estate of an intestate devolves without distinction between heritable and moveable property, so that the special position of the heir-at-law has for nearly all purposes[3] disappeared. The need in at least most cases for collation *inter haeredes* has also disappeared though the doctrine has not been abolished.

Forisfamiliation

A child may be forisfamiliated by having renounced his right gratuitously or onerously,[4] or by having discharged it in return for an *inter vivos* payment. The children may as a class be forisfamiliated by conventional provisions in their favour by their parents' ante-nuptial marriage contract.[5]

Payments to account of legitim

Sums paid by a parent during his lifetime to a child must be deemed advances of legitim, particularly if an obligation of debt be taken therefor.[6] Advances may be made expressly on such terms.[7] There is no case for imputation of advances where only one of several children claims legitim.[8]

Collation inter liberos

In order to maintain equality among children claiming legitim any child who has in the parent's lifetime received advances must in general collate the advances, i.e. add them to the legitim fund and have them set against the share falling to that child on equal division.[9] Whether a particular benefit to a child is to be held an advance requiring to be collated depends on its nature and the circumstances in which it was made.[10] Thus collation is

[1] *Adam's Exrx.* v. *Maxwell*, 1921 S.C. 418; *Waddell's J.F.*, *supra*.

[2] Ersk. III, 9, 3; *Anstruther*, *supra*.

[3] For exceptions see 1964 Act, S. 37.

[4] *Obers* v. *Paton's Trs.* (1897) 24 R. 719; *Scott's Trs.* v. *S.* (1902) 40 S.L.R. 133.

[5] Ersk. III, 9, 23.

[6] *Nisbet's Trs.* v. *N.* (1868) 6 M. 567; *Trevelyan* v. *T.* (1873) 11 M. 516.

[7] *Gilmour's Trs.* v. *G.*, 1922 S.C. 753.

[8] *Coat's Trs.* v. *C.*, 1914 S.C. 744.

[9] If the child has already received more than its share, it is doubtful if the excess can be recovered.

[10] Stair III, 8, 45; Ersk. III, 9, 24; Bell, *Prin.* §1588; *Fisher* v. *Dixon* (1840) 2 D. 1121; 2 Bell, 63; see also *Duncan* v. *Crichton's Trs.*, 1917 S.C. 728.

necessary in cases of advances to set the child up in trade, for a settlement in the world or for a marriage portion,[1] to enable him to purchase an Army commission,[2] advances to account of legitim,[3] an interest settled on a daughter on marriage,[4] a trust provision for a child's maintenance till majority and her subsequent liferent,[5] but not of sums paid to aliment or educate the child,[6] of remuneration for services rendered,[7] of a provision of a heritable right, which does not affect the legitim fund,[8] of a legacy, which comes out of dead's part of the estate,[9] nor of a loan or debt, which is owed to the whole estate.[10]

But no advance will fall to be collated if the intention adequately appears that the parent's intention had been that the child should have it as a gift in addition to his share of legitim.[11] It is competent for a parent to agree with a child that certain advances are to be taken as payments to account of legitim and set against the sum ultimately payable to the child.[12]

Collation applies only between claimants on the legitim fund; it has no application where there is only one child, or only one claiming legitim, in which case neither the trustees nor any other children can require the claiming child to collate advances, nor can the claiming child require non-claiming children to collate advances.[13] Trustees representing a residuary legatee cannot require collation.[14] It has no application between a surviving spouse and children.[15]

Where collation applies, interest on the advance from its date need not be added to the capital, in the absence of contrary indication from the parent.[16]

Collation by child's representatives

A grandchild, or more remote issue, of the deceased, who claims legitim under the Succession (Sc.) Act, 1964, S. 11,

1 Bell, *Prin.* §1588; *Douglas* v. *D.* (1876) 4 R. 105.
2 *Nisbet's Trs.* v. *N.* (1868) 6 M. 567.
3 *Young* v. *Y's Trs.*, 1910 S.C. 275; *Gilmour's Trs.* v. *G.*, 1922 S.C. 753.
4 *Monteith* v. *M's Trs.* (1882) 9 R. 982.
5 *Elliot's Exrx.* v. *E.*, 1953 S.C. 43.
6 Ersk. III, 9, 24; *Elliot's Exrx.*, *supra.*
7 *Minto* v. *Kirkpatrick* (1833) 11 S. 632.
8 Ersk. III, 9, 25.
9 *Ibid.*
10 *Webster* v. *Rettie* (1859) 21 D. 915.
11 Ersk. III, 9, 24; *Douglas* v. *D.* (1876) 4 R. 105.
12 *Young* v. *Y's Trs.*, 1910 S.C. 275; *Gilmour's Trs.* v. *G.*, 1922 S.C. 753.
13 *Monteith* v. *M's Trs.* (1882) 9 R. 982; *Coat's Trs.* v. *C.*, 1914 S.C. 744; *Gilmour's Trs.*, *supra.*
14 *Collins* v. *Collins' Trs.* (1898) 5 S.L.T. 256.
15 Ersk. III, 9, 25.
16 *Gilmour's Trs.*, *supra.*

must collate any advances made to him, and the proportion appropriate to him of any advances made to any person through whom he derives such entitlement.[1]

Alteration or defeat of legal rights

The deceased might in his lifetime alter the rights of his relatives to legal rights by converting most of his property into heritage, thereby formerly increasing terce or courtesy at the expense of *jus relictae vel relicti* and legitim, and now diminishing the fund for relict and issue. He might also alienate his estate in whole or in part, gratuitously or onerously, and so leave little or nothing to bear these claims.[2] But if any deed of alienation, though *ex facie* divesting the deceased, in fact left property under his command, or if there be any trust or arrangement whereby he retains the benefit of the property or is entitled to require its reconveyance, he is not divested and the arrangement is ineffectual to exclude claims to legal rights,[3] though he may do so effectively by alienating his property outright reserving his own liferent,[4] and that even though the disposition were effected for the express purpose of excluding claims to legal rights.[5]

Renunciation of legal rights

A spouse or child may, *stante matrimonio*, renounce his or her legal rights, but only by clear expression of intention,[6] or by clear implication, as by acceptance by a wife in her husband's lifetime of a liferent provided for her by a post-nuptial marriage contract, acceptance being inconsistent with a claim to part of the fee as *jus relictae*.[7]

Discharge of legal rights

The legal rights of a spouse or children might both, prior to 1964, be discharged in the lifetime of the spouses and parents,

[1] Succession (Sc.) Act, 1964, S. 11(3).

[2] e.g. *Skinner* v. *Beveridge* (1872) 10 S.L.R. 12; *Allan* v. *Stark* (1901) 8 S.L.T. 468.

[3] Bell, *Prin.* §1584–5; Fraser, *H. & W.*, II, 1000; *Lashley* v. *Hog* (1804) 4 Pat. 581; *Nicolson's Assignee* v. *Hunter*, 3 March 1814, F.C.; *Buchanan* v. *B.* (1876) 3 R. 556; *Boustead* v. *Gardner* (1879) 7 R. 139; *Allan* v. *Stark* (1901) 8 S.L.T. 468; *Fann* v. *McDonald*, 1913 S.C. 937; *Hutton's Trs.* v. *H's Trs.*, 1916 S.C. 860; *Drysdale's Trs.* v. *D.*, 1940 S.C. 85.

[4] *Collie* v. *Pirie's Trs.* (1851) 13 D. 506.

[5] *Skinner* v. *Beveridge* (1872) 10 S.L.R. 12; *Boustead* v. *Gardner* (1879) 7 R. 139; *Scott* v. *S.*, 1930 S.C. 903.

[6] *Scott's Trs.* v. *S.* (1902) 10 S.L.T. 122.

[7] *Riddel* v. *Dalton* (1781) Mor. 6457; *Edward* v. *Cheyne* (1888) 15 R. (H.L.) 33; *Taylor's* v. *T's Trs.* (1897) 5 S.L.T. 125; *Smart* v. *S.*, 1926 S.C. 392.

in their ante-nuptial marriage contract, either expressly,[1] or impliedly, as by settlement of the settler's whole estate at his death on his wife and children,[2] or by a wife's acceptance *stante matrimonio* of a liferent provided in a post-nuptial marriage contract or other deed.[3] It appeared that a discharge was effectual if no provision were made for the children or only an illusory provision.[4] The effect of discharge was that that person was treated as dead,[5] and the sum released by his discharge increased the sum available for other claimants to legal rights. If all claims to legal rights were discharged the sum released increased the dead's part of free estate. By the Succession (Sc.) Act, 1964, S. 12, nothing in an ante-nuptial marriage contract executed after the commencement of that Act is to operate on the death of either spouse to exclude the right of any child or more remote issue of the marriage to legitim out of the estate of that party unless such child or issue shall elect to accept in lieu of legitim the provision made in his favour under the contract. The liberty of a spouse to discharge legal rights by marriage contract is unaffected.

A child may also, *stante matrimonio*, discharge his parent or parents of any claim to legitim he could otherwise make. This may be gratuitous,[6] or onerous,[7] express or implied, but conduct will not raise an implication of discharge if parties were in ignorance of their legal rights.[8] A spouse may by post-nuptial marriage contract discharge *jus relictae* expressly or impliedly.[9]

An inference of discharge is not necessarily to be drawn from long delay in claiming.[10]

Satisfaction of legal rights

Prima facie any testamentary provision for or bequest to a surviving spouse or child is additional to any claims to legal

1 *Maitland* v. *M.* (1843) 6 D. 244; *Sim* v. *S.* (1901) 4 F. 944; *Dunbar Dunbar* v. *D.D.* (1905) 7 F. (H.L.) 92.

2 McLaren, *Wills*, I, 136; *Home* v. *Watson* (1757) 5 B.S. 330; *Fisher's Trs.* v. *F.* (1844) 7 D. 129; *Durrant Steuart's Trs.* v. *D.S.* (1891) 18 R. 1114; *Buntine* v. *B's Trs.* (1894) 21 R. 714; *Murray's Trs.* v. *M.* (1901) 3 F. 820; contrast *Lyon's Trs.* v. *Miller* (1903) 5 F. 1096; *Douglas* v. *D's Trs.* (1906) 13 S.L.T. 749.

3 *Edward* v. *Cheyne* (1888) 15 R. (H.L.) 33; *Smart* v. *S.*, 1926 S.C. 392. A claim thereto was inconsistent with a claim to part of the fee *jure relictae*.

4 *E. Kintore* v. *Dowager Countess of Kintore* (1884) 11 R. 1013; affd. (1886) 13 R. (H.L.) 93; *Simpson's Tr.* v. *Taylor*, 1912 S.C. 280; *Ramsay* v. *R's Trs.* (1905) 12 S.L.T. 654; *Galloway's Trs.* v. *G.*, 1943 S.C. 339.

5 Ersk. III, 9, 20.

6 *Obers* v. *Paton's Trs.* (1897) 24 R. 719.

7 *Scott's Trs.* v. *S.* (1902) 10 S.L.T. 122; *Ramsay*, *supra.*

8 *Countess Dowager of Kintore* v. *E. Kintore* (1886) 13 R. (H.L.) 93; see also *Rait* v. *Arbuthnot* (1892) 19 R. 687.

9 *Smart* v. *S.*, 1926 S.C. 392.

10 *Mackenzie* v. *M's Trs.* (1873) 11 M. 681; *Wick* v. *W.* (1898) 1 F. 199.

rights competent to that person. But a testator may provide that such a bequest is given in satisfaction of legal rights, and if the spouse or child elects to accept the provision, that bars any claim for legal rights as well, the sum released going to increase the dead's part of the estate out of which the bequest has been paid.[1]

A provision that a legacy is given in satisfaction of legal rights prevents the legatee, if he accepts, from making any claim on the estate which conflicts with the scheme of the testator's settlement, and may be held to be intended to protect the interests not only of the beneficiaries under the settlement but also of the heirs on intestacy. In this case acceptance wholly bars a claim for legal rights.[2] But the declaration may be held intended to exclude claims to legal rights only in so far as necessary for the protection of the settlement, in which case a claim to legal rights may be made in the event of any of the estate falling into intestacy.[3]

If the bequest to a child in satisfaction of legal rights is a bequest in liferent, the fee going to his issue, and the child elects to claim legitim, his forfeiture of the liferent does not in general involve forfeiture of his issue's right to the fee, the bequests of liferent and fee being deemed independent.[4] If, however, the deed is interpreted as directing that the fee is dependent on or inseparable from the bequest of liferent, the election to take legitim involves forfeiture of the issue's right to the fee also.[5]

Formerly a legacy, if intended to be in satisfaction of legal rights, had to be stated expressly to be so, but in the case of settlements made since 10th September 1964, a declaration that a provision made in favour of a spouse or issue of the testator is made in full and final satisfaction of legal rights is implied unless expressly excluded.[6]

An express provision of legal rights may be made to an entitled person in a will and may be held to be a legacy and not merely a direction to pay legal rights.[7]

[1] *Fisher's Trs.* v. *Dixon* (1842) 2 D. 1121; affd. (1843) 2 Bell 63; *Dunbar Dunbar* v. *D.D.* (1905) 7 F. (H.L.) 92; *Johnstone's Trs.* v. *J.*, 1936 S.C. 766.

[2] *Sim* v. *S.* (1902) 4 F. 944.

[3] *Naismith* v. *Boyes* (1899) 1 F. (H.L.) 79; *McGregor's Trs.* v. *Kimbell*, 1911 S.C. 1196; *Petrie's Trs.* v. *Manders's Trs.*, 1954 S.C. 430.

[4] *Fisher* v. *Dixon* (1831) 10 S. 55; 6 W. & S. 431; *Jack* v. *Marshall* (1879) 6 R. 543; *Brown's Trs.* v. *Gregson*, 1916 S.C. 97.

[5] *Campbell's Trs.* v. *C.* (1889) 16 R. 1007; *McCaull's Trs.* v. *McC.* (1900) 3 F. 222.

[6] Succession (Sc.) Act, 1964, S. 13.

[7] *Galt's Trs.* v. *G.*, 1945 S.C. 183.

CHAPTER 111
INTESTATE SUCCESSION

THE rules of intestate succession apply to determine the devolution of a deceased's property, so far as it is not required to pay debts and government duties, and to implement claims for statutory prior rights,[1] or for legal rights,[2] where the deceased (a) left no testamentary directions for the disposal of his property, or (b) any directions are ineffectual or fail of effect, or (c) in so far as they do not dispose of the deceased's whole estate. The part of the estate not required for prior rights and legal rights and hence freely disposable is frequently known as dead's part. The rights of relatives on the deceased's death cannot be excluded merely by disinheriting them, but only by giving by will to other persons what would otherwise go to them.[3]

Debts

The deceased's debts are a first charge against his estate. Formerly, though a creditor might pursue either heir in heritage or executor of moveables,[4] *inter se* the former was liable for debts heritable or secured over heritage and the latter for moveable debts,[5] either having a right of relief against the other.[6] Under the Succession (Sc.) Act, 1964, the whole estate vests for the purposes of administration in the executor[7] and claims may be brought against him, but the Act does not alter any rule whereby any particular debt of a deceased falls to be paid out of any particular part of his estate.[7] Hence debts in the form of heritable securities[8] and annuities[9] are still payable out of heritable estate. The price of land bought but not conveyed is payable out of the moveable estate, the land falling into the heritable estate[10] and conversely.[11]

1 *Infra.*
2 Ch. 110, *supra.*
3 *Cowan's Trs.* v. *C.* (1887) 14 R. 670.
4 *B.L. Co.* v. *Reay* (1850) 12 D. 949.
5 Ersk. III, 9, 48; *Duncan* v. *D.* (1882) 10 R. 1042.
6 Ersk., *supra.*
7 S. 14.
8 *Bell's Trs.* v. *B.* (1884) 12 R. 85.
9 *Breadalbane's Trs.* v. *Jamieson* (1873) 11 M. 912.
10 *Ramsay* v. *R.* (1887) 15 R. 25; *Fairlie's Trs.* v. *F's C.B.*, 1932 S.C. 216.
11 *Heron* v. *Espie* (1856) 18 D. 917; *McArthur's Exors.* v. *Guild*, 1908 S.C. 743.

Relatives entitled to claim

The persons entitled fall to be ascertained as at the date of the intestate's death or, if intestacy results from the failure of a testamentary provision, the testator's death.[1] A person claiming to be the deceased's spouse must, if there is doubt, prove the marriage.[2] At common law only legitimate relatives might succeed on intestacy. By the Legitimacy Act, 1926, S. 9, an illegitimate child, or, if deceased, his issue, became entitled, if the mother died intestate and without leaving legitimate issue, to the same interest in her estate as would belong to the child or its issue if legitimate, and if an illegitimate child died intestate, his mother became entitled to any interest to which she would have been entitled if the child had been legitimate and she had been the only surviving parent. By the Law Reform (Misc. Prov.) (Sc.) Act, 1968, S. 1, an illegitimate child now has practically the same rights in succession as one legitimate. Legitimated children have the same rights in succession as children born legitimate. Adopted children had prior to 1964 no rights of succession to their adoptive parents but retained any rights they might have in the estates of their natural parents. By the Succession (Sc.) Act, 1964, Ss. 23—4, an adopted person has to be treated as the child of the adopter for all purposes of succession, except (S. 37(1)) as regards titles, honours and dignities, and (S. 23(3)) where a deed prescribes that property is to devolve along with such a title.

COMMON LAW SYSTEM

In the case of deaths prior to 10th September 1964 a common law system, latterly amended in detail by statutes, applied. A distinction had to be drawn between heritable and moveable property and, after satisfying claims to prior rights[3] and to legal rights,[4] separate, though similar, rules of devolution applied to the two bodies of property, with further provisions where a person might claim under both heads. In both cases the broad scheme of devolution was, firstly to descendants, whom failing to collaterals, whom failing to ascendants and their collaterals. The common law system still applies to any title, coat of arms, honour

[1] *Lord* v. *Colvin* (1865) 3 M. 1083; *Gregory's Trs.* v. *Alison* (1889) 10 R. (H.L.) 10; *Wilson's Trs.* v. *W's Trs.* (1894) 22 R. 62.

[2] cf. *Wallace* v. *Fife Coal Co.*, 1909 S.C. 682.

[3] Ch. 110, *supra*.

[4] Ch. 110, *supra*.

or dignity transmissible on the death of the holder thereof,[1] and applied to the succession to the tenancy of any croft, within the Crofters (Sc.) Act, 1955, S. 3(1), until 1968.[2]

Succession to heritage

Succession to heritage at common law depended on the feudal principle of the devolution, if possible, of land undivided to one male heir, the heir-at-law, who would be responsible for the feudal military services due from the land. Only failing males did the succession open to females and then equally to all females related in the same degree, as heirs-portioners.

The succession opened successively to (A) the descendants, (B) the collaterals, and (C) the ascendants of the deceased. At every stage a single male heir was preferred to females; among males, except where the devolution was to a collateral, the estate devolved on the eldest to the exclusion of the younger; and there was an infinite right of representation, so that one who would have been heir had he not predeceased was represented in the succession by his own heir or heirs in preference to a later-ranking relative of the same degree who had survived. When the estate, failing males, devolved on females, all females of the same degree of propinquity took equally in common,[3] as heirs-portioners, with representation, save that the eldest heir-portioner was held entitled to certain subjects as her *praecipuum*, without liability to compensate her sisters;[4] these included titles of honour, as being indivisible; the principal mansion house or family seat with necessary adjuncts, but not villas or country-houses;[5] and a superiority with its casualties, but subject to compensating her sisters for feuduties yielded by the superiority.[6] Among collaterals the full-blood excluded the half-blood, but failing the full-blood, collaterals of the half-blood consanguinean (by the same father) succeeded; collaterals of the half-blood uterine (by the same mother) had no right of succession.

The inheritance to heritage accordingly opened successively to (A) (1) the deceased's eldest son, with representation by his children if he had predeceased; (2) his younger sons in order of seniority, with representation; (3) his daughters, as heirs-portioners, with representation of any who had predeceased by her

1 Succession (Sc.) Act, 1964, S. 37(1).
2 Law Reform (Misc. Prov.) (Sc.) Act, 1968, S. 8.
3 *Cargill* v. *Muir* (1837) 15 S. 408.
4 Stair III, 5, 11; Ersk. III, 8, 5.
5 *Callendar* v. *Harvey*, 1916 S.C. 420.
6 Ersk. III, 8, 13; *McNeight* v. *Lockhart* (1843) 6 D. 128.

sons, in their order; (B) (4) the deceased's next younger brother, with representation; (5) other younger brothers in descending order, with representation; (6) his next elder brother, with representation; (7) other elder brothers in ascending order, with representation; (8) his sisters, as heirs-portioners, with representation of any who had predeceased; (C) (9) his father; (10) his father's younger brothers in descending order, with representation; (11) his father's elder brothers in ascending order, with representation; (12) his father's sisters as heirs-portioners; (13) his paternal grandfather; (14) his paternal grandfather's brothers, and so on. The intestate's mother and her relatives had no right of succession to heritable rights. Failing any person entitled as heir the heritage fell to the Crown as *ultimus haeres*.

Succession to moveables

In succession to moveables the moveable estate was divisible, subject to prior rights and legal rights, equally among the next-of-kin of the deceased. Primogeniture and the preference of males over females did not apply.

The succession opened successively to (A) the descendants, (B) the collaterals, and (C) the ascendants. At common law no right of representation was recognized. In each group relatives of the full-blood excluded those of the half-blood, though the half-blood consanguinean (i.e. by the same father) succeeded in preference to the full-blood of a postponed group. Accordingly, the succession opened successively to (A) (1) the surviving children equally; (2) the surviving grandchildren equally; (B) (3) surviving brothers and sisters equally; (C) (4) the father; (5) the father's surviving brothers and sisters equally; (6) the paternal grandfather; (7) the paternal grandfather's surviving brothers and sisters equally; and so on. The deceased's mother and relatives through her had no claim.

The Intestate Moveable Succession (Sc.) Act, 1855, introduced representation of any of the next of kin who had predeceased by their children, but not beyond brothers' and sisters' descendants.[1] The widened group of next of kin was known as the heirs *in mobilibus*, and such heirs succeeded, if all of the same degree, *per capita*,[2] and if of different degrees, *per stirpes*.

[1] 1855 Act, S. 1; *Ormiston* v. *Broad* (1862) 1 M. 10; *Finlayson's Exor.* v. *Hastie*, 1916 1 S.L.T. 123.

[2] *Turner* (1869) 8 M. 222; *Macmillan* v. *M.*, 1909 1 S.L.T. 35; *Finlayson's Exor.* v. *Hastie*, 1916 1 S.L.T. 123.

Where there were no descendants the father, and subsequently the mother, had right to a half of the moveables in preference to collaterals or their descendants.[1] Where there were no descendants, failing collaterals consanguinean and their descendants and parents, collaterals uterine and their descendants had right to half of the moveables.[2] A widow was never among the heirs *in mobilibus*.[3]

The Intestate Husband's Estate (Sc.) Acts, 1911 and 1919, as later amended, gave a surviving spouse a statutory prior right, in addition to legal rights, where there was no lawful issue, which in many cases excluded the claims of the heirs *in mobilibus*.[4] Failing any entitled person the moveables fell to the Crown as *ultimus haeres*.[5]

Mixed estates—collation inter haeredes

Where an estate comprised both heritage and moveables the heir-at-law was not entitled to share in the moveables also, either in legitim or in dead's part.[6] He might, however, share if he collated, i.e. put the heritage into a common fund with the moveables and shared it equally with those entitled to legitim and/or as next-of-kin. He could not collate with a surviving spouse taking *jus relictae vel relicti*. No case for collation arose if the heir-at-law were also the sole heir *in mobilibus*,[7] or heirs-portioners the only heirs *in mobilibus*. Nor was an heir-at-law entitled to collate if he were not also one of the heirs *in mobilibus*.[8] Heirs-portioners, if not the only heirs *in mobilibus*, had to collate if they wished to share in the moveable estate.[9]

The heir-at-law had to collate not only the heritage to which he succeeded as such, but whatever he might have received by will or by deed *inter vivos* or *mortis causa* if he would otherwise have succeeded to it as heir-at-law.[10]

To effect collation it was sufficient to bring the value of the heritage into account for the division of the estate,[11] but it was not

[1] 1855 Act, S. 3, amended by Intestate Moveable Succession (Sc.) Act, 1919, S. 1.
[2] 1855 Act, S. 5.
[3] *Inglis* v. *I.* (1869) 7 M. 435.
[4] Ch. 110, *supra*.
[5] Stair IV, 31, 1; Ersk. III, 10, 2; Bell, *Prin.* §1669.
[6] *McCaw* v. *McC.* (1787) Mor 2383; *Anstruther* v. *A.* (1836) 14 S. 272, 282.
[7] *Anstruther*, *supra*; affd. (1836) 2 S. & McL. 369.
[8] *Jamieson* v. *Walker* (1896) 23 R. 547; *Robertson* v. *R.* (1907) 15 S.L.T. 249; *Colville's J.F.* v. *Nicoll*, 1914 S.C. 62.
[9] *Anstruther*, *supra*.
[10] *Murray* v. *M.* (1678) Mor. 2374.
[11] McLaren, *Wills*, I, 156; *Fisher's Trs.* v. *F.* (1850) 13 D. 245; but see *Waddell's J.F.* v. *W.*, 1924 S.C. 877.

competent to accept the heritage, sell it, and offer to bring in the price.[1] If the heir died without having elected, his testamentary representative might elect in his stead.[2]

The obligation to collate might also arise where a mixed estate was destined to persons 'legally entitled thereto' or in similar terms.[3]

Collation by representatives

The Intestate Moveable Succession (Sc.) Act, 1855, provided that where the person predeceasing would have been the heir in heritage of the intestate, his child, being heir in heritage of the intestate, was entitled to collate the heritage to the effect of claiming for himself, or for himself and other issue, the share of the moveable estate of the intestate which might have been claimed by the predeceaser on collation if he had survived the intestate. This right is confined to those taking by representation under the Act, i.e. to descendants of the deceased or of his brothers and sisters.[4]

STATUTORY SCHEME OF INTESTATE SUCCESSION

In the case of the death of a person, wholly or partly intestate, on and after 10 September 1964 the scheme of succession enacted by the Succession (Scotland) Act, 1964, applies, but not (S. 37(1)(a)) to any title, coat of arms, honour or dignity transmissible on the death of the holder thereof, nor (b) until 1968, to the tenancy of any croft within S. 3(1) of the Crofters (Sc.) Act, 1955, in relation to which matters the common law still applies.[5]

The statutory scheme includes (a) revised forms of statutory prior rights of a spouse, and of (b) legal rights, as well as (c) a modified list of relatives entitled to succeed to dead's part. In relation to the disposal of dead's part the scheme aggregates heritage and moveables, and removes for the future the privileged position of heir-at-law in respect of heritage and consequently the doctrine of collation *inter haeredes*.

A decree of judicial separation held by a wife extinguishes all rights of her husband in her intestate succession.[6]

[1] *McCall's Tr.* v. *McC's C.B.* (1901) 3 F. 1065. [2] *Waddell's J.F., supra.*

[3] *Waddell's J.F., supra*; *Grant's Trs.* v. *Slimon*, 1925 S.C. 261.

[4] *Innes* v. *Coghill* (1897) 25 R. 23; *Colville's J.F.* v. *Nicoll*, 1914 S.C. 62; *Waddell's J.F.* v. *Waddell*, 1924 S.C. 877.

[5] Exception (b) was deleted by the Law Reform (Misc. Prov.) (Sc.) Act, 1968, S. 8.

[6] Conjugal Rights (Sc.) Amdt. Act, 1861, S. 6.

Prior rights—dwelling house

A surviving spouse is entitled,[1] if the intestate estate included an interest as owner or tenant[2] (not being a tenancy to which the Rent Acts, 1920–39 apply), but subject in either case to any heritable debt secured over the interest, in any dwelling-house,[3] including a part of a building occupied (at the date of the intestate's death) as a separate dwelling, in which the surviving spouse was ordinarily resident at the date of the intestate's death, (a) where the value of the interest does not exceed £15,000, to the relevant interest, or to the value of the relevant interest if the dwelling house forms part only of the subjects comprised in one tenancy or lease under which the intestate was the tenant,[4] or formed the whole or part of subjects used by the intestate for carrying on a trade, profession or occupation, and the value of the estate as a whole would be likely to be substantially diminished if the dwelling-house was disposed of otherwise than with the assets of the trade, profession or occupation,[5] and (b) in any other case, to the sum of £15,000.[1] If the intestate estate comprises a relevant interest in two or more dwelling-houses the entitlement is effective in relation to such one as the surviving spouse may elect for the purpose within six months of the death of the intestate.[6] Where a question arises as to the value of any interest in a dwelling house the question shall be determined by a single arbiter appointed by the sheriff.[7]

Prior rights—furniture and plenishing

A surviving spouse is also entitled,[8] where the intestate estate includes the furniture and plenishings[9] of a dwelling-house[10] in which the surviving spouse was ordinarily resident at the date of death of the intestate (whether or not the dwelling-house is comprised in the intestate estate), to receive out of the intestate estate the whole of the furniture and plenishings if the value does not exceed £5000, or in any other case, such part of the furniture and plenishings, to a value not exceeding £5000, as the surviving

1 1964 Act, S. 8(1), (2), (4) and (6)(a) and (d).
2 Defined, S. 8(6)(d).
3 Defined, S. 8(6)(a).
4 e.g. a farmhouse.
5 e.g. a farmhouse or a doctor's house-cum-surgery.
6 S. 8(1), proviso.
7 S. 8(5).
8 1964 Act, S. 8(3), (4), (5) and (6)(b) and (c).
9 Defined, S. 8(6)(b) and (c).
10 Defined, S. 8(6)(a).

spouse may choose. If the intestate estate comprises the furniture and plenishings of two or more such houses, the entitlement applies only to the furniture and plenishing of such one as the surviving spouse may elect within six months of the intestate's death.

Questions as to the value of any furniture or plenishing, or of any interest in a dwelling-house, for the purpose of the provisions are to be determined by a single arbiter appointed, failing agreement, by the sheriff.[1]

These entitlements arise only where an interest in a dwelling-house, or furniture and plenishing, is included in the *intestate* estate;[2] if accordingly a person dies, having disposed of his dwelling-house, or furniture and plenishing, by will, but intestate *quoad ultra*, the surviving spouse has no entitlement under this section.

The surviving spouse is only 'entitled' to these rights; if she elects not to take a dwelling-house which she might have taken, she is entitled to £15,000, irrespective of the value of the house. If she elects not to take furniture and plenishing which she might have claimed she is entitled to nothing in lieu.

The surviving spouse may in an appropriate case elect to take one house and the furnishings of another. The surviving spouse must, though the deceased need not, have been 'ordinarily resident' in a dwelling house before either right under S. 8 applies. The provisos to subsections (1) and (3) imply that a spouse may be 'ordinarily resident' in more than one house.

If the deceased possessed no interest of ownership or tenancy of a house, or no furniture or plenishings,[3] the surviving spouse has no claim under S. 8.

Prior rights—financial provision

The surviving spouse of a person dying wholly or partly intestate is entitled[4] to receive out of the intestate estate,[5] if the intestate is survived by issue,[6] £2500, or if not survived by issue,[6] £5000, in either case with interest at 4% from the date of death until payment. But if the surviving spouse is entitled to a legacy[7]

[1] 1964 Act, S. 8(5).
[2] As defined by S. 36.
[3] e.g. if he lived in a hotel.
[4] 1964 Act, S. 9(1).
[5] Defined, S. 9(6)(a) as the net intestate estate remaining after satisfaction of claims to house and furniture under S. 8.
[6] i.e. by S. 36, lawful issue however remote. By the Law Reform (Misc. Prov.) (Sc.) Act, 1968, S. 3, the smaller sum only is now due if there is illegitimate issue.
[7] Defined, S. 9(6)(b).

(other than a legacy of any dwelling-house to which S. 8 applies or of any furniture and plenishings of any such dwelling-house) he or she, unless renouncing the legacy, is entitled only to such sum, if any, as is required to bring the legacy up to £2500 or £5000. If the intestate estate is less than the sum which the surviving spouse is entitled to, he or she is entitled to the whole of the intestate estate.[1]

The amount which the surviving spouse is entitled to receive is payable from heritage and moveables in proportion to the respective amounts of those parts of the intestate estate.[2]

This right is postponed to the rights to house and furniture conferred by S. 8.[3]

This prior right is to money out of the intestate estate (as defined) only, and if that should be only a small amount, the major part of the whole estate having been disposed of by will, the surviving spouse has no claim to have the estate so disposed of reduced to satisfy his or her claim, unlike a claim to legal rights.

Statutory legal rights

The 1964 Act[4] abolishes the rights of terce and courtesy,[5] but preserves the legal rights of *jus relictae*, *jus relicti* and legitim.[6] These continue to be exigible from moveable estate only, and from so much of the moveable estate as remains after the satisfaction of any claims thereon under Ss. 8 and 9, i.e. they are postponed to the statutory prior claims under Ss. 8 and 9.[7]

The Act[8] provides for representation in claims for legitim; if a child who would have been entitled to legitim has predeceased leaving issue surviving the deceased, such issue have the same right to legitim as their parent would have had if he had survived the deceased. If two or more persons have right to legitim and are all in the same degree of relationship to the deceased, it is divided among them equally *per capita*; if they are in two or more degrees of relationship, it is divided *per stirpes*.

If a person dies survived by a spouse and persons who claim legitim by representation, e.g. children of a predeceased child, the proportion due to the spouse as *jus relictae vel relicti* is to be

[1] S. 9(2).
[2] S. 9(3).
[3] See definition of 'intestate estate' in S. 9(6)(a).
[4] S. 10(1).
[5] See Ch. 110, *supra*.
[6] See Ch. 110, *supra*.
[7] S. 10(2).
[8] S. 11(1) and (2).

ascertained as if the deceased had been survived by that child, i.e. it is one-third.[1]

The requirement of collation of advances (*collatio inter liberos*)[2] is maintained. A person claiming legitim by representation must collate any advances made by the deceased to him, and the proportion appropriate to him of any advances so made to any person through whom he derives such entitlement.[3]

Legitim may no longer be discharged by an ante-nuptial marriage contract executed after the commencement of the Act unless the child or issue elect to accept the provision made in his favour under the contract in lieu of legitim.[4]

Testamentary dispositions executed after the commencement of the Act by which provision is made in favour of a spouse or of any issue of the testator, if not containing a declaration that the provision so made is in full and final satisfaction of claims competent by way of *jus relictae vel relicti* or legitim, are to have effect as if they contained such a declaration, unless the disposition contains an express provision to the contrary.[5]

Disposal of dead's part

Under the 1964 Act the whole intestate estate of a deceased, after deduction of prior rights and legal rights, devolves, without distinction between heritable and moveable property, in accordance with Ss. 1–7 of the Act, and any rule of law previously in force not inconsistent with those provisions and which, apart from the Act, would apply to the deceased's moveable intestate estate, if any.[6]

The succession to dead's part opens successively to the following groups of relatives:[7]

(a) children,[8] taking the whole estate;
(b) a parent or parents and brothers or sisters:[9] half to the parent(s), half to the siblings;
(c) brothers or sisters,[9] the whole estate;

[1] S. 11(4). [2] Ch. 110, *supra*. [3] S. 11(3). [4] S. 12.

[5] S. 13. It seems that in consequence the doctrine of equitable compensation (Ch. 112, *infra*) will not arise further, save possibly where the disposition does contain express provision that provisions are *not* in full satisfaction of legal rights. But the section does not abolish the doctrine.

[6] 1964 Act, S. 1. The privileged position of the heirs-at-law accordingly disappears, and with it the necessity for, and doctrine of, collation *inter haeredes*.

[7] S. 2.

[8] No distinction is drawn between children of first and of other marriages of the deceased.

[9] i.e. brothers and sisters of the whole blood, or of the half-blood: S. 2(2), but see S. 3.

(d) one or both parents, the whole estate;
(e) surviving spouse, the whole estate;
(f) uncles or aunts, on either paternal or maternal side, the whole estate;
(g) grandparent or grandparents, on either side, the whole estate;
(h) brothers or sisters[1] of any of the grandparents, the whole estate;
(i) ancestors of the intestate, generation by generation successively, without distinction between paternal or maternal lines, the brothers and sisters of any ancestors having right before ancestors of the next more remote generation, the whole estate.

Where brothers and sisters of an intestate or of an ancestor of the intestate have right to the whole[2] or half[3] of the free intestate estate, collaterals of the whole blood are entitled to succeed in preference to collaterals of the half-blood; if collaterals of the half-blood have right, no distinction is drawn between half-blood consanguinean and half-blood uterine.[4]

Succession in cases of illegitimacy

Formerly where a woman died intestate and was not survived by any legitimate issue, however remote, but was survived by illegitimate children,[5] they had right to the whole of the intestate estate. If an illegitimate person died intestate not survived by any legitimate issue or, being a woman, by any person entitled to succeed to her estate, as being her own illegitimate child, but was survived by his or her mother, the mother had right to the whole of the intestate estate. Apart from these provisions there was no rule of succession through illegitimate relationship.[6] By virtue of the Law Reform (Misc. Prov.) (Sc.) Act, 1968, S. 1, substituting a new S. 4 for the original S. 4 of the 1964 Act, legitimate and illegitimate children together have right to the whole of an intestate's estate, and the parents or surviving parent of an illegitimate child have right to the whole of his estate if he dies intestate. An illegitimate person is to be presumed not to be survived by his father unless the contrary is shown. By S. 10A of the 1964 Act, added to it by the Law Reform (Misc. Prov.)

[1] i.e. brothers and sisters of the whole blood, or of the half-blood: S. 2(2), but see S. 3.

[2] S. 2(1)(c), (f) (h), and (i), *supra*.

[3] S. 2(1)(b), *supra*.

[4] S. 3.

[5] Or, by S. 5, issue of a predeceasing illegitimate child or children.

[6] 1964 Act, S. 4, replacing Legitimacy Act, 1926, S. 9. Hence there was no succession to or by the bastard's father.

(Sc.) Act, 1968, S. 2, illegitimate children now have the same right to legitim from either parent as if legitimate, but cannot represent their parent in a claim for legitim from a grandparent,[1] and, by S. 3 of the 1968 Act, a surviving spouse's prior right to financial provision and to *jus relicti vel relicti* is restricted if there is an illegitimate child, just as if there had been a legitimate one. By S. 4 of the 1968 Act an illegitimate child has right to aliment from the deceased's estate or from anyone *lucratus* by the succession, just as if legitimate, but has no preference over the legitimate children,[2] and the court may modify agreements for aliment accordingly.

Representation

Where a person, if he had survived an intestate, would have had right, otherwise than as a parent or spouse of the intestate, to any part of the free intestate estate, but has predeceased leaving issue who survive the intestate, such issue have the same right as their parent would have had if he had survived the intestate.[3] There being no representation of parents or spouses, half-blood collaterals cannot claim by representation, but only if themselves entitled, and step-children cannot claim at all.

Division of dead's part among entitled claimants

Where two or more persons have right to a half or the whole of the free intestate estate,[4] then the half or whole is divided equally among them if all are in the same degree of relationship,[5] and in other cases *per stirpes*.[6]

Right of Crown as ultimus haeres

The Act preserves the right of the Crown to succeed as *ultimus haeres* to any estate to which no person is entitled to succeed by virtue of the Act.[7]

COMPLETION OF TITLE ON INTESTACY

Both at common law and under statute the rules of succession merely determine which person or persons have right to certain portions of the deceased's estate. It remains for the claimant to

[1] Because in S. 11 of the 1964 Act 'issue' means legitimate issue only.
[2] Altering law stated in *S.* v. *P's Trs.*, 1941 S.L.T. 35.
[3] 1964 Act, S. 5(1). [4] Under S. 2(1)(b).
[5] Irrespective of whether on the paternal or maternal side, and of how many on each.
[6] S. 6.
[7] S. 7.

establish his right and to complete his title to the property to which he has a recognized right.

Heritage prior to Succession (Sc.) Act, 1964

At common law no right to any estate in land descendible to heirs vested in the heir merely by his survivance of the deceased owner. But by statute[1] a personal right to every estate in land descendible to heirs, without service or other procedure, vests or is held to have vested in the heir entitled to succeed thereto by his survivance of the person to whom he is entitled to succeed. Such an heir may complete title by petition to the Sheriff of the county for general service as heir in general of the deceased, or for special service as heir in special of the deceased in the lands described in the petition and in which the deceased died vest and seised, or by writ of *clare constat* granted by the subject-superior of the lands. The petition for service set out the facts and had to be supported by affidavit from two persons who know the facts, and particularly the relationship of the petitioner to the deceased.[2]

Moveables at common law

At common law right to moveables did not vest in next-of-kin by mere survivance, and if any died before confirmation of the executor was expede, their rights lapsed as if they had predeceased. By the Confirmation of Executors (Sc.) Act, 1823, S. 1, the right of next-of-kin dying before confirmation transmitted to their representatives, and by survivance they acquired a right assignable and transmissible.[3] But confirmation of the executor remained necessary to give him a title to ingather and administer the moveable estate.

Under the Succession (Sc.) Act, 1964

By the 1964 Act, S. 14, the former rules as to the administration and winding up of the moveables of a deceased have effect, with certain amendments, to both heritage and moveables. On the death of a person, testate or intestate, every part of his estate, heritable or moveable, by virtue of confirmation, vests for the purposes of administration in the executor thereby confirmed and falls to be administered and disposed of according to law by him.[4]

1 Conveyancing (Sc.) Act, 1874, S. 9; *McAdam* v. *McA.* (1879) 6 R. 1256.
2 On service of heirs, see Craigie, *Heritable*, 836 *et seq.*
3 *Frith* v. *Buchanan* (1837) 15 S. 729; *Elder* v. *Watson* (1859) 21 D. 1122.
4 On obtaining confirmation see Ch. 114, *infra*.

Confirmation granted, if including heritage adequately described, entitles the executor to transfer that heritable property to a person in satisfaction of a claim to prior rights or to legal rights, or to a person entitled under the Act to share in the estate, or to a person entitled to take the property under a will by the deceased, by endorsing on the confirmation or certificate thereof a docket in favour of that person,[1] which may be specified as a midcouple or link in title in any deduction of title, but without prejudice to the competence of any other mode of transfer.[2] An English probate or letters of administration can also be used as links in title.[3]

Leases

Leases also vest in the executor. The executor may, notwithstanding a prohibition of assignation of the lease, transfer the deceased's interest therein to any one of those entitled to prior rights or legal rights or a share of the free estate in or towards satisfaction of that claim, but not to anyone else without the landlord's consent. Alternatively the executor may terminate the lease.[4]

Protection of persons acquiring title from executor

Where a person has in good faith and for value acquired title to any interest in or security over heritable property which has vested in an executor, directly or indirectly from the executor, or from a person deriving title directly from the executor, the title so acquired is not challengeable on the ground that the confirmation was reducible or has in fact been reduced, or that the title should not have been transferred to the person who did derive title from the executor.[5]

A trustee or executor may distribute property or make payments without having ascertained that no illegitimate person exists or has existed, entitled or whose existence is relevant to the ascertainment of persons entitled to property, and the trustee or executor is not personally liable to an entitled person of whose claim he had no notice at the time of payment, but the person may recover the property from any one who received it.[6]

[1] Form in 1964 Act, Sched. 1.

[2] 1964 Act, S. 15. Other modes could be a disposition by the executor, recorded, or a notice of title specifying the docket as a link in title, also recorded.

[3] Law Reform (Misc. Prov.) (Sc.) Act, 1968, S. 19.

[4] 1964 Act, S. 16.

[5] 1964 Act, S. 17.

[6] Law Reform (Misc. Prov.) (Sc.) Act, 1968, S. 7.

Entails and special destinations

Entailed property vests in the executor only for conveyance to the heir of entail next entitled.

On the death of a person entitled to heritable property subject to a special destination in favour of another being a destination which the deceased could not have, or had not, evacuated, the property vests in the executor only for conveyance to the person next entitled.[1]

PAYMENT OF CERTAIN FUNDS TO PERSONS DEEMED ENTITLED

Various statutory provisions[2] authorize certain bodies, on the death intestate of a member, to pay over sums standing to the credit of the deceased member, not exceeding £500, without confirmation of any executor, to persons appearing to be beneficially entitled thereto, to relatives or dependants of the deceased, or to such persons as appear to the committee of the body, on such evidence as they deem satisfactory, to be entitled by law to receive it, and such payments are statutorily validated.[3] The evidence need not be full legal evidence. The committee may not pay to one of the persons legally entitled on intestacy merely by direction of the majority of the persons so entitled.[4] It is questionable if these provisions authorize payment in a manner disregarding priority of prior rights, legal rights and of relatives set out in the table in the Succession (Sc.) Act, 1964, S. 2, but they possibly justify payment to persons entitled thereunder in ignorance of the existence of persons with a preferential right under that Act.[5]

[1] 1964 Act, S. 18.
[2] Listed in Schedule 1 of Administration of Estates (Small Payments) Act, 1965.
[3] Ibid., S. 1. By S. 6 the Treasury may by order increase the maximum sum.
[4] *Symington* v. *Galashiels Co-op. Store Co.* (1894) 21 R. 371.
[5] *Symington, supra*, 376.

CHAPTER 112

TESTATE SUCCESSION

It is competent to provide by writing,[1] usually entitled a will, testament or settlement, for the disposal of one's property, after payment of debts and government duties, after one's death, and such a declaration of wishes will normally be given effect to. A will cannot trench on the legal rights of any surviving relatives entitled thereto[2] and may accordingly freely dispose only of the deceased's whole heritage and one-third, if he leaves both a spouse and issue, or one-half, if he leave only either spouse or issue, of his moveables. In so far as a will fails of effect for any reason, or leaves estate undisposed of, that estate falls into intestacy and must be disposed of according to the rules of prior rights and intestate succession, to the testator's heirs on intestacy at the time of his death.[3]

The right to challenge titles to property completed on the basis of the deceased's intestacy prescribes in twenty years and it is thereafter too late to found on an alleged testamentary writing.[4]

Debts

As in the case of intestacy, the first charge on the deceased's estate are his debts. The incidence of liability therefor was and is the same as in cases of intestacy,[5] save that the testator may by his will indicate an intention to modify these principles. If he bequeaths heritage burdened with debt to a legatee, that legatee is liable for the debt notwithstanding a general direction to his executors to pay his debts.[6] The same principle may also apply to a specific bequest of a moveable subject which has been pledged or assigned in security for a debt.[7]

[1] A nuncupative or verbal bequest of property is valid to the value of £100 Scots (£8 6s. 8d.): *Kelly* v. *Kelly* (1861) 23 D. 703; cf. *Thomson* v. *Dunlop* (1884) 11 R. 453; *Turner's Trs.* v. *McFadyen* (1906) 14 S.L.T. 57; *Jackson* v. *Ogilvie*, 1933 S.L.T. 533.

[2] Prior to 1964 it could do so only subject to terce or courtesy, where applicable. The surviving spouse's claims to house and furniture, and to financial provision, under the Succession (Sc.) Act, 1964, Ss. 8–9, arise only in cases of total or partial intestacy.

[3] *Wilson's Trs.* v. *W's Trs.* (1894) 22 R. 62.

[4] *Pettigrew* v. *Harton*, 1956 S.C. 67.

[5] Ch. 111, *supra*.

[6] *Douglas's Trs.* v. *D.* (1868) 6 M. 223; *Macleod's Trs.* (1871) 9 M. 903.

[7] *Stewart* v. *S.* (1891) 19 R. 310; *Heath* v. *Grant's Trs.*, 1913 S.C. 78; *Reid's Trs.* v. *Dawson*, 1915 S.C. (H.L.) 47, 50.

THE MAKING OF WILLS

Capacity to test

Any person of sound mind and full age has testamentary capacity. A pupil has no testamentary capacity;[1] a minor could at common law test on his moveables, without his curator's consent,[2] and may now test on heritage also.[3] A person mentally incapacitated may not test if unable to understand the nature of the act, the extent of his property, and appreciate the disposition he is making of it.[4] But testamentary capacity may exist if the person were not generally and completely insane, but had lucid intervals, and the will were made during such an interval.[5]

Obligation to test

A person is normally under no duty, moral or legal, to make a will, or a will in particular terms, and may choose to die intestate, his spouse and children, if any, being adequately provided for by prior and legal rights and the rules of intestate succession. But he may validly promise, or contract with a party, onerously or gratuitously, to make him an heir or leave him a legacy,[6] and such an undertaking, if proveable in writing,[7] is effectual against the deceased's estate. In particular circumstances the undertaking to make a will as agreed might be specifically enforceable during his life, or a will in contravention be reduced.[8] An expressed intention to make a will in particular terms is not enforceable.[9]

So too a bequest may be made to a person on condition that he undertakes to make a prescribed testamentary provision; any such condition is strictly construed, as a limitation on a person's *prima facie* freedom of testation.[10]

Requisites of will

Apart from nuncupative or verbal legacies not exceeding £100 Scots,[11] a will must be in writing. No particular words or forms are

1 Stair III, 8, 37; Ersk. III, 9, 5.

2 Ersk. I, 7, 33; McLaren, I, 262; *Brown's Tr.* v. *B.* (1897) 24 R. 962.

3 Succession (Scotland) Act, 1964, S. 28.

4 *Graeme* v. *G's Trs.* (1869) 7 M. 1062; *Nisbet's Trs.* v. *N.* (1871) 9 M. 937; *Sivewright* v. *S's Trs.*, 1920 S.C. (H.L.) 63. See also *Manson* v. *Edinburgh Royal Inst.*, 1947 S.L.T. (Notes) 14; *McNaughton* v. *Smith*, 1949 S.L.T. (Notes) 54.

5 Bell, *Prin.* §2103; *Nisbet, supra*; *Sivewright, supra.*

6 cf. *Paterson* v. *P.* (1893) 20 R. 484; *McLachlan* v. *Seton's Trs.*, 1937 S.C. 206.

7 *Gray* v. *Johnston*, 1928 S.C. 659.

8 *Rollo's Trs.* v. *R.*, 1940 S.C. 578, 580.

9 *Gray, supra.*

10 *Murray* v. *Macfarlane's Trs.* (1895) 22 R. 927.

11 McLaren, I, 573; *Kelly* v. *K.* (1861) 23 D. 703. The Roman law doctrine of *testamentum militare*, which dispensed with formalities, does not appear to be Scots law: *Stuart* v. *S.*, 1942 S.C. 510.

essential to a valid will.[1] But ideally a will should identify the maker, clearly identify those persons whom the testator wishes to benefit, identify the bequests intended for each, include a residue clause disposing of all estate otherwise undisposed of, appoint one or more executors to give effect to the will, revoke all prior wills, and be validly executed. The only absolute essentials are evidence of testamentary intention in relation to certain property, and authentication.[2] A will is valid though it disposes only of part of the testator's property, in which case the balance falls to be distributed in accordance with the rules of prior rights and intestate succession, or though parts of it fail of effect, as by the predecease of a named legatee. An effective will may be couched in the form of a letter.[3]

The date and place of execution of a will are usual, but unnecessary,[4] though the *locus acti* may be important for formal validity and the date may be important in a question whether one will has revoked another.[5]

No particular heading, style or words are requisite for or automatically secure the validity of a writing as a will. Prior to 1868 a *mortis causa* conveyance of heritage was invalid unless the word 'dispone' was used[6] but no particular word is now necessary.[7]

No testamentary effect attaches to undated cheques to be delivered to payees after the granter's death,[8] nor to a mandate to a bank to pay all the granter's money to a named person on the day of the granter's death,[9] nor to a holograph declaration that the writer held deposit receipts in trust for a named person.[10]

Testamentary intention

Any writing propounded as a will must be fairly capable of interpretation as evidencing present testamentary intention of

[1] *Hamilton* v. *White* (1882) 9 R. (H.L.) 53, 56; *Colvin* v. *Hutcheson* (1885) 12 R. 947; *Cameron's Trs.* v. *Mackenzie*, 1915 S.C. 313, 318.

[2] *Cameron's Trs., supra.*

[3] *Scott* v. *Sceales* (1864) 2 M. 613; *Ritchie* v. *Whish* (1880) 8 R. 101; *McAra's Exors.* v. *Moore*, 1949 S.L.T. (Notes) 62; *Eadie's Trs.* v. *Lauder*, 1952 S.L.T. (Notes) 16; *Draper* v. *Thomason*, 1954 S.C. 136.

[4] Ersk. III, 2, 18; *Duncan* v. *Scrimzeour* (1706) Mor. 16914; *Ogilvie* v. *Bailie* (1711) Mor. 16896; *Wemyss* (1825) 1 W. & S. 140; *Taylor's Exces.* v. *Thom*, 1914 S.C. 79, 82.

[5] *Tait's Trs.* v. *Chiene*, 1911 S.C. 743.

[6] *Kirkpatrick's Trs.* v. *K.* (1874) 1 R. (H.L.) 37; *McLeod's Trs.* v. *McL.* (1875) 2 R. 481.

[7] Titles to Land Consolidation (Sc.) Act, 1868, S. 20.

[8] *Stewart's Trs.*, 1953 S.L.T. (Notes) 26.

[9] *Baird's Trs.* v. *B.*, 1955 S.C. 286.

[10] *Graham's Trs.* v. *Gillies*, 1956 S.C. 437.

giving the testator's estate in whole or in part on his death to some person or persons.[1] Questions have frequently arisen whether a writing, whatever its heading[2] or literary form,[3] evidences such an intention, and can be regarded as a completed deed, or whether it is rather only a jotting,[4] a personal memorandum,[5] a draft,[6] a tentative list of possibilities,[7] instructions for a will,[8] an expression of wish,[9] or intention,[10] a temporary codicil,[11] a mandate,[12] a declaration of trust,[13] or otherwise not testamentary. Evidence of surrounding circumstances is competent as to whether a document was intended as an interim will or a memorandum of instructions for a will.[14] A document described as a preliminary will may be effective if no final will is made.[15]

A writing in an envelope to be opened only on the testator's death, if not having testamentary effect, does not make a bequest of deposit receipts referred to therein.[16]

In such a case of doubt extrinsic evidence, written and parole, is competent[17] as to the circumstances in which the document was

1 *Colvin* v. *Hutchison* (1885) 12 R. 947; *Draper* v. *Thomason*, 1954 S.C. 136.

2 *Forsyth's Trs.* v. *F.* (1872) 10 M. 616; *Low's Exors.* (1873) 11 M. 744; *Hamilton* v. *White* (1882) 9 R. (H.L.) 53; *Murdoch's J.F.* v. *Thomson* (1896) 4 S.L.T. 155; *Tait's Trs.* v. *Chiene*, 1911 S.C. 743.

3 e.g. letters, *Ritchie* v. *Whish* (1880) 8 R. 101; *Richardson* v. *Macdonald's Exor.* (1899) 7 S.L.T. 14; *Eadie's Trs.* v. *Lauder*, 1952 S.L.T. (Notes) 16; *Draper* v. *Thomason*, 1954 S.C. 136; *MacLaren's Trs.* v. *Mitchell and Brattan*, 1959 S.C. 183; cf. *Simson* v. *S.* (1883) 10 R. 1247; *Mitchell's Trs.* v. *Pride*, 1912 S.C. 600; contrast *Allison* v. *Anderson* (1907) 15 S.L.T. 529.

4 *Muir's Trs.* (1869) 8 M. 53; *Waddell's Trs.* v. *W.* (1896) 24 R. 189; contrast *Simson*, *supra*.

5 *Cunningham* v. *Murray's Trs.* (1871) 9 M. 713; *Colvin* v. *Hutchison* (1885) 12 R. 947; *Tait's Trs.* v. *Chiene*, 1911 S.C. 743.

6 *Forsyth's Trs.* v. *F.* (1872) 10 M. 616; *Sprot's Trs.* v. *S.*, 1909 S.C. 1272; contrast *Murdoch's J.F.* v. *Thomson* (1896) 4 S.L.T. 155.

7 *Cameron's Trs.* v. *Mackenzie*, 1915 S.C. 313.

8 *Munro* v. *Coutts* (1813) 1 Dow 437; *Wilson* v. *Hovell*, 1924 S.C. 1; *Stuart* v. *S.*, 1942 S.C. 510; contrast *McAra's Exors.* v. *Moore*, 1949 S.L.T. (Notes) 62; *Eadie's Trs.* v. *Lauder*, 1952 S.L.T. (Notes) 16.

9 *Beattie* v. *Bain's Trs.* (1899) 6 S.L.T. 277; cf. *Low's Exors.* (1873) 11 M. 744.

10 *Ferrier's Trs.* v. *F.* (1899) 1 F. 610; *Allison* v. *Anderson* (1907) 15 S.L.T. 529.

11 *Butler's Exors.* v. *Walker*, 1935 S.N. 85.

12 *Aitchison's Trs.* v. *Somerville*, 1949 S.L.T. (Notes) 8; *Baird's Trs.* v. *B.*, 1955 S.C. 286; contrast *McAra's Exors.* v. *Moore*, 1949 S.L.T. (Notes) 62.

13 *Graham's Trs.* v. *Gillies*, 1956 S.C. 437.

14 *Young's Trs.* v. *Henderson*, 1925 S.C. 749; *McLaren's Trs.* v. *Mitchell and Brattan*, 1959 S.C. 183.

15 *Flockhart's Trs.* v. *Bourlet*, 1934 S.N. 23.

16 *Graham's Trs.* v. *Gillies*, 1956 S.C. 437.

17 *Munro* v. *Coutts* (1813) 1 Dow 437; *Scott* v. *Sceales* (1864) 2 M. 613; *Lowson* v. *Ford* (1866) 4 M. 631; *Forsyth's Trs.* v. *F.* (1872) 10 M. 616; *Sprot's Trs.* v. *S.*, 1909 S.C. 272; *Wilson* v. *Hovell*, 1924 S.C. 1; *Young's Trs.* v. *Henderson*, 1925 S.C. 749; *Stuart* v. *S.*, 1942 S.C. 510.

found, the way it was transmitted, by whom it had been prepared, and other similar facts which cast light on the issue of whether the document was meant to be a will or not.

It is favourable to the writing being deemed testamentary that it has been found with or attached to a writing which is undeniably testamentary.[1]

Apart from authentication the main factor is whether or not the writing contains words importing gift or testamentary purpose.[2] The word 'to' prefacing names, even with a mention of sums of money or items of property, is not sufficient,[3] nor is a verb such as 'give' or 'to have',[3] though the verb 'bequeath' and the word 'residue',[4] are indicative of testamentary intention.

Wills in several documents

A deceased's testamentary intention may be contained in several documents of different kinds and dates. Every writing held to be testamentary must be taken into account.[5] The testamentary writings may be of different kinds, such as a formal attested will, a holograph codicil, and a letter addressed to a solicitor.[6]

Formalities and execution

A will may be written,[7] typed,[8] printed or otherwise marked, by any kind of instrument, on any kind of surface, in any language or code whereby the testator's wishes may be communicated.[9]

It may be executed in any way in which a deed may be validly authenticated.[10] Alterations and additions must be authenticated.[11]

[1] *Low's Exors.* (1873) 11 M. 744; *Tait's Trs.* v. *Chiene,* 1911 S.C. 743; *Roberts* v. *Burns' Exor.*, 1914 1 S.L.T. 509.

[2] *Colvin, supra*; *Waddell's Trs.* v. *W.* (1896) 24 R. 189.

[3] *Cameron's Trs.* v. *Mackenzie,* 1915 S.C. 313.

[4] *Gillies* v. *Glasgow R.I.*, 1960 S.C. 438.

[5] e.g. *Low's Exors.* (1873) 11 M. 744 (will and later writing); *Ritchie* v. *Whish* (1880) 8 R. 107 (will, codicils, and letter); *Richardson* v. *Macdonald's Exor.* (1899) 7 S.L.T. 14 (will and letter); *Tait's Trs.* v. *Chiene,* 1911 S.C. 743 (will and list of legacies).

[6] *MacLaren's Trs.* v. *Mitchell and Brattan,* 1959 S.C. 183.

[7] Pencil will suffice: *Muir's Trs.* (1869) 8 M. 53; *Simsons* v. *S.* (1883) 10 R. 1247; *Lamont* v. *Glasgow Mags.* (1887) 14 R. 603; *Currie's Trs.* v. *C.* (1904) 7 F. 364; *Tait's Trs.* v. *Chiene,* 1911 S.C. 743. But see *Walker's Trs.* v. *W.*, 1923 S.L.T. 387.

[8] *Simpson's Trs.* v. *Macharg* (1902) 39 S.L.R. 562.

[9] Wills in Braille and in shorthand have been recorded; wills in a foreign language are competent.

[10] As to these see Ch. 6, *supra.*

[11] *Brown* v. *Stirling-Maxwell's Exors.* (1884) 11 R. 821; *Pettigrew's Trs.* v. *P.* (1884) 12 R. 249; *Currie's Trs., supra*; holograph and signed writings on a typed copy of a duly executed formal will have been held effective: *Manson* v. *Edinburgh Royal Inst.*, 1948 S.L.T. 196.

Postscripts and matter after the signature cannot be held part of the will.[1]

A holograph letter containing an adequate expression of testamentary intention has been held adequately authenticated by the writer's Christian name only.[2]

Holograph wills

A will may competently be written entirely by the hand of the testator and, if signed by him, is valid though unwitnessed.[3] If unsigned it is ineffectual.[4] Similarly a document printed, typed, or written by another, if docqueted as 'Adopted as holograph' (or in words to the same effect) and signed by the testator is valid though unwitnessed.[5] A holograph and signed docquet referring to a writing as the writer's will has been held a valid testamentary writing.[6] By statute[7] every holograph writing of a testamentary character is presumed, in the absence of contrary evidence, to be of the date it bears. Alterations or interlineations on a holograph will are valid though not authenticated, if proved to be in the handwriting of the granter.[8]

Where the genuineness of a holograph writing is in question, the onus of proving that it is holograph of the subscriber rests on those proponing it,[9] and a statement *in gremio* that the writing is holograph of the subscriber has no evidential value unless the subscription is admitted or proved to be genuine.[10]

The practice of the Commissary Courts for long was to grant confirmation in unopposed petitions on a writing which contained a statement in *gremio* that it was holograph of the subscriber without further evidence,[11] but the Succession (Sc.) Act, 1964,

[1] *Fraser's Exrx.* v. *F's C.B.*, 1931 S.C. 536; *McLay* v. *Farrell*, 1950 S.C. 149; *Burnie's Trs.* v. *Lawrie* (1894) 21 R. 1015 is not now good law.

[2] *Draper* v. *Thomason*, 1954 S.C. 136.

[3] e.g. *Lorimer's Exors.* v. *Hird*, 1959 S.L.T. (Notes) 8. A holograph addition above the signature is authenticated thereby: *Reid's Exors.* v. *R.*, 1953 S.L.T. (Notes) 52. Signature on the backing of a holograph will is inadequate: *Boyd* v. *Buchanan*, 1964 S.L.T. (Notes) 108.

[4] *Skinner* v. *Forbes* (1883) 11 R. 88; *Goldie* v. *Shedden* (1885) 13 R. 138; *Foley* v. *Costello* (1904) 6 F. 365; *Taylor's Exces.* v. *Thom*, 1914 S.C. 79; *Roberts* v. *Burn's Exor.*, 1914 1 S.L.T. 509; *Stenhouse* v. *S.*, 1922 S.C. 370.

[5] For special cases see *McBeath's Trs.* v. *McB.*, 1935 S.C. 471; *Chisholm* v. *C.*, 1949 S.C. 434.

[6] *Campbell's Exors.* v. *Maudslay*, 1934 S.L.T. 420; *Muir* v. *M.*, 1950 S.L.T. (Notes) 40.

[7] Conveyancing (Sc.) Act, 1874, S. 40.

[8] *Robertson* v. *Ogilvie's Trs.* (1844) 7 D. 236; *Grant* v. *Stoddart* (1849) 11 D. 860.

[9] *Turnbull* v. *Doods* (1844) 6 D. 896; *Anderson* v. *Gill* (1858) 20 D. 1326; (1858) 3 Macq. 180; *Frederick* v. *Craig*, 1932 S.L.T. 315.

[10] *Harper* v. *Green*, 1938 S.C. 196.

[11] *Cranston* (1890) 17 R. 410.

S. 21, has enacted that confirmation should not be granted unless the court is satisfied by evidence consisting at least of affidavits by two persons that the writing and signature are in the handwriting of the testator.

Wills partly printed, partly written

A will may validly be made by completing by hand blanks in a form printed, typed or written by another. If executed before witnesses, or docqueted as 'adopted as holograph' and signed, such a will is completely valid. If not thus authenticated but merely signed the document is valid as a holograph will if the holograph portions read by themselves contain the essentials, and sufficiently express testamentary intention, and the printed portions are inessential or superfluous,[1] but if essentials, such as words of gift, and the subjects of the gifts, are not holograph, the document cannot receive testamentary effect.[2] If unsigned, it is wholly ineffective. Effect cannot be given to particular clauses such as a clause revoking earlier wills, as a separate holograph writing, though they are holograph and the whole signed.[3]

Incorporation of other documents

Other documents, though themselves inadequately authenticated, may be incorporated into an adequately authenticated testamentary writing if it contains clear indications that it is the testator's intention that such other documents should be incorporated in the will and have testamentary effect.[4] The incorporation may be retrospective[5] or prospective;[6] it may refer to a specific other document, or provide for the incorporation of any document identifiable in a specified way; it may dispense with any or all formalities of authentication of the other document,[7] or even, very exceptionally, with any signature

[1] *Carmichael's Exors.* v. *C.*, 1909 S.C. 1387; *Bridgeford's Exors.* v. *B.*, 1948 S.C. 416; *Gillies* v. *Glasgow R.I.*, 1960 S.C. 438; cf. *Murdoch's J.F.* v. *Thomson* (1896) 4 S.L.T. 155. Testamentary intention may be sufficiently indicated by the word 'residue': *Gillies, supra.*

[2] *Macdonald* v. *Cuthbertson* (1891) 18 R. 101; *Tucker* v. *Canch's Tr.*, 1953 S.C. 270.

[3] *Tucker, supra.*

[4] *Taylor's Exces.* v. *Thom*, 1914 S.C. 79.

[5] *Macintyre* v. *Macfarlane's Trs.*, 1 Mar. 1821, F.C.,; *Cross's Trs.* v. *C.*, 1921 1 S.L.T. 244; *Craik's Exrx.* v. *Samson*, 1929 S.L.T. 592; *Fraser's Exrx.* v. *Fraser's C.B.*, 1931 S.C. 536; *Macphail's Trs.* v. *Macphail*, 1940 S.C. 560; *Muir* v. *M.*, 1950 S.L.T. (Notes) 40.

[6] *Waterson's Trs., infra.*

[7] *Baird* v. *Jaap* (1856) 18 D. 1246 ('any jotting under my hand'). *Crosbie* v. *Wilson* (1866) 3 M. 870 ('writing under my hand or any writing subscribed by me'); *Bannatyne's Trs.* v. *Cunninghame* (1869) 7 M. 993; *Lamont* v. *Glasgow Mags.* (1887) 14 R. 603; *Fraser* v. *Forbes's Trs.* (1899) 1 F. 513; *Hamilton's Trs.* v. *H.* (1901) 4 F. 260; *Butler's Exors.* v. *Walker*, 1935 S.N. 85; *Waterson's Trs.* v. *St. Giles Boys' Club*, 1943 S.C. 369 ('any writing under my hand . . . however informal'); *Russel's Exor.* v. *Duke*, 1946 S.L.T.

at all.[1] Undated cheques to be delivered to payees after the writer's death cannot be incorporated by anticipation, as they lapse on death.[2]

Reduction of will on ground of mental capacity

Whether the testator was at the time of executing his will of sound and disposing mind, capable of understanding the nature of his deed and its effect, may be challenged by an action of reduction of the will at the instance of a spouse seeking to claim prior rights on intestacy, or an heir on intestacy, or a beneficiary under a prior will which the will challenged purports to revoke.

If the testator were generally and completely insane at the time, his will is null.[3] If he were subject to periods of insanity, his will is reducible if it was executed during a period of such incapacity.[4] If he were subject to delusions it is reducible if it appears that his dispositions were affected by those delusions.[5]

Similarly if a testator be shown to have been, at the time, incapacitated, by drink, drugs or otherwise, from understanding the nature and effect of his will, effect cannot be given to it.[6]

Reduction on ground of facility or undue influence

A will is also reducible on the ground of facility and circumvention or fraud, if the testator was at the time so weak in body or mind, not amounting to insanity, as left him susceptible to influence and persuasion, and he was in fact prevailed upon to make the disposition he did,[7] or if he were subjected to force and fear,[8] or to undue influence in relation to the will by a person in whom he reposed trust and who exercised a dominating influence,[9]

242; *Snailum's Trs.* v. *Edinburgh R.I.*, 1948 S.L.T. (Notes) 26; *Stewart's Trs.*, 1953 S.L.T. (Notes) 26.

1 *Waterson's Trs., supra*, 376; cf. *Hamilton's Trs.* v. *H.* (1901) 4 F. 266; *Ronald's Trs.* v. *Lyle*, 1929 S.C. 104, overruled by *Waterson's Trs.*

2 *Stewart's Trs.*, 1953 S.L.T. (Notes) 26.

3 *Nisbet's Trs.* v. *N.* (1871) 9 M. 937.

4 *Nisbet Trs., supra*; *Houston* v. *Aitken*, 1913 S.C. 1037.

5 *Morrison* v. *Maclean's Trs.* (1862) 24 D. 625, 633; *Maitland's Trs.* v. *M.* (1871) 10 M. 79; *Ballantyne* v. *Evans* (1886) 13 R. 652; *Hope* v. *H's Trs.* (1898) 1 F. (H.L.) 1; *Sivewright's Trs.* v. *S.*, 1920 S.C. (H.L.) 63.

6 *Laidlaw* v. *L.* (1870) 8 M. 882.

7 *Morrison* v. *Maclean's Trs.* (1862) 24 D. 625; *Munro* v. *Strain* (1874) 1 R. 1039; *McCallum* v. *Graham* (1894) 21 R. 824; *Rooney* v. *Cormack* (1895) 22 R. 761; *Williams* v. *Philip* (1907) 15 S.L.T. 396; *Horsburgh* v. *Thomson's Trs.*, 1912 S.C. 267; *McDougal* v. *McD.'s Trs.*, 1931 S.C. 102; *Cleugh* v. *Fleming*, 1948 S.L.T. (Notes) 60.

8 *Boyse* v. *Rossborough* (1856) 6 H.L.C. 1, 48; *Love* v. *Marshall* (1870) 9 M. 291; *Weir* v. *Grace* (1899) 2 F. (H.L.) 30; *McLachlan* v. *Seton's Trs.*, 1937 S.C. 206.

9 *Munro, supra*; *Gray* v. *Binnie* (1879) 6 R. 332; *Weir* v. *Grace* (1899) 2 F. (H.L.) 30; *Forrest* v. *Low's Trs.*, 1907 S.C. 1240; *McKechnie* v. *McK.'s Trs.*, 1908 S.C. 93 (mistress); *Horsburgh, supra*; *L.A.* v. *Davidson's J.F.*, 1921 2 S.L.T. 267; *Ross* v. *Gosselin's Exors.*, 1926 S.C. 325; *McDougal* v. *McD.'s Trs.*, 1931 S.C. 102.

or if the testator were fraudulently, or possibly even negligently or innocently, deceived as to some matter material to his intestamentary dispositions, and thereby influenced,[1] or if the testator were under essential error as to some such matter, even though uninduced.[2] A will benefiting the solicitor who drew it up or other person in a fiduciary capacity throws on him the onus of establishing that no undue influence had been used.[3] A will in favour of a paramour is not reducible merely because granted for an immoral consideration.[4]

Law of deathbed—Reduction ex capite lecti

A deed conveying or burdening heritable estate to the prejudice of the granter's lawful heir was formerly reducible if executed by the granter while ill of the sickness from which he died, on the presumption that he had acted from importunity. The presumption did not hold if a supervening accident or disease caused death.[5]

The presumption was rebutted if the deed had been granted in liege poustie,[6] which was evidenced by surviving the granting of the deed for sixty days,[7] or by going to kirk or market unsupported.[8]

This rule was possibly abolished by the Reduction *ex capite lecti* Abolition Act, 1871,[9] but the abolition affected only the challenge of deeds, instruments or writings executed on deathbed and may not cover all cases.[10]

Revocability and revocation

A will does not operate till death and is revocable by the testator at any time,[11] notwithstanding a statement *in gremio* that it is irrevocable,[12] or its delivery to a beneficiary or agent for

[1] e.g. if it appeared that he had been influenced to cut his son out by reason of reports that the son was a worthless rotter; cf. *Munro* v. *Strain, supra.*

[2] e.g. if he mistakenly stated in the will that his son was dead and he therefore made other dispositions of his property.

[3] *Weir, supra*; *Forrest, supra*; *Stewart* v. *McLaren*, 1920 S.C. (H.L.) 148.

[4] *Troussier* v. *Matthew*, 1922 S.L.T. 670.

[5] Stair I, 12, 34; Ersk, III. 8, 95; Bell, *Prin.* §1786–1816.

[6] i.e. *in legitima potestate.*

[7] Bell, *Prin.* §1788–9.

[8] Bell, *Prin.* §1790–5.

[9] Itself repealed by Statute Law Revision Act, 1883. See also *Thain* v. *T.* (1891) 18 R. 1196.

[10] cf. Bell, *Prin.* §1786; Fraser, *H. & W.*, II, 1008; *Hay* v. *Coutts's Trs.* (1890) 18 R. 244.

[11] Ersk. III, 9, 5.

[12] Menzies, *Conv.*, 425; *Dougall's Trs.* v. *D.* (1789) Mor. 15949.

beneficiaries.[1] Even a specific bequest in a writing delivered to the legatee during life is revocable by a later general settlement.[2] But if the testator has promised[3] or bound himself contractually[3] to leave his estate, or a particular bequest, to a particular person a later will in contravention thereof is reducible and null so far as in breach of obligation.[4]

Express and implied revocation

A will may be revoked in whole or in part by a subsequent authenticated writing,[5] most commonly by another will, either expressly,[6] by a declaration therein revoking prior wills, or impliedly, by complete inconsistency between the later and earlier wills, in which case the later or latest prevails.[7] So far as not inconsistent, both or all wills fall to be read together.[8] Whether there is such inconsistency as to imply revocation is a question of interpretation in each case.[9] A will revoked by a later will is revived by the revocation of the revoking will by a third will, either expressly or if it is still extant.[10]

If the revoking deed is invalid[11] or ineffectual[12] the earlier will stands. If the clause of revocation is inconsistent with the rest of

[1] Ersk. III, 3, 91; Bell, *Prin.* §1866; *Somerville* v. *S.*, 18 May 1819, F.C.; *Miller* v. *Dickson* (1825) 4 S. 822; *Romanes* v. *R's Trs.*, 1933 S.N. 112; *Clark's Exor.* v. *C.*, 1943 S.C. 216.

[2] *Clark's Exor.* v. *C.*, 1943 S.C. 216.

[3] *Duguid* v. *Cadell's Trs.* (1831) 9 S. 844; such an undertaking is proveable as obligatory only by writ or oath, and the latter will be impossible by reason of the testator's death.

[4] Stair III, 8, 28–33; Ersk. III, 9, 6; *Paterson* v. *P.* (1893) 20 R. 484; *Mackenzie's Trs.* v. *Kilmarnock's Trs.*, 1909 S.C. 472. If he has not made a will at all his estate is liable in damages for breach of contract.

[5] Ersk. III, 9, 5; *Stewart* v. *Neilson* (1860) 22 D. 646.

[6] In *Clarke's Trs.* v. *C's Exors.*, 1925 S.C. 431, an express revocation was held ineffective as the latter will as a whole treated the earlier will as subsisting.

[7] e.g. *Beattie* v. *Thomson* (1861) 23 D. 1163 (later will disposing of whole estates); *Sibbald's Trs.* v. *Greig* (1871) 9 M. 399; *Dick's Tr.* v. *D.*, 1907 S.C. 953; *Perrett's Trs.* v. *P.*, 1909 S.C. 522; *Clark's Exor.* v. *Clark*, 1943 S.C. 216; *Cadger* v. *Ronald's Trs.*, 1946 S.L.T. (Notes) 24; *Lawrie's Trs.* v. *Church of Scotland*, 1962 S.C. 497.

[8] *Horsburgh* v. *H.* (1847) 9 D. 329; *Stoddart* v. *Grant* (1852) 1 Macq. 163, 170; *Kenmore's Trs.* (1869) 7 M. 771; *Low's Exors.* v. *Macdonald* (1873) 11 M. 744; *Gordon's Exor.* v. *Macqueen*, 1907 S.C. 373; *Taylor's Tr.* v. *Robinson*, 1911 S.C. 334; *Lumsden's Trs.* v. *L.* 1921 1 S.L.T. 155.

[9] See e.g. *Maclean* v. *M.* (1891) 18 R. 874; *McGaw's Trs.* v. *King* (1902) 10 S.L.T. 83; *Gordon's Exor.* v. *Macqueen*, 1907 S.C. 373; *Tait's Trs.* v. *Chiene*, 1911 S.C. 743; *Lennie* v. *L's Trs.*, 1914 1 S.L.T. 258.

[10] *Blackwood* (1875) 12 S.L.R. 384; *Ferguson* v. *Russell's Trs.*, 1919 S.C. 80; *Bruce's J.F.* v. *L.A.*, 1964 S.L.T. 316; 1968 S.L.T. 242.

[11] *Stirling Stuart* v. *Stirling Crawfurd's Trs.* (1885) 12 R. 610; *Cullen's Exor.* v. *Elphinstone*, 1948 S.C. 662; *Tucker* v. *Canch's Tr.*, 1953 S.C. 270.

[12] *Kirkpatrick's Trs.* v. *K.* (1874) 1 R. (H.L.) 37; *Sutherland's Trs.* v. *S's Tr.* (1893) 20 R. 925; *Thomson's Trs.* v. *Bowhill Baptist Church*, 1956 S.C. 217.

the deed in which it appears and the rest of that deed assumes the continuance of the earlier will, it will stand and the revoking clause be ignored.[1]

Revocation by cancellation or destruction

A will may also be revoked, in whole or in part, by the testator obliterating or scoring out part of the deed,[2] or tearing up or destroying the deed in whole or in part[3] or instructing this to be done.[4] But unless the obliteration or scoring out is authenticated by the testator's signature or initials, it will be ineffective[5] unless so completely done that the writing cannot be made out at all. If still legible it remains effective, unless the cancellation is authenticated. If a will, known to have existed, cannot be found on the testator's death, it is presumed to have been destroyed *animo revocandi*.[4]

For destruction to be effective it must have been done *animo revocandi*[6] and if it appears that this was done *sine animo revocandi*, by accident,[7] in anger,[8] when drunk or insane,[9] or by another person without the testator's authority or consent,[10] the will is not revoked,[11] and will receive effect if its terms can be established by piecing together the fragments, or from a draft or copy, by an action of proving of the tenor.

No revocation by marriage

A will is not revoked by the testator's subsequent marriage or remarriage, the spouse being provided for, at least to some extent, by the doctrine of legal rights.[12]

Revocation under conditio si testator

By the principle of the *conditio si testator sine liberis decesserit* a will which makes no provision for subsequently born children

1 *Clarke's Trs.* v. *C's Exors.*, 1925 S.C. 431.
2 *Ogilvie's Trs.* (1870) 8 M. 427; *Kirkpatrick's Trs.* v. *K.* (1874) 1 R. (H.L.) 37; *Stirling Stuart* v. *Stirling Crawfurd's Trs.* (1885) 12 R. 610; *Sutherland's Trs.* v. *S's Tr.* (1893) 20 R. 925; *Cullen's Exor.* v. *Elphinstone*, 1948 S.C. 662.
3 *Falconer* v. *Stephen* (1848) 11 D. 220; *Winchester* v. *Smith* (1863) 1 M. 685.
4 *Bonthrone* v. *B.* (1883) 10 R. 779.
5 *Gemmell's Exor.* v. *Stirling*, 1923 S.L.T. 384.
6 *Cunningham* v. *Mouat's Tr.* (1851) 13 D. 1376.
7 *Irvine* v. *Lang* (1840) 2 D. 804; *Cunningham, supra.*
8 *Winchester, supra.*
9 *Laing* v. *Bruce* (1838) 1 D. 59.
10 *Cullen's Exor., supra.*
11 *Fotheringham's Tr.* v. *Reid*, 1936 S.C. 831; *Cullen's Exor., supra.*
12 cf. *Mitchell's Administratrix* v. *Edinburgh R.I.*, 1928 S.C. 47.

may be presumed revoked by the subsequent birth of a child to the testator. The presumption is based on the implied condition that his will contemplated his death without children, or further children; if this condition is defeated the basis for the will disappears and it is deemed revoked, it being presumed that the testator would not have wished to make no provision for the later child.[1] Whether the presumption applies or not depends entirely on the circumstances of the case.[2] The strongest cases for the application are where a testator subsequently has a child and dies without having had an adequate opportunity to alter his will, or a child is born posthumously, but it applies equally though he survives the birth for some time.[3]

This presumption may however be rebutted and its operation excluded by circumstances which evidence an intention that the will should stand despite the subsequent birth of a child,[4] such as the testator's having made an *inter vivos* provision for the child, or having provided for it by marriage contract,[5] or having made the will in the knowledge of his wife's pregnancy.[6] It is not rebutted merely by the facts that the testator had living children at the date of the will,[7] nor that he survived the birth of the later child for a substantial time but did not alter his will,[8] nor by mere lapse of time after the birth of the child,[9] nor because separate provision is made by marriage contract.[10] Proof of declarations of intention by the testator is not competent to fortify or rebut the presumption.[11]

The presumption does not apply *ipso jure* but must be invoked, if necessary in a process of reduction; it may be invoked only by the after-born child and not by any other party.[12] The *conditio* may be invoked by an illegitimate child.[13]

1 *Stevenson's Trs.* v. *S.*, 1932 S.C. 657, 667.

2 *Hughes* v. *Edwardes* (1892) 19 R. (H.L.) 33; *Millar's Trs.* v. *M.* (1893) 20 R. 1040.

3 *A's Exors.* v. *B.* (1874) 11 S.L.R. 259; *McKie's Tutor* v. *McKie* (1897) 24 R. 526; *Rankin* v. *R's Tutor* (1902) 4 F. 979; *Rankine* v. *R's Trs.* (1904) 6 F. 581; *Milligan's J.F.* v. *M.*, 1910 S.C. 58.

4 *Millar's Trs.* v. *M.* (1893) 20 R. 1040; *Elder's Trs.* v. *E.* (1895) 21 R. 704; 22 R. 505; *Stuart Gordon* v. *S.G.* (1898) 1 F. 1005.

5 *Millar's Trs.*, *supra*; *Stuart Gordon*, *supra*.

6 *Adamson's Trs.* v. *A's Exors.* (1891) 18 R. 1133.

7 *Elder's Trs.*, *supra*; *Knox's Tr.* v. *K.*, 1907 S.C. 1123.

8 *Rankin* v. *R's Tutor* (1902) 4 F. 979; *Nicolson* v. *N's Tutrix*, 1922 S.C. 649.

9 *A's Exors.* v. *B.* (1874) 11 S.L.R. 259; *McKie's Tutor* v. *McKie* (1897) 24 R. 526; *Rankin* v. *R's Tutor* (1902) 4 F. 979; *Rankine* v. *R's Trs.* (1904) 6 F. 581; *Milligan's J.F.* v. *M.*, 1910 S.C. 58.

10 *Dobie's Tr.* v. *Pritchard* (1887) 15 R. 2.

11 *Smith's Trs.* v. *Grant* (1897) 5 S.L.T. 190.

12 *Smith's Trs.* v. *Grant* (1897) 35 S.L.R. 129; *Stevenson's Trs.* v. *S.*, 1932 S.C. 657.

13 Law Reform (Misc. Prov.) (Sc.) Act, 1968, S. 6.

If the presumption is successfully invoked, the whole will challenged is held revoked,[1] but earlier wills expressly revoked by that will are not thereby revived.[2] If the presumption is rebutted by proven intention that it should receive effect notwithstanding the birth, the will stands as a whole.[3] A will revoked by the *conditio* is not restored by alterations made thereon subsequent to the birth, if not authenticated.[4]

Codicils

Codicils are subsequent testamentary writings which add to, revoke in part, or otherwise modify a will. They must be executed in the same way as a will, unless validated *ab ante*, though not authenticated, by anticipatory adoption in the will itself. The will and all the valid codicils have to be read together and, so far as possible, interpreted consistently with one another, to ascertain the testator's final intention.[5]

Apart from formal codicils writings held to be codicils include holograph and signed alterations to a copy of a will,[6] and a holograph addition inserted above the signature.[7]

An unsigned holograph list of the names of intended beneficiaries put up with, though not attached to, a codicil has been held part of the testator's testamentary writings so far as adopted by that codicil.[8]

Mutual Wills

A mutual will is a single deed whereby two or more persons dispose of their own separate estates in whole or in part to the survivor(s) of them.[9] If not validly executed by both or all testators, it is effective as a disposition only of the estate of the one who has validly executed it,[10] and similarly if one testator is found to be incapacitated.[11] Such a will may give rise to problems, as where both testators die in a common calamity,[12] but particularly

1 *Knox's Trs., supra.*
2 *Elder's Trs., supra; Crow* v. *Cathro* (1903) 5 F. 950.
3 *Crow, supra.*
4 *Munro's Exors.* v. *M.* (1890) 18 R. 122.
5 e.g. *Miller's Trs.* v. *M.*, 1958 S.C. 125.
6 *Lawson* v. *L.*, 1954 S.L.T. (Notes) 60.
7 *Reid's Exors.* v. *R.*, 1953 S.L.T. (Notes) 52.
8 *Macphail's Trs.* v. *M.*, 1940 S.C. 560.
9 *Craich's Trs.* v. *Mackie* (1870) 8 M. 898 is a case of a mutual will by three testators. Dispositions by two or more persons of their separate estates to the same third parties, even if contained in one deed, do not constitute a mutual will.
10 *Millar* v. *Birrell* (1876) 4 R. 87.
11 *Graeme* v. *G's Trs.* (1869) 7 M. 1062.
12 *Ross's J.F.* v. *Martin*, 1955 S.C. (H.L.) 56.

of revocability, especially where it is not exhausted by the first death. It may be held to be no more than two or more wills contained in one deed, in which case either party may freely alter or revoke it *quoad* his own estate either before[1] or after[2] the death of the other, or *quoad* the estate carried to him by the will on the death of the other.[3] Alternatively, where there is a gift to the survivor, and subsequently to a third party, such a deed may be held to be, in whole or in part, contractual and to confer a *jus quaesitum tertio* on the third party, so that it is not revocable before[4] or after[5] the death of the predeceaser. If a will is contractual *quoad* one testator it is contractual *quoad* the other. A codicil may be revocable though the main will is contractual.[6]

In every case the question is one of the fair meaning of the will. The presumption is that a mutual will is merely two wills in one deed and revocable.[7] Power to revoke may be expressly conferred on the survivor[8] or the survivor may be given absolute power of disposal of the joint estate[9] or the settlement may be declared wholly or partly irrevocable by the survivor.[10] Where the parties are spouses the court may more readily hold that provisions in favour of each other or of their children are contractual and non-revocable than in the case of provisions in favour of third parties.[11] The court is also rather more willing to hold that the survivor may

1 *Gibson's Trs.* v. *G.* (1877) 4 R. 867; *Main* v. *Lamb* (1880) 7 R. 688; *Saxby* v. *Saxby' Exor.*, 1952 S.C. 352.

2 *Traquair* v. *Martin* (1872) 11 M. 22; *Milne* v. *M.* (1876) 13 S.L.R. 223; *Melville* v. *M's Trs.* (1879) 6 R. 1286; *Lang's Trs.* v. *L.* (1885) 12 R. 1265; *Boath's Trs.* v. *Machardy* (1902) 10 S.L.T. 446; *Scott's Tr.* v. *S.*, 1919 1 S.L.T. 78; *Stirling's Trs.*, 1948 S.L.T. (Notes) 69; *Dewar* v. *D's Trs.*, 1950 S.L.T. 191.

3 *Davidson* (1870) 8 M. 807; *U.F. Church* v. *Black*, 1909 S.C. 25; *Garioch's Trs.* v. *G's Exors.*, 1917 S.C. 404. Contrast *Welsh's Trs.* v. *W.* (1871) 10 M. 16; *Kay's Tr.* v. *Stalker* (1892) 19 R. 1071.

4 *Wood's Trs.* v. *Findlay*, 1909 1 S.L.T. 156.

5 *Kerr* v. *Ure* (1873) 11 M. 780; *Croll's Trs.* v. *Alexander* (1895) 22 R. 677; *Robertson's Trs.* v. *Bond's Trs.* (1900) 2 F. 1097; *Corrance's Trs.* v. *Glen* (1903) 5 F. 777; *Johnstone's Trs.* v. *J's Trs.* (1907) 15 S.L.T. 382; *Lawrie's Exor.* v. *Haig*, 1913 S.C. 1159; *Craig's Trs.* v. *C's Trs.*, 1927 S.C. 367; *Duthie* v. *Keir's Exor.*, 1930 S.C. 645; *Thomson's Trs.* v. *Lockhart*, 1930 S.C. 674.

6 *Mackie's Trs.* v. *M.*, 1914 1 S.L.T. 203.

7 *Traquair* v. *Martin* (1872) 11 M. 22; *Croll's Trs.* v. *Alexander* (1895) 22 R. 677; *Corrance's Trs.* v. *Glen* (1903) 5 F. 777. It is almost impossible to establish that a mutual will is irrevocable *stante matrimonio*: *Saxby* v. *S's Exors.*, 1952 S.C. 352.

8 e.g. *Kay's Tr.* v. *Stalker* (1892) 19 R. 1071; *Corrance's Trs.*, *supra*; *U.F. Church*, *supra*; *Lawrie's Exor.*, *supra*; *Scott* v. *Thomson's Exor.*, 1925 S.L.T. 226; *Duthie* v. *Keir's Exor.*, 1930 S.C. 645; see also *Wood's Trs.* v. *Findlay*, 1909 1 S.L.T. 156.

9 e.g. *Berwick's Exor.* (1885) 12 R. 565.

10 e.g. *Mitchell* v. *M's Trs.* (1877) 4 R. 800; *Whyte* v. *Paul* (1879) 7 R. 321.

11 *U.F. Church*, *supra*; *Lawrie's Exor.*, *supra*; contrast *Hanlon's Exor.* v. *Baird*, 1945 S.L.T. 304.

revoke when he is given only a liferent than when given the fee of the predeceaser's estate.[1] A survivor is not normally prevented from testing separately on savings from income of the rights under the mutual will.[2]

DISPOSAL OF THE TESTATOR'S ESTATE

A will may dispose of the testator's estate by direct gift or bequest to designated persons or other objects of his benevolence, or by creation of a trust, conveyance of the estate to trustees, and statement of the objects and purposes of the trust. Where the conveyance is to trustees, there may be directions as to the way in which property is to be conveyed or settled in particular circumstances. When trustees are directed to carry out the testator's intention by a definite method they must conform exactly to his directions even though it may be apparent that he had some object in mind which cannot be effectually attained by the methods prescribed.[3]

Subjects affected by will

A testator's will can effectively dispose of only those subjects in which he had at his death a right of property,[4] save that in some case he may thereby deal also with property as to which he has a power of appointment.[5]

Bequests contrary to public policy

The court will not enforce a bequest deemed contrary to public policy, such as one promoting illegality, immorality,[6] of no utility, merely extravagant, wasteful, futile, or conferring no benefit on any person or class of persons,[7] or otherwise contrary to public policy.[8] But a bequest in favour of a paramour is not reducible as granted in consideration of adultery.[9] The bequest of the whole estate for the erection of a burial vault may be so

[1] *Corrance's Trs., supra*; *Craig's Trs.* v. *C.*, 1927 S.C. 367; *Duthie, supra.*

[2] *Morris* v. *Anderson* (1882) 9 R. 952; *Nicol's Exors.* v. *Hill* (1887) 14 R. 384.

[3] *Sandys* v. *Bain's Trs.* (1897) 25 R. 261.

[4] *Carruthers* v. *Crawford*, 1945 S.C. 82.

[5] See further *infra.*

[6] cf. *Young* v. *Johnson* (1880) 7 R. 760.

[7] *McCaig* v. *Glasgow University*, 1907 S.C. 231 (towers and statues); *McCaig's Trs.* v. *Lismore U.F. Kirk Session*, 1915 S.C. 426; *Aitken's Trs.* v. *A.*, 1927 S.C. 374 (statue); *Lindsay's Exor.* v. *Forsyth*, 1940 S.C. 568 (flowers for grave in perpetuity); *Sutherland' Tr.* v. *Verschoyle*, 1968 S.L.T. 43.

[8] *Sutherland's Trs., supra.*

[9] *Troussier* v. *Matthew*, 1922 S.L.T. 670.

extravagant as to be contrary to public policy,[1] but a bequest for a monument to commemorate a regiment has been held valid, when the sum was not so excessive as to render the bequest extravagant, wasteful or irrational.[2]

A bequest to a person to look after the deceased's animals, even though bearing to be in favour of the animals themselves, is valid.[3] A bequest of the income of a sum for saying masses for persons named is not contrary to public policy.[4]

INTERPRETATION OF WILL

In interpreting a will the court's object is to ascertain the testator's intention and to give effect to it. It is presumed that a will is to be construed according to the law of the testator's domicile.[5] That intention falls to be discovered from the language of the deed itself, not from outside sources, nor even from other expressions of intention, not amounting to testamentary writings, by the testator. But to a limited extent the court may receive evidence from outside sources.

Extrinsic evidence is admissible to help the court to decide whether a writing was intended to be testamentary, or merely instructions, a note or memorandum, or otherwise not testamentary.[6] Extrinsic evidence is also admissible to aid in deciphering the text of the will, or to translate any part of it in a foreign language, and also as to the facts, such as the testator's family and his property, presumed known to him and with regard to which he made his will.[7]

The leading principle of interpretation proper in that the court should give each word the natural and ordinary meaning which it bears in everyday usage, and not any artificial, secondary or technical meaning,[8] though technical legal terms, such as 'next-of-kin' will normally, particularly in a deed prepared professionally, be given their legal meaning. The court will, *in dubio*, prefer an interpretation which avoids intestacy.[9]

1 *Mackintosh's J.F.* v. *L.A.*, 1935 S.C. 406.
2 *Campbell Smith's Trs.* v. *Scott*, 1944 S.L.T. 198.
3 *Flockhart's Trs.* v. *Bowlet*, 1934 S.N. 23.
4 *Lindsay's Exor.* v. *Forsyth*, 1940 S.C. 568.
5 *McBride's Trs.*, 1952 S.L.T. (Notes) 59.
6 On this see *supra*.
7 *Dunsmure* v. *D.* (1879) 7 R. 261; *Free Church Trs.* v. *Maitland* (1887) 14 R. 333; *Hannay's Trs.* v. *Keith*, 1913 S.C. 482.
8 *Young* v. *Robertson* (1862) 4 Macq. 314; *Miller's Trs.* v. *Brown*, 1933 S.C. 669.
9 *Ainslie's Trs.* v. *Imlach's Exors.*, 1926 S.L.T. 28; *Johnston's Trs.* v. *Gray*, 1949 S.L.T. (Notes) 16.

Patent and latent ambiguities

Where there is ambiguity or doubt as to which persons or things the testator had in mind, if it is patent or apparent on the face of the deed, it must be resolved by examination of the context and the whole scheme of the will, and if no meaning emerges from this examination the will to that extent fails from uncertainty. But if the ambiguity is latent, not apparent on the face of the deed but emerging only when the testator's language is sought to be applied to the circumstances, extrinsic evidence is admissible to help resolve the ambiguity.[1] Thus evidence is admissible as to which of two persons, neither of whose names correspond exactly to a beneficiary named, is truly intended;[2] this may include parole evidence of other statements by the testator as to which he intended, if the language of the will is equally applicable to two competing claimants.[3]

A provision in a codicil may be referred to to discover the meaning of an expression used by the testator, even though that provision has subsequently been revoked.[4]

If a description or designation accurately names one beneficiary, the strong presumption that he was the one intended can be overcome only by cogent positive evidence that another claimant, whose designation does not exactly correspond, was the legatee intended.[5]

Revoked wills of the testator and the wills of other members of the family cannot be referred to to assist interpretation of the subsisting will,[6] nor is it competent to lead evidence of the testator's orally expressed opinion of the effect of the will.[7]

Where a reference in a will to an earlier clause was clearly to the wrong clause, the court has interpreted the will as if it referred to the clause obviously intended.[8]

Date from which will speaks

A will, whatever its date of execution, speaks from the date of the testator's death. Consequently legatees who predecease can claim nothing and beneficiaries designated as 'children' or

[1] McLaren I, 392; cf. Bell, *Prin.* §1885; *Hay* v. *Duthie's Trs.*, 1956 S.C. 511.

[2] *Johnstone's Exors.* v. *J.* (1902) 10 S.L.T. 42; *Cathcart's Trs.* v. *Bruce*, 1923 S.L.T. 722.

[3] *Charter* v. *C.* (1874) L.R. 7 H.L. 364.

[4] *Currie's Trs.* v. *Collier*, 1939 S.C. 247.

[5] *Nasmyth's Trs.* v. *N.S.P.C.C.*, 1914 S.C. (H.L.) 76.

[6] *Devlin's Trs.* v. *Breen*, 1945 S.C. (H.L.) 27.

[7] *Devlin's Trs.* v. *Breen*, 1943 S.C. 556.

[8] *Reid's Trs.* v. *Bucher*, 1929 S.C. 615.

by other similar descriptive terms are normally ascertained as at the date of death.[1]

No right under the will can vest in any person before the date of the testator's death.

Testamentary writings construed together

All the deceased's testamentary writings must be construed, so far as possible, as one and an attempt made to give effect to all such writings.[2] In case of inconsistency a later provision on any matter is deemed to supersede an earlier provision on the matter.[3]

Repugnancy

Where a testator confers an initial gift of fee and in a later will or codicil does not revoke that gift but seeks to fetter or restrain the fiar's enjoyment by any provision which is inconsistent with an estate in fee, the later restrictions fall to be disregarded as repugnant to the initial gift.[4] It is a question of interpretation whether the later deed effects an express or implied revocation or is merely an attempt to fetter the initial gift.[5]

CLAIMS TO LEGAL RIGHTS

Legal rights

As on intestacy, a testator's surviving spouse and issue are entitled to their legal rights as established at common law and modified by the Succession (Sc.) Act, 1964, Ss. 10–11.[6] A testator having such relatives is not entitled, unless they have discharged their claims to legal rights,[7] to test, nor is his will free to operate, on more than dead's part or so much of his estate as

1 But see, exceptionally, *Macdonald's Trs.* v. *M.* (1900) 8 S.L.T. 226.

2 e.g. *Coxe* v. *Cox* (1874) 2 R. 41; *Gore Booth's Tr.* v. *G.B.* (1898) 25 R. 803; *Taylor's Tr.* v. *Robinson*, 1911 S.C. 334.

3 *Low's Exors.* (1873) 11 M. 744; *Tronson* v. *T.* (1884) 12 R. 155; *Storrar* v. *Smail* (1888) 26 S.L.R. 43; *Jamieson's Trs.* v. *J.* (1899) 2 F. 258.

4 *Miller's Trs.* v. *M.* (1890) 18 R. 301; *Yuill's Trs.* v. *Thomson* (1902) 4 F. 815; *Macculloch* v. *McCulloch's Trs.* (1903) 6 F. (H.L.) 3, 6; *Graham* v. *G's Trs.*, 1927 S.C. 388; *Ironside's Exor.* v. *I's Exor.*, 1933 S.C. 116.

5 *Ford's Trs.* v. *F.*, 1940 S.C. 426.

6 Ch. 110, *supra.* The surviving spouse is not, however, entitled to prior rights to house, furniture, and plenishing, nor to financial provision, under the 1964 Act, Ss. 8–9, unless there is total or partial failure of the will and consequent total or partial intestacy.

7 Legitim could formerly, but cannot now, be discharged by antenuptial marriage contract: Succession (Sc.) Act, 1964, S. 12. *Jus relictae vel relicti* can still be so discharged.

is not required to satisfy these claims.[1] If the will does not provide for legal rights, any party entitled thereto who has not discharged his or her rights may claim against the will, and the testamentary provisions must abate so far as necessary to pay legal rights.[2]

Testamentary provisions made to parties who can claim legal rights

Where testamentary provisions are made for persons entitled to claim legal rights the provision is *prima facie* deemed given in satisfaction of legal rights and not in addition thereto, if it is expressed to be so,[3] or if payment of the provision in addition to legal rights would conflict with other provisions of the will which disposes of the whole estate,[4] but it is *prima facie* additional to legal rights is expressed to be so, or if payment of the provision can be made without prejudice to other provisions of the will, which disposes of only dead's part or of some lesser part of the estate.[5] A provision expressed to be in full of legal rights protects only the testator's estate from such claims; it does not exclude such claims against the other parent's estate.[6]

Statutorily implied declaration that provision in satisfaction of legal rights

Every testamentary disposition executed after the commencement of the Succession (Sc.) Act, 1964, by which provision is made in favour of the spouse or of any issue of the testator, and which does not contain a declaration that the provision so made is in full and final satisfaction of the right to any share in the testator's estate to which such party is entitled by way of legal rights has effect as if it contained such a declaration, unless it contains an express provision to the contrary.[7]

Election

The principle of approbate and reprobate, or of election,[8] is to the effect that a person cannot both repudiate a deed, as by claiming legal rights in conflict with a will, and claim under it,

[1] He can accordingly test on his heritage and one half of his moveables (if he leaves a spouse or issue) or one-third of his moveables (if he leaves both a spouse and issue).

[2] e.g. *Urquhart's Exors.* v. *Abbott* (1899) 1 F. 1149 (where held that children were also entitled to the expense of their upbringing and education out of the estate, in so far as their legitim was inadequate).

[3] e.g. *McLaren* v. *Howie* (1869) 8 M. 106; *Moon* v. *M's Trs.*, 1909 S.C. 185.

[4] *Caithness' Trs.* v. *C.* (1877) 4 R. 937.

[5] *White* v. *Finlay* (1861) 24 D. 38.

[6] *Buckle* v. *B's Curator* (1907) 15 S.L.T. 98; *Moon* v. *M's Trs.*, 1909 S.C. 185.

[7] Succession (Sc.) Act, 1964, S. 13.

[8] The doctrine of approbate and reprobate in Scots Law is identical with that of election in English law: *Crum Ewing's Trs.* v. *Bayly's Trs.*, 1911 S.C. (H.L.) 18.

as by claiming a provision thereunder, but must elect which claim to pursue. A case for election arises only if the provision is expressed to be in full of legal rights, or if the claim thereto would conflict with the scheme of the will, or if the will is statutorily deemed to declare that the provision is in full of legal rights,[1] but not where legal rights and the provision can both be claimed within the testator's scheme of disposal.

A case for election may also arise where there has been a marriage contract containing provisions in lieu of, and discharging, legal rights, and a will also provides for the person so entitled.[2]

Where claimants not put to election

A claimant is not put to his election if the surrender of the claim to legal rights will not benefit the other purposes of the will but that property will be treated as undisposed of.[3]

Nor is there a case for election where the claimant is entitled to a provision independently of the testator's settlement, such as from a pension fund,[4] or an insurance policy.[5]

Conditions of election

A party put to his election must have a free choice and have a right absolutely to whichever he chooses. The necessity of electing must arise from the wishes of someone who has power to bind the person put to election, and the result of election must be to give effect to the testator's desire, express or implied.[6] The party must also have full knowledge of the alternative rights and the facts relevant to the choice;[7] election once made in these circumstances is final, but not if made in ignorance, or under error, or in circumstances showing it not to be a free and deliberate choice.[8] If children have enjoyed conventional provisions for

1 Succession (Sc.) Act, 1964, S. 13.

2 *Darling's Exor.* v. *D.* (1869) 41 Sc. Jur. 545; *Crum Ewing's Trs.* v. *Bayly's Trs.* (1888) 15 R. 507. If the marriage contract does not discharge the claims, legal rights may be claimed as well as any provision made under the marriage contract: *Murray's Trs.* v. *M.* (1888) 18 S.L.R. 690.

3 *Hewit's Trs.* v. *Lawson* (1891) 18 R. 793; *Brown's Trs.* v. *Gregson*, 1920 S.C. (H.L.) 87.

4 *Craigie's Trs.* v. *C.* (1904) 6 F. 343.

5 *Hay's Trs.* v. *H.* (1904) 6 F. 978.

6 *Douglas's Trs.* v. *D.* (1862) 24 D. 1191, 1208; *Brown's Trs.* v. *Gregson*, 1920 S.C. (H.L.) 87.

7 *Logan* v. *L.* (1869) 7 S.L.R. 40; *Dawson's Trs.* v. *D.* (1896) 23 R. 1006; *Walker* v. *Orr's Trs.*, 1958 S.L.T. 220.

8 *Inglis* v. *Brown* (1890) 17 R. (H.L.) 76; *Dawson's Trs.*, *supra*; *Stewart* v. *Bruce's Trs.* (1898) 25 R. 965; *Duff* (1899) 7 S.L.T. 46; *Younger* v. *Y's Trs.* (1900) 7 S.L.T. 453.

some time the onus is on them to prove that they had not elected.[1]

Election must be made without unreasonable delay but there may be no necessity for immediate election.[2] An election by a person under curatory without the curator's consent is revocable during the ward's lifetime[3]. A curator bonis may be authorized to elect on behalf of the ward.[4] Questions may also arise whether conduct amounts to an election.[5] A person may approbate the testator's will as an individual and reprobate it in a representative capacity, or conversely.[6]

A person may be held, by long delay, to elect and by silence, despite knowledge of the possible claim, to have abandoned a claim to legal rights.[7]

Forfeiture

It may be expressly provided that if a person given a provision in full of legal rights claims legal rights against the will he is to forfeit all claim to the provision. A clause of forfeiture affects the interest only of the person who has claimed against the will, not of anyone having a separate, even though dependent, claim.[8] If a claimant claims legal rights and incurs the forfeiture the provision forfeited goes to those beneficiaries under the will whose interests have been prejudiced by the election,[9] unless the will expressly provides to whom the forfeited interest is to go.[10] A child claiming legitim against the will cannot found on the forfeiture clause to the effect of causing partial intestacy and claiming

[1] *Walker* v. *Orr's Trs.*, 1958 S.L.T. 63, 220.

[2] *Watson's Trs.* v. *W.*, 1910 S.C. 975; *Robinson* v. *R's Trs.*, 1934 S.L.T. 183; see also *Turner's Trs.* v. *T.*, 1943 S.C. 389.

[3] *Lawson* v. *Cook*, 1928 S.L.T. 411.

[4] *Morrison's C.B.* v. *Morrison's Trs.* (1880) 8 R. 205; *McCall's Tr.* v. *McCall's C.B.* (1901) 3 F. 1055; *Skinner's C.B.* (1903) 5 F. 914.

[5] *McFadyen* v. *McF's Trs.* (1882) 10 R. 285; *Donaldson* v. *Tainsh's Trs.* (1886) 13 R. 967; *Crellin* v. *Muirhead's J.F.* (1892) 20 R. 51.

[6] *MacGregor's Exrx.* v. *M's Trs.*, 1935 S.C. 13.

[7] *Pringle's Exces.* (1870) 8 M. 622; *Countess of Kintore* v. *E. Kintore* (1886) 13 R. (H.L.) 93; cf. *Lawson* v. *Cook*, 1928 S.L.T. 411; *Walker* v. *Orr's Trs.*, 1958 S.L.T. 63.

[8] *Fisher* v. *Dixon* (1833) 6 W. & S. 431; *Snody's Trs.* v. *Gibson's Trs.* (1883) 10 R. 599; *Gunn's Trs.* v. *Macfarlane* (1897) 4 S.L.T. 334; *Paton's Trs.* v. *Rowan*, 1947 S.C. 466; *Nicholson's Trs.* v. *N.*, 1960 S.C. 186; *Hurll's Trs.* v. *H.*, 1964 S.C. 12. Contrast *Jack* v. *Marshall* (1879) 6 R. 543; *Gillies* v. *G's Trs.* (1881) 8 R. 505; *Campbell's Trs.* v. *C.* (1889) 16 R. 1007; *Hannah's Trs.* v. *H.*, 1924 S.C. 494; *Tindall's Trs.* v. *T.*, 1933 S.C. 419; where interests held not separate and forfeiture affected claimant's children also.

[9] *Davidson's Trs.* v. *D.* (1871) 9 M. 995; *Jack* v. *Marshall* (1879) 6 R. 543; *Snody's Trs.*, *supra*. In *Tindall* v. *T.*, 1933 S.C. 419 they fell into intestacy.

[10] *Campbell's Trs.* v. *C.* (1889) 16 R. 1007; *Brown's Trs.* v. *Gregson*, 1916 S.C. 97; *Ballantyne's Trs.* v. *B.*, 1952 S.C. 458.

as heir *ab intestato*.[1] If there is no beneficiary in whose favour the forfeiture clause can operate it does not take effect.[2]

Even if there is no express clause of forfeiture, where a provision is given in full satisfaction of legal rights, a party claiming legal rights forfeits the testamentary provision.[3]

Equitable compensation

If a declaration that a testamentary provision is given in full satisfaction of legal rights is excluded, and formerly also where there was no such declaration but that intention appeared, but there is no express condition or declaration of forfeiture, the provision is not wholly forfeited but is applied firstly to restoring what has been taken out of the estate by the claim for legal rights, so as to compensate claimants on dead's part, and thereafter may be claimed by the party taking legal rights.[4]

Claims to legal rights notwithstanding election of provision

Where a person entitled to legal rights has elected to accept a testamentary provision in lieu thereof, this election does not preclude a claim to legal rights[5] from any part of the estate which falls into intestacy, since such a claim does not conflict with the testator's settlement,[6] unless the person accepting has granted a full discharge of claims to legal rights.[7]

So too an election does not in an appropriate case prevent a claim as an heir on intestacy to part of the estate which falls into intestacy.[8]

1 *Gillies*, *supra*; *Hannah's Trs.* v. *H.*, 1924 S.C. 494; *Macnaughton* v. *M's Trs.*, 1954 S.C. 312.

2 *Gillies* v. *Gillies' Trs.* (1881) 8 R. 505.

3 *Breadalbane's Trs.* v. *Buckingham* (1840) 2 D. 731; *Macfarlane's Trs.* v. *Oliver* (1882) 9 R. 1138; *Rose's Trs.* v. *R.*, 1916 S.C. 827; *Wingate* v. *W's Trs.*, 1921 S.C. 857; *Hannah's Trs.* v. *H.*, 1924 S.C. 494; *Gray's Trs.* v. *G.*, 1907 S.C. 54 and *Nixon's Trs.* v. *Kane*, 1915 S.C. 496 are overruled.

4 *Macfarlane's Trs.* v. *Oliver* (1882) 9 R. 1138; *Russell's Trs.* v. *R.* (1886) 13 R. 989; *Somervell* v. *S.* (1884) 11 R. 1004; *Ross* v. *R.* (1896) 23 R. 1024; *Rose's Trs.* v. *R.*, 1916 S.C. 827; *Thomson's Trs.* v. *T.*, 1946 S.C. 399; *Orchardson's Trs.* v. *Kelly*, 1947 S.L.T. (Notes) 35; see also *Jack's Trs.* v. *J.*, 1913 S.C. 815; *McLeod* v. *Love*, 1914 S.C. 983.

5 Nor, presumably, to a claim by a widow for prior rights under the Succession (Sc.) Act, 1964, Ss. 8–9, on the basis that there is now a partial intestacy.

6 *Naismith* v. *Boyes* (1899) 1 F. (H.L.) 79; *Moon's Trs.* v. *M.* (1899) 2 F. 201; *Farquharson* v. *Kelly* (1900) 2 F. 863; *McGregor's Trs.* v. *Kimbell*, 1911 S.C. 1196; *Walker* v. *Orr's Trs.*, 1958 S.L.T. 63; *Petrie's Trs.* v. *Mander's Tr.*, 1954 S.C. 430.

7 *Melville's Trs.* v. *M's Trs.*, 1964 S.C. 105.

8 *Crawford's Trs.* v. *C.* (1899) 7 S.L.T. 205; *Scott* v. *Gowans*, 1916 1 S.L.T. 404; *Symmer's Trs.* v. *S.*, 1918 S.C. 337; *Tindall's Trs.* v. *T.*, 1933 S.C. 419; cf. *Bowie's Trs.* v. *McIntosh* (1905) 13 S.L.T. 72.

LEGACIES

Legacies

Part or all of the estate on which the testator can test freely is normally disposed of by giving legacies or bequests, i.e. gifts of specified subjects to specified persons or objects. A legacy may be a direct gift, or the gift of a claim the testator had against a third party,[1] or the release of the legatee from a debt owed to the testator.[2]

Kinds of legacies

Legacies are distinguished into (a) special or specific legacies, gifts of a determinate object or investment, which confer on the legatee a personal right to delivery or transfer of the subject of the bequest;[3] of this category a sub-group are demonstrative legacies, gifts of an object or sum from a designated source;[4] and (b) general legacies, which are gifts not having a character distinct from other things of the same kind belonging to the deceased.[5] Questions may arise whether a legacy is specific or demonstrative, or merely general which may be satisfied by paying money.[6]

Ademption of special legacies

Where the subject of a special legacy had ceased to be part of the testator's estate by the time of his death it is held adeemed and nothing is due to the legatee.[7] Ademption is a question, not of intention, but of fact, whether the thing specially bequeathed was still part of the testator's estate at the time of death.[8] Ademption may take place by the testator's having previously alienated the subject,[9] or its having perished, or been realized and converted

[1] e.g. *Cobban's Exors.* v. *C.*, 1915 S.C. 82.

[2] e.g. *Reid* v. *Hope's Trs.* (1825) 1 W. & S. 172.

[3] e.g. my Bentley motor-car; my holding in A.B. Ltd.; see e.g. *Anderson* v. *Thomson* (1877) 4 R. 1101; *Cobban's Exors.* v. *C.*, 1915 S.C. 82; *Sommerville's Trs.* v. *S's Exors.*, 1952 S.L.T. 251.

[4] e.g. £500 of the War Stock bequeathed to me by X.Y.; such of my books as the legatee may choose; see e.g. *Douglas's Exors.* (1869) 7 M. 504; *Chivas' Tr.* v. *McLeod* (1881) 9 R. 86; *McKenzie* v. *Barker's Trs.* (1905) 13 S.L.T. 501; *Reid's Trs.* v. *Dawson*, 1915 S.C. (H.L.) 47.

[5] e.g. £1000.

[6] See e.g., *Sym's Tr.* v. *Ayr Hospital* (1897) 25 R. 40; *Barr's Trs.* v. *Ardrossan Castle Curling Club* (1901) 3 F. 903; *Maclean* v. *M's Exrx.*, 1908 S.C. 838.

[7] *Anderson* v. *Thomson* (1877) 4 R. 1101; *McArthur's Exors.* v. *Guild*, 1908 S.C. 743.

[8] *McArthur's Exors.*, *supra*; *Cobban's Exors.* v. *C.*, 1915 S.C. 82.

[9] *Congreve's Trs.* v. *C.* (1874) 1 R. 1102; *Thomson's Trs.* v. *Lockhart*, 1930 S.C. 674; *Tennant's Tr.* v. *T.*, 1946 S.C. 420.

into another form,[1] or been taken from him under compulsory powers,[2] but is not held to have taken place by mere change in name or form, as where company shares are converted into stock or otherwise altered by the company.[3]

Ademption has been held not to have been effected where the testator was incapacitated before his death and his curator bonis, in the course of ordinary administration, sold the subject of the special legacy.[4]

Uncertainty

A legacy fails from uncertainty if it proves impossible to ascertain the subject matter of the bequest, or the object to which it is given, or the way in which the testator's wish is to be implemented.[5] The court is reluctant to reach such a conclusion if it can reasonably arrive at a result consistent with the testator's intentions.[6]

Certainty of subject matter does not require that the bequest be of a definite amount if the will furnishes sufficient means of qualifying it,[6] but there is uncertainty if there is no criterion for ascertaining the amount, or it is not certain what interest the beneficiary is to take,[7] or a specific bequest is not identifiable.[8]

Uncertainty of object may arise from misdescription or description of the legatee insufficient to enable him or it to be identified,[9] or vagueness, such as the promotion of free thought,[10] or the benefit of relations, friends or acquaintances,[11] or indefiniteness, as where residue was to be applied in increasing charitable bequests or for other objects of a similar nature.[12]

Uncertainty of manner of implement exists where the testator's directions are deemed too vague to be able to be implemented.[13]

1 *Anderson* v. *Thomson* (1877) 4 R. 1101; *Davidson's Trs.* v. *D.* (1901) 4 F. 107; *Maclean* v. *M's Exor.*, 1908 S.C. 838; *Cobban's Exors.* v. *C.*, 1915 S.C. 82; *Ballantyne's Trs.* v. *B.*, 1941 S.C. 35; *Ogilvie-Forbes' Trs.* v. *O.F.*, 1955 S.C. 405.

2 *Chalmers* v. *C.* (1857) 14 D. 57; cf. *Pollock's Trs.* v. *Anderson* (1902) 4 F. 455.

3 *Mitchell's Trs.* v. *Fergus* (1889) 16 R. 902; *Macfarlane's Trs.* v. *M.*, 1910 S.C. 325.

4 *Kennedy* v. *K.* (1843) 6 D. 40; *Moncrieff* v. *Miln* (1856) 18 D. 1286; *McAdam's Exor.* v. *Souter* (1904) 7 F. 179; *Macfarlane's Trs.* v. *M.*, 1910 S.C. 325.

5 *Dodds* v. *McBain*, 1933 S.N. 16 (bequest to A for any purpose he may think proper).

6 *Dundee Mags.* v. *Morris* (1858) 3 Macq. 134; *Barr's Trs.* v. *Ardrossan Castle Curling Club* (1901) 3 F. 903; cf. *Macduff* v. *Spence's Trs.*, 1909 S.C. 178.

7 *Hamilton's Trs.* v. *H.* (1901) 4 F. 266.

8 *Barr's Trs.* v. *Ardrossan Castle Curling Club* (1901) 3 F. 903.

9 *Shepherd's Trs.* v. *S.*, 1945 S.C. 60; *Guthrie's Exor.* v. *G.*, 1945 S.C. 138.

10 *Hardie* v. *Morison* (1899) 7 S.L.T. 42; contrast *McLean* v. *Henderson's Trs.* (1880) 7 R. 601 (advancement of phrenology).

11 *Salvesen's Trs.* v. *Wye*, 1954 S.C. 440.

12 *Campbell's Trs.* v. *Edinburgh R.I.*, 1932 S.N. 10.

13 *Hamilton's Trs.*, *supra*; cf. *Campbell Smith's Trs.* v. *Scott*, 1944 S.L.T. 198.

Conditions attached to bequests

A testator may attach a condition, suspensive or resolutive, to a bequest and the legatee must, in general, accept the condition or forfeit the bequest.[1] The condition may be to any effect, such as not to allow the beneficiary's mother to reside on his estate,[2] or provided that the beneficiary was living with her husband,[3] or on condition that the beneficiary occupies a house given in liferent,[4] or providing for forfeiture if the legatee remarried,[5] or provided that the legatee was of a stated religion.[6]

Thus it may be provided that heirs succeeding to lands must assume the name and arms of the testator,[7] or that a liferenter may not sell or mortgage lands,[8] or that a liferenter should not have any communication with a certain child,[9] or that a charity is to take if not subject to government control.[10]

The legatee is deemed to have implemented the condition if he has done all in his power to implement the condition and the non-implement is attributable to factors outwith his control.[11] And there is no forfeiture if the condition is not timeously intimated to the beneficiaries, so as to give them a fair opportunity to elect whether to implement the condition or not.[12]

Description of a beneficiary as the testator's wife[13] or fiancée[14] may imply the condition that she still possessed that character when the will operated, so that the bequest is defeated if the person has ceased to possess that character.

A conditional bequest is frequently fenced with a clause of forfeiture or of devolution or destination-over, to take effect in the event of the condition not being implemented at a later date.[15]

1 *Sturrock* v. *Rankin's Trs.* (1875) 2 R. 850.

2 *Wemyss* v. *W's Trs.*, 1921 S.C. 30.

3 *Barker* v. *Watson's Trs.*, 1919 S.C. 109.

4 *Veitch's Exor.* v. *V.*, 1947 S.L.T. 17.

5 *Beaton's J.F.* v. *Beaton*, 1950 S.L.T. (Notes) 63.

6 *Innes's Trs.* v. *I.*, 1963 S.C. 339.

7 *Hunter* v. *Weston* (1882) 9 R. 492; *E. Caithness* v. *Sinclair*, 1912 S.C. 79; *Munro's Trs.* v. *Spencer*, 1912 S.C. 933; *McFarlane* v. *McF's J.F.*, 1955 S.L.T. (Notes) 68; *Munro's Trs.* v. *Monson*, 1962 S.C. 414; 1965 S.C. 84.

8 *Kirkland* v. *K's Tr.* (1886) 13 R. 798; *Chaplin's Trs.* v. *Hoile* (1890) 18 R. 27.

9 *Balfour's Trs.* v. *Johnston*, 1936 S.C. 137; cf. *Wemyss* v. *W's Trs.*, 1921 S.C. 30.

10 *Connell's Trs.* v. *Milngavie District Nursing Assocn.*, 1953 S.C. 230; *Mollison's Trs.* v. *Aberdeen General Hospitals*, 1953 S.C. 264.

11 Stair I, 3, 8; Ersk. III, 3, 85; *Pirie* v. *P.* (1873) 11 M. 941; *Simpson* v. *Roberts*, 1931 S.C. 259; cf. *Dunbar* v. *Scott's Tr.*, (1872) 10 M. 982; *Reid* v. *McPhedran* (1881) 9 R. 80; *Robertson's Trs.* v. *White* (1903) 11 S.L.T. 566; *Simpson* v. *Roberts*, 1931 S.C. 259; *Cumming's Trs.*, 1960 S.L.T. (Notes) 96; *Munro's Trs.* v. *Monson*, 1965 S.C. 84.

12 *Rodger's Trs.* v. *Allfrey*, 1910 S.C. 1015; *Balfour's Trs.* v. *Johnstone*, 1936 S.C. 137.

13 *Ritchie* v. *R's Trs.* (1874) 1 R. 987; *Pirie's Trs.* v. *P.*, 1962 S.C. 43.

14 *Ormiston's Exor.* v. *Laws*, 1966 S.L.T. 110.

15 e.g. *Chaplin's Trs.* v. *Hoile* (1890) 18 R. 27; (1891) 19 R. 237; *E. Caithness* v. *Sinclair*, 1912 S.C. 79; *Munro's Trs.* v. *Spencer*, 1912 S.C. 933; cf. *Collins's Trs.* v. *C.*, 1913 S.C. 588.

If a condition attached to a gift of income has become impossible of fulfilment the gift lapses and falls into residue.[1]

If executors or trustees are directed to pay a bequest if satisfied as to certain facts, the exercise of their discretion is not challengeable unless unreasonable, or possibly even unless *in mala fide* or *ultra vires*.[2]

Conditions ineffective

If, however, a condition attached to a bequest is legally objectionable, the condition falls to be disregarded and the legatee is entitled to the bequest unconditionally.

A condition is void from uncertainty if the legatee, and the court, cannot decide with reasonable certainty whether or not particular conduct contravenes the condition.[3]

A condition is void for impossibility if in the nature of things it cannot be performed at all, or at least at the time when the legacy vests,[4] but not merely because the legatee cannot satisfy it,[5] nor because satisfaction is merely improbable.[6]

It is void for illegality if the implement of the condition would require, or tend to promote, illegal conduct.

It is void for immorality if conducive to immoral conduct or given on account of immoral conduct.[7]

It is void as *contra bonos mores* if deemed contrary to the requirements of good morals, such as a condition that a child should not reside with her own parents, against whose character no allegation could be made.[8]

Voidness as being contrary to public policy is the most general ground of objection, striking at anything deemed reprehensible or undesirable, such as a condition wholly prohibiting marriage,[9] though not at a condition prohibiting

[1] *Young's Tr.* v. *Deacons of Perth* (1893) 20 R. 778.

[2] *Dundee Hospitals* v. *Bell's Trs.*, 1952 S.C. (H.L.) 78.

[3] *Wemyss* v. *W's Trs.*, 1921 S.C. 30; *Campbell Smith's Trs.* v. *Scott*, 1944 S.L.T. 198; *Veitch's Exor.* v. *V.*, 1947 S.L.T. 17; *Beaton's J.F.* v. *B.*, 1950 S.L.T. (Notes) 63.

[4] Inst. II, 14, 10; Stair III, 8, 24; Ersk. III, 3, 85; Bell, *Prin.* §1785; *Dunbar* v. *Scott's Trs.* (1872) 10 M. 982; cf. *Sutherland's Trs.* v. *S.* (1870) 8 M. 716.

[5] e.g. if he runs a mile in five minutes; cf. *Barker* v. *Watson's Trs.*, 1919 S.C. 109; *Pennie's Trs.* v. *R.N.L.I.*, 1924 S.L.T. 520; *Forrest's Trs.* v. *Alexander*, 1925 S.N. 80.

[6] cf. *Egerton* v. *Brownlow* (1853) 4 H.L.C. 1; *Barker* v. *Watson's Trs.*, 1919 S.C. 109.

[7] *Johnston* v. *McKenzie's Exors.* (1875) 14 S. 106; *Young* v. *Johnston & Wright* (1880) 7 R. 760; *Troussier* v. *Matthew*, 1922 S.L.T. 670.

[8] *Fraser* v. *Rose* (1840) 11 D. 1466; *Grant's Trs.* v. *G.* (1898) 25 R. 929; cf. *Barker* v. *Watson's Trs.*, 1919 S.C. 109; *Wemyss* v. *W's Trs.*, 1921 S.C. 30; *Balfour's Trs.* v. *Johnston*, 1936 S.C. 137; see also *Innes's Trs.* v. *I.*, 1963 S.C. 339, 346.

[9] Stair I, 3, 7; III, 8, 24; Ersk. III, 3, 85; Bell, *Prin.* §1785; Fraser, *H. & W.*, I, 467; McLaren, I, 601; cf. *Sturrock* v. *Rankin's Trs.* (1875) 2 R. 850; see also *Aird's Exors.* v. *A.*, 1949 S.C. 154.

marriage with a particular person or persons of a particular class,[1] nor at a clause of devolution in the event of succeeding to a peerage.[2]

Repugnancy

Repugnancy arises where conditions are attached to a bequest which are inconsistent with it. Thus where an unqualified and indefeasible gift of fee is given and has vested the beneficiary is entitled to payment notwithstanding a later direction to trustees to hold the capital and pay only the income, or to apply the bequest for the beneficiary's behoof in some manner directed.[3] Similarly if there is a direction to purchase an annuity for a beneficiary, the latter may elect to take the capital value thereof,[4] so long as if purchased the annuity would be at the beneficiary's absolute disposal, but not if alimentary.[5]

The subject of bequest

The subject of a bequest must be designated so as to be identifiable; it matters not whether it is designated by any appropriate legal or technical term, nor whether there is misdescription, if the testator's intention adequately appears.[6] But if the subject of bequest cannot be identified the bequest must lapse from uncertainty.

Questions may arise whether a general word such as 'money'

[1] *Ommanney* v. *Bingham* (1796) 3 Pat. 448; *Graham* v. *G.* (1822) 1 Sh. App. 365; *Kidd* v. *Kidd's Trs.* (1863) 2 M. 227; *Sturrock, supra,* 852; *Forbes* v. *F's Trs.* (1882) 9 R. 675; *Smith's Trs.* v. *S.* (1883) 10 R. 1144; cf. Stair III, 8, 24; Fraser, *H. & W.*, I, 474.

[2] *E. Caithness* v. *Sinclair,* 1912 S.C. 79.

[3] *Jamieson* v. *Lesslie's Trs.* (1889) 16 R. 807; *Christie's Trs.* v. *Murray's Trs.* (1889) 16 R. 913; *Duthie's Trs.* v. *Forlong* (1889) 16 R. 1002; *Brown* v. *B's Trs.* (1890) 17 R. 517; *Miller's Trs.* v. *M.* (1890) 18 R. 301; *Greenlees' Trs.* v. *G.* (1894) 22 R. 136; *Hargrave's Trs.* v. *Schofield* (1900) 3 F. 14; *Yuill's Trs.* v. *Thomson* (1902) 4 F. 815; *Forrest's Trs.* v. *Reid* (1904) 7 F. 142; *Veitch's Trs.* v. *Rutherford,* 1914 S.C. 182; *Graham* v. *G's Trs.*, 1927 S.C. 388; *Ironside's Exor.* v. *I's Exor.*, 1933 S.C. 116; see also *Ford's Trs.* v. *F.*, 1940 S.C. 426.

[4] *Tod* v. *T's Trs.* (1871) 9 M. 728; *Kippen* v. *K's Trs.* (1871) 10 M. 134; *Dow* v. *Kilgour's Trs.* (1877) 4 R. 403; *Turner's Trs.* v. *Fernie,* 1908 S.C. 883; *Murray* v. *Macfarlane's Trs.* (1895) 22 R. 927; *Kennedy's Trs.* v. *Warren* (1901) 3 F. 1087; *Hutchinson's Trs.* v. *Young* (1903) 6 F. 26; *Turner's Trs.* v. *Fernie,* 1908 S.C. 883; *Brown's Trs.* v. *Thom,* 1916 S.C. 32; *Dempster's Trs.* v. *D.*, 1921 S.C. 332; *Forbes's Trs.* v. *Tennant,* 1926 S.C. 294.

[5] *Dempster's Trs., supra*; *Branford's Trs.* v. *Powell,* 1924 S.C. 439.

[6] *Wright's Trs.* (1870) 8 M. 708; *Bruce's Trs.* v. *B.* (1875) 2 R. 775; *Smith's Trs.* v. *S.* (1883) 10 R. 1144; *Neilson's Trs.* v. *N.* (1903) 5 F. 938; cf. *Gellatly's Trs.* v. *Edinburgh R.I.* (1905) 13 S.L.T. 38.

or 'capital' carries heritage[1] and whether a particular phrase includes a particular subject.[2]

Where subjects of bequest are subject to burdens, such as rights in security, the legatee must take the bequest *cum onere* and cannot, unless such intention appears from the will, require the executor to disburden the bequest.[3]

Legatum rei alienae

Where the testator has bequeathed something not belonging to him, he is presumed to have believed (erroneously) that it did belong to him, and the legacy accordingly fails. But if it can be shown that he knew that the subject of the legacy did not belong to him, the bequest falls to be interpreted as a direction to the executor to purchase the subject of the bequest and transfer it to the legatee, subject to the legatee's power to elect to take the value in lieu; if the subject cannot be acquired by the executor, the legatee must be content with the fair value thereof.[4]

Designation of legatee

The overriding principle is *falsa demonstratio non nocet dummodo constet de persona*: if the legatee is clearly identifiable from the deed and the circumstances, it matters not that he is not properly named or designed, and extrinsic evidence is competent to help determine what person or body was intended to be legatee.[5] A reference back in a settlement *prima facie* refers to the nearest sensible antecedent.[6]

[1] See e.g. *Urquhart* v. *Dewar* (1879) 6 R. 1026; *Aim's Trs.* v. *A.* (1880) 8 R. 294; *Farquharson* v. *F.* (1883) 10 R. 1253; *McLeod's Tr.* v. *McLuckie* (1883) 10 R. 1056; *Oag's Curator* v. *Corner* (1885) 12 R. 1162; *Campbell* v. *C.* (1887) 15 R. 103; *Forsyth* v. *Turnbull* (1887) 15 R. 172; *Copland's Exors.* v. *Milne*, 1908 S.C. 426; *Jack's Exor.* v. *Downie*, 1908 S.C. 718; *Smith's Exors.* v. *S.*, 1918 S.C. 772; *Woodward's J.F.* v. *W.*, 1919 S.C. 350; *Craw's Tr.* v. *Blacklock*, 1920 S.C. 22; *Simson's Trs.* v. *S.*, 1922 S.C. 14; *Ord* v. *O.*, 1927 S.C. 77; *Fraser's Exrx.* v. *Fraser's C.B.*, 1931 S.C. 536; *Auld's Trs.* v. *A's Trs.*, 1933 S.C. 176; contrast *Pitcairn* v. *P.* (1870) 8 M. 604; *McInnes* v. *Hill*, 1912 1 S.L.T. 80; *Mair's Tr.* v. *Aberdeen R.I.*, 1946 S.L.T. 88.

[2] e.g. *Harper's Trs.* (1903) 5 F. 716; *Marson* v. *Smellie* (1903) 6 F. 148; *Denholm's Trs.* v. *D.*, 1908 S.C. 43; *Guthrie's Exor.* v. *G.*, 1945 S.C. 138 ('remainder'); *Thomson* v. *T.*, 1962 S.C. (H.L.) 28 (whether universal legacy nominated widow to partnership).

[3] *Carter* v. *Macarthur* (1870) 8 M. 480; *Park's Curator* v. *Black* (1871) 9 M. 1078; *Murray* v. *Parlane's Trs.* (1890) 18 R. 287; *Stewart* v. *S.* (1891) 19 R. 310; *Brand* v. *Scott's Trs.* (1892) 19 R. 768; *Adam's Trs.* v. *Wilson* (1899) 1 F. 1042.

[4] Ersk. III, 9, 10; *Traquair* v. *Martin* (1872) 11 M. 22; *Meeres* v. *Dowell's Exor.*, 1923 S.L.T. 184.

[5] *Keiller* v. *Thomson's Trs.* (1824) 3 S. 396; (1826) 4 S. 724; *Scottish Missionary Socy.* v. *Home Mission Cttee.* (1858) 20 D. 634; *Donald's Trs.* v. *D.* (1864) 2 M. 922; *Wilson's Exors.*

Note 5 continued and note 6 on page 1805.

The description of a legatee may, however, be held to import a condition, so that the legatee is entitled to the legacy only if satisfying the condition.[1]

A bequest to persons so vaguely described as not to be ascertainable with any certainty, such as to 'dependents' is void from uncertainty.[2]

Where the legatee is an entity or body the question may arise whether it has perished or continues, albeit changed in name, function or management. If the purpose is to benefit the work of the entity and that continues, the legacy is payable to the body now responsible for its management.[3]

Date when legatee ascertained

When legatees are designated as the testator's heirs or nearest of kin, or otherwise by description, the persons who occupy that category fall to be ascertained at the date of death of the testator[4] or of the other person whose life suspends vesting.[5]

In the construction of a family settlement by a parent, however, the presumption is for the inclusion of all children, so that the issue of a predeceasing child are included.[6]

v. *Scottish Socy. for Conversion of Israel* (1869) 8 M. 233; *Bogie's Trs.* v. *Swanston* (1878) 5 R. 634; *Bryce's Tr.* (1878) 5 R. 722; *Macfarlane's Trs.* v. *Henderson* (1878) 6 R. 288; *Millar's Trs.* v. *Rattray* (1891) 18 R. 989; *Johnstone's Exors.* v. *J.* (1902) 10 S.L.T. 42; *Jaffrey's Trs.* v. *S.P.C.A.* (1903) 10 S.L.T. 651; *Allison* v. *Anderson* (1907) 15 S.L.T. 529; *McGrouther's Trs.* v. *L.A.* (1907) 15 S.L.T. 652; *Lumsden's Trs.* v. *L.*, 1921 1 S.L.T. 155; *Cathcart's Trs.* v. *Bruce*, 1923 S.L.T. 722.

6 *Shepherd's Trs.* v. *S.*, 1945 S.C. 60.

1 *Shairp* v. *Henderson*, 1930 S.L.T. 743; *Ormiston's Exor.* v. *Laws*, 1966 S.L.T. 110.

2 *Robertson's J.F.* v. *R.*, 1968 S.L.T. 32.

3 *McClements' Trs.* v. *Campbell*, 1951 S.C. 167; *Thomson's Tr.* v. *Leith Hospital*, 1951 S.C. 523; *Connell's Trs.* v. *Milngavie District Nursing Assocn.*, 1953 S.C. 230; *Mollison's Trs.* v. *Aberdeen General Hospitals*, 1953 S.C. 264; contrast *Dewar's Trs.* v. *Glasgow Children's Hospitals*, 1962 S.C. 100, where trustees had discretion.

4 *Todd* v. *Mackenzie* (1874) 1 R. 1203; *Ferguson* v. *F.* (1875) 2 R. 627; *Ferrier* v. *Angus* (1876) 3 R. 396; *Maule* (1876) 3 R. 831; *Gregory's Trs.* v. *Alison* (1889) 16 R. (H.L.) 10; *Howe's Trs.* v. *Howe's J.F.* (1903) 5 F. 1099; *McDonald's Trs.* v. *McD.*, 1907 S.C. 65; *Muirhead's Trs.* v. *Torrie*, 1913 S.C. 85; *Waddell's J.F.* v. *W.*, 1924 S.C. 877; *G's Trs.* v. *G.*, 1937 S.C. 141; *Murray's Trs.* v. *Watts*, 1939 S.C. 382; *Campbell's Trs.* v. *Lamont's Exor.*, 1941 S.C. 564; *Grant's Trs.* v. *Crawford's Tr.*, 1949 S.L.T. 374; *Davidson's Trs.* v. *D.*, 1952 S.L.T. (Notes) 52.

5 *Haldane's Trs.* v. *Murphy* (1881) 9 R. 269; *Gollan's Trs.* v. *Booth* (1901) 3 F. 1035; *Johnstone's Trs.* v. *Dewar*, 1911 S.C. 722; *Brown* v. *B's Trs.*, 1912 1 S.L.T. 474; *Calder* v. *Crawford's Trs.*, 1948 S.L.T. (Notes) 37; *Grant's Trs.* v. *Crawford's Tr.*, 1949 S.L.T. 374.

6 *Sturrock* v. *Binny* (1843) 6 D. 117; *Rhind's Trs.* v. *Leith* (1866) 5 M. 104; *Stewart's Trs.* v. *Walker* (1905) 12 S.L.T. 801; *Baird's Trs.* v. *Crombie*, 1926 S.C. 518; *Muir's Trs.* v. *Coats*, 1942 S.C. 65.

Interpretation of terms descriptive of legatees

The common terms descriptive of classes of legatees have generally settled meanings, which may, however, always be displaced by the wording of particular testamentary writings, or the context in which the terms have been used, either of which may show that the term was intended to have an unusual or extended meaning. Thus normally 'children' includes immediate legitimate[1] and adopted[2] descendants, and now also illegitimate descendants unless they are expressly excluded,[3] but not grandchildren or more remote descendants;[4] 'issue' includes all direct descendants;[5] 'family' includes sons and daughters only;[6] 'relatives' and 'relations' are wider, but ordinarily limited to blood relations, and may cover nephews and nieces, a sister-in-law, and the like;[7] 'nephews and nieces' include those of the half-blood;[8] "heir-at-law' is the person entitled at common law to succeed on intestacy to heritage;[9] 'next-of-kin' are those entitled at common law to succeed on intestacy to moveables;[10]

[1] *Mitchell's Trs.* v. *Cables* (1893) 1 S.L.T. 156; *Govenlock's Trs.* v. *G.* (1895) 3 S.L.T. 163; *McDonald's Trs.* v. *Gordon*, 1909 2 S.L.T. 321; *Scott's Trs.* v. *Smart*, 1954 S.C. 12; contrast *Sharp's Trs.* v. *S.* (1894) 2 S.L.T. 124; *Gentle's Trs.* v. *Bunting* (1908) 16 S.L.T. 437; *Allan* v. *Adamson* (1902) 9 S.L.T. 404; *Burn's Trs.* v. *B.*, 1917 S.C. 117; *Purdie's Trs.* v. *Doolan*, 1929 S.L.T. 273.

[2] Succession (Sc.) Act, 1964, S. 23(2); see also Law Reform (Misc. Prov.) (Sc.) Act, 1966, S. 5.

[3] Law Reform (Misc. Prov.) (Sc.) Act, 1968, S. 5.

[4] *Ranken* (1870) 8 M. 878; *Buchan* v. *Porteous* (1879) 7 R. 211; *Whittet's Trs.* v. *W.* (1892) 19 R. 975; *Perth Mags.* v. *Irvine* (1895) 3 S.L.T. 23; *Marquis* v. *Prentice* (1896) 23 R. 595; *Adam's Trs.* v. *Carrick* (1896) 23 R. 828; *Adam's Trs.* v. *Maxwell*, 1921 S.C. 418; *Craik's Trs.* v. *Anderson*, 1932 S.C. 61; *Hay* v. *Duthie's Trs.*, 1956 S.C. 511 (adopted child excluded); contrast *Lindsay's Trs. and L.*, 1954 S.L.T. (Notes) 52.

[5] *Turner's Trs.* v. *T.* (1887) 14 R. 458; *Macdonald* v. *Hall* (1893) 20 R. (H.L.) 88; *McMurdo's Tr.* v. *McM.* (1897) 24 R. 458; *Bowie's Trs.* v. *Black* (1899) 36 S.L.R. 475; *Cattanach's Trs.* v. *C.* (1901) 4 F. 205; *Dalziel* v. *D's Trs.* (1905) 7 F. 545; *Bannerman* v. *B's Trs.* (1906) 13 S.L.T. 754; *Stewart's Trs.* v. *Whitelaw*, 1926 S.C. 701; *Craik's Trs.*, *supra*; *McKinnon's Trs.* v. *Brownlie*, 1947 S.C. (H.L.) 27; *Bailey's Trs.* v. *B.*, 1954 S.L.T. 282; *Stirling's Trs.* v. *Legal & General Assce. Socy. Ltd.*, 1957 S.L.T. 73; *Murray's Trs.* v. *Mackie*, 1959 S.L.T. 129. The Law Reform (Misc. Prov.) (Sc.) Act, 1968, S. 5 makes 'issue' include illegitimate issue, unless they are expressly excluded.

[6] *Low's Trs.* v. *Whitworth* (1892) 19 R. 431; *Searcy's Trs.* v. *Allbuary*, 1907 S.C. 823; *Phillips' Trs.* v. *Davies*, 1910 2 S.L.T. 161; *Greig's Trs.* v. *Simpson*, 1918 S.C. 321.

[7] *Cunningham's Trs.* v. *C.* (1891) 18 R. 380; *Stewart's Trs.* v. *S.*, 1917 2 S.L.T. 267; see also *Johnson's Trs.* v. *J.* (1891) 18 R. 823; *Tait's Trs.* v. *Bannatyne* (1894) 2 S.L.T. 168; *Thomson's Trs.* v. *T.* (1903) 11 S.L.T. 67.

[8] *Jean's Trs.* v. *Walker*, 1933 S.L.T. 500; *Clow's Trs.* v. *Bethune*, 1935 S.C. 754.

[9] *Glen* v. *Stewart* (1874) 1 R. (H.L.) 48; cf. *Paton's Trs.* v. *P.*, 1947 S.C. 250.

[10] *Young's Trs.* v. *Janes* (1880) 8 R. 242; *Gregory's Trs.* v. *Alison* (1889) 16 R. (H.L.) 10; *Fulton's Trs.* v. *F.* (1900) 8 S.L.T. 465; *Honeyman's Tr.* v. *Donaldson* (1900) 2 F. 539; *Murray's Factor* v. *Melrose*, 1910 S.C. 924; *Steedman's Trs.* v. *S.*, 1916 S.C. 857; *Andrew's Trs.* v. *A.*, 1918 2 S.L.T. 12; contrast *Thomson* v. *T.* (1884) 12 R. 155; *Rutherford's Trs.*

heirs *in mobilibus*' are those entitled at common law, as extended formerly by the Intestate Moveable Succession Act, 1855, and now by the Succession (Sc.) Act, 1964, to succeed on intestacy to moveables;[1] 'heirs' meant the heir-at-law in the case of a heritable subject, the heirs *in mobilibus* in the case of a moveable subject, and both in the case of a mixed subject, the former taking the heritable part and the latter the moveable part;[2] since the Succession (Sc.) Act, 1964, it may be a general term for the heirs on intestacy;[3] 'heirs and executors' means heirs *in mobilibus* and does not include executors nominate;[4] 'assignees' are those to whom a legatee has assigned his interest, provided he has acquired a vested right therein;[5] 'survivors' includes only those who outlive the deceased or the date of vesting;[6] 'predeceasing me' includes those predeceasing the will as well as these merely predeceasing the testator;[7] 'unmarried' does not include widows;[8] 'wife' is the person's wife when the will operates, not his wife at the date of the will.[9]

Such general descriptive terms as 'servants' have a less settled meaning, and it must be interpreted according to the circumstances of the case.[10] The term 'dependents' has no settled meaning and a bequest to dependants is void from uncertainty.[11]

In interpreting such words as 'child' or 'issue' a child *in utero* is fictionally deemed already born if the result of applying the fiction is to benefit that child; the fiction cannot be invoked in the interest of any third party.[12]

v. *Dickie*, 1907 S.C. 1280; *Borthwick's Trs.* v. *B.*, 1955 S.C. 227. The next of kin must be determined by reference to the *lex loci contractus*: *Stuart's Tr.* v. *Goold's Tr.*, 1947 S.L.T. 221.

[1] *Young's Trs.*, *supra*; *Gregory's Trs.*, *supra*; *Rutherford's Trs.*, *supra*.

[2] *Mitchell's Trs.* v. *Waddell* (1872) 11 M. 206; *Paton's Trs.* v. *P.*, 1947 S.C. 250; heirs are those who are heirs by the law of the legatee's domicile: *Smith's Trs.* v. *Macpherson*, 1926 S.C. 983.

[3] 1964 Act, Ss. 1(1) and 37.

[4] *Kinnaird's Trs.* v. *Ogilvy*, 1911 S.C. 1136.

[5] *Barr* v. *Parnie* (1903) 11 S.L.T. 426; *Montgomerie Fleming's Trs.* v. *Carre*, 1922 S.C. 688.

[6] *Swan's Trs.* v. *S.*, 1912 S.C. 273; *Stevenson's Trs.* v. *S.*, 1913 1 S.L.T. 292; *Leiper's Trs.* v. *Forrest*, 1930 S.C. 892; contrast *Curle's Trs.* v. *Millar*, 1922 S.C. (H.L.) 15.

[7] *Baird's Trs.* v. *Crombie*, 1926 S.C. 518.

[8] *Soutar's Trs.* v. *Spence*, 1937 S.L.T. 207.

[9] *Burns' Trs.*, 1961 S.C. 17.

[10] *Brown* v. *Maxwell's Exors.* (1884) 11 R. 821; *Stirling Maxwell's Exors.* v. *Grant* (1886) 13 R. 854; *Young* v. *Dick's Trs.* (1904) 12 S.L.T. 20.

[11] *Robertson's J.F.* v. *R.*, 1968 S.L.T. 32.

[12] *Elliot* v. *Joicey*, 1935 S.C. (H.L.) 57; *Johnstone's Trs.* v. *J.*, 1936 S.C. 766; *Cox's Tr.* v. *C.*, 1950 S.C. 117.

Predecease of the legatee

A bequest to a determinate person falls if the legatee predeceases the testator, and does not pass to the legatee's issue, unless provision to that effect is made.

Conditio si institutus sine liberis decesserit

In the case, however, of a bequest by a testator to his own descendants,[1] or to his nephews and nieces to whom the testator appears from his will to have placed himself *in loco parentis*, as by making a will in their favour such as a parent might have made in favour of his own children,[2] the condition may be implied that a predeceasing legatee's issue should take their parent's legacy in preference to a conditional institute, or residuary legatee, or the heirs on intestacy. The implied condition is justified by the presumption that the testator, if he had foreseen the legatee's predecease, would have given the bequest to the legatee's issue. It accordingly has no application where the legatee (parent of the issue claiming) predeceased the execution of the will,[3] nor where it cannot be shown that the legatee has predeceased the testator.[4] The *conditio* applies to a gift of revenue as much as of capital.[5] Whether the *conditio* should be implied in a particular case is a question of interpretation, but the testator's assumption of the position of a parent in relation to a nephew, niece, or their descendants, will be presumed unless it appears that the provision was made from personal favour.[6] It may be implied though the child is illegitimate.[7]

Facts which favour the implication are that the settlement disposes of the whole estate, that the provision is of the nature of a family settlement, or that the beneficiaries are a class.[8] It is not elided by the fact that the nephews and nieces are called *nominatim*, that the legacies varied in amounts, that legacies were also given to the testator's wife's nephews and nieces, or that the favoured nephews had also been given a share of residue[9] nor

1 *Hall* v. *H.* (1891) 18 R. 690.

2 *Bogie's Trs.* v. *Christie* (1882) 9 R. 453; *Hall, supra*; *Waddell's Trs.* v. *W.* (1896) 24 R. 189; *Alexander's Trs.* v. *Paterson*, 1928 S.C. 371; *Miller's Trs.* v. *M.*, 1958 S.C. 125.

3 *Rhind's Trs.* v. *Leith* (1866) 5 M. 104; *Low's Trs.* v. *Whitworth* (1892) 19 R. 431.

4 *Mitchell's Trs.* v. *Gordon's Factor*, 1953 S.C. 176.

5 *Pattinson's Trs.* v. *Motion*, 1941 S.C. 290.

6 *Knox's Exor.* v. *K.*, 1941 S.C. 532.

7 Law Reform (Misc. Prov.) (Sc.) Act, 1968, S. 6.

8 *Blair's Exors.* v. *Taylor* (1876) 3 R. 362; *Mackinnon's Trs.* v. *Watt*, 1933 S.L.T. 192; *Devlin's Trs.* v. *Breen*, 1945 S.C. (H.L.) 27.

9 *Alexander's Trs.* v. *Paterson*, 1928 S.C. 371; *Mair's Trs.* v. *M.*, 1936 S.C. 731; *Devlin's Trs.*, *supra*; *Reid's Trs.* v. *Drew*, 1960 S.C. 46.

by the fact that the gift is of revenue and not of capital.[1] It does not apply to relationship by affinity, such as testator to stepson.[2]

Facts unfavourable to the implication of the *conditio* are that the bequest springs purely from *delectus personae* and not from relationship,[3] that the failure to mention the legatee's issue was not oversight of the possibility of his predecease but intention, and the express mention in other bequests of the issue of a legatee who may predecease.[4]

The *conditio* does not apply where the parent had never been an institute under the settlement,[5] but may apply even though the parent was only a conditional institute.[6] It has been applied also to marriage contracts,[7] but not to *inter vivos* deeds[8] nor to bequests of specific articles. It does not apply to bequests to relatives by affinity.[9]

Where the *conditio* applies, the issue take only their parent's original share.[10]

The courts have indicated that the scope of the *conditio* will not readily be extended because it is an artificial rule of construction.[11]

Where legatees listed in succession

A testator may provide for the possibility of the legatee's predeceasing him by naming others to take the property failing the legatee. This may raise questions of the nature of the right of a later-named person if the first named legatee dies, or after he has taken the property and died.

The person first called to take is an institute.[12] The person first named to take if a certain condition is satisfied is a proper conditional institute. The person who first takes the succession because those called before him have predeceased the testator is a constructive conditional institute. The person named to take after the institute or a prior substitute is a substitute. The person

[1] *Renwick's Trs.* v. *Russell*, 1938 S.C. 855; *Pattinson's Trs.* v. *Motion*, 1941 S.C. 290.

[2] *Sinclair's Trs.* v. *S.*, 1942 S.C. 362.

[3] *Keith's Trs.* v. *K.* (1908) 16 S.L.T. 390; *Traver's Trs.* v. *Macintyre*, 1934 S.C. 520.

[4] *Greig* v. *Malcolm* (1835) 13 S. 607; *Mc Nab* v. *Brown's Trs.*, 1926 S.C. 387; *Travers's Trs.*, *supra*; *Paterson* v. *P.*, 1935 S.C. (H.L.) 7.

[5] *Barr* v. *Campbell*, 1925 S.C. 317.

[6] *Greig's Trs.* v. *Simpson*, 1918 S.C. 321.

[7] *Hughes* v. *Edwardes* (1892) 19 R. (H.L.) 33.

[8] *Halliday* v. *McCallum* (1869) 8 M. 112; *Crichton's Trs.* v. *Howat's Tutor* (1890) 18 R. 260; *Spalding* v. *S's Curator*, 1963 S.C. 141.

[9] *Alexander's Trs.* v. *Paterson*, 1928 S.C. 371.

[10] *Young* v. *Robertson* (1862) 4 Macq. 337; *Henderson* v. *H.* (1890) 17 R. 293; *Crosbie's Trs.* v. *C.*, 1927 S.C. 159; *Miller's Trs.* v. *Brown*, 1933 S.C. 669.

[11] *Hall* v. *H.* (1891) 18 R. 690; *Halliday*, *supra*; *Spalding*, *supra*.

[12] Bell, *Convg.* II, 844.

called after the institute or a prior substitute and whose right to take is subject to a certain condition being satisfied is a conditional substitute.

In considering whether a destination is a conditional institution or a substitution the testator's intention disclosed by his will and the nature of the subject are the main factors; there is a strong presumption for conditional institution in moveables,[1] and for substitution in the case of heritage,[2] though converse cases are possible.[3] In mixed estate the presumption is for conditional institution.[4] A substitution includes a conditional institution in the same character.

In either case if the institute predeceases the testator he takes nothing and the next-named acquires right under the destination.

If the subject of bequest vests on the testator's death in the institute, a conditional institution is thereby defeated but a substitution remains effectual and the substitute takes the subject on the institute's death, unless the institute has in the meantime defeated the substitution by onerous or gratuitous disposition of the subject, *inter vivos* or *mortis causa*,[5] or in the case of moveables by inmixing the subjects of bequest with his own.[6]

Delegation of choice of beneficiaries

It is not essential that the testator himself nominate the beneficiaries under his bequest. He may confer on executors, trustees or other selected persons power to select the beneficiaries from a general class or categories prescribed in the will.[7] If the class is defined with sufficient accuracy, or an intelligible and workable criterion for selection prescribed, such a delegation is valid,[8]

1 *Greig* v. *Johnston* (1833) 6 W. & S. 406; *Fyffe* v. *F.* (1841) 3 D. 1205; *Sutherland* v. *Douglas's Tr.* (1865) 4 M. 105; *Crumpton's J.F.* v. *Barnardo's Homes*, 1917 S.C. 713.

2 Ersk. III, 8, 44; Bell, *Prin.* §1693; *Watson* v. *Giffen* (1884) 11 R. 444.

3 *Dyer* v. *Carruthers* (1874) 1 R. 943; *McClymont's Exors.* v. *Osborne* (1895) 22 R. 411; *Marshall* v. *M.* (1900) 37 S.L.R. 775.

4 *Greig, supra*; *Allan* v. *Fleming* (1845) 7 D. 908; *Henderson* v. *Hamilton* (1858) 20 D. 473.

5 Ersk. III, 8, 44; *Baine* v. *Craig* (1845) 7 D. 845.

6 *McDowall* v. *McGill* (1847) 9 D. 1284; *Buchanan's Trs.* v. *Dalziel's Trs.* (1868) 6 M. 536; *Bell's Exor.* v. *Borthwick* (1897) 24 R. 1120.

7 *Crichton* v. *Grierson* (1828) 3 W. & S. 329, 338; *Hill* v. *Burns* (1826) 2 W. & S. 80; *Reid's Trs.* v. *Cattanach's Trs.*, 1929 S.C. 727.

8 *Mitchell's Trs.* v. *Waddell* (1872) 11 M. 206; *Warrender* v. *Anderson* (1893) 1 S.L.T. 304; *Smellie's Trs.* v. *Glasgow R.I.* (1905) 13 S.L.T. 450; *Mitchell's Trs.* v. *Fraser*, 1915 S.C. 350; *Bannerman's Trs.* v. *B.*, 1915 S.C. 398; *Emslie's Trs.* v. *Aberdeen Female Society*, 1949 S.L.T. (Notes) 61; *Jowett's Trs.* v. *J's Heirs*, 1952 S.L.T. 131; *Milne's Trs.* v. *Davidson*, 1956 S.C. 81; *Craig's Trs.* v. *Hunter*, 1956 S.L.T. (Notes) 15.

but the bequest fails from uncertainty if the class is so vaguely or indefinitely prescribed that the executors or others are in effect being allowed to make the testator's will for him, and this is not allowed.[1] Thus, it is ineffectual to empower trustees to dispose of the testator's estate as they think proper,[2] or best,[3] or prudent,[4] or to give it to persons whom they may choose.[5] Nor does Scots law recognize the secret trust, i.e. a bequest to objects privately communicated by truster to trustee.[6]

Uncertainty is particularly important where the testator empowers trustees or others to select the objects of benefit from a class described as 'charitable', 'charitable and beneficial', or in similar ways. It is settled that 'charitable' objects or purposes are a definite class and not uncertain,[7] even though the testator may not have considered what kind of charity was to benefit.[8] Educational purposes may be valid, but the advancement of art, science or literature is too vague.[9] But 'public' purposes are too indefinite to receive effect,[10] as are 'religious' purposes.[11] Where objects or purposes are described by conjoined adjectives such as 'Christian and benevolent purposes' the bequest is prima facie sufficiently certain to be upheld.[12] Where, however, the objects

[1] *Grimond* v. *G's Trs.* (1905) 7 F. (H.L.) 90; *Fraser's Trs.*, 1947 S.L.T. (Notes) 56; *Dunlop's Trs.* v. *Farquharson*, 1955 S.L.T. (Notes) 80; *Craig's Trs.* v. *Hunter*, 1956 S.L.T. (Notes) 15; a direction to divide 'among charities, infirmaries, etc.' is not void from uncertainty, 'etc.' having to be construed *ejusdem generis*: *Milne's Trs., supra.*

[2] *Sutherland's Trs.* v. *S's Tr.* (1893) 20 R. 925; *McGregor's Trs.* v. *Bosomworth* (1896) 3 S.L.T. 231; *Anderson* v. *Smoke* (1898) 25 R. 493; *Bannerman's Trs., supra.*

[3] *Shaw's Trs.* (1893) 1 S.L.T. 308.

[4] *Wilson's Trs.* v. *W's Trs.* (1894) 1 S.L.T. 548.

[5] *Playfair's Trs.* v. *P.* (1900) 2 F. 686.

[6] *Shaw's Trs.* v. *Greenock Medical Aid Socy.*, 1930 S.L.T. 39.

[7] *Hill* v. *Burns* (1826) 2 W. & S. 80; *Dick's Trs.* v. *D.*, 1907 S.C. 953; *Weir* v. *Crum Brown*, 1908 S.C. (H.L.) 3; *Macduff* v. *Spence's Trs.*, 1909 S.C. 178; *Wordie's Trs.* v. *W.*, 1916 S.C. (H.L.) 126.

[8] *Dick's Trs., supra*; cf. *Anderson's Trs.* v. *A's Factor* (1901) 9 S.L.T. 174; *Cameron's Trs.* v. *Mackenzie*, 1915 S.C. 313.

[9] *Harper's Trs.* v. *Jacobs*, 1929 S.C. 345.

[10] *Turnbull's Trs.* v. *L.A.*, 1918 S.C. (H.L.) 88; *Reid's Trs.* v. *Cattanach's Trs.*, 1929 S.C. 727.

[11] *McConochie's Trs.* v. *McC.*, 1909 S.C. 1046; *Shaw's Trs.* v. *Weir*, 1927 S.L.T. 641.

[12] *Cobb* v. *C's Trs.* (1894) 21 R. 638 ('useful, benevolent, and charitable institutions'); *Brown's Trs.* v. *Young* (1898) 6 S.L.T. 32 ('charitable, religious, educational, and public institutions'); *Hay's Trs.* v. *Baillie*, 1908 S.C. 1224 ('institutions of a benevolent or charitable nature'); *Dick* v. *Audsley*, 1908 S.C. (H.L.) 27 ('local or Scottish charitable institutions'); *Paterson's Trs.* v. *P.*, 1909 S.C. 485 ('charities, or benevolent or beneficent institutions'); *Mackinnon's Trs.* v. *M.*, 1909 S.C. 1041 ('charitable or philanthropic institutions'); *Smith's Trs.* v. *S's Trs.*, 1910 2 S.L.T. 74 ('Christian and benevolent purposes'); *McPhee's Trs.* v. *McP.*, 1912 S.C. 75 ('religious and charitable institutions'); *Bannerman's Trs.* v. *B.*, 1915 S.C. 398 ('religious or charitable institutions'); *Caldwell's*

or purposes are described disjunctively, as 'charitable or religious' 'charitable or public', so that the whole bequest might be applied to non-charitable purposes, the bequest may well fail from uncertainty if one alternative object is uncertain.[1] A later adjective conjoined by 'or' may, however, be merely exegetic of the former one, and not disjunctive or indicative of an alternative category.[2]

A limitation of the area from within which the objects are to be selected makes for certainty,[3] but does not necessarily make a bequest certain.[4] A list of examples also makes for certainty.[5]

A bare bequest to 'charities' without appointment of a trustee or executor, or instructions as to the choice of charities, is void for uncertainty, as the court cannot appoint a trustee and give him power of selection.[6] Where the trustees have not selected and a judicial factor is appointed, he may not exercise the power of selection.[7]

The legatee's interest

What interest a legatee acquires under a bequest is a matter of interpretation. The gift to him may be beneficial or merely in

Trs. v. *C.*, 1921 S.C. (H.L.) 82 ('charitable and benevolent institutions'); *Edgar's Trs.* v. *Cassells*, 1922 S.C. 395 ('benevolent, charitable, and religious institutions'); *Macrae's J.F.* v. *Martin*, 1937 S.L.T. 209 ('religious and charitable purposes'); *Brough* v. *B's Trs.*, 1950 S.L.T. 117 ('religious and educational work, missionary operations, and charitable or benevolent schemes').

1 *Blair* v. *Duncan* (1901) 4 F. (H.L.) 1 ('charitable or public purposes'); *Jaffrey's Trs.* v. *L.A.* (1903) 11 S.L.T. 119 ('charitable or other institutions'); *Macintyre* v. *Grimond's Trs.* (1905) 7 F. (H.L.) 90 ('charitable or religious institutions'); *Brown's Trs.* v. *McIntosh* (1905) 13 S.L.T. 72 ('religious, charitable or educational institutions'); *Shaw's Trs.* v. *Esson's Trs.* (1905) 8 F. 52 ('charitable, benevolent or religious objects'); *McGrouther's Trs.* v. *L.A.* (1907) 15 S.L.T. 652 ('religious or charitable purposes'); *McConochie's Trs.* v. *McC.*, 1909 S.C. 1046 ('educational, charitable, and religious purposes'—held to be construed disjunctively); *Turnbull's Trs.* v. *L.A.*, 1918 S.C. (H.L.) 88 ('public, benevolent or charitable purposes'); *Symmer's Trs.* v. *S.*, 1918 S.C. 337 ('charitable institutions or deserving agencies'); *Campbell's Trs.* v. *C.*, 1921 S.C. (H.L.) 12 ('charitable or other deserving institution'); *Shaw's Trs.* v. *Weir*, 1927 S.L.T. 641 ('for the benefit of religion, education or the poor'); *Rintoul's Trs.* v. *R.*, 1949 S.C. 297 ('charitable or social institutions'); *Shaw's Trs.* v. *Greenock Medical Aid Socy.*, 1930 S.L.T. 39; *Salvesen's Trs.* v. *Wye*, 1954 S.C. 440 ('poor relations, friends or acquaintances').

2 *Paterson's Trs.* v. *P.*, 1909 S.C. 485; *Mackinnon's Trs.* v. *M.*, 1909 S.C. 1041; *Wink's Exors.* v. *Tallent*, 1947 S.C. 470.

3 *Cleland's Trs.* v. *C.*, 1907 S.C. 591; *Adam's Trs.* v. *A.* (1908) 16 S.L.T. 144; *McPhee's Trs.*, *supra*; *Caldwell's Trs.*, *supra*; *Edgar's Trs.*, *supra*.

4 *Low's Exors.* (1873) 11 M. 744; *Shaw's Trs.*, *supra*; *McConochie's Trs.*, *supra*; *Turnbull's Trs.*, *supra*; *Symmer's Trs.*, *supra*.

5 *Smellie's Trs.* v. *Glasgow R.I.* (1905) 13 S.L.T. 450.

6 *Angus's Exrx.* v. *Batchan's Trs.*, 1949 S.C. 335.

7 *Vollar's J.F.* v. *Boyd*, 1952 S.L.T. (Notes) 84.

trust, the presumption being for outright beneficial gift.[1] Precatory bequests, qualified by expressions of the testator's wishes, limit the legatee's right to one in trust only if the wishes amount to a command and appear intended to impose a trust.[2] If the gift is to hold in trust only the further question arises of what the trust purposes are, the objects to be benefited, and of the powers conferred to effect the purposes.[3]

A beneficial bequest may be either in liferent only or in fee. It is a matter of interpretation in each case.[4] The presumption is that the interest conferred is the fee of heritage or the absolute ownership of moveables, but it may be a liferent interest only.[5] There is now no interest intermediate between fee and liferent.[6]

If the gift is in liferent it may be an ordinary liferent or, provided there is a trust, an alimentary liferent.[7]

Nominal liferents interpreted as fee

In two cases a gift, nominally in liferent, is construed as a gift of the fee. The first is where the legatee is given a liferent with an absolute *jus disponendi* superadded, when the legatee is in effect fiar,[8] provided that the liferent and the power of disposal are unqualified[9] and the power of disposal absolute and not merely a power of appointment,[10] and that no other parties are

[1] *Jamieson* v. *Clark* (1872) 10 M. 399; *Macpherson* v. *M's C.B.* (1894) 21 R. 386; *Chalmer's J.F.* v. *C.* (1903) 5 F. 1154; *Miller* v. *M.* (1906) 13 S.L.T. 770; contrast *Urquharts' Exors.* v. *Abbott* (1899) 1 F. 1149; see also *Romanes* v. *R's Trs.*, 1933 S.N. 112.

[2] *Wilson* v. *Lindsay* (1878) 5 R. 539; *Barclay's Exor.* v. *McLeod* (1880) 7 R. 477; *Hamilton's Trs.* v. *H.* (1901) 4 F. 266; *Garden's Exor.* v. *More*, 1913 S.C. 285; *Campbell's Trs.* v. *Kinsey-Morgan's Trs.*, 1915 S.C. 298; *Smart* v. *S.*, 1926 S.C. 392.

[3] See e.g. *Mackenzie's Trs.* v. *M's Exors.*, 1948 S.C. (H.L.) 53; *Hood* v. *Macdonald's Tr.*, 1949 S.C. 24.

[4] *Sim* v. *Duncan* (1900) 2 F. 434.

[5] *Sanderson's Exors.* v. *Kerr* (1860) 23 D. 227; *Fulton's Trs.* v. *F.* (1880) 7 R. 566; *Lawson's Trs.* v. *L.* (1890) 17 R. 1167; *Spink's Exors.* v. *Simpson* (1894) 21 R. 551; *Mackenzies' Trs.* v. *M.* (1899) 2 F. 330; *Gillies' Trs.* v. *Hodge* (1900) 3 F. 238; *Brash's Trs.* v. *Phillipson*, 1916 S.C. 271; *Riddoch's Trs.* v. *Calder's Tr.*, 1947 S.C. 281; *Parlane's Exrx.* v. *Dunlop*, 1948 S.L.T. (Notes) 22; *Innes's Tr.* v. *I.*, 1948 S.C. 406; *Lashmar's Trs.*, 1951 S.L.T. (Notes) 55.

[6] *Cochrane's Exrx.* v. *C.*, 1947 S.C. 134; overruling *Denholm's Trs.* v. *D's Trs.*, 1908 S.C. 255; *Heavyside* v. *Smith*, 1929 S.C. 68; *Ironside's Tr.* v. *I's Exor.*, 1933 S.C. 116 and *Duncan* v. *Edinburgh R.I.*, 1936 S.C. 811; *Innes's Tr.* v. *I.*, 1948 S.C. 406.

[7] e.g. *Miller* v. *M's Trs.*, 1953 S.L.T. 225.

[8] *Alves* v. *A.* (1861) 23 D. 712; *Pursell* v. *Elder* (1865) 3 M. (H.L.) 59; *Cumstie* v. *C's Trs.* (1876) 3 R. 921; *Rattray's Trs.* v. *R.* (1899) 1 F. 510.

[9] *Douglas's Trs.* v. *D.* (1902) 5 F. 69; *Ewing's Trs.* v. *E.*, 1909 S.C. 409; *Mackenzie's Trs.* v. *Kilmarnock's Trs.*, 1909 S.C. 472.

[10] *Alves, supra*; *Miller's Trs.* v. *Findlay* (1896) 24 R. 114; *Rattray's Trs., supra*; *Reid* v. *R's Trs.* (1899) 1 F. 969; *Howe's Trs.* v. *Howe's J.F.* (1903) 5 F. 1099; *Miller Richard's Trs.* v. *M.R.* (1903) 5 F. 909; *Tait's Trs.* v. *Neill* (1903) 6 F. 138; *Mackenzie's Trs., supra.*

called in default of the liferenter's exercise of the powers of disposal granted him; if another party is called in default the interpretation as a gift of fee is excluded.[1]

The second case is where the gift is to one in liferent and his issue unnamed or unborn in fee, in which case the fee is deemed to be in the parent, the issue having only a *spes successionis*, on the ground that a fee cannot be left *in pendente*.[2] This rule might yield to adequate expressions of contrary intention,[3] and this rule is inapplicable where the liferent is stated to be a liferent allenarly, or only, in which case there is deemed to be a fiduciary fee in the parent for behoof of the children, which passes to them when they come into being.[4] By the Trusts (Sc.) Act, 1921, S. 8, a liferent is not to be deemed a fee by reason only of the absence of the word 'allenarly' and in all cases that word is to be read into the deed.[5] The doctrine of fiduciary fee has not been extended beyond the cases of holding for a child or an heir.[6] In such cases there is no difficulty where a continuing trust is established.

Restrictions on liferents

A testator may grant a liferent estate of heritage in Scotland in favour only of a party in life at the date of the grant; land held in liferent by a party of full age born after the date of the deed is empowered by petition to acquire the fee of the estate.[7]

He may grant or reserve by a trust or otherwise a liferent in moveable estate in Scotland in favour only of a person in life at the date of the deed, and any moveable estate held in liferent for a person of full age born after the date of the deed belongs

1 *Morris* v. *Tennant* (1855) 18 D. (H.L.) 42; *Alves, supra*; *Rattray's Trs., supra*; *Tait's Trs.* v. *Neill* (1903) 6 F. 138; *Forrest's Trs.* v. *Reid* (1904) 7 F. 142; *Murray's Trs.* v. *MacGregor's Trs.*, 1931 S.C. 516.

2 *Frog's Creditors* v. *His Children* (1735) Mor. 4262; *Dewar* v. *McKinnon* (1825) 1 W. & S. 161; the rule applies also to moveables: *Mure* v. *M.* (1786) Mor. 4288; *Macintosh* v. *Gordon* (1845) 4 Bell 105; *Ralston* v. *Hamilton* (1862) 4 Macq. 397. It applies only to gifts to parents and children: *Cumstie* v. *C's Trs.* (1876) 3 R. 921.

3 *Watson* v. *W.* (1854) 16 D. 803; *Maule* (1876) 3 R. 831; *Rait* v. *Arbuthnott* (1892) 19 R. 687; *Gifford's Trs.* v. *G.* (1903) 5 F. 723; *Studd* v. *Cook* (1887) 10 R. (H.L.) 53.

4 *Newlands* v. *N's Crs.* (1794) Mor. 4289; *Beattie's Trs.* v. *Cooper's Trs.* (1862) 24 D. 519; *Douglas* v. *Thomson* (1870) 8 M. 374; *Cumstie, supra*; *Beveridge* v. *B's Trs.* (1878) 5 R. 1116; description of the liferent as 'alimentary' has the same effect.

5 Applicable only to liferents taking effect after that Act, and not to those created by English trust deeds: *Cripps's Trs.* v. *C.*, 1926 S.C. 188.

6 *Colville's Trs.* v. *Marinden*, 1908 S.C. 911; *Devlin* v. *Lowrie*, 1922 S.C. 255; *Cripps's Trs., supra.*

7 Entail Amdt. Act, 1848, S. 48; *Crichton-Stuart's Tutrix*, 1921 S.C. 840.

absolutely to him and the trustees are bound to convey it to him.[1] This does not apply to annuities.[2]

Where by any deed executed after the commencement of the Law Reform (Misc. Prov.) (Sc.) Act, 1968, there is created a liferent interest in any property and a person who was not living or *in utero* at the date of the coming into operation of the said deed becomes entitled to that interest, then (a) if that person is of full age at the date on which he becomes entitled to the liferent interest, as from that date, or (b) if that person is not of full age at that date, as from the date on which, being still entitled to the liferent interest, he becomes of full age, the said property, subject to subsec. (2), belongs absolutely to that person, and if the property is vested in trustees those trustees are bound to convey the property to that person.[3] By subsec. (2) the fact that by virtue of the foregoing provisions any property has come to belong absolutely to any person shall not affect (a) the rights in the property of any person holding a security over the property, (b) any rights in the property created independently of the deed by which the liferent interest in question was created, (c) in the case of heritable property, the rights therein of the superior of the property. The Entail Amendment Act, 1848, S. 48, and the Trusts (Sc.) Act, 1921, S. 9 are not to have effect in relation to any deed executed after the commencement of the 1968 Act.

Restrictions on accumulations

No testator may[4] dispose of any property so that the income shall be wholly or partially accumulated for longer than one of the following, namely: (a) the life of the grantor;[5] or (b) twenty-one years from the death of the grantor;[6] or (c) the duration of the minority or respective minorities of any person or persons living or *in utero* at the death of the grantor; or (d) the minority

[1] Trusts (Sc.) Act, 1921, S. 9, replacing Entail Amdt. Act, 1868, S. 17; *Stewart's Trs.* v. *Whitelaw*, 1926 S.C. 701; *Reid's Trs.* v. *Dashwood*, 1929 S.C. 748; see also *Burn's Trs.* v. *McKenna*, 1940 S.C. 489; *Muir's Trs.* v. *Williams*, 1943 S.C. (H.L.) 47.

[2] *Dryburgh's Trs.*, 1912 S.C. 939.

[3] 1968 Act, S. 18(1); 'date of coming into operation' and 'date of execution or of coming into operation' are defined by subsec. (5). The commencement of the Act was 25th November, 1968.

[4] Trusts (Sc.) Act, 1961, S. 5, replacing (Thellusson) Accumulations Act, 1800; (e) and (f) were added by Law Reform (Misc. Prov.) (Sc.) Act, 1966, S. 6, and apply only in relation to instruments taking effect under the Act, or where the instrument creating the power of appointment takes effect after the Act.

[5] This provision applies only to *inter vivos* dispositions: *Stewart's Trs.* v. *S.*, 1927 S.C. 350; *Union Bank* v. *Campbell*, 1929 S.C. 143; *Russell's Trs.* v. *R.*, 1959 S.C. 148; *Gibson's Trs.*, 1963 S.C. 350.

[6] *Stewart's Trs.* v. *Whitelaw*, 1926 S.C. 701; *Carey's Trs.* v. *Rose*, 1957 S.C. 252.

or respective minorities of any person or persons who, under the deed directing the accumulation would for the time being, if of full age, be entitled to the income directed to be accumulated, or (e) a term of 21 years from the date of the making of the settlement, or other disposition, or (f) the duration of the minority or respective minorities of any person living or in utero at that date; and a direction to accumulate income during a period specified in (e) or (f) is not void, nor the accumulation contrary to the Trusts (Sc.) Act, 1961, S. 5 solely by reason of the fact that the period begins during the life of the grantor and ends after his death. Directions in other terms express or implied[1] are void, and the income directed to be accumulated, so long as to be accumulated contrary to the Act, is to go to and be received by the person or persons who would have been entitled thereto if accumulation has not been directed.[2] The restrictions imposed by the 1961 Act, S. 5, as amended, apply in relation to a power to accumulate income whether or not there is a duty to exercise that power, and whether or not the power to accumulate extends to income produced by the investment of income previously accumulated.[3]

A testator cannot circumvent the statutory prohibition by bequeathing income to *inter vivos* trustees to add to the capital of their trust.[4]

The restrictions imposed by the 1800 (now 1961) Act do not prevent holding income undistributed for later distribution, so long as it is not directed to form a capital fund.[5]

A direction to accumulate is a burden on a gift and fixes the capital of that gift, but does not make the gift fail.[6]

The Accumulation Act, 1892, provides that no person shall settle or dispose of any property in such manner that the rents, issues, profits or income thereof shall be wholly or partially accumulated for the purchase of land only, for any longer period than the minority or respective minorities of any person or persons who under the uses or trusts of the instrument directing such accumulation would for the time being, if of full age, be entitled

1 *Watson's Trs.* v. *Brown*, 1923 S.C. 228; *Carey's Trs.* v. *Rose*, 1957 S.C. 252.

2 *Maxwell's Trs.* (1877) 5 R. 248; *Elder's Trs.* v. *Free Church of Scotland* (1892) 20 R. 2; *Watson's Trs.* v. *Brown*, 1923 S.C. 228; *Stewart's Trs.* v. *Whitelaw*, 1926 S.C. 701; *Pyper's Trs.* v. *Leighton*, 1946 S.L.T. 255; *Carey's Trs., supra*; *Russell's Trs.* v. *R.*, 1959 S.C. 148; see also *Lindsay's Trs.* v. *L.*, 1931 S.C. 586.

3 Law Reform (Misc. Prov.) (Sc.) Act, 1966, S. 6(2).

4 *Gibson's Trs.*, 1963 S.C. 350.

5 *Lindsay's Trs.*, 1911 S.C. 584; *Mitchell's Trs.* v. *Fraser*, 1915 S.C. 350; see also *Barbour* v. *Budge*, 1947 S.N. 100.

6 *Donaldson's Trs.* v. *L.A.*, 1938 S.L.T. 106.

to receive the rents, etc., so directed to be accumulated. The Act does not annul the provisions of a will relative to the purchase of lands, but merely prevents accumulation, and the income falls to the heir at law (now to the testator's executor).[1]

Perpetuities

There is no rule of Scots law against perpetuities as such,[2] other than the statutory limitations on liferents and on accumulations of income,[3] and a direction to invest and pay income in perpetuity is valid; the object of such perpetual benefit need not be a charity, but the bequest must not be unreasonable or wholly lacking in public benefit.[4] If the object is a valid charity the bequest is clearly valid.[5]

Annuities

The testator's gift may take the form of an annuity, or gift of an annual sum of £x, payable for a determinate time, or for life, or for the life of a third party. If no special conditions are attached an annuity is deemed payable for life.[6]

Such a gift may, if such appears to be the intention, continue to the annuitant's representatives after his death.[7]

Prima facie an annuity falls to be paid under deduction of income tax,[8] but the gift may be expressly or impliedly made free of income tax, in which case the tax must be paid from the residue of the estate.[9]

Options to legatees

A testator may confer on beneficiaries certain options.[10] It is a question of interpretation when the option can or must be exercised,[11] and whether any conditions have to be satisfied.[12]

1 *Robertson's Trs.* v. *R's Trs.*, 1933 S.C. 639.

2 McLaren I, 304; *Suttie's Trs.* v. *S.* (1846) 18 S. Jur. 462; *Stewart's Trs.* v. *Whitelaw*, 1926 S.C. 701, 716.

3 *Supra.*

4 *Lindsay's Exor.* v. *Forsyth*, 1940 S.C. 568.

5 *Lindsay's Exor., supra* (masses for the dead in perpetuity).

6 *McDonald's Trs.* v. *McD.'s Exrx.*, 1940 S.C. 433; *Reid's Exrx.* v. *R.*, 1944 S.C. (H.L.) 25.

7 *Young's Trs.* v. *Shelton's Exors.*, 1937 S.C. 28; *McDonald's Trs., supra*; *Reid's Exrx., supra.*

8 *Wilson's Trs.* v. *W.*, 1919 S.C. 359; *Hunter's Trs.* v. *Mitchell*, 1930 S.C. 978.

9 *Smith's Trs.* v. *Gaydon*, 1919 S.C. 95; *Union Bank* v. *Campbell*, 1929 S.C. 143; *Milne's Tr.*, 1936 S.C. 706; *Rowan's Trs.* v. *R.*, 1940 S.C. 30. This may include surtax: *Smith's Trs.* v. *S.*, 1924 S.C. 485; *Baird's Trs.* v. *B.*, 1933 S.C. 553; *Prentice's Trs.* v. *P.*, 1935 S.C. 211; *Turner's Trs.* v. *T.*, 1943 S.C. 389; *Richmond's Trs.* v. *R.*, 1935 S.C. 585.

10 cf. *Hood* v. *Macdonald's Tr.*, 1949 S.C. 24.

11 *Coat's Trs.* v. *C.* (1903) 5 F. 401.

12 *Fraser's Trs.* v. *F.* (1894) 21 R. 790.

An option may transmit to and be exercisable by the legatee's representatives.[1]

Whether double legacies cumulative or substitutional

Where a deceased's testamentary writings provide more than one bequest to the same legatee the question may arise whether both or all are due, or whether a later provision should be held mere repetition of, or in substitution for, the first. Failing adequate expression of the testator's intention, the court may draw an inference from the writings themselves. The presumption is that, if the testator bequeaths the same sums to the same legatee in separate testamentary writings, (assuming that the later writing does not alter the earlier) the legacies fall to be regarded as cumulative,[2] but a thrice-given legacy of a stated sum has been held substitutional.[3] If he bequeaths different sums in separate writings they are more readily presumed cumulative.[4] Separate and different special provisions for a person in separate writings have been held substitutional[5] though a legacy and an annuity in separate deeds have been held cumulative.[6]

Where two bequests of the same amount are made to a legatee in one deed, the presumption is that this is mere repetition,[7] but if bequests of different amounts are made they are presumed cumulative.[8] So too if a motive is stated for one bequest and not for the other they are presumed cumulative.[9]

In considering whether bequests are intended to be cumulative or substitutional, the court may consider the history of the bequests to arrive at the testator's intention.[10]

Joint or several legacies: Accretion

A gift to a group or number of legatees will normally, subject to any indication in the will, be held to be joint, in which case, if any of the group predecease, his share accresces to the others

1 *Adam's Trs.* v. *Russell*, 1955 S.C. 232.

2 *Horsburgh* v. *H.* (1847) 9 D. 329; *Edinburgh R.I.* v. *Muir's Trs.* (1881) 9 R. 352; *Fraser* v. *Forbes' Trs.* (1899) 1 F. 513; *McLachlan* v. *Seton's Trs.*, 1937 S.C. 206; but contrast *Tennent* v. *Dunsmure* (1878) 6 R. 150; *Free Church* v. *Maitland* (1887) 14 R. 333; *Miller's Trs.* v. *Kirkcaldy* (1905) 13 S.L.T. 73.

3 *Brander's Trs.* v. *Anderson* (1883) 10 R. 1258.

4 *Hood's Exors.* (1869) 7 M. 774.

5 *Arres' Trs.* v. *Mather* (1881) 9 R. 107.

6 *Bryce's Tr.* (1878) 5 R. 722; cf. *Milne* v. *Scott* (1880) 8 R. 83.

7 *Edinburgh R.I.*, *supra*, 355; *Gillies* v. *Glasgow R.I.* 1960 S.C. 438; cf. *Rennie's Trs.* v. *Watt* (1904) 12 S.L.T. 195.

8 cf. *Gillies*, *supra*.

9 *Horsburgh* v. *H.* (1848) 10 D. 824.

10 *McLachlan* v. *Seton's Trs.*, 1937 S.C. 206.

and the whole legacy will fall to be divided equally among the survivors,[1] but it may be several, in which case each is entitled to his own share and no more, accretion is excluded, and the share of any who may predecease will fall into residue or intestacy as the case may be.[2] The words 'equally', 'in equal shares', 'equally among them', 'share and share alike' or 'divide among' import severance.[3] This rule applies whether the gift is in liferent or in fee, whether moveables, a sum of money or residue. But the terms of the will may indicate an intention, despite words of severance, that accretion should apply.[4]

Where the gift is, however, made to a class, called as such, notwithstanding words of equality, accretion applies in the event of predecease of one of the class.[5]

In the absence of indication in the will, there is no implication that any conditions or limitations affecting the original gift attach also to any share falling to a beneficiary by accretion.

Group bequests

Where a bequest is made to a number of individuals, in the absence of contrary indication, all who survive the testator take equal shares. But where a bequest is made to persons described as members of a group or groups, the question may arise whether division is to be made *per stirpes* or *per capita*. The presumption is for division *per capita* but this may be overcome by contrary indications in the will.[6] Where relations of different degrees are beneficiaries the presumption is for division *per stirpes*.[7]

[1] Stair III, 8, 27; *Andrew's Exors.* v. *A's Trs.*, 1925 S.C. 844; *Young's Trs.* v. *Y.*, 1927 S.C. (H.L.) 6; *Beveridge's Trs.* v. *B.*, 1930 S.C. 378; *Miller's Trs.* v. *Brown*, 1933 S.C. 669; *McDonald's Trs.* v. *McD.'s Exrx.*, 1940 S.C. 433; *McKinlay's Trs.* v. *Smith*, 1960 S.L.T. (Notes) 87.

[2] *Ross's Trs.* v. *Porteous*, 1954 S.C. 239.

[3] *Paxton's Trs.* v. *Cowie* (1886) 13 R. 1191; *Menzies' Factor* v. *M.* (1898) 1 F. 128; *Cochrane's Trs.* v. *C.*, 1914 S.C. 403; *Young's Trs.* v. *Y.*, 1927 S.C. (H.L.) 6; *Paterson* v. *Aberdeen Sailors Inst.*, 1953 S.L.T. (Notes) 34; *White's Tr.*, 1957 S.C. 322.

[4] e.g. *Bartholomew's Trs.* v. *B.* (1904) 6 F. 322.

[5] *Muir's Trs.* v. *M.* (1889) 16 R. 954; *Menzies' Factor*, *supra*; *Roberts's Trs.* v. *R.* (1903) 5 F. 541. See also *Blair's Exors.* v. *Taylor* (1876) 3 R. 362, criticised in *Farquharson* v. *Kelly* (1900) 2 F. 863.

[6] *MacDougall* v. *McD.* (1868) 6 M. (H.L.) 18; *Haldane's Trs.* v. *Murphy* (1881) 9 R. 269; *Bogie's Trs.* v. *Christie* (1882) 9 R. 453; *Hogg* v. *Bruce* (1887) 14 R. 887; *Inglis* v. *McNeil* (1892) 19 R. 924; *Searcy's Trs.* v. *Allbuary*, 1907 S.C. 823; *Hay Cunningham's Trs.* v. *Blackwell*, 1909 S.C. 219; *Robertson's Trs.* v. *Horne*, 1921 S.C. 817; *Campbell's Trs.* v. *Welsh*, 1952 S.C. 343.

[7] *Laing's Trs.* v. *Samson* (1879) 7 R. 244; *Cunningham's Trs.* v. *C.* (1891) 18 R. 380; *Galloway's Trs.* v. *G.* (1897) 25 R. 28; *Still's Trs.* v. *Hall* (1899) 36 S.L.R. 390; *Campbell's Tr.* v. *Dick*, 1915 S.C. 100; *Robertson's Trs.*, *supra*; *Mair's Exrx.* v. *M.*, 1950 S.L.T. (Notes) 16; *Boyd's Tr.* v. *Shaw*, 1958 S.C. 115; contrast *Cobban's Exors.* v. *C.*, 1915 S.C. 82.

Bequests to A 'and' B

A bequest to one person 'and' another is *prima facie* a joint bequest rather than a conditional institution of the second-named, failing the first.[1] But there may be contrary indications, particularly where the persons named are parent and child.[2]

Legacies in satisfaction of provisions

A legacy may be given in satisfaction of a provision due to the legatee under an obligation, such as a marriage contract, but there is no presumption against a gratuitous testamentary provision being in addition to and not in satisfaction of a previous provision *in obligatione*.[3] At most the fact that the testator is already bound to give so much raises a presumption of fact that the bequest is in satisfaction of the provision.[4] The question is always one of intention.[4] A legacy has been held to have been given in satisfaction of an obligation when declared to be so given,[5] or when the legacy was greater than the provision due,[6] or where it appears intended to implement the obligation,[7] but in other circumstances to be additional thereto.[8]

Satisfaction of legacies by advances

Questions may also arise whether legacies given by will have been satisfied by advances made to the legatee in the testator's lifetime. Satisfaction has been held established where the advances are of the same amount as the legacy and particularly where receipts for the payments bear that they are in satisfaction of the share of the estate falling to be paid on the testator's death,[9] or the testator had advanced money to his son-in-law's firm, his will providing that advances should be imputed to the shares in his estate,[10] or the testator directed equal division of his estate and made a payment to his son greater than that made to his daughters by the amount of a legacy to the son.[11]

1 *Cobban's Exors.* v. *C.*, 1915 S.C. 82; *Munro* v. *M.*, 1962 S.C. 599.

2 *Murray* (1873) 45 Sc. Jur. 574; *Black's Trs.* v. *Nixon*, 1931 S.C. 590; *Clow's Trs.* v. *Bethune*, 1935 S.C. 754.

3 *Cowan* v. *Dick's Trs.* (1873) 1 R. 119.

4 *Kippen* v. *K's Trs.* (1874) 1 R. 1171.

5 *Scott* v. *Graham*, 1913 S.C. 467; cf. *Proctor's Trs.* v. *P.* (1905) 13 S.L.T. 114.

6 *Thomson* v. *T's Trs.* (1868) 5 S.L.R. 742; *Buttery's Trs.* v. *McClelland* (1879) 6 R. 564; *Campbell's Trs.* v. *Adamson*, 1911 S.C. 1111.

7 *Meiklam's Trs.* v. *M.* (1868) 6 S.L.R. 2.

8 *Elliot* v. *Bowhill* (1873) 11 M. 735; *Keith Johnstone's Trs.* v. *Johnston's Trs.* (1894) 22 R. 28; *Johnstone* v. *Haviland* (1896) 23 R. (H.L.) 6; cf. *Hope Johnstone* v. *H.J.* (1880) 7 R. 766.

9 *McLaren* v. *Howie* (1869) 8 M. 106.

10 *Smith's Trs.* v. *Sellar* (1894) 21 R. 633.

11 *Johanson* v. *J's Trs.* (1898) 1 F. 244.

Abatement of legacies

If the testator's estate is insufficient to satisfy all his bequests in full then, unless the testator has provided for priorities in the will itself, legacies must abate or be cut down. Residuary bequests abate first, not being payable at all unless all other legatees have been paid in full. Then general legacies abate *pari passu* and finally demonstrative and other special legacies.[1] It may therefore be important whether a bequest is a general legacy or a share of residue.[2] Unless the will so provides no priority as to payment is conferred by the mere order or numbering of bequests or classes of bequests in the will,[3] but any indication of priority in the will may be acted on.[4]

An annuity payable out of capital has been held preferable to legacies payment of which was postponed till the annuitant's death.[5]

Where a testator left one will dealing with his whole estate and a later will dealing with his moveables, it was held that the legacies left by the earlier will were chargeable only against heritage and must abate proportionally.[6]

Lapse of legacies

A legacy may be held to have lapsed if the legatee has predeceased,[7] or if the designated purpose of the bequest has failed, or if any condition attached to it is not implemented.[8] The subject of the legacy in such a case falls into residue.[9]

A specific legacy fails if the deceased did not at his death possess an object answering the description.[10]

Where the bequest is to an institution the legacy lapses only if there has been such a change in its identity as to make it a different entity from that in the testator's mind.[11]

1 *Tait's Trs.* v. *Lees* (1886) 13 R. 1104.
2 e.g. *Chivas' Tr.* v. *McLeod* (1881) 9 R. 86.
3 *McConnel* v. *McC.'s Trs.*, 1931 S.N. 31.
4 *Adamson's Trs.* v. *A's Exors.* (1891) 18 R. 1133 (provision 'if my estate will permit').
5 *Kinmond's Trs.* v. *K.* (1873) 11 M. 381; as to abatement of annuities, see *Isaac's J.F.* v. *I.*, 1935 S.C. 243.
6 *Hood's Exors.* (1869) 7 M. 774.
7 Subject to the application of the *conditio si institutus* rule.
8 *Sutherland's Trs.* v. *S.* (1870) 8 M. 716; *Dunbar* v. *Scott's Trs.* (1872) 10 M. 982; *Graham's Trs.* v. *G.* (1899) 2 F. 232.
9 *White's Trs.* v. *W.*, 1936 S.L.T. 562.
10 *Stark's Trs.* v. *S.*, 1948 S.C. 41.
11 *Pope's Trs.* v. *Scott*, 1927 S.N. 122.

Payment of legacies

The date when legacies are to be paid may be expressly stated[1] or be implied in the terms of the will.[2] Failing such indication the executor may normally pay after the expiry of six months from the testator's death.

Payment may be expressly postponed, in which case payment may be anticipated if the reason for the postponement has disappeared,[3] but not at the request of the legatee if the estate might be insufficient to pay the provisions in full at the due date.[4]

A claim against an executor for payment of a legacy will be excluded by the long negative prescription.[5]

Interest on legacies

Legacies of money bear interest from the death until payment[6] unless the legacy is given without interest,[7] or unless the capital of the legacy was not in the executor's hands whence to pay the legacy.[8]

The rate of interest is normally that earned on average by the estate while awaiting distribution, but a higher rate may be exacted where the executor or trustee has delayed unreasonably to pay.[9]

Whether bequests free of duty or not

Legacies are frequently given expressly 'free of duty', in which case estate duty applicable thereto must be paid from residue.[10] If not so expressed each legacy must bear the rateable proportion of the total estate duty exigible from the estate. A question of interpretation may arise in case of doubt as to which of the bequests the words 'free of duty' apply.[11] Where legacies are given free of duty and a codicil adds other legacies it is not implied that they also are free of duty.[12] An express bequest of

1 *Campbell's Trs.* v. *Cazenove* (1880) 8 R. 21.
2 e.g. *Haldane's Trs.* v. *Murphy* (1881) 9 R. 269.
3 *Finlay's Trs.* v. *F.* (1886) 13 R. 1052.
4 *Haldane's Trs.* v. *H.* (1895) 23 R. 276.
5 *Jamieson* v. *Clark* (1872) 10 M. 399.
6 *Kirkpatrick* v. *Bedford* (1878) 6 R. (H.L.) 4; *McLean's Trs.* v. *McL.* (1891) 18 R. 892; *May's Trs.* v. *Paul* (1900) 2 F. 657.
7 e.g. *Scott's Trs.* v. *Hoare*, 1942 S.C. 455.
8 *Ewing* v. *Mathieson* (1904) 41 S.L.R. 594; *Waddell's Trs.* v. *Crawford*, 1926 S.C. 654.
9 *Inglis' Trs.* v. *Breen* (1891) 18 R. 487.
10 *Dunn's Trs.* v. *D.*, 1924 S.C. 613.
11 *Kirkpatrick* v. *Bedford* (1878) 6 R. (H.L.) 4; *Macdonald's Trs.* v. *Aberdeen Mags.* (1902) 4 F. 907.
12 *Melville's Trs.* v. *Duncan*, 1950 S.L.T. (Notes) 27; cf. *Christie's Trs.* v. *C's Trs.*, 1943 S.C. 97.

legal rights and a provision that legacies are to be paid free of duty may make legal rights also free of duty.[1] There is a presumption that a testator intends to provide only for death duties payable on his own death.[2]

Whether bequests free of burdens

When the subjects of bequest are burdened with debts, annuities or other payments, the legatee *prima facie* must take the subject with the burden, even where the testator has directed his trustee to pay debts affecting his property.[3]

FACULTIES AND POWERS

Apart from making a beneficial gift to a donee, a testator may convey property to another, such as a liferenter or trustee, and confer on him a faculty or power or authority to confer on others rights in that property.

The power may be proprietary, where the donee of the power may use the power for his own benefit, or fiduciary, where the power is a trust to be exercised for the benefit of others.[4] Again, it may be general, where the donee has liberty of choice whom to benefit by exercising the power (including liberty to benefit himself),[5] or special, where his power is limited by the terms of the will, such as to divide among the members of a prescribed class only.[6] A distinction may also be drawn between a power to appoint, and a power to apportion a gift among the members of a prescribed class.[7] The nature of the power in each case depends on the intention of the testator as disclosed in his settlement. A power conferred may be too indefinite to receive effect, in which case a purported exercise will be invalid.[8]

Creation of power

A power may be created by reservation, where the testator reserves to himself power to confer rights in property being

[1] *Galt's Trs.* v. *G.*, 1945 S.C. 183.

[2] *Scott's Trs.* v. *Hoare*, 1942 S.C. 455; *Purvis's Trs.* v. *P.*, 1942 S.C. 560; *Connel's Trs.* v. *C.*, 1949 S.C. 231.

[3] *Muir's Tr.* v. *M.*, 1916 1 S.L.T. 372. See also *Caithness' J.F.* v. *Sinclair-Gerold*, 1929 S.N. 100.

[4] *Bannerman's Trs.* v. *B.*, 1915 S.C. 398, 408.

[5] *Hyslop* v. *Maxwell's Trs.* (1834) 12 S. 413.

[6] e.g. *Allan's Exor.* v. *A.*, 1908 S.C. 807.

[7] *Alexander's Trs.* v. *A's Trs.*, 1917 S.C. 654, 659.

[8] *Sutherland's Trs.* v. *S's Tr.* (1893) 20 R. 925; *Anderson* v. *Smoke* (1898) 25 R. 493; *Campbell's Trs.* v. *Edinburgh R.I.*, 1932 S.N. 10.

disposed of, or by constitution, where the power is conferred on another, such as trustees, or a liferenter. The difference does not affect the interpretation or mode of exercise of the power.

It may be created by *inter vivos* deed, such as marriage contract, or *mortis causa* deed, such as will or trust disposition.

In the case of a limited power the date of creation of the power is the date of constitution of liferents created thereunder for the purpose of the statutory limitations on liferents.[1]

Implied power

In the case of a provision in their parents' marriage contract destined to the children of the marriage as a class the father has an implied power to apportion the provision among the children.[2]

Who may exercise power

A power conferred on trustees may be personal to them and not exercisable by assumed trustees,[3] or exercisable only by nominees jointly.[4] Where the power is conferred by will the donee of the power must survive the testator.[5] A power conferred by marriage contract may remain unaffected though one spouse has been divorced and thereby forfeited the provisions therein in her favour.[6]

Power not delegable

The exercise of a power must be done by the donee of the power, and cannot be delegated to a third party.[7] It is questionable whether a testator may give his trustees a power to apportion a fund, or to convey the fund to third parties to act as trustees for apportioning the fund,[8] but an objection to delegation does not prevent a testator with a reserved power from conferring on another the right to exercise the power.[9] If a power is conferred on one, whom failing on another, exercise by the first donee evacuates the power.[10] It may be possible to separate a delegated,

[1] *Muir's Trs.* v. *Williams*, 1943 S.C. (H.L.) 67; *Malcolm's Trs.* v. *M.*, 1950 S.C. (H.L.) 17.

[2] Ersk. III, 8, 49; Bell, *Prin.* §1971, 1988; *Thomson* v. *His Children* (1762) Mor. 13018; *Ponton* v. *P.* (1837) 15 S. 554; *Moir's Trs.* (1871) 9 M. 848.

[3] *Hill's Trs.* v. *Thomson* (1874) 2 R. 68.

[4] *Paterson's Trs.* v. *Findlay*, 1918 S.C. 713.

[5] *Penny's Trs.* v. *P's Trs.*, 1925 S.C. 175.

[6] *McGrady's Trs.* v. *McG.*, 1932 S.C. 191.

[7] *Marshall's Trs.* v. *Findlay*, 1928 S.L.T. 560; *Monies* v. *M.*, 1939 S.C. 344; *Burn's Trs.* v. *McKenna*, 1940 S.C. 489; *Cathcart's Trs.* v. *Valentine*, 1940 S.C. 588; *Coats's Trs.* v. *Tillinghast*, 1944 S.C. 466.

[8] *Potter's Trs.* v. *Allan*, 1918 S.C. 173.

[9] *Miller* v. *M.* (1906) 13 S.L.T. 770.

[10] *Darling's Exor.* v. *D.* (1869) 41 S. Jur. 545.

and therefore invalid, exercise from a valid part, and so not destroy the scheme which the appointer had in mind.[1] But if an invalid exercise is inseparable from a valid part, the whole appointment is invalid.[2]

Over what property power extends

It is a question of interpretation over what property a power extends. It may not cover the whole estate conveyed.[3]

Manner of exercise of power

A power must be exercised strictly in the manner, if any, prescribed by the testator.[4] Thus a power to dispose of heritage 'during his life' did not entitle a person to dispose of it by *mortis causa* deed.[5] Failing prescription it may be exercised in any way.[6] It is not essential that a deed whereby a power is exercised should refer thereto, but if it does not, it is a question of the interpretation of that deed whether or not it purports to exercise the power.[7] Hence a general power may be exercised by the donee's own general settlement of his property,[8] as also may a special power.[9] It may even be held exercised by a general settlement executed prior to acquiring the power in question.[10] An express exercise of one power may suggest that a general residuary bequest does not impliedly exercise another power.[11] A conveyance of property including property over which the testator has a power of appointment may be held to imply exercise of the power by the residue clause.[12] It is competent to appoint

[1] *Cathcart's Trs.*, *supra*.

[2] *Mackenzie's Trs.* v. *M.*, 1927 S.C. 424; *Monies* v. *M.*, 1939 S.C. 344; *Burns's Trs.* v. *McKenna*, 1940 S.C. 489; *Coats's Trs.* v. *Tillinghast*, 1944 S.C. 466.

[3] *Campbell* v. *C.* (1887) 15 R. 103.

[4] *Campbell's Trs.* v. *C.* (1903) 5 F. 366.

[5] *Miller's Trs.* v. *Findlay* (1896) 24 R. 114; contrast *McLean* v. *Henderson's Trs.* (1880) 7 R. 601; *Watt's Trs.* v. *Jamieson*, 1912 S.C. 1320; *Stirling's Trs.* v. *Legal and General Assce. Socy.*, 1957 S.L.T. 73; cf. *Durie's Trs.* v. *Osborne*, 1960 S.C. 444.

[6] *Jack* v. *Rennie* (1874) 1 R. 828. It may be exercised in a marriage contract: *Buchanan's Trs.* v. *Whyte* (1890) 17 R. (H.L.) 53; *Thomson's Trs.* v. *Pringle* (1901) 9 S.L.T. 11; contrast *Montgomerie's Trs.* v. *Alexander's Trs.*, 1911 S.C. 856.

[7] *Brodie's J.F.* v. *B.* (1900) 2 F. 1105; *Dick's Trs.* v. *Cameron*, 1907 S.C. 1018; *Ramsay's Trs.* v. *R.*, 1909 S.C. 628; *Smart* v. *S.*, 1926 S.C. 392.

[8] *Hyslop* v. *Maxwell's Trs.* (1834) 12 S. 413; *Mackenzie* v. *Gillanders* (1874) 1 R. 1050; *Dalgleish's Trs.* v. *Young* (1893) 20 R. 904; *Clark's Trs.* v. *C's Exors.* (1894) 21 R. 546; *Bray* v. *Bruce's Exors.* (1906) 8 F. 1078.

[9] *Tarratt's Trs.* v. *Hastings* (1904) 6 F. 968; *Alexander's Trs.* v. *A's Trs.*, 1917 S.C. 654; *Burns's Trs.* v. *B's Tr.*, 1935 S.C. 906; *Gemmell's Trs.* v. *Shields*, 1936 S.C. 717. But see also *Dick's Trs.* v. *Cameron*, 1907 S.C. 1018.

[10] *White's Tr.* v. *Mathie* (1899) 7 S.L.T. 81; *McTavish's Trs.* v. *Ogston's Exors.* (1903) 5 F. 641; contrast *Bertram's Trs.* v. *Matheson's Tr.* (1885) 15 R. 572.

[11] *Ramsay's Trs.* v. *R.*, 1909 S.C. 628; contrast *Bray*, *supra*.

[12] *Alexander's Trs.*, *supra*.

the property to be distributed in the same way as the testator's own estate.[1]

Revocable and irrevocable appointments

An appointment in an *inter vivos* deed, if valid, may be irrevocable, if made in a contractual deed.[2] It is probably also irrevocable if the deed is delivered[3] or if infeftment is taken in heritage pursuant thereto.[4] A declaration *in gremio* that the appointment is irrevocable, certainly if combined with intimation to the appointee or delivery, probably implies irrevocability.

An appointment in a *mortis causa* deed is normally revocable, like the rest of the deed, until the appointer's death, and a fresh appointment may be made instead.[5]

Objects of power

The objects of a power are those persons, usually designated by class or relationship, who may be benefited.[6] An exercise of a power which will, or may, benefit non-objects is invalid.[7] If valid and invalid appointments cannot be separated the whole appointment is invalid.[8]

It is questionable whether the class of 'children' includes the issue of a deceased child, under the principle *conditio si institutus sine liberis decesserit*.[9]

Release of power

The donee of a power normally has a discretion whether to exercise the power or not and accordingly may by deed release or extinguish it and so bring into effect the destination-over provided in the will to apply in default of appointment.[10] But he may have

1 *Mackie* v. *M's Trs.* (1885) 12 R. 1230; *Dalziel* v. *D's Trs.* (1905) 7 F. 545.

2 cf. *MacGillivray's Trs.* v. *Watson's Trs.*, 1911 S.C. 1103.

3 *Wylie's Trs.* v. *W.* (1902) 10 S.L.T. 395; cf. *Moncreiff's Trs.* v. *Balfour*, 1928 S.N. 139, where revocation was made with the appointee's consent.

4 *Murray's Trs.* v. *M.* (1872) 10 M. 778.

5 *Crosbie's Trs.* v. *Wylie* (1902) 10 S.L.T. 395; *Henderson's Trs.* v. *H.*, 1930 S.L.T. 346.

6 cf. *Potter's Trs.* v. *Allan*, 1918 S.C. 173.

7 *Wright's Trs.* v. *W.* (1894) 21 R. 568; *Darling's Trs.* v. *D's Trs.*, 1909 S.C. 445; *Inverclyde's Trs.* v. *I.*, 1910 S.C. 420; *Burns's Trs.* v. *McKenna*, 1940 S.C. 489; *Middleton's Trs.* v. *Borwick*, 1947 S.C. 517; *Simpson's M/C Trs.* v. *Wilkie*, 1948 S.L.T. 46; *Macdonald's J.F.* v. *M.*, 1950 S.L.T. (Notes) 56; *Wight's Trs.* v. *Milliken*, 1960 S.C. 137.

8 *Cathcart's J.F.* v. *Stewart*, 1948 S.C. 456; *MacLaren's Trs.* v. *Wilkie*, 1948 S.C. 652; *Wight's Trs.* v. *Milliken*, 1960 S.C. 137.

9 See *Gillon's Trs.* v. *G.* (1890) 17 R. 435; *Hughes* v. *Edwardes* (1892) 19 R. (H.L.) 33; *Blackburn's Trs.* v. *B.* (1896) 23 R. 698; *Cuming's Tr.* v. *C.* (1896) 24 R. 153; *Matthews Duncan's Trs.* v. *M.D.* (1901) 3 F. 533; *Cattanach's Trs.* v. *C.* (1901) 4 F. 205; *Cathcart's Trs.* v. *Valentine*, 1940 S.C. 588.

10 *Lawson* v. *Cormack's Trs.*, 1940 S.C. 210.

a duty to exercise it, as where the power is vested in trustees who have accepted the duties of the trust, in which case the power cannot be extinguished save by its exercise.[1]

Validity of exercise

The validity of the exercise of a power depends on its conforming with the terms in which it has been conferred.[2] An exercise of a power is valid notwithstanding that any object of such power has been altogether excluded,[3] unless the deed constituting the power declares the amount or share from which no object of the power shall be excluded, or that some one or more object or objects shall not be excluded.[4] A power to deal with subjects during life does not entitle the donee to dispose of the subjects by *mortis causa* deed.[5]

If the power conferred includes power to impose conditions or restrictions on the share allocated to the objects of the power, that may justify restriction to a liferent,[6] but a restriction not authorized is an invalid exercise of the power.[7]

The power may not be exercised in a way obviously designed to frustrate a pre-existing obligation to deal with the funds in a certain way.[8]

It is sometimes possible to separate valid and invalid parts of the exercise of a power, but if they are inseparable the whole appointment is invalid.[9]

Ultra vires *exercise*

A power must be exercised within the limits set by the donor thereof; if exercised to benefit non-objects of the power,[10] or subject to restrictions or conditions not authorised by the donor

[1] *Walker* v. *Ker* (1866) L.R. 1 Sc. & D. 11.

[2] cf. *Strathmore's Trs.* v. *L. Glamis*, 1932 S.C. 458.

[3] Powers of Appointment Act, 1874, S. 1; and see *Mackie* v. *Gloag's Trs.* (1883) 10 R. 746; *Mackie* v. *M's Trs.* (1885) 12 R. 1230; but see now *Henderson's Trs.* v. *H.*, 1930 S.L.T. 346; *Robertson's Trs.* v. *Smith's Trs.*, 1941 S.C. 439.

[4] Ibid., S. 2.

[5] *Miller's Trs.* v. *Findlay* (1896) 24 R. 114.

[6] *Warrand's Trs.* v. *W.* (1901) 3 F. 369; *Ewing's Trs.* v. *E.*, 1909 S.C. 409; *Pringle's Trs.* v. *Basta*, 1913 S.C. 172; *Angus's Trs.* v. *Monies*, 1939 S.C. 509; *Burn's Trs.* v. *McKenna*, 1940 S.C. 489; contrast *MacEwan's Trs.* v. *McE.*, 1917 S.C. 50; *Mackenzie's Trs.* v. *M.*, 1927 S.C. 424.

[7] *Gavin's Trs.* v. *Johnston*, 1926 S.L.T. 187.

[8] *Murray's Trs.* v. *MacGregor's Trs.*, 1931 S.C. 576.

[9] *Wight's Trs.* v. *Milliken*, 1960 S.C. 137.

[10] *Wright's Trs.* v. *W.* (1894) 21 R. 568; *Cattanach's Trs.* v. *C.* (1901) 4 F. 205; *Neill's Trs.* v. *Neill* (1902) 4 F. 636; *Dalziel* v. *D's Trs.* (1905) 7 F. 545; *Darling's Trs.* v. *D's Trs.*, 1909 S.C. 445; *Inverclyde's Trs.* v. *I.*, 1910 S.C. 420; *Burn's Trs.* v. *McKenna*, 1940 S.C. 489.

of the power,[1] the exercise is to that extent *ultra vires* and invalid. In the latter category an exercise in favour of objects of the power may be valid, notwithstanding *ultra vires* restrictions, the latter only being held *pro non scripto*,[2] but if the invalid conditions are not separable the whole appointment is invalidated.[3] It is questionable whether the consent of the objects can validate an *ultra vires* exercise.[4]

Failure to exercise

If a power is not exercised the fund is divided equally among the objects alive at the date of vesting, and similarly if a fund is partly not appointed, or invalidly appointed.[5] If there is only a partial appointment it is a question of intention how the unappointed fund falls to be paid.[6] To appoint to those who were conditionally instituted, failing appointment, has been held a non-exercise of the power.[7]

Fraud on a power

A fraud on a power is the exercise of the power for a purpose or with an intention beyond the scope of or not justified by the instrument creating the power. It does not necessarily involve any deceit or conduct dishonest or immoral.[8] Such an exercise is invalid unless the benefit *bona fide* intended to be conferred can be distinguished from that unjustifiably intended. It may consist in using the power in pursuance of a bargain with the object of the power;[9] such a bargain is probably not specifically enforceable.[10] Or it may consist in any exercise with an ulterior motive.[11] The donee of a power is prohibited from purchasing for her own behoof the interest in the fund of one of the objects of the power.[12]

1 *Dalziel's Trs., supra*, 553.
2 *McDonald* v. *McD's Trs.* (1875) 2 R. (H.L.) 125.
3 *Baikie's Trs.* v. *Oxley and Cowan* (1862) 24 D. 589; *McDonald, supra*; *Gillon's Trs.* v. *G.* (1890) 17 R. 435; *Mackenzie's Trs.* v. *M.*, 1927 S.C. 424; *Coats's Trs.* v. *Tillinghast*, 1944 S.C. 466; *Torrance's Tr.* v. *Weddell*, 1947 S.C. 96.
4 *Mackie* v. *M's Trs.* (1885) 12 R. 1230; *Macleod's Trs.* v. *M's Trs.*, 1914 S.C. 10; (yes); *MacGillivray's Trs.* v. *Watson's Trs.*, 1911 S.C. 1103 (no).
5 *Stirling's Trs.* v. *S.* (1898) 1 F. 215; *Mackenzie's Trs.* v. *Kilmarnock's Trs.*, 1909 S.C. 472.
6 *Macrae's Trs.* v. *M.*, 1927 S.C. 210.
7 *L.A.* v. *Routledge's Trs.*, 1907 S.C. 327.
8 *Vatcher* v. *Paull* [1915] A.C. 372.
9 *Smith Cunninghame* v. *Anstruther's Trs.* (1872) 10 M. (H.L.) 39; *McDonald* v. *McGrigor* (1874) 1 R. 817.
10 *Rollo's Trs.* v. *R.*, 1940 S.C. 578.
11 *Craig* v. *C's Trs.* (1904) 12 S.L.T. 136, 620; *Dick's Trs.* v. *Cameron*, 1907 S.C. 1018.
12 *McDonald* v. *McGrigor* (1874) 1 R. 817.

RESIDUE

The residue is the balance of the testator's estate, capital and income, not required for satisfying debts, death duties, any claims to legal rights, and the antecedent purposes of his testamentary deeds.[1] It is necessarily an indefinite and uncertain amount until the estate is ascertained at death. A residuary legatee may be regarded as taking the whole estate under the burden of debts, claims to legal rights, and all the antecedent purposes of the will.[2] The residuary legatee is entitled to everything left and his right is not defeated by the plea of confidentiality.[3] The residue may be marked off from legacies by such phrases as 'the rest', 'what is left', or 'then divided'.[4]

So far as legacies have failed by predecease of the legatees, or subsequently fail, the subjects thereof normally fall into residue.[5] Property carried by a direction held invalid falls into residue.[6] Similarly any part of the testator's estate not disposed of, such as surplus income accruing before a legacy vested,[7] falls into residue.

If, as is common, some or all of the testator's bequests are made payable free of duty, the duty thereon diminishes the residue. Similarly, where a large part of the estate consisted of bonds taken with special destinations in favour of the testator or his wife or the survivor it was held that legitim was payable out of the residue *primo loco* and only if that were insufficient out of the sums in the bonds.[8]

Disposal of residue

Residue may be disposed of by bequest in the same way as the subject matter of a legacy, specific or general, and most of the principles relative to legacies apply equally to gifts of residue.

[1] *Sturgis* v. *Campbell* (1865) 3 M. (H.L.) 70; *Gunn's Trs.* v. *Macfarlane* (1900) 37 S.L.R. 499.

[2] *Jamieson* v. *Clark* (1872) 10 M. 399; *Storie's Trs.* v. *Gray* (1874) 1 R. 953; *Samson* v. *Raynor*, 1928 S.C. 899.

[3] *Robertson* v. *R's Exors.*, 1925 S.C. 606.

[4] *McAulay's Trs.* v. *R.N.L.I.*, 1961 S.C. 307.

[5] *Dymock's Trs.* (1873) 10 S.L.R. 263; *Lawrence* v. *Stewart*, 1924 S.C. 934; *White's Trs.* v. *W.*, 1936 S.L.T. 562; *McCrorie's C.B.* v. *McC.*, 1909 1 S.L.T. 544.

[6] *Aitken's Trs.* v. *A.*, 1927 S.L.T. 308 (point not reported in 1927 S.C. 374).

[7] *Stobie's Trs.* (1888) 15 R. 340; *Brodie* v. *B's Trs.* (1893) 20 R. 795; *Adam's Trs.* v. *Wilson* (1899) 1 F. 1042; *Gibson's Trs.* v. *Lamb*, 1931 S.L.T. 22; contrast *McLean's Trs.* v. *McL.* (1891) 18 R. 892.

[8] *Farmer's Trs.* v. *Taylor*, 1917 S.C. 366; cf. *Tait's Trs.* v. *Lees* (1886) 13 R. 1104.

Residue undisposed of

If the residue in whole or in part is not destined to anyone, or if a legacy of the residue fails, the residue falls into intestacy and has to be distributed according to the rules of intestate succession to the heirs on intestacy ascertained at the date of the testator's death.[1] Thus if a liferent is given and the fee undisposed of it is undisposed of residue and falls into intestacy.[2] If bequests are made of shares of residue and one lapses, the lapsed share *prima facie* falls into intestacy rather than accruing to the other legatees of residue,[3] but this presumption may be displaced by the wording of a particular will.[4]

OTHER PROVISIONS HAVING TESTAMENTARY EFFECT

Deeds other than wills may in some cases have testamentary effect.

Donation mortis causa

A donation *mortis causa* is a gift made *intuitu mortis*, i.e. in contemplation, though not necessarily under immediate apprehension, of death,[5] by *de presenti* act or deed, so that the right of property is immediately transferred to the grantee, and the subject of gift or document of title thereto representing it must, at least normally, be delivered to the donee or to someone on his behalf.[6] Such a donation is effective on death but is revocable if the donor recovers.[7] It falls if the donee predeceases. If not solely for the donee's benefit but partly for administrative purposes it is ineffectual.[8] It differs from a legacy in not requiring writing, unless the kind of right donated requires writing for its transfer,

1 *Lord* v. *Colvin* (1865) 3 M. 1083.
2 *Reid's Trs.* v. *Bucher*, 1929 S.C. 615.
3 *Lawrence* v. *Stewart*, 1924 S.C. 934.
4 *Alves* v. *A.* (1861) 23 D. 712; *Lawrence, supra.*
5 *L.A.* v. *Galloway* (1884) 11 R. 541; *Blyth* v. *Curle* (1885) 12 R. 674.
6 Bankt. I, 9, 18; Ersk. II, 7, 1; *Morris* v. *Riddick* (1867) 5 M. 1036; *Young* v. *Donald's Trs.* (1881) 18 S.L.R. 372; *McSkimming* v. *Stenhouse* (1883) 21 S.L.R. 3; *Blyth* v. *Curle* (1885) 12 R. 674; *Martin's Trs.* v. *M.* (1887) 24 S.L.R. 484; *Rose* v. *Cameron's Exor.* (1901) 3 F. 337; *National Bank* v. *Mackie's Trs.* (1905) 13 S.L.T. 383; *Scott's Trs.* v. *Macmillan* (1905) 8 F. 214; *Hutchieson's Exrx.* v. *Shearer*, 1909 S.C. 15. Delivery was held not essential in *Gibson* v. *Hutchison* (1872) 10 M. 923; *Crosbie's Trs.* v. *Wright* (1880) 7 R. 823; *Blyth, supra*; *Scott's Trs., supra.* It is probably essential in the case of corporeal moveables.
7 *Macfarquhar* v. *McKay* (1869) 7 M. 766; see also *Scott's Trs.* v. *Macmillan* (1905) 8 F. 214.
8 *Sharp* v. *Paton* (1883) 10 R. 1000; *Thomson* v. *Dunlop* (1884) 11 R. 453.

and in being preferable to legacies, but resembles a legacy in being revocable, in not affecting *jus relictae* or legitim, in being liable for the donor's debts if there is insufficiency of funds to pay them, and in being subject to estate duty.[1]

The subject matter of gift may be heritage, or corporeal moveables, but has been most frequently been a claim to money, frequently evidenced by a deposit receipt.[2] A cheque payable after death does not operate as a donation *mortis causa* or *inter vivos*,[3] nor does a letter intimating intention to send a cheque for known purposes.[4]

A deposit receipt in the donor's name only may be validly donated *mortis causa* by indorsement and delivery.[5] If in the donee's name, or in joint names of donor and donee, or taken in joint names and to the survivor, the deposit receipt is better evidence of *animus donandi* and may help to evidence donation *mortis causa*[6] but the presumption in case of deposit in joint names is joint ownership and this must be overcome.[7]

There must always be evidence of *animus donandi* sufficient to overcome the legal presumption against donation, as by declaration of wish to make a gift to the donee.[8]

Obligations by legatee

A legatee having a vested right may undertake unilaterally or for consideration, to deal with his legacy, when it comes to be paid over to him, in a particular way, either voluntarily or as giving effect to an understood wish of the testator. If the legatee predeceases the date of payment the obligation does not fall to be construed as a *mortis causa* settlement, but, if sufficiently specific, is enforceable in its terms.[9]

1 *Morris, supra.*

2 In *Taggart* v. *Higgins' Exor.* (1900) 8 S.L.T. 139, entry of a name in a savings bank pass book, undelivered, failed to establish donation *mortis causa*.

3 *Milne* v. *Grant's Exors.* (1884) 11 R. 887.

4 *Hutcheson* v. *Potter* (1901) 9 S.L.T. 214.

5 *Macfarquhar* v. *McKay* (1869) 7 M. 766; *McNicol* v. *McDougall* (1889) 17 R. 25.

6 *McCubbin's Exors.* v. *Tait* (1868) 6 M. 310; *Crosbie's Trs.* v. *Wright* (1880) 7 R. 823; *Young* v. *Donald's Trs.* (1881) 18 S.L.R. 372; *McSkimming* v. *Stenhouse* (1883) 21 S.L.R. 3; *Macdonald* v. *M.* (1889) 16 R. 758; *Penman's Trs.* v. *P.* (1896) 4 S.L.T. 66; *Macfarlane's Trs.* v. *Miller* (1898) 25 R. 1201; *Lind* v. *Dalrymple's Exor.* (1900) 8 S.L.T. 308; contrast *Watt's Trs.* (1869) 7 M. 930; *Durie* v. *Ross* (1871) 9 M. 969; *Jamieson* v. *McLeod* (1880) 7 R. 1131; *Connell's Trs.* v. *C's Trs.* (1886) 13 R. 1175; contrast *Morrison* v. *Forbes* (1890) 17 R. 958; *Rose* v. *Cameron's Exor.* (1901) 3 F. 337.

7 *Jamieson* v. *McLeod* (1880) 7 R. 1131; *Trotter* v. *Spence* (1885) 22 S.L.R. 353.

8 *Ross* v. *Mellis* (1871) 10 M. 197; *Sharp* v. *Paton* (1883) 10 R. 1000; *Trotter* v. *Spence* (1885) 22 S.L.R. 353; *Morrison* v. *Forbes* (1890) 17 R. 958; cf. *Robertson* v. *Taylor* (1868) 6 M. 917; *Gibson* v. *Hutchison* (1872) 10 M. 923.

9 *Denny's Trs.* v. *Dumbarton Mags.*, 1945 S.C. 147.

Nominations

A person having money standing to his credit with certain kinds of benevolent bodies[1] may nominate a person to receive on his death the sum at his credit, subject to compliance with the relevant statute and regulations,[2] without the need for confirmation of an executor. The limit of sum is £500.[3] A nomination is a document of a testamentary nature[4] and has the character of a special destination.[5] It may be revoked but has been held not revoked by a subsequent will disposing of the nominator's whole estate.[6] The nomination must be delivered or sent to the appropriate office, or made in the appropriate book, as required by the statute governing the kind of body concerned in a particular case. Certain such statutes formerly permitted nomination only in cases of intestacy but have been extended to cases of testacy.[7]

Special destinations in titles of property

A testator may, before or after making his will, have taken property, heritable or moveable, in the name of another, or of himself and another, or of himself, whom failing, another, or in similar terms. Or he may have acquired property as substitute or as conditional institute under the will of another and wish to dispose thereof *mortis causa*. Special destinations of heritage originated prior to 1868 at least partly because of the impossibility before then of conveying heritage by testamentary writing, and their continued use now is productive more of difficulty than of benefit.[8] Titles containing special destinations are not, strictly speaking, writings of a testamentary character.[9]

Destinations—heritage

Where heritage is specially destined, the destination, unless evacuated, carries the property on the death of the institute to the substitute named as heir of provision in the destination of the

[1] Listed in Administration of Estate (Small Payments) Act, 1965, Sched. 2.

[2] Where 'writing under hand' was required, authentication by mark was held inadequate: *Morton* v. *French*, 1908 S.C. 171.

[3] Administration of Estates (Small Payments) Act, 1965, S. 2. This limit may be raised by the Treasury: ibid., S. 6.

[4] *Gill* v. *G.*, 1938 S.C. 65.

[5] *Ford's Trs.* v. *F.*, 1940 S.C. 426.

[6] *Clark's Exors.* v. *Macaulay*, 1961 S.L.T. 109.

[7] Administration of Estates (Small Payments) Act, 1965, S. 3 and Sched. 3.

[8] *Murray's Exors.* v. *Geekie*, 1929 S.C. 633; *Hay's Tr.* v. *H's Trs.*, 1951 S.C. 329, 334.

[9] *Connell's Trs.* v. *C's Trs.* (1886) 13 R. 1175; *Murray's Exors., supra.*

title. Where it is destined to two persons jointly and to the survivor they are joint fiars and the whole fee vests in the survivor.[1]

Destinations—moveables

Stock certificates, bonds, mortgage debentures, and certificates of debt issued by public companies or trustees of public utilities, if taken with a destination, pass thereunder on the taker's death.[2] Similarly with destinations in a moveable bond,[3] or a policy of assurance.[4]

But a destination in a deposit receipt or promissory note has no testamentary effect,[5] nor has a cheque made payable after death,[6] though extrinsic evidence may in the case of a deposit receipt prove donation *mortis causa*.

Clause of return

A clause of return is one whereby the granter takes a special destination providing that in certain circumstances the title shall revert to himself and his heirs.[7] Though mainly found in destinations of heritage, it is not confined thereto.[8] To be valid as a clause of return, the destination must be ultimately to the granter and his heirs, or possibly to the granter's heir *eo nomine*.[9] If the conditions for being regarded as a clause of return apply the property will return to the granter in preference to the gratuitous disponees of the institute or his heirs.[10]

Evacuation of special destinations—destination created by testator

Difficult questions may arise as to whether a subsequent universal settlement evacuates or revokes a destination of

[1] *Walker* v. *Galbraith* (1896) 23 R. 347; *Perrett's Trs.* v. *P.*, 1909 S.C. 522.

[2] *Buchan* v. *Porteous* (1874) 7 R. 211; *Walker's Exors.* v. *W.* (1878) 5 R. 965; *Thomson's Trs.* v. *T.* (1879) 6 R. 1227; *Milne* v. *Scott* (1880) 8 R. 83; *Connell's Trs.* v. *C's Trs.* (1886) 13 R. 1175; *Paterson's J.F.* v. *P's Trs.* (1897) 24 R. 499; *Fraser* v. *McKillican* (1905) 13 S.L.T. 81; *Ferguson* v. *L.A.* (1906) 13 S.L.T. 724; *Colenso's Exor.* v. *Davidson*, 1930 S.L.T. 359.

[3] *Paterson's J.F.* v. *Paterson's Trs.* (1897) 24 R. 499.

[4] *Dickie's Trs.* v. *D.* (1892) 29 S.L.R. 908.

[5] *Cuthill* v. *Burns* (1862) 24 D. 849; *Watt's Trs.* (1869) 7 M. 930; *Miller* v. *M.* (1874) 1 R. 1107; *Crosbie's Trs.* v. *Wright* (1880) 7 R. 823; *Connell's Trs.*, *supra*; *Dinwoodie's Exrx.* v. *Carruther's Exor.* (1895) 23 R. 234; *Fraser* v. *McKillican* (1905) 13 S.L.T. 81; *Sillars* v. *McAlpine* (1907) 15 S.L.T. 365.

[6] *Milne* v. *Grant's Exors.* (1884) 11 R. 887.

[7] Ersk. III, 8, 45; Bell, *Prin.* §1075.

[8] *Scott of Mangerton* v. *Scott of Ancrum* (1683) Mor. 4341; *McDowall* v. *Hannay* (1847) 9 D. 1284; *Bell's Exor.* v. *Borthwick* (1897) 24 R. 1120.

[9] *Robertson* v. *Hay-Boyd*, 1928 S.C. (H.L.) 8.

[10] *Dyer* v. *Carruthers* (1874) 1 R. 943.

property to another previously made by the testator. The matter is one of intention, and it is legitimate to take into account circumstances extraneous to the writings in judging whether or not a general revocation revokes destinations.[1] A destination may be indefeasible if involving a contractual element.[2] The presumption is that a subsequent general settlement does not evacuate a prior special destination of the property taken by the testator himself[3] (the destination and the settlement being both expressions of his will and to receive effect as such). But this presumption may be rebutted, if the subsequent general settlement is inconsistent with, and cannot be wholly effective in the face of, the prior special destination.[4] The presumption is also rebutted by a contractual element, as where joint owners had each paid for the property in part.[5] A clause revoking in general terms all prior testamentary writings is not normally sufficient by itself to evacuate a prior special destination.[6] It is otherwise if the revocation expressly mentions special destinations. The testator's conveyance of his estate, expressly including property held under special destinations, to trustees evidences intention to evacuate the destinations.[7]

A special destination taken by the testator subsequently to a general settlement by him, being later, is not superseded by the general settlement,[8] but a destination of property subsequently acquired to one spouse in liferent and the other in fee is not a special destination and is accordingly carried by an antecedent settlement.[9]

1 *Glendonwyn* v. *Gordon* (1873) 11 M. (H.L.) 33; *Bryden's C.B.* v. *B's Trs.* (1898) 25 R. 708; *Minto's Trs.* v. *M.* (1898) 1 F. 62; *Morrison's Trs.* v. *M.* (1905) 7 F. 810; *Perrett's Trs.* v. *P.*, 1909 S.C. 522; *Murray's Exors.* v. *Geekie*, 1929 S.C. 633.

2 *Perrett's Trs., supra*; *Renouf's Trs.* v. *Haining*, 1919 S.C. 497; *Chalmers's Tr.* v. *Thomson's Exrx.*, 1923 S.C. 271; *Taylor's Exors.* v. *Brunton* 1939 S.C. 444; *Shand's Trs.* v. *S's Trs.*, 1966 S.L.T. 306.

3 *Glendonwyn, supra*; *Walker's Exor.* v. *W.* (1878) 5 R. 965; *Campbell* v. *C.* (1880) 7 R. (H.L.) 100; *Lang's Trs.* v. *L.* (1885) 12 R. 1265; *Connell's Trs.* v. *C.* (1886) 13 R. 1175; *Currie* v. *McLennan* (1899) 1 F. 684; *Morrison's Tr.* v. *M.* (1905) 7 F. 810; *Perrett's Trs., supra*; *Chalmers's Tr.* v. *Thomson*, 1923 S.C. 271; *Cunningham's Trs.* v. *C.*, 1924 S.C. 581; *Murray's Exors., supra*; *Brown's Tr.* v. *B.*, 1943 S.C. 488.

4 *Perrett's Trs., supra*; *Dennis* v. *Aitchison*, 1924 S.C. (H.L.) 122; *Murray's Exors.* v. *Geekie*, 1929 S.C. 633; *Brown's Tr., supra.*

5 *Perrett's Trs., supra*; *Chalmers's Trs.* v. *Thomson's Exrx.*, 1923 S.C. 271.

6 *Connell's Trs.* v. *C.* (1886) 13 R. 1175; *Paterson's J.F.* v. *Paterson's Trs.* (1897) 24 R. 499; *Murray's Exors., supra*; though see *Turnbull's Trs.* v. *Robertson*, 1911 S.C. 1288; *Drysdale's Trs.* v. *D.*, 1922 S.C. 741.

7 *Drysdale's Trs.* v. *D.*, 1922 S.C. 741.

8 *Perrett's Trs., supra.*

9 *Webster's Trs.* v. *W.* (1876) 4 R. 101; *Philip* v. *P.* (1885) 13 R. 329; *Farquharson* v. *F.* (1883) 10 R. 1253; *Haddow's Exors.* v. *H.*, 1943 S.C. 44.

Destination created by third party

The opposite presumption applies where the destination was not taken by the testator himself but by a third party, and his settlement is presumed to evacuate a special destination.[1] Thus where the testator holds property under a special destination taken by another party, and to which he has succeeded, a subsequent general settlement by him revokes that destination, though this may have the effect of defeating the expectations of conditional institutes or substitutes under that destination.[2] This result does not follow where joint institutes accepted a gift conditioned by the terms of the destination imposed by the donor.[3]

The power to evacuate extends only to property so far as vested in the testator, such as the testator's *pro indiviso* share of property destined to him and to another.[4]

A testamentary disposition executed on or after 10 September 1964 does not have the effect of evacuating a special destination (being one which could competently be evacuated by testamentary disposition) unless it contains a specific reference to the destination and a declared intention on the part of the testator to evacuate it.[5] This provision does not distinguish between destinations created by the testator and one created by a third party.

Marriage contracts

Marriage contracts are intended to regulate the property rights of the spouses and particularly to protect certain property from the acts of the donor or of the other spouse or the diligence of that spouse's creditors, and to make provision for the surviving spouse and the children of the marriage. They are less important and common than formerly because of the greater capacity of married women today, both in law and in fact, to own and manage property independently, and the decline of family wealth and property.

Marriage contracts may be ante-nuptial or post-nuptial. Either may be created by bilateral contractual undertakings by each party in favour of the other and of the children, or, and

[1] *Gray* v. *G's Trs.* (1878) 5 R. 820; *Campbell* v. *C.* (1880) 7 R. (H.L.) 100; *Watson's Trs.* v. *Hamilton* (1894) 21 R. 451.

[2] *Glendonwyn, supra*; *Gray* v. *G's Trs.* (1878) 5 R. 820; *Campbell* v. *C.* (1880) 7 R. (H.L.) 100; *Perrett's Trs., supra.*

[3] *Renouf's Exors.* v. *Haining*, 1919 S.C. 497; *Taylor's Exors.* v. *Brunton*, 1939 S.C. 444; *Brown's Tr.* v. *B.*, 1943 S.C. 488.

[4] e.g. *Hay's Tr., supra.*

[5] Succession (Sc.) Act, 1964, S. 30.

usually, by creation of a trust and dispositions by each party, and sometimes by their parents also, of estate, heritable and/or moveable, to the trustees for declared purposes, which include provisions for the spouses *stante matrimonio*, for the survivor and for the children, and for the disposal of the property failing children. The undertakings of each prospective spouse may be contained in a separate deed.[1]

The court has no power to supply defects or deficiencies in a marriage contract,[2] and if a *casus improvisus* arises the settlement may fail.

A prospective wife may, by ante-nuptial marriage contract, create in her own favour an alimentary liferent protected against both her husband and the diligence of creditors, provided that there is a trust.[3] If the liferentrix later acquires the fee, her liferent continues and remains alimentary for her own protection.[4] It was formerly possible to discharge the legal rights of the yet unconceived children of the marriage[5] but this is no longer competent,[6] but it is still competent for either prospective spouse to discharge his or her legal rights in the other's estate on death, accepting a conventional provision in satisfaction.

In a post-nuptial contract neither party can create an alimentary liferent in favour of himself or herself. An agreement for a liferent of a settled fund implies a discharge of the liferenter's claim to any part of the capital of that fund by way of legal rights, if the capital is destined to other parties by the deed.[7] Legitim cannot be discharged by post-nuptial deed unless with the consent of children who are *sui juris*.

Ante-nuptial contracts

Two major questions in determining the rights and obligations under marriage contracts are whether the provisions are contractual or testamentary, and whether any claimants are within the consideration of marriage. The first depends on the intention

[1] cf. *Williamson* v. *Boothby* (1890) 17 R. 927; *Wilken's Trs.* v. *Wilken* (1904) 6 F. 655.

[2] *Dolphin's Trs.* v. *Baxter* (1888) 15 R. 733; *Ferguson's C.B.* v. *F's Trs.* (1893) 20 R. 835; *Scott's Trs.* v. *S.* (1902) 10 S.L.T. 122.

[3] *Dewar's Trs.* v. *D.*, 1910 S.C. 730; *Forbes' Trs.* v. *Tennant*, 1926 S.C. 294; *Arnold's Trs.* v. *Graham*, 1927 S.C. 353. As to phrases in marriage contracts held ineffectual to confer alimentary protection, see *Douglas, Gardiner & Mill* v. *Mackintosh's Trs.*, 1916 S.C. 125; *Dunsmure's Trs.* v. *D.*, 1920 S.C. 147; *Mackie's J.F.*, 1920 2 S.L.T. 95.

[4] *Eliott's Trs.* v. *E.* (1894) 21 R. 975; *Howat's Trs.* v. *H.*, 1922 S.C. 506.

[5] e.g. *Panmure* v. *Crokat* (1856) 18 D. 703; *Bell* v. *B.* (1897) 25 R. 310; *Simpson's Trs.* v. *Taylor*, 1912 S.C. 280; *Galloway's Trs.* v. *G.*, 1943 S.C. 339.

[6] Succession (Sc.) Act, 1964, S. 12.

[7] *Smart* v. *S's Trs.*, 1926 S.L.T. 227.

of parties as disclosed by their deed. Under the second the spouses and issue of the intended marriage are certainly within the marriage consideration, while third parties are not.

Revocability

Whether a marriage contract is revocable or not *stante matrimonio* depends on its terms. If truly contractual, it will be irrevocable, even by common consent,[1] unless there is an express reserved power to revoke,[2] but if it is primarily testamentary it will be revocable, notwithstanding a declaration of irrevocability.[3] An ante-nuptial marriage contract is presumed contractual *quoad* the spouses and the children of the marriage,[4] but not *quoad* third parties.[5]

Mortis causa *provisions in marriage contracts*

Marriage contracts commonly include provisions becoming applicable only when the marriage has been dissolved by the death of one spouse. These commonly include provisions in substitution for the claims to legal rights the surviving spouse and children would otherwise have had, and expressly given in satisfaction thereof, but possibly confer provisions additional to legal rights. The rights of surviving parties depend primarily on the terms of the particular deed and on the circumstances which have arisen. There is no presumption that a marriage contract is primarily or substantially testamentary.[6]

The first question is of what property is carried by the marriage contract conveyances; this is a question of intention.[7] It may be specific property only, or the spouse's whole means and estate, and may extend also to property acquired during the subsistence of the marriage.[8] It normally covers only capital sums and does not include annuities or liferents.[9] Savings from that spouse's

[1] *Pringle* v. *Anderson* (1868) 6 M. 982; *Hope* v. *H.* (1870) 8 M. 699; *Menzies* v. *Murray* (1875) 2 R. 507.

[2] *Fowler's Trs.* v. *F.* (1898) 25 R. 1034; *Simpson's Trs.* v. *Taylor*, 1912 S.C. 280.

[3] *Byre's Trs.* v. *Gemmell* (1895) 23 R. 332.

[4] *Mackie* v. *Gloag's Trs.* (1884) 11 R. (H.L.) 10; *Burgh Smeaton* v. *Whitson*, 1907 S.C. 1009; *Leslie's Trs.* v. *L.*, 1921 S.C. 940.

[5] McLaren, I, 424.

[6] *McOnie* v. *Whyte* (1890) 17 R. (H.L.) 53.

[7] *Campbell* v. *C.* (1887) 15 R. 103.

[8] On *acquirenda* see *Boyd's Trs.* v. *B.* (1877) 4 R. 1082; *Young's Trs.* (1885) 12 R. 968; *Russell's Trs.* (1887) 14 R. 849; *Simson's Trs.* v. *Brown* (1890) 17 R. 581; *Neish's Trs.* v. *N.* (1897) 24 R. 306; *Neilson's Trs.* v. *Henderson* (1897) 24 R. 1135; *Campbell* v. *C's Trs.* (1899) 1 F. 999; *Boyd's Trs.* v. *B.* (1905) 7 F. 576; as to *spes successionis* see *McEwan's Trs.* v. *Macdonald*, 1909 S.C. 57.

[9] *Ramsay's Trs.* v. *R.* (1899) 1 F. 495; *Murdoch's Trs.* v. *Stocks*, 1923 S.C. 906.

income and investments made therefrom do not fall into the marriage contract funds under an *acquirenda* clause if the origin of the investments be established.[1]

Rights of surviving spouse

The rights of the surviving spouse depend primarily on the interpretation of the deed in question in the circumstances which have arisen. A widow is normally given a sum for mournings[2] and for interim aliment. She is frequently also given an annuity or liferent.[3] Provisions for the survivor may be secured so as to confer a preference, or merely give a *jus crediti* entitling the survivor to rank with the predeceaser's creditors, or be of the nature of a right in succession, giving no such *jus crediti*.[4]

Rights of children or remoter issue

This also is primarily a question of the interpretation of the deed in question in the circumstances.

The heir of the marriage may under the marriage contract be given a fee, importing a preference as against creditors, if the father dispones lands to himself in liferent only and to the heirs of the marriage in fee,[5] or transfers property to trustees to hold for himself in liferent and for the heirs of the marriage in fee,[6] and infeftment is taken in the fee.

The heir may have only a *jus crediti* which entitles him to compete with the father's creditors, if there is an obligation to infeft the heir in lands at a stated date or age, or restricting the father's right to a liferent and conferring a fee on the heir but not followed by infeftment.[7]

Or the heir may have the still lesser right of a *spes successionis in obligatione*, as where the father dispones lands to himself and the heirs male of the marriage, whom failing to other persons. The marriage contract is deemed onerous in relation to the heirs-male but gratuitous in relation to the substitutes.[8] In such a case the father cannot in a question with the heir burden the estate

[1] *Young's Trs.* v. *Y's Trs.* (1892) 20 R. 22; *Dunbar's Trs.* v. *D.* (1902) 5 F. 191; cf. *Ramsay's Trs., supra.*

[2] A discharge of legal rights does not cover mournings: *Griffith's Trs.* v. *G.*, 1912 S.C. 626.

[3] cf. *Milne's Tr.* v. *M.*, 1920 S.C. 456.

[4] *Grant* v. *Robertson* (1872) 10 M. 804.

[5] Bell, *Convg.* II, 885; *Newlands* v. *N's Crs.* (1798) 4 Pat. 43; *Maule* (1876) 3 R. 831.

[6] Bell, *supra*; *Ross* v. *King* (1847) 9 D. 1327.

[7] Ersk. III, 8, 40; Bell, *Convg.* II, 883; Fraser, *H. & W.* II, 1421.

[8] *Wilson* v. *Reid* (1827) 6 S. 198.

or evacuate the destination gratuitously,[1] nor restrict the heir's interest to a liferent or an annuity.[2] The father may, however, reserve power to burden the estate or evacuate the destination, either onerously or gratuitously.

Heirs under the destination, not of the marriage, have usually no more than a *spes successionis in destinatione*.

Provisions for other children

The provisions made for other children also depend on the terms of the particular marriage contract. The provisions may confer a preference over the parents' creditors, if the parent is wholly divested, as by vesting the funds in trustees, or has granted security, properly completed, for payment of the provisions.

They may confer a *jus crediti* when the parent's obligation is to transfer assets to the children or trustees for them during his lifetime.[3] They may confer no *jus crediti*, as where the obligation is not enforceable during the granter's life,[4] but even in such a case the children have a protected right of succession, which cannot be defeated by the parent's will.[5] Lastly, they may affect property from which the general body of creditors is already excluded, as where property had been previously conveyed subject to a reserved faculty to create provisions in favour of the children of a future marriage.[6]

Provisions for second marriage

Express provisions may be made for the possibility of the surviving spouse contracting a second marriage and of having children thereby. An express reserved power may be inserted permitting provisions in such a case.

A husband has implied power to encroach on provisions made on a former marriage for the benefit of the wife and children of a later marriage, provided that the provisions on the later marriage are reasonable in amount, and that the husband has no other source from which to make the provisions for the later marriage.[7]

1 *Grahame* v. *Ewen's Trs.* (1824) 2 S. 612; *Gillon's Trs.* v. *G.* (1890) 17 R. 435; *Livingstone* v. *Waddell's Trs.* (1899) 1 F. 831.

2 *Ormiston* v. *O.* (1809) Hume 531.

3 *Goddard* v. *Stewart's Children* (1844) 6 D. 1018; *Cruickshank's Trs.* v. *C.* (1853) 16 D. 7; *Greenock* v. *G.* (1870) 8 M. 386; *Black* v. *B's Trs.*, 1912 2 S.L.T. 68; *Mackinnon's Trs.* v. *Dunlop*, 1913 S.C. 232.

4 *Goddard, supra*; *Gillon's Trs.* v. *G.* (1890) 17 R. 435; *Mackinnon's Trs., supra.*

5 *Gillon's Trs., supra.*

6 See Stair II, 3, 54; Ersk. II, 3, 50; Bell, *Comm.* I, 39; *Prin.* §924.

7 Ersk. III, 8, 42; *Arthur & Seymour* v. *Lamb* (1870) 8 M. 928.

Postnuptial marriage contracts

At common law a donation *inter virum et uxorem* was revocable, but such donations are now irrevocable unless sequestration follows within a year and a day of the donation.[1] Formerly, accordingly, a postnuptial marriage contract, so far as benefiting the other spouse, might be regarded as a donation rather than a provision, and to that extent was revocable and not protected against the donor's creditors. Nevertheless a right taking effect before the donor's death cannot be deemed a matrimonial provision.[2]

A postnuptial contract is not always revocable by the spouses jointly,[3] and not if alimentary rights have been created[4] or the interests of children or other issue may be affected,[5] or the wife is being protected against her own acts.[6]

Creditors challenging a postnuptial contract may invoke a presumption of the grantor's insolvency at the date when the provision was constituted, which may be rebutted by proof of solvency.[7] If the husband was in fact insolvent it is difficult to see how any provisions for his wife can be reasonable.[8]

1 Married Women's Property (Sc.) Act, 1920, S. 5.

2 *Anderson* v. *A.* (1903) 5 F. 323.

3 See *Peddie* v. *P's Trs.* (1891) 18 R. 491; *Gillon's Trs.* v. *G.* (1903) 5 F. 533.

4 *Mackenzie* v. *Banks* (1886) 24 S.L.R. 230.

5 *Allan* v. *Kerr* (1869) 8 M. 34; *Low* v. *L's Trs.* (1877) 5 R. 185.

6 *Barras* v. *Scottish Widows Fund Socy.* (1900) 2 F. 1094.

7 *Campbell's Trs.* v. *Whyte* (1884) 11 R. 1078; *Dunn's Trs.* (1896) 4 S.L.T. 46; *McLay* v. *McQueen* (1899) 1 F. 804; *Corbidge* v. *Somerville's Trs.*, 1911 S.C. 1326.

8 *Guthrie* v. *Cowan* (1846) 9 D. 124; *Robertson's Trs.* v. *R.* (1901) 3 F. 359.

CHAPTER 113

VESTING OF INTERESTS IN SUCCESSION

An interest, whether on intestacy or under a will, vests[1] when the person entitled thereto acquires full legal right of property in the share of estate or subjects of bequest, so that they become part of his estate, disposable by him *inter vivos* or *mortis causa*, attachable by his creditors, and passing on his death to his executor.[2] A vested interest is accordingly distinct from a contingent interest, an expectancy or a *spes successionis*. Vesting does not necessarily depend on actual possession, enjoyment or payment, as these may be held up by prior interests, nor is it necessarily postponed by the existence of a trust. In some contexts, however, the word may connote vesting in possession.

Vesting of prior rights on intestacy

Statutory prior rights exigible on intestacy vest on the predeceasing spouse's death, provided that that spouse has left no will disposing of the whole of his or her estate. The vesting is possibly subject to defeasance in the event of a will disposing of the whole estate being subsequently found within the long prescriptive period.

Vesting of legal rights

All legal rights vest on the death of the spouse or parent and are fixed as regards share, and, unless the estate is actually realized, monetary value, at that date.[3]

Vesting of shares in succession on intestacy

The whole estate, heritable and moveable, of a deceased, falling to be administered under the law of Scotland, by virtue of confirmation thereto, vests on death for the purposes of

[1] Generally, McLaren, *Wills*, II, 783; Henderson, *Vesting in Succession*.

[2] *Kilgour* v. *K.* (1845) 7 D. 451; *Newton* v. *Thomson* (1849) 11 D. 452; *Haldane's Trs.* v. *Murphy* (1881) 9 R. 269.

[3] (*Jus relictae*) Stair III, 8, 50; Bankt. III, 8, 40; Ersk. III, 9, 30; Bell, *Prin.* §1591; Fraser *H. & W.*, II, 1060; *McIntyre* v. *McI's Trs.* (1865) 3 M. 1074; *Mackenzie* v. *M's Trs.* (1873) 11 M. 681; *Russell* v. *A.G.*, 1917 S.C. 28.

(*Jus relicti*) Married Women's Property (Sc.) Act, 1881, S. 4; *Simon's Tr.* v. *Neilson* (1890) 18 R. 135, 138.

(Legitim) *Fisher* v. *Dixon* (1843) 2 Bell 63; *McMurray* v. *McM's Trs.* (1852) 14 D. 1048; *Macdougal* v. *Wilson* (1858) 20 D. 658.

administration in the executor thereby confirmed.[1] But the persons entitled under S. 2 of the 1964 Act to succeed to the free estate are ascertained, and their rights to shares vest, on the intestate's death.[2]

Vesting of rights under testamentary dispositions

Under the Succession (Sc.) Act, 1964, S. 14, on a testator's death, every part of his estate, heritable and moveable, falling to be administered under the law of Scotland, by virtue of confirmation thereto, vests for the purposes of administration in the executor thereby confirmed, but the right of property in anything bequeathed by the testator's will may vest in the person entitled to it thereunder at the date of death or at another time.

No distinction in principle is drawn between gifts of heritable and gifts of moveable rights in respect of vesting.[3] Different parts of an estate may vest at different times.

Though the amount of residue is uncertain until the testator's death and possibly till later, vesting is not thereby prevented, and the time of vesting of residue is determined by the same considerations as in other bequests.[4]

General rule—intention

The date of vesting of any bequest is determined by the testator's intention as disclosed in his will, but, failing any clear expression of such intention, falls to be determined by presumptions.[5] Where the will purports to dispose of the testator's whole estate, the court is averse to an interpretation which results in total or partial intestacy, though it may feel driven to that conclusion.[6]

There may be an express declaration in the will as to the date at which a particular bequest is to vest. Such a declaration is decisive unless the rest of the will demands that another time be

[1] Succession (Sc.) Act, 1964, S. 14.

[2] *Mann* v. *Thomas* (1830) 8 S. 468; *Frith* v. *Buchanan* (1837) 15 S. 729; *Elder* v. *Watson* (1859) 21 D. 1122; *Lord* v. *Colvin* (1865) 3 M. 1083.

The rights excepted from the operation of the 1964 Act by S. 37(1)(a) and (b) thereof vest in the heir by mere survivance of his ancestor.

[3] *Hay's Trs.* v. *H.* (1890) 17 R. 961, 962.

[4] *Storie's Trs.* v. *Gray* (1874) 1 R. 953; *Yule's Trs.* v. *Dean*, 1919 S.C. 570.

[5] *Carleton* v. *Thompson* (1867) 5 M. (H.L.) 151; *Bowman* v. *B.* (1899) 1 F. (H.L.) 69.

[6] *Gillies' Trs.* v. *G.* (1900) 3 F. 238; *Lawrence* v. *Stewart*, 1924 S.C. 934; *Beveridge's Trs.* v. *B.*, 1930 S.C. 578; *Mowbray's Trs.* v. *M's Exor.*, 1931 S.C. 595.

selected, in which case the general scheme of the will may defeat the express declaration.[1]

Presumption for early vesting

There is a presumption in favour of early vesting, or vesting *a morte testatoris*,[2] which is the earliest possible date for vesting under a will, and an unconditional bequest *prima facie* vests then.[3] Among unconditional bequests are included bequests which are payable on a future day certain to arrive, such as a fixed date, or on the death of a liferenter or other party.[4] But bequests dependent on the happening of an event or the coming of a time which may never happen or come are deemed conditional: *dies incertus pro conditione habetur*.[5]

Vesting may take place even though payment is postponed[6] to a time certain to arrive, and a gift of fee normally vests *a morte* though payment be deferred till the expiry of a liferent.[7] The existence of a trust does not prevent vesting *a morte*,[8] unless the trust is a discretionary one, when there is no vesting until the discretion to order payment is exercised.[9] Similarly a gift vests *a morte* though burdened with payment of an annuity.[10]

Vesting at the time of payment

The last possible time for vesting is the time at which the testator has directed that possession be given or payment made to the legatee,[11] and if vesting does not take place *a morte testatoris* the time for payment is the most likely alternative.[12]

[1] See e.g. *Popham's Trs.* v. *Parker's Exors.* (1882) 10 R. 888; *Smith's Trs.* (1894) 31 S.L.R. 538; *Carruther's Trs.* v. *Eales* (1894) 21 R. 492; *Dewar's Trs.* v. *Glasgow Children's Hospitals*, 1962 S.C. 100.

[2] *Stoddart* v. *Grant* (1852) 1 Macq. 163; *Carleton*, *supra*; *Taylor's Trs.* v. *Gilbert's Trs.* (1878) 5 R. (H.L.) 217; *Webster's Trs.* v. *Neill* (1900) 2 F. 695; *Mowbray's Trs.* v. *M's Exor.*, 1931 S.C. 595; but see *Wylie's Trs.* v. *Bruce*, 1919 S.C. 211.

[3] *Hamilton* v. *Ritchie* (1894) 21 R. (H.L.) 35; *Hay Cunningham's Trs.* v. *Blackwell*, 1909 S.C. 219.

[4] *Fraser's Trs.* v. *Cunninghame*, 1928 S.L.T. 425; *Mowbray's Trs.* v. *M's Exor.*, 1931 S.C. 595.

[5] *Wylie's Trs.* v. *Bruce*, 1919 S.C. 211.

[6] *Jackson* v. *McMillan* (1876) 3 R. 627; *Cunningham* v. *C.* (1889) 17 R. 218; *Hay's Trs.* v. *H.* (1890) 17 R. 961; *Wylie's Trs.*, *supra*.

[7] *Carleton*, *supra*; *Robertson's Trs.* v. *Mitchell*, 1930 S.C. 970.

[8] *Carleton*, *supra*.

[9] *Paterson's Trs.* v. *P.* (1870) 8 M. 449.

[10] *Young* v. *Stewart* (1875) 13 S.L.R. 5; *Henderson's Trs.* v. *H.* (1876) 3 R. 320.

[11] *Popham's Trs.* v. *Parker's Exors.* (1883) 10 R. 588.

[12] *Marshall* v. *King* (1888) 16 R. 40.

Vesting of conditional bequests

If a bequest is conditional, the condition may be suspensive or resolutive. A suspensive condition renders the gift contingent and prevents vesting until the condition is satisfied;[1] among such are conditions that the legatee attain a certain age, survive a stated time or event, get married, or obtain some qualification.[2] But a mere proviso postponing payment till such a time or event does not postpone vesting, but only payment.[3] The existence of a destination-over in the event of the legatee's death before the condition is satisfied strongly indicates postponed vesting.[4]

Where the condition is one of survivorship, vesting cannot take place till it is determined who is the survivor.[5] Words of survivorship are presumed to refer to the period of payment.

Resolutive conditions attached to bequests

A resolutive condition attached to a bequest permits immediate vesting, subject to defeasance if the condition happens which terminates entitlement to the bequest.[6] Among categories of cases to which vesting subject to defeasance applies are

(a) cases of a gift, with a destination-over failing issue of the institute, in which case the substitute takes a vested right subject to defeasance if and when the institute has issue,[7] though not where the substitute's right is itself conditional.[8]

(b) Also in this class are cases of an initial gift, with a subsequent direction that it is to be held by trustees for the beneficiary in liferent and his issue in fee; in such a case it is presumed that the testator, having made an initial gift outright did not intend to revoke it by his later decision, and the beneficiary takes a vested interest in the fee subject to defeasance in favour of his issue to a liferent, only if and when he has any issue.[9] This principle does

1 *Wylie's Trs.* v. *Bruce*, 1918 S.C. 211.

2 *Ralston* v. *R.* (1842) 4 D. 1496; *Alves' Trs.* v. *Grant* (1874) 1 R. 969; *Mackinnon's Trs.* v. *Watt*, 1933 S.L.T. 192; *Freeborn's Trs.* v. *Bennett*, 1940 S.C. 517.

3 *Ralston*, *supra*; *Allardice's Trs.* v. *Ritchie* (1866) 1 S.L.R. 225.

4 *Johnston's Trs.* v. *J.* (1891) 18 R. 823; *Pattinson's Trs.* v. *Motion*, 1941 S.C. 290.

5 *Young* v. *Robertson* (1862) 4 Macq. 314.

6 *Taylor's Trs.* v. *Gilbert's Trs.* (1878) 5 R. (H.L.) 217; see also *Johnston's Trs.* v. *Dewar*, 1911 S.C. 722.

7 e.g. to A in liferent and his issue in fee, whom failing to B in fee: B takes a vested right in the fee until issue is born to A: *Taylor's Trs.*, *supra*; *Steel's Trs.* v. *S.* (1888) 16 R. 204.

8 e.g. . . . whom failing to B if he survives A, whom failing to C; *Lees's Trs.* v. *L.*, 1927 S.C. 886.

9 *Lindsay's Trs.* v. *L.* (1880) 8 R. 281; *Dalglish's Trs.* v. *Bannerman's Exors.* (1889) 16 R. 559; *Milne's Trs.* v. *M's Exor.*, 1937 S.C. 149.

not apply if it appears that the testator's intention was to confer only a liferent.[1]

(c) Also in this category are cases where trustees are directed to hold a fund for a legatee and, if he predeceases a certain event, for his issue, in which case the legatee takes a vested right subject to defeasance in the event of his both predeceasing and leaving issue.[2]

Vesting subject to defeasance is excluded where there is a double contingency, such as a gift in liferent to A, then a liferent to B.[3]

Gifts to heirs and other relatives

A bequest to the children or other relatives, not of the testator, but of another living person is susceptible of various meanings,[4] but it is generally taken to mean the relatives at the time when the gift is to be paid over,[5] who may be those in existence at the testator's death,[6] or those in existence at the date of distribution, such as the expiry of a liferent, in which case there is partial defeasance of vesting of the fee as each post-natus is born.[7] Relatives born after the date of distribution are excluded.[8]

Where the bequest is to children at a stated age or satisfying some condition, there is vesting in the child first to attain that age or satisfy that condition subject to partial defeasance as each other child qualifies.[9] But if the gift is directed to be payable when the children attain an age or marry the class is fixed when the first child qualifies for payment and post-nati are excluded.[10]

Where the bequest is to a class, some of whom are dead at the date of the will, it seems to depend entirely on the deed in question whether their representatives share or not.[11]

[1] *Muir's Trs.* v. *M's Trs.* (1895) 22 R. 553; *Nicol's Trs.* v. *Farquhar*, 1918 S.C. 358; *Smith's Trs.* v. *Clark*, 1920 S.C. 161.

[2] *Snell's Trs.* v. *Morrison* (1877) 4 R. 709; *Allan's Trs.* v. *A.*, 1918 S.C. 164; *Gibson's Trs.* v. *G.*, 1925 S.C. 477; *Moss's Trs.* v. *Moss's Trs.*, 1958 S.C. 501.

[3] *Nicolson's Trs.* v. *N.*, 1960 S.C. 186.

[4] *Biggar's Trs.* v. *B.* (1858) 21 D. 4.

[5] *Ross* v. *Dunlop* (1878) 5 R. 833.

[6] *Wood* v. *W.* (1861) 23 D. 338; *Stopford Blair's Exors.* v. *Heron Maxwell's Trs.* (1872) 10 M. 760; *Hayward's Exors.* v. *Young* (1895) 22 R. 757 (children born after will but before testator's death included).

[7] *Douglas* v. *D.* (1864) 2 M. 1008; *Carleton* v. *Thomson* (1867) 5 M. (H.L.) 151.

[8] *Wood, supra*; *Ross* v. *Dunlop* (1878) 5 R. 833; *Potter's Trs.* v. *Allan*, 1918 S.C. 173; *Murray's Tr.* v. *M.*, 1919 S.C. 552.

[9] *Burnett* v. *B.* (1854) 16 D. 780.

[10] *Buchanan's Trs.* v. *B.* (1877) 4 R. 754; *Scott's Trs.* v. *S.*, 1909 S.C. 773; *Howden's Trs.* v. *Macpherson*, 1911 2 S.L.T. 308.

[11] *Sturrock* v. *Binny* (1843) 6 D. 117; *Stewart's Trs.* v. *Walker* (1905) 12 S.L.T. 801; *Rhind's Trs.* v. *Leith* (1866) 5 M. 104; *Baird's Trs.* v. *Crombie*, 1926 S.C. 518.

Gifts-over in case of death without issue

Where there is a gift to one and his issue, and if he dies without issue to others, the gift-over is defeated whenever issue is born.[1] But such a gift may be interpreted as a gift to one and his issue even if the issue predecease the legatee, in which case the children take a vested right even if they predecease their parent.[2]

If the bequest is to one, and if he die without issue, to another, the vesting date is the date of death of the legatee, but in such a case predeceasing issue as well as surviving issue may be held to have acquired a vested right.[3]

Survivorship clauses and destinations-over

Where a gift is made to several persons or the survivors of them, in the absence of specialties vesting takes place at the time or occasion by which it is ascertained who are the survivors;[4] this is usually the date of payment.[5] Sometimes a provision as to survivorship has in particular contexts been held to connote survivorship *inter se* with consequent vesting in whoever is the longer or longest liver, as soon as he becomes the survivor, but all are exceptional cases.[6]

Where a gift is given to one, whom failing to another, vesting takes place at the time fixed for payment, which may be at the testator's death,[7] or postponed.[8] If the destination-over is a substitution, it does not normally prevent vesting, but if a conditional institution, it normally suspends vesting until the time or event, the survivance of which entitles the institute to take the gift.[9] There is a presumption for substitution in the case of heritage,[10] and for conditional institution in the case of moveables,[11] or mixed estate.[12] A gift to one with a destination-over to

[1] *Carleton* v. *Thomson* (1867) 5 M. (H.L.) 151; *Scott's Trs.* v. *Brown* (1882) 9 R. 798; *Cunningham* v. *C.* (1889) 17 R. 218.

[2] *Scott's Trs.* v. *Dunbar* (1900) 2 F. 516; *Currie's Trs.* v. *Collier*, 1939 S.C. 247.

[3] *Hickling's Trs.* v. *Garland's Trs.* (1898) 1 F. (H.L.) 7; but contrast *Graham's Trs.* v. *Lang's Trs.*, 1916 S.C. 763; *Craik's Trs.* v. *Anderson*, 1932 S.C. 61.

[4] *Walker* v. *Park* (1859) 21 D. 286.

[5] *Young* v. *Robertson* (1862) 4 Macq. 314; *Nolan* v. *Hartley's Trs.* (1866) 5 M. 153; *Muirhead* v. *M.* (1890) 17 R. (H.L.) 45; *Laing's Trs.* v. *Horsburgh*, 1965 S.C. 339.

[6] *Lindsay's Trs.* (1885) 12 R. 964; *Gardner* v. *Hamblin* (1900) 2 F. 679; *Ferguson's Trs.* v. *Readman's Exors.* (1903) 10 S.L.T. 697; *Macfarlane's Trs.* v. *M's C.B.*, 1934 S.C. 476.

[7] *Sanderson* v. *Wardrop* (1873) 1 R. 96; *Dalrymple's Trs.* v. *Watson's Trs.*, 1932 S.L.T. 480.

[8] *Bryson's Trs.* v. *Clark* (1880) 8 R. 142; *Baillie's Trs.* v. *Whiting*, 1910 S.C. 891.

[9] *Robertson* v. *Davidson* (1846) 9 D. 152.

[10] *Watson* v. *Giffen* (1884) 11 R. 444.

[11] *Crumpton's J.F.* v. *Barnardo's Homes*, 1917 S.C. 713.

[12] *Paul* v. *Home* (1872) 10 M. 937; *McLay* v. *Chalmers* (1903) 11 S.L.T. 223.

his heirs, children, successors, descendants or executors is a conditional institution of such persons, and they take if the legatee named predeceases;[1] such a gift suspends vesting.[2]

Clauses of devolution

Where there is a clause of devolution, as where there is a gift to one, but if he predeceases, to his issue, or failing issue, to the survivors of his class, the issue take their parents' share only,[3] unless the consequence would be intestacy.[4]

Vesting of class-gifts

Unless the will yields a contrary indication, the members of a class are settled at the time when payment is due, and only those then in life, including children *in utero*, may participate, and not any subsequently born.[5]

Where, however, payment is postponed as by the existence of a liferent, the class is not closed until the date of payment. The right vests in the fiars as a class, though the birth of further members of the class will alter the shares which each will receive when payment becomes possible.[6]

In the case where the bequest is to children, and is payable as and when they attain majority, it has been held that the class is limited to the children alive at the date when the eldest child attains majority and becomes entitled to payment, as otherwise there would be no way of determining what share is payable to each.[7]

Gifts subject to double contingencies

Where a gift is subject to a double contingency, such as a gift of fee on the expiry of the liferent and provided the beneficiary has attained majority, vesting is postponed until attainment of majority if this appears to be a condition of entitlement to the

[1] *Grant* v. *G's Trs.* (1862) 24 D. 1211; *Findlay* v. *Mackenzie* (1875) 2 R. 909; *Scott's Trs.* v. *Methven's Exors.* (1890) 18 R. 389; *Macleod* v. *Wilson* (1903) 6 F. 213.

[2] *Bowman* v. *B.* (1899) 1 F. (H.L.) 69; *Wylie's Trs.* v. *Bruce*, 1919 S.C. 211.

[3] *Young* v. *Robertson* (1862) 4 Macq. 337; *Henderson* v. *H.* (1890) 17 R. 293; *Miller's Trs.* v. *Brown*, 1933 S.C. 669.

[4] *Beveridge's Trs.* v. *B.*, 1930 S.C. 578.

[5] *Wood* v. *Wood* (1861) 23 D. 338; *Stopford Blair's Exors.* v. *Heron Maxwell's Trs.* (1872) 10 M. 760; *Hayward's Exors.* v. *Young* (1895) 22 R. 757.

[6] *Douglas* v. *D.* (1864) 2 M. 1008; *Carleton* v. *Thompson* (1867) 5 M. (H.L.) 151; *Christie* v. *Wiseley* (1874) 1 R. 436; *Ross* v. *Dunlop* (1878) 5 R. 833; *Hickling's Trs.* v. *Garland's Trs.* (1898) 1 F. (H.L.) 7; *Potter's Trs.* v. *Allan*, 1918 S.C. 173; *Murray's Trs.* v. *M.*, 1919 S.C. 552.

[7] *Scott's Trs.* v. *S.*, 1909 S.C. 773.

bequest, but not if it be merely for the protection of the beneficiary during his minority.[1]

Vesting subject to defeasance

Under this principle a right may vest in one person, subject to the right being defeated and shifting in the event of a particular resolutive condition being purified. The classes of cases where this principle has been applied have been mainly gifts to one in liferent and to his issue in fee, whom failing to another,[2] where the fee vests in the other until the birth of issue of the liferenter, in which case defeasance takes place and the fee vests in the issue; or gifts to one with a direction to trustees to hold for him in liferent and for his issue in fee,[3] where the fee vests in the institute subject to defeasance in favour of the issue if and when any are born; or gifts to one in fee with the condition that if he predeceases, leaving issue, his issue shall take, where the fee vests subject to defeasance in the event of predecease without issue.[4]

Gifts subject to powers of appointment

Where a gift is made subject to a power of appointment no right vests in any object of the power until or unless the power is exercised.

If there is a gift to a class subject to apportionment, and with a gift-over to the class in default of apportionment, there is vesting in the members of the class, subject to defeasance if the power is exercised.[5] If in such a case there is no gift-over, there is again vesting subject to defeasance, but if the power is not exercised the gift will lapse,[6] unless there is an evident intention to benefit the class, when equal division will be applied.[7] A general power of disposal, as the donee of the power thinks fit, does not suspend vesting, but it is subject to defeasance if and when the power is

[1] *Matthew* v. *Scott* (1844) 6 D. 718; *Boyd's Trs.* v. *B.* (1905) 7 F. 576; *Bogle's Trs.* v. *Cochrane* (1892) 20 R. 108; *Swan's Trs.* v. *S.*, 1912 S.C. 273.

[2] *Taylor* v. *Gilbert's Trs.* (1878) 5 R. (H.L.) 217; *Steel's Trs.* v. *S.* (1888) 16 R. 204; *Munro's Trs.* v. *Monson*, 1962 S.C. 414; contrast *Corbett's Trs.* v. *Pollock* (1901) 3 F. 963.

[3] *Lindsay's Trs.* v. *L.* (1880) 8 R. 281; *Dalglish's Trs.* v. *Bannerman's Exors.* (1889) 16 R. 559; *Tweeddale's Trs.* v. *T.* (1905) 8 F. 264.

[4] *Snell's Trs.* v. *Morrison* (1877) 4 R. 709; *Dalhousie's Trs.* v. *Young* (1889) 16 R. 681; *Wylie's Trs.* v. *W.* (1906) 8 F. 617; *Allan's Trs.* v. *A.*, 1918 S.C. 164.

[5] *Sivright* v. *Dallas* (1824) 2 S. 643; *Beattie's Trs.* v. *Cooper's Trs.* (1862) 24 D. 519; *Romanes* v. *Riddell* (1865) 3 M. 348.

[6] *Robbie's J.F.* v. *McCrae* (1893) 20 R. 358.

[7] *Weir* v. *Young* (1898) 5 S.L.T. 233.

exercised.[1] Nor does a power to encroach on the capital of a fund liferented.[2]

Acceleration of vesting or payment

If a legatee has a vested right, as of a fee, payment may be accelerated if the liferenter renounces the liferent,[3] but not if the vesting of the fee has been postponed, or is subject to possible defeasance,[4] or if there are trust purposes which require the continuance of the trust.[5]

[1] *Haldane's Trs.* v. *Murphy* (1881) 9 R. 269; *Howe's Trs.* v. *H's J.F.* (1903) 5 F. 1099.

[2] *Reddie's Trs.* v. *Lindsay* (1890) 17 R. 558; *Ross's Trs.* v. *R.* (1897) 25 R. 65.

[3] *Finlay's Trs.* v. *F.* (1886) 13 R. 1052; *McMurdo's Trs.* v. *McM.* (1897) 24 R. 458; contrast *Middleton's Trs.* v. *M.*, 1955 S.C. 51; *Chrystal's Trs.* v. *Haldane*, 1960 S.C. 127.

[4] *Muirhead* v. *M.* (1890) 17 R. (H.L.) 45; *Hughes* v. *Edwardes* (1892) 19 R. (H.L.) 33; *Chrystal's Trs., supra.*

[5] *Haldane's Trs.* v. *H.* (1895) 23 R. 276; *Macculloch* v. *McCulloch's Trs.* (1903) 6 F. (H.L.) 3.

CHAPTER 114

EXECUTORS AND THE ADMINISTRATION OF ESTATES

Who are executors[1]

THE term executors was formerly applied to the person or persons who were next-of-kin at common law and entitled thereby to succeed on intestacy to a deceased's moveable estate, as distinct from his heir-at-law entitled to succeed to his heritage.[2] The word has, however, in some contexts been held to mean universal legatory.[3] The term later came to be used for any person or persons, nominated by a testator or entitled by law, and confirmed in office by the court, to wind up a deceased's affairs and distribute his estate according to law or as directed by his will.[4] Such persons require judicial confirmation, formerly to complete their right to the estate, and latterly to entitle them to intromit with it, complete title to it, and transfer it to beneficiaries.[5]

The office of executor does not, however, prevent the holder, if entitled, from claiming prior rights and/or legal rights, or a share on intestacy, or a legacy.

Position of executor

The office is an administrative appointment, not a benefit;[6] the executor is the representative of the deceased, *eadem persona cum defuncto*, but with liability limited to the extent of the estate.[7] An executor is not a trustee for the deceased's creditors,[7] though he is for the beneficiaries,[8] but interim proprietor of the deceased's estate under burden of the debts due to the deceased's creditors, of the claims of those entitled on intestacy, and of the bequests of the deceased's will.

A person while acting as executor acts in a capacity independent of his personal capacity as an individual, though actings

1 Generally McLaren, *Wills*, II, 853 *et seq.*; Currie on *Confirmation of Executors*.

2 Ersk. III, 9, 1; *Nimmo* v. *Murray's Trs.* (1864) 2 M. 1144; *Stodart's Trs.* (1870) 8 M. 667; *Ewart* v. *Cotton* (1870) 9 M. 232.

3 *Jamieson* v. *Clark* (1872) 10 M. 399.

4 cf. *Manson* v. *Hutcheon* (1874) 1 R. 371.

5 Bell, *Prin.* §1889–92.

6 *Smart* v. *S.*, 1926 S.C. 392.

7 *Globe Ins. Co.* v. *Mackenzie* (1850) 7 Bell 296; *Stewart* v. *S's Exrx.* (1890) 23 R. 739; *Mitchell* v. *Mackersy* (1905) 8 F. 198.

8 *Smart, supra*; Trusts (Sc.) Act, 1921, S. 2; Succession (Sc.) Act, 1964, Ss. 14, 20.

in the one capacity may affect the person in his individual capacity.[1]

The office is gratuitous and an executor is entitled to no fee for his services,[2] save that an institution, such as a bank, which acts, may take reasonable fees for its services. An executor may be left, and may accept, a legacy for his services.

The office differs from that of trustee in that the executor's function is to ingather and distribute the deceased's estate, that of the trustee to ingather and then hold and administer it for the trust purposes.[3] But in a *mortis causa* trust disposition the truster usually appoints the same persons to be executors and trustees, and it may be doubtful at what point the one office ends and the other begins. Moreover, executors nominate have the powers, privileges and immunities of trustees,[4] but an executor dative, though having these powers, cannot resign, nor assume new trustees.[5]

Persons entitled to seek confirmation as executor

The recognized grounds entitling a person to be confirmed executor are nomination by the deceased, propinquity, or direct interest in the estate.[6]

Executors nominate: Where there is a will any person or persons nominated, expressly,[7] or impliedly,[8] or by reference,[9] thereby as executors[10] are entitled to the office, failing whom testamentary trustees, nominated by the deceased, or assumed, or appointed by the court, failing whom any general disponee,[11] or universal legatory or residuary legatee, is entitled.[12] Any of these persons is entitled to confirmation as executor nominate.[12] The will founded

1 *MacGregor's Exrx.* v. *MacGregor's Trs.*, 1935 S.C. 13.

2 *Malcolm's Exors.* v. *M.* (1869) 8 M. 272. The executor's right under the Act 1617, c. 14, to keep a third of dead's part for himself was abolished by the Intestate Moveable Succession Act, 1855, S. 8; see also *Lowndes* v. *Douglas* (1862) 24 D. 1391.

3 *Jamieson* v. *Clark* (1872) 10 M. 399.

4 Executors (Sc.) Act, 1900, S. 2; Trusts (Sc.) Act, 1921, S. 2.

5 Succession (Sc.) Act, 1964, S. 20.

6 *Whiffin* v. *Lees* (1872) 10 M. 797.

7 *Dundas* v. *D.* (1837) 15 S. 427; as to recall of nomination see *Scott* v. *Peebles* (1870) 8 M. 959.

8 *Mackenzies* v. *M.* (1886) 13 R. 507; *Tod* (1890) 18 R. 152; *Martin* v. *Ferguson's Trs.* (1892) 19 R. 474; *Jerdon* v. *Forrest* (1897) 24 R. 395.

9 *Martin* v. *Ferguson's Trs.* (1892) 19 R. 474.

10 The word 'executor' is not essential: *Tod* (1890) 18 R. 152.

11 *Jamieson* v. *Clark* (1872) 10 M. 399; *Christison* v. *C.* (1881) 18 S.L.R. 528; *Reid* v. *Dobie*, 1921 S.C. 662.

12 Executors (Sc.) Act, 1900, S. 3; see also *McGown* v. *McKinlay* (1835) 14 S. 105; *Easson* v. *Thomson's Trs.* (1879) 7 R. 251; *Dunsmure* v. *D.* (1879) 7 R. 261; *Keith* v. *Fraser* (1883) 20 S.L.R. 785; *Forsyth* v. *Turnbull* (1887) 15 R. 172; *Macintyre* v. *Miller*

on must be validly executed according to the system of law which regulates its formal validity. Nomination of persons as trustees does not necessarily imply their appointment as executors,[1] though appointment as executors may imply appointment as trustees.[2] A nomination may be revoked expressly or impliedly by a later testamentary writing.[3]

If a person or persons nominated as executor(s) be described by some characteristic other than by name there must be averment and proof that the petitioner satisfies the description.[4]

A person nominated may decline to act. The court may refuse to confirm an executor-nominate and appoint a judicial factor on the estate if there is risk of injury to the estate if it were entrusted to the petitioner,[5] or if litigation is in prospect.[6]

Executor-dative: Where there is no executor-nominate or the deceased died intestate, a person may be appointed executor-dative on petition to the sheriff of the sheriffdom in which the deceased was domiciled, or if he had no fixed domicile, or was domiciled furth of Scotland, the Sheriff of the Lothians. The following persons in order are entitled to claim the office:[7] (a) the surviving spouse, where that spouse's prior rights under Ss. 8 and 9 of the 1964 Act exhaust the whole estate;[8] (b) any universal legatee;[9] (c) next-of-kin at common law;[10] (d) persons having a

(1900) 7 S.L.T. 435; *Maclagan's Trs.* v. *L.A.* (1903) 11 S.L.T. 227; *Letham* v. *Evans*, 1918 1 S.L.T. 27; *Reid* v. *Dobie*, 1921 S.C. 662. If there is application for confirmation of a universal legatory or residuary legatee and the will is challenged, a judicial factor may be appointed: *Henderson* v. *H.*, 1930 S.L.T. 23; *Piries' Trs.* v. *P.*, 1962 S.C. 43. Failing any prior claimant the assignee of a legatee is entitled to be confirmed: *Macpherson* v. *M.* (1855) 17 D. 358.

1 *Martin* v. *Ferguson's Trs.* (1892) 19 R. 474.

2 *Ainslie* v. *A.* (1886) 14 R. 209.

3 *Scott* v. *Peebles* (1870) 8 M. 959; *Sibbald's Trs.* v. *Greig* (1871) 9 M. 399; *Tronsons* v. *T.* (1884) 12 R. 155; *Mellis* v. *M's Tr.* (1898) 25 R. 720; cf. *Tegner* v. *Henderson*, 1930 S.L.T. 23. As to nominations under different settlements see *Jones* v. *Pursey* (1886) 23 S.L.R. 628; *MacHardy* v. *Steele* (1902) 4 F. 765.

4 Currie on Confirmation, 76.

5 *Hamilton* v. *Hardie* (1889) 16 R. 192; *Campbell* v. *Barber* (1895) 23 R. 90; *Simpson's Exor.* v. *S's Trs.*, 1912 S.C. 418.

6 *Tegner* v. *Henderson*, 1930 S.L.T. 23.

7 Bell, *Prin.* §1894; *Stewart* v. *Kerr* (1890) 17 R. 707, 708.

8 1964 Act, S. 9(4), replacing similar provisions under Intestate Husband's Estate (Sc.) Acts, 1911–59. If the surviving spouse's prior rights do not exhaust the estate, S. 9(4) is inapplicable. The former rule, that a spouse entitled to *jus relicti vel relictae* had a right postponed to the next-of-kin: *Stewart* v. *Kerr* (1890) 17 R. 707; *Campbell* v. *Falconer* (1892) 19 R. 563; suggests that in such a case the surviving spouse's claim is under class (d); see also *Inglis* v. *I.* (1869) 7 M. 435.

9 *Stewart, supra.*

10 *Stewart, supra*; *Campbell* v. *Falconer* (1892) 19 R. 563; *Denman, supra*; if the next of kin has no beneficial interest his claim is postponed to that of anyone who has: *Bones* v. *Morrison* (1866) 5 M. 240.

right of succession to the free estate of the intestate under the 1964 Act, Ss. 1–6, according to the order set out in S. 2;[1] (e) issue of persons who would, if they had survived the intestate, have had rights to the whole or any part of the intestate estate under the 1964 Act, Ss. 1–6;[2] (f) creditors of the deceased;[3] (g) legatees;[4] (h) the procurator-fiscal of court or a judicial factor.[5] The petition must state in what capacity the petitioner claims decerniture as executor-dative.

An alien[6] or a person under detention in wartime[7] may be decerned executor-dative. Pupils or minors may be decerned executors with their tutor or curators or alone.[8] The curator bonis of a ward who is entitled may seek confirmation as representing the ward, but has no title in competition with other persons who have a title in themselves.[9] Where one person has been decerned executor-dative, another person may petition in the same court to be conjoined as executor.[10] The consul in this country of an alien dying here may be appointed.[11]

Petition for confirmation

A person entitled to the office of executor by nomination or by decerniture as executor-dative has no authority to intromit with the deceased's estate until he has obtained confirmation. This is obtained by petition to the sheriff of the county in which the deceased had his last domicile; if he had no fixed domicile, or it was furth of Scotland, the petition is to the Sheriff of the Lothians.[12] Confirmation constitutes judicial ratification of the nomination, or judicial appointment, and confers a title to possess, administer,

[1] Replacing Intestate Moveable Succcession (Sc.) Act, 1855, S. 4. Under this class father and mother may claim the office; see also *Dowie* v. *Barclay* (1871) 9 M. 726; *Muir* (1876) 4 R. 74; *Webster* v. *Shiress* (1878) 6 R. 102.

[2] 1964 Act, S. 5(2), replacing Intestate Moveable Succession (Sc.) Act, 1855, S. 1.

[3] *Stewart* v. *Kerr* (1890) 17 R. 707.

[4] *Stewart, supra*; including the assignee of a beneficiary: *McPherson* v. *McP.* (1855) 17 D. 358.

[5] *Stewart, supra*; *Johnston* v. *Lowden* (1838) 16 S. 541; *Martin* v. *Ferguson's Trs.* (1892) 19 R. 474. A judicial factor may be apppointed under the Bankruptcy (Sc.) Act, 1913, S. 163.

[6] *Schulze*, 1917 S.C. 400.

[7] *Crolla*, 1942 S.C. 21.

[8] *Reid* v. *Turner* (1830) 8 S. 960; *Keith* v. *Archer* (1836) 15 S. 116; *Johnstone* v. *Lowden* (1838) 16 S. 541.

[9] *Martin* v. *Ferguson's Trs.* (1892) 19 R. 474; see also *Johnston's Exor.* v. *Dobie*, 1907 S.C. 31.

[10] *Webster* v. *Shiress* (1878) 6 R. 102.

[11] *Schulze*, 1917 S.C. 400.

[12] Procedure is prescribed by Confirmation of Executors (Sc.) Act, 1858, Ss. 1–7; A.S. (Confirmation of Executors) 1964. See also *Hamilton* v. *Hardie* (1888) 16 R. 192.

and dispose of the deceased's estate.[1] Where confirmation is granted to more than one executor-dative, the powers accrue to the survivor or survivors, and while more than two survive a majority is a quorum, and each is liable only for his own acts and omissions.[2]

The only function of commissary proceedings is to determine who is entitled to be executor, and vest him with a title to act as such. That is not the forum to determine questions of the validity of a will for other purposes, or of its interpretation, or of succession generally.[3]

The court may dismiss a petition for confirmation and appoint a judicial factor if there is *prima facie* risk of injury to the estate if left in the petitioner's hands.[4]

Inventory

Before any person can be confirmed executor he must exhibit a full and true inventory of all the estate and effects of the deceased,[5] distinguishing items situated in Scotland, in England and Wales, and elsewhere,[6] and it must be stamped indicating that estate duty due thereon has been paid. The petitioner must also make an oath or affirmation that he has made a true disclosure of the deceased's estate.[7]

As confirmation now[8] confers an administrative title to heritage as well as moveables the inventory of estate must include a description, acceptable for a conveyance of lands or an estate in land, of any heritable property or interest therein forming part of the estate of the deceased.

The confirmation granted has appended thereto an inventory of the estate in respect of which confirmation has been granted.[9]

Confirmation of an executor-nominate is a testament-testamentar; that of an executor-dative is a testament-dative.

The will or other testamentary writing, if any, must be produced.[10] No difficulty arises if the will is probative. The practice

[1] For form of confirmation see A.S. (Confirmation of Executors) 1967.

[2] Executors (Sc.) Act, 1900, S. 4.

[3] *Jones* v. *Pursey* (1886) 23 S.L.R. 628; *Hamilton* v. *Hardie* (1888) 16 R. 192; *Martin* v. *Ferguson's Trs.* (1892) 19 R. 474; *MacHardy* v. *Steele* (1902) 4 F. 765.

[4] *Campbell* v. *Barber* (1895) 22 R. 90; *Simpson's Exor.* v. *S's Trs.*, 1912 S.C. 418.

[5] Prior to the Succession (Sc.) Act, 1964, only moveable property was included in a confirmation, but since and by virtue of that Act (S. 14) both heritable and moveable property falling to be administered by the law of Scotland must be included.

[6] Probate and Legacy Duties Act, 1808, S. 38; Finance Act, 1894, S. 6.

[7] Executors (Sc.) Act, 1900, S. 8.

[8] Succession (Sc.) Act, 1964, Ss. 14–15.

[9] Executors (Sc.) Act, 1900, S. 5.

[10] Probate and Legacy Duties Act, 1808, S. 38.

long was to grant confirmation on a holograph will even though it was not attested by witnesses. If the will did not contain a declaration *in gremio* that it was in the testator's handwriting proof was required, the affidavit of two persons who knew the deceased's writing that it was holograph of him being normally accepted. If the will did contain such a declaration it was accepted as *ex facie* valid and entitled to confirmation without such evidence, unless challenged.[1] The Wills Act, 1963, S. 5,[2] provided that any testamentary instrument should be treated as probative for the purpose of the conveyance of heritage if certain conditions were satisfied.

By the Succession (Sc.) Act, 1964, S. 21, confirmation of an executor to property disposed of in a holograph will shall not be granted unless the court is satisfied by evidence consisting at least of an affidavit by each of two persons that the writing and signature of the disposition are in the handwriting of the testator. By S. 32, replacing S. 5 of the Wills Act, 1963,[3] for the purpose of any question arising as to entitlement to any property by virtue of a testamentary disposition, it shall (if not otherwise probative) be treated as probative if (a) confirmation of an executor to property disposed of in the disposition has been granted in Scotland, or (b) probate, letters of administration or other grant of representation issued outwith Scotland in respect of property disposed of in the disposition has been certified in Scotland under the Confirmation of Executors (Sc.) Act, 1858, S. 14, or sealed in Scotland under the Colonial Probates Act, 1892, S. 2.

Caution

As a condition of confirmation an executor-dative must find caution, usually from an insurance company, to make the estate forthcoming to parties entitled thereto.[4]

Confirmation ad omissa

Except as executor-creditor, no executor may confirm to other than the whole estate of the deceased. If the whole estate

[1] *Cranston* (1890) 17 R. 410. For any purpose other than confirmation the validity of a holograph will whether containing such a declaration or not, required to be established judicially: *Frederick* v. *Craig*, 1932 S.L.T. 315; *Harper* v. *Green*, 1938 S.C. 198.

[2] Effective 1 January 1964.

[3] With effect from 10th September, 1964.

[4] Confirmation of Executors (Sc.) Act, 1823, S. 2. A personal cautioner is competent but the practice for long was, at least normally, not to accept a woman as cautioner: *French* (1871) 9 M. 741. There seems no justification for this today.

be not included in the inventory or it be undervalued, the executor must lodge a corrective inventory and obtain an eik to the confirmation.[1] More than one eik may be obtained. Or an interested party may apply to have the executor compelled to confirm the omission, or himself to be confirmed executor *ad omissa vel male appretiata*.[2]

Resignation

An executor-nominate may resign office. If a trustee resigns that implies resignation also from the office of executor.[3]

An executor-dative has no power to resign, nor to assume a new trustee.[4]

Removal

An executor or co-executor may be removed by the court, e.g. if causing obstruction bringing about an administrative deadlock,[5] but it is not a sufficient ground that he has a personal interest conflicting with his duty as executor.[6] If all are removed a judicial factor will be appointed to wind up the estate.[7]

Death of executor

The office of executor is personal to the person confirmed and does not pass on the holder's death to his heirs, or executors,[8] nor can it be assigned or carried by will, nor are the representatives or universal legatees of a deceased executor liable to account for the executor's intromissions with the deceased's estate.[9]

Where several persons are nominated, or are equally entitled by statute, and are confirmed as joint-executors, they act jointly; if one dies, the office accresces to the survivor.[10]

When any sole or last surviving trustee or executor-nominate has died with any property (whether heritable or moveable) in Scotland vested in him as trustee or executor, confirmation by his executors-nominate, if any, to the proper estate of such person,

[1] Executors (Sc.) Act, 1823, S. 3.
[2] Ersk. III, 9, 36; Bell, *Prin.* §1897; cf. *Smith* v. *S.* (1880) 7 R. 1013.
[3] Trusts (Sc.) Act, 1921, S. 28.
[4] Succession (Sc.) Act, 1964, S. 20.
[5] *Wilson* v. *Gibson*, 1948 S.C. 52.
[6] *Birnie* v. *Christie* (1891) 19 R. 334, 338; see also *Fleming* v. *Anderson*, 1948 S.L.T. (Notes) 43.
[7] *Birnie*, *supra*.
[8] Executors (Sc.) Act, 1900, S. 7; *Hutcheson & Co.'s Adminr.* v. *Taylor's Exor.*, 1931 S.C. 484.
[9] *Hutcheson & Co.'s Adminr.*, *supra*.
[10] Executors (Sc.) Act, 1900, S. 4 (executors-dative only) resolving doubt in *Anderson* v. *Kerr* (1866) 5 M. 32.

or the probate granted in England or Ireland to his executors, and produced and certified by the commissary clerk of Edinburgh, is valid and available to such executors for recovering such property, and for assigning and transferring them to the person who may be authorized to continue the administration of the estate, or directly to the beneficiaries thereto or to anyone whom the beneficiaries may appoint to receive and discharge, realize, and distribute it. A statement of such funds must be appended to any inventory of the estate of the deceased trustee or executor, given up by his executors, and duly confirmed, but executors of a deceased trustee or executor are not bound to make up title to such property, and other persons may complete a title to such funds by any means otherwise competent.[1]

Confirmation ad non executa

Where any confirmation has become inoperative by the death or incapacity of all the executors confirmed, no title to intromit with the estate, save as authorized by S. 6, transmits to the representatives of the executors, but confirmation *ad non executa* may be granted to any estate in the original confirmation remaining unuplifted or untransferred to the persons entitled thereto, to the persons previously entitled to confirmation *ad omissa*, which is a sufficient title to continue and complete the administration of the estate contained therein, and this confirmation may be specified as a midcouple or link for the purposes of any deduction of title in relation to such estate from the former executors.[2] Executors *ad non executa* do not assume responsibility for their predecessor but may be bound to require his representatives to account for his intromissions with the estate.[3]

Executor-creditors

If no person with a prior entitlement to the office petitions for decerniture and confirmation, any creditor whose debt is liquid or has been constituted by decree during the debtor's lifetime[4] may do so, and be confirmed as executor-creditor;[5] if one applies, other creditors may apply to be conjoined with him in the office. Notice of the application for confirmation must be given in the *Edinburgh Gazette* and anyone with a preferable claim may

[1] Executors (Sc.) Act, 1900, S. 6, amd. Succession (Sc.) Act, 1964, S. 34.
[2] Executors (Sc.) Act, 1900, S. 7, amd. Succession (Sc.) Act, 1964, S. 34.
[3] *Nicol Wilson* (1856) 18 D. 1000.
[4] *McWhirter* v. *McCulloch's Trs.* (1887) 14 R. 918; *McNab* v. *Clarke* (1889) 16 R. 610; cf. *Stiven* v. *Myer* (1868) 6 M. 370 (English judgment-debt).
[5] Ersk. III, 9, 34–35; Bell, *Prin.* §1895; Graham Stewart, *Diligence*, 441.

exclude the creditor from the office. Such confirmation is in effect a form of diligence, and the creditor need confirm only to the amount of his debt.[1] If the debt was not constituted in the debtor's lifetime, the creditor may charge the deceased's next of kin to confirm as executor within twenty days after the charge, thereby imposing liability, as vitious intromitters, for the debt. They may renounce the succession, in which case the charging creditor may constitute his debt and obtain decree *cognitionis causa* against the *haereditas jacens* of the estate and then obtain confirmation as executor-creditor.[2] The charge may be dispensed with if the creditor claims only a decree *cognitionis causa tantum*.[3]

The creditor's right to confirmation is excluded by confirmation by anyone having a prior claim, or by sequestration of the deceased[4] but not by mere decerniture as executor-dative,[5] by possession by the deceased's trustees, executors-nominate or dative, or a beneficial successor,[6] or by another creditor obtaining a decree in a multiplepoinding.[7]

Confirmation as executor creditor creates a burden on the subject confirmed, leaving it in the *haereditas jacens* of the deceased, but subject to the burden.[8] As a diligence it is preferable to an arrestment, even though prior in date, as being only an inchoate diligence,[9] and to a decree of preference in a multiplepoinding.[10] It does not affect a special legacy.[11] All creditors doing legal diligence within six months of the debtor's death are entitled to rank *pari passu* on the estate.[12]

Property furth of Scotland

If the confirmation of an executor granted in Scotland, and showing that the deceased died domiciled in Scotland, but including estate in England and Wales, is produced and a copy deposited in the Principal Probate Registry of the High Court in

1 Confirmation of Executors (Sc.) Act, 1823, S. 4; *Smith's Trs.* v. *Grant* (1862) 24 D. 1142, 1169. This is the only case in which partial confirmation is competent.

2 Confirmation Act, 1695, amd. Succession (Sc.) Act, 1964; *Davidson* v. *Clark* (1867) 6 M. 151.

3 *Forrest* v. *F.* (1868) 1 M. 806.

4 Bankruptcy (Sc.) Act, 1913, Ss. 29, 106.

5 Bell, *Comm.* II, 81.

6 *Smith's Trs., supra.*

7 *Anderson* v. *Stewart* (1831) 10 S. 49.

8 *Smith's Trs.* v. *Grant* (1862) 24 D. 1142, 1169.

9 *Wilson* v. *Fleming* (1823) 2 S. 430.

10 *Anderson* v. *Stewart* (1831) 10 S. 49.

11 *Bell* v. *Willison* (1831) 9 S. 266; *Innerarity* v. *Gilmore* (1840) 2 D. 813.

12 A.S. 28 Feb. 1662.

England, and is sealed with the seal of the Principal Probate Registry, it has the like effect in England as a grant of probate by the High Court.[1] Confirmation may similarly be resealed in Northern Ireland.

Conversely, where probate or letters of administration have been granted in England and show that the deceased died domiciled in England, their effect may be extended to Scotland by a certificate thereon, and have the same force as confirmation.[2] Such a certificate may be reduced if later found to have been issued under a misapprehension.[3]

By the Colonial Probates Act, 1892, provision was made for reciprocity between the United Kingdom countries and countries in the Commonwealth to which the Act has been applied by Order in Council.

Certificates

Provision is made for the issue to any interested person of a certificate certifying that the confirmation covered, *inter alia*, the item of estate in Scotland thereafter specified.[4]

Confirmation in Small Estates

By the Intestates' Widows and Children (Sc.) Act, 1875, and the Small Testate Estates (Sc.) Act, 1876, both amended by the Small Estates (Representation) Act, 1961, where the estate has a net value of less than £1000 and a gross value of less than £3000, application may be made to the sheriff clerk who completes an inventory, has it deponed to and recorded, and issues confirmation to the applicant. By the Executors (Sc.) Act, 1900, S. 9, applications for confirmation under the Small Estates Acts may also be made to officers of Customs and Excise at certain places.

Effect of confirmation

Confirmation vests in the executor the rights of property in the deceased's heritable and moveable estate contained in the inventory thereof for the purposes of administration, and empowers him to uplift, receive, administer, and dispose of the estate, to grant discharges, to pursue actions, and to do whatever else is necessary subject to accounting for his intromissions when this is required.

1 Supreme Court of Judicature (Consolidation) Act, 1925, S. 168.
2 Confirmation of Executors (Sc.) Act, 1858, S. 14.
3 *Baines' Exor.* v. *Clark*, 1957 S.C. 342.
4 A.S. 3 Feb. 1933 and 11 Dec. 1936; *Watt*, 1942 S.C. 214.

In general executors have no title to deal with the estate in any way until confirmed, but in emergency may exceptionally deal with property, their title to do so being validated retrospectively when confirmation is granted.[1] Executors-nominate who had not yet confirmed may be sued.[2]

Vesting of estate in executor

At common law no estate, heritable or moveable, vested in an heir on intestacy or legatee under a will merely by his survivance of the deceased. This has been gradually modified by legislation.

Prior to 1964

Prior to the Succession (Scotland) Act, 1964, the position was:

Heritage

A personal right to every estate in land descendible to heirs vested in the heir entitled to succeed thereto by his survivance of the person to whom he was entitled to succeed.[3] The heir was thereby entitled to dispose of the estate *inter vivos* or *mortis causa*, and on his death it would pass to his heir-at-law. He was not liable for his ancestor's debts beyond the value of the ancestor's estate to which he succeeded.[4]

To complete title to the lands he had to obtain a writ of *clare constat* from the superior and record it in the General Register of Sasines, or obtain, on petition to the sheriff, decree of special service as heir, an extract of which was recorded, or a decree of general service as heir, followed by a notarial instrument or notice of title to the particular property, also recorded in the General Register of Sasines.[5]

Where heritage was bequeathed by will, the will conferred a personal right to the heritage on the legatee named, and he completed title by expeding a notarial instrument or notice of title on the will, and recording it in the Register of Sasines.[6]

[1] *Mackay* v. *M.*, 1914 S.C. 200.

[2] *Emslie* v. *Tognarelli's Exors.*, 1967 S.L.T. (Notes) 66.

[3] Conveyancing (Sc.) Act, 1874, S. 9; *McAdam* v. *McA.* (1879) 6 R. 1256. Prior to 1874 the heir acquired no transmissible right by mere survivance, but only when he established his right by writ of *clare constat* from the superior or by decree of service. Till then if he did not take up the succession the lands were *in haereditate jacente*.

[4] 1874 Act, S. 12.

[5] For procedure in petitions for service see Titles to Land Consolidation (Sc.) Act, 1868, Ss. 27–50; Conveyancing (Sc.) Act, 1874, S. 10.

[6] Titles to Land Consolidation (Sc.) Act, 1868, S. 19 and Sched. L; Conveyancing (Sc.) Act, 1924, S. 4 and Sched. B(1).

Where the intestate was not infeft the legatee recorded a notarial instrument or notice of title,[1] or a notarial instrument or notice of title along with the disposition in favour of the deceased.[2]

Moveables

At common law no right vested in next-of-kin by mere survivance. By the Confirmation of Executors (Sc.) Act, 1823, S. 1, a personal right to moveables vested on the death of the intestate, but confirmation as executor remained necessary to give the executor a title to recover and administer the estate.[3] A legatee of moveables obtained by survivance of the testator only a personal claim against the executor for payment or transfer to him of his legacy.

Since 1964—heritage and moveables

Under the Succession (Scotland) Act, 1964, S. 14, the rules previously applicable to the administration and winding-up of an estate of moveable estate have effect, as modified by that Act,[4] in relation to the whole estate, heritable and moveable, and on a person's death, testate or intestate, every part of his estate falling to be administered under the law of Scotland,[5] by virtue of confirmation thereto, vests for the purpose of administration in the executor thereby confirmed, and has to be administered and disposed of by him according to law. Accordingly, thereunder, an administrative title to heritage and powers in connection with leases vests in the executor on confirmation, as well as title to moveable property, and an executor may complete title to heritage in his own name as executor, if for administrative reasons it is desired to do so, by expeding and recording a notice of title, using the confirmation or the will as a link in the title.[6] But debts continue[7] to attach to heritage or moveables as formerly.

Estate which was vested in deceased solely in trust

If a sole trustee or executor has died, his executor-nominate or dative may include in the inventory of his estate any property

[1] Ibid., Sched. J and Sched. B(1).

[2] Ibid., Sched. N and Sched. 13(2).

[3] *Frith* v. *Buchanan* (1837) 15 S. 729; *Elder* v. *Watson* (1859) 21 D. 1122.

[4] See 1964 Act, Sched. 2.

[5] Heritable or real property furth of Scotland will fall to be administered according to the *lex situs*. The moveable or personal estate of one dying in Scotland domiciled elsewhere will be regulated by his *lex domicilii*.

[6] Titles to Land Consolidation (Sc.) Act, 1868, S. 20, amd. 1964 Act, Sched. 2.

[7] 1964 Act, S. 14(3).

fiduciarily vested in him and confirmation vests such property in the executor for administrative purposes.[1] The executor may then transfer the trust property to new trustees, whether appointed by the court or by the truster, using the confirmation as a link in title. Alternatively, an executor *ad non executa* may in the case of testamentary trusts be appointed to the original testator, and that confirmation used as a link in title.[1]

Powers and duties

Unless the contrary is expressly provided in the trust deed all executors nominate have the powers, privileges, and immunities and are subject to the limitations and restrictions applicable to gratuitous trustees at common law and under statute.[2] An executor dative has now the same powers and disabilities, save that he must find caution for his intromissions and has no power to resign or to assume new trustees.[3]

The executor is not a trustee for the deceased's creditors, but stands in the deceased's place in relation to them, being debtor to them but with his liability limited to the extent of the deceased's estate.[4] Hence creditors may acquire preference by diligence even after the deceased's death,[5] and may set off debts due by the deceased against debts to the executor.[6] The executor is not bound to account to creditors for profits made by use of the assets of the estate.[7]

He owes to beneficiaries under the deceased's will the duty to carry out the testator's directions completely.[8]

A majority of co-executors have a right to manage and realize the estate as they think best and the court will protect them unless it is shown that their action will dilapidate the estate or prejudice the interests of beneficiaries.[9] If a majority act adversely to those interests they may be removed by the court.[10]

1 Executors (Sc.) Act, 1900, S. 6–7, extended by Succession (Sc.) Act, 1964, Sched. 2.

2 Executors (Sc.) Act, 1900, S. 2; Trusts (Sc.) Act, 1921, S. 2; cf. *Pettigrew's Exors.* (1890) 28 S.L.R. 14; *Jack's Exor.* v. *Downie*, 1908 S.C. 718.

3 Successsion (Sc.) Act, 1964, S. 20.

4 *Stewart's Tr.* v. *Stewart's Exrx.* (1896) 23 R. 739; *Mitchell* v. *Mackersy* (1905) 8 F. 198; *Taylor* v. *Ferguson* v. *Glass's Trs.*, 1912 S.C. 165.

5 *Globe Ins. Co.* v. *Mackenzie* (1849) 11 D. 618; 7 Bell, 296.

6 *Mitchell, supra.*

7 *Stewart's Tr., supra.*

8 *Robertson* v. *R's Exors.*, 1925 S.C. 606; *Beveridge* v. *B's Exrx.*, 1938 S.C. 160.

9 *Mackenzies* v. *M.* (1886) 13 R. 507.

10 *Birnie* v. *Christie* (1891) 19 R. 334.

Ingathering assets

An unconfirmed executor may sue for a debt due to the deceased[1] but a debtor is not bound to pay until the executor has confirmed,[2] and only a confirmed executor can obtain an extract of decree for, or enforce payment of, a debt, or grant an effectual discharge therefor.[3] Only very exceptionally has heir or residuary legatee a title to sue persons indebted to the deceased.[4]

An executor who has not included the claim in the inventory of the deceased's estate has no title to sue for money due to the deceased.[5]

An executor is allowed twelve months to ingather and realize the estate and though bound to exercise due diligence in ingathering will not be liable in interest on debts of the estate beyond what he actually recovers until that period has expired. If by failure in diligence debts remain unrealized after that time he may be held liable therefor.[6] He is also entitled to a reasonable time to realize investments.[7]

An executor may require a surviving spouse or housekeeper to account for intromissions with the deceased's funds during his last illness and down to the date of confirmation, but allowances must be made for aliment and housekeeping expenses.[8] An executor may also disburse money for the maintenance and education of children, even though the surviving spouse was able to do so out of his own funds, if that course was reasonable in the circumstances.[9]

Whether assets part of the deceased's estate

Questions of fact may arise whether particular assets or claims belong to the estate of the deceased or to his relatives personally[10] or to his firm[11] or otherwise. Questions may also arise as to whether a business has a realisable goodwill or not.[12]

[1] *Bain* v. *Munro* (1878) 5 R. 416; *Adamson's Trs.* v. *A's Exors.* (1891) 18 R. 1133.

[2] *Chalmers' Trs.* v. *Watson* (1860) 22 D. 1060; *Bones* v. *Morrison* (1866) 5 M. 240; *Mackay* v. *Mackay*, 1914 S.C. 200.

[3] *Fraser* v. *Gibb* (1784) Mor. 3921; *Buchanan* v. *Royal Bank* (1842) 5 D. 211.

[4] *Mackay, supra.*

[5] *Hinton* v. *Connell's Trs.* (1883) 10 R. 1110; *Teulon* v. *Seaton* (1885) 12 R. 971, 1179; *Rae* v. *Meek* (1889) 16 R. (H.L.) 31, 33; *Morrison* v. *M's Exor.*, 1912 S.C. 892.

[6] *Landale's Trs.* v. *Nicol*, 1918 2 S.L.T. 10.

[7] cf. *Forman* v. *Burns* (1853) 15 D. 362.

[8] *Buchan* v. *City of Glasgow Bank* (1879) 6 R. (H.L.) 44.

[9] *McPherson* v. *Walker* (1869) 8 M. 246.

[10] *Polland* v. *Sturrock's Exors.*, 1952 S.C. 535.

[11] *Forrester* v. *Robson's Trs.* (1875) 2 R. 755.

[12] *Bell's Tr.* v. *B.* (1884) 12 R. 85; *Reid* v. *Reid*, 1938 S.L.T. 415; cf. *Bain, supra.*

Property belonging to a deceased which is subject to a special destination is not part of the estate of the deceased for the purposes of the Succession (Sc.) Act, 1964, unless the destination could be, and has been, evacuated by the deceased.[1]

Continuing business

An executor may continue a deceased's business pending its sale or transfer to a beneficiary.[2]

If subsequently the deceased's estate is sequestrated the executor is liable only to account to the trustee in bankruptcy for the value of the business take over, including goodwill, but not for any profits made by continuing it.[3]

Title to sue and liability to be called to defend

In general an executor may initiate or continue an action, or defend an action, if the estate has any financial interest in the merits.[4] A residuary legatee or other beneficiary has no title to sue a debtor of the testator.[5] All co-executors should normally sue, but a single executor has been held to have a title to sue for recovery of a debt to the estate without the concurrence of the others.[6] The confirmation of executors in one sheriffdom does not subject executors to the jurisdiction of that sheriff court unless they are subject to it on another ground.[7] An executor who defends does not thereby render his personal estate liable to arrestment on the dependence[8] or to diligence.[9]

Executors have a title to support on appeal a judgment in the deceased's favour in a divorce action[10] or to pursue an alternative conclusion for damages.[11]

In the case of contracts not involving *delectus personae* the executor may tender performance and complete the deceased's contracts, recovering payment therefor, or may require perform-

1 1964 Act, S. 36(2) proviso (a).

2 *Matheson's C.B.* v. *Mathesons* (1889) 16 R. 701.

3 *Philp's Exor.* v. *P's Exor.* (1894) 21 R. 482; *Stewart's Tr.* v. *S's Exrx.* (1896) 23 R. 739; *Brown* v. *Robertson* (1896) 4 S.L.T. 17; *Morrison's Tr.* v. *M.*, 1915 2 S.L.T. 296; but see *Macdonald, Fraser & Co.* v. *Cairn's Exrx.*, 1932 S.C. 699.

4 *Carron Co.* v. *Hunter* (1868) 6 M. (H.L.) 106; *Brand* v. *Shaw* (1888) 15 R. 449; *Martin's Exrx.* v. *McGhee*, 1914 S.C. 628.

5 *Hinton* v. *Connell's Trs.* (1883) 10 R. 1110; cf. *Addison* v. *Whyte* (1870) 8 M. 909.

6 *Ballantyne* v. *B.* (1899) 7 S.L.T. 3.

7 *Robson* v. *Walsham* (1867) 6 M. 4; *Halliday's Exor.* v. *H's Exors.* (1886) 14 R. 251.

8 *Macfarlane* v. *Sanderson & Muirhead* (1868) 40 S. Jur. 189; *Wilson* v. *Mackie* (1875) 3 R. 18.

9 *McMahon* v. *Matheson* (1899) 1 F. 896.

10 *Ritchie* v. *R.* (1874) 1 R. 826.

11 *Green* v. *Borthwick* (1896) 24 R. 211.

ance by the other party, making payment therefor.[1] If the contract involves *delectus personae* it falls on the death of one party, whether creditor or debtor in the obligation.[1]

In the case of delicts the executor does not have a title to claim solatium for personal injuries sustained by the deceased,[2] though the executor is entitled to carry on for the benefit of the estate an action for such injuries already commenced before his death by the deceased.[3] Such an action is inconsistent with,[4] but may be abandoned to permit, an action by the deceased's surviving relatives to be brought.[5] But the executor always has a title to sue for patrimonial loss to the deceased's estate caused by delict,[6] and for wrongs to him generally,[7] and may seek to recover earnings lost by the deceased prior to his death, notwithstanding a concurrent action by his surviving relatives for loss of support caused them after and by reason of the death.[8] An executor is always liable to be sued for a wrong committed by the deceased.[9]

If a majority of executors consent to the settlement of an action, any non-consenting executor has no title to continue the action if there is no allegation of unfairness on the part of the majority.[10]

If beneficiaries are dissatisfied with an executor's decision not to prosecute a claim, they may ask the executor for the use of his name to do so themselves, giving him an indemnity against expenses.[11] Where an executor, who was also a beneficiary, alleged that the deceased owed him money under a bond, the other beneficiary was held to have title to sue a reduction of the bond.[12]

Beneficiaries have no title to sue a debtor of the executry estate.[13]

[1] *Hoey* v. *McEwan & Auld* (1867) 5 M. 814.

[2] *Bern's Exor.* v. *Montrose Asylum* (1893) 20 R. 859; *Boyce's Exor.* v. *McDougall* (1903) 5 F. 452; *Stewart* v. *L.M.S. Ry.*, 1943 S.C. (H.L.) 19; *Smith* v. *Stewart*, 1960 S.C. 329; overruling *Leigh's Exrx.* v. *Caledonian Ry.*, 1913 S.C. 838.

[3] *Neilson* v. *Rodger* (1854) 16 D. 325; *Darling* v. *Gray* (1891) 19 R. (H.L.) 31; *Riley* v. *Ellis*, 1910 S.C. 934; *Reid* v. *Lanarkshire Traction Co.*, 1934 S.C. 79; *Smith* v. *Stewart*, 1960 S.C. 329.

[4] *Darling*, *supra*.

[5] *Bruce* v. *Stephen*, 1957 S.L.T. 78.

[6] *Auld* v. *Shairp* (1875) 2 R. 191; *Smith* v. *Stewart*, 1961 S.C. 91.

[7] *Green* v. *Borthwick* (1896) 24 R. 211.

[8] *McGhie* v. *B.T.C.*, 1964 S.L.T. 25; but see *Darling* v. *Gray* (1891) 19 R. (H.L.) 31.

[9] e.g. *Dalziel* v. *Coulthurst's Exors.*, 1934 S.C. 564; *Bourhill* v. *Young*, 1942 S.C. (H.L.) 78.

[10] *Scott* v. *Craig's Reps.* (1897) 24 R. 462.

[11] *Blair* v. *Stirling* (1894) 1 S.L.T. 599; *Morrison* v. *M's Exrs.*, 1912 S.C. 892.

[12] *Strachan* v. *S.* (1894) 1 S.L.T. 498.

[13] *Hinton* v. *Connell's Trs.* (1883) 10 R. 1110.

As there is no passive representation in crime or criminal proceedings an executor cannot be sisted to prosecute an appeal to the High Court in a criminal cause.[1]

Estate duty

The executor is accountable for all estate duty which may be payable on the death of the deceased in respect both of heritable and moveable property which vests in him.[2]

Prima facie the proportion of estate duty applicable to each item of estate, heritable or moveable, is a burden on that item and payable by the recipient thereof under the will or intestacy. But not infrequently some or all bequests are made payable free of duty, in which case the duty applicable thereto is payable by the residue or the portion of the estate falling into intestacy, as the case may be.

The deceased's debts

The executor is bound to pay the deceased's debts; it is customary to advertise in the press for claims against the estate. He is not liable personally and, as executor, only to the extent of the executry estate.[3] He may require formal constitution of the debt when the estate is small, the amount of claims uncertain and the existence of the debt at all doubtful.[4] If the creditor fails within the due time to claim against the executry he has no claim against beneficiaries to refund.[5]

All creditors using legal diligence by citation of the executors, or by having themselves confirmed executors-creditors, or by citing other executors-creditors within six months after the debtor's death rank *pari passu*.[6] Hence an executor cannot be compelled to pay any creditor or beneficiary until six months have elapsed, nor is it prudent to do so as till then the full extent of debts is not known.[7] After six months he may pay *primis venientibus*, is indeed bound to pay any just debt produced, and is not liable to creditors appearing only thereafter.[8] He is not, however, entitled to pay a deferred creditor leaving a preferred creditor unsatisfied.[7]

1 *Keane* v. *Adair*, 1941 J.C. 77.
2 Finance Act, 1894, S. 6; Succession (Sc.) Act, 1964, S. 19(1).
3 *E. Rosslyn* v. *Lawson* (1872) 9 S.L.R. 291.
4 *McGaan* v. *McG.'s Trs.* (1883) 11 R. 249; as to liability in expenses for unreasonably opposing a claim see *Law* v. *Humphrey* (1876) 3 R. 1192.
5 *St. Andrew's Mags.* v. *Forbes* (1893) 1 S.L.T. 340.
6 A.S. 28 Feb. 1662.
7 Bell, *Prin.* §1900; McLaren II, 2159.
8 *Laird* v. *Hamilton*, 1911 1 S.L.T. 27; *Taylor & Ferguson* v. *Glass's Trs.*, 1912 S.C. 165.

Preferential claims

The only preferential debts[1] are the expenses of confirmation, deathbed, and funeral expenses,[2] widow's and family mournings,[3] aliment for the widow and family,[4] and wages of farm and domestic servants for the current term.[5] Then come debts for which the creditor holds security; these rank *pari passu* and in preference to all unsecured creditors. If a preferential creditor cannot be paid by reason of the executor's carelessness in paying ordinary creditors first and not retaining enough, he is personally liable to make good that creditor's claim.[6] The claim of the executor's solicitor for professional charges is not preferable to that of a surviving spouse for legal rights,[7] but as solicitor for the executor he may claim retention of funds ingathered, in extinction of a debt due to him by the deceased, even though the estate is insolvent, the executor being *eadem persona cum defuncto*.[8]

Where a widow's legal or conventional provisions are quite insufficient for her maintenance, she has a claim for aliment against the estate, which ranks as a debt and may be paid out of capital.[9] A widow is similarly entitled to interim aliment, pending payment of her legal rights or other provision.[10] A marriage contract provision for a widow is a debt for which she is entitled to decree for payment, even though there may be doubt whether the estate is sufficient to cover debts and legacies.[11]

The maintenance of an incapax widow,[12] or child[13] is not a burden on the executry estate, beyond their legal claims.

The executor, if himself a creditor, is not entitled to satisfy his debt out of the executry funds to the prejudice of the other creditors, if he knows that the estate is insolvent,[14] but if no other creditor has done diligence he may after six months pay himself.

1 Stair III, 8, 64, and 72; Ersk. III, 9, 43; Bell, *Comm.* II, 147; *Prin.* §1402–9.
2 *Sanders* v. *Hewat* (1822) 1 S. 333.
3 *Sheddon* v. *Gibson* (1802) Mor. 11855; *Barlass* v. *B's Trs.*, 1916 S.C. 741.
4 *Barlass, supra.*
5 *McLean* v. *Sheriffs* (1832) 10 S. 217.
6 *Lamond's Trs.* v. *Croom* (1871) 9 M. 662.
7 *Stirling Waterworks Commrs.* v. *Gall* (1903) 11 S.L.T. 87.
8 *Mitchell* v. *Mackersy* (1905) 8 F. 198.
9 *Anderson* v. *Grant* (1899) 1 F. 484.
10 *Barlass* v. *B's Trs.*, 1916 S.C. 741.
11 *Ctss. Galloway* v. *Stewart* (1903) 11 S.L.T. 188.
12 *Howard's Exor.* v. *H's C.B.* (1894) 21 R. 787.
13 *Mackintosh* v. *Taylor* (1868) 7 M. 67; *Edinburgh Parish Council* v. *Couper*, 1924 S.C. 139.
14 *Salaman* v. *Sinclair's Trs.*, 1916 S.C. 698.

Duty to preserve estate and account

An executor must keep executry funds separate from his own funds, and be able to account to creditors for his intromissions with the estate. If he cannot account for executry money, a claim lies against him and his cautioner, if any.[1] It is imprudent but not necessarily a misapplication of executry funds to pay himself in respect of a debt disputed by the beneficiaries.[2]

Where an executor died insolvent, having inmixed executry estate with his own funds, an heir *in mobilibus* of the deceased was held entitled to sue the executor's cautioner for the value of her share in the estate, without the need for all the family interested in the estate to join in the action.[1]

An executor is bound to take reasonable care of executry funds, but not bound as strictly as a trustee to invest them;[3] he is not necessarily in fault even if he retains money in his own hands uninvested,[4] though executors have been held liable in interest on their intromissions where they had not banked the executry money separately.[5] He should keep proper accounts showing how much, to whom and for what purpose payments have been made.[6]

An executor is not justified in leaving funds ingathered in the hands of his solicitor and he is responsible for loss occasioned thereby, as by the solicitor's bankruptcy.[7]

Distribution of deceased's estate

The executor is not entitled to distribute the estate to the beneficiaries or persons entitled by law without having first provided for payment of all debts due by the executry estate.[8]

Six months after the deceased's death the executor is entitled, unless he has, or should have, reason to believe the estate to be insolvent, to distribute the estate.[9] He must pay in the following order: prior rights of a surviving spouse on intestacy, to house, furnishing and plenishing, and financial provision;[10] claims to

[1] *Scott* v. *McNab* (1902) 10 S.L.T. 288.
[2] *Watson* v. *B.L. Bank*, 1941 S.C. 43.
[3] cf. *Buchan* v. *City of Glasgow Bank* (1879) 6 R. (H.L.) 44.
[4] *Russell* v. *Mackie's Trs.* (1869) 7 S.L.R. 99.
[5] *Malcolm's Exor.* v. *M.* (1869) 8 M. 272.
[6] *Polland* v. *Sturrock's Exors.*, 1955 S.L.T. (Notes) 77.
[7] *E. Dalhousie* v. *Crokat* (1868) 8 M. 659; *Kintore Mags.* v. *Tait's Exors.* (1873) 10 S.L.R. 397.
[8] *Lamond's Trs.* v. *Croom* (1871) 9 M. 662.
[9] *Laird* v. *Hamilton*, 1911 1 S.L.T. 27; *Taylor & Ferguson, Ltd.* v. *Glass's Trs.*, 1912 S.C. 165.
[10] Under Succession (Sc.) Act, 1964, Ss. 8–9.

legal rights, so far as not discharged, or satisfied by other provisions; special legacies and general legacies, observing any order or priority of payment prescribed by the testator; residue; and any amount falling into intestacy. Interest is due on a financial provision[1] and on legal rights.[2] The executor is entitled to proceed on reasonable evidence of relationship, or legitimacy.[3] He is not obliged to retain money to meet a merely contingent claim, such as under a guarantee.[4]

An executor, who, after six months and reasonable inquiry for claims, pays known claims *primis venientibus*, may plead *bona fide* payment which excludes personal liability.[5] A creditor who first claims thereafter must look to the beneficiaries, not the executor,[5] but if the estate has not yet been distributed he is entitled to be ranked *pari passu* with other creditors, even if they hold decrees.[6] Executors have been held personally liable for paying beneficiaries without retaining sufficient to satisfy a creditor, though misled by a wrong estimate of the value of the estate.[7] An executor is not entitled to withhold business books from the legatee to whom they were destined on a plea of confidentiality.[8]

The long negative prescription applies to a claim against an executor for a legacy.[9]

Payment in error

If payment be made under error as to fact, or as to the interpretation of the will, it is recoverable by the executor from the overpaid beneficiary, on the basis of *condictio indebiti*, but not if made under error as to the general law, nor under judicial authority subsequently held to be unsound in law.[10] Unpaid or underpaid beneficiaries cannot recover money direct from wrongly paid beneficiaries, without the intervention of the executors.[11]

[1] Succession (Sc.) Act, 1964, S. 9(1): the rate is 4%.

[2] *Kearon* v. *Thomson's Trs.*, 1949 S.C. 287; the rate is what is reasonable in the circumstances.

[3] *Flett* v. *Brown's Exor.*, 1915 2 S.L.T. 261.

[4] *Taylor & Ferguson, Ltd.* v. *Glass's Trs.*, 1912 S.C. 165; cf. *Edinburgh Parish Council* v. *Couper*, 1924 S.C. 139.

[5] *Stewart's Trs.* v. *Evans* (1871) 9 M. 810; *Beith* v. *Mackenzie* (1875) 3 R. 185; *Laird* v. *Hamilton*, 1911 1 S.L.T. 27.

[6] *Russell* v. *Sunio* (1791) Bell's Oct. Cas. 217.

[7] *Lamond's Trs.* v. *Croom* (1871) 9 M. 662.

[8] *Robertson* v. *R's Exors.*, 1925 S.C. 606.

[9] *Jamieson* v. *Clark* (1872) 10 M. 399.

[10] *Pattison* v. *McVicar* (1886) 13 R. 550.

[11] *Armour* v. *Glasgow R.I.*, 1909 S.C. 916.

Power of executor to transfer heritage

An executor requiring to transfer heritage in satisfaction of prior rights, legal rights, or to a person entitled to share in the estate on intestacy, or under a testamentary disposition,[1] may do so by means of a docket endorsed on the confirmation, or on a certificate of confirmation relating to the heritage in question, identifying the item or items in the confirmation being transferred, and signed by the executor and attested by two witnesses.[2] Any such docket may be specified as a mid-couple or link in any deduction of title; it may be competent to record the docketed confirmation or certificate direct, but is preferable to expede and record a notice of title specifying the docketed confirmation as the link between deceased and person now entitled.

For the purpose of any question as to the entitlement to any property by virtue of a testamentary disposition, it must be treated as probative, apart from any other grounds, if (a) confirmation of an executor to property disposed of in it has been granted in Scotland, or (b) probate, letters of administration or other grant of representation issued outwith Scotland has been certified in Scotland.[3] Taken along with S. 21 this makes confirmation conclusive evidence of the validity of a will as a link in the title of heritable property.

The executor may sell heritage and convey it by disposition in the usual form, deducing his title from the deceased by reference to the confirmation.

Executor's powers in relation to leases

Where a deceased's interest of tenancy under a lease vests in an executor and (a) is not the subject of a valid bequest, or (b) is the subject of a bequest not accepted, or (c) is an interest under an agricultural lease and the subject of a bequest which is declared null under statute,[4] the executor may, notwithstanding an express or implied prohibition of assignation, transfer the interest to a person entitled to prior rights or legal rights, or to succeed on intestacy, but not to anyone else without the landlord's consent.[5]

In certain circumstances either executor or landlord may, on

[1] It must be clear that there is an intention to convey heritage and the beneficiary must be adequately ascertained.

[2] 1964 Act, S. 15(2) and Sched. 1.

[3] 1964 Act, S. 32.

[4] Crofters Holdings (Sc.) Act, 1886, S. 16; Agricultural Holdings (Sc.) Act, 1949, S. 20.

[5] 1964 Act, S. 16(1) and (2).

giving notice, terminate the lease, notwithstanding any contrary provision, enactment or rule.[1] Such termination does not prejudice any claim for compensation or damages for the termination of the lease.[2]

Where the interest is one under an agricultural lease and an application is made under the Small Landholders and Agricultural Holdings (Sc.) Act, 1931, S. 3 for an order for removal or a reference is made under the Agricultural Holdings (Sc.) Act, 1949, S. 27(2) to an arbiter to determine any question which has arisen under s. 25(2) in connection with a notice to quit, the Land Court shall not make the order nor the arbiter an award in favour of the landlord, unless the court or arbiter is satisfied that it is reasonable, having regard to the fact that the interest is vested in the executor in his capacity as such, that it should be made.[3] If such an interest is the subject of a valid bequest by the deceased the fact that it is vested in the executor under S. 14 of the 1964 Act does not prevent the operation in relation to the legatee of specified parts of the 1886 and 1949 Acts.[4]

Where the interest is not under an agricultural lease and the landlord brings an action of removing against the executor in respect of a breach of a condition of the lease, the court shall not grant decree unless satisfied that the condition alleged to have been breached is one which it is reasonable to expect the executor to have observed, having regard to the fact that the interest is vested in him in his capacity as an executor.[5]

Protection of persons acquiring title from executor

Where any person has in good faith and for value acquired title to any interest in or security over heritable property[6] which has vested in an executor, directly or indirectly from the executor, or from a person deriving title directly from the executor, the title so acquired is not challengeable on the ground that the confirmation was reducible or has in fact been reduced, or, in the latter case, that the title should not have been transferred to the person deriving title directly from the executor.[7] Moreover, executors, both nominate and dative, have the powers of trustees[8]

[1] 1964 Act, S. 16(3) and (4).
[2] 1964 Act, S. 16(5).
[3] 1964 Act, S. 16(6).
[4] 1964 Act, S. 16(8).
[5] 1964 Act, S. 16(7).
[6] Including heritage subject to entail or special destination.
[7] 1964 Act, S. 17.
[8] 1964 Act, S. 20.

and by the Trusts (Sc.) Act, 1961, S. 2, a title acquired by a person who transacts with a trustee is not challengeable on the ground that the transaction is at variance with the terms or purposes of the trust.

Entails and special destinations

On the death of an heir of entail in possession, the entailed property vests in his executor, if confirmed thereto, only to enable it to be conveyed to the heir of entail next entitled thereto.[1]

On the death of a person entitled to heritage subject to a special destination in favour of someone else which the deceased could not competently, or in fact had not, evacuated by testamentary disposition or otherwise, if the deceased's executor is confirmed to the property, it vests in the executor only for conveyance to the person next entitled thereto under the destination. The modes of transfer of heritage introduced by S. 15 are applicable.[2] The title of a person acquiring title in good faith and for value to any interest vested in an executor is protected, as it is under S. 17.[3]

Powers of executor to transfer moveables

The executor may transfer moveables to any person entitled thereto by delivery, or payment, transfer of shares, or assignation, as may be appropriate to the particular moveables.

Right of beneficiaries to make up title

If an executor has died without granting a conveyance of property, heritable or moveable, standing in his name, any person entitled thereto for his own absolute use or deriving right from a person so entitled, may on petition to the court be authorized to complete a title thereto in his own name.[4]

Personal liability of executor

An executor may be held liable for loss of executry funds or of interest therein, as where he allowed funds to remain in the hands of his agent and part of them were lost,[5] or failed to keep executry funds separate from his own,[6] but an executor is not so strictly bound to invest as is a trustee.

[1] 1964 Act, S. 18(1). [2] 1964 Act, S. 18(2)–(3). [3] 1964 Act, S. 18(4).

[4] Trusts (Sc.) Act, 1921, S. 24; *Cowper* (1897) 5 S.L.T. 85.

[5] *E. Dalhousie* v. *Crokat* (1868) 6 M. 659; *Mags. of Kintore* v. *Tait's Exors.* (1873) 10 S.L.R. 397.

[6] *Malcolm's Exors.* v. *M.* (1869) 8 M. 272; *Matheson's C.B.* v. *M.* (1889) 16 R. 701.

The executor of a deceased executor is not liable to account for the latter's intromissions with the deceased's estate.[1]

Discharge of executor

Creditors or beneficiaries may call an executor to account by an action of court, reckoning, and payment. Such an action is competent in respect of part of the estate allegedly intromitted with, even though not given up in the inventory.[2]

An executor who defended an action unreasonably has been held personally liable in expenses, but with a right of relief against the free executry estate, if any.[3]

If an executor dies without having exhausted his function, his own executor is not liable to account for the deceased's intromissions as executor.[4]

There is no practice of executors obtaining a discharge, other than receipts from individual beneficiaries or persons entitled by law, for items of estate transferred to them. When the whole estate has been administered, the executor's office is exhausted.[5]

Where Crown succeeds

Where the Crown is entitled as *ultimus haeres* the Queen's and Lord Treasurer's Remembrancer takes possession of the estate without confirmation.[6]

Payments without confirmation

Various statutes[7] authorize the disposal of property not exceeding £500 held for the deceased's credit by various benevolent bodies, on death, testate or intestate, to persons appearing to be beneficially entitled thereto, or to relatives or dependants of the deceased or other persons mentioned in the statutes, without the necessity for confirmation or other proof of title.[8]

Winding up under Bankruptcy Act

A creditor of, or person interested in the succession to, a deceased, if no trustees have been nominated or other parties having power to manage the estate, or if they have not accepted

[1] *Hutcheson & Co.'s Adminr.* v. *Taylor's Exrx.*, 1931 S.C. 484.
[2] *Smith* v. *S.* (1880) 7 R. 1013.
[3] *Law* v. *Humphrey* (1875) 3 R. 1192.
[4] *Hutcheson & Co.'s Adminr.* v. *Taylor's Exrx.*, 1931 S.C. 484.
[5] Ersk. III, 9, 47; *Johnston's Exor.* v. *Dobie*, 1907 S.C. 31.
[6] See also, as to estate in England, Law Reform (Misc. Prov.) (Sc.) Act, 1940, S. 6(1).
[7] Listed in Schedule 1 to Administration of Estates (Small Payments) Act, 1965.
[8] 1965 Act, S. 1.

or do not act, may apply for the appointment of a judicial factor to wind up the estate.[1]

PASSIVE TITLES

At common law a person to whom a deceased's estate transmitted was deemed *eadem persona cum defuncto* and he incurred liability for the deceased's obligations and debts, not limited by the amount of estate taken by the succession.[2] The rules whereby such a person incurred a passive title in heritage have been rather superseded than abolished. The only passive title in moveables was, and is, vitious intromission.

Passive representation in heritage

Universal passive representation was incurred by one who took an inheritance from the deceased, the liability being for the full amount of the debt, for the benefit of creditors, in the cases (a) where the heir entered as heir by service,[3] or (b) took gratuitously a right to heritage to which he would otherwise have succeeded (*praeceptio haereditatis*),[4] or (c) where the apparent heir obtained possession of heritage to which he would otherwise have succeeded, or bought it otherwise than at public sale or intromitted with its rents or writs (*gestio pro haerede*).[5]

Limited representation, inferring only a limited responsibility, was imported by taking as heir of provision under a particular deed or destination,[6] as heir under a destination in a lease,[7] taking as a gratuitous disponee, and in certain other cases,[8] particularly where the heir served heir *cum beneficio inventarii*, i.e. with reference to an inventory lodged within a year of the ancestor's death.[9]

Possession of an estate as apparent heir for three years inferred liability for debts to the value of the lands,[10] but possession on

1 Bankruptcy (Sc.) Act, 1913, S. 163.
2 Ersk. III, 8, 50.
3 Ersk. III, 8, 50; Bell, *Prin.* §1916; *E. Fife* v. *Duff* (1828) 6 S. 698; *Mackay* v. *Campbell's Trs.* (1835) 13 S. 246; *Nisbet's Trs.* v. *Halket* (1839) 1 Rob. 53; *Storeys* v. *Paxton* (1878) 6 R. 293.
4 Stair III, 7, 1; Bankt. III, 7, 1; Ersk. III, 8, 87; Bell, *Comm.* I, 704; *Prin.* §1917–18.
5 Stair III, 6, 6; Ersk. III, 8, 83; Bell, *Prin.* §1919–20; *Montgomerie* v. *Boswell* (1841) 4 D. 332. For exceptions to liability see Bell, *Prin.* §1920.
6 *Leslie* v. *McLeod* (1870) 8 M. (H.L.) 99.
7 *Bain* v. *Mackenzie* (1896) 23 R. 528.
8 Ersk. III, 8, 51; Bell, *Prin.* §1922–8.
9 Act, 1695, c. 24 (repealed S.L.R. Act, 1906); see Bell, *Prin.* §1926–8.
10 Ersk. III, 8, 93; Bell, *Prin.* §1929–30; *Morris* v. *Beveridge* (1867) 6 M. 60.

apparency disappeared by virtue of the Conveyancing (Sc.) Act, 1874, S. 9, which conferred a personal right on an heir by mere survivance.[1]

By statute the ancestor's creditors had preference on his estate over the heir's creditors.[2]

Though liable universally to creditors heirs were responsible only in a particular order, and there were rules as to discussion and relief.[3] The heir might evade liability by renouncing the succession.

Modern law

The Conveyancing (Sc.) Act, 1874, S. 12, provided that an heir in heritage should not be liable for the debts of his ancestors beyond the value of the estate to which he succeeded,[4] and this limitation included liability under bonds secured over the estate.[5] This probably abolished *praeceptio haereditatis*.

In moveables the executor is *eadem persona cum defuncto* and becomes proprietor as the deceased was, but his liability does not extend beyond the estate vested in him by confirmation.[6]

The Succession (Sc.) Act, 1964, S. 14, vests the whole property of a deceased, heritable and moveable, in the executor confirmed by the court, and repeals the provision of the 1874 Act, so that now the executor's liability appears to be limited in respect both of heritage and of moveables to the extent of the estate vested in him by confirmation.

Passive representation in moveables—Vitious intromission

The liability of the vitious intromitter, who is anyone[7] who, without having been confirmed executor, takes possession of or intromits with the moveables of the deceased, remains.[8] It is liability for all the debts due by the deceased. There is no liability

[1] cf. *McAdam* v. *McA.* (1879) 6 R. 1256.

[2] (heritage) Act, 1661, c. 24 (repealed Succession (Sc.) Act 1964, S. 34(2)); Ersk. III, 8, 102; Bell, *Prin.* §1931–3; *Macalpine* v. *Lang* (1885) 12 R. 604; (moveables) Act 1695, c. 24 (repealed Statute Law Revision Act, 1906); Stair III, 8, 71; Ersk. III, 9, 43; Bell, *Prin.* §1934; *Orr* (1871) 9 M. 500; *Glen* v. *Scale's Trs.* (1881) 9 R. 317; *Fleming's Trs.* v. *F's Tutors* (1882) 9 R. 1013.

[3] Stair III, 5, 17; Bankt. III, 5, 69; Ersk. III, 8, 52; Bell, *Prin.* §1935–6.

[4] cf. *Welch's Exors.* v. *Edinburgh Life Assce. Co.* (1896) 23 R. 772.

[5] Ibid., S. 47; *Welch's Exors., supra.*

[6] *Globe Ins. Co.* v. *Scott's Trs.* (1850) 7 Bell 296; *Stewart's Trs.* v. *Stewart's Exor.* (1896) 23 R. 739; *Mitchell* v. *Mackersy* (1905) 8 F. 198.

[7] Stair III, 9, 1; Ersk. III, 9, 49; Bell, *Comm.* I, 705; *Prin.* §1921; *Forbes* v. *F.* (1823) 2 S. 395; *Wilson* v. *Taylor* (1865) 3 M. 1060.

[8] Stair III, 9, 9; Ersk. III, 9, 49; Bell, *Prin.* §1921.

unless the subject meddled with was truly part of the deceased's estate[1] and any *bona fide* title of intromission which removes the suspicion of fraud and affords a check on the intromission relieves from the universal liability.[2] The character of the intromission rather than its extent matters.[3] Where several persons are involved their liability is joint and several.[4] The plea is competent by way of action only to creditors holding an obligation from the deceased and legatees may only call for an accounting from the intromitter.[5]

Universal liability for all the debts of the deceased is not an inevitable consequence of vitious intromission and liability may be held less as where the intermeddling has been done *bona fide*.[6] But good faith, honest belief or mistake afford no complete defence though it is a defence that the creditors approved the intromissions and accepted payments.[7] The legal presumption is more readily enforced where there are suspicious circumstances.[8]

The liability of a vitious intromitter, where it exists, does not transmit to his executor except in so far as the latter was lucratus by the succession.[9] It is also elided if the intromitter becomes confirmed as executor nominate or dative (but not as executor creditor) within a year and a day, or before action is brought against him, but he thereby renders himself liable to account as an executor.[10]

As the executor is now[11] the deceased's representative in both heritage and moveables the liability for vitious intromission probably attaches to intromission with either heritage or moveables.

1 Stair III, 9, 12; Ersk. III, 9, 51; *Greig* v. *Christie*, 1908 S.C. 370.

2 Bell, *Prin.* §1921; *Thomson* v. *Miller* (1834) 13 S. 143; *Wilson* v. *Taylor* (1865) 3 M. 1060, 1061; *Greig, supra.*

3 *Simpson* v. *Barr* (1854) 17 D. 33, 478.

4 Stair III, 9, 4; Bell, *Prin.* §1921; *Wilson, supra.*

5 Ersk. III, 9, 54.

6 *Thomson* v. *Miller* (1834) 13 S. 143; *Adam* v. *Campbell* (1854) 16 D. 964; *Simpson* v. *Barr* (1854) 17 D. 33, 478; *Wilson* v. *Taylor* (1865) 3 M. 1060; *Greig, supra.*

7 *French* v. *Muirkirk Iron Co.* (1797) Hume 435.

8 Bell, *Comm.* I, 705.

9 Stair III, 9, 14; Ersk. III, 9, 54; Bell, *Prin.* §1921.

10 Ersk. III, 9, 52.

11 Succession (Sc.) Act, 1964, S. 14.

BOOK IX

CIVIL REMEDIES

CHAPTER 115

CIVIL REMEDIES

WHILE the substantive part of the private law defines what rights, claims, and other advantages attach to particular persons, and what duties, liabilities, and other disadvantages attach to other persons, vis-a-vis one another, in particular circumstances, and what remedial or consequential rights and duties arise from the infringement of a substantive right or the non-implement of a substantive duty, the adjective law defines, *inter alia*, what means must be resorted to, in case of doubt or dispute, to have the infringement established and the remedy declared or defined, granted, and enforced.[1] The antithesis between 'right' and 'remedy' is a false one in that remedial rights are as much legal rights as substantive rights, though the latter are logically prior.

Remedial rights arise only if and when there is breach of a primary right vested in the complainer, or breach of a correlative primary duty owed to him. If there is no primary right or no infringement thereof there can be no remedy, but, in general, if there is a primary right infringed there is a consequential remedy. Nor can the distinction between substantive and adjective law be equated to the distinction between 'law' and 'procedure'. The competency of a claim of damages, and the rules affecting the claim and any award made, are rules of law and distinct from the rules of procedure regulating how the claim is presented, established, and enforced.

A breach of legal duty does not always give rise to a civil remedial right; the remedy may have been excluded or limited by contract[2] or statute, and the only sanction for a breach of some statutory duties may be criminal prosecution.[3] One breach may give rise to more than one remedial right,[4] or there may be doubt

[1] Adjective law is therefore not synonymous with procedure, but wider. Adjective law includes also, as well as procedure, the rules of evidence, and of pleading and practice in civil causes, of diligence, of representation and legal aid, and expenses, but these latter subjects are, for reasons of space, omitted from this book.

[2] e.g. *McKay* v. *Scottish Airways*, 1948 S.C. 254.

[3] e.g. *Cutler* v. *Wandsworth Stadium* [1949] A.C. 398; *Pullar* v. *Window Clean Ltd.*, 1956 S.C. 13.

[4] e.g. an injury to a person may give him claims of damages for personal injury, for Industrial Injury benefit, and under a personal accident insurance policy.

which of possible remedial rights should appropriately be claimed.[1] A legal remedy normally, but not always, is granted by a court on the application of the aggrieved party.

The recognized classes of legal remedies are:

(1) self-help, without resort to legal process;
(2) judicial declaration of the rights of parties, by declarator or reduction;
(3) judicial stopping of wrongful conduct, by suspension or interdict;
(4) judicial assistance to recover possession of property;
(5) judicial compulsion of performance of duties, by specific implement, or payment of debt, with or without interest;
(6) the right to rescind a contract for material breach;
(7) judicial enforcement of agreed compulsitors, such as provisions for irritancies or liquidate damages;
(8) judicial grant of substitutional redress or compensation, by award of pecuniary damages;
(9) judicial appointment of a person to administer the property in dispute.

These kinds, and categories of remedial rights, do not correspond exactly to the various categories or forms of actions allowed, nor to particular procedure followed.[2]

SELF-HELP

In a limited number of cases the aggrieved individual may lawfully resort to self-help and need not resort to legal procedure. Self-help is not favoured and should not be resorted to unnecessarily or in unprecedented cases.[3]

Self-help is, however, permissible by way of self-defence against assault, so long as no greater force is used than is reasonably necessary;[4] it may extend to the defence of spouse or child,

[1] e.g. *Goldie* v. *Christie and Petrie* (1868) 6 M. 541; *Arnott* v. *L.A.*, 1932 S.L.T. 46.

[2] The standard procedural classification is into actions rescissory, declaratory, petitory or possessory: Ersk. IV, 1, 18. To this list is sometimes added penal, competitive, and actions relative to execution. Consistorial actions and maritime actions are also treated separately by some authorities. Actions may also be classed as real or personal, *in rem* or *in personam*. Whether an action is commenced by summons or petition is a procedural matter.

[3] *Ashburton* v. *Mackenzie* (1829) 7 S. 849; *Lagan Navigation Co.* v. *Lambeg Bleaching Co.* [1927] A.C. 226, 244.

[4] Bankt. I, 10, 23; Bell, *Prin.* §2032; *Hallowell* v. *Niven* (1843) 5 D. 759; *McDiarmid* v. *Barrie* (1901) 18 Sh. Ct. Rep. 47; cf. Hume, *Crimes*, I, 218.

or even of a third party;[1] it is also permissible to eject trespassers,[2] to poind straying animals until payment of the statutory penalty therefor,[3] to shoot dogs if necessary to stop sheepworrying or a resumption of it,[4] to protect property, but only by fencing or measures to frighten, not by shooting,[5] mantraps, or electrified fences,[6] to protect lands against the sea or floods[7] but not deliberately to cast flood water on a neighbour's lands,[8] to abate a nuisance, if this can be done without going on the neighbour's land and so long as no more harm is done than is necessary,[9] and to retake goods in the hands of another,[10] unless that other obtained and holds the goods with the consent of the owner now seeking repossession,[11] and unless there is a difficult issue of law as to ownership.[12]

DECLARATOR

A declarator merely declares the pursuer's legal right, but requires nothing further to be done unless, as is usual, other conclusions are annexed.[13] The pursuer must have a material patrimonial interest in having the right in question declared.[14]

A bare declarator of facts without any consequential right flowing from it,[15] or of an abstract legal proposition,[16] is generally

[1] *H.M.A.* v. *Carson*, 1964 S.L.T. 21.

[2] *E. Eglinton* v. *Campbell* (1770) Maclaurin 505; *Bell* v. *Shand* (1870) 7 S.L.R. 267; *Aitchison* v. *Thorburn* (1870) 7 S.L.R. 347; *Wood* v. *N.B. Ry.* (1899) 2 F. 1.

[3] Winter Herding Act, 1686; *Shaw* v. *Ewart*, 2 Mar. 1809, F.C.; *McArthur* v. *Miller* (1873) 1 R. 248; *McArthur* v. *Jones* (1878) 6 R. 41; *Fraser* v. *Smith* (1899) 1 F. 487.

[4] *Blackie* v. *Stewart* (1920) 37 Sh. Ct. Rep. 60; *Wilson* v. *Buchanan* (1943) 59 Sh. Ct. Rep. 54; *Gott* v. *Measures* [1947] 2 All E.R. 609; *Cresswell* v. *Sirl* [1947] 2 All E.R. 730; *Leven* v. *Mitchell* (1949) 65 Sh. Ct. Rep. 225.

[5] cf. *H.M.A.* v. *Phipps* (1905) 4 Adam 616.

[6] *Bird* v. *Holbrook* (1828) 4 Bing. 628.

[7] *Lagan Navigation Co.* v. *Lambeg Bleaching Co.* [1927] A.C. 226.

[8] *Menzies* v. *E. Breadalbane* (1828) 3 W. & S. 235; *Tennent* v. *E. Glasgow* (1864) 2 M. (H.L.) 22; *Orr-Ewing* v. *Colquhoun* (1877) 4 R. (H.L.) 116.

[9] *Lemmon* v. *Webb* [1895] A.C. 1; *Butler* v. *Standard Telephones* [1940] 1 K.B. 399. As to statutory nuisance see Public Health (Sc.) Act, 1897, Ss. 16–27.

[10] cf. *Strachan* v. *Gordon* (1671) Fol. Dict. 115.

[11] As to protection of goods on hire-purchase from *brevi manu* repossession see Hire-Purchase (Sc.) Act, 1965, Ss. 33–40.

[12] cf. *Morrisson* v. *Robertson*, 1908 S.C. 332; *MacLeod* v. *Kerr*, 1965 S.C. 253.

[13] Stair IV, 3, 47; Ersk. IV, 1, 46; cf. *Barbour* v. *Grierson* (1827) 5 S. 565; *E. Mansfield* v. *Stewart* (1846) 5 Bell 139.

[14] *Forbes* v. *Eden* (1867) 5 M. (H.L.) 36; *Skerret* v. *Oliver* (1896) 23 R. 468; *Orr* v. *Alston*, 1912 1 S.L.T. 95; *Drennan* v. *Associated Ironmoulders*, 1921 S.C. 151; *Griffin* v. *L.A.*, 1950 S.C. 448; *Macnaughton* v. *M's Trs.*, 1953 S.C. 387.

[15] *Gifford* v. *Trail* (1829) 7 S. 854; *Bosville* v. *Macdonald*, 1910 S.C. 597; *Menzies* v. *McKenna*, 1914 S.C. 272.

[16] *N.B. Ry.* v. *Birrell's Trs.*, 1918 S.C. (H.L.) 33, 47; cf. *Callendar's Cable Co.* v. *Glasgow Corpn.* (1900) 2 F. 397, 401; *Sinclair Lockhart's Trs.* v. *Central Land Board*, 1951 S.C. 258, 262.

incompetent, though not if the declarator effectively determines a live practical issue between the parties.[1] Thus declarator is incompetent as to the meaning of a statute[2] or as to general legal relations of persons placed as were the parties,[3] or as to an undisputed fact or obligation,[4] or for a purely collateral purpose.[5] So too it is incompetent if in substance an appeal when the statutory mode of appeal had not been invoked.[6]

Declarator may be granted in more limited terms than sought, but only by omitting parts of the conclusions, not by rewriting the pursuer's conclusions.[7]

Declarator is also generally incompetent where another form of redress is prescribed but has not been utilised.[8]

A declarator may be positive or negative;[9] some states of rights which one may wish declared are essentially negative, e.g. declarator of nullity or bastardy.

In general a declarator as to future or hypothetical rights is incompetent, particularly if any contingency is not yet satisfied,[10] but it is competent where a pursuer is excusably ignorant of his rights which he wishes to have clarified,[11] or if the right is in danger of being lost by the passage of time if not now declared.[12]

Applications of declarator

A main application of declarator is to declare existing personal status, as by declarators of marriage,[13] of nullity of marriage,[14] of

[1] *Sullivan* v. *Close* (1898) 6 S.L.T. 2; *Stewart* v. *Sillars* (1906) 13 S.L.T. 800; *Griffin* v. *L.A.*, 1950 S.C. 448; *B.O.C.* v. *S.S.E.B.*, 1958 S.C. 53, 63; *Macnaughton, supra.*

[2] *Todd & Higginbotham* v. *Burnet* (1854) 16 D. 794; *Orr* v. *Alston*, 1912 1 S.L.T. 95; but contrast *Hogg* v. *Parochial Board of Auchtermuchty* (1880) 7 R. 986; *Glasgow District Ry.* v. *Glasgow Mags.* (1884) 11 R. 1110.

[3] *Rothfield* v. *N.B. Ry.*, 1920 S.C. 805, 830, 836, 838.

[4] *Sime* v. *Grimond*, 1920 1 S.L.T. 270; *Drennan* v. *Assoc. Ironmoulders*, 1921 S.C. 151.

[5] *Menzies* v. *McKenna*, 1914 S.C. 272.

[6] *Dante* v. *Ayr Assessor*, 1922 S.C. 109; contrast *Hope* v. *Edinburgh Mags.* (1897) 5 S.L.T. 195.

[7] *Assets Co.* v. *Ogilvie* (1897) 24 R. 400; *Howard de Walden Estates* v. *Bowmaker*, 1965 S.C. 163.

[8] *Dante* v. *Ayr Assessor*, 1922 S.C. 109; contrast *Hope* v. *Edinburgh Mags.* (1897) 5 S.L.T. 195.

[9] *N.B. Ry.* v. *Birrell's Trs.*, 1918 S.C. (H.L.) 33, 47; cf. *Home* v. *Young* (1846) 9 D. 286; *Perth General Stn. Committee* v. *Ross* (1897) 24 R. (H.L.) 44; *Howard de Walden Estates* v. *Bowmaker*, 1965 S.C. 163.

[10] *Millar* v. *M's Trs.* (1896) 4 S.L.T. 122; *Murray* v. *M.*, 1909 1 S.L.T. 122.

[11] *Mackenzie* v. *M's Tutors* (1846) 8 D. 964; *Chaplin's Trs.* v. *Hoile* (1890) 18 R. 27.

[12] *Central S.M.T. Co.* v. *Lanarkshire C.C.*, 1949 S.C. 450.

[13] e.g. *Steuart* v. *Robertson* (1875) 2 R. (H.L.) 80; *De Thoren* v. *Wall* (1876) 3 R. (H.L.) 28; *Petrie* v. *P.*, 1911 S.C. 360; *Davidson* v. *D.*, 1921 S.C. 341.

[14] e.g. *McLeod* v. *Adams*, 1920 1 S.L.T. 229; *Courtin* v. *Elder*, 1930 S.C. 68 (void); *C.B.* v. *A.B.* (1885) 12 R. (H.L.) 36; *F.* v. *F.*, 1945 S.C. 202 (voidable).

legitimacy,[1] of bastardy,[2] of illegitimacy and putting to silence,[3] or of the validity of a foreign divorce.[4] A declarator of marriage may be necessary as a preliminary to a divorce,[5] or to a prosecution for bigamy.[6]

Another application is as to the personal rights of the pursuer, e.g. of membership of a trade union.[7]

Property

In relation to heritable property declarator may be sought of the existence of a servitude[8] or of a public right of way,[9] of the incurring of a legal irritancy of a feu *ob non solutum canonem*[10] or the incurring of a conventional irritancy, if it is convenient and expedient to have the rights of parties judicially found,[11] but not if the incurring of the irritancy is admitted or the facts are so simple and notorious as to admit of instant verification.[12] Declarator should also normally precede a decree of extraordinary removing.[13]

Where lands have been adjudged for debt by a creditor the latter's right is redeemable until the expiry of the legal period for redemption (ten years) or until the expiry of the negative prescriptive period from the date of recording of the decree of adjudication in the Register of Sasines, which cuts off the right of redemption, unless the creditor after the ten years brings a declarator of expiry of the legal, whereupon he obtains an irredeemable title, which may be made the foundation of prescriptive possession.[14]

In relation to moveable rights declarator has been held the proper remedy in a dispute as to the disposal of the goodwill of a partnership.[15]

1 *Bosville* v. *Lord Macdonald*, 1910 S.C. 597; *Smijth* v. *S.*, 1918 1 S.L.T. 156.
2 *Tennent* v. *T.* (1890) 17 R. 1205; *Imre* v. *Mitchell*, 1958 S.C. 439.
3 *A.B.* v. *C.D.* (1901) 8 S.L.T. 406; *Williams* v. *Forsythe*, 1909 2 S.L.T. 252.
4 *Arnott* v. *L.A.*, 1932 S.L.T. 46.
5 *Nicol* v. *Bell*, 1954 S.L.T. 314.
6 cf. *Reid* v. *H.M.A.*, 1934 J.C. 7.
7 *Berry* v. *T. & G.W.U.*, 1933 S.N. 10; *Martin* v. *S.T.G.W.U.*, 1952 S.C. (H.L.) 1.
8 *Malcolm* v. *Lloyd* (1886) 13 R. 512.
9 *Mackintosh* v. *Moir* (1871) 9 M. 574.
10 *D. Argyll* v. *Campbeltown Coal Co.*, 1924 S.C. 844, 850. Irritancy of a lease for non-payment of rent does not require declarator: *D. Argyll, supra.*
11 *Stewart* v. *Watson* (1864) 2 M. 1414; *Wylie* v. *Heritable Securities Investment Assocn.* (1871) 10 M. 253; *D. Argyll, supra*; *McDouall's Trs.* v. *Macleod*, 1949 S.C. 593.
12 *D. Argyll, supra*, 852.
13 *D. Argyll, supra*, 850.
14 Bell. *Prin.* §829–30; *Hinton* v. *Connell's Trs.* (1883) 10 R. 1110.
15 *Mackenzie* v. *Macfarlane*, 1934 S.N. 16.

Declarator is also proper if it is contended that possession, *ex facie* as owner, is truly in trust.[1]

Miscellaneous cases

Declarator has also been sought in many miscellaneous cases, such as that a typewritten will was holograph,[2] that a notarially executed will was valid and effective,[3] that a committee had failed to administer a charity and were bound to make a scheme for doing so,[4] as to the construction to be put on a decree,[5] that despite a decree on the footing that the deceased had died intestate he had made a valid bequest in the pursuer's favour,[6] as to the jurisdiction of burgh magistrates under a Crown charter,[7] that an annuity fell to be paid under deduction of tax,[8] that the conduct of a public inquiry was irregular and mistaken,[9] and that spouses could renounce rights under a marriage contract.[10]

Dissolution of marriage

Akin to declarators of status are decrees dissolving a marriage and thereby judicially altering the status of parties henceforth.

Presumption of death

The various provisions for finding that a person must be presumed dead[11] are similarly akin to declarators but have future effect only.

REDUCTION

Reduction is the remedy of annulling a deed or contract under which the defender claims rights prejudicial to the pursuer's right.[12] It has never been competent in the sheriff court. It is

1 *L. Elibank* v. *Hamilton* (1827) 6 S. 69; *Anstruther* v. *Mitchell and Cullen* (1857) 19 D. 674; *Robertson* v. *R.*, 1929 S.L.T. 510.

2 *Chisholm's Trs.* v. *C.*, 1949 S.C. 434.

3 *Gorrie's Tr.* v. *Stiven's Exrx.*, 1952 S.C. 1.

4 *Fraser* v. *McNeill*, 1948 S.C. 517.

5 *Park's Curator* v. *Black* (1870) 8 M. 671; cf. *Morton, Whitehead & Greig* v. *Smith* (1864) 3 M. 29.

6 *Dundee Mags.* v. *Morris* (1856) 19 D. 168.

7 *Edinburgh Mags.* v. *Officers of State* (1825) 4 S. 319.

8 *David Allen & Sons Billposting* v. *Bruce*, 1933 S.C. 253.

9 *Ayr Mags.* v. *L.A.*, 1950 S.C. 102.

10 *Hamilton* v. *H's Trs.*, 1961 S.C. 205.

11 Common law: *Greig* v. *Edinburgh Merchant Co.*, 1921 S.C. 76; Presumption of Life Limitation (Sc.) Act, 1891; Dissolution of marriage on the ground of presumed death, under Divorce (Sc.) Act, 1938, S. 5.

12 Stair IV, 20, 1; Ersk. IV, 1, 18; Mackay, *Manual*, 391.

necessary only where there is some deed or document; if there be none such, declaratory or petitory conclusions alone suffice. The deed must, if allowed to stand, prejudice the pursuer's rights and not merely be distasteful to him.[1] It may be reduced in part[2] or *quoad* the pursuer's interest only.[3] If reduction is granted the deed is thereafter ineffectual against the party who has obtained the decree of reduction.

Reduction is competent by itself and further conclusions to give effect to the pursuer's rights, though common, are unnecessary.[4]

The defender may demur to producing the deed challenged,[5] and may be required to satisfy production under reservation of objections to the competency and relevancy of the action.[6]

The defender may be called on to produce only deeds which are or should be under his care[7] and not those belonging to a third party. Exceptionally, production has been satisfied by production of a copy of a disposition.[8]

Non-production: certification

There may be annexed to the conclusion a certification that if the deed is not produced, it will be held void; if later produced, this lapses and the deed may be founded on.[9]

Scope of reduction

Reduction is strictly necessary only where the deed or obligation is voidable, not where it is totally void, in which case declarator would suffice. But it may be prudent to have the nullity of a deed or an obligation declared by reduction if it is not clear or certain whether it is void or merely voidable. Thus where a will had possibly been revoked by a later writing, the position might be clarified by a reduction of one deed.[10]

[1] *Agnew* v. *Laughlan*, 1948 S.C. 656.
[2] *Adams* v. *G.N.S. Ry.* (1889) 16 R. 843.
[3] *McConechy* v. *McIndoe* (1853) 16 D. 315; *Bain* v. *Seafield* (1887) 14 R. 939; *Balls* v. *Macdonald*, 1909 2 S.L.T. 310.
[4] *Beattie* v. *McLellan* (1844) 6 D. 1088; *Ferguson* v. *Malcolm* (1850) 12 D. 732; *Graham* v. *N.B. Bank* (1850) 12 D. 907; *Rachkind* v. *Donald*, 1916 S.C. 751; *Bruce* v. *British Motor Trading Corpn.*, 1924 S.C. 908.
[5] *E. Perth* v. *Willoughby de Eresby's Trs.* (1869) 7 M. 642, 654; cf. *Rixon* v. *Edinburgh Northern Tramways* (1889) 16 R. 653.
[6] *Pattison* v. *Dunn's Trs.* (1863) 1 M. 647; *Cochran* v. *Dunlop* (1872) 9 S.L.R. 597; *Whyte* v. *Forbes* (1890) 17 R. 895.
[7] *Elder* v. *Smith* (1829) 7 S. 656; *Miller* v. *Oliver and Boyd* (1901) 9 S.L.T. 287.
[8] *Law* v. *Law's Trs.* (1903) 11 S.L.T. 155.
[9] Ersk. IV, 1, 19–24.
[10] *Tucker* v. *Canch's Tr.*, 1953 S.C. 270.

Lack of title to grant deed

Deeds by a person having no title to grant such are null and require no reduction; among such are obligations by pupils,[1] or by minors, having curators, without their consent.[2] Deeds and obligations by a person cognosced as insane, or to whom a *curator bonis* has been appointed, are null but reduction has always been held necessary.[3] It is the more necessary if the incapax has not been so found or placed under curatory.[4]

Minority and lesion: drunkenness

Deeds and obligations granted by minors without curators, or with the consent of their curators, are voidable *infra quadriennium utile* on proof of minority and lesion,[5] probably at the instance of the minor only.

A person alleging incapacity by drink at the time of granting a deed must reduce it.[6]

Deeds or obligations contrary to law or public policy

Deeds or obligations contrary to law[7] or morality[8] or public policy[9] or calculated to impede the course of justice[10] are null and require no reduction. The nullity may be pleaded in defence to an action and will be judicially noticed even if not pleaded.

Deeds granted in fraud of creditors in bankrupty can be set aside by reduction or exception.[11]

Where statute renders no action maintainable on an agreement, it can be ignored and no reduction is necessary.[12]

1 Bell, *Prin.* §2067.

2 Bell, *Prin.* §2088; *Bell* v. *Sutherland* (1728) Mor. 8985; *Thomson* v. *Pagan* (1781) Mor. 8985.

3 Stair I, 10, 3; Ersk. I, 7, 51; III, 1, 16; Bell, *Convg.* I, 125; *Towal* v. *Sellers* (1817) 5 Dow 131.

4 *Johnston* v. *J.* (1857) 19 D. 706; *Nisbet* v. *N's Trs.* (1871) 9 M. 937.

5 *McFeetridge* v. *Stewarts & Lloyds*, 1913 S.C. 773.

6 *Johnston* v. *Clark* (1854) 17 D. 228; *Pollok* v. *Burns* (1875) 2 R. 497.

7 e.g. *Mackenzie* v. *M's Trs.* (1877) 4 R. 902; *Smyth's Trs.* v. *Kinloch* (1880) 7 R. 1176; *Cathcart's Trs.* v. *Heneage's Trs.* (1883) 10 R. 1205; *Campbell's Trs.* v. *C.* (1891) 18 R. 992.

8 Stair I, 10, 8; Ersk. I, 3, 10; Bell, *Prin.* §37; *Durham* v. *Blackwood* (1622) Mor. 9469; *Stewart* v. *E. Galloway* (1752) Mor. 9465; *Hamilton* v. *Main* (1823) 2 S. 313; but see *Young* v. *Johnson & Wright* (1880) 7 R. 760; *Webster* v. *W's Trs.* (1886) 14 R. 90.

9 *Wedderburn* v. *Monorgan* (1612) Mor. 9453; *Gibson* v. *Stewart* (1828) 6 S. 733.

10 Bell, *Comm.* I, 301.

11 Bankruptcy Acts, 1621 (c. 18) and 1696 (c. 5).

12 *McKernan* v. *Operative Masons Assocn.* (1874) 1 R. 453; *Shanks* v. *Operative Masons* (1874) 1 R. 823.

Deeds lacking proper execution

A deed *ex facie* lacking the requisite solemnities is null and no reduction is necessary,[1] but if *ex facie* property authenticated reduction is necessary.[2] It is also necessary where there is doubt whether or not a statutory solemnity has been complied with,[3] or a defect cured by a subsequent writing,[4] or an erasure in a material place.[5]

Forged deeds

If *ex facie* probative, the deed impugned must be reduced,[6] but otherwise it may be challenged by exception in defence, or by suspension.[7]

Cases where reduction essential

Reduction is essential in cases of obligations and wills impetrated by facility and circumvention,[8] by undue influence,[9] and generally necessary in cases of deeds obtained by force and fear.[10] It is also normally necessary where a deed or obligation has allegedly been obtained by fraud,[11] though the validity may be raised incidentally in other processes,[12] or obtained under essential error common to both parties.[13] Reduction has also been granted of discharges granted under essential error as to facts or legal rights, particularly if gratuitous.[14]

1 *Ferrie* v. *F's Trs.* (1863) 1 M. 291; contrast *Newstead* v. *Dansken*, 1918 1 S.L.T. 136.

2 e.g. *Walker* v. *Whitwell*, 1916 S.C. (H.L.) 75 (one witness signing after testator's death); *Finlay* v. *F's Trs.*, 1948 S.C. 16 (notary disqualified); *Hynd's Tr.* v. *H's Trs.*, 1955 S.C. (H.L.) 1 (notarial docquet and witnesses' signatures adhibited later).

3 *Johnston* v. *Pettigrew* (1865) 3 M. 954; *Thomson* v. *McCrummen* (1856) 18 D. 470; *Hynd's Tr., supra.*

4 *Callander* v. *C's Trs.* (1863) 2 M. 291.

5 *Peddie* v. *Doig's Trs.* (1857) 19 D. 820; *Strathmore* v. *S.* (1837) 15 S. 449; affd. (1840) 1 Rob. 109.

6 *Ferrie, supra.*

7 *Gellatly* v. *Jones* (1851) 13 D. 961; *E. Galloway* v. *Grant* (1857) 19 D. 865.

8 e.g. *Taylor* v. *Tweedie* (1865) 3 M. 928; *Horsburgh* v. *Thomson's Trs.*, 1912 S.C. 267; *Donald* v. *D.*, 1913 S.C. 274; *McDougal* v. *McD's Trs.*, 1931 S.C. 102; *Mackay* v. *Campbell*, 1967 S.L.T. 337.

9 *Tennent* v. *T's Trs.* (1870) L.R. 2 Sc. App. 6; *Gray* v. *Binny* (1879) 3 R. 332; *Menzies* v. *M.* (1893) 20 R. (H.L.) 108; *Ross* v. *Gosselin's Exors.*, 1926 S.C. 325; *Allan* v. *A.*, 1961 S.C. 200.

10 *Dickie* v. *Gutzmer* (1829) 8 S. 147; *Priestnell* v. *Hutcheson* (1857) 19 D. 495; *Gelot* v. *Stewart* (1870) 8 M. 649.

11 *Smyth* v. *Muir* (1891) 29 S.LR. 99; cf. *Rodger (Builders) Ltd.* v. *Fawdry*, 1950 S.C. 483.

12 *Gibb and MacDonald* v. *Baghott* (1827) 5 S. 690; *City of Edinburgh Brewery Co.* v. *Gibson's Trs.* (1869) 7 M. 886.

13 *Fletcher* v. *L.A.*, 1923 S.C. 27; *Anderson* v. *Lambie*, 1954 S.C. (H.L.) 43.

14 *Purdon* v. *Rowatt's Trs.* (1856) 19 D. 206; *Dickson* v. *Halbert* (1854) 16 D. 586; *Johnston* v. *Goodlet* (1868) 6 M. 1067; *Cunninghame* v. *Anstruther's Trs.* (1869) 7 M. 689;

Challenge ope exceptionis

A party challenging the validity of a deed founded on by his opponent may sometimes have it set aside *ope exceptionis* in the action in which it is produced, without need for a separate reduction.[1] A decree of court cannot be set aside *ope exceptionis*.[2]

Reduction of administrative actings

Reduction is a competent mode of challenge of orders issued by administrative authorities,[3] and of decisions of administrative tribunals,[4] on such grounds as defective procedure or being reached in disregard of natural justice.

Reduction of arbiters' awards

An arbiter's award which is *ultra fines compromissi*[5] or where he has not acted fairly between the parties[6] is reducible.

Reduction of decrees of court

Reduction may be invoked to set aside a judgment of a court when other means of review are not competent, but generally not where ordinary means of appeal or review are prescribed and have either not been exhausted or parties have neglected to utilize them.[7]

The Court of Session may reduce its own decrees[8] on such grounds as inherent nullity of the proceedings,[9] lack of jurisdiction,[10] fraud,[11] collusion, vitiation *in essentialibus*,[12] or suborna-

Mercer v. *Anstruther's Trs.* (1872) 10 M. (H.L.) 39; contrast *Russell* v. *Farrell* (1900) 2 F. 892.

1 A.S. 20 Mar. 1907; C.A.S. IV, 4(d); R.C. 174. *Oswald* v. *Fairs*, 1911 S.C. 257; *Jarvie's Trs.* v. *Bannatyne*, 1927 S.C. 34.

As to Sheriff Court see Sheriff Courts (Sc.) Act, 1907, Sched. I, R. 50; *D. Argyll* v. *Muir*, 1910 S.C. 96; *Donald* v. *D.*, 1913 S.C. 274.

2 *Leggat Bros.* v. *Gray*, 1912 S.C. 230.

3 *Alexander* v. *Min. of Transport*, 1936 S.L.T. 553; *Ayr Burgh* v. *Secy. of State*, 1950 S.C. 102.

4 *McGeehen* v. *Knox*, 1913 S.C. 688; *Moss' Empires* v. *Glasgow Assessor*, 1917 S.C. (H.L.) 1; *Barrs* v. *British Wool Marketing Board*, 1957 S.C. 72; *McDonald* v. *Lanarkshire Fire Brigade Cttee.*, 1959 S.C. 141; *Palmer* v. *Inverness Hospitals Board*, 1963 S.C. 311.

5 *Thomson's Trs.* v. *Muir* (1867) 6 M. 145; *Lockerby* v. *City of Glasgow Improvement Trs.* (1872) 10 M. 971; *Adams* v. *G.N.S. Ry.* (1889) 16 R. 843.

6 *Mitchell* v. *Cable* (1848) 10 D. 1297; cf. *Black* v. *Williams*, 1924 S.C. (H.L.) 22, 27.

7 *Adair* v. *Colvilles*, 1926 S.C. (H.L.) 51, 56.

8 In *Jarvie's Trs.* v. *Bannatyne*, 1927 S.C. 34, 38, a decree in absence was set aside *ope exceptionis*.

9 *Munro* v. *Rose* (1855) 18 D. 292.

10 *Longworth* v. *Yelverton* (1868) 7 M. 70; *Corbidge* v. *Somerville*, 1913 S.C. 858.

11 *McCarroll* v. *McKinstrey*, 1926 S.C. (H.L.) 1.

12 Maclaren, *Practice*, 695.

tion of perjury (but not perjury),[1] but may not reduce a decree granted *in foro* on the merits, on grounds which could have been but were not adduced,[2] or grounds repelled,[3] unless there are facts amounting to *res noviter*.[4]

Reduction is competent where judgment has been obtained by some fraud practised on the court.[5]

A decree in absence may be reduced on the merits or on grounds which infer nullity, such as lack of jurisdiction,[6] fundamental irregularity in procedure, or fraud.[7] Reduction of an unextracted decree is not competent, except in the case of decrees enforceable without extract,[8] but if it has become final and been extracted,[9] or even been implemented, it can be reduced. The reduction must be brought before it has become equivalent to a decree *in foro*.

Reduction is also competent of decrees of inferior courts,[10] but not of the Small Debt courts,[11] or of licensing courts.[12]

Administration functions of sheriff

Decrees of the sheriff serving persons as heirs to deceased ancestors are reducible,[13] as are decrees of confirmation of executors.[14]

SUSPENSION

Suspension is the remedy of stopping some act not yet completed,[15] complained of as injurious. Its main uses are to stay diligence, and as a method of review of decrees of court.

1 *Lockyer* v. *Ferryman* (1876) 3 R. 882, 887, 912; *Forster* v. *F.* (1871) 8 M. 445; *Bell* v. *B.* (1889) 17 R. (H.L.) 68.

2 *Carmichael* v. *Anstruther* (1866) 4 M. 842.

3 cf. *Acutt* v. *A.*, 1935 S.C. 525.

4 *Munro, supra*; *McCarroll, supra*; see also *Campbell* v. *C.* (1865) 3 M. 501.

5 *Adair, supra.*

6 *Acutt, supra.*

7 *Graham* v. *G.* (1881) 9 R. 327; *Walker* v. *W.*, 1911 S.C. 163; *Corbidge* v. *Somerville*, 1913 S.C. 858.

8 *Jack* v. *Umpherston* (1837) 15 S. 833.

9 *McLeod* v. *Collie* (1889) 42 Sc. Jur. 62; *Broom* v. *Anderson* (1837) 15 S. 977.

10 Ersk. IV, 3, 8; *Mathewson* v. *Yeoman* (1900) 2 F. 873; *Graham* v. *Stirling*, 1922 S.C. 90; *Adair* v. *Colvilles*, 1926 S.C. (H.L.) 51, 56; contrast *Philp* v. *Reid*, 1927 S.C. 224.

11 Small Debt (Sc.) Acts, 1825, S. 14; 1837, S. 30.

12 *Ashley* v. *Rothesay Mags.* (1873) 11 M. 708; *Milne* v. *Aberdeen District Cttee.* (1899) 2 F. 220; *Goodall* v. *Bilsland*, 1909 S.C. 1152, but see *Walsh* v. *Pollokshaws Mags.*, 1907 S.C. (H.L.) 1.

13 *Whyte* v. *Stewart* (1805) 3 Pat. 100; *Hunter* v. *H.* (1823) 1 Sh. App. 459; *Officers of State* v. *Alexander* (1839) 1 D. 1188.

14 *Davie* v. *Barclay* (1871) 9 M. 726; *Baines' Exor.* v. *Clark*, 1957 S.C. 342.

15 *McDougall* v. *Galt* (1863) 1 M. 1012.

The Court of Session[1] may suspend diligence on its own decrees or those of inferior courts.[2] The Sheriff Court of the defender's domicile may suspend charges on decrees of that court or proceedings on bills, bonds, or other obligations registered in the Books of Council and Session or Sheriff Court books where the debt does not exceed £50, and such suspensions are excluded from the Court of Session.[3]

Suspension may be sought of a charge on a decree, threatened[4] or served, but it suffices if decree has been obtained on which diligence may follow.[5] The ground may be defect in the extract decree, or defect in the charge itself,[6] or because an excessive sum has been charged for,[7] or because the sum charged for has been paid,[8] or because in the case of a decree *ad factum praestandum* there is vagueness or doubt as to the act required.[9]

Suspension will not, however, be granted merely because of trivial or immaterial errors in a charge.[10]

Summary diligence on a bill of exchange or note[11] may be suspended if there has been any illegality or nonconformity to procedure.[12]

Suspension is sometimes granted only if caution is found.[13]

1 Stair IV, 52, 8; Ersk. IV, 3, 8, and 18–22.

2 *Aitchison* v. *Macdonald*, 1911 S.C. 174. Suspension of Small Debt decrees is incompetent.

3 Sheriff Courts (Sc.) Act, 1907, Sched. I, R. 123–5; see *Bryce* v. *Belhaven Eng. Co.* (1908) 15 S.L.T. 1043; *Stevenson* v. *Sharpe*, 1910 S.C. 580; *Abrahams* v. *Campbell*, 1911 S.C. 353; *Brown & Critchley* v. *Decorative Art Journals, Ltd.*, 1922 S.C. 192.

4 Ersk. IV, 3, 20; *Templeton* v. *T.* (1837) 16 S. 100; *Watson* v. *Merrilees* (1848) 10 D. 370.

5 *Lowson* v. *Reid* (1861) 23 D. 1089.

6 *Beattie* v. *McLellan* (1844) 6 D. 1088; *Gillespie* v. *McLinnachie and Ellis* (1894) 2 S.L.T. 291; *Craig* v. *Hogg* (1896) 24 R. 6; *Mackay* v. *Parish Council of Resolis* (1899) 1 F. 521; *Hardie* v. *Brown, Barker & Bell* (1907) 15 S.L.T. 539; *Aitchison* v. *McDonald*, 1911 S.C. 174; *Paterson* v. *Sc. Insurance Commrs.*, 1915 2 S.L.T. 178; *Dunbar* v. *Mitchell*, 1928 S.L.T. 225.

7 *Dick* v. *Morrison* (1845) 8 D. 1; *Wilson* v. *Stronach* (1862) 24 D. 271; *Haughhead Coal Co.* v. *Gallacher* (1903) 11 S.L.T. 156.

8 *Paul* v. *Henderson* (1867) 5 M. 1120; *Gibb* v. *Edinburgh Brewery Co.* (1873) 11 M. 705; *MacRobbie* v. *McLellan's Trs.* (1891) 18 R. 470.

9 cf. *Middleton* v. *Leslie* (1892) 19 R. 801; *McKellar* v. *Dallas, Ltd.*, 1928 S.C. 503.

10 *Oakeley* v. *Campbell* (1867) 6 M. 12; *Henderson* v. *Rollo* (1871) 10 M. 104; *McLintock* v. *Prinzen and Van Glabbeek* (1902) 4 F. 948.

11 But not competent if granted in favour of a moneylender: Moneylenders Act, 1927, S. 18(h); nor competent on a cheque: *Glickman* v. *Linda*, 1950 S.C. 18; nor against a party not subject to the Scottish court's jurisdiction: *Charteris* v. *Clydesdale Banking Co.* (1882) 19 S.L.R. 602; *Davis* v. *Cadman* (1897) 24 R. 297.

12 *Goodwin* v. *Industrial and General Trust* (1890) 18 R. 193; *Kechans* v. *Barr* (1893) 21 R. 75; *Neill* v. *Dobson, Molle & Co.* (1902) 4 F. 625.

13 *Simpson* v. *Taylor* (1874) 2 R. 75; *Simpson* v. *Brown* (1888) 15 R. 716; *Kinloch, Campbell & Co.* v. *Cowan* (1890) 27 S.L.R. 870; *Renwick* v. *Stamford, Spalding & Boston Banking Co.* (1891) 19 R. 163.

Suspension of decrees

Suspension may also be invoked in some cases as a form of review of a judgment, provided it has not been implemented or acquiesced in.[1] In the Court of Session suspension of decrees *in foro* is incompetent,[2] but diligence on such a decree may be suspended if the debt has been consigned or paid, or the diligence been irregular,[3] and an extracted decree in absence may be suspended[4] where extract has been issued or the period for appeal has expired.[5] Suspension of a decree in absence may be incompetent, unless on grounds of essential nullity.[6]

Suspension of a decree of the Small Debt Court is excluded,[7] save in cases of essential illegality in procedure.[8]

INTERDICT

Interdict is a remedy by decree of court, either against a wrong in course of being done or against an apprehended violation of a party's rights, only to be awarded on evidence of the wrong or on reasonable grounds of apprehension that such violation is intended.[9] It proceeds on the basis that prevention is better than cure. The conduct must amount to some appreciable wrong or harm; interdict is inappropriate to a case of negligible or trivial harm.[10] Actual injury need not be proved so long as reasonable grounds for apprehension of injury are set out.[11] It is also a remedy incompetent to a statutory body or board empowered to utilise statutory remedies.[12]

1 *Macintosh* v. *Robertson* (1830) 9 S. 75; *Ewing* v. *Cheape* (1835) 13 S. 515; *Wotherspoon* v. *Winning* (1849) 11 D. 371.

2 *Young* v. *List and McHardie* (1862) 24 D. 587; *Maule* v. *Tainsh* (1878) 6 R. 44; but contrast *McCarroll* v. *McKinstery*, 1923 S.C. 94.

3 Stair I, 18, 4; Ersk. III, 4, 5; *Paul* v. *Henderson* (1867) 5 M. 1121.

4 Court of Session (No. 1) Act, 1838, S. 5; see also *Lowson* v. *Cooper* (1861) 23 D. 1089.

5 Ibid., S. 4; see also *Fletcher* v. *Davidson* (1874) 2 R. 71; *Paul* v. *Henderson* (1867) 5 M. 1120; *Campbell's Trs.* v. *O'Neill*, 1911 S.C. 188; *Macdonald* v. *Denoon*, 1928 S.L.T. 439.

6 *Aitchison* v. *McDonald*, 1911 S.C. 174; *Christie Bros.* v. *Remington Typewriting Co.*, 1912 1 S.L.T. 123.

7 Small Debt Act, 1837, S. 30.

8 *Manson* v. *Smith* (1871) 9 M. 492; *Shiell* v. *Mossman* (1872) 10 M. 58; *Brown* v. *Rodger* (1884) 12 R. 340; *Gray* v. *Smart* (1892) 19 R. 692.

9 *Hay's Trs.* v. *Young* (1877) 4 R. 398; *Macleod* v. *Davidson* (1886) 14 R. 92.

10 *Steuart* v. *Stephen* (1877) 4 R. 875; *Winans* v. *Macrae* (1885) 12 R. 1051.

11 *King* v. *Hamilton* (1844) 6 D. 399; *Hoyle* v. *Shaws Water Co.* (1854) 17 D. 83; *Singer Mfg. Co.* v. *Kimball & Morton* (1873) 11 M. 267; contrast *Hood* v. *Traill* (1884) 12 R. 362.

12 *Tay District Fishery Board* v. *Robertson* (1888) 15 R. 40; *Buckhaven & Methil Mags.* v. *Wemyss Coal Co.*, 1932 S.C. 201; cf. *Inst. of Patent Agents* v. *Lockwood* (1894) 21 R. (H.L.) 61; *Scottish Milk Marketing Board* v. *Paris*, 1935 S.C. 287, 296.

Conclusions for interdict must be precise and the interdict, if granted, also precise, leaving the defender in no doubt as to what he may not do.[1] If interdict cannot be granted in accordance with the prayer of the petition it cannot be granted at all.

Interdict is incompetent against a breach of duty completed.[2]

Interdict is an equitable remedy[3] and the court is never bound to grant it unless certain that the result of the decision will not be to cause another wrong,[4] but this consideration is rarely important in cases of enforcing a contractual undertaking.[5] The court may decline to grant interdict and make declaratory findings.[6]

By the Court of Session Act, 1868, S. 89, where the respondent in an application has, before or after the institution thereof, done any act which the court might have prevented by interdict, the court may in the interdict proceedings ordain the respondent to perform any act which may be necessary for reinstating the complainer in his possessory right or for granting specific relief against the illegal act complained of.[7]

Interdict on caution

Interdict is sometimes granted only if caution is found for loss which may be caused to the respondent in the event that the interdict is ultimately found unjustifiable.[8] In this event the interdict is ineffectual until caution is found.[9] Similarly it may be refused only on caution being found by the respondent for any damage done to the complainer.[10]

Interim and perpetual interdict

Interdict may be granted *ad interim*, to preserve the *status quo* or prevent any further action of the kind complained of, pending

[1] *Kelso School Board* v. *Hunter* (1874) 2 R. 228; *Cairns* v. *Lee* (1892) 20 R. 16; *Perth General Station Cttee.* v. *Ross* (1896) 23 R. 885; modified 24 R. (H.L.) 44.

[2] *Hoyle* v. *Shaws Water Co.* (1854) 17 D. 83; *Lawson's Trs.* v. *Cramond* (1863) 3 M. 53; *Glen* v. *Caledonian Ry.* (1868) 6 M. 797; *Buchanan* v. *Glasgow Waterworks Commrs.* (1869) 7 M. 853; *Begg* v. *Jack* (1874) 1 R. 366.

[3] *Ben Nevis Distillery* v. *British Aluminium Co.*, 1948 S.C. 592.

[4] *Maclure* v. *M.*, 1911 S.C. 200, 206.

[5] *Bank of Scotland* v. *Stewart* (1891) 18 R. 957; cf. *Campbell* v. *Watt* (1795) Hume 788; *Davie* v. *Stark* (1876) 3 R. 1114.

[6] *Perth General Station Cttee.* v. *Ross* (1897) 24 R. (H.L.) 44.

[7] *Incandescent Gas Light Co.* v. *McCulloch* (1897) 5 S.L.T. 190; *Clippens Oil Co.* v. *Edinburgh and District Water Trs.* (1897) 25 R. 370; *Heriot's Trust* v. *Carter* (1903) 10 S.L.T. 514; *Caledonian Ry.* v. *G.S.W. Ry.*, 1903 11 S.L.T. 510.

[8] e.g. *Williams* v. *Fairbairn* (1899) 1 F. 944.

[9] *Wilson* v. *Gilchrist* (1900) 2 F. 391.

[10] *Caledonian Ry.* v. *Buchanan* (1855) 17 D. 996; *Ferguson* v. *D. Sutherland* (1866) 2 S.L.R. 38; *Graham* v. *D. Hamilton* (1868) 6 M. 965; *Fergusson-Buchanan* v. *Dunbartonshire C.C.*, 1923 S.C. 42; cf. *Bernard* v. *B.* (1893) 1 S.L.T. 29; *Incandescent Gas Light Co.* v. *McCulloch* (1897) 5 S.L.T. 190.

the elucidation of the parties' rights and duties.[1] The grant or refusal of interim interdict is very much a matter of judicial discretion, frequently to be exercised in the light of a *prima facie* view of the facts and of an *ex parte* application. The court has to consider the apparent cogency of the need for interim interdict,[2] the uncertainty of the respondent's right,[3] the balance of convenience,[4] and the public interest.[5]

The court is, however, hesitant by interdict to interfere with the operation of a statutory scheme,[6] and will not normally grant interim interdict where the complainer could have availed himself of some other remedy or mode of appeal.[7]

If granted,[8] interim interdict remains in force until recalled and does not lapse automatically when answers are lodged,[9] or an appeal is lodged.[10] It may be recalled after report as to remedial action taken.[11] Otherwise any further action of the kind complained of may not be taken, but the *status quo* maintained.[12]

If granted, interim interdict is granted *periculo petentis* and the complainer is liable for having wrongfully stopped the respondent's actings if in the end interdict is not made perpetual.[13]

Interdict against exercise of statutory duties and powers

The court cannot interdict the doing of anything in implement of statutory duty to do so, nor anything empowered by statute if done within the terms of the authority granted,[14] but may interdict actings authorised by statute if done without taking all reasonable precautions to avoid harm.[15]

[1] *Innes* v. *I.* (1829) 7 S. 762; cf. *Brodie* v. *E. Dalhousie's Trs.* (1895) 3 S.L.T. 150; *Innes* v. *Kirkcaldy Mags.*, 1963 S.L.T. 325.

[2] *Rankin* v. *McLachlan* (1864) 3 M. 128.

[3] *Edinburgh Mags.* v. *Edinburgh, Leith & Granton Ry.* (1847) 19 S. Jur. 421.

[4] *Baird* v. *Monkland Iron Co.* (1862) 24 D. 1418, 1425; cf. *Lindsay* v. *Robertson* (1867) 5 M. 864, 866; *Tennant* v. *Thomson* (1870) 8 S.L.R. 15.

[5] *Johnston* v. *Dumfriesshire Road Trs.* (1867) 5 M. 1127; *Fergusson-Buchanan* v. *Dunbartonshire C.C.*, 1924 S.C. 42; *Scottish Milk Marketing Board* v. *Paris*, 1935 S.C. 287; cf. *Ben Nevis Distillery* v. *British Aluminium Co.*, 1948 S.C. 592.

[6] *Scottish Milk Board*, *supra*; *Anderson* v. *Kirkintilloch Mags.*, 1948 S.C. 27.

[7] *Cumming* v. *Inverness Mags.*, 1953 S.C. 1; contrast *Innes* v. *Kirkcaldy Mags.*, 1963 S.L.T. 325.

[8] It is effective once the interlocutor has been signed: *Stent* v. *Edinburgh P.F.* (1845) 17 Sc. Jur. 535.

[9] *Clippens Oil Co.* v. *Edinburgh Water Trs.* (1906) 8 F. 731, 748; *Home Drummond* v. *McLachlan*, 1908 S.C. 12.

[10] *Edwards* v. *Begbie* (1847) 9 D. 1384, 1388.

[11] *Crawford* v. *Paisley Mags.* (1870) 8 M. 693. Recall may be from a future date: *Dundee Gas Light Co.* v. *Dundee New Gas Light Co.* (1844) 7 D. 109.

[12] cf. *Henderson* v. *Maclellan* (1874) 1 R. 920.

[13] *Fife* v. *Orr* (1895) 23 R. 8.

[14] *Buchanan* v. *Glasgow Waterworks Commrs.* (1869) 7 M. 853.

[15] *Gillespie* v. *Lucas & Aird* (1893) 20 R. 1035.

Breach of contract

Interdict is competent to enforce any negative contractual undertaking, such as a contractual stipulation restrictive of future employment[1] or business,[2] or to stop any conduct in breach of an implied term of, or inconsistent with the good faith of, the contract.[3]

It is doubtful if a positive undertaking can be enforced by interdict against conduct inconsistent therewith, but probably this is not competent in any case where the court would refuse a decree for specific implement of the contract.[4]

Interdict is not excluded by a provision in the contract for a penalty for contravention, the provision thereof inferring no licence to contravene on payment.[5]

Delict

Interdict is also competent against any delict threatened,[6] or being committed,[7] such as nuisance.[8] Previous commission of the same delict is good evidence of the reasonableness of apprehension that a particular delict will be committed.[9] Intention to commit delict cannot, however, be inferred from the mere assertion of a claim of legal right to do what is objected to, and interdict is inappropriate in such a case.[10] Nor is interdict competent where there is no reasonable apprehension that the delict will be repeated or continued,[11] nor where the delict is past and completed,[11] nor where the conduct objected to does not amount to a wrong to the complainer.[12]

Obligations in regard to heritage

Actings in contravention of the conditions of a feu-contract[13] or lease may be interdicted.

1 *Berlitz School* v. *Duchene* (1903) 6 F. 181.

2 *Davie* v. *Stark* (1876) 3 R. 1114; *Stewart* v. *S.* (1899) 1 F. 1158; *B.M.T.A.* v. *Gray*, 1951 S.C. 586.

3 cf. *Hivac* v. *Park Royal Scientific Instruments, Ltd.* [1946] Ch. 169.

4 cf. *Cormack* v. *Keith & Murray* (1893) 20 R. 977; *Murray* v. *Dunbarton C.C.*, 1935 S.L.T. 239.

5 Ersk. III, 3, 86; Bell, *Prin.* §34; *Gold* v. *Houldsworth* (1870) 8 M. 1006; *Dalrymple* v. *Herdman* (1878) 5 R. 847.

6 *Hay's Tr.* v. *Young* (1877) 4 R. 398; *Martin* v. *Nisbet* (1893) 1 S.L.T. 371; *Brocket Estates* v. *McPhee*, 1949 S.L.T. (Notes) 36; *Inverurie Mags.* v. *Sorrie*, 1956 S.C. 175.

7 *Inverurie Mags., supra.*

8 *Inglis* v. *Shotts Iron Co.* (1881) 8 R. 1006; (1882) 9 R. (H.L.) 78; *Fleming* v. *Hislop* (1886) 13 R. (H.L.) 45; *Ben Nevis Distillery* v. *N.B. Aluminium Co.*, 1948 S.C. 592.

9 *Inverurie Mags., supra.*

10 *Warrand* v. *Watson* (1905) 8 F. 253, 1098; *Inverurie Mags.* v. *Sorrie*, 1956 S.C. 175.

11 *Hay's Trs.* v. *Young* (1877) 4 R. 398.

12 *Steuart* v. *Stephen* (1877) 4 R. 873.

13 *Naismith* v. *Cairnduff* (1876) 3 R. 863.

Regulation of possession of heritage

Interdict is commonly used to regulate possession of heritage where the complainer shows title and possession, and interference with that possession, or, as against a competing title, possession for seven years.[1] The possession relied on must not be attributable to force, illegality or permission; it must be *nec vi, nec clam, nec precario*.[2]

Thus interdict may be granted to protect an exclusive right of possession and prevent trespass,[3] to prevent removal of a weir in a river erected more than seven years earlier,[4] to prevent interference with passage along an alleged right of way pending a declarator that there is no such right.[5]

So too a person having title to possess, as owner, liferenter, tenant, bondholder in possession, or party in right of a servitude, may by interdict seek to maintain or recover his possession. The title must be one to which possession can be imputed,[6] and it is unavailing if it excludes or is inconsistent with the possessory right claimed.[7]

The effect of a possessory judgment is to secure the possessor in his right until his title be reduced or avoided; till then he has the rights of a *bona fide possessor*.[8]

Non-compliance with interdict

If interdict is granted but not obeyed, the complainer may bring a petition and complaint, and the court, if it finds the non-compliance proved, may deal with the party in breach by way of censure, fine,[9] imprisonment,[10] or otherwise.

POSSESSION OF PROPERTY

A person entitled to the possession of heritable property may seek to obtain or recover it from those in possession by action of removing or of ejection.[11] Interdict is inappropriate to dispossess

[1] Ersk. II, 1, 15; *Colquhoun* v. *Paton* (1859) 21 D. 996, 1001; cf. *Maxwell* v. *G.S.W. Ry.* (1866) 4 M. 447, 456.

[2] *McKerron* v. *Gordon* (1876) 3 R. 429, 433–4.

[3] *Colquhoun, supra.*

[4] *Maxwell, supra.*

[5] *McKerron, supra,* 437.

[6] *Calder* v. *Adam* (1870) 8 M. 645, 647; *McKerron* v. *Gordon* (1876) 3 R. 429, 434.

[7] *Bridges* v. *Elder* (1822) 1 S. 373; see also *Warrand* v. *Watson* (1905) 8 F. 253.

[8] *Irvine* v. *Robertson* (1873) 11 M. 298; *Hagart* v. *Fyfe* (1870) 9 M. 127.

[9] *Kelso School Board* v. *Hunter* (1874) 2 R. 228, 232; *Johnson* v. *Grant,* 1923 S.L.T. 501.

[10] *Kelso, supra.*

[11] As to these see Ch. 88, *supra.*

bankrupt tenants,[1] but is competent against ejected tenants or squatters who threaten to take possession of or to return to subjects from which they have been ejected.[2]

SPECIFIC IMPLEMENT

It is a general rule of Scots law that a person who is entitled by contract to performance may obtain decree requiring the defender specifically to implement his undertaking.[3] A decree *ad factum praestandum*, once extracted, warrants imprisonment of the party wilfully failing to implement it.[4] In view of the stringency of this sanction it is essential that a conclusion for this decree, and any decree granted, be clearly and precisely framed.[5]

It is always in the discretion of the court to grant or refuse specific implement according as they deem it proper or not in the circumstances,[6] and in some circumstances the courts will normally not grant decree of specific implement. These are:

(1) where the obligation is to pay money, because imprisonment for civil debt has, in general, been abolished,[7] though it remains competent to imprison for failure to consign money in court,[8] and a contract to take and pay for debentures in a company is specifically enforceable.[9]

(2) where performance is impossible, even though by reason of the defender's fault;[10]

1 *Borrows* v. *Colquhoun* (1852) 14 D. 791; revd. (1854) 1 Macq. 691; *Rankin* v. *McLachlan* (1864) 3 M. 128; *Johnston* v. *Thomson* (1897) 4 R. 868.

2 *Baillie* v. *Mackintosh* (1882) 19 S.L.R. 352; *Boswell's Trs.* v. *Pearson* (1886) 24 S.L.R. 32.

3 Stair I, 17, 16; Bell, *Prin.* §29; *Seaforth's Trs.* v. *Macaulay* (1844) 7 D. 180; *McArthur* v. *Lawson* (1877) 4 R. 1134; *Hendry* v. *Marshall* (1878) 5 R. 687; *Stewart* v. *Kennedy* (1890) 17 R. (H.L.) 1; cf. *Beardmore* v. *Barry*, 1928 S.C. 101.

4 *Wilson* v. *McKellar* (1896) 24 R. 254; Law Reform (Misc. Prov.) (Sc.) Act, 1940, S. 1.

5 *Middleton* v. *Leslie* (1892) 19 R. 801.

6 *Moore* v. *Paterson* (1881) 9 R. 337; *Grahame* v. *Kirkcaldy Mags.* (1882) 9 R. (H.L.) 91; *Aurdal* v. *Estrella*, 1916 S.C. 882.

7 Debtors (Sc.) Act, 1880, S. 4. There are exceptions for (1) (as amended by Crown Proceedings Act, 1947, S. 49) death duties and purchase tax, fines or penalties due to Her Majesty, and rates and assessments; (2) sums decerned for aliment.

8 *Mackenzie* v. *Balerno Paper Mill Co.* (1883) 10 R. 1147.

9 Companies Act, 1948, S. 92; cf. *Beardmore* v. *Barry*, 1928 S.C. (H.L.) 47.

10 *Petrie* v. *Forsyth* (1874) 2 R. 214; *Macarthur* v. *Lawson* (1877) 4 R. 1134; *Waterson* v. *Stewart* (1881) 9 R. 155; *Sinclair* v. *Caithness Flagstone Co.* (1898) 25 R. 703; *Faill* v. *Wilson* (1899) 36 S.L.R. 941; *Rudman* v. *Jay*, 1908 S.C. 552; *D. Portland* v. *Wood's Trs.*, 1926 S.C. 640. But a charge on such a decree does not become incompetent merely because delayed till performance is impossible: see *McKellar* v. *Dallas's, Ltd.*, 1928 S.C. 503; cf. also *Leitch* v. *Edinburgh Ice Co.* (1900) 2 F. 904; *Rodger (Builders) Ltd.* v. *Fawdry*, 1950 S.C. 483.

(3) where enforcement of the decree would be impossible;[1]

(4) where the grant of the remedy would cause exceptional hardship.[2]

But specific implement is competent in the case of a contract to sell a specific thing,[3] or a specific piece of land,[4] to build houses of a particular class,[5] to rebuild premises,[6] to put a tenant in possession of subjects let,[7] to subscribe for shares in a company,[8] to enter into and remain in possession of subjects leased,[9] and to furnish and heat, though not to carry on a stated business in, a shop.[10]

Where a defender refuses to implement a contract by signing and delivering a deed, such as a disposition of heritage, the court may authorise a clerk of court to sign it in his stead.[11]

An alternative conclusion for damages, failing decree for specific implement, is commonly annexed. The defender's consent to decree for damages passing does not bar the pursuer's claim to decree for implement.[12]

Orders to restore possession or to implement statutory duty

By the Court of Session Act, 1868, S. 91, the court may order the restoration of possession of any real or personal property, of the possession of which the petitioner has been violently or fraudulently deprived, and also the specific performance of any statutory duty, under such conditions and penalties (including fine and imprisonment, where consistent with the statute) in the event of the order not being implemented, as seem proper to the

1 *Gall* v. *Loyal Glenbogie Lodge of Oddfellows* (1900) 2 F. 1187; Crown Proceedings Act, 1947, S. 21; see also *Delaney* v. *Edinburgh Children's Refuge* (1889) 16 R. 753; (1891) 19 R. 8; (1893) 20 R. 506; *Whyte* v. *W.*, 1913 2 S.L.T. 85.

2 *Jack* v. *Begg* (1875) 3 R. 35; *Moore* v. *Paterson* (1881) 9 R. 337; *Grahame* v. *Kirkcaldy Mags.* (1882) 9 R. (H.L.) 91; *Winans* v. *Mackenzie* (1883) 10 R. 941; *Wilson* v. *Pottinger*, 1908 S.C. 580.

3 *Sutherland* v. *Montrose Shipbuilding Co.* (1860) 22 D. 665, 671; *Purves* v. *Brock* (1867) 5 M. 1003; *Henry* v. *Morrison* (1881) 8 R. 692; Sale of Goods Act, 1893, S. 52. It is unlikely to be granted in the case of sale of a generic thing: *Sutherland*, *supra*; *Davidson* v. *Macpherson* (1889) 30 S.L.R. 2; *Union Electric Co.* v. *Holman*, 1913 S.C. 954.

4 *Stewart* v. *Kennedy* (1890) 17 R. (H.L.) 1; *Petrie* v. *Forsyth* (1874) 2 R. 214.

5 *Middleton* v. *Leslie* (1892) 19 R. 801; *McKellar* v. *Dallas's Ltd.*, 1928 S.C. 503.

6 *Marshall* v. *Callander Hydro Co.* (1897) 24 R. 712.

7 *Seaforth's Trs.* v. *Macaulay* (1844) 7 D. 180.

8 *Beardmore* v. *Barry*, 1928 S.C. (H.L.) 47.

9 *Robertson* v. *Cockburn* (1875) 3 R. 21.

10 *Whitelaw* v. *Fulton* (1871) 10 M. 27.

11 *Mackay* v. *Campbell*, 1966 S.L.T. 329; 1967 S.L.T. 337.

12 *Mackay* v. *Campbell*, 1967 S.L.T. 337.

court.[1] Such a decree is incompetent against a Minister of the Crown.[2]

DEBT

A claim of debt arises where there is delay or failure to pay a liquid sum of money due under a contract, express or implied, such as money borrowed, money due as the price or otherwise as payment for performance of a contract,[3] money due as overpaid or paid for an object which has failed, money due as legal rights or a share of an estate or a legacy. Thus in a sale of goods an action for the price may be brought if the property has passed and the buyer wrongfully neglects or refuses to pay according to the terms of the contract, or if the price is payable on a day certain irrespective of delivery, even though the property has not passed and the goods not been appropriated to the contract.[4]

In the special cases of a heritable creditor, or owner of a ground annual, seeking to enforce his right to exact from the tenants payment of their rents the action appropriate is an action of maills and duties.[5]

The right to claim arises as soon as the debt has become due for payment, which time may be fixed by the contract or be settled by legal implication. Thus legacies are not payable until six months after death,[6] and the date for repayment of a loan may be fixed by reference to a date or the happening of an uncertain event.

INTEREST

A claim for interest is the proper remedy for the improper withholding, or undue delay in the payment, of money,[7] and is frequently conjoined with a claim of debt. Interest may be

[1] See *Adamson* v. *Edinburgh Street Tramways Co.* (1872) 10 M. 533; *Annan* v. *Leith Licensing Authy.* (1901) 9 S.L.T. 63; *Sons of Temperance Friendly Socy.*, 1926 S.C. 418; *Langlands* v. *Manson*, 1962 S.C. 493; cf. *Macandrew*, 1925 S.L.T. 78; see also *Carlton Hotel Co.* v. *L.A.*, 1921 S.C. 237; *Kelso Mags.* v. *Alexander*, 1939 S.C. 78.

[2] Crown Proceedings Act, 1947, S. 21; in lieu the court may declare the rights of parties.

[3] *White & Carter (Councils)* v. *McGregor*, 1962 S.C. (H.L.) 1.

[4] Sale of Goods Act, 1893, S. 49.

[5] *Scottish Heritable Security Co.* v. *Allan Campbell & Co.* (1876) 3 R. 333; *Somerville* v. *Johnston* (1899) 1 F. 726.

[6] Ersk. III, 9, 43; *Barlass* v. *B's Trs.*, 1916 S.C. 741.

[7] Bell, *Comm.* I, 690; *Prin.* §32; *Carmichael* v. *Caledonian Ry.* (1870) 8 M. (H.L.) 119, 131; *Durie's Trs.* v. *Ayton* (1894) 22 R. 34, 38; *Roissard de Bellet* v. *Scott's Trs.* (1897) 24 R. 861; *Greenock Harbour Trs.* v. *G.S.W. Ry.*, 1919 S.C. (H.L.) 49.

expressly stipulated for, and if stipulated for from a stated date this may imply that it is not earlier due.[1] In other cases it depends very much on the circumstances of each case whether interest is due by legal implication.[2]

When interest normally due by agreement

Interest is normally due by express agreement on bonds,[3] I.O.U.'s,[4] and on sums payable by instalments,[5] in which cases, failing express provision, it is exigible only from the date of citation in an action for repayment,[4] but it may be stipulated for in any agreement.

When interest due by statute

It is due by statute on bills and promissory notes.[6]

When interest impliedly due

It is due by legal implication, unless excluded, on loans of money,[7] advances of money,[8] cash balances in the hands of an agent,[9] on the price of goods from the date when they were tendered or the due date of payment,[10] on accounts for goods supplied, or services rendered,[11] on the price of heritage sold, from the date when possession is taken,[12] till payment or consignation to await settlement,[13] on *jus relictae*,[14] *jus relicti*, or

[1] *Baird's Trs.* v. *B.* (1877) 4 R. 1005.

[2] *Blair's Trs.* v. *Payne* (1884) 12 R. 104.

[3] *Blair's Trs., supra*; *Forbes* v. *Welsh and Forbes* (1894) 21 R. 630; *Gatty* v. *Maclaine*, 1921 S.C. (H.L.) 1.

[4] *Winestone* v. *Wolifson*, 1954 S.C. 77.

[5] *Baird's Trs.* v. *B.* (1877) 4 R. 1005; *Ewing & Co.* v. *E.* (1882) 10 R. (H.L.) 1; contrast *McArthur* v. *Scott* (1898) 6 S.L.T. 162.

[6] Bills of Exchange Act, 1882, Ss. 9, 57.

[7] *Garthland's Trs.* v. *McDowall*, 26 May 1820, F.C.; *Cunninghame* v. *Boswell* (1868) 6 M. 890; *Blair's Trs., supra*; *Galashiels Provident Bldg. Socy.* v. *Newlands* (1893) 20 R. 821; *Hope Johnstone* v. *Cornwall* (1895) 22 R. 314; *United Collieries* v. *L.A.*, 1950 S.C. 458; but the implication was displaced in the circumstances in *Christie* v. *Matheson* (1871) 10 M. 9; *Smellies' Exrx.* v. *S.*, 1933 S.C. 725; cf. *Shaw's Trs.* v. *S.* (1870) 8 M. 419.

[8] *Hill* v. *Gilroy* (1821) 1 S. 33; *Findlay, Bannatyne & Co.'s Assignee* v. *Donaldson* (1864) 2 M. (H.L.) 86; *Graham's Exors.* v. *Fletcher's Exors.* (1870) 9 M. 298; *Forbes* v. *F.* (1867) 8 M. 85; *Christie* v. *Matheson* (1871) 10 M. 9; *Blair's Trs., supra.*

[9] *Mill's J.F.* (1904) 10 S.L.T. 444; *Jopp* v. *Johnston's Trs.* (1905) 13 S.L.T. 522.

[10] Bell, *Comm*, I, 692; *Prin.* §32; Sale of Goods Act, 1893, Ss. 49(3), 54, 61(2).

[11] *Blair's Trs., supra*; *Bunten* v. *Hart* (1902) 9 S.L.T. 476; *Somervell's Trs.* v. *Edinburgh Life Assce. Co.*, 1911 S.C. 1069.

[12] Ersk. III, 3, 79; Bell, *Comm.* I, 693; Bell, *Convg.* II, 724; *Wallace* v. *Oswald* (1825) 3 S. 525; *Dickson* v. *Munro* (1855) 17 D. 524; *W. Highland Ry.* v. *Place* (1894) 21 R. 576; *Greenock Harbour Trs.* v. *G.S.W. Ry.*, 1909 S.C. 49.

[13] *Traill* v. *Connon* (1877) 5 R. 25; *Grandison's Trs.* v. *Jardine* (1895) 22 R. 925; *Prestwick Cinema Co.* v. *Gardiner*, 1951 S.C. 98.

[14] *Henderson* v. *H's Trs.*, 1916 2 S.L.T. 292; *Reid* v. *R's Trs.*, 1927 S.L.T. 18.

legitim,[1] on legacies from the date of death[2] (though beneficiaries who have received advances to account of legal rights or share in an estate may be liable for interest thereon),[3] on trust funds lost or improperly paid away,[4] or left uninvested,[5] on money paid in error and recovered.[6]

Interest on damages

Interest runs *ex lege* on a sum of damages from the date of decree,[7] and is usually concluded for; if not, it runs only from the affirmance of the decree, if reclaimed.[8] It may be awarded from only a later date, such as the date when a jury verdict would normally have been applied,[9] or may be refused.[10]

The Interest on Damages (Sc.) Act, 1958, empowers the court to award interest on damages from an earlier date, not earlier than the date the action was commenced, at the rate specified in the interlocutor, till decree. The discretion to award must be exercised in a selective and discriminating manner,[11] and an award from a date earlier than the decree can be allowed only on damages for loss suffered before the decree where such loss could be definitely ascertained.[11]

1 *McMurray* v. *McM's Trs.* (1852) 14 D. 1048; *Gilchrist* v. *G's Trs.* (1889) 16 R. 1118; *Bishop's Trs.* v. *B.* (1894) 21 R. 728; *Mason* v. *Mitchell* (1895) 3 S.L.T. 3; *Ross* v. *R.* (1896) 23 R. 802; *Grant* v. *G's Trs.* (1898) 25 R. 948; *Smith's Trs.* v. *S.*, 1912 1 S.L.T. 484; *Henderson* v. *H's Trs.*, 1916 2 S.L.T. 292; *Duncan* v. *Crichton's Trs.*, 1917 S.C. 728; *Kearon* v. *Thomson's Trs.*, 1949 S.C. 287.

2 *Kilpatrick* v. *Bedford* (1878) 6 R. (H.L.) 4; *Inglis's Trs.* v. *Breen* (1891) 18 R. 487; *McLean's Trs.* v. *McL.* (1891) 18 R 892; *Campbell's Exor.* v. *C's Trs.* (1898) 25 R. 687; *May's Trs.* v. *Paul* (1900) 2 F. 657; *Waddell's Trs.* v. *Crawford*, 1926 S.C. 654.

3 *Baird's Trs.* v. *Duncanson* (1892) 19 R. 1045; *Matthew's Trs.* v. *M.* (1905) 13 S.L.T. 470; *Gilmour's Trs.* v. *G.*, 1922 S.C. 753.

4 *Heritable Securities Inv. Assoc.* v. *Miller's Trs.* (1893) 20 R. 675; *Melville* v. *Noble's Trs.* (1896) 24 R. 243; *Ferrie's Curator* (1897) 5 S.L.T. 62; *Lees's Tr.* v. *Dun*, 1913 S.C. (H.L.) 12; cf. *Mills* v. *Brown's Trs.* (1901) 3 F. 1012.

5 *Malcolm's Exors.* v. *M.* (1869) 8 M. 272; *Graham's Trs.* v. *G.* (1870) 8 S.L.R. 107; *Morrison* v. *Dryden* (1890) 17 R. 704; *Bryson* v. *B's Trs.* (1907) 14 S.L.T. 750; *Miller's Exrx.* v. *M's Trs.*, 1922 S.C. 150.

6 *Gwyder* v. *L.A.* (1894) 2 S.L.T. 280.

7 *Dalmahoy* v. *Brechin Mags.* (1859) 21 D. 210; *Taylor* v. *Macfarlane* (1868) 5 S.L.R. 797; *Flensburg S.S. Co.* v. *Seligmann* (1871) 9 M. 1011; *Martin* v. *Robertson, Ferguson & Co.* (1872) 10 M. 949.

8 *Rogers* v. *Cochrane*, 1910 S.C. 1; *McGovern* v. *Nimmo*, 1938 S.C. (H.L.) 18; *McCormack* v. *N.C.B.*, 1957 S.C. 277.

9 *Clancy* v. *Dixon's Ironworks*, 1955 S.C. 17.

10 *Kolbin* v. *Kinnear*, 1931 S.C. (H.L.) 128.

11 *Macrae* v. *Read and Mallik, Ltd.*, 1961 S.C. 68; see also *Killah* v. *Aberdeen Milk Marketing Board*, 1961 S.L.T. 232; *Dempster* v. *Motherwell Bridge Co.*, 1964 S.C. 308.

When interest due only by stipulation

Interest does not run, unless expressly stipulated for, on arrears of feuduties,[1] ground annuals,[2] rents,[3] a tradesman's current account,[4] charges for professional services.[5]

Rate of interest

There is no legal rate of interest,[6] and the rate awarded varies according to circumstances, though 5% has commonly been awarded as a penal rate.

Compound interest, unless expressly stipulated for,[7] is only exceptionally allowed, and usually only as a penalty for breach of duty.[8]

RESCISSION OF CONTRACT

Rescission is not a judicial remedy but the act of a party who claims to be entitled to rescind or set aside a contract or undertaking as not binding.[9] But the assistance of the court is frequently necessary to determine whether the party is entitled to rescind or not, or to set aside a formal document,[9] or to obtain restitution of property handed over by him pursuant to that transaction. Rescission is effected by communicating clearly to the other party the decision to treat the contract as at an end. If, failing such intimation, the other party is allowed to act on the assumption that the contract still stands, the innocent party may be held barred.[10]

[1] Bell, *Comm.* I, 691; *Prin.* §32; *Tweeddale's Trs.* v. *Haddington* (1880) 7 R. 620; *Blair's Trs., supra*; *Maxwell's Trs.* v. *Bothwell School Board* (1893) 20 R. 958.

[2] *Moncreiff* v. *L. Dundas* (1835) 14 S. 61.

[3] *Moncreiff, supra*; *Advocate General* v. *Sinclair's Trs.* (1855) 17 D. 290; *Stirling and Dunfermline Ry.* v. *Edinburgh and Glasgow Ry.* (1857) 19 D. 598; *Blair's Trs., supra.*

[4] *Cardno & Darling* v. *Steuart* (1869) 7 M. 1026.

[5] *Bunten* v. *Hart* (1902) 9 S.L.T. 476; *Somervell's Tr.* v. *Edinburgh Life Assce. Co.*, 1911 S.C. 1069; it is otherwise with outlays: *Graham's Exors.* v. *Fletcher's Exors.* (1870) 9 M. 298; *Blair's Trs., supra.*

[6] *Greenock Harbour Trs.* v. *G.S.W. Ry.*, 1909 S.C. (H.L.) 49; *Waddell's Trs.* v. *Crawford*, 1926 S.C. 654; *Kearon* v. *Thomson's Trs.*, 1949 S.C. 287; *Prestwick Cinema Co.* v. *Gardiner*, 1951 S.C. 98. For limits on interest rate see Moneylenders Act, 1927, S. 7.

[7] *Gilmour* v. *Bank of Scotland* (1880) 7 R. 734; *Commercial Bank* v. *Pattison's Trs.* (1891) 18 R. 476.

[8] Ersk. III, 3, 81; Bell, *Comm.* I, 695; *Prin.* §32; *Maclean* v. *Campbell* (1856) 18 D. 609; *Douglas* v. *D's Trs.* (1867) 5 M. 827; *Graham's Exors.* v. *Fletcher's Exors.* (1870) 9 M. 298.

[9] *Westville S.S. Co.* v. *Abram S.S. Co.*, 1923 S.C. (H.L.) 68.

[10] *Dunford & Elliot* v. *Macleod* (1902) 4 F. 912; *Sanderson* v. *Armour*, 1922 S.C. (H.L.) 117.

To rescind or not is in the option of the innocent party, provided that the other party has committed a material breach of the contract; if the breach was in the circumstances immaterial he may not rescind but may only claim damages.[1] He cannot be forced to rescind and, where performance on his part alone is required to complete the contract, may elect to perform the contract and claim the contract price.[2]

Where the right arises

The right to rescind arises where the party discovers that he has been induced to enter into the contract by the misrepresentations, innocent or fraudulent, of the other party,[3] where he discovers that he has been induced to contract by force and fear, facility and circumvention, or under error common to both parties, or where the other party, by anticipation, or at the due date for performance, has expressly repudiated the contractual obligations incumbent on him, or so acted as to justify the inference that he has so repudiated;[4] or where the contract has been performed by the other party and the aggrieved party finds the performance tendered fundamentally disconform to contract.[5] If questions arise whether one party has or has not the right to rescind they may be solved by an action of reduction of the contract.

Loss of right to rescind

The right to rescind may be lost by acquiescence after discovery of the facts which justified rescission, or by affirming the contract in the full knowledge of circumstances justifying rescission. Lapse of time may be evidence of waiver of the right to rescind.[6] It is also lost where the parties cannot make mutual restoration *in integrum*,[7] though this rule is not applied too strictly,[8] nor where third parties have, in good faith, and for value, acquired rights under the contract.[9]

1 *Wade* v. *Waldon*, 1909 S.C. 571.

2 *White & Carter* (*Councils*) v. *McGregor*, 1962 S.C. (H.L.) 1. But this should be subject to the rule that a pursuer must minimize his loss, and a party should not be allowed to perform and recover the full price of unwanted performance but only his loss of profit.

3 Ch. 33, *supra*; *Westville, supra.*

4 *White & Carter, supra.*

5 *Pollock* v. *Macrae*, 1922 S.C. (H.L.) 92; cf. *Mechans* v. *Highland Marine Charters*, 1964 S.C. 48.

6 *Re Scottish Petroleum Co.* (1883) 23 Ch. D. 434.

7 *Manners* v. *Whitehead* (1898) 1 F. 171; *Boyd & Forrest* v. *G.S.W. Ry.*, 1915 S.C. (H.L.) 20.

8 *Adam* v. *Newbigging* (1888) 3 App. Cas. 308; *Spence* v. *Crawford*, 1939 S.C. (H.L.) 52.

9 *Westville Shipping Co.* v. *Abram*, 1923 S.C. (H.L.) 68.

Effect of rescission

A person who rescinds a contract is entitled to be restored to the position he would have been in if the contract had not been made. Hence there must be mutual *restitutio in integrum* of property transferred, but the rescinding party is released from his further obligations under the contract.[1] Damages may also be claimed for the loss resulting from the repudiation and failure of the contract.[2]

Even justified rescission does not release the party rescinding from liability for debts to the other party which have accrued.[3]

Nor does rescission affect real rights in property which have passed under the contract to the party in breach[4] though it gives a right to retain goods for the price thereof.[5]

IRRITANCIES

An irritancy is a provision, express or legally implied, in a contract entitling one party in certain circumstances to irritate or determine the contract.[6]

LIQUIDATE DAMAGES

Parties may legitimately by contract provide that, in the event of failure to perform certain specified obligations of the contract, the party in breach shall pay a predetermined sum by way of compensation for the loss caused thereby.[7]

PENALTIES

Parties may not lawfully agree, the one to impose and the other to pay, a penalty in the event of a breach of obligation. In whatever terms it may be set out, a provision which is held to be in substance a penalty is unenforceable according to its terms, but does not preclude, or limit, a claim for damages for loss actually sustained.[8]

1 *Johannesburg Municipal Council* v. *Stewart*, 1909 S.C. 860; revd. 1909 S.C. (H.L.) 53.

2 *Duff* v. *Iron Buildings Co.* (1891) 19 R. 199; *Dunford & Elliot* v. *Macleod* (1902) 4 F. 912; *Johannesburg, supra.*

3 *Gibson* v. *McNaughton* (1861) 23 D. 358; *Christie* v. *Wilson*, 1915 S.C. 645.

4 *Richmond* v. *Railton* (1854) 16 D. 403.

5 Sale of Goods Act, 1893, S. 39(1)(a).

6 See Ch. 34, *supra.*

7 See Ch. 34, *supra.*

8 *Dingwall* v. *Burnett*, 1912 S.C. 1097.

The common clause in charter-parties 'penalty for non-performance estimated amount of freight' is unenforceable in its terms.[1]

DAMAGES

Damages is an award of money claimed as compensation for the loss sustained in consequence of the defender's breach of a duty incumbent on him, by contract, or by law,[2] and owed to the pursuer. The award is intended, so far as possible, to effect *restitutio in integrum* and to restore the pursuer to the position he would have been in if the contract had been duly performed, or the legal duty to him duly implemented.[3] Hence the pursuer's loss, and not the defender's position or plight, must be considered.[4]

Where there is breach of legal duty, damages are due *ex lege*, but liability for damages may in certain cases be excluded or limited, by an express term of contract,[5] or by statute.[6] Apart from such cases, at least nominal damages are due if there is breach of contract[7] but in the case of damage to person or property or business some actual loss must be proved or be capable of being inferred to justify damages.[8]

Damnum sine injuria

No award of damages may be made merely because a pursuer has suffered loss unless there were breach of duty by the defender and that breach caused the loss for which compensation is sought. Any such loss is *damnum sine injuria*.[9]

Claim must be once and for all

Both in contract and in delict, the pursuer must claim in one action for the whole loss which he sustained and is likely to

1 *Godard* v. *Gray* (1870) L.R. 6 Q.B. 139; *Dingwall, supra*.

2 Including obligations arising from the duty of restitution, from the commission of delict, from certain cases of non-implement of a statutory duty, and from breach of trust.

3 Ersk. III, 3, 86; *Houldsworth* v. *Brand's Trs.* (1877) 4 R. 369; *D. Portland* v. *Wood's Trs.*, 1926 S.C. 640; 1927 S.C. (H.L.) 1; *A/B Karlshamns Oljefabriker* v. *Monarch S.S. Co.*, 1949 S.C. (H.L.) 1 (breach of contract); *Livingstone* v. *Rawyards Coal Co.* (1880) 7 R. (H.L.) 1; *Watson, Laidlaw & Co.* v. *Pott, Cassels & Williamson*, 1914 S.C. (H.L.) 18, 29; *Pomphrey* v. *Cuthbertson*, 1951 S.C. 147; *Cruikshank* v. *Shiels*, 1951 S.C. 741 (delict).

4 *Somerville* v. *Thomson* (1896) 23 R. 576.

5 *Houldsworth* v. *Brand's Trs.* (1876) 3 R. 304, 319; *Wallis* v. *Pratt* [1910] 2 K.B. 1003, 1076; *McKay* v. *Scottish Airways*, 1948 S.C. 254.

6 Ch. 64, *supra*.

7 *Webster* v. *Cramond Iron Co.* (1875) 2 R. 752.

8 *Cassidy* v. *Connochie*, 1907 S.C. 1112; *Aarons* v. *Fraser*, 1934 S.C. 137; *Rankin* v. *Waddell*, 1949 S.C. 555, 558.

9 *Crofter Co.* v. *Veitch*, 1942 S.C. (H.L.) 1, 7; *Bourhill* v. *Young*, 1942 S.C. (H.L.) 78, 89.

sustain from the one cause of action;[1] subsequent loss, or subsequent discovery of more serious loss, if flowing from the same ground of action, does not permit of a fresh action.[2] But a later claim may be made for separate breaches of a continuing contract,[3] or separate harms from one wrong.[4] A single incident may give rise to more than one cause of action, such as for personal injuries and for property damage, or to claims by several persons.

Causal connection between breach of duty and harm

It must always be established that the breach of duty founded on was a main cause of the loss complained of.[5] If causal connection is not established the case is one of *damnum sine injuria*. If the loss were caused or made worse by the conduct of the pursuer he cannot recover for loss attributable to his own fault.[6]

Limitation by rules of remoteness of damage

The main limitation on any claim of damages is the rule excluding compensation for loss or damage which is deemed too remote from the wrong initiating the losses. In breach of contract this rule is that if there is established breach of contract, there is liability for the consequences of the breach which were reasonably foreseeable by the wrongdoer at the time of making the contract, having regard to his then state of knowledge, both that imputed to him by law and that actually possessed by him, of the likely consequences of the breach.[7] In delict the rule is that, if there is established breach of duty of care to the pursuer, there is liability for the harm immediately caused, and for all the natural and direct consequences thereof, whether these were reasonably foreseeable or not.[8]

Minimization of loss

The injured party must take reasonable steps to minimize his loss and cannot recover for loss reasonably avoidable by prudent

[1] *Stevenson* v. *Pontifex & Wood* (1887) 15 R. 125 (contract).

[2] Ersk. III, 1, 15; *Delaney* v. *Stirling* (1893) 20 R. 506; *Steven* v. *Broady Norman & Co.*, 1928 S.C. 351; *Balfour* v. *Baird*, 1959 S.C. 64.

[3] *Jackson* v. *Cowie* (1872) 9 S.L.R. 617.

[4] In damage caused by subsidence each fresh subsidence is a fresh ground of action though caused by the same extraction of material: *Darley Main Colliery* v. *Mitchell* (1886) 11 App. Cas. 127; *D. Abercorn* v. *Merry & Cunninghame*, 1919 S.C. 750.

[5] *Seton* v. *Paterson* (1880) 8 R. 236; *Wilson* v. *Carmichael* (1894) 21 R. 732; *Millar* v. *Bellvale Chemical Co.* (1898) 1 F. 297 (contract); *Macfarlane* v. *Colam*, 1908 S.C. 56; *Howie* v. *Ailsa Shipbuilding Co.*, 1912 S.C. 1225; *Leyland Shipping Co.* v. *Norwich Fire Ins. Socy.* [1918] A.C. 350; *Yorkshire Dale S.S. Co.* v. *M.O.W.T.* [1942] A.C. 691 (delict).

[6] *Stephen* v. *Swayne* (1861) 24 D. 158.

[7] Ch. 36, *supra*.

[8] Ch. 61, *supra*.

action on his part.[1] But he is not bound to take exceptional measures or incur substantial expense in minimizing the loss,[2] though it may be proper to accept a compromise offer from the other party.[3]

Quantum of damages—contract

Subject to the limitation imposed by the rule against too remote harm the main principle is that the pursuer should be awarded fair compensation for the loss sustained by reason of the defender's breach of contract, including such factors as trouble and inconvenience,[4] necessary expenses and outlays,[5] loss of business or profits, as by late delivery,[6] loss of market,[7] loss caused by having to sell off non-accepted goods cheaply,[8] the extra cost of supply from an alternative source,[9] the extra cost of performance by an alternative means,[10] the loss of a known or foreseeable sub-contract,[11] damages paid for default on a sub-contract, if known or foreseeable,[12] the expense of necessary litigation with third parties,[13] damages paid to third parties in consequence of the defender's breach.[14]

Quantum of damages—restitution

Where a person subject to an obligation of restitution or of *negotiorum gestio* has failed to implement that duty with due diligence he is liable in damages for the loss thereby sustained.[15]

1 *Warin & Craven* v. *Forrester* (1876) 4 R. 190; affd. 4 R. (H.L.) 75; *Connal, Cotton & Co.* v. *Fisher, Renwick & Co.* (1883) 10 R. 824; *Ross* v. *Macfarlane* (1894) 21 R. 396; *British Westinghouse Co.* v. *Underground Ry.* [1912] A.C. 673; *Cazalet* v. *Morris*, 1916 S.C. 952 (contract); *Jones* v. *Watney, Combe Reid & Co.* (1912) 28 T.L.R. 399; *Admiralty Commrs.* v. *S.S. Chekiang* [1926] A.C. 637; *Liesbosch* v. *Edison* [1933] A.C. 449; *Pomphrey* v. *Cuthbertson*, 1951 S.C. 147 (delict).

2 *Henderson* v. *Turnbull*, 1909 S.C. 510; *Banco de Portugal* v. *Waterlow* [1932] A.C. 452.

3 *Payzu* v. *Saunders* [1919] 2 K.B. 581.

4 *Webster* v. *Cramond Iron Co.* (1875) 2 R. 752; *Murray* v. *Marr* (1892) 20 R. 119.

5 *Duff* v. *Iron Buildings Co.* (1891) 19 R. 199.

6 *Fletcher* v. *Tayleur* (1855) 17 C.B. 21; *Lindsay* v. *Scholefield* (1897) 24 R. 530; *Victoria Laundry* v. *Newman* [1949] 2 K.B. 528.

7 *Wilson* v. *L. & Y. Ry.* (1861) 9 C.B. (N.S.) 632.

8 *Warin & Craven* v. *Forrester* (1877) 4 R. (H.L.) 75; Sale of Goods Act, 1893, S. 50.

9 Sale of Goods Act, 1893, S. 51; *Marshall* v. *Nicoll*, 1919 S.C. (H.L.) 129.

10 e.g. *Seaton Brick Co.* v. *Mitchell* (1900) 2 F. 550; *Stroms Brüks A/B* v. *Hutchison* (1905) 7 F. (H.L.) 131.

11 *Keddie Gordon & Co.* v. *N.B. Ry.* (1886) 14 R. 233; *Stroms Brüks, supra.*

12 *Grebert Borgnis* v. *Nugent* (1885) 15 Q.B.D. 85; *Biggin* v. *Permanite* [1951] 2 K.B. 314.

13 *Munro* v. *Bennet*, 1911 S.C. 337.

14 *Buchanan & Carswell* v. *Eugene*, 1936 S.C. 160.

15 *Kolbin* v. *Kinnear*, 1931 S.C. (H.L.) 128.

Quantum of damages—delict—personal injuries

In cases of personal injuries, whether intentional, negligent, or in circumstances of strict liability, the pursuer is entitled firstly to a sum in name of solatium for the pain and suffering occasioned by the injuries, and for loss of limbs or faculties, impaired senses or bodily and mental powers.[1] The award must have regard to present and also future disability, and evaluate the prospects of recovery or of deterioration.[2] Loss of expectation of life is relevant for consideration.[3]

The court or jury must try to make a fair award of compensation having regard to the pursuer's sufferings and losses in the circumstances.[4] If some physical injury is proved, some award must be made for solatium.[5] In cases of serious injuries the award under this head may run to thousands of pounds.

Secondly, an injured pursuer is entitled to compensation for patrimonial loss, and particularly for loss of earnings past[6] and prospective.[7] In assessing future earnings probable rises or falls in earnings must be considered[8] and allowance made for actual or possible earnings from an alternative occupation.[9]

Earnings must be taken on the basis of net earnings, after deduction of tax,[10] but without deduction for national insurance contributions.[11] It is wrong to award under this head such a capital sum as would produce an annuity income equal to the lost earnings.[12] Allowances must be made for contingencies, such as the pursuer's death or injury from any other causes, but not for anything recovered under an insurance policy.[13] Unemployment benefit received during incapacity falls to be deducted.[14]

1 *Young* v. *Glasgow Tramways Co.* (1882) 10 R. 242–3; *Burns* v. *Allan* (1892) 30 S.L.R. 57; *McLaurin* v. *N.B. Ry.* (1892) 19 R. 346; *Thoms* v. *Caledonian Ry.*, 1913 S.C. 804; *Lewis* v. *Laird Line*, 1925 S.L.T. 316; *Traynor's Exrx.* v. *Bairds & Scottish Steel*, 1957 S.C. 311; *Waddell's C.B.* v. *Lindsay*, 1960 S.L.T. 189; *McCallum* v. *Paterson*, 1968 S.L.T. (Notes) 57; *Steen* v. *McNicol*, 1968 S.L.T. (Notes) 77.

2 *Aitken* v. *Laidlay*, 1938 S.C. 303.

3 *Neilson* v. *Rodger* (1853) 16 D. 325, 327; *McMaster* v. *Caledonian Ry.* (1885) 13 R. 252; *Reid* v. *Lanarkshire Traction Co.*, 1934 S.C. 79.

4 *Traynor's Exrx.* v. *Bairds & Scottish Steel*, 1957 S.C. 311.

5 cf. *Gibson* v. *Kyle*, 1933 S.C. 30.

6 *Reid* v. *Morton* (1902) 4 F. 438.

7 *Johnston* v. *G.W. Ry.* [1904] 2 K.B. 250.

8 *Smith* v. *Comrie's Exrx.*, 1944 S.C. 499.

9 *Billingham* v. *Hughes* [1949] 1 K.B. 643.

10 *McDaid* v. *C.N. Trs.*, 1946 S.C. 462; *B.T.C.* v. *Gourley* [1956] A.C. 185; overruling *Blackwood* v. *Andre*, 1947 S.C. 333.

11 *McCreadie* v. *Clydebank Co-operative Socy.*, 1966 S.C. 71.

12 *McKechnie* v. *Henderson* (1858) 20 D. 551; *Lewis* v. *Laird Line*, 1925 S.L.T. 316.

13 *Bradburn* v. *G.W. Ry.* (1874) L.R. 10 Ex. 1.

14 *McPherson* v. *Kelsey Roofing Industries, Ltd.*, 1967 S.L.T. (Notes) 93.

By statute there must be taken into account,[1] as against any loss of earnings or profits, half of the value of any rights which have accrued or probably will accrue[2] to the injured person in respect of industrial injury benefit, industrial disablement benefit or sickness benefit for the five years beginning when the cause of action accrued. There must be disregarded any increase of an industrial disablement pension in respect of the need of constant attendance.[3]

Thirdly, an injured pursuer is entitled to compensation for outlays and expenses necessarily and reasonably incurred, as on medical treatment.[4] No deduction may be made from damages because of the possibility of avoiding these expenses by relying on the National Health Service.[5]

If the injured person has died and the action is being continued by his executor the executor can recover under the same heads as the injured man could have done, but for the period of survivance only.[6] In such cases the court has allowed an extra amount of solatium on account of the shortening of the injured person's life.[7]

Death of relative

Where surviving relatives sue for the loss caused them by the death of a relative, between whom and them there existed a recognized close relationship and a mutual obligation of support during life,[8] each entitled relative must conclude for a separate award of damages. The court is not obliged to make an award under any head if there is no evidence of loss under that head.[9]

Firstly, the court must award a moderate sum of solatium,[10] more in recognition of grief caused by the death than in compensation for the loss,[11] provided some evidence is given of grief felt.[12]

1 See *Flowers* v. *Wimpey* [1956] 1 Q.B. 73.

2 *Ferguson* v. *Durastic, Ltd.* [1951] 1 Lloyd's Rep, 324; *Harris* v. *Brights Asphalt Contractors, Ltd.* [1953] 1 Q.B. 617; *Stott* v. *Arrol* [1953] 2 Q.B. 92.

3 Law Reform (Personal Injuries) Act, 1948, S. 2(1) and (2). As to industrial disablement gratuity see S. 2(6)(c).

4 *Young* v. *Glasgow Tramway Co.* (1882) 10 R. 242; *Aitken* v. *Laidlay*, 1938 S.C. 303; *Rubens* v. *Walker*, 1946 S.C. 215.

5 Law Reform (Personal Injuries) Act, 1948, S. 2(4).

6 *McEnaney* v. *Caledonian Ry.*, 1913 2 S.L.T. 293; *Russell's Exrx.* v. *B.R. Board*, 1965 S.C. 422.

7 *McMaster* v. *Caledonian Ry.* (1885) 13 R. 252; *McEnaney, supra*; *Reid* v. *Lanarkshire Traction Co.*, 1934 S.C. 79.

8 *Eisten* v. *N.B. Ry.* (1870) 8 M. 980.

9 *Rankin* v. *Waddell*, 1949 S.C. 555.

10 *Quin* v. *Greenock Tramways*, 1926 S.C. 544; *Gibson* v. *Kyle*, 1933 S.C. 30.

11 *Elliot* v. *Glasgow Corpn.*, 1922 S.C. 146; *Quin* v. *Greenock Tramways*, 1926 S.C. 544; *Smith* v. *Comrie's Exrx.*, 1944 S.C. 499.

12 *Rankin* v. *Waddell*, 1949 S.C. 555.

It is doubtful if an award exceeding £1000 under this head is ever justified.[1]

Secondly, an award must be made for loss of the financial support which the deceased was affording to the claimant and would probably have continued to afford. Loss of even a contingent right of support is relevant[2] and it is not necessary that the pursuer be in actual need of support if he was in fact getting it.[3] The annual loss must be multiplied by a number of years, depending on the period for which the loss may be assumed to continue, to arrive at the total award under this head.[4] Allowance must be made for foreseeable increases or decreases in the support likely to be given.[5] The award under this head should not be a sum which, if invested, would produce the same, or nearly the same, income as the claimants had lost by the death.[6]

Some deduction must be made from this sum if the loss of support is partly made up by estate inherited from the deceased,[7] or by a pension awarded in respect of the deceased's death,[8] or if a widow has remarried or is likely to do so.[9] But it is irrelevant that the survivor had adequate means if in fact he had lost support by the death.[10]

Thirdly, by custom, the cost of funeral expenses is paid to one of the entitled relatives.[11]

In assessing the sum due the grossness of the defender's fault is irrelevant[12] as are allegations of specific injury to a widow's health.[13] There must not be taken into account any right to benefit under the National Insurance or Industrial Injuries Acts resulting from the deceased's death.[14]

A jury customarily makes a lump sum award to each pursuer to cover all heads of claim, but a sheriff or judge is expected to particularize his award.

[1] *McKinlay* v. *Glasgow Corpn.*, 1951 S.C. 495; *McLeish* v. *Fulton*, 1955 S.C. 46.

[2] *Sagar* v. *N.C.B.*, 1955 S.C. 424.

[3] *Dickson* v. *N.C.B.*, 1957 S.C. 157.

[4] See e.g. *Wason* v. *B.T.C.*, 1960 S.C. 261; *Urquhart* v. *Baxter*, 1961 S.C. 149.

[5] *Brennan* v. *Gale* [1949] N.I.L.R. 178.

[6] *Love* v. *N.C.B.*, 1956 S.C. 459.

[7] *Smith* v. *Comrie's Exrx.*, 1944 S.C. 499.

[8] *Moorcraft* v. *Alexander*, 1946 S.C. 466; *Johnson* v. *Hill* (1945) 61 T.L.R. 398; *Smith* v. *B.E.A.* [1951] 2 K.B. 893.

[9] cf. *Donnelly* v. *Glasgow Corpn.*, 1949 S.L.T. 362.

[10] *Cruikshank* v. *Shiels*, 1953 S.C. (H.L.) 1.

[11] e.g. *McLeish* v. *Fulton*, 1955 S.C. 46. But see *McEnaney* v. *Caledonian Ry.*, 1913 2 S.L.T. 293.

[12] *Black* v. *N.B. Ry.*, 1908 S.C. 444.

[13] *Kirkpatrick* v. *Anderson*, 1948 S.C. 251; *Nicolson* v. *Cursiter*, 1959 S.C. 350.

[14] Law Reform (Personal Injuries) Act, 1953, overruling *Adams* v. *Spencer*, 1951 S.C. 175.

Reconsideration of awards on appeal

An award of damages may be reconsidered on appeal but the Inner House will not allow a substantial error made by a Lord Ordinary or sheriff to go uncorrected.[1] A jury award may be challenged by way of motion for a new trial, but the Inner House allows a greater margin of error, and will not allow a new trial merely because the award is substantially larger or smaller than it should have been[2] but only if it is such as no reasonable jury could properly have made.[3] In cases of solatium only the working rule has sometimes been applied that a new trial will be allowed only if the award were less than half or more than double what the Inner House considered reasonable.[4] In other cases the standard is one of comparison with other awards made in current practice.

It has been suggested that in actions for the death of a relative the proper comparison is between the aggregate of the sums awarded to the several pursuers and the aggregate which in the view of the court should properly have been awarded.[5]

Dishonour and harm to reputation

In cases such as assault, defamation, malicious prosecution, and the like, where the essence of the wrong is the hurt to feelings and reputation, the whole award is of the nature of solatium, and must be assessed by regard to the nature and extent of the dishonour done, the evidence of injury to feelings and reputation, and the whole circumstances.[6]

If in addition to hurt to feelings and reputation there is evidence of patrimonial loss, as of loss of business, damages may be given for this also on the basis of a fair estimate of the loss caused by the conduct in question.[7]

Damage to property

In cases of injury to or destruction of property, heritable or moveable, the basic measure of damages is the diminution in value

1 *King* v. *B.L. Co.* (1899) 1 F. 928; *Inglis* v. *L.M.S. Ry.*, 1941 S.C. 551; *Purdie* v. *Allan*, 1949 S.C. 477; *Butler* v. *Lynn*, 1965 S.C. 137.

2 *Houlden* v. *Couper* (1871) 9 S.L.R. 169; *Potter* v. *N.B. Ry.* (1873) 11 M. 664; *Gibson* v. *Anderson* (1897) 24 R. 556; *Casey* v. *United Collieries*, 1907 S.C. 690.

3 *Landell* v. *L.* (1841) 3 D. 819; *Adamson* v. *Whitson* (1849) 11 D. 680; *Houlden, supra*; *McGinley* v. *Pacitti*, 1950 S.C. 364.

4 *Elliot* v. *Glasgow Corpn.*, 1922 S.C. 146; *Inglis* v. *L.M.S. Ry.*, 1941 S.C. 551; *McGinley, supra*.

5 *Hewitt* v. *West's Gas Improvement Co.*, 1955 S.C. 162; *Love* v. *N.C.B.*, 1956 S.C. 459. But see also *McLeish* v. *Fulton*, 1955 S.C. 46.

6 *Ritchie* v. *Barton* (1883) 10 R. 813; *Fletcher* v. *Wilsons* (1885) 12 R. 683; *Cunningham* v. *Duncan & Jamieson* (1889) 16 R. 383; cf. *Cassidy* v. *Connochie*, 1907 S.C. 1112.

7 *Ritchie, supra*; cf. *Lamond* v. *Daily Record*, 1923 S.L.T. 512.

of the property,[1] which may amount to its total pre-injury value. In some cases the cost of repair is a guide to the diminution in value.[2]

Quantum of damages—other kinds of delicts

In other cases of delicts the basic question is the same: what loss has the pursuer suffered?[3]

Quantum of damages—breach of statute

If the breach of statutory duty is held civilly actionable[4] and has resulted in personal injuries or death the measure of damages therefore is the same as in a case of breach of common law duty causing such losses.

Quantum of damages—breach of trust

The basic measure of damages is the loss sustained by the trust estate in consequence of the trustee's breach of duty, namely the sum misapplied or wrongly paid away, or lost by negligent investment,[5] or the loss sustained by the beneficiary.[6]

ADMINISTRATIVE REMEDIES

The seeking of an administrative remedy is only the seeking of machinery whereby the rights and claims of parties may be enforced. Under this head falls applications to the courts for the appointment of curators, new trustees, of a judicial factor, or of an executor-dative, petitions for the sequestration of a debtor, or for the winding up of a company. Applications made to the *nobile officium* of the Court of Session also fall within this class.

ACCESSORY ACTIONS

Apart from the main substantive remedies there are certain actions which are normally merely accessory to particular remedies. These are wakening, exhibition *ad probandum*, transumpt, and proving the tenor of a lost document.

[1] *Hutchison* v. *Davidson*, 1945 S.C. 395; *Pomphrey* v. *Cuthbertson*, 1951 S.C. 147.
[2] *Hamilton* v. *Galloway S.P. Co.* (1894) 1 S.L.T. 432; *Gibson* v. *Farie*, 1918 1 S.L.T. 404; *Gilmour* v. *Simpson*, 1958 S.C. 477.
[3] *Arneil* v. *Paterson*, 1931 S.C. (H.L.) 117; *Aarons* v. *Fraser*, 1934 S.C. 137; *Stewart* v. *Brechin*, 1959 S.C. 306; *Yeoman's Exrx.* v. *Ferries*, 1967 S.L.T. 332.
[4] Ch. 62, *supra*; cf. *Millar* v. *Galashiels Gas Co.*, 1949 S.C. (H.L.) 31.
[5] *Millar's Trs.* v. *Polson* (1897) 24 R. 1038; cf. *Raes* v. *Meek* (1889) 16 R. (H.L.) 31.
[6] *Hood* v. *Macdonald's Trs.*, 1949 S.C. 24.

INDEX

Lost property:
abandonment of, 1500
belongs to Crown, 1221
duty to restore, 989, 1462